Office 2007 Bible

Office 2007 Bible

John Walkenbach
Herb Tyson
Faithe Wempen
Cary N. Prague
Michael R. Groh
Peter G. Aitken
Michael R. Irwin
Gavin Powell
Lisa A. Bucki

Wiley Publishing, Inc.

Office 2007 Bible

Published by
Wiley Publishing, Inc.
10475 Crosspoint Boulevard
Indianapolis, IN 46256
www.wiley.com

Published simultaneously in Canada

ISBN: 978-0-470-04691-3

Manufactured in the United States of America

10 9 8 7 6 5 4 3 2 1

For general information on our other products and services or to obtain technical support, please contact our Customer Care Department within the U.S. at (800) 762-2974, outside the U.S. at (317) 572-3993 or fax (317) 572-4002.

Library of Congress Cataloging-in-Publication Data

Office 2007 bible / John Walkenbach . . . [et al.].
p. cm.
Includes index.
ISBN 978-0-470-04691-3 (paper/website)
1. Microsoft Office. 2. Business—Computer programs. I. Walkenbach, John.
HF5548.4.M525O3342 2007
005.5—dc22

2007014969

About the Authors

John Walkenbach is a bestselling Excel author and has published more than 50 spreadsheet books. He lives amid the saguaros, javelinas, and gila monsters in Southern Arizona. For more information, Google him.

Herb Tyson is an economist and computer consultant and trainer in the Washington, D.C., area. He earned an interdisciplinary doctorate from Michigan State University in 1977 and an undergraduate degree in Economics and Sociology from Georgetown University in 1973.

He is the author of many computer magazine and ezine articles, as well as more than a dozen computing books, including *Teach Yourself Outlook 2000 in 24 Hours*, *Word for Windows Super Book*, *Teach Yourself Web Publishing with Microsoft Word*, *XyWrite Revealed*, *Word for Windows Revealed*, *Your OS/2 Consultant*, and *Navigating the Internet with OS/2 Warp*. Herb is also joint author and technical editor for many other books.

He has received the Microsoft MVP (Most Valuable Professional) award each year for more than ten years in recognition for helping thousands of Microsoft Word users. Widely recognized for his expertise, Herb's clients have included IBM, Wang, the federal government, the World Bank, as well as numerous law firms and publishers.

Herb is also a singer and songwriter, currently working on his second CD. He and his guitar are no strangers to musical venues in the Washington, D.C., area. He has performed at the Birchmere, the Kennedy Center, Jammin' Java, and coffeehouses, and is a frequent performer at the Mount Vernon Unitarian Church (where he serves as Webmaster).

You can visit Herb's Web site at `www.herbtyson.com`. Questions about this book and Microsoft Office can be pursued at Herb's Word 2007 blog, at `word2007bible.blogspot.com`. You can also e-mail Herb Tyson at `herbsbooks@herbtyson.com`.

Faithe Wempen, M.A., is an A+ Certified hardware guru, Microsoft Office Specialist Master Instructor, and software consultant with more than 90 computer books to her credit. She has taught Microsoft Office applications, including PowerPoint, to more than a quarter of a million online students for corporate clients including Hewlett Packard, CNET, Sony, Gateway, and eMachines. When she is not writing, she teaches Microsoft Office classes in the Computer Technology department at Indiana University–Purdue University at Indianapolis (IUPUI), does private computer training and support consulting, and owns and operates Sycamore Knoll Bed and Breakfast in Noblesville, Indiana (`www.sycamoreknoll.com`).

Cary N. Prague is an internationally best-selling author and lecturer in the database industry. He owns Database Creations, Inc., the world's largest Microsoft Access add-on company. Their products include a line of financial software; Business! for Microsoft Office, a mid-range accounting system, POSitively Business! Point of Sale software, the Inventory Barcode manager for mobile data collection, and the Check Writer and General Ledger. Database Creations also produces a line of developer tools including the appBuilder, an application generator for Microsoft Access, the EZ Access Developer Tools for building great user interfaces, appWatcher for maintaining code bases among several developers, and Surgical Strike, the only Patch Manager for Microsoft Access.

Cary also owns Database Creations Consulting, LLC., a successful consulting firm specializing in Microsoft Access and SQL Server applications. Local and national clients include many Fortune 100 companies including manufacturers, defense contractors, insurance, health-care, and software industry companies. His client list includes Microsoft, United Technologies, ABB, Smith & Wesson Firearms, Pratt and Whitney Aircraft, ProHealth, OfficeMax, Continental Airlines, and other Fortune 500 companies.

Formerly, he has held numerous management positions in corporate information systems, including Director of Managed Care Reporting for MetraHealth, Director of Corporate Finance and Software Productivity at Travelers Insurance, where he was responsible for software support for 35,000 end users, and Manager of Information Systems support for Northeast Utilities.

He is one of the top bestselling authors in the computer database management market, having written more than 40 books that have sold more than one million copies on software including Microsoft Access, Borland (Ashton-Tate) dBASE, Paradox, R:Base, Framework, and graphics. Cary's books include 11 books in the *Access Bible* series (recently number one on the Ingram Bestselling Database Titles list and in the Amazon.com top 100), *Access 97 Secrets, dBASE for Windows Handbook, dBASE IV Programming* (winner of the Computer Press Association's Book of the Year award for Best Software Specific Book), and *Everyman's Database Primer Featuring dBASE IV.* He recently completed several books for Access 2003 including *Weekend Crash Course in Office Access 2003 Programming*. Cary recently sold a product line named eTools for Microsoft Access to MightyWords, a division of FatBrain.com and Barnes and Noble.

Cary is certified in Access as a Microsoft Certified Professional and has passed the MOUS test in Access and Word. He is a frequent speaker at seminars and conferences around the country. He is on the exclusive Microsoft Access Insider Advisory Board and makes frequent trips to Microsoft headquarters in Redmond, WA. He has been voted the best speaker by the attendees of several national conferences. Recently, he was a speaker for Microsoft-sponsored conferences in New Orleans, Hawaii, Phoenix, Chicago, Toronto, Palm Springs, Boston, and Orlando. He has also spoken at Borland's Database Conference, Digital Consulting's Database World, Microsoft's Developer Days, Computerland's Technomics Conference, COMDEX, and COMPAQ Computer's Innovate. He was a contributing editor to *Access Advisor* magazine and has written for the *Microsoft Office Developer's* journal.

He is active in local town politics serving on the South Windsor, Connecticut, Board of Education, Parks and Recreation Commission, and the Board of Assessment Appeals.

Cary holds a master's degree in computer science from Rensselaer Polytechnic Institute, and an MBA and a Bachelor of Accounting from the University of Connecticut. He is also a Certified Data Processor.

Michael R. Groh is a well-known author, writer, and consultant specializing in Windows database systems. His company, PC Productivity Solutions, provides information-management applications to companies across the country. Over the last 25 years, Mike has worked with a wide variety of programming languages, operating systems, and computer hardware, ranging from programming a DEC PDP-8A using the Focal interpreted language to building distributed applications under Visual Studio .NET and Microsoft SharePoint.

Mike was one of the first people outside Microsoft to see Access in action. He was among a select group of journalists and publishers invited to preview the Access 1.0 beta (then called Cirrus) at the 1992 Windows World Conference in Chicago. Since then, Mike has been involved in every Microsoft Access beta program, as an insider and as a journalist and reporter documenting the evolution of this fascinating product.

Mike has authored parts of more than 20 different computer books and is a frequent contributor to computer magazines and journals. Mike has written more than 200 articles and editorials over the last 15 years, mostly for Advisor Media (San Diego, CA). He frequently speaks at computer conferences virtually everywhere in the world, and is technical editor and contributor to periodicals and publications produced by Advisor Media.

Mike holds a master's degree in Clinical Chemistry from the University of Iowa (Iowa City, IA) and an MBA from Northeastern University (Boston, MA).

Mike can be reached at `AccessBible@mikegroh.com`. Please prefix the e-mail subject line with "AccessBible:" to get past the spam blocker on this account.

Peter G. Aitken has been writing about computers and programming for over 15 years, with more than 45 books to his credit and more than 1.5 million copies in print. He has also contributed hundreds of articles and product reviews to magazines and Web sites such as *Visual Developer Magazine*, *PC Magazine*, DevX, Microsoft Office Pro, Builder.com, and DevSource. Peter is the proprietor of PGA Consulting, providing custom application development and technical writing services to business, academia, and government since 1994.

Michael R. Irwin is considered one of the leading authorities on automated database and Internet management systems today. He is a noted worldwide lecturer, winner of national and international awards, bestselling author, and developer of client/server, Internet, intranet, and PC-based database-management systems.

Michael has extensive database knowledge, gained by working with the Metropolitan Police Department in Washington, D.C., as a developer and analyst for the Information Systems Division for more than 20 years and assorted Federal Agencies of the United States Government. Since retiring in June 1992, he has run his own consulting firm, named The Irwin Group, and is principal partner in the company - IT in Asia, LLC, specializing in Internet database integration and emphasizing Client/Server and Internet solutions. With consulting offices in Cincinnati, Ohio, Bangkok, Thailand, and Manila, Philippines, his companies offer training and development of Internet and database applications. His company has the distinction of being one of the first Microsoft Solution's Providers (in 1992). His local, national, and international clients include many software companies, manufacturers, government agencies, and international companies.

His range of expertise includes database processing and integration between mainframe, minicomputer, and PC-based database systems, as well as B-2-B and B-2-C integration between back-end databases. He is a leading authority on PC-based databases.

He is one of the top bestselling authors in the computer database-management market, having authored numerous database books, with several of them consistently on the bestseller lists. His books, combined, have sold nearly a million copies worldwide. His most recent works include *The OOPs Primer* (Borland Press), *dBASE 5.5 for Windows Programming* (Prentice Hall), *Microsoft Access 2002 Bible*, *Microsoft Access 2002 Bible Gold Edition* (co-authored), and *Working with the Internet*. The *Access Bible* series have constantly been number one on the Ingram Best-selling Database Titles list and is consistently in the Amazon.com and Buy.com top 10. He has also written several books on customs and cultures of the countries of Asia (including China, Japan, Thailand, and India). Two of his books have won international acclaim. His books are published in more than 24 languages worldwide. He has been a contributing editor and author to many well-known magazines and journals.

He is a frequent speaker at seminars and conferences around the world and has been voted the best speaker by the attendees of several international conferences.

Michael has developed and markets several add-on software products for the Internet and productivity-related applications. Many of his productivity applications can be obtained from several of his Internet sites or on many common download sites. Many of his application and systems are distributed as freeware and careware. He has also developed and distributes several development tools and add-ins for a wide range of developer applications.

Gavin Powell is a computer consultant and a writer, with more than 20 years of IT experience and more than 10 titles to his credit. He has worked as a programmer, analyst, data modeler, database administrator, and Unix administrator. Gavin is also a semiprofessional musician, songwriter, and recording engineer, playing multiple instruments and writing prolifically. Gavin can be reached by e-mail at `info@oracledbaexpert.com` or `ezpowell@ezpowell.com`.

Lisa A. Bucki is an author, trainer, and consultant and has been writing and teaching about computers and software for more than 15 years. She wrote *Teach Yourself Visually Microsoft Office PowerPoint 2007*, *Microsoft Office Project 2007 Survival Guide*, *Learning Photoshop CS2*, *Dell Guide to Digital Photography: Shooting, Editing, and Printing Pictures*, *Learning Computer Applications: Projects & Exercises* (multiple editions), and *Adobe Photoshop 7 Fast & Easy*. Lisa has written or contributed to dozens of additional books and multimedia tutorials covering a variety of software and technology topics, including FileMaker Pro 6 for the Mac, iPhoto 2, Fireworks and Flash from Adobe, Microsoft Office applications, and digital photography. She also spearheaded or developed more than 100 computer and trade titles during her association with the former Macmillan Computer Publishing (now a division of Pearson).

To homeless and neglected pets everywhere, in the hope that you will find a better life and the loving care that you deserve. And to the many compassionate people involved in animal rescue work, in thanks for the selfless work that you do.

Credits

Senior Acquisitions Editor
Jim Minatel

Senior Development Editor
Adaobi Obi Tulton

Technical Editors
Dian Chapman
Todd Meister

Copy Editor
Susan Christophersen

Editorial Manager
Mary Beth Wakefield

Production Manager
Tim Tate

Vice President and Executive Group Publisher
Richard Swadley

Vice President and Executive Publisher
Joseph B. Wikert

Project Coordinator
Bill Ramsey

Graphics and Production Specialists
Jonelle Burns
Carrie A. Foster
Jennifer Mayberry
Barbara Moore
Heather Pope

Quality Control Technicians
Laura Albert
John Greenough

Proofreading and Indexing
Aptara

Anniversary Logo Design
Richard Pacifico

Contents

Part III: Making the Numbers Work with Excel

Part IV: Persuading and Informing with PowerPoint

Part V: Organizing Messages, Contacts, and Time with Outlook

Part VI: Designing Publications with Publisher

Part VII: Tracking Detailed Data with Access

Acknowledgments

Thanks to Acquisitions Editor Jim Minatel for offering me (Lisa A. Bucki) the opportunity to work on this monster book. Jim, you're a good friend, and I value your support and professionalism. Thanks also to Adaobi Obi Tulton, Senior Development Editor par excellence. An image of her standing proudly, head held high and shoulders squared, hands planted firmly on her hips, and a large cape billowing behind her in the wind sticks firmly in my mind.

The authors who contributed chapters from their individual *Bible* books provided the granite from which this edifice was built. Thanks to these folks for their excellence and expertise:

- Herb Tyson, *Word 2007 Bible*
- John Walkenbach, *Excel 2007 Bible*
- Faithe Wempen, *PowerPoint 2007 Bible*
- Peter G. Aitken, *Outlook 2007 Bible*
- Michael R. Groh, Gavin Powell, Cary N. Prague, and Michael R. Irwin, *Access 2007 Bible*

I thank Technical Editor Dian Chapman for vetting my new material and tying up some other loose ends on this project. Check out all the Office expertise Dian offers at her Web site, `www.mousetrax.com`. I also appreciate some last-minute expertise kicked in by Technical Editor Todd Meister.

Introduction

Welcome to *Office 2007 Bible*. This book provides the information you need to get up and running with the applications in the latest version of the Microsoft Office 2007 suite. Inside, you get coverage of these members of the various versions of the Office Suite:

- Microsoft Office Word 2007
- Microsoft Office Excel 2007
- Microsoft Office PowerPoint 2007
- Microsoft Office Outlook 2007
- Microsoft Office Publisher 2007
- Microsoft Office Access 2007
- Microsoft Office OneNote 2007
- Microsoft Office InfoPath 2007

This book brings together chapters from the new versions of the Word, Excel, PowerPoint, Outlook, and Access *Bibles*. You get the best information from experts in each program so that you can get to work and be productive quickly.

Who Should Read This Book

Office 2007 brings some sweeping changes to the user interface in Word, Excel, PowerPoint, Access, and parts of Outlook. As a result, even experienced Office users can use this book to get up to speed with using the new interface quickly. Because this book presents information using the friendly, accessible *Bible* format that combines straightforward steps and concise reference information, beginners with Office can use it to learn Office quickly and expand their skills beyond the basics.

How This Book Is Organized

Office 2007 Bible organizes information into several parts. In most cases, a part focuses on a particular application in the suite, so you can jump right to the part for the application you're currently using.

Part I: Common Office Features

The chapters in this part provide the first introduction to the new user interface in the major Office applications, as well as show how to perform fundamental operations such as working with files.

Part II: Creating Documents with Word

This part covers using the Microsoft Office Word 2007 word processing program to create and format text-based documents. In addition to learning how to format words, paragraphs, and pages, you get a shot at working with more sophisticated features such as tables and mail merge, and even the new SmartArt diagrams. You also see how document security settings can help protect information.

Part III: Making the Numbers Work with Excel

The chapters here show you how to use the spreadsheet program Microsoft Office Excel 2007 to organize and calculate data. After getting a preview of the new features in the program, you learn how to enter, format, and calculate information. You also see how to create powerful charts that tell a story about your data, and how to manage lists of information.

Part IV: Persuading and Informing with PowerPoint

In this part, you learn how to get the word out with the Microsoft Office PowerPoint 2007 presentation graphics program. This part explains how to add information, charts, SmartArt diagrams, and graphics to slides. You also see how to animate and automate a slide show and get expert tips about going live with your presentation.

Part V: Organizing Messages, Contacts, and Time with Outlook

The basics for using Microsoft Office Outlook 2007 appear in this part. Learn to set up an e-mail account; compose, send, and respond to messages; organize messages and deal with junk mail and security issues; manage your contacts, appointments, and to-do list; and get new online content by setting up and using an RSS feed.

Part VI: Designing Publications with Publisher

This part introduces you to the Microsoft Office Publisher 2007 page layout and design program. Learn how to not only create great-looking publications with Publisher's flexible tools but also prep your publications for professional printing.

Part VII: Tracking Detailed Data with Access

If you manage detailed lists—with customer or product data, for example—Microsoft Office Access 2007 and this part's chapters are for you. Get a roadmap here for designing a good database. Learn how to create tables, fields, and forms, and how to select and present data with queries and reports.

Part VIII: Gathering Information

Get efficient with the programs introduced in this part—Microsoft Office OneNote 2007 and Microsoft Office InfoPath 2007. Get an overview about using OneNote to track notes and project details, and then see how to use InfoPath to create fill-in forms for gathering responses from others.

Part IX: Sharing and Collaboration

This part explains not only how to share information between Office applications, but also how to use Office 2007 applications with SharePoint and Groove on a network or the Internet.

What Is on the Web Site

On the *Office 2007 Bible* Web site at `www.wiley.com/go/office2007bible`, you can find the databases needed to create the examples used for Chapters 35 and 36.

The Web site also includes three appendixes to provide supplementary information: Appendix A, "Customizing Office"; Appendix B, "Optimizing Your Office Installation"; and Appendix C, "International Support and Accessibility Features."

Conventions and Features

As you work your way through the text, be on the lookout for these icons that bring your attention to important information:

CAUTION This information is important and is set off in a separate paragraph with a special icon. Cautions provide information about things to watch out for, whether simply inconvenient or potentially hazardous to your data or systems.

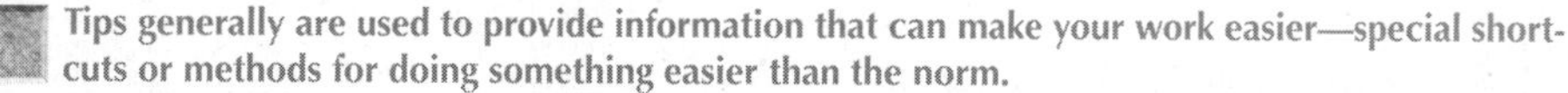

TIP Tips generally are used to provide information that can make your work easier—special shortcuts or methods for doing something easier than the norm.

NOTE Notes provide additional, ancillary information that is helpful but somewhat outside of the current presentation of information.

CROSS-REF Cross-references point you to other areas in the book that give more detail about the current topic.

The text also uses specific shortcuts for choosing commands:

- **Mouse.** When the text instructs you to choose a command from a menu or the Ribbon (in the new interface), the command is presented like this: "Choose Home ➪ Copy." That means to click the Home tab on the Ribbon and click the Copy choice. For another example, "Choose Office Button ➪ Save" means to click the Office Button and then click Save in the menu that appears. Some command sequences also may include a specific group after the Ribbon tab.
- **Keyboard.** Any keyboard shortcuts appear like this: Ctrl+C. That means to press the Ctrl key and C key simultaneously and then release them.

Where to Go from Here

Microsoft has released several versions of the Microsoft Office 2007 suite, with different versions including different applications. You can jump right to the parts that offer coverage for the applications offered in the flavor of Office that you own.

Part I

Common Office Features

IN THIS PART

Chapter 1

Welcome to Microsoft Office 2007

Microsoft Office 2007 provides a comprehensive toolkit for tackling your business and personal information and communication tasks. This chapter introduces the individual Office applications and teaches you skills for getting started using them.

Learning About Top Office Applications

Microsoft Office 2007 offers a robust set of applications, each tailor made to provide the best tools for a particular job. For example, if you're creating a letter, you may need to work with commands for formatting text. If you need to total sales figures, you'll need an automated way to sum the numbers.

Office provides an application to enable you to handle each of those scenarios and more. Read on to learn which Office applications to use for creating text-based documents, crunching numbers, presenting your ideas, or communicating with others via e-mail.

NOTE Microsoft offers eight different versions of the Microsoft Office 2007 software suite. Each version includes a different combination of the individual Office programs. Only Microsoft Office Word 2007 and Microsoft Office Excel 2007 are included in all eight versions. So, depending on the Office version you're using, you may not have all the applications described in this chapter and the book as a whole available to you.

Word

Word processing—typing, editing, and formatting letters, reports, fax cover sheets, and so on—is perhaps the most common activity performed with computers. Whether you need to create a memo at the office or a letter at home, using a computer and a word processing program can save you time and help you achieve polished results.

Microsoft Office Word has long been the leading word processing program. As one of the anchor applications in the Office suite, Word provides a host of document-creation tools that have been refined to be easy to use yet comprehensive. Using Word to apply just a minor bit of text formatting and a graphic can make even a simple document such as the meeting agenda shown in Figure 1-1 have more impact and Wow! appeal.

Word enables you to do even more than simply make your documents look great. Its features can help you create document text more quickly, create sophisticated documents with features such as footnotes, and more. You'll learn about these powerful Word features, among others, later in this book:

- **Templates.** A *template* is a starter document that supplies the document design, text formatting, and, often, placeholder text or suggested text. Add your own text and your document is finished!
- **Styles.** If you like a particular combination of formatting settings that you've applied to text, you can save the combination as a style that you can easily apply to other text.
- **Tables.** Add a table grid to organize text in a grid of rows and columns to which you can apply terrific formatting.
- **Graphics.** You can add all types of pictures into your documents and even create diagrams like the one in Figure 1-2 using the new SmartArt feature.

FIGURE 1-1

Microsoft Office Word 2007 enables you to create eye-catching documents.

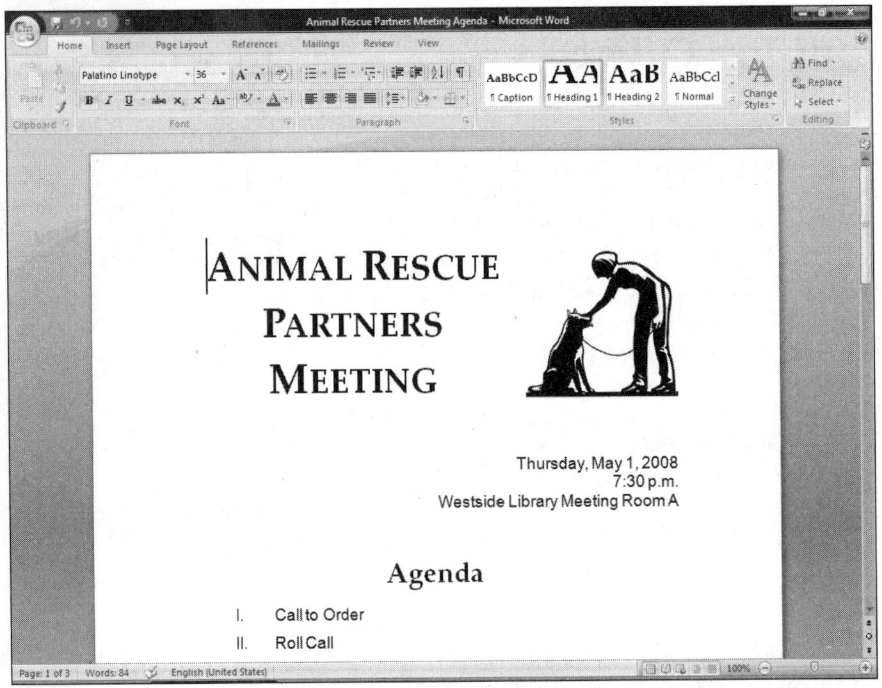

FIGURE 1-2

SmartArt diagrams illustrate information in a document.

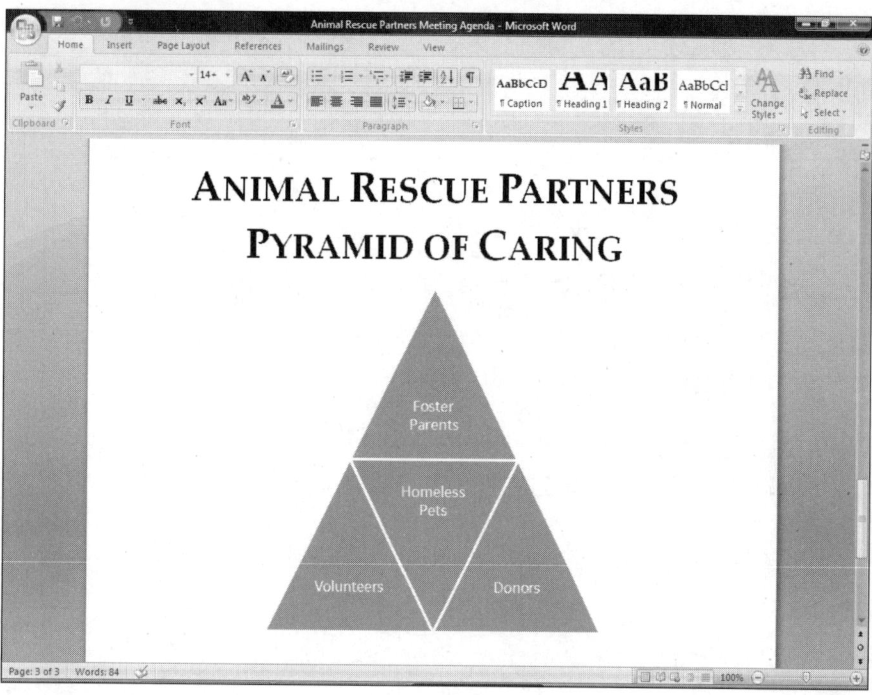

- **Mail Merge.** Create your own, customized "form letter" documents, for which each copy is automatically customized for a particular recipient (or list entry). Word's merge feature even enables you to create matching envelopes and labels.
- **Document Security and Review.** Word enables you to protect a document against unwanted changes, as well as to track changes made by other users. In this way, you can control the document content through a collaboration process.

Excel

Spreadsheet programs—which provide formulas and functions that make it easy to calculate numerical data—provided a critical technology leap in business computing. Business people no longer need to rely on adding machines, scientific calculators, or accountants to perform detailed sales or financial calculations. Even a beginning salesperson could plug some numbers into the spreadsheet grid and type a few formulas to calculate data. Microsoft Office Excel 2007, shown in Figure 1-3, performs the spreadsheet duties in the Microsoft Office suite.

FIGURE 1-3

Use the Microsoft Office Excel 2007 program to organize and calculate numerical data.

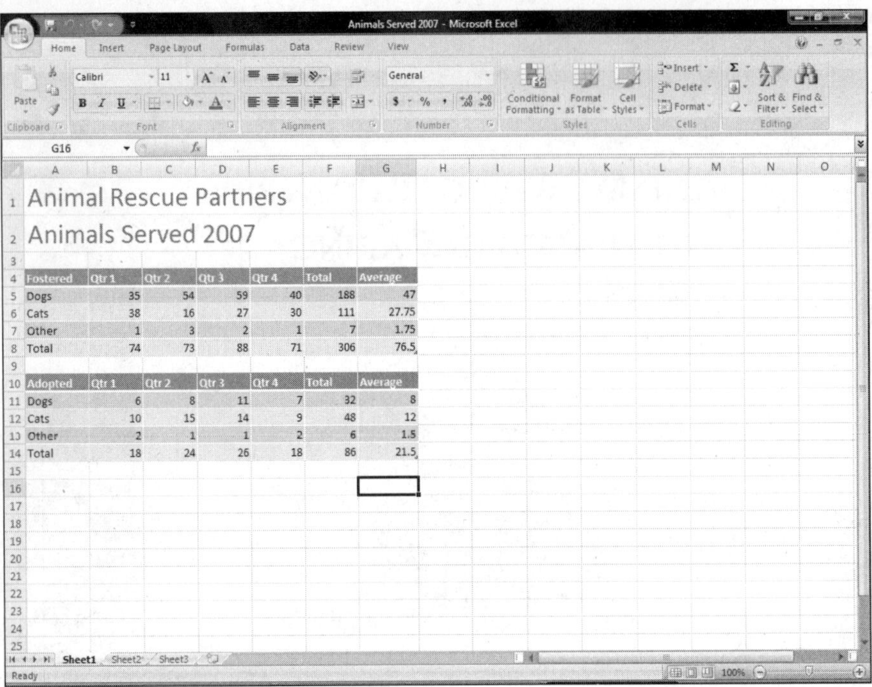

Excel enables you to build a calculation by creating a *formula* that specifies what values to calculate and what mathematical operators to use to perform the calculation. Excel also offers *functions*, predesigned formulas that perform more complex calculations, such as calculating accrued interest. Excel not only provides tools to assist you in building and error-checking spreadsheet formulas but also gives you many easy choices for formatting the data to make it more readable and professional. You'll learn these Excel essentials later in the book, as well as more about these key Excel features:

- **Worksheets.** Within each file, you can divide and organize a large volume of data across multiple *worksheets* or pages of information in the file.
- **Ranges.** You can assign a name to a section of data on a worksheet so that you can later select that area by name, or use the name in a formula to save time.
- **Number and Date Value Formatting.** You can apply a number format that defines how Excel should display a number, indicating details such as how many decimal points should appear and whether a percentage or dollar sign should be included. You also can apply a date format to determine how a date appears.
- **Charts.** Translate your data into a meaningful image by creating a chart in Excel (Figure 1-4). Excel offers dozens of chart types, layouts, and formats to help you present your results in the clearest way.

FIGURE 1-4

Excel's charting features help you make data more compelling and easier to evaluate.

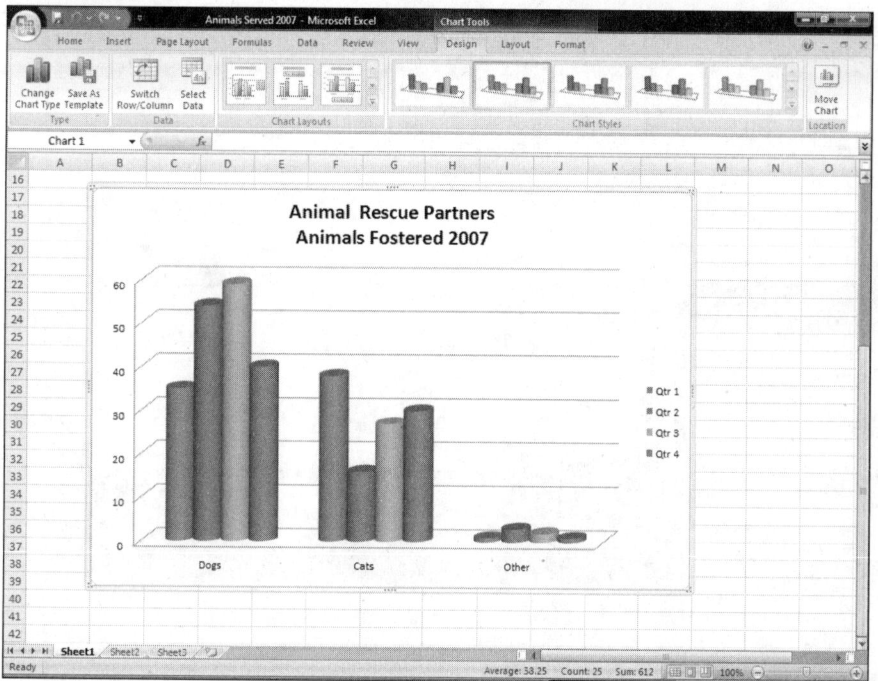

- **Lists.** You may need to manage and sort lists that combine text and numerical values, such as a list of product orders, and Excel can handle that job, too. Excel offers other powerful data features, such as the capability to apply a *filter* to see list entries with matching information.

PowerPoint

Persuading customers to buy. Convincing your company's leadership to invest in developing a new product you've conceived. Training members of your team to follow a new operating procedure. Making sure that a group of volunteers understands program requirements. To achieve positive outcomes in situations like these, you must deliver your message in a clear, concise, and convincing way.

The Microsoft Office PowerPoint 2007 *presentation graphics program* (Figure 1-5) enables you to communicate information and ideas via an onscreen *slide show* or printed pages. Each slide should present a key topic that you want to convey, along with a few supporting points or a graphical reinforcement such as a chart or picture. In this way, PowerPoint helps you to divide information into chunks that audience members can more easily absorb.

FIGURE 1-5

Use PowerPoint to present your message in informative slides.

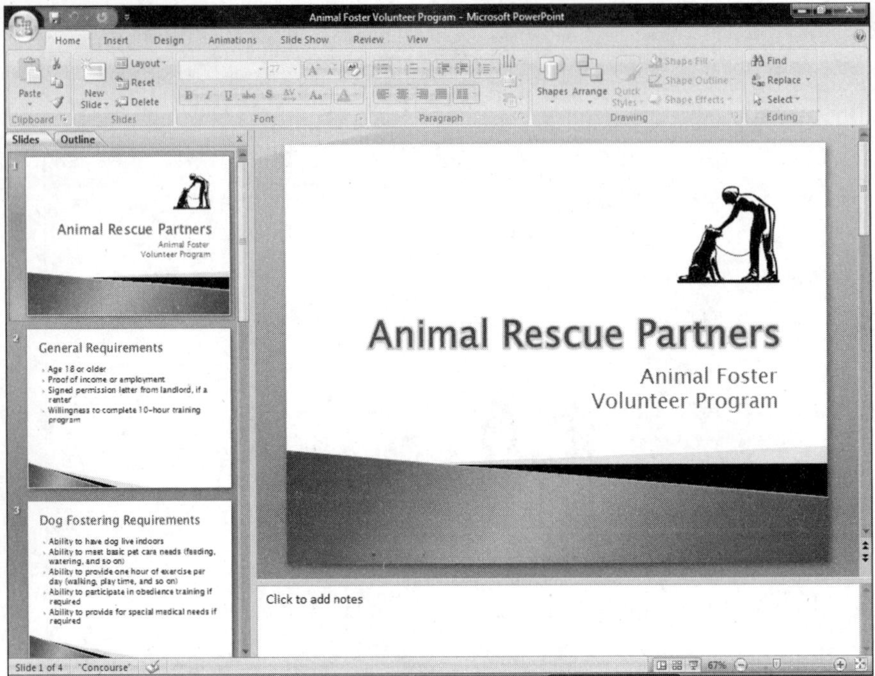

Later in the book, you learn not only how to create the basic presentation structure and add information but also to use the following PowerPoint features:

- **Layouts, Themes, and Masters.** These PowerPoint features control the content that appears on a slide and its arrangement, as well as the appearance of all the slides. You can quickly redesign a single slide or the whole presentation.
- **Tables and Charts.** As do Word and Excel, PowerPoint enables you to arrange information in an attractively formatted grid of rows and columns. PowerPoint works with Excel to deliver charted data, so the Excel charting skills you build make developing charts in PowerPoint even easier.
- **Animations and Transitions.** You can set up the text and other items on the slide to make a special entrance, such as fly onto the screen, when you play the slide show. In addition to applying *animations* to objects, you can apply a *transition* that animates how the overall slide appears onscreen, such as dissolving or wiping in.
- **Live Presentations.** PowerPoint offers a number of different ways in which you can customize and control how the presentation looks when played as an onscreen slide show. You learn tricks such as hiding slides or jumping between slides onscreen.

Outlook

Technology improvements naturally lead to business environments that move at a faster and faster pace. No one has the luxury to have a face-to-face conversation about every issue anymore, and everyone faces the challenge of tracking more and more contacts and to-dos. The Microsoft Office Outlook 2007 program in the Microsoft Office suite can handle your e-mail messages (Figure 1-6), appointment scheduling, contact information, and your to-do list. This program helps you stay in the loop, organized, and up-to-date with all the action in your work life.

FIGURE 1-6

Send and receive e-mail messages in Microsoft Outlook.

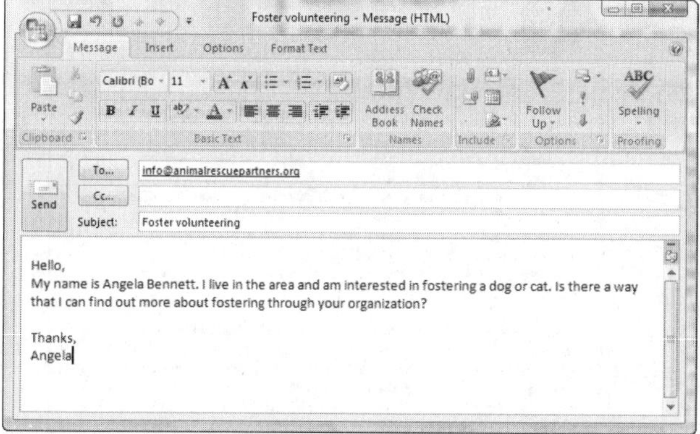

In addition to learning Outlook e-mail, scheduling, contact management, and to-do list basics later in the book, you also explore two additional but timely topics:

- **Security.** Learn which Outlook settings and tools help prevent messages with *viruses* from infecting your computer. Also learn how Outlook can automatically manage annoying yet pervasive junk mail messages.
- **RSS Feeds.** Outlook now enables you to subscribe to and read *RSS feeds* — online content posted by its authors for automatic download to your system (Figure 1-7). This capability stores the feed information for later reading or offline reading.

FIGURE 1-7

Outlook solves the need to read your RSS feed.

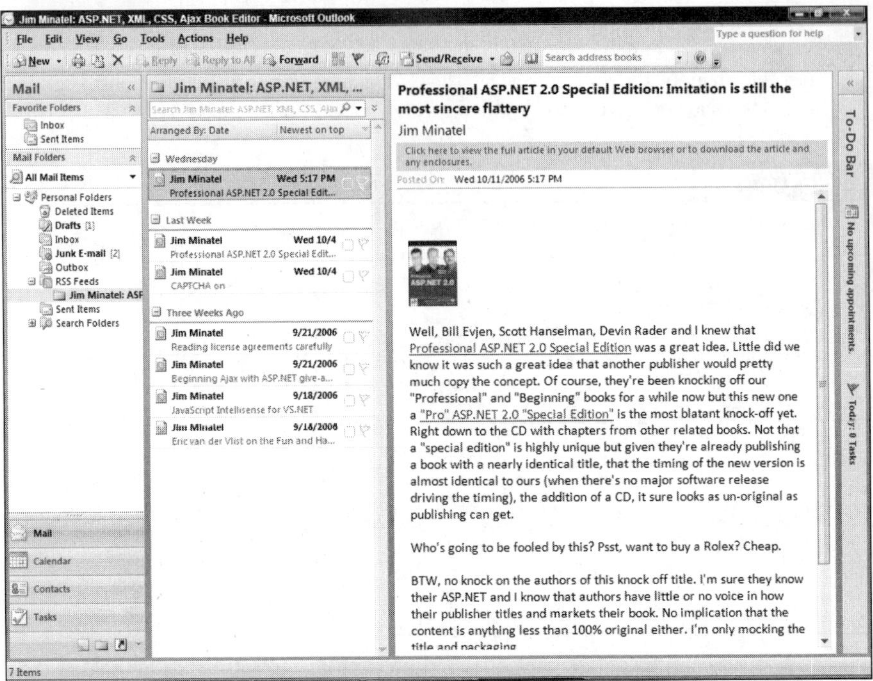

Taking Advantage of Other Office Applications

You may be a user whose needs extend beyond letter writing and number crunching. If you routinely take on special tasks such as creating printed publications or tracking extensive customer data, you may find yourself working with some of the other applications that are part of some editions of Microsoft Office 2007. This section gives you a snapshot of those other applications; later chapters of the book revisit these topics.

Publisher

Microsoft Office Publisher 2007 enables you to create publications, which have a greater emphasis on design than do word processing documents. To dummy-proof the creative process, Publisher includes attractive publication designs with placeholders for text and images and other features such as decorative rules and backgrounds already in place, as shown in Figure 1-8.

FIGURE 1-8

Publisher provides placeholders and design elements so that you can create interesting publications with minimal design know-how.

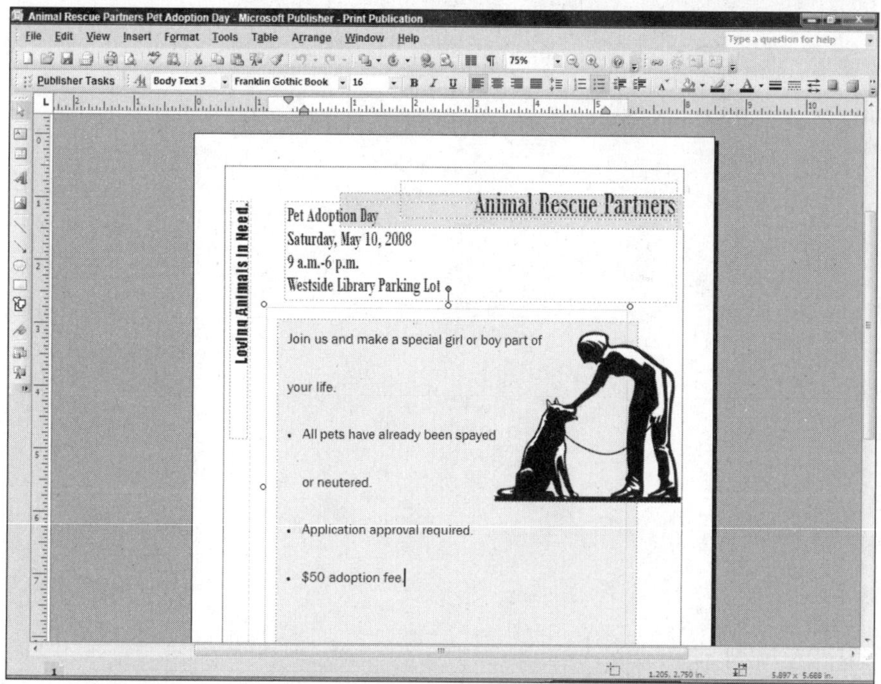

TIP **The distinction between documents and publications may seem fuzzy, but you can roughly think of a document as anything you'd print from an office printer — such as a report or proposal — compared to something you might have professionally printed, such as a business card or brochure.**

A later chapter shows you how to handle the Publisher basics of choosing a publication design and adding text and graphics. Then you'll learn to throw in snazzier effects such as drop caps and Design Gallery objects, and even how to prep a publication for professional printing.

Access

The Microsoft Office Access 2007 *database program* can certainly do the heavy lifting when it comes to managing detailed mountains of data such as customer, inventory, and order lists that may have hundreds or thousands of entries. The file that holds such lists is called a *database*. Each Access database file actually can hold multiple lists of data, each stored in a separate *table*, such as the Current Foster Animals table shown in Figure 1-9.

FIGURE 1-9

An Access database organizes lists of information in tables.

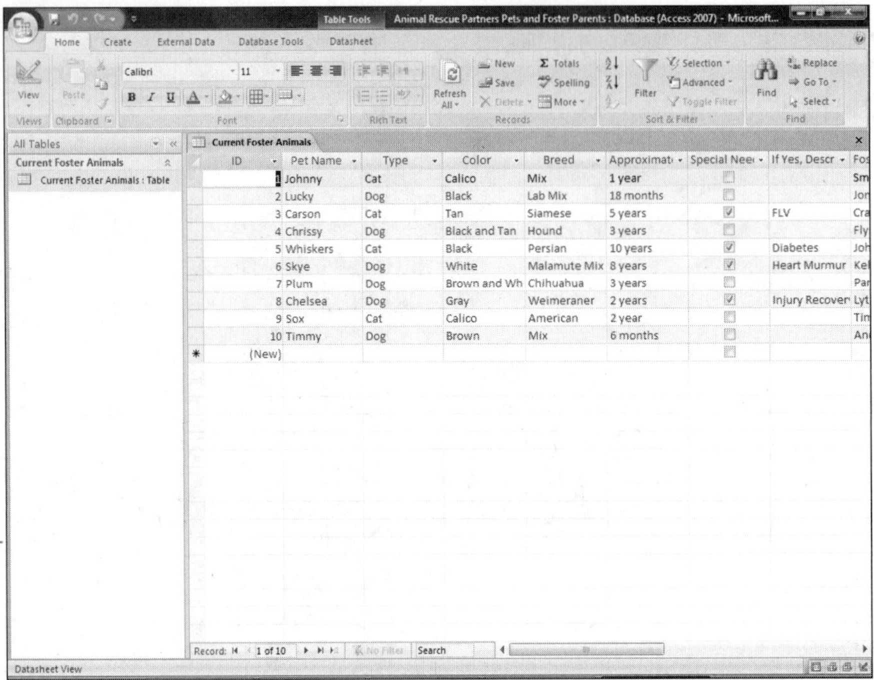

Access enables you to enter and view data using a *simple* form. You also can set up *queries* to pull sets of matching data out of the database and generate *reports* that consolidate and analyze data. Later chapters introduce you to these Access skills.

OneNote

It's a risky proposition to track your professional or educational life via notes scribbled on various scraps of paper or notebook pages. As the notes pile up, it becomes harder and harder to find relevant information, making you look as though you can't keep up. If you lose a scrap of paper containing a critical piece of information, you can put a project in jeopardy.

Microsoft Office OneNote 2007 (Figure 1-10) serves as a type of electronic scrapbook for notes, reference materials, and files related to a particular activity or project. Then, when you need to find all the "stuff" related to a particular project, you can flip right to the applicable notebook tab. You learn to get yourself together with OneNote in a later chapter.

FIGURE 1-10

Organize notes, files, pictures, and other material in a OneNote notebook.

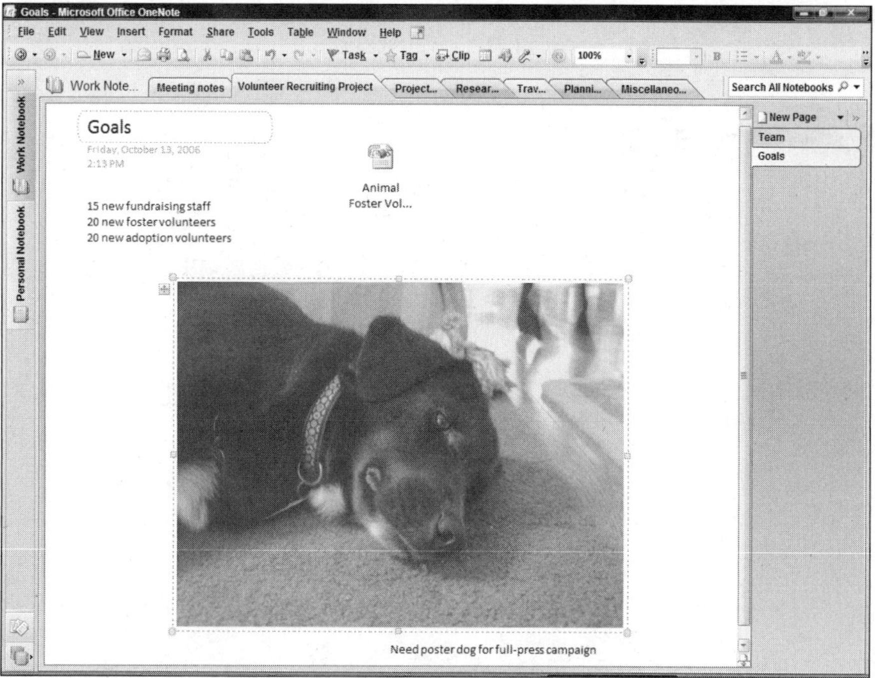

InfoPath

The Microsoft Office InfoPath 2007 application included with the higher-end Office versions may actually move us closer to that mythical land known as the "paperless office." InfoPath enables you to design electronic fill-in forms based on a template like the one shown in Figure 1-11. Each time a user fills in the form, the unique user data is stored in a separate location called a data source, in essence adding a new entry to that list. You'll get started with InfoPath forms later in the book, too.

FIGURE 1-11

Collect and store data via an InfoPath form template.

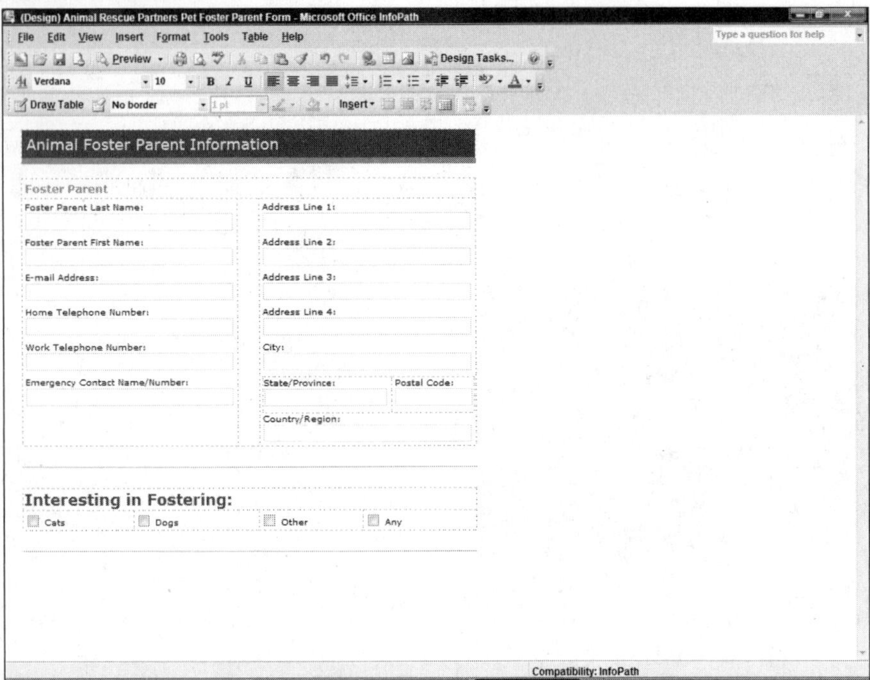

Starting an Application

Starting one of the Office applications loads that program and its tools into your computer system's *RAM* (working memory) so that you can begin working. If you've started an application in Windows XP or Windows Vista before, you'll probably be able to find the startup commands for the Office applications and load the program of your choice on your own (but skip ahead in this section for a new trick that applies in Vista).

Otherwise, use these steps to start an Office application in either Windows XP or Windows Vista:

1. **Click the Start button at the left end of the Windows taskbar.** The taskbar appears along the bottom of the Windows desktop. The Start menu opens.
2. **Click All Programs.** A list of available programs appears. In XP, it appears as a submenu of the Start menu. In Vista, the list appears in the left column of the Start menu.
3. **Click Microsoft Office.** The available Office programs appear.
4. **Click the desired Office program (Figure 1-12).** The program window appears onscreen.

FIGURE 1-12

Use the Start menu to start an Office program.

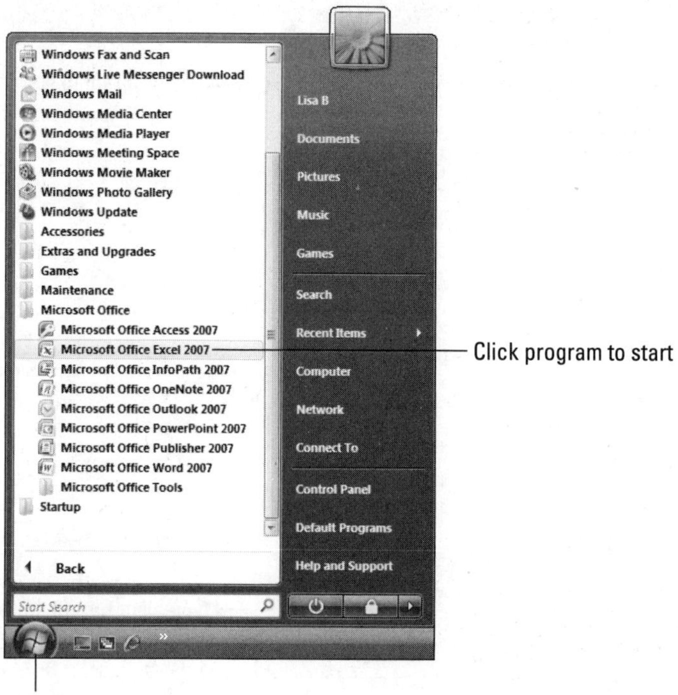

NOTE Some applications automatically open a new, blank file when you start them. Others prompt you to create a new file. Outlook automatically displays personal folder information, whereas OneNote opens the notebook page that you last worked with.

Vista provides you with a quick-and-dirty way to start any application, including the Office applications, as follows:

1. **Click the Start button on the taskbar.** The Start menu opens with the blinking insertion point in the Start Search text box at the bottom of the menu.
2. **Type all or part of the name of the application you want to start.** As shown in Figure 1-13, a list of matching applications (and files with the typed information in them) appears.
3. **Click the desired Office program.** The program window appears onscreen.

FIGURE 1-13

Typing a name in the Start Search text box lists matching programs.

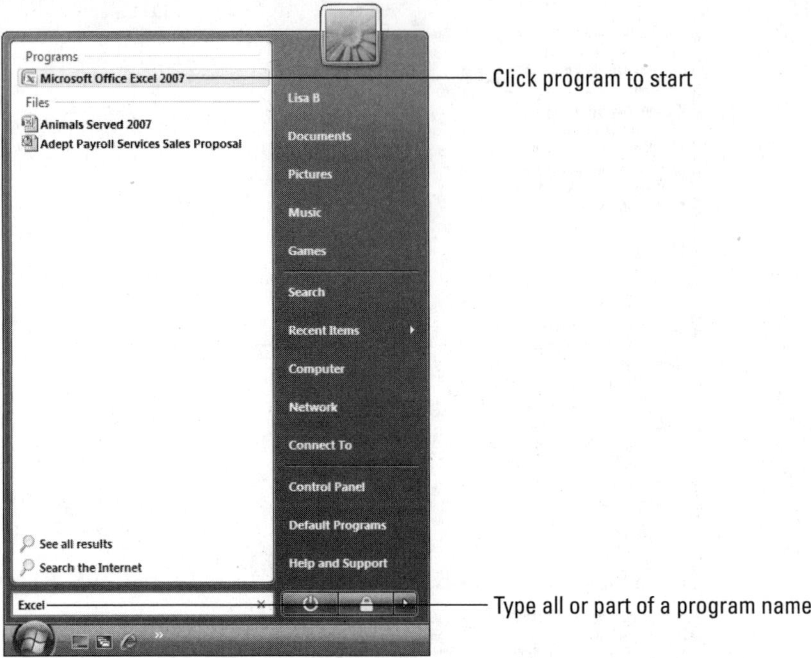

You also can create a desktop shortcut icon to use for program startup. To do so, drag the application name from the Start menu to the desktop. A shortcut icon will appear. You then can double-click that icon to start the program.

Closing an Application

When you finish your work in an application, shutting the application down removes it from system memory, freeing that memory for other uses. Closing the application also provides the benefit of closing any possibly sensitive open files to prevent unwanted viewing by others.

You can use one of three methods to shut down any program:

- Press Alt+F4.
- Click the Microsoft Office (File menu) Button (again, abbreviated in this book as *Office Button*), in the upper-left corner of the program window (see Figure 1-14); then, click Exit *Program Name*.
- Click the program window Close (X) button in the upper-right corner.

If you see a message box like the one in Figure 1-14, it means you haven't saved all your changes to the file. Click Yes to save your changes. Both the application and file close.

FIGURE 1-14

A prompt appears to remind you to save file changes.

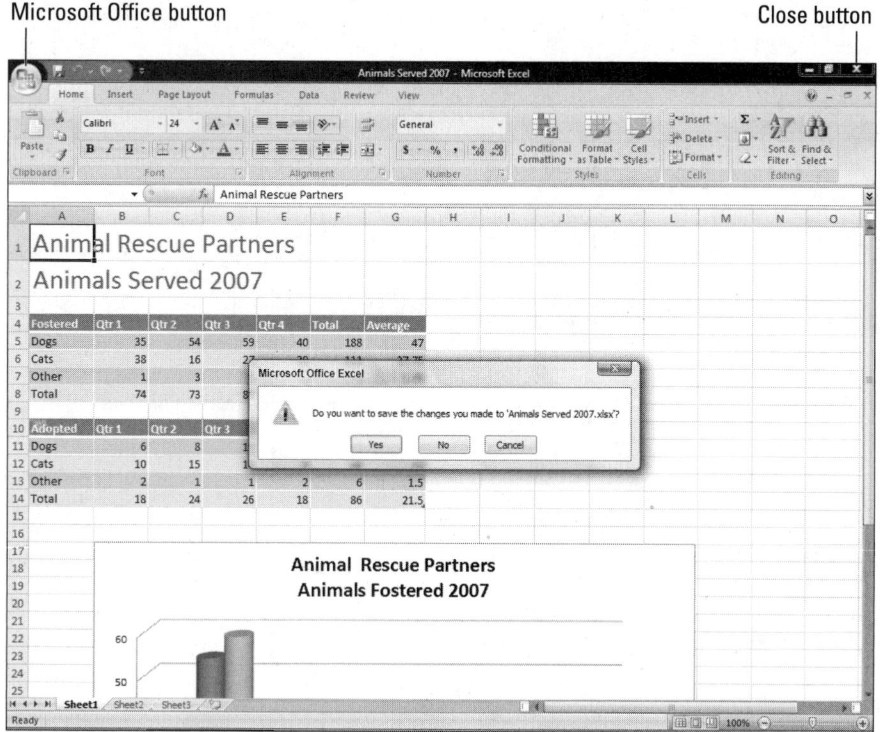

Finding Files

Searching through *folders* (named storage locations) on a computer's hard disk to try to find the file you want to work with sure can eat into your quality working time. If you're using Office with Windows Vista, you can take advantage of a couple of shortcuts that help you find a file on your system.

As shown back in Figure 1-13, making an entry in the Start Search text box displays not only matching programs but also files with the search text in the filename or file contents. So, you can enter all or part of the filename or topic in the Start Search text box on the file menu and then click the name of the file to open. The application used to create the file opens with the specified file in it.

Alternatively, you can work in the Open dialog box for any Office program to search for a file. Use these steps when you're already working in the application used to create the file:

1. **Click Office Button ➪ Open.** The Open dialog box appears.
2. **Click the up arrow button beside the Folders heading.** The folder tree appears.
3. **Select the folder that you think holds the file to find.** Its contents appear in the dialog box.

TIP **If you're not sure even of what folder holds the file, choose a higher-level folder or even a disk icon. Doing so will search more locations but means that the search may take more time.**

4. **Type the name of the file to search for in the Search text box in the upper-right corner of the dialog box.** As you type, the Open dialog box lists files with matching names or contents, as shown in Figure 1-15.

FIGURE 1-15

You can search for a file in the Open dialog box for any Office application running in Windows Vista.

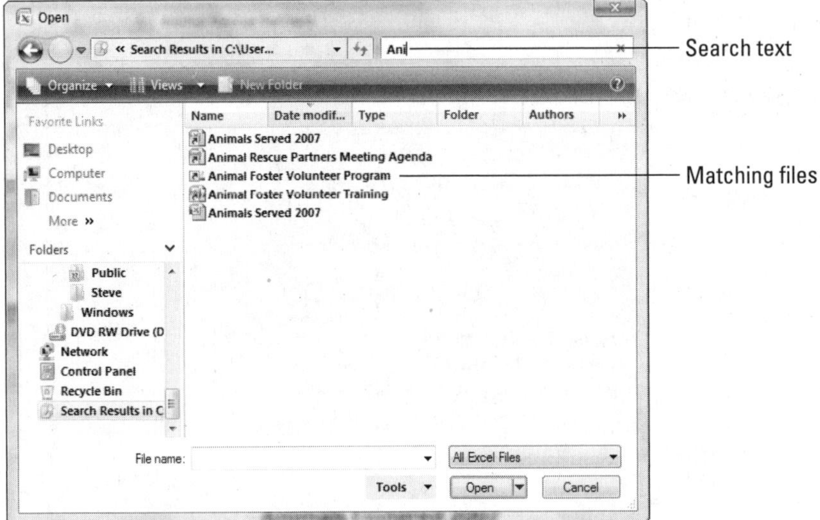

5. **Double-click the name of the file to open.** The file appears in the application.

NOTE **In Windows XP, you will still have search capabilities, too. Click the Start button and then click Search in the right column of the menu. Then click the Documents link under What Do You Want to Search For? to display the controls where you can enter information about the file you need. If you've already displayed the Open dialog box in an Office application running under XP, you can right-click any folder in the Open dialog box and then click Search in the shortcut menu to search for a file.**

Getting Help

Program features sometimes can seem a little obscure, and because the interface has been heavily redesigned in the Microsoft Office 2007 applications, you may get stuck from time to time when you're trying out a feature that you don't use every day. If you don't have this book handy, it's time to turn to another resource — the Help system for the application that you're using.

Browsing Help contents

Whether you have an Internet connection or not, you can explore and browse the basic Help that installs with each of the Office applications. To open the application's Help window, click the round Help (question mark) button at the right end of the Ribbon or press F1.

OneNote and InfoPath don't have a Help button, so in those applications, choose Help ➪ Microsoft Office *Program Name* Help to launch Help.

The Help window for the program appears and lists general help categories. Click a category to view available Help topics in that category (see Figure 1-16). In some cases, you may need to click a subcategory to display the topic you need. When you see the topic you need, you can click the Print button to print it. To move around to additional topics, use the Back and Forward buttons, as well as click additional links.

When you finish working in the Help window, click the window's Close button to finish.

FIGURE 1-16

Browse by clicking categories, subcategories, and topics.

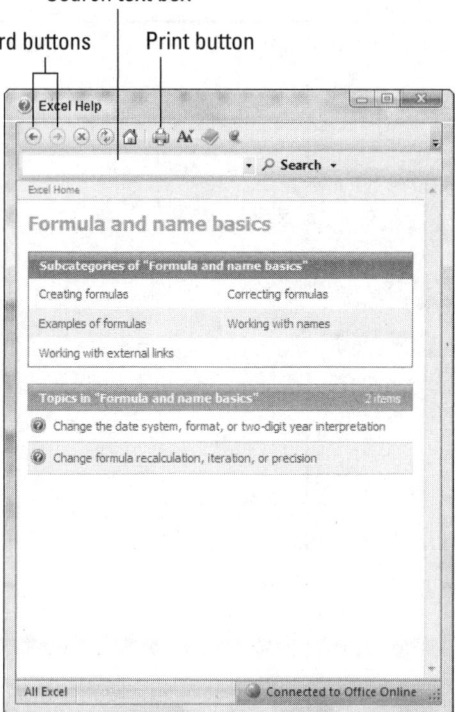

Searching Office online

You can search for help about a particular topic or question using the text box near the top of the Search window. If your system is already connected to the Internet, all you need to do is type the topic to search for into the text box and press Enter.

However, if you see Offline displayed in the right end of the status bar at the bottom of the Help window, you need to make sure that you're connected to search the online Help. Follow these steps to search in that way:

1. **Click the drop-down arrow for the Search button and click a choice under Content from Office Online in the menu (Figure 1-17).** The All *Program Name* choice searches all the online Help resources for that application, whereas any of the other choices under Content from Office Online target the Help search to a specific type of information.
2. **Type the search topic into the Search text box.**
3. **Press Enter.** The list of matching Help topics appears.
4. **Click the desired topic.** The Help for the topic appears in the Help window.

FIGURE 1-17

You can request that Office go back online for Help.

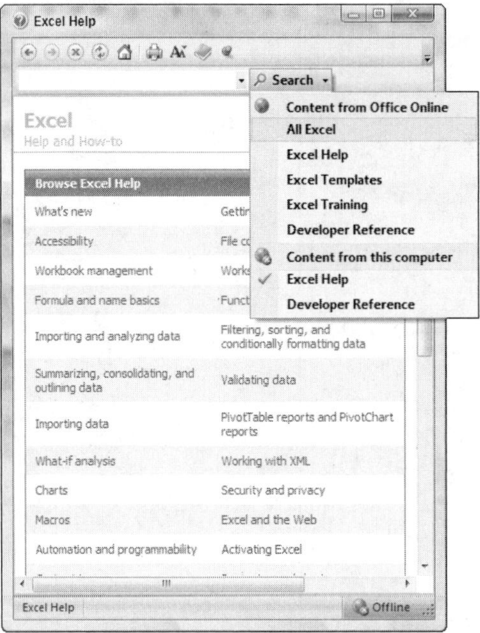

NOTE **Whether you browsed for Help while already connected to the Internet or you forced the Help window to search online, in some cases clicking a Help topic link will launch your system's Web browser and display the Help and resources there, rather than in the Help window.**

TIP If you click the Search button drop-down arrow as noted in the preceding Step 1, you can click the Word Help choice under Content From This Computer to search only help installed on your system with Word. For simple questions, this method might display the right Help topic a bit more quickly.

Summary

This chapter introduced the programs that are part of the Microsoft Office 2007 system. You learned about core features in the Word (word processing), Excel (spreadsheet), PowerPoint (presentation graphics), and Outlook (e-mail and scheduling) programs. You also learned that you can perform more specialized business functions with Publisher (publication design), Access (database), OneNote (information management), and InfoPath (forms). You moved on to learn how to start and close any application in Microsoft Office, how to find a file that's not quite at your fingertips, and how to use offline and online Help when you need to learn more.

Chapter 2

Navigating in the New Office

Welcome to Oz. Whether you're a brand-new user to the Office applications or a veteran Office user, this chapter bids you welcome to the 2007 version. If you're new to Office 2007, this chapter provides an overview of what very likely is a user interface unlike any you've encountered previously.

If you're completely new to Office and have been using other applications such as WordPerfect or 1-2-3, you're likely more accustomed to toolbars and menus than you are to Office 2007's Ribbons, so when I contrast Office 2007's Ribbons with the previous interface, you'll likely immediately grasp just how different the primary Office 2007 applications are, even if you never touched an Office 2003 program.

The Ribbon is a completely new way of presenting tools and features to users of Word, Excel, PowerPoint, and Access. (Outlook message windows use the Ribbon, too.) Briefly, the *Ribbon* is a set of contextual tools designed to put what you need where you need it when you need it. When you click one of the major *tabs* on the Ribbon, the tools you need for specific tasks should mostly be right where you need them. The ideal result is that you don't need to go looking for what you want.

In fact, the Ribbon might actually be considered a new kind of toolbar. Instead of a list of different toolbars accessed from the View menu, however, the different parts of the Ribbon are organized into tabs and groups. The result is that more of the tools are exposed to you, making it more likely that you'll discover what you need.

If you've used other versions of the main Office applications in the past, the 2007 versions will seem strange and different. Imagine that you left earth in the year 1994 — the last time that the Office interface was overhauled — and returned in the year 2007. Over the ensuing thirteen years, the interface slowly morphed from menus and toolbars into the Ribbon.

IN THIS CHAPTER

When considered from an evolutionary perspective, perhaps the 2007 versions of Word, Excel, PowerPoint, and Access don't look so different. What you, the space traveler, do not realize, however, is that the radical changes occurred not slowly and gradually over more than a decade, but in one giant leap from Office 2003 to Office 2007, only 15 minutes before you landed. Everybody who stayed right here on Earth is just as stunned as you are.

NOTE **The other Office 2007 applications covered in this book — Publisher, OneNote, and InfoPath — retain the old menu and toolbar interface. Outlook retains the old interface for its main window, but uses the Ribbon in message windows.**

Discoverability

If past versions of Office were driven mostly by *functionality* and *usability*, Office 2007's catchwords are *discoverability* and *results*. For example, studies show that typical Word users use only a fraction of the myriad features contained in Word. Yet, the same studies show that users often employ the wrong feature. For example, rather than use an indent setting, a user might press the spacebar five times (gasp!) or press the Tab key once (again gasp, but not quite as loud).

Microsoft's challenge, therefore, was to design an interface that made discovering the right features easier, more direct, and more deliberate.

Have they succeeded? Well, you'll have to be the judge. To some, the new interface succeeds only in being different and in making Office novices out of those who previously were Office experts. Whether it makes things easier for beginners, ultimately easier for casual users, or simply more difficult for veteran users, remains to be seen.

Let's suppose you want to create a table. Assuming for the moment that you even know that a table is what you want, in Word 2003 and earlier you might choose Table ➪ Draw Table or Table ➪ Insert ➪ Table from the menu. Or, perhaps you would click the Table tool on the Standard toolbar, assuming you recognize the icon as possessing that functionality.

The point is that you had to navigate sometimes dense menus or toolbars in order to find the needed functionality — perhaps not even knowing what that functionality was called. It's akin to wandering through a hardware store looking for something that will twist a spiraling piece of metal into a piece of wood, without knowing whether such a tool actually exists. You don't even know what the piece of metal is called, so you wander about, and finally discover, to your utter delight, the perfect tool . . . a hammer. Oops! There's an old saying: When the only tool you have is a hammer, everything looks like a nail.

Like a hammer, the time-proven spacebar has been used countless times to perform chores for which it was never intended. Yes, a hammer can compel a screw to join two pieces of wood together; and a spacebar can be used to move text around so it looks like a table. However, just as a hammered screw makes for a shaky wooden table, a word processing table fashioned together using spaces is equally fragile. Add something to the table and it doesn't hold together. Which table? Take your pick.

In the main Office 2007 applications, there are no dense menus and toolbars. To insert a table in Word — again assuming you even know a table is what you're looking for — you stare at the Home Ribbon and see nothing that looks remotely like a table.

Thinking "insert" may be what you need, you click on the Insert tab, and there you see a grid with the word Table under it. You click Table, move the mouse, and perhaps you see what's shown in Figure 2-1, as an actual table is previewed inside your document, changing as the mouse moves. Epiphany!

FIGURE 2-1

Office 2007's "Live Preview" shows the results of the currently selected Ribbon action.

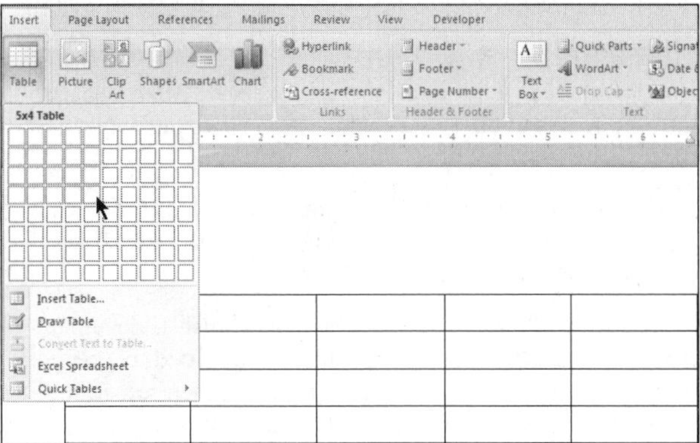

Epiphany? Perhaps, or maybe just a new wrinkle. Be that as it may, the new Office 2007 apps bring with them a number of improvements in performance, stability, design elements, interoperability, and document integrity that ultimately can improve the quality of your documents and make them faster and easier to create. Whether the new interface excites you or annoys you, the fact that the new format makes it harder to corrupt documents should make you smile.

If you've ever spent endless hours wrestling with a document because its numbering is haunted by ghosts that won't let you do what you need to do, you will find relief in Office 2007. More on this in Chapter 3, but for now, you might be happy to know that some of the proprietary file formats in Office applications have been replaced by formats that use XML (eXtensible Markup Language). XML is an open format in the public domain. At its heart are plain text commands that can be resolved by Office applications and a variety of other programs. The bottom line for the user is that the mysterious so-called *binary* format is gone, meaning that Office documents are now harder to corrupt. When and if they do get corrupted, your work is easier to salvage.

NOTE **If you're a glutton for punishment or you like taking risks, the Word, Excel, and PowerPoint 2007 applications still support the legacy file formats. You can even tell the applications to always save documents in earlier formats. This is a good option when you share your work with users of 2003 versions and earlier. For those same 2003 users (as well as 2000 and 2002 version users), however, Microsoft provides a free compatibility pack that enables them to read and write Word, Excel, and PowerPoint 2007 documents (although 2007–specific enhancements will be lost in the translation). To find the compatibility pack, visit** `http://office.microsoft.com`**.**

The "Results-Oriented" User Interface

If you're like most users, when you begin a letter or a report, the first thing you do is check whether you've ever written a letter or report like the one you are about to write. If you have written something similar, then you very likely will open it and use it as a starting point.

When my daughter needs a written excuse for school, rather than write a brand-new letter each time, I search my stock of documents for whatever I have that is closest to the current need.

If you don't have a document to use as a starting point, then you check whether there's an existing template in the Office application's repertoire. Failing there, you might search online. Indeed, it's not uncommon to come across questions in online communities or newsgroups asking if anyone has a particular type of template, e.g., "Does anyone have a template for a resignation letter?" I just love replying to that kind of request: *Dear Meat for Brains Boss* . . . but, I digress.

Knowing that most people don't prefer to begin documents with a clean slate, so to speak, Microsoft has redesigned Office to give users what they want. The goal is to offer users a collection of results they are probably seeking, to save time and guesswork.

They have done this in a variety of ways. One of the most prominent ways is the expanded use of galleries of already formatted options. Coupled with this is something called *Live Preview,* which instantly shows the user the effect of a given option in the current document — not in a preview window!

Rather than focus on a confusing array of tools, the Ribbon instead shows a variety of finished document parts or building blocks. It then goes on to provide context-sensitive sets of effects — also tied to Live Preview. These are designed to help you sculpt those into, if not exactly what you want, then something close. The objective at each step is to help you achieve results quickly, rather than combing through myriad menus and toolbars to discover possibilities. If nothing else, the new interface eliminates several steps in what necessarily has been a process of trial and error.

In addition, with each result, Office 2007's new context-sensitive Ribbon changes to show you additional tools that seem most likely appropriate for or relevant to the current document part that is selected. For example, if a picture is selected in Word, then the Format tab on the Ribbon displays context-sensitive Picture Tools, as shown in Figure 2-2.

FIGURE 2-2

When a picture is selected, the Format tab of the Ribbon displays context-sensitive Picture Tools; the result of the Picture Style gallery selection (Bevel Perspective, in this case) is previewed in the document.

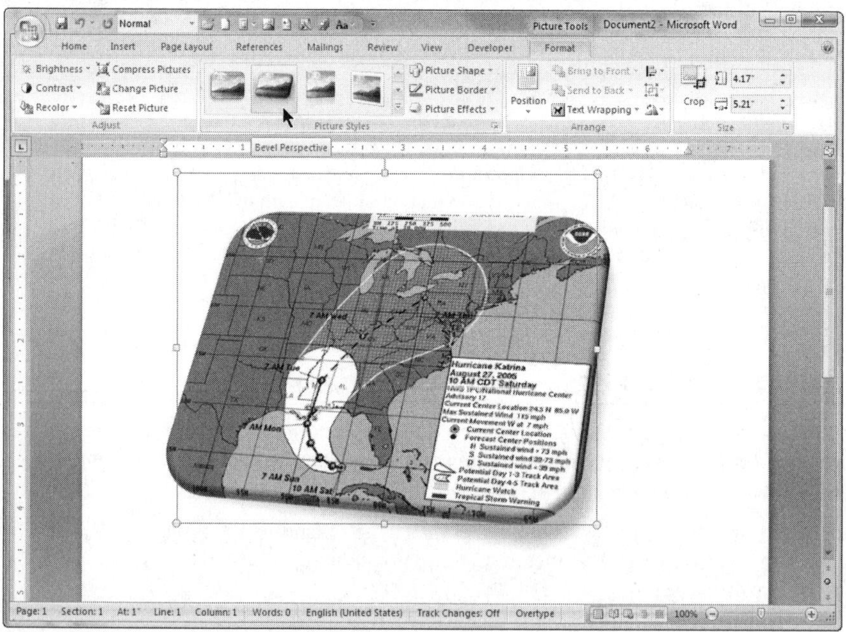

With each action, the Office application displays a likely set of applicable tools on the Ribbon. As the mouse pointer moves over different gallery options, such as the picture styles shown here, the image in the actual document shows a Live Preview of the effect of that choice. As you navigate the Ribbon to additional formatting options and special effects, the Live Preview changes to reflect the currently selected choice, as shown in Figure 2-3.

FIGURE 2-3

Live Preview shows the result of the selected formatting or effect.

In addition to providing a Live Preview of many formatting options, Microsoft has also greatly enhanced and expanded the range of different effects and options. The result, optimally, is documents that look more polished and professional than was possible previously.

Ribbons and Things

At the heart of Office 2007's results-oriented interface is the *Ribbon*. The Ribbon is the area above the document workspace, as shown in the example from Word 2007 (Figure 2-4). Technically, I suppose, the Ribbon is just the area below the tabs for Home, Insert, and so on. Clicking a tab with Home, Insert, Page Layout, and so on controls which Ribbon tab is displayed.

FIGURE 2-4

Word 2007's Ribbon, shown with the Home tab displayed, on a 19-inch monitor using normal-size fonts.

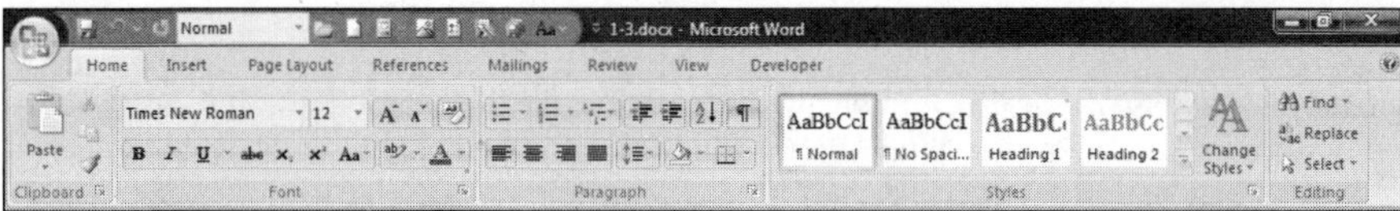

Exactly what you see in any given Ribbon tab is determined by a number of factors, including the size of your monitor, your screen resolution, the size of the current Office program window, as well as whether you're using Windows' display settings to accommodate low vision. Hence, what *you* see might not always be what you see pictured in this book. If you have a very large monitor operating at comparatively high resolution, you will see many more of the available options, such as on the Word Home tab shown in Figure 2-5.

FIGURE 2-5

At the highest resolution and largest screen size, the Ribbon displays additional gallery options and text labels.

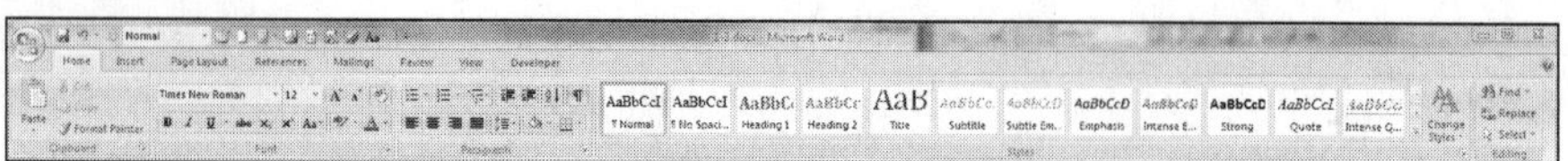

NOTE In Figure 2-5 Word's Home tab Ribbon shows 12 styles from the style gallery, as well as additional tools and text labels in the Clipboard and Editing groups. This is the maximum amount of information you will ever see in the Home tab Ribbon. To "shoot" this picture, Word was stretched across two 19-inch monitors, and additional detail stopped appearing when Word was 35 inches wide. Therefore, if you're wondering whether you need a 52-inch monitor for Office 2007, you'll be happy to know that a 42-inch model would work just fine.

TIP Ctrl+F1 toggles the Ribbon on and off. At times — especially at first — the Ribbon is going to look overly large to you. It will also seem imposing when you're simply reading a document or when you're trying to develop formulas in a worksheet. The Ribbon might also be distracting if all you're doing is entering and formatting information and are fluent in the keystrokes you need to perform basic formatting. For those times, there is Ctrl+F1. To turn the Ribbon off using the mouse, double-click the current tab; click any tab to turn it back on temporarily. It will automatically hide when you're done using it. Double-click any tab or press Ctrl+F1 to turn it back on full-time.

Title bar

The top bar of the current Office application window is called the *title bar,* exhibited in Figure 2-6. Double-clicking the title bar toggles the Office application between maximized and restored states. It's the equivalent of alternately clicking the Maximize and Restore buttons at the right end of the title bar.

FIGURE 2-6

The title bar

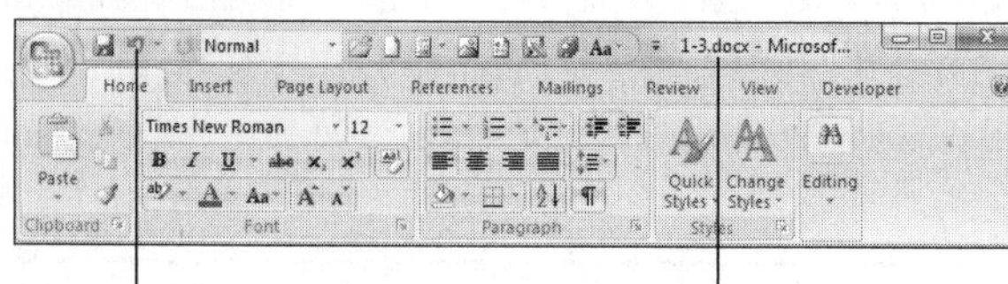

The title bar contains the *Quick Access Toolbar* (optionally), the name of the document in the current application window, and buttons for controlling the application window. If you've turned off the "Show all windows in the Taskbar" option (Office Button ➪ *Program Name* Options ➪ Advanced ➪ Display section), then these buttons control all of the application, rather than just the current document window. In your own installation, the title bar might contain other elements as well, such as items placed there by various Office and Windows add-ins.

TIP **Right-click different areas of the title bar for available options. For example, if you right-click the Quick Access Toolbar (QAT), you'll see that it can be customized or placed below the Ribbon; any tool on it can be instantly removed as well. If you right-click the middle area of the title bar, you'll see a shortcut menu with commands for working with the window (Move, Size, Minimize, etc.). You also can display this menu by pressing Alt+spacebar.**

The tab row

Shown below the title bar in Figure 2-6 is a row with the Ribbon tabs. I'm not sure if it has an official name, so I'll use "tab row" here. In addition to the tabs themselves, which control which Ribbon is displayed, this line contains the Help button (which replaces Help ➪ Microsoft *Application Name* Help from Office 2003 and earlier). If you've turned off the "Show all windows in the Taskbar" option (Office Button ➪ *Program Name* Options ➪ Advanced ➪ Display section), addition document and window control buttons will be present.

You can select a Ribbon tab using the mouse or using hot keys. Unlike in previous versions of the Office applications, however, there are no underlined letters showing you the hot keys.

As noted earlier, double-clicking the currently selected tab hides the Ribbon. Double-click any tab to unhide it. Ctrl+F1 toggles the Ribbons on and off as well. Once the Ribbon has been turned off, you can temporarily turn it back on by clicking a tab (or pressing its hot key). Once you've used a tool in that tab, the Ribbons automatically go back into hiding.

Key Tips

If there are no underlined letters, then how do you know which keys to press? Tap the Alt key. As shown in Figure 2-7, when you tap the Alt key, shortcut keys that work in the current context are displayed. "In the current context" might seem like an odd way to phrase it. Why context is relevant will become clear when we talk more about the Ribbon (described in the following section). For now, however, if you're working in a Word document, pressing Alt+H will display the Home Ribbon, Alt+N displays the Insert Ribbon, and so on.

FIGURE 2-7

Tap the Alt key to display the Ribbon tab's context-sensitive hot keys.

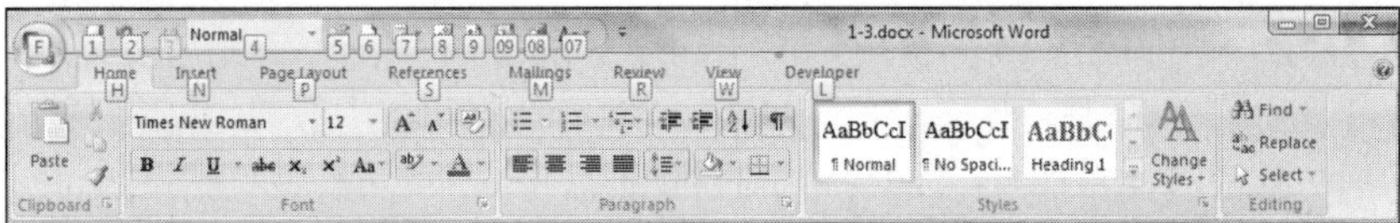

Note that I've added some additional tools to the QAT shown in Figure 2-7, and that numbered hot keys are associated with them. In addition to the first nine being accessible using Alt+1 through Alt+9, the last three are accessible using Alt+09, Alt+08, and Alt+07.

Ribbon

The Ribbon is divided into a number of different tabs that ostensibly correspond to each application's former menus. Unlike 2003's menus, however, there are no expanded drop-down lists under each main menu item. Instead, each tab exposes a different set of command buttons. Note that in Figure 2-4, the Home tab's choices are exposed. Contrast that with Figure 2-8, which displays the Insert tab of the Ribbon.

FIGURE 2-8

Each of the tabs exposes a different set of commands; the Insert tab is shown here.

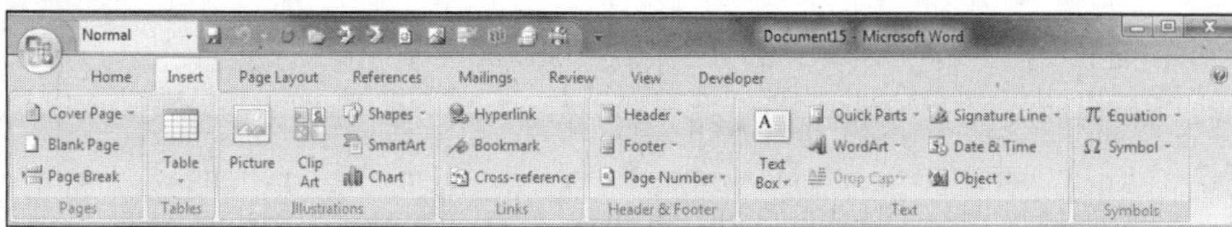

Note that the number of Ribbon tabs you see also varies according to user settings. In Figure 2-8 you can see the Developer tab. On your own setup, that tab might not appear.

Groups

We've already talked about the Ribbon — now it's time to explore a few tricks and some odd nomenclature. At the bottom of the Ribbon tab shown in Figure 2-7, note the names Clipboard, Font, Paragraph, Styles, and Editing. These are known as *groups*. Each group contains individual tools or controls.

If you're a veteran Office user — perhaps even if not — you've probably been wondering what to do, for example, if the Ribbon is displaying the Page Layout tab, and you really want to access the Home tab's Editing tools (the group that contains Find, Replace, Go To, and Select).

NOTE **In this book, Ribbon command sequences typically name the Ribbon tab, the group, and then the specific button or option. So, for example, "Select Page Layout ⇨ Page Setup ⇨ Orientation" is telling you to choose the Orientation drop-down in the Page Setup group on the Page Layout tab of the Ribbon.**

In previous incarnations of Office applications, access to commonly used commands was always available via the menu, and often via the Standard and Formatting toolbars. Indeed, they are always available here as well, sort of. When the Page Layout tab (or any other) is displayed, you can access any of the Home tab items simply by pressing Alt, H (in sequence), or by clicking the Home tab.

What if you want to remained focused on Page Layout?

Any item on the Ribbon — individual tools, groups, and even dialog box launchers — can be added to the QAT. For example, right-click Bold and choose Add to Quick Access Toolbar. Now Bold will be available all the time, regardless of which Ribbon tab is displayed. Did I mention that Q stands for Quick? Don't want Bold there? Right-click it and choose Remove from Quick Access Toolbar.

Let's try another navigation trick. Tap Alt+P (Page Layout tab). Now press the arrow keys. If you're unsteady with the mouse, you can use the four arrow keys to navigate. You can also use Tab and Shift+Tab to move forward or backward through all of the Ribbon commands. When you get to a command you want to use, press either the spacebar or the Enter key.

NOTE In the previous section, I mentioned that hot keys are context-sensitive. Shouldn't hot keys work the same way all the time? One would think so. Alas, Microsoft does not agree, so while 1 might activate the first QAT command when the Home tab in Word is displayed, you cannot count on it always doing the same thing. If you press Alt+H, now the 1 key applies bold formatting. Hence, context is vital. If you're a touch typist who hardly ever looks at the screen, good luck. Meanwhile, press Alt+P and try not to laugh (or cry) when you notice that some commands have two — not one — hot keys. Any idea why AY means Rotate? Me neither.

Contextual tools

In addition to the default set of main tabs, additional context-sensitive or *contextual tabs* appear depending on what kind of document part or object is selected. For example, if you choose Insert ➪ Header and insert a header from the Header gallery in Word, the Design tab displays contextual Header &Footer tools, as shown in Figure 2-9.

FIGURE 2-9

When a header is selected, the Design tab displays Header & Footer contextual tools.

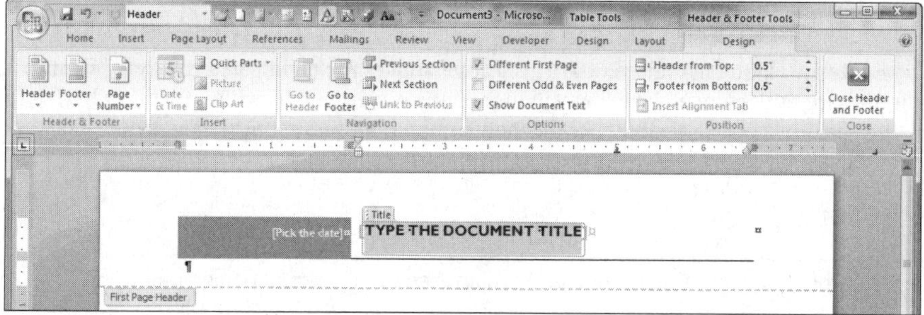

Notice that because this particular header format is enclosed in a table, the Table Tools tab is also exposed. The Table Tools tab has Design and Layout subtabs, each of which is also available in the current view.

TIP As you are becoming acclimated to Office 2007, whenever a new tab appears, you should click it to explore what it has to offer. Think of contextual tabs as hidden drawers that might contain money! This is an aspect of Office 2007's *discoverability*. If you don't like the design choice in a given gallery, you very likely can change it (and even add new or changed items to the gallery for future use — more on this later).

Quick Access Toolbar

If you are a veteran Office user, you might be asking, "Where have all the toolbars gone?" If you're a long-time veteran, in fact, you might be screaming that question at the top of your lungs, perhaps adding a colorful expletive or two. All of the toolbars have been collapsed into the single and less flexible Quick Access Toolbar, or QAT, as it is rapidly becoming known (the exact pronunciation is still under negotiation). Shown above the Ribbon in Figure 2-10, the QAT can also be placed below the Ribbon, where there is more room.

FIGURE 2-10

The Quick Access Toolbar (QAT) replaces all of Office's earlier user-customizable toolbars.

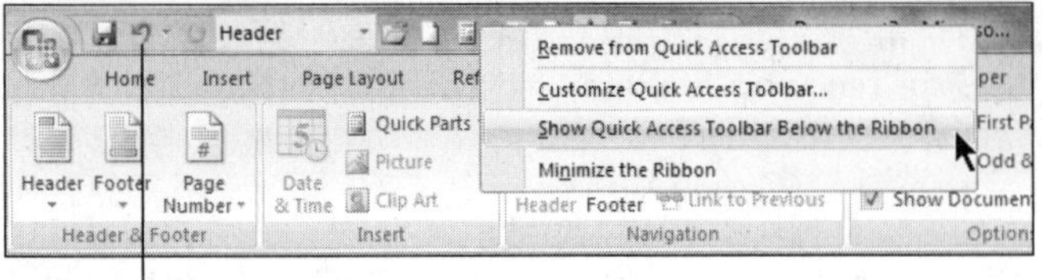

NOTE **If you have custom templates that rely heavily upon carefully crafted custom toolbars and menus, there's good news and bad news. The good news is that some of those toolbars might actually still work in Office 2007. Look for them in the Add-Ins Ribbon. The bad news is that Office 2007 no longer contains customization tools that let you create and modify multiple toolbars.**

Live Preview

Live Preview is a brand-new feature in Office 2007. This feature applies the highlighted gallery formatting to the selection in the current document, enabling you to instantly see the results without actually having to apply that formatting, as shown in Figure 2-11. As the mouse pointer moves among the different gallery options, the formatting displayed in the body of the document instantly changes.

FIGURE 2-11

Live Preview, showing the results of the Intense Quote style in Word applied to the current paragraph.

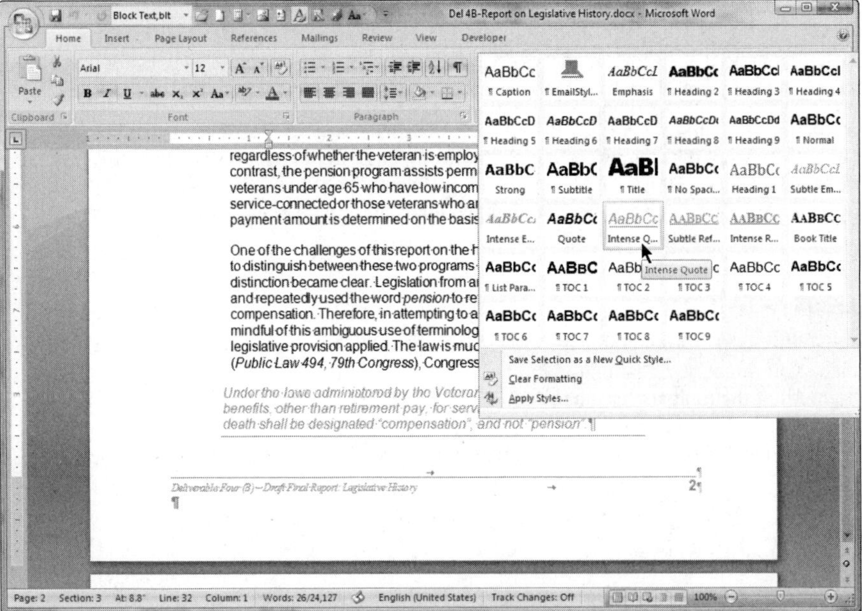

Note that not all galleries and formatting options produce Live Preview results. For example, in the Page Layout tab in Word, none of the Page Setup items produce Live Previews, nor do the paragraph settings on that tab.

Another time you won't see Live Preview is when working with dialog boxes, such as the Paragraph dialog box in Word. Many of those offer internal Preview sections but do not take advantage of Office 2007's new Live Preview capability.

A gotcha in all this newfangled functionality is that sometimes the gallery itself covers up all or part of the Live Preview. This gets old quickly, and can negate much of the functionality, unless you're blessed with unlimited screen real estate. Maybe that 52-inch monitor isn't such a bad idea after all.

Fortunately, some galleries and controls have draggable borders that enable you to see more of what you're trying to preview, as shown in Figure 2-12. If a control's border is draggable, this is indicated by three dots. Notice the three dots in the lower-right corner of the Styles Gallery in Figure 2-11, and in the bottom border of Theme Fonts in Figure 2-12. On the lower-right corner, the three dots indicate that the border can be rolled up and to the left. On the bottom, the three dots indicate that the border can be rolled up.

FIGURE 2-12

Some Live Preview controls can be rolled up to reveal document details that otherwise would be covered.

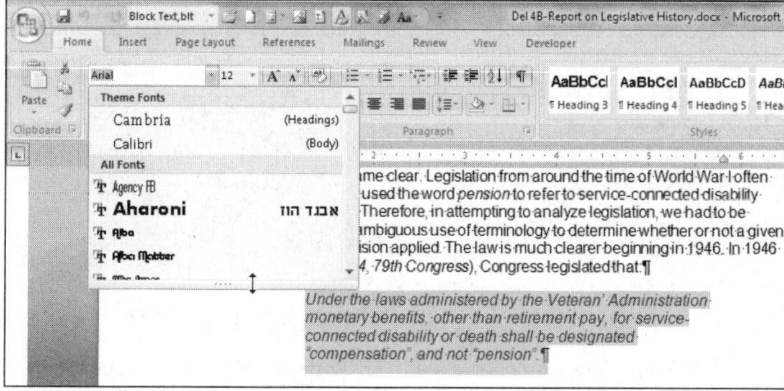

Sometimes, however, it's easiest simply to go ahead and apply the formatting, rather than jump through hoops. If necessary, you can always use the venerable Ctrl+Z (Undo) if you don't like the result.

CAUTION **When using Live Preview, it's very easy to forget to click the desired gallery or formatting command when you come to it. Particularly in extensive lists (such as lists of fonts, colors, or styles), it's possible to get exactly the right effect without noticing what it's called. In the case of colors, you usually don't even have a name to use as a guide. Sometimes, the hand really *is* quicker than the eye. Once you move your mouse away from your selection, it's lost. You might have to re-inspect that entire list to find exactly what you already found, so once you find what you're looking for, don't forget to click! Ctrl+Z is your friend!**

Galleries

Up to now, I've thrown around the word *gallery* as if it were a common everyday word. Well, it is — but it's taken on expanded meaning in Office 2007. Simply put, a gallery is a set of formatting results or preformatted object parts. Virtually every set of formatting results or object parts in Office 2007 might be called a gallery, although Office itself does not use the word *gallery* to refer to every feature set. Some, such as the list of bullets in Word, are called *libraries* instead.

Galleries include document styles, themes, headers, footers, page colors, tables, WordArt, equations, symbols, and more. The Word Styles Gallery is shown in the previous section, in Figure 2-11. Galleries often work hand-in-hand with the Live Preview feature. Imagine paging through a coffee-table volume of paintings, and each time you point to a different painting, your own house and garden are transformed to reflect the style and period of the painting. Point at a different painting, and your house and garden are retransformed.

As noted earlier, however, not every gallery results in a Live Preview. As you begin to take advantage of this new feature, you will quickly start to miss it when it's not available. Perhaps galleries will become more prevalent in future releases!

The Mini toolbar

Another new feature in some of the Office 2007 applications is the *Mini toolbar*. The Mini toolbar is a set of formatting tools that appears when you first select text. It is not context sensitive and always contains the identical set of formatting tools. There is no Mini toolbar for graphics and other non-text objects.

When you first select text, the Mini toolbar appears as a ghostly apparition. When you move the mouse pointer closer to it, it becomes more solid, as shown in Figure 2-13. If you move the mouse pointer far enough away from it, it fades away completely. Click a button on the Mini toolbar to apply formatting to the selection.

FIGURE 2-13

The Mini toolbar appears when text is first selected.

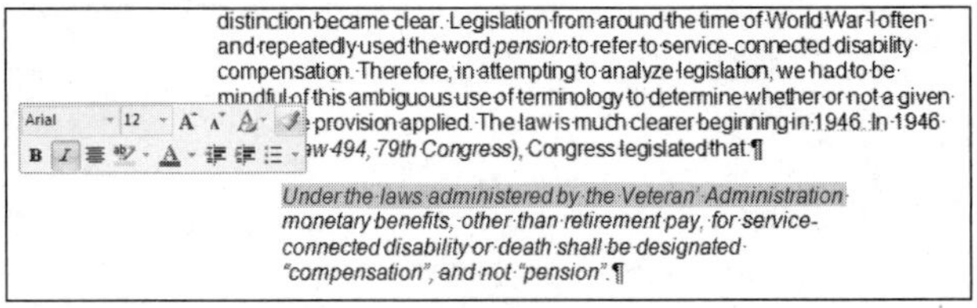

distinction became clear. Legislation from around the time of World War I often and repeatedly used the word *pension* to refer to service-connected disability compensation. Therefore, in attempting to analyze legislation, we had to be mindful of this ambiguous use of terminology to determine whether or not a given provision applied. The law is much clearer beginning in 1946. In 1946 aw 494, 79th Congress), Congress legislated that:¶

Arial 12

Under the laws administered by the Veteran' Administration monetary benefits, other than retirement pay, for service-connected disability or death shall be designated "compensation", and not "pension".¶

NOTE **Once the Mini toolbar disappears, you cannot resurrect it by hovering the mouse over the selection. You can, however, display the Mini toolbar and the current context-sensitive pop-up menu by right-clicking the selection. Note also that only the mouse triggers the Mini toolbar. If you display the pop-up context menu by pressing Shift+F10 or by tapping the Menu button on a Windows keyboard, the Mini toolbar will not appear.**

Some users will love the Mini toolbar, others will hate it. I recommend that you give it a try. It exists to provide convenient and discoverable access to commands that are otherwise less convenient and less accessible than they were in Office 2003 (with the disappearance of toolbars and menus).

When the Home tab is displayed, the Mini Toolbar might seem superfluous, as all of the Mini toolbar's components are replicated in that tab. However, consider for a moment how far the mouse has to travel to access those formatting commands. With the Mini toolbar, the mouse pointer usually has to travel less than an inch or so. For those with repetitive motion injuries, this can save a lot of wear and tear on the wrist.

If you decide that the Mini toolbar gets in the way, you can turn it off. Even when turned off, however, it can still be summoned by right-clicking the current selection. To turn it off, see Appendix A.

Unlike many Ribbon tools, the Mini toolbar tools do not produce Live Previews of formatting and other effects. If you need to see a Live Preview, use the Ribbon instead.

Shortcut or contextual menus

While the Office applications' main menu system has been almost entirely replaced by Ribbon tabs, Office's shortcut menus, often called contextual or pop-up menus, remain. Shown in Figure 2-14, shortcut menus remain largely unchanged from Office 2003, except for the fact that when text is selected, the Mini toolbar sometimes accompanies the menu.

FIGURE 2-14

When you right-click a selection, a context-sensitive shortcut menu appears, along with the Mini toolbar.

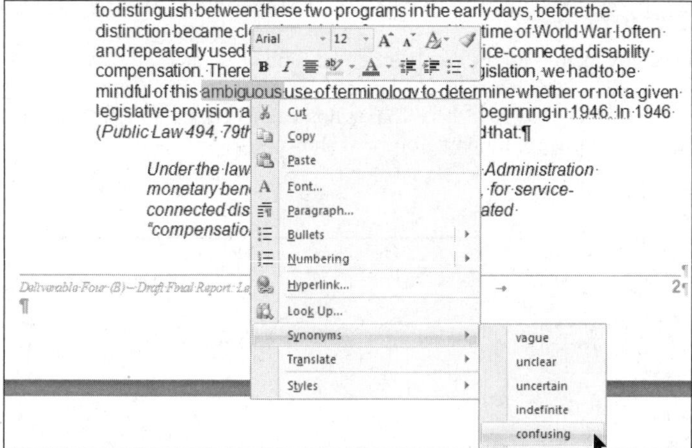

While shortcut menus remain in Office 2007, the ability to customize them is gone.

Enhanced ScreenTips

Another new addition to Office 2007 is *Enhanced ScreenTips*. The very name makes you want to leap over tall buildings! In Office 2003 and earlier, ScreenTips showed only the name of the command under the mouse pointer. Enhanced ScreenTips, instead, are expanded feature descriptions designed to make features more discoverable, as well as to reduce the frequency with which you'll need to press the F1 key for Help. (As it turns out, this is a blessing, because Office 2007's Help system isn't exactly what the doctor ordered.)

Shown in Figure 2-15, an Enhanced ScreenTip magically appears when you hover the mouse pointer over a tool. If you hover the mouse pointer over an exposed gallery item (such as a style), however, you will see a Live Preview of the gallery item instead of an Enhanced ScreenTip. Even better!

FIGURE 2-15

Enhanced ScreenTips explain the selected feature, reducing the need to press F1.

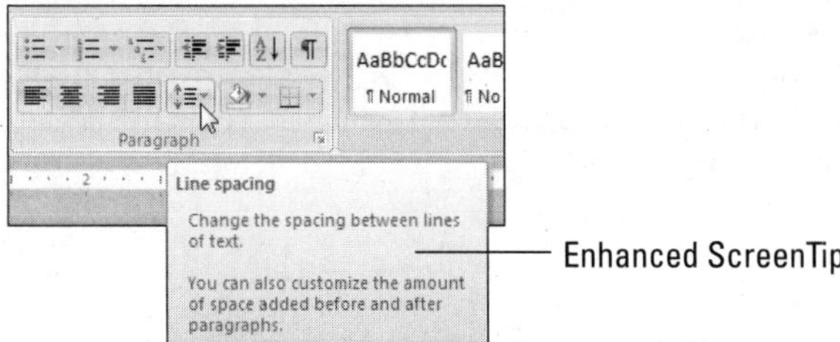

Dialog boxes and launchers

Even though Office 2007's new philosophy focuses on the results-oriented Ribbon, some features and functions remain tied to traditional dialog boxes. Dialog boxes can be launched in several ways, including by direct keystrokes and what Microsoft calls *Dialog Box Launchers*. Dialog Box Launchers are indicated by an arrow pointing southeast in the lower-right corner of Ribbon groups, as shown in Figure 2-16.

FIGURE 2-16

Clicking a Dialog Box Launcher displays a dialog box.

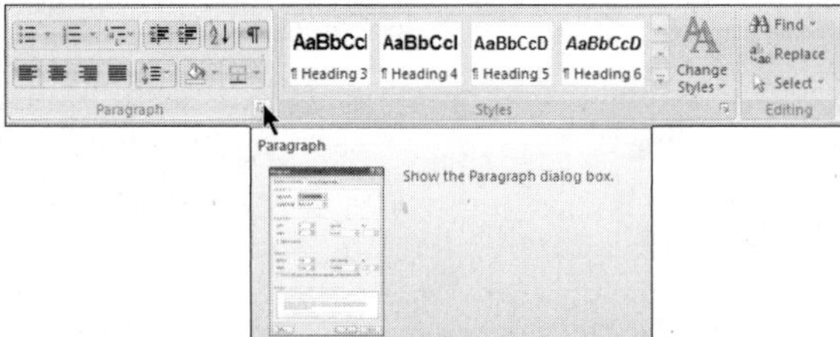

In many instances, Office's dialog boxes have not been overhauled or greatly enhanced for this release. However, if you look closely, you often will see a number of changes, some subtle and others not so subtle. Figure 2-17 contrasts the Paragraph dialog boxes from Word 2007 and 2003. Sometimes, if you look really closely, new features will leap out at you!

FIGURE 2-17

Can you spot the differences between the Word 2007 and Word 2003 dialog boxes? Without running the two versions side by side, you might never notice Word 2007's new feature: Mirror Indents!

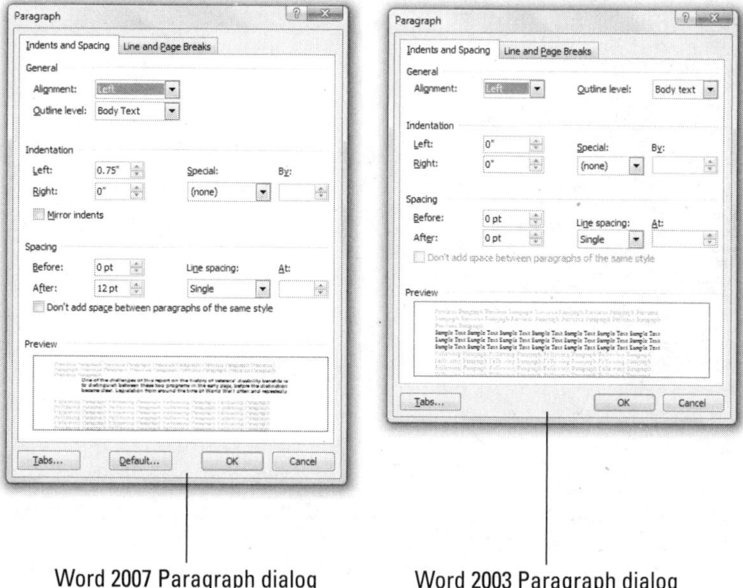

Task panes

Word 2003 sported a collection of 14 task panes (or more, depending on what features are installed and in use), and the other Office apps had numerous task panes, as well. The task pane was activated by pressing Ctrl+F1. As noted earlier in this chapter, in Office 2007, Ctrl+F1 now toggles the Ribbon on and off.

If Ctrl+F1 is now used for something else, how do you activate the task panes in Office 2007? The short answer is that task panes, as a cohesive concept, have been mostly abandoned. Office 2007 still has some task panes, but you can't access them using a drop-down menu as you could in Office 2003, and you can't access the entire collection of task panes using a single keystroke. Instead, they will appear as needed (and possibly when you aren't expecting them). Think of them as dialog boxes that enable you to type while they're onscreen.

For example, on the Home tab in Word, click the Styles Dialog Box Launcher. This displays the Styles task pane. Now click the drop-down arrow to the left of the X in the upper-right corner of the task pane, as shown in Figure 2-18. Instead of a list of task panes, you get three options that control only this task pane. Like their counterparts in earlier versions of Office, task panes in Office 2007 can be dragged away from the right side of the Word window and displayed wherever it's convenient—including completely out of the application's window frame. Just move the mouse pointer over the task pane title bar and drag. To return it, just drag it back, or double-click the floating task pane's title bar.

FIGURE 2-18

Office 2007's task panes are independent of each other and can't be selected from a common pull-down control.

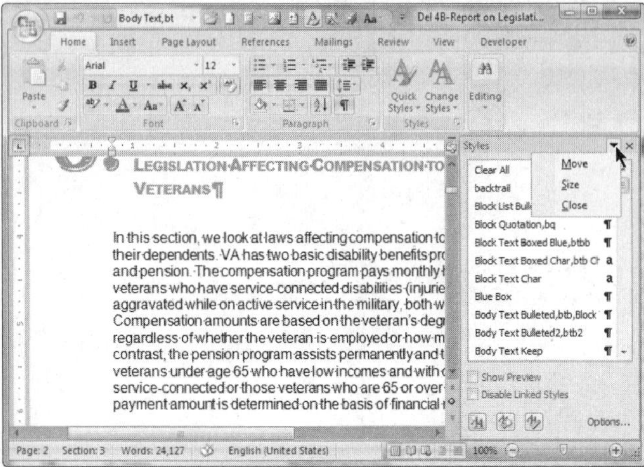

While it might seem a bit odd for Microsoft to have unbundled the task panes, a quick look at Figure 2-19 demonstrates a decided advantage of the new approach. While you probably won't need to have them all onscreen at the same time, it's nice to know that you're no longer limited to just one at a time.

FIGURE 2-19

With Office 2007, you can display multiple task panes at the same time, should you feel a compelling need for clutter.

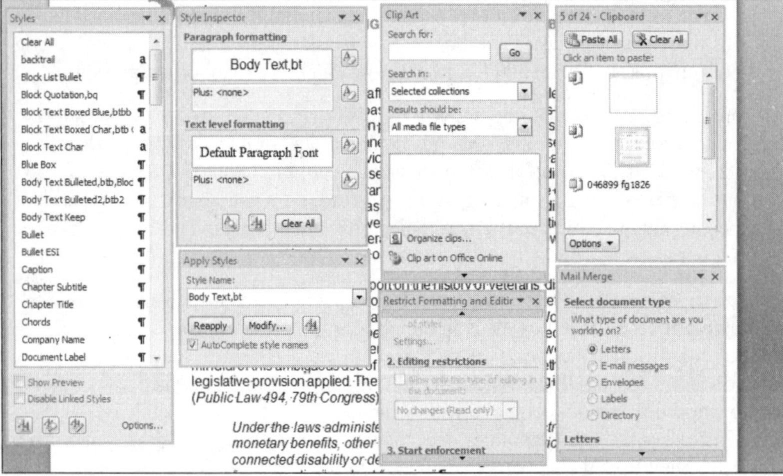

Status bar

Now we turn to the status bar, neglected until now. Shown in Figure 2-20, the status bar is the bar at the bottom of the application window. Depending on the application in use, the status bar provides dozens of optional pieces of information about the current document. Right-click the status bar to display the status bar's configuration options.

FIGURE 2-20

Status bar display options have been greatly expanded in some Office 2007 applications.

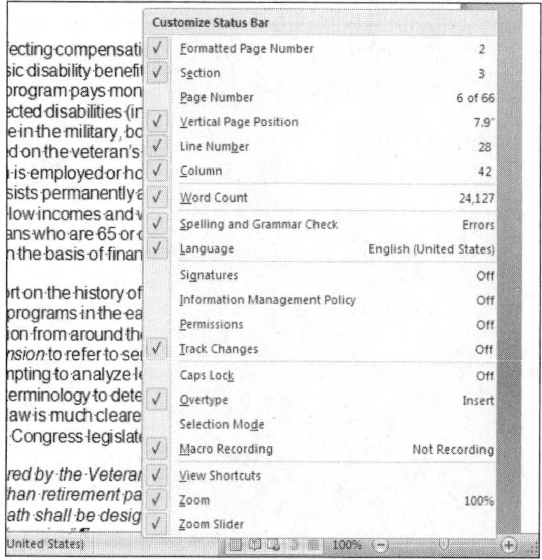

As an example of the type of information the status bar might display, not only does Word 2007 update the Word count continuously, but if you select text, it tells you how many words are selected: 180/5,644 means that 180 words are selected out of a total of 5,644.

NOTE **The status bar configuration menu stays onscreen until you explicitly dismiss it. That means that you can enable/disable as many options as you want without having to repeatedly right-click the status bar. Notice also that the configuration menu displays the current status too, so if you just want to quickly refer to it to find out what language you're using — but don't really want Language on the status bar — you don't have to put it on the status bar and then remove it. Note additionally that the status items aren't just pretty pictures. For example, clicking the Page item shown in Figure 2-20 takes you to the Go To Page dialog box in Word. Clicking the Macro Recording item opens the Record Macro dialog box.**

To dismiss the configuration menu, simply click on the status bar or in the document, or press Esc, Enter, or the spacebar.

The Office Button (File)

The Office Button is that large, round control in the upper-left corner of some of Office 2007 applications. I say *some* because the Office Button has not found its way into the 2007 version of the main Outlook window, the Office Picture Manager, InfoPath, OneNote, or Publisher. The Office Button, which has been clicked in Figure 2-21, displays a number of top-level commands that you ordinarily might expect to find in the File menu. Just in case you didn't notice, the Office Button design is the Office logo, the detail of which might be hard to discern on some computers.

FIGURE 2-21

The Office Button replaces the File menu in the major Office 2007 applications.

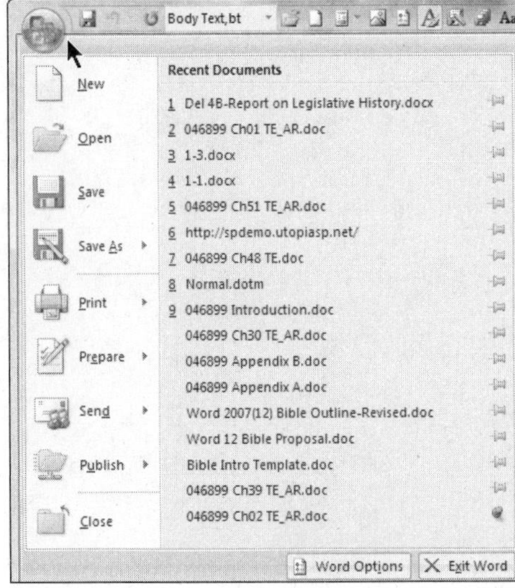

Why the Office button? Why not File? Microsoft was looking for a unifying new theme for Office 2007. It's as simple as that. Moreover, many of the functions contained therein really have nothing to do with files per se.

In the Office (File) menu some of the commands — Save As, Print, Prepare, Send, and Publish — have right-pointing triangles. These triangles indicate the presence of additional subcommands.

As shown in Figure 2-22, it pays to explore in Office 2007. By clicking each of the expandable commands in Word's Office menu, the seasoned Word user will quickly discover a number of new features: PDF files, XPS files, the Document Inspector, the compatibility checker, and blogging, to name a few. You'll also find legacy features hiding there. Similar menus appear in the other Office 2007 applications.

NOTE **Depending on what features are being used, your Office (File) menu might include additional items. For example, if the current document is located on a SharePoint server, you'll also see a Server Tasks button, between Publish and Close.**

In addition, because of a dispute between Microsoft and Adobe on the inclusion of PDF publishing in Word 2007, the capability to publish in PDF and XPS format is excluded from the default installation of Office 2007. However, you can download a free patch for Office 2007 by clicking Find Add-Ins for Other File Formats on the Save As submenu shown in Figure 2-22.

FIGURE 2-22

Save As, Print, Prepare, Send, and Publish reveal a number of capabilities new in Word 2007.

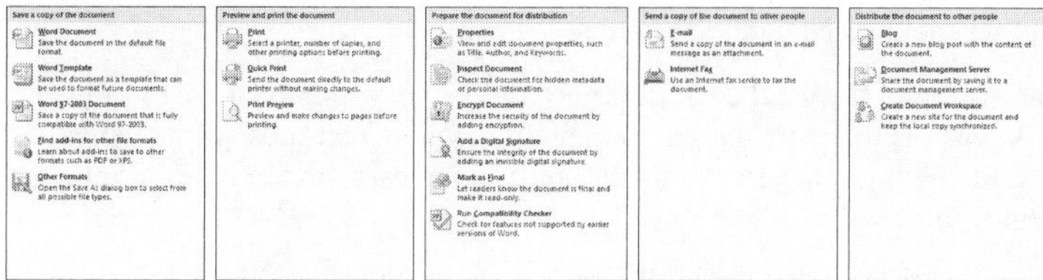

Options

When you wanted to change something about Word 2003 or earlier, you had multiple places to look, including Tools ➪ Options, Tools ➪ Customize, Help ➪ About ➪ Disabled Items, Help ➪ Check for Updates, File ➪ Permission, Tools ➪ Protect, and Tools ➪ AutoCorrect Options, to name but a few. In Office 2007, "change central" is now located in one place: the application's Options dialog box. To get there, choose Office Button ➪ *Program Name* Options to display a dialog box like the one shown in Figure 2-23. Click any information icon (the letter i in a circle) to get more help about an option.

FIGURE 2-23

The Options dialog box for any Office application features Information icons to clarify selected options.

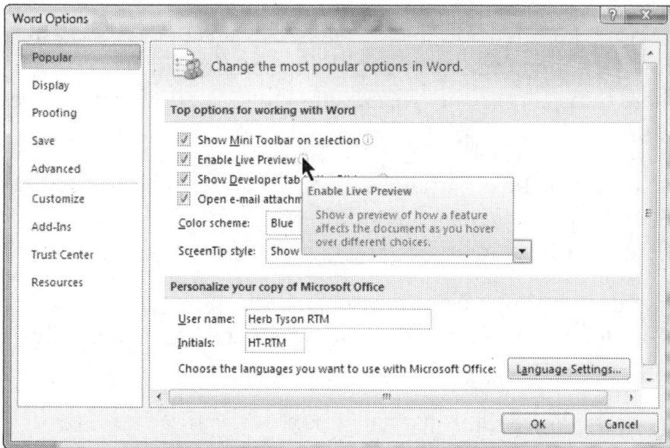

NOTE **Figure 2-23 is a bit fraudulent, I have to admit. In order not to waste a lot of space, I've neatly resized the dialog box so it's no longer larger than the state of Rhode Island. That you can resize it is the good news. The bad news is that Office refuses to remember that you resized it, and the next time you open it, it's back just as big as ever. In fact, in some dual-monitor configurations, it's possible that Options won't obey Windows' normal rules, and Options will span both monitors each and every time you open it.**

Although all of an Office application's options are now in one place, so to speak, that doesn't necessarily make them any easier to find. Navigating the Options dialog box can be daunting.

Truth in advertising, or, what's in a name?

Each application's Options dialog box displays multiple sections, or tabs, on the left. Do not be fooled by the labels. Note that one of the choices is called Advanced. Microsoft's idea of *Advanced* might not be the same as yours. What's optional for someone else might be essential for you.

Microsoft's logic is to try to put at the top of the list the controls and options they think you are most likely to want to change. The first set, Popular, is therefore the group they think will matter most to the typical user. If you're reading the Office 2007 Bible, however, you might not be a typical user. Keep this in mind as you look at the category or section names.

Another "don't be fooled by the labels" caveat is that the labels aren't even objectively accurate. For example, there is a tab labeled Display. If you don't find the display option you're looking for there, don't give up. Some "Display" options actually reside in Popular, such as Show Mini Toolbar on Selection, Enable Live Preview, Show Developer tab in the Ribbon, and Open e-mail attachments in Full Screen Reading View. Oh, wait. That's *all* of the top options!

A number of Word's "display" options are also sheltered under the Advanced umbrella, including great favorites such as the Show Document Content options, the Display options (duh!), and Provide Feedback with Animation (under General). Still other display options are to be found hiding in various other dark corners and recesses. If you can't find something you *know* must be there, check the index in this book.

Options are covered in more detail in Appendix A. I urge you to click each of the nine tabs to explore the different options that are available. Mostly, this is so you can learn the answer to "Where did they hide it?" Additionally, however, it will enable you to learn about new options that correspond to new features.

Advanced . . . versus not advanced?

If you're at all like me, you might be wondering "How did Microsoft decide what's advanced and what's not advanced?" We'll probably never know. More important than understanding the logic is simply becoming familiar with the lay of the land so you know where things are, rather than having to look all over the place each time you want to know how to change a setting.

For example, the Advanced tab in the Word Options dialog box, partially shown in Figure 2-24, has 10 major sections (depending on how you count them, of course). Also depending on how you count, Word Options' Advanced tab offers more than 150 different settings, including the Layout Options.

Remember those nice information icons so prevalent in the Popular category? The Advanced category in Word has only four of them! Out of more than 150 different settings, there are information icons for only four!

If you scroll down a bit in the Advanced category of the Word Options dialog box, you can see both the Save and Preserve Fidelity sections at the same time. Is there any doubt in your mind what "Prompt before saving Normal template" means? Not in mine either.

Now look at "Embed linguistic data." Do you really know exactly what that means? I didn't (I looked it up, so I know now, but there's no cute information button to tell you). Why, do you suppose, did Microsoft choose to provide cute little information buttons for the options whose meanings, for the most part, are already patently obvious? Clearly, they must not know what "Embed linguistic data" means either!

To find out what these advanced options are, simply select the option and press F1. Not much help, right? Okay, then, type "embed linguistic data" into the Search box (including the quotes) and click Search for the really helpful view shown in Figure 2-25.

FIGURE 2-24

Word's Advanced options contain over 150 settings.

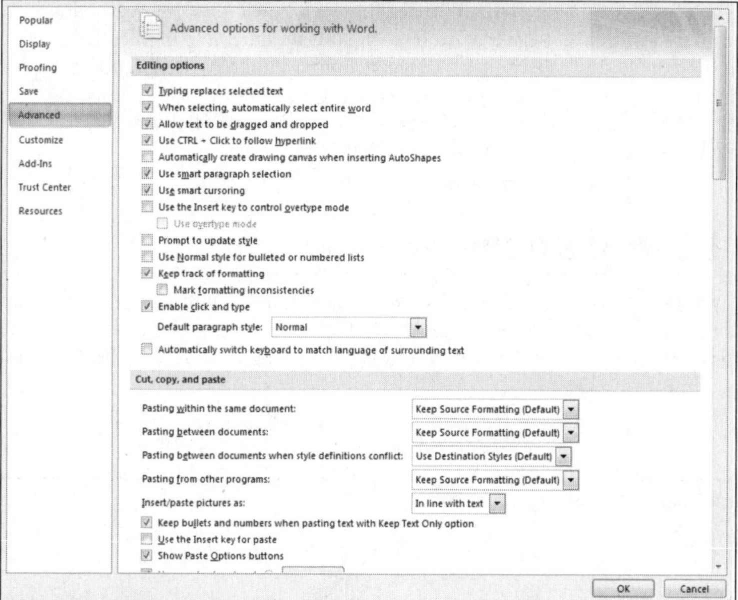

FIGURE 2-25

Office 2007's Help system leaves a lot to be desired.

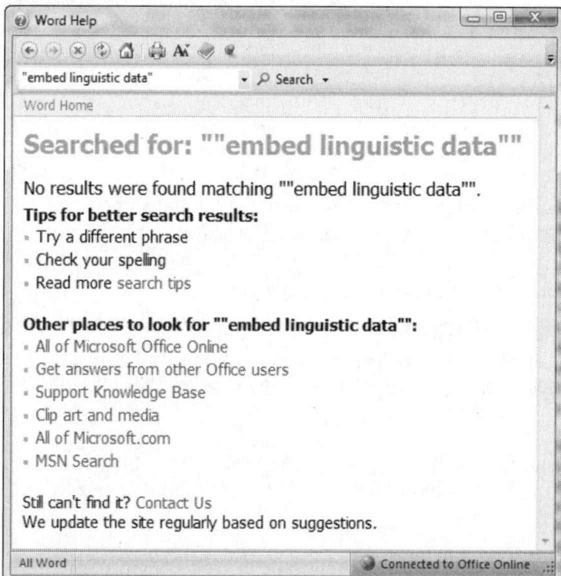

TIP **In many instances, but not always, you can find Help on what you want by typing the exact feature name (e.g., "embed linguistic data") into the Search box, pressing Enter (which usually returns "No results"), and then clicking the Support Knowledge Base link.**

Clearly, Help needs Help. You will find useful help much more quickly by following the tip shown above, or simply by "Googling" the feature in question. Note that even when you can find Help in Microsoft's Knowledge Base, that help often is couched in Microsoftese, a clever circular kind of writing that repeatedly uses the mystery feature's name in lieu of actually telling you what the feature does or means. Searching other sources online often nets you more useful information because the very existence of such sources likely is the result of someone's frustration in trying to parse the "official" sources.

Working with Dialog Boxes

Many Office commands display a dialog box, which is simply a way of getting more information from you. For example, if you choose Review ➪ Changes ➪ Protect Sheet from Excel's Ribbon, Excel can't carry out the command until it finds out from you what parts of the sheet you want to protect. Therefore, it displays the Protect Sheet dialog box, shown in Figure 2-26.

FIGURE 2-26

A dialog box is used to get additional information about a command.

The Excel dialog boxes vary in how they work. Some of them show the result of your actions immediately. For example, if you're applying formatting to a chart, changes you make in the Format dialog box are shown immediately. Generally speaking, if a dialog box has an OK button, then it must be dismissed before anything happens. If the dialog box has a Close button, then it shows the result of your actions while the dialog box remains open.

When a dialog box appears, you make your choices by manipulating the controls. When you're finished, click the OK button (or the Close button) to continue. If you change your mind, click the Cancel button (or press Esc), and nothing further happens.

Most people find working with dialog boxes to be quite straightforward and natural. If you've used other programs, you'll feel right at home. The controls can be manipulated either with your mouse or directly from the keyboard.

Navigating dialog boxes

Navigating dialog boxes is generally very easy — you simply click the control you wish to activate.

Although dialog boxes were designed with mouse users in mind, you can also use the keyboard. Every dialog box control has text associated with it, and this text always has one underlined letter (a *hot key* or *accelerator key*). You can access the control from the keyboard by pressing the Alt key and then the underlined letter. You also can use Tab to cycle through all the controls on a dialog box. Shift+Tab cycles through the controls in reverse order.

When a control is selected, it appears with a darker outline. You can use the spacebar to activate a selected control.

Using tabbed dialog boxes

Many of the dialog boxes are "tabbed" dialog boxes. A *tabbed dialog box* includes notebook-like tabs, each of which is associated with a different panel.

When you click a tab, the dialog box changes to display a new panel containing a new set of controls. The Format Cells dialog box in Excel is a good example. This dialog box is shown in Figure 2-27; it has six tabs, which makes it functionally equivalent to six different dialog boxes.

FIGURE 2-27

Use the dialog box tabs to select different functional areas in the dialog box.

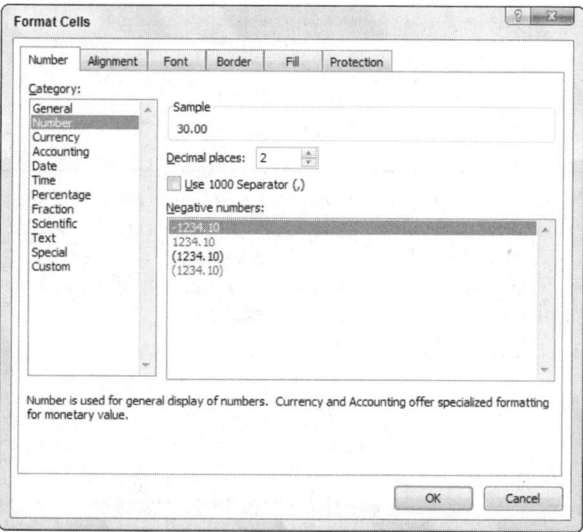

Tabbed dialog boxes are quite convenient because you can make several changes in a single dialog box. After you make all of your setting changes, click OK or press Enter.

TIP

To select a tab by using the keyboard, use Ctrl+PgUp or Ctrl+PgDn, or simply press the first letter of the tab that you want to activate.

Office 2007 introduced a new style of tabbed dialog box in which the tabs are on the left, rather than across the top. An example from Excel is shown in Figure 2-28. To select a tab using the keyboard, use the up and down arrow keys, then press Enter.

FIGURE 2-28

A "new style" tabbed dialog box with tabs on the left.

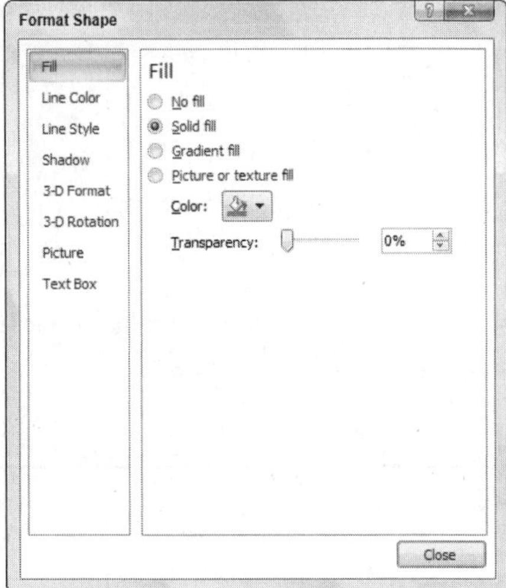

Summary

In this chapter, you've had a look at many of the exciting, new, and different facets of Office 2007. You've seen the philosophy behind the changes (discoverability) and the implementation (the Ribbon). You've also learned a number of ways in which Office 2007 is similar to earlier versions, and a number of ways in which it's different. You should now know what people are talking about when they mention Ribbon tabs, the Quick Access Toolbar (QAT), Live Preview, Enhanced ScreenTips, and Galleries.

Chapter 3

Mastering Fundamental Operations

Years ago, computer program developers began to standardize some commands and functions, even in programs with significantly different purposes. Early versions of the Microsoft Office suite were pioneers in meeting the need to give users standard names for menus and commands and familiar tools in all the suite applications. This chapter discusses features, commands, and tasks that many of the Microsoft Office 2007 applications have in common.

IN THIS CHAPTER

Working with Files

Computer *files* are part of a framework for managing the data you create and store on your computer. When you create information in a program, such as a letter, you save that information in a file and assign the file a memorable name. When you want to work with the file at a later time, you can identify the file by its name and open the file in the program. Although the ins and outs of creating and using files differ somewhat among the Office programs, after you learn to work with files in one Office application, you will for the most part be able to work with files in the other Office applications. The skills you learn next will come in handy when you need to work with files in various Office programs.

Understanding Office 2007 file formats

Every program saves data in a particular *file format* that reflects how the program identifies, organizes, and interprets information. You can typically identify what program was used to create a file in two ways:

- The file's icon in a Windows folder window or a dialog box such as the Open dialog box identifies the program used to create the file. That is, all files created in a particular program use the same icon. Figure 3-1 shows the file icons for some of the key Office programs.

FIGURE 3-1

A file's icon reflects the program used to create the file.

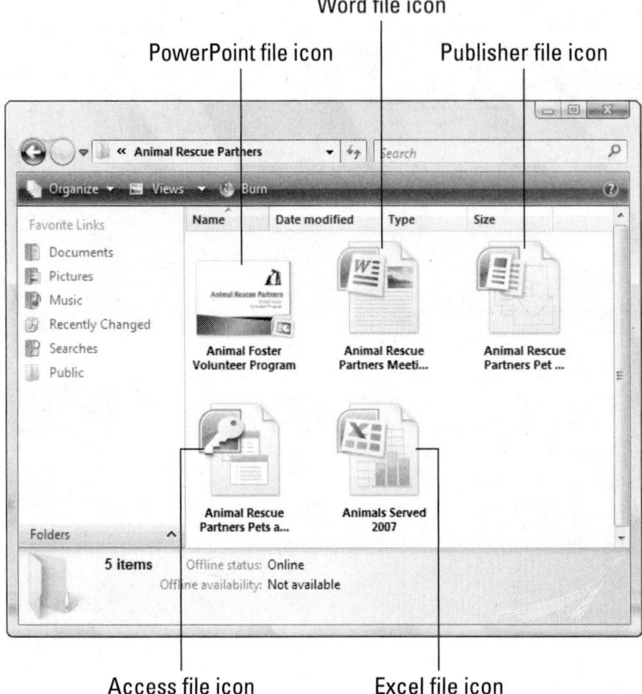

- A three- to five-letter filename extension (such as `.docx` for Word 2007 files) also identifies the program used to create the file. Although filename extensions often are hidden, you may see the extension when viewing information about a file or browsing to find a file in Windows.

The file formats for the 2007 releases of Word, Excel, and PowerPoint have been dramatically changed to use the Microsoft Office Open XML Formats. Microsoft Office Open XML Format is based on a wider standard called eXtensible Markup Language (XML), a method of describing data that was designed to facilitate sharing data between different systems. To signify their XML roots, the filename extensions for Word, Excel, and PowerPoint now include an *x*: `.docx` for Word documents, `.xlsx` for Excel workbooks, and `.pptx` for PowerPoint presentations. The change to XML-based file formats enables the applications to create smaller, more secure files that corrupt less easily but can be shared more easily.

If an Office 2007 file has been saved in a special macro-enabled format, it will have the `.docm` (Word), `.xlsm` (Excel), or `.pptm` (PowerPoint) filename extension.

Access 2007 also features a new `.accdb` database file format rather than the old `.mdb` file format. The new Access file format and the database engine that drives it give tighter integration with SharePoint Services and Outlook 2007. There are also some special variations of the Access file format, including an execute-only database file (`.accde`) and a runtime version (`.accdr`) of the database file. Although Access can read tables from database files created in earlier Access versions so that you don't have to recreate those tables, older Access versions cannot read tables from an Access 2007 database file. Publisher 2007 files continue to use the `.pub` filename extension.

Creating a new, blank file

When you start some of the Office applications — such as Word, Excel, and PowerPoint — the application automatically opens a new, blank file for you. You can then begin adding and formatting the content you want to preserve for yourself or other readers or viewers.

If you're working with an existing file and need to create another blank file, you can do so at any time, using one of the following two methods:

- Press Ctrl+N. The blank file appears immediately.
- Click the Office Button (File menu) in the upper-left corner of the program window and then click New. The New *Document Type* dialog box, like the one for Excel shown in Figure 3-2, appears. Double-click the Blank *Document Type* icon, which closes the dialog box and immediately opens the new document onscreen.

FIGURE 3-2

You can create a blank file using the New dialog box.

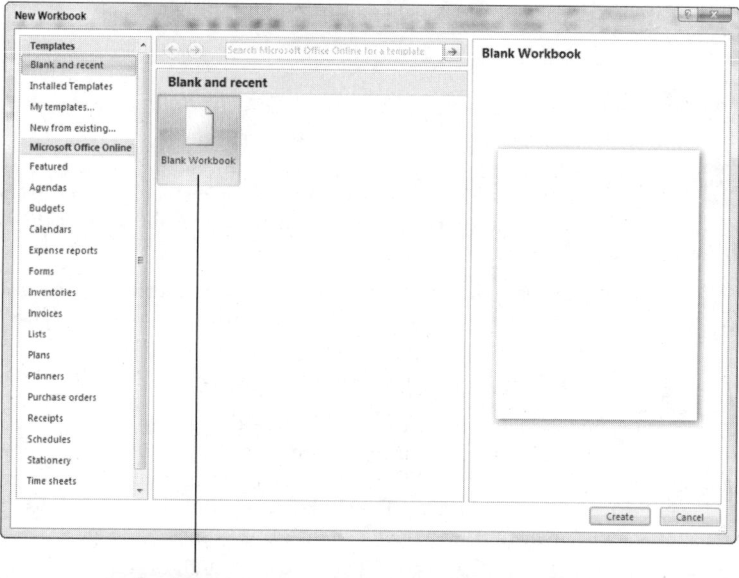

Because of its more complicated file structure, Access requires you to take a few more set up steps when you create a new database file. If you double-click the Blank Database icon after starting Access or choosing the New command, Access prompts you to enter a name for the file. After you click Create (Figure 3-3), you then must set up the first table that will hold the data you'll enter. Chapter 34 covers the process for creating an Access table.

FIGURE 3-3

Access prompts you to enter a filename immediately.

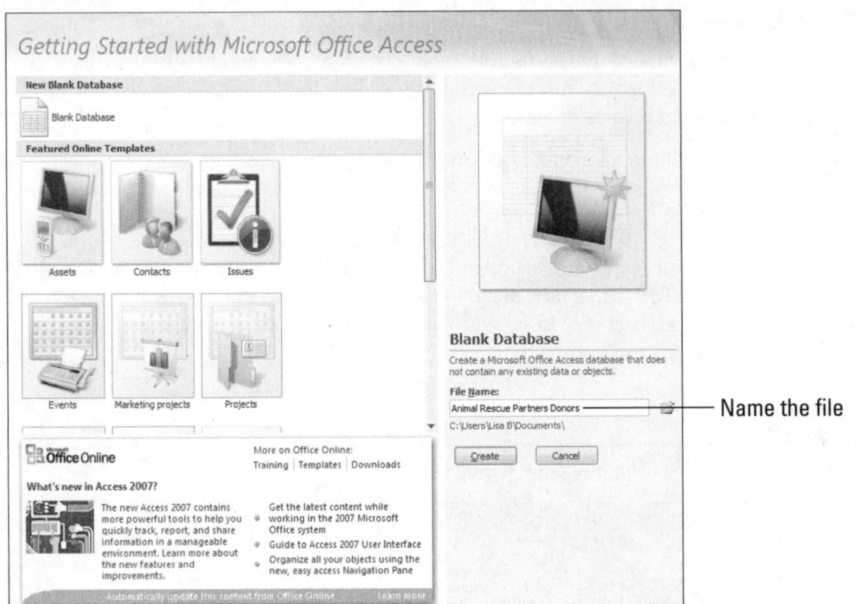

TIP **Outlook doesn't use files, so you'll learn how to work with its messages and information in the later part that covers that program. As does Access, the Publisher, OneNote, and InfoPath programs each have a somewhat unique process for setting up a new file, and you'll learn about each process in the applicable later chapters.**

NOTE **Rather than the Office Button, some Office applications instead still offer a File menu that contains the New command and other commands for working with files, such as the Print command.**

Creating a file with a document template

You can avoid starting from scratch when creating a file by selecting a *template*. A template includes starter content and attractive formatting, both of which you can adapt for your own uses. For example, Excel includes a Loan Amortization template that includes all the formulas required to calculate payments on a loan; you plug in the loan terms, and presto! The worksheet presents you with precise principal and payment information for any payment date in the life of the loan. As shown in Figure 3-4, this template also includes the formatting needed to organize and highlight the information.

FIGURE 3-4

Templates include starter information and formatting.

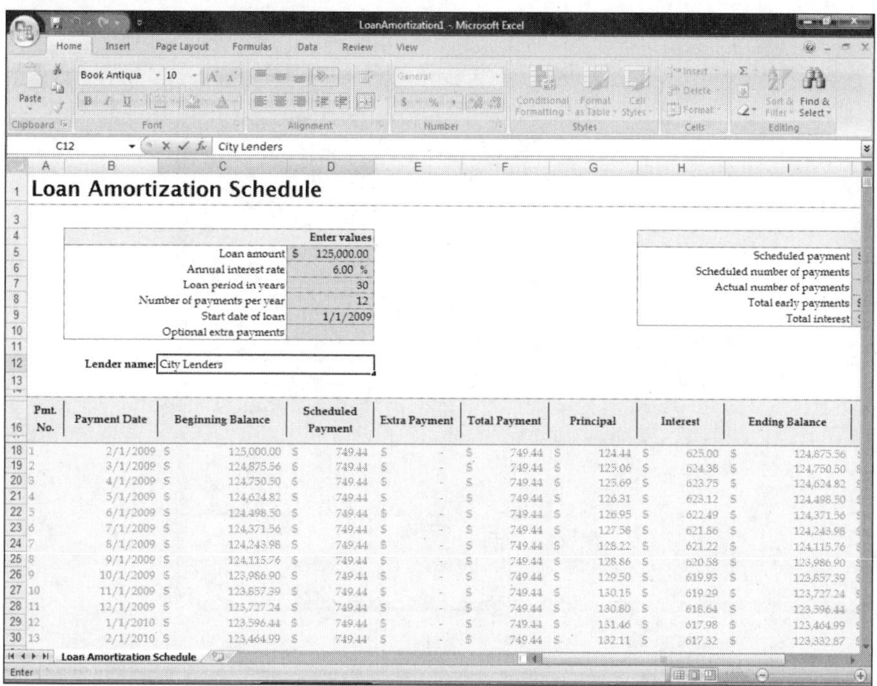

Some templates install on your system's hard disk when you install Office. Microsoft also enables you to browse and download templates stored on Office Online, giving you the opportunity to take advantage of new templates as Microsoft adds them to the site.

Whether you choose an installed template or download a new template, the process for using a template to create a new file is roughly the same:

1. **Click Office Button ⇨ New.** The New *Document Type* dialog box appears.

2a. **Click Installed Templates in the Templates section of the list at the left.**

OR

2b. **Click a template category in the Microsoft Office Online section of the list at the left.**

3. **Click a template thumbnail.** As shown in Figure 3-5, a preview of the template appears at the right side of the dialog box.

FIGURE 3-5

The Office application displays a preview of the selected template.

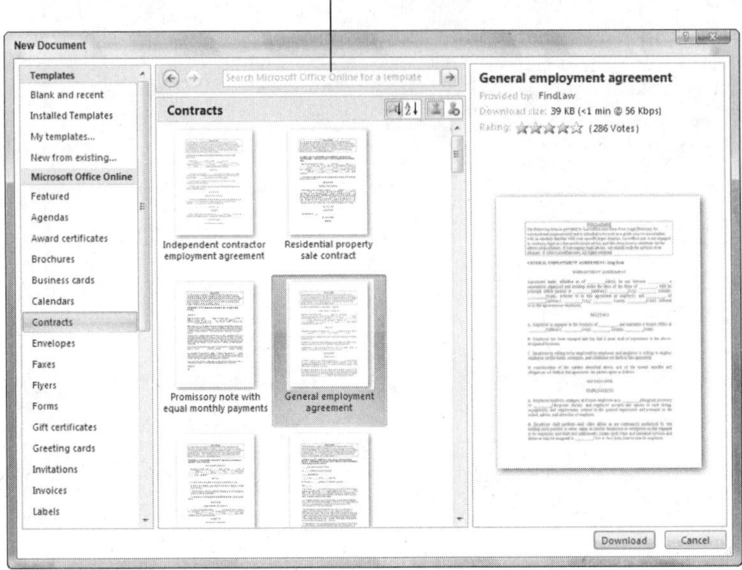

TIP If you don't see the template you want in one of the available categories, type a keyword or description for the type of template that you need into the Search Microsoft Office Online for a Template text box. Then click the Start Searching (right arrow) button beside it to find matching templates.

4. **Click Create (for an installed template) or Download.** If you selected a template installed on your system, the new file appears. An online template will take a few moments to a few minutes to download, and then the new file will appear.

NOTE The first time you download a template, the Microsoft Office Genuine Advantage message box will appear to inform you that Microsoft will verify that you have a legitimate copy of Office as a requirement of the download process. To turn off this message for future downloads, click the Do Not Show This Message Again checkbox to check it before clicking Continue.

NOTE PowerPoint also enables you to create a file by applying a design *theme*. Although themes don't include any content, they do provide attractive, consistent formatting for all the slides in a presentation. To create a file with a theme, click Installed Themes in the Templates list of the New Presentation dialog box, click a theme icon to see its preview, and then click Create.

Saving and naming a file

When you create a new file, the application assigns it a temporary name, numbering names sequentially when you create more than one new file. If you create more than one new file in Excel, for example, the program assigns the temporary filenames *Book1*, *Book2*, and so on. To replace the temporary filename and to make sure your work in a file gets preserved on your computer's hard disk or a network drive, you need to *save* the file. The application you're saving with will automatically apply the file format extension to whatever filename you specify during the save process.

Follow these steps to save a file in an Office application running in Windows Vista:

1. **Click Office Button ➪ Save or press Ctrl+S.** The Save As dialog box appears.
2. **Click the Browse Folders button.** This expands the dialog box to include a pane where you can choose a disk or folder in which to save the file. The Browse Folders button changes to the Hide Folders button, which you can click at any later time to suppress the folder display.
3. **Click the up arrow to the right of Folders in the left pane.** The Folders list with the folder tree for navigating to disks and folders expands.
4. **Click the triangle to the left of any disk or folder to display its contents, if needed.** A triangle appears beside only folders that have subfolders within them, so you may not see any triangles beside folder icons.
5. **Click the desired folder in the tree.** This selects the folder as the save location. Figure 3-6 displays a selected folder.

NOTE **If you're using Windows XP, select File ➪ Save to open the Save As dialog box. You can use the Save In drop-down list and the list of folders in the Save As dialog box to navigate to the folder in which you want to save the file. Enter a filename in the File Name Text box and then click Save.**

FIGURE 3-6

Choose a save location and enter a filename.

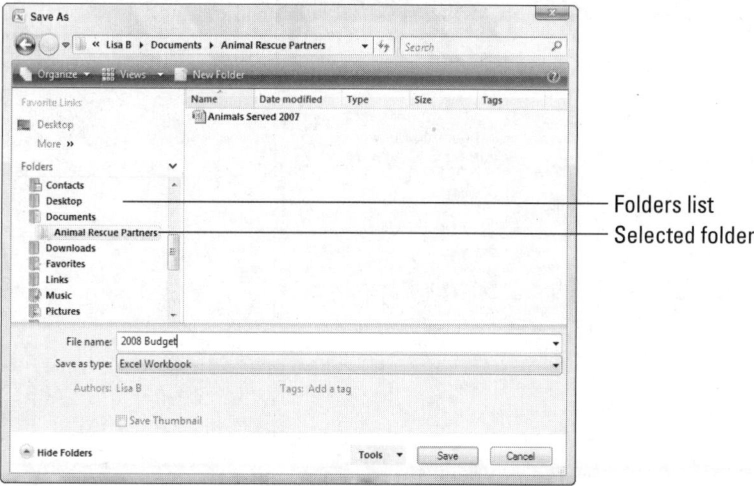

6. **Drag over the contents of the File Name text box and type a new name.** Make sure your filename not only describes the file's contents but also includes information such as a date to distinguish it from other similar files.
7. **Click Save.** The program saves the file and displays the new filename in the title bar onscreen.

As you continue working with a file, you should save it periodically to ensure that your latest changes are included in the stored version. That way, in the event of a power surge or problem with your computer, you won't lose much work. Saving every 10 minutes proves good insurance for your file. To save your latest changes, click the Save button on the Quick Access toolbar or press Ctrl+S. If you must, you can click the Microsoft Office button and then click Save, but why choose two steps when you can choose one?

TIP **The top Office applications offer an AutoRecover feature that can automatically save your work at an interval you specify. This feature is enabled by default to save every 10 minutes. Appendix A, "Customizing Office," discusses how to work with this feature.**

Files created in the 2007 versions of Word, Excel, PowerPoint, and Access cannot be opened with older versions of those programs by default. (They can download and install a compatibility pack to handle the files; information is available by going to the main Office Web site at `http://office.microsoft.com` and searching for "office compatibility pack," with or without quotation marks.) If a user running an older version of one of these applications needs to open one of your files, you may need to save a copy of the file in a compatible format. Here's how:

1. **Click Office Button ⇨ Save As right arrow.** A list of other file formats that you can select for the copy you're creating appears, like the one shown in Figure 3-7.

FIGURE 3-7

Choose an alternative format for the file copy.

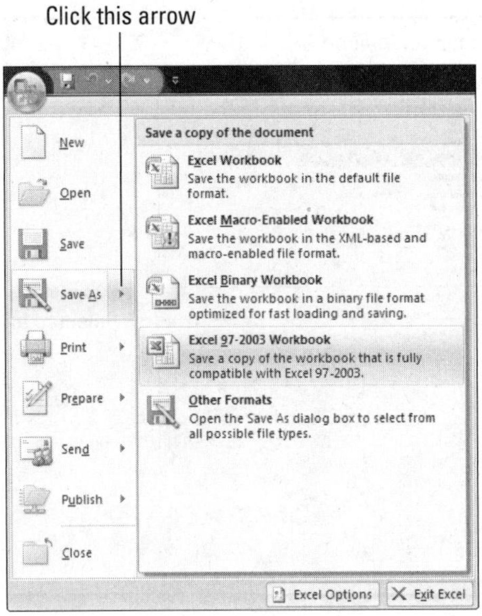

2. **Click the desired "save as" format.**
3. **Specify a save location and filename in the Save As dialog box.** The process works just as described in the previous set of steps about saving a new file.
4. **Click Save.**

TIP When working in Windows XP, you can choose File ➪ Save As and select the file format to use from the Save As Type drop-down list. The Save As dialog box for Office apps running under Windows Vista also offers a Save As Type list.

Opening a file

Opening a file you've previously saved loads the file back into the program so that you can review, change, or print it. The open process works a lot like the save process. You select the folder in which you stored the file and then select the file to open, as follows:

1. **Click Office Button ➪ Open or press Ctrl+O.** The Open dialog box appears.
2. **Click the up arrow to the right of Folders in the left pane.** The Folders list with the folder tree for navigating to disks and folders expands.
3. **Click the triangle to the left of any disk or folder to display its contents, if needed.** A triangle appears beside only folders that have subfolders within them, so you may not see any triangles beside folder icons.
4. **Click the folder that holds the file to open in the tree.** The files stored in the folder appear in the dialog box.
5. **Click the file to open.**
6. **Click Open.** The file loads in the program.

NOTE If you're using Windows XP, select File ➪ Open to open the Open dialog box. You can use the Look In drop-down list and the list of folders in the dialog box to navigate to the folder that holds the file to open. Click the file and then click Open.

TIP In some Office applications, the Open button includes a drop-down list arrow. Click a file to select it. You can then click the Open button drop-down arrow to see additional options for opening the file, such as the Open and Repair command.

TIP Double-click a file's icon in any Windows folder window to open the file within the application in which it was created.

Closing a file

Closing a file that you've finished working on removes the file from the system's working memory. Only a few years ago, closing a file was a necessity because most computers had limited amounts of working memory. Today's powerful computers make that less of an issue, but there are some other equally important reasons to close a file after you finish making changes. For example, you may want to close a file so that it's not visible onscreen for security or privacy reasons. Closing a file also reduces the chances of the file's being corrupted by a power fluctuation or a system error; it also gives you a reminder to save your changes to the file if you haven't already done so.

Some Office applications offer a Close (X) button for the file window itself, located below the application Close (X) button near the upper-right corner of the program window. Clicking the file window Close button closes the file. Other Office applications may not include a file window Close button. If that's the case, you can close the current file by clicking the Microsoft Office Button or File menu and then clicking Close. The keyboard shortcut Alt+F+C will close the current file as well in some Office applications.

If you haven't saved your most recent changes to the file being closed, a reminder message like the one shown in Figure 3-8 appears.

FIGURE 3-8

Click Yes to save the file before closing it.

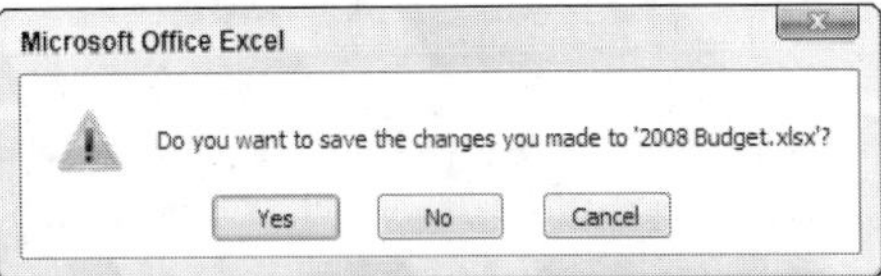

Printing a File

With the crisp, vibrant output produced by today's cheap color printers, who would want a paperless office? Although the Internet and faster computer networks have made electronic transmission a common and accepted means of sharing documents, many circumstances still call for — if not require — that information be shared on paper:

- Legal documents such as contracts that need to be signed, initialed, dated, or otherwise stamped are still largely handled on paper. Standards for digital signatures are still evolving, and most users still print a hard copy of a contract or agreement for official filing.
- When a reader or viewer won't have a computer or connection at hand and will need to take notes, you need to provide a hard copy. For example, participants in seminars typically don't bring along a notebook and prefer to take their notes on a hard copy of a presentation.
- When you want to make a strong impression, hard copy is still preferred. Although e-mail is increasingly accepted as a standard business practice for many communications, sometimes it doesn't measure up. For example, it might be acceptable to e-mail a proposal to a potential new client, but hand-delivering a hard copy and then following up by e-mail shows that you still care enough to make a personal effort to get the business.
- When you need a fresh perspective on a document, you can get it by working from hard copy. Reading through a printed copy of a document can help you catch text and formatting mistakes you previously missed, while also enabling you to make additional notes and engage in proofreading tricks such as reading the document backwards.
- When you want to provide a more constant, visible reminder, you need hard copy. Whether it's putting up a flyer at the grocery store about a found cat or giving a recognition certificate to a valued volunteer, hard copy is still the only useful format.

With all the great documents you can create in Office, you'll be proud to publish and share hard copies. This section explains how to set up and print your files.

Of course, this section on printing assumes that a printer is installed on your system or network and that the printer is powered on and has ample paper and ink or toner in it.

Performing a quick print

A *quick print* operation prints the file as it stands, sending the job directly to the default printer and using the current settings for the printer. When you use this printing method, you do not have the opportunity to make changes such as specifying how many copies of the file to print. On the other hand, if you have previously set up all the desired document and printer settings, you don't need to repeat the whole process for every print job.

Not all of the Office 2007 applications offer the quick print capability, but for those that do, performing a quick print is easy:

1. **Click Office Button ⇨ Print right arrow.** A list of print commands appears, as shown in Figure 3-9.

FIGURE 3-9

Perform a quick print with this command.

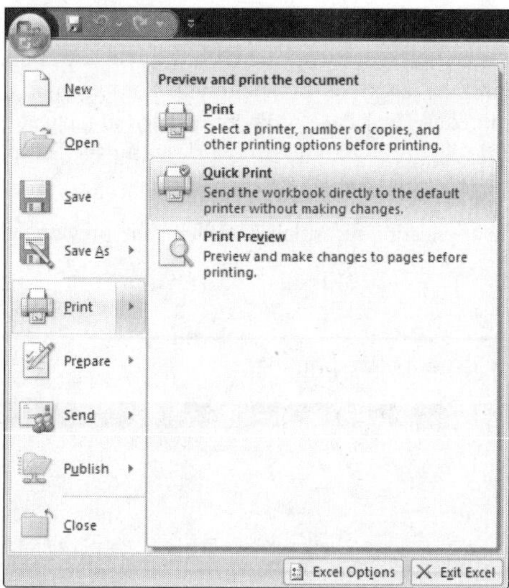

2. **Click Quick Print.** The document prints.

If you prefer the keyboard to the mouse, you can use this rather long keyboard shortcut for performing a quick print: Alt+F+W+Q.

TIP **In Office applications that use the Ribbon, you can add a Quick Print button to the Quick Access toolbar. Clicking that button then prints the current file directly. To add the button, click the Customize Quick Access Toolbar drop-down arrow at the right end of the Quick Access toolbar; then, click Quick Print.**

Previewing a print job

You can check out how a document will look before committing it to paper by using the *Print Preview* feature. Print Preview is a special view designed to provide you with a more accurate view of how a particular file will look when you print it. Print Preview can help you diagnose issues that are matters of preference, such as having a text heading appear at the bottom of one page rather than at the top of the next page in a Word document, as well as issues that can save paper, such as squeezing one more column of an Excel worksheet onto the page to reduce a printout from two pages to one. The Print Preview includes buttons for sending the document to the printer and for working with the page design, although the latter choices vary depending on which application you're using.

To view and use Print Preview in an Office application:

1. **Click Office Button ➪ Print right arrow.** A list of print commands appears.
2. **Click Print Preview.** The Print Preview appears, as in the example shown in Figure 3-10.

NOTE In some applications, you just select File ➪ Print Preview to display the Print Preview.

3. **Click with the magnifying glass pointer as needed.** Clicking the document the first time zooms in; clicking again zooms back out.
4. **Click other choices as available to work with the preview and document.** Beyond giving you the ability to zoom in and out, the choices for working with the preview and the document vary depending on the application and the length of the document. For example, if the document includes multiple pages, you can click Next Page or Previous Page to navigate between pages. In the example from Word shown in Figure 3-10, you can work with Page Setup settings or change the display to show Two Pages or the full Page Width.
5. **Click Close Print Preview.** The application redisplays the file in the previous view you were using.

FIGURE 3-10

Preview a document to identify issues before printing.

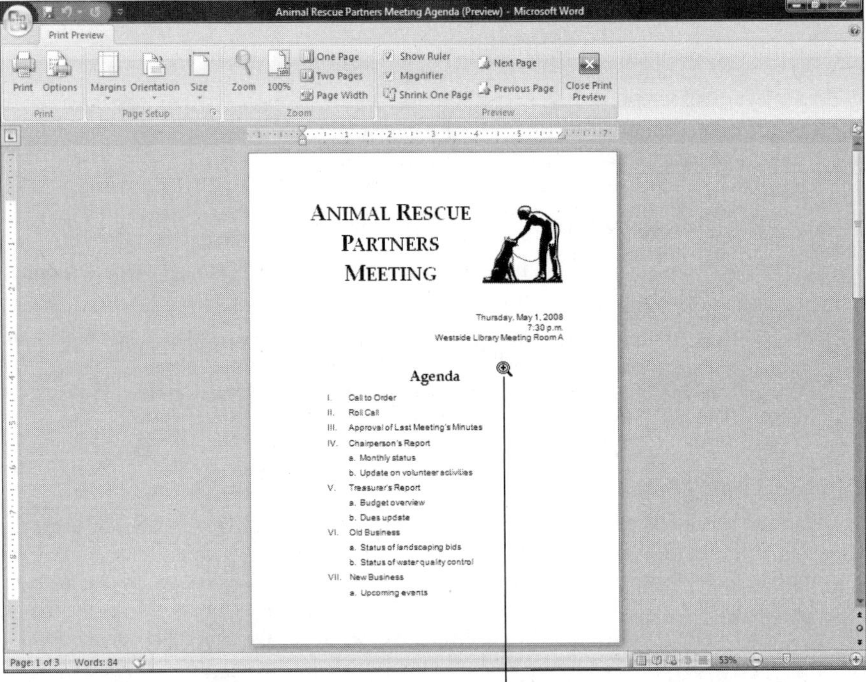

Understanding page design settings

Some document settings affect the overall page design not only in terms of its look but also in making the document print correctly from the printer. The most important page settings you need to specify when it comes to printing fall into three categories:

- **Margins.** The *margin* is the white space between the edge of the paper and the information printed on the page. Most printers require at least .25 inches of margin on each edge of the document; specifying a smaller margin than required by your printer could cause some of the printed information to appear "cut off." In some cases, you need to specify special-purpose margins such as *mirrored margins*, for which the inside (center) margins of each two-page spread are wider to allow for binding the pages.
- **Orientation.** You can choose to present information from a file in *portrait* (tall) or *landscape* (wide) format. When you choose a portrait orientation such as that used for a typical letter, the printer prints the text parallel to the shorter edges of the paper. When you choose a landscape orientation such as that often used for worksheets or presentation slides, the printer rotates the information and prints horizontal to the longer edges of the paper.
- **Size.** If you want to print on paper other than a standard letter-sized sheet, you need to choose that paper size for the document's page design or setup. This choice automatically adjusts the document contents to fit within the margins on the specified sheet size.

Because page design settings vary quite a bit between applications, it's not possible to cover each and every choice here. Later chapters detail some of the settings that pertain to particular Office applications. So, here's an idea of where you can find the page settings you need to check or change them before sending a file to the printer:

- **On the Page Layout or Design tab of the Ribbon.** The Ribbon tab used to format the page or design typically includes a Page Layout section with the options for changing crucial page settings. Clicking a choice here typically displays a menu or gallery (Figure 3-11) of specific settings; click the one you want to apply to the document.
- **In the Print Preview.** As shown previously in Figure 3-10, the Print Preview Ribbon or toolbar often offers settings for working with the page layout. These settings work just like the corresponding settings found on the Ribbon.
- **In the Page Setup dialog box.** The Page Setup dialog box for an application offers general page formatting options such as margin settings, as well as choices specific to the application that you're using. For example, the Page Setup dialog box for Excel includes a Sheet tab, on which you can indicate such details as whether gridlines should print (Figure 3-12). To open the Page Setup dialog box, you can click the Dialog Box Launcher for the Page Setup group on the Page Layout or Design tab of the Ribbon (Figure 3-13). Or, for applications that don't use the Ribbon, you can select File ➪ Page Setup. After you make your choices in the dialog box, click OK to apply them to the document.

FIGURE 3-11

The Page Layout or Design tab of the Ribbon offers page design settings.

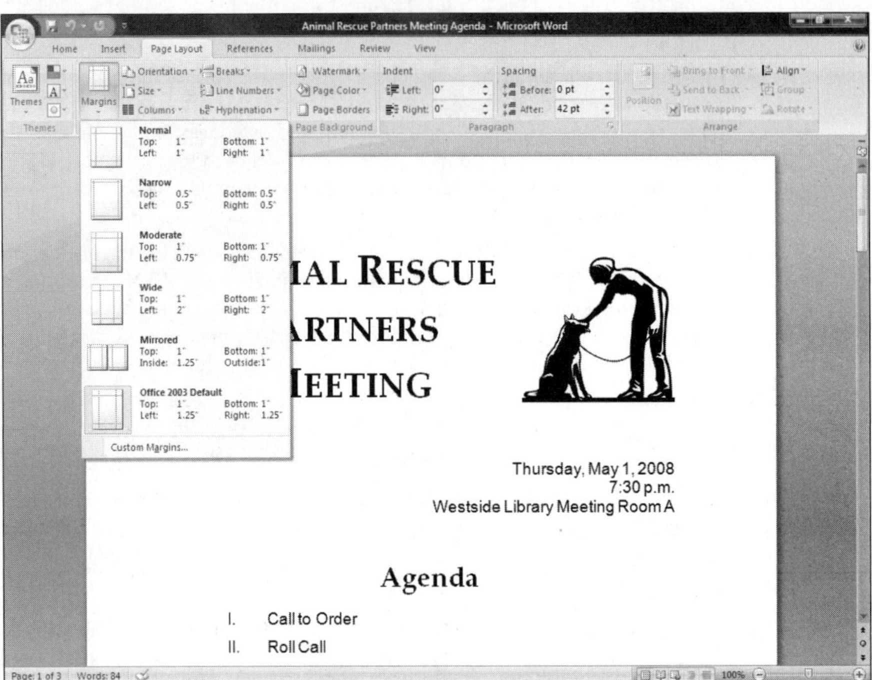

FIGURE 3-12

Page Setup options vary from application to application.

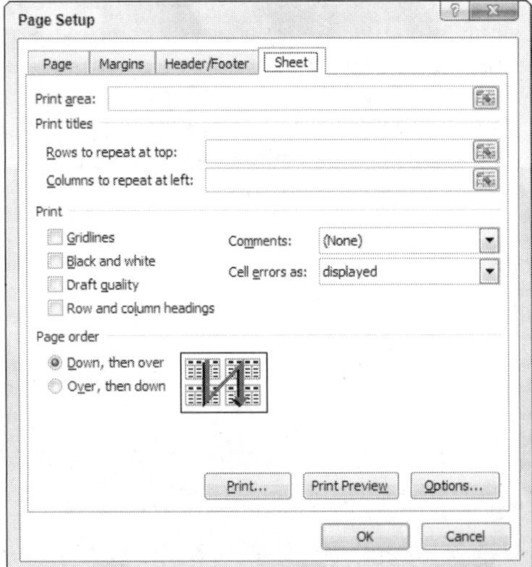

FIGURE 3-13

Click the Dialog Box Launcher for the Page Setup group.

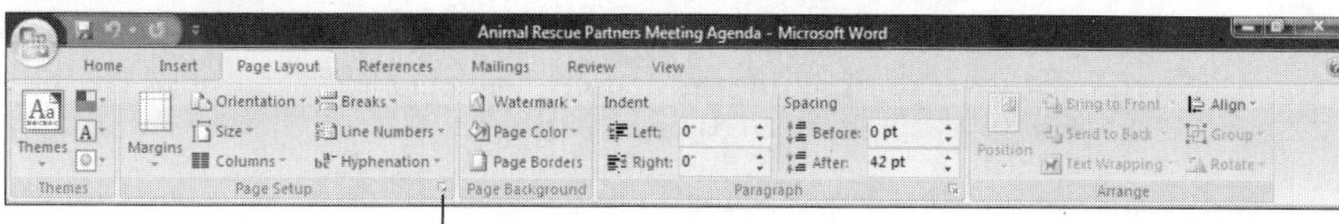

Choosing print settings and printing

As opposed to being specific to the design of the pages of the document to be printed, additional settings pertain to the nature of the hard copy produced, such as which printer to use, which pages of the file to print, how many copies to print, what print quality to use, and so on. You choose all these types of settings in the Print dialog box.

Although settings such as which pages to print and how many copies to print are the same in all circumstances, other choices vary depending on the application or the selected printer. For example, Excel has additional options for enabling you to print only the current worksheet or the entire workbook file. And choosing an inkjet printer generally enables you to select whether you want to print in just black ink or in full color.

Despite those types of differences, the process for choosing a printer and print settings and finishing the print job is about the same in every application:

1. **Click Office Button ➪ Print or press Ctrl+P.** The Print dialog box appears.
2. **Select the printer to use from the Name drop-down list.** The printer becomes the current or active printer (see Figure 3-14).

FIGURE 3-14

Choose printout settings in the Print dialog box.

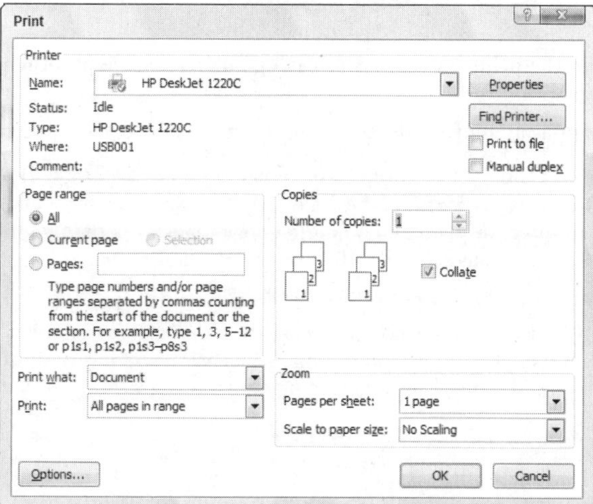

3. **Specify what pages to print in the Page Range area of the dialog box.** Figure 3-14 shows how these choices look in Word's Print dialog box.
4. **Specify how many copies to print in the Copies area of the dialog box.** In some cases, you also can choose to collate the printed pages.
5. **Choose other print settings as desired.** For example, you might be able to change zoom settings or print to a file rather than paper.

Clicking the Options button in the lower-left corner of the dialog box opens another dialog box that includes additional print options, such as whether to print hidden text in Word.

6. **Click the Properties button beside the selected printer.** The dialog box that appears has additional print quality settings, as in the example shown in Figure 3-15.

FIGURE 3-15

Properties for the selected printer enable you to fine-tune the print job even further.

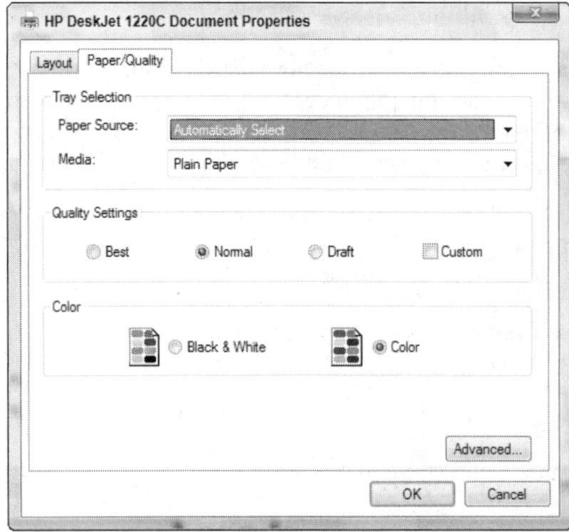

7. **Choose settings in the printer's Properties dialog box as needed and then click OK.** The Print dialog box reappears.
8. **Click Print.** The application prints the file to the specified printer.

TIP

You can download add-ins that "print" a document as a PDF (Portable Document Format) or XPS (XML Paper Specification) file. These special file formats preserve all the file's formatting while making the file easier to share. In Word 2007, find the downloads by choosing Office Button ⇨ Save As right arrow ⇨ Find Add-Ins for Other File Formats. (This command is not available if you've already installed the add-ins.)

TIP

If you *insist* on doing things the easy way and prefer to e-mail a file rather than print it, you can send it from right within the application. Select Microsoft Office Button ⇨ Send ⇨ E-mail File ⇨ Send To ⇨ E-Mail Recipient in some applications to begin the process.

Working with Multiple Windows

Every time you open another file in an Office application, the file opens in its own file window. You can have multiple programs and files open to help you *multitask* — to jump between different jobs you're working on and to look at information stored in a number of different files and applications.

The *taskbar* is a band or bar that appears by default along the bottom of the Windows desktop. A button for each file or program that you open appears on the taskbar. The Office 2007 applications work with Windows Vista to provide you with multiple options for navigating between open file and application windows, including using the taskbar.

Switching to another file or application window

Switching to another open file makes it the active file in its application. When you use the taskbar to switch between open files, Windows switches to the application for that file, if applicable. You can use one of the following techniques to navigate to another file or application in Office and Windows:

- **View tab on Ribbon.** To switch to another open file window in an application, click the View tab on the Ribbon, click Switch Windows, and then click the name of the file to select, as shown in the example in Figure 3-16. The selected file becomes the active file.

FIGURE 3-16

Using the Ribbon to switch between open files.

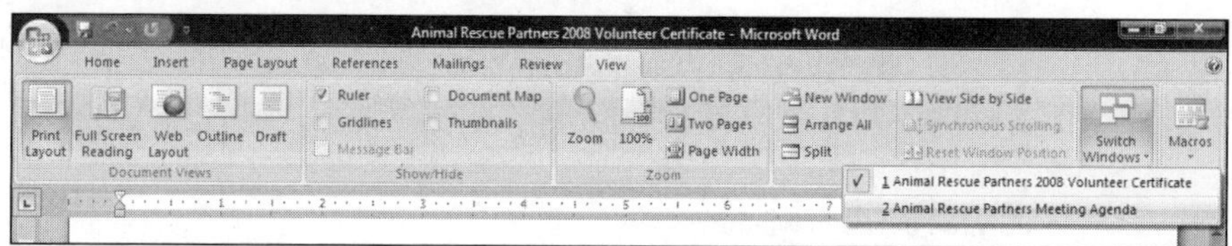

- **Taskbar.** Click the taskbar button for the file to open, which immediately makes the file appear in its application. If the taskbar button represents more than one open file, clicking it displays a menu with the name for each open file. Click the file you want to open to select it.
- **Shortcut key combination.** If you press and hold the Alt+Tab key combination, a task-switching box with an icon for each open file, as well as for the Windows desktop, appears. Continue holding down the Alt key as you press and release the Tab key until you've highlighted the desired file icon; then, release both keys. The file you last selected opens onscreen in its application.
- **Quick Launch toolbar.** Click the Switch Between Windows button on the Windows Vista Quick Launch toolbar to "stack" the open windows, as shown in Figure 3-17. Then click the window for the file (and application) you want to switch to.

NOTE **Many of the actions described previously work nearly the same under Windows XP.**

FIGURE 3-17

Windows Vista provides a visual way to switch between open file and application windows.

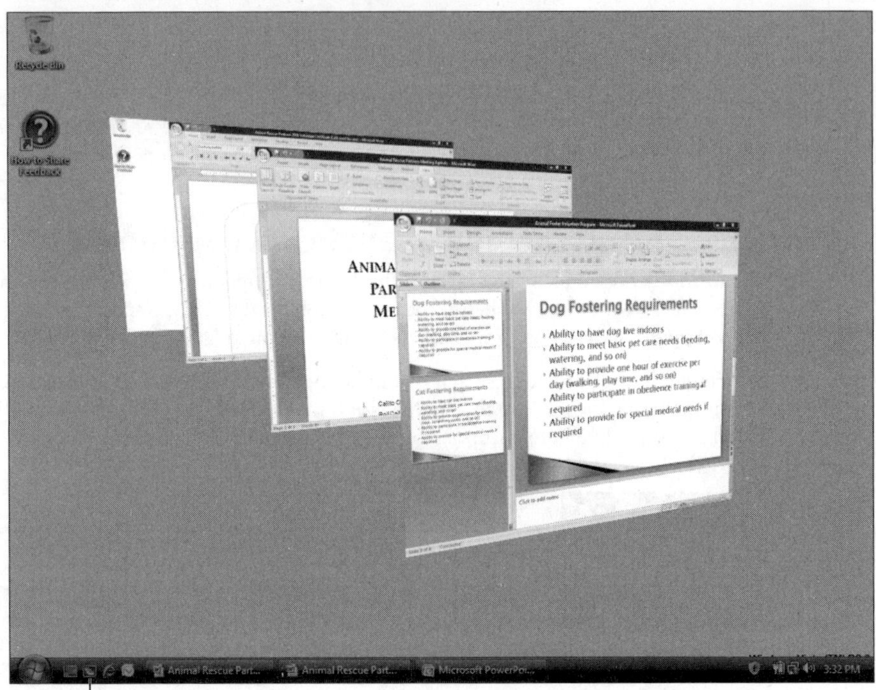

Arranging windows

Arranging windows sizes all the open files in an application and positions them so that the files fill the available space in the application window without overlapping. (Word actually sizes multiple instances of the Word application window to fill the screen.) This feature enables you to review and compare the information in multiple files more easily, or to perform an action such as moving or copying information from one file to another, as described in the next section.

The View tab of the Ribbon includes an Arrange All button. Click that button to arrange the open file windows, as in the example shown in Figure 3-18. Note that some applications also include Cascade, which stacks the open windows so that you can switch to another window by clicking its title bar.

To arrange all the open file and program windows on the Windows desktop, right-click a blank area of the taskbar (not a taskbar button) and then click Show Windows Side by Side.

In some of the Office applications, such as Publisher, use the Window menu to switch between open files within the application and to arrange open Windows.

FIGURE 3-18

Arranging file windows makes file contents more accessible.

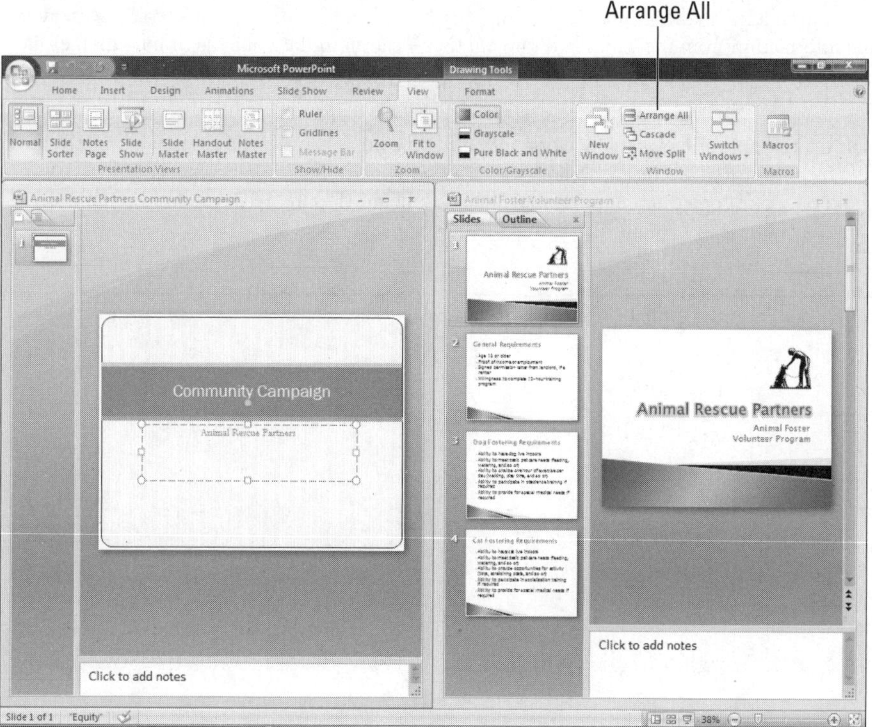

Moving and Copying Information

A template can save you time by providing starter content for a document, but that starter content is not your own, unique information. When needed, you can reuse information you've created in one file in a new file by moving or copying that information.

Microsoft has dedicated significant effort over time to ensure that the Office applications can accept information from one another so that users can build documents that integrate content created from different applications. For example, you can use an Excel worksheet to perform complicated calculations and then reuse that information in Word or PowerPoint.

This section shows you how simple techniques enable you to work quickly and have consistent content by moving and copying information.

See Chapter 42, "Integration with Other Office Applications," to learn more specifics about reusing information between applications.

Understanding the Clipboard

The *Windows Clipboard* enables users to copy information between virtually any two applications, as long as the applications are relatively compatible in terms of the file formats they use. Windows transfers information you *copy* or *cut* from a file to the Clipboard, a temporary holding area in the system's working memory. You can *paste* the information from the Clipboard into another location in the same file or into another file altogether. The information stays on the Clipboard until you copy or paste something else or shut down the computer.

The top Microsoft Office applications actually work with Office's own version of the Clipboard, called the *Office Clipboard*, which improves on the capabilities of the Windows Clipboard. Whereas the Windows Clipboard can hold only one copied or cut item, the Office Clipboard (Figure 3-19) can hold up to 24.

FIGURE 3-19

Multiple cut or copied items appear on the Office Clipboard for pasting.

Selecting information

Before you can copy or cut information to place it in the Clipboard, you have to *select,* or highlight, the information. Most users today prefer to use the mouse to select text or other onscreen content by clicking it or dragging over it. Although selection methods vary a bit between Office applications, here are some basic techniques to know:

- In Word, drag over text to select it. Word also offers a variety of shortcut techniques, such as double-clicking a word to select it, or triple-clicking a paragraph to select the whole paragraph.
- In applications that use text placeholders, such as PowerPoint and Publisher, click the placeholder to select or activate it and then drag over the specific text to select.
- In Excel worksheets and Access tables, drag diagonally over cells to select the group of cells. For example, in Figure 3-20, you can see that the range A4:38 is selected because the heavy black cell selector appears around the selected range and the row and column headings for the selected cells appear highlighted.

FIGURE 3-20

Drag diagonally to select worksheet cells.

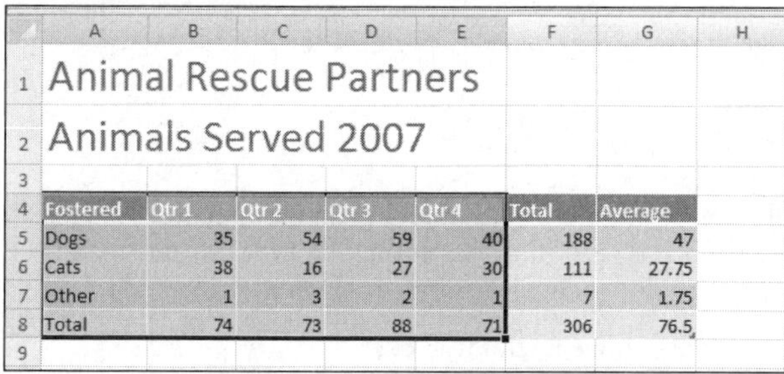

	A	B	C	D	E	F	G	H
1	Animal Rescue Partners							
2	Animals Served 2007							
3								
4	Fostered	Qtr 1	Qtr 2	Qtr 3	Qtr 4	Total	Average	
5	Dogs	35	54	59	40	188	47	
6	Cats	38	16	27	30	111	27.75	
7	Other	1	3	2	1	7	1.75	
8	Total	74	73	88	71	306	76.5	
9								

- To select another type of item such as a graphic, click it. Black selection handles and a selection box appear around the object. You can Shift+click additional objects to add them to the selection.

Copying

Copy a selection when you want to reuse information from one location in one or more other locations. Copying a selected item leaves the original intact and places a duplicate on the Clipboard. You can use one of three methods to copy a selection that you've already made:

- Press Ctrl+C.
- Click the Home tab on the Ribbon and then click the Copy button. (In some Office applications, select Edit ➪ Copy.) Figure 3-21 shows the Ribbon buttons for copying, cutting, and pasting.

FIGURE 3-21

Check the Home tab to find the tools for copying and moving text.

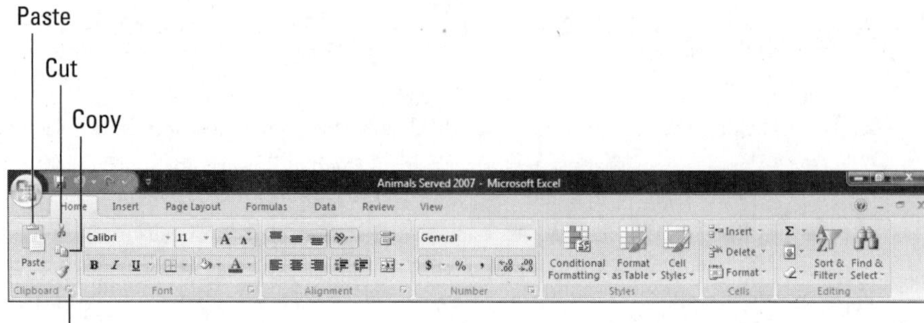

- Right-click the selection and click Copy in the shortcut menu.

NOTE **After you copy or cut a range of cells in Excel, a flashing marquee appears around the selected range to remind you to paste. Press Esc to clear the marquee if you decide not to paste the information.**

Cutting

Cutting also places the selection on the Clipboard but removes the selection from its original location rather than make a duplicate. So, when you want to *move* information from one file to another, you first cut the selection from its original location and then paste it into position in another file.

As with copying, you can use one of three methods to cut:

- Press Ctrl+X.
- Click the Home tab on the Ribbon and then click the Cut button.
- Right-click the selection and click Cut in the shortcut menu.

CAUTION **After you cut information from a text document or placeholder, be sure to take a look at the location from which you cut. In many instances, you might need to delete extra line spaces or add new spaces between words.**

Pasting

Pasting places an item from the Clipboard into a new location within the same file or in a completely different file or application. For example, Figure 3-22 shows the selection from Figure 3-20 pasted from Excel onto a PowerPoint slide. Pasting finishes the overall activity of either copying or moving information between locations. The method you use to paste in Office depends on whether you need to use the Office Clipboard, which enables you to paste multiple selections or a selection other than the most recent item you cut or copied.

FIGURE 3-22

Pasting to finish copying and moving text enables you to deliver a powerful, consistent message by combining information you've developed in a variety of applications.

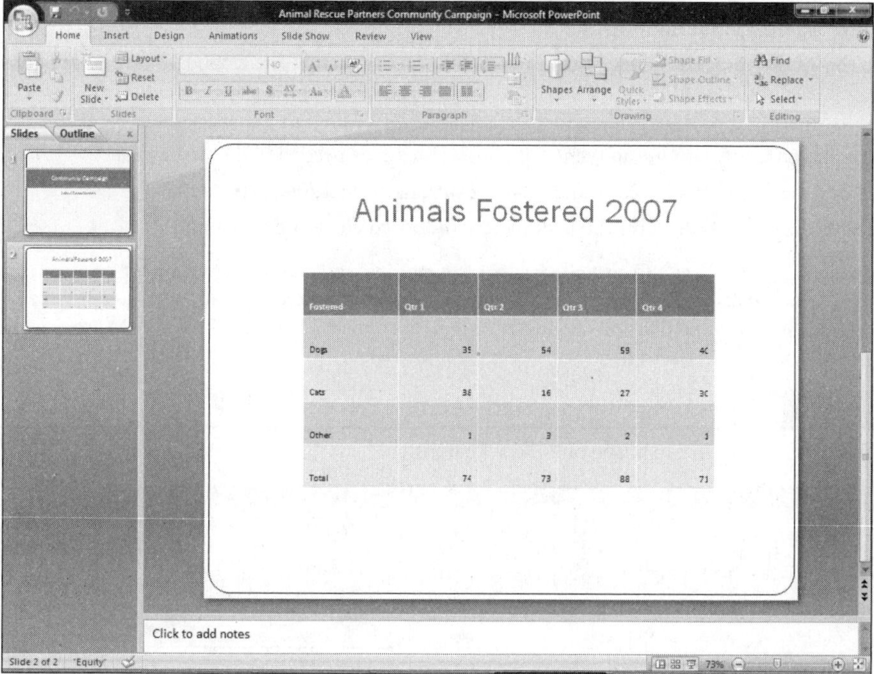

To paste directly:

1. **Click to position the insertion point at the location in which you want to paste the item.** Switch to the file first, if needed. In some cases, you might have to click within a text placeholder first. In Excel, click the upper-left cell in the range to paste to.
2. **Perform the paste.** As when copying or cutting, you can use one of three techniques to issue the Paste command:
   - Press Ctrl+V.
   - Click the Home tab on the Ribbon and then click the top portion of the Paste button.
   - Right-click the location where you want the selection inserted and then click Paste in the shortcut menu.

TIP **In Excel, you also can press Enter to paste after selecting a destination cell. This method clears the blinking marquee from the copied or cut material, in contrast to the three techniques listed in the previous step.**

Using the Office Clipboard enables you to take advantage of multiple selections that you've copied or cut. To paste using the Office Clipboard:

1. **Click to position the insertion point at the location in which you want to paste the item.** Again, switch to the destination file first, if needed.
2. **Click the Home tab on the Ribbon.**
3. **Click the Dialog Box Launcher button in the Clipboard group.** The Clipboard task pane opens at the left side of the window.
4. **Click the item to paste in the task pane.** As shown in Figure 3-23, the pasted item appears in the destination location. You can then resize and format it as needed in the destination.
5. **Select additional paste locations and paste additional selections as needed.**
6. **Click the Close (X) button on the task pane window to close the task pane.**

TIP **If you plan to use the Office Clipboard to paste multiple selections in a document, copy or cut all the selections before opening the Clipboard and pasting. Doing so can save you a bit of moving back and forth between files.**

FIGURE 3-23

Use the Office Clipboard to paste multiple selections.

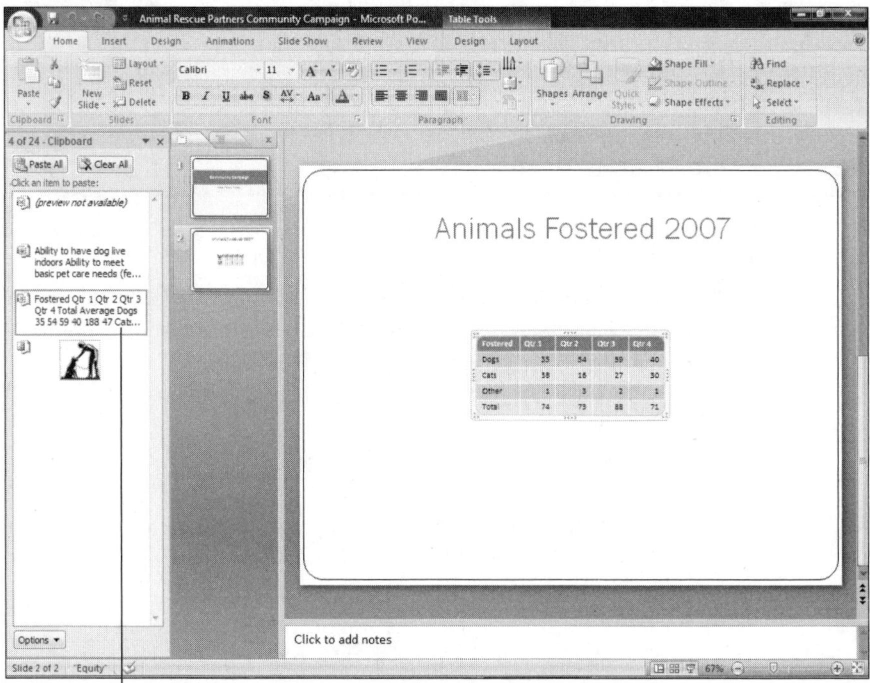

Finding and Replacing

Lengthy, complex business files can hold a ton of information, and who wants to spend all day using the PgDw key and scrolling to try to find one bit of information? Luckily, you can use the Find feature to search for a particular word or phrase. For example, if you need to find the section of a construction contract that deals with site remediation, you can find the phrase "site remediation." Even better, you can use the Replace feature to correct words you've misspelled or to change phrases or names. For example, if you've mistakenly spelled "Artur Consulting" as "Arthur Consulting" throughout a proposal for a new client, you can replace all instances of the spelling boo-boo with the correction.

Finding and replacing work in a very similar fashion, so you can use the following steps for either operation:

1. **Press Ctrl+Home.** This step moves the cursor to the beginning of the document so that the Find or Replace operation starts from there.
2. **Click the Home tab on the Ribbon.**
3. **Click either Find or Replace in the Editing Group.** The Find and Replace dialog box appears. The Find tab that appears for a find includes a Find What text box, whereas the Replace tab that appears for a replace also includes a Replace With text box.

NOTE In Excel, click the Find & Select button on the Home tab and then click either Find or Replace. In other applications, you may need to choose Find or Replace from the Edit menu or may be able to press Ctrl+F to start a find. The Find and Replace dialog box varies in appearance from application to application.

4. **Type the entry to find in the Find What text box.**
5. **Type the replacement entry, if any, in the Replace With text box.**
6. **Specify additional options, if needed.** The available options vary depending on the application. For example, in Word, you can click the More button and then specify choices such as matching case or matching a prefix or suffix.
7. **Click Find Next.** The application highlights the first matching instance of the search word or phrase, as shown in Figure 3-24.
8. **Click a button for replacing the found text, if applicable:**
   - Replace: Replaces only the highlighted instance of the matching word or phrase.
   - Replace All: Replaces all instances of the matching word or phrase.
   - Find Next: Skips to the next match without making a replacement.
9. **Repeat Steps 7 and 8 as needed to proceed through the find or replace operation.**
10. **Click OK in the message that tells you that the search has been completed.**

TIP Some Office applications offer special methods for finding information. For example, Outlook enables you to find messages from a particular sender or having a particular subject. And Access enables you to save and reuse a *query*, which finds information matching one or more criteria.

FIGURE 3-24

The found match is selected (highlighted).

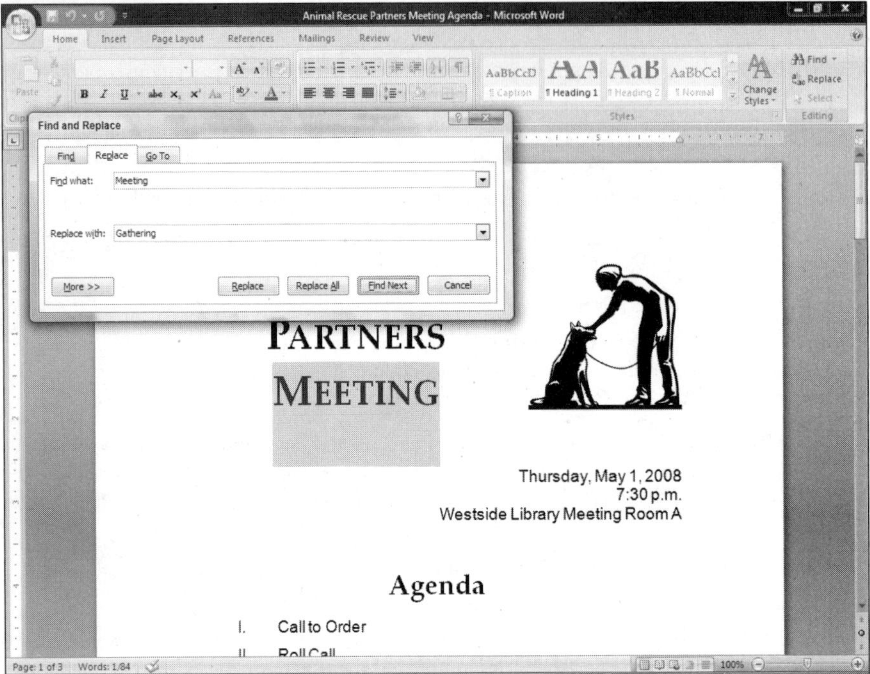

Spell Checking

Typos have no place in professional business documents, whether delivered electronically or in hard copy form. You always want to put your best foot forward and make sure that your files are attractive, clear and easy to follow, and typo free.

By default, many of the Office applications quietly check your spelling for you as you type. If you see a telltale red squiggle appear underneath a word, that means that the application thinks you've misspelled the word — according to the application's own dictionary, anyway. If you see a wavy red underline underneath a word, right-click the word. As shown in Figure 3-25, you can then click a correction in the shortcut menu that appears to replace the typo with the correction, or click Add to Dictionary so that the word is no longer flagged as a misspelling.

FIGURE 3-25

Right-click any word with a red wavy outline and then click a correction.

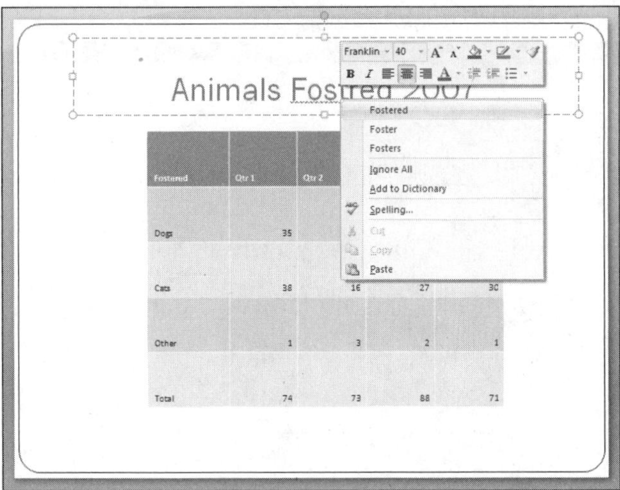

If you've finished creating the document and have moved on to the fine-tuning stage, you should always run a complete spell check to catch any typos that you may have missed earlier. Use these steps to run the check, and use the most common options for dealing with potential misspellings:

1. **Press Ctrl+Home.** This step moves to the beginning of the document so that the spell checking operation will start from there.
2. **Click the Review tab on the Ribbon.**
3. **Click Spelling & Grammar (Word) or Spelling (other apps) in the Proofing Group.** The Spelling dialog box appears with the first potential misspelling highlighted, as shown in Figure 3-26. Some applications enable you to start a spelling check simply by pressing F7.

NOTE **Word can check grammar in addition to spelling every time you run a spell check. A green squiggle may appear under any potential grammar error in the document. Appendix A explains where you can find the settings for controlling how spelling and grammar checking behave in Word.**

4. **Click a button to tell the spelling check how to proceed:**
   - Ignore: Skips only the currently found instance of the suspected word without replacing it.
   - Ignore All: Skips all instances of the suspected word without replacing it.
   - Change: Replaces only the currently found instance of the suspected word with the current selection in the Suggestions list. (Click another suggestion before clicking this button, if needed.)
   - Change All: Replaces all instances of the suspected word with the current selection in the Suggestions list. (Click another suggestion before clicking this button, if needed.)
   - Add: Adds the suspected word to the dictionary so that it will be skipped in future spelling checks.

FIGURE 3-26

The spelling check highlights the suspected word and displays it in the Not in Dictionary text box of the Spelling dialog box.

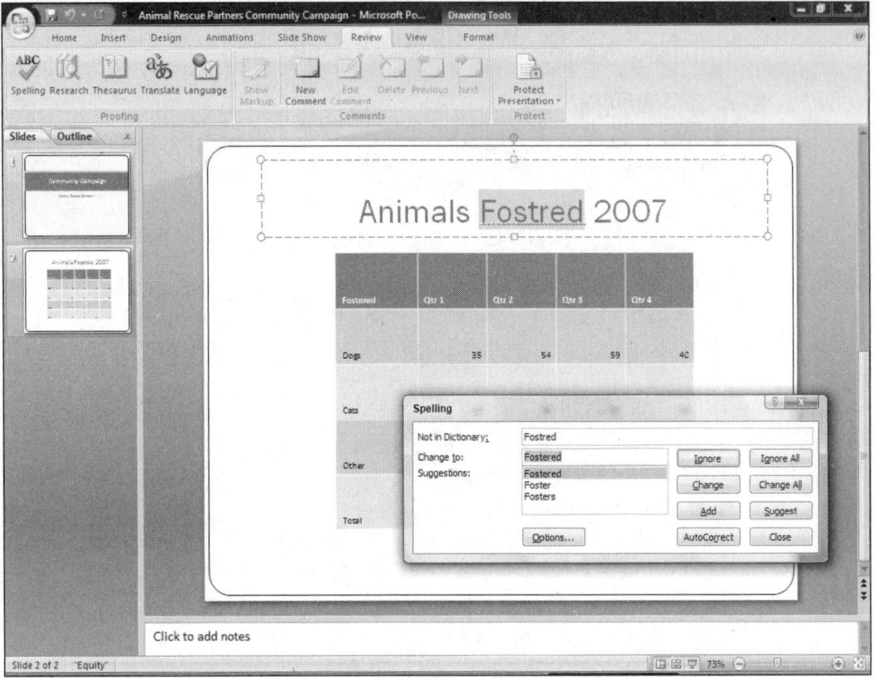

5. **Repeat Step 4 as needed to proceed through the spelling check.**
6. **Click OK in the message that tells you that the spelling check has been completed.**

TIP **It's critical to proofread your files even after spell checking. Because no spelling checker can pick up on every wrong word choice — such as when you use "then" instead of "than" or "their" instead of "there," you still need to apply your own intelligence in perfecting your documents.**

AutoCorrect, AutoFormat, and Smart Tags

These three features provide a trio of conveniences that many users have come to take for granted. The AutoCorrect feature makes certain corrections as you type. For example, it capitalizes the first word of a sentence if you've failed to do so, or it can change a typo such as "acessories" to "accessories." The AutoFormat feature supplies automatic formatting, such as creating true fraction characters or automatic numbered lists. And the Smart Tags feature displays a red dotted underline under particular types of data such as a date. Click the button that appears with the data and you see a menu of special operations pertaining to that data, such as seeing your calendar for an underlined date.

Most users will want to keep these features working as they were originally installed. However, in other cases, you may want to turn off one or more aspects of these features, such as whether AutoFormat converts Web or e-mail addresses to hyperlinks or whether the Smart Tags feature flags dates.

You can access the settings for all three of these features in the AutoCorrect dialog box. To display the dialog box, click the Microsoft Office Button and then click the *Program Name* Options button that appears at the bottom of the menu. Click the Proofing category in the list at the left side of the Options dialog box that appears and then click the AutoCorrect Options button. The AutoCorrect dialog box appears. (In Publisher, choose Tools ➪ AutoCorrect Options.)

Change settings on each of the tabs as needed and then click OK to apply your changes. Here's a look at the tabs and the changes you might want to make:

- **AutoCorrect.** Clear the checkbox beside any of the standard corrections that you want the program to stop making. If you want to add your own correction to the list of typos that AutoCorrect fixes, type entries in the Replace and With text boxes (see Figure 3-27) and then click Add.

FIGURE 3-27

You can create a new typo correction for AutoCorrect.

- **AutoFormat As You Type.** On this tab (Figure 3-28), clear the checkbox beside any of the formatting changes to disable that change.
- **Smart Tags.** As on the other two tabs, clear or check checkboxes as needed to disable or enable Smart Tag features. The Label Text with Smart Tags checkbox turns smart tags on and off altogether.

FIGURE 3-28

Choose which AutoFormatting changes the application will make.

Styles and Live Preview

The 2007 versions of Word, Excel, and PowerPoint in particular offer powerful new formatting choices loosely known as *styles* and are typically found on a contextual Design tab that appears when you select an element such as a table onscreen. The styles might be found in a Ribbon group or gallery named "Styles" or something similar. For example, Figure 3-29 shows the gallery of styles available in the Table Styles group of the Design tab that you can use when you've selected a collection of cells on an Excel worksheet.

Style choices work with a new Office feature called *Live Preview*. When you move your mouse pointer over a choice in a gallery like the one shown in Figure 3-29, the selected object temporarily changes to show you how it would look if you applied the highlighted style. In this way, you can quickly "try on" various looks for the selected item. When the Live Preview shows you the look you want, you can click the selected style to apply it to the selected item.

If you prefer not to use the Live Preview feature, you can turn it off. See Appendix A to learn how to change this and other program options.

FIGURE 3-29

Click a style to apply all its formatting choices to the selected object.

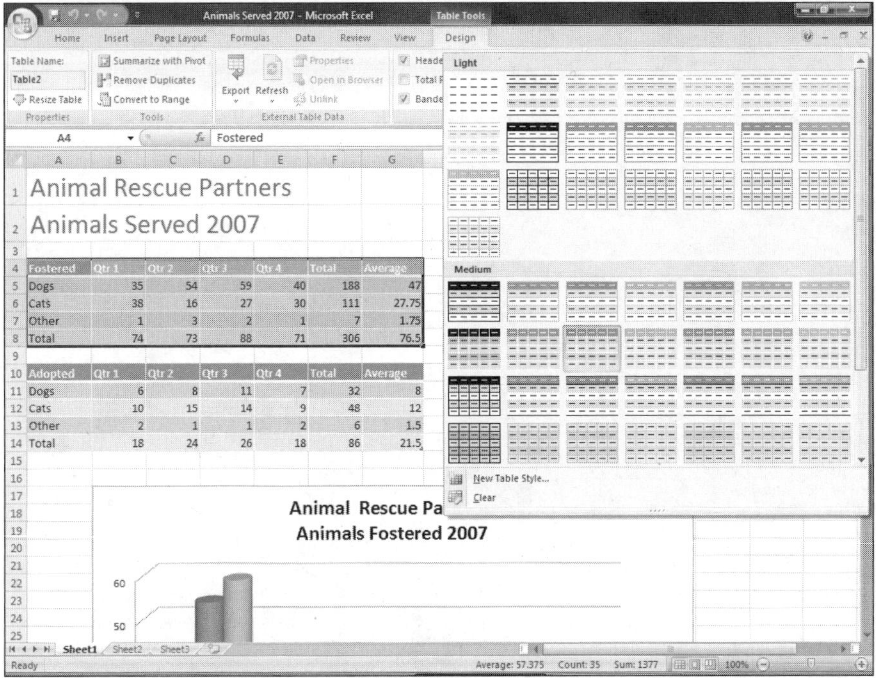

Summary

You now should have a good grounding in tasks common to most of the Office applications. In this chapter, you learned how to create, save, open, and close files. You learned how to check out how a file will look when printed, how to tweak page and printer settings, and how to print. The chapter also showed you how you can work in multiple files and applications, move easily between different files and programs, and how to move or copy information from one file or program to another. Finally, you saw how you can polish a document by replacing text, spell checking, making automatic corrections and formatting changes, and viewing and using the sophisticated styles offered in some Office 2007 applications.

Part II

Creating Documents with Word

IN THIS PART

Chapter 4

Making a Document

IN THIS CHAPTER

Creating a blank file

Using a template

Saving

Word's new "XML"-based documents

Stick with .doc or upgrade to .docx?

Navigation tricks

Getting to the view you want

Regardless of your background with prior generations of Word, this chapter will help you get started quickly. If you're new to Word, this chapter escorts you through the basics, so you're ready to begin your journey toward becoming an expert. If you've been using Word for years, there are many new wrinkles that I'll point out along the way. This chapter explores navigation nuances, view variations, and saving options. You'll also learn some navigation tricks and take a tour of Word's views.

Creating a Blank File

When you start the Word application using the Start menu, it by default creates a new, blank document file for you. This document file has the placeholder name *Document1* until you save it to assign a more specific name, as described later in the chapter. You can immediately start entering content into this blank document.

If you need another blank document, you can create it at any time by following these steps:

1. **Select Office Button ⇨ New.** The New Document dialog box appears.
2. **Click the Blank Document icon if it isn't selected by default.**
3. **Click Create.** The new, blank document appears.

Typing text

When you create a new, blank document, you can begin typing text to fill the page. As you type, each character appears to the right of the blinking vertical insertion point. You can use the Backspace and Delete keys to delete text, the Spacebar to enter spaces, and all the other keys that you're using for typing.

Word also enables you to start a line of text anywhere on the page using the Click and Type feature. (This feature only works in the Print Layout view, so to learn more about that view, see the later section describing Word 2007's views.) To take advantage of Click and Type, move the mouse pointer over a blank area of the page. If you don't see formatting symbols below the I-beam mouse pointer, click once. This enables Click and Type and displays its special mouse pointer. Then, you can double-click to position the pointer on the page and type your text. Figure 4-1 shows snippets of text added to a page using Click and Type.

Using word wrap

By default, the margins for a blank document in Word 2007 are 1" on the left and right, which is a quarter inch less than previous versions of Word. When you type enough text to fill each line, hitting the right margin boundary, Word automatically moves the insertion point to the next line. This automated feature is called *word wrap*, and it's a heck of a lot more convenient than having to make a manual carriage return at the end of this line.

If you adjust the margins for the document, word wrap always keeps your text within the new margin boundaries. Similarly, if you apply a right indent, divide the document into columns, or create a table and type in a table cell, word wrap automatically creates a new line of text at every right boundary. Just keep typing until you want or need to start a new paragraph (covered shortly). Later chapters cover changing margins and indents and working with tables.

FIGURE 4-1

Double-click and type anywhere on the page.

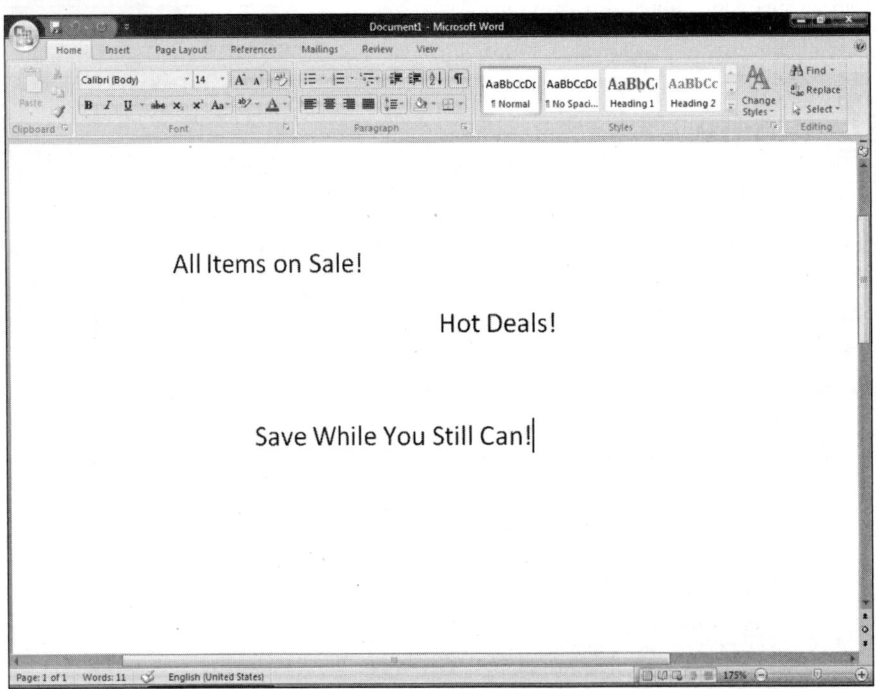

Inserting versus overtyping

Like its prior versions, Word 2007 offers two modes for entering text: *insert mode* and *overtype mode*. In the default mode, insert mode, if you click within existing text and type, Word inserts the added text between the existing characters, moving text to the right of the insertion point farther right to accommodate your additions, and rewrapping the line as needed. In contrast, when you switch to overtype mode, any text you type replaces text to the right of the insertion point.

Overtyping is a fine method of data entry — when it's the mode that you want. Unfortunately, in previous Word versions, the Insert key on the keyboard toggled between insert and overtype modes by default. Because the Insert key is found above or right next to the Delete key on the keyboard, many a surprised user would accidentally hit the Insert key and then unhappily type right over their text.

In Word 2007, the Insert key's control of overtype mode is turned off by default. You can use the Word Options dialog box to turn overtype mode on and off, and also to enable the Insert key's control of overtype mode. Select Office Button ⇨ Word Options, and then click Advanced in the list at the left side of the Word Options dialog box. Use the Use Overtype Mode checkbox (Figure 4-2) to toggle overtype mode on and off, and the Use the Insert Key to Control Overtype Mode checkbox to toggle the Insert key's control of overtype mode on and off. Click OK to apply your changes.

FIGURE 4-2

The Word Options dialog box enables you to turn overtype mode on and off.

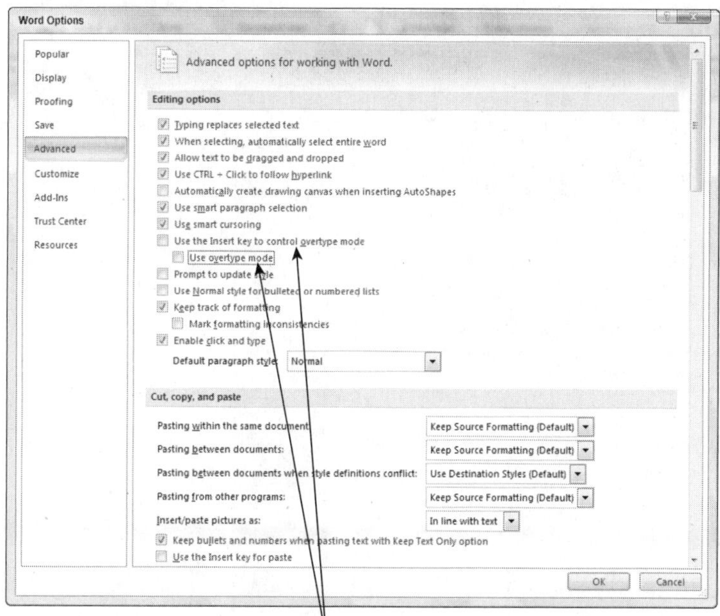

Using default tabs

Every new, blank document has default tab stops already set up for you. These tabs are set at 1/2 inch (.5") intervals along the whole width of the document between the margins. To align text to any of these default tab stops, press the Tab key. You can press Tab multiple times if you need to allow more width between the information that you're using the tab stops to align.

TIP **To display the rulers so that you can better work with text alignment features like tabs in a document, click the View Ruler button that appears at the top of the vertical scroll bar at the right side of the Word window.**

Making a new paragraph

In previous versions of Word, when you wanted to create a new paragraph in a blank document, you had to press the Enter key twice. That's because the default body text style didn't provide for any extra spacing after a paragraph mark, which is a hidden symbol inserted when you press Enter.

In Word 2007, pressing Enter by default not only inserts the paragraph mark to create a new paragraph, but also inserts extra spacing between paragraphs to separate them visually and eliminate the need to press Enter twice. As shown in Figure 4-3, when you press Enter after a paragraph the insertion point moves down to the beginning of a new paragraph, and Word includes spacing above the new paragraph.

FIGURE 4-3

Press Enter to create a new paragraph in Word.

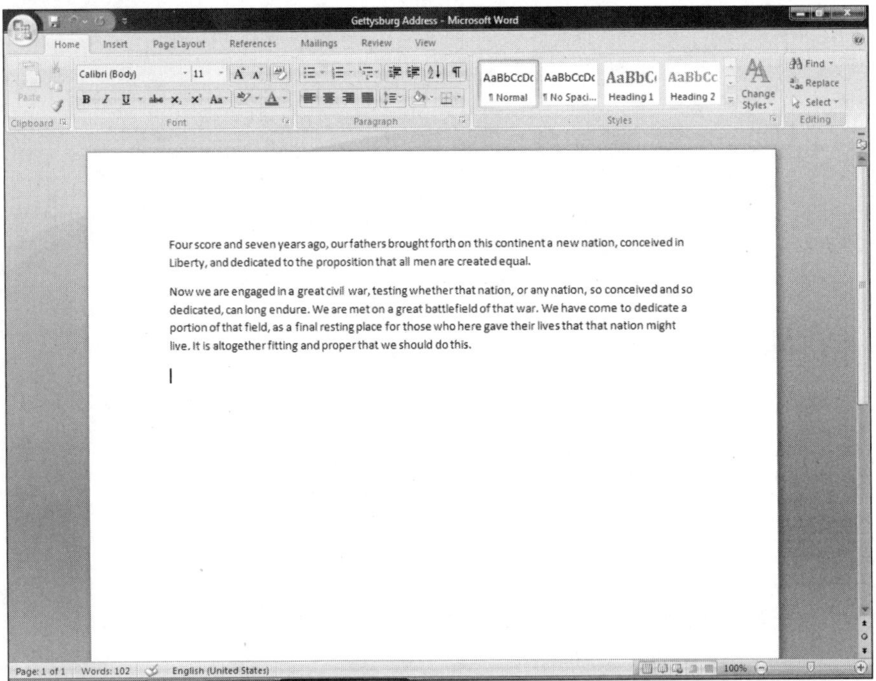

Creating a File from a Template

You need not start every document that you create from scratch. You can instead select a *template* that supplies design settings and in many cases starter text on which you can base your own document content. The Office applications offer many templates, both installed on your system and available online. In Word, you can choose from a variety of different templates to get your document started.

Understanding templates

Every new document you create in Word — even a blank document — is based on a template that specifies basic formatting for the document such as margin settings and default text styles. When you create a blank document, Word automatically applies the default global template, *Normal.dotm*.

In other instances, you can select a specific template to use as the basis for a new document. A template can include not only design elements, but also labels and starter text and placeholders for your information. For example, you can select a fax template that holds predefined labels and positions for recipient name, fax number, and more. Or, you can choose resume template that defines a nice layout has placeholders that you select and replace to add your own resume information.

Installing Word 2007 installs a variety of letter, resume, fax, and report templates on your system. Word also enables you to download templates from dozens of different categories from Office Online. There are downloadable templates for brochures, business cards, memos, purchase orders, and more.

Creating the file from the template

Using a template for a new file starts out just like creating a blank file. The New Document dialog box enables you to browse for an select a template and in most cases to see a preview before you select the template to use. Follow these steps to create a new document based on a template:

1. **Select Office Button ⇨ New.** The New Document dialog box opens.
2. **Click either Installed Templates in the Templates section in the left-hand list, or click a template category under Microsoft Office Online.** Thumbnails and names for the available templates in the selected category appear in the middle section of the dialog box.
3. **Click the thumbnail for the desired template.** A preview for the template appears at the right, as shown in Figure 4-4.
4. **Click the Create button to create the new file from an installed template, or click Download to create the new document from a selected online template.** If you're downloading a template, the Microsoft Office Genuine Advantage dialog box appears.
5. **Click Continue to validate your software installation and download the template.**

The new document appears onscreen.

NOTE **Some of the templates available via Office Online were created in earlier Word versions. Those documents will open in compatibility mode, which is described later in this chapter.**

FIGURE 4-4

Preview a template before making a new document from it.

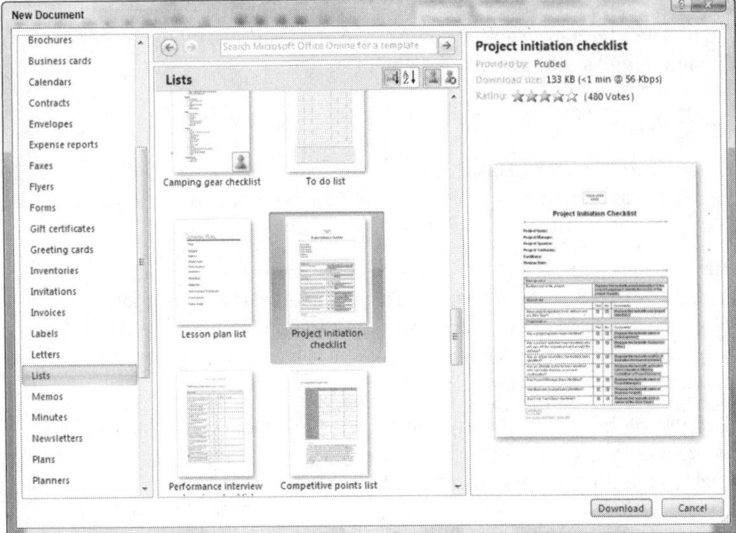

Working with template content

As shown in Figure 4-5, a template might hold a variety of different sample content and placeholders.

You can work with these placeholders and other contents as follows to finish your document:

- **Graphics placeholders.** The box at the top of Figure 4-5 that says Your Logo Here is a placeholder for a graphic. Click the placeholder to select it, click the Insert tab on the Ribbon, and then click the Picture or Clip Art choice in the Illustrations group to select a replacement item. Chapter 9, "Tables and Graphics," provides more information about working with artwork in your Word documents.
- **Labels for text.** If you were to click to the right of the colon for any of the label items listed immediately below Project Initiation Checklist in Figure 4-5, the insertion point would appear at a precise position, ready for you to enter the text to go with the label.
- **Gray field placeholders.** Template text that appears with square brackets and gray shading are *text form fields*. Clicking one of these placeholders selects the entire placeholder, and then any text you type replaces the placeholder contents.
- **Other text.** You can supplement the template's contents by adding your own text anywhere in the document.
- **Styles.** Templates also include predefined styles (formatting) that you can apply to text that you add. See Chapter 7 to learn more about applying styles to text.

FIGURE 4-5

Replace template placeholders with your own content.

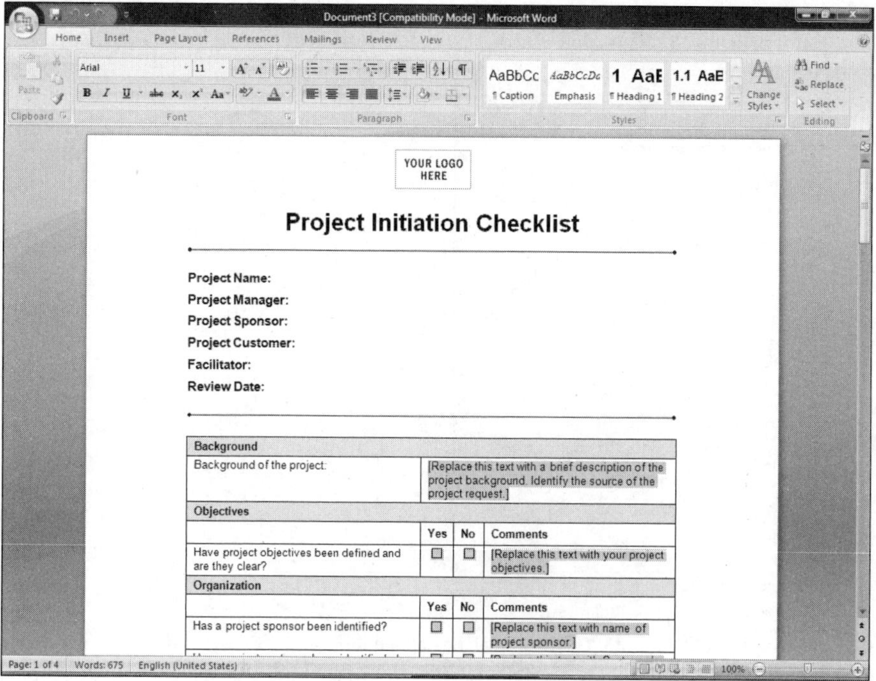

Saving and File Formats

What good are any of these tools if the information never leaves the Word window? At the end of the day, the goal is to create letters, reports, brochures, pamphlets, books, web pages, blogs, and other publications that take on some kind of semi-permanent existence. As long as you see "Document1" in Word's title bar, you run the risk of losing your investment of time and creativity.

Word is like most other Windows programs. When you're ready to commit your work to disk, just choose Office Button ➪ Save.

Like most other Windows programs, you also can press Ctrl+S to save the current document. If it is new and hasn't been named, you'll see the Save As dialog box shown in Figure 4-6, or something similar. If the document isn't new, Ctrl+S does an immediate Save using the existing filename. For a new file, navigate to the save location, enter a filename in the File Name text box, and then click Save.

FIGURE 4-6

Choose a folder and specify a filename when saving.

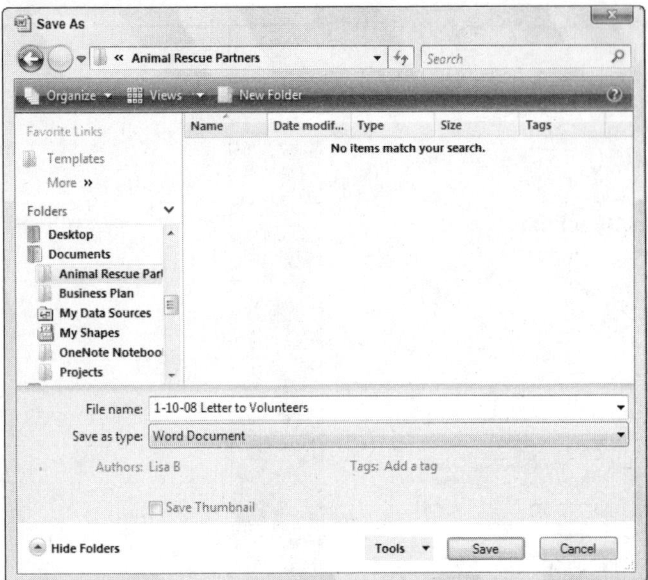

TIP **If you're working in Windows XP, the Places Bar at the left makes it easy to navigate to a folder for saving. To add a folder to the Places Bar, select the folder in the list of files and folders. Right-click in the Places Bar itself and choose Add [*folder name*]. Notice the Move Up and Move Down commands. You can reorganize your places by right-clicking a place and choosing the appropriate command. Most of the default places can be shuffled to the bottom if you don't use them, but they can't be removed. The Trusted Templates place, however, can't be moved *or* removed. Windows Vista does not use the Places Bar in Save As or Open dialog boxes. Instead, you'll see a Favorite Links list at the left. You can drag links into the Favorite Links list and use the resulting shortcuts much as you use the Places Bar in Windows XP, only more easily and more directly.**

Note also the Save as Type drop-down list under File Name. The list of formats you will see varies depending on how much of Office was installed. To have the fullest array of save options, you should do two things.

First, in Word or Office setup (start the process for changing program settings in the Add or Remove Programs section in Windows' Control Panel), navigate to Office 2007's (or Word 2007's) Installation Options section, and set Converters and Filters to Run All from My Computer, as shown in Figure 4-7. Click Continue, as needed, to complete the installation. Note that you need do this only if the full set of converters isn't already installed.

The second thing to do is to go to the Microsoft Office Web site and download the converter pack. Installed, this pack adds the fullest range of converters to your Office 2007 setup. Note that the location and name of this free add-on varies. At this writing, however, it is located here:

`www.microsoft.com/downloads/details.aspx?FamilyID=cf196df0-70e5-4595-8a98-370278f40c57&DisplayLang=en`

You can also search Microsoft's Web site for `OCONVPCK.EXE`.

FIGURE 4-7

To maximize your Save and Open options, install the full set of converters.

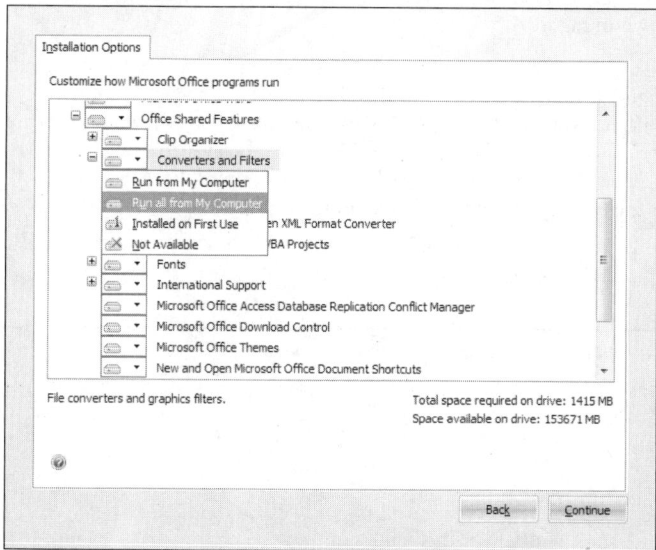

If, instead of pressing Ctrl+S, you click the Office button, you will see — among other options — Convert, Save (same as having pressed Ctrl+S), Save As, and Publish options. Note that only Save works exactly as it did in Office 2003.

Convert

You will see the Convert option on the Office Button (File) menu only if the current file is from an earlier Word format (e.g., Word 97–Word 2003, also known as *compatibility mode*), such as when you use an older template from Office Online as the basis for your document. Clicking the Convert menu choice converts the current file into Word 2007 format so that you can then save it.

WARNING **Make a copy of the file or save the file under a new name *before* clicking Convert. The Convert option renames the original file. The first time you convert, Word does alert you to what it's doing, but if you're like most users, you won't read the fine print and you'll click "Do not ask me again about converting documents." If you do happen to click that option, in the future there will be no warning; and if you're like me, you will forget it was ever there the first time.**

When you convert, Word converts the document currently displayed to Word 2007 format. At that point, the notation "(Compatibility Mode)" disappears from Word's title bar, but the displayed name still shows `.doc` instead of a new Word 2007 document extension. Even so, at this point you can still recover the original file by closing the file without saving the changes. Until you save, the converted file exists only in the current window.

However, if you now save the file, Word immediately renames it using Word's new extension (`.docx` for a plain vanilla Word 2007 document file, or `.docm` for a Word 2007 document file that contains macros). Once converted, the original `.doc` file is gone forever! After the fact, you can perform a Save As and resave the file in the original format. However, I'm not going to guarantee that it will be byte-for-byte identical to the original.

Word 2007's confusing Save As

Word 2007's Save As option is a bit confusing. You really have two choices embedded in that option, even though it might look like you have only one. If you click Save As itself — not the right-pointing triangle — you will get the Save As dialog box shown in Figure 4-6.

When you hover over the right-pointing triangle, however, the two options shown in Figure 4-8 are displayed. Most users at first overlook the first option (clicking on Save As itself) and conclude that the five options shown in Figure 4-8 are the only ones offered. Not only is that not the case, but the options shown actually are redundant. That's because all of those formats (Word 97–2003, PDF, and XPS) are also available from the Save As dialog box. Why did Microsoft do it this way? It was to highlight the typical user's most likely Save As choices. Unfortunately, it often confuses the user who thinks that the number of Save As options has been greatly reduced.

FIGURE 4-8

Save As... and the triangle to the right of it are two distinct options that can be clicked.

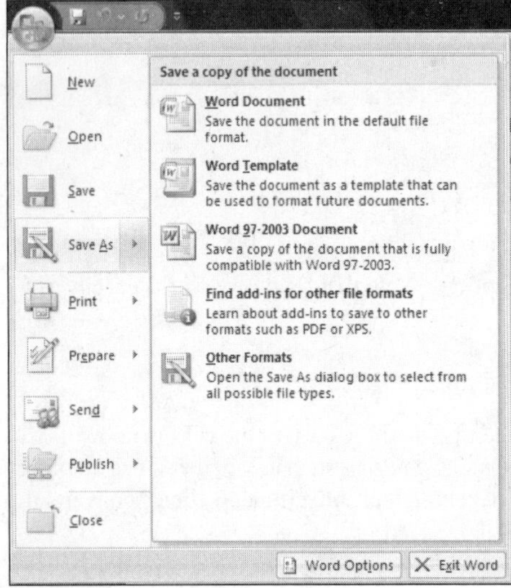

The PDF or XPS option appears only if you install the free patch available from Microsoft.

Publish

Word 2007's other new save-related option contains three options that have been termed *publish*. Many Internet users ordinarily think of publish in terms of Web sites. Well, that's really what this is, albeit perhaps different from the way some users think about publishing. Shown in Figure 4-9, these options all result in Word content ending up online. I'm going to talk about the Blog feature here. To learn more about the latter two options, Document Management Server and Create Document Workspace, see Chapter 40, "SharePoint."

FIGURE 4-9

Word 2007 has three new Publish options: Blog, Document Management Server, and Create Document Workspace.

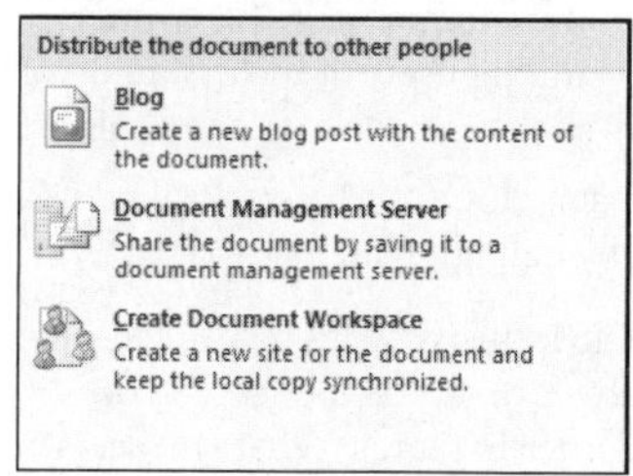

Blogging

New in Word 2007 is the Blog feature, which enables you to publish directly from Word to supported blogs. Which blogs are supported? At this time, MSN Spaces, SharePoint 2007, Blogger, and Community Server are supported. You might also have success with some services that support the metaweblog and ATOM APIs.

Compatibility with Previous Versions of Word

With Office 2007's new interface and powerful new tools also comes a new file format. Word 2003's previous file format has been basically unchanged since Word 97. Feature enhancements have necessitated the modification of Word's binary format over the years, such as when document versioning and floating tables were introduced.

Even so, you can still open most Word 2003 files in Word 97 and the document looks basically the same. Only if you use newer features will you see a difference, and usually that just means reduced functionality rather than lost data and formatting.

Word 2007 and Word 2003 users will continue to see interoperability. However, Word 2007's new "native" format is radically different — and better — than the old format. Word 2007's new format boasts a number of improvements over the older format:

- **Open format** — The basic file is ZIP format, an open standard, which serves as a container for `.docx` and `.docm` files. Additionally, many (but not all) components are in XML format (eXtensible Markup Language). Microsoft makes the full specifications available free, and they may be used by anyone royalty-free. In time, this should improve and expand interoperability with products from software publishers other than Microsoft.
- **Compressed** — The ZIP format is compressed, resulting in files that are much smaller. Additionally, Word's "binary" format has been mostly abandoned (some components such as VBA macros are still written in binary format), resulting in files that ultimately resolve to plain text, and are much smaller.
- **Robust** — ZIP and XML are industry standard formats with precise specifications that offer fewer opportunities to introduce document corruption. Hence, the frequency of corrupted Word files should be greatly reduced.

- **Backward compatibility**—While Word 2007 has a new format, it still fully supports opening and saving files in legacy formats. A user can opt to save all documents in an earlier format by default. Moreover, Microsoft makes available a *compatibility pack* that enables Word 2000–2003 users to open and save in the new format. In fact, Word 2000–2003 users can make the Word 2007 format their default, providing considerable interoperability among users of the different versions.
- **New extensions**—Word 2007 now has three new native file formats: `.docx` (ordinary documents), `.docm` (macro-enabled documents), and `.dotm` (templates, which by definition are macro enabled).

Calling Word 2007's new file format XML actually is a bit of a misnomer. The industry news media calls it XML format. That's not exactly true. While XML is at the heart of Word's new format, the files saved by Word are not XML files. You can verify this by trying to open one using Internet Explorer. What you see decidedly is not XML.

As indicated, Word 2007 and 2000–2003 users will still be able to read and write to each others' files, assuming that the Word 2000–2003 user installs the free Office 2007 compatibility pack. Even so, Word will sometimes warn you that features might be lost when converting between the different formats.

Word itself runs an automatic compatibility check when you attempt to save a document in a format that's different from the current one. You can, without attempting to save, run this check yourself at any time from Word 2007. To see whether features might be lost when moving from one version of Word to another, open the document in Word 2007. Choose Office Button ➪ Prepare ➪ Run Compatibility Checker.

For the most part, Word 2007 does a good job at checking compatibility when trying to save a native `.docx` file in `.doc` format. For example, if you run the compatibility checker on a Word 2007 document containing advanced features, you will be alerted, as shown in Figure 4-10.

FIGURE 4-10

Use the Compatibility Checker to determine whether converting to a different Word version will cause a loss of information or features.

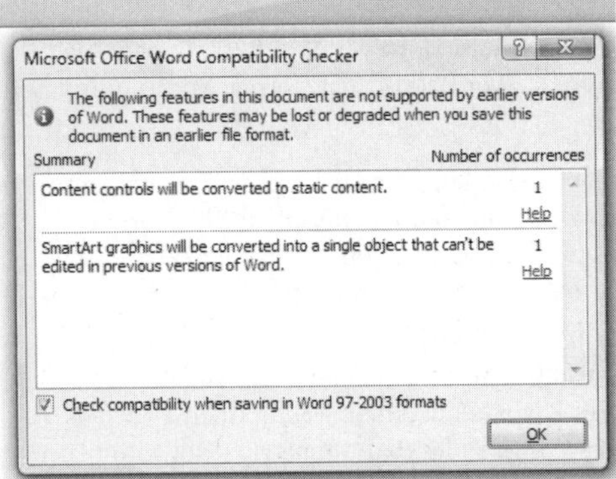

When moving in the other direction—checking a Word 2003 (or earlier) document for compatibility with Word 2007—it usually will inform you that "No compatibility issues were found." Note however, that the Compatibility Checker doesn't check when you first open a document formatted for Word 2003 (or earlier).

Nor does it check when you convert a file. It's not until you try to save the file that it warns you, as shown in Figure 4-11.

FIGURE 4-11

Word 2007 warns you when saving a document that contains multiple versions saved in Word 2003 or earlier.

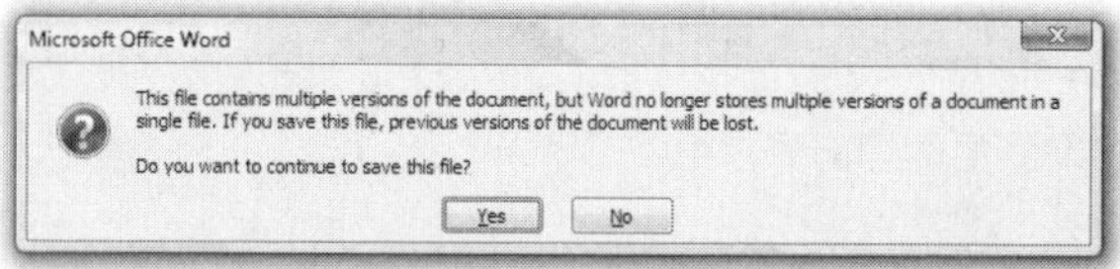

CAUTION **At this time, the Compatibility Checker does not warn you if you open a file that uses Word's versioning feature. Word 2007 does come with a tool for dealing with multiple document versions that were saved in a single file, but Word will not alert you to the fact that the current file contains versioned changes until or unless you try to save the file in .docx format. Note also that Word 2007 itself cannot fully access or properly save a versioned file, even if you tell Word 2007 to work in Word 2003 format. Hence, if you save such a file from Word 2007 — even if you tell it to save in Word 2003 format — all versioning information will be lost!**

To .doc or not to .doc

If you have the option to use Word's old format, rather than the new format, why shouldn't you do that? Isn't old usually more reliable and well tested than new? Well, that's certainly a plausible argument, but consider the fragility of Word's binary .doc format. Have you ever experienced document corruption? With a proprietary binary file format, the larger and more complex the document, the more likely corruption becomes. It doesn't take much for a Word file to become inaccessible to Word's default Open command.

Another issue is document size. Consider a simple Word document that contains just the phrase "Hello, Word." Here, when saved in Word 97–2003 format, that basic file is 26K. That is to say, to store those 11 characters, it takes Word about 26,000 characters!

The same phrase stored in Word 2007's .docx format requires just 10K. Make no mistake. That's still a lot of storage space for just those 11 characters, but it's a lot less than what's required by Word 2003. The storage savings you get won't always be that dramatically different, but over time you will notice a difference. Smaller files means not only lower storage requirement, but faster communication times as well.

Still another issue is interoperability. When a Word user gives a .doc file to a WordPerfect or other word processor user, it's a very sure bet that something is going to get lost in the translation, even though WordPerfect claims to be able to work with Word's .doc format. Such documents seldom look and print identically, and the larger and more complex they are, the more different they look.

With Word's adoption of an open formatting standard, it will now be possible for WordPerfect and other programs to more correctly interpret how any given .docx file should be displayed. Just as the same web page looks and prints nearly identically when viewed in different web browsers, Word's new .docx files should look and print nearly identically regardless of which program you use to open it (assuming it supports XML-based formats).

Persistent Save As

If, despite the advantages of using the new format, you choose to use Word's .doc format, you can do so. Choose Office Button ➪ Word Options ➪ Save. As shown in Figure 4-12, open the Save Files in This Format drop-down list and select Word 97–2003 Document (*.doc).

FIGURE 4-12

You can tell Word to save in any of a variety of formats by default.

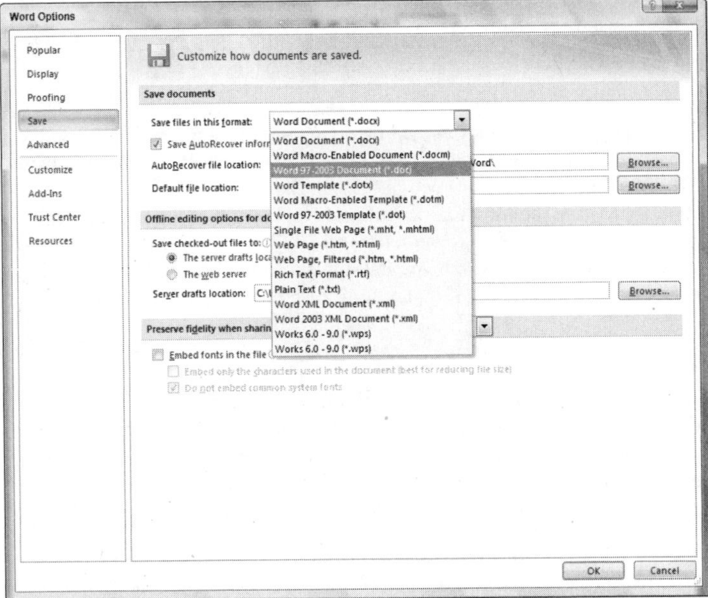

Note that even if you set .doc or some other format as your default, you can still override that setting at any time by using Save As and saving to .docx or any other supported format. Setting one format as the default does not lock you out of using other formats as needed.

Microsoft Office Compatibility Pack

As noted earlier, Microsoft makes available a free enhancement that enables Word 2003 users to open and save files in the new format. In fact, it also works with Word 2002.

Instructions are in flux regarding how to download and install the converters, as is the location of the compatibility pack. Try the following search in Google:

```
site:microsoft.com "office compatibility pack"
```

At this time, the first hit listed is the correct location.

.docx Versus .docm

With Word 2007 comes not one new format, but two — or four, depending on how you count:

- .docx — An ordinary document containing no macros
- .docm — A document that either contains macros or is macro enabled
- .dotx — A template that does not contain macros
- dotm — A template that either contains macros or is macro enabled

It is important for some purposes for users to be able to include macros not just in document templates, but in documents as well. This makes documents that contain automation a lot more portable. Rather than having to send both document and template, or worse, a template masquerading as a document, you can send a document that has macros enabled.

NOTE **When Word macro viruses first started appearing, ordinary Word documents could not contain macros — only templates could. Therefore, one of the most popular ways of "packaging" macro viruses was in a `.dot` file that had been renamed with a `.doc` extension. The virus itself often was an automatic macro (typically, AutoExec) that performed some combination of destruction and propagation when the rogue `.dot` file was first opened. A common precaution was to press Shift as you opened any Word file — `.doc` or `.dot` — to prevent automatic macros from running. In fact, even with various advances in security and antivirus software, pressing Shift when you open an unfamiliar Word document is still not being overcautious. In recent versions of Word, `.doc` files can legitimately contain macros, so I'm not really sure the situation has improved much. I still reach for the Shift key, do a quick inspection to determine whether any macros are hiding inside, and then proceed. Often, though, Word 2007 will warn you when a document contains macros.**

Because Word 2003 documents can contain legitimate macros, there is no outward way to know whether any given `.doc` document file contains macros. If someone sends you a `.doc` file, is opening it safe?

While it's not clear that the new approach — distinct file extensions for documents and templates that are macro-enabled — is going to improve safety a lot, it does provide more information for the user. This is true especially in business environments, where people don't deliberately change file extensions. If you see a file with a `.docm` or `.dotm` extension, then you know that they contain macros and might warrant careful handling.

Moreover, if the document filename extension has been deliberately changed, Word will refuse to open the document. Whether it's a `.docx` file that's been renamed to `.docm`, or vice versa, you will see the message box shown in Figure 4-13.

FIGURE 4-13

Word 2003 refuses to open a `.docx` or `.docm` file when the filename extension has been deliberately changed.

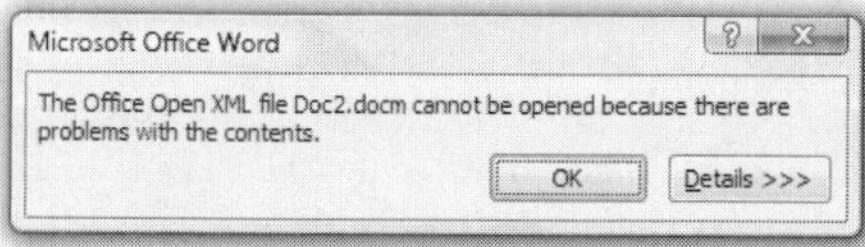

Converting a .docx file into a .docm

If you want to convert a `.docx` file so that it can contain macros, you must use Save As and choose "Word macro-enabled document (*.docm)" as the file type. You can do this at any time — it doesn't have to be when the document is first created. You can also remove any macros from a `.docm` file by saving it as Word document (*.docx).

Even so, you can create or record a macro while editing a `.docx` file, and even tell Word to store it in a `.docx` file. There will be no error message, and the macro will be available for running in the current session. However, when you first try to save the file, you will be prompted to change the target format or risk losing the VBA project. If you save it as a `.docx` anyway and close the file, the macro will not be saved.

Understanding .docx

As indicated earlier, Word's new `.docx` format doesn't itself use XML format. Rather, the main body of your document is stored in XML format, but that file isn't stored directly on disk. Instead, it's stored inside a ZIP file, which gets a `.docx`, `.docm`, `dotm`, or `dotx` file extension.

To verify this, create a simple Word 2007 file, and save and close it. Next, rename it to add a `.zip` extension. Finally, use Windows Explorer to display the contents of that ZIP file, as shown in Figure 4-14.

FIGURE 4-14

When viewed as a ZIP file, most `.docx` files contain three main folders and a Content Types XML document.

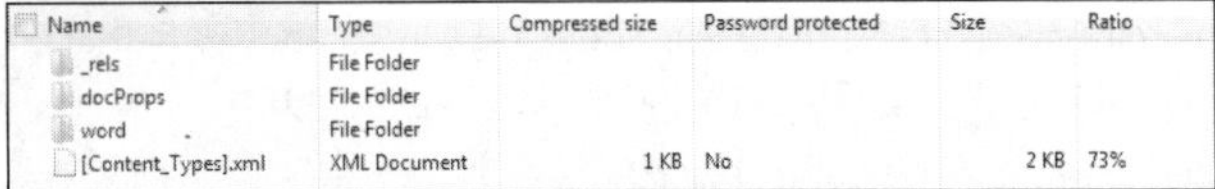

Name	Type	Compressed size	Password protected	Size	Ratio
_rels	File Folder				
docProps	File Folder				
word	File Folder				
[Content_Types].xml	XML Document	1 KB	No	2 KB	73%

Word `.docx` files can contain additional folders as well, such as one named `customXml`. This folder would be used if the document contains content control features that are linked to document properties, an external database or forms server, etc.

The main parts of the Word document are inside the folder named word. A typical word folder for a simple document appears in Figure 4-15.

FIGURE 4-15

The Word document's main components are stored inside the `.docx` file in the folder named "word."

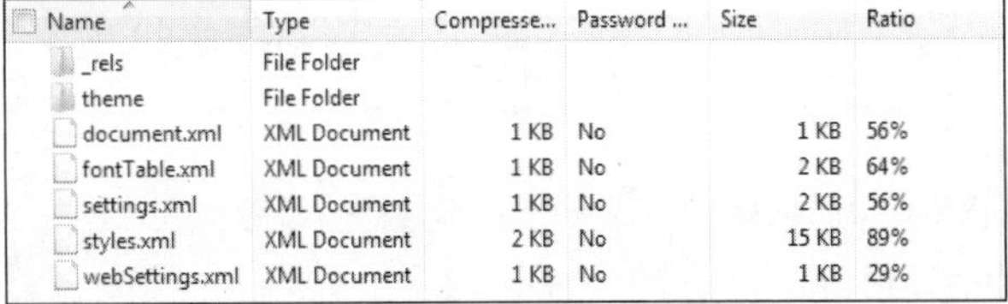

Name	Type	Compresse...	Password ...	Size	Ratio
_rels	File Folder				
theme	File Folder				
document.xml	XML Document	1 KB	No	1 KB	56%
fontTable.xml	XML Document	1 KB	No	2 KB	64%
settings.xml	XML Document	1 KB	No	2 KB	56%
styles.xml	XML Document	2 KB	No	15 KB	89%
webSettings.xml	XML Document	1 KB	No	1 KB	29%

The main text of the document is stored in `document.xml`. Using an XML editor, you could actually make changes to the text in `document.xml`, replace the original file with the changed one, rename the file so that it has a .docx extension instead of `.zip`, and open the file in Word, and those changes would appear.

Q: What's an XML editor? When I double-click on an XML file, it just opens Internet Explorer, which doesn't let me edit anything.

A. There are specialized XML editors. You can also use a Web site builder like FrontPage or SharePoint Designer. You can also use anything that edits plain text files, such as Notepad.

More complex Word files contain additional elements. Shown in Figure 4-16 is an expanded folder view of a .docx file that contains clip art, an embedded Excel chart, several pictures, some SmartArt, as well as custom XML links to document properties.

FIGURE 4-16

In a .docx file, images are stored in the word\media folder.

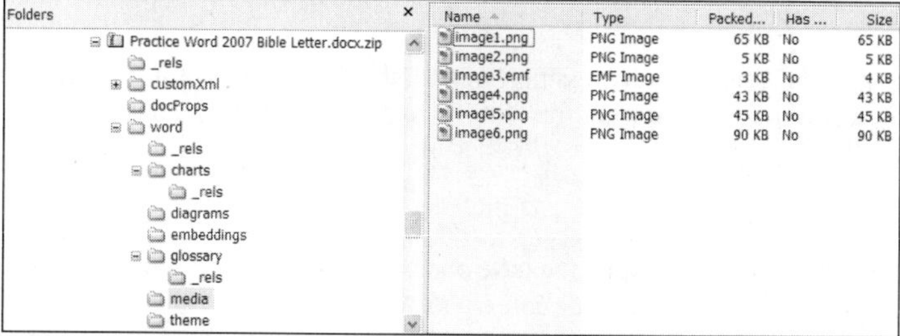

TIP

You can replace the images in a .docx file without editing the file in Word. Rename the .docx file so that it has a .zip extension. Extract the images stored in the word\media folder so you can see what's what. Give the replacement images the same respective names as the existing ones. Replace the contents of the word\media folder with the new images. Finally, replace the .zip extension with the original extension. Presto! And you never touched Word! This might not make ergonomic sense for just a few images, but if you have dozens it could save you a substantial amount of time.

Navigation Tips and Tricks

Bible readers already know the basics of using the Windows interface, so this book skips the stuff that I think every Windows user already knows about, and instead covers aspects of Word you might not know about. In our great hurry to get things done, ironically, we often overlook simple tricks and tips that might otherwise make our computing lives easier and less harried, or, at the very least, more entertaining.

Tricks with clicks

We all know about double-clicking, but not everyone knows the benefits of triple-clicking, Ctrl+clicking, and Alt+clicking.

Triple-clicking

When you triple-click inside a paragraph, Word selects the entire paragraph. However, *where* you click makes a difference. If you triple-click in the left margin, rather than in a paragraph, and the mouse pointer's shape is the arrow shown in Figure 4-17, the entire document is selected.

FIGURE 4-17

A hollow mouse pointer in the left margin indicates a different selection mode.

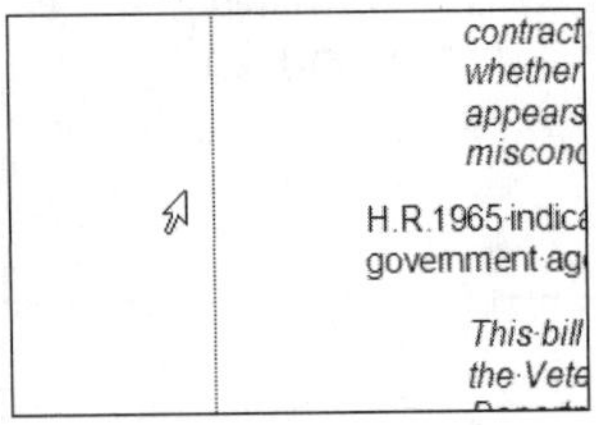

Is triple-clicking in the left margin faster and easier than pressing Ctrl+A? Not necessarily, but it might be if your hand is already on the mouse. In addition, if you want the MiniBar to appear, the mouse method will summon it, whereas Ctrl+A won't.

Ctrl+clicking

Want something faster than triple-clicking? If you just happen to have one hand on the mouse and another on the keyboard, Ctrl+click in the left margin. That also selects the entire document, and displays the MiniBar.

If you Ctrl+click in a paragraph, the current sentence is selected. This can be handy when you want to move, delete, or highlight a sentence. As someone who sometimes highlights as I read, this can also help focus on a particular passage when you're simply reading, rather than editing.

Alt+clicking

If you Alt+click a word or a selected passage, that looks up the word or selection using Office 2007's Research pane. Do you ever accidentally invoke the Research pane? Want a good way to turn it off? Well . . . stop looking, because it doesn't exist.

NOTE **If you're an advanced Word user, you probably don't want to accept this. You're probably thinking "Herb doesn't know that you can intercept the built-in Research command and replace it with a dummy macro, thereby disabling this behavior." Well, you caught me. Go ahead and try it. I'll wait.**

Back already? That's right. You can indeed prevent the Research command on the Review tab from doing anything, but that doesn't tame the Alt+click shortcut. It's more persistent than a horsefly.

Alt+dragging

You can use Alt+drag to select a vertical column of text — even if the text is not column oriented. This can be useful when working with monospaced fonts and there is a de facto columnar setup. Once selected, any character- or font-oriented formatting can be applied to the selection, as shown in Figure 4-18. The selection can also be deleted. Note that if the text is proportionally spaced, then anything that affects the size and therefore the ostensible columnar orientation will undo the selection. The effect can be rather bizarre.

FIGURE 4-18

With the Alt key pressed, you can drag to select a vertical swath of text.

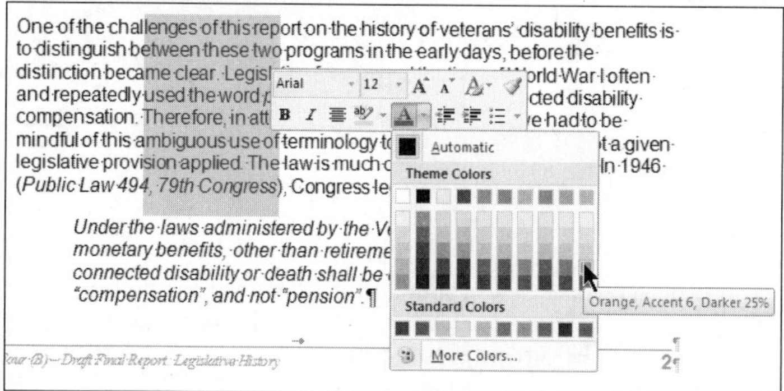

Shift+click

Click where you want a selection to start, and then Shift+click where you want it to end. You can continue Shift+clicking to expand or reduce the selection. This technique can be really useful if you have difficulty dragging exactly the selection you want.

Multi-selecting

A few versions of Word ago, it became possible to make multiple noncontiguous selections in a document. While many know this, many more don't. To do it, make your first selection. Then, hold down the Ctrl key to make additional selections. Once you've made as many selections as you want, you can then apply the desired formatting to the selections.

Seldom screen

I've already reviewed a number of new features that you'll see on the Word screen. Word 2007's new interface is so overwhelming, however, that you might never notice a few features — new and old. In this section, I point out features that are either new or often overlooked (even by long-time users), and which you might find useful.

Split box

Shown in Figure 4-19, the split box is used to divide the current document into two horizontal views of the same document. Move the mouse over the top of the vertical scroll bar so that the pointer changes (refer to Figure 4-19). At that point, you can drag down to divide the window into two panes. Alternatively, you can double-click the split box to divide the window into two equal panes.

Why would you want to do that? Well, you might not have two monitors but you need to look at a table or a figure while you write about it. In a single pane, this can be challenging, especially if what you type keeps causing the figure to move out of view.

FIGURE 4-19

Double-click or drag the split box to display the current document in two panes.

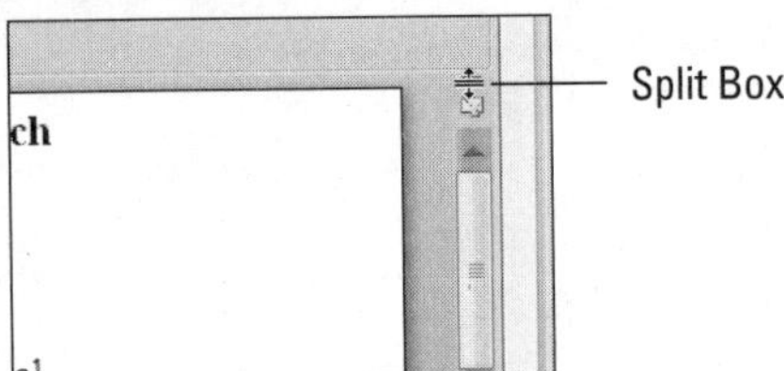

As another example, you might want to have an Outline view of your document in one pane while maintaining a Print Layout view in the other, as shown in Figure 4-20. When viewing a document in two split panes, note that the status bar reflects the status of the currently active pane. Not only can you display different views in multiple panes, but at different zoom levels as well.

You can remove the split by dragging it up or down, leaving the desired view in place, or double-click anywhere on the split line. Alternatively, if the ribbon's View tab is displayed, click Remove Split in the Window group.

FIGURE 4-20

Split panes can be displayed in different views, enabling you to see Outline and Print Layout at the same time.

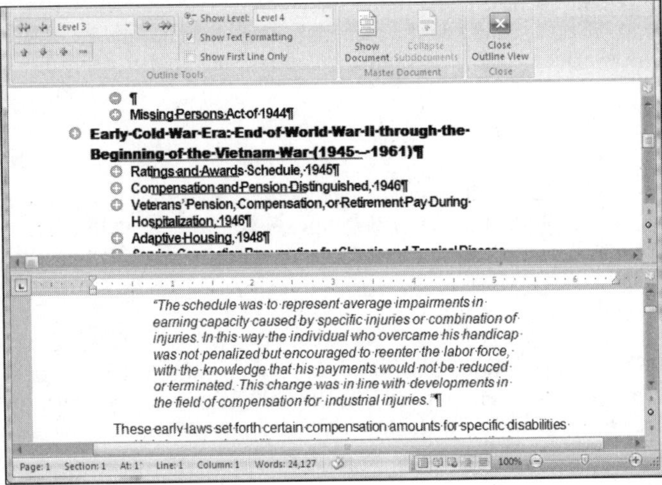

View rulers

New in Word 2007 is the rulers toggle control, also shown in Figure 4-20. This control toggles the horizontal and vertical (if it's on) rulers on and off. It cannot control them separately.

The presence of the ruler toggle on both panes of a split document window might lead you to assume that the upper and lower rulers can be toggled independently. They cannot.

Select Browse Object

While we're visiting over there on that side of the Word screen, let's take a look at another sometimes overlooked control — Select Browse Object. Shown in Figure 4-21, this control determines what happens when you click the Previous or Next buttons that are immediately above and below the Select Browse Object control. It also determines what happens when you press Ctrl+Page Up or Ctrl+Page Down.

FIGURE 4-21

Select Browse Object determines the actions performed by the Previous and Next buttons.

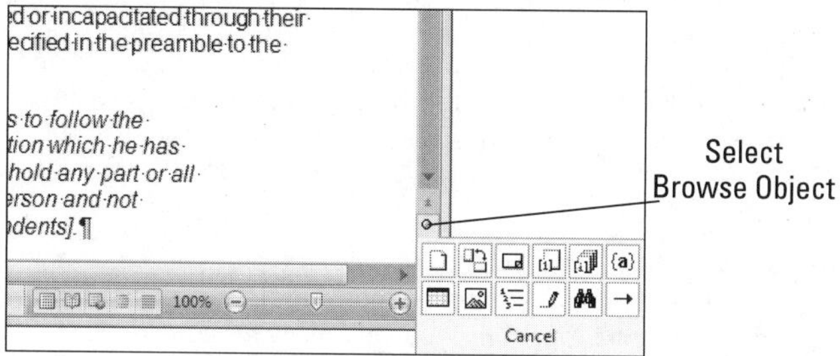

By default, the browse object is set to Page. Clicking the Previous or Next button performs Page Up or Page Down actions. When the default object type is active, the browse buttons (Up and Down) are black. When a non-default object type is active, the browse buttons change to blue.

For example, click the Select Browse Object button, and choose Browse by Table. If you hear an error beep, that means the current document does not contain any tables between the insertion point and the end of the document. Nonetheless, the browse buttons turn blue, and they now "mean" previous table and next table.

If you ever click a browse button and don't get the expected default Page Up/Page Down behavior, take a look at the color. If it's blue, then that's the problem. To reset the browse behavior to the default, click the Select Browse Object button and choose Page.

What makes this a little tricky is that there are ways other than clicking that button to change browse behavior. For example, if you perform a search, the browse buttons now become Find Previous and Find Next. If you perform a Go To and go to the next field, then Previous Field/Next Field become the browse actions. Hover your mouse pointer over each of the twelve object types to explore the possibilities. If you keep these objects in mind, then this feature can become a tool, rather than just an annoyance.

NOTE **Edit browse object? One browse feature is the Edit object. Word remembers the current and previous three places where editing occurred (anything that changes the status of the document from Saved to Dirty). Hence, when Edit is the browse behavior, the Previous and Next buttons cycle the insertion point among those four locations. The Shift+F5 keystroke (assigned to the GoBack command) performs the same action as the Previous button when the browse object is set to Edit.**

Keyboard

With a new version of Word comes some new keystrokes and new keyboard behavior. At the same time, some old keystrokes now work differently. Surprisingly, as you'll see, a number of old keystrokes still work, even though Word's menus are gone.

What works differently? One of my favorite keystrokes is Ctrl+Shift+S, which in Word 2003 and earlier moves the focus to the Style control on the Formatting toolbar. Given that there *is* no Formatting toolbar in Word 2007 and that there is no comparable Style control on the Ribbon, Ctrl+Shift+S pretty much has to be at least a little different. If you still have Word 2003, open it, press Ctrl+Shift+S, tap the first letter of a style that's not currently selected, and then use the down-arrow key to go to the style you had in mind. Press Enter to apply the style.

Now, try the same thing in Word 2007. Pressing Ctrl+Shift+S activates the Apply Styles task pane, and the keystrokes otherwise seem to work the same way. However, the Apply Styles task pane doesn't go away. Well, neither did the Style control in Word 2003, but pressing Ctrl+Shift+S doesn't activate a task pane either.

How do you dismiss the Apply Styles task pane? Well, you could click its X. Unfortunately, pressing the Esc key simply returns the focus to the document without dismissing Apply Styles. To dismiss it (as well as any other task pane) using the keyboard, press Ctrl+spacebar, C. Note that for this to work, the task pane must have the focus, so you might need to press Ctrl+Shift+S and then Ctrl+spacebar, C to get it to work.

Other built-in keystrokes

Word boasts a broad array of keystrokes to make writing faster. If you're a fast touch typist, you might not care to have to reach for the mouse to make a word **bold** or *italic*. You might not want to reach for the mouse to create a hyperlink. If you've been using Word for a long time, you very likely have memorized a number of keystrokes (some of them that apply only to Word, and others not) that make your typing life easier. You'll be happy to know that most of those keystrokes still work in Word 2007.

Rather than provide a list of all of the key assignments in Word, I'm going to show you how to make one yourself. Start by pressing Alt+F8. In Macro name: type **listcommands** and press Enter. In the List Commands dialog box, choose Current Keyboard Settings, and press Enter.

Presto! You now have a table showing all of Word's current keyboard settings. If you've reassigned any built-in keystrokes to other commands or macros, your own assignments are shown in place of Word's built-in assignments. If you've redundantly assigned any keystrokes, all assignments will be shown. For example, Word assigns Alt+F8 to ToolsMacro. I also assigned Ctrl+Shift+O to it. Therefore, my ListCommands table shows both assignments. The table also shows those assignments and commands you haven't customized.

If you want a list of Word's default built-in assignments, open Word in safe mode (hold down Ctrl as Word is starting and then click Yes), and repeat this exercise.

Office 2003 menu keystrokes

One of Microsoft's aims was to assign as many legacy menu keystrokes as possible to the equivalent commands in Word 2007, so if you're used to pressing Alt+IB to choose Insert ➪ Break in Word 2003, you'll be glad to know it still works. So does Alt+OP, for Format ➪ Paragraph. Liking this so far, are you? Great!

Now try Alt+HA for Help ➪ About. It doesn't work. In fact, none of the Help shortcuts work, because that Alt+H shortcut is reserved for the Ribbon's Home tab. Some others don't work either, but at least Microsoft tried.

Some key combinations can't be assigned because the corresponding commands have been eliminated. There are very few in that category. Some other legacy menu assignments haven't been made in Word 2007 because Microsoft is grappling with some conflicts between how the new and old keyboard models work. There are, for example, some problems with Alt+F because that keystroke is used to select the Office button. For now at least, Microsoft has resolved to use a different approach for the Alt+F assignments. Press Alt+I and then press Alt+F to compare the different approaches.

Custom keystrokes

You can also make your own keyboard assignments. To give you a sneak peak, choose Office Button ➪ Word Options ➪ Customize, and then click the Customize button to open the Customize Keyboard dialog box and make the desired changes.

TIP If you're a keyboard aficionado, to simplify your life, assign Alt+K (it's unassigned by default) to the ToolsCustomizeKeyboard command. Then, whenever you see something you want to assign, press Alt+K and you're off and running. To assign Alt+K, choose Office ➪ Word Options ➪ Customization ➪ Customize. Set Categories to All Commands. In Commands, tap the T key to accelerate to the Ts. Find and select ToolCustomizeKeyboard. Click Press New Keyboard Shortcut Key and then press Alt+K (or whatever other assignment you might find preferable or more memorable). Make sure that Save Changes In is set to `Normal.dotm` (assuming you don't want it saved somewhere else). Click Assign, and then click Close. If you've told Word to prompt before saving changes in `Normal.dotm`, then make sure you say Yes to saving this change.

Views

To expand the ways of working with documents, Word offers a number of different environments you can use, called *views*. For reading and performing text edits on long documents with a minimum of UI (user interface) clutter, you can use Full Screen Reading view. For composing documents and reviewing text and basic text formatting, you can choose a fast-display view called Draft view.

For working with documents containing graphics, equations, and other non-text elements, where document design is a strong consideration, there's Page Layout view. If the destination of the document is online (Internet or intranet), Word's Web Layout view removes paper-oriented screen elements, enabling you to view documents as they would appear in a Web browser.

For organizing and managing a document, Word's Outline view provides powerful tools that enable you to move whole sections of the document around without having to copy, cut, and paste. An extension of Outline view, Master Document view enables you to split large documents into separate components for easier management and workgroup sharing.

Draft view is the new Normal view

If you're someone who ordinarily works with Word in Normal view, you might be alarmed to see the view options in Word 2007. Shown in Figure 4-22, they include Print Layout, Full Screen Reading, Web Layout, Outline, and Draft. Where's Normal?

"Normal" as a view name is history. What was Normal is now called Draft.

Did you ever find it confusing that earlier Word versions used the word *normal* in at least three ways that really had nothing to do with each other? Users, especially new or casual users, often were confused by the differences between Normal view, Normal style, and Normal.dot. In Word 2007, what used to be called Normal view is now called Draft view, so maybe there will be less confusion.

FIGURE 4-22

"Normal" view is now called "Draft" view.

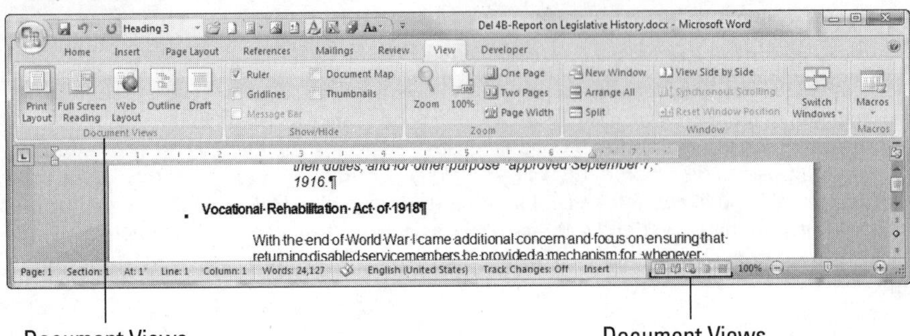

Internally, when you click on Draft either in the View ribbon or on the status bar, Word still uses the ViewNormal command. You can confirm this with the following tip.

TIP **You can determine Word's name for most ribbon or status bar–based commands with a simple keystroke and a click. First, switch to Print Layout view so that the Draft view command will have an effect. Next, press Ctrl+Alt and the plus (+) sign on the number pad. This turns the mouse pointer into the cloverleaf pattern shown in Figure 4-23. Use that pointer to click on (just about) any tool. Word responds by displaying the Customize Keyboard dialog box. The Commands box displays the actual command's name, as shown in Figure 4-24. (I'll have more to say about the amazingly useful cloverleaf tool in subsequent chapters.) When in "cloverleaf" mode, Word returns to normal when the Customize Keyboard dialog box is closed, or you can hasten the return to normal by pressing the Esc key.**

FIGURE 4-23

The cloverleaf mouse pointer indicates that ToolsCustomizeKeyboardShortcut mode is active.

If Word is really running ViewNormal, what happened to Draft view? It's still there. In the Word Options dialog box, choose Advanced. Near the bottom of the Show Document Content options, notice the option to Use Draft Font in Draft and Outline Views. You can also choose the font and point size to use for Draft.

TIP **When you need to distinguish between an uppercase i (I), a lowercase L (l), the number one (1) and the vertical line segment (|, usually typed using shift \ on most U.S. keyboards), the single best font I've discovered that makes the distinction clearest is Comic Sans. It's also a very comfortable and readable font, its nonprofessional-sounding name notwithstanding. If after applying Comic Sans you're still uncertain as to what's what, try toggling the case. Properly distinguishing among these characters, as well as between 0 (zero) and O (capital o), can make a world of difference when you are trying to convey part numbers, serial numbers, user names, and passwords.**

FIGURE 4-24

"Cloverleaf" mode (ToolsCustomizeKeyboardShortcut) displays the next Word command or macro you perform in Word; it responds to mouse and keyboard actions.

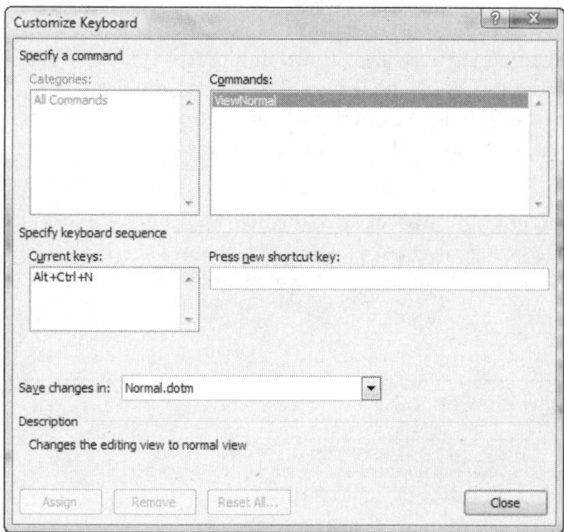

For editors and writers, Normal view was the workhorse view in many prior versions of Word. It enabled them to focus on just words. When coupled with wrapping text to fit the window, you could take off the reading glasses and zoom to any magnification you like. You don't have to monkey around with the horizontal scroll bar or bothersome floating pictures to see what's written. It's also faster. Let the layout editors worry about the placement of pictures and other formatting nuances. If you're used to thinking Normal view, then in Word 2007, think Draft view with the Draft Font view turned off.

If you plan to toggle between Draft and Draft Fonts views very often, you should know that Word has a built-in ViewDraft command that toggles the Use Draft Font setting on and off. To make it more accessible, you might either assign it to a keyboard shortcut or put it onto the Quick Access Toolbar (QAT) for ready access. In the QAT customization dialog box, it's in the All Commands list.

CAUTION **If you do use the ViewDraft command, be advised that font and point size changes will not be reflected in what you see onscreen. This can be good if the original is a legal contract written in 4-point type. It can be bad, however, if you don't toggle out of draft mode before sending a `.doc` file to someone else for review, particularly if you've been careless with the font and point size formatting.**

Print Layout

If Normal view (now Draft view) was the workhorse view for Word 2003, it appears that Print Layout is destined to be the workhorse view for Word 2007. That's because one of Word 2007's strongest new features, live preview, does not work in Draft view. Live preview works in Print Layout and Web Layout. If you could actually display the Formatting tab Ribbon components when in Print Preview mode, it might work there, as well. However, you can't do that (at least not using the tools and techniques that come with Office 2007).

NOTE It is possible that some Ribbon behavior is not fully carved into stone. At this writing, however, there are no Live Preview–enabled tools on Word's Print Preview tab on the Ribbon, so whether it works or not is moot.

Full Screen Reading

Full Screen Reading view is similar to Word 2003's Reading Layout view. Shown in Figure 4-25, the Word 2007 view now uses more of the screen than the comparable Word 2003 view did. It also provides a number of new features, as well. For example, by default, reading mode does not permit editing. Often, this is exactly what you want. But, not always. Switch a document into Full Screen Reading view and peruse the different options.

TIP Full Screen Reading view offers a variety of ways to scroll up and down: Page Down/Page Up, Space/Shift+Space, Enter/Shift+Enter, Right/Left arrow keys, Down/Up arrow keys, the Next/Previous graphic controls at the bottom of the window, and the scroll wheel on your mouse.

FIGURE 4-25

Word 2007's Full Screen Reading view features a number of new View options.

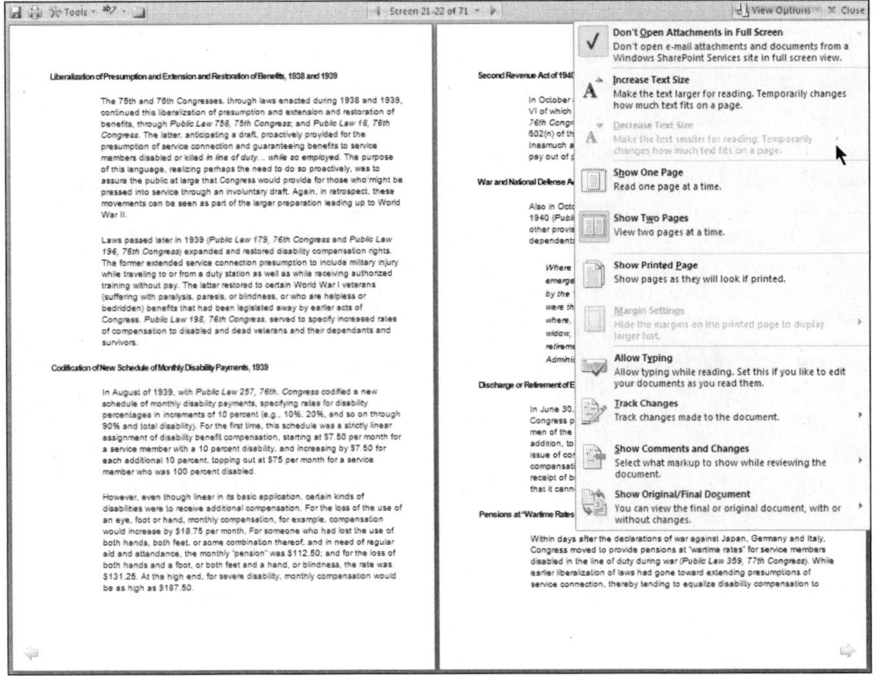

Web Layout

Web Layout is designed for composing and reviewing documents that will not be printed. Hence, information such as page and section numbers are excluded from the status bar. If the document contains hyperlinks, they are displayed underlined by default, as shown in Figure 4-26. Background colors, pictures, and textures are also displayed.

FIGURE 4-26

Web Layout suppresses paper-oriented information such as pages and section numbers, and includes Web-oriented features such as underlined hyperlinks and background colors and textures.

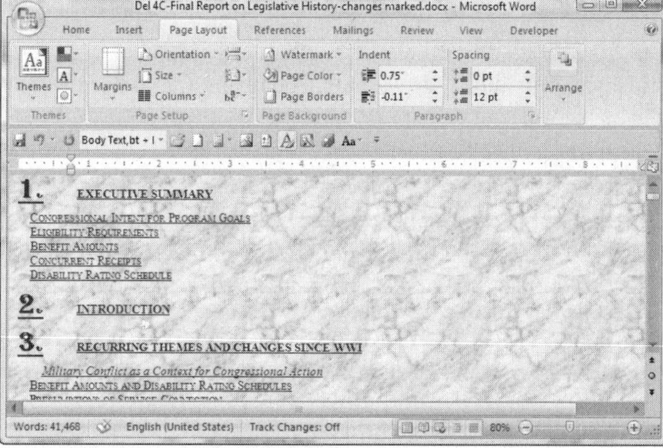

Outline (Master Document tools)

The final distinct Word view is Outline. Outlining is one of Word's most powerful and least utilized tools for writing and organizing your documents. To avail yourself of this tremendous resource, the easiest way is simply to use Word's Heading styles. Heading levels 1 through 9 are available using styles named Heading 1 through Heading 9. You don't need to use all nine levels — most users find that the first three or four levels are adequate for most structured documents. If your document is organized using the built-in heading levels, then a wonderful world of document organization is at your fingertips.

As suggested by the title of this section, Outline view has a split personality, of sorts. As an outline manager, this view can be used on any document with heading styles that are tied to outline levels. If you don't want to use Word's built-in Heading styles, you can use other styles and assign them to different outline levels. Outline view's other personality is the Master Document manager. Compare the two Ribbons shown in Figure 4-27. Both say Outlining, yet the lower Ribbon contains additional tools. To display the additional tools, click Show Document.

FIGURE 4-27

Click Show Document to display the Master Document tools.

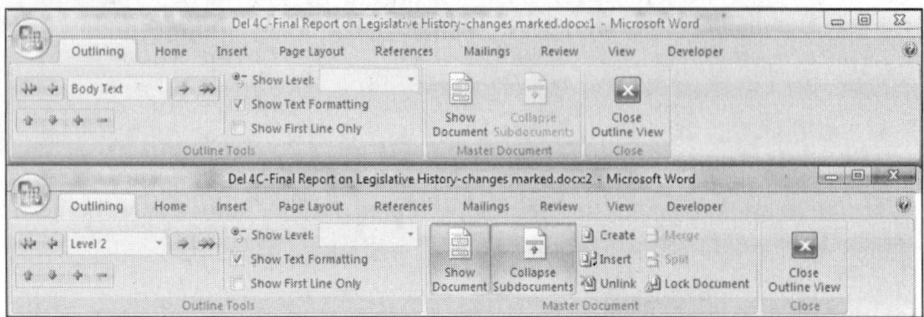

With regard to the Master Document feature, I'll just dish out a little warning. Potentially, this is an extremely powerful document control feature for users who are working on parts of the same document. It provides a way to carefully control checking out and checking in of document parts, as well as to manage problems inherent in working with very large documents.

In previous versions of Word, the Master Document feature was quite unstable, leading to the adage "There are two kinds of master document users: those whose documents are corrupted, and those whose documents will soon be corrupted." Is this harsh assessment still true or does the existence of the new Word document format based on XML relegate those concerns to history? The jury is still out.

Summary

In this chapter, you've seen a variety of ways to start Word 2007 as well as a number of navigation techniques that might be new to you. You've also explored how to modify Word's view to fit your work style and needs, and some of the finer points about saving, converting, and publishing in Word 2007. Finally, putting it all together, you should now have no problem doing the following:

- Creating a blank file or one using a template
- Saving a file
- Converting Word 2003 documents to Word 2007, and vice versa
- Impressing your friends with cool navigation trick and tips
- Viewing your work in different ways for different kinds of writing and editing

Chapter 5

Formatting 101: Font/Character Formatting

IN THIS CHAPTER

- Character styles versus direct character formatting
- Character formatting techniques
- Character formatting tools
- Character formatting keyboard shortcuts

One of the more difficult conceptual hurdles in understanding Word is the way formatting is conceived. Some people think about formatting as a stream. You turn it on here, and it remains on until you turn it off later.

However, Word's formatting "mindset" is not stream oriented, it's object oriented. Rather than turn formatting on in one place and off in another in order to format a block of text, you format objects such as letters, words, paragraphs, tables, pictures, and so on. However, once you say the O word (object), that causes some brains to glaze over.

Another way to think about formatting is in *units*. Formatting can be applied to any unit you can select. The smallest unit that can be formatted is a single character. Discrete units larger than characters are words, sentences, paragraphs, document sections, and the whole document.

The Big Picture

Word has four levels of formatting: *character/font*, *paragraph*, *section,* and *document*. Things such as bold, italic, points, and superscript are called character or font formatting and can be applied to as little as a single character. I'll talk about the other levels of formatting in later chapters.

Personally, I don't like the adjective "font" formatting, because most people — including me — think of fonts as things like Times New Roman, Arial, and Tahoma. For me, character formatting is a lot clearer and less confusing, but because Word has a Ribbon with this chunk (or group) called Font, as shown in Figure 5-1, we're kind of stuck with that terminology. We're all stuck with another term, too: text-level formatting, which really means the same thing as font and character formatting. It helps, however, to think in terms of character formatting, as a character is the smallest thing you can format in Word.

FIGURE 5-1

Much, but not all, character (or font) formatting is accessible from the Home tab's Font group.

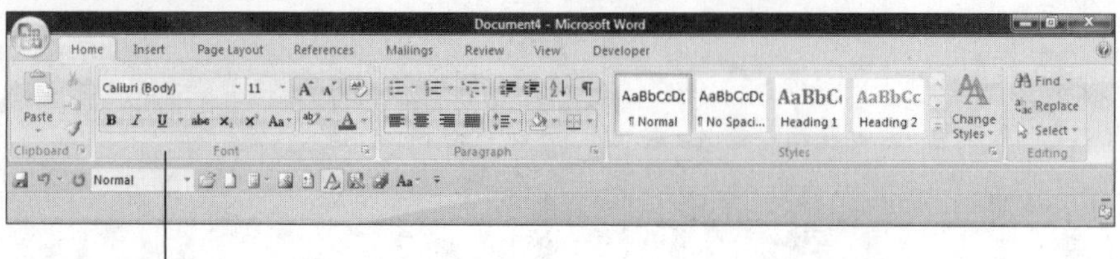

The Font Group

NOTE **Okay. I lied. Technically, the smallest thing you can "format" is a point between two characters, but the word "format" is debatable. To split hairs, you can insert a bookmark at a point so that no characters are enclosed. Is that formatting? I don't think so, but somebody else might.**

Note also that the Font group on the Home tab does not contain access to all character-level formatting. Language, which can be applied down to a single character, is not shown there. Moreover, the Font group contains case (upper, lower, title, etc.), which isn't formatting at all. This should be distinguished from small caps and all caps, both of which are considered character formatting.

Styles and Character/Font Formatting

A few Word versions ago, possibly while many users weren't watching, Microsoft added to Word a new type of style. Before that, there was just one type of style — the paragraph style — and styles could be applied only to a whole paragraph. It soon became clear, however that a more flexible, sophisticated style was needed — one that could be applied to characters within a paragraph.

The character style was born. Using this new invention, it was suddenly possible to create styles for formatting book titles, article titles, names, phone numbers, Internet links — you name it.

Later in this book (Chapter 7) you'll find an entire chapter on styles, but to understand character formatting, there's a little you need to know at the outset, so please bear with me for another couple of paragraphs.

Even if you yourself never apply a style using Word's vast array of formatting tools, two styles are always in effect: a *paragraph* style and a *character* style. To demonstrate this, display the Style Inspector by clicking the Styles Dialog Box Launcher at the bottom-right corner of the Styles group. Then, click the middle icon at the bottom of the Styles task pane to display the Style Inspector, shown in Figure 5-2. You can dismiss the Styles pane if it's distracting.

Here, the two styles applied are *Normal* (the default paragraph style) and *Default Paragraph Font* (the default character style for normal). The latter is the name of the Normal style's default character style.

FIGURE 5-2

Use the Style Inspector when you want to fully examine the styles and direct formatting in use (direct formatting is identified by *Plus* in the Style Inspector).

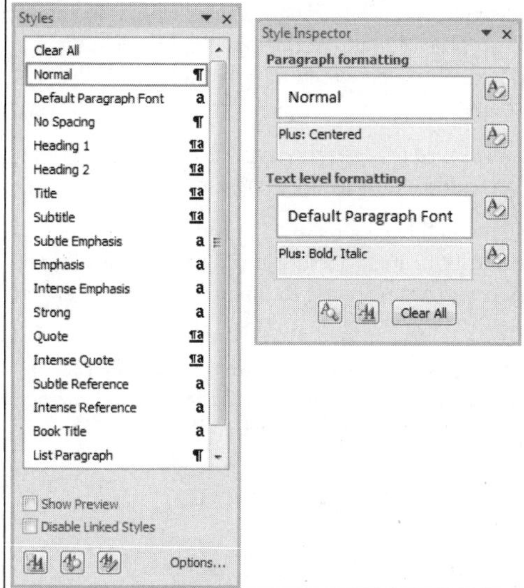

Style versus direct

I just went through that whole rigmarole so that I could explain that you have two ways to apply character formatting. You can use a style to apply character formatting, or you can apply character formatting directly. As you're typing along, it's really quite easy to apply bold, italic, or underlining to text. That's called *direct* formatting, and often there's no reason for you to do it any other way. After all, the goal is to create a functional document in as short a time as possible.

Given that creating and applying styles involves more thought, preparation, and work than using direct formatting, it would appear that using direct formatting works better for my twin goals of speed and functionality. However, a shortcut is only as good as the time it saves you. If it ends up taking more time, then it wasn't really a shortcut at all.

For example, suppose each time I need to type a book title, I press Ctrl+B (bold), type the book title, and then press Ctrl+B again to toggle bold off. That doesn't seem too onerous, right? Suppose my editor now tells me that they don't like book titles formatted that way. Instead, they want me to use bold small caps. Now I have to change the book title references so that they match the editor's requirements. If all book titles and only book titles were formatted as bold, I could use Word's Replace feature to simply replace bold with bold and small caps, but what if I've applied bold to something other than a book title? (The chances are good that I did!) Now I'm left carefully plodding through the document looking for things that look like book titles.

Or worse, suppose I needed to correct the formatting error not in just one document file, but in dozens of files? I would have a lot of work to do, right? That Ctrl+B shortcut doesn't seem like a very good shortcut anymore, does it?

If, instead, each time I wanted a book title, I had applied a character style named *Book Title*, I'd be in much better shape. That way, I could simply modify the Book Title style, and all of my book titles would obediently change. Even if the formatting "error" were propagated over dozens of different documents, I could change the definition of the style in the template on which those documents were based, use the Automatically Update Document Styles feature, and I'd be done.

The commandment is this: *If the formatting is something you will need to repeatedly apply to certain categories of text (such as book titles, programming commands, jargon, etc.), create a character style and use it.*

If, conversely, the use is ad hoc and not something for which you'll have a recurring need, then go ahead and use direct formatting. For example, when I'm writing a letter or memo and want to use bold for emphasis, I use direct formatting. When I'm writing a formal report and am referring to the name of a journal and a journal article, I use a style.

TIP **To make using styles less onerous, you can assign keyboard shortcuts to them. From Word Options, click the Customize choice in the list at the left, and click the Customize button. Set Categories to Styles. Choose the style, click in Press New Shortcut Key, press the desired key(s), and then click Assign ⇨ Close. Don't forget to click Assign!**

Character Formatting

There are at least six ways of directly applying various kinds of character formatting:

- Using the Font group on the Home tab
- The Font dialog box (Ctrl+D or Ctrl+Shift+F, or click the Font group Dialog Box Launcher)
- The Mini Toolbar (hover the mouse over selected text)
- Using shortcut keys
- With the Font group or components placed on the QAT
- Using the Language tool on the status bar

In this section, I'll describe these methods and try to give you a sense of which ones to use. A lot depends on your working style, but it can also depend on what you happen to be doing. On any given day, I'll probably use at least five of the six methods.

Formatting techniques

To apply character formatting, you have three basic options:

- **Stream method** — Apply formatting before you start typing a word or passage, and then turn it off when you're done. For example, click the Bold tool, type a word, and then click the Bold tool again.
- **Selection method** — Select the text you want formatted by dragging over it or using a keyboard shortcut and/or the mouse, and then apply the formatting.
- **Whole-word method** — Click anywhere in a word and then choose the desired formatting.

NOTE The whole-word method is settings dependent. It will work by default, but it will not work if you've turned off "When selecting, automatically select entire word" in the Editing Option section of the Advanced category in the Word Options dialog box.

It would be redundant to repeat the basic steps for each and every formatting type. The techniques described here apply to all character formatting described in this chapter.

Repeat formatting (F4)

A tremendous time saver in Word is the Repeat Formatting command, invoked by pressing F4. Actually, F4 will repeat typing and many other actions too, but I find it most useful for repeating formatting.

Suppose, for example that you're scanning a newsletter looking for people's names, which need to be made bold. There's John Smith, so you select his name and press Ctrl+B. Thereafter, however, it might be faster to position one hand on the mouse and the other at the F4 key. Click on Jane; press F4. Click on Doe; press F4. Or, click to select Jane Doe as a phrase, and then press F4. The F4 key enables you to temporarily forget about pressing Ctrl+B, right-clicking, or traveling to the top of the Word menu in search of a formatting tool.

Now, let's try something else. Click on a word and press Ctrl+B to make it bold. Now press Ctrl+I. Now the text is bold and italic. Click on another word and press F4. It's only italic! That's because F4 repeats only the most recent formatting (or other action).

Note that F4 and Ctrl+Y both do the same thing. Which you use is your choice. Many prefer F4 because it can be pressed with one finger. Others prefer Ctrl+Y because it doesn't involve as much of a stretch as F4.

TIP If you have multiple or compound character formatting to repeatedly apply to a non-style-formatted series of words or selections, use the Font dialog box instead of individual commands. When you use the Font dialog box, all changes applied when you click OK become a single formatting event to the F4 key, so F4 can now apply multiple types of character formatting all at once.

Copy formatting

Sometimes, the moment for using F4 has passed, yet you're still left needing to reapply compound formatting. I'm assuming that for whatever reason you're not using a character style. Be that as it may, there are two common methods for copying formatting: the Format Painter and the Copy Formatting keystroke. Note that these techniques aren't limited to character formatting. They'll work with many other kinds of formatting as well.

Format Painter

To use the Format Painter, click or select the item whose formatting you want to copy. If you want to clone that formatting just once, click the Format Painter in the Clipboard group on the Home Ribbon, shown in Figure 5-3. If you want to apply that formatting multiple times, then double-click the Format Painter.

Note that the mouse pointer turns into a paintbrush. Honestly! That's what it's supposed to be!

Next, if you're copying formatting to a whole word, click the word you want formatted. Presto! If you're copying to any other group of characters, then use the mouse pointer to select the destination text. If you double-clicked the Format Painter, continue this until you're done. Press Esc or click the Format Painter again to exit format painting mode.

FIGURE 5-3

Use the Format Painter in the Clipboard group to copy formatting.

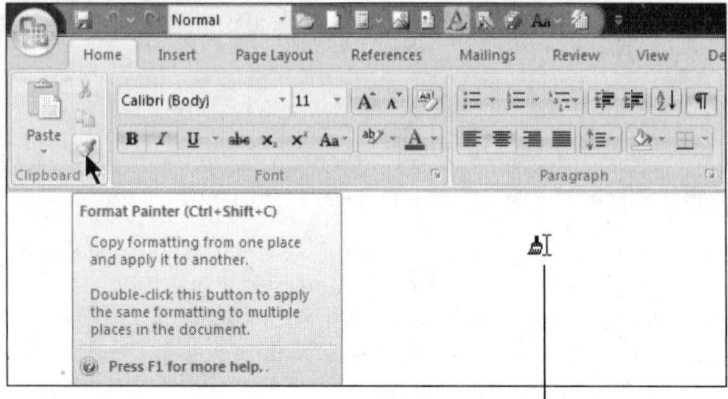

Format Painter Mouse Pointer

Keyboard method

If you don't care for the Format Painter, that's perfectly okay. You'll need to know about two keystrokes:

- **Ctrl+Shift+C** — Copy Format
- **Ctrl+Shift+V** — Paste Format

You might have noticed Ctrl+Shift+C in the Format Painter's tooltip in Figure 5-3. This works very similarly to the Format Painter. Click in or select the text whose formatting you want to copy, and press Ctrl+Shift+C. Observe the mouse pointer. It's the Format Painter pointer! Now, move to or select the text where you want the formatting copied and press Ctrl+Shift+V. Note that there is no keyboard equivalent for the multi-copy method (double-clicking on the Format Painter), but you can combine the two methods, initiating the process by double-clicking the Format Painter and then following through using Ctrl+Shift+V.

Clear formatting

There are several degrees of clearing formatting. Here, I'll talk about two of them:

- Clear direct character formatting (ResetChar)
- Clear all formatting (ClearAllFormatting)

The first is the venerable Ctrl+Spacebar command known and loved by many in every version of Word they can remember. It's also a widely misunderstood command. This command does not remove all character formatting. It removes all *direct* character formatting. So, if the selected text's formatting all comes from styles applied to the text — regardless of how bizarre or compound the formatting might be — Ctrl+Spacebar will have no effect whatsoever.

For example, when you apply Heading 1 to a section of text, it becomes bold. Ctrl+Spacebar can't touch that bold formatting since it was applied though the style rather than by pressing Ctrl+B or clicking the bold tool. If you use direct formatting to italicize a word in an otherwise non-italicized heading, however, now Ctrl+spacebar can remove it.

New feature alert!

The second type of format removal is completely new to Word 2007. It is accessible using the Clear Formatting tool on the Home Ribbon, shown in Figure 5-4. This command is quite different from Ctrl+spacebar.

FIGURE 5-4

The Clear Formatting tool is actually misplaced in the Ribbon. It affects not only character/font formatting but paragraph and style formatting as well.

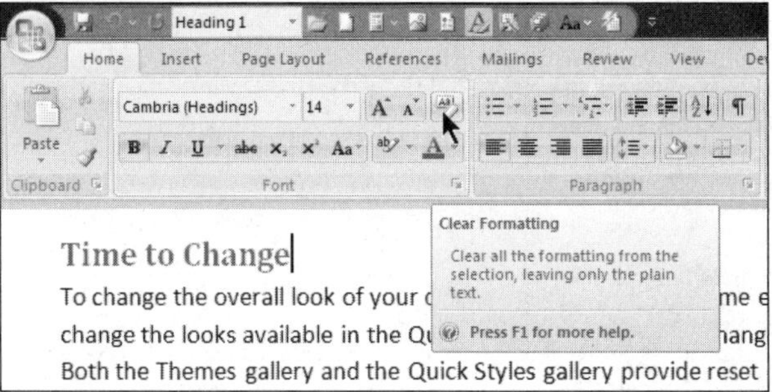

This new command is the moral equivalent of copying a selection to the Clipboard and then using Paste Special ➪ Unformatted Text to paste it back into the document. It strips out all formatting.

The Font group

The Font group (or *chunk* as it's more affectionately called) on the Home tab is shown in Figure 5-5. The Font group is compressed or expanded depending on the width of the current Word window. In its full glory, the Font group can display up to 14 separate controls.

FIGURE 5-5

The Font group is Word 2007's "discoverable" new way of applying character formatting.

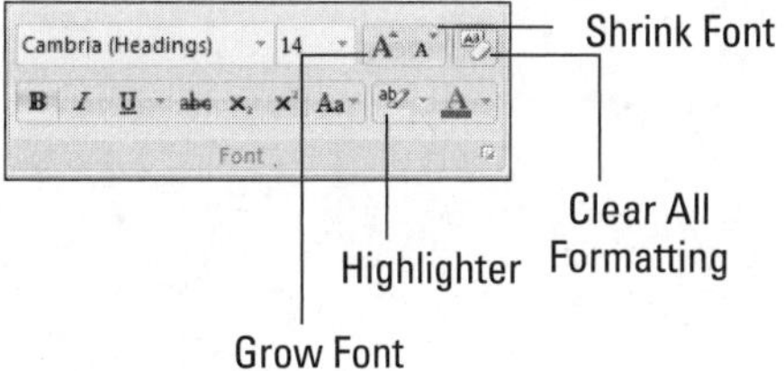

Four of the Font tools feature Live Preview:

- Font (e.g., typeface name, such as Calibri)
- Size
- Highlight color
- Text color

As shown in Figure 5-6, Live Preview shows you the results of the selected (but not yet applied) formatting. Two of the Live Preview controls — font and size — can be rolled up and out of the way, as shown in Figure 5-6. The other two cannot.

FIGURE 5-6

Dots at the bottom of a Live Preview control indicate that it can be rolled up and out of the way.

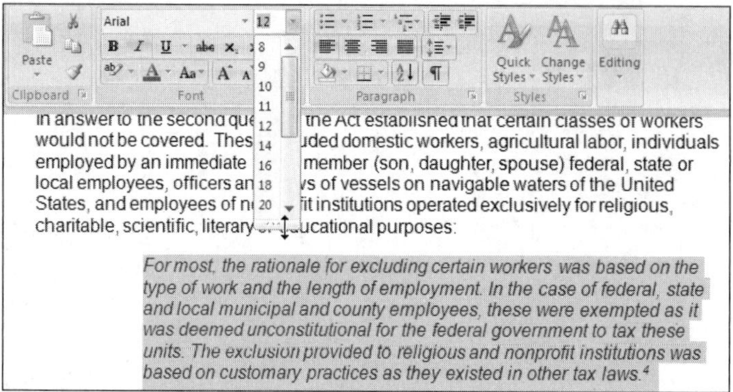

As shown in Figure 5-7, there's also a fifteenth control — the Font Dialog Box Launcher. The Font dialog box is nearly identical to its counterpart from Word 2003, with most of the differences owing to the removal of the Text Effects tab.

FIGURE 5-7

Use the Font Dialog Box Launcher to display the nearly full-service dialog box.

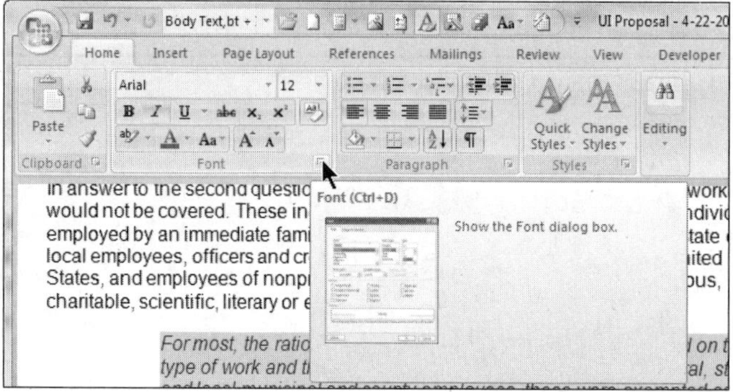

Some of the icons in the Font group might seem a bit obscure and indistinct. Hover the mouse pointer over each of the controls to see what they do. Notice that for many of the controls, if shortcut keys exist, they are indicated in the Enhanced ScreenTip. However, this is not the end of the story. Some tools, for whatever reason, might not show the shortcuts. Jump ahead to the section "Character formatting shortcut keys" later in this chapter if you're just dying to know what's assigned to what.

Typeface or font

Some call it font, some call it typeface. Some skirt the nomenclature issue simply by saying what typeface or font they want (Times New Roman, Arial, etc.). Whatever you call it, it's key to a document's appearance.

NOTE **In Word 2003, you could move the focus to the Font tool in the toolbar by pressing Ctrl+Shift+F. That precise functionality no longer exists in Word 2007. Instead, that keystroke now does the same thing as Ctrl+D, which is to show the Font dialog box.**

Point size

Size controls the height of the font, generally measured in points. A point is 1/72 of an inch, so 12 points would be 12/72 of an inch. For Word, a font set's point size is the vertical distance from the top of the highest ascending character to the bottom of the lowest descending character.

You aren't limited to the range of sizes you see in the Home tab of the Ribbon. Word can go as low as 1 point and as large as 1,638 points. Plus, you can set the height in increments of .5. Hence, a point size of 1637.5 is perfectly valid.

As with typeface, Word 2007 will no longer let you make a key assignment that takes you directly to the exposed size control. While Ctrl+Shift+P did that in Word 2003 and earlier, Ctrl+Shift+P now simply takes you to the Font dialog box, where size is highlighted.

Grow/Shrink tools and keyboard shortcuts

Text size can also be controlled using the Grow Font and Shrink Font tools (refer to Figure 5-5). If you hover the mouse pointer over each, you'll also learn that they both have shortcuts, Ctrl+Shift+> and Ctrl+Shift+<, respectively.

NOTE **The ScreenTip actually says Ctrl+> and Ctrl+<, and technically that's right because > and < are a shifted period and comma, respectively. Personally, though, I'd rather have you understand exactly what keys to press than to stand on ceremony.**

If you click the drop-down arrow next to the Point Size tool, you'll notice that the fonts listed are not all even increments of 2. Instead, they go from 8 to 28 in steps of 2, but then they leap to 32, 48, and 72. The Grow and Shrink font tools follow the listed increments.

If you want a finer degree of control (for example, when you're trying to make text as large as possible without spilling onto an additional page), you should know about two additional default shortcut keys: Ctrl+[and Ctrl+]. These two commands shrink or grow the selected characters by 1 point. The extra granularity often is just what you need to find the largest possible font you can fit inside a given space, such as a page, table, or text box.

Color

Word has three color settings that can be applied at the character level:

- **Text color** — The color of the characters themselves
- **Shading** — The color of the background immediately behind text
- **Highlighting** — The electronic equivalent to those neon-colored felt markers you use to annoy people who ask you to read things you don't want to read

Text color

Text color is pretty self-explanatory, except when it's not. Most of us know what red, black, and blue are, but what is Automatic? Automatic can be Black or White and is based on the shading. If the shading is so dark that black text can't be read without difficulty, Word automatically switches the display color to white.

Shading

We'll talk about design considerations in a later chapter. For now, note a few things about shading that sometimes escape notice. Looking at the Home tab and the placement of Shading (second from the right under Paragraph), you might be tempted to believe that shading is paragraph-level formatting. Indeed, it sure acts that way. With nothing selected, Shading acts on the entire current paragraph. (You'll learn more about this later.)

However, if you select a single word or character, Shading suddenly acts like a character formatting attribute. Well, that's what it is. Because people seldom vary the shading within any given paragraph, it is treated as a paragraph attribute by Word's interface. Yet, just like font, point size, bold, and italic, shading is a character attribute.

As shown in Figure 5-8, shading also affects the display of text color. In this case, the shading color is maroonish, which you can't tell in the printed version of this book. Keep the character aspect of shading in mind when we look at the Font dialog box, coming up shortly.

FIGURE 5-8

Despite its placement in the Paragraph group of the Home tab, shading can be applied to a selection of characters.

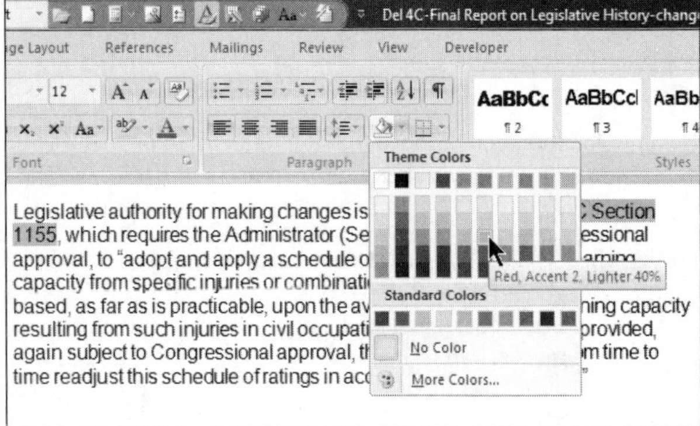

Highlighting

The Text Highlight Color control — more generally known as the *highlighter* — is shown in Figure 5-5. It actually has four modes of operation. Most people are aware of one mode or another, but not all four.

One mode is to select text and then click the highlighter. This is the mode that most users are aware of. It's pretty effective, but it might not reflect the actual highlighting process.

A second mode is to turn the highlighter on by clicking the Text Highlight Color tool and then use the mouse to drag areas you want highlighted. The highlighter mouse pointer stays active until you click the Text Highlight Color tool again, or until you press the Esc key.

A third mode can be used to apply highlighting to all occurrences of a given word or phrase in a document, using the most recently applied highlighting color. Press Ctrl+F to open the Find dialog box. Type the word or phrase of interest, and then choose Reading Highlight ➪ Highlight All, as shown in Figure 5-9.

FIGURE 5-9

Use Find to apply a *reading highlight* to every occurrence of a word or phrase in your document.

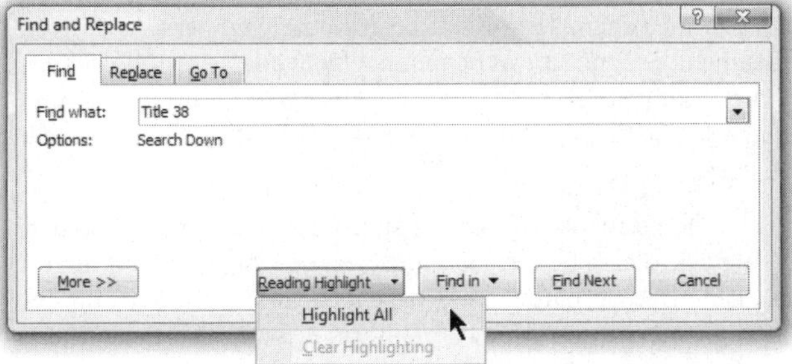

A fourth highlight method is one I find a bit more useful than the Reading Highlight feature. It works from the Replace dialog box. Press Ctrl+H (Replace). In Find What, type the word or phrase you want to highlight. Clear the contents of the Replace With field, and in Replace's lower-left corner, choose Format ➪ Highlight. Click Replace All to apply highlighting to all occurrences of the Find What text. Highlighting inserted this way is more robust than that inserted using the Reading Highlight and will not disappear if you choose to manually manipulate highlighting.

Note that when the Replace With field is blank but has associated formatting, the formatting is applied to text that matches the Find What text. If both formatting and Replace With text are absent, then Replace deletes all occurrences of the matching text.

You can also choose not to print highlighting. This gives you the best of both worlds. You can mark up a document for your own benefit, and then — if desired — print it out without the highlighting. Not only is this good for keeping internal guides private, but it also saves money on yellow ink. To prevent printing (or displaying) highlighting, choose Office Button ➪ Word Options, select the Display tab, and remove the check next to Show Highlighter Marks. If you hover over the information while you're here, the tip informs you that this controls both display and printing. Click OK when you're done.

TIP **One very annoying thing about highlighting is that if you use the select-and-highlight method, Word undoes the selection after you apply highlighting. This can be really irritating if you use the wrong color, but if you immediately press Ctrl+Z or click Undo, Word not only undoes the highlighting, it also reselects that section of text so you can take another stab at highlighting.**

Change case

Change case doesn't really fit in here, but that's precisely why it's included. Case is not formatting. Case is a choice of which characters to use — uppercase, lowercase, or some combination thereof. Why does Microsoft put it in the Font group? I don't know for sure, but it's probably because it can affect groups of characters and doesn't really fit anywhere else.

The first thing you need to know is that you cannot use any variation of this command to affect style definitions in your document. For example, you can't apply lowercase to text, turn it into a style, and then use that style to format Internet keywords. It could be useful, but this feature must await some distant version of Word as yet unannounced. For now, you can include All Caps or Small Caps as elements of a Word style, not that that helps with Internet addresses.

Language

Note that language is not included in the Home tab's Font group. You'll also notice that it's not present in the Font dialog box either, so how do you know it's a character formatting attribute? Two reasons: First, it can be applied to a single character in a document. Second, it can be included in a character style definition, as shown in Figure 5-10. (To display the Modify Style dialog box, click the Styles group Dialog Box Launcher button on the Home tab. In the Styles pane that appears, point to any style with the mouse, click the drop-down list arrow that appears, and click **Modify**.)

You set the language using the Language tool on the status bar. Click the status bar area that displays the language (the Language tool) to open the Language dialog box. If you don't see the Language tool, then right-click the status bar and click to enable Language. Among the language tools' more useful features is that Do Not Check Spelling or Grammar setting you can apply to text. This can be handy for technical jargon and programming keywords that you might not want checked.

Conversely, Detect Language Automatically, the last feature, shown in Figure 5-11, can be a real troublemaker. With that setting turned on, it's possible for text to unintentionally be tagged as some other language, resulting in large sections of text being flagged as misspelled. You should turn that setting off unless you actually need it. It is enabled by default!

FIGURE 5-10

Language is included among the attributes associated with a character style.

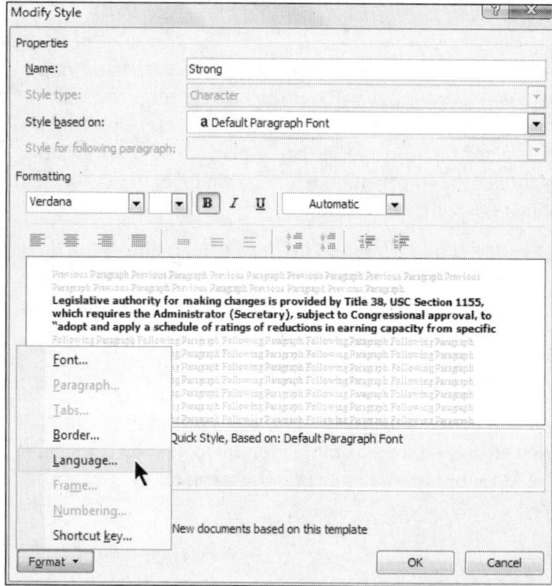

FIGURE 5-11

The Do Not Check Spelling or Grammar option can be useful for technical writers. Detect Language Automatically can cause problems for chronically bad spellers!

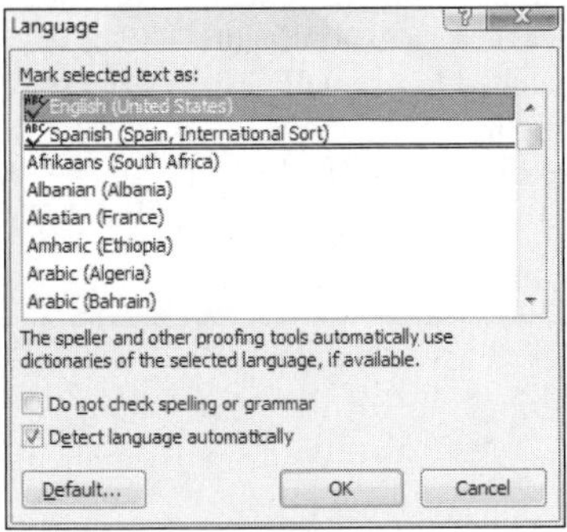

To set the default for all documents based on the current template, choose the desired language as well as the desired settings for the last two options, and then click Default. Confirm the settings by clicking Yes. Note that even though the confirmation box doesn't mention the latter two settings, they are included in the changes made to the underlying template.

The Font dialog box

The Font dialog box, shown in Figure 5-12, can be a useful tool when applying multiple character format changes at the same time. Note, however, that the Font dialog box and the Font group on the Home tab of the Ribbon do not provide identical capabilities. Not only doesn't the Font dialog provide any live preview at all (just the static preview box), it contains different commands and settings.

FIGURE 5-12

Only some of the functionality of the Font dialog's two tabs is replicated on the Home tab of the Ribbon.

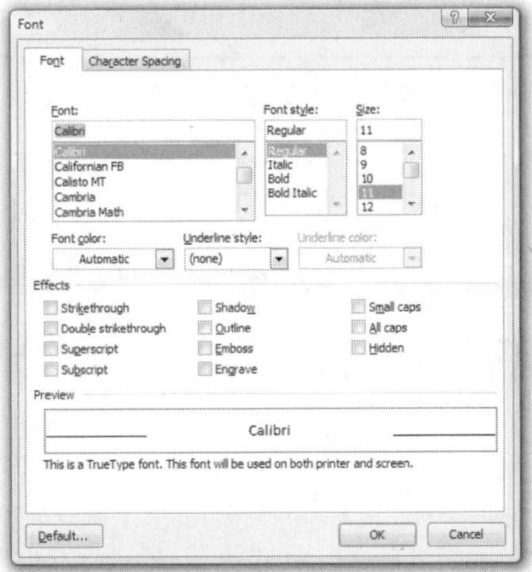

Most font attributes are largely self-explanatory. Experiment with them to see the different effects. Conspicuously missing from the Home Ribbon are the controls in the Font dialog box's Character Spacing tab, shown in Figure 5-12. Note the Scale and Spacing controls.

Scale is used to stretch or compress the actual characters. Spacing is used to expand or condense only the spacing. Scaling and spacing expansion are demonstrated on the identical text shown in Figure 5-13. The top sample was scaled up 150%. The characters and spaces were all stretched horizontally. The bottom sample was expanded by 2.8 points. An additional 2.8 points of spacing were inserted between each character. Even though both samples are nearly identical in height and width, the top sample actually looks larger.

FIGURE 5-13

Scaling and horizontal spacing can yield text of identical length and height, but with a very different appearance.

Costs and Benefits of Compensation

C o s t s   a n d   B e n e f i t s   o f   C o m p e n s a t i o n

Position is used to raise or lower the selected characters by a specified number of points. Unlike spacing, which can vary by as little as .1 points, position's smallest gradation is .5 points. This is sometimes used to adjust subscripts and superscripts if the built-in versions don't accomplish the desired effect or you need the subscripts and superscripts to be the identical size as the surrounding text.

If you have a chronic need to adjust subscripts and superscripts, you might consider creating a character style that gives you the desired formatting.

The Mini Toolbar

Yet another tool for applying formatting is the Mini Toolbar. New in Word 2007, this feature is fully explained in Chapter 2. Shown in Figure 5-14, The Mini Toolbar has a sampling of character formatting tools from the Home tab of the Ribbon. Unlike the Ribbon tools, however, none of the Mini Toolbar's tools provide Live Preview.

FIGURE 5-14

The Mini Toolbar has a sampling of character formatting tools from the Home tab of the Ribbon.

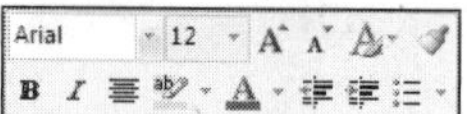

The Mini Toolbar's singular but important claim to fame for many users will be its ergonomic utility. When you need something on it, it's right there, close to the text. Just select the text, move the mouse pointer over the upper-right corner of the selection, and then move the mouse over the faint version of the toolbar that appears. Conversely, many of its tools are easily accessible with direct keystrokes, as you'll see in the next and final section in this chapter.

Character formatting shortcut keys

Many of the character formatting commands discussed in this chapter are accessible via built-in keyboard shortcuts. Longtime users of Word undoubtedly have many of them committed to memory. Newcomers, however, might need a quick guide. As you navigate your way through Word 2007, keep your eyes open. Quite often, Word will show you its built-in key assignments. To make sure this happens, do the following:

- In Office Button ➪ Word Options ➪ Popular, set the ScreenTip Style setting to Show Feature Descriptions in ScreenTips.
- In Office Button ➪ Word Options ➪ Advanced ➪ Display section, enable (check) Show Shortcut Keys in ScreenTips.

Table 5-1 provides a quick reference of keyboard shortcuts related to character formatting. This list might not be exhaustive.

TABLE 5-1

Default Character Formatting Keyboard Shortcuts

Command	Keystroke
All Caps	Ctrl+Shift+A
Bold	Ctrl+B, Ctrl+Shift+B
Copy formatting	Ctrl+Shift+C
Font dialog box	Ctrl+D, Ctrl+Shift+F
Highlighting	Alt+Ctrl+H
Hyperlink	Ctrl+K
Italics	Ctrl+I
Paste formatting	Ctrl+Shift+V
Point size: decrease by 1 point	Ctrl+[
Point size: decrease to next preset	Ctrl+Shift+<
Point size: increase by 1 point	Ctrl+]
Point size: increase to next preset	Ctrl+Shift+>
Remove non-style character formatting	Ctrl+Space
Small capital letters	Ctrl+Shift+K
Subscript	Ctrl+=
Superscript	Ctrl+Shift+=
Symbol font	Ctrl+Shift+Q
Toggle case of selected text	Shift+F3
Underline	Ctrl+U
Word underline	Ctrl+Shift+W

Summary

For most of us, the most important thing about the documents we create is the choice of words. Character formatting is mostly about formatting words. In this chapter, you've seen the variety of things you can do to words and characters, as well as a variety of ways to treat them in Word. You should now be able to do the following:

- Apply character formatting to any size selection of text, from a single character up to a complete document
- Choose whether to apply formatting directly or to use a character style
- Distinguish between character formatting and characters
- Decide among the variety of formatting tools which one to use in any given formatting situation
- Remove unwanted character formatting
- Save time by using shortcut keystrokes and shortcut techniques

Chapter 6

Paragraph Formatting

Everything you type in Word resides in paragraphs. Even if you type nothing at all, in fact, every Word document — even one that you believe is completely empty — contains at least one paragraph. The key to knowing that a paragraph is present is the ubiquitous paragraph mark: ¶. If you don't see them in Word right now, perhaps you have them turned off. Pressing Ctrl+Shift+8 toggles it and the other nonprinting characters on and off.

Also called a *pilcrow* or an *alinea,* in Word the paragraph mark is the repository of paragraph formatting. Delete a paragraph's pilcrow, and you've extinguished its soul. A little dramatic? Perhaps, but Word is filled with drama. Just ask anybody who ever wrestled with numbering in Word 2000.

In this chapter, I'll go into detail about paragraph formatting, and along the way, try to demystify aspects that seem to leave people scratching their heads. You'll also learn about the interaction between selected Word options and the nuances of paragraph formatting.

IN THIS CHAPTER

Styles and Paragraph Formatting

One of Word's challenges is that there often are multiple ways to do the same thing. For any given set of circumstances, however, only one way is the most efficient. The challenge is to see through the clutter and determine which way is best.

"I don't use styles" is something I hear quite frequently, but that can't be true. If you're using Word, you're always using two styles: a paragraph style and a character style. When people say "I don't use styles," of course, that doesn't mean that they don't use styles at all. It's that they use just a single paragraph style, called Normal, and a single character style called Default Paragraph Font. More to the point, it means that they simply ignore the existence of styles.

Any formatting variation such "astylists" might achieve is by applying variant or direct formatting. I'm not going to snobbishly sit here and tell you that paying no attention to styles is a sin. Although, come to think of it, this is a Bible . . . Even so, there are times when you have to do something ASAP, and if ignoring styles gets that "The building is on fire!" memo finished sooner than fumbling with unfamiliar tools and concepts, then so be it.

This chapter will tell style shunners what paragraph formatting is, what it's for, and how to use it. It also will tell style users the same things, but the latter will have a broader context for it all as well as a strategy, because paragraph formatting is integral to paragraph style formatting.

When to use styles

The same commandment that applies to character style formatting applies with respect to paragraph style formatting. If it's a one-time ad hoc need, direct paragraph formatting is entirely appropriate. For example, if it's a centered heading on a one-time announcement you're going to tack to a bulletin board, feel free to simply press Ctrl+E.

On the other hand, if it's formatting that you're going to need again and again, then use a style. For example, if it's one of a number of headings in a monthly newsletter you're going to be assembling for the next five years, either adopt and adapt built-in heading styles to suit the need, or create your own styles. The more work styles can do for you, the less time you're going to have to spend formatting and reformatting.

What Exactly Is a Paragraph, Anyway?

With apologies to Mrs. Hewitt, my eighth-grade English teacher, a paragraph is everything between two different paragraph marks. Shown in Figure 6-1, the shaded block near the bottom is a complete paragraph. Note, however, that so is the solitary paragraph marker that follows the shaded paragraph. Moreover, the bordered block of italicized text above the shaded block is also a single paragraph, despite the fact that there is white space between the upper and lower portions.

FIGURE 6-1

A paragraph is everything between two paragraph marks. A paragraph mark without any text is called an *empty* paragraph.

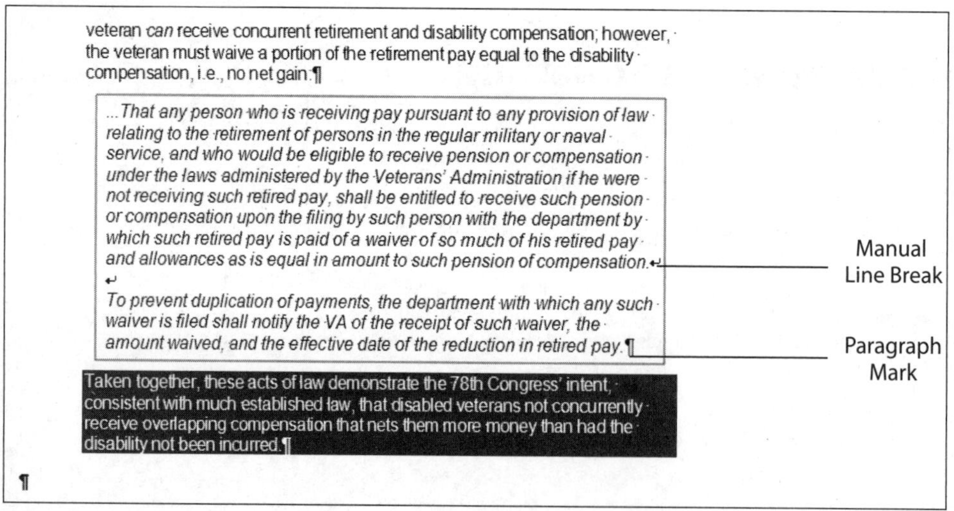
veteran can receive concurrent retirement and disability compensation; however, the veteran must waive a portion of the retirement pay equal to the disability compensation, i.e., no net gain.¶

...That any person who is receiving pay pursuant to any provision of law relating to the retirement of persons in the regular military or naval service, and who would be eligible to receive pension or compensation under the laws administered by the Veterans' Administration if he were not receiving such retired pay, shall be entitled to receive such pension or compensation upon the filing by such person with the department by which such retired pay is paid of a waiver of so much of his retired pay and allowances as is equal in amount to such pension of compensation.↵
↵
To prevent duplication of payments, the department with which any such waiver is filed shall notify the VA of the receipt of such waiver, the amount waived, and the effective date of the reduction in retired pay.¶

Taken together, these acts of law demonstrate the 78th Congress' intent, consistent with much established law, that disabled veterans not concurrently receive overlapping compensation that nets them more money than had the disability not been incurred.¶

¶

Note that many new Word users often are distracted by the display of nonprinting characters (such as paragraph marks, manual line breaks, spaces, and tabs). As shown here, however, displaying them can give you essential clues about what's going on in a document.

Sometimes it's useful to break a paragraph horizontally, while still keeping it as a solitary paragraph. That way, any paragraph formatting you do to any part of the paragraph is done to the entire paragraph, despite its disjoint appearance. If the paragraphs are numbered or bulleted, it also prevents a new number or bullet from being assigned to what logically is a continuation, not a new item.

If you're in the habit of working with nonprinting characters turned off, you might sometimes find that it's useful to occasionally turn them on when trying to diagnose the behavior of text. They can be toggled by pressing Ctrl+Shift+8. If any marks don't toggle, then check Word Options ➪ Display to see whether any are checked to be displayed all the time.

Another useful diagnostic aid in analyzing paragraph formatting is the Reveal Formatting pane, shown in Figure 6-2. You display it by pressing Shift+F1. It shows all of the formatting that's common to the selected text, or that's applied at the insertion point. It has three segments: Font (character formatting), Paragraph, and Section. (Thanks to Word's thesaurus, I just neatly sidestepped having to refer to the bottom segment as the "section section.") It also displays the selected text, if any, using the current common formatting, as best it can. If nothing is selected, then it displays the words "Sample Text" using common current formatting.

FIGURE 6-2

Press Shift+F1 to toggle the Reveal Formatting pane. It shows all of the formatting in effect for the selection.

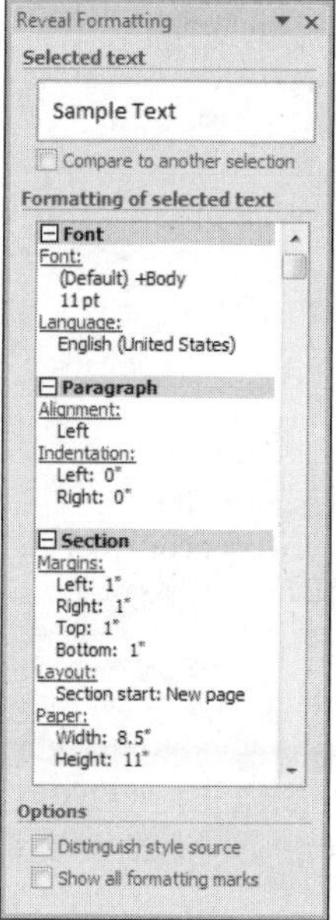

Why do I say that it displays the common formatting? That's because the selected text might not be formatted homogeneously. In this case, although you can't see it, the sentence in the text was "It was a **dark** and *stormy* night." Because bold and italic aren't common to the entire selection, you can't use Reveal Formatting to determine whether a given selection contains any formatting of a particular type.

Notice that the Reveal Formatting pane does not tell you what style is applied. We will look at other tools later on that help us with styles. In this chapter, we focus only on the paragraph segment.

TIP **The Reveal Formatting pane is not accessible from the Ribbon interface. If you want to be able to access it from the Quick Access Toolbar (QAT), you can add it. To do so, right-click the QAT and choose Customize Quick Access Toolbar. Choose Commands Not in the Ribbon from the Choose Commands From drop-down list. Click in the list and tap the S key to accelerate to the S's, and then tap the up-arrow key seven times or so to select Reveal Formatting. Click Add ⇨ OK, and you're done.**

Paragraph formatting attributes

Paragraph formatting, like character formatting, can be applied using a wide variety of tools that apply certain paragraph attributes. Many of those attribute controls, but not all, can be found on the Paragraph group in the Home tab of the Ribbon, shown in Figure 6-3. Indent and Spacing, both of which are paragraph attributes, are located on the Paragraph group in the Page Layout tab of the Ribbon, also shown in Figure 6-3. A number of attributes missing from the Ribbon are on the horizontal rulers: left and right indent, hanging and paragraph indent, and tab settings.

FIGURE 6-3

The Paragraph section in the Home tab of the Ribbon contains a number of paragraph formatting controls.

Many paragraph attributes, but again not all, are also found in the Paragraph dialog box, shown in Figure 6-4. You can display the Paragraph dialog box by clicking the Dialog Box Launcher in the lower-right corner of the Home tab's Paragraph groups, by double-clicking any of the indent controls on the horizontal ruler, or by pressing the legacy keystrokes Alt+O, P.

Missing from the dialog box, of course, are tab settings, which can be accessed by clicking Tabs in the Indents and Spacing tab of the dialog box. Also missing are borders and shading, which can be accessed by clicking Borders and Shading from the bottom of the menu that appears when you click the Border tool's drop-down list arrow (in the Home tab), shown in Figure 6-5.

FIGURE 6-4

The Paragraph dialog box contains controls for most, but not all, of Word's paragraph attributes.

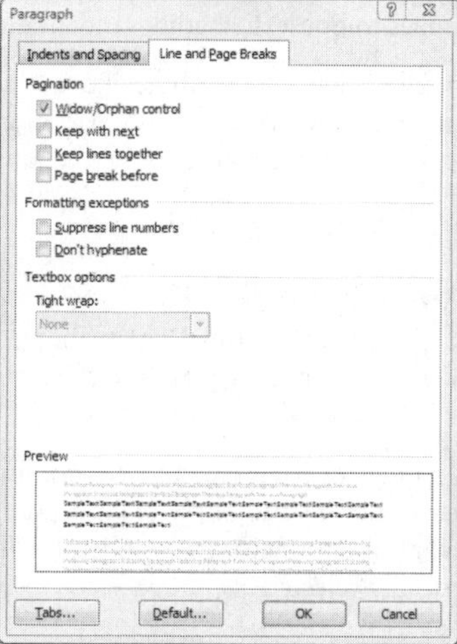

FIGURE 6-5

The Borders and Shading dialog box can be accessed from the bottom of the Borders control in the Home tab.

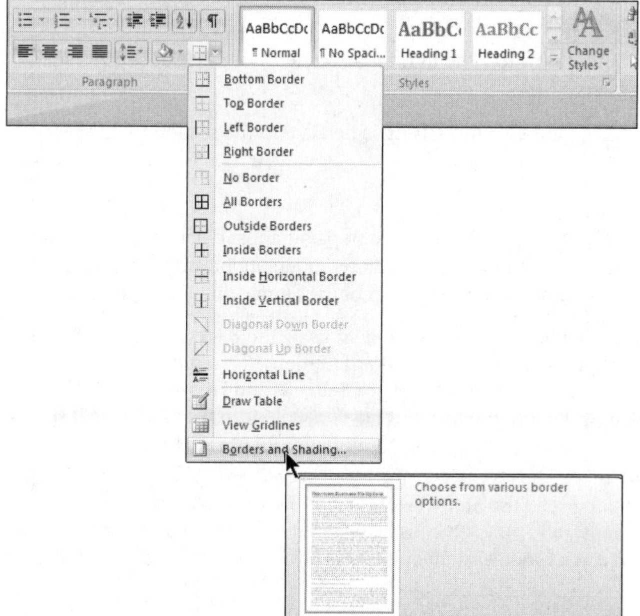

You might be wondering from all this how to determine whether a setting is a paragraph formatting attribute. One way is to see whether the attribute can be applied to a paragraph without selecting the whole paragraph. For example, if you click anywhere inside a paragraph and click the Center tool on the Home tab, the whole paragraph is centered. The same anywhere-in-the-paragraph rule is true for each of the other alignment options. The same applies to borders, shading, indentation, bullets, numbering, and line spacing.

Note, however, that two "paragraph formatting" attributes behave according to the *if nothing is selected, format the whole paragraph* rule, but behave differently if only part of a paragraph is selected. These two are shading and borders. While they generally are considered paragraph formatting, they also can be character formatting.

Paragraph formatting techniques

Two techniques can be used for all paragraph formatting attributes. As noted, you can simply place the insertion point in the paragraph you want and then choose the attribute (using the Ribbon, a dialog box, a keystroke, the context menu, or the Mini Toolbar).

The other technique is to select a range of paragraphs (up to and including the entire document). Note that even though shading and border formatting can apply to a selection of characters/words, if the selection includes or spans a paragraph mark, the formatting is applied to all of the full paragraphs in the selection, even those paragraphs that aren't fully selected.

Structural Formatting

Paragraph formatting can be thought of as encompassing two concepts:

- **Structural formatting**—Attributes that affect the overall structure of the text, such as alignment, indentation, tabs, etc.
- **Decorative formatting**—Attributes that affect the interior appearance of the text, such as shading, borders, numbering, and bullets

This section deals with structural formatting. Decorative formatting is detailed in the section that follows.

Indentation

Indentation typically is used for automatically indenting the first line of paragraphs, block indenting quotes, and setting up hanging indentation for bulleted or numbered text. Preset indentation can be set using the Decrease Indent and Increase Indent controls in the Paragraph group of the Home tab on the Ribbon.

TIP You can also perform Decrease Indent and Increase Indent using the Backspace and Tab keys, respectively. To do this, first choose Office Button ⇨ Word Options ⇨ Proofing ⇨ AutoCorrect Options. In AutoFormat As You Type, in the bottom set of options, click Set Left- and First-Indent with Tabs and Backspaces to enable it. This is enabled by default in Word, but many people turn it off because it sometimes appears to be "broken." I should also note that it does not perform identically to the Ribbon's Decrease Indent and Increase Indent controls.

When this setting is enabled, the Tab and Backspace (also Shift+Tab, if you prefer symmetry) work as advertised, but only when the paragraph is not empty, and only if the insertion point is as far left as it can go (in any line in the paragraph). If the insertion point is anywhere else, then the keys have their normal effects. Note

that the first press of the Tab key (if the insertion point is at the beginning of the paragraph) indents only the first line of the paragraph. Subsequent presses indent the entire paragraph.

Special rules apply for the Backspace key. Backspace decreases the indent only when an indentation is actually set. If there is a negative indent and a first-line or hanging indent, the first press of Backspace removes the hanging or first-line indent. If there is a negative indent and no hanging/first-line indent, then Backspace resets the indent to 0.

This is all potentially confusing enough that you might want to turn the setting off. In any case, if you turn it on, watch the ruler and the text when you press Tab or Backspace. One last thing: To insert an actual tab at the beginning of a paragraph when this setting is enabled, press Shift+Tab. This is also how you insert a tab into a table.

More precise indentation can be set using the Indent Left and Right settings controls in the Page Layout tab of the Ribbon. First-line indent or hanging indent typically are set using the mouse drag controls on the horizontal ruler, as shown in Figure 6-6.

FIGURE 6-6

The ruler provides GUI controls for indentation.

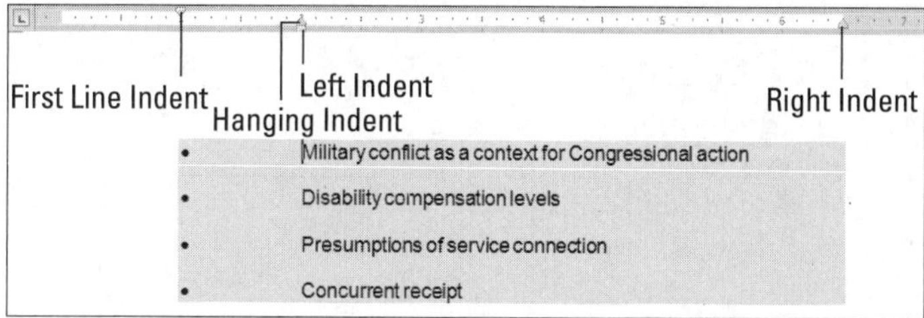

TIP **If you have trouble grabbing the ruler's tiny indent controls, you can use the tab/indent selection control at the left end of the horizontal ruler. Click the L-shaped (usually) control to cycle through the different tabs and indents and stop at the indent control that's giving you problems. With that control selected, you can now set first indent or hanging indent by clicking the desired position on the ruler.**

If you press the Alt key while manipulating the ruler's indent controls, Word displays the measurement, allowing for more informed positioning. Depending on your mouse's resolution, however, you might sometimes need to use the Paragraph dialog box's Special settings, shown in Figure 6-7. Here, the settings are identical to those shown in Figure 6-6.

Mirror Indents

Word 2007 isn't all just a flashy new interface. Keen observers who've used Word 2003 or earlier versions no doubt notice the Mirror Indents addition to the Paragraph dialog box. When enabled, left and right become Inside and Outside, as shown in Figure 6-8. This enables your indent settings to accommodate book style printing. Note that this is different from Mirror Margins, which is a Page Setup setting discussed in Chapter 8, "Page Setup and Sections."

FIGURE 6-7

The Paragraph dialog box is ideally suited to users who need more precision for exact settings.

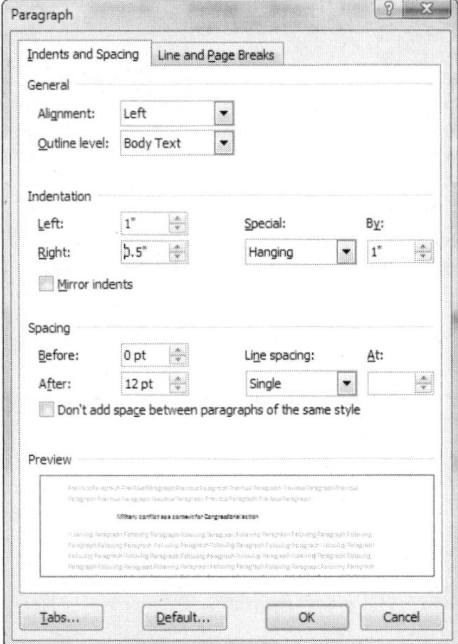

FIGURE 6-8

Mirror Indents is a new feature in Word 2007.

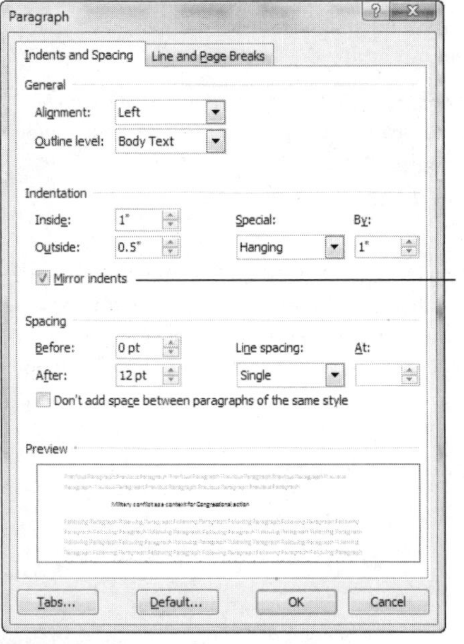

Alignment

Horizontal alignment determines how any given paragraph is oriented. The four options are Left, Right, Centered, and Justified. Settings can be made using the respective controls in the Paragraph group in the Home tab of the Ribbon. They can also be made using the four Alignment options in the Paragraph dialog box. And finally, they can be set using Ctrl+L, Ctrl+R, Ctrl+E (don't ask), and Ctrl+J. How Ctrl+E ever came to mean "center" is a mystery to me, but it seems to mean "center" in a wide variety of Windows programs. Maybe it's because it contains two e's.

Tabs

Tab is largely passé for many modern computer users. That's because better control can be effected using tables. Ever wonder about why we call them tabs and tables? We call them tabs because that's short for tabulation. And we call them tables for the same reason. (If you want the exact etymology, try the Oxford English Dictionary [OED].)

By default, a new document doesn't have any explicit tabs set. However, when no explicit tabs are set, Word uses default preset tabs every .5". When you set a tab, all of the built-in preset tabs to the left of the one you set are removed, leaving the manually inserted tab and all remaining preset tabs to the right.

Tabs can be set using the horizontal ruler line or the Tabs dialog box. Using the ruler line, you first determine the type of tab by clicking the tab control at the left end of the ruler. As indicated earlier, this control cycles not only among Word's built-in five tabs, but among first and hanging indent controls as well. The five built-in tab types are shown in Figure 6-9. When the desired tab type is displayed, click the lower portion of the ruler (below the ⅛-inch notches) to set the desired tab(s). You can drag them for better placement; holding the Alt key while dragging shows you the exact location.

FIGURE 6-9

Tabs can be set visually using the ruler line.

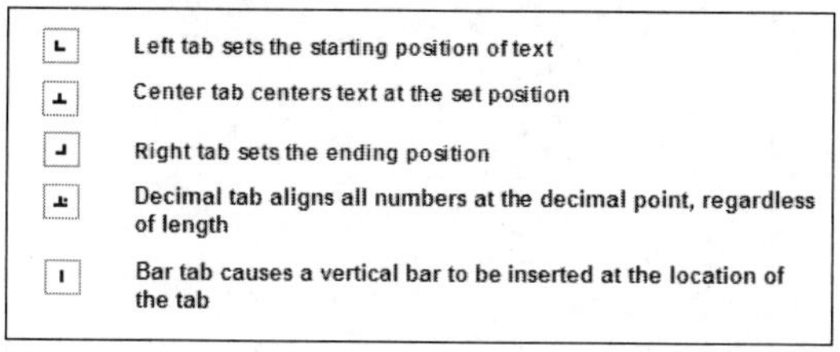

Left tab sets the starting position of text

Center tab centers text at the set position

Right tab sets the ending position

Decimal tab aligns all numbers at the decimal point, regardless of length

Bar tab causes a vertical bar to be inserted at the location of the tab

To remove a tab using the ruler, simply drag it down and away from the ruler until the mouse pointer is no longer in the ruler area.

If you prefer the steadiness and precision of being able to type the settings you want, use the Tabs dialog box, shown in Figure 6-10. Activate the Tabs dialog box by choosing Tabs from the Paragraph dialog box, or by double-clicking any existing tab in the ruler line.

Notice that the Tab dialog box also lets you set tab leaders, typically used to help the reader visually line up text and numbers. Tab leaders often are used in tables of contents and indexes, such as the one shown in Figure 6-11.

FIGURE 6-10

Use the Tabs dialog box to set and clear tabs, set the default tab stop interval, and set a tab leader.

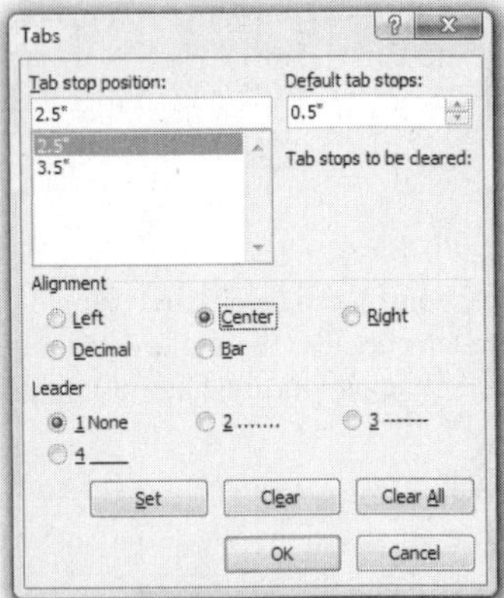

FIGURE 6-11

Tab leaders are a visual aid that help the reader correctly align associated text.

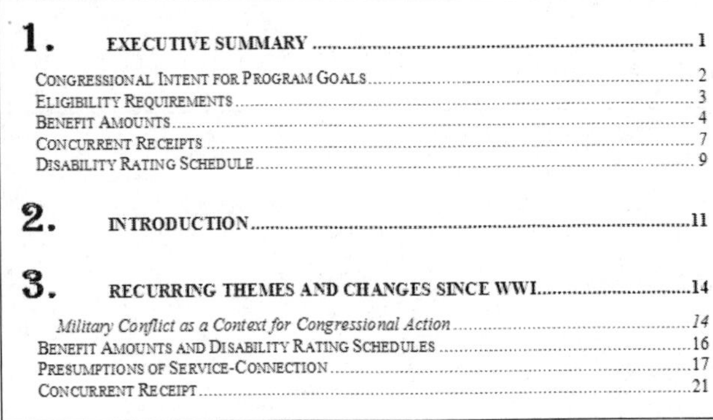

1. EXECUTIVE SUMMARY 1

Congressional Intent for Program Goals 2
Eligibility Requirements 3
Benefit Amounts 4
Concurrent Receipts 7
Disability Rating Schedule 9

2. INTRODUCTION 11

3. RECURRING THEMES AND CHANGES SINCE WWI 14

Military Conflict as a Context for Congressional Action *14*
Benefit Amounts and Disability Rating Schedules 16
Presumptions of Service-Connection 17
Concurrent Receipt 21

Tabs versus tables

If you can use tabs, and you can use tables, when should you use which? Years of using Word has convinced me that pseudo tables, as I like to call tables that are created using tabs, are a lot more fragile than actual tables. They're also a lot less flexible.

Even so, there are times when tabs give you precisely what you want, and in a way that a table either can't or can't without jumping through hoops. If you want tab leader lines, while there are other ways to accomplish the same effect, it's almost always faster and easier to use tab leaders.

If you need to create an underscored area for a signature or other fill-in information on a paper form, the solid tab leader line is definitely the way to go, even though you could draw lines where you want them instead (holding down the Shift key to keep it horizontal, of course). However, graphical lines have a way of not always staying where you put them, so you'll usually find that it's much more efficient and predictable to just use a leader line.

TIP **To create a signature or other fill-in area, type the prompt (Name:, Phone:, etc.). Use the tab selection tool at the left end of the horizontal ruler to choose a right tab, and then click on the horizontal ruler line where you want the fill-in line to end to insert a right tab. Double-click the tab you just created. In the Tabs dialog box, choose Leader option 4 (solid underscore), and click OK. This creates something like what is shown in Figure 6-12. (If you accidentally inserted a new tab when you tried to double-click, make sure you zap it while visiting the Tabs dialog box.)**

FIGURE 6-12

Tab leader lines are ideal for creating underscored fill-in areas for paper forms.

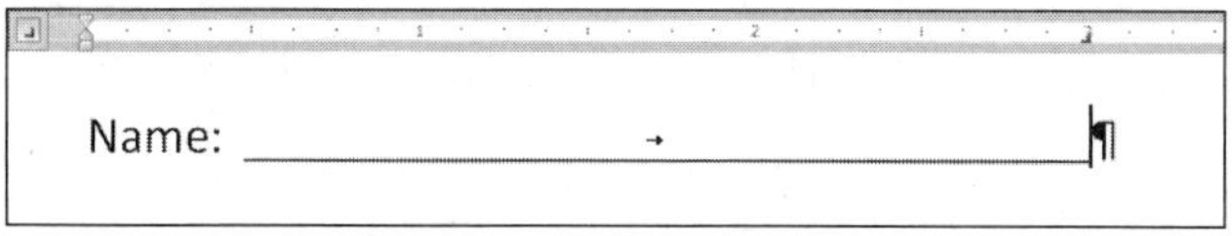

Name: ________________________________

Incidentally, using a table, you can create a fill-in area that looks identical to that one. Create a table with one row. Size it so that Name is a narrower column and the second column ends where you want the fill-in area to end. Next, use the Borders tool to turn off all borders in the table. Finally, use the Bottom Border tool to turn on just the bottom border in the second column's cell. For me, however, this is a lot more work just to prove a point.

Another situation when tabs give you what you want is with simple document headers. The default header for Word 2007 documents contains a center tab and a right-align tab. This enables you to easily create a header with text to the left, centered text, and right-aligned text, simply by separating those three components with tabs. Tabs also can be useful inside actual tables for aligning numbers at the decimal point. (As noted earlier, to insert a tab inside a table, press Ctrl+Tab.)

However, for more complex presentations of information, particularly when you might need organizational control (copying and moving rows and columns), it's much better and much more natural to use a table.

Paragraph Decoration

A second kind of paragraph formatting is something that might be termed *paragraph decoration*. This includes shading, boxes, bullets, and other semi-graphical elements that help the writer call attention to particular paragraphs, or that help the reader understand the text better.

Numbering/bullets

Numbering in Word has always been a bit of a sore point. That's because historically, it has proven to be both confusing and fraught with odd quirks. Let's pretend for the moment that numbering and bullets work perfectly and never give the user grief. To make that assumption pass the Sarcastic Giggle Test, let's assume we're using the Word 2007 `.docx` format, rather than Word 2003's (or earlier) legacy `.doc` format.

Numbering or bullets can be applied simply by clicking the Numbering or Bullets tool in the Home tab of the Ribbon. You can click the Numbering or Bullets tool and just start typing. When you're done with your list, simply press Enter twice.

NOTE **If Automatic bulleted lists or Automatic numbered lists are enabled, then you don't even need to click the Numbering or Bullets tool. To begin a numbered list, simply type 1. and press the spacebar, and Word automatically replaces what you typed with automatic number formatting. Other variations work, too, such as 1<tab>. To begin a bulleted list, simply type * and press the spacebar. When you want to end either kind of list, press Enter twice.**

You can also apply numbering or bullets to an existing list. Just select the list and click either tool. If the list has levels (for example, created by pressing tab before certain sub-items), then the Numbering tool uses different and appropriate numbering schemes for each level.

Note that Bullets and Numbering both offer live preview of the resulting list. Multilevel List, however, does not.

Line numbering

Line numbering, which is different from numbered lists, often is used in legal documents such as affidavits. The numbering allows for ready reference to testimony by page and line number. Line numbering itself, however, is not a paragraph formatting attribute. It is a section formatting attribute. Line numbering is turned on using the Line Numbers tool in the Page Layout tab of the Ribbon or by using the Line Numbers option in the Layout tab of the Page Setup dialog box, shown in Figure 6-13.

FIGURE 6-13

Line numbering is a section formatting attribute, but it can be turned off in any given paragraph.

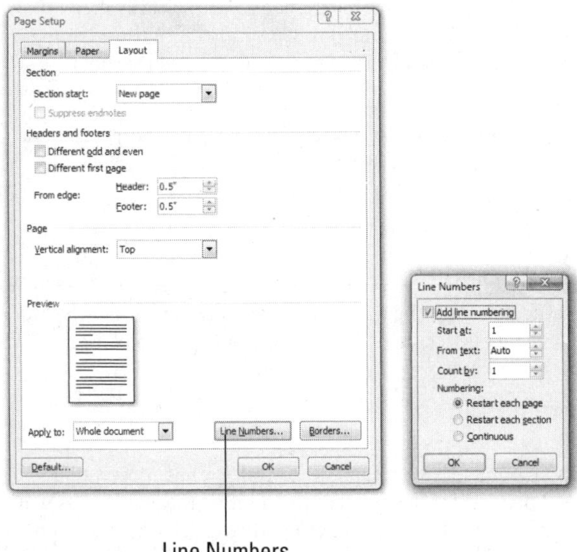

So, why am I talking about line numbering here if it's not a paragraph formatting attribute? I'm talking about it here because although line numbering isn't a paragraph attribute, suppressing line numbering *is* a paragraph attribute, as shown in Figure 6-14. (Note that line numbers do not display in Draft or Outline views.) Here, I've also displayed the Reveal Formatting pane so that you can see that Suppress Line Numbers is indeed a paragraph formatting attribute.

FIGURE 6-14

While line numbering is a section formatting attribute, the ability to suppress it is a paragraph attribute.

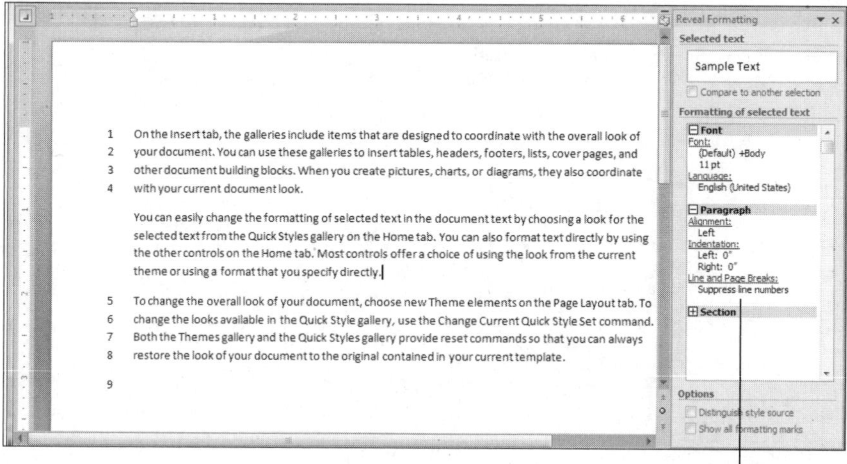

To suppress line numbering in any given paragraph, put the insertion point in that paragraph, display the Paragraph dialog box (double-click any of the indent controls on the horizontal ruler), and enable Suppress Line Numbers in the Line and Page Breaks tab, as shown in Figure 6-15.

Additional paragraph controls

Figure 6-15 shows additional paragraph-level formatting controls:

- **Widow/Orphan control** — Prevents a solitary paragraph line from being "stranded" on a page all by itself (widows precede the main portion of the paragraph, while orphans follow it).
- **Keep with next** — Forces a paragraph to appear with the paragraph that follows. This is used to keep headings together with at least the first few lines of the first paragraph under that heading. It is also used to keep captions and pictures, figures, tables, and so on, on the same page.
- **Keep lines together** — Prevents a paragraph from breaking across two pages.
- **Page break before** — Forces an automatic page break before the paragraph. This often is used to force each chapter to begin on a new page.
- **Don't hyphenate** — Instructs Word not to perform hyphenation in a given paragraph. This often is done when trying to reproduce a quote and maintain its integrity with respect to the words and position of the original being quoted.

FIGURE 6-15

Line numbers can be suppressed on a paragraph-by-paragraph basis.

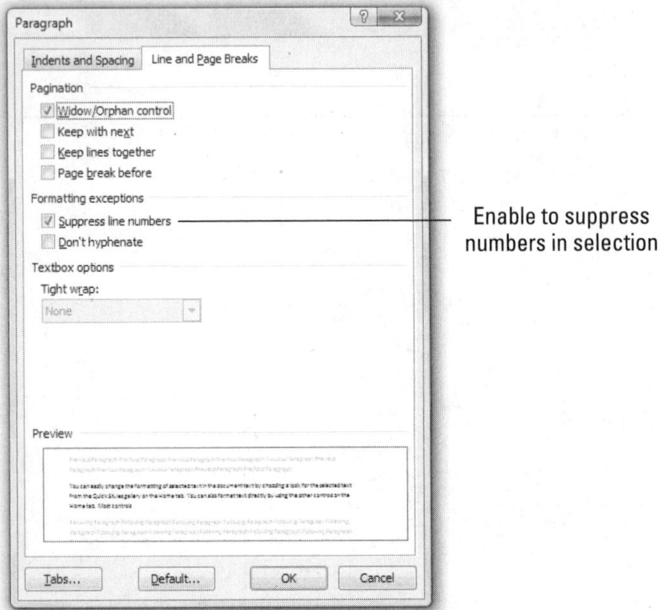

Shading

Paragraph shading, as well as shading of individual words, can be performed graphically with live preview using the Shading control in the Home tab of the Ribbon, shown in Figure 6-16.

Additional shading options can be viewed using the Shading tab in the Borders and Shading dialog box. In addition to color shading, you can also choose to apply patterns. Patterns often are more useful when preparing documents for grayscale printing in which shading variations might be too subtle. To display the Borders and Shading dialog box, click the drop-down arrow next to the Border tool in the Home tab of the Ribbon, and select Borders and Shading (at the bottom of the list).

CONFUSION ALERT **Note that the Border tool changes to the last border option you picked using the drop-down arrow. Therefore, if the last option you picked was Borders and Shading, then that's what the main Border tool becomes (for now, anyway).**

FIGURE 6-16

When nothing is selected, shading is applied to the whole paragraph. Unlike many other paragraph formatting attributes, shading can be a character formatting attribute as well.

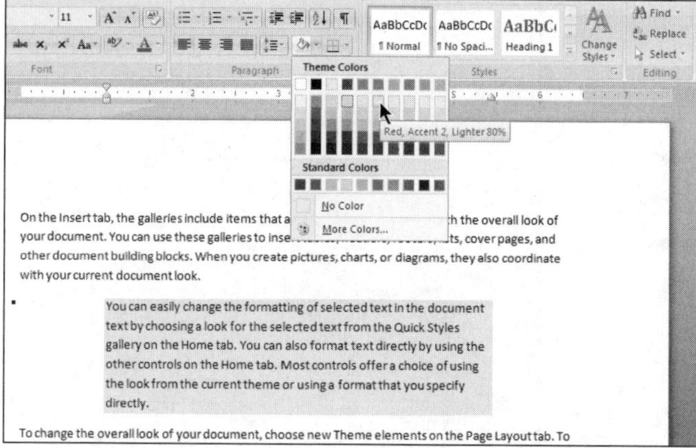

What's that dot?

When a square dot appears to the left of a paragraph, any of the following attributes are assigned to that paragraph:

- Keep with next
- Keep lines together
- Page break before
- Suppress line numbers

These options can all be found in the Line and Page Breaks tab of the Paragraph dialog box, shown in Figure 6-15.

Borders and boxes

Some call them borders, some call them boxes. I call them . . . borders and boxes. Unlike shading, Borders does not provide Live Preview. You can choose from the Border control's drop-down options, or you can instead display the Borders and Shading option at the end of the drop-down list to display the dialog box shown in Figure 6-17.

FIGURE 6-17

The Borders and Shading dialog box provides complete control over a paragraph's border.

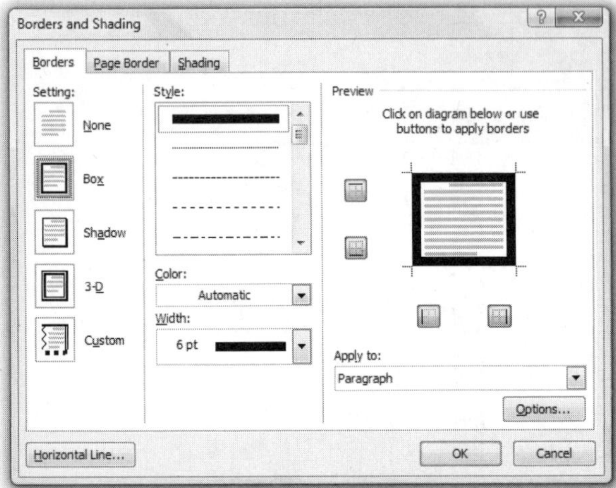

Because the drop-down doesn't provide live preview, I often find working in the dialog box to involve a bit less trial-and-error. The basic technique is to choose a box/border design (Box, Shadow, or 3-D), and then customize as you see fit. You can click the boxes or the borders in the Preview area to turn individual sides on or off. By alternately clicking Style, Color, or Width and the line segments you want to format, you can even create a box with four completely different sides. (Did I fail to mention that this chapter is about formatting, not tacky design?)

Additionally, the distance between the border and paragraph text can be adjusted by clicking Options in the southeast corner of the dialog box. You can individually adjust the distance for any of the four sides.

Random Bonus Tip #1 — Sort Paragraphs That Aren't in a Table

You've seen Sort in the Paragraph group and in the Table Layout Ribbon, but you might not know that it works on any list — even one that's not in a table. Select the items you want sorted and click the Sort tool in the Home Ribbon's Paragraph group. Or, if you're a keyboard junkie, try using the same menu keystrokes you used in earlier versions of Word (Alt+A, S).

Random Bonus Tip #2 — Move Paragraphs Easily

If you ever have two paragraphs that you need to quickly swap, don't reach for the mouse. Instead, put the insertion point into either paragraph, and use Shift+Alt+Up or Shift+Alt+Down to "drag" the current paragraph up or down so that it changes places with the other paragraph. These are outlining keystrokes, but they work great for this sort of thing as well. You can also quickly move rows around in tables.

Summary

In this chapter, we've explored the ins and outs of direct paragraph formatting. You should have also learned that anything you can do to a paragraph, you can enshrine in a style. You should now be able to do the following:

- Decide when to use direct formatting, and when to use a style
- Distinguish between paragraph formatting attributes and other kinds of attributes
- Properly indent and align any paragraph, as well as determine how to find and use the appropriate tools
- Apply and remove bullets and numbering
- Use shading and boxes to highlight paragraphs
- Explain at the next cocktail party what those strange square dots are at the left side of certain paragraphs
- Decide when to use tabs versus when to use a table

Chapter 7

Styles

Styles are the seat of power in Word — any version, not just Word 2007. Word 2007 includes additional tools that make using styles for formatting more powerful and more flexible. The dizzying array of options might leave you scratching your head in wonder and amazement, but perhaps in confusion as well. In fact, much of how Word 2007 goes about its business might seem shrouded in mystery, since there are so many unfamiliar elements.

This chapter sorts things out, solving the mysteries, reducing the confusion, and giving you a handle on which tools to use for what. It looks at new concepts and tools, such as Quick Styles and Quick Style sets, the Style Inspector, the Apply Styles task pane, and the Styles task pane. It ties these features together and shows how they relate to legacy Word tools, such as the Modify Styles dialog box and the Organizer.

IN THIS CHAPTER

Styles Group

The most visible Ribbon control for applying and changing styles is the Styles group in the Home tab of the Ribbon. Seemingly simple, the Styles group is the tip of a rather large iceberg.

On its face are four controls, shown in Figure 7-1: the Quick Styles Gallery, Change Styles (for selecting Style sets), More, and the Styles Dialog Box Launcher.

NOTE **The word "quick" very likely will confuse many users. You might also notice that the term "Quick Style" also applies to the gallery used for SmartArt. These are not related. One way to deal with the disconnect is to think of them as different kinds of styles — one you apply to text elements, the other you apply to certain kinds of graphic elements. We will look at SmartArt "styles" in Chapter 9.**

FIGURE 7-1

The Styles group is the command and control center for styles.

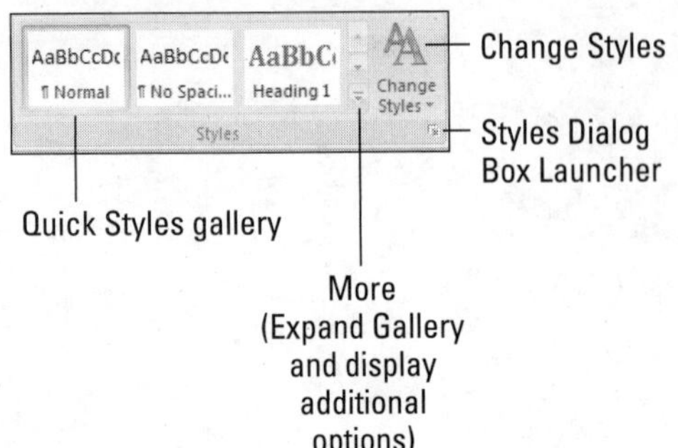

In a normal screen configuration and resolution, the Quick Styles gallery shows only three to five styles. In a very high resolution setup with a sufficiently wide monitor, it can show up to a dozen styles without having to use the More control. Clicking the More button shows more of the styles in the Quick Styles gallery, as shown in Figure 7-2. If there are still more styles in the gallery, they can be accessed using the vertical scroll bar or by dragging the right corner control to expand or shrink the size of the gallery.

FIGURE 7-2

The Style Gallery can be scrolled and made larger or smaller.

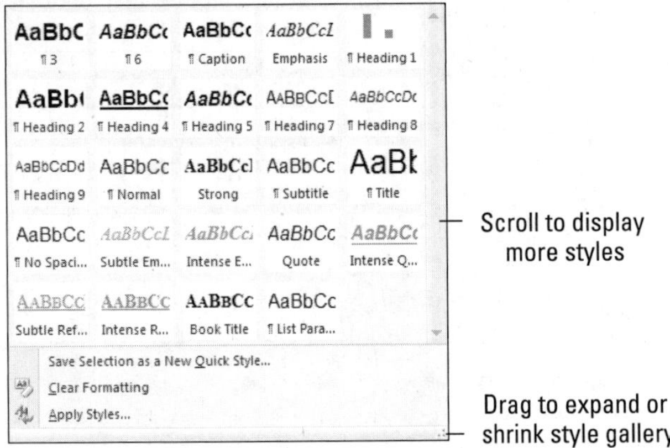

The Styles group also provides access to Quick Style sets. If you click Change Styles and then click Style Set, you see additional new toys, shown in Figure 7-3. The options shown — Default (Black and White), Distinctive, and so on, are carefully constructed sets of styles that are coordinated to help you quickly change the look of your document. (You'll see where those Quick Style sets come from later in this chapter.)

FIGURE 7-3

Quick Style sets offer additional coordinated styles to help achieve a different "look" for your documents.

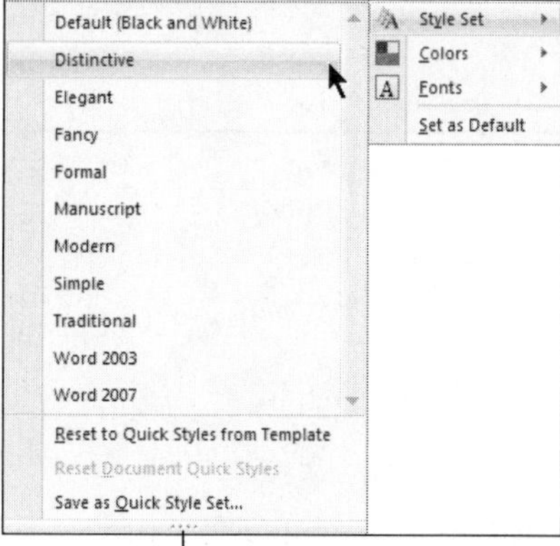

Notice also the Colors and Fonts controls. These tools work with themes, which aren't the same thing as styles. Like Quick Style sets, themes can be used to dramatically change the appearance of your document. Unlike Quick Style sets, however, they are tied to the use of theme elements in your document.

NOTE **Theme is a feature new to Word 2007, and does not work with compatibility mode documents. In the Change Styles list, Style Set is available, but Colors and Fonts are not. These features are available, however, not only when working with Word 2007 documents, but also when working with web-oriented documents (*.`mht`, *.`htm`, *.`html`, etc.). Themes are explored in Chapter 8, "Page Setup and Sections."**

The effect of different style sets — indeed, seeing any effect at all — depends on your having used styles in your document. If you simply use the style Normal, then at most applying a new Quick Style set will change the font. For maximum benefit from Word's new style features, you need to lay the proper foundation, which means using styles to differentiate different kinds of text (headings, body, captions, etc.).

Using styles

When you first start typing in any Word document, you're automatically using the default style. Ordinarily, that would be Normal.

NOTE **The style named Normal is wholly independent of the fact that there is a Word template named `Normal.dotm`. `Normal.dotm` contains many different styles, and one of them happens to be named Normal. In fact, every Word template contains a style named Normal. This is nothing more than an unfortunate, confusing, and creativity-challenged choice of names. They could have named Word's default style Base or Body, and I really wish they had. It would make notes like this one unnecessary. Fortunately, Normal view has been renamed Draft view, so at least we no longer have to deal with that added bit of creativity-challenged confusion.**

As you type different parts of any document, you should consider applying an appropriate style. For example, if you type a heading, consider applying a heading style to it, such as Heading 1, 2, or 3. To do this, click the heading style in the Quick Styles gallery, as shown in Figure 7-4. If Heading 1 isn't showing, then click the More button to the right of the Styles, also shown in Figure 7-4.

FIGURE 7-4

Click a style in the Quick Styles gallery to apply it to the current paragraph or selection.

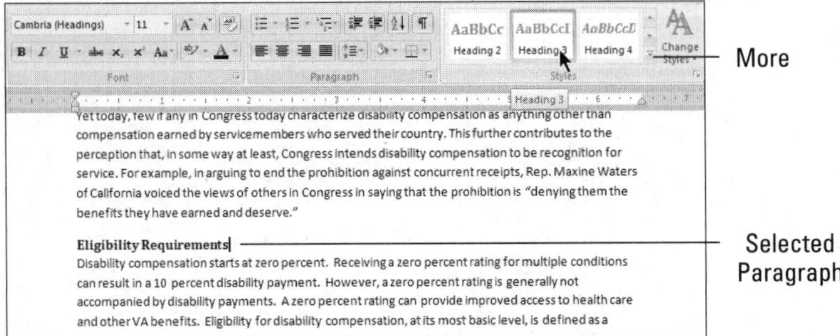

Apply styles task pane

If you're accustomed to Word 2003 or earlier, you can also apply a style in a way that's similar. In Word 2003, you could either click in the Style drop-down tool or press Ctrl+Shift+S. There is no default Style drop-down in Word 2007, but Ctrl+Shift+S activates the Apply Styles task pane, shown in Figure 7-5. Once the Apply Styles task pane is visible, it can be used in a way that's similar but not identical to Word 2003's Style tool.

FIGURE 7-5

Press Ctrl+Shift+S to activate the Apply Styles task pane, which is Word 2007's substitute for Word's earlier Style tool in the Formatting toolbar.

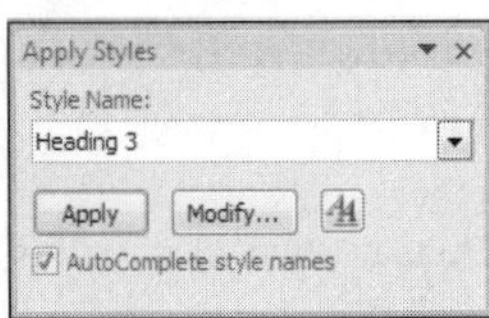

TIP

In the preceding paragraph, I said there is no *default* Style drop-down tool. There isn't. However, there is one you can add to the Quick Access Toolbar. Unfortunately, you can't assign a keystroke to it, but you can at least use it for setting the style using the mouse. More important, it displays the style assigned to the insertion point all the time, unlike the Quick Styles gallery.

To put this tool onto your QAT, right-click the QAT and choose Customize Quick Access Toolbar. Set Customize Quick Access Toolbar to For All Documents (default). Choose Commands Not in the Ribbon from the Choose Commands From drop-down list. Click in the list of commands and tap the T key. This displays the first command starting with T, but also exposes all of the commands beginning with "Style." Click on the command named just Style. When you hover the mouse over it, the tooltip says "Style (StyleGalleryClassic)." With Style selected, click Add to add it to the QAT. Click OK, and you're done.

Creating and modifying styles

Often, when you use a built-in heading style, it does not suit your needs. The font or point size might be wrong, or, the spacing might be off. No problem. Change it. Or, if you still need the existing style but want a slightly different version for another purpose, create a new style.

To change an existing style, right-click the style in the Quick Styles gallery and choose Modify. This displays the Modify Style dialog box shown in Figure 7-6. Make the desired change to the style. If the formatting you need to change isn't shown, click Format in the southwest corner and choose from the seven different categories of formatting.

FIGURE 7-6

Use the Modify Style dialog box to make changes to a style.

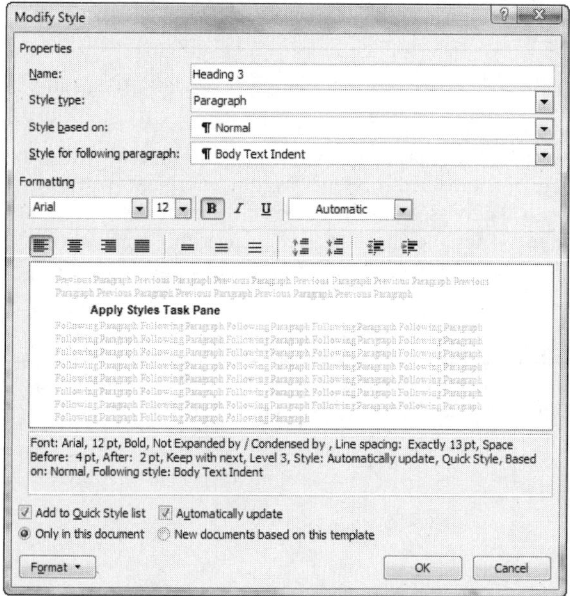

CAUTION Keep Automatically Update turned off unless you absolutely need it (for example, if your company's policy requires it be used). The Automatically Update setting can bring much joy or much sorrow. If enabled, when you make changes to Heading 3, for example, those changes are automatically incorporated in the style's definition. All other text in the document formatted using that style will automatically change to reflect the changes in the style's definition. If you're using styles correctly, this can bring great joy.

If, on the other hand, you've misused Body Text throughout the document, applying direct formatting in various locations to make it "look right," then you could be in for an unpleasant shock. Suppose a modified Body Text style sometimes is used on a heading, other times used for a caption, and other times for other purposes. Each time you modify the Body Text style in one place, all other instances in your document also change, undoing your careful direct formatting. This can happen without you realizing it, because the updated instances may be miles away in another part of the document. By the time you see what's happening, it might be too late for a Ctrl+Z miracle. On the bright side, the Automatically Update option does not exist for the Normal style. This option was the cause of much grief in Word 2003 and earlier. Its removal from the Normal style in Word 2007 will prevent a great many self-inflicted mishaps!

While there is a special New Style dialog box you can use (available from the bottom of the Styles task pane and the Manage Styles dialog box, for example), you aren't limited to that method. In Figure 7-6, where it says Heading 3, you can type a new style name. When you click OK, the style is created!

Style by example

Another way to modify a style assumes that Automatically Update is *not* enabled, and that Prompt to Update Style *is* enabled in the Advanced section of the Word Options dialog box. Choose Office Button ➪ Word Options ➪ Advanced, and in the Editing Options section, click to enable Prompt to Update Style. Assuming that Automatically Update is not enabled for a given style, you can now perform what's sometimes called *style-by-example*. We also need to assume that you're not using the Normal style, as it plays by different rules (Automatically Update doesn't work for Normal).

Use whatever formatting controls you like — Ribbon, keyboard shortcuts, dialog boxes, and so on — to tweak text so that it looks the way you want. When you've got it looking just so, you can either create a new style or modify the current one. Note that you should modify a given style only if you want all other text formatted with that style to be formatted the same way.

To create a new style, type the new style name in the Style Name box in the Apply Styles task pane, and then press Enter to apply it.

To modify the existing style, click Reapply on the Apply Styles task pane. Or, reapply the current style using some other method such as the Quick Style Gallery or a keyboard shortcut. Word now prompts you with the dialog box shown in Figure 7-7. Note that you will never see this dialog box if the current style is Normal. Normal marches to a different drummer and is designed to resist easy changes that might have major unintended consequences.

FIGURE 7-7

When enabled, the Advanced Word option Prompt to Update Style tells Word to prompt you when you attempt to reapply a style (other than Normal) to text that contains formatting that differs from the current style's settings.

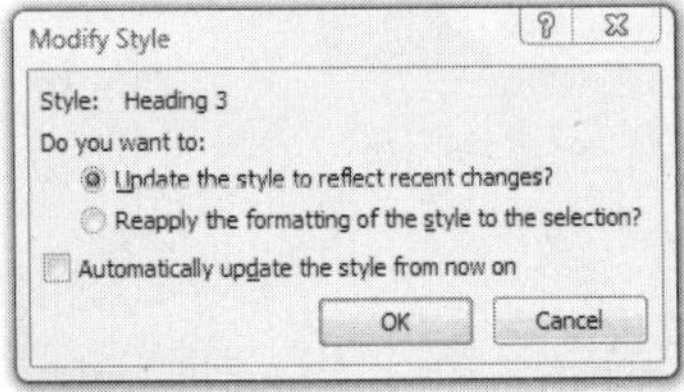

Choose the Update the Style to Reflect Current Changes option to redefine the current style according to the formatting in the current selection (that's what "recent changes" really means — it doesn't mean "in the last week or two"). The Reapply the Formatting of the Style to the Selection option will undo your direct formatting and reapply the original style. Note that Automatically Update the Style From Now On enables (checks) the Automatically Update checkbox in the Modify Style dialog box. Think long and hard before you ever check that checkbox!

CAUTION Furthermore, redefining a style works on the Normal style! This can be good or bad. Consider, for example, that many styles are based on Normal. If you change the font, for example, every style that gets its font definition from Normal changes too. If you change the Before or After spacing, the indentations, the alignment, and so on, then every style that inherits those attributes from Normal will also change. Only rarely will that be exactly what you want.

Quick Style sets

Quick Style sets are a potentially confusing new addition to Word's formatting arsenal. Quick Style sets get their information from a set of `.dotx` (not macro-enabled) templates. In the Styles group of the Home tab on the Ribbon, choose Change Styles ➪ Style Set and look at the names: Default (Black and White), Distinctive, Elegant, and so on.

These sets correspond to `.dotx` files stored in `C:\Program Files\Microsoft Office\OFFICE12\1033\QuickStyles`, as shown in Figure 7-8.

FIGURE 7-8

The Quick Style sets are stored as .dotx files, and can be changed or customized by the user.

Name	Type	Size
Classic.dotx	Microsoft Office Word Template	9 KB
Default.dotx	Microsoft Office Word Template	9 KB
DefaultBlackAndWhite.dotx	Microsoft Office Word Template	9 KB
Distinctive.dotx	Microsoft Office Word Template	9 KB
Elegant.dotx	Microsoft Office Word Template	9 KB
Fancy.dotx	Microsoft Office Word Template	9 KB
Formal.dotx	Microsoft Office Word Template	9 KB
Manuscript.dotx	Microsoft Office Word Template	9 KB
Modern.dotx	Microsoft Office Word Template	9 KB
Simple.dotx	Microsoft Office Word Template	9 KB
Traditional.dotx	Microsoft Office Word Template	9 KB

NOTE These `.dotx` files contain no text or other formatting, but only style information for 135 built-in styles (no, this is not the entire list; a few notable missing styles are footnote, endnote, header, and footer).

When you apply a new Quick Style set by choosing Change Styles ➪ Style Set and clicking on one of the displayed sets, Word replaces the style definitions in the current document with those contained in the corresponding `.dotx` file. It effectively overlays a new document template on top of what you're already using (even though the name of the underlying document template does not change). All *style-formatted* text that uses any of the styles in the replaced Quick Style set is affected.

I emphasize *style-formatted* because if paragraphs have direct formatting applied, then that formatting will not be overridden. The attributes of the selected text that are applied only through a style are changed. For example, if you manually change the alignment of a series of paragraphs from centered to left aligned, then any alignment formatting in a Quick Style set you apply will be ignored.

Modifying and creating quick style sets

Quick Style sets are not carved into stone. You can modify the ones that Microsoft provides, and you can create your own.

You should modify the ones that Microsoft provides, by the way, only when a built-in Quick Style set's original form is something you wouldn't be caught dead using. While you can recover the original, it's easier to simply use a different name, such as Classic Bert, so you recognize it as your own variation (assuming your name is Bert).

To easily modify a set that Microsoft provides, open a document that is affected by a Quick Style set, and apply the style set you want to use, using Change Styles ➪ Style Set on the Home tab. Next, modify any styles you want changed. Finally, choose Change Styles ➪ Style Set ➪ Save as Quick Style Set, as shown in Figure 7-9.

FIGURE 7-9

You can modify the built-in Quick Style sets or add your own.

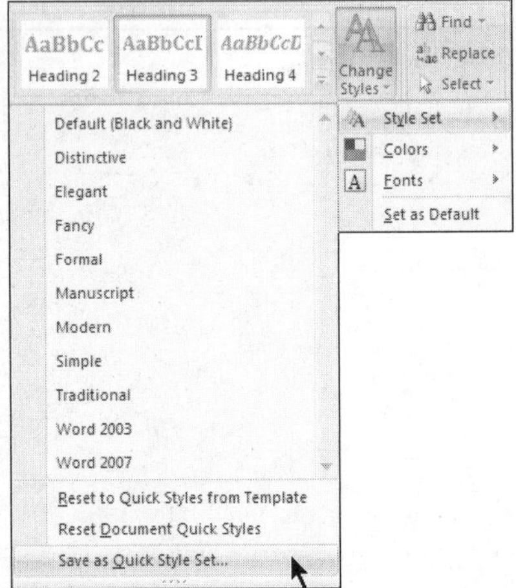

In the Save Quick Style Set dialog, specify the name of the built-in set you want to modify or override. Suppose, for example, that you want a custom version of the Elegant Quick Style Set. In File Name, type **Elegant** (you don't need to type the `.dotx` extension). Note that this will not actually modify or overwrite the original file. Then click Save. Or, to create your own Quick Style Set, type a new name (such as **My Elegant**) and choose Save.

If creating your own style set named Elegant doesn't overwrite Word's version, then how does Word know to use yours instead of its own? As indicated earlier in this chapter, Word keeps its own Quick Style sets in one of the Microsoft Office Program Files folders. It saves *your* Quick Style sets, however, to the `C:\Documents and Settings\user name\Application Data\Microsoft\QuickStyles` folder (in XP) or C:\Users*user name*\AppData\Roaming\Microsoft\QuickStyles (in Vista). When you display the Quick Style sets list by choosing Change Styles ➪ Style Set on the Home tab, Word builds the list from a combination of the user folder and its "own" folder, giving priority to any user Quick Style set names that are the same as the Quick Style set names that ship with Word.

To revert to a Quick Style set that comes with Word, simply delete or rename your own. In general, however, you increase your options by not giving your Quick Style sets the same names as those that come with Word.

TIP **Do you have customized styles in your `Normal.dotm` file? If so, before working with Quick Style sets, protect your original `Normal.dotm` Quick Style set by saving it as a unique Quick Style set. To do this, press Ctrl+N to create a new document window based on `Normal.dotm`. On the Home tab of the Ribbon, choose Change Styles ⇨ Style Set ⇨ Save as Quick Style Set. In File Name, choose a name that's unambiguously clear, such as `My Favorite QuickStyles`.**

Changing your mind

If you've been experimenting with Quick Style sets but now want to revert either to the document's own styles or to those of the underlying template, you probably can. To be able to revert to the document's own original styles, the document must not have been saved and closed. Even when the document has been saved, you can revert to the document's original styles as of when the document was opened.

To revert to the document styles that were in effect at the beginning of the current editing session, choose Home ⇨ Change Styles ⇨ Style Set. As shown in Figure 7-10, click Reset Document Quick Styles.

FIGURE 7-10

As long as the current document hasn't been saved and closed since the last Quick Style set change, you can revert to the document's original set of Quick Styles.

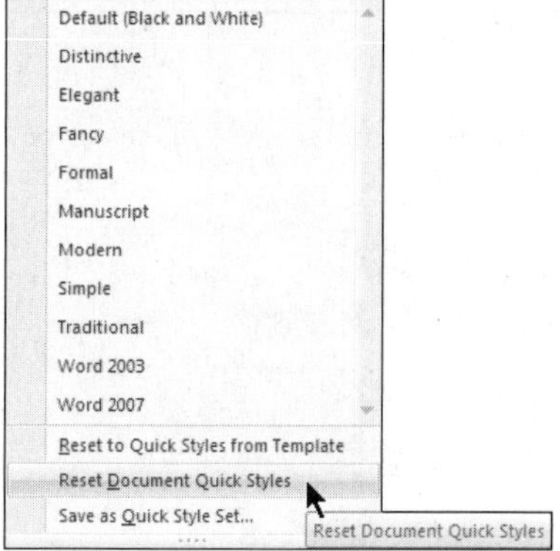

To be able to revert to the styles of the underlying template, you must not have saved Quick Style set changes to the template. Otherwise, reverting won't do anything other than reapply styles that are already in effect. Unlike the document itself, where a mere save doesn't prevent you from being able to go back to square one, a mere save to the underlying template *does* commit the style changes in that case. If you did that, see the tip at the end of the preceding section.

Assuming that you haven't saved a Quick Style set to your current document template, you can revert to its styles. Choose Change Styles ⇨ Style Set ⇨ Reset to Quick Styles from Template on the Home tab (refer to Figure 7-10).

Styles Task Pane

Conceptually, the Styles task pane is the replacement for Word 2003's Styles and Formatting task pane. Shown in Figure 7-11, the Styles task pane provides some of the same functionality, but not all. It also offers some new functionality that Word's earlier task pane didn't have.

NOTE

In Figure 7-11, notice that styles have three kinds of icons next to them: ¶, a, or ¶a.

The ¶ means that it's a paragraph style only. You cannot apply it to only part of a paragraph, and you can apply it by placing the insertion point anywhere in the target paragraph.

The a icon means that it's a character/text style. It is applied only to selected text. You can apply it to a single word (assuming that "When selecting, automatically select entire word" is enabled in the Editing Options section of Word Options). You can also apply it to a single character or an entire document.

The ¶a icon means that the style can be used as either a character style or a paragraph style. If nothing is selected or if parts of two or more paragraphs are selected, the style is applied to the entire paragraph(s) touched by the selection. If only part of a single paragraph is selected, the style is applied only to selected text.

Does this mean that Heading styles, which use ¶a, can be applied to something less than a full paragraph? You betcha! This can be exceedingly useful when you want to include headings at the beginning of paragraphs, particularly when you want to save vertical space in the document. This is not a new feature, by the way; you could do it as far back as Word 2000.

FIGURE 7-11

Right-click a style in the Styles task pane for style-specific options.

The options you get when you right-click or use the drop-down arrow vary according to Word's Options settings as well as to whether the selected style is a built-in style or a user-created style. In Figure 7-11, the built-in Heading 1 style excludes the Delete option. You cannot delete a built-in style. You can hide it, but you can't deep-six it.

The Update option at the top of the menu appears even if the option Prompt to Update Styles is not enabled (Office Button ➪ Word Options ➪ Advanced ➪ Editing Options). If you have that option turned off but need the capability, the Styles task pane provides ad hoc access to it.

Two extremely useful options, one of them new in Word 2007, are Select All # Instance(s) and Remove All # Instance(s). The Remove All option is new and extremely useful when cleaning up a document's extraneous formatting. Remove does not delete the text in question. Instead, it removes the style wherever it is used and resets the formatting of those occurrences to the default style for the current document. Ordinarily, that would be Normal.

The Select option is equally useful. Typically, to change a given style to a different style, you might consider using Find and Replace. Indeed, that is an option. However, it's not necessary. Click Select All # Instances, and then click the desired style in the Styles task pane. Or, once the instances are selected, use manual/direct formatting to "sculpt" the text just the way you want it, and then choose New Style at the bottom of the Styles task pane.

NOTE **In Figure 7-11, why would Select All and Remove All say Not Currently Used when the style is in fact in use? This is an artifact of a Word Options setting. Choose Office Button ➪ Word Options ➪ Advanced ➪ Editing Options section and click to disable Keep Track of Formatting. Now Select All and Remove All will work. The problem stems from the way in which Word keeps track of formatting, which it does by making tiny incremental changes to the underlying style. The result is that when Keep Track of Formatting is used, Word disallows the Select All and Remove All features.**

Remove from Quick Gallery does not remove the style from the document. Instead, it removes the style from the Quick Gallery listing of styles. If the style is not currently in the Quick Style Gallery, the command in the pop-up will be Add to Quick Gallery instead.

Manage styles

Another option available from the Styles task pane is the Manage Styles button. Shown in Figure 7-12, Manage Styles is your master control and grand central station for styles. Use this dialog box to create, modify, and delete styles (the latter, only user-created styles).

Use the manager also as a launch pad for the Organizer, via the Import/Export button, which enables you to copy styles between different templates and documents, as well as rename and delete styles (again, only user-created styles can be deleted).

Recommended styles

The Recommend tab, shown in Figure 7-13, controls which styles show up on the list of recommended styles. The "recommended" option shows up in each of the style-related task panes and applies to the styles that are displayed in the Quick Style Gallery. For any style, you can choose to Show, Hide Until Used, or Hide. It's a great way to focus the options when you want to exercise strong control over document formatting. It's better than a whip!

FIGURE 7-12

Manage Styles gives you complete control over styles.

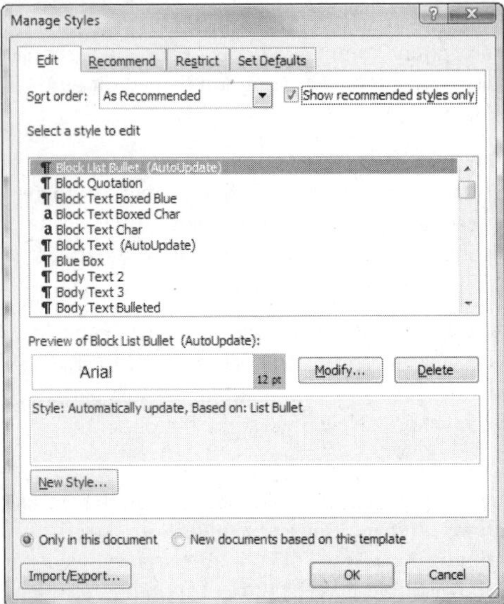

FIGURE 7-13

Use the Recommend tab to control what styles show up when you restrict style controls to displaying "recommended" styles.

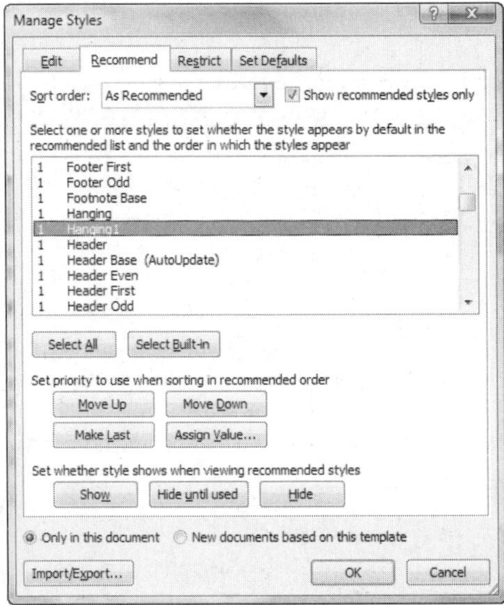

In the recommended list of styles, you can apply your changes one at a time or by using standard Windows selection techniques to select multiple styles. Note the Select All and Select Built-in buttons, too, which enable you to quickly distinguish between Word's standard styles and user-created styles.

Use the Move Up/Move Down/Make Last/Assign Value tools to determine the recommended order. You can even alphabetize them, if that makes more sense to you!

Restricted styles

You've heard of the style police? Well, grab your badge! For even stronger style enforcement, the Restrict tab lets you restrict which styles can be used. This is a good tool when designing templates and forms in which you want extremely tight control over the formatting of content. It's also useful in setting up training classes for Word, for which you might want to tame the options a bit to prevent the novice user from being overwhelmed.

Additionally, if you want to enforce the use of only styles—and not direct formatting—the restricted styles capability provides a way to do it. Use Limit Formatting to Permitted Styles, shown at the bottom of Figure 7-14, to accomplish this feat. This can be useful when setting up forms and templates for specific tasks in which the resulting document formatting must adhere to strict requirements.

By restricting formatting only to certain styles, you effectively prevent the use of direct formatting tools. As shown in Figure 7-15, when formatting is restricted to Normal and Heading 1 through Heading 5, most of the Font and Paragraph controls on the Home tab of the Ribbon are dimmed as unavailable.

FIGURE 7-14

The Restrict tab enables you to make direct formatting off-limits.

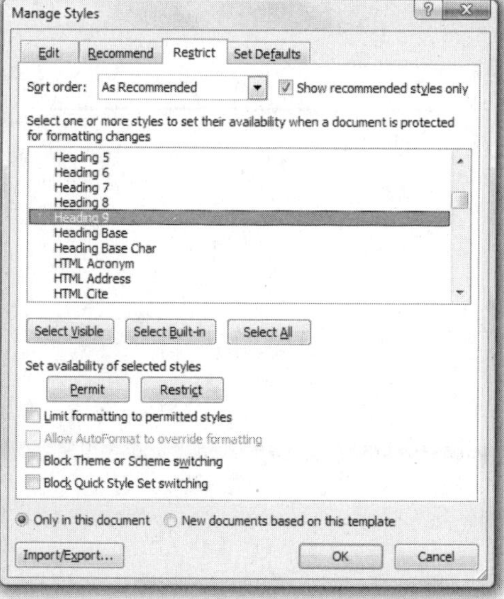

FIGURE 7-15

In this scenario, formatting is limited to Normal and Heading 1 through 5, which puts the Font and Paragraph direct formatting controls off-limits.

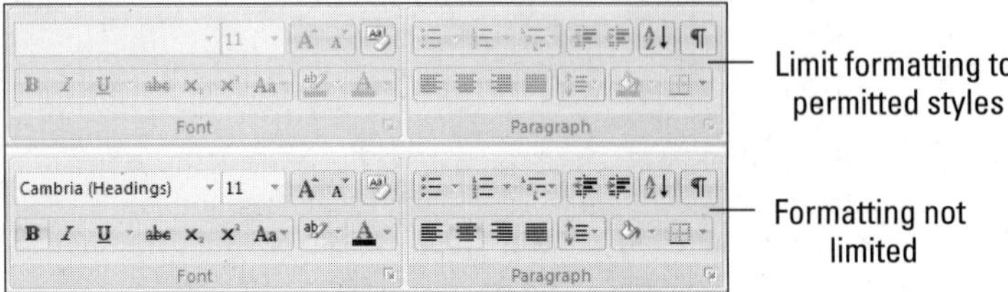

Note that not only can you limit formatting only to permitted styles, you can block Theme and Quick Style switching. If you want to tame "artistic" tendencies of users whose mission statement doesn't include using up all of the colored ink or toner, this provides an avenue of attack. Did I mention that this stuff is better than a whip?

Style Inspector

The Style Inspector enables you to quickly determine whether the current formatting is applied wholly through a style, or whether direct formatting is in effect. In Figure 7-16, notice that under the paragraph and text (character) styles there is a box with the word "Plus." In the lower panel, it says Plus: <none>, which indicates that no direct text/character formatting has been applied. In the upper panel, however, it shows that left alignment has been applied directly, along with a left indent of .38", and line spacing of 1.5 lines. In the current mystery, it appears that someone mistakenly applied the Heading 3 style to regular body text and then tried to compensate using direct formatting.

FIGURE 7-16

The Style Inspector can help you diagnose formatting mysteries.

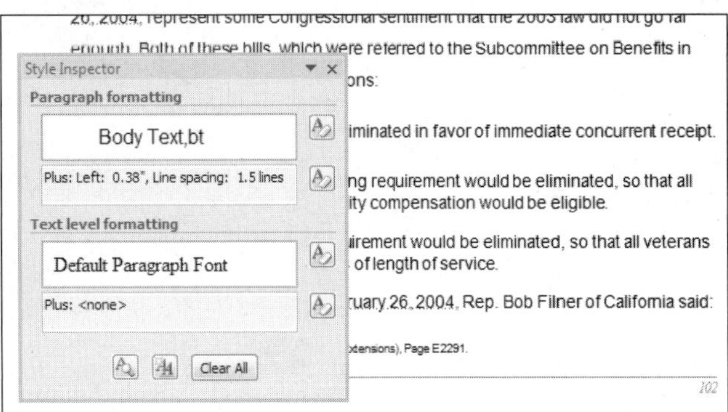

Summary

In this chapter, we've explored a variety of features, old and new, but mostly new. You now know how to apply Quick Styles, choose and modify Quick Style sets (as well as create your own), and how to create, modify, and delete user-created styles. In addition, when a style can't be deleted, you now know why. You should also be able to do the following:

- Use the Manage Styles dialog box to hide and restrict styles and direct formatting
- Use Apply Styles to apply, create, and modify styles
- Use the Styles pane to quickly select all occurrences of any given style
- Use the Style Inspector to solve formatting mysteries

Chapter 8

Page Setup and Sections

IN THIS CHAPTER

- Section formatting
- Page layout
- Working with section breaks
- Page borders
- Understanding the header/footer layer
- Header and footer navigation
- Header and footer design
- Page numbers
- Work with themes

This chapter examines some concepts that might be a bit challenging if you're new to Word, perhaps even if you're not new to Word. Grasping these concepts, however, opens up the marvelous and potential-filled world of section formatting, themes, and headers and footers, which enable you to do wonderfully creative things with your documents.

Page Setup Basics

To fully grasp what this chapter is about, you're going to have to make sure that you can see section breaks and other nonprinting formatting characters. Although some users think these characters are an eyesore and distract from the basic business of putting words into the computer, they should instead be viewed as flashlights that illuminate otherwise dark corners that are home to the secret and mysterious powers of Microsoft Word. Wow!

It's time to turn on those flashlights, assuming they're not already on. Looking at Figure 8-1, the upper paragraph has nonprinting formatting marks turned On, whereas the lower paragraph has them turned off. You press Ctrl+Shift+8 to toggle them on and off, or click the Show/Hide (¶) button in the Paragraph section of the Home tab on the Ribbon. To truly understand what's happening in this chapter, as well as what's happening in your documents, you should toggle those nonprinting formatting characters on — at least for now. From here on out in this chapter, it's assumed that you can actually see what's being talked about. Otherwise, you'll miss out on all the fun and you won't be in on the mystery.

Page setup is an interesting concept in Word. It's interesting because the phrase really isn't about setting up a page. It's really about setting up section formatting. We've talked earlier about distinct units of formatting — letters, words, sentences, paragraphs. For Word, section formatting is large-scale formatting that usually affects the entire document. The scale of section formatting is so encompassing, in fact, that it can't be contained in styles. To contain section formatting, you need a whole document or a whole document template.

FIGURE 8-1

These two paragraphs are identical, but in the upper one, Ctrl+Shift+8 was pressed to toggle nonprinting formatting marks on.

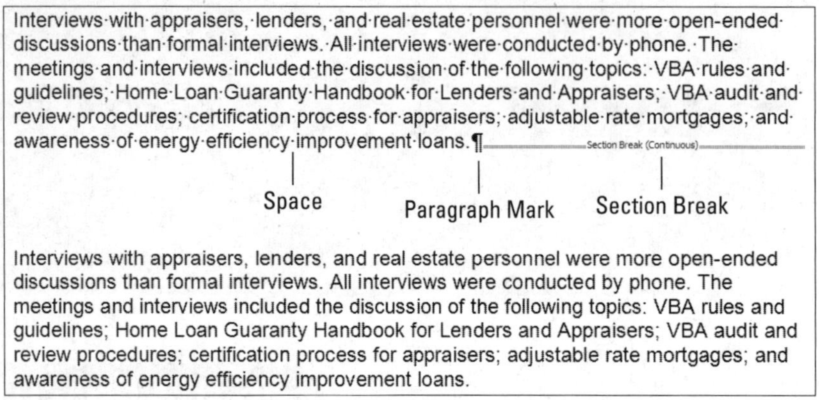

Interviews·with·appraisers,·lenders,·and·real·estate·personnel·were·more·open-ended·
discussions·than·formal·interviews.·All·interviews·were·conducted·by·phone.·The·
meetings·and·interviews·included·the·discussion·of·the·following·topics:·VBA·rules·and·
guidelines;·Home·Loan·Guaranty·Handbook·for·Lenders·and·Appraisers;·VBA·audit·and·
review·procedures;·certification·process·for·appraisers;·adjustable·rate·mortgages;·and·
awareness·of·energy·efficiency·improvement·loans.¶ Section Break (Continuous)
Space
Paragraph Mark
Section Break
Interviews with appraisers, lenders, and real estate personnel were more open-ended
discussions than formal interviews. All interviews were conducted by phone. The
meetings and interviews included the discussion of the following topics: VBA rules and
guidelines; Home Loan Guaranty Handbook for Lenders and Appraisers; VBA audit and
review procedures; certification process for appraisers; adjustable rate mortgages; and
awareness of energy efficiency improvement loans.

Section formatting

Word uses section breaks to separate distinctly formatted parts of a document. Most documents, in fact, have just a single section. Only when you need to apply different section formatting within the same document do you need to create a document that contains more than one section. Different sections are necessary for variations in the following kinds of formatting:

- **Headers and footers** — Includes changes in page numbering style (except for Different First Page settings)
- **Footnotes** — Can be set to be numbered continuously or set to restart numbering on every new page or every new section
- **Changes in line numbering style** — Except for suppression on a paragraph-by-paragraph basis
- **Margins** — Indentation can vary within a section, but not margins.
- **Orientation** — Landscape versus portrait (actually done through paper size)
- **Paper size** — 8.5 × 11 (letter), 8.5 × 14 (legal), 7.25 × 10.5 (Executive), A4 (210.03 × 297.03 mm), and so on.
- **Paper source** — Upper tray, envelope feed, manual feed, and so on
- **Columns** — Snaking newspaper-style columns, the number of which cannot vary within a document section

Them's the breaks (section breaks, that is)

Word uses four kinds of section breaks. What kind of break you use depends on why you're breaking:

- **Next Page** — Causes the new section to begin on the next page.
- **Continuous** — Enables the current and next section to coexist on the same page. Not all kinds of formatting can coexist on the same page, so even if you choose Continuous, Word will sometimes force the differently formatted content onto a new page. Section formatting that can be different on different parts of the same page include the number of columns, left and right margins, and line numbering.

- **Even Page** — Causes the new section to begin on the next even page. If the following page would have been odd, then that page will be blank (unless it has header/footer content, which can include watermarks).
- **Odd Page** — Causes the new section to begin on the next odd page. If the following page would have been even, then that page will be blank, except as noted for the Even Page break.

If you set up a letter in which the first page is to be printed on letterhead, but subsequent pages are to be printed onto regular stock (using different paper feed methods), the first page must be in a separate document section. If you set up a letter for which the first or last page is an envelope, the envelope must be in a separate section — for multiple reasons, because envelopes typically would use a different printer paper source, different orientation (landscape), and different margin settings.

Inserting section breaks

To insert a section break, in the Page Setup group of the Page Layout tab on the Ribbon, as shown in Figure 8-2, click Breaks. Word displays a variety of different kinds of breaks, including the four types of section breaks. Click on the desired section break.

FIGURE 8-2

The icons next to the four section break types provide a graphic hint of what the different breaks do.

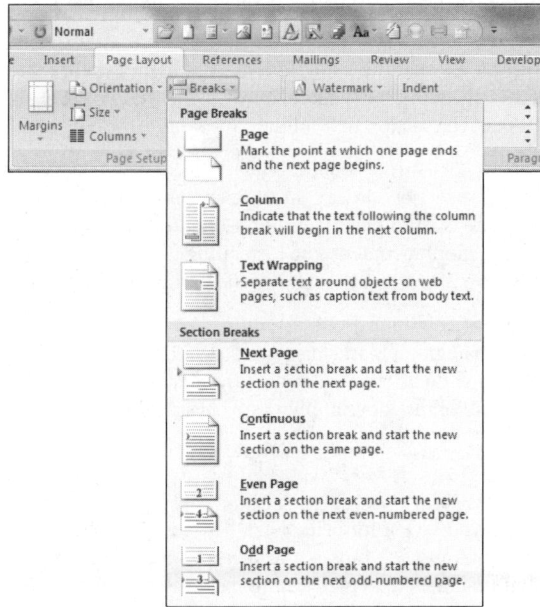

TIP **If you're inserting multiple breaks of the same kind to section-off part of a document to be formatted, after inserting the first section break, you can use F4 (Repeat) to insert subsequent breaks. Keep in mind that if you do something else after inserting a break, that F4 will now repeat that other action, rather than insert another break.**

Automatic section breaks

Because some kinds of formatting require a section break in order to vary within a document, Word automatically inserts one or more section breaks when you apply "qualifying" formatting to selected text. Sometimes it gets those breaks right, sometimes not. You'll have to be vigilant if you're going to rely on this feature.

For example, suppose you want an interior set of paragraphs to be formatted in three columns, while the adjacent areas are formatted as a single column. Select the paragraph you want to differentiate and in the Page Layout tab, choose Columns ➪ Three Columns. Word automatically inserts continuous section breaks before and after the selected text to cordon it off for the distinct formatting. If you're lucky, that's what it does, that is.

Sometimes, but not always, Word will insert the wrong kind of section break before and/or after the selected text. It's never quite clear why, but when that happens, the best recourse is to press Ctrl+Z to undo the attempt, bracket the target text with the desired type of section breaks, and then apply the formatting to the section you want formatted differently.

Styles, section formatting, and paragraph formatting

Styles can contain font/character formatting attributes and paragraph formatting attributes. However, they cannot contain section formatting attributes. Therefore, for example, you cannot create a style that would enable you to format a given selection with three columns and 1.5-inch left and right margins. Stand by for a few minutes, however, and you'll see how you can indeed effectively create a style for section formatting, although it's not really a style.

Recall that in Chapter 6, "Paragraph Formatting," you learned that the paragraph mark is the repository of paragraph formatting. Similarly, the section break is the repository for section formatting. If you delete a section break, the current section adopts the formatting of the section that follows, the section whose section break is still intact.

Where is the section break in a document that has only one section? In fact, most documents have only a single section, so this is a serious and valid question. There is an implied section break at the end of the document, so if you insert a section break into a single-section document, the formatting for section 1 resides in that section break, and the formatting for section 2 effectively resides in the permanent paragraph mark at the end of the document.

Permanent? Yes, permanent. If you don't believe it, with paragraph marks displayed, delete everything in a document. Now delete that last paragraph mark. You can't do it! (You can hide it by clicking the Show/Hide button in the Paragraph group in the Home tab of the Ribbon, but that's cheating, because it's not really gone.)

Saving section formatting for reuse

If section formatting can't reside in a style, then how can you save it for using later? Suppose you often use a very precise set of section formatting attributes — margins and columns, for example — and want to save them for using in other documents. There is a way, but it's not using what's traditionally called a style. Instead, use a Quick Part or a Building Block.

To do this, insert section breaks — continuous or next page, as needed — to bracket the area to be formatted. Format the first section break in as vanilla or as typical a way as possible. This first section break will be used to shield existing text from the new formatting when the Building Block or Quick Part is inserted into an existing document. If it's inserted at the beginning of a document, the vestigial section break can then be deleted.

Format the area between the first section break and the second as needed (see the next section, "Page setup choices," for a handy all-in-one-place location to set section formatting, or display the Page Layout tab of the Ribbon).

Finally, select both section breaks and the interior matter (it doesn't have to contain text because section formatting resides in the section break), and choose Insert ➪ Quick Parts ➪ Save Selection to Quick Part Gallery. In Create New Building Block, in the Name box, type a descriptive name for the item as well as a longer Description. If you'll need this item frequently, save it to the Quick Part Gallery. Otherwise, you might as well save it as AutoText. Use the Category drop-down setting to choose Create New Category. In the Create New Category dialog box, as shown on the right in Figure 8-3, type a category name that you can later recall for accessing all of your custom section formatting. Click OK, twice.

FIGURE 8-3

Use Quick Parts or Building Blocks to create reusable section "styles."

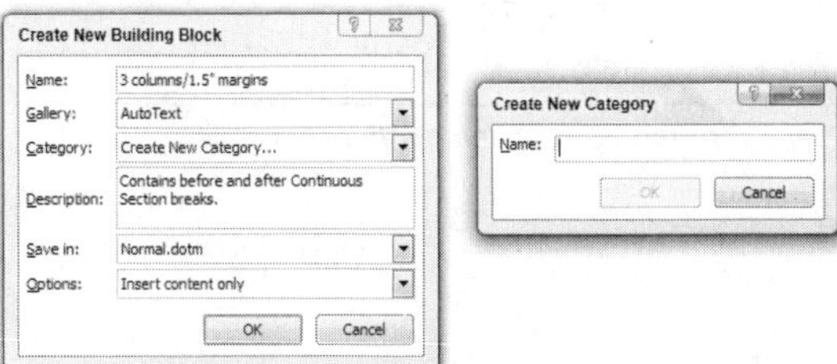

Now, whenever you want this particular kind of formatting, it's there waiting for you. Choose Insert ➪ Quick Parts, and if it's in the Quick Parts Gallery, click on it to insert it. If it's in AutoText or elsewhere, choose Building Blocks Organizer. Click the Category heading to sort by category, select the item, and then click Insert. Or, if it's a simple name, type it and press F3.

Page setup choices

For access to section formatting, click the Page Layout tab on the Ribbon. The Page Setup section provides access to a number of section formatting attributes, as well as to the Page Setup dialog box, as shown in Figure 8-4. The Page Setup section of the tab also contains Hyphenation, which is not a section formatting attribute. As discussed in Chapter 6, hyphenation is a paragraph formatting attribute. (The Margin tab of the Page Setup dialog box is shown in Figure 8-8. The Paper tab is shown in Figure 8-10.)

TIP **If the Page Layout tab isn't showing, you can also activate the Page Setup dialog box by double-clicking the vertical ruler, if it's displayed, or even by double-clicking the left edge of the Word window in the document area (i.e., anywhere below the horizontal ruler and above the horizontal scroll bar).**

If you click the Line Numbers drop-down arrow in the Page Setup group of the Page Layout tab, note that the fifth option — Suppress for Current Paragraph, shown in Figure 8-5 — actually is incomplete. The feature should say Suppress for *Selected* Paragraphs. If you choose this option, line numbers for the current paragraph (even if no text is selected) or for the entire selection are suppressed.

FIGURE 8-4

The Page Setup section of the Page Layout tab provides access to section formatting and the Page Setup dialog box.

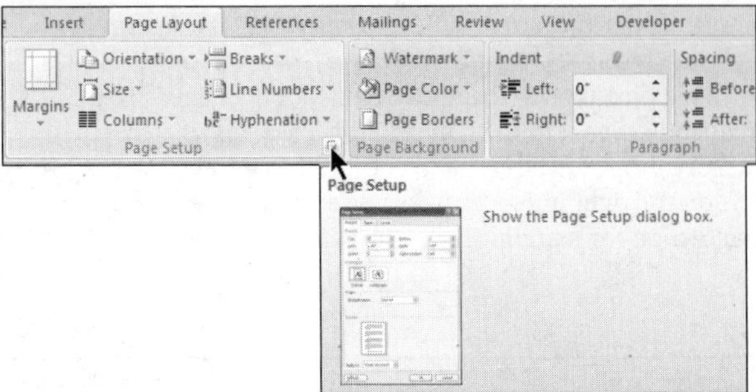

FIGURE 8-5

Suppress for Current Paragraph actually suppresses line numbering for the current *selection,* not *section.*

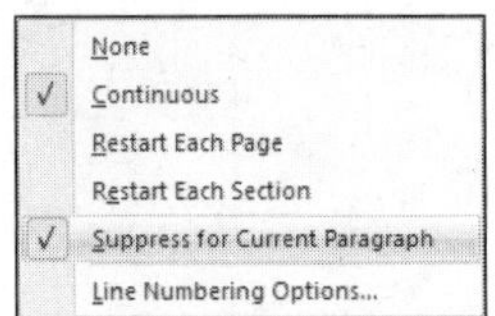

Margins

Using the Margins drop-down of the Page Setup group on the Page Layout tab, shown in Figure 8-6, you can apply a variety of different preset margin settings. If the document contains multiple sections, each of the presets would be applied only to the current document section if nothing is selected, or only to the selected sections if multiple sections are included in the selection.

If you want more precise control, choose Custom Margins, which opens the Page Setup dialog box to the Margins tab, shown in Figure 8-7. From here, you can control all margins as needed, and apply the change where you want. If text is selected, then Selected Sections and Selected Text replace This Section and This Point Forward, respectively.

You can also adjust the top and bottom margins by dragging the blue and white boundary in the vertical ruler to the left of the document window (depending on your Personalize settings, you might see shades of gray or some other color rather than blue), also shown in Figure 8-7. To increase the top margin, drag the top border down. To increase the bottom margin, draw the bottom border up. In both cases, press the Alt key to display the margin setting as you're dragging.

FIGURE 8-6

The Margins drop-down offers a selection of preset margins, including Office 2003 Default, just in case you want to reminisce.

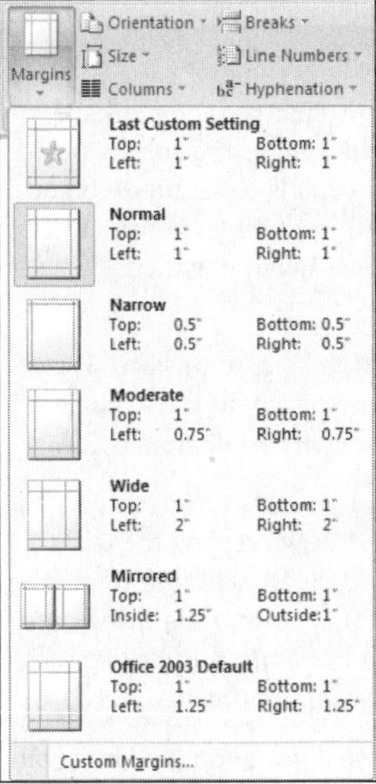

FIGURE 8-7

Using the Margins tab of the Page Setup dialog box, you can control how/where the new formatting is applied.

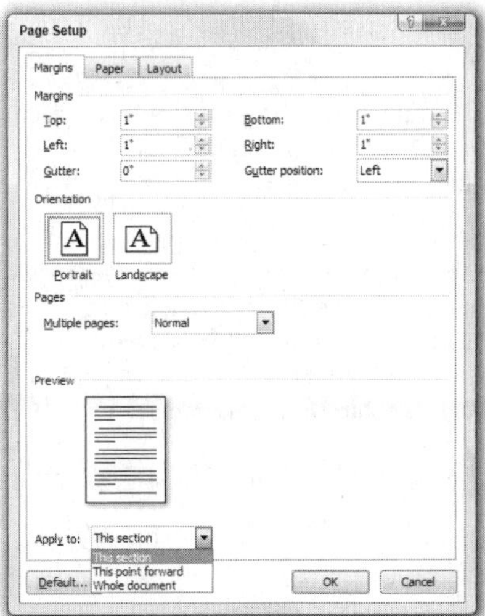

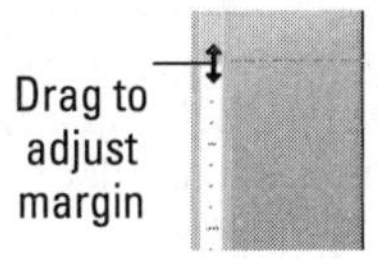

Orientation

Orientation refers to whether the page is laid out horizontally (landscape) or vertically (portrait — the default orientation). You might sometimes need to rotate a page to landscape in order to fit a particular picture, chart, table, or other object. It should be emphasized, however, that changing a page to landscape orientation carries with it a number of consequences that might be considerably worse and harder to deal with than trying to find a way to rotate the object itself.

Consider page numbers and other header and footer content. If the whole page is changed to landscape, then the header and footer now rotate as well. To have the headers and footers located in the correct position relative to portrait-oriented pages takes a bit of strategizing. The usual approach is to set up different headers and footers for the solitary landscape page. To get the orientation correct, you might consider putting the header and footer material either into a text box or a single-cell borderless table, in which the text has been rotated 90 degrees.

Alternatively, you can keep the orientation as portrait, and rotate the table, chart, or picture instead. For pictures and charts, rotation isn't challenging. With Wrapping (Picture Tools Format tab, in the Arrange group) set to anything other than In line with Text, simply rotate the pictures or chart 90 degrees by dragging the green rotation handle at the top of the selected object.

Tables are a bit more challenging, but you have several possibilities. If you're just now creating the table, select the entire table and in the Table Tools Layout tab, Alignment group, click Text Direction to rotate the text so that it can be read by tilting your head to the right or left. Keep in mind that columns and rows are reversed. It's not necessarily easy to work this way, but it can be done, as shown in Figure 8-8. Notice that the header and footer are properly oriented to conform with the rest of the [unseen] document.

Another option would be to copy the table to the Clipboard, choose Paste ➪ Paste Special on the Home tab, and paste the table into the document as a picture. Because it's now a picture, you can choose any floating wrapping style and then rotate it as needed so that it fits comfortably, but sideways, in a portrait-oriented Word document page. As above, headers and footers will display in portrait mode because you haven't changed the paper orientation.

The downside is that sometimes the graphics resolution of this technique isn't perfect. You'll have to decide if it's acceptable and legible. Plus, to make changes in the table, you need to maintain a copy of the actual table and remake the "conversion" as needed.

Another negative is that once you've done this to a table, you won't be able to edit it anymore. If you decide to go this route, you might consider saving the nongraphic version of the table as a Building Block in the current template. If you need to modify it, it would still be accessible.

A variation of this approach, if the table fits into a window from which you can copy it, is to use screen capture software to take a picture of the table. This often yields more predictable and better-quality graphics, but it suffers from the same maintenance issues as the previous approach, and achieving it depends on having a sufficiently large monitor. To make a screen capture of a table under Windows XP, you'll get the best results using an amenable screen capture program(such as SnagIt, from www.TechSmith.com, which is highly flexible). Under Vista, you can use the new Snipping Tool feature (Start ➪ All Programs ➪ Accessories ➪ Snipping Tool.

FIGURE 8-8

With all text in a table rotated 90 degrees, it's possible to create a sideways table, rather than have to change orientation within a document.

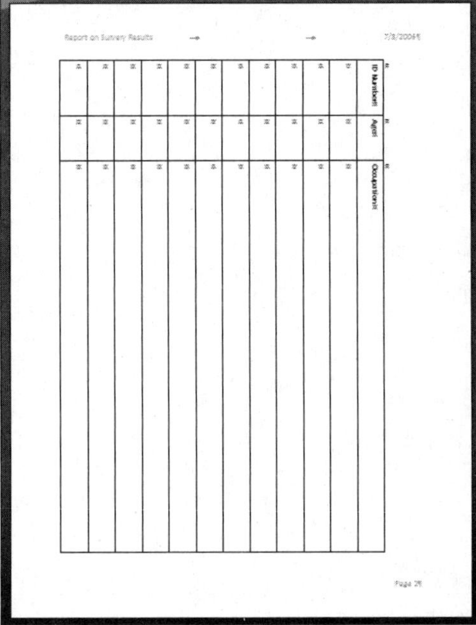

Size

Size refers to paper size. A number of preset standard sizes are available by clicking the Size drop-down arrow in the Page Setup group of the Page Layout tab, shown in Figure 8-9. Clicking More Paper Sizes displays the Paper tab in the Page Setup dialog box. While it says "More Paper Sizes," that's not actually what you get. The "more" refers to the Custom Size setting at the bottom of the Paper Size list, which enables you to set any size up to 22 inches. This assumes that your printer supports something that large.

Columns

Use the Columns tool in the Page Setup group on the Page Layout tab of the Ribbon to set the number of columns either in the current section or in all sections in the current selection if text is selected.

FIGURE 8-9

Click More Paper Sizes to display the Paper tab in the Page Setup dialog box.

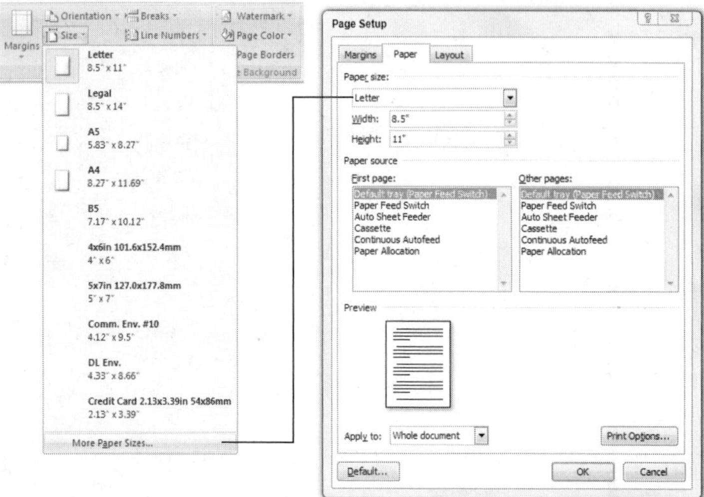

Page layout settings

We've already looked at the Margins and Paper tabs in the Page Setup dialog box. The Layout tab, visible in Figure 8-10, houses additional settings, some of which often go unnoticed. Headers and Footers settings are also set using the Layout tab; a full discussion of headers and footers comes later in this chapter.

If the Page Layout tab is showing, the quickest way to display the Layout tab of the Page Setup dialog box is by clicking Line Numbers ➪ Line Numbering Options in the Page Setup group, even if you're not interested in line numbering. If the Page Layout tab of the Ribbon isn't showing, you can double-click on the vertical ruler or between the horizontal ruler and the bottom of the Ribbon area to display the Page Setup dialog box, and then click the Layout tab.

Fixing or changing a section break

The Section Start setting shown in Figure 8-10 is a bit cryptic and confusing to many users, but it can be extremely useful. Have you ever ended up with the wrong kind of section break? For example, suppose you want a Continuous section break, but you have a New Page, Odd, or Even section break, instead. This can happen either because *you* inserted the wrong kind of break, or because *Word* inserted the wrong kind of break automatically.

The ordinary impulse is to delete the wrong one and insert the kind you want. Sometimes, however, despite your best efforts, you still end up with the wrong kind of break.

Section Start to the rescue! Put the insertion point into the section that is preceded by the wrong kind of break. Activate the Page Setup dialog box using any of the techniques described earlier. Click the Layout tab to display the dialog box view shown in Figure 8-10. Set Section Start to the kind of section break you want and click OK.

FIGURE 8-10

The Different Odd and Even and Different First Page heading/footer settings enable you to have different headers and footers without using another section break.

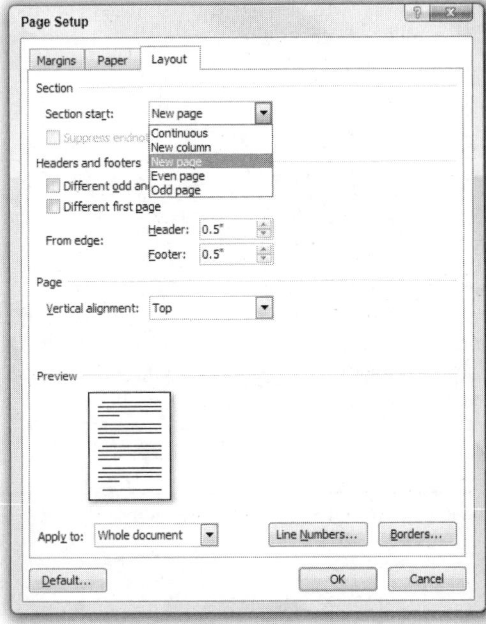

Vertical page alignment

Another often unnoticed feature in Word is the Vertical Alignment setting (found on the Layout tab of the Page Setup dialog box). By default, Word sets vertical alignment to Top, and most users never discover the additional options shown in Figure 8-11. As a section formatting attribute, you can set vertical alignment for the whole document or just for selected sections.

FIGURE 8-11

Word provides four different types of vertical page alignment.

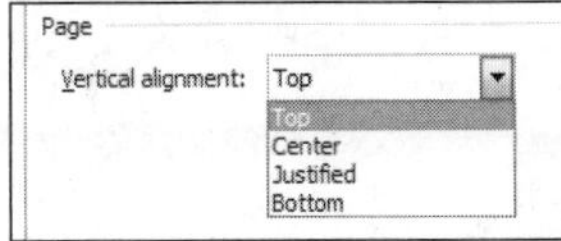

Vertical alignment can be extremely useful for particular parts of a publication — such as the title page for a format report, booklet, or book — as well as for short letters, brochures, newsletters, and flyers. For title pages, setting vertical alignment to Centered is almost always more efficient than trying to insert the right number of empty paragraphs above the top line, or trying to set the Before spacing to just the right amount. For one-page notices, vertical alignment is also often just what the doctor ordered.

For some newsletters and other page-oriented publications, setting the alignment to Justified serves a couple of purposes. Not only does it make the most use of the whole sheet of paper, it adjusts line spacing to do it. Hence, the appearance is smoother than it might be otherwise. This also lets you optimize the point size if you want to make the font as large as possible without spilling onto another page.

Page Borders

The last page setup setting we'll look at is page borders. A page border is a line, set of lines, or decorative artwork that appears around the perimeter of the page. You see them a lot on title pages as well as on flyers and brochures.

To insert a page border, in the Page Layout tab, and choose Page Borders in the Page Background group, which displays the dialog box shown in Figure 8-12. The dialog box offers the same options you saw earlier in Chapter 6, "Paragraph Formatting," under "Borders and boxes." In addition, however, you have over 150 Art options you can use to create decorative borders, although some of these might look pretty cheesy compared to the professional graphics you can create with SmartArt.

FIGURE 8-12

For page borders, you can insert a variety of different lines, or choose from over 150 built-in "Art" items.

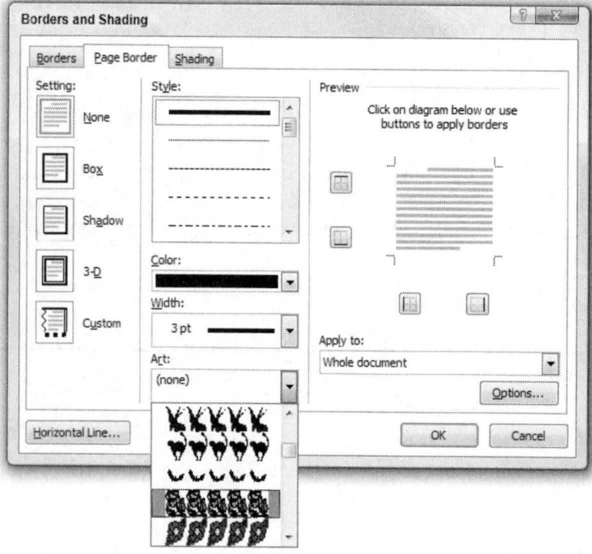

For placing a border around a title page, you can set Apply To This section — First page only. Other options here are Whole Document, This section, and This section — All except first page.

To control the placement of the page border with respect to the edge of the text or paper, click Options for the Border and Shading Options dialog box shown in Figure 8-13. Note that when setting page borders, paragraph-related options are grayed out. Using the Measure From box, you can set the distance of the page border either from the text or from the edge of the paper.

FIGURE 8-13

Use Border and Shading Options if your page border crowds the text too much.

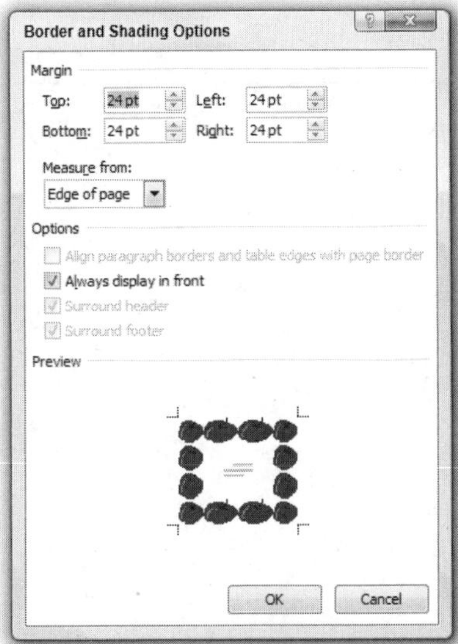

The Header and Footer Layer

Like that crazy aunt and uncle who live in Montana — or was it Idaho — headers and footers are often misunderstood. Most folks think they know what they do and where they live, but they don't fully understand them. The next sections will remove the veil and give you the full truth about headers and footers in a way that not only puts you fully in the driver's seat, but helps you understand when something unexpected suddenly shows up.

Seemingly, headers and footers are the areas in the top and bottom margins of each page, but that's not the whole story. In Word, headers and footers are distinct layers in your document, usually behind the text area. They usually appear at the top or bottom of the page, respectively, but that's just a convention. Once you're in Word's header or footer layer, text and graphics can be placed anywhere on the page.

This means that in addition to titles, page numbers, dates, and other essential bits of information, headers and footers are also ripe for containing things such as watermarks, side margin material, or even those full-bleed markers that are visible when you look at the edge of the pages of a closed book. (the concept is there, the actual implementation requires a type of printer most of us can't afford and don't need).

A second area of misunderstanding concerns how headers and footers are inserted into your Word documents. They aren't inserted. They've been there right from the start. When you "insert" or "create" a header, you're really doing neither. Instead, you're merely using what was already there, but was previously empty or unused.

When you're working in Print Layout view, any text in the header and footer layer usually shows up as grayish text at the top, bottom, or side of your document. To access those areas, double-click where you want to edit — even if you don't see any text there. This brings the header and footer areas to the surface, as shown in Figure 8-14.

FIGURE 8-14

Header and Footer tabs clarify what and where headers and footers are. With headers and footers open editing, the document body text turns gray.

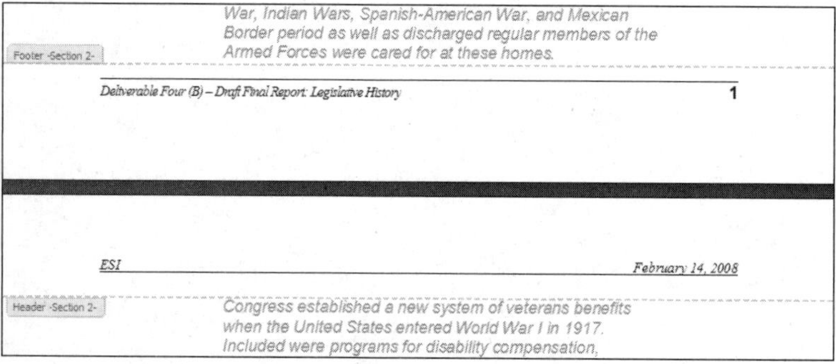

Headers and footers also display in Print Preview. There, however, because the view is supposed to represent what you'll see when the document is printed, the header/footer areas aren't gray and isolated. By default, headers and footers don't show up in Full Screen Reading view unless you use the Show Printed Page option. Unlike normal document text, however, headers and footers cannot be edited or changed in Full Screen Reading view. For that honor and privilege, you need to be in Print Layout view or Print Preview. This chapter assumes that you are working in Print Layout view. If you don't see what's shown in the screen shots, then check your view setting.

Document sections

Figure 8-14 indicates the document section number in the header and footer tabs at the left end of each area. Word documents can be single-section or multi-section. You might use multiple sections for a variety of reasons, particularly in long documents. Some users place each chapter of a document in a separate section, with additional sections being used for front matter (tables of contents, tables of figures, forward, etc.) and back matter (index, glossary, etc.).

Section formatting allows for different sections to have different kinds of numbering. It also allows different header and footer text in different sections. For example, the header or footer might include the name of each chapter, or the word *Index* or *Glossary*.

Section formatting is also used for other reasons that have nothing in particular to do with headers and footers. See the earlier sections in this chapter for more uses for section formatting.

Header and Footer Navigation and Design

Word provides a number of different tools that enable you to control the way headers and footers are displayed and formatted. In this section, you'll learn what those are and where to find them in the new Word 2007.

Editing the header/footer areas

The main set of controls are contained in the Header & Footer Tools Design tab of the Ribbon, shown in Figure 8-15. To display the Design tab, double-click the header or footer area in a document. Or, from the Insert tab, choose Header ➪ Edit Header (or Footer ➪ Edit Footer). Once the header/footer layer is open for editing, either header or footer can be edited, as can items inserted into the side area (e.g., page numbers in the side margins), as well as watermarks.

FIGURE 8-15

The Header & Footer Tools Design tab on the Ribbon provides complete control over headers and footers.

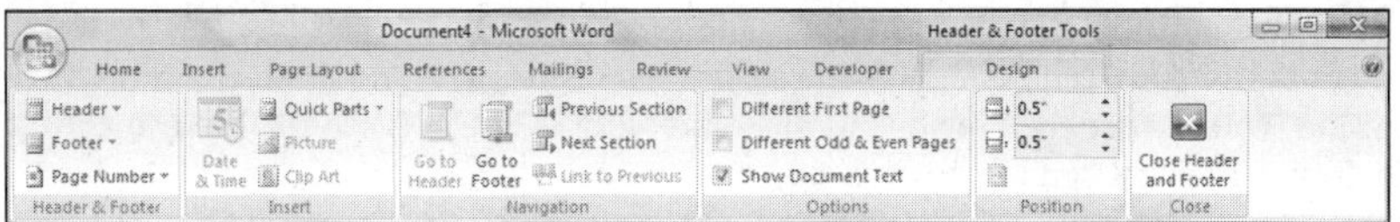

Notice the Go To Header and Go To Footer commands in the Navigation group on the Design tab. You can use those commands to quickly switch back and forth between the header and footer areas, but as suggested by Figure 8-14, both areas are equally accessible at the same time.

NOTE **While header and footer material can reside in the side margins, you cannot open the header/footer areas for editing by double-clicking in the side margins. The double-click method for opening headers and footers only works in the top and bottom margin areas.**

Header and footer styles

By default, Word's headers and footers use built-in paragraph styles named Header and Footer. Both are formatted with a center tab and a right-aligned tab to facilitate placement of text and other items inside headers or footers. This enables you to have three distinct components that reside at the left, center, and right within the header or footer without having to resort to using a table, text box, or other devices (although tables and text boxes are perfectly acceptable in headers and footers).

For example, to create a header with a left-adjusted date, a centered document name, and a right-adjusted author's name, you would enter the date, press Tab, enter the document name, press Tab, and finally type the author's name, as shown in Figure 8-16.

FIGURE 8-16

The default header style makes three-part headers easy.

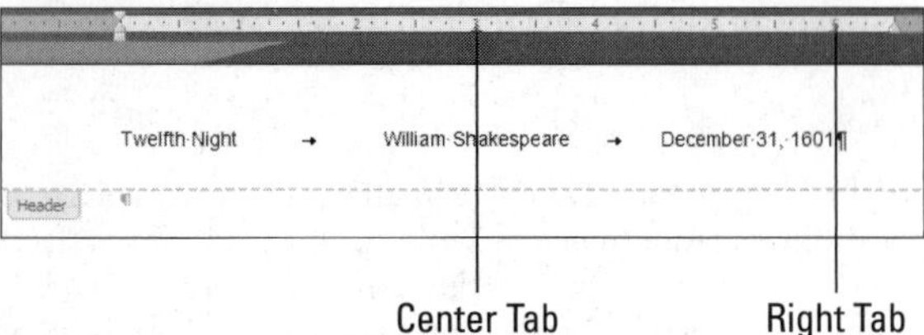

Section surfing

When editing the header/footer layer of a document, you can use the mouse or keyboard keys to navigate as needed. As long as you don't double-click in the text area of the document, the header and footer area remains open for business.

In a long document that contains many sections, however, scrolling can be tedious and imprecise. For greater control and precision, you can use the Previous Section and Next Section tools in the Navigation section of the Header & Footer Tools Design tab.

NOTE **When the header and footer area is open for editing, the Browse Object's Next Section and Previous Section buttons located at the base of the vertical scroll bar will not have the expected effect. Yes, they move you to the next and previous sections, but they also switch the focus back to the main text layer.**

Link to previous

Different document sections can contain different headers and footers. When Link to Previous is selected (in the Navigation group of the Header & Footer Tools Design tab) for any given header or footer, that header or footer is the same as that for the previous section. By default, when you add a new document section, its headers and footers inherit the header and footer settings of the previous section.

To unlink the currently selected header or footer from the header or footer in the previous section (which will allow the current section to maintain a distinct header or footer), click Link to Previous to toggle it off. Observe the difference between the upper and lower Link to Previous buttons shown in Figure 8-17.

FIGURE 8-17

Link to Previous is a toggle that can be turned on or off independently in each header and footer in every document section.

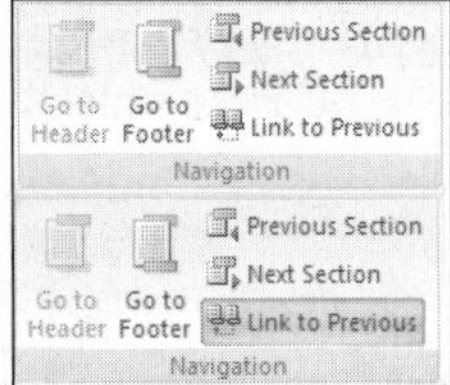

Note that headers and footers in any section have independent Link to Previous settings. While Link to Previous initially is turned on for all new sections that are created, when you turn it off for any given header, the corresponding footer remains linked to the previous footer. This gives you additional control over how document information is presented.

Different first page

Most formal reports and indeed many other formal documents typically do not use page numbers on the first page. To keep users from almost always having to make such documents multi-section documents, Word lets you set an exception for the first page of each document section. To enable this option for any given document section, display a header or footer in that section, and click the Different First Page option in the Options group of the Header & Footer Tools Design tap (refer to Figure 8-15).

In a way, this is like a "link to previous" option that you can apply to different document sections. Unlike Link to Previous, there is no telltale toggle tool to tell you the setting for the current section. Instead, there's a checkbox that indicates whether the option is turned on or off. As you navigate across different header/footer areas in a multi-section document, the checkmark appears or disappears to indicate the setting for the current section. Also unlike the Link to Previous option, Different First Page cannot be different for header and footer. You cannot suppress just one. To accomplish that, you would need distinct document sections (separated by a section break).

Different odd and even pages

You can, without using section breaks, instruct Word to maintain different headers and footers on odd and even pages. A common application is for use in book/booklet printing, where the header/footer always appears closest to the outside edge of the paper — left for left pages, and right for right pages. This checkbox feature, also in the Options group in the Header & Footer Tools Design tab, works in the same way as the Different First Page option and is set per section and not individually for headers and footers.

Show document text

Sometimes, having document text showing is useful, and helps provide a frame of reference for headers and footers. Other times, however, it can be distracting and can make it harder to identify header and footer text, particularly if you're actually using gray fonts in the header/footer area. Displayed text also can make it difficult to access graphics that are stored in the header or footer layer.

By default, Show Document Text is enabled. To hide document text, click to remove the check next to Show Document Text in the Options group of the Header & Footer Tools Design tab.

Distance from edge of paper

Headers and footers are printed in the margin area. The margin is the area between the edge of the paper and the edge of the text layer in the body of the document. If the header or footer is too "tall" for a given page, Word reduces the height of the text layer on-the-fly so that the header or footer can be printed. This assumes that the distances between the top/bottom of the header/footer and respective edge of the paper are kosher with respect to the nonprintable areas of the paper.

Printers have a nonprintable area around the perimeter of the paper. This is an area in which it is mechanically impossible for a given printer to print. Windows' printer drivers do a good job of calculating the margin so that the printer does not try to print in the nonprintable region. When the margin is too small, Word will warn you.

Word does not warn you, however, if the header or footer extends too far into the margin. When this happens, all or part of the header or footer is cut off. Everything might look fine in Print Preview, and there is no warning, but part of the footer or header will be printed in the Twilight Zone.

You can rein the document in using the Header from Top and Footer from Bottom settings in the Header & Footer Design tab's Position group. If you find that the header or footer is being cut off, determine how much is being cut off and make that much additional allowance. For example, if .25" of text is being cut off of the footer, then increase Footer from Bottom by that amount.

Adding Header and Footer Material

You can put a variety of things into headers and footers, ranging from filenames and various other document properties (author, title, date last printed/modified, etc.) to page numbers and even watermarks. Inserting most text and graphics that will actually be printed in the top or bottom margin is straightforward. There are some special cases, however, such as page numbers, side margin matter, and background images and watermarks, that require special attention.

Page numbers

A common use for headers and footers is to display page numbers. To include page numbers in Word 2007, several methods are available — some new, and some old. This section focuses mostly on the new ways because they provide extraordinary ease, flexibility, and variety not found in any previous version of Word. When the old ways are best, however, that's where we'll turn.

Insert page numbers

Inserting page numbers in Word has never been easier. First, decide where you want the page numbers to appear (top, bottom, or side margin). Then click anywhere on the first page in the document section where you want the number to appear. As noted earlier, documents can contain multiple sections, and each section can have independent headers and footers, which means they also can be numbered independently.

In the Insert tab's Header & Footer group, click the Page Number button to open its menu, as shown in Figure 8-18, and choose one of the top for items.

To see the gallery that corresponds to where you want the page number to appear, click the applicable choice in the Page Number menu:

- Top of Page
- Bottom of Page
- Page Margins (see "Where do page margin numbers really go?" a little later in this section)
- Current Position (use this option, for example, when the insertion point is already exactly where you want the page number to appear)

The bottom of the page is the most common choice for word processing documents, but there are times when the top or side works better for a particular publication. Select the desired destination. Word displays a number of preset page number options.

When you find a page number gallery item that suits your fancy, click on it to insert the page number into the header or footer (according to which option you chose to get here). Note that you can also right-click the gallery item to see additional options, which are shown in Figure 8-19.

FIGURE 8-18

Word 2007 has extensive new galleries with a variety of page number formats from which to choose.

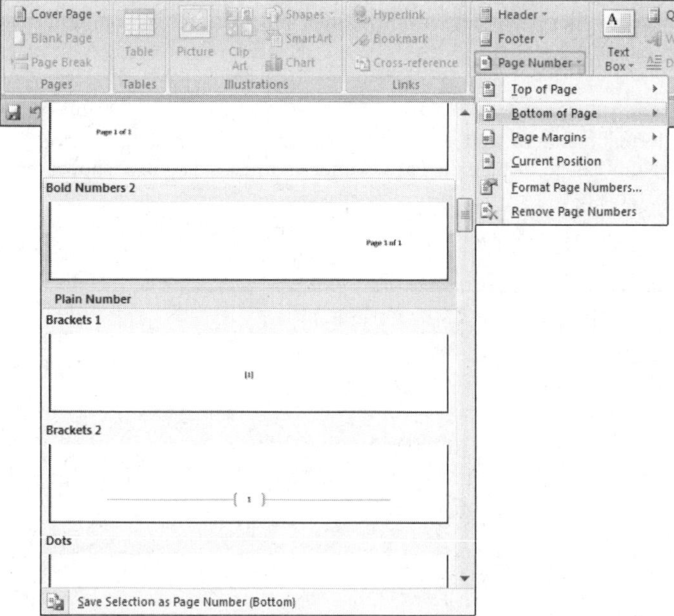

FIGURE 8-19

Right-click a page number gallery item for additional options.

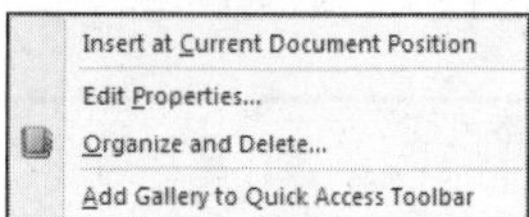

To see the true nature of a page number gallery item, right-click it and choose Edit Properties.

Where do page margin numbers really go?

When you insert the page number in the page margin, Word 2007 inserts it into the header as a floating shape to which a page field code was added. If you try to double-click on that page number, nothing happens! In fact, you can even try the Select Objects tool (in the Editing group in the Home tab, choose Select ➪ Select Objects), which normally can grasp any graphic. It can't grab it either. The reason is because it's out of reach, located below the text in the header/footer layer.

To bring it into reach, in the Insert tab, choose Header ➪ Edit Header. You can now click on the side page number and edit to your heart's content.

Deleting page numbers

To delete page numbers, move to the document section that contains the numbering you want to remove. In the Insert tab, click Page Numbers ➪ Remove Page Numbers.

Remove Page Numbers removes all page numbers from headers and footers in the current section. It does not remove page numbers from other document sections.

Formatting page numbers

You can choose the page numbering format before or after you insert a page number. On the Insert tab, choose Page Number ➪ Format Page Numbers, to display the Page Number Format dialog box, shown in Figure 8-20. Options are explained in Table 8-1.

FIGURE 8-20

Word provides flexible page numbering options.

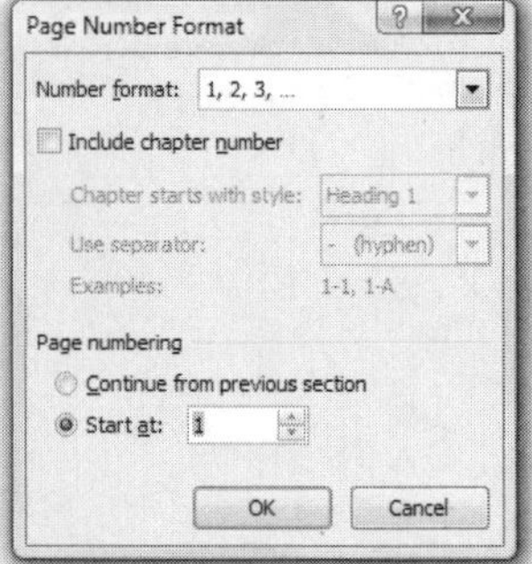

TABLE 8-1

Page Number Options

Option	Purpose
Number format	Numbering using 1, 2, 3; A, B, C; a, b, c; I, II, III; or i, ii, iii. Provides an additional option to bracket Arabic numbers with dashes (to bracket others, edit the header or footer directly, as shown later in this chapter).
Include chapter number	Use a chapter numbering scheme such as I-1, II-5, III-43, where I, II, and III are chapter numbers, and chapters are formatted using a Heading 1–9 style with numbering applied.
Chapter starts with style	Available only if Include Chapter Number is enabled. For this option to work, chapter numbers must be formatted using a Heading 1 through Heading 9 style, and numbering must be included in the style.
Use separator	Specify the separator to use between chapter and page numbers.

Option	Purpose
Continue from previous section	Indicates whether the current section's numbering is connected with that of the previous section. Use this option when distinct sections are being used for a reason other than to create distinct numbering, such as when switching sections to accommodate changes from portrait to landscape and back again.
Start at	Use this to specify a starting number other than 1.

Additional options that affect page numbers, such as whether headers or footers are displayed on the first page of a document or document section, are discussed earlier in this chapter, under "Different first page."

Themes

Before you leave the overall topic of formatting Word documents, you should consider one last formatting "quick change" you can make in a document — changing its theme.

What are themes?

In Word 2007, the applied *theme* determines the overall color, font, and style choices for items in a document such as tables, shapes, and SmartArt. Changing the theme updates the colors for these items and others in the document, so that the document maintains a consistent overall look. The theme even works with the styles supplied by the document template; changing the theme updates the fonts for the styles.

Each overall Theme encompasses three different elements:

- **Theme colors.** Controls the colors used in tables, graphic objects, and some other documents elements like headers and footers.
- **Theme fonts.** Controls the heading and body fonts used in the document.
- **Theme effects.** Controls whether certain document elements use effects like glows or shadows.

Using built-in themes

The themes appear in a gallery, and when Live Preview is enabled, you can "try on" themes for the document before applying the one you want. To change the theme. click the Page Layout tab on the Ribbon, and then click the Themes button in the Themes group. Move the mouse pointer over various themes to preview the look each applies (Figure 8-21), and then click the theme to apply.

Notice that there are three additional buttons in the Themes group. These are the Theme Colors, Theme Fonts, and Theme Effects buttons, respectively, and you can use them to change overall factors of the document's appearance without changing the whole theme. You can save any combination of Theme Colors, Theme Fonts, and Theme Effects settings as a new overall document theme; to start the process, click the Themes button and then click the Save Current Theme choice at the bottom of the gallery that appears.

FIGURE 8-21

Choosing a theme updates the colors and fonts in the document.

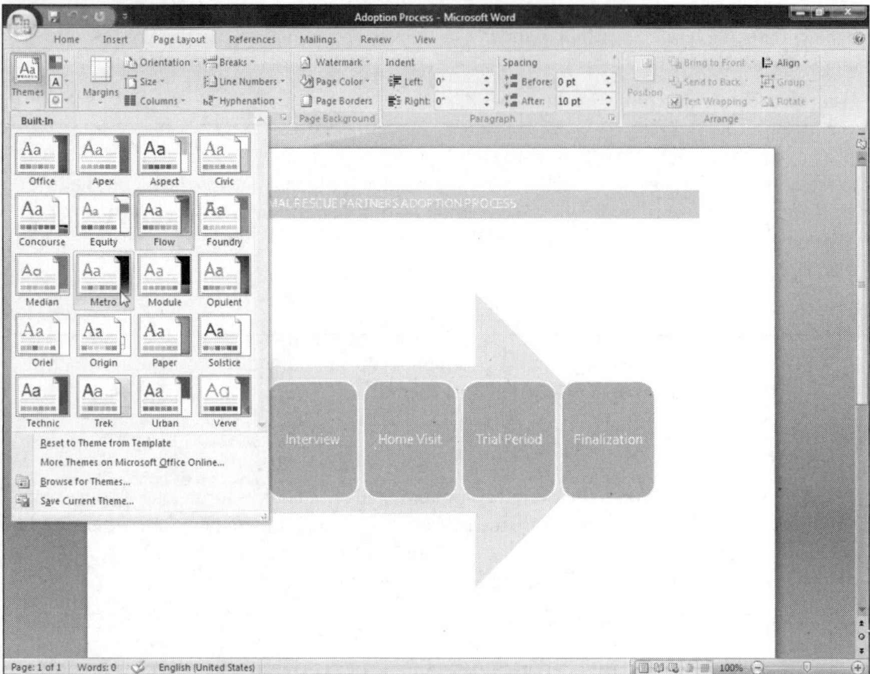

Summary

In this chapter, you've learned about the difference between section and paragraph formatting, and exactly what section formatting is. You now know how to create new document sections, as well as why you might want to. You've also learned what headers and footers are, what they're used for, how to use them, and how to navigate them. You finished by seeing how applying a new theme can polish the look of your document. You should now be able to do the following:

- Convert a next page section break into a continuous section break, and vice versa
- Vertically align a section of a document
- Change the paper size and paper feed for the envelope section of a document
- Place decorative or line borders around specific pages
- Create page numbers in your documents
- Edit headers and footers
- Set up different page numbering systems in different parts of a document
- Access side-margin material in the header/footer layer
- Apply a new theme

Chapter 9

Tables and Graphics

Tables are one of Word's most powerful and useful tools. They're extremely flexible and easy to create and manipulate, both directly and by using the Ribbon. Thanks to a gaggle of galleries, it's now easier than ever to create professional-looking tables quickly and with minimal effort. Live Preview comes to life when it comes to working with tables.

This chapter won't help you decide whether to include pictures. It won't tell you what pictures to use. This chapter will, however, show you where to find pictures if you don't have any, how to insert pictures and other graphics, how to work with pictures once they're in your document, and how to negotiate the precarious relationship between pictures and text.

So, pull up a chair!

IN THIS CHAPTER

Quick Start

The quickest way to create a table in Word is to use one that already exists. It might not be exactly what you want, but it often will be closer to what you want than if you create one from scratch. It helps if you can see a picture, of course, and Word 2007 includes many images of tables. From the Insert tab of the Ribbon, choose Table ➪ Quick Tables for a view similar to what is shown in Figure 9-1.

Stroll through the gallery to see if there's something you like — something that compares favorably with the table in your mind's eye. If there is, then click on it. If it has too many rows, you can delete the ones you don't need. If it has too few columns, you can add a few more. If the proportions and other attributes aren't quite right, you can use Word's table tools to make them right. The point is that you hit the ground running.

FIGURE 9-1

The Quick Tables Gallery offers a number of preformatted tables.

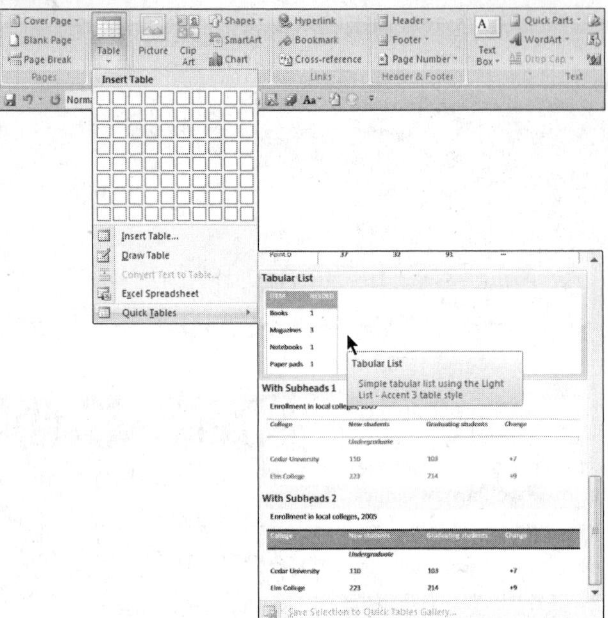

Table Basics

One way to think about a table is as a container for information. The container consists of vertical columns and horizontal rows. If someone speaks of a five-by-four (5 × 4) table, by convention and agreement, they mean a table that's five columns wide and four rows high.

If the terminology is foreign to you, think of rows as you would rows of seats in a theater. Think of columns as vertical columns on a building. Rows go across, and columns go up and down.

Inserting tables from scratch

There are three basic methods for creating a table from scratch. One is to use the Table tool to select the numbers of rows and columns you want. In the Insert tab of the Ribbon, click Table. Release the mouse button and then draw the mouse down through the table grid. As you move the mouse, the selected table dimensions change, and Word shows a Live Preview in the document window, as shown in Figure 9-2.

Cell Markers and Gridlines

When nonprinting formatting marks are displayed (Ctrl+Shift+8), cell markers display in each cell, showing where the cells are, as indicated in Figure 9-2. You might wonder why cell markers are needed if the table borders show the location of cells. That's because not every table has borders. If a borderless table's gridlines aren't displayed, you might not even know a table is there! Toggling the cell markers might provide just the clue you need. Cell markers, incidentally, display whenever paragraph marks do.

When a table has no border, it's a good idea to display table gridlines. These are nonprinting marks that show the cell's dimensions. To display gridlines, click the Show Gridlines tool at the left end of the Table Tools Layout tab on the Ribbon.

FIGURE 9-2

When a 5 × 4 table is selected in the Table tool grid, a 5 × 4 Live Preview appears in the document window.

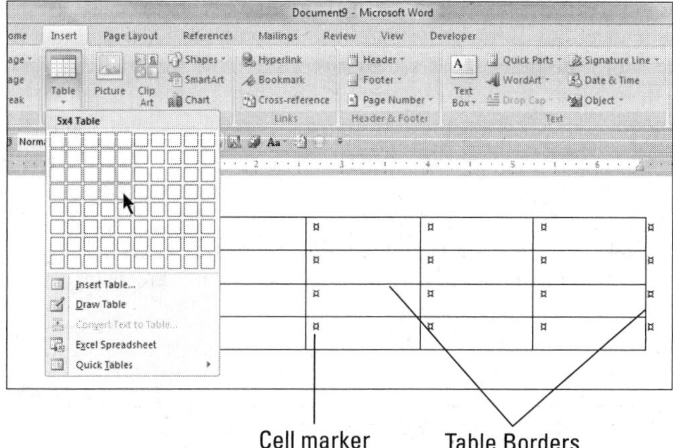

A second method for creating a table from scratch is by using the Insert Table dialog box. To get its attention, choose Table ➪ Insert Table on the Insert tab of the Ribbon. As shown in Figure 9-3, you choose the number of columns and rows, select an AutoFit behavior, and click OK. If you'd like Word to remember to default to the dimensions you choose, then click the Remember Dimensions for New Tables option.

FIGURE 9-3

If your hands aren't steady, use the old-fashioned dialog box to choose the number of columns and rows using spin controls.

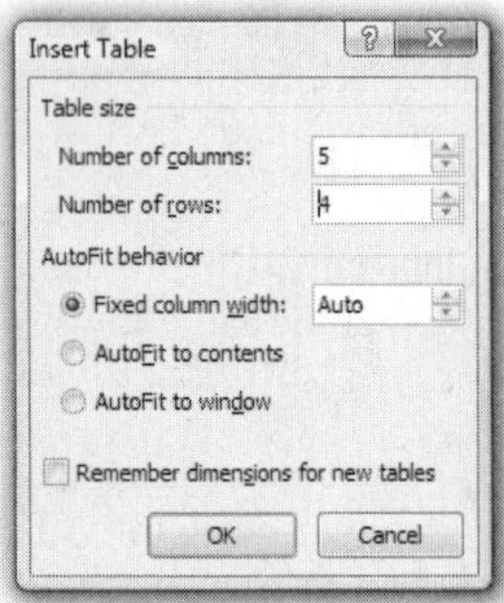

The third method for inserting a table from scratch is to draw it using the Draw Table tool. To begin, choose Insert ➪ Table ➪ Draw Table. Drag a rectangle to inscribe the outer boundary of your table shell, and then use the Draw Table tool (or pen) to carve out the desired cells. Use the tools in the Table Tools ➪ Design Ribbon's Draw Borders group to set line style, weight, and color for the table borders. Use the Eraser tool to remove unwanted table parts. See the sections "Borders and table drawing" and "The Table Eraser" later in this chapter for additional information.

AutoFit behavior

Notice the AutoFit behavior options shown in Figure 9-3. These same AutoFit options are also available from the shortcut (right-click menu), as shown in Figure 9-4. Keep this in mind if you need to change the formatting once a table is fully populated.

FIGURE 9-4

When the insertion point is inside a table, table-related options are displayed on the shortcut menu.

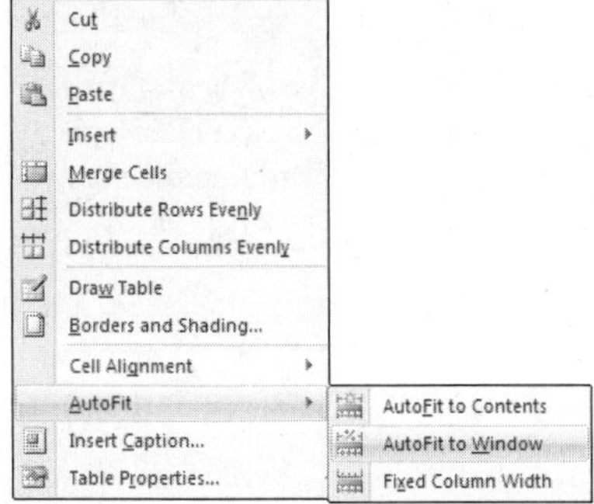

The Fixed Column Width option is straightforward enough. When you choose this option, the column widths remain fixed unless you explicitly change them by dragging or by using some other method. Note that *fixed* is not the same as *equal*. They might be equal also, but that's a different concept.

The middle option — AutoFit to Contents — is a formatting attribute that causes a table to automatically resize as you add or remove material. It's not a temporary setting, so don't freak out when it acts like it's made out of elastic when you add or remove text in existing cells.

The third option — AutoFit to Window — is misnamed. It should be AutoFit to Left And Right Margins. This option means that the table will remain as wide as the document text itself, regardless of how much text you stuff into the cells. If you add text disproportionately to any given column, that column will automatically resize, making the other columns correspondingly narrower. But the table itself will maintain the width of the document text.

Inserting tables based on existing data

As suggested elsewhere in this book, there is a correspondence between the word *tab* and the word *table*. While the proportion of the word processing population that was raised on typewriters is rapidly dwindling, many of us still survive in the wild. Those who took typing classes learned how to fashion tables using the tab stops and the tab key. Tab stops are metal hardware on a typewriter that literally stop the carriage when you press the Tab key.

Microsoft knows that tab and table both have the same root. As a result, Word can readily convert your tab-delineated tables into real tables. The easiest way is to select the "table" (although it might look like a table, Word doesn't agree). On the Insert tab of the Ribbon, click Table ⇨ Insert Table. Word instantly determines how many rows and columns there are and encloses your data in a table. As shown in Figure 9-5, the results are basic, but functional. For example, you often end up with the expected number of rows and columns, but one or both columns might be too wide. In this case, it's so wide that you can't see where it ends on the right.

FIGURE 9-5

Word easily converts a tabbed "table" into an actual Word table.

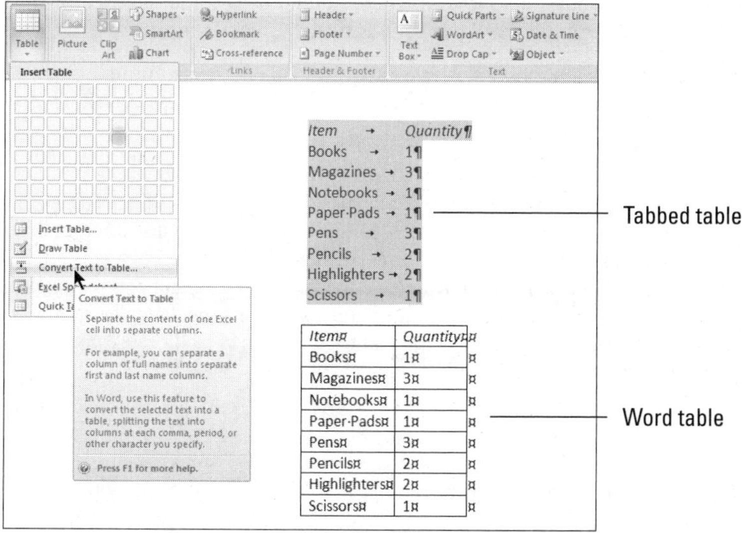

You can fix the width problem easily. Right-click anywhere in the table and choose AutoFit ➪ AutoFit to Contents (refer to Figure 9-4).

NOTE There are other methods for converting text to tables, but they all take more effort. For example, you can create a table *shell* (an empty table) that fits the dimensions of the data you have, select it, and then drag your tabbed data into it.

Convert text to table

Alternatively, you can use the Convert Text to Table dialog box as an intermediary. Select the data to be converted and choose Table ➪ Convert text to table on the Insert tab. This displays the Convert Text to Table dialog box, shown in Figure 9-6.

FIGURE 9-6

The Convert Text to Table dialog box guesses how many rows and columns to create.

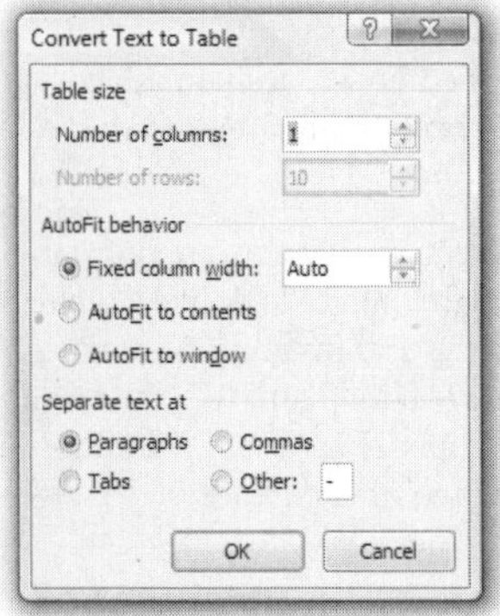

This method doesn't produce instant results, but it does let you set the AutoFit behavior ahead of time, as well as choose a different column delimiter if the one Word guesses (usually Tabs) is incorrect.

It's also a useful diagnostic tool when the quick method illustrated above yields unexpected results, such as more or fewer columns than you expected. When you get the wrong table dimensions, press Ctrl+Z, investigate the data, make any corrections, and try again.

You can get the wrong number of columns if there are too many tabs (sometimes obscured due to formatting issues) or if some rows use spaces instead of tabs to accomplish the table "look." Figure 9-5 demonstrates the utility of displaying nonprinting formatting characters, such as tabs. In this case, the user relied upon built-in tab stops rather than setting a custom tab in the tabbed table. As a result, alignment required two tabs for some of the shorter items (Books, Pens, and Pencils), and only one tab for the rest. The result confuses Word, which assumes there are three columns, rather than two. When this happens, dismiss the dialog box, find and remove the extra tabs, and try again. Don't worry about setting a properly aligned tab because you're converting the tabbed data into a table anyway; the table will handle the alignment for you.

Converting tables to text

What goes around, comes around. Sometimes it's necessary or useful to convert an existing table to text. You might want to do this if the data needs to be provided to someone else in a different form. Some statistical programs will accept CSV (comma-separated value) data, but not Word tables, so you might need to convert a table to text to use the data in such a statistical program. Or, you might simply find it easier to manipulate the data in text form, and then transform it back into a table. Whatever the reason, it's easy.

First, save your document (because it's easy to make mistakes, too). Next, select the table you want to convert. This activates the Table Tools tab on the Ribbon. Click Layout, and on the right end, choose Convert to Text. In the Convert Table to Text dialog box, choose the desired horizontal delimiter and then click OK. Note that if the table contains nested tables, then the Convert Nested Tables option will be available.

Handling tables

Word tables feature several kinds of handles and mouse pointers that enable you to manipulate and select cells, rows, columns, and entire tables. The table handle, shown in Figure 9-7, is displayed only when part of the table is selected, and only when All Formatting Marks are displayed (Office Button ➪ Word Options ➪ Display). Row and column sizing handles, on the other hand, are not affected by the display setting.

FIGURE 9-7

Handles enable you to resize rows and columns by dragging, as well as to select and move whole tables.

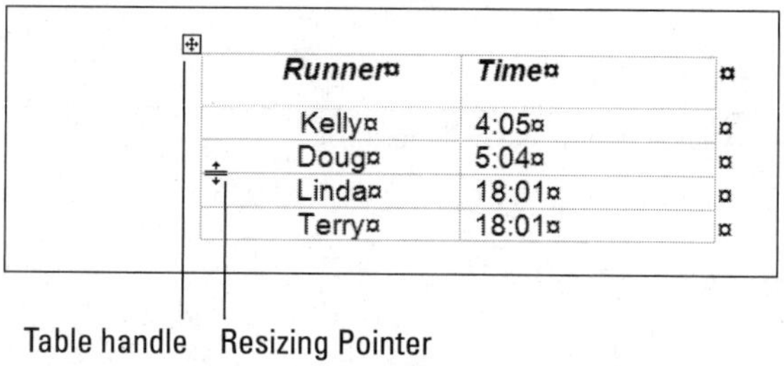

Runner¤	*Time*¤	¤
Kelly¤	4:05¤	¤
Doug¤	5:04¤	¤
Linda¤	18:01¤	¤
Terry¤	18:01¤	¤

Table handle Resizing Pointer

Use the resizing mouse pointer that appears when you point to a row border to drag the row to make it larger or smaller. Press the Alt key while dragging to display the measurements on the vertical ruler (even if the vertical ruler currently is not displayed).

Columns can be resized in a similar way by dragging a vertical resizing pointer (it looks like the row resizing pointer, but flipped 90 degrees). Again, adding the Alt key displays the measurements, this time on the horizontal ruler, enabling you to drag with a little more precision. You can modify the results by pressing the Ctrl or Shift keys while dragging. Experiment to see which method yields the desired results. Remember: Ctrl+Z is your friend.

The entire table can be resized proportionally using the resize table handle. Hover the mouse pointer over it until you see a diagonal arrow and drag to expand or shrink the table.

Selecting tables, rows, and columns

Click on the table handle to select the entire table. You can also select an entire table by right-clicking anywhere in the table and choosing Select Table. If you're Ribbon-oriented, you can always select the table by clicking anywhere in it to reveal the Table Tools tab of the Ribbon, shown in Figure 9-8, and then clicking Select ➪ Select Table in the Layout tab.

FIGURE 9-8

Use Table Tools ➪ Layout tab to access a number of table selection and manipulation tools.

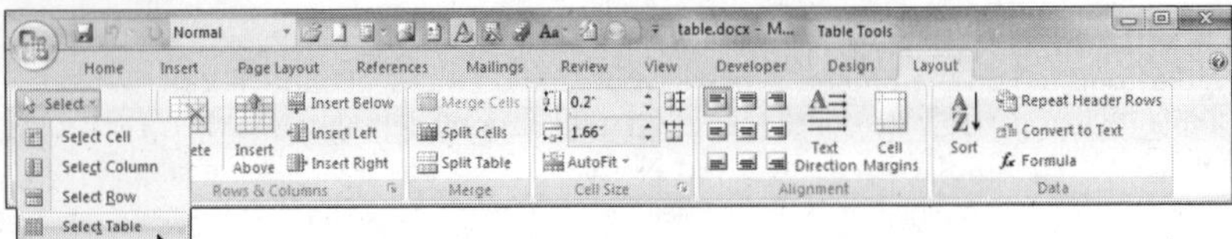

There is also a keyboard method for selecting tables, but it's a nuisance to remember and to use. With the insertion point anywhere in the table, and NumLock engaged, press Alt+Shift+5 on the number pad. If NumLock isn't engaged, then press Shift+5 on the number pad instead. Unless it's Thursday, of course, in which case. . . .

To select a cell, you can use the method illustrated in Figure 9-8. Using the keyboard, selecting the cell marker selects the cell. Hold down the Shift key and use the arrow keys to expand the selection to other cells. Using the direct mouse method, move the mouse pointer so that it is the diagonal black arrow indicated in Figure 9-9. You can drag to expand the selection to include additional cells. Or, hold the Ctrl key and use the select cell pointer to select additional discrete cells.

FIGURE 9-9

Word's mouse pointer changes shapes to indicate what action a click will perform.

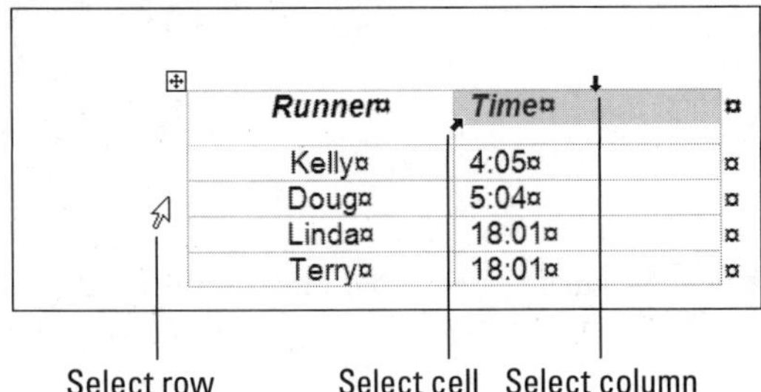

To select a row without using the Ribbon, move the mouse pointer so that it assumes the Select Row shape, and click. Drag to expand the selection to include contiguous rows, or Ctrl+Click using the Select Row pointer to select additional noncontiguous rows.

To select a column without using the Ribbon, move the mouse pointer so that it takes on the Select Column shape, and click. Again, drag to expand the selection to include additional contiguous columns, or Shift+Click using the Select Column pointer to select additional discrete/noncontiguous columns.

Copying table matter

When copying all or part of a table from one table to another, you need to consider the dimensions of the source and the target. Sometimes, when you paste into the new table, the whole table is pasted into a single cell! That's hardly ever what you want!

As a general rule, when pasting table matter, the receiving dimensions should match the sending dimensions. If you're trying to paste a 4 × 5 set of cells into a table whose dimensions are 6 × 8, then copy the 4 × 5 source to the Clipboard, then select the desired 4 × 5 location in the receiving table, and then paste. Pasting without first selecting sometimes works, but sometimes doesn't. The situation can get ever weirder when pasting between Word and Excel, so have that Ctrl+Z (Undo) key standing by.

To control what happens with respect to formatting, see Office ⇨ Word Options ⇨ Advanced ⇨ Cut, Copy, and Paste section. Use the top four Pasting options to specify what happens when you paste under a variety of circumstances. If necessary, temporarily enable the desired behavior, perform the paste, and then go back to reset the defaults.

Moving and copying columns

To move one or more adjacent columns, select them and then drag to the desired column. Release the mouse button anywhere in the destination column. The selected column(s) will move to the position of the destination column, which will scoot to the right. To move one or more selected columns to the right of the right-most column, drop the selection at what appears to be outside the right edge of the table. As shown in Figure 9-9, there are cell markers to the right of the table's right boundary. When moving columns to the right side of the table, drop them on those exterior markers.

To copy one or more columns, hold the Ctrl key as you drop. The selection will be inserted at the drop point, using the same location rules that apply when moving columns.

Moving and copying rows

Rows can be moved and copied in the same way as columns, except with respect to last row. The last row does not have exterior cell markers. If you drop a selection of one or more rows onto the last row of a table, the selection will be placed above the last row. If you drop it after the last row, the selection will be appended to the table, but the formatting will often change.

Instead, when you want to move rows after the last current row, drop them on the last row. Then, put the insertion point anywhere in the last row and press Ctrl+Shift+Up Arrow to move the stubborn last row up to where you want it.

TIP **Anytime you want to move table rows around, Ctrl+Shift+Up and Ctrl+Shift+Down can be used to push the current row up or down in the table. If you're moving a single row, you don't need to select anything. If you're moving multiple contiguous rows, select them first.**

Table properties

If you prefer to manipulate tables nongraphically, click Properties in the Table Tools ⇨ Layout tab, or right-click a table and choose Table Properties to display the dialog box shown in Figure 9-10. Use the Table tab to control overall layout and behavior; use the other tabs to control row, column, and cell characteristics.

Preferred width

Preferred width sets a target width for the table. Preferred width can't be absolute, however, because tables contain text and data, and are further constrained by paper and margin settings. Note that preferred width is overridden by AutoFit settings.

FIGURE 9-10

Use Table Properties to control overall alignment, indentation, and positioning of tables.

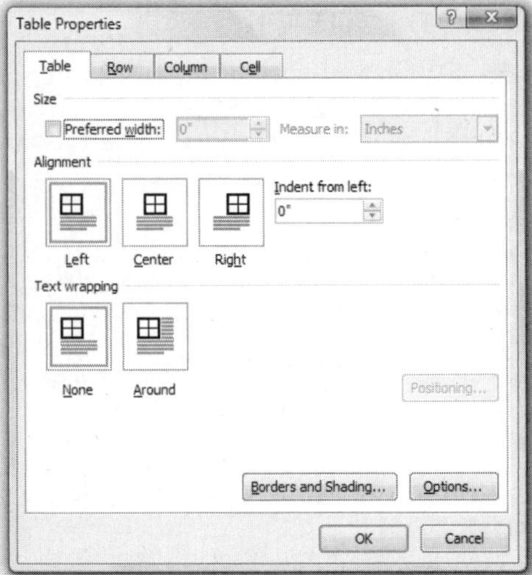

Alignment

Table alignment affects the entire table with respect to the current left and right margins. If the table extends from the left margin to the right margin, which is the default for tables inserted in Word, then the alignment controls seemingly will have no effect. This makes it easy not to notice if they're changed. If you later narrow the table, its placement on the page might suddenly seem askew. That's the time to visit the Table Properties dialog box to see what's going on.

Table alignment is a sore spot for some users due to the fact that table alignment and text alignment within cells are different things. Whereas table alignment can be set using the Alignment tools in the Ribbon, if the entire table is not selected, then the Home tab's Paragraph alignment tools affect only the selected portion of the table.

The Cell Alignment option, shown in Figure 9-11, affects only selected cells. The Alignment tools in the Table Tools ➪ Layout tab also affect only selected cells.

The bottom line is that if you're having trouble centering your table, center it using the Alignment control in the Table tab of the Table Properties dialog box. You can't go wrong.

Table indent from left

This setting controls how far the table is from the left margin. There is no Ribbon control for this setting, and it cannot be set using the ruler line.

Note that Indent from Left is available only when Text Wrapping is set to None (see Figure 9-10). When Around Wrapping is enabled, use Table Positioning to set the distance from the left, as shown in the section that follows.

FIGURE 9-11

Cell Alignment affects only the text inside cells, even if the entire table is selected.

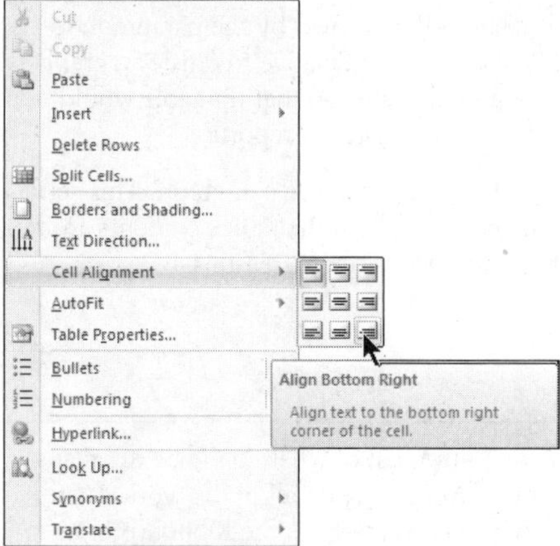

Text wrapping

Tables can be inserted in line with other text, or they can be moved/dragged so that text outside the table wraps around them, as shown in Figure 9-12. You can achieve wrapping by selecting the appropriate option in the Table Properties dialog box, or you can force it by dragging a table to the desired location, using its handle. This automatically changes the setting from None to Around.

FIGURE 9-12

Tables can be positioned for text wrapping, like graphics.

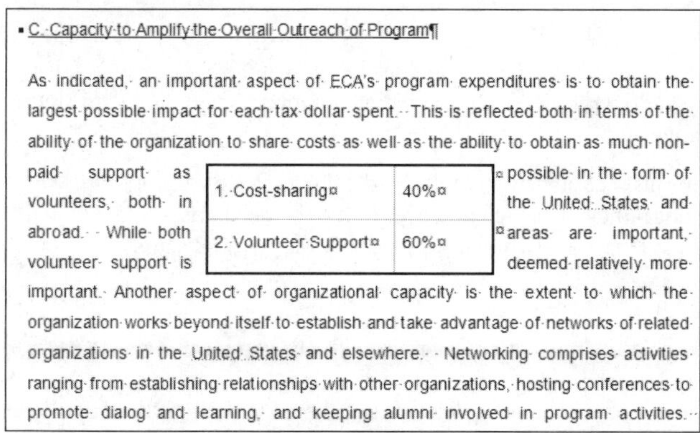

C. Capacity to Amplify the Overall Outreach of Program¶

As indicated, an important aspect of ECA's program expenditures is to obtain the largest possible impact for each tax dollar spent. This is reflected both in terms of the ability of the organization to share costs as well as the ability to obtain as much non-paid support as possible in the form of volunteers, both in the United States and abroad. While both areas are important, volunteer support is deemed relatively more important. Another aspect of organizational capacity is the extent to which the organization works beyond itself to establish and take advantage of networks of related organizations in the United States and elsewhere. Networking comprises activities ranging from establishing relationships with other organizations, hosting conferences to promote dialog and learning, and keeping alumni involved in program activities.

1. Cost-sharing¤	40%¤
2. Volunteer Support¤	60%¤

Positioning

Table Positioning is used much like the positioning settings for graphics. Most of the settings here need no further explanation.

The Move with Text option controls whether the table's vertical position is governed by the paragraph to which it is anchored. If Move with Text is enabled, the Vertical Position can be Relative to only Paragraph. Use this setting if the paragraph's content and the table's content are intertwined so that the table would not make sense except in that paragraph. This often is the setting you want for research reports.

Turn off Move with Text if the location of the table is not logically tied to a particular paragraph. This setting might be more in keeping with the design of a brochure or a newsletter in which the table's contents are relative to the entire document, and should appear in a particular location for aesthetic reasons.

Table Layout and Design

Word 2007's Table Tools contextual tab of the Ribbon provides you with most of what you need to create tables that are both aesthetically appealing and functional. Naturally, Word can't do all of the work. It's up to you to decide on presentation. When you get stuck for ideas, however, sometimes the Ribbon provides just the touch of inspiration, or just the right suggestion or hint to speed you along your way.

Word's Table Tools tab has Design and Layout tabs. In many ways, although Design comes first in the Ribbon, Layout logically comes first. Layout determines whether or not your presentation is logical, meaningful to the reader, and ultimately whether it helps whatever point you're trying to make. After all that, design is icing on the cake.

So far, we've looked at a number of basic tools that help you achieve the right structure for your tables. In this section, we're going to look at how to mold tables into shape and then polish them for presentation.

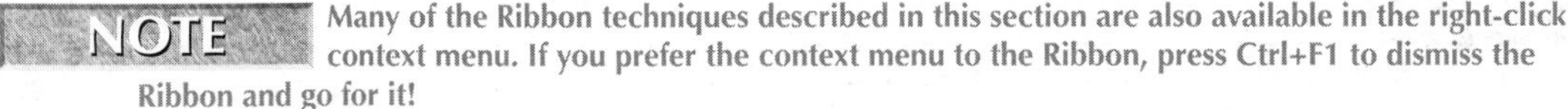

Many of the Ribbon techniques described in this section are also available in the right-click context menu. If you prefer the context menu to the Ribbon, press Ctrl+F1 to dismiss the Ribbon and go for it!

Modifying table layout

Once you have your basic table, what do you do with it? We all know that situations, ideas, and data change. Let's look at how to cope with change.

Note that all references to the Layout tab in this section actually refer to the Table Tools ➪ Layout tab. We can save ink and trees by saying that up front rather than each and every time the need arises. Note that none of the layout tools provide Live Preview. Live Preview must wait for the Design tab discussion.

Deleting tables and table parts

Sometimes you need to trim your tables by deleting rows or columns. Sometimes you have to delete the entire table. Sometimes this simple act can prove more daunting and challenging than you expect. If you select a table and tap the Delete key, the data inside the table is deleted, but the table shell itself is still there! "Good trick! Now, make it go away!" you exclaim. The same thing sometimes happens when you try to delete a cell, a row, or a column.

When the Delete key doesn't do what you want, try the Backspace key instead.

Rather than say this a half dozen times, let's just say it once. If you want to remove the contents of a cell, row, column, or table, select what you want to remove and tap the Delete key. In what follows, we'll be looking at table structure, not contents.

Deleting tables

As you've seen, you can't just select a table and tap the Delete key. That would be too logical and easy. Instead, select the table and tap the Backspace key. Goodbye table. Why? Who knows. It works.

Alternately, click anywhere in the table (no need to select anything) and in the Layout tab, choose Delete ➪ Delete Table, as shown in Figure 9-13. Again, the table is gone. If you absolutely positively need to know how to do it using the Delete key, insert a paragraph above or below the table (but outside the table) and include it in the selection. Now when you press Delete, the table departs.

You can also kiss the table goodbye by cutting it to the Clipboard. Select the table and click the Cut tool, or press Ctrl+X (or Shift+Delete). Of course, this clutters the Clipboard, which you might not want cluttered.

FIGURE 9-13

Delete the current cell, column, row, or table using the Layout tab's Delete tool.

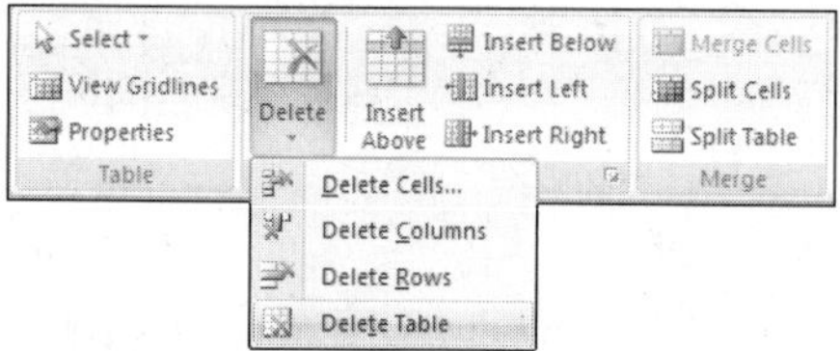

Deleting rows, columns, and cells

To delete the current row or column, you have the same options: select the offending rows or columns and press Backspace, or choose Delete ➪ Delete Columns, Delete ➪ Rows, or Delete ➪ Cells from the Layout tab's Delete tool (refer to Figure 9-13).

When deleting cells, Word needs a little more information. You are prompted as shown in Figure 9-14. Make your selection and click OK. Now you know how those rag-eared tables you sometimes see lost their corner cells!

FIGURE 9-14

Word prompts to find out how to handle the rest of the column or row when you delete a single cell.

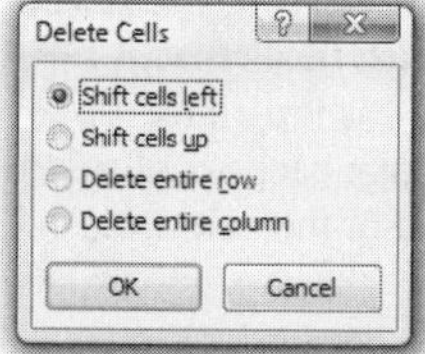

Inserting rows, columns, and cells

To insert a row or column into a table, click in the row or column adjacent to where you want to insert, and then click Insert Above, Insert Below, Insert Left, or Insert Right, depending on where you want the new row or column to appear. If you miss, you can always drag the new row or column where you want it.

TIP **To add a new row to the end of an existing table, put the insertion point in the bottom right cell and press the Tab key. To add additional rows, press F4 (Repeat). Or, hold the Tab key until it repeats, and then continue holding until the table has the desired number of new rows. To add a new interior row, click outside the right side of the table above where you want the new row to appear, and press Enter.**

To insert multiple rows or columns, you have a couple of options. Select the number of rows or columns you want to insert, and then click the appropriate Insert tool. Word will insert as many rows or columns as you have selected. Alternatively, insert a single row or column, and then press the F4 (Repeat) key for each additional row or column you need.

To insert cells, select the cell(s) adjacent to where you want the new one(s) to appear, and click the Insert Cells launcher in the bottom right corner of the Rows and Columns group in the Layout tab. You'll see a dialog box with the identical options shown in Figure 9-14. Choose the desired action and click OK.

Controlling how tables break

Sometimes you don't particularly care how tables break across pages, but sometimes you do. When you have an opinion, select the row or rows in question and click Properties in the Layout tab (or right-click the selection and choose Table Properties from the shortcut menu). In the Row tab under Options, Allow Row to Break Across Pages is enabled by default. Clear this option if you absolutely positively don't want the selected row(s) to break.

To force a table to break at a particular point, move the insertion point to anywhere in the row where you want the break to occur, and then press Ctrl+Enter. Note that this doesn't simply force the table to break at that point, it actually breaks the table into two tables. If the Repeat As Header Row At The Top of Each Page setting is enabled, it won't be inherited by the "new" table. You'll need to copy the heading row to the new table and reinstate the setting, if needed.

Merge

Sometimes you need to merge columns, rows, or cells. Merging cells is easy. Select the cells you want to merge and click Merge Cells in the Layout tab (refer to Figure 9-13).

TIP **You want it even easier? Use the Table Eraser, in the Table Tools ⇨ Design tab. Click the Eraser button, and then click on the table line segment that stands between Romeo and Juliet. Instant marital bliss. Click the Eraser button again, or press the Esc key to turn it off. Jump ahead to the section "The Table Eraser" near the end of this chapter for more exciting details.**

Word can't really merge rows or columns. Suppose, for example, that your table has three columns, and you need to merge each of the cells in two adjoining rows. What you want to end up with is one new row with three new combined cells. If you select both rows and click Merge Cells, however, Word treats that as a request to merge all of the cells in the selection, and you end up with one big cell. This is illustrated in Figure 9-15. There is no way around this. If you want the middle result, you must merge each set of cells separately (in other words, merge A and F, and then merge B and G). To effect a merge of the columns, while retaining the rows, you would need to merge A and B, and then F and G.

FIGURE 9-15

Word cannot merge into multiple cells.

What you have...

A	B
F	G

What you want...

A F	B G

What you get...

A B F G

Splitting cells, row, and columns

At first, it seemed that one cell, row, or column was fine, but later you decide that the logic of the presentation calls for two (or more) where there once was one. In any divorce, amicable or not, one has to divvy up the jointly held property. Like a few of the shadier attorneys, Word seems to think that everything should go to one party, the other getting nothing.

If we reverse the situation illustrated in Figure 9-15, to make a long story short, we end up with all of the data in the upper row, as shown in Figure 9-16.

FIGURE 9-16

When you split cells, Word's distribution logic probably won't agree with yours.

What you get...

A B	F G

When you split cells using Word's default divorce attorney, you're going to have to manually redistribute the goodies after the split. You get to be the judge!

A better solution to managing and controlling split-ups is to use the Draw Table tool, described later in this chapter. In Table Tools ⇨ Design, click on the Draw Table tool to set it in motion. Use the tool to draw a line in a cell between the items you want to separate. The items above the new line go north, and the ones below the line head south.

Horizontal splits are often harder to control. The trick is to make sure that items are horizontally displayed and separated either by at least two spaces or by a tab (press Ctrl+Tab to insert a tab inside a table). It can still be tedious, but it's a bit more direct than using the dialog box, and you have a bit more control and precision, your honor.

Cell size

When using a table to lay out a form, cell measurements sometimes have to be precise, especially when trying to align a Word document with preprinted forms. When cell height and width need to be controlled precisely, click in the corresponding boxes in the Cell Size group on the Layout tab, shown in Figure 9-17. Note that cell height cannot vary for any cell within any given row.

FIGURE 9-17

Use the Cell Size group to specify the precise height and width of rows and columns.

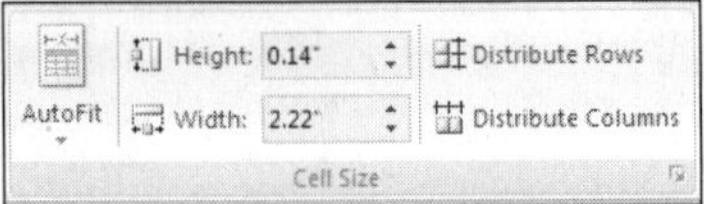

When you need rows to all have the identical height, click the Distribute Rows button. If rows are of different heights — as sometimes happens when converting part of an Excel spreadsheet into a Word table — this command determines the optimal height and equalizes the height of all selected rows, or of all rows in the table if no rows are selected.

Similarly, click Distribute Columns to set selected or all columns to the same width. If columns in different rows have different widths, this command will not equalize the whole table. It works only when all the rows have the identical width. If any differ (e.g., if row 2 is 4" and all of the other rows are 3.5", giving the table a ragged left and/or right edge), it won't equalize them all. To remedy this, drag the right border(s) of shorter or longer rows so that they all align on the left and right.

Cell alignment

Cell alignment offers nine options, as shown in Figure 9-18. To set or change cell alignment, click in or select the cells you want to change, and then click the desired tool. As noted elsewhere, many users confuse cell alignment with table alignment. With the whole table selected, this tool will at most set the individual alignment of each cell, and won't have any effect on table alignment. Instead, select the whole table and use the Paragraph Alignment tool in the Home tab of the Ribbon, or use the Alignment setting in the Table Properties dialog box.

FIGURE 9-18

Word offers nine options for cell alignment.

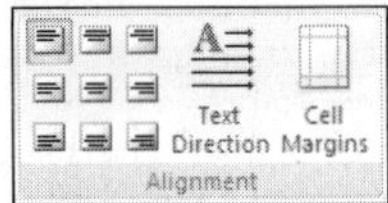

Text direction

To control Text direction in table cells, click the Text Direction tool in the Layout tab. This option often makes possible the portrait presentation of tables that otherwise might need to reside in separate landscape document sections.

Cell margins and cell spacing

Word provides several different kinds of controls for cell margins. Cell margin is the distance between cell contents and the imaginary lines that divide cells. Proper margins can keep cells from becoming too crowded. Additional spacing sometimes helps achieve a precise look. It can also prevent data from printing over the borders when using a table to format data for printing on preprinted forms. To set cell margins and cell spacing, click Cell Margins in the Layout tab, shown in Figure 9-18. This displays the Table Options dialog box shown in Figure 9-19.

FIGURE 9-19

If your table is too crowded, increase the default cell margins.

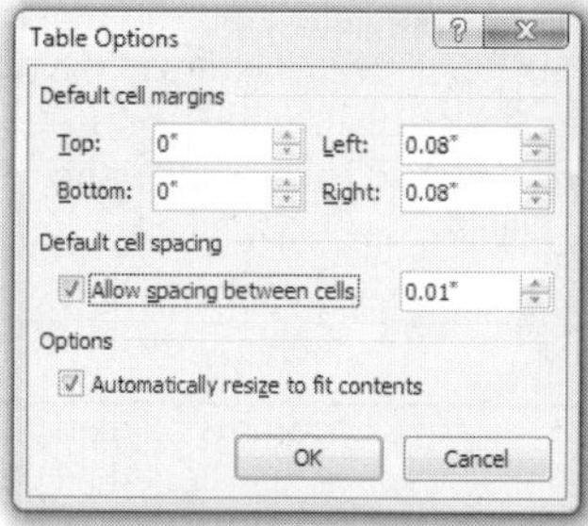

Despite the text in the dialog box, this does not set the *default* cell margins or spacing for tables. It sets those only for the currently selected table.

Cell spacing can be used to create the rather cool effect shown in Figure 9-20. This gives the table the appearance of having a distinct box inside each table cell.

FIGURE 9-20

Cell spacing can give tables a more dramatic appearance.

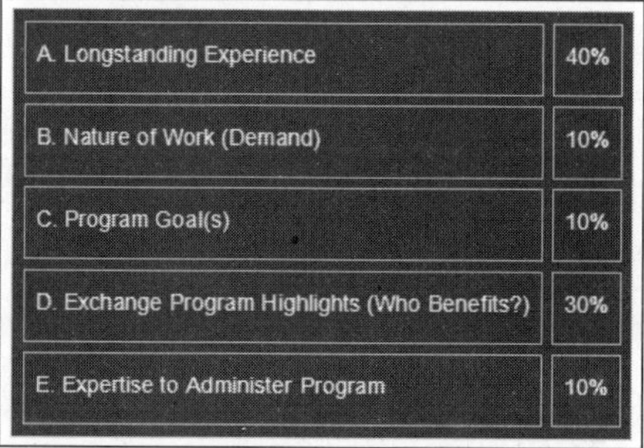

Tables that span multiple pages

When a table spans multiple pages, Word can automatically repeat one or more heading rows to make the table more manageable. When the need arises, select the target table's heading rows (you can have multiple heading rows), and click Repeat Heading Rows in the Layout tab. The selected heading rows are then repeated where necessary. The setting can be toggled on or off for each individual table. Because the number of heading rows can vary, this setting cannot be made the default for all tables, nor incorporated into a style definition.

This setting has no observable effect on tables that display or print on a single page. It also has no effect on pages displayed in Web view, because Web pages are seamless and pageless in concept.

Sorting tables

Word provides a flexible and fast way to sort data in tables. As noted in Chapter 6, "Paragraph Formatting," it can also sort lists that aren't in tables. To sort a table, click anywhere in the table and click the Sort tool in the Layout tab. Word displays the Sort dialog box, shown in Figure 9-21. If the table has headings at the top of each column, enabling the Header Row setting does two things. First, it provides labels in the Sort By and Then By drop-down lists. Second, it excludes the header row from being included in the sort. Unlike the previous feature, this one allows only a single header row.

FIGURE 9-21

The Sort command lets you sort by up to three fields.

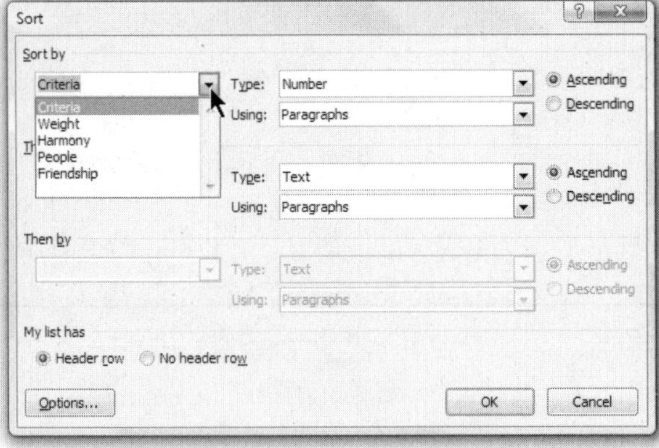

To sort, set Sort By to the first field. Setting Type to Text, Number, or Date affects the way data is sorted. For Weight, shown here, sorting by number ensures that the correct sorting order will be used. Choose the desired order, Ascending or Descending. If you have additional sort fields, use Then By to include up to two of them. Click Options for additional settings, including how fields are separated (for non-table sorts) and additionally whether to make the sort case sensitive, and to set the sorting language. Click OK to close Sort Options, and then click OK to do the sort.

Table math

Word can perform some calculations using the Formula tool shown in the Layout tab in Figure 9-18. It is limited, however, and is subject to hard-to-spot errors. If you use Word for math, double-check all calculations using a calculator or Excel. But if you have Excel and you need math in tables, then use Excel, period. You can then link the results to Word. See Chapter 44, "Integration with Other Office Applications," for additional information on using Excel with Word.

Modifying table design

Word 2007 provides a number of powerful new tools to help you quickly enhance the look and feel of your tables. One of these tools, Table Styles, features Live Preview. In this section, we'll look only at the features contained in the Table Tools ➪ Design tab, shown in Figure 9-22.

FIGURE 9-22

The Table Tools ➪ Design tab provides access to six preset Table Style Options and a gallery of Table Styles.

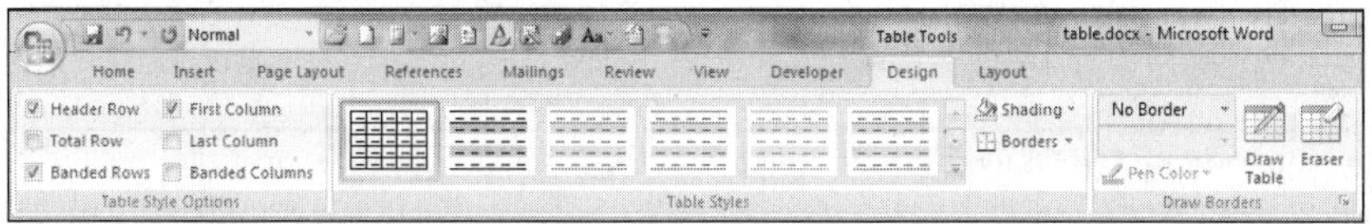

Table styles

Word 2007 has a number of preset table styles that you can apply to any table. They provide a wide variety of different kinds of formatting that can be previewed live in your table. You can use these styles to ensure a consistent, professional look to your tables. You can also modify them and save the modified version for later use.

To use a table style, click anywhere in the target table to activate the Table Tools tab. Under Table Tools, click Design. In Table Styles, hover the mouse over different styles and observe the changes to your table. As you move the mouse, ScreenTips display the name of the selected table style (such as Table Colorful 2), as shown in Figure 9-23.

If you see a style you like, click on it to apply it to your table. If it's not perfect, you can modify it. If you don't see a style you like, click the More button to the right of the table styles that are showing. Word displays the full Table Style Gallery, showing Custom, Plain, and Built-In table styles, as shown in Figure 9-24.

FIGURE 9-23

As you move the mouse over different table styles, the currently selected table displays a Live Preview of the formatting.

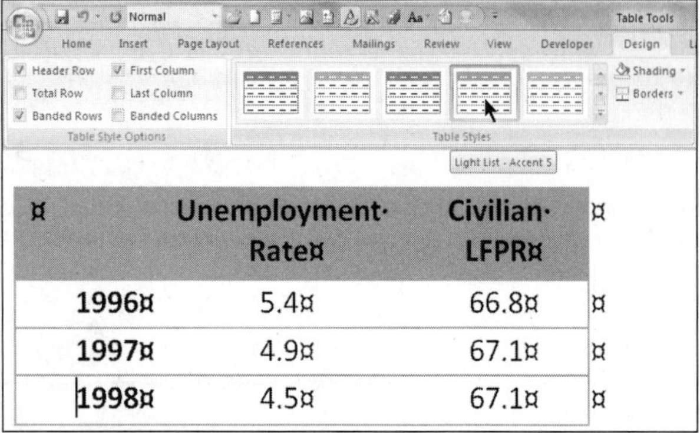

FIGURE 9-24

The Table Style Gallery enables you to test-drive dozens of built-in table styles.

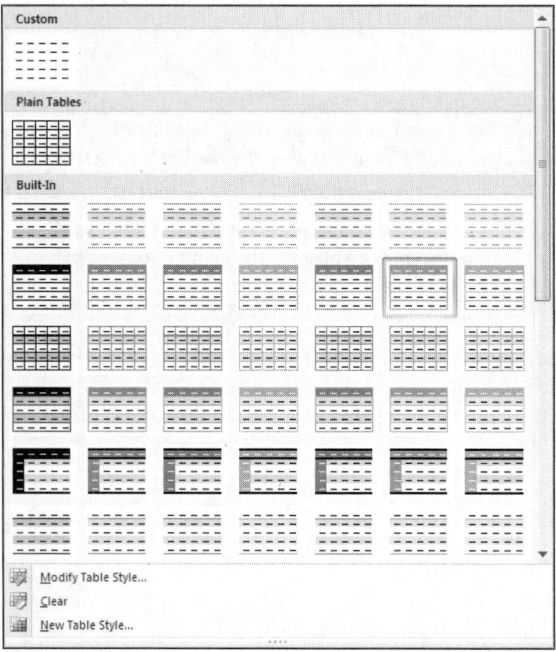

To modify the currently displayed table style, click Modify Table Style just below the Table Style Gallery, to display the Modify Style dialog box, shown in Figure 9-25. You can use the Modify Style dialog box to apply style formatting, as described in Chapter 7, "Styles."

FIGURE 9-25

If you type a new name, the style will be saved as a custom style in the Table Styles Gallery.

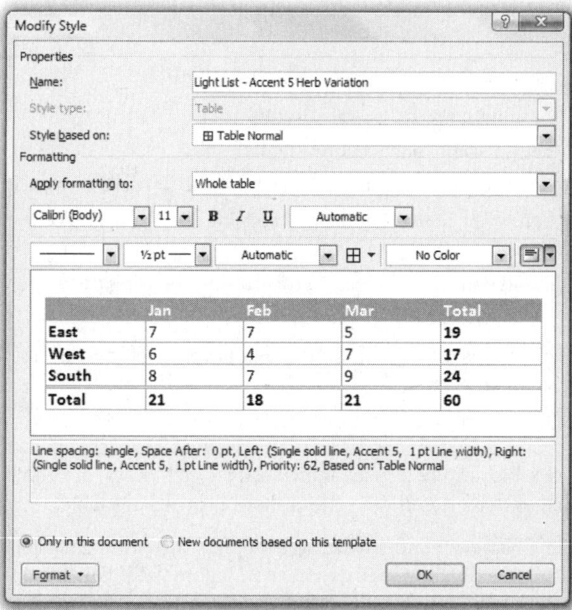

For additional options, right-click a table style in the gallery for the menu shown in Figure 9-26. Note the Set as Default option. This option enables you to set the selected table style as the default for all tables in the current document, or as the default for all future tables in documents based on the current template. This enables you to easily achieve a consistent look for tables you add to your documents.

FIGURE 9-26

For additional options, right-click any table style in the gallery.

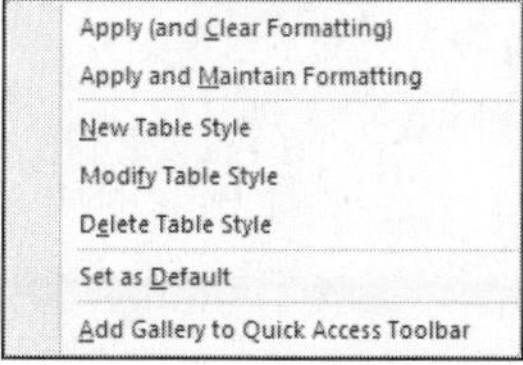

NOTE **Making this your default table style does not apply the style to existing tables. You would need to do that using the method described above (albeit one table at a time). Note also that the Modify Style dialog box for table styles lacks the Automatically Update option. That denies you the potential utility or the disastrous consequences (take your pick) to which that might lead given the preponderance of documents based on the `normal.dot` or `normal.dotm` templates.**

Table style options

Word provides access to six options, shown in Figure 9-22, that it can automatically apply to your table. For these to work, the table must have been formatted using one of the Built-In table styles instead of Plain Table, shown in Figure 9-24. Click to check or uncheck to apply those features to your tables. Table style options provided are as follows:

- **Header Row** — Applies special formatting to the entire top row in your table.
- **First Column** — Applies special formatting to the entire first column.
- **Total Row** — Applies special formatting the last row, except for the first cell.
- **Last Column** — Applies special formatting to the last column, except for the top cell.
- **Banded Rows** — Alternates shading in rows to create a horizontal striping effect. This helps the reader focus on specific rows.
- **Banded Columns** — Alternates shading in columns to create vertical strips, focusing the reader on columnar comparisons.

Each of the style options works together with Table Styles. Each Table Style might have any of these attributes enabled. Use the checkboxes to add or remove attributes.

Shading

Shading refers to the background color for tables, which can be applied individually to cells, rows, or columns, or to a complete table. Shading sometimes is used to draw attention to one or more elements of a table.

Shading is a Live Preview attribute. As shown in Chapters 5 and 6, shading is applied by selecting the part of the document you want shaded, and then using the Shading tool, as shown in Figure 9-27. You can use either of the Shading tools in the Ribbon to shade a table, not just the one in the Design tab. The Home tab's Shading tool also works.

FIGURE 9-27

If you apply one of the Theme Colors to shade a table, the table shading will change when different themes are applied.

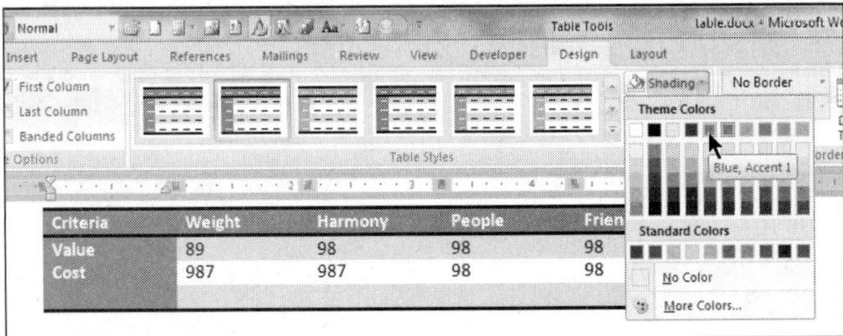

Borders and table drawing

Borders refers to lines that separate a table into cells, rows, and columns. You've seen in other chapters that borders are not unique to tables, and can be applied to characters and paragraphs as well. They also can be applied to other Word document elements, such as text boxes, frames, and graphics. Any of the border tools can be used to control borders in tables. None of the border tools offer Live Preview, although the Borders and Shading dialog box does provide a generic preview.

You have two strategies for working with borders. You can use the holistic approach by launching the Borders and Shading dialog box. For a detailed description of how to apply borders using the Borders and Shading dialog box, see the "Borders and boxes" section in Chapter 6.

The second strategy uses an ad hoc approach, by using the Borders, Line Style, Line Weight, Pen Color, Draw Table, and Eraser tools in the Design tab, shown in Figure 9-28. Much, if not all, of what you can do using the Borders and Shading dialog box, you can also do using the Borders tool, in combination with the Draw Borders group in the Design tab. Use whichever method works better for you, and it doesn't have to be the same method or set of tools each time.

FIGURE 9-28

Use the Borders tool and its friends to perform ad hoc editing on table borders.

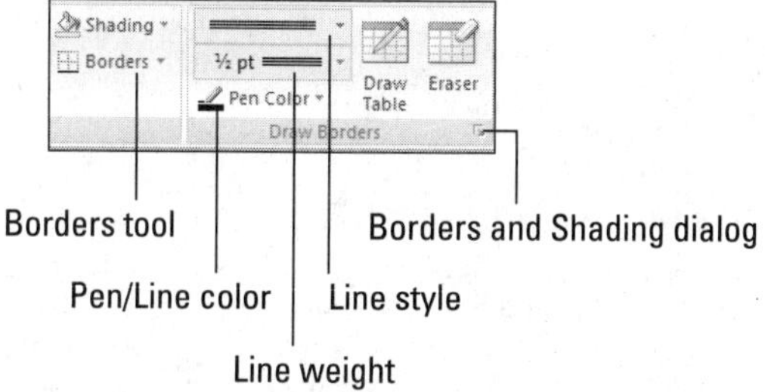

You should experiment with the Borders tools to get a feel for how they work. Even if you generally prefer the dialog box approach, the individual tools are great when you want to touch up or polish the look of a table. Keep in mind that you can use Ctrl+Z to remove the last effect applied, and F4 to reapply the most recent effect to a new selection.

When you use the Borders tool, it applies the current style, weight, and color shown in the Draw Borders group. For example, if you use the Borders tool in the configuration shown in Figure 9-29, the line style will be the triple line shown, 2¼ points, and black (which might be hard to see in a book with grayscale pictures). Therefore, to apply a black, 2¼ point triple line to the outside perimeter of the currently selected table cells, rows, columns, or complete table, choose Borders ➪ Outside Borders, as shown in Figure 9-29.

You can also change existing borders using the Draw Table tool. Like the Borders tool, the Draw Table tool also takes its cue from the currently selected style, weight, and color.

To change a particular border to blue without changing the other border attributes, for example, use the style and weight controls to reset those controls so that they match the current border settings. Use the Pen Color control to choose the shade of blue that you want. Finally, click Draw Table to turn the tool on (it will look pushed-in), and then click each of the borders you want dyed blue. Note that the Draw Table tool affects only one border at a time.

FIGURE 9-29

Use the Borders tool to apply borders by name, remove borders (No Border), draw a horizontal line, display gridlines, as well as launch the Borders and Shading dialog box.

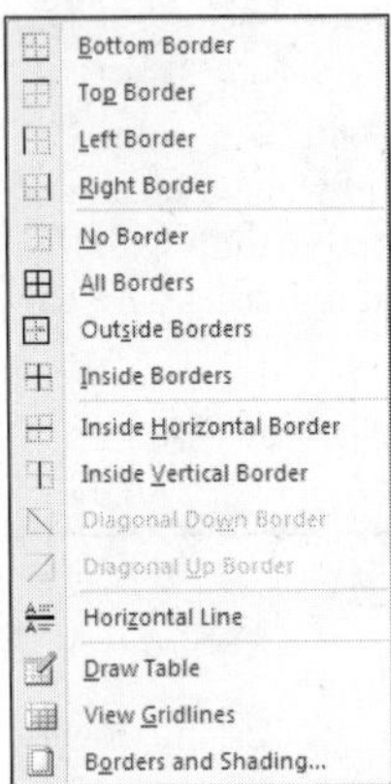

To turn the Draw Table tool off, either click it again (it's a toggle) or press the Esc key.

NOTE **Using either the Draw Table tool or the Borders tool, it's possible to place *ugly* diagonal lines in table cells. Unfortunately, the effect is purely visible, not functional. You cannot place data above and below those lines. Some folks use these ugly lines to indicate that the cells contain no data. Some might well imagine that emptiness or subtle shading conveys the same information, and somewhat more elegantly and eloquently. It's all a matter of style and aesthetics. If you want ugly diagonal lines and X's in your tables (yes, the diagonals can go both ways at the same time), it's entirely up to you. It's your table.**

Drawing tables from scratch

You can also use the Draw Table tool to draw tables from scratch. In the Insert tab, choose Table ➪ Draw Table. Use the table pen to drag to form an overall outline of the table. Then use the pen to add rows or columns, as shown in Figure 9-30. If necessary, you can use the Layout tools later to touch up any cell, row, or column dimensions that need to be adjusted.

FIGURE 9-30

Use the Draw Table tool to create tables from scratch, as well as to expand, extend, and modify existing tables.

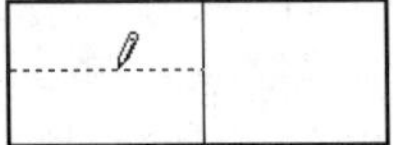

The Table Eraser

The Table Eraser is a powerful tool, and perhaps misunderstood. The Eraser actually erases parts of tables. It doesn't merely remove border lines. It actually deletes the table structure it touches. To turn the Table Eraser on, click the Eraser button at the far right end of the Table Tools ➪ Design tab.

No, it won't leave a hole in the middle of the table where non-table text can leak through (although that would be really cool). What it can do, however, is turn interior cells into a larger interior cell. Or, if you've ever wanted to knock a table's block off, now's your chance. You can use the Table Eraser to remove corner cells from tables. In some presentations, the top left corner cell serves no purpose, so why tolerate its presence? Erase it!

To dismiss the Eraser, either click the Eraser tool again to toggle it off, or press the Esc key. The Table Eraser also goes away if you click outside a table (i.e., in regular text).

Inserting Pictures from Files

Is a picture really worth a thousand words? It's up to you. Pictures for their own sake might simply clutter up a document and make it more time consuming to send to somebody and more expensive to print. Used carefully, pictures enable you to show the reader what you mean. Yes, used the right way, pictures can save many paragraphs of explanation, so perhaps a picture *is* worth a thousand words — maybe more. If not, there wouldn't be so many pictures in this book, helping to illustrate ideas.

You can insert pictures in Word in several ways, using pictures from a variety of different graphics formats. We'll look at formats shortly.

If you have pictures on removable media — such as SD (secure digital), CF (compact flash), CD, or DVD — it's usually best if those pictures have been copied to your hard drive before proceeding. While you can insert directly from such sources, or from a LAN or over the Internet, you have more options available to you if the files are on your own computer in a location that is always accessible.

You might also have pictures available from a webcam, other camera, or a scanner connected to your computer. Assuming the formats are supported, those also can be inserted into Word.

While it's not necessary, computing life is usually easier when pictures, sounds, and other files are where Word and other programs expect them to be. In the case of pictures, the expected location is your My Pictures subfolder of the My Documents folder (Windows XP) or Pictures folder (Windows Vista). You'll see why in this chapter. I'm going to assume that you've either copied the picture(s) you want to use to the applicable folder, or that you otherwise know where to find them.

I'm also going to assume that you're working with Word 2007 `.docx` files, and not Word 97–2003 compatibility mode files. This matters because things are a bit different in compatibility mode. In compatibility mode, linking of picture files is accomplished using the INCLUDEPICTURE field. In Word 2007 mode, linking is accomplished using XML relationships.

To insert a picture at the current insertion point, choose Insert ➪ Picture, which displays the Insert Picture dialog box. Assuming the picture is listed there, select it, but don't double-click it yet. Word displays a sometimes blurry preview (see Figure 9-31). As shown, click the drop-down arrow next to Insert to view the Insert options.

FIGURE 9-31

When you insert a picture, Word's default location is the \My Documents\My Pictures folder in Windows XP or Pictures folder in Windows Vista (shown here).

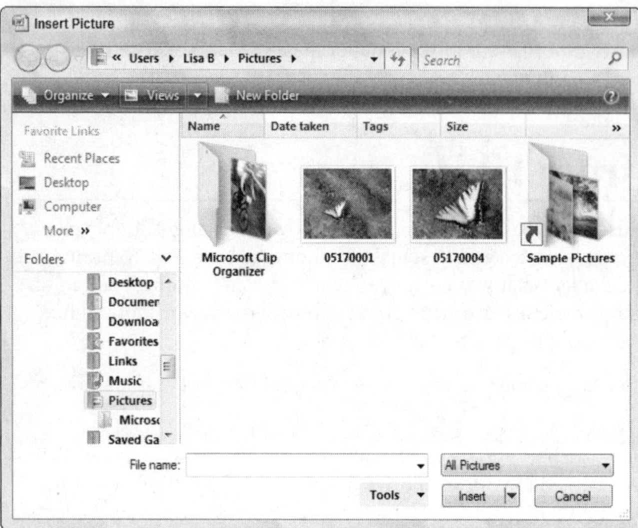

When inserting a picture this way, Word offers three options:

- **Insert** — The picture is embedded in the current document. If the original is ever deleted or moved, it will still exist in your document. If the original is ever updated, however, your document will not reflect the update. The document file will be larger because the original image is stored in the .docx file. If neither file size nor updates are important, this is the best option.
- **Link to File** — A link to the picture is inserted, and the picture is displayed in the document. The document file will be smaller — often dramatically smaller — because the image is external to the Word document. If the original file is moved or deleted, it will no longer be available for viewing in the document the next time you start Word and reopen the document, and you will see the upsetting and confusing message shown in Figure 9-32 (see the following Caution for more information). On the other hand, if the image is updated (press F9), the update will be available and displayed in Word. If file size is an issue but the availability of the image file is not, then this is the best option.
- **Insert and Link** — The image is both embedded in the document and linked to the original file. If the original file is updated, the picture in the document will be updated to reflect changes in the original. Because the file is embedded, the document will be larger than it would be if only linked. However, the document will not be larger than it would be if only inserted. If file size is not an issue but updates are, then this is the best option.

FIGURE 9-32

If a linked, non-embedded picture is moved, renamed, or deleted, Word will not be able to display it the next time you start Word and open the document.

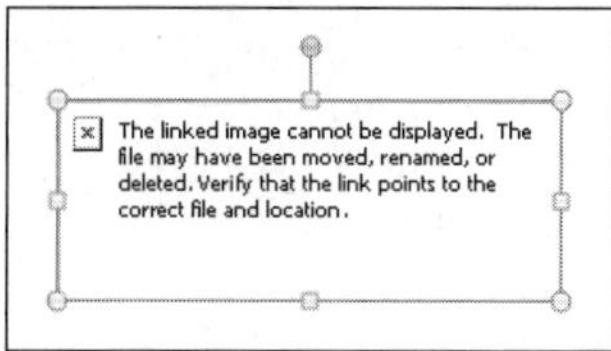

CAUTION If a link is broken, it can be confusing to discover the name of the missing file(s), especially if you're accustomed to Word 2003 or earlier. That's because linked files are not linked using field codes. You can't toggle field codes to discover the name. If you right-click the picture, there is no menu item that will tell you the name of the file. To discover the name, choose Office Button ➪ Prepare ➪ Edit Links to Files. (The command only appears when links exist in the document.) In the Links dialog box, the name of the file is shown next to Source File.

If your picture format isn't supported

If the picture you want doesn't appear in Word's Insert Picture dialog box but you know that it's really there, open the Files of Type drop-down list shown in Figure 9-33 to verify that Word supports the format. If your picture format isn't supported, there are several possible reasons.

FIGURE 9-33

Word supports a number of popular graphics formats, but some formats do not come with Word 2007.

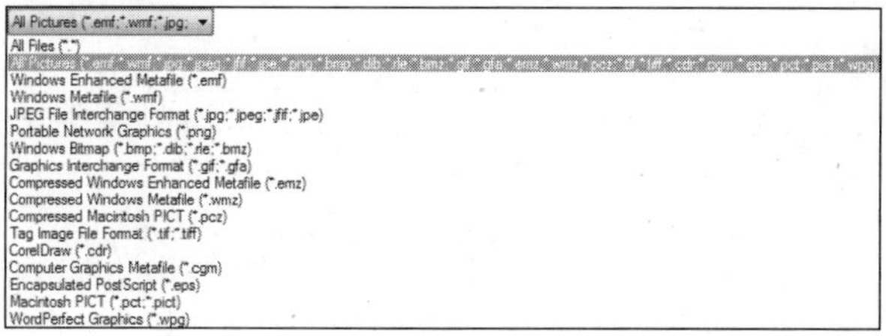

All Pictures (*.emf;*.wmf;*.jpg;
All Files (*.*)
Windows Enhanced Metafile (*.emf)
Windows Metafile (*.wmf)
JPEG File Interchange Format (*.jpg;*.jpeg;*.jfif;*.jpe)
Portable Network Graphics (*.png)
Windows Bitmap (*.bmp;*.dib;*.rle;*.bmz)
Graphics Interchange Format (*.gif;*.gfa)
Compressed Windows Enhanced Metafile (*.emz)
Compressed Windows Metafile (*.wmz)
Compressed Macintosh PICT (*.pcz)
Tag Image File Format (*.tif;*.tiff)
CorelDraw (*.cdr)
Computer Graphics Metafile (*.cgm)
Encapsulated PostScript (*.eps)
Macintosh PICT (*.pct;*.pict)
WordPerfect Graphics (*.wpg)

The most popular picture format used by most digital cameras is JPG, which stands for Joint Photographic Experts Group (so if you didn't know before, you do now). Word 2007 comes with a converter that supports `.JPG` files. Other Word 2007–supported popular formats include `.GIF`, which is heavily used on the Internet (because of support for transparent backgrounds, which makes such images better suited for web page design), `.PNG`, `.WMF`, and `.BMP`. Note that the latter two are natively supported by Word and do not require special converters.

Which formats are supported by your installation of Word depends on several things. Several graphics converters are installed as part of Office 2007's Shared Features. Other converters installed by other programs might also be available. If you had Office 2000 or Office XP installed on your computer and upgraded to Office 2007, additional converters possibly were installed as well.

If your file uses any of the formats that come with Office 2007 but they don't show up in the Insert Picture dialog box, then it's probable that you didn't install all of the converters. To add the missing converters, from Windows Control Panel, run Add or Remove Programs (Windows XP) or Programs ➪ Installed Programs (Windows Vista), and locate Microsoft Office 2007. The precise name depends on which flavor of Office 2007 you have.

Click Change ➪ Add or Remove Features ➪ Continue. Expand Office Shared Features ➪ Converters and Filters ➪ Graphic Filters. Click the drop-down arrow by Graphic Filters and choose Run All from My Computer. While you're here, you might want to install all of the text filters as well. You never know when they might come in handy. Click Continue and follow any instructions (which might or might not include inserting the original Office 2007 DVD or CD). When you're done, go back and check whether your picture format is now supported.

If your file format isn't supported natively by Word 2007, try searching for a "converter pack" on Microsoft's support site for Office and see what you can find. Choose Office ➪ Word Options ➪ Resources ➪ Check for Updates. Once there, type **converter pack** in the Search box, and click Go. At this writing, several are listed.

Pictures from the Clipboard and Internet

You can also insert pictures from the Clipboard and from your Internet browser (usually, but not always). To use the Clipboard, display the picture in any Windows program that supports graphics, and use that program's controls to select and copy the picture to the Clipboard. If all else fails, try right-clicking the picture and choosing Copy or Copy Picture. Then, in Word, move to where you want the picture, and press Ctrl+V (or click Paste in the Home tab of the Ribbon).

Sometimes the copy and paste method works from Internet Explorer, Firefox, Netscape, and other popular browsers, other times not. When the Clipboard method fails, or when you want a copy of the file itself (not simply the embedded version in a Word document), you can try several things.

In Firefox, right-click the picture and choose Save Image As. In Save Image, navigate to where you want to store the file, accept the name shown or type a new one (no need to type an extension — Firefox automatically supplies the extension), and click Save. In Internet Explorer, right-click the picture and choose Save Picture. Again, navigate to the desired location, pick a file name, and click Save.

TIP **If you're harvesting a number of files from an Internet browser, open a copy of Windows Explorer and navigate to where you want to store the pictures. Using the left mouse button, drag the pictures from Internet Explorer and drop them into Windows Explorer. Click Yes to confirm copying the file, and then continue.**

There are a number of ways to find pictures on the Internet, from surfing to explicitly searching. Google itself has an image Search feature. From Google's home page, click Images. In the Image Search page, type the search text (enclose in "quotes" to search for a whole name), and click Search Image. Another common technique is to search for "gallery," although, these days, you'd probably find a lot of Office 2007 gallery hits!

Manipulation 101

Now that you've got those pictures, what are you going to do with them? Word 2007 provides a number of cool new tools that really expand your presentation options. What you can do with pictures depends on how they "live" in the Word document. We'll look at the various wrapping options and their implications, and then move on to working with pictures, knowing that there are some constraints. Keep in mind also that this discussion is about working with Word 2007 format documents. If we were to deal with Word 97–2003 format, this book might need another 900 pages because the methods are so different.

Wrapping

Wrapping is the term used to classify the various ways in which pictures (as well as other graphics) are used in a Word document. It helps to understand that a Word document has several different *layers*. Where you normally compose text is called the *text layer*. There are also *drawing layers* that are both in front of and behind the text layer. A graphic inserted in front of the text layer will cover text up, unless the graphic is semi-transparent, in which case it will modify the view of the text. Graphics inserted behind the text layer act as a backdrop, or background, for the text.

Additionally, there is the *header and footer layer*. This is where headers and footers reside. This area is behind the text area. If you place a graphic into a header or footer, the graphic will appear behind the text. Dim graphics placed in the header/footer layer often serve as watermarks. Sometimes, the word CONFIDENTIAL will be used in the header/footer layer, branding each page of the document as a caution to readers.

Setting wrapping and wrapping defaults

Wrapping determines how graphics interact with each other and with text. Different wrapping settings are shown in Table 9-1. To set the wrapping behavior of a graphic, double-click it and then click the Wrapping tool in the Arrange group (in Picture Tools ➪ Format tab, or in the Page Layout tab). Choose the desired wrapping from the list shown.

You can also set the default wrapping. If you're a long-time Word user, you likely already have a default wrapping style that suits your generic needs. If not, then in time you likely will find that you frequently change the wrapping from the default to something else. If that happens a lot, you can save yourself a step by setting the wrapping default to your usual setting.

To set the default wrapping style for most graphic objects you insert, paste, or create, choose Office Button ➪ Word Options ➪ Advanced. In the Cut, Copy, and Paste section, use Insert/Paste Pictures As to set wrapping to any of the options shown in Figure 9-34. This setting determines the default for most, but not all, graphics inserted into Word.

Notable exceptions are Shapes (the leftmost group in the Insert tab) and Text Boxes. Shapes and Text Boxes can be set to any wrapping style after the fact, but they are always inserted as In Front of Text. Another exception, of sorts, stems from the fact that if you copy a picture from one part of a document and paste it elsewhere, then it will inherit the wrapping style of the original picture and won't use your default.

FIGURE 9-34

Wrapping behavior determines what you can do with a picture in Word.

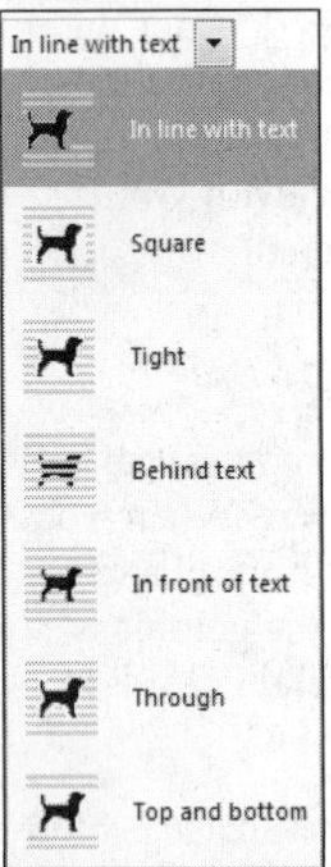

Knowing how you plan to use a picture and what you need to do to it should determine the wrapping setting. Wrapping effects and typical uses are shown in Table 9-1. Wrapping comes in two basic flavors: in line with text and floating. Floating means that the picture can be dragged anywhere in the document and isn't constrained in the way that in line with text graphics are.

TABLE 9-1

Wrapping Styles

Wrapping Setting	Effect/Application
In line with text	Inserted into text layer. Graphic can be dragged, but only from one paragraph marker to another. Typically used in simple presentations and formal reports.
Square	Creates a square "hole" in the text where the graphic is. Text wraps around the graphic, leaving a gap between the text and the graphic. The graphic can be dragged anywhere in the document. Typically used in newsletters and flyers with a fair amount of white space.
Tight	Effectively creates a "hole" in the text where the graphic is, the same shape as the overall outline of the graphic, so that text flows around the graphic. Wrapping points can be changed to reshape the "hole" that text flows around. The graphic can be dragged anywhere in the document. Typically used in denser publications in which paper space is at a premium, and where irregular shapes are acceptable and even desirable.
Behind text	Inserted into the bottom or back drawing layer of a document. The graphic can be dragged anywhere in the document. Typically used for watermarks and page background pictures. Text flows in front of the graphic. Also used when assembling a picture from different vector elements.
In front of text	Inserted into the top drawing layer of a document. The graphic can be dragged anywhere in the document. Text flows behind the graphic. Typically used only on top of other pictures or when assembling a vector drawing, or when you deliberately need to cover or veil text in some way to create a special effect.

Wrapping Setting	Effect/Application
Through	Text flows around the graphic's wrapping points, which can be adjusted. Text is supposed to flow into any open areas of the graphic, but evidence that this actually works is in short supply. For all practical purposes, this appears to have the same effects and behavior as Tight wrapping.
Top and bottom	Effectively creates a rectangular hole the same width as the margin. Text flows above and below, but not beside, the graphic. The picture can be dragged anywhere in the document. Typically used when the graphic is the focal point of the text.

Changing Wrap Points

For Tight and Through wrapping, you can change the wrap points. To edit the wrap points, click the picture (you might need to click twice), and then choose Text Wrapping ➪ Edit Wrap Points from the Arrange group in the Picture Tools ➪ Format tab, or from the Arrange group in the Page Layout tab, as shown in Figure 9-35. If too much white space is showing, you can reduce it by moving the wrap points closer to the object. If you want a special effect by creating a starburst or other pattern, you can drag the wrap points outward and inward.

FIGURE 9-35

Use Edit Wrap Points to change the way text flows around a picture.

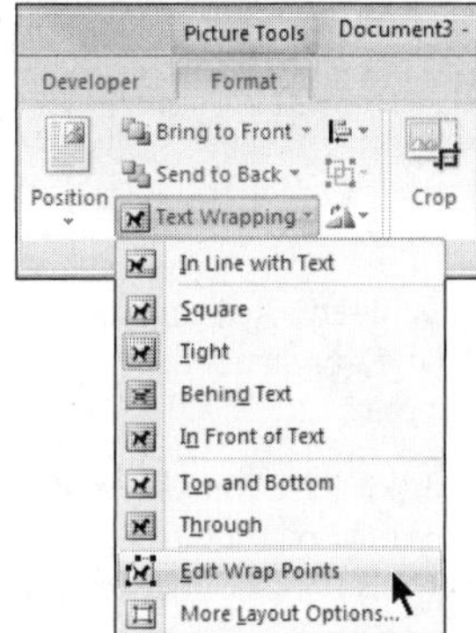

Dragging and nudging

You can move any graphic by dragging it, and some graphics can be dropped anywhere in the document. Graphics inserted as In Line with Text, however, can be dropped only at a paragraph mark. All other graphics can be dragged and dropped anywhere. The techniques described in this section apply only to floating graphics (i.e., not In Line with Text). As described earlier, what happens when you drag a graphic is determined by the wrapping that is applied.

To drag a graphic, click to select it, and then drag it where you want it to go. You can also *nudge* a selected floating graphic. Select it, and then use the cursor keys to nudge it in any of the four directions.

To drag in discrete steps using Word's built-in invisible drawing grid, hold the Alt key as you drag. If you make Word's gridlines visible (View ➪ Gridlines), however, the effect of the Alt key is reversed. Now, holding Alt while dragging ignores the grid, shown in Figure 9-36. With the grid displayed, cursor key nudging also changes. Now, the cursor keys move the picture in grid steps. Press the Ctrl key to nudge in smaller gradations. Each grid mark is ⅛ of an inch.

FIGURE 9-36

Enable Gridlines in the View Ribbon for help in planning graphic placement.

Note that gridlines is a Wordwide display setting. If you have other documents open in the same Word session, they too will be gridded. Waffles, anyone?

Resizing and cropping

Resizing changes the physical dimensions of the picture as it is displayed in your document. Resizing in Word will not make the associated file (or the image stored in the `.docx` file) any larger or smaller. If you make it smaller and then later make it larger, you still retain the original file resolution.

Cropping refers to blocking out certain portions of a picture by changing its exterior borders. You can crop out distracting or unnecessary details. Again, cropping in Word does not affect the actual picture itself, only the way it is displayed in Word. The fact that Word doesn't change the actual image is a big plus, because you preserve your options if you later change your mind.

CAUTION **Resizing and cropping in Microsoft Picture Manager and other graphics programs does change the picture itself. Keep this distinction in mind. Once you've saved a cropped or resized picture in Picture Manager, you can't get the original back (unless you saved a backup copy, of course).**

Resizing

You can resize a picture by typing the measurements or by dragging. To resize by dragging, click on the picture and then move the mouse pointer so that it's over one of the eight sizing handles. The mouse pointer changes into a double arrow, as shown in Figure 9-37. Drag until the picture is the desired size and then release the mouse button. Note that dragging the corner handles maintains the aspect ratio of the picture, while dragging the side handles can be used to stretch or compress the picture.

FIGURE 9-37

Resize a picture or other graphic by dragging any of the eight sizing handles.

Hold down the Ctrl and/or Alt keys while dragging to modify the way resizing occurs:

- To resize symmetrically, causing the picture to increase or decrease by the same amount in opposite directions, hold down the Ctrl key while dragging.
- To drag in discrete steps, hold down the Alt key while dragging; if gridlines are displayed, the Alt key's behavior is reversed, as indicated earlier.

You can combine these options. For example, holding down the Alt and Ctrl keys at the same time forces Word to resize in discrete steps while resizing symmetrically.

NOTE **Use the solitary green handle above the center of the picture to rotate the picture.**

To specify the size of the picture exactly, click in the Height and/or Width boxes in the Size group in the Picture Tools ➪ Format tab. By default, these settings maintain the aspect ratio automatically. To distort the picture, click the Size dialog box launcher in the Size group. Remove the check next to Lock aspect ratio, as shown in Figure 9-38. The Alt Text tab in the Size dialog box is for specifying descriptive alternative text to be displayed in a browser if the picture is not available or the user has disabled displaying pictures.

Cropping

To crop a picture, click the Crop button in the Size group in the Picture Tools ➪ Format tab, shown in Figure 9-39. The selected picture sprouts cropping handles, as does the mouse pointer. Move the pointer over any of the eight cropping handles and drag to remove the part of the picture you want to hide. Note that the Alt key crops in discrete steps. You can also crop using the Size dialog box, as shown in Figure 9-38.

FIGURE 9-38

Lock aspect ratio is enabled by default; to distort a picture's dimensions, turn it off.

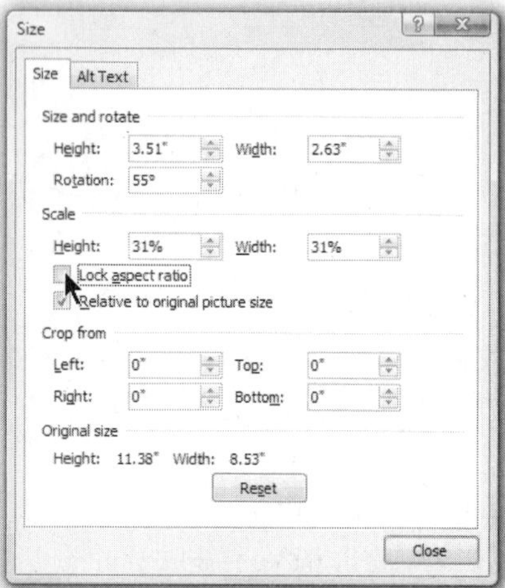

FIGURE 9-39

Crop to hide part of a picture to focus the reader's attention.

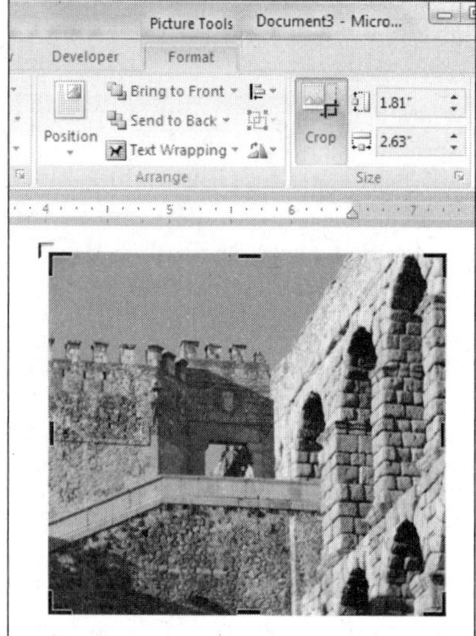

Picture Styles

Word 2007 provides a variety of tools for controlling the presentation of graphics. To the extent possible, use the Ribbon to apply the basic effects, then use additional tools to refine the effect for more precision, if needed. The Picture Styles Gallery provides a variety of different presentation styles. Double-click a picture to activate the Picture Tools ➪ Format tab. In the Picture Styles group, shown in Figure 9-40, click the More tool to expose more of the gallery.

FIGURE 9-40

Picture Styles are previewed in your document when you move the mouse.

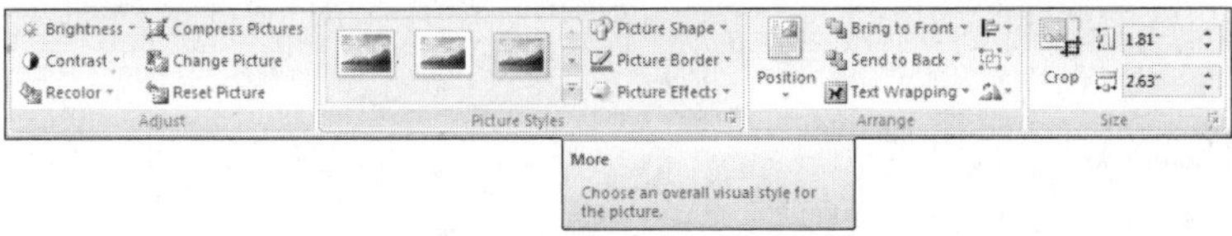

As shown in Figure 9-41, when you move the mouse, each style is applied to the selected picture (or pictures). Note that the speed of Live Preview is heavily affected by the size of the graphic file. If the picture is 2MB, then Live Preview is going to be a lot slower than if the file is only 50K in size.

FIGURE 9-41

Effects of each style are previewed as you move the mouse.

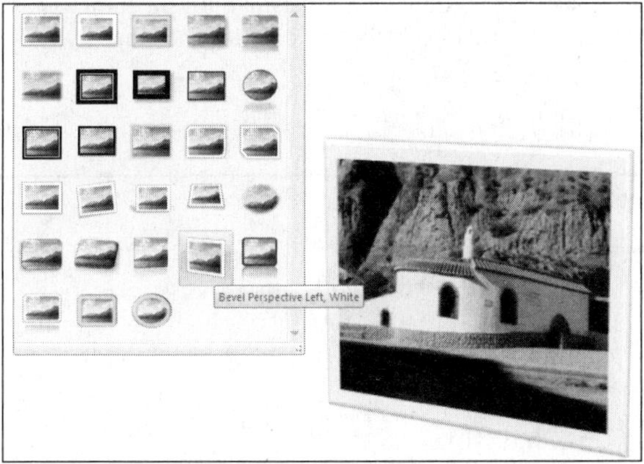

Picture Effects

Additional effects can be applied and refined using the Picture Effects tool, also contained in the Picture Styles group. There literally are millions of different permutations of effects you can apply, a small sampling of which is shown in Figure 9-42. Take a few years off to explore the different combinations.

FIGURE 9-42

Applying multiple picture effects and Picture Style Gallery choices provides myriad combinations of formatting.

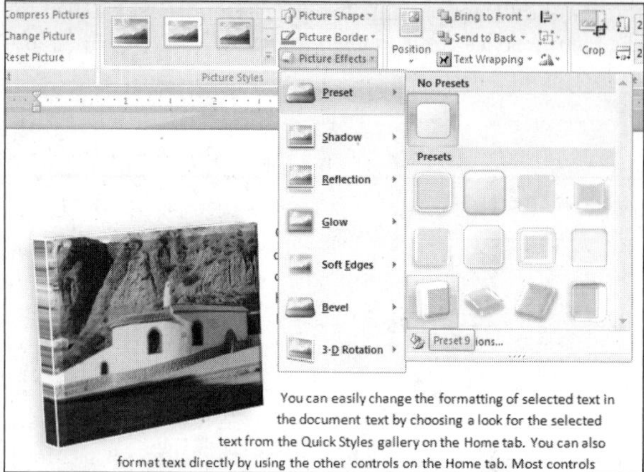

Format picture/shape

You can hone many picture styles and effects using the Format Picture/Format Shape dialog box. Like many other picture tools, although this is a dialog box, it nonetheless features Live Preview of effects. To display the Format Picture/Shape dialog box, right-click on a picture or shape and choose Format Picture or Format Shape. The Format Picture/Format Shape dialog box, which does duty for a variety of different graphic types, is displayed, like the one shown in Figure 9-43. If you've applied formatting using the other style implements, you can hone those effects here.

FIGURE 9-43

Refine your pictures further using the Format Shape (Picture) tool set.

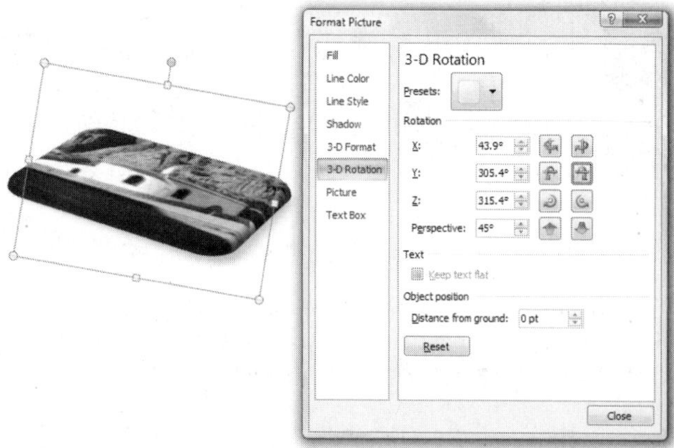

Adjust

Word also features six tools for adjusting picture attributes, shown in Figure 9-40. Use the tools to accomplish a number of common tasks:

- **Brightness and Contrast** — Tweak images for better printing or onscreen presentation (Live Preview).
- **Recolor** — Apply different color masks to achieve antiquing, sepia tone, grayscale, and a variety of other color effects (Live Preview).
- **Compress Pictures** — Reduce the size of the picture stored in the file to the minimum needed for a given application.
- **Change Picture** — Replace the picture with a different one. Picture Style and Effects applied carry over to the replacement picture, as do changes applied using other tools in the Adjust group. Cropping and resizing, however, do not.
- **Reset Picture** — Removes formatting applied using Picture Styles, Picture Effects, and other Adjust tools (except for Change and Compress).

Arranging pictures on the page

Word has additional tools for quickly controlling the position of pictures, both two-dimensionally on the document page, as well as with respect to other objects in the graphical layer. In the Arrange group (see Figure 9-40), click Position. Shown in Figure 9-44, In Line with Text is identical to the In Line with Text option listed under Text Wrapping. The other options, however, aren't duplicated elsewhere, except indirectly through use of the Advanced Layout dialog box.

FIGURE 9-44

Position gives you a Live Preview of nine fixed positions.

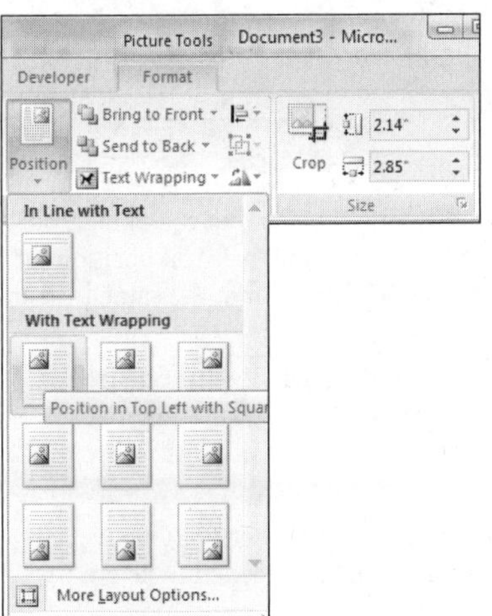

Some pictures need to be in a particular location in order to make sense. In laying out newsletters, brochures, and many other publications, however, some pictures are intended as general illustrations. Position on the page can be decided on the basis of aesthetics and balance rather than purely on logic and the relationship between a given picture and a particular passage in the text.

The More Layout Options invokes the Advanced Layout dialog box, shown in Figure 9-45. Users of earlier versions of Word will recognize this as the result of clicking the Advanced button in the Layout tab of the Format Picture dialog box. The settings shown here correspond to the center position available in the preset positions (absolute center of the page both vertically and horizontally).

FIGURE 9-45

Advanced Layout enables you to precisely control and set the position of graphics on the page.

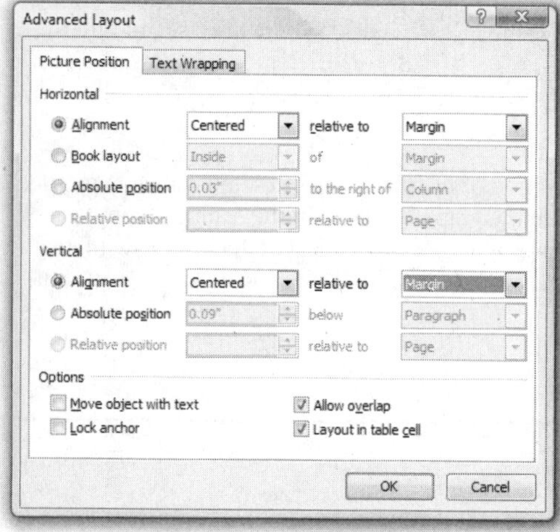

Additional options of interest include the following:

- **Move object with text** — Associates a picture with a particular paragraph so that the paragraph and the picture will always appear on the same page. This setting affects only vertical position on the page. Although Word will allow you to check this option and Lock anchor at the same time in the dialog box, once you click OK, the Move object with text option is cleared.
- **Lock anchor** — This setting locks the picture's current position on the page. If you have trouble dragging a picture, verify that it is set to one of the floating wrapping options (anything but In Line), and that Lock anchor is turned off. Pictures that have been positioned using the nine Position presets will also resist dragging.
- **Allow overlap** — Use this setting to allow graphical objects to cover each other up. One use for this is to create a stack of photographs or other objects. This feature is also needed in layered drawings.
- **Layout in table cell** — This setting enables you to use tables for positioning graphics on the page.

Inserting Clip Art

Clip Art provides another source of decoration for your documents, frequently used in newsletters and flyers when visuals are useful. Part of Office's Shared Features set, depending on what Office program you have and how much of them you have installed, Clip Art has hundreds or even thousands of little pieces of royalty-free topical art that you can use anywhere.

To insert Clip Art at the insertion point, click Insert ⇨ Clip Art, in the Illustrations group. To accept the defaults, type a search term (for example, **medicine**) and click Go, shown in Figure 9-46. When clip art appears, scroll through the list. When you find something you want to use, click on it to insert it into your document.

FIGURE 9-46

The Clip Art pane uses local clip art as well as clip art from Office Online.

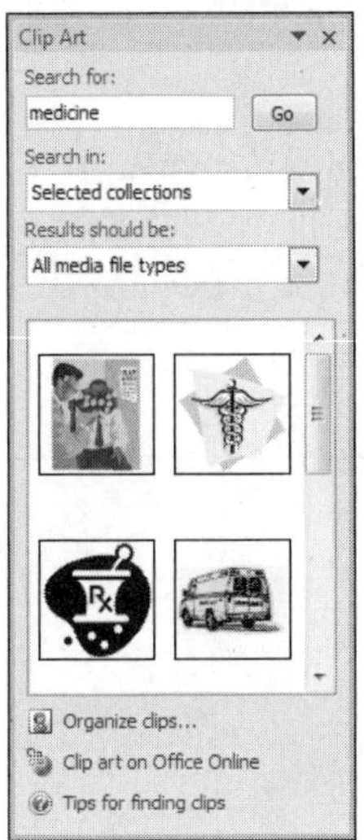

To control where Clip Art searches, use the drop-down Search In list, shown in Figure 9-47. To search only your local collection, remove the check next to Everywhere, and enable only My Collections and Office Collections. To include searching online, leave Web Collections checked. You can further control the scope of the search by limiting the search to only a particular kind of media. By default, Word searches for all media types — including movies and sounds! Note also that we talked earlier about where to find photographs on the web. Now you know another source. With Search In set only to Web Collections and Results Should Be set only to Photographs, you can quickly see a list of photographs available for download from Microsoft.

NOTE **As shown in the section "If your picture format isn't supported," earlier in this chapter, if you lack local clip art, check Office 2007's Setup settings and verify that Clip Art was actually fully installed; check Clip Organizer under Office Shared Features.**

FIGURE 9-47

Use the Search In drop-down list to control the scope of a search for clip art.

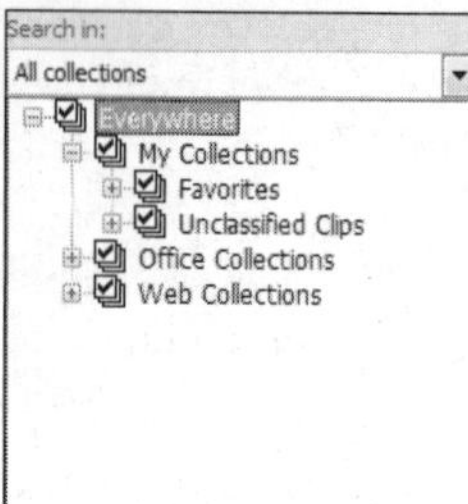

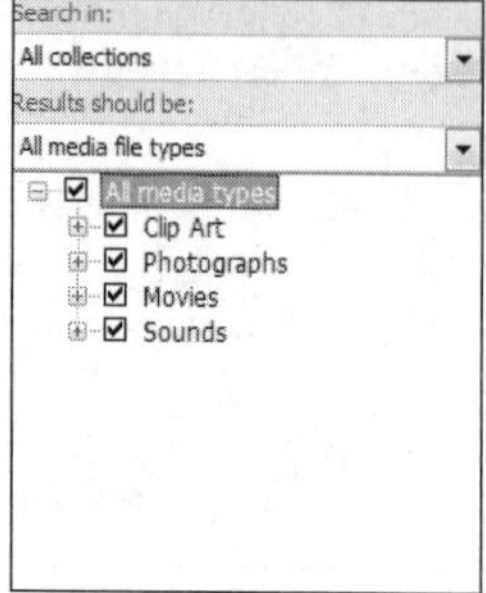

Microsoft Clip Organizer

At the bottom of the Clip Art pane (refer to Figure 9-46), notice the Organize Clips option. This runs Microsoft Clip Organizer, which is a separate application that comes with Office. I won't go into a lot of detail about it except to say that it can be very useful. As shown in Figure 9-48, if you choose File ➪ Add Clips to Organizer, it can search your hard disk(s) and add items to the Clip Organizer. These added items will also be available from Word's Clip Art pane.

FIGURE 9-48

The Clip Organizer can vastly expand the supply of clips to which Word has access.

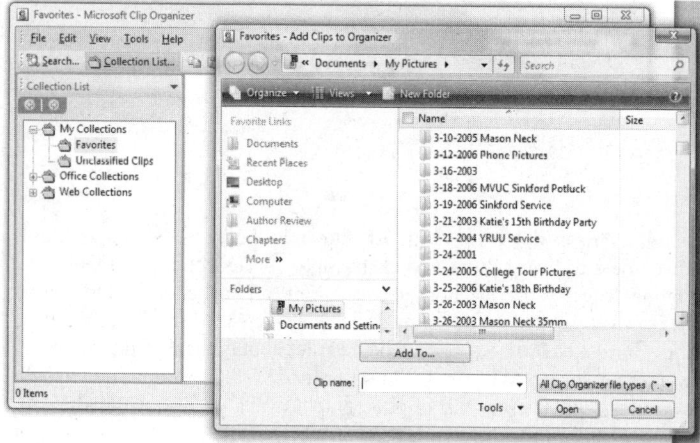

CAUTION **If you have a lot of media files on your computer, this can take a long time, and it might appear that your computer has stopped. It hasn't (not usually, anyway). Go out for some lunch and it might be done by the time you return.**

SmartArt

Thanks to SmartArt, there's now a whole new level of professional graphics available for use in Word. If this book had color screen shots, you would be dazzled by the kinds of sparkling, shiny, bubbly diagrams you can now make with Word. Best of all, although the SmartArt is seemingly bottomless in variety, the techniques are intuitive and simple to use.

SmartArt replaces Word 2003's (and earlier) Insert Diagram and Insert Organization Chart feature. The six-item Diagram Gallery has been completely revamped and replaced with SmartArt. Moreover, the plain two-dimensional formatting has been replaced by 3-D formatting that's so slick it looks like something you'd find in the pages of a major magazine. Let's just hope that Word users have some excellent data and content to go with all this newfound slickness.

Inserting SmartArt

To insert SmartArt, on the Insert tab, click SmartArt. As shown in Figure 9-49, there are seven categories, plus All, which enables you to peruse the entire gallery. Clicking on a thumbnail preview in the middle panel reveals a larger preview displayed on the right. A description lists the intended use. When you find something that looks appropriate, either double-click it or click on it and then choose OK. Note that SmartArt is inserted like other graphics, such as pictures, and will use your default wrapping style. See "Wrapping" earlier in this chapter.

FIGURE 9-49

Word 2007 has more than 100 different SmartArt gallery items distributed in seven different categories.

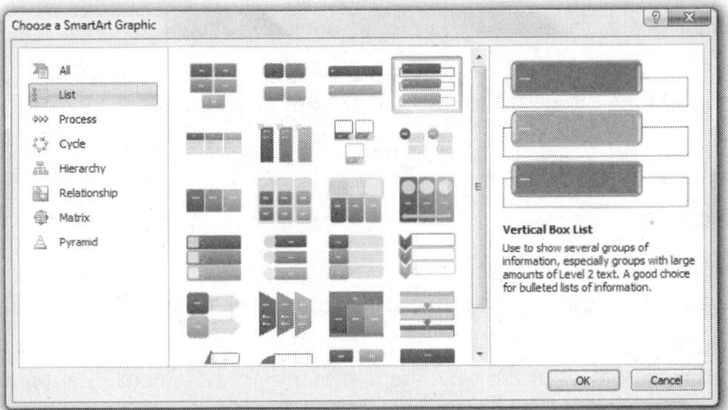

Word inserts the shape into your document with the text entry area ready to accept information, as shown in Figure 9-50. To enter text for the SmartArt diagram, click in the Type Your Text Here box (the Text Pane) and start typing. As you type on the left, text is displayed in the corresponding SmartArt component on the right.

FIGURE 9-50

A new SmartArt chart begins with the SmartArt Tools ➪ Design tab.

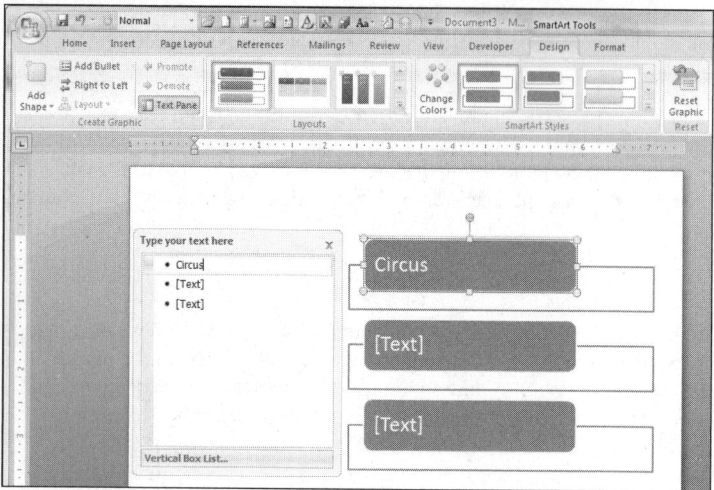

There are a variety of different ways to enter and format text. The following is not intended to be exhaustive; it's simply a list of things that work. Note that some actions can also be performed using the Create Graphic group in the SmartArt Tools ➪ Design tab, shown at the left in Figure 9-50.

- To move to the next item, press the down arrow. Use the other arrow keys to navigate in the text entry box as well.
- To add a new item to the list, press Enter, either at the end of the list of items, or above an existing item.
- To demote the current item, press the Tab key.
- To promote the current item, press Shift+Tab.
- To delete an item, select it and press the Backspace key.
- To change the font for an item, select the text you want to change, mouse over the selection, and use the Mini toolbar.
- The Text Pane can be moved and resized if it's in the way; drag it to a more convenient location or drag any of the four sides to resize the text area.
- To dismiss the Text Pane, click the X. To redisplay the Text Pane, click either of the arrows at the left end of the diagram (see Figure 9-51).

FIGURE 9-51

The Text Pane isn't the only way to enter text.

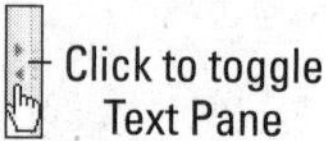

You can also enter text directly, without using the Text Pane. Click in the SmartArt item and type. Right-click the item to see a list of options, shown in Figure 9-52. To add a shape above the selected item, right-click and choose Add Shape ➪ Add Shape Before.

FIGURE 9-52

When working directly with the SmartArt item, right-click to see actions and formatting options.

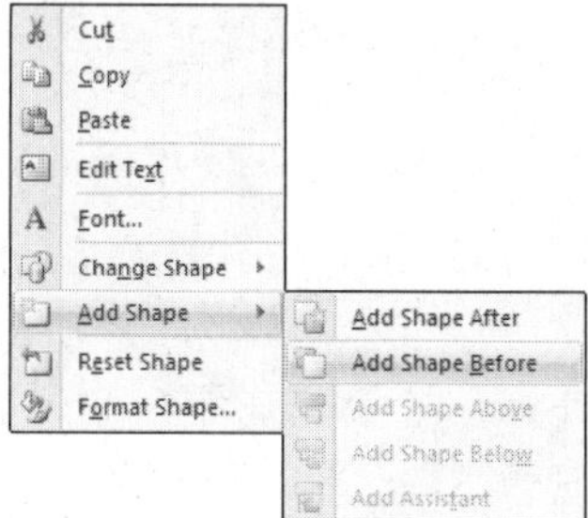

Note that basic paragraph and character formatting can be applied to SmartArt shapes. Indents, bullets, and numbering cannot be, nor can styles. You can assign a style to the overall diagram; however, effects are limited unless the SmartArt item is In Line with Text.

To change the font used in all of the text in a SmartArt object, display the Text Pane, click in it, press Ctrl+A to select the contents of the text area, and then right-click and set the desired font.

You're not limited to the shapes you start out with, nor must each item be the same shape. To change the shape of any given item, select the item, right-click it, choose Change Shape, and select an alternative. Keep in mind, however, that not every shape works for every type of diagram.

TIP **If you have a list — hierarchical or not — that you would like to convert into a SmartArt object, select the list and copy it to the Clipboard before choosing the SmartArt tool. Once your SmartArt object appears, click in the Text Pane. Press Ctrl+A to select the placeholder list, and then press Ctrl+V to paste the list over the placeholder.**

Changing layout

You can change layout at any time. Select the SmartArt graphic and use the Layouts Gallery, shown in Figure 9-53, to choose a different layout. Note that the gallery provides a Live Preview. You aren't limited to applying the same class (List, Hierarchy, Process, Cycle, etc.). SmartArt will adapt the different designs using the relationship levels currently applied.

FIGURE 9-53

SmartArt will apply any layout to any hierarchical list.

SmartArt Quick Styles

SmartArt Quick Styles apply a variety of preset formatting to your SmartArt diagrams — again, using Live Preview. As suggested by Figure 9-54, a great deal of care, thought, and artistry has gone into the design of SmartArt Quick Styles.

SmartArt formatting

SmartArt provides a number of additional tools for further sculpting your diagrams. Shown in Figure 9-55, use the SmartArt Tools ➪ Format tab to add the finishing touches.

FIGURE 9-54

The Quick Style Gallery puts a basic spin on your graphics; you can refine these further using the SmartArt Tools ➪ Format tab.

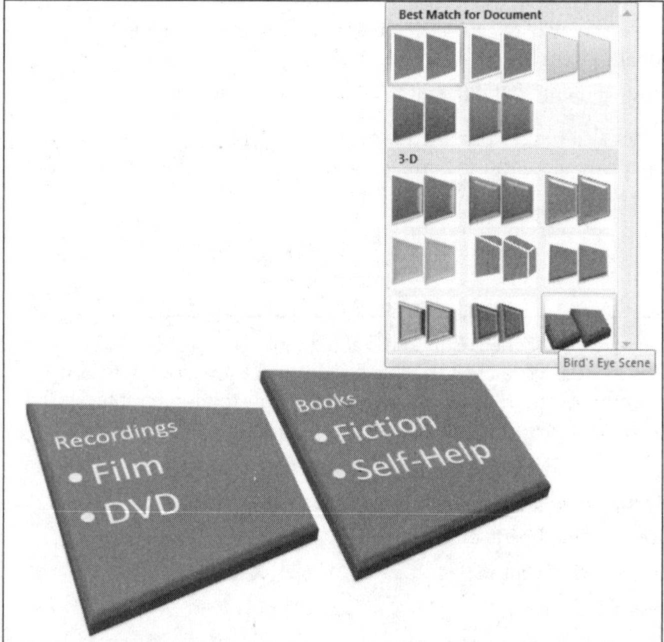

FIGURE 9-55

Formatting tools include Shapes, Shape Styles, and WordArt Styles.

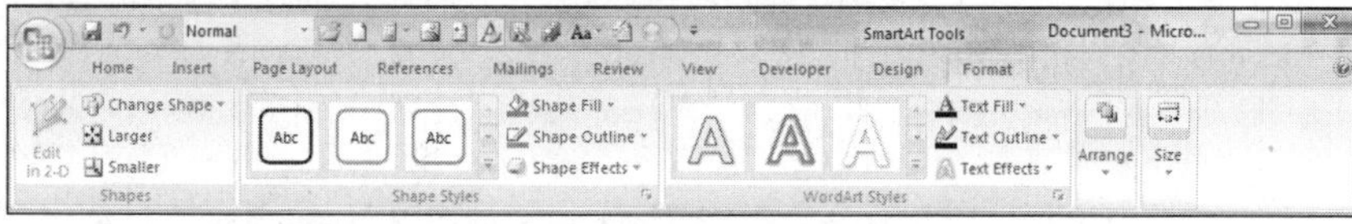

Use the Format tools as follows:

Shapes

- **Edit in 2-D** — When you click on a shape, a 2-D version appears for more direct editing.
- **Change Shape** — Change the selected shape into any of dozens of Word's shapes.
- **Make Larger or Smaller** — Expand or shrink the selected shape.

Shape styles

- **Shape Style Gallery** — Choose from three dozen different patterns of outlines and fill.
- **Shape Fill** — Choose your own custom fill for the selected shape.
- **Shape Outline** — Choose a custom outline for the selected shape.
- **Shape Effects** — Choose from a variety of effects — shadow, reflection, glow, soft edges, bevel, and 3-D — to change individual shapes.
- **WordArt Styles** — Choose from a number of different filled-block lettering styles.

In addition to these tools, SmartArt shapes also can be formatted using the Format Shape dialog box that you can display by right-clicking the SmartArt and clicking Format Shape. This tool is especially useful for honing rotation in 3-D objects.

Summary

In this chapter, you've learned just about everything there is to know about tables and graphics. You know a quick way to insert a whole table and several ways to create a table from scratch. You also know how to modify and format tables using a variety of tools and techniques. You learned how to insert graphics, Clip Art, and SmartArt, and how to work with the formatting for those objects. You should now be able to do the following:

- Copy material from one table into another, even if the dimensions don't match
- Use the table eraser to remove unwanted parts of tables
- Use table styles to add zest and color to your tables
- Create tables from existing non-tabular data
- Use the Ribbon tools to modify table layout and design
- Determine whether Word supports the graphic format of your pictures
- Achieve any wrapping effect when working with text and graphics
- Use the Clip Organizer to add media files on your hard disk to the Clip Art Pane
- Present a hierarchical text list as SmartArt

Chapter 10

Mail Merge

IN THIS CHAPTER

Attaching a data source to a data document

Editing data

Assembling a data document

Merging to a printer

Using the Mail Merge Wizard

Let's face it. The term *mail merge* is entirely too narrow to fully reflect the range of what can be done using Word's "mail merge" features.

Setting up a mail merge or data document involves a number of steps, some of which must be done before others can happen:

1. Set the document type: letter, e-mail, envelope, labels, and directory.
2. Associate a data source with the document: new, Outlook contact, or some other source.
3. Design your data document by combining ordinary document features with Word merge fields.
4. Preview the finished document by testing to see how it looks with different data records.
5. Finish the process by merging the data document with the data source, creating a printed result, a saved document, or an e-mailed document.

Understanding Data Sources

When you perform a mail merge, Word inserts an individual set of information (such as a recipient's name and mailing address) into a copy of a document to customize or personalize the document. The sets of information come from a *data source* — a file that organizes information into fields and records of information. For example, for a mailing address, the person's first name, last name, street number, city, state, and ZIP represent the different *fields*; all the field entries for a single recipient comprise a single *record*.

In most cases, the data source that you use for a merge will be a file created in another application, most typically in Excel or Access. You also can use the contact information from Outlook. You even can use information from a Word file or other Word processing file. The key with data sources is that the information in the data source file must be properly divided into fields and records. In Excel, you can enter the field names in row 1 and each record below the field names. In Access, the table will already define the field names and records. In a word processing file, you can enter the field names on the first line, and press Enter to start each new record; you include a *delimiter* such as a comma or tab between each field name and field entry so that Word can correctly separate the information to perform the merge.

Chances are, your data source may be a file that's already been created for another purpose. If not, many users create a data source file first, but Word can accommodate creating a data source "on the fly" during the merge process described in this chapter.

Choosing the Type of Data Document

The data *document* holds the text that repeats for all the merged documents. For example, for a merged letter, the data document consists of every thing *except* the individual records merge in to personalize each copy of the letter. In Word, you can set up an existing document as your data document, or a new, blank document.

To choose the type of data document, in the Mailings tab of the Ribbon, click Start Mail Merge, as shown in Figure 10-1. Some of the options are obvious, others are not. There are basically two kinds of data documents you can design. For one kind, each data record (a set of data items or fields describing a person, company, product, etc.) will result in a single document, such as a form letter, a mass e-mail, a product specification sheet, or an invoice. For the other kind, a single document is produced in which multiple records can appear on any given page. This approach is needed for creating directories, catalogs, and sheets of labels.

FIGURE 10-1

Letters, e-mail messages, and envelopes use one record per output document, while labels and directories use multiple records for each output document.

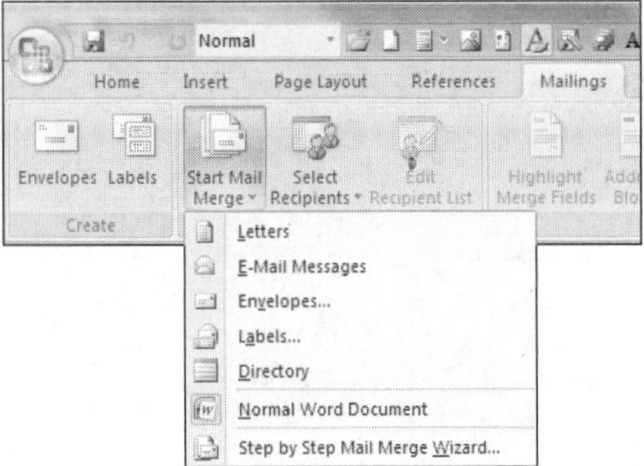

Contrast, for example, using an envelope (with a different address on each envelope) with using a sheet of labels (with a different address on each label). If you have only one address and want to print only one envelope or label, you don't need a data document. When you plan to crank out stacks of envelopes, each with a different address, or sheets of labels for which no two contain the same information, then you need the approach described in this chapter.

As shown in Figure 10-1, Word offers five flavors of the two basic types of data documents:

- **Letters** — Use this option for composing and designing mass mailings for which only the recipient information varies from page to page. Use this approach too when you're preparing sheets containing product or other item specifications with one piece of paper per product or item. You might use this approach, for example, not only when sending out a form letter or invoices, but also when producing a job manual wherein each page describes a different job title, and job information is stored in a database.
- **E-mail messages** — This is identical in concept to the form letter, except that it is geared to paperless online distribution. Contrast this with using multiple e-mail addresses in the To, Cc, or Bcc fields. Using E-mail *merge*, each recipient can receive a personalized e-mail. Using multiple addresses, each recipient receives the identical e-mail.
- **Envelopes** — This is also identical in concept to the form letter, except that the resulting document will be envelopes. As a result, when you choose this option, Word begins by displaying the Envelope Options dialog box.
- **Labels** — Use this option to print to one or more sheets of labels. This combines Word's capability to print to any of hundreds of different label formats with the capability to associate a database with a document, printing many addresses (data records) on the same page, rather than the same address on each label.
- **Directory** — This is similar in concept to labels, in that you print from multiple data records on a single page. Use the directory approach when printing a catalog or any other document that requires printing multiple records per page.

To choose the kind of document, choose Start Mail Merge in the Mailings tab, and click on the kind of document you want to create.

If you want step-by-step guidance through the process, note an additional option at the bottom of the Start Mail Merge list — Step by Step Mail Merge Wizard. Use this option if you're unfamiliar with the mail merge process. The Mail Merge Wizard process is described later in this chapter.

Restoring a Word document to normal

Sometimes, either by accident, temporary need, or whatever, a Word document becomes associated with a data file, and you want to restore a document to normal non-mail-merge status. To restore a Word document to normal, in the Mailings tab, choose Start Mail Merge ⇨ Normal Word Document. Note that when you restore a document to normal status, a number of tools on the Mailings toolbar that were formerly available are now grayed out as unavailable. If you later decide that you need to again make the document into a data document, you will need to reestablish the data connection.

TIP **If there's a chance that you'll later need to restore a data connection, and if document storage space isn't a concern, rather than break the data connection for a document, save a copy of the document, giving it a name that lets you know that it has a data connection, such as *Sales Letter Merge with Data Connection.* While establishing a data connection isn't all that difficult or time-consuming, you can usually save some time and guesswork by not having to reinvent that particular wheel.**

Attaching a Data Source

After you establish the type of data document for the merge, you need to attach a data source to it. In the Mailings tab, choose Select Recipients, as shown in Figure 10-2. If you choose Use Existing List, the Select Data Source dialog box appears so that you can navigate to and select a data source file. If you choose Type a New List, click Create, and then use the dialog box that appears to enter names and addresses.

FIGURE 10-2

A document isn't really a data document until you attach a data source to it using one of the Select Recipient options.

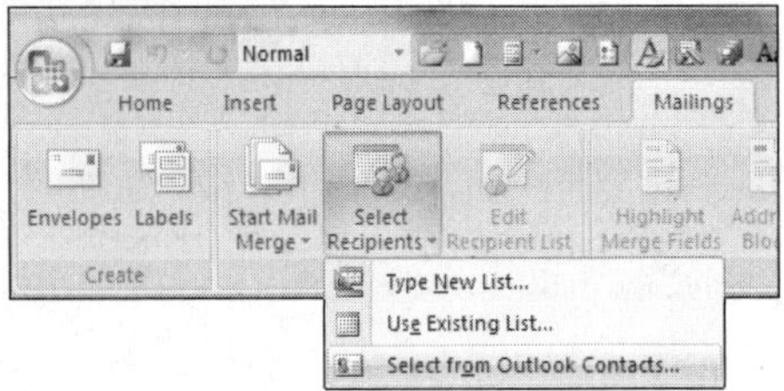

Note that once you've attached a data source to the document, Edit Recipient List and a number of other tools on the Mailings tab are no longer grayed out. If you plan to use the entire database, you can skip following section.

Selecting recipients

If you don't plan to use the entire database, you can use the Mail Merge Recipients dialog box, shown in Figure 10-3, to select just the recipients you want to use. To open the dialog box, click Edit Recipient list in the Start Mail Merge group of the Mailings tab. Use the check boxes shown to include or exclude records. To quickly deselect all records, clear or select the checkbox at the top of the list, just to the right of Data Source.

Editing data

Depending on your data source, you sometimes can edit it by clicking the database in the Mail Merge Recipients dialog box and then clicking Edit. When your data source is Outlook contacts, note that Edit is not an option. To change your Outlook data, you must use Outlook. Once you've made your change in Outlook, you can then refresh the records you see in the Mail Merge Recipients list by highlighting the data source and clicking Refresh.

FIGURE 10-3

Select just the target recipients using the Mail Merge Recipients dialog box.

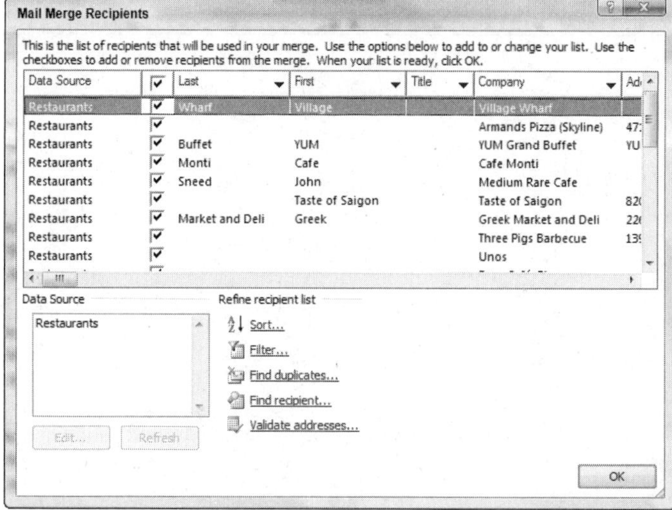

Sorting records

When editing non-Outlook data, you can sort using Word controls. Click the down arrow for a field name in the Mail Merge Recipients dialog box to drop down a list of sort options, shown in Figure 10-4. For example, if you want to filter out records for which company name is blank, click the Company drop-down arrow and choose Blanks. To select only records for which the e-mail address is *not* blank, click Nonblanks. To restore the list to show all records, choose the All option.

FIGURE 10-4

Quickly select records for which the current field is blank or nonblank by choosing Blanks or Nonblanks.

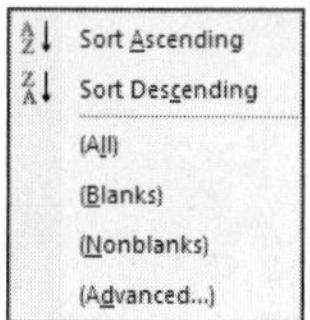

To sort by multiple fields at the same time, in the Mail Merge Recipients dialog box, choose Sort under Refine Recipient List. This displays the Filter and Sort dialog box, shown in Figure 10-5.

FIGURE 10-5

You can sort by up to three fields.

Use this dialog box to sort by multiple criteria. For example, if letters are being hand-delivered within a company, it might be useful to sort by floor and then by room number, assuming those are separate fields. (Often, sorting just by room number accomplishes both at the same time.)

Filtering records

Word also enables you to filter records to either include or exclude records with data fields matching specific criteria. To filter records, click Filter under Refine Recipient List. Here, you again get the Filter and Sort dialog box, but the Filter Records tab this time, as shown in Figure 10-6. Use the options shown to filter by specific values. As shown here, you can use it to include specific zip codes. While the dialog box initially shows just six filter fields, you are not limited to that many. It's not clear what the upper limit is, but you can specify at least 45 (that's the point at which I got bored trying to discover an upper limit).

FIGURE 10-6

You can specify multiple filter criteria.

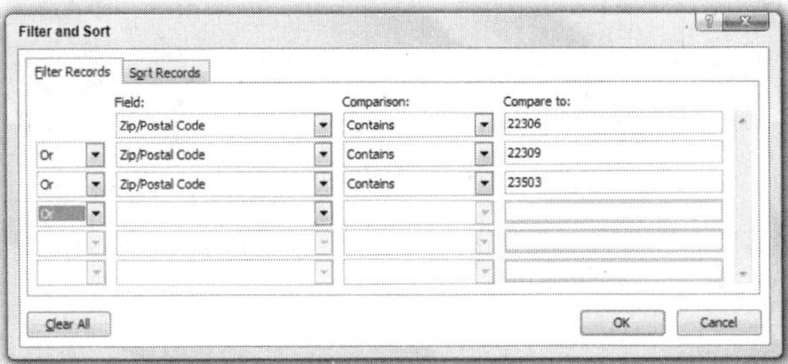

While the dialog box shown in Figure 10-6 shows just the Contains comparison, you can make a total of 10 comparisons (see Figure 10-7).

FIGURE 10-7

Include records based on 10 comparison operators.

Equal to
Not equal to
Less than
Greater than
Less than or equal
Greater than or equal
Is blank
Is not blank
Contains
Does not contain

TIP When filtering by ZIP code, if your database contains nine-digit ZIP codes, use the Contains filter rather than the Equal To filter. Using Equal To, you would need to specify all nine digits in the filter, and specifying as many as 9,999 different filters doesn't seem like a productive use of your time.

Understanding And and Or

When setting up filters, there are two kinds of comparisons you can make: *And* and *Or*. If all we had were one or the other, there would be no problem, but we have both, and we don't have parentheses to help clarify the comparisons.

It helps to understand that *And* and *Or* apply to each pair of rules. You also need to understand that the *And* rule is harder to satisfy, in that it requires that two conditions be met. Depending on what comes before or follows, each and/or effectively divides the list of filters into sets of filters that are being evaluated. However, by being careful with filters, you can avoid combinations that are impossibly difficult to understand.

Suppose the filters contained the comparisons shown in Table 10-1. The first *And* applies to the Alexandria and VA filters. The second *And* applies to the Hampton and VA filters. This set of filters requires that records must be in Alexandria, VA, *or* in Hampton, VA.

TABLE 10-1

Understanding Or and And Operators

Operator	Field	Comparison	Compare to
	City	Equal to	Alexandria
And	State	Equal to	VA
Or	City	Equal to	Hampton
And	State	Equal to	VA

Finally, understand that it's perfectly possible to set up filters that make no logical sense. Hence, Table 10-1 could have been set up with all of the Operators set to *And*. There would be no matching records, of course. It's up to you to examine the collection of resulting data records to make sure that your logic is being applied as you think it should be.

Duplicates

Databases often contain duplicate records. When mailing or e-mailing, especially, you want to avoid sending the same person duplicate messages. When sending invoices to large companies, this can cause problems, especially if they are received and processed by different people, resulting in double payment and further paperwork downstream.

To find duplicates, click the Find Duplicates link in the lower section of the Mail Merge Recipients dialog box. Word now displays the Find Duplicates dialog box, shown in Figure 10-8. If you identify duplicates, remove the checks next to them to exclude them from the data merge. Look carefully, however, because Word's criteria for what constitutes a duplicate might be different from your own.

FIGURE 10-8

Beware of Word's ability to find duplicates. Some "duplicates" aren't duplicates at all!

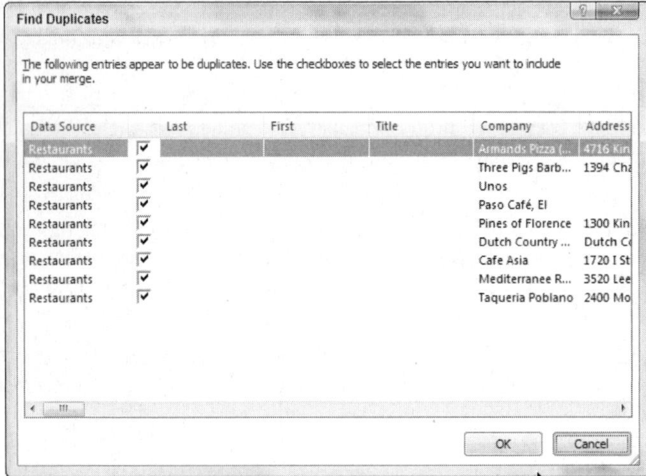

CAUTION **Caveat duplicates! In Figure 10-8, Word identified nine entries as duplicates, which they clearly aren't. Word uses First and Last name to identify duplicates. If your database contains only company names and no First and Last name fields (which isn't unexpected when all you have is the name of the establishment), you cannot use this feature to reliably identify duplicates.**

Find Recipient

If your database is especially large, using Find Recipient can be faster than pawing through the listings manually. Click the Find Recipient link in the lower portion of the Mail Merge Recipients dialog box to display the Find Entry dialog box shown in Figure 10-9. Alternatively, click the Find Recipient tool in the Preview Results section of the Mailings tab.

Type the search text in the Find field, choose All fields or a specific field, and then click Find Next. Note that the search is not case sensitive. If there are matches, Word highlights the first match in the Mail Merge Recipients dialog, and the Find Entry dialog box stays onscreen. Click Find Next to move to successive matches in the database.

Return to this tool later, after your data document has been constructed, to preview specific data records. It's better to iron out problems before committing your merge to paper or e-mail.

FIGURE 10-9

Use Find Entry to search for text in any or all data fields.

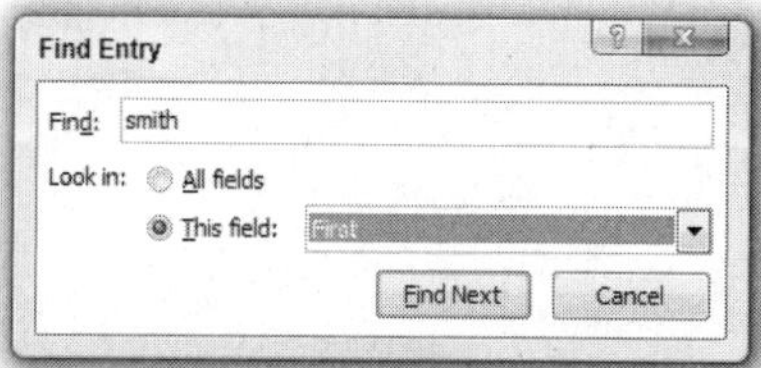

Validate Addresses

The Validate Addresses link works with third-party software, such as that provided with stamps.com and other electronic postage services. If you don't have such software installed, you'll see the message shown in Figure 10-10. These services vary, but basically they check against a huge database of valid street addresses to determine whether the selected address and zip code combination really exists. This can save considerably on costs, as it can prevent you from mailing to addresses that might actually be somewhere in the middle of a lake (if the street were extended to where an address logically would fall). Unless you are targeting fish, you might find having such a capability handy.

FIGURE 10-10

If you don't have address validation software installed, Word invalidates your attempt to run the Validate Address command.

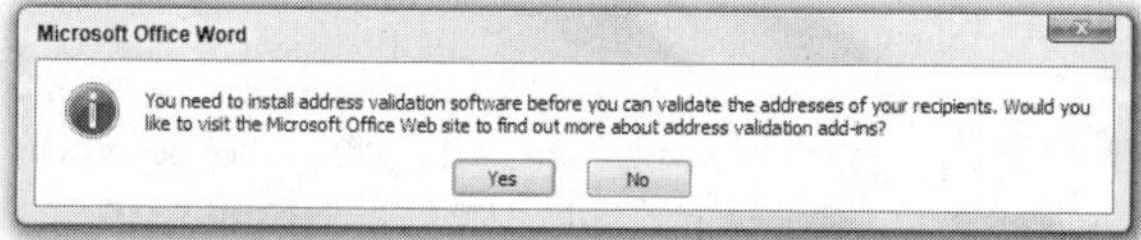

Assembling a Data Document

Regardless of which data document type you choose (letter, e-mail, envelopes, labels, or directory), the process is similar. There are some additional considerations for multi-record-per-page documents, however, so we will look at those separately after discussing the common elements.

When designing a letter or e-mail you plan to send to multiple recipients using the merge feature, it's often a good idea to draft the document as you want it to appear, using placeholders for information pertaining to the intended recipient, as shown in the following example:

Dear [name]:

We are writing to inform you that the warranty for:

[product]

which you purchased on:

[purchase date]

will expire on [expirationdate].

If you would like to extend your warranty, you must take advantage of our extended warranty coverage plans before [expirationdate]. Costs for extending the warranty are:

1 Year: [oneyearwarranty]

2 Years: [twoyearwarranty]

3 Years: [threeyearwarranty]

Please use the enclosed card and envelope to extend your warranty before it's too late!

Yours truly,

[salesagent]

When you're done, edit your document and substitute *merge fields* for the placeholders.

Merge fields

After setting the data document type (using Start Mail Merge), associating a database with it (using Select Recipients), narrowing the list of recipients or records just to those records you plan to use, and drafting the data document, the next step is to insert *merge fields* into your document where you want the corresponding data fields to appear.

NOTE **Merge fields are special Word fields that correspond to the data fields in your database. For example, if you have a data field called Company, then you would insert the company name into your data document by using a MergeField field code with the name Company in it: { MERGEFIELD Company }. In your data document, that field displays either as «Company» or as the name of the company associated with the current record in the data set. Use the ribbon's Preview Results button to toggle between the merge field name and actual data.**

To insert a merge field, position the insertion point where you want the field to appear (or select the placeholder if you're replacing a placeholder with a merge field). In the Mailings tab on the Ribbon, choose Insert Merge Field in the Write & Insert Fields group, as shown in Figure 10-11. Click on the field you want to insert. Using a combination of text, punctuation, and merge fields that you insert, complete the assembly and wording of your document. Note that in addition to individual merge fields that you can insert using the Insert Merge Field tool, you can use special sets of merge fields to save time: Address Block and Greeting Line.

FIGURE 10-11

Merge fields are data tokens that you use where you want actual data fields to appear in the data document.

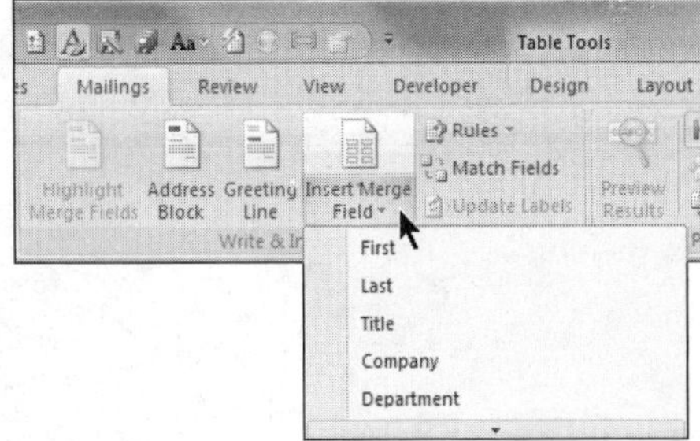

Address Block

The address block contains a number of elements that you can select from the Insert Address Block dialog box. To determine the contents of the address block, click Address Block in the Mailings ribbon, as shown in Figure 10-12.

FIGURE 10-12

Use the Address Block tool to launch the Insert Address Block dialog box.

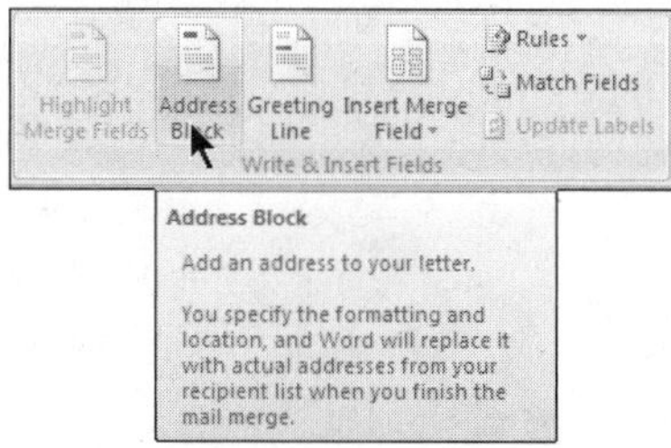

When you click Address Block, the Insert Address Block dialog box, shown in Figure 10-13, appears. Notice that it contains three sections for selecting, previewing, and correcting your address block information (if there are problems). Make your selections as indicated, and then click OK.

FIGURE 10-13

Use the Insert Address Block dialog box to choose the address block elements for the current data document.

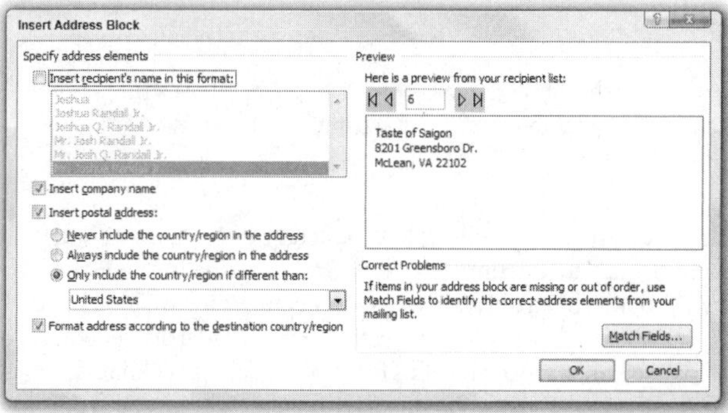

- **Specify address elements** — Use this section to tell Word how to define the address block. You can include the recipient's name (in a variety of formats), the company name, the postal address, as well as the country or region. If desired, you can suppress the country or region, always include it, or include it only if it's different from the country selected. You can also tell Word to format the address according to the destination country or region.
- **Preview** — Use the First, Previous, Next, and Last buttons to preview different addresses as they will appear with the selected options. It's a good idea to preview a good sampling in case some

parts of the address are treated differently from how you expect, or if there are problems with missing data that will leave "holes" in the address block.

- **Correct Problems** — If the preview isn't what you expect, click Match Fields to change the different data elements with which each of the fields listed is associated, as shown in Figure 10-14.

FIGURE 10-14

Use the Match Fields dialog box to associate each of the listed items with data fields from your database for the Address Block.

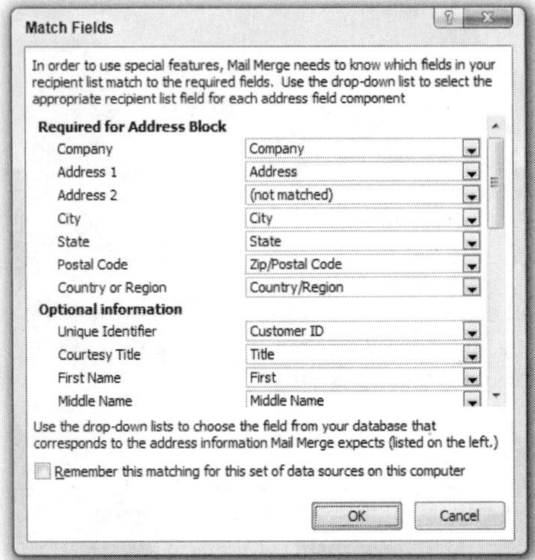

If you plan to reuse the address block data either for the same database or for other databases that contain the same field names, click to enable the "Remember this matching . . ." setting.

Greeting Line

The Greeting Line merge field, like the Address Block field, is a collection of different data elements and plain text designed to save you entry time when composing data documents. Click Greeting Line in the Write & Insert Fields section of the Mailings tab of the Ribbon. This displays the Insert Greeting Line dialog box shown in Figure 10-15. Proper operation of a number of aspects of the greeting line merge field depends upon your having several potentially obscure data elements available and filled out, such as nickname, spouse's nickname, and the color of their children's socks. Unless you or someone with whom you work is obsessively compulsive about data entry, you're not likely to find some aspects of this terribly useful.

Use the Preview buttons to test your selected greeting line options against your actual data. If something doesn't look quite right, click Match Fields and use the controls shown in Figure 10-16 to associate the Greeting Line components with the correct merge data fields.

FIGURE 10-15

Set and preview greeting line components.

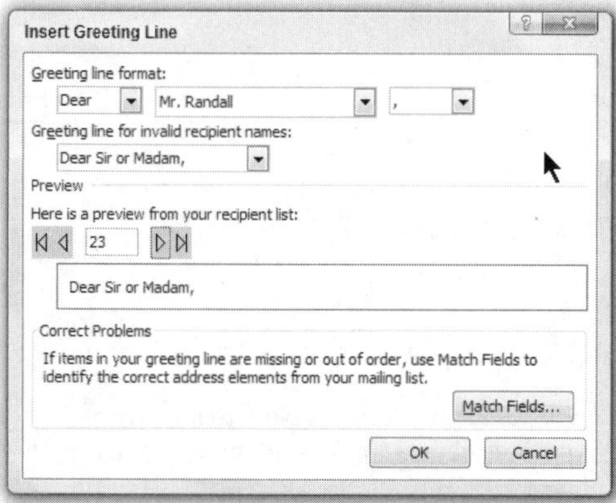

FIGURE 10-16

Use the Match Fields dialog box to associate Greeting Line merge field components with data elements from your database.

Rules

In assembling a data document, you sometimes need to control or modify how data and records are processed. Word provides nine commands to help you do that, as shown in Figure 10-17. The entries shown in the Rules drop-down menu (click Rules in the Write & Insert Fields group of the Mailings tab) show how those rule keywords are displayed in the data document.

FIGURE 10-17

Use the Rules drop-down list of Word fields to control how data is merged with the data document.

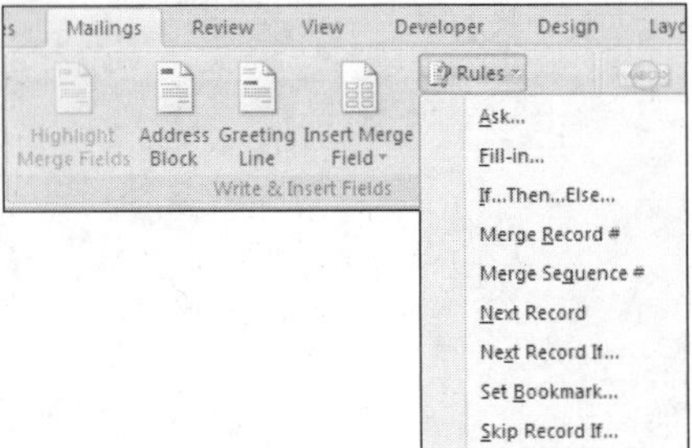

These rules are tied to specific Word field codes, and are explained in Table 10-2. Note that many of these are supported by dialog boxes that guide you through proper syntax, making them easy to use and understand.

TABLE 10-2

Merge Rules

Field	Usage/Purpose
Ask	This field prompts you to provide information and assigns a bookmark to the answer you provide; the information is stored internally. A reference to the bookmark can then be used in the mail merge document to reproduce the information you type. A default response to the prompt can also be included in the field. The Ask field displays as an empty bookmark in the mail merge document. You might use this field in conjunction with an IF field to prompt for missing information during a merge.
Fill-in	This field prompts you to enter text, and then uses your response in place of the field in the mail merge document. This is similar to the Ask field, except that the information can be used only in one place.
If...Then...Else...	This is used in mail merge documents to control the flow and to create a conditional statement that controls whether specific mail merge fields are printed or included in the merged document.
Merge Record #	When doing a mail merge, the Merge Record # field serves as a counter of records in the data file and doesn't count the number of documents actually printed. This field is incremented by the presence of Next Record and Next Record If fields. If you skip records using Skip Record If, Merge Record # is incremented nonetheless.
Merge Sequence #	This field provides a counter of mail merge documents that actually result from a merge. If you merge the entire database and do not change the base sorting, and if no records are skipped, then Merge Sequence # and Merge Record # will be identical.
Next Record	The Next Record field is used to include more than one record in a given document. Ordinarily, when doing a mail merge, one document is printed for each record. With the Next Record field, however, you can include multiple records in a single document. This can be useful when you need to refer to several addresses from a data file. When doing a label merge, the Next Record field is provided automatically, and appears as « Next Record ».

Field	Usage/Purpose
Next Record If	The Next Record If statement works like the Next field except that it advances to the next record only if an expression being evaluated is true. A typical use is to skip a given record if a particular key field is blank. For example, in an e-mail merge, if you haven't otherwise excluded records with blank e-mail addresses, you can use Next Record If to do it.
Set Bookmark	The Set Bookmark field is used to change the text referred to by a bookmark. Set Bookmark often is used in conjunction with If...Then...Else... to conditionally change how particular text is defined based on external factors, such as the current date, or internal factors, such as the value(s) of particular fields.
Skip Record If	The Skip Record If field is used to cancel processing of the current database record during a mail merge. For example, you might use it to screen out a particular zip code.

Match Fields

The Match Fields button in the Write & Insert Fields group of the Mailings tab on the Ribbon displays the Match Field dialog box shown in Figure 10-18. If the dialog box and fields look familiar, it's no accident. The "special features" notation referred to at the top of the Match Fields dialog box refers to the Address Block and Greeting Line. If you've already visited the Match Fields dialog boxes in those respective dialogs, you can forego the pleasure of another visit. In addition, if you aren't using Address Block and Greeting Line fields, you can safely ignore this tool.

FIGURE 10-18

When launched from the Mailings tab, the Match Fields dialog box is a marriage of the Match Field dialogs available from within the Insert Address Block and Insert Greeting Line dialog boxes.

Preview Results

At any time as you go along, if you want to see what actual data will look like in your document, click the Preview Results button in the Preview Results group of the Mailings tab to toggle between a data token (merge field name) and actual data, shown in Figure 10-19. Note that because the merge fields actually are field codes, they can also be displayed in a third way, also shown in Figure 10-19.

FIGURE 10-19

Data merge fields can be displayed in three different ways in your document.

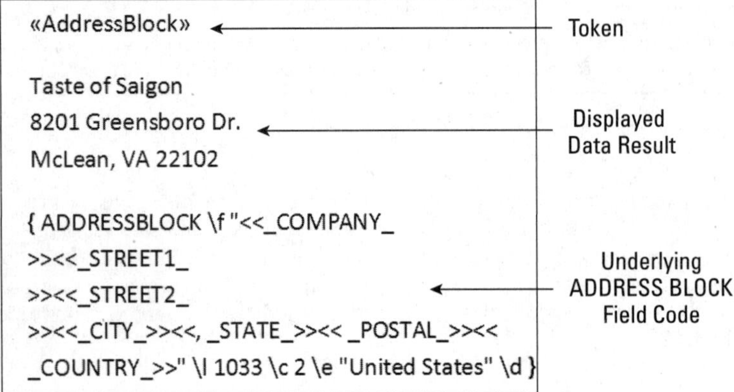

In the Preview Results section of the Mailings tab, shown in Figure 10-20, you can use the First Record, Previous Record, Next Record, Last Record, and Go To Record tools to display any data record.

FIGURE 10-20

Use the Preview Results tools to ensure that the merge will produce the results you want.

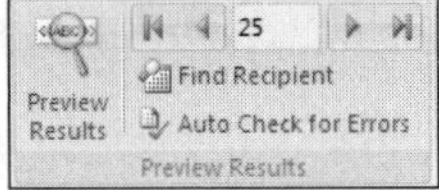

Find Recipient

To search for a specific data record or for records whose data you want to preview, click the Find Recipient button in the Preview Results group. This displays the Find Entry dialog box shown earlier in Figure 10-9. Refer to the discussion earlier in this chapter.

Update Labels

When the data document type is Labels, there are two ways to proceed. The easy way is to carefully edit just the first label cell by inserting whatever merge fields you need. When you're finished, click Update Labels in the Write & Insert Fields group of the Mailings tab. Word copies all text, merge fields, and formatting from the first cell into each of the other cells, after the Next Record control. The result is that each sheet of labels will contain data from the same number of label cells. A sheet containing nine labels will use data from nine database records.

The hard way to do labels is to ignore the existence of the Update Labels tool and to carefully edit each of the table cells, inserting the merge fields you want to use. Note that Word automatically provides the NEXT (Next Record) field in each of the table cells, as shown in Figure 10-21. If you manually populate the cells, additional merge fields should be inserted *after* the Next Record control. If you insert merge fields before the Next Record control, data from the same record used for the first cell will be used.

FIGURE 10-21

When you insert a merge field into the first label cell, Word automatically puts the Next Record control into each of the other cells.

«AddressBlock»	«Next Record»	«Next Record»
«Next Record»	«Next Record»	«Next Record»

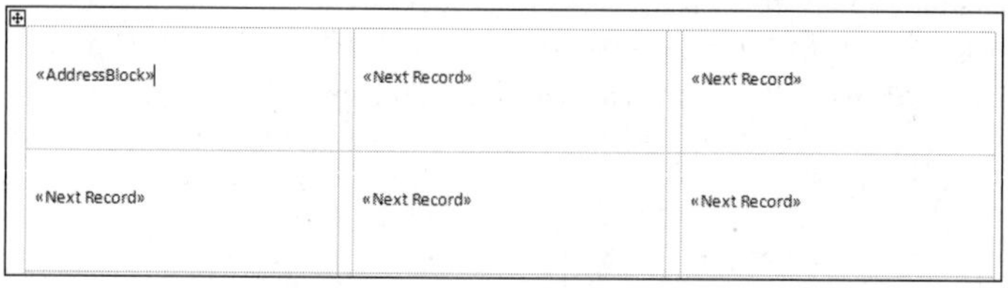

Why would you choose to do it the hard way? You might do it that way if you need to do something else in each data field that can't be accomplished by Word automatically copying the first table cell to each of the other label cells. What might that be? Who knows? After all, they're *your* labels!

Highlight Merge Fields

Use the Highlight Merge Fields button in the Write & Insert Fields group of the Mailings tab to highlight all of the merge fields in your data. This can be useful if you're working on a complex document and need to recheck the logic and placement of merge fields. This is especially true if you've turned on Preview Results and are looking at actual data results, rather than the merge fields themselves.

If, for example, you expect a given merge field result to appear in two places in the document, this tool enables you to find those locations more easily so you can verify that the correct text appears. If you're using conditional rules, such as Skip Record If, Next Record If, and If, this also helps you focus on the results so you can verify that the rules are working as expected.

Auto Check for Errors

To avoid wasting paper and other resources, when you think you're done, click Auto Check for Errors in the Preview Results group on the Mailings tab to display the options shown in Figure 10-22.

FIGURE 10-22

Rather than waste paper or send out errant e-mails, use the error checking tool to avoid logical errors or other unwanted surprises.

Options are as follows:

- **Simulate the Merge and Report Errors in a New Document** — Use this option to examine any and all errors in a new document.
- **Complete the Merge, Pausing To Report Each Error As It Occurs** — Use this option once you've determined that there are errors, so you can observe the error in action.
- **Complete the Merge Without Pausing. Report Errors in a New Document** — Use this option to go ahead and complete the merge without stopping at each error, sending the error report to a new document.

Finishing the merge

Once the data document is ready and has been thoroughly debugged and certified as error free, it's time to go through the final motions. The Finish & Merge button in the Finish group on the Mailings tab provides three options, shown in Figure 10-23, *regardless of the type of data document chosen*. Think twice before accidentally clicking Send E-mail Messages if the document is a set of labels or a directory!

FIGURE 10-23

It's usually a good idea *not* to send a merge directly to a printer until the results have been thoroughly examined.

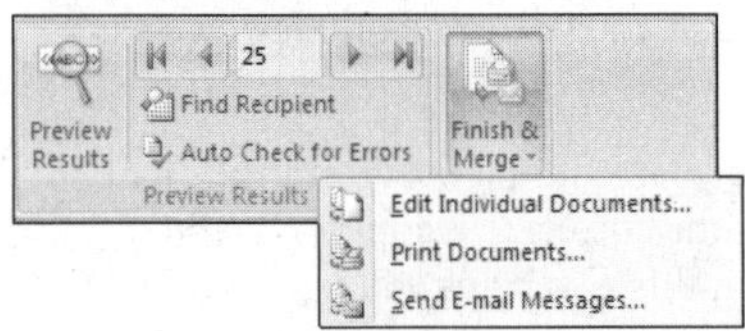

Edit Individual Documents

Use the Edit Individual Documents choice if you want to save your merged results for future use. For example, suppose you have a set of labels that seldom changes and which you need to print out every week. Rather than go through the mail merge exercise each week, save a copy of the labels and then print them each time you need them. That way, you don't need to go through the whole mail merge routine unless the underlying database has changed.

You might also choose this option if you don't trust other ways of proofing the results. Instead of printing from the Mailings ribbon controls, send the results to a new document where you can examine each of them, and then print when you're ready.

When you choose this option, Word displays the Merge to New Document dialog box shown in Figure 10-24. If you want Word to create a limited number of output documents, choose either Current Record or indicate a From/To range. Click OK to commit those electrons to a Word window that displays your results.

FIGURE 10-24

Even if you're sure you're ready, Word wants to make sure you're sure.

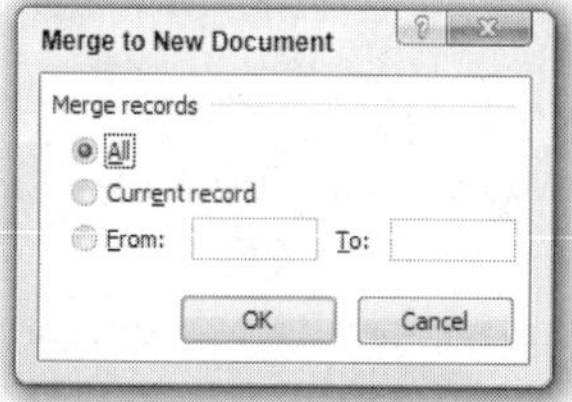

NOTE If you choose this option for an e-mail merge, the resulting document(s) will not be useful except for proofing the e-mails. To actually send the e-mails, you have to choose the Send E-mail Messages option.

Print Documents

Choose the Print Documents option when you're certain that the merge will give you the results you want, and your boss is at the door asking "Where are those letters?" When you click Print Documents, Word displays the dialog box shown earlier in Figure 10-24, this time sporting a Merge to Printer title bar. The same options prevail. Choose wisely and click OK to immediately . . . launch yet another dialog box, the Print dialog box. Make any additional choices and decisions, including which printer to use, cross your fingers, and click OK.

TIP If you don't trust all of the previews and error checks at this stage, you've probably been burned by mail merge in the past. If you still want to be sure before wasting a tree, use the Name drop-down list to see whether you have an option that produces electronic images of printed pages, rather than actual printed pages. If you have Adobe Acrobat, Microsoft Office Document Image Writer, SnagIt, or a host of other options, choose one of those. Then you can review what actually amounts to your best possible print preview.

Send E-mail Messages

Choose the Send E-Mail Messages option if you're working on an e-mail merge. When you click Send E-mail Messages, Word displays the Merge to E-mail dialog box, shown in Figure 10-25.

FIGURE 10-25

Make sure you fill out the Subject Line field!

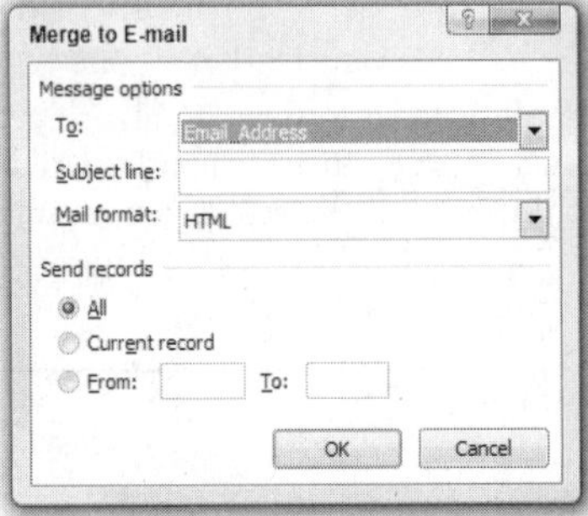

In addition to the Send Records options (All, Current Record, and From/To), Word provides three additional options:

- **To:** — If the proposed e-mail address data field is not correct, use the drop-down arrow to replace it with the correct address field.
- **Subject line** — This is very important. Studies show that 73.4% of all non-spam e-mail merges sent omit the subject line.[1] Don't become a statistic! Replace that blank Subject line.
- **Mail format** — Many e-mail recipients wisely have their e-mail options set up to read all e-mail as plain text (this gives them a shot at preventing any automatic naughtiness from being executed when e-mail is opened). Options provided are Attachment, Plain Text, and HTML, the latter being the default. While Attachment seems like a good compromise for formatted e-mail, this option provides no way for you to include any message text for the body of the e-mail. When and if you use that option, make sure the Subject line isn't blank.

Mail Merge Task Pane/Wizard

YAHOO stands for *you always have other options*. YAHOO applies here, as well. Your other option is to use the Mail Merge Wizard, rather than the individual tools in the Mailings tab of the Ribbon. If you need a little more hand-holding when doing a mail merge, Word has the hand ready and waiting, in the form of the Mail Merge Wizard. To travel this particular yellow brick road, start a new blank document (or open a document you want to use as the basis for a data document). In the Start Mail Merge group of the Mailings tab on the Ribbon, click the Start Mail Merge button and choose Step by Step Mail Merge Wizard. This opens the Mail Merge task pane, shown in Figure 10-26.

[1] This statistic was made up by the author. Nonetheless, don't send subjectless e-mails!

FIGURE 10-26

Choosing the Mail Merge Wizard opens the Mail Merge task pane.

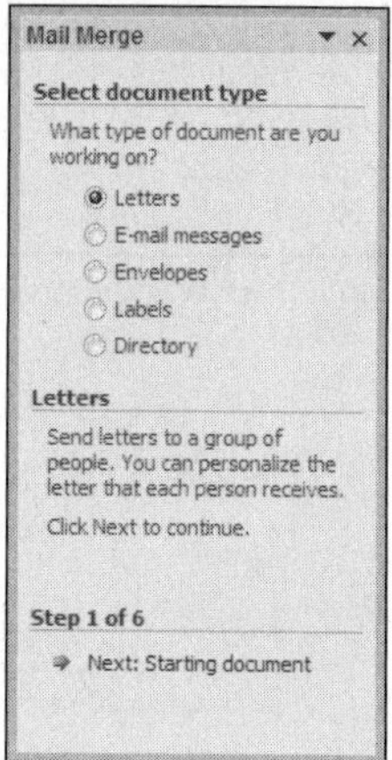

Step 1: Document Type

In Step 1, shown in Figure 10-26, choose the type of data document you want to create. Later, if you need to restore this to a normal document, in the Start Mail Merge group of the Mailings tab, choose Start Mail Merge ⇨ Normal Word Document. In the Mail Merge task pane, click Next: Starting Documents.

Step 2: Starting Document

In Starting Document, Word provides three options. Note that when you choose any of these options, Word explains the option in the lower part of the task pane. The options are as follows:

- **Use the Current Document** — Start from the current document and use the Mail Merge Wizard to add recipient information (merge fields).
- **Start from a Template** — Start from a template, which you can customize as needed by adding merge fields and/or other contents. If you choose this option, click Select Template to be shown a list of all of the available templates (at least the ones that Word knows about). Note that despite the option's wording, it does *not* present you with a list of "ready-to-use mail merge" templates.
- **Start from Existing Document** — Open an existing mail merge or other document and change it to fit the current need by changing the contents or recipients. Recent mail merge documents, if any, will be listed. If the one you want isn't listed, click Open to navigate to the one you want, select it, and then click Open.

After homing in on the starting document, click Next: Select Recipients at the bottom of the task pane.

Step 3: Select Recipients

In Step 3, select from Use an Existing List, Select from Outlook Contacts, and Type a New List. If you select Use an Existing List, you will need to select a file that holds the recipients in the dialog box that appears. If you choose Type a New List, click Create, and then use the dialog box that appears to enter names and addresses. These options appear in Figure 10-27.

FIGURE 10-27

Choose whether to use the existing document or a new document, and then choose the data source (list of recipients).

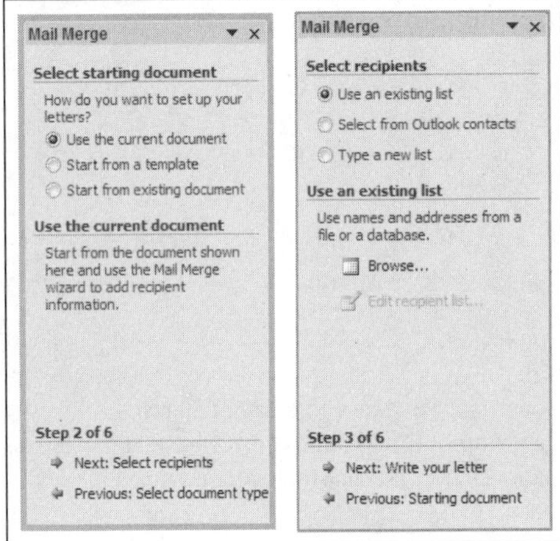

After selecting the data source and the data, it is ready. Click Next: Write Your Letter at the bottom .

Step 4: Write Your Letter

In Step 4, shown in Figure 10-28, you are greeted with four options:

- **Address block** — This leads to the dialog box shown in Figure 10-13. See the discussion under "Address Block" for additional details.
- **Greeting line** — The Greeting line option displays the dialog box shown in Figure 10-15. See the "Greeting Line" heading for more information.
- **Electronic postage** — As indicated previously, the functioning of this option requires the installation of third-party software that enables you to apply postage to items you send.
- **More items** — This option displays the dialog box shown in Figure 10-28. It is a shame that this thoroughly confusing dialog box appears as part of the Mail Merge Wizard. If you choose Address Fields, the dialog box shows you a list of all of the fields in its vocabulary, many or most of which are probably irrelevant to the attached database. Choose Database Fields instead to see a list of what's actually available for use in this merge.

TIP In theory, you move the insertion point to where you want a merge field to appear, click More items, select the field, and click Insert. Dismiss the dialog box and repeat this series of actions for each merge field. In practice however, if you know which fields you want to insert, go ahead and insert them all at once, and then cut and paste them where you want them to go.

Use a combination of text and merge fields to write the data document, inserting merge fields where you want database fields to appear. When you're done, click Step 5: Preview Your Letter at the bottom of the Mail Merge task pane.

FIGURE 10-28

Ignore the Address Fields option. The associated database fields are listed when you choose Database Fields.

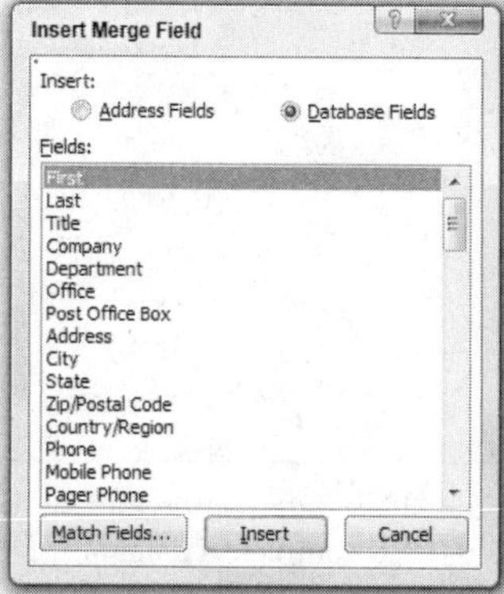

Step 5: Preview Your Letter

In Step 5, shown in Figure 10-29, use the controls shown to move from record to record in your database. Note that the << and >> tools correspond to the Previous and Next button in the Preview Results group in the Mailings tab. There's no reason you can't use the far more flexible and useful tools in the ribbon.

Notice that the Find a Recipient and Edit Recipient list perform identical actions, respectively, as the Find Recipient and Edit Recipient List ribbon tools discussed earlier in this chapter. About the only useful tool in this set is the Exclude This Recipient button, which is the equivalent of choosing Edit Recipient List from the Ribbon and removing the check next to the currently selected record.

Step 6: Complete the Merge

The contents of the Step 6 panel vary depending on the document type. As shown in Figure 10-29, when the document type is a letter, the options are to send the merged results to the printer or to send them to "individual letters." Actually, that's not at all what the option does. Instead, it sends all of the merged letter results to a single new document, in which the individual letters are separated by section breaks.

FIGURE 10-29

Use Steps 5 and 6 to preview the data document and complete the merge.

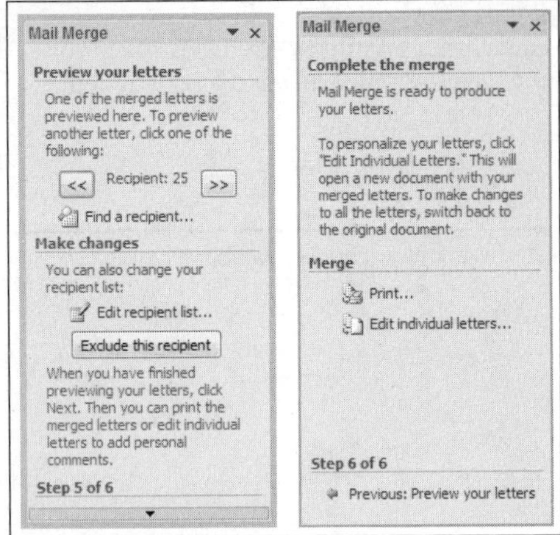

Summary

In this chapter, you've learned how to use each of the mail merge tools in the Mailings tab of the Ribbon to begin a mail merge, attach a database to a data document, insert merge fields, and complete a data merge. You've also seen that this feature isn't just for mail merge, but has many other uses as well. You should now be able to do the following:

- Attach a data source to a Word document and select just the records you want
- Within limits, use Word tools to discover duplicate data records
- Insert composite merge fields, such as the Address Block and Greeting Line, as well as control how those fields are constituted
- Use the Mail Merge Wizard

Chapter 11

Document Security

Not too terribly long ago, about the only way you could protect a Word document was to password-protect it using a password technology that was decidedly easy to crack. Password-cracking solutions abounded and were available free or practically free. Word has come a long way since then and now offers a variety of different kinds of protection that are a lot better than what was available for Word 97 and earlier, although nothing is 100% secure.

Not only does improved technology make protection stronger, but the variety of types of protection has expanded as well. This chapter looks at the types of document protection available to Word users and describes how to use them.

IN THIS CHAPTER

Protection Types

One of the unfortunate things about a piece of software as complicated as Word 2007 is that privacy settings aren't centrally located. This makes discovering the full range of what's available a bit difficult. To save you the trouble of searching all over to find what you can control, here's the definitive list of the different types of protection (and pseudo-protection) Word 2007 offers and where to find them (more details about the settings will follow later in the chapter):

- **Permission** — Restrict a document so it can be opened and/or changed only by specific individuals. Select Review tab ➪ Protect ➪ Protect Document ➪ Restricted Access. You then need to specify whether to restrict formatting or editing (or both), click Yes, Start Enforcing Protection, and then create a password when prompted.
- **Digital signature** — Sign a document with a digital signature to provide assurance that you are the source of the document. Select Office Button ➪ Prepare ➪ Add a Digital Signature.

- **Inspect Document** — Inspect the document to see if it contains private or sensitive information or data. Select Office Button ➪ Prepare ➪ Inspect Document.
- **Mark as Final** — Mark a document as final to let recipients know that the document is considered the final revision. This setting makes the document read-only and makes it unavailable for additional typing, editing, proofing, or tracking changes. Note that this setting is advisory only. Recipients with Word 2007 can remove the Mark as Final setting. Recipients with earlier versions of Word who have installed the Office 2007 Compatibility Pack won't even see the file as read-only. Hence, this kind of gentle protection would have to be combined with something more substantial to be meaningful. Select Office Button ➪ Prepare ➪ Mark as Final.
- **Style formatting restrictions** — Limit formatting to a selection of styles, as well as block Theme, Scheme, or Quick Style Set switching. Protection here is by password, and is therefore less secure and robust than when using permissions. Select Review tab ➪ Protect Document ➪ Limit Formatting to a Selection of Styles.
- **Editing restrictions-No Changes (Read Only)** — This offers password protection, which is not very secure, along with exceptions of specific areas of the document. Exceptions can be made wholesale, or you can limit them to individuals with specific .NET Passport–associated e-mail addresses. Select Review tab ➪ Protect Document ➪ Allow Only This Type of Editing in the Document ➪ No Changes (Read Only).
- **Editing restrictions-Tracked Changes** — This type of protection allows only tracked changes to be made. Select Review tab ➪ Protect Document ➪ Allow Only This Type of Editing in the Document ➪ Tracked Changes.
- **Editing restrictions-Filling In Forms** — This type of protection allows filling in of form fields and content controls. Select Review tab ➪ Protect Document ➪ Allow Only This Type of Editing in the Document ➪ Filling In Forms.
- **Editing restrictions-Comments** — This type of protection allows only comments. Exceptions can be made for selected areas of the document, for everyone, or for specific individuals (using .NET Passport–associated e-mail addresses). Select Review tab ➪ Protect Document ➪ Allow Only This Type of Editing in the Document ➪ Comments.
- **Password to open/modify** — This type of protection lets you specify a password to open and/or modify the document. This protection is not the same as the Editing restrictions' No Changes setting. You must choose one or the other. Select Office Button ➪ Save As. In the Save As dialog box, select Tools ➪ General Options.

The rest of this section looks at each of these, showing how you enable protection and assessing the degree of protection provided.

Restricting permission (Information Rights Management)

A relatively new and strong way to protect your documents uses an Information Rights Management server to authenticate users who create or receive documents or e-mail that have restricted permissions. As noted in Figure 11-1, some enterprises have their own rights management servers. To use Information Rights Management with Word 2007, you have to have the Windows Rights Management client software installed. It should be installed automatically if you're using Word with Windows Vista, but you do need to install the client when using Windows XP. Word will prompt you to download and install this software if you open a document that's protected with Information Rights Management.

If you don't have access to one, you can use Microsoft's free trial Information Rights Management service.

FIGURE 11-1

If you don't already have access to an Information Rights Management service, you can sign up to use a free trial service.

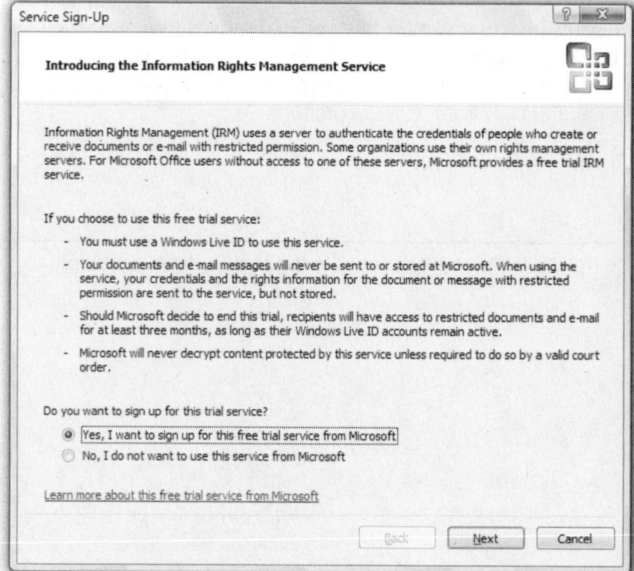

To use this service, you and all users with whom you share rights-managed documents or e-mail must have .NET Passport–registered e-mail addresses. (These are also called Windows Live IDs.) The biggest risk is that Microsoft might at some point end the free trial service. You'll then have three months in which to move to a different rights management server, subscribe to whatever service Microsoft offers (assuming they replace the free trial service with a for-pay service), or remove rights management protection from your documents so you don't lose access to them.

To restrict permission by using Information Rights Management, choose Office Button ➪ Prepare ➪ Restrict Permission ➪ Restricted Access. If you do not have Rights Management software installed on your computer, the dialog box shown in Figure 11-1 appears. If you choose to proceed, a five-step wizard walks you through the process of setting up rights management and associating your .NET Passport account or Windows Live ID.

CAUTION **You may not see the Office Button ➪ Prepare ➪ Restrict Permission command and its subcommands in your Word 2007 installation. If that happens, ask a colleague to send you a document protected with IRM. When you try to open the document, you'll be prompted to set up your system to use IRM.**

If you are not logged on to the rights management server account you want to use, or if you need to specify, add, or remove a user account, choose Office Button ➪ Prepare ➪ Restrict Permission ➪ Manage Credentials, which displays the Select User dialog box, shown in Figure 11-2. If you need to add a .NET Passport or Windows Live ID, click Add. To remove an account, select the one you want to remove and then click Remove. Select the account you want to use (if desired, enable Always Use This Account), and then click OK.

Signing Up for Your Information Rights Management Free Trial

In the Service Sign-Up dialog box, choose "Yes, I want to sign up for this free trial service from Microsoft" and click Next. In the Welcome to the Windows RM Account Certification Wizard, specify whether you have a .NET Passport or need to sign up for one, and then follow the wizard steps that appear to complete the trial sign up and download an RM (rights management) certificate to your computer

FIGURE 11-2

While most rights management users have only one rights management account, it is possible to have multiple accounts.

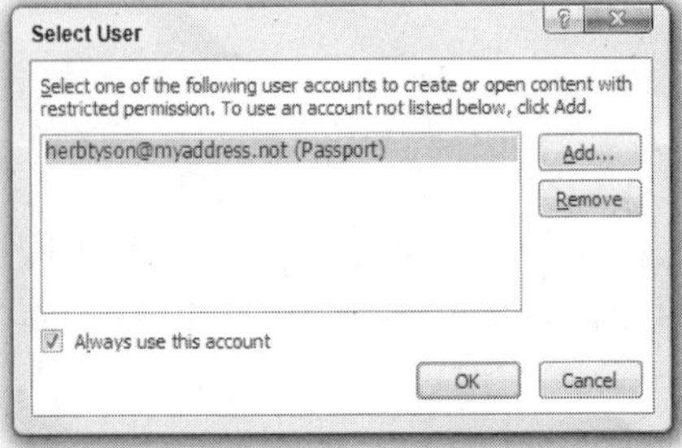

If credentials are already associated, and/or when you click OK in the dialog box shown in Figure 11-2, Word displays the Permission dialog box shown in Figure 11-3. Type the e-mail addresses of people with permission to read and change the document in the boxes provided. E-mail addresses should be separated with semicolons. Note that the Read and Change boxes use your Outlook e-mail address cache as a source of potential e-mail addresses to enter. When you type the first character of an address, cached addresses beginning with that character are listed.

To see more options, click More Options, not surprisingly, which displays the different Permission dialog box shown in Figure 11-4. Note that you can set an expiration date for permissions you grant. In addition, recipients of the document will not be able to print, copy, or access document content programmatically (for example, use a program to extract XML data) unless the corresponding options are checked. For additional protection, if you don't want to receive requests for additional permission, remove the check next to Users Can Request Additional Permissions From. Once you've selected permissions, click Set Defaults to make the selected permissions the default for future documents on which you restrict permissions.

Click Require a Connection To Verify A User's Permission to require that individuals to whom you are granting permissions be connected to the rights management server, either over the Internet or over the respective intranet. Note that if you have not installed the Windows RMS client for Rights Management Services, this option will be grayed out as unavailable.

FIGURE 11-3

You can use rights management to limit who can read and change a document.

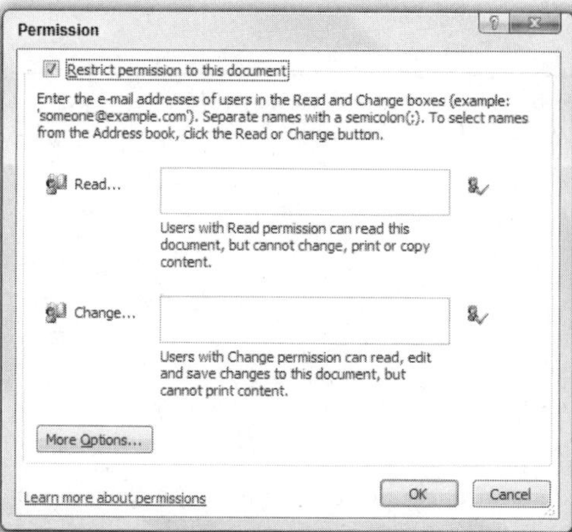

FIGURE 11-4

You can set an expiration date as well as restrict permission to copy or print a document.

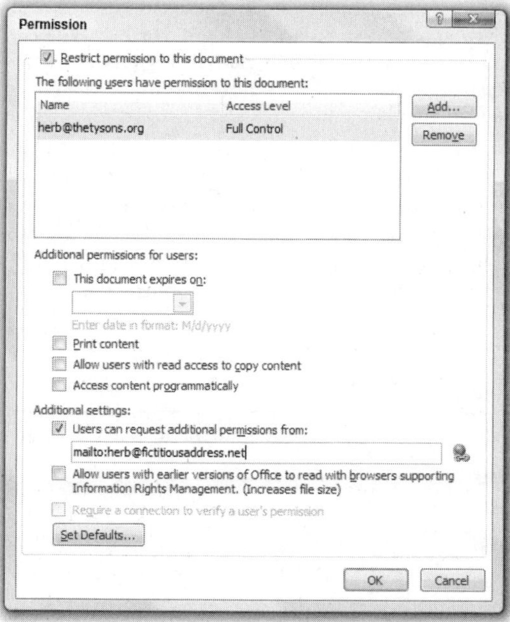

When you click OK in either of the dialog boxes shown in Figure 11-3 or Figure 11-4, Word adds the Do Not Distribute bar at the top of the document window. Clicking Change Permissions redisplays the dialog box shown in Figure 11-5.

FIGURE 11-5

The Do Not Distribute message bar is not affected by the Message Bar setting in the Trust Center.

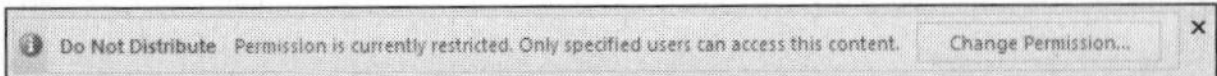

Removing access restrictions

When and if there is no longer a need to restrict access to a document, choose Office Button ➪ Prepare ➪ Restrict Permission ➪ Unrestricted Access. Click Yes to the prompt that asks if you're sure you want to remove permission. Note that you're not removing permission. Rather, you're removing permission restrictions.

Digital signatures

A *digital signature* is an electronic certificate that provides a way for recipients to verify that a document or e-mail actually came from the sender. Can these certificates really provide such verification? That's an article of faith, perhaps — an appropriate enough concept for a Bible, one supposes. Use and trust digital signatures according to your own personal beliefs. You assume any and all risks.

NOTE **Personally, I don't trust digital signatures. They seem like a gimmick to get potentially billions of Internet users to fork over a few dollars a year for something that, at present, provides no assurance at all (to skeptics, at any rate). When I receive e-mail containing a digital signature, warning bells immediately go off because nobody with whom I exchange e-mail actually uses digital signatures. Hence, the only e-mails I ever get that have digital signatures have been part of some scam to try to convince me to share various account numbers. The bottom line? If you receive something important and the validity of the signature is an issue, then you are going to pick up the telephone and call the sender to verify the contents. You aren't going to take a digital signature at face value, and neither am I.**

How to digitally sign a Word document

To digitally sign a Word document, choose Office Button ➪ Prepare ➪ Add a Digital Signature. If this is the first time you've used this feature, or if you didn't previously choose "Don't show this message again," Word displays the dialog box shown in Figure 11-6. If you already have a digital signing certificate, click Yes. Otherwise, you can dismiss the dialog box (if you've changed your mind) or click Signature Services from the Office Marketplace.

FIGURE 11-6

If you don't already have a digital signing certificate, click Signature Services from the Office Marketplace to learn about for-fee and free services.

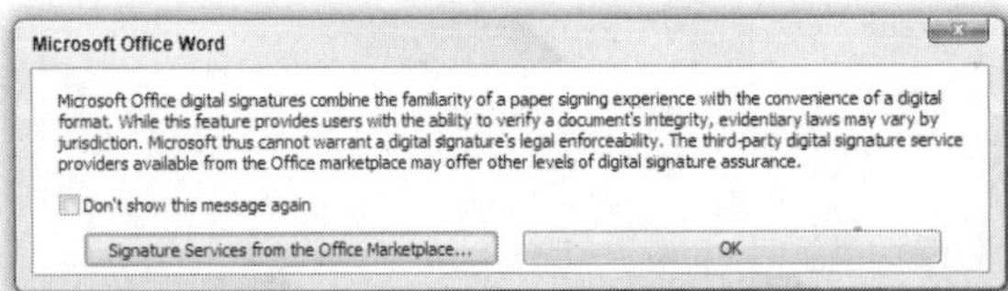

If you choose the Signature Services option, Word takes you to a Digital Signing site on the Microsoft Office website. There, you can use a commercial service to buy a digital certificate. As this is being written, at least one certificate authority is offering a free digital signature to private individuals (non-business).

If you choose OK, and the document has not been saved, you are prompted to save the file as a Word document. Word then displays the Sign dialog box, shown in Figure 11-7. You do not need to provide a purpose for signing the document, but you can if you want. To see exactly what you are signing and what information is provided along with the signature, click the link at the top of the dialog box: See additional information about what you are signing. If the Signing As identity/certificate isn't the one you want to use, click Change. If everything is as you want it, click Sign, and the Signature Confirmation message appears, as shown in Figure 11-8.

FIGURE 11-7

If you're not sure about the signing identity, click Change to see additional signing certificates as well as information about this one.

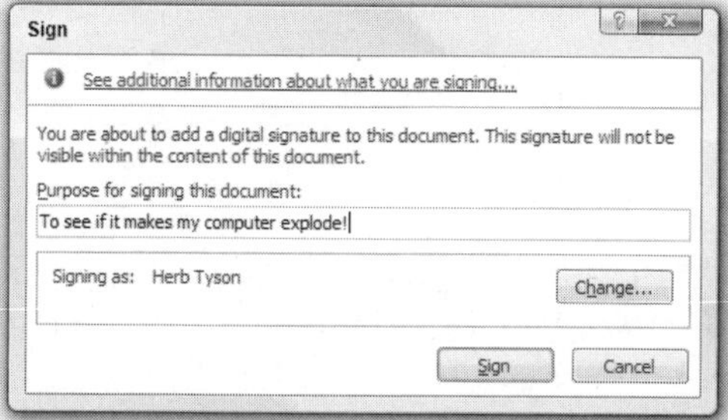

FIGURE 11-8

Don't sign a document until you're finished making changes to it.

Removing a signature

Once you've signed a document, the document is locked against further changes until the signature is removed. Unlike document permissions, a digital signature can be removed from a Word document by anyone with the appropriate version of Word. Once removed, however, it can be signed only by the owner of a signing certificate. Hence, if you remove my signature, you can edit the file I sent you and make any changes you want to. However, you will not be able to restore my signature.

CAUTION **Let's be honest here. You can use a free service to obtain a certificate with my name on it and affix that signature to a document and claim that I signed it. However, if it comes from the same CA (Certificate Authority) I used, it can't be associated with my e-mail address, which proves it's not really my signature; and if it doesn't come from the same CA, I can use that as proof that it's not really my signature. Presumably, there are ways to determine whether a signature is valid, but there are ways to make a forged signature look valid, and not everyone is sufficiently skeptical. Forewarned is forearmed.**

To remove a signature from a document, choose Office Button ➪ Prepare ➪ View Signatures (unless the Signatures pane is already showing). Right-click the signature and choose Remove Signature. At the prompt shown in Figure 11-9, click Yes.

FIGURE 11-9

"Permanently" and "This action cannot be undone" don't mean the document can't be signed again, just that Ctrl+Z won't do it.

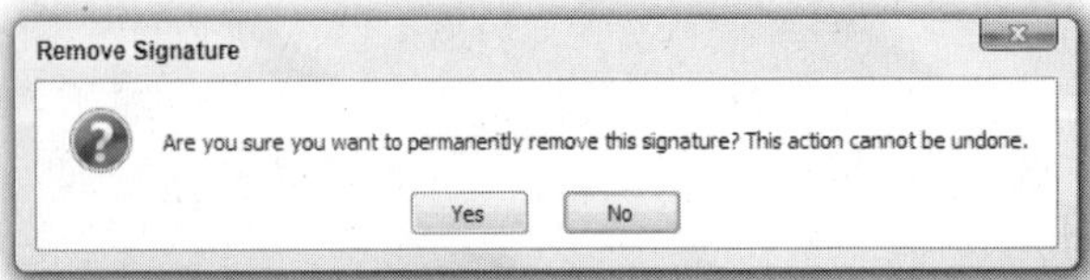

Don't let the words "permanently" and "cannot be undone" throw you. This simply means that you can't remove someone's signature, change that $1,000 fee to $100,000, and then reaffix their signature. Once you remove someone's signature, only they can put it back.

Document Inspector (Removing private/personal information)

You can use the Document Inspector to see what private or personal information resides in a file, and remove it. The Document Inspector checks for the kinds of information and content shown in Figure 11-10. To display the Document Inspector, choose Office Button ➪ Prepare ➪ Inspect Document. By default, all five areas are checked. Remove checks if you don't want those kinds of information removed. For example, if the purpose for sending a document to someone is to convey the XML data it contains, then remove the check next to Custom XML Data. On the other hand, if the document might contain "colorful" comments about someone's draft, you probably do want to inspect it for those. When the right checks are checked and the wrong checks are unchecked, click Inspect.

FIGURE 11-10

Use the Document Inspector to remove private/proprietary information before passing a document along to someone else.

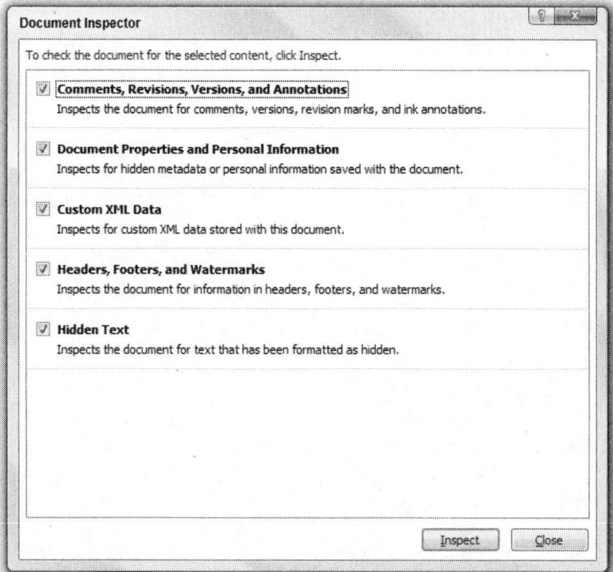

The Document Inspector inspects the current document for each of the types of material or data indicated. If it finds any, the Document Inspector dialog box is redisplayed, with Remove All buttons next to each type of content that was found, as shown in Figure 11-11.

CAUTION **Make a backup copy of the document before using Remove All. Once you remove the content using the Document Inspector, you can't get it back using Undo. Particularly for comments and data, if they are content you need to preserve, make a backup copy of the document.**

There is no facility in the Document Inspector for further inspecting to see exactly what it found. You have two options: click Remove All to do exactly that, or click Close and conduct a closer personal inspection. You can remove the content yourself manually or you can return to the Document Inspector and use Remove All once you're satisfied that you really want it removed.

FIGURE 11-11

A red exclamation mark means that the Document Inspector found potentially sensitive content, while the check mark indicates that the specified type of content was not found.

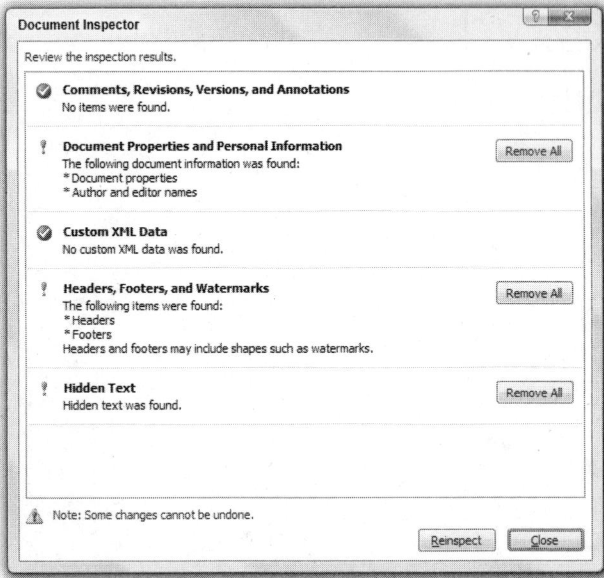

Formatting and editing restrictions

Rights management represents one general area of document protection, and it is certainly more formidable and secure than most of what you can do using formatting and editing restrictions. However, if you choose not to install and use rights management software, the Restrict Formatting and Editing settings can provide a measure of protection.

Limit formatting to a selection of styles

To limit formatting to certain styles, in the Review or Developer tabs, choose Protect Document, which displays the Restrict Formatting and Editing task pane. Click to place a check next to Limit Formatting to a Selection of Styles. To choose which styles, click Settings. The Formatting Restrictions dialog box now appears, also shown in Figure 11-12.

FIGURE 11-12

With "Limit formatting to a selection of styles" checked, click Settings to choose those limits.

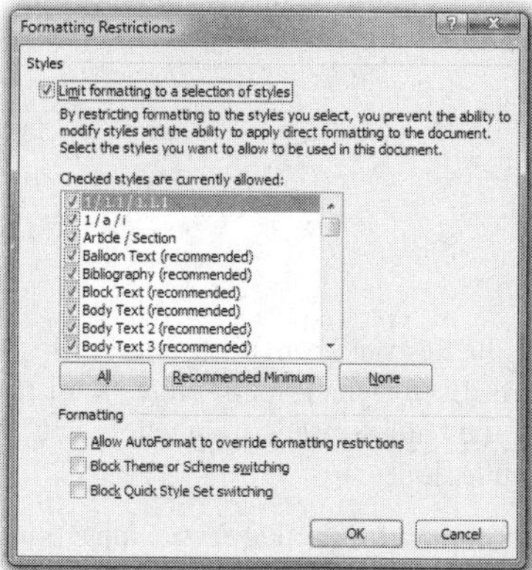

The Formatting Restrictions dialog box provides the following options:

- **Checked styles** — Place a check next to each style you want to allow. Remove checks for styles you want to disallow. Note that the styles listed might be limited based on settings in the Manage Styles dialog box. Note that Normal is not included in the list. As much as you might like to, you can't deny access to the Normal style.
- **Recommended Minimum** — If the list is too inclusive, click Recommended Minimum, and then add or remove checks as needed.
- **None** — If the style list is way too inclusive, then choose None, and place a check next to just those you want to allow.
- **All** — If the style list is way too restrictive, then click All and remove the check next to those you want to disallow.
- **Allow AutoFormat to Override Formatting Restrictions** — If AutoFormat's rules and practices are sufficiently rigorous for your purposes, click to allow this option.
- **Block Theme or Scheme Switching** — Choose this option to limit formatting to the currently applied theme or scheme.
- **Block Quick Style Set Switching** — Choose this option to use style definitions from the current document and template only.

When you're ready to proceed, click OK in the Formatting Restrictions dialog box. Word next displays the message box shown in Figure 11-13. Click Yes if you want disallowed styles or formatting removed. Note that if any styles are removed, text will be reformatted using Normal (even if the default paragraph style, set in Office Button ➪ Word Options ➪ Advanced ➪ Editing options, is set to something else).

FIGURE 11-13

If the document contains styles you want to disallow, you can remove them.

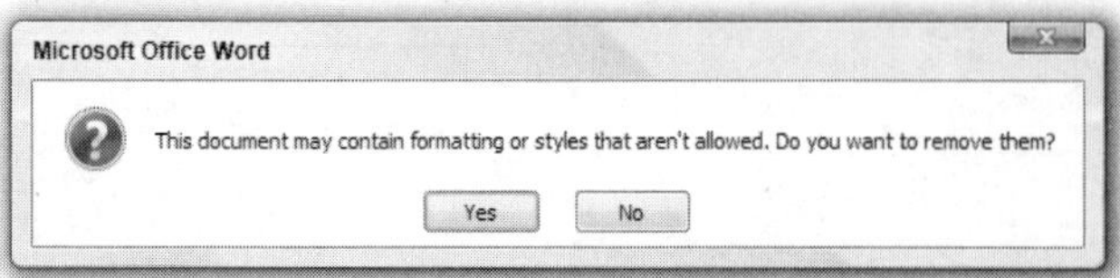
Microsoft Office Word
This document may contain formatting or styles that aren't allowed. Do you want to remove them?
Yes
No

When you're ready to proceed, click Yes, Start Enforcing Protection in the Restrict Formatting and Editing pane. Optionally, you can password-protect your formatting restrictions. Even if the level of protection isn't as strong as rights management, it's still better than nothing, assuming the hapless users upon whom you are imposing the restrictions can't be trusted. Sniff. Click OK when you're done.

NOTE **Other than being an ornery cuss, why would you want to impose formatting restrictions? Some publishing processes depend upon only certain styles being used. There are macros or other programs that process files so that they can be fed into other parts of the publishing process. If other styles are used, then the process breaks down and requires manual intervention. Hence, it's better if only the allowed styles are used. In other cases, enterprise-wide formatting standards are strictly imposed to ensure that all documents have a consistent and professional look. Enforcing style restrictions is one way to do that.**

With formatting restrictions in place, a number of formatting tools, commands, and keystrokes are grayed out as unavailable, as shown in Figure 11-14. Notice that the Change Case "formatting" tool isn't grayed out, however. That's because case is not formatting; it's simply a choice of which characters to use.

FIGURE 11-14

With style formatting restrictions applied, all direct formatting tools are grayed out, and only allowed styles can be applied.

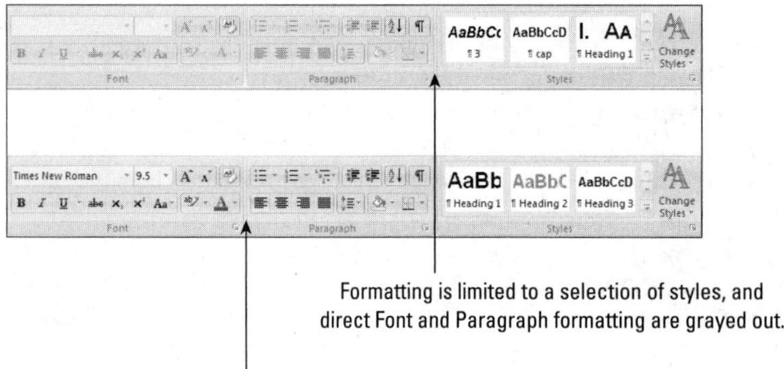
Formatting is limited to a selection of styles, and direct Font and Paragraph formatting are grayed out.
With formatting not limited, direct Font and Paragraph formatting are available.

No changes (Read-only)

You can protect all or part of a document against changes. You can make different exceptions for different users. Suppose, for example, that you have a document that has been written by a group of people. You want each individual to be able to edit his or her own section, but not that of others. At the same time, you don't want to have to manage different documents.

The solution is to create a document with a specific area for each individual. You make the entire document read-only, but you make an exception for each individual's section so that the individual responsible can make changes as needed.

To set a document as read-only, click Protect Document on the Review tab to display the Restrict Formatting and Editing pane. In the Editing restrictions section, click the check box to Allow Only This Type of Editing in the Document, and use the drop-down arrow to set it to No changes (Read only).

To make an exception, select the part of the document to which you want to allow changes by someone (or everyone). This selection can be any part of the document — a single letter, word, sentence, line, paragraph, and so on. If you want the exception to apply to everyone, click the check box next to Everyone. Or, if other groups are listed, you can place a check next to any of them.

To make an exception for individuals, if they are listed, click to place a check by their names. If the individuals aren't listed (or if no individuals are listed at all), click More Users. In Add Users, type the user IDs or e-mail addresses for the individuals you want to exempt from the read-only proscription, as shown in Figure 11-15. When you click OK, Word attempts to verify the names/address you added. If they are verified, then they are added to the list of individuals.

FIGURE 11-15

You can combine network and Internet e-mail addresses.

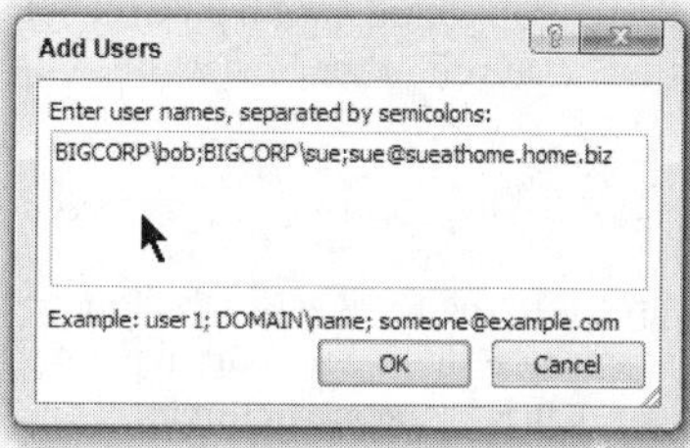

Back in the Restrict Formatting and Editing pane, you need to place a check by the name(s) and e-mail address(es) you added, and then click Yes, Start Enforcing Protection. Add and confirm a password if desired, as shown in Figure 11-16, noting that the document is not encrypted and is susceptible to hacking by malicious users. If you enabled User authentication, the top part of the dialog box becomes unavailable, and Word will use Information Rights Management to control the permissions. The document is encrypted, and users are authenticated using .NET Passport or Windows Live ID.

FIGURE 11-16

Choose the degree of protection desired.

Comments

This protection option is identical to the No changes (Read only) type of protection except that all users can insert comments wherever they want to. Refer to the preceding discussion, adding to it that comments are enabled everywhere.

Tracked Changes

Another option is to allow editing, but only tracked changes. That way, you can see who changed what, and when. This is an important feature in controlling the editing/revision process. To protect a document for tracked changes, click Protect Document in the Review or Developer tabs of the Ribbon. In the Restrict Formatting and Editing pane, click to enable Allow Only This Type of Editing in the Document, and set the drop-down type to Tracked Changes.

To turn protection on, click Yes, Start Enforcing Protection. The Start Enforcing Protection dialog box appears, where you can set and confirm a password. Note that User authentication is not available for this kind of protection. When you click OK, protection is enabled, and the document switches into Track Changes mode. To turn protection off — which is necessary for accepting/rejecting tracked changes — click Stop Protection. If the Restrict Formatting and Editing pane has long since disappeared, and the time comes to turn protection off; you can toggle it back on using the Protect Document button in the Review or Developer tab.

Filling in Forms

To protect a fill-in form that you've created in Word, click Protect Document in the Review or Developer tabs of the Ribbon. In the Restrict Formatting and Editing pane, click to enable Allow Only This Type of Editing in the Document, and set the drop-down type to Filling In Forms. Click Yes, Start Enforcing Protection.

Password to open/modify

A final kind of protection is well hidden in Word 2007. It was a bit less hidden in Word 2003 and earlier, although still not overly conspicuous. This legacy feature offers the same weak protection already noted, in that passwords aren't impossibly difficult to hack and crack. It suffers from other fatal flaws, as well, described below. The bottom line: Use this kind of protection at your own risk. It is essentially worthless and offers minimal, if any, protection. Worse, it offers the illusion of protection, and thinking a document is well protected when it's not is perhaps worse than no protection at all, because you are unlikely to be as careful with the document as you would be if you knew it were completely unprotected.

Applying passwords to open and/or modify a Word document

You can set two different passwords: one that enables a user to open the document and another that enables the user to make changes. To enable this kind of password protection, choose Office Button ➪ Save As. In the lower-left corner of the Save As dialog box, choose Tools ➪ General Options to display the General Options dialog box shown in Figure 11-17. Type a password in Password to Open, and/or in Password to Modify. Both are optional.

FIGURE 11-17

File encryption options are no longer available when applying Open and Modify passwords to a Word document.

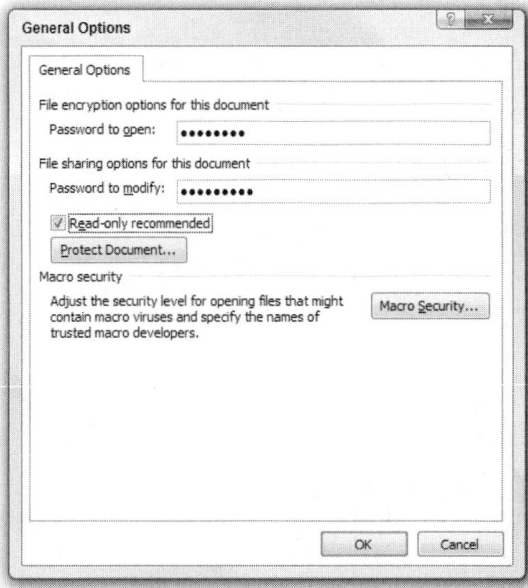

The Read-only Recommended option applies only if there is no password for modifying the document. If this option is enabled, the user is provided a read-only recommendation when the file is opened, and an easy way to select read-only.

When you click OK, you are prompted to confirm any passwords and are returned to the Save As dialog box. Click Save to save the document with the password settings.

NOTE **The Protect Document button is really irrelevant to this dialog box and serves mostly to let the user know that there are other and better protection options. If you click this button and the Restrict Formatting and Editing pane is not already showing, it is displayed behind the Save As dialog box, and the General Options dialog box goes away. If the Restrict Formatting and Editing pane is *not* already showing, clicking the Protect Document button simply causes the General Options dialog box to close, leaving users scratching their heads.**

When you try to open the file, you are prompted for the relevant passwords. If you know the password to open but not the password to modify, you can click Read Only to open the document in "read only" mode. Why the quotes? Because it's only the file itself that is read only. The document window can be edited willy-nilly, unlike when using other kinds of protection discussed earlier. If you save the file under a new name, the new file will inherit the password settings, but if you copy the file to the Clipboard and save under a new name, the protection is history.

Protecting Documents for Review

When you send a document to someone, you can protect it so that any changes they make are marked as changes. You can protect it for Tracked Changes or for Comments, but not both at the same time. See the "Comments" and "Tracked Changes" sections earlier in this chapter in the material on document protection.

Summary

In this chapter, you've learned about the many different and potentially confusing kinds of document protection and security available in Word. You should now have a good idea about which forms of protection and security are useful and which ones give only a false sense of security. You've also learned about tracking changes and commenting on Word documents. You should now be able to do the following:

- Use Information Rights Management to set strong protection for Word documents
- Use Word's legacy password protection, while understanding that it's feeble protection at best

Part III

Making the Numbers Work with Excel

IN THIS PART

Chapter 12

Using Excel Worksheets and Workbooks

IN THIS CHAPTER

- Understanding what Excel is used for
- Seeing what's new in Excel 2007
- Learning the parts of Excel's window
- Introducing the Ribbon user interface, shortcut menus, and dialog boxes
- Navigating Excel worksheets
- Introducing Excel with a quick hands-on session

This chapter serves as an introductory overview of Excel 2007. If you're already familiar with a previous version of Excel, reading this chapter is still a good idea. Excel 2007 is different from every previous version — *very* different.

What Is Excel Good For?

Excel, as you probably know, is the world's most widely used spreadsheet program and is part of the Microsoft Office suite. Other spreadsheet programs are available, but Excel is by far the most popular and has become the world standard.

Much of the appeal of Excel is due to the fact that it's so versatile. Excel's forte, of course, is performing numerical calculations, but Excel is also very useful for non-numerical applications. Here are just a few of the uses for Excel:

- **Number crunching:** Create budgets, analyze survey results, and perform just about any type of financial analysis you can think of
- **Creating charts:** Create a wide variety of highly customizable charts
- **Organizing lists:** Use the row-and-column layout to store lists efficiently
- **Accessing other data:** Import data from a wide variety of sources
- **Creating graphics and diagrams:** Use Shapes and the new SmartArt to create professional-looking diagrams
- **Automating complex tasks:** Perform a tedious task with a single mouse click with Excel's macro capabilities

What's New in Excel 2007?

If you've used a previous version of Excel, this section is for you. Here you'll find a quick overview of what's new and what's changed in Excel 2007.

A new user interface

The first thing you notice about Excel 2007 is its new look. The time-honored menu-and-toolbar user interface has been scrapped and replaced with a new "tab-and-ribbon" interface. Although the new interface kind of resembles menus and toolbars, you'll find that it's radically different.

Long-time Excel users have probably noticed that, with each new version, the menu system has gotten increasingly complicated. In addition, the number of toolbars had become almost overwhelming. After all, every new feature must have a way to be accessed. In the past, access meant adding more items to the menus and building new toolbars. The Microsoft designers set out to solve the problem, and the new Ribbon interface is their solution.

CROSS-REF **Chapter 2 contains more information about the new Ribbon interface, including a description of its components.**

Many experienced Excel users might suffer from a mild case of bewilderment as they realize that all their familiar command sequences no longer work. Beginning users, on the other hand, will be able to get up to speed much more quickly because they won't be overwhelmed with irrelevant menus and toolbars.

Other elements that comprise the new look include

- **Six new modern-looking fonts:** The default workbook font is now 11-point Calibri, which, I think, is much more readable than the old 10-point Arial, especially in smaller sizes.
- **Quick Access toolbar:** A personal toolbar, to which you can add commands that you use regularly. This toolbar is the only part of the Excel 2007 interface that the user can customize.
- **The Mini Toolbar:** This toolbar contains commonly used formatting icons, displayed near your mouse pointer for quick access.

Larger worksheets

Over the years, perhaps the most common complaint about Excel was the size of a worksheet. Users who required more rows or columns were simply out of luck. Microsoft finally, responded, and Excel 2007 has upped the ante significantly. A worksheet now has 1,048,576 rows and 16,384 columns, which works out to more than 17 billion cells — almost three cells for every man, woman, and child on the planet. Stated differently, an Excel 2007 worksheet has more than 1,000 times as many cells as an Excel 2003 worksheet.

NOTE **Having more rows and columns doesn't mean that you can actually use them all. If you attempted to fill up all cells in a worksheet, you would soon run out of memory. The advantage to having more rows and columns is the flexibility it provides.**

In addition to a larger worksheet grid, Excel 2007 has also increased some other limits that have frustrated users. Table 12-1 summarizes some of these changes.

TABLE 12-1

By the Numbers: Excel 2003 versus Excel 2007

	Excel 2003	Excel 2007
Number of rows	65,536	1,048,576
Number of columns	256	16,384
Amount of memory used	1GB	Maximum allowed by Windows
Number of colors	56	4.3 billion
Number of conditional formats per cell	3	Unlimited
Number of levels of sorting	3	64
Number of levels of undo	16	100
Number of items shown in the Auto-Filter dropdown	1,000	10,000
The total number of characters that can display in a cell	1,000	32,000
Number of unique styles in a workbook	4,000	64,000
Maximum number of characters in a formula	1,000	8,000
Number of levels of nesting in a formula	7	64
Maximum number of function arguments	30	255

New file formats

Over the years, Excel's XLS file format has become an industry standard. Excel 2007 still supports that format, but it now uses new default "open" file formats that are based on XML (Extensible Markup Language).

CROSS-REF **Find out more about the new Office file formats in Chapter 3.**

For compatibility, Excel 2007 still supports the old file formats so that you can continue to share your work with those who haven't upgraded to Excel 2007.

Worksheet tables

Excel, of course, has always been able to deal with tables. A *table* is just a rectangular range of cells that (usually) contain column headers. The designers of Excel 2007 realized that such tables are widely used in Excel, and they've taken the concept to a new level. Working with tables is easier than ever.

Once you designate a particular range to be a table (using the Insert ➪ Tables ➪ Table command), Excel provides you with some very efficient tools that work with the table. For example:

- You can apply attractive formatting with a single click.
- You can easily insert summary formulas in the table's total row.
- If each cell in a column contains the same formula, you can edit one of the formulas, and the others change automatically.
- You can easily toggle the display of the table's the header row and totals row.

- Removing duplicate entries is easy.
- AutoFiltering and sorting options have been expanded.
- If you create a chart from a table, the chart will always reflect the data in the table — even if you add new rows.
- If you scroll a table downwards so that the header row is no longer visible, the column headers now display where the worksheet column letters would be.

Figure 12-1 shows a table in a worksheet.

FIGURE 12-1

Working with tables of data has never been easier.

State	July 2005 Population	July 2004 Population	Change	Pct Change
Alabama	4,557,808	4,525,375	32,433	0.71%
Alaska	663,661	657,755	5,906	0.89%
Arizona	5,939,292	5,739,879	199,413	3.36%
Arkansas	2,779,154	2,750,000	29,154	1.05%
California	36,132,147	35,842,038	290,109	0.80%
Colorado	4,665,177	4,601,821	63,356	1.36%
Connecticut	3,510,297	3,498,966	11,331	0.32%
Delaware	843,524	830,069	13,455	1.60%
District of Columbia	550,521	554,239	-3,718	-0.68%
Florida	17,789,864	17,385,430	404,434	2.27%
Georgia	9,072,576	8,918,129	154,447	1.70%
Hawaii	1,275,194	1,262,124	13,070	1.02%
Idaho	1,429,096	1,395,140	33,956	2.38%
Illinois	12,763,371	12,712,016	51,355	0.40%
Indiana	6,271,973	6,226,537	45,436	0.72%
Iowa	2,966,334	2,952,904	13,430	0.45%
Kansas	2,744,687	2,733,697	10,990	0.40%
Kentucky	4,173,405	4,141,835	31,570	0.76%
Louisiana	4,523,628	4,506,685	16,943	0.37%
Maine	1,321,505	1,314,985	6,520	0.49%
Maryland	5,600,388	5,561,332	39,056	0.70%
Massachusetts	6,398,743	6,407,382	-8,639	-0.14%
Michigan	10,120,860	10,104,206	16,654	0.16%
Minnesota	5,132,799	5,096,546	36,253	0.71%
Mississippi	2,921,088	2,900,768	20,320	0.70%
Missouri	5,800,310	5,759,532	40,778	0.70%
Montana	935,670	926,920	8,750	0.94%
Nebraska	1,758,787	1,747,704	11,083	0.63%
Nevada	2,414,807	2,332,898	81,909	3.39%

NST03

Styles and themes

Excel has always supported named styles, which can be applied to cells and ranges. Excel 2007 brings this feature to the forefront by providing a good assortment of predefined styles, easily accessible by choosing Home ➪ Styles ➪ Cell Styles.

With the introduction of document themes, Excel 2007 makes it easy to create good-looking worksheets. A theme consists of a color palette, font set, and effects. You now have one-click access to a gallery of professionally designed themes that can dramatically change the look of your entire spreadsheet — almost always for the better. Access the theme gallery by choosing Page Layout ➪ Themes ➪ Themes. And yes. You can still create ugly Excel documents if you try hard enough.

Better-looking charts

There is both good news and bad news relating to the charting features in Excel 2007. First the bad news: Excel 2007 offers no new chart types, and many of the long-time chart-related feature requests have been ignored by Microsoft. The good news? Excel charts now look better than ever. For the first time, you can honestly use the term "boardroom quality" to describe Excel charts

I discuss charts in Chapter 18.

Page layout view

As an option, you can display your worksheet as a series of pages. This new Page Layout view ensures there are no surprises when it's time to print your work. Even better, the Page Layout view includes "click and type" page headers and footers — which is much more intuitive than the old method. Unlike the standard print preview, Page Layout view is fully functional in terms of spreadsheet editing.

Figure 12-2 shows a spreadsheet displayed in Page Layout view. The display is zoomed out to show multiple pages.

FIGURE 12-2

Excel's new Page Layout view makes it easy to see how your printed work will appear.

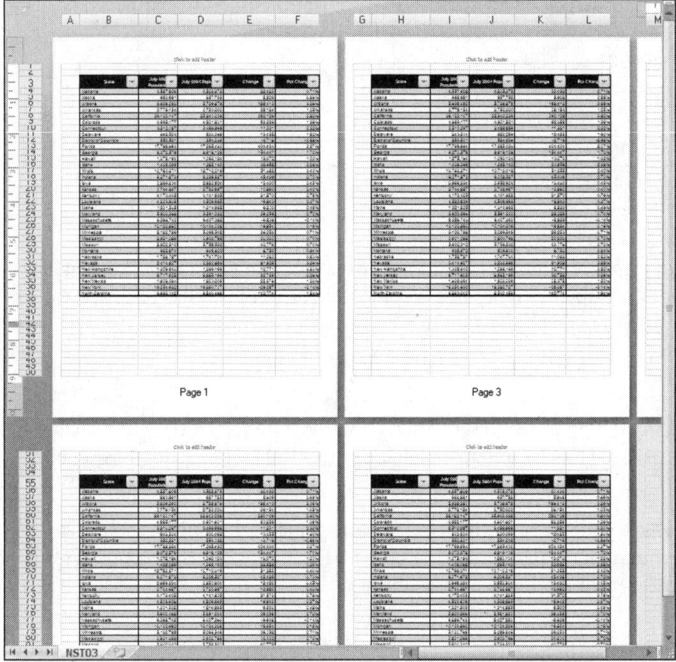

Enhanced conditional formatting

Conditional formatting refers to the ability to format a cell based on its value. Conditional formatting makes it easy to highlight certain values so that they stand out visually. For example, you may set up conditional formatting so that if a formula returns a negative value, the cell background displays green.

In the past, a cell could have at most three conditions applied. With Excel 2007, you can format a cell based on an unlimited number of conditions. But that's the least of the improvements. Excel 2007 provides a number of new data visualizations: data bars, color scales, and icon sets. Figure 12-3 shows an example of a range that uses conditional formatting to display data bars directly in the cells. The size of each data bar is proportional to the value in the cell.

FIGURE 12-3

Data bars are just one of the new conditional formatting options.

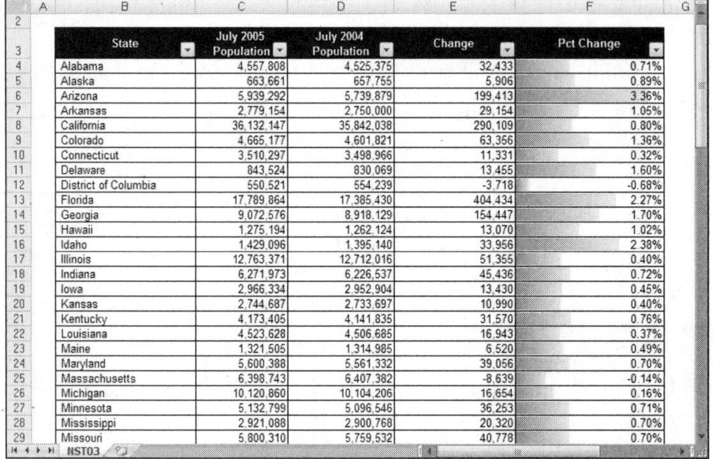

State	July 2005 Population	July 2004 Population	Change	Pct Change
Alabama	4,557,808	4,525,375	32,433	0.71%
Alaska	663,661	657,755	5,906	0.89%
Arizona	5,939,292	5,739,879	199,413	3.36%
Arkansas	2,779,154	2,750,000	29,154	1.05%
California	36,132,147	35,842,038	290,109	0.80%
Colorado	4,665,177	4,601,821	63,356	1.36%
Connecticut	3,510,297	3,498,966	11,331	0.32%
Delaware	843,524	830,069	13,455	1.60%
District of Columbia	550,521	554,239	-3,718	-0.68%
Florida	17,789,864	17,385,430	404,434	2.27%
Georgia	9,072,576	8,918,129	154,447	1.70%
Hawaii	1,275,194	1,262,124	13,070	1.02%
Idaho	1,429,096	1,395,140	33,956	2.38%
Illinois	12,763,371	12,712,016	51,355	0.40%
Indiana	6,271,973	6,226,537	45,436	0.72%
Iowa	2,966,334	2,952,904	13,430	0.45%
Kansas	2,744,687	2,733,697	10,990	0.40%
Kentucky	4,173,405	4,141,835	31,570	0.76%
Louisiana	4,523,628	4,506,685	16,943	0.37%
Maine	1,321,505	1,314,985	6,520	0.49%
Maryland	5,600,388	5,561,332	39,056	0.70%
Massachusetts	6,398,743	6,407,382	-8,639	-0.14%
Michigan	10,120,860	10,104,206	16,654	0.16%
Minnesota	5,132,799	5,096,546	36,253	0.71%
Mississippi	2,921,088	2,900,768	20,320	0.70%
Missouri	5,800,310	5,759,532	40,778	0.70%

Excel 2007 includes quite a few other improvements to conditional formatting. In general, conditional formatting is much more flexible, easier to set up, and relies less on creating custom formulas to define the formatting rules.

Consolidated options

In the past, Excel provided far too many dialog boxes to set various options. In Excel 2007, most dialog boxes have been consolidated into a massive Excel Options dialog box. To display this dialog box, choose Office Button ➪ Excel Options.

The options are grouped into tabs, which you select on the left. Locating some of the options still isn't easy, but the new implementation is much better than it used to be. The Excel Options dialog box is also resizable — just click and drag the lower-right corner to change the size.

SmartArt

Excel 2007 still includes a wide assortment of Shapes that you can use to create visual diagrams, such as flow charts, org charts, or diagrams that depict relationships. But the new SmartArt feature is a much better tool for such tasks. You can quickly add shadows, reflection, glow, and other special effects.

Figure 12-4 shows two SmartArt diagrams. The diagram on the left is the original, and the one on the right is the same diagram after a single mouse click that changed the layout and style.

NOTE SmartArt works in Excel just as it does in Word. Chapter 9 covers the SmartArt in more detail. In Excel, click the Insert tab on the Ribbon and then click SmartArt to begin inserting a SmartArt graphic.

FIGURE 12-4

Diagrams created with SmartArt.

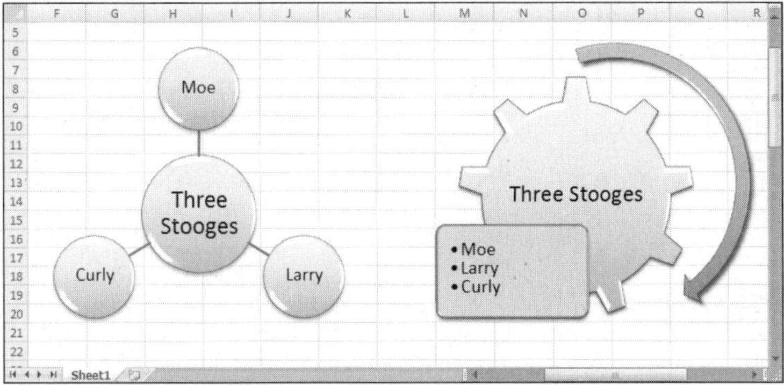

Formula AutoComplete

Entering formulas in Excel 2007 can be a bit less cumbersome, thanks to the new Formula AutoComplete feature. When you begin typing a formula, Excel displays a continually updated drop-down list of matching items (see Figure 12-5), including a description of each item. When you see the item you want, press Tab to enter it into your formula. The items in this list consist of functions, defined names, and table references.

FIGURE 12-5

The Formula AutoComplete feature can speed up formula entry.

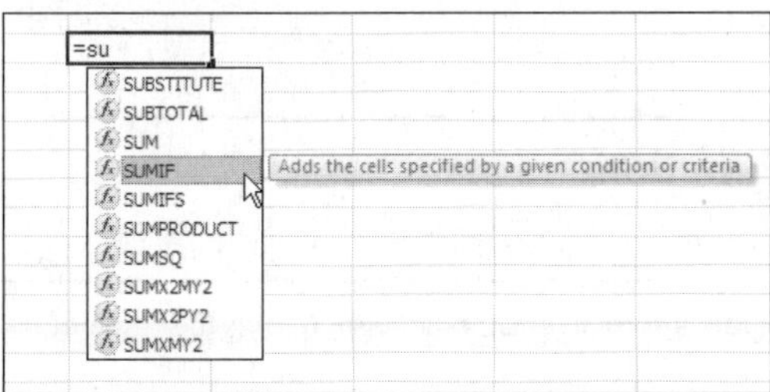

CROSS-REF Refer to Chapter 15 for more information about Formula AutoComplete.

Compatibility Checker

Given all the new features in Excel 2007, you may be hesitant to share a workbook with others who use an earlier version of Excel. To find out how your workbook will function with previous versions, use the compatibility checker. Choose Office Button ➪ Prepare ➪ Run Compatibility Checker. Figure 12-6 shows an example.

FIGURE 12-6

Use the Compatibility Checker if you plan to share your workbooks with people who use an earlier version of Excel.

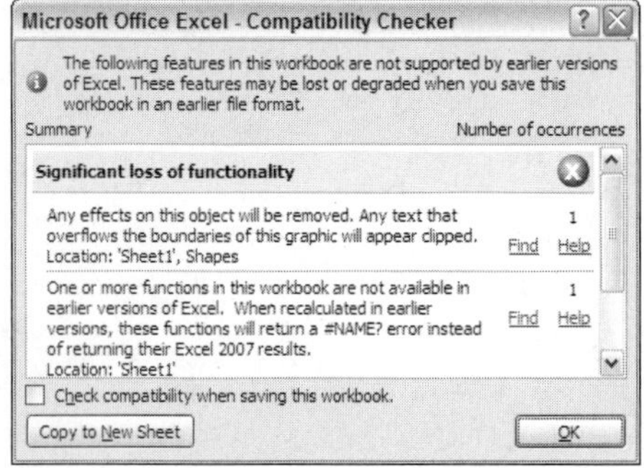

Improved PivotTables

Excel's PivotTable feature is probably one of its most underutilized features. A *PivotTable* can turn a large range of raw data into a useful interactive summary table with only a few mouse clicks. Microsoft hopes to make this feature more accessible by improving just about every aspect of pivot tables in Excel 2007.

One other thing worth noting: Charts created from PivotTables (*PivotCharts*) now retain their formatting when they're updated. This loss of formatting had been a frustration for hundreds of thousands of users, and Microsoft finally did something about it.

New Worksheet functions

Excel 2007 has five new worksheet functions, described in Table 12-2.

TABLE 12-2

New Worksheet Functions

Function	Use
`IFERROR`	Returns a value you specify if a formula evaluates to an error; otherwise, returns the result of the formula
`AVERAGEIF`	Calculates a conditional average (similar to `SUMIF` and `COUNTIF`)
`AVERAGEIFS`	Calculates a conditional average using multiple criteria
`SUMIFS`	Calculates a conditional sum using multiple criteria
`COUNTIFS`	Calculates a conditional `COUNT` using multiple criteria

In addition, 39 worksheet functions that used to require the Analysis Toolpak add-in are now built in.

Excel 2007 also includes seven new CUBE functions that retrieve data from SQL Server Analysis Services.

CROSS-REF Chapter 15 covers formulas and functions.

Other new features

Other new features in Excel 2007 worth noting are:

- **Trust Center:** Protecting yourself from malicious macros is a bit easier with Excel 2007. For example, you can disable all macros, except those in workbooks that are stored in trusted locations on your computer.
- **PDF add-in:** You can create an industry-standard Adobe PDF file directly from Excel using an add-in available from Microsoft. Search Excel's Help system for "PDF" to learn more.
- **Improved zooming:** Use the Zoom control or Zoom slider on the right side of the status bar to quickly zoom in or zoom out on your worksheet.
- **More control over the status bar:** You can now control the type of information that appears in the status bar.
- **Color Schemes:** Change the appearance of Excel by applying one of three color schemes that ship with Excel (Blue, Silver, or Black).
- **Resizable formula bar:** When editing lengthy formulas, you can increase the height of the formula bar so that it doesn't obscure your worksheet. Just click and drag on the bottom border of the formula bar.
- **Lots of new templates:** Why reinvent the wheel? Choose Office Button ➪ New, and you can choose from a variety of templates. One of them may be exactly (or at least close) to what you need.

Understanding Workbooks and Worksheets

The work you do in Excel is performed in a workbook file, which appears in its own window. You can have as many workbooks open as you need. By default, Excel 2007 workbooks use an XLSX file extension.

Each *workbook* is comprised of one or more worksheets, and each *worksheet* is made up of individual *cells*. Each cell contains a value, a formula, or text. A worksheet also has an invisible *draw layer*, which holds charts, images, and diagrams. Each worksheet in a workbook is accessible by clicking the *tab* at the bottom of the workbook window. In addition, workbooks can store chart sheets. A *chart sheet* displays a single chart and is also accessible by clicking a tab.

Newcomers to Excel are often intimidated by all the different elements that appear within Excel's window. Once you become familiar with the various parts, it all starts to make sense.

Figure 12-7 shows you the more important bits and pieces of Excel. As you look at the figure, refer to Table 12-3 for a brief explanation of the items shown in the figure.

FIGURE 12-7

The Excel screen has many useful elements that you will use often.

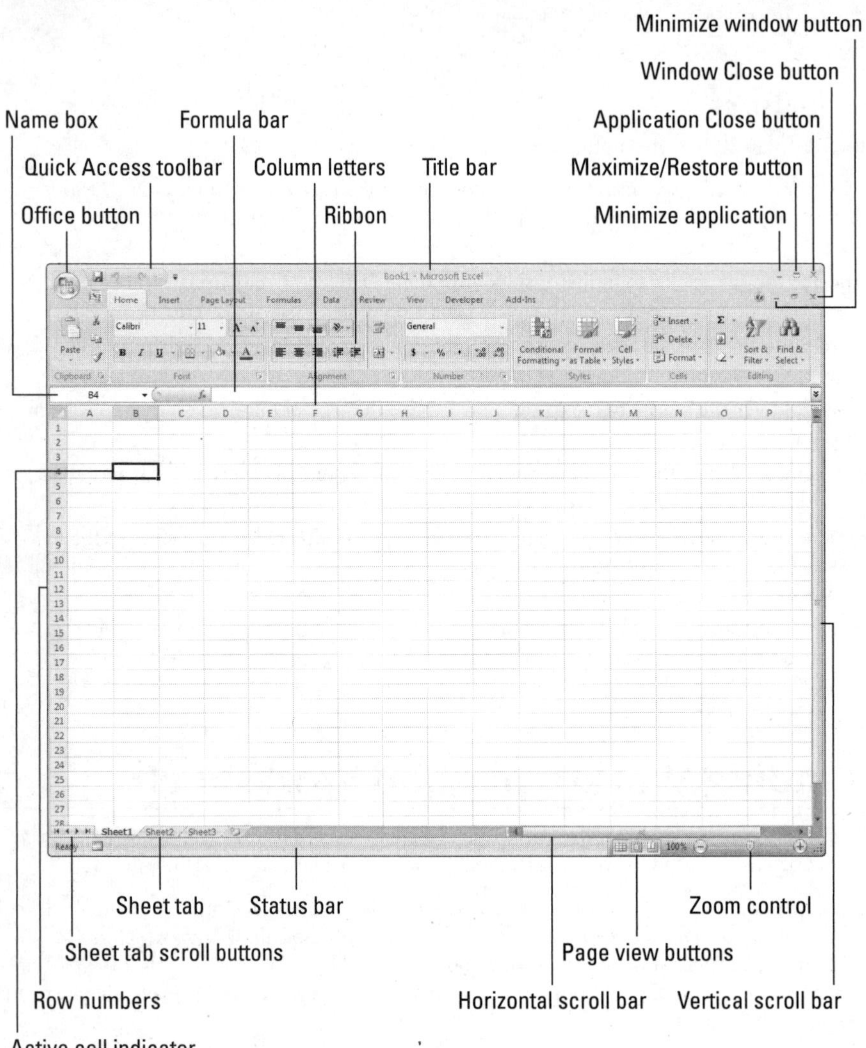

TABLE 12-3

Parts of the Excel Screen That You Need to Know

Name	Description
Active cell indicator	This dark outline, also called the cell selector, indicates the currently active cell (one of the 17,179,869,184 cells on each worksheet).
Application close button	Clicking this button closes Excel.
Window close button	Clicking this button closes the active workbook window.
Column letters	Letters range from A to XFD — one for each of the 16,384 columns in the worksheet. You can click a column heading to select an entire column of cells.
Office button	This button leads to lots of commands for working with your document, or Excel in general.
Formula bar	When you enter information or formulas into Excel, they appear in this line.
Horizontal scrollbar	Enables you to scroll the sheet horizontally.
Maximize/Restore button	Clicking this button increases the workbook window's size to fill your monitor's workspace. If the window is already maximized, clicking this button Restores Excel's window down to its previous window size so that it no longer fills the entire screen.
Minimize application button	Clicking this button minimizes Excel's window down to the Windows taskbar.
Minimize window button	Clicking this button minimizes the workbook window.
Name box	Displays the active cell address or the name of the selected cell, range, or object.
Page view buttons	Change the way the worksheet is displayed by clicking one of these buttons.
Quick Access Toolbar	A toolbar that you customize to hold commonly-used commands
Ribbon	The main location to find Excel's commands. Clicking a tab changes the Ribbon buttons that appear.
Row numbers	Numbers range from 1 to 1,048,576 — one for each row in the worksheet. You can click a row number to select an entire row of cells.
Sheet tabs	Each of these notebook-like tabs represents a different sheet in the workbook. A workbook can have any number of sheets, and each sheet has its name displayed in a sheet tab. By default, each new workbook that you create contains three sheets. Add a new sheet by clicking the Insert Worksheet button (which is displayed after the last sheet tab).
Sheet tab scroll buttons	These buttons let you scroll the sheet tabs to display tabs that aren't visible.
Status bar	This bar displays various messages as well as the status of the Num Lock, Caps Lock, and Scroll Lock keys on your keyboard. It also shows summary information about the range of cells that is selected. Right-click the status bar to change the information that's displayed
Title bar	All Windows programs have a title bar, which displays the name of the program and the name of the current workbook and also holds some control buttons that you can use to modify the window.
Vertical scrollbar	Lets you scroll the sheet vertically.
Zoom control	A slider control that lets you zoom your worksheet in and out.

Moving Around a Worksheet

This section describes various ways to navigate through the cells in a worksheet. Every worksheet consists of rows (numbered 1 through 1,048,576) and columns (labeled A through XFD). After column Z comes column AA, which is followed by AB, AC, and so on. After column AZ comes BA, BB, and so on. After column ZZ is AAA, AAB, and so on.

The intersection of a row and a column is a single cell. At any given time, one cell is the *active cell.* You can identify the active cell by its darker border, as shown in Figure 12-8. Its *address* (its column letter and row number) appears in the Name box. Depending on the technique that you use to navigate through a workbook, you may or may not change the active cell when you navigate.

Notice that the row and column headings of the active cell appear in different colors to make it easier to identify the row and column of the active cell.

FIGURE 12-8

The active cell is the cell with the dark border — in this case, cell C8.

	A	B	C	D	E	F
1		Last Year	This Year			
2	January	89	121			
3	February	94	143			
4	March	91	130			
5	April	104	127			
6	May	115	135			
7	June	98	135			
8						
9						
10						
11						
12						

Sheet1 Sheet2 Sheet3

Navigating with your keyboard

As you probably already know, you can use the standard navigational keys on your keyboard to move around a worksheet. These keys work just as you'd expect: The down arrow moves the active cell down one row, the right arrow moves it one column to the right, and so on. PgUp and PgDn move the active cell up or down one full window. (The actual number of rows moved depends on the number of rows displayed in the window.)

TIP **You can use the keyboard to scroll through the worksheet without changing the active cell by turning on Scroll Lock, which is useful if you need to view another area of your worksheet and then quickly return to your original location. Just press Scroll Lock and use the direction keys to scroll through the worksheet. When you want to return to the original position (the active cell), press Ctrl+Backspace. Then, press Scroll Lock again to turn it off. When Scroll Lock is turned on, Excel displays** `Scroll Lock` **in the status bar at the bottom of the window.**

The Num Lock key on your keyboard controls how the keys on the numeric keypad behave. When Num Lock is on, Excel displays `Num Lock` in the status bar, and the keys on your numeric keypad generate numbers. Most keyboards have a separate set of navigational (arrow) keys located to the left of the numeric keypad. The state of the Num Lock key doesn't affect these keys.

Table 12-4 summarizes all the worksheet movement keys available in Excel.

TABLE 12-4

Excel's Worksheet Movement Keys

Key	Action
Up arrow	Moves the active cell up one row
Down arrow	Moves the active cell down one row
Left arrow or Shift+Tab	Moves the active cell one column to the left
Right arrow or Tab	Moves the active cell one column to the right
PgUp	Moves the active cell up one screen
PgDn	Moves the active cell down one screen
Alt+PgDn	Moves the active cell right one screen
Alt+PgUp	Moves the active cell left one screen
Ctrl+Backspace	Scrolls the screen so that the active cell is visible
Up arrow*	Scrolls the screen up one row (active cell does not change)
Down arrow*	Scrolls the screen down one row (active cell does not change)
Left arrow*	Scrolls the screen left one column (active cell does not change)
Right arrow*	Scrolls the screen right one column (active cell does not change)

* With Scroll Lock on

Navigating with your mouse

To change the active cell by using the mouse, click another cell; it becomes the active cell. If the cell that you want to activate isn't visible in the workbook window, you can use the scrollbars to scroll the window in any direction. To scroll one cell, click either of the arrows on the scrollbar. To scroll by a complete screen, click either side of the scroll bar's scroll box. You also can drag the scroll box for faster scrolling.

TIP **If your mouse has a wheel on it, you can use the mouse wheel to scroll vertically. Also, if you click the wheel and move the mouse in any direction, the worksheet scrolls automatically in that direction. The more you move the mouse, the faster the scrolling.**

Press Ctrl while you use the mouse wheel to zoom the worksheet. If you prefer to use the mouse wheel to zoom the worksheet without pressing Ctrl, choose Office Button ➪ Excel Options and select the Advanced section. Place a check mark next to the Zoom On Roll With Intellimouse checkbox.

Using the scroll bars or scrolling with your mouse doesn't change the active cell. It simply scrolls the worksheet. To change the active cell, you must click a new cell after scrolling.

Creating Your First Excel Worksheet

This section presents an introductory hands-on session with Excel. If you haven't used Excel, you may want to follow along on your computer to get a feel for how this software works.

In this example, you create a simple monthly sales projection table along with a chart.

Getting started on your worksheet

Start Excel and make sure that you have an empty workbook displayed. To create a new, blank workbook, press Ctrl+N.

The sales projection will consist of two columns of information. Column A will contain the month names, and column B will store the projected sales numbers. You start by entering some descriptive titles into the worksheet. Here's how to begin:

1. **Move the cell pointer to cell A1 by using the direction keys.** The Name box displays the cell's address.
2. **Enter** Month **into cell A1.** Just type the text and then press Enter. Depending on your setup, Excel either moves the cell pointer to a different cell, or the pointer remains in cell A1. (You can change this behavior in the Advanced category of the Excel Options dialog box. Appendix A, "Customizing Office," explains how to find and work with options.)
3. **Move the cell pointer to B1, type** Projected Sales, **and press Enter.**

Filling in the month names

In this step, you enter the month names in column A.

1. **Move the cell pointer to A2 and type** Jan **(an abbreviation for January).** At this point, you can enter the other month name abbreviations manually, but we'll let Excel do some of the work by taking advantage of the AutoFill feature.
2. **Make sure that cell A2 is selected.** Notice that the active cell is displayed with a heavy outline. At the bottom-right corner of the outline, you'll see a small square known as the *fill handle.* Move your mouse pointer over the fill handle, click, and drag down until you've highlighted from A2 down to A13.
3. **Release the mouse button, and Excel will automatically fill in the month names.**

Your worksheet should resemble the one shown in Figure 12-9.

FIGURE 12-9

Your worksheet, after entering the column headings and month names.

Entering the sales data

Next, you provide the sales projection numbers in column B. Assume that January's sales are projected to be $50,000, and that sales will increase by 3.5 percent in each of the subsequent months.

1. **Move the cell pointer to B2 and type** 50000**, the projected sales for January.**
2. **To enter a formula to calculate the projected sales for February, move to cell B3 and enter the following:** =B2*103.5%. When you press Enter, the cell will display 51750. The formula returns the contents of cell B2, multiplied by 103.5%. In other words, February sales are projected to be 3.5% greater than January sales.
3. **The projected sales for subsequent months will use a similar formula.** But rather than retyping the formula for each cell in column B, once again take advantage of the AutoFill feature. Make sure that cell B3 is selected. Click the cell's fill handle, drag down to cell B13, and release the mouse button.

At this point, your worksheet should resemble the one shown in Figure 12-10. Keep in mind that, except for cell B2, the values in column B are calculated with formulas. To demonstrate, try changing the projected sales value for the initial month, January (in cell B2). You'll find that the formulas recalculate and return different values. But these formulas all depend on the initial value in cell B2.

FIGURE 12-10

Your worksheet, after creating the formulas.

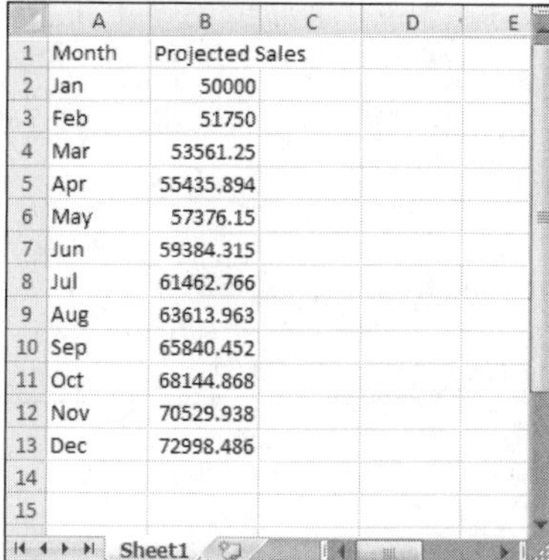

	A	B	C	D	E
1	Month	Projected Sales			
2	Jan	50000			
3	Feb	51750			
4	Mar	53561.25			
5	Apr	55435.894			
6	May	57376.15			
7	Jun	59384.315			
8	Jul	61462.766			
9	Aug	63613.963			
10	Sep	65840.452			
11	Oct	68144.868			
12	Nov	70529.938			
13	Dec	72998.486			
14					
15					

Formatting the numbers

The values in the worksheet are difficult to read because they aren't formatted. In this step, you apply a number format to make the numbers easier to read and more consistent in appearance:

1. **Select the numbers by clicking cell B2 and dragging down to cell B13.**
2. **Choose Home ➪ Number, click the drop-down Number Format control (it initially displays** `General`**), and select** `Currency` **from the list.** The numbers now display with a currency symbol and two decimal places. Much better!

Making your worksheet look a bit fancier

At this point, you have a functional worksheet — but it could use some help in the appearance department. Converting this range to an "official" (and attractive) Excel table is a snap:

1. **Move to any cell within the range.**
2. **Choose Insert ➪ Tables ➪ Table.** Excel displays its Create Table dialog box to make sure that it guessed the range properly.
3. **Click OK to close the Create Table dialog box.** Excel applies its default table formatting and also displays its Table Tools ➪ Design contextual tab. Your screen should look like Figure 12-11.

FIGURE 12-11

Your worksheet, after converting the range to a table.

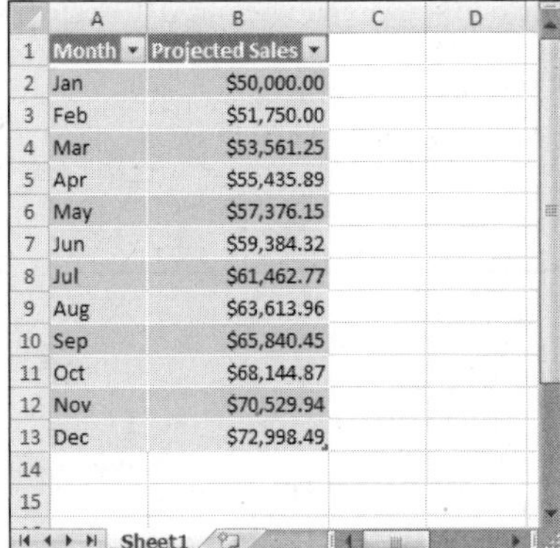

	A	B	C	D
1	Month	Projected Sales		
2	Jan	$50,000.00		
3	Feb	$51,750.00		
4	Mar	$53,561.25		
5	Apr	$55,435.89		
6	May	$57,376.15		
7	Jun	$59,384.32		
8	Jul	$61,462.77		
9	Aug	$63,613.96		
10	Sep	$65,840.45		
11	Oct	$68,144.87		
12	Nov	$70,529.94		
13	Dec	$72,998.49		
14				
15				

4. **If you don't like the default table style, just select another one from the Table Tools ➪ Design ➪ Table Styles group.** Notice that you can get a preview of different table styles by moving your mouse over the ribbon. When you find one you like, click it, and that style will be applied to your table.

Summing the values

The worksheet displays the monthly projected sales, but what about the total sales for the year? Because this range is a table, it's simple:

1. **Activate any cell in the table.**
2. **Choose Table Tools ➪ Design ➪ Table Style Options ➪ Totals Row.** Excel automatically adds a new row to the bottom of your table, including a formula that calculates the total of the Projected Sales column.
3. **If you'd prefer to see a different summary formula (for example, average), click cell B14 and choose a different summary formula from the drop-down list.**

Creating a chart

How about a chart that shows the projected sales for each month?

1. **Activate any cell in the table.**
2. **Choose Insert ➪ Charts ➪ Column and then select one of the 2-D column chart types. Excel inserts the chart in the center of your screen.**
3. **To move the chart to another location, click its border and drag it.**
4. **To change the appearance and style of the chart, use the commands in the Chart Tools context tab.**

Figure 12-12 shows the worksheet after creating the chart. Your chart may look different, depending on the chart layout or style you selected.

FIGURE 12-12

The table and chart.

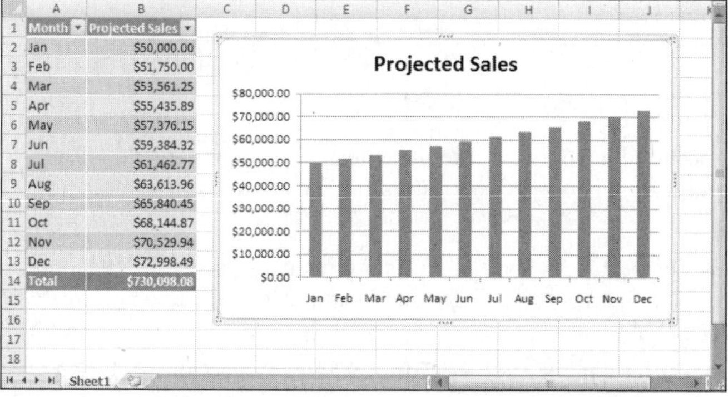

Month	Projected Sales
Jan	$50,000.00
Feb	$51,750.00
Mar	$53,561.25
Apr	$55,435.89
May	$57,376.15
Jun	$59,384.32
Jul	$61,462.77
Aug	$63,613.96
Sep	$65,840.45
Oct	$68,144.87
Nov	$70,529.94
Dec	$72,998.49
Total	$730,098.08

Printing your worksheet

Printing your worksheet is very easy (assuming that you have a printer attached and that it works properly).

1. **First, make sure that the chart isn't selected.** If a chart is selected, it will print on a page by itself. To deselect the chart, just press Esc or click any cell.
2. **To make use of Excel's handy new page layout view, click the Page Layout View button on the right side of the status bar.** Excel will then display the worksheet page by page (see Figure 12-13) so that you can easily see how your printed output will look. For example, you can tell immediately if the chart is too wide to fit on one page. If the chart is too wide, click and drag its lower-right corner to resize it.
3. **When you're ready to print, choose Office Button ➪ Print ➪ Quick Print.**

   The worksheet is printed using your default settings.

FIGURE 12-13

Viewing the worksheet in Page Layout mode.

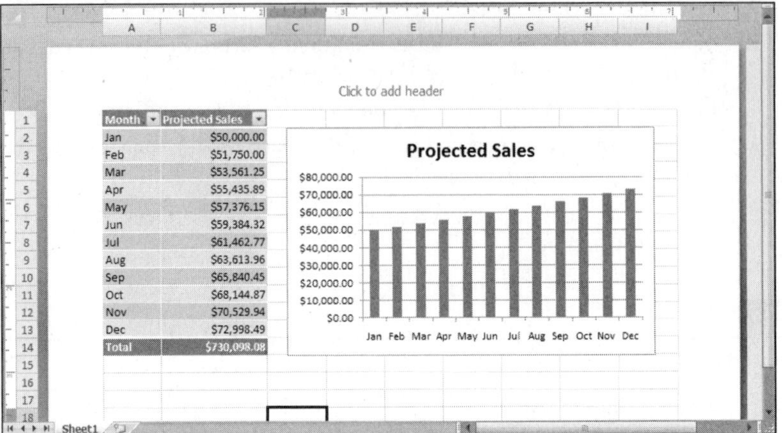

Saving your workbook

Until now, everything you've done has occurred in your computer's memory. If the power should fail, all may be lost — unless Excel's AutoRecover feature happened to kick in. It's time to save your work to a file on your hard drive.

1. **Click the Save button on the Quick Access Toolbar.** (This button looks like an old-fashioned floppy disk.) Because the workbook hasn't been saved yet and still has its default name, Excel responds with the Save As dialog box.
2. **In the box labeled File Name, enter a name such as Monthly Sales Projection, and then click Save or press Enter.** Excel saves the workbook as a file. The workbook remains open so that you can work with it some more.

NOTE **By default, Excel saves a copy of your work automatically every 10 minutes. To adjust this setting (or turn it off), use the Save tab of the Excel Options dialog box. To display this dialog box, choose Office Button ➪ Excel Options. However, you should never rely on Excel's AutoRecover feature. Saving your work frequently is a good idea.**

If you've followed along, you may have realized that creating this workbook was not at all difficult. But, of course, you've barely scratched the surface. The remainder of this book will cover these tasks (and many, many more) in much greater detail.

Summary

This chapter introduced you to the new version of Excel 2007. You learned about many of the new features in this version of the spreadsheet program, such as the new file format, new table features, SmartArt, new functions, and more. You learned the difference between a workbook and a worksheet, as well as how to navigate around Excel. You finished up by creating your first spreadsheet, including adding labels and values, building a simple sum formula, treating your information as a table, and even charting and printing. Well done!

Chapter 13

Entering and Editing Worksheet Data

This chapter describes what you need to know about entering, using, and modifying data in your worksheets. You see, Excel doesn't treat all data equally. Therefore, you need to learn about the various types of data that you can use in an Excel worksheet.

IN THIS CHAPTER

Understanding the types of data you can use

Entering text and values into your worksheets

Entering dates and times into your worksheets

Modifying and editing information

Using built-in number formats

Exploring the Types of Data You Can Use

An Excel workbook can hold any number of worksheets, and each worksheet is made up of more than 17 billion cells. A cell can hold any of three basic types of data:

- Numerical values
- Text
- Formulas

A worksheet can also hold charts, diagrams, pictures, buttons, and other objects. These objects aren't contained in cells. Rather, they reside on the worksheet's *draw layer,* which is an invisible layer on top of each worksheet.

About numerical values

Numerical values represent a quantity of some type: sales amounts, number of employees, atomic weights, test scores, and so on. Values also can be dates (such as Feb-26-2007) or times (such as 3:24 a.m.).

CROSS-REF Excel can display values in many different formats. Later in this chapter, you will see how different format options can affect the display of numerical values (see the section "Applying Number Formatting").

Excel's Numerical Limitations

You may be curious about the types of values that Excel can handle. In other words, how large can numbers be? And how accurate are large numbers?

Excel's numbers are precise up to 15 digits. For example, if you enter a large value, such as 123,456,789,123,456,789 (18 digits), Excel actually stores it with only 15 digits of precision. This 18-digit number displays as 123,456,789,123,456,000. This precision may seem quite limiting, but in practice, it rarely causes any problems.

One situation in which the 15-digit accuracy can cause a problem is when entering credit-card numbers. Most credit-card numbers are 16 digits long. But Excel can handle only 15 digits, so it will substitute a zero for the last credit-card digit. Even worse, you may not even realize that Excel made the card number invalid. The solution? Enter the credit-card numbers as text. The easiest way is to preformat the cell as Text (choose Home ⇨ Number and choose Text from the drop-down Number Format list). Or you can precede the credit-card number with an apostrophe. Either method prevents Excel from interpreting the entry as a number.

Here are some of Excel's other numerical limits:

Largest positive number: 9.9E+307

Smallest negative number: –9.9E+307

Smallest positive number: 1E–307

Largest negative number: –1E-307

These numbers are expressed in scientific notation. For example, the largest positive number is "9.9 times 10 to the 307th power." (In other words, 99 followed by 306 zeros.) But keep in mind that this number has only 15 digits of accuracy.

About text entries

Most worksheets also include text in their cells. You can insert text to serve as labels for values, headings for columns, or instructions about the worksheet. Text is often used to clarify what the values in a worksheet mean.

Text that begins with a number is still considered text. For example, if you type **12 Employees** into a cell, Excel considers the entry to be text rather than a value. Consequently, you can't use this cell for numeric calculations. If you need to indicate that the number 12 refers to employees, enter **12** into a cell and type **Employees** into the cell to the right.

About formulas

Formulas are what make a spreadsheet a spreadsheet. Excel enables you to enter powerful formulas that use the values (or even text) in cells to calculate a result. When you enter a formula into a cell, the formula's result appears in the cell. If you change any of the values used by a formula, the formula recalculates and shows the new result.

Formulas can be simple mathematical expressions, or they can use some of the powerful functions that are built into Excel. Figure 13-1 shows an Excel worksheet set up to calculate a monthly loan payment. The worksheet contains values, text, and formulas. The cells in column A contain text. Column B contains four values and two formulas. The formulas are in cells B6 and B10. Column D, for reference, shows the actual contents of the cells in column B.

FIGURE 13-1

You can use values, text, and formulas to create useful Excel worksheets.

	A	B	C	D	E
1	**Loan Payment Calculator**				
2					
3				Column B Contents	
4	Purchase Amount:	$475,000		475000	
5	Down Payment Pct:	20%		0.2	
6	Loan Amount:	$380,000		=B4*(1-B5)	
7	Term (months):	360		360	
8	Interest Rate (APR):	6.25%		0.0625	
9					
10	**Monthly Payment:**	**$2,339.73**		=PMT(B8/12,B7,-B6)	
11					
12					
13					

Sheet1

CROSS-REF **You can find out much more about formulas in Chapter 15.**

Entering Text and Values into Your Worksheets

To enter a numerical value into a cell, move the cell pointer to the appropriate cell, type the value, and then press Enter or one of the arrow keys. The value is displayed in the cell and also appears in Excel's Formula bar when the cell is active. You can include decimal points and currency symbols when entering values, along with plus signs, minus signs, and commas. If you precede a value with a minus sign or enclose it in parentheses, Excel considers it to be a negative number.

Entering text into a cell is just as easy as entering a value: Activate the cell, type the text, and then press Enter or an arrow key. A cell can contain a maximum of about 32,000 characters — more than enough to hold a typical chapter in this book. Even though a cell can hold a huge number of characters, you'll find that it's not possible to actually display all these characters.

TIP **If you type an exceptionally long text entry into a cell, the Formula bar may not show all the text. To display more of the text in the Formula bar, click the bottom of the Formula bar and drag down to increase the height (see Figure 13-2).**

What happens when you enter text that's longer than its column's current width? If the cells to the immediate right are blank, Excel displays the text in its entirety, appearing to spill the entry into adjacent cells. If an adjacent cell isn't blank, Excel displays as much of the text as possible. (The full text is contained in the cell; it's just not displayed.) If you need to display a long text string in a cell that's adjacent to a nonblank cell, you can take one of several actions:

- Edit your text to make it shorter.
- Increase the width of the column.
- Use a smaller font.
- Wrap the text within the cell so that it occupies more than one line. Choose Home ➪ Alignment ➪ Wrap Text to toggle wrapping on and off for the selected cell or range.

FIGURE 13-2

The Formula bar, expanded in height to show more information in the cell.

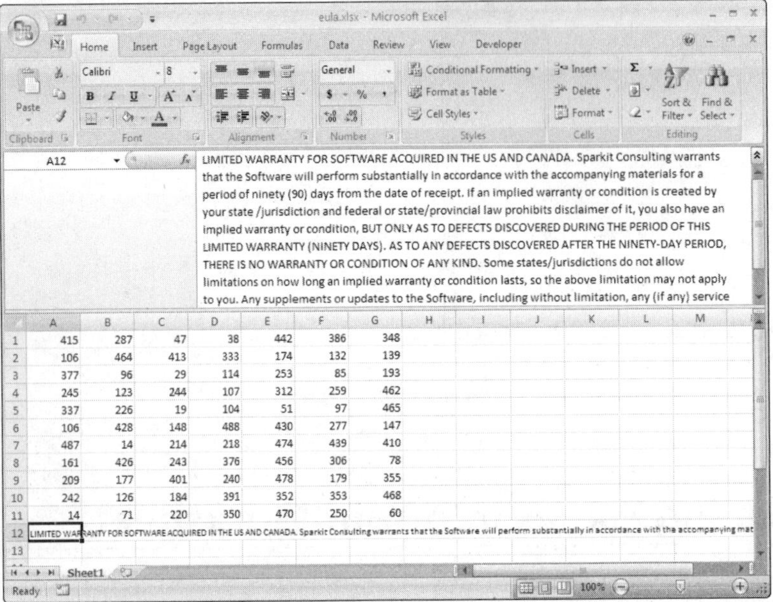

Entering Dates and Times into Your Worksheets

Excel treats dates and times as special types of numeric values. Typically, these values are formatted so that they appear as dates or times because we humans find it far easier to understand these values when they appear in the correct format. If you work with dates and times, you need to understand Excel's date and time system.

Entering date values

Excel handles dates by using a serial number system. The earliest date that Excel understands is January 1, 1900. This date has a serial number of 1. January 2, 1900, has a serial number of 2, and so on. This system makes it easy to deal with dates in formulas. For example, you can enter a formula to calculate the number of days between two dates.

Most of the time, you don't have to be concerned with Excel's serial number date system. You can simply enter a date in a familiar date format and Excel takes care of the details behind the scene.

For example, if you need to enter June 1, 2007, you can simply enter the date by typing **June 1, 2007** (or use any of several different date formats). Excel interprets your entry and stores the value 39234, which is the date serial number for that date.

NOTE **The date examples in this book use the U.S. English system. Depending on your regional settings, entering a date in a format (such as June 1, 2007) may be interpreted as text rather than a date. In such a case, you need to enter the date in a format that corresponds to your regional date settings — for example, 1 June, 2007.**

 For more information about working with dates and times, refer to Chapter 16.

Entering time values

When you work with times, you simply extend Excel's date serial number system to include decimals. In other words, Excel works with times by using fractional days. For example, the date serial number for June 1, 2007, is 39234. Noon on June 1, 2007 (halfway through the day), is represented internally as 39234.5 because the time fraction is simply added to the date serial number to get the full date/time serial number.

Again, you normally don't have to be concerned with these serial numbers (or fractional serial numbers, for times). Just enter the time into a cell in a recognized format.

 Refer to Chapter 16 for more information about working with time values.

Modifying Cell Contents

After you enter a value or text into a cell, you can modify it in several ways:

- Erase the cell's contents
- Replace the cell's contents with something else
- Edit the cell's contents

Erasing the contents of a cell

To erase the contents of a cell, just click the cell and press Delete. To erase more than one cell, select all the cells that you want to erase and then press Delete. Pressing Delete removes the cell's contents but doesn't remove any formatting (such as bold, italic, or a different number format) that you may have applied to the cell.

For more control over what gets deleted, you can choose Home ➪ Editing ➪ Clear. This command's drop-down list has four choices:

- **Clear All:** Clears everything from the cell
- **Clear Formats:** Clears only the formatting and leaves the value, text, or formula
- **Clear Contents:** Clears only the cell's contents and leaves the formatting
- **Clear Comments:** Clears the comment (if one exists) attached to the cell

NOTE Clearing formats doesn't clear the background colors in a range that has been designated as a table, unless you've replace the table style background colors manually.

Replacing the contents of a cell

To replace the contents of a cell with something else, just activate the cell and type your new entry, which replaces the previous contents. Any formatting that you previously applied to the cell remains in place and is applied to the new content.

TIP You can also replace cell contents by dragging and dropping or by pasting data from the Clipboard. In both cases, the cell formatting will be replaced by the format of the new data. To avoid pasting formatting, choose Home ➪ Clipboard ➪ Paste and select Formulas or Paste Values.

Editing the contents of a cell

If the cell contains only a few characters, replacing its contents by typing new data usually is easiest. But if the cell contains lengthy text or a complex formula and you need to make only a slight modification, you probably want to edit the cell rather than re-enter information.

When you want to edit the contents of a cell, you can use one of the following ways to enter cell-edit mode:

- **Double-clicking the cell** enables you to edit the cell contents directly in the cell.
- **Selecting the cell and pressing F2** enables you to edit the cell contents directly in the cell.
- **Selecting the cell that you want to edit and then clicking inside the Formula bar** enables you to edit the cell contents in the Formula bar.

You can use whichever method you prefer. Some people find editing directly in the cell easier; others prefer to use the Formula bar to edit a cell.

NOTE **The Advanced tab of the Excel Options dialog box contains a section called Editing Options. These settings affect how editing works. (To access this dialog box, choose Office Button ⇨ Excel Options.) If the option labeled Allow Editing Directly In Cells isn't enabled, you aren't able to edit a cell by double-clicking. In addition, pressing F2 allows you to edit the cell in the Formula bar (not directly in the cell).**

All these methods cause Excel to go into *edit mode*. (The word `Edit` appears at the left side of the status bar at the bottom of the screen.) When Excel is in edit mode, the Formula bar displays two new icons: the X and Check Mark (see Figure 13-3). Clicking the X icon cancels editing, without changing the cell's contents. (Pressing Esc has the same effect.) Clicking the Check Mark icon completes the editing and enters the modified contents into the cell. (Pressing Enter has the same effect.)

FIGURE 13-3

While editing a cell, the Formula bar displays two new icons.

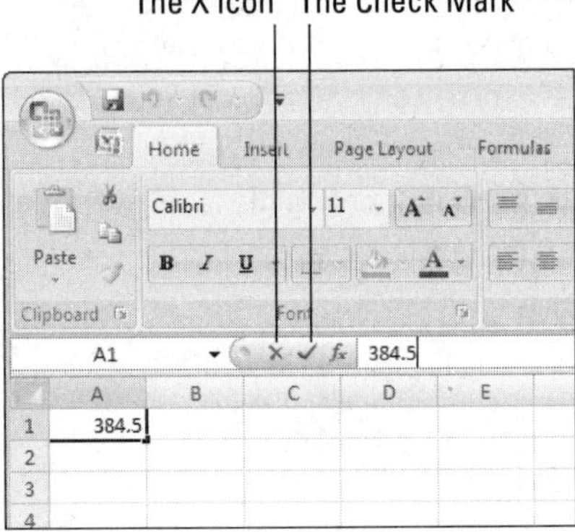

When you begin editing a cell, the insertion point appears as a vertical bar, and you can move the insertion point by using the arrow keys. Use Home to move the insertion point to the beginning of the cell and use End to move the insertion point to the end. You can add new characters at the location of the insertion point. To select multiple characters, press Shift while you use the arrow keys. You also can use the mouse to select characters while you're editing a cell. Just click and drag the mouse pointer over the characters that you want to select.

Learning some handy data-entry techniques

You can simplify the process of entering information into your Excel worksheets and make your work go quite a bit faster by using a number of useful tricks, described in the following sections.

Automatically moving the cell pointer after entering data

By default, Excel automatically moves the cell pointer to the next cell down when you press the Enter key after entering data into a cell. To change this setting, choose Office Button ➪ Excel Options and click the Advanced item (see Figure 13-4) in the list at the left. The checkbox that controls this behavior is labeled After Pressing Enter, Move Selection. You can also specify the direction in which the cell pointer moves (down, left, up, or right).

Your choice is completely a matter of personal preference. I prefer to keep this option turned off. When entering data, I use the arrow keys rather than the Enter key (see the next section).

FIGURE 13-4

You can use the Advanced choices in the Excel Options dialog box to select a number of helpful input option settings.

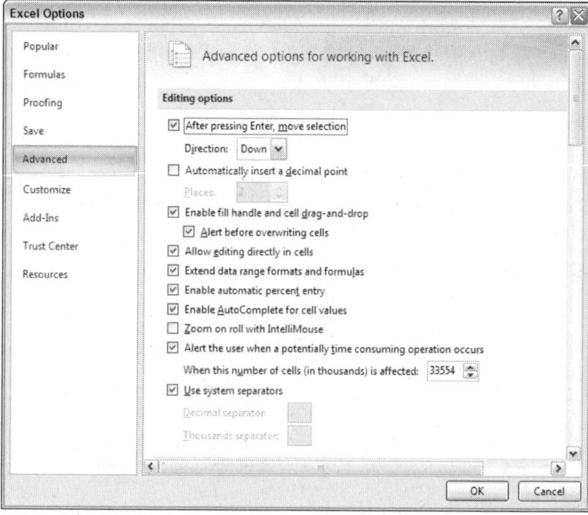

Using arrow keys instead of pressing Enter

Instead of pressing the Enter key when you're finished making a cell entry, you also can use any of the directional keys to complete the entry. Not surprisingly, these directional keys send you in the direction that you indicate. For example, if you're entering data in a row, press the right-arrow (→) key rather than Enter. The other arrow keys work as expected, and you can even use PgUp and PgDn.

Selecting a range of input cells before entering data

Here's a tip that most Excel users don't know about: When a range of cells is selected, Excel automatically moves the cell pointer to the next cell in the range when you press Enter. If the selection consists of multiple rows, Excel moves down the column; when it reaches the end of the selection in the column, it moves to the first selected cell in the next column.

To skip a cell, just press Enter without entering anything. To go backward, press Shift+Enter. If you prefer to enter the data by rows rather than by columns, press Tab rather than Enter.

Using Ctrl+Enter to place information into multiple cells simultaneously

If you need to enter the same data into multiple cells, Excel offers a handy shortcut. Select all the cells that you want to contain the data; type the value, text, or formula, which will appear in the formula bar; and then press Ctrl+Enter (instead of Enter). The same information is inserted into each cell in the selection.

Entering decimal points automatically

If you need to enter lots of numbers with a fixed number of decimal places, Excel has a useful tool that works like some adding machines. Open the Excel Options dialog box (Office Button ➪ Excel Options) and click the Advanced choice. Select the checkbox Automatically Insert a Decimal Point and make sure that the Places box is set for the correct number of decimal places for the data you need to enter.

When this option is set, Excel supplies the decimal points for you automatically. For example, if you've specified two decimal places, entering **12345** into a cell is interpreted as 123.45. To restore things to normal, just uncheck the Automatically Insert a Decimal Point checkbox in the Excel Options dialog box. Changing this setting doesn't affect any values that you have already entered.

CAUTION **The fixed-decimal-places option is a global setting and applies to all workbooks (not just the active workbook). If you forget that this option is turned on, you can easily end up entering incorrect values — or some major confusion if someone else uses your computer.**

Using AutoFill to enter a series of values

Excel's AutoFill feature makes inserting a series of values or text items in a range of cells easy. It uses the AutoFill handle (the small box at the lower right of the active cell). You can drag the AutoFill handle to copy the cell or automatically complete a series.

If you drag the AutoFill handle while you press the right mouse button, Excel displays a shortcut menu with additional fill options.

Figure 13-5 shows an example. I entered 1 into cell A1 and 3 into cell A2. Then I selected both cells and dragged the fill handle down to create a linear series of odd numbers.

FIGURE 13-5

This series was created using AutoFill.

	A	B	C	D	E
1	1				
2	3				
3	5				
4	7				
5	9				
6	11				
7	13				
8	15				
9	17				
10	19				
11	21				
12	23				
13	25				
14	27				
15	29				

Sheet1

Using AutoComplete to automate data entry

Excel's AutoComplete feature makes entering the same text into multiple cells easy. With AutoComplete, you type the first few letters of a text entry into a cell, and Excel automatically completes the entry based on other entries that you've already made in the column. Besides reducing typing, this feature also ensures that your entries are spelled correctly and are consistent.

Here's how it works. Suppose that you're entering product information in a column. One of your products is named Widgets. The first time that you enter Widgets into a cell, Excel remembers it. Later, when you start typing Widgets in that same column, Excel recognizes it by the first few letters and finishes typing it for you. Just press Enter, and you're done. It also changes the case of letters for you automatically. If you start entering widget (with a lowercase *w*) in the second entry, Excel makes the *w* uppercase to be consistent with the previous entry in the column.

TIP **You also can access a mouse-oriented version of AutoComplete by right-clicking the cell and selecting Pick From Drop-Down List from the shortcut menu. Excel then displays a drop-down box that has all the entries in the current column, and you just click the one that you want.**

Keep in mind that AutoComplete works only within a contiguous column of cells. If you have a blank row, for example, AutoComplete identifies only the cell contents below the blank row.

If you find the AutoComplete feature distracting, you can turn it off by using the Advanced settings of the Excel Options dialog box. Remove the check mark from the checkbox labeled Enable AutoComplete For Cell Values. (See Appendix A, "Customizing Office," for more information about changing options.)

Forcing text to appear on a new line within a cell

If you have lengthy text in a cell, you can force Excel to display it in multiple lines within the cell. Use Alt+Enter to start a new line in a cell.

NOTE **When you add a line break, Excel automatically changes the cell's format to Wrap Text. But unlike normal text wrap, your manual line break forces Excel to break the text at a specific place within the text, which gives you more precise control over the appearance of the text than if you rely on automatic text wrapping.**

TIP **To remove a manual line break, edit the cell and press Delete when the insertion point is located at the end of the line that contains the manual line break. You won't see any symbol to indicate the position of the manual line break, but the text that follows it will move up when the line break is deleted.**

Using AutoCorrect for shorthand data entry

You can use Excel's AutoCorrect feature to create shortcuts for commonly used words or phrases. For example, if you work for a company named Consolidated Data Processing Corporation, you can create an AutoCorrect entry for an abbreviation, such as cdp. Then, whenever you type cdp, Excel automatically changes it to Consolidated Data Processing Corporation.

Excel includes quite a few built-in AutoCorrect terms (mostly common misspellings), and you can add your own. To set up your custom AutoCorrect entries, access the Excel Options dialog box (choose Office Button ➪ Excel Options) and click the Proofing tab. Then click the AutoCorrect Options button to display the AutoCorrect dialog box. In the dialog box, click the AutoCorrect tab, check the option labeled Replace Text As You Type, and then enter your custom entries. (Figure 13-6 shows an example.) You can set up as many custom entries as you like. Just be careful not to use an abbreviation that might appear normally in your text.

TIP **Excel shares your AutoCorrect list with other Office applications. For example, any AutoCorrect entries you created in Word also work in Excel.**

FIGURE 13-6

AutoCorrect allows you to create shorthand abbreviations for text you enter often.

Entering numbers with fractions

To enter a fractional value into a cell, leave a space between the whole number and the fraction. For example, to enter 6⅞, enter **6 7/8** and then press Enter. When you select the cell, 6.875 appears in the Formula bar, and the cell entry appears as a fraction. If you have a fraction only (for example, ⅛), you must enter a zero first, like this: **0 1/8**—otherwise, Excel will likely assume that you're entering a date. When you select the cell and look at the Formula bar, you see 0.125. In the cell, you see ⅛.

Simplifying data entry by using a form

Many people use Excel to manage lists in which the information is arranged in rows. Excel offers a simple way to work with this type of data through the use of a data entry form that Excel can create automatically. This data form works with either a normal range of data or with a range that has been designated as a table (choosing Insert ➪ Tables ➪ Table). Figure 13-7 shows an example.

FIGURE 13-7

Excel's built-in data form can simplify many data-entry tasks.

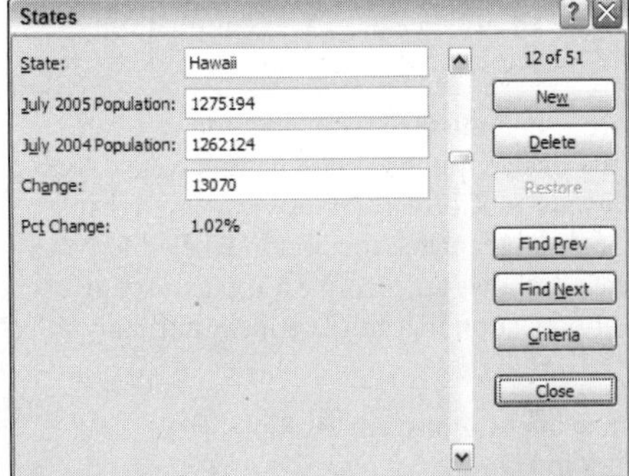

Unfortunately, the command to access the data form is not in the Ribbon. To use the data form, you must add it to your Quick Access toolbar (QAT):

1. **Right-click the QAT and select Customize Quick Access Toolbar.** The Customize panel of the Excel Options dialog box appears.
2. **In the Choose Commands From drop-down list, select Commands Not In The Ribbon.**
3. **In the list box on the left, select Form.**
4. **Click the Add button to add the selected command to your QAT.**
5. **Click OK to close the Excel Options dialog box.**

After performing these steps, a new button appears on your QAT.

To use a data entry form, you must arrange your data so that Excel can recognize it as a table. Start by entering headings for the columns in the first row of your data entry range. Select any cell in the table and click the Form button on your QAT. Excel then displays a dialog box customized to your data. You can use Tab to move between the text boxes and supply information. If a cell contains a formula, the formula result appears as text (not as an edit box). In other words, you can't modify formulas using the data entry form.

When you complete the data form, click the New button. Excel enters the data into a row in the worksheet and clears the dialog box for the next row of data.

Entering the current date or time into a cell

If you need to date-stamp or time-stamp your worksheet, Excel provides two shortcut keys that do this task for you:

- **Current date:** Ctrl+; (semicolon)
- **Current time:** Ctrl+Shift+; (semicolon)

NOTE **When you use either of these shortcuts to enter a date or time into your worksheet, Excel enters a static value into the worksheet. In other words, the date or time entered doesn't change when the worksheet is recalculated. In most cases, this setup is probably what you want, but you should be aware of this limitation. If you want the date or time display to update, use one of these formulas:**

```
=TODAY()
=NOW()
```

Applying Number Formatting

Number formatting refers to the process of changing the appearance of values contained in cells. Excel provides a wide variety of number formatting options. In the following sections, you see how to use many of Excel's formatting options to quickly improve the appearance of your worksheets.

TIP **Remember that the formatting you apply works with the selected cell or cells. Therefore, you need to select the cell (or range of cells) before applying the formatting. Also remember that changing the number format does not affect the underlying value. Number formatting affects only the appearance.**

Values that you enter into cells normally are unformatted. In other words, they simply consist of a string of numerals. Typically, you want to format the numbers so that they're easier to read or are more consistent in terms of the number of decimal places shown.

Figure 13-8 shows a worksheet that has two columns of values. The first column consists of unformatted values. The cells in the second column are formatted to make the values easier to read. The third column describes the type of formatting applied.

FIGURE 13-8

Use numeric formatting to make it easier to understand what the values in the worksheet represent.

Unformatted	Formatted	Type
1200	$1,200.00	Currency
0.231	23.1%	Percentage
2/3/2008	2/3/2008	Short Date
2/3/2008	Sunday, February 03, 2008	Long Date
123439832	123,439,832.00	Accounting
5559832	555-9832	Phone Number
434988723	434-98-8723	Social Security Number
0.552	1:14:53 PM	Time
0.25	1/4	Fraction
12332354090	1.23E+10	Scientific

TIP If you move the cell pointer to a cell that has a formatted value, the Formula bar displays the value in its unformatted state because the formatting affects only how the value appears in the cell — not the actual value contained in the cell.

Using automatic number formatting

Excel is smart enough to perform some formatting for you automatically. For example, if you enter 12.2% into a cell, Excel knows that you want to use a percentage format and applies it for you automatically. If you use commas to separate thousands (such as 123,456), Excel applies comma formatting for you. And if you precede your value with a dollar sign, the cell is formatted for currency (assuming that the dollar sign is your system currency symbol).

TIP A handy default feature in Excel makes entering percentage values into cells easier. If a cell is formatted to display as a percent, you can simply enter a normal value (for example 12.5 for 12.5%). If this feature isn't working (or if you prefer to enter the actual value for percents), open the Excel Options dialog box and click the Advanced choice in the list at the left. In the Editing Options section, locate the checkbox labeled Enable Automatic Percent Entry and remove the check mark.

Formatting numbers by using the Ribbon

The Home ➪ Number group in the Ribbon contains controls that let you quickly apply common number formats (see Figure 13-9).

The Number Format drop-down list contains 11 common number formats. Additional options include an Accounting Number Format drop-down list (to select a currency format), plus a Percent Style and a Comma Style button. In addition, the group contains a button to increase the number of decimal places, and another to decrease the number of decimal places.

When you select one of these controls, the active cell takes on the specified number format. You also can select a range of cells (or even an entire row or column) before clicking these buttons. If you select more than one cell, Excel applies the number format to all the selected cells.

FIGURE 13-9

You can find number formatting commands in the Number group of the Home tab.

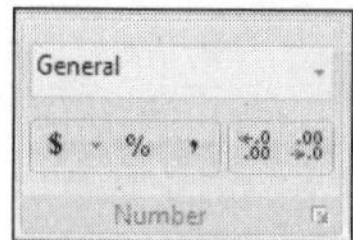

Using shortcut keys to format numbers

Another way to apply number formatting is to use shortcut keys. Table 13-1 summarizes the shortcut key combinations that you can use to apply common number formatting to the selected cells or range. Notice that these Ctrl+Shift characters are all located together, in the upper-left part of your keyboard.

TABLE 13-1

Number-Formatting Keyboard Shortcuts

Key Combination	Formatting Applied
Ctrl+Shift+~	General number format (that is, unformatted values)
Ctrl+Shift+$	Currency format with two decimal places (negative numbers appear in parentheses)
Ctrl+Shift+%	Percentage format, with no decimal places
Ctrl+Shift+^	Scientific notation number format, with two decimal places
Ctrl+Shift+#	Date format with the day, month, and year
Ctrl+Shift+@	Time format with the hour, minute, and AM or PM
Ctrl+Shift+!	Two decimal places, thousands separator, and a hyphen for negative values

Formatting numbers using the Format Cells dialog box

In most cases, the number formats that are accessible from the Number group on the Home tab are just fine. Sometimes, however, you want more control over how your values appear. Excel offers a great deal of control over number formats through the use of the Format Cells dialog box, shown in Figure 13-10. For formatting numbers, you need to use the Number tab.

You can bring up the Format Cells dialog box in several ways. Start by selecting the cell or cells that you want to format and then do the following:

- Choose Home ➪ Number and click the small Dialog Box Launcher icon.
- Choose Home ➪ Number, click the Number Format drop-down list, and select More Number Formats from the drop-down list.
- Right-click and choose Format Cells from the shortcut menu.
- Press the Ctrl+1 shortcut key.

The Number tab of the Format Cells dialog box displays 12 categories of number formats from which to choose. When you select a category from the list box, the right side of the tab changes to display the appropriate options.

FIGURE 13-10

When you need more control over number formats, use the Number tab of the Format Cells dialog box.

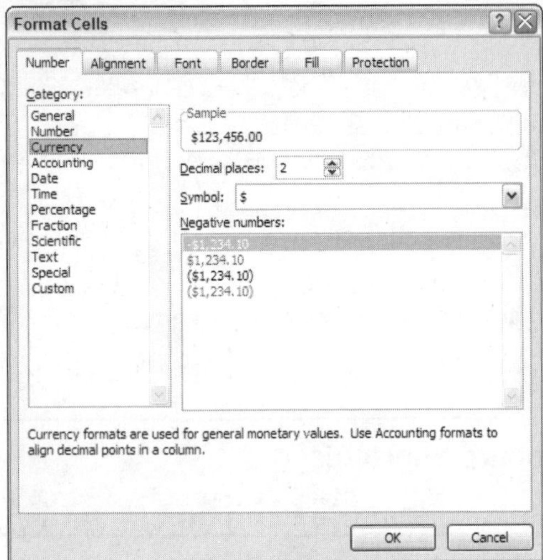

The Number category has three options that you can control: the number of decimal places displayed, whether to use a thousand separator, and how you want negative numbers displayed. Notice that the Negative Numbers list box has four choices (two of which display negative values in red), and the choices change depending on the number of decimal places and whether you choose to separate thousands.

The top of the tab displays a sample of how the active cell will appear with the selected number format (visible only if a cell with a value is selected). After you make your choices, click OK to apply the number format to all the selected cells.

CAUTION **Selecting the Precision As Displayed option changes the numbers in your worksheets to permanently match their appearance onscreen. This setting applies to all sheets in the active workbook. Most of the time, this option is *not* what you want. Make sure that you understand the consequences of using the Set Precision As Displayed option.**

CROSS-REF **Chapter 15 discusses** ROUND **and other built-in functions.**

The following are the number-format categories, along with some general comments:

- **General:** The default format; it displays numbers as integers, as decimals, or in scientific notation if the value is too wide to fit in the cell.
- **Number:** Enables you to specify the number of decimal places, whether to use a comma to separate thousands, and how to display negative numbers (with a minus sign, in red, in parentheses, or in red and in parentheses).
- **Currency:** Enables you to specify the number of decimal places, whether to use a currency symbol, and how to display negative numbers (with a minus sign, in red, in parentheses, or in red and in parentheses). This format always uses a comma to separate thousands.

When Numbers Appear to Add Up Incorrectly

Applying a number format to a cell doesn't change the value — only how the value appears in the worksheet. For example, if a cell contains 0.874543, you may format it to appear as 87%. If that cell is used in a formula, the formula uses the full value (0.874543), not the displayed value (87%).

In some situations, formatting may cause Excel to display calculation results that appear incorrect, such as when totaling numbers with decimal places. For example, if values are formatted to display two decimal places, you may not see the actual numbers used in the calculations. But because Excel uses the full precision of the values in its formula, the sum of the two values may appear to be incorrect.

Several solutions to this problem are available. You can format the cells to display more decimal places. You can use the `ROUND` function on individual numbers and specify the number of decimal places Excel should round to. Or you can instruct Excel to change the worksheet values to match their displayed format. To do so, open the Excel Options dialog box and click the Advanced choice. Check the Set Precision As Displayed checkbox (which is located in the section named When Calculating This Workbook).

- **Accounting:** Differs from the Currency format in that the currency symbols always line up vertically.
- **Date:** Enables you to choose from several different date formats.
- **Time:** Enables you to choose from several different time formats.
- **Percentage:** Enables you to choose the number of decimal places and always displays a percent sign.
- **Fraction:** Enables you to choose from among nine fraction formats.
- **Scientific:** Displays numbers in exponential notation (with an E): 2.00E+05 = 200,000; 2.05E+05 = 205,000. You can choose the number of decimal places to display to the left of E.
- **Text:** When applied to a value, causes Excel to treat the value as text (even if it looks like a number). This feature is useful for such items as part numbers.
- **Special:** Contains four additional number formats (Zip Code, Zip Code +4, Phone Number, and Social Security Number).
- **Custom:** Enables you to define custom number formats that aren't included in any other category.

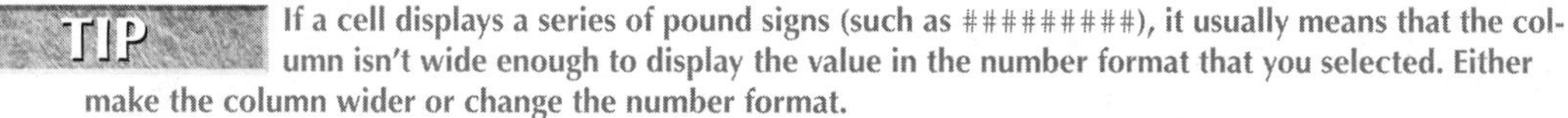

TIP **If a cell displays a series of pound signs (such as #########), it usually means that the column isn't wide enough to display the value in the number format that you selected. Either make the column wider or change the number format.**

Summary

This chapter showed you the techniques you need to know to enter the contents for any worksheet in Excel. You learned how Excel treats different types of information — text, numbers, and formulas. You saw how to enter each type of information into a cell, as well as how to edit or replace a cell entry. The chapter shared handy data-entry shortcuts such as AutoFill, and finished by explaining what number formats are and how to apply them. Continue in the book to learn how to work with groups of cells called ranges.

Chapter 14

Essential Worksheet and Cell Range Operations

IN THIS CHAPTER

- Understanding Excel worksheet essentials
- Controlling your views
- Manipulating the rows and columns
- Understanding Excel's cells and ranges
- Selecting cells and ranges
- Copying or moving ranges
- Using names to work with ranges
- Adding comments to cells

This chapter covers some basic information regarding workbooks, worksheets, and windows. You will discover tips and techniques to help you take control of your worksheets. Most of the work you do in Excel involves cells and ranges. Understanding how best to manipulate cells and ranges will save you time and effort. This chapter discusses a variety of techniques that you can use to master worksheets, cells, and ranges. The result? You'll be a more efficient Excel user.

Learning the Fundamentals of Excel Worksheets

In Excel, each file is called a *workbook,* and each workbook can contain one or more *worksheets.* You may find it helpful to think of an Excel workbook as a notebook and worksheets as pages in the notebook. As with a notebook, you can view a particular sheet, add new sheets, remove sheets, and copy sheets.

The following sections describe the operations that you can perform with worksheets.

Working with Excel's windows

An Excel workbook file can hold any number of sheets, and these sheets can be either worksheets (sheets consisting of rows and columns) or *chart sheets* (sheets that hold a single chart). A worksheet is what people usually think of when they think of a spreadsheet. You can open as many Excel workbooks as necessary at the same time.

Figure 14-1 shows Excel with four workbooks open, each in a separate window. One of the windows is minimized and appears near the lower-left corner of the screen. (When a workbook is minimized, only its title bar is visible.) Worksheet windows can overlap, and the title bar of one window is a different color. That's the window that contains the active workbook.

FIGURE 14-1

You can open several Excel workbooks at the same time.

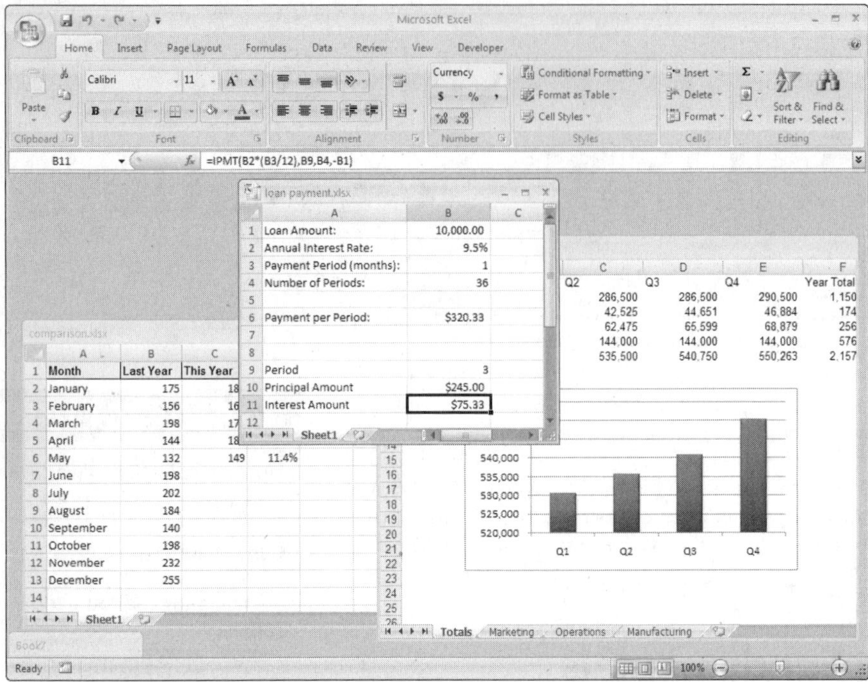

The workbook windows that Excel uses work much like the windows in any other Windows program. Each window has three buttons at the right side of its title bar. From left to right, they are Minimize, Maximize (or Restore), and Close. When a workbook window is maximized, the three buttons appear directly below Excel's title bar.

Excel's windows can be in one of the following states:

- **Maximized:** Fills Excel's entire workspace. A maximized window doesn't have a title bar, and the workbook's name appears in Excel's title bar. To maximize a window, click its Maximize button.
- **Minimized:** Appears as a small window with only a title bar. To minimize a window, click its Minimize button.
- **Restored:** A nonmaximized size. To restore a maximized or minimized window, click its Restore button.

If you work with more than one workbook simultaneously (which is quite common), you have to know how to move, resize, and switch among the workbook windows.

Moving and resizing windows

To move a window, make sure that it's not maximized. Then drag its title bar with your mouse.

To resize a window, drag any of its borders until it's the size that you want it to be. When you position the mouse pointer on a window's border, the mouse pointer changes to a double-sided arrow, which lets you know that you can now drag to resize the window. To resize a window horizontally and vertically at the same time, drag any of its corners.

You can't move or resize a workbook window if it's maximized. You can move a minimized window, but doing so has no effect on its position when it's subsequently restored.

If you want all your workbook windows to be visible (that is, not obscured by another window), you can move and resize the windows manually, or you can let Excel do it for you. Choosing View ➪ Window ➪ Arrange All displays the Arrange Windows dialog box, shown in Figure 14-2. This dialog box has four window-arrangement options. Just select the one that you want and click OK. Windows that are minimized aren't affected by this change.

FIGURE 14-2

Use the Arrange Windows dialog box to quickly arrange all open workbook windows.

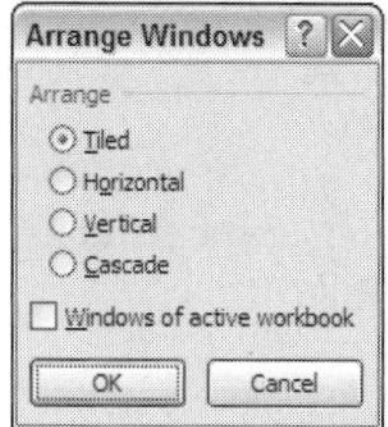

Switching among windows

At any given time, one (and only one) workbook window is the active window. The active window accepts your input and is the window in which your commands work. The active window's title bar is a different color, and the window appears at the top of the stack of windows. To work in a different window, you need to make that window active. You can make a different window the active workbook in several ways:

- Click another window, if it's visible. The window you click moves to the top and becomes the active window. This method isn't possible if the current window is maximized.
- Press Ctrl+Tab (or Ctrl+F6) to cycle through all open windows until the window that you want to work with appears on top as the active window. Shift+Ctrl+Tab (or Shift+Ctrl+F6) cycles through the windows in the opposite direction.
- Choose View ➪ Window ➪ Switch Windows and select the window that you want from the drop-down list (the active window has a check mark next to it). This menu can display up to nine windows. If you have more than nine workbook windows open, choose More Windows (which appears below the nine window names).
- Click the icon for the window in the Windows taskbar. This technique is available only if the Show All Windows In The Taskbar option is turned on. You can control this setting by clicking the Advanced choice in the Excel Options dialog box (the setting is in the Display section).

TIP

Most people prefer to do most of their work with maximized workbook windows, which enables you to see more cells and eliminates the distraction of other workbook windows getting in the way. At times, however, viewing multiple windows is preferred. For example, displaying two windows is more efficient if you need to compare information in two workbooks or if you need to copy data from one workbook to another.

When you maximize one window, all the other windows are maximized, too (even though you don't see them). Therefore, if the active window is maximized and you activate a different window, the new active window is also maximized.

TIP **You also can display a single workbook in more than one window. For example, if you have a workbook with two worksheets, you may want to display each worksheet in a separate window in order to compare the two sheets. All the window-manipulation procedures described previously still apply. Choose View ➪ Window ➪ New Window to open an additional window in the active workbook.**

Closing windows

If you have multiple windows open, you may want to close those windows that you no longer need. Excel offers several ways to close the active window:

- Choose Office Button ➪ Close.
- Click the Close button (the *X* button) on the workbook window's title bar. If the workbook window is maximized, its title bar is not visible, so its Close button appears directly below Excel's Close button.
- Press Ctrl+W.

When you close a workbook window, Excel checks whether you have made any changes since the last time you saved the file. If not, the window closes without a prompt from Excel. If you've made any changes, Excel prompts you to save the file before it closes the window.

Activating a worksheet

At any given time, one workbook is the active workbook, and one sheet is the active sheet in the active workbook. To activate a different sheet, just click its sheet tab, located at the bottom of the workbook window. You also can use the following shortcut keys to activate a different sheet:

- **Ctrl+PgUp:** Activates the previous sheet, if one exists
- **Ctrl+PgDn:** Activates the next sheet, if one exists

If your workbook has many sheets, all its tabs may not be visible. Use the tab-scrolling controls (see Figure 14-3) to scroll the sheet tabs. The sheet tabs share space with the worksheet's horizontal scroll bar. You also can drag the tab split control to display more or fewer tabs. Dragging the tab split control simultaneously changes the number of tabs and the size of the horizontal scroll bar.

When you right-click any of the tab-scrolling controls, Excel displays a list of all sheets in the workbook. You can quickly activate a sheet by selecting it from the list.

FIGURE 14-3

Use the tab controls to activate a different worksheet or to see additional worksheet tabs.

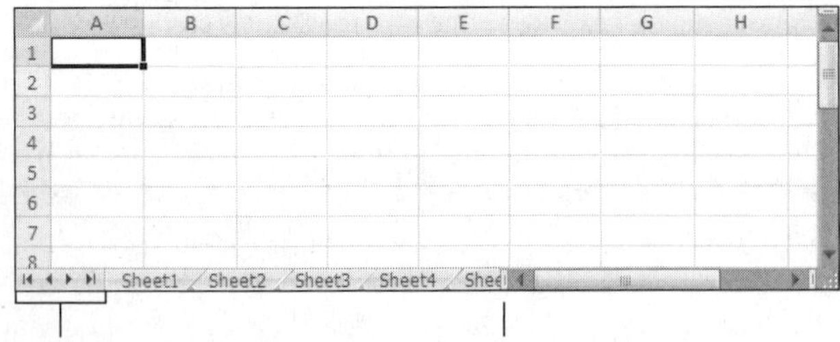

Changing the Default Number of Sheets in Your Workbooks

By default, Excel automatically creates three worksheets in each new workbook. You can change this default behavior. For example, I prefer to start each new workbook with a single worksheet. After all, you can easily add new sheets if and when they're needed. To change the default number of worksheets:

1. **Select Office Button ➪ Excel Options to display the Excel Options dialog box.**
2. **In the Excel Options dialog box, click Popular in the list at the left.**
3. **Change the value for the Include This Many Sheets setting and click OK.**

Making this change affects all new workbooks but has no effect on existing workbooks.

Adding a new worksheet to your workbook

Worksheets can be an excellent organizational tool. Instead of placing everything on a single worksheet, you can use additional worksheets in a workbook to separate various workbook elements logically. For example, if you have several products whose sales you track individually, you may want to assign each product to its own worksheet and then use another worksheet to consolidate your results.

The following are three ways to add a new worksheet to a workbook:

- Click the Insert Worksheet control, which is located to the right of the last sheet tab. This method inserts the new sheet after the last sheet in the workbook.
- Press Shift+F11. This method inserts the new sheet before the active sheet.
- Right-click a sheet tab, choose Insert from the shortcut menu, and click the General tab of the Insert dialog box. Then click the Worksheet icon and click OK. This method inserts the new sheet before the active sheet.

Deleting a worksheet you no longer need

If you no longer need a worksheet, or if you want to get rid of an empty worksheet in a workbook, you can delete it in either of two ways:

- Right-click the sheet tab and choose Delete from the shortcut menu.
- Choose Home ➪ Cells ➪ Delete ➪ Delete Sheet. If the worksheet contains any data, Excel asks you to confirm that you want to delete the sheet. If you've never used the worksheet, Excel deletes it immediately without asking for confirmation.

TIP **You can delete multiple sheets with a single command by selecting the sheets that you want to delete. To select multiple sheets, press Ctrl while you click the tabs for the sheets that you want to delete. To select a group of contiguous sheets, click the first sheet tab, press Shift, and then click the last sheet tab. Then use either method to delete the selected sheets.**

CAUTION **When you delete a worksheet, it's gone for good. Deleting a worksheet is one of the few operations in Excel that can't be undone.**

Changing the name of a worksheet

The default names Excel uses for worksheets — Sheet1, Sheet2, and so on — aren't very descriptive. If you don't change the worksheet names, remembering where to find things in multiple-sheet workbooks can be a bit difficult. That's why providing more meaningful names for your worksheets is often a good idea.

To change a sheet's name, double-click the sheet tab. Excel highlights the name on the sheet tab so that you can edit the name or replace it with a new name.

Sheet names can be up to 31 characters, and spaces are allowed. However, you can't use the following characters in sheet names:

: colon
/ slash
\ backslash
? question mark
* asterisk

Keep in mind that a longer worksheet name results in a wider tab, which takes up more space on the screen. Therefore, if you use lengthy sheet names, you won't be able to see very many sheet tabs without scrolling the tab list.

Changing a sheet tab's color

Excel allows you to change the color of your worksheet tabs. For example, you may prefer to color-code the sheet tabs to make identifying the worksheet's contents easier.

To change the color of a sheet tab, right-click the tab and choose Tab Color. Then select the color from the color selector box.

Rearranging your worksheets

You may want to rearrange the order of worksheets in a workbook. If you have a separate worksheet for each sales region, for example, arranging the worksheets in alphabetical order or by total sales may be helpful. You may want to move a worksheet from one workbook to another. (To move a worksheet to a different workbook, both workbooks must be open.) You can also create copies of worksheets.

You can move or copy a worksheet in the following ways:

- Right-click the sheet tab and choose Move or Copy to display the Move or Copy dialog box (see Figure 14-4). Use this dialog box to specify the operation and the location for the sheet.
- To move a worksheet, drag the worksheet tab to the desired location (either in the same workbook or in a different workbook). When you drag, the mouse pointer changes to a small sheet, and a small arrow guides you.
- To copy a worksheet, press and hold Ctrl while dragging the tab to its desired location (either in the same workbook or in a different workbook). When you drag, the mouse pointer changes to a small sheet with a plus sign on it.

TIP **You can move or copy multiple sheets simultaneously. First select the sheets by clicking their sheet tabs while holding down the Ctrl key. Then you can move or copy the set of sheets by using the preceding methods.**

Preventing Sheet Actions

To prevent others from unhiding hidden sheets, inserting new sheets, renaming sheets, copying sheets, or deleting sheets, protect the workbook's structure:

1. **Choose Review ➪ Changes ➪ Protect Workbook.**
2. **In the Protect Workbook dialog box, click the Structure option.**
3. **Provide a password, if you like.**

After performing these steps, several commands will no longer be available when you right-click a sheet tab: Insert, Delete, Rename, Move or Copy, Hide, and Unhide. Be aware, however, that this is a very weak security measure. Cracking Excel's protection features is relatively easy.

You can also make a sheet "very hidden." A sheet that is very hidden doesn't appear in the Unhide dialog box. To make a sheet very hidden:

1. **Activate the worksheet.**
2. **Choose Developer ➪ Controls ➪ Properties.** The Properties dialog box, shown in the following figure, appears. (If the Developer tab isn't available, you can turn it on from the Popular category in the Excel Options dialog box.)
3. **In the Properties box, select the Visible option and choose 2 - xlSheetVeryHidden.**

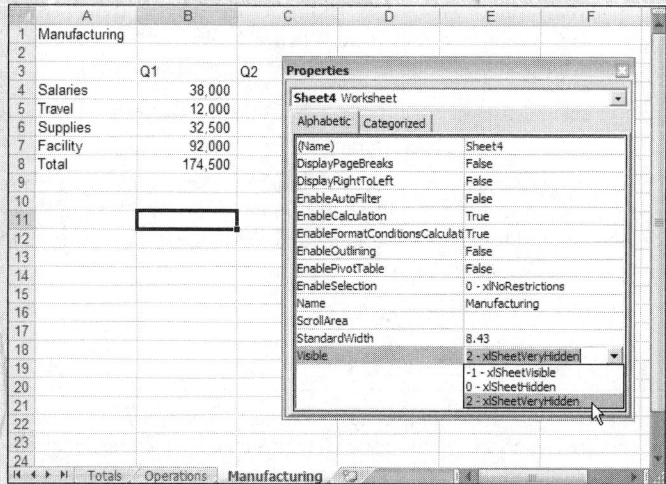

After performing these steps, the worksheet is hidden and doesn't appear in the Unhide dialog box.

Be careful! After you make a sheet very hidden, you can't use the Properties box to unhide it because you aren't able to select the sheet! In fact, the only way to unhide such a sheet is to use a VBA macro. For example, this VBA statement unhides Sheet1 in the active workbook:

```
ActiveWorkbook.Worksheets("Sheet1").Visible = True
```

FIGURE 14-4

Use the Move or Copy dialog box to move or copy worksheets in the same or another workbook.

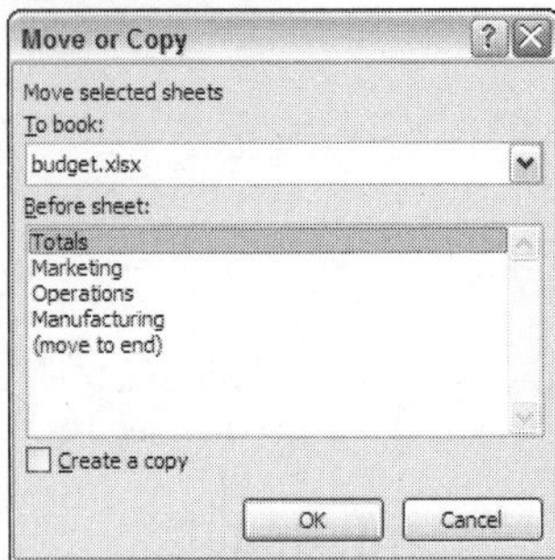

If you move or copy a worksheet to a workbook that already has a sheet with the same name, Excel changes the name to make it unique. For example, `Sheet1` becomes `Sheet1 (2)`.

When you move or copy a worksheet to a different workbook, any defined names and custom formats also get copied to the new workbook.

Hiding and unhiding a worksheet

In some situations, you may want to hide one or more worksheets. Hiding a sheet may be useful if you don't want others to see it or if you just want to get it out of the way. When a sheet is hidden, its sheet tab is also hidden. You can't hide all the sheets in a workbook, so at least one sheet must remain visible.

To hide a worksheet, right-click its sheet tab and choose Hide. The active worksheet (or selected worksheets) will be hidden from view.

To unhide a hidden worksheet, right-click any sheet tab and choose Unhide. Excel opens its Unhide dialog box that lists all hidden sheets. Choose the sheet that you want to redisplay and click OK. You can't select multiple sheets from this dialog box, so you need to repeat the command for each sheet that you want to unhide.

Controlling the Worksheet View

As you add more information to a worksheet, you may find that navigating and locating what you want gets more difficult. Excel includes a few options that enable you to view your sheet, and sometimes multiple sheets, more efficiently. This section discusses a few additional worksheet options at your disposal.

Zooming in or out for a better view

Normally, everything you see on-screen is displayed at 100 percent. You can change the *zoom percentage* from 10 percent (very tiny) to 400 percent (huge). Using a small zoom percentage can help you to get a bird's-eye view of your worksheet to see how it's laid out. Zooming in is useful if your eyesight isn't quite what it used to be and you have trouble deciphering tiny type. Zooming doesn't change the font size, so it has no affect on printed output.

CROSS-REF Excel contains separate options for changing the size of your printed output. (Use the controls in the Page Layout ➪ Scale To Fit group on the Ribbon.)

Figure 14-5 shows a window zoomed to 10 percent and a window zoomed to 400 percent.

FIGURE 14-5

You can zoom in or out for a better view of your worksheets.

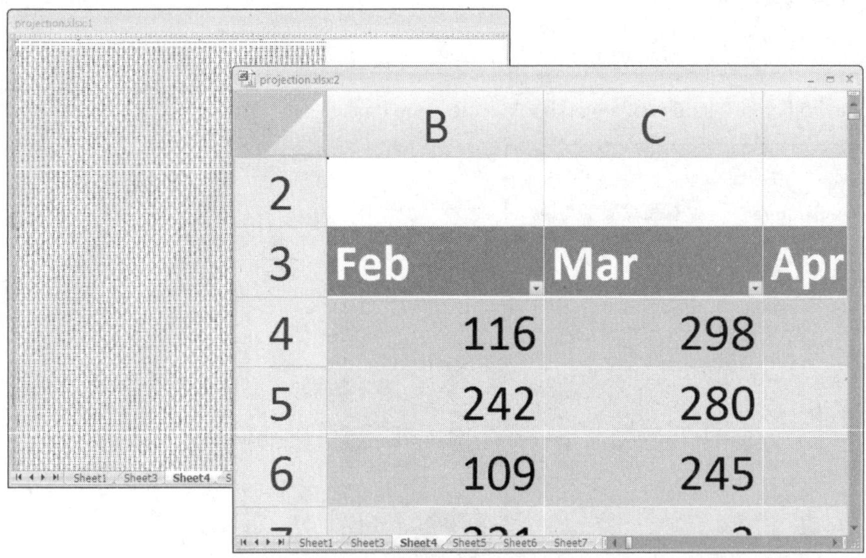

You can easily change the zoom factor of the active worksheet by using the Zoom slider located on the right end of the status bar. Drag the slider, and your screen transforms instantly.

Another way to zoom is to choose View ➪ Zoom ➪ Zoom, which displays a dialog box. Choosing View ➪ Zoom ➪ Zoom To Selection zooms the worksheet to display only the selected cells (useful if you want to view only a particular range).

TIP Zooming affects only the active worksheet, so you can use different zoom factors for different worksheets. Also, if you have a worksheet displayed in two different windows, you can set a different zoom factor for each of the windows.

CROSS-REF If your worksheet uses named ranges, zooming your worksheet to 39 percent or less displays the name of the range overlaid on the cells. Viewing named ranges in this manner is useful for getting an overview of how a worksheet is laid out.

Viewing a worksheet in multiple windows

Sometimes, you may want to view two different parts of a worksheet simultaneously — perhaps to make referencing a distant cell in a formula easier. To create and display a new view of the active workbook, choose View ➪ Window ➪ New Window.

Excel displays a new window for the active workbook, similar to the one shown in Figure 14-6. In this case, each window shows a different worksheet in the workbook. Notice the text in the windows' title bars: `climate data.xls:1` and `climate data.xls:2`. To help you keep track of the windows, Excel appends a colon and a number to each window.

TIP **If the workbook is maximized when you create a new window, arrange the windows to see them both. Choose View ➪ Window ➪ Arrange and choose one of the Arrange options in the Arrange Windows dialog box. If you select the Windows Of Active Workbook check box, only the windows of the active workbook are arranged.**

FIGURE 14-6

Use multiple windows to view different sections of a workbook at the same time.

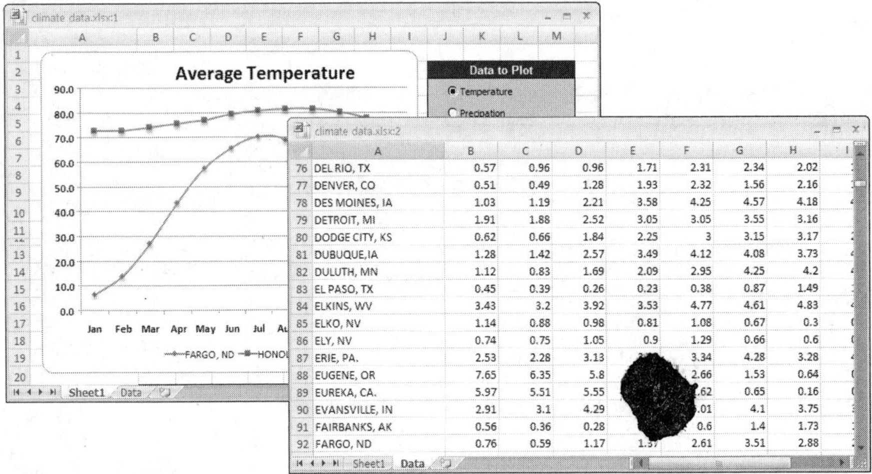

	A	B	C	D	E	F	G	H
76	DEL RIO, TX	0.57	0.96	0.96	1.71	2.31	2.34	2.02
77	DENVER, CO	0.51	0.49	1.28	1.93	2.32	1.56	2.16
78	DES MOINES, IA	1.03	1.19	2.21	3.58	4.25	4.57	4.18
79	DETROIT, MI	1.91	1.88	2.52	3.05	3.05	3.55	3.16
80	DODGE CITY, KS	0.62	0.66	1.84	2.25	3	3.15	3.17
81	DUBUQUE,IA	1.28	1.42	2.57	3.49	4.12	4.08	3.73
82	DULUTH, MN	1.12	0.83	1.69	2.09	2.95	4.25	4.2
83	EL PASO, TX	0.45	0.39	0.26	0.23	0.38	0.87	1.49
84	ELKINS, WV	3.43	3.2	3.92	3.53	4.77	4.61	4.83
85	ELKO, NV	1.14	0.88	0.98	0.81	1.08	0.67	0.3
86	ELY, NV	0.74	0.75	1.05	0.9	1.29	0.66	0.6
87	ERIE, PA.	2.53	2.28	3.13	[illegible]	3.34	4.28	3.28
88	EUGENE, OR	7.65	6.35	5.8	[illegible]	2.66	1.53	0.64
89	EUREKA, CA.	5.97	5.51	5.55	[illegible]	.62	0.65	0.16
90	EVANSVILLE, IN	2.91	3.1	4.29	[illegible]	.01	4.1	3.75
91	FAIRBANKS, AK	0.56	0.36	0.28	[illegible]	0.6	1.4	1.73
92	FARGO, ND	0.76	0.59	1.17	1.3[illegible]	2.61	3.51	2.88

A single workbook can have as many views (that is, separate windows) as you want. Scrolling to a new location in one window doesn't cause scrolling in the other window(s).

You can close these additional windows when you no longer need them. Clicking the Close button on the active window's title bar closes the active window but doesn't close the other windows for the workbook.

TIP **Multiple windows make copying or moving information from one worksheet to another easier. You can use Excel's drag-and-drop procedures to copy or move ranges.**

Comparing sheets side by side

In some situations, you may want to compare two worksheets that are in different windows. The View Side By Side feature makes this task a bit easier.

First, make sure that the two sheets are displayed in separate windows. (The sheets can be in the same workbook or in different workbooks.) Activate the first window; then choose View ➪ Window ➪ View Side by Side. If more than two windows are open, you see a dialog box that lets you select the window for the comparison. The two windows appear next to each other.

When using the View Side by Side feature, scrolling in one of the windows also scrolls the other window. If, for some reason, you don't want this simultaneous scrolling, choose View ➪ Window ➪ Synchronous Scrolling (which is a toggle). If you have rearranged or moved the windows, choose View ➪ Window ➪ Reset Window Position to restore the windows to the initial side-by-side arrangement. To turn off the side-by-side viewing, choose View ➪ Window ➪ View Side by Side again.

Keep in mind that this feature is for manual comparison only. Unfortunately, Excel doesn't provide a way to show you the differences between two sheets.

Splitting the worksheet window into panes

If you prefer not to clutter your screen with additional windows, Excel provides another option for viewing multiple parts of the same worksheet. Choosing View ➪ Window ➪ Split splits the active worksheet into two or four separate panes. The split occurs at the location of the cell pointer. If the cell pointer is in row 1 or column A, this command results in a two-pane split. Otherwise, it gives you four panes. You can use the mouse to drag the individual panes to resize them.

Figure 14-7 shows a worksheet split into two panes. Notice that row numbers aren't continuous. In other words, splitting panes enables you to display in a single window widely separated areas of a worksheet. To remove the split panes, choose View ➪ Window ➪ Split again or just double-click on the split bar you want removed.

FIGURE 14-7

You can split the worksheet window into two or four panes to view different areas of the worksheet at the same time.

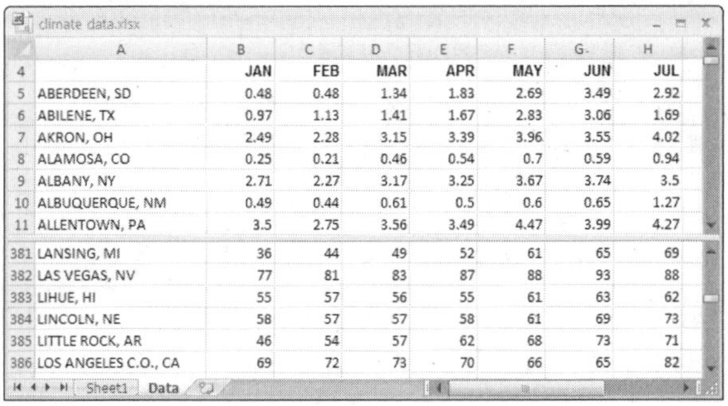

climate data.xlsx

	A	B	C	D	E	F	G	H
4		JAN	FEB	MAR	APR	MAY	JUN	JUL
5	ABERDEEN, SD	0.48	0.48	1.34	1.83	2.69	3.49	2.92
6	ABILENE, TX	0.97	1.13	1.41	1.67	2.83	3.06	1.69
7	AKRON, OH	2.49	2.28	3.15	3.39	3.96	3.55	4.02
8	ALAMOSA, CO	0.25	0.21	0.46	0.54	0.7	0.59	0.94
9	ALBANY, NY	2.71	2.27	3.17	3.25	3.67	3.74	3.5
10	ALBUQUERQUE, NM	0.49	0.44	0.61	0.5	0.6	0.65	1.27
11	ALLENTOWN, PA	3.5	2.75	3.56	3.49	4.47	3.99	4.27
381	LANSING, MI	36	44	49	52	61	65	69
382	LAS VEGAS, NV	77	81	83	87	88	93	88
383	LIHUE, HI	55	57	56	55	61	63	62
384	LINCOLN, NE	58	57	57	58	61	69	73
385	LITTLE ROCK, AR	46	54	57	62	68	73	71
386	LOS ANGELES C.O., CA	69	72	73	70	66	65	82

Sheet1 Data

Keeping the titles in view by freezing panes

If you set up a worksheet with row or column headings, these headings will not be visible when you scroll down or to the right. Excel provides a handy solution to this problem: freezing panes. Freezing panes keeps the headings visible while you're scrolling through the worksheet.

To freeze panes, start by moving the cell pointer to the cell below the row that you want to remain visible as you scroll vertically, and to the right of the column that you want to remain visible as you scroll horizontally. Then, choose View ➪ Window ➪ Freeze Panes and select the Freeze Panes option from the drop-down list. Excel inserts dark lines to indicate the frozen rows and/or columns. The frozen area remains visible as you scroll throughout the worksheet. To remove the frozen panes, choose View ➪ Window ➪ Freeze Panes, and select the Unfreeze Panes option from the drop-down list.

Figure 14-8 shows a worksheet with frozen panes. In this case, rows 1:3 and column A are frozen in place. This technique allows you to scroll down and to the right to locate some information while keeping the column titles and the column A entries visible.

NEW FEATURE **The vast majority of the time, you'll want to freeze either the first row or the first column. Excel 2007 makes it a bit easier. The View ➪ Window ➪ Freeze Panes drop-down list has two additional options: Freeze Top Row and Freeze First Column. Using these commands eliminates the need to position the cell pointer before freezing panes.**

NEW FEATURE **If you have designated a range to be a table (by choosing Insert ➪ Tables ➪ Table), you may not even need to freeze panes. When you scroll down, Excel displays the table column headings in place of the column letters. Figure 14-9 shows an example. The table headings replace the column letters only when a cell within the table is selected.**

FIGURE 14-8

By freezing certain columns and rows, they remain visible while you scroll the worksheet.

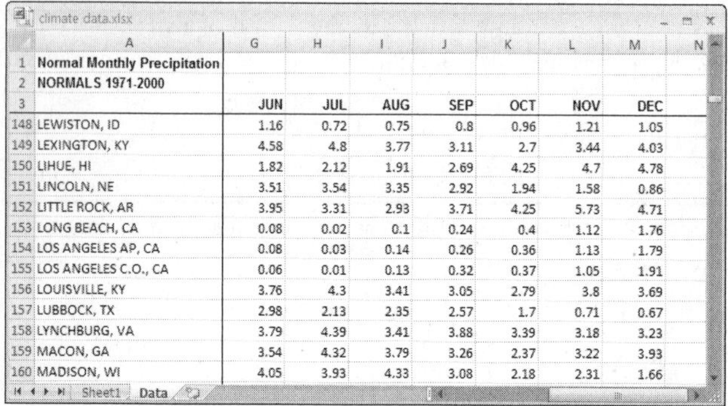

climate data.xlsx

	A	G	H	I	J	K	L	M	N
1	**Normal Monthly Precipitation**								
2	**NORMALS 1971-2000**								
3		JUN	JUL	AUG	SEP	OCT	NOV	DEC	
148	LEWISTON, ID	1.16	0.72	0.75	0.8	0.96	1.21	1.05	
149	LEXINGTON, KY	4.58	4.8	3.77	3.11	2.7	3.44	4.03	
150	LIHUE, HI	1.82	2.12	1.91	2.69	4.25	4.7	4.78	
151	LINCOLN, NE	3.51	3.54	3.35	2.92	1.94	1.58	0.86	
152	LITTLE ROCK, AR	3.95	3.31	2.93	3.71	4.25	5.73	4.71	
153	LONG BEACH, CA	0.08	0.02	0.1	0.24	0.4	1.12	1.76	
154	LOS ANGELES AP, CA	0.08	0.03	0.14	0.26	0.36	1.13	1.79	
155	LOS ANGELES C.O., CA	0.06	0.01	0.13	0.32	0.37	1.05	1.91	
156	LOUISVILLE, KY	3.76	4.3	3.41	3.05	2.79	3.8	3.69	
157	LUBBOCK, TX	2.98	2.13	2.35	2.57	1.7	0.71	0.67	
158	LYNCHBURG, VA	3.79	4.39	3.41	3.88	3.39	3.18	3.23	
159	MACON, GA	3.54	4.32	3.79	3.26	2.37	3.22	3.93	
160	MADISON, WI	4.05	3.93	4.33	3.08	2.18	2.31	1.66	

Sheet1 Data

FIGURE 14-9

When using a table, scrolling down displays the table headings where the column letters normally appear.

climate data.xlsx

	City	JAN	FEB	MAR	APR	MAY	JUN	JUL	AUG	SEP
268	WAKE ISLAND, PC	1.4	1.89	2.38	2.11	1.7	1.95	3.44	5.62	4.82
269	WALLA WALLA WASHINGTON	2.25	1.97	2.2	1.83	1.95	1.15	0.73	0.84	0.83
270	WASHINGTON DULLES AP, D.C.	3.05	2.77	3.55	3.22	4.22	4.07	3.57	3.78	3.82
271	WASHINGTON NAT'L AP, D.C.	3.21	2.63	3.6	2.77	3.82	3.13	3.66	3.44	3.79
272	WATERLOO, IA	0.84	1.05	2.13	3.23	4.15	4.82	4.2	4.08	2.95
273	WEST PALM BEACH, FL	3.75	2.55	3.68	3.57	5.39	7.58	5.97	6.65	8.1
274	WICHITA FALLS, TX	1.12	1.57	2.27	2.62	3.92	3.69	1.58	2.38	3.19
275	WICHITA, KS	0.84	1.02	2.71	2.57	4.16	4.25	3.31	2.94	2.96
276	WILLIAMSPORT, PA	2.85	2.61	3.21	3.49	3.79	4.45	4.08	3.38	3.98
277	WILLISTON, ND	0.54	0.39	0.74	1.05	1.88	2.36	2.28	1.48	1.35
278	WILMINGTON, DE	3.43	2.81	3.97	3.39	4.15	3.59	4.28	3.51	4.01
279	WILMINGTON, NC	4.52	3.66	4.22	2.94	4.4	5.36	7.62	7.31	6.79
280	WINNEMUCCA, NV	0.83	0.62	0.86	0.85	1.06	0.69	0.27	0.35	0.53
281	WINSLOW, AZ	0.46	0.53	0.61	0.27	0.36	0.3	1.18	1.31	1.02
282	WORCESTER, MA	4.07	3.1	4.23	3.92	4.35	4.02	4.19	4.09	4.27
283	YAKIMA, WA	1.17	0.8	0.7	0.53	0.51	0.62	0.22	0.36	0.39
284	YAKUTAT, AK	13.18	10.99	11.41	10.8	9.78	7.17	7.88	13.27	20.88

Sheet1 Data

Monitoring cells with a Watch Window

In some situations, you may want to monitor the value in a particular cell as you work. As you scroll throughout the worksheet, that cell may disappear from view. A feature known as Watch Window can help. A *Watch Window* displays the value of any number of cells in a handy window that's always visible.

To display the Watch Window, choose Formulas ➪ Formula Auditing ➪ Watch Window. The Watch Window appears in the task pane, but you can also drag it and make it float over the worksheet.

To add a cell to watch, click Add Watch and specify the cell that you want to watch. The Watch Window displays the value in that cell. You can add any number of cells to the Watch Window, and you can move the window to any convenient location. Figure 14-10 shows the Watch Window monitoring four cells.

Double-click a cell in the Watch Window to jump to that cell.

FIGURE 14-10

Use the Watch Window to monitor the value in one or more cells.

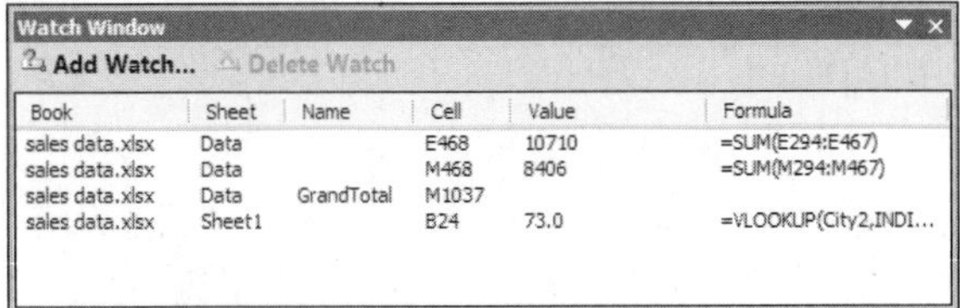

Book	Sheet	Name	Cell	Value	Formula
sales data.xlsx	Data		E468	10710	=SUM(E294:E467)
sales data.xlsx	Data		M468	8406	=SUM(M294:M467)
sales data.xlsx	Data	GrandTotal	M1037		
sales data.xlsx	Sheet1		B24	73.0	=VLOOKUP(City2,INDI...

Working with Rows and Columns

This section discusses worksheet operations that involve rows and columns. Rows and columns make up an Excel worksheet. Every worksheet has exactly 1,048,576 rows and 16,384 columns, and these values can't be changed.

NOTE **If you open a workbook that was created in a previous version of Excel, the workbook is opened in "compatibility mode." These workbooks have 65,536 rows and 256 columns. To increase the number of rows and columns, save the workbook as an Excel 2007 `XLSX` file and then reopen it.**

Inserting rows and columns

Although the number of rows and columns in a worksheet is fixed, you can still insert and delete rows and columns if you need to make room for additional information. These operations don't change the number of rows or columns. Rather, inserting a new row moves down the other rows to accommodate the new row. The last row is simply removed from the worksheet if it's empty. Inserting a new column shifts the columns to the right, and the last column is removed if it's empty.

NOTE **If the last row isn't empty, you can't insert a new row. Similarly, if the last column contains information, Excel doesn't let you insert a new column. Attempting to add a row or column displays a warning dialog box shown. Click OK and then move or eliminate the contents of the nonblank cells to continue.**

To insert a new row or rows, you can use any of these techniques:

- Select an entire row or multiple rows by clicking the row numbers in the worksheet border. Right-click and choose Insert from the shortcut menu.
- Move the cell pointer to the row that you want to insert and then choose Home ➪ Cells ➪ Insert ➪ Insert Sheet Rows. If you select multiple cells in the column, Excel inserts additional rows that correspond to the number of cells selected in the column and moves the rows below the insertion down.

The procedures for inserting a new column or columns is similar, but you choose Home ➪ Cells ➪ Insert ➪ Insert Sheet Columns.

You also can insert cells, rather than just rows or columns. Select the range into which you want to add new cells and then choose Home ➪ Cells ➪ Insert ➪ Insert Cells (or right-click the selection and choose Insert). To insert cells, the existing cells must be shifted to the right or shifted down. Therefore, Excel displays the Insert dialog box shown in Figure 14-11 so that you can specify the direction in which you want to shift the cells.

FIGURE 14-11

You can insert partial rows or columns by using the Insert dialog box.

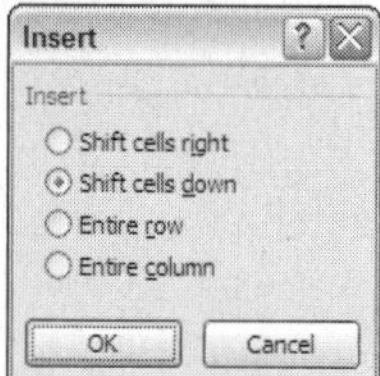

Deleting rows and columns

You may also want to delete rows or columns in a worksheet. For example, your sheet may contain old data that is no longer needed.

To delete a row or rows, use either of these methods:

- Select an entire row or multiple rows by clicking the row numbers in the worksheet border. Right-click and choose Delete from the shortcut menu.
- Move the cell pointer to the row that you want to delete and then choose Home ➪ Cells ➪ Delete ➪ Delete Sheet Rows. If you select multiple cells in the column, Excel deletes all rows in the selection.

Deleting columns works in a similar way. If you discover that you accidentally deleted a row or column, select Undo from the Quick Access Toolbar (or press Ctrl+Z) to undo the action.

Hiding rows and columns

In some cases, you may want to hide particular rows or columns. Hiding rows and columns may be useful if you don't want users to see certain information or if you need to print a report that summarizes the information in the worksheet without showing all the details.

To hide rows or columns in your worksheet, select the row or rows that you want to hide by clicking in the row or column header. Then right-click and choose Hide from the shortcut menu. Or, you can use the commands on the Home ⇨ Cells ⇨ Format drop-down list.

TIP **You also can drag the row or column's border to hide the row or column. You must drag the border in the row or column heading. Drag the bottom border of a row upward or the border of a column to the left.**

A hidden row is actually a row with its height set to zero. Similarly, a hidden column has a column width of zero. When you use the arrow keys to move the cell pointer, cells in hidden rows or columns are skipped.

Unhiding a hidden row or column can be a bit tricky because selecting a row or column that's hidden is difficult. The solution is to select the columns or rows that are adjacent to the hidden column or row. (Select at least one column or row on either side.) Then right-click and choose Unhide. For example, if column G is hidden, select columns F and H.

Another method is to choose Home ⇨ Find & Select ⇨ Go To (or its F5 equivalent) to select a cell in a hidden row or column. For example, if column A is hidden, you can press F5 and specify cell A1 (or any other cell in column A) to move the cell pointer to the hidden column. Then you can choose Home ⇨ Cells ⇨ Format ⇨ Hide & Unhide ⇨ Unhide Columns.

Changing column widths and row heights

Often, you'll want to change the width of a column or the height of a row. For example, you can make columns narrower to accommodate more information on a printed page. Or you may want to increase row height to create a "double-spaced" effect.

Excel provides several different ways to change the widths of columns and the height of rows.

Changing column widths

Column width is measured in terms of the number of characters of a *fixed pitch font* that will fit into the cell's width. By default, each column's width is 8.43 units, which equates to 64 pixels.

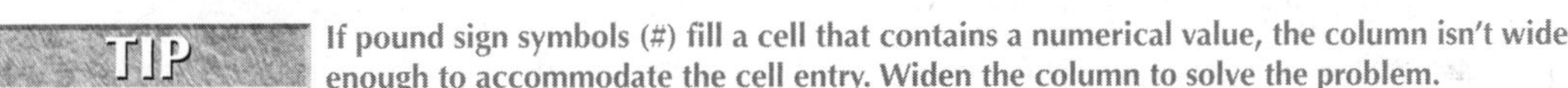

TIP **If pound sign symbols (#) fill a cell that contains a numerical value, the column isn't wide enough to accommodate the cell entry. Widen the column to solve the problem.**

Before you change the column width, you can select multiple columns so that the width will be the same for all selected columns. To select multiple columns, either drag in the column border or press Ctrl while you click individual columns. To select all columns, click the button where the row and column headers intersect (or press Ctrl+A). You can change the width for the selected columns by using any of the following techniques.

- Drag the right column border with the mouse until the column is the desired width.
- Choose Home ⇨ Cells ⇨ Format ⇨ Column Width and enter a value in the Column Width dialog box.
- Choose Home ⇨ Cells ⇨ Format ⇨ AutoFit Column Width to adjust the width of the selected column so that the widest entry in the column fits. Rather than selecting an entire column, you can just select cells in the column, and the column is adjusted based on the widest entry in your selection.
- Double-click the right border of a column header to set the column width automatically to the widest entry in the column.

TIP To change the default width for all columns, choose Home ➪ Cells ➪ Format ➪ Default Width. This command displays a dialog box into which you enter the new default column width. All columns that haven't been previously adjusted take on the new column width.

After you manually adjust a column's width, Excel will no longer automatically adjust the column to accommodate longer numerical entries.

Changing row heights

Row height is measured in points (a standard unit of measurement in the printing trade — 72 points is equal to 1 inch). The default row height using the default font is 15 points, or 20 pixels.

The default row height can vary, depending on the font defined in the Normal style. In addition, Excel automatically adjusts row heights to accommodate the tallest font in the row. So, if you change the font size of a cell to 20 points, for example, Excel makes the column taller so that the entire text is visible.

Changing the row height is useful for spacing out rows and is almost always preferable to inserting empty rows between lines of data. You can set the row height manually by using any of the following techniques. As with columns, you can select multiple rows to size them all at once.

- Drag the lower row border with the mouse until the row is the desired height.
- Choose Home ➪ Cells ➪ Format ➪ Row Height and enter a value (in points) in the Row Height dialog box.
- Double-click the bottom border of a row to set the row height automatically to the tallest entry in the row. You also can choose Home ➪ Cells ➪ Format ➪ AutoFit Row Height for this task.

Understanding Cells and Ranges

A *cell* is a single element in a worksheet that can hold a value, some text, or a formula. A cell is identified by its *address* or *reference,* which consists of its column letter and row number. For example, cell D12 is the cell in the fourth column and the twelfth row.

A group of cells is called a *range.* You designate a range address by specifying its upper-left cell address and its lower-right cell address, separated by a colon.

Here are some examples of range addresses:

C24	A range that consists of a single cell.
A1:B1	Two cells that occupy one row and two columns.
A1:A100	100 cells in column A.
A1:D4	16 cells (four rows by four columns).
C1:C1048576	An entire column of cells; this range also can be expressed as C:C.
A6:XFD6	An entire row of cells; this range also can be expressed as 6:6.
A1:XFD1048576	All cells in a worksheet.

Selecting ranges

To perform an operation on a range of cells in a worksheet, you must first select the range. For example, if you want to make the text bold for a range of cells, you must select the range and then choose Home ➪ Font ➪ Bold (or press Ctrl+B).

When you select a range, the cells appear highlighted. The exception is the active cell, which remains its normal color. Figure 14-12 shows an example of a selected range (B5:C11) in a worksheet. Cell B5, the active cell, is selected but not highlighted.

FIGURE 14-12

When you select a range, it appears highlighted, but the active cell within the range is not highlighted.

	A	B	C	D	E
1	**Product**	**Sold By**	**Month**		
2	Widget	Jones	January		
3	Widget	Jones	January		
4	Sprocket	Gomez	January		
5	Widget	Gomez	January		
6	Widget	Gomez	January		
7	Sprocket	Jones	January		
8	Widget	Jones	January		
9	Sprocket	Gomez	January		
10	Sprocket	Jackson	February		
11	Sprocket	Jones	February		
12	Widget	Jackson	February		
13	Widget	Jackson	February		
14	Sprocket	Smith	February		
15	Widget	Jackson	February		

Sheet1 Sheet2 Sheet3

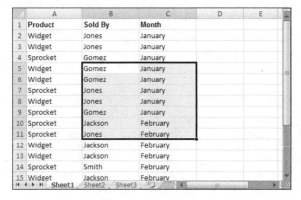

You can select a range in several ways:

- Drag diagonally, highlighting the range. If you drag to the end of the screen, the worksheet will scroll.
- Press the Shift key while you use the arrow keys to select a range.
- Press F8 and then move the cell pointer with the arrow keys to highlight the range. Press F8 again to return the arrow keys to normal movement.
- Type the cell or range address into the Name box and press Enter. Excel selects the cell or range that you specified.
- Choose Home ➪ Editing ➪ Find & Select ➪ Go To (or press F5) and enter a range's address manually into the Go To dialog box. When you click OK, Excel selects the cells in the range that you specified.

TIP **As you're selecting a range, Excel displays the number of rows and columns in your selection in the Name box (located on the left end of the Formula bar). As soon as you finish the selection, the Name box reverts to showing the address of the active cell.**

Selecting complete rows and columns

Often, you'll need to select an entire row or column. For example, you may want to apply the same numeric format or the same alignment options to an entire row or column. You can select entire rows and columns in much the same manner as you select ranges:

- Click the row or column border to select a single row or column.
- To select multiple adjacent rows or columns, drag over the row or column borders.
- To select multiple (nonadjacent) rows or columns, press Ctrl while you click the row or column borders that you want.
- Press Ctrl+spacebar to select a column. The column holding the active cell (or columns of the selected cells) is highlighted.
- Press Shift+spacebar to select a row. The row holding the active cell (or rows of the selected cells) is highlighted.

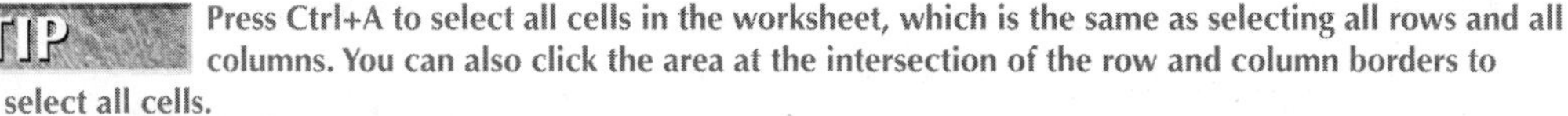

Press Ctrl+A to select all cells in the worksheet, which is the same as selecting all rows and all columns. You can also click the area at the intersection of the row and column borders to select all cells.

Selecting noncontiguous ranges

Most of the time, the ranges that you select are *contiguous* — a single rectangle of cells. Excel also enables you to work with *noncontiguous ranges,* which consist of two or more ranges (or single cells) that aren't next to each other. Selecting noncontiguous ranges is also known as a *multiple selection.* If you want to apply the same formatting to cells in different areas of your worksheet, one approach is to make a multiple selection. When the appropriate cells or ranges are selected, the formatting that you select is applied to them all. Figure 14-13 shows a noncontiguous range selected in a worksheet. (Three ranges are selected.)

FIGURE 14-13

Excel enables you to select noncontiguous ranges.

	A	B	C	D	E	F
1	Last Name	First Name	Department	Extension	Date Hired	
2	Allen	Yolanda	Sales	4465	03/05/98	
3	Baker	Nancy	Operations	4498	11/24/98	
4	Bunnel	Ken	Marketing	4422	05/12/98	
5	Charles	Larry	Administration	3988	06/30/06	
6	Cramden	Oliver	Administration	4421	01/04/01	
7	Davis	Rita	Administration	4441	09/19/98	
8	Dunwell	James	Operations	3321	04/16/99	
9	Ellis	Pamela	Data Processing	3398	02/01/05	
10	Endow	Ed	Data Processing	4448	02/01/99	
11						
12						

Sheet1

You can select a noncontiguous range in several ways:

- Select the first range (or cell). Then press Ctrl as you drag the mouse to highlight additional cells or ranges.
- From the keyboard, select a range as described previously (using F8 or the Shift key). Then press Shift+F8 to select another range without canceling the previous range selections.

- Enter the range (or cell) addresses in the Name box, typing a comma between each address. Press Enter.
- Choose Home ➪ Editing ➪ Find & Select ➪ Go To (or press F5) to display the Go To dialog box. Enter the range (or cell) addresses in the Reference box, adding a comma between each range address. Click OK, and Excel selects the ranges.

Noncontiguous ranges differ from contiguous ranges in several important ways. One obvious difference is that you can't use drag-and-drop methods to move or copy noncontiguous ranges.

Selecting multisheet ranges

In addition to two-dimensional ranges on a single worksheet, ranges can extend across multiple worksheets to be three-dimensional ranges.

Suppose that you have a workbook set up to track budgets. A common approach is to use a separate worksheet for each department, making it easy to organize the data. You can click a sheet tab to view the information for a particular department.

Say you have a workbook with four sheets, named Totals, Marketing, Operations, and Manufacturing. The sheets are laid out identically. The only difference is the values. The Totals sheet contains formulas that compute the sum of the corresponding items in the three departmental worksheets.

Assume that you want to apply formatting to the sheets — for example, make the column headings bold with background shading. One (not so efficient) approach is simply to format the cells in each worksheet separately. A better technique is to select a multisheet range and format the cells in all the sheets simultaneously. The following is a step-by-step example of multisheet formatting, using the example workbook described above.

1. **Activate the Totals worksheet by clicking its tab.**
2. **Select the range holding the column headings, B3:F3 in the example.**
3. **Press Shift and click the sheet tab labeled Manufacturing.** This step selects all worksheets between the active worksheet (Totals) and the sheet tab that you click — in essence, a three-dimensional range of cells (see Figure 14-14). Notice that the workbook window's title bar displays `[Group]` to remind you that you've selected a group of sheets and that you're in Group edit mode.

FIGURE 14-14

In Group mode, you can work with a three-dimensional range of cells that extends across multiple worksheets.

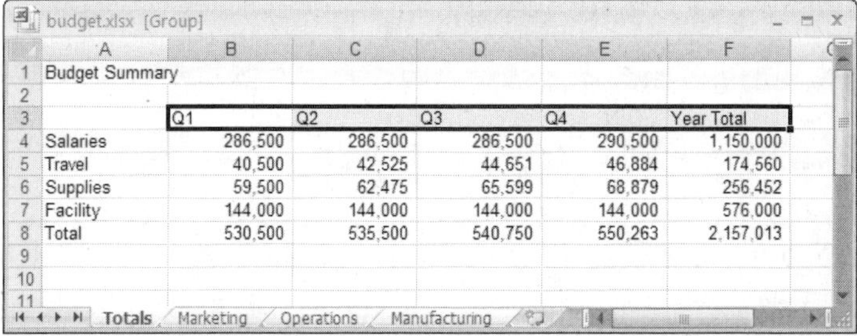

	A	B	C	D	E	F
1	Budget Summary					
2						
3		Q1	Q2	Q3	Q4	Year Total
4	Salaries	286,500	286,500	286,500	290,500	1,150,000
5	Travel	40,500	42,525	44,651	46,884	174,560
6	Supplies	59,500	62,475	65,599	68,879	256,452
7	Facility	144,000	144,000	144,000	144,000	576,000
8	Total	530,500	535,500	540,750	550,263	2,157,013
9						
10						
11						

4. **Choose Home ➪ Font ➪ Bold and then choose Home ➪ Font ➪ Fill Color to apply a colored background.**
5. **Click one of the other sheet tabs.** This step selects the sheet and also cancels Group mode; `[Group]` is no longer displayed in the title bar. Excel applies the formatting to the selected range across the selected sheets.

When a workbook is in Group mode, any changes that you make to cells in one worksheet also apply to all the other grouped worksheets. You can use this to your advantage when you want to set up a group of identical worksheets because any labels, data, formatting, or formulas you enter are automatically added to the same cells in all the grouped worksheets.

When Excel is in Group mode, some commands are "grayed out" and can't be used. In the preceding example, you can't convert all these ranges to tables by choosing Insert ➪ Tables ➪ Table.

In general, selecting a multisheet range is a simple two-step process: Select the range in one sheet and then select the worksheets to include in the range. To select a group of contiguous worksheets, you can press Shift and click the sheet tab of the last worksheet that you want to include in the selection. To select individual worksheets, press Ctrl and click the sheet tab of each worksheet that you want to select. If all the worksheets in a workbook aren't laid out the same, you can skip the sheets that you don't want to format. When you make the selection, the sheet tabs of the selected sheets appear with a white background, and Excel displays `[Group]` in the title bar.

To select all sheets in a workbook, right-click any sheet tab and choose Select All Sheets from the shortcut menu.

Selecting special types of cells

As you use Excel, you may need to locate specific types of cells in your worksheets. For example, wouldn't it be handy to be able to locate every cell that contains a formula — or perhaps all the cells whose value depends on the current cell? Excel provides an easy way to locate these and many other special types of cells. Simply choose Home ➪ Select & Find ➪ Go To Special to display the Go To Special dialog box, shown in Figure 14-15.

FIGURE 14-15

Use the Go To Special dialog box to select specific types of cells.

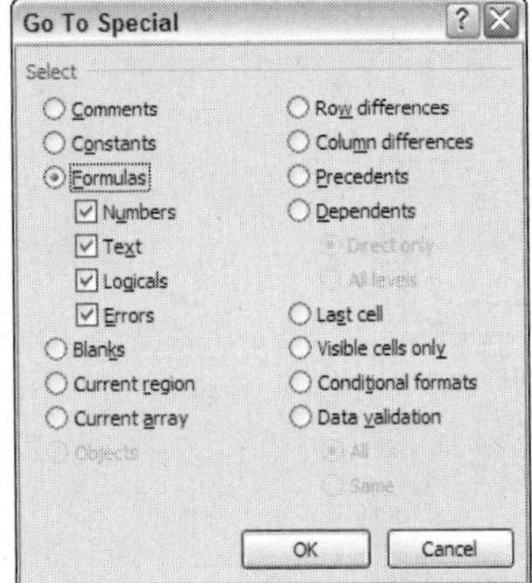

After you make your choice in the dialog box, Excel selects the qualifying subset of cells in the current selection. Usually, this subset of cells is a multiple selection. If no cells qualify, Excel lets you know with the message `No cells were found`.

TIP If you bring up the Go To Special dialog box with only one cell selected, Excel bases its selection on the entire used area of the worksheet. Otherwise, the selection is based on the selected range.

TIP When you select an option in the Go To Special dialog box, be sure to note which suboptions become available. For example, when you select Constants, the suboptions under Formulas become available to help you further refine the results. Likewise, the suboptions under Dependents also apply to Precedents, and those under Data Validation also apply to Conditional formats.

Selecting cells by searching

Another way to select cells is to use Excel's Home ➪ Editing ➪ Find & Select ➪ Find command (or press Ctrl+F), which enables you to select cells by their contents. Click the Options button to display additional choices for refining the search.

Enter the text that you're looking for; then click Find All. The dialog box expands to display all the cells that match your search criteria. For example, Figure 14-16 shows the dialog box after Excel has located all cells that contain the text Tucson. You can click an item in the list, and the screen will scroll so that you can view the cell in context. To select all the cells in the list, first select any single item in the list. Then press Ctrl+A to select them all.

FIGURE 14-16

The Find And Replace dialog box, with its results listed.

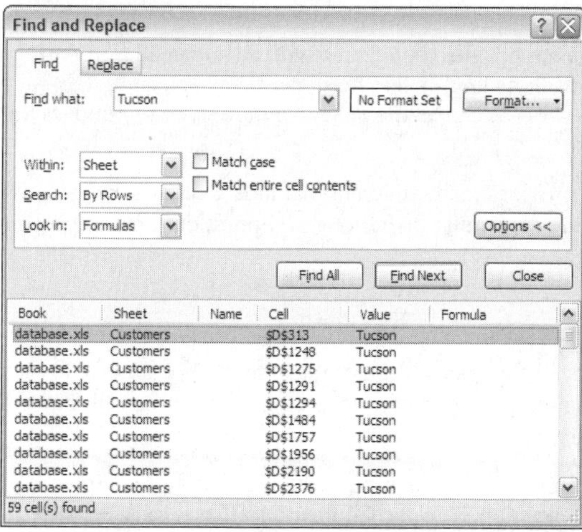

Note that the Find and Replace dialog box allows you to return to the worksheet without dismissing the dialog box.

Copying or Moving Ranges

As you create a worksheet, you may find it necessary to copy or move information from one location to another. Excel makes copying or moving ranges of cells easy. Here are some common things you might do:

- Copy a cell to another cell.
- Copy a cell to a range of cells. The source cell is copied to every cell in the destination range.
- Copy a range to another range. Both ranges must be the same size.
- Move a range of cells to another location.

The primary difference between copying and moving a range is the effect of the operation on the source range. When you copy a range, the source range is unaffected. When you move a range, the contents are removed from the source range.

NOTE Copying a cell normally copies the cell's contents, any formatting that is applied to the original cell (including conditional formatting and data validation), and the cell comment (if it has one). When you copy a cell that contains a formula, the cell references in the copied formulas are changed automatically to be relative to their new destination.

Copying or moving consists of two overall steps (although shortcut methods do exist):

1. **Select the cell or range to copy (the source range) and copy it to the Clipboard.** To move the range instead of copying it, cut the range rather than copying it.
2. **Move the cell pointer to the range that will hold the copy (the destination range) and paste the Clipboard contents.**

CAUTION When you paste information, Excel overwrites any cells that get in the way without warning you. If you find that pasting overwrote some essential cells, choose Undo from the Quick Access Toolbar (or press Ctrl+Z).

NOTE When you copy a cell or range, Excel surrounds the copied area with an animated border (sometimes referred to as "marching ants"). As long as that border remains animated, the copied information is available for pasting. If you press Esc to cancel the animated border, Excel removes the information from the Clipboard.

Because copying (or moving) is used so often, Excel provides many different methods. I discuss each method in the following sections. Copying and moving are similar operations, so I point out only important differences between the two.

Copying by using Ribbon commands

Choosing Home ➪ Clipboard ➪ Copy transfers a copy of the selected cell or range to the Windows Clipboard and the Office Clipboard. After performing the copy part of this operation, select the cell that will hold the copy and choose Home ➪ Clipboard ➪ Paste.

Rather than using Home ➪ Clipboard ➪ Paste, you can just activate the destination cell and press Enter. If you use this technique, Excel removes the copied information from the Clipboard so that it can't be pasted again.

NOTE If you click the Copy button more than once before you click the Paste button, Excel may automatically display the Office Clipboard task bar. To prevent this task bar from appearing, click the Options button at the bottom and then remove the check mark from Show Office Clipboard Automatically.

Understanding the Office Clipboard

Whenever you cut or copy information from a Windows program, Windows stores the information on the Windows Clipboard, which is an area of your computer's memory. Each time that you cut or copy information, Windows replaces the information previously stored on the Clipboard with the new information that you cut or copied. The Windows Clipboard can store data in a variety of formats. Because Windows manages information on the Clipboard, it can be pasted to other Windows applications, regardless of where it originated.

Office has its own Clipboard, the Office Clipboard, which is available only in Office programs. Whenever you cut or copy information in an Office program, such as Excel, the program places the information on both the Windows Clipboard and the Office Clipboard. However, the program treats information on the Office Clipboard differently than it treats information on the Windows Clipboard. Instead of replacing information on the Office Clipboard, the program appends the information to the Office Clipboard. With multiple items stored on the Clipboard, you can then paste the items either individually or as a group.

Find out more about this feature in the section "Using the Office Clipboard to paste," later in this chapter.

If you're copying a range, you don't need to select an entire same-sized range before you click the Paste button. You need only activate the upper-left cell in the destination range.

Copying by using shortcut menu commands

If you prefer, you can use the following shortcut menu commands for copying and pasting:

- Right-click the range and choose Copy (or Cut) from the shortcut menu to copy the selected cells to the Clipboard.
- Right-click and choose Paste from the shortcut menu that appears to paste the Clipboard contents to the selected cell or range.

Rather than using Paste, you can just click the destination cell and press Enter. If you use this technique, Excel removes the copied information from the Clipboard so that it can't be pasted again.

Copying by using shortcut keys

The copy and paste operations also have shortcut keys associated with them:

- Ctrl+C copies the selected cells to both the Windows and Office Clipboards.
- Ctrl+X cuts the selected cells to both the Windows and Office Clipboards.
- Ctrl+V pastes the Windows Clipboard contents to the selected cell or range.

TIP Most other Windows applications also use these shortcut keys.

Copying or moving by using drag-and-drop

Excel also enables you to copy or move a cell or range by dragging. Be aware, however, that dragging and dropping does not place any information on either the Windows Clipboard or the Office Clipboard.

Using Options Buttons When Inserting and Pasting

Some cell and range operations — specifically inserting, pasting, and filling cells by dragging — result in the display of a pop-up Options button. Clicking the Options button displays choices for completing the insert or paste, such as whether to keep the original formatting for the copied material. For example, if you copy a range and then paste it to a different location, a Paste Options button appears at the lower-right corner of the pasted range. Click the Paste Options button to see the detailed options for pasting.

Some users find these options buttons helpful, while others think that they're annoying. (Count me in the latter group.) To turn off these buttons, choose Office Button ➪ Excel Options and click the Advanced choice. Clear the check mark from the two options labeled Show Paste Options Buttons and Show Insert Options Buttons.

NOTE **The drag-and-drop method of moving does offer one advantage over the cut -and-paste method — Excel warns you if a drag-and-drop move operation will overwrite existing cell contents. However, you do *not* get a warning if a drag-and-drop copy operation will overwrite existing cell contents.**

To copy using drag-and-drop, select the cell or range that you want to copy and then press Ctrl and move the mouse to one of the selection's borders (the mouse pointer is augmented with a small plus sign). Then, simply drag the selection to its new location while you continue to press the Ctrl key. The original selection remains behind, and Excel makes a new copy when you release the mouse button. To move a range using drag-and-drop, don't press Ctrl while dragging the border.

TIP **If the mouse pointer doesn't turn into an arrow when you point to the border of a cell or range, you need to make a change to your settings. Access the Excel Options dialog box, click the Advanced choice in the list at the left, and place a check mark on the option labeled Enable Fill Handle And Cell Drag-And-Drop.**

Copying to adjacent cells

Often, you'll find that you need to copy a cell to an adjacent cell or range. This type of copying is quite common when working with formulas. For example, if you're working on a budget, you might create a formula to add the values in column B. You can use the same formula to add the values in the other columns. Rather than re-enter the formula, you can copy it to the adjacent cells.

Excel provides additional options for copying to adjacent cells. To use these commands, select the cell that you're copying and the cells that you're copying to. Then issue the appropriate command from the following list for one-step copying:

- Home ➪ Editing ➪ Fill ➪ Down (or Ctrl+D) copies the cell to the selected range below.
- Home ➪ Editing ➪ Fill ➪ Right (or Ctrl+R) copies the cell to the selected range to the right.
- Home ➪ Editing ➪ Fill ➪ Up copies the cell to the selected range above.
- Home ➪ Editing ➪ Fill ➪ Left copies the cell to the selected range to the left.

None of these commands places information on either the Windows Clipboard or the Office Clipboard.

TIP **You also can use AutoFill to copy to adjacent cells by dragging the selection's *fill handle* (the small square in the bottom-right corner of the selected cell or range). Excel copies the original selection to the cells that you highlight while dragging. For more control over the AutoFill operation, drag the fill handle with the right mouse button, and you'll get a shortcut menu with additional options.**

Copying a range to other sheets

You can use the copy procedures described previously to copy a cell or range to another worksheet, even if the worksheet is in a different workbook. You must, of course, activate the other worksheet before you select the location to which you want to copy.

Excel offers a quicker way to copy a cell or range and paste it to other worksheets in the same workbook. Start by selecting the range to copy. Then, press Ctrl and click the sheet tabs for the worksheets to which you want to copy the information. (Excel displays `[Group]` in the workbook's title bar.) Choose Home ➪ Editing ➪ Fill ➪ Across Worksheets, and a dialog box appears to ask you what you want to copy (All, Contents, or Formats). Make your choice and then click OK. Excel copies the selected range to the selected worksheets; the new copy occupies the same cells in the selected worksheets as the original occupies in the initial worksheet.

CAUTION **Be careful with the Home ➪ Editing ➪ Fill ➪ Across Worksheets command because Excel doesn't warn you when the destination cells contain information. You can quickly overwrite lots of cells with this command and not even realize it.**

Using the Office Clipboard to paste

Whenever you cut or copy information in an Office program, such as Excel, you can place the data on both the Windows Clipboard and the Office Clipboard. When you copy information to the Office Clipboard, you append the information to the Office Clipboard instead of replacing what is already there. With multiple items stored on the Office Clipboard, you can then paste the items either individually or as a group.

To use the Office Clipboard, you first need to open it. Use the dialog launcher on the bottom right of the Home ➪ Clipboard group to toggle the Clipboard task pane on and off.

TIP **To make the Clipboard task pane open automatically, click the Options button near the bottom of the task pane and choose the Show Office Clipboard Automatically option.**

After you open the Clipboard task pane, select the first cell or range that you want to copy to the Office Clipboard and copy it by using any of the preceding techniques. Repeat this process, selecting the next cell or range that you want to copy. As soon as you copy the information, the Office Clipboard task pane shows you the number of items that you've copied and a brief description (it will hold up to 24 items). Figure 14-17 shows the Office Clipboard with five copied items.

When you're ready to paste information, select the cell into which you want to paste information. To paste an individual item, click it in the Clipboard task pane. To paste all the items that you've copied, click the Paste All button.

You can clear the contents of the Office Clipboard by clicking the Clear All button.

The following items about the Office Clipboard and its functioning are worth noting:

- Excel pastes the contents of the Windows Clipboard when you paste either by choosing Home ➪ Clipboard ➪ Paste, by pressing Ctrl+V, or by right-clicking to choose Paste from the shortcut menu.
- The last item that you cut or copied appears on both the Office Clipboard and the Windows Clipboard.
- Clearing the Office Clipboard also clears the Windows Clipboard.

WARNING **The Office Clipboard, however, has a serious problem that makes it virtually worthless for Excel users: If you copy a range that contains formulas, the formulas are not transferred when you paste to a different range. Only the values are pasted. Furthermore, Excel doesn't even warn you about this fact.**

FIGURE 14-17

Use the Clipboard task pane to copy and paste multiple items.

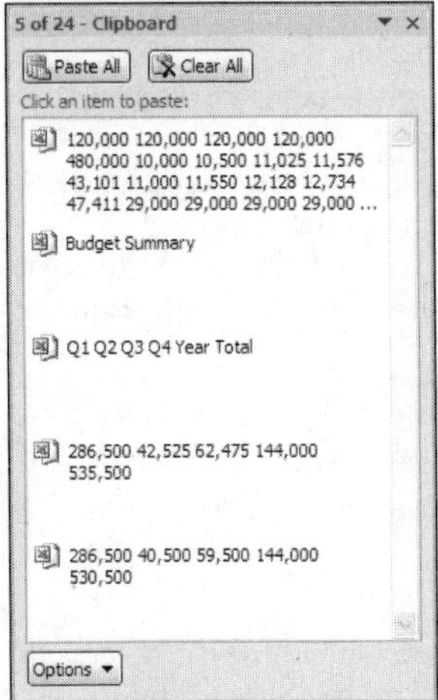

Pasting in special ways

You may not always want to copy everything from the source range to the destination range. For example, you may want to copy only the formula results rather than the formulas themselves. Or you may want to copy the number formats from one range to another without overwriting any existing data or formulas.

To control what is copied into the destination range, choose Home ➪ Clipboard, and then click the bottom half of the Paste button to open the drop-down menu shown in Figure 14-18. Options are:

- **Paste:** Pastes the cell's contents, formats, and data validation from the Windows Clipboard.
- **Formulas:** Pastes formulas, but not formatting.
- **Paste Values:** Pastes the results of formulas. The destination for the copy can be a new range or the original range. In the latter case, Excel replaces the original formulas with their current values.
- **No Borders:** Pastes everything except any borders that appear in the source range.
- **Transpose:** Changes the orientation of the copied range. Rows become columns, and columns become rows. Any formulas in the copied range are adjusted so that they work properly when transposed.
- **Paste Link:** Creates formulas in the destination range that refer to the cells in the copied range.
- **Paste Special:** Displays the Paste Special dialog box (described in the next section).
- **Paste As Hyperlink:** Creates a clickable hyperlink to the copied cell or range, which can be in the same workbook or in a different workbook. The Paste As Hyperlink command is not available if the workbook has not been saved.
- **As Picture:** Pastes the copied information as a picture. If you use the Paste Picture Link option, Excel creates a "live" picture that is updated if the source range is changed.

FIGURE 14-18

Excel offers several pasting options.

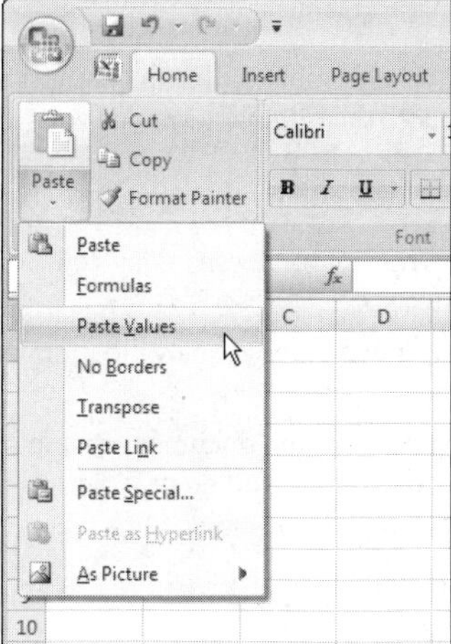

Using the Paste Special Dialog box

For maximum flexibility in what gets pasted, choose Home ➪ Clipboard ➪ Paste (bottom half of button) ➪ Paste Special to display the Paste Special dialog box (see Figure 14-19). You also can right-click and select Paste Special to display this dialog box. This dialog box has several options, which I explain in the following list.

NOTE **Excel actually has several different Paste Special dialog boxes. The one displayed depends on what's copied. This section describes the Paste Special dialog box that appears when a range or cell has been copied.**

FIGURE 14-19

The Paste Special dialog box.

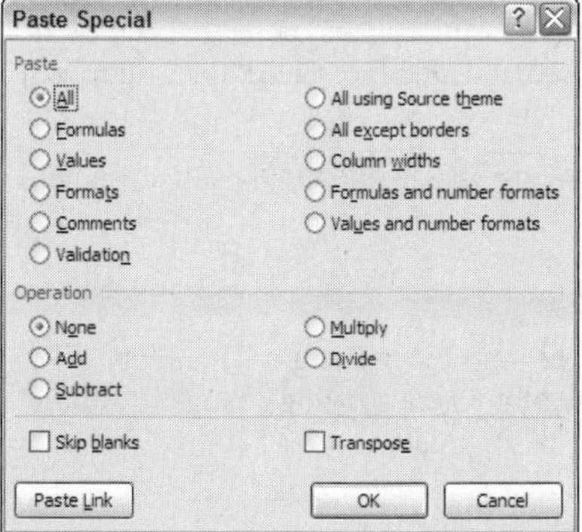

For the Paste Special command to be available, you need to copy a cell or range. (Choosing Home ➪ Clipboard ➪ Cut doesn't work.)

- **All:** Pastes the cell's contents, formats, and data validation from the Windows Clipboard.
- **Formulas:** Pastes values and formulas, with no formatting.
- **Values:** Pastes values and the results of formulas (no formatting). The destination for the copy can be a new range or the original range. In the latter case, Excel replaces the original formulas with their current values.
- **Formats:** Copies only the formatting.
- **Comments:** Copies only the cell comments from a cell or range. This option doesn't copy cell contents or formatting.
- **Validation:** Copies the validation criteria so the same data validation will apply. Data validation is applied by choosing Data ➪ Data Tools ➪ Data Validation.
- **All Using Source Theme:** Pastes everything, but uses the formatting from the document theme of the source. This option is relevant only if you're pasting information from a different workbook, and the workbook uses a different document theme than the active workbook.
- **All Except Borders:** Pastes everything except borders that appear in the source range.
- **Column Widths:** Pastes only column width information.
- **Formulas And Number Formats:** Pastes all values, formulas and number formats (but no other formatting).
- **Values And Number Formats:** Pastes all values and numeric formats, but not the formulas themselves.

In addition, the Paste Special dialog box enables you to perform other operations, described in the following sections.

Performing mathematical operations without formulas

The option buttons in the Operation section of the Paste Special dialog box let you perform an arithmetic operation. For example, you can copy a range to another range and select the Multiply operation. Excel multiplies the corresponding values in the source range and the destination range and replaces the destination range with the new values.

This feature also works with a single copied cell, pasted to a range. Assume that you have a range of values, and you want to increase each value by 5 percent. Enter **105%** into any blank cell and copy that cell to the Clipboard. Then select the range of values and bring up the Paste Special dialog box. Select the Multiply option, and each value in the range is multiplied by 105 percent.

If the destination range contains formulas, the formulas are also modified. In many cases, this is *not* what you want.

Skipping blanks when pasting

The Skip Blanks option in the Paste Special dialog box prevents Excel from overwriting cell contents in your paste area with blank cells from the copied range. This option is useful if you're copying a range to another area but don't want the blank cells in the copied range to overwrite existing data.

Transposing a range

The Transpose option in the Paste Special dialog box changes the orientation of the copied range. Rows become columns, and columns become rows. Any formulas in the copied range are adjusted so that they work properly when transposed. Note that you can use this check box with the other options in the Paste Special dialog box. Figure 14-20 shows an example of a horizontal range (A1:F1) that was transposed to a vertical range (A3:A8).

FIGURE 14-20

Transposing a range changes the orientation as the information is pasted into the worksheet.

If you click the Paste Link button in the Paste Special dialog box, you create formulas that link to the source range. As a result, the destination range automatically reflects changes in the source range.

Using Names to Work with Ranges

Dealing with cryptic cell and range addresses can sometimes be confusing. (This confusion becomes even more apparent when you deal with formulas, which I cover in Chapter 15.) Fortunately, Excel allows you to assign descriptive names to cells and ranges. For example, you can give a cell a name such as Interest_Rate, or you can name a range JulySales. Working with these names (rather than cell or range addresses) has several advantages:

- A meaningful range name (such as Total_Income) is much easier to remember than a cell address (such as AC21).
- Entering a name is less error-prone than entering a cell or range address.
- You can quickly move to areas of your worksheet either by using the Name box, located at the left side of the Formula bar (click the arrow to drop down a list of defined names) or by choosing Home ➪ Editing ➪ Find & Select ➪ Go To (or F5) and specifying the range name.
- Creating formulas is easier. You can paste a cell or range name into a formula by using Formula Autocomplete, a new feature in Excel 2007.
- Names make your formulas more understandable and easier to use. A formula such as =Income — Taxes is more intuitive than =D20 — D40.

Creating range names in your workbooks

Excel provides several different methods that you can use to create range names. Before you begin, however, you should be aware of some important rules about what is acceptable:

- Names can't contain any spaces. You may want to use an underscore character to simulate a space (such as Annual_Total).
- You can use any combination of letters and numbers, but the name must begin with a letter. A name can't begin with a number (such as 3rdQuarter) or look like a cell reference (such as QTR3). If these are desirable names, you can precede the name with underscore: _3rd Quarter and _QTR3.
- Symbols, except for underscores and periods, aren't allowed.
- Names are limited to 255 characters, but it's a good practice to keep names as short as possible yet still meaningful and understandable.

Excel also uses a few names internally for its own use. Although you can create names that override Excel's internal names, you should avoid doing so. To be on the safe side, avoid using the following for names: Print_Area, Print_Titles, Consolidate_Area, and Sheet_Title.

Using the New Name dialog box

To create a range name, start by selecting the cell or range that you want to name. Then, choose Formulas ➪ Defined Names ➪ Define Name. Excel displays the New Name dialog box, shown in Figure 14-21. Note that this is a resizable dialog box. Drag a border to change the dimensions.

FIGURE 14-21

Create names for cells or ranges by using the New Name dialog box.

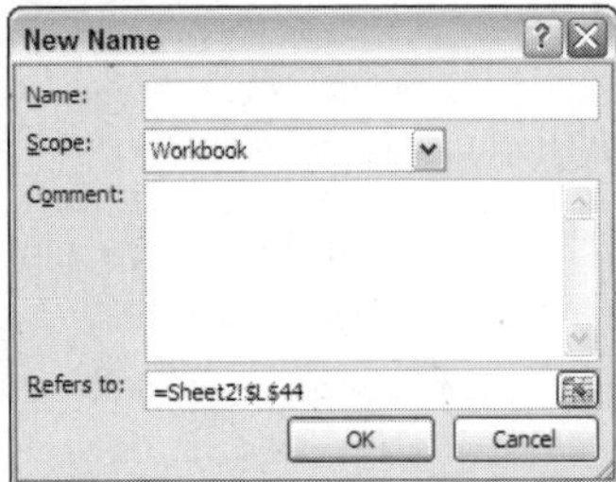

Type a name in the box labeled Name (or use the name that Excel proposes, if any). The selected cell or range address appears in the box labeled Refers To. Use the Scope drop-down to indicate the scope for the name. The scope indicates where the name will be valid, and it's either the entire workbook, or a particular sheet. If you like, you can add a comment that describes the named range or cell. Click OK to add the name to your workbook and close the dialog box.

Using the Name box

A faster way to create a name is to use the Name box (to the left of the Formula bar). Select the cell or range to name, click the Name box, and type the name. Press Enter to create the name. (You must press Enter to actually record the name; if you type a name and then click in the worksheet, Excel doesn't create the name.) If a name already exists, you can't use the Name box to change the range to which that name refers. Attempting to do so simply selects the range.

The Name box is a drop-down list and shows all names in the workbook. To choose a named cell or range, click the Name box and choose the name. The name appears in the Name box, and Excel selects the named cell or range in the worksheet.

Using the Create Names From Selection dialog box

You may have a worksheet that contains text that you want to use for names for adjacent cells or ranges. For example, you may want to use the text in column A to create names for the corresponding values in column B. Excel makes this task easy to do.

To create names by using adjacent text, start by selecting the name text and the cells that you want to name. (These items can be individual cells or ranges of cells.) The names must be adjacent to the cells that you're naming. (A multiple selection is allowed.) Then, choose Formulas ➪ Defined Names ➪ Create From Selection. Excel displays the Create Names From Selection dialog box, shown in Figure 14-22. The check marks in this dialog box are based on Excel's analysis of the selected range. For example, if Excel finds text in the first row of the selection, it proposes that you create names based on the top row. If Excel didn't guess correctly, you can change the check boxes. Click OK, and Excel creates the names.

FIGURE 14-22

Use the Create Names From Selection dialog box to name cells using labels that appear in the worksheet.

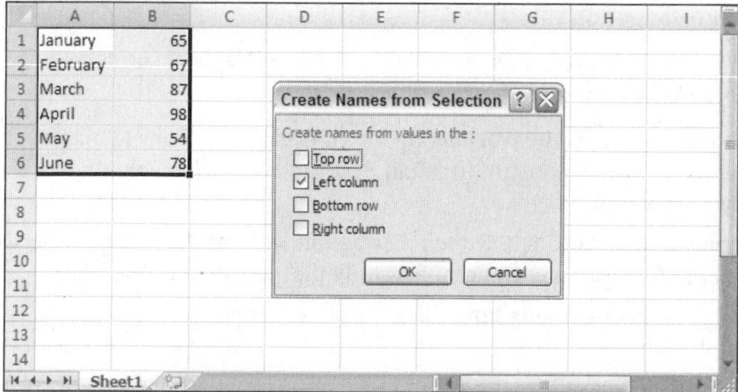

NOTE If the text contained in a cell would result in an invalid name, Excel modifies the name to make it valid. For example, if a cell contains the text Net Income (which is invalid for a name because it contains a space), Excel converts the space to an underscore character. If Excel encounters a value or a numeric formula where text should be, however, it doesn't convert it to a valid name. It simply doesn't create a name — and does not inform you of that fact.

CAUTION If the upper-left cell of the selection contains text and you choose the Top Row and Left Column options, Excel uses that text for the name of the entire data excluding the top row and left column. So, before you accept the names that Excel creates, take a minute to make sure that they refer to the correct ranges. If Excel creates a name that is incorrect, you can delete or modify it by using the Name Manager (described next).

Managing names

A workbook can have any number of names. If you have many names, you should know about the Name Manager, shown in Figure 14-23.

FIGURE 14-23

The Name Manager is new in Excel 2007.

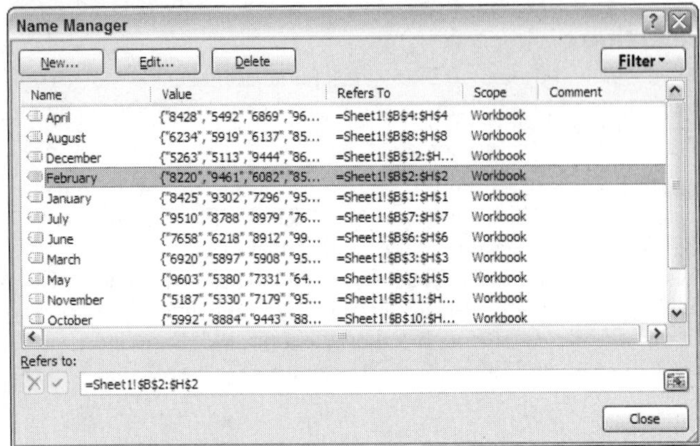

NEW FEATURE **The Name Manager is a new feature in Excel 2007.**

The Name Manager appears when you choose Formulas ➪ Defined Names ➪ Name Manager (or press Ctrl+F3). The Name Manager has the following features:

- **Displays information about each name in the workbook.** You can resize the Name Manager dialog box and widen the columns to show more information. You can also click a column heading to sort the information by the column.
- **Allows you to filter the displayed names.** Clicking the Filter button lets you show only those names that meet a certain criteria. For example, you can view only the worksheet level names.
- **Provides quick access to the New Name dialog box.** Click the New button to create a new name without closing the Name Manager.
- **Lets you edit names.** To edit a name, select it in the list and then click the Edit button. You can change the name or the Refers To range or edit the comment.
- **Lets you quickly delete unneeded names.** To delete a name, select it in the list and click Delete.

CAUTION **Be extra careful when deleting names. If the name is used in a formula, deleting the name causes the formula to become invalid. (It displays `#NAME?`.) However, deleting a name can be undone, so if you find that formulas return `#NAME?` after you delete a name, choose Undo from the Quick Access Toolbar (or press Ctrl+Z) to get the name back.**

If you delete the rows or columns that contain named cells or ranges, the names contain an invalid reference. For example, if cell A1 on Sheet1 is named Interest and you delete row 1 or column A, the name Interest then refers to `=Sheet1!#REF!` (that is, to an erroneous reference). If you use Interest in a formula, the formula displays `#REF`.

TIP **The Name Manager is useful, but it has a shortcoming: It doesn't let you display the list of names in a worksheet range so you can view or print them. Such a feat is possible, but you need to look beyond the Name Manager.**

To create a list of names in a worksheet, first move the cell pointer to an empty area of your worksheet— the list is created at the active cell position and overwrites any information at that location. Press F3 to display the Paste Name dialog box, which lists all the defined names. Then click the Paste List button. Excel creates a list of all names in the workbook and their corresponding addresses.

Adding Comments to Cells

Documentation that explains certain elements in the worksheet can often be helpful. One way to document your work is to add comments to cells. This feature is useful when you need to describe a particular value or explain how a formula works.

To add a comment to a cell, select the cell and then choose Review ➪ Comments ➪ New Comment. Alternatively, you can right-click the cell and choose Insert Comment from the shortcut menu. Excel inserts a comment that points to the active cell. Initially, the comment consists of your name. Enter the text for the cell comment and then click anywhere in the worksheet to hide the comment. You can change the size of the comment by clicking and dragging any of its borders. Figure 14-24 shows a cell with a comment.

FIGURE 14-24

You can add comments to cells to help clarify important items in your worksheets.

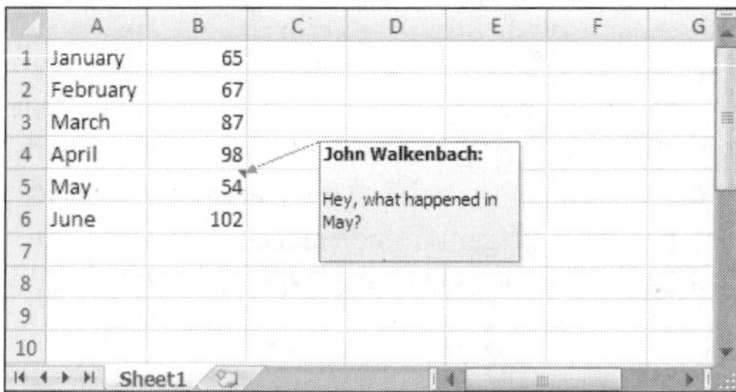

Cells that have a comment display a small red triangle in the upper-right corner. When you move the mouse pointer over a cell that contains a comment, the comment becomes visible.

You can control how comments are displayed. Access the Advanced tab of the Excel Options dialog box. In the Display section, an option lets you turn off the comment indicators if you like.

Formatting comments

If you don't like the default look of cell comments, select the comment text and use the Home ➪ Font and Home ➪ Alignment groups to make changes to the comment's appearance.

For even more formatting options, right-click the comment's border and choose Format Comment from the shortcut menu. Excel responds by displaying the Format Comment dialog box, which allows you to change many aspects of its appearance.

TIP

You also can display an image inside of a comment. Select the Colors and Lines tab in the Format Comment dialog box. Click the Color drop-down list in the Fill section and select Fill Effects. In the Fill Effects dialog box, click the Picture tab and then click the Select Picture Button to specify a graphics file. Figure 14-25 shows a comment that contains a picture.

FIGURE 14-25

This comment contains a graphic image.

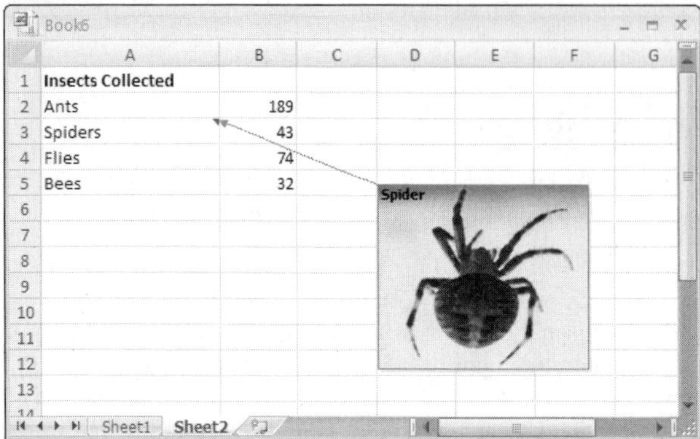

Reading comments

To read all of the comments in a workbook, choose Review ➪ Comments ➪ Next. Click this command repeatedly to cycle through all the comments in a workbook. Choose Review ➪ Comments ➪ Previous to view the comments in reverse order.

Hiding and showing comments

If you want all cell comments to be visible (regardless of the location of the cell pointer), choose Review ➪ Comments ➪ Show All Comments. This command is a toggle; select it again to hide all cell comments. To toggle the display of an individual comments, select its cell and then choose Review ➪ Comments ➪ Show/Hide Comment.

Editing comments

To edit a comment, activate the cell, right-click, and then choose Edit Comment from the shortcut menu. When you've made your changes, click any cell.

Deleting comments

To delete a cell comment, activate the cell that contains the comment and then choose Review ➪ Comments ➪ Delete. Or, right-click and then choose Delete Comment from the shortcut menu.

Summary

This chapter taught essential skills dealing with worksheets, cells, and ranges. Among the wide variety of skills covered, you learned to create, copy, move, rename, and change the view of worksheets. You also learned to work with rows and columns within sheets, performing actions including resizing, inserting, and deleting rows and columns. The chapter moved on to teach you about cells and ranges, covering how to make various kinds of selections, to naming ranges and adding comments to cells. The next chapter moves on to covering formulas and functions to perform calculations.

Chapter 15

Introducing Formulas and Functions

Formulas are what make a spreadsheet program so powerful. If it weren't for formulas, a spreadsheet would simply be a glorified word-processing document that has great support for tabular information. You use formulas in your Excel worksheets to calculate results from the data stored in the worksheet. When data changes, those formulas calculate updated results with no extra effort on your part. This chapter introduces formulas and functions and helps you get up to speed with this important element.

IN THIS CHAPTER

Understanding Formula Basics

A formula is entered into a cell. It performs a calculation of some type and returns a result, which is displayed in the cell. Formulas use a variety of operators and worksheet functions to work with values and text. The values and text used in formulas can be located in other cells, which makes changing data easy and gives worksheets their dynamic nature. For example, you can see multiple scenarios quickly by changing the data in a worksheet and letting your formulas do the work.

A formula can consist of any of these elements:

- Mathematical operators, such as + (for addition) and * (for multiplication)
- Cell references (including named cells and ranges)
- Values or text
- Worksheet functions (such as `SUM` or `AVERAGE`)

NEW FEATURE **When you're working with a table, a new feature in Excel 2007 enables you to create formulas that use column names from the table — which can make your formulas much easier to read. I discuss table formulas later in this chapter. (See the section "Using Formulas in Tables.")**

After you enter a formula, the cell displays the calculated result of the formula. The formula itself appears in the Formula bar when you select the cell, however.

Following are a few examples of formulas:

`=150*.05`	Multiplies 150 times 0.05. This formula uses only values and isn't all that useful because it always returns the same result. You may as well just enter the value 7.5 into the cell.
`=A1+A2`	Adds the values in cells A1 and A2.
`=Income-Expenses`	Subtracts the value in the cell named `Expenses` from the value in the cell named `Income`.
`=SUM(A1:A12)`	Adds the values in the range A1:A12.
`=A1=C12`	Compares cell A1 with cell C12. If they are identical, the formula returns `TRUE`; otherwise it returns `FALSE`.

Formulas always begin with the equal sign so that Excel can distinguish them from text.

Using operators in formulas

Excel lets you use a variety of *operators* in your formulas. Operators are symbols that indicate the type of mathematical operation you want the formula to perform. Table 15-1 lists the operators that Excel recognizes. In addition to these, Excel has many built-in functions that enable you to perform additional calculations.

TABLE 15-1

Operators Used in Formulas

Operator	Name
+	Addition
–	Subtraction
*	Multiplication
/	Division
^	Exponentiation
&	Concatenation
=	Logical comparison (equal to)
>	Logical comparison (greater than)
<	Logical comparison (less than)
>=	Logical comparison (greater than or equal to)
<=	Logical comparison (less than or equal to)
<>	Logical comparison (not equal to)

You can, of course, use as many operators as you need to perform the desired calculation.

Following are some examples of formulas that use various operators.

Formula	What It Does
="Part-"&"23A"	Joins (concatenates) the two text strings to produce Part-23A.
=A1&A2	Concatenates the contents of cell A1 with cell A2. Concatenation works with values as well as text. If cell A1 contains 123 and cell A2 contains 456, this formula would return the value 123456.
=6^3	Raises 6 to the third power (216).
=216^(1/3)	Returns the cube root of 216 (6).
=A1<A2	Returns TRUE if the value in cell A1 is less than the value in cell A2. Otherwise, it returns FALSE. Logical-comparison operators also work with text. If A1 contained Bill and A2 contained Julia, the formula would return TRUE, because Bill comes before Julia in alphabetical order.
=A1<=A2	Returns TRUE if the value in cell A1 is less than or equal to the value in cell A2. Otherwise, it returns FALSE.
=A1<>A2	Returns TRUE if the value in cell A1 isn't equal to the value in cell A2. Otherwise, it returns FALSE.

Understanding operator precedence in formulas

When Excel calculates the value of a formula, it uses certain rules to determine the order in which the various parts of the formula are calculated. You need to understand these rules if you want your formulas to produce the desired results.

Table 15-2 lists the Excel operator precedence. This table shows that exponentiation has the highest precedence (it's performed first) and logical comparisons have the lowest precedence (they're performed last).

TABLE 15-2

Operator Precedence in Excel Formulas

Symbol	Operator	Precedence
^	Exponentiation	1
*	Multiplication	2
/	Division	2
+	Addition	3
–	Subtraction	3
&	Concatenation	4
=	Equal to	5
<	Less than	5
>	Greater than	5

You can use parentheses to override Excel's built-in order of precedence. Expressions within parentheses are always evaluated first.

The following formula uses parentheses to control the order in which the calculations occur. In this case, cell B3 is subtracted from cell B2 and the result is multiplied by cell B4:

```
=(B2-B3)*B4
```

If you enter the formula without the parentheses, Excel computes a different answer. Because multiplication has a higher precedence, cell B3 is multiplied by cell B4. Then this result is subtracted from cell B2, which isn't what was intended.

The formula without parentheses looks like this:

```
=B2-B3*B4
```

It's a good idea to use parentheses even when they aren't strictly necessary. Doing so helps to clarify what the formula is intended to do. For example, the following formula makes it perfectly clear that B3 should be multiplied by B4, and the result subtracted from cell B2. Without the parentheses, you would need to remember Excel's order of precedence.

```
=B2-(B3*B4)
```

You can also *nest* parentheses within formulas—that is, put them inside other parentheses. If you do so, Excel evaluates the most deeply nested expressions first—and then works its way out. Here's an example of a formula that uses nested parentheses:

```
=((B2*C2)+(B3*C3)+(B4*C4))*B6
```

This formula has four sets of parentheses—three sets are nested inside the fourth set. Excel evaluates each nested set of parentheses and then sums the three results. This result is then multiplied by the value in B6.

Although the preceding formula uses four sets of parentheses, only the outer set is really necessary. If you understand operator precedence, it should be clear that you can rewrite this formula as:

```
=(B2*C2+B3*C3+B4*C4)*B6
```

Again, using the extra parentheses makes the calculation much clearer.

Every left parenthesis, of course, must have a matching right parenthesis. If you have many levels of nested parentheses, keeping them straight can sometimes be difficult. If the parentheses don't match, Excel displays a message explaining the problem—and won't let you enter the formula.

In some cases, if your formula contains mismatched parentheses, Excel may propose a correction to your formula. Figure 15-1 shows an example of the Formula AutoCorrect feature. You may be tempted simply to accept the proposed correction, but be careful—in many cases, the proposed formula, although syntactically correct, isn't the formula you intended, and it will produce an incorrect result.

FIGURE 15-1

Excel's Formula AutoCorrect feature often suggests a correction to an erroneous formula.

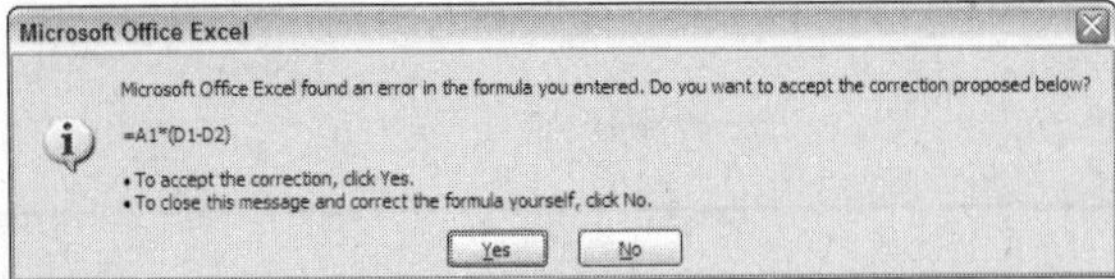

TIP Excel lends a hand in helping you match parentheses. When the insertion point moves over a parenthesis while you're editing a cell, Excel momentarily bolds it — and does the same with its matching parenthesis.

Using functions in your formulas

Most formulas you create use worksheet functions. These functions enable you to greatly enhance the power of your formulas and perform calculations that are difficult (or even impossible) if you use only the operators discussed previously. For example, you can use the `TAN` function to calculate the tangent of an angle. You can't do this calculation by using only the mathematical operators.

Examples of formulas that use functions

A worksheet function can simplify a formula significantly. To calculate the average of the values in 10 cells (A1:A10) without using a function, you'd have to construct a formula like this:

```
=(A1+A2+A3+A4+A5+A6+A7+A8+A9+A10)/10
```

Not very pretty, is it? Even worse, you would need to edit this formula if you added another cell to the range. Fortunately, you can replace this formula with a much simpler one that uses one of Excel's built-in worksheet functions:

```
=AVERAGE(A1:A10)
```

The following formula demonstrates how using a function can enable you to perform calculations that would not be possible otherwise. If (for example) you need to determine the largest value in a range, a formula can't tell you the answer without using a function. Here's a simple formula that returns the largest value in the range A1:D100:

```
=MAX(A1:D100)
```

Functions also can sometimes eliminate manual editing. Assume that you have a worksheet that contains 1,000 names in cells A1:A1000, and all names appear in all-capital letters. Your boss sees the listing and informs you that the names will be mail-merged with a form letter — so all uppercase is not acceptable; for example, `JOHN F. SMITH` must appear as `John F. Smith`. You *could* spend the next several hours re-entering the list — or you could use a formula such as the following, which uses a function to convert the text in cell A1 to the proper case:

```
=PROPER(A1)
```

Enter this formula once in cell B1 and then copy it down to the next 999 rows. Then select B1:B1000 and use Home ➪ Clipboard ➪ Copy to copy the range. Next, with B1:B1000 still selected, use Home ➪ Clipboard ➪ Paste Values to convert the formulas to values. Delete the original column, and you've just accomplished several hours of work in less than a minute.

One last example should convince you of the power of functions. Suppose you have a worksheet that calculates sales commissions. If the salesperson sold more than $100,000 of product, the commission rate is 7.5 percent; otherwise the commission rate is 5.0 percent. Without using a function, you would have to create two different formulas and make sure that you used the correct formula for each sales amount. A better solution is to write a formula that uses the `IF` function to ensure that you calculate the correct commission, regardless of sales amount:

```
=IF(A1<100000,A1*5%,A1*7.5%)
```

This formula performs some simple decision-making. The formula checks the value of cell A1. If this value is less than 100,000, the formula returns cell A1 multiplied by 5 percent. Otherwise it returns what's in cell A1, multiplied by 7.5 percent.

New Functions in Excel 2007

Excel 2007 contains five new functions:

- IFERROR — Used to check for an error, and display a message or perform a different calculation.
- AVERAGEIF — Used to calculate a conditional average (similar to SUMIF and COUNTIF).
- AVERAGEIFS — Used to calculate a conditional average using multiple criteria.
- SUMIFS — Used to calculate a conditional sum using multiple criteria.
- COUNTIFS — Used to calculate a conditional COUNT using multiple criteria.

In addition, worksheet functions that formerly required the Analysis ToolPak add-in (which is shipped with Excel) are now built into Excel. So you have access to dozens of additional functions without installing the add-in.

These new functions are described in detail in the Excel Help.

Keep in mind that if you use any of these new functions, you may not be able to share your workbook with someone who uses an earlier version of Excel, unless that person has installed the Analysis ToolPak add-in.

Function arguments

In the preceding examples, you may have noticed that all the functions used parentheses. The information inside the parentheses is called the *list of arguments.*

Functions vary in how they use arguments. Depending on what it has to do, a function may use

- No arguments
- One argument
- A fixed number of arguments
- An indeterminate number of arguments
- Optional arguments

An example of a function that doesn't use an argument is the NOW function, which returns the current date and time. Even if a function doesn't use an argument, you must still provide a set of empty parentheses, like this:

```
=NOW()
```

If a function uses more than one argument, you must separate each argument with a comma. The examples at the beginning of the chapter used cell references for arguments. Excel is quite flexible when it comes to function arguments, however. An argument can consist of a cell reference, literal values, literal text strings, expressions, and even other functions.

NOTE **A comma is the list-separator character for the U.S. version of Excel. Some other versions may use a semicolon. The list separator is a Windows setting, which can be adjusted in the Windows Control Panel (the Regional and Language Options dialog box).**

More about functions

All told, Excel includes 340 functions. And if that's not enough, you can purchase additional specialized functions from third-party suppliers — and even create your own custom functions (by using VBA) if you're so inclined.

Some users feel a bit overwhelmed by the sheer number of functions, but you'll probably find that you use only a dozen or so on a regular basis. And as you'll see, Excel's Insert Function dialog box (described later in this chapter) makes it easy to locate and insert a function, even if it's not one that you use frequently.

You'll find examples of Excel's built-in functions in Chapters 16 and 17.

Entering Formulas into Your Worksheets

As I mentioned earlier, a formula must begin with an equal sign to inform Excel that the cell contains a formula rather than text. Excel provides two ways to enter a formula into a cell: manually or by pointing to cell references. The following sections discuss each way in detail.

NEW FEATURE **Excel 2007 provides additional assistance when you create formulas by displaying a drop-down list that contains function names and range names. The items displayed in the list are determined by what you've already typed. For example, if you're entering a formula and type the letter T, you'll see the drop-down list shown in Figure 15-2. If you type an additional letter, the list is shortened to show only the matching functions. To have Excel *AutoComplete* an entry in that list, use the arrow keys to highlight the entry, and then press Tab. Notice that highlighting a function in the list also displays a brief description of the function. See the sidebar "Using Formula AutoComplete" for an example of how this new feature works.**

FIGURE 15-2

Excel 2007 displays a drop-down list when you enter a formula.

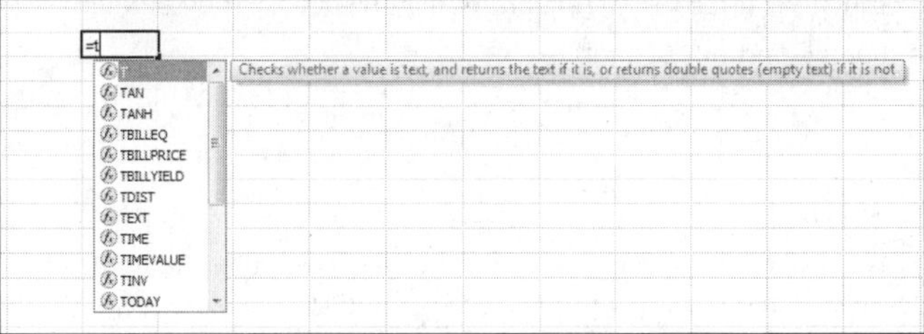

Entering formulas manually

Entering a formula manually involves, well, entering a formula manually. In a selected cell, you simply type an equal sign (=) followed by the formula. As you type, the characters appear in the cell and in the Formula bar. You can, of course, use all the normal editing keys when entering a formula.

Using Formula AutoComplete

The Formula AutoComplete feature in Excel 2007 makes entering formulas easier than ever. Here's a quick walk-through that demonstrates how it works. The goal is to create a formula that uses the `SUBTOTAL` function to calculate the average value in a range named `TestScores`.

1. **Activate an empty cell and type an equal sign (=) to signal the start of a formula.**
2. **Type the letter S, and you'll get a list of functions and names that begin with *S*.** This feature is not case-sensitive, so you can use either uppercase or lowercase characters.
3. **Type the second letter,** U. The list is filtered to show only functions and names that begin with *SU*.
4. **`SUBTOTAL` is second on the list, so use the Down Arrow to highlight the function and press Tab.** Excel adds the opening parenthesis and displays another list that contains options for the first argument for `SUBTOTAL`.
5. **Use the Down Arrow to select `AVERAGE` and press Tab.** Excel inserts `101`, the code for calculating the average.
6. **Type a comma to separate the next argument.**
7. **Type a T, and you get a list of functions and names that begin with *T*. You're looking for `TestScores`, so narrow it down a bit by typing the second character (e).**
8. **Highlight `TestScores` and press Tab.**
9. **Finally, type a closing parenthesis and press Enter.**

Formula AutoComplete includes the following items (and each type is identified by a separate icon):

- Excel built-in functions
- User defined functions (Functions defined by the user through VBA or other methods)
- Defined Names (named using the Formulas ➪ Defined Names ➪ Define Name command).
- Enumerated Arguments (only a few functions use such arguments, and `SUBTOTAL` is one of them)
- Table structure references (used to identify portions of a table)

Entering formulas by pointing

Even though you can enter formulas by typing in the entire formula, Excel provides another method of entering formulas that is generally easier, faster, and less error-prone. This method still involves some manual typing, but you can simply point to the cell references instead of typing their values manually. For example, to enter the formula =A1+A2 into cell A3, follow these steps:

1. **Move the cell pointer to cell A3.**
2. **Type an equal sign (=) to begin the formula.** Notice that Excel displays `Enter` in the status bar (bottom left of your screen).
3. **Press the up arrow twice.** As you press this key, Excel displays a faint moving border around cell A1, and the cell reference appears in cell A3 and in the Formula bar. In addition, Excel displays `Point` in the status bar.
4. **Type a plus sign (+). A solid-color border replaces the faint border, and Enter reappears in the status bar.**

5. **Press the up arrow again, which puts the moving border around cell A2, and adds that cell address to the formula.**
6. **Press Enter to end the formula.**

You also can point to the data cells by using your mouse.

Pasting range names into formulas

If your formula uses named cells or ranges, you can either type the name in place of the address or choose the name from a list and have Excel insert the name for you automatically. Two ways to insert a name into a formula are available:

- **Select the name from the drop-down list:** To use this method, you must know at least the first character of the name. When you're entering the formula, type the first character and then select the name from the drop-down list that appears.
- **Press F3:** This key displays the Paste Name dialog box. Select the name from the list and click OK (or just double-click the name). Excel will enter the name into your formula. If no names are defined, pressing F3 has no effect.

Figure 15-3 shows an example. The worksheet contains two defined names: `Expenses` and `Sales`. The Paste Name dialog box is being used to insert a name (`Sales`) into the formula being entered in cell B11.

CROSS-REF **Refer to Chapter 14 for information about defining names.**

FIGURE 15-3

You can use the Paste Name dialog box to quickly enter a defined name into a formula.

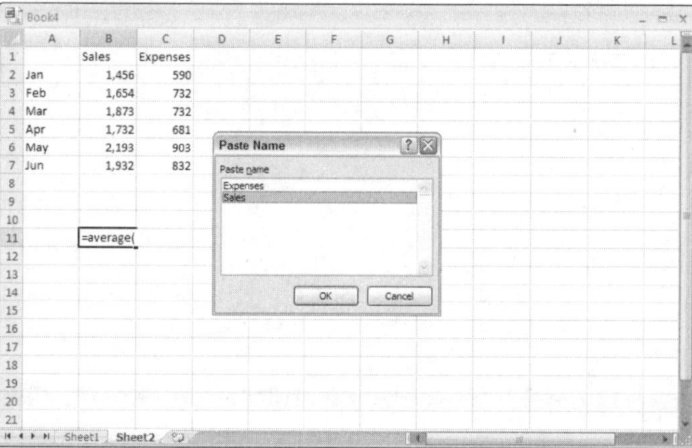

Inserting functions into formulas

The easiest way to enter a function into a formula is to use the drop-down list that Excel displays while you type a formula. In order to use this method, however, you must know at least the first character of the function's name.

Another way to insert a function is to use the Function Library group on the Formulas tab (see Figure 15-4). This is especially useful if you can't remember which function you need. Click the function category (Financial, Logical, Text, etc.) and you'll get a list of the functions in that category. Click the function you want, and Excel displays its Function Arguments dialog box. This is where you enter the function's arguments. In addition, you can click the **Help On This Function** link to learn more about the selected function.

FIGURE 15-4

You can insert a function by selecting it from one of the function categories.

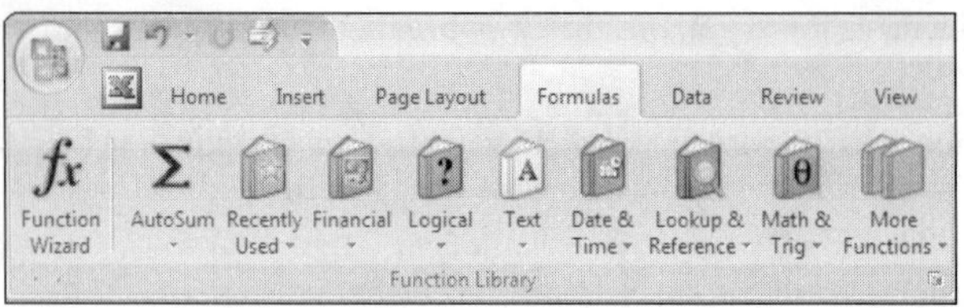

Yet another way to insert a function into a formula is to use Excel's Insert Function dialog box (see Figure 15-5). You can access this dialog box in several ways:

- By using the Formulas ➪ Function Library ➪ Insert Function command.
- By clicking the Insert Function icon, which is directly to the left of the Formula bar. This button displays `fx`.
- By pressing Shift+F3.

FIGURE 15-5

The Insert Function dialog box.

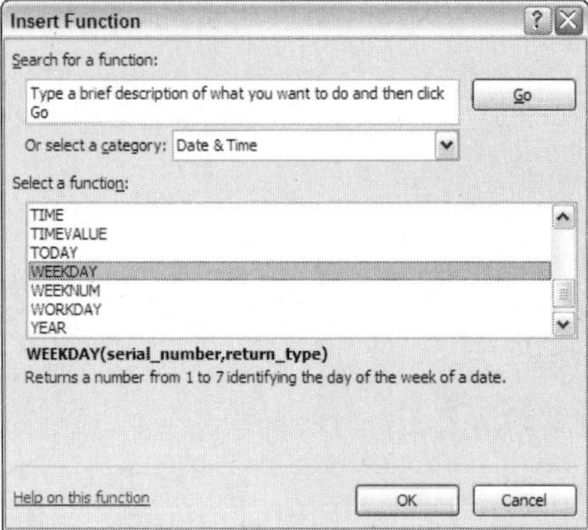

The Insert Function dialog box shows a drop-down list of function categories. Select a category, and the functions in that category are displayed in the list box. To access a function that you've used recently, select Most Recently Used from the drop-down list.

If you're not sure which function you need, you can search for the appropriate function by using the Search For A Function box at the top of the dialog box. Enter your search terms, click Go, and you'll get a list of relevant functions. When you select a function in the Select A Function list box, Excel displays the function (and its argument names) in the dialog box along with a brief description of what the function does.

When you locate the function you want to use, highlight it and click OK. Excel then displays its Function Arguments dialog box, as shown in Figure 15-6. Use this dialog box to specify the arguments for the function. The dialog box will vary, depending on the function you're inserting, and it will show one text box for each of the function's arguments. To use a cell or range reference as an argument, you can enter the address manually or click inside the argument box and then select (that is, point to) the cell or range in the sheet). After you've specified all the function arguments, click OK.

FIGURE 15-6

The Function Arguments dialog box.

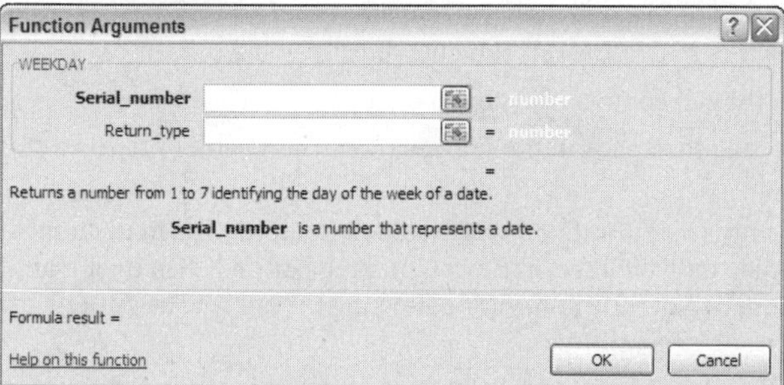

TIP **Yet another way to insert a function while you're entering a formula is to use the Function List to the left of the Formula bar. When you are entering or editing a formula, the space normally occupied by the Name box displays a list of the functions you've used most recently. After you select a function from this list, Excel displays the Function Arguments dialog box.**

Function entry tips

Following are some additional tips to keep in mind when you use the Insert Function dialog box to enter functions:

- You can use the Insert Function dialog box to insert a function into an existing formula. Just edit the formula and move the insertion point to the location at which you want to insert the function. Then open the Insert Function dialog box (using any of the methods described above) and select the function.
- You can also use the Function Arguments dialog box to modify the arguments for a function in an existing formula. Click the function in the Formula bar and then click the Insert Function button (the *fx* button, to the left of the Formula bar).
- If you change your mind about entering a function, click the Cancel button.
- How many boxes you see in the Function Arguments dialog box depends on the number of arguments used in the function you selected. If a function uses no arguments, you won't see any boxes. If the function uses a variable number of arguments (such as the `AVERAGE` function), Excel adds a new box every time you enter an optional argument.

- As you provide arguments in the Function Argument dialog box, the value of each argument is displayed to the right of each box.
- A few functions, such as `INDEX`, have more than one form. If you choose such a function, Excel displays another dialog box that lets you choose which form you want to use.
- As you become familiar with the functions, you can bypass the Insert Function dialog box and enter the function directly. Excel prompts you with argument names as you enter the function.

Editing Formulas

After you've entered a formula, you can (of course) edit that formula. You may need to edit a formula if you make some changes to your worksheet and then have to adjust the formula to accommodate the changes. Or the formula may return an error value, in which case you edit the formula to correct the error.

The following are some of the ways to get into cell edit mode:

- Double-click the cell, which enables you to edit the cell contents directly in the cell.
- Press F2, which enables you to edit the cell contents directly in the cell.
- Select the cell that you want to edit, and then click in the Formula bar. This enables you to edit the cell contents in the Formula bar.
- If the cell contains a formula that returns an error, Excel will display a small triangle in the upper-left corner of the cell. Activate the cell, and you'll see an Error Checking button. Click the Error Checking button, and you can choose one of the options for correcting the error. (The options will vary according to the type of error in the cell.)

TIP **You can control whether Excel displays error indicators in the Formulas section of the Excel Options dialog box. To display this dialog box, select Office Button ⇨ Excel Options. Click Formulas. If you remove the check mark from Enable Background Error Checking, Excel no longer displays the error indicators or the Error Checking button.**

While you're editing a formula, you can select multiple characters either by dragging the mouse cursor over them or by pressing Shift while you use the direction keys.

TIP **If you have a formula that you can't seem to edit correctly, you can convert the formula to text and tackle it again later. To convert a formula to text, just remove the initial equal sign (=). When you're ready to try again, type the initial equal sign to convert the cell contents back into a formula.**

Using Cell References in Formulas

Most formulas you create include references to cells or ranges. These references enable your formulas to work dynamically with the data contained in those cells or ranges rather than being restricted to fixed values. For example, if your formula refers to cell A1 and you change the value contained in A1, the formula result changes to reflect the new value. If you didn't use references in your formulas, you would need to edit the formulas themselves in order to change the values used in the formulas.

Using relative, absolute, and mixed references

When you use a cell (or range) reference in a formula, you can use three types of references:

- **Relative:** The row and column references can change when you copy the formula to another cell because the references are actually offsets from the current row and column.
- **Absolute:** The row and column references do not change when you copy the formula because the reference is to an actual cell address.
- **Mixed:** Either the row or column reference is relative, and the other is absolute.

An absolute reference uses two dollar signs in its address: one for the column letter and one for the row number (for example, $A$5). Excel also allows mixed references in which only one of the address parts is absolute (for example, $A4 or A$4).

By default, Excel creates relative cell references in formulas. The distinction becomes apparent when you copy a formula to another cell.

Figure 15-7 shows a simple worksheet. The formula in cell D2, which multiplies the quantity by the price, is:

```
=B2*C2
```

This formula uses relative cell references. Therefore, when the formula is copied to the cells below it, the references adjust in a relative manner. For example, the formula in cell D3 is:

```
=B3*C3
```

FIGURE 15-7

Copying a formula that contains relative references.

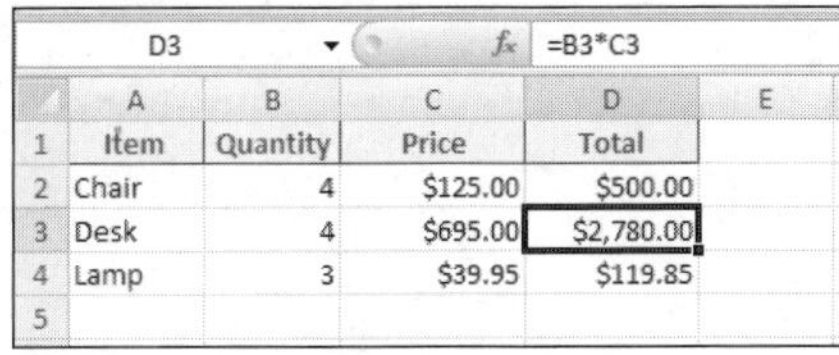

D3 =B3*C3

	A	B	C	D	E
1	Item	Quantity	Price	Total	
2	Chair	4	$125.00	$500.00	
3	Desk	4	$695.00	$2,780.00	
4	Lamp	3	$39.95	$119.85	
5					

But what if the cell references in D2 contained absolute references, like this?

```
=$B$2*$C$2
```

In this case, copying the formula to the cells below would produce incorrect results. The formula in cell D3 would be exactly the same as the formula in cell D2.

Now I'll extend the example to calculate sales tax, which is stored in cell B7 (see Figure 15-8). In this situation, the formula in cell D2 is:

```
=B2*C2*$B$7
```

The quantity is multiplied by the price, and the result is multiplied by the sales-tax rate stored in cell B7. Notice that the reference to B7 is an absolute reference. When the formula in D2 is copied to the cells below it, cell D3 will contain this formula:

```
=B3*C3*$B$7
```

Here, the references to cells B2 and C2 were adjusted, but the reference to cell B7 was not—which is exactly what I want.

FIGURE 15-8

Formula references to the sales tax cell should be absolute.

E2 =B2*C2*$B$7

	A	B	C	D	E	F	G
1	Item	Quantity	Price	Total	Sales Tax	Total	
2	Chair	4	$125.00	$500.00	$37.50		
3	Desk	4	$695.00	$2,780.00			
4	Lamp	3	$39.95	$119.85			
5							
6							
7	Sales Tax:	7.50%					
8							

Figure 15-9 demonstrates the use of mixed references. The formulas in the C3:F7 range calculate the area for various lengths and widths. The formula in cell C3 is:

```
=$B3*C$2
```

FIGURE 15-9

Using mixed cell references.

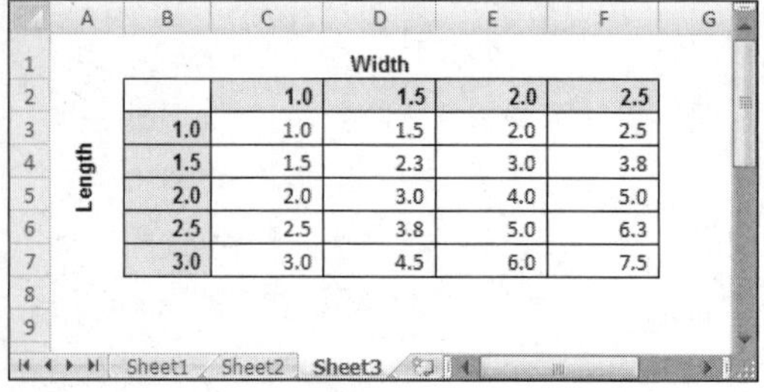

	A	B	C	D	E	F	G
1				Width			
2			1.0	1.5	2.0	2.5	
3	Length	1.0	1.0	1.5	2.0	2.5	
4		1.5	1.5	2.3	3.0	3.8	
5		2.0	2.0	3.0	4.0	5.0	
6		2.5	2.5	3.8	5.0	6.3	
7		3.0	3.0	4.5	6.0	7.5	
8							
9							

Sheet1 Sheet2 Sheet3

Notice that both cell references are mixed. The reference to cell B3 uses an absolute reference for the column ($B), and the reference to cell C2 uses an absolute reference for the row ($2). As a result, this formula can be copied down and across, and the calculations will be correct. For example, the formula in cell F7 is:

```
=$B7*F$2
```

If C3 used either absolute or relative references, copying the formula would produce incorrect results.

NOTE **When you cut and paste a formula (move it to another location), the cell references in the formula aren't adjusted. Again, this is usually what you want to happen. When you move a formula, you generally want it to continue to refer to the original cells.**

Changing the types of your references

You can enter nonrelative references (that is, absolute or mixed) manually by inserting dollar signs in the appropriate positions of the cell address. Or you can use a handy shortcut: the F4 key. When you've entered a cell reference (by typing it or by pointing), you can press F4 repeatedly to have Excel cycle through all four reference types.

For example, if you enter **=A1** to start a formula, pressing F4 converts the cell reference to `=$A$1`. Pressing F4 again converts it to `=A$1`. Pressing it again displays `=$A1`. Pressing it one more time returns to the original `=A1`. Keep pressing F4 until Excel displays the type of reference that you want.

NOTE **When you name a cell or range, Excel (by default) uses an absolute reference for the name. For example, if you give the name `SalesForecast` to A1:A12, the Refers To box in the New Name dialog box lists the reference as `$A$1:$A$12`. This is almost always what you want. If you copy a cell that has a named reference in its formula, the copied formula contains a reference to the original name.**

Referencing cells outside the worksheet

Formulas can also refer to cells in other worksheets — and the worksheets don't even have to be in the same workbook. Excel uses a special type of notation to handle these types of references.

Referencing cells in other worksheets

To use a reference to a cell in another worksheet in the same workbook, use this format:

```
SheetName!CellAddress
```

In other words, precede the cell address with the worksheet name, followed by an exclamation point. Here's an example of a formula that uses a cell on the `Sheet2` worksheet:

```
=A1*Sheet2!A1
```

This formula multiplies the value in cell A1 on the current worksheet by the value in cell A1 on `Sheet2`.

TIP **If the worksheet name in the reference includes one or more spaces, you must enclose it in single quotation marks. (Excel does that automatically if you use the point-and-click method.) For example, here's a formula that refers to a cell on a sheet named `All Depts`:**

```
=A1*'All Depts'! A1
```

Referencing cells in other workbooks

To refer to a cell in a different workbook, use this format:

```
=[WorkbookName]SheetName!CellAddress
```

In this case, the workbook name (in square brackets), the worksheet name, and an exclamation point precede the cell address. The following is an example of a formula that uses a cell reference in the `Sheet1` worksheet in a workbook named `Budget`:

```
=[Budget.xlsx]Sheet1!A1
```

If the workbook name in the reference includes one or more spaces, you must enclose it (and the sheet name) in single quotation marks. For example, here's a formula that refers to a cell on `Sheet1` in a workbook named `Budget For 2008`:

```
=A1*'[Budget For 2008.xlsx]Sheet1'!A1
```

When a formula refers to cells in a different workbook, the other workbook doesn't have to be open. If the workbook is closed, however, you must add the complete path to the reference so that Excel can find it. Here's an example:

```
=A1*'C:\My Documents\[Budget For 2008.xlsx]Sheet1'!A1
```

A linked file can also reside on another system that's accessible on your corporate network. The formula below, for example, refers to a cell in a workbook in the files directory of a computer named `DataServer`.

```
='\\DataServer\files\[budget.xlsx]Sheet1'!$D$7
```

TIP **To create formulas that refer to cells not in the current worksheet, point to the cells rather than entering their references manually. Excel takes care of the details regarding the workbook and worksheet references. The workbook you're referencing in your formula must be open if you're going to use the pointing method.**

NOTE **If you point to a different worksheet or workbook when creating a formula, you'll notice that Excel always inserts absolute cell references. Therefore, if you plan to copy the formula to other cells, make sure that you change the cell references to relative before you copy it.**

Using Formulas in Tables

One of the most significant new features in Excel 2007 is its support for tables. In this section I describe how formulas work with tables.

Summarizing data in a table

Figure 15-10 shows a simple table with three columns. I entered the data, and then converted the range to a table by choosing Insert ➪ Tables ➪ Table. Note that I didn't define any names, but the table is named `Table1` by default.

FIGURE 15-10

A simple table with three columns.

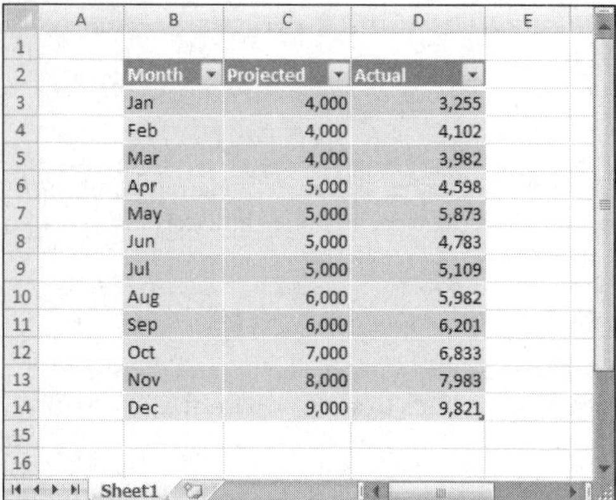

Month	Projected	Actual
Jan	4,000	3,255
Feb	4,000	4,102
Mar	4,000	3,982
Apr	5,000	4,598
May	5,000	5,873
Jun	5,000	4,783
Jul	5,000	5,109
Aug	6,000	5,982
Sep	6,000	6,201
Oct	7,000	6,833
Nov	8,000	7,983
Dec	9,000	9,821

If you'd like to calculate the total projected and total actual sales, you don't even need to write a formula. Simply click a button to add a row of summary formulas to the table:

1. **Activate any cell in the table.**
2. **Place a check mark next to Table Tools ➪ Design ➪ Table Style Options ➪ Total Row.**

3. **Activate a cell in the Total Row and use the drop-down list to select the type of summary formula to use (see Figure 15-11).** For example, to calculate the sum of the Actual column, select `SUM` from the drop-down list in cell D15. Excel creates this formula:

```
=SUBTOTAL(109,[Actual])
```

For the `SUBTOTAL` function, 109 is an enumerated argument that represents `SUM`. The second argument for the `SUBTOTAL` function is the column name, in square brackets. Using the column name within brackets is a new way to create "structured" references within a table. (I discuss this further in an upcoming section, "Referencing data in a table.")

FIGURE 15-11

A drop-down list enables you to select a summary formula for a table column.

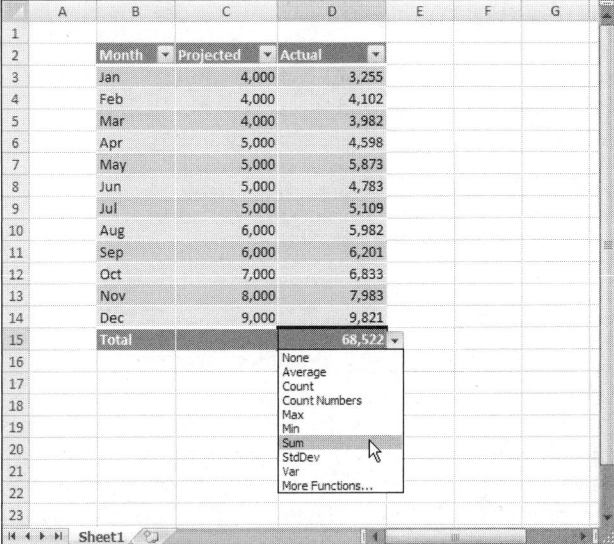

NOTE You can toggle the Total Row display on and off by using Table Tools ➪ Design ➪ Table Style Options ➪ Total Row. If you turn it off, the summary options you selected will be remembered when you turn it back on.

Using formulas within a table

In many cases, you'll want to use formulas within a table. For example, in the table shown in Figure 15-11, you may want a column that shows the difference between the Actual and Projected amounts. As you'll see, Excel 2007 makes this very easy.

1. **Activate cell E2 and type** Difference **for the column header.** Excel automatically expands the table for you.
2. **Next move to cell E3 and type an equal sign to signify the beginning of a formula.**
3. **Press the left arrow key.** Excel displays `[Actual]`, which is the column heading, in the Formula bar.

4. **Type a minus sign and then press left arrow twice.** Excel displays `[Projected]` in your formula.

5. **Press Enter to end the formula. Excel copies the formula to all rows in the table.**

Figure 15-12 shows the table with the new column.

FIGURE 15-12

The Difference column contains a formula.

	A	B	C	D	E	F
1						
2		Month	Projected	Actual	Difference	
3		Jan	4,000	3,255	-745	
4		Feb	4,000	4,102	102	
5		Mar	4,000	3,982	-18	
6		Apr	5,000	4,598	-402	
7		May	5,000	5,873	873	
8		Jun	5,000	4,783	-217	
9		Jul	5,000	5,109	109	
10		Aug	6,000	5,982	-18	
11		Sep	6,000	6,201	201	
12		Oct	7,000	6,833	-167	
13		Nov	8,000	7,983	-17	
14		Dec	9,000	9,821	821	
15		Total	68,000	68,522		
16						
17						

Sheet1

If you examine the table, you'll find this formula for all cells in the `Difference` column:

```
=[Actual]-[Projected]
```

Although the formula was entered into the first row of the table, that's not necessary. Any time a formula is entered into an empty table column, it will automatically fill all the cells in that column. And if you need to edit the formula, Excel will automatically copy the edited formula to the other cells in the column.

The steps listed above used the pointing technique to create the formula. Alternatively, you could have entered it manually using standard cell references. For example, you could have entered the following formula in cell E3:

```
=D3-C3
```

If you type the cell references, Excel will still copy the formula to the other cells automatically.

One thing should be clear, however, about formulas that use the column headers: They are much easier to understand.

Referencing data in a table

Excel 2007 adds some new ways to refer to data that's contained in a table by using the table name and column headers. There is no need to create names for these items. The table itself has a name (for example, `Table1`), and you can refer to data within the table by using column headers.

You can, of course, use standard cell references to refer to data in a table, but the new method has a distinct advantage: The names adjust automatically if the table size changes by adding or deleting rows.

Refer to the table shown in Figure 15-11. This table was given the name `Table1` when it was created. To calculate the sum of all the data in the table, use this formula:

```
=SUM(Table1)
```

This formula will always return the sum of all the data, even if rows or columns are added or deleted. And if you change the name of Table1, Excel will adjust formulas that refer to that table automatically. For example, if you renamed `Table1` to be `AnnualData` (by using the Name Manager), the preceding formula would be changed to:

```
=SUM(AnnualData)
```

Most of the time, you'll want to refer to a specific column in the table. The following formula returns the sum of the data in the `Actual` column:

```
=SUM(Table1[Actual])
```

Notice that the column name is enclosed in square brackets. Again, the formula adjusts automatically if you change the text in the column heading.

Even better, Excel provides some helpful assistance when you create a formula that refers to data within a table. Figure 15-13 shows formula `AutoComplete` helping to create a formula by showing a list of the elements in the table.

FIGURE 15-13

The formula AutoComplete feature is useful when creating a formula that refers to data in a table.

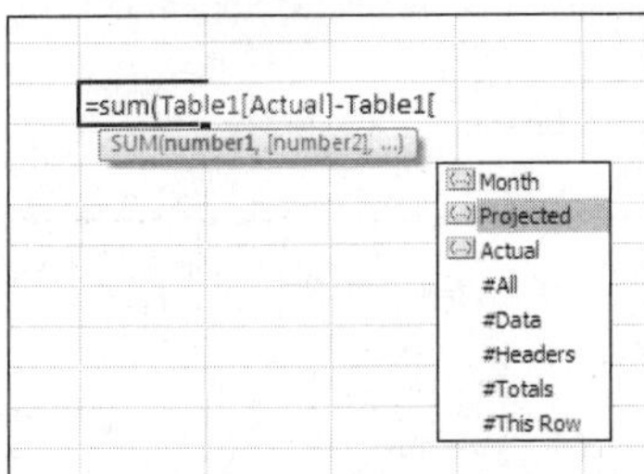

Correcting Common Formula Errors

Sometimes, when you enter a formula, Excel displays a value that begins with a pound sign (#). This is a signal that the formula is returning an error value. You have to correct the formula (or correct a cell that the formula references) to get rid of the error display.

If the entire cell is filled with pound sign characters, this means that the column isn't wide enough to display the value. You can either widen the column or change the number format of the cell.

In some cases, Excel won't even let you enter an erroneous formula. For example, the following formula is missing the closing parenthesis:

```
=A1*(B1+C2
```

If you attempt to enter this formula, Excel informs you that you have unmatched parentheses, and it proposes a correction. Often, the proposed correction is accurate, but you can't count on it.

Table 15-3 lists the types of error values that may appear in a cell that has a formula. Formulas may return an error value if a cell to which they refer has an error value. This is known as the *ripple effect* — a single error value can make its way into lots of other cells that contain formulas that depend on that one cell.

TABLE 15-3

Excel Error Values

Error Value	Explanation
#DIV/0!	The formula is trying to divide by zero. This also occurs when the formula attempts to divide by what's in a cell that is empty (that is, by nothing).
#NAME?	The formula uses a name that Excel doesn't recognize. This can happen if you delete a name that's used in the formula or if you have unmatched quotes when using text.
#N/A	The formula is referring (directly or indirectly) to a cell that uses the NA function to signal that data is not available. Some functions (for example, VLOOKUP) can also return #N/A.
#NULL!	The formula uses an intersection of two ranges that don't intersect. (This concept is described later in the chapter.)
#NUM!	A problem with a value exists; for example, you specified a negative number where a positive number is expected.
#REF!	The formula refers to a cell that isn't valid. This can happen if the cell has been deleted from the worksheet.
#VALUE!	The formula includes an argument or operand of the wrong type. An *operand* is a value or cell reference that a formula uses to calculate a result.

Handling circular references

When you're entering formulas, you may occasionally see a Circular Reference Warning message, shown in Figure 15-14, indicating that the formula you just entered will result in a *circular reference*. A circular reference occurs when a formula refers to its own value — either directly or indirectly. For example, you create a circular reference if you enter **=A1+A2+A3** into cell A3 because the formula in cell A3 refers to cell A3. Every time the formula in A3 is calculated, it must be calculated again because A3 has changed. The calculation could go on forever.

FIGURE 15-14

If you see this warning, you know that the formula you entered will result in a circular reference.

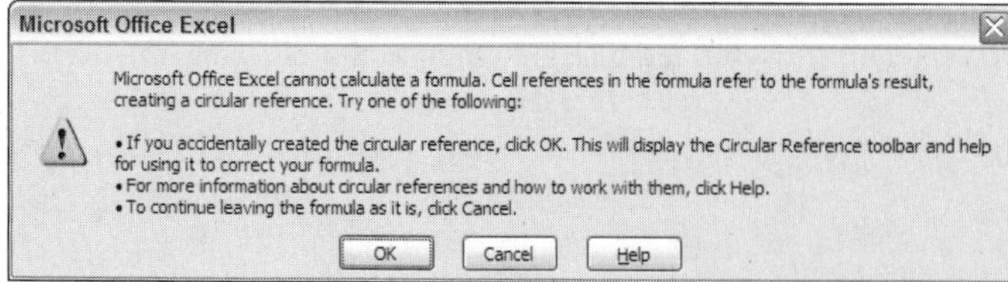

Intentional Circular References

You can sometimes use a circular reference to your advantage. For example, suppose a company has a policy of contributing 5 percent of its net profit to charity. The contribution itself, however, is considered an expense — and is therefore subtracted from the net profit figure. This produces a circular reference.

The `Contributions` cell contains the following formula:

```
=5%*Net_Profit
```

The `Net Profit` cell contains the following formula:

```
=Gross_Income-Expenses-Contributions
```

These formulas produce a resolvable circular reference. If the Enable Iterative Calculation setting is on, Excel keeps calculating until the `Contributions` value is, indeed, 5 percent of `Net Profit`. In other words, the result becomes increasingly accurate until it converges on the final solution.

When you get the circular reference message after entering a formula, Excel gives you two options:

- Click OK, and Excel displays a Help screen that tells you more about circular references.
- Click Cancel to enter the formula as is.

Regardless of which option you choose, Excel displays a message in the left side of the status bar to remind you that a circular reference exists.

WARNING **Excel won't tell you about a circular reference if the Enable Interactive Calculation setting is in effect. You can check this setting in the Formulas section of the Excel Options dialog box. (To display this dialog box, select Office Button ➪ Excel Options.) If Enable Interactive Calculation is turned on, Excel performs the circular calculation exactly the number of times specified in the Maximum Iterations field (or until the value changes by less than 0.001 or whatever value is in the Maximum Change field). In a few situations, you may use a circular reference intentionally. In these cases, the Enable Interactive Calculation setting must be on. However, it's best to keep this setting turned off so you're warned of circular references. Usually a circular reference indicates an error that you must correct.**

Usually, a circular reference is quite obvious — easy to identify and correct. But when a circular reference is indirect — as when a formula refers to another formula that refers to yet another formula that refers back to the original formula — it may require a bit of detective work to get to the problem.

Specifying when formulas are calculated

You've probably noticed that Excel calculates the formulas in your worksheet immediately. If you change any cells that the formula uses, Excel displays the formula's new result with no effort on your part. All this happens when Excel's Calculation mode is set to Automatic. In Automatic Calculation mode (which is the default mode), Excel follows these rules when it calculates your worksheet:

- When you make a change — enter or edit data or formulas, for example — Excel calculates immediately those formulas that depend on new or edited data.
- If Excel is in the middle of a lengthy calculation, it temporarily suspends the calculation when you need to perform other worksheet tasks; it resumes calculating when you're finished with your other worksheet tasks.

- Formulas are evaluated in a natural sequence. In other words, if a formula in cell D12 depends on the result of a formula in cell D11, Excel calculates cell D11 before calculating D12.

Sometimes, however, you may want to control when Excel calculates formulas. For example, if you create a worksheet with thousands of complex formulas, you'll find that processing can slow to a snail's pace while Excel does its thing. In such a case, set Excel's calculation mode to Manual — which you can do by choosing Formulas ➪ Calculation ➪ Calculation Options ➪ Manual (see Figure 15-15).

FIGURE 15-15

You can control when Excel calculates formulas.

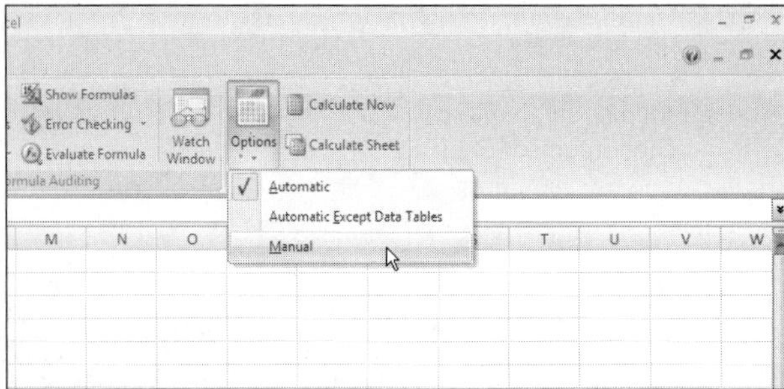

TIP **If your worksheet uses any data tables, you may want to select the option labeled** `Automatically Except For Data Tables`**. Large data tables calculate notoriously slowly. Note: A data table is not the same as a table created by choosing Insert ➪ Tables ➪ Table.**

When you're working in Manual Calculation mode, Excel displays `Calculate` in the status bar when you have any uncalculated formulas. You can use the following shortcut keys to recalculate the formulas:

- **F9:** Calculates the formulas in all open workbooks.
- **Shift+F9:** Calculates only the formulas in the active worksheet. Other worksheets in the same workbook aren't calculated.
- **Ctrl+Alt+F9:** Forces a complete recalculation of all formulas.

NOTE **Excel's Calculation mode isn't specific to a particular worksheet. When you change the Calculation mode, it affects all open workbooks, not just the active workbook.**

Tips for Working with Formulas

In this section, I offer a few additional tips and pointers relevant to formulas.

Don't hard-code values

When you create a formula, think twice before you use any specific value in the formula. For example, if your formula calculates sales tax (which is 6.5 percent), you may be tempted to enter a formula, such as the following:

```
+A1*.065
```

A better approach is to insert the sales tax rate in a cell — and use the cell reference. Or you can define the tax rate as a named constant, using the technique presented earlier in this chapter. Doing so makes modifying and maintaining your worksheet easier. For example, if the sales tax rate changed to 6.75 percent, you would have to modify every formula that used the old value. If you store the tax rate in a cell, however, you simply change that one cell — and Excel updates all the formulas.

Using the Formula bar as a calculator

If you simply need to perform a calculation, you can use the Formula bar as a calculator. For example, enter the following formula — but don't press Enter:

```
=(145*1.05)/12
```

If you press Enter, Excel enters the formula into the cell. But because this formula always returns the same result, you may prefer to store the formula's *result* rather than the formula itself. To do so, press F9 — and watch the result appear in the Formula bar. Press Enter to store the result in the active cell. (This technique also works if the formula uses cell references or worksheet functions.)

Making an exact copy of a formula

When you copy a formula, Excel adjusts its cell references when you paste the formula to a different location. Sometimes, you may want to make an exact copy of the formula. One way to do this is to convert the cell references to absolute values, but this isn't always desirable. A better approach is to select the formula in Edit mode and then copy it to the Clipboard as text. You can do this in several ways. Here's a step-by-step example of how to make an exact copy of the formula in A1 — and copy it to A2:

1. **Double-click A1 (or press F2) to get into Edit mode.**
2. **Drag the mouse to select the entire formula.** You can drag from left to right or from right to left. To select the entire formula with the keyboard, press Shift+Home.
3. **Choose Home ➪ Clipboard ➪ Copy(or press Ctrl+C).** This copies the selected text (which will become the copied formula) to the Clipboard.
4. **Press Esc to get out of Edit mode.**
5. **Select cell A2.**
6. **Home ➪ Clipboard ➪ Paste (or press Ctrl+V) to paste the text into cell A2.**

You also can use this technique to copy just *part* of a formula, if you want to use that part in another formula. Just select the part of the formula that you want to copy by dragging the mouse, and then use any of the available techniques to copy the selection to the Clipboard. You can then paste the text to another cell.

Formulas (or parts of formulas) copied in this manner won't have their cell references adjusted when they are pasted to a new cell. That's because the formulas are being copied as text, not as actual formulas.

TIP **You can also convert a formula to text by adding an apostrophe (') in front of the equal sign. Then, copy the formula as usual and paste it to its new location. Remove the apostrophe from the pasted formula, and it will be identical to the original formula. And don't forget to remove the apostrophe from the original formula as well.**

Converting formulas to values

If you have a range of formulas that will always produce the same result (that is, *dead formulas*), you may want to convert them to values. If, say, range A1:A20 contains formulas that have calculated results that will never change — or that you don't want to change. For example, if you use the RANDBETWEEN function to create a set of random numbers and you don't want Excel to recalculate those random numbers each time you press Enter, you can convert the formulas to values. Just follow these steps:

1. **Select A1:A20.**
2. **Choose Home ➪ Clipboard ➪ Copy (or press Ctrl+C).**
3. **Choose Home ➪ Clipboard ➪ Paste Values.**
4. **Press Esc to cancel Copy mode.**

Summary

This chapter taught you what you need to learn to enter formulas to perform calculations in cells. You learned about formula operators and the correct precedence in formulas, as well as how built-in functions help you perform sophisticated calculations. You also learned a host of techniques and shortcuts that will make your formula building faster and easier than ever.

Chapter 16

Working with Dates and Times

IN THIS CHAPTER

An overview of using dates and times in Excel

Excel's date-related functions

Excel's time-related functions

Beginners often find that working with dates and times in Excel can be frustrating. To work with dates and times, you need a good understanding of how Excel handles time-based information. This chapter provides the information you need to create powerful formulas that manipulate dates and times.

NOTE The dates in this chapter correspond to the U.S. English date format: month/day/year. For example, the date 3/1/1952 refers to March 1, 1952, not January 3, 1952. I realize that this setup may seem illogical, but that's the way Americans have been trained. I trust that the non-American readers of this book can make the adjustment.

How Excel Handles Dates and Times

This section presents a quick overview of how Excel deals with dates and times. It includes coverage of the Excel program's date and time serial number system, and it offers tips for entering and formatting dates and times.

Understanding date serial numbers

To Excel, a date is simply a number. More precisely, a date is a *serial number* that represents the number of days since the fictitious date of January 0, 1900. A serial number of 1 corresponds to January 1, 1900; a serial number of 2 corresponds to January 2, 1900, and so on. This system makes it possible to deal with dates in formulas. For example, you can create a formula to calculate the number of days between two dates (just subtract one from the other).

Excel supports dates from January 1, 1900, through December 31, 9999 (serial number = 2,958,465).

You may wonder about January 0, 1900. This *nondate* (which corresponds to date serial number 0) is actually used to represent times that aren't associated with a particular day. This nondate business becomes clear later in this chapter (see the section "Entering times").

Choose Your Date System: 1900 or 1904

Excel actually supports two date systems: the 1900 date system and the 1904 date system. Which system you use in a workbook determines what date serves as the basis for dates. The 1900 date system uses January 1, 1900, as the day assigned to date serial number 1. The 1904 date system uses January 1, 1904, as the base date. By default, Excel for Windows uses the 1900 date system, and Excel for Macintosh uses the 1904 date system. Excel for Windows supports the 1904 date system for compatibility with Macintosh files. You can choose the date system for the active workbook in the Advanced section of the Excel Options dialog box. (It's in the subsection titled "When Calculating This Workbook.") You can't change the date system if you use Excel for Macintosh.

Generally, you should use the default 1900 date system. And you should exercise caution if you use two different date systems in workbooks that are linked together. For example, assume that Book1 uses the 1904 date system and contains the date 1/15/1999 in cell A1. Assume that Book2 uses the 1900 date system and contains a link to cell A1 in Book1. Book2 displays the date as 1/14/1995. Both workbooks use the same date serial number (34713), but they're interpreted differently.

One advantage to using the 1904 date system is that it enables you to display negative time values. With the 1900 date system, a calculation that results in a negative time (for example, 4:00 PM–5:30 PM) cannot be displayed. When using the 1904 date system, the negative time displays as –1:30 (that is, a difference of 1 hour and 30 minutes).

To view a date serial number as a date, you must format the cell as a date. Choose Home ➪ Number ➪ Number Format. This drop-down control provides you with two date formats. To select from additional date formats, see the section "Formatting dates and times," later in this chapter.

Entering dates

You can enter a date directly as a serial number (if you know it), but more often, you enter a date using any of several recognized date formats. Excel automatically converts your entry into the corresponding date serial number (which it uses for calculations), and it also applies the default date format to the cell so that it displays as an actual date rather than as a cryptic serial number.

For example, if you need to enter June 18, 2007, you can simply enter the date by typing **June 18, 2007** (or any of several different date formats). Excel interprets your entry and stores the value 39251, the date serial number for that date. It also applies the default date format so that the cell contents may not appear exactly as you typed them.

NOTE **Depending on your regional settings, entering a date in a format, such as June 18, 2007, may be interpreted as a text string. In such a case, you'd need to enter the date in a format that corresponds to your regional settings, such as 18 June, 2007.**

When you activate a cell that contains a date, the Formula bar shows the cell contents formatted by using the default date format — which corresponds to your system's *short date format.* The Formula bar doesn't display the date's serial number. If you need to find out the serial number for a particular date, format the cell using a nondate number format.

TIP To change the default date format, you need to change a system-wide setting. Access the Windows Control Panel and select Regional and Language Options. Then click the Customize button to display the Customize Regional Options dialog box. Select the Date tab. The item selected in the Short Date Format drop-down list box determines the default date format used by Excel. These instructions apply to Windows XP and may vary with other versions of Windows.

Table 16-1 shows a sampling of the date formats that Excel recognizes (using the U.S. settings). Results will vary if you use a different regional setting.

TABLE 16-1

Date Entry Formats Recognized by Excel

Entry	Excel's Interpretation (U.S. Settings)
6-18-07	June 18, 2007
6-18-2007	June 18, 2007
6/18/07	June 18, 2007
6/18/2007	June 18, 2007
6-18/07	June 18, 2007
June 18, 2007	June 18, 2007
Jun 18	June 18 of the current year
June 18	June 18 of the current year
6/18	June 18 of the current year
6-18	June 18 of the current year
18-Jun-2007	June 18, 2007
2007/6/18	June 18, 2007

As you can see in Table 16-1, Excel is rather intelligent when it comes to recognizing dates entered into a cell. It's not perfect, however. For example, Excel does *not* recognize any of the following entries as dates:

- June 18 2007
- Jun-18 2007
- Jun-18/2007

Rather, it interprets these entries as text. If you plan to use dates in formulas, make sure that Excel can recognize the date you enter as a date; otherwise, the formulas that refer to these dates will produce incorrect results.

If you attempt to enter a date that lies outside of the supported date range, Excel interprets it as text. If you attempt to format a serial number that lies outside of the supported range as a date, the value displays as a series of pound signs (#########).

Searching for Dates

If your worksheet uses many dates, you may need to search for a particular date by using the Find And Replace dialog box (which you can access by choosing Home ⇨ Editing ⇨ Find & Select ⇨ Find or by pressing Ctrl+F). Excel is rather picky when it comes to finding dates. You must enter a full four-digit year into the Find What field in the Find dialog box. In addition, you must enter the date in the same format used to display dates in the Formula bar.

Understanding time serial numbers

When you need to work with time values, you simply extend the Excel date serial number system to include decimals. In other words, Excel works with times by using fractional days. For example, the date serial number for June 1, 2007, is 39234. Noon (halfway through the day) is represented internally as 39234.5.

The serial number equivalent of one minute is approximately 0.00069444. The formula that follows calculates this number by multiplying 24 hours by 60 minutes, and dividing the result into 1. The denominator consists of the number of minutes in a day (1,440).

```
=1/(24*60)
```

Similarly, the serial number equivalent of one second is approximately 0.00001157, obtained by the following formula: 1 divided by 24 hours times 60 minutes times 60 seconds. In this case, the denominator represents the number of seconds in a day (86,400).

```
=1/(24*60*60)
```

In Excel, the smallest unit of time is one one-thousandth of a second. The time serial number shown here represents 23:59:59.999 (or one one-thousandth of a second before midnight):

```
0.99999999
```

Table 16-2 shows various times of day along with each associated time serial number.

TABLE 16-2

Times of Day and Their Corresponding Serial Number

Time of Day	Time Serial Number
12:00:00 AM (midnight)	0.00000000
1:30:00 AM	0.06250000
3:00:00 AM	0.12500000
4:30:00 AM	0.18750000
6:00:00 AM	0.25000000
7:30:00 AM	0.31250000
9:00:00 AM	0.37500000

Time of Day	Time Serial Number
10:30:00 AM	0.43750000
12:00:00 PM (noon)	0.50000000
1:30:00 PM	0.56250000
3:00:00 PM	0.62500000
4:30:00 PM	0.68750000
6:00:00 PM	0.75000000
7:30:00 PM	0.81250000
9:00:00 PM	0.87500000
10:30:00 PM	0.93750000

Entering times

As with entering dates, you normally don't have to worry about the actual time serial numbers. Just enter the time into a cell using a recognized format. Table 16-3 shows some examples of time formats that Excel recognizes.

TABLE 16-3

Time Entry Formats Recognized by Excel

Entry	Excel's Interpretation
11:30:00 am	11:30 AM
11:30:00 AM	11:30 AM
11:30 pm	11:30 PM
11:30	11:30 AM
13:30	1:30 PM

Because the preceding samples don't have a specific day associated with them, Excel (by default) uses a date serial number of 0, which corresponds to the nonday January 0, 1900. Often, you'll want to combine a date and time. Do so by using a recognized date-entry format, followed by a space, and then a recognized time-entry format. For example, if you enter **6/18/2007 11:30** in a cell, Excel interprets it as 11:30 AM on June 18, 2007. Its date/time serial number is 39251.4791666667.

When you enter a time that exceeds 24 hours, the associated date for the time increments accordingly. For example, if you enter **25:00:00** into a cell, it's interpreted as 1:00 AM on January 1, 1900. The day part of the entry increments because the time exceeds 24 hours. Keep in mind that a time value without a date uses January 0, 1900 as the date.

Similarly, if you enter a date *and* a time (and the time exceeds 24 hours), the date that you entered is adjusted. If you enter **9/18/2007 25:00:00**, for example, it's interpreted as 9/19/2007 1:00:00 AM.

If you enter a time only (without an associated date), into an unformatted cell, the maximum time that you can enter into a cell is 9999:59:59 (just under 10,000 hours). Excel adds the appropriate number of days. In this case, 9999:59:59 is interpreted as 3:59:59 PM on 02/19/1901. If you enter a time that exceeds 10,000 hours, the entry is interpreted as a text string rather than a time.

Formatting dates and times

You have a great deal of flexibility in formatting cells that contain dates and times. For example, you can format the cell to display the date part only, the time part only, or both the date and time parts.

You format dates and times by selecting the cells and then using the Number tab of the Format Cells dialog box, as shown in Figure 16-1. To display this dialog box, click the Dialog Box Launcher icon in the Number group of the Home tab. Or, you can click the Number Format control and select More Number Formats from the list that appears.

The Date category shows built-in date formats, and the Time category shows built-in time formats. Some formats include both date and time displays. Just select the desired format from the Type list and click OK.

FIGURE 16-1

Use the Number tab in the Format Cells dialog box to change the appearance of dates and times.

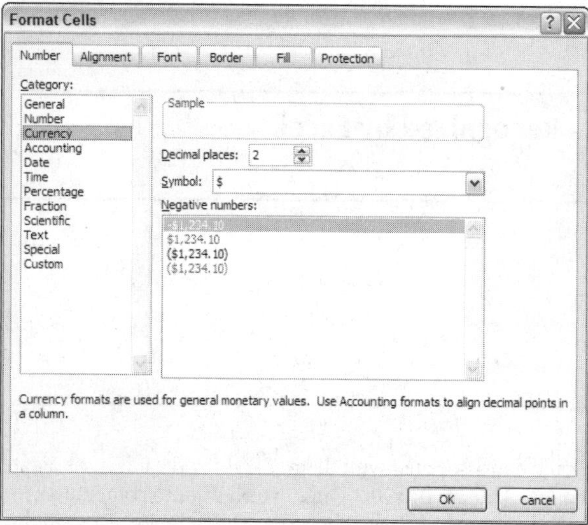

TIP **When you create a formula that refers to a cell containing a date or a time, Excel automatically formats the formula cell as a date or a time. Sometimes, this automation is very helpful; other times, it's completely inappropriate and downright annoying. To return the number formatting to the default General format, choose Home ⇨ Number ⇨ Number Format, and select General from drop-down list Or, use this shortcut-key combination: Ctrl+Shift+~.**

If none of the built-in formats meets your needs, you can create a custom number format. Select the Custom category and then type the custom format codes into the Type box.

Problems with dates

Excel has some problems when it comes to dates. Many of these problems stem from the fact that Excel was designed many years ago, before the acronym *Y2K* was even thought of. And, as I describe, the Excel designers basically emulated the Lotus 1-2-3 program's limited date and time features, which contain a nasty bug duplicated intentionally in Excel.

If Excel were being designed from scratch today, I'm sure it would be much more versatile in dealing with dates. Unfortunately, users are currently stuck with a product that leaves much to be desired in the area of dates.

Excel's leap year bug

A leap year, which occurs every four years, contains an additional day (February 29). Although the year 1900 was not a leap year, Excel treats it as such. In other words, when you type **2/29/1900** into a cell, Excel interprets it as a valid date and assigns a serial number of 60.

If you type **2/29/1901**, however, Excel correctly interprets it as a mistake and doesn't convert it to a date. Rather, it simply makes the cell entry a text string.

How can a product used daily by millions of people contain such an obvious bug? The answer is historical. The original version of Lotus 1-2-3 contained a bug that caused it to consider 1900 as a leap year. When Excel was released some time later, the designers knew of this bug and chose to reproduce it in Excel to maintain compatibility with Lotus worksheet files.

Why does this bug still exist in later versions of Excel? Microsoft asserts that the disadvantages of correcting this bug outweigh the advantages. If the bug were eliminated, it would mess up millions of existing workbooks. In addition, correcting this problem would possibly affect compatibility between Excel and other programs that use dates. As it stands, this bug really causes very few problems because most users don't use dates before March 1, 1900.

Pre-1900 dates

The world, of course, didn't begin on January 1, 1900. People who use Excel to work with historical information often need to work with dates before January 1, 1900. Unfortunately, the only way to work with pre-1900 dates is to enter the date into a cell as text. For example, you can enter **July 4, 1776** into a cell, and Excel won't complain.

You can't, however, perform any manipulation on dates entered as text. For example, you can't change its numeric formatting, you can't determine which day of the week this date occurred on, and you can't calculate the date that occurs seven days later.

NOTE **My Power Utility Pak add-in includes eight new worksheet functions that enable you to work with any date in the years 0100 through 9999. Figure 16-2 shows a worksheet that uses these extended date functions in columns E though H to perform calculations that involve pre-1900 dates. You can download a trial version of Power Utility Pak from my Web site (`http://j-walk.com/ss`).**

FIGURE 16-2

The author's Extended Date Functions add-in enables you to work with pre-1900 dates.

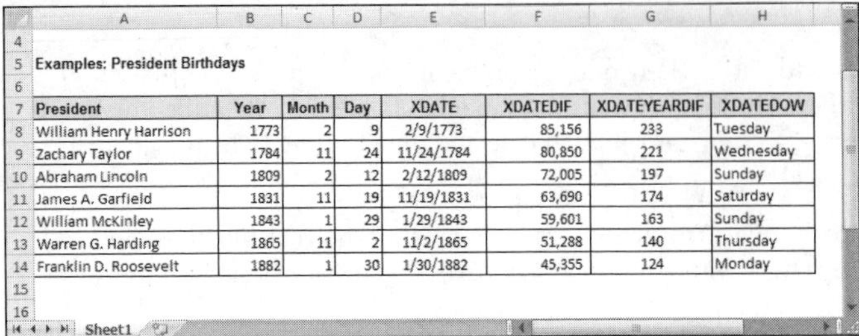

Examples: President Birthdays

President	Year	Month	Day	XDATE	XDATEDIF	XDATEYEARDIF	XDATEDOW
William Henry Harrison	1773	2	9	2/9/1773	85,156	233	Tuesday
Zachary Taylor	1784	11	24	11/24/1784	80,850	221	Wednesday
Abraham Lincoln	1809	2	12	2/12/1809	72,005	197	Sunday
James A. Garfield	1831	11	19	11/19/1831	63,690	174	Saturday
William McKinley	1843	1	29	1/29/1843	59,601	163	Sunday
Warren G. Harding	1865	11	2	11/2/1865	51,288	140	Thursday
Franklin D. Roosevelt	1882	1	30	1/30/1882	45,355	124	Monday

Inconsistent date entries

You need to exercise caution when entering dates by using two digits for the year. When you do so, Excel has some rules that kick in to determine which century to use. And those rules vary, depending on the version of Excel that you use.

Two-digit years between 00 and 29 are interpreted as twenty-first century dates, and two-digit years between 30 and 99 are interpreted as twentieth-century dates. For example, if you enter 12/15/28, Excel interprets your entry as December 15, 2028. But if you enter 12/15/30, Excel sees it as December 15, 1930, because Windows uses a default boundary year of 2029. You can keep the default as is or change it by using the Windows Control Panel. In Windows XP, display the Regional And Language Options dialog box. Then click the Customize button to display the Customize Regional Options dialog box. Select the Date tab and then specify a different year. This procedure may vary with different versions of Windows.

The best way to avoid any surprises is to simply enter *all* years using all four digits for the year.

Date-Related Functions

Excel has quite a few functions that work with dates. These functions are accessible by choosing Formulas ➪ Function Library ➪ Date & Time.

Table 16-4 summarizes the date-related functions available in Excel.

TABLE 16-4

Date-Related Functions

Function	Description
`DATE`	Returns the serial number of a particular date
`DATEVALUE`	Converts a date in the form of text to a serial number
`DAY`	Converts a serial number to a day of the month
`DAYS360`	Calculates the number of days between two dates based on a 360-day year

Function	Description
EDATE*	Returns the serial number of the date that represents the indicated number of months before or after the start date
EOMONTH*	Returns the serial number of the last day of the month before or after a specified number of months
MONTH	Converts a serial number to a month
NETWORKDAYS*	Returns the number of whole work days between two dates
NOW	Returns the serial number of the current date and time
TODAY	Returns the serial number of today's date
WEEKDAY	Converts a serial number to a day of the week
WEEKNUM*	Returns the week number in the year
WORKDAY*	Returns the serial number of the date before or after a specified number of workdays
YEAR	Converts a serial number to a year
YEARFRAC*	Returns the year fraction representing the number of whole days between start_date and end_date

* In versions prior to Excel 2007, these functions are available only when the Analysis ToolPak add-in is installed.

Displaying the current date

The following function displays the current date in a cell:

```
=TODAY()
```

You can also display the date combined with text. The formula that follows, for example, displays text, such as *Today is Monday, April 9, 2007*.

```
="Today is "&TEXT(TODAY(),"dddd, mmmm d, yyyy")
```

It's important to understand that the TODAY function is updated whenever the worksheet is calculated. For example, if you enter either of the preceding formulas into a worksheet, the formulas display the current date. But when you open the workbook tomorrow, they will display the current date (not the date when you entered the formula).

TIP **To enter a date stamp into a cell, press Ctrl+; (semicolon). This action enters the date directly into the cell and does not use a formula. Therefore, the date will not change.**

Displaying any date

You can easily enter a date into a cell by simply typing it while using any of the date formats that Excel recognizes. You also can create a date by using the DATE function, which takes three arguments: the year, the month, and the day. The following formula, for example, returns a date comprised of the year in cell A1, the month in cell B1, and the day in cell C1:

```
=DATE(A1,B1,C1)
```

NOTE **The** DATE **function accepts invalid arguments and adjusts the result accordingly. For example, the following formula uses 13 as the month argument and returns January 1, 2008. The month argument is automatically translated as month 1 of the following year.**

```
=DATE(2007,13,1)
```

Often, you'll use the DATE function with other functions as arguments. For example, the formula that follows uses the YEAR and TODAY functions to return the date for Independence Day (July 4th) of the current year:

```
=DATE(YEAR(TODAY()),7,4)
```

The DATEVALUE function converts a text string that looks like a date into a date serial number. The following formula returns 39316, the date serial number for August 22, 2007:

```
=DATEVALUE("8/22/2007")
```

To view the result of this formula as a date, you need to apply a date number format to the cell.

CAUTION **Be careful when using the** DATEVALUE **function. A text string that looks like a date in your country may not look like a date in another country. The preceding example works fine if your system is set for U.S. date formats, but it returns an error for other regional date formats because Excel is looking for the eighth day of the twenty-second month!**

Generating a series of dates

Often, you want to insert a series of dates into a worksheet. For example, in tracking weekly sales, you may want to enter a series of dates, each separated by seven days. These dates will serve to identify the sales figures.

The most efficient way to enter a series of dates doesn't require any formulas. Use the Excel AutoFill feature to insert a series of dates. Enter the first date and drag the cell's fill handle while pressing and holding the right mouse button. Release the mouse button and select an option from the shortcut menu (see Figure 16-3)— either Fill Days, Fill Weekdays, Fill Months, or Fill Years.

The advantage of using formulas (instead of the AutoFill feature) to create a series of dates is that you can change the first date, and the others update automatically. You need to enter the starting date into a cell and then use formulas (copied down the column) to generate the additional dates.

The following examples assume that you entered the first date of the series into cell A1 and the formula into cell A2. You can then copy this formula down the column as many times as needed.

To generate a series of dates separated by seven days, use this formula:

```
=A1+7
```

To generate a series of dates separated by one month, use this formula:

```
=DATE(YEAR(A1),MONTH(A1)+1,DAY(A1))
```

To generate a series of dates separated by one year, use this formula:

```
=DATE(YEAR(A1)+1,MONTH(A1),DAY(A1))
```

To generate a series of weekdays only (no Saturdays or Sundays), use the formula that follows. This formula assumes that the date in cell A1 is not a weekend day.

```
=IF(WEEKDAY(A1)=6,A1+3,A1+1)
```

FIGURE 16-3

Using Excel's AutoFill feature to create a series of dates.

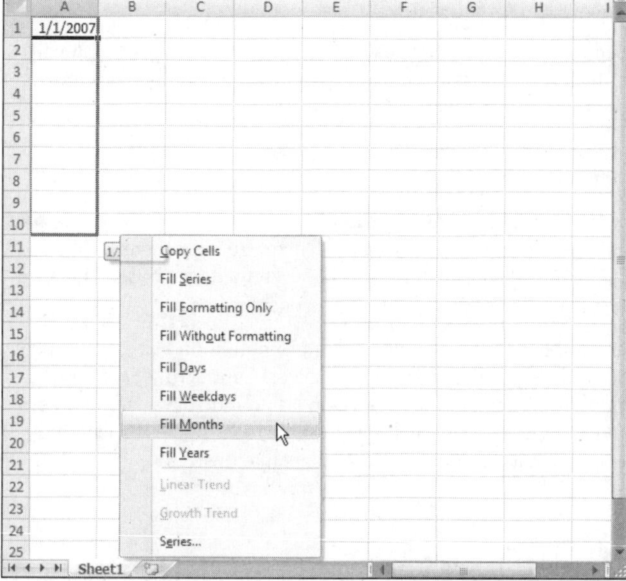

Converting a nondate string to a date

You may import data that contains dates coded as text strings. For example, the following text represents August 21, 2007 (a four-digit year followed by a two-digit month, followed by a two-digit day):

```
20070821
```

To convert this string to an actual date, you can use a formula, such as this one. (It assumes that the coded data is in cell A1.)

```
=DATE(LEFT(A1,4),MID(A1,5,2),RIGHT(A1,2))
```

This formula uses text functions (`LEFT`, `MID`, and `RIGHT`) to extract the digits, and then it uses these extracted digits as arguments for the `DATE` function.

Calculating the number of days between two dates

A common type of date calculation determines the number of days between two dates. For example, you may have a financial worksheet that calculates interest earned on a deposit account. The interest earned depends on the number of days the account is open. If your sheet contains the open date and the close date for the account, you can calculate the number of days the account was open.

Because dates are stored as consecutive serial numbers, you can use simple subtraction to calculate the number of days between two dates. For example, if cells A1 and B1 both contain a date, the following formula returns the number of days between these dates:

```
=A1-B1
```

Excel automatically formats this formula cell as a date rather than as a numeric value. Therefore, you will need to change the number format so that the result is displayed as a nondate. If cell B1 contains a more recent date than the date in cell A1, the result will be negative.

NOTE **If this formula does not display the correct value, make sure that A1 and B1 both contain actual dates — not text that *looks* like a date.**

Sometimes, calculating the difference between two days is more difficult. To demonstrate, consider the common *fence-post analogy.* If somebody asks you how many units make up a fence, you can respond with either of two answers: the number of fence posts or the number of gaps between the fence posts. The number of fence posts is always one more than the number of gaps between the posts.

To bring this analogy into the realm of dates, suppose that you start a sales promotion on February 1 and end the promotion on February 9. How many days was the promotion in effect? Subtracting February 1 from February 9 produces an answer of eight days. Actually, the promotion lasted nine days. In this case, the correct answer involves counting the fence posts, not the gaps. The formula to calculate the length of the promotion (assuming that you have appropriately named cells) appears like this:

```
=EndDay-StartDay+1
```

Calculating the number of work days between two dates

When calculating the difference between two dates, you may want to exclude weekends and holidays. For example, you may need to know how many business days fall in the month of November. This calculation should exclude Saturdays, Sundays, and holidays. The `NETWORKDAYS` function can help out.

NEW FEATURE **In versions prior to Excel 2007, the `NETWORKDAYS` function was available only when the Analysis ToolPak add-in was installed. The function is now part of Excel 2007.**

The `NETWORKDAYS` function calculates the difference between two dates, excluding weekend days (Saturdays and Sundays). As an option, you can specify a range of cells that contain the dates of holidays, which are also excluded. Excel has absolutely no way of determining which days are holidays, so you must provide this information in a range.

Figure 16-4 shows a worksheet that calculates the work days between two dates. The range A2:A11 contains a list of holiday dates. The two formulas in column C calculate the work days between the dates in column A and column B. For example, the formula in cell C15 is:

```
=NETWORKDAYS(A15,B15,A2:A11)
```

This formula returns 4, which means that the seven-day period beginning with January 1 contains four work days. In other words, the calculation excludes one holiday, one Saturday, and one Sunday. The formula in cell C16 calculates the total number of work days in the year.

FIGURE 16-4

Using the `NETWORKDAYS` function to calculate the number of working days between two dates.

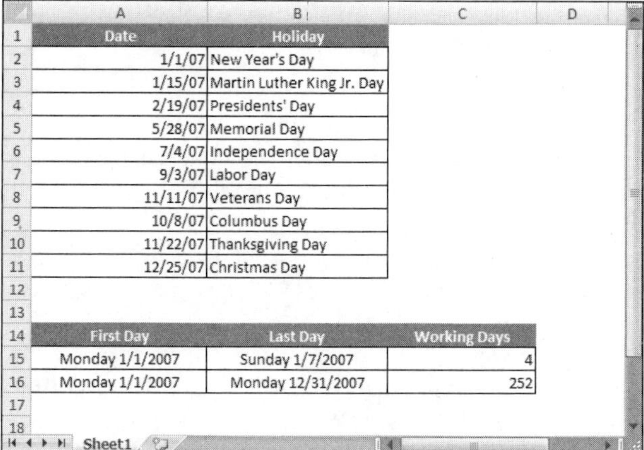

	A	B	C
1	Date	Holiday	
2	1/1/07	New Year's Day	
3	1/15/07	Martin Luther King Jr. Day	
4	2/19/07	Presidents' Day	
5	5/28/07	Memorial Day	
6	7/4/07	Independence Day	
7	9/3/07	Labor Day	
8	11/11/07	Veterans Day	
9	10/8/07	Columbus Day	
10	11/22/07	Thanksgiving Day	
11	12/25/07	Christmas Day	
12			
13			
14	First Day	Last Day	Working Days
15	Monday 1/1/2007	Sunday 1/7/2007	4
16	Monday 1/1/2007	Monday 12/31/2007	252

Offsetting a date using only work days

The `WORKDAY` function is the opposite of the `NETWORKDAYS` function. For example, if you start a project on January 4, and the project requires ten working days to complete, the `WORKDAY` function can calculate the date you will finish the project.

NEW FEATURE **In versions prior to Excel 2007, the `WORKDAY` function was available only when the Analysis ToolPak add-in was installed. The function is now part of Excel 2007.**

The following formula uses the `WORKDAY` function to determine the date that is 10 working days from January 4, 2008. A working day consists of a week day (Monday through Friday).

```
=WORKDAY("1/4/2008",10)
```

The formula returns a date serial number, which must be formatted as a date. The result is January 18, 2008 (four weekend dates fall between January 4 and January 18).

CAUTION **The preceding formula may return a different result, depending on your regional date setting. (The hard-coded date may be interpreted as April 1, 2008.) A better formula is:**

```
=WORKDAY(DATE(2008,1,4),10)
```

The second argument for the `WORKDAY` function can be negative. And, as with the `NETWORKDAYS` function, the `WORKDAY` function accepts an optional third argument (a reference to a range that contains a list of holiday dates).

Calculating the number of years between two dates

The following formula calculates the number of years between two dates. This formula assumes that cells A1 and B1 both contain dates:

```
=YEAR(A1)-YEAR(B1)
```

This formula uses the YEAR function to extract the year from each date and then subtracts one year from the other. If cell B1 contains a more recent date than the date in cell A1, the result will be negative.

Note that this function doesn't calculate *full* years. For example, if cell A1 contains 12/31/2007 and cell B1 contains 01/01/2008, the formula returns a difference of one year, even though the dates differ by only one day. See the next section for another way to calculate the number of full years.

Calculating a person's age

A person's age indicates the number of full years that the person has been alive. The formula in the previous section (for calculating the number of years between two dates) won't calculate this value correctly. You can use two other formulas, however, to calculate a person's age.

The following formula returns the age of the person whose date of birth you enter into cell A1. This formula uses the YEARFRAC function.

```
=INT(YEARFRAC(TODAY(),A1,1))
```

NEW FEATURE **In versions prior to Excel 2007, the** YEARFRAC **function was available only when the Analysis ToolPak add-in was installed. The function is now part of Excel 2007.**

The following formula uses the DATEDIF function to calculate an age. (See the sidebar, "Where's the DATEDIF Function?")

```
=DATEDIF(A1,TODAY(),"Y")
```

Determining the day of the year

January 1 is the first day of the year, and December 31 is the last day. But what about all those days in between? The following formula returns the day of the year for a date stored in cell A1:

```
=A1-DATE(YEAR(A1),1,0)
```

The following formula returns the number of days remaining in the year after a particular date (assumed to be in cell A1):

```
=DATE(YEAR(A1),12,31)-A1
```

When you enter either of these formulas, Excel applies date formatting to the cell. You need to apply a non-date number format to view the result as a number.

To convert a particular day of the year (for example, the ninetieth day of the year) to an actual date in a specified year, use the formula that follows. This formula assumes that the year is stored in cell A1 and the day of the year is stored in cell B1:

```
=DATE(A1,1,B1)
```

Determining the day of the week

The WEEKDAY function accepts a date argument and returns an integer between 1 and 7 that corresponds to the day of the week. The following formula, for example, returns 3 because the first day of the year 2008 falls on a Tuesday:

```
=WEEKDAY(DATE(2008,1,1))
```

Where's the DATEDIF Function?

One of Excel's mysteries is the `DATEDIF` function. You may notice that this function does not appear in the drop-down function list for the Date & Time category, nor does it appear in the Insert Function dialog box. Therefore, when you use this function, you must always enter it manually.

The `DATEDIF` function has its origins in Lotus 1-2-3, and apparently Excel provides it for compatibility purposes. For some reason, Microsoft wants to keep this function a secret. The function has been available since Excel 5, but Excel 2000 is the only version that ever documented it in its Help system.

`DATEDIF` is a handy function that calculates the number of days, months, or years between two dates. The function takes three arguments: start_date, end_date, and a code that represents the time unit of interest. The following table displays valid codes for the third argument. (You must enclose the codes in quotation marks.)

Unit Code	Returns
`"y"`	The number of complete years in the period.
`"m"`	The number of complete months in the period.
`"d"`	The number of days in the period.
`"md"`	The difference between the days in start_date and end_date. The months and years of the dates are ignored.
`"ym"`	The difference between the months in start_date and end_date. The days and years of the dates are ignored.
`"yd"`	The difference between the days of start_date and end_date. The years of the dates are ignored.

The start_date argument must be earlier than the end_date argument, or the function returns an error.

The `WEEKDAY` function uses an optional second argument that specifies the day numbering system for the result. If you specify 2 as the second argument, the function returns 1 for Monday, 2 for Tuesday, and so on. If you specify 3 as the second argument, the function returns 0 for Monday, 1 for Tuesday, and so on.

TIP **You can also determine the day of the week for a cell that contains a date by applying a custom number format. A cell that uses the following custom number format displays the day of the week, spelled out:**

```
dddd
```

Determining the date of the most recent Sunday

You can use the following formula to return the date for the previous Sunday. If the current day is a Sunday, the formula returns the current date:

```
=TODAY()-MOD(TODAY()-1,7)
```

To modify this formula to find the date of a day other than Sunday, change the 1 to a different number between 2 (for Monday) and 7 (for Saturday).

Determining the first day of the week after a date

This next formula returns the specified day of the week that occurs after a particular date. For example, use this formula to determine the date of the first Monday after June 1, 2007. The formula assumes that cell A1 contains a date and cell A2 contains a number between 1 and 7 (1 for Sunday, 2 for Monday, and so on):

```
=A1+A2-WEEKDAY(A1)+(A2<WEEKDAY(A1))*7
```

If cell A1 contains June 1, 2007 (a Friday), and cell A2 contains 2 (for Monday), the formula returns June 4, 2007. This is the first Monday after June 1, 2004.

Determining the *n*th occurrence of a day of the week in a month

You may need a formula to determine the date for a particular occurrence of a week day. For example, suppose that your company payday falls on the second Friday of each month, and you need to determine the paydays for each month of the year. The following formula will make this type of calculation:

```
=DATE(A1,A2,1)+A3-WEEKDAY(DATE(A1,A2,1))+
(A4-(A3>=WEEKDAY(DATE(A1,A2,1))))*7
```

The formula in this section assumes that:

- Cell A1 contains a year.
- Cell A2 contains a month.
- Cell A3 contains a day number (1 for Sunday, 2 for Monday, and so on).
- Cell A4 contains the occurrence number (for example, 2 to select the second occurrence of the weekday specified in cell A3).

If you use this formula to determine the date of the second Friday in November 2007, it returns November 11, 2007.

NOTE **If the value in cell A4 exceeds the number of the specified day in the month, the formula returns a date from a subsequent month. For example, if you attempt to determine the date of the fifth Friday in November 2007 (there is no such date), the formula returns the first Friday in December.**

Calculating dates of holidays

Determining the date for a particular holiday can be tricky. Some, such as New Year's Day and U.S. Independence Day are no-brainers because they always occur on the same date. For these kinds of holidays, you can simply use the `DATE` function. To enter New Year's Day (which always falls on January 1) for a specific year in cell A1, you can enter this function:

```
=DATE(A1,1,1)
```

Other holidays are defined in terms of a particular occurrence of a particular week day in a particular month. For example, Labor Day falls on the first Monday in September.

Figure 16-5 shows a workbook with formulas that calculate the date for 10 U.S. holidays. The formulas, which reference the year in cell A1, are listed in the sections that follow.

FIGURE 16-5

Using formulas to determine the date for various holidays.

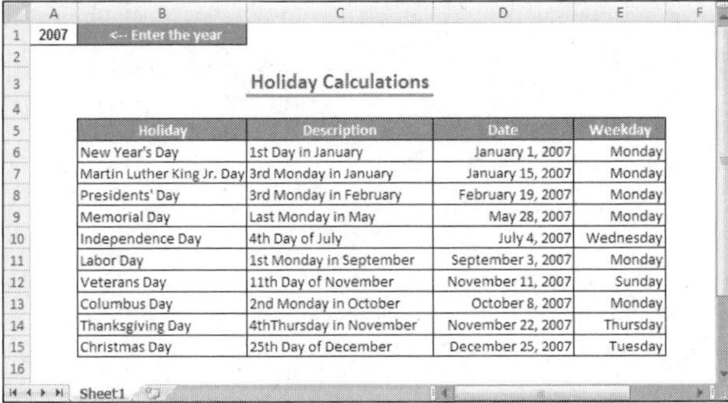

2007 <-- Enter the year

Holiday Calculations

Holiday	Description	Date	Weekday
New Year's Day	1st Day in January	January 1, 2007	Monday
Martin Luther King Jr. Day	3rd Monday in January	January 15, 2007	Monday
Presidents' Day	3rd Monday in February	February 19, 2007	Monday
Memorial Day	Last Monday in May	May 28, 2007	Monday
Independence Day	4th Day of July	July 4, 2007	Wednesday
Labor Day	1st Monday in September	September 3, 2007	Monday
Veterans Day	11th Day of November	November 11, 2007	Sunday
Columbus Day	2nd Monday in October	October 8, 2007	Monday
Thanksgiving Day	4thThursday in November	November 22, 2007	Thursday
Christmas Day	25th Day of December	December 25, 2007	Tuesday

Sheet1

New Year's Day

This holiday always falls on January 1:

```
=DATE(A1,1,1)
```

Martin Luther King, Jr. Day

This holiday occurs on the third Monday in January. This formula calculates Martin Luther King, Jr. Day for the year in cell A1:

```
=DATE(A1,1,1)+IF(2<WEEKDAY(DATE(A1,1,1)),7-WEEKDAY
(DATE(A1,1,1))+2,2-WEEKDAY(DATE(A1,1,1)))+((3-1)*7)
```

Presidents' Day

Presidents' Day occurs on the third Monday in February. This formula calculates Presidents' Day for the year in cell A1:

```
=DATE(A1,2,1)+IF(2<WEEKDAY(DATE(A1,2,1)),7-WEEKDAY
(DATE(A1,2,1))+2,2-WEEKDAY(DATE(A1,2,1)))+((3-1)*7)
```

Memorial Day

The last Monday in May is Memorial Day. This formula calculates Memorial Day for the year in cell A1:

```
=DATE(A1,6,1)+IF(2<WEEKDAY(DATE(A1,6,1)),7-WEEKDAY
(DATE(A1,6,1))+2,2-WEEKDAY(DATE(A1,6,1)))+((1-1)*7)-7
```

Notice that this formula actually calculates the first Monday in June and then subtracts 7 from the result to return the last Monday in May.

Independence Day

This holiday always falls on July 4:

```
=DATE(A1,7,4)
```

Labor Day

Labor Day occurs on the first Monday in September. This formula calculates Labor Day for the year in cell A1:

```
=DATE(A1,9,1)+IF(2<WEEKDAY(DATE(A1,9,1)),7-WEEKDAY
(DATE(A1,9,1))+2,2-WEEKDAY(DATE(A1,9,1)))+((1-1)*7)
```

Veterans Day

This holiday always falls on November 11:

```
=DATE(A1,11,11)
```

Columbus Day

This holiday occurs on the second Monday in October. This formula calculates Columbus Day for the year in cell A1:

```
=DATE(A1,10,1)+IF(2<WEEKDAY(DATE(A1,10,1)),7-WEEKDAY
(DATE(A1,10,1))+2,2-WEEKDAY(DATE(A1,10,1)))+((2-1)*7)
```

Thanksgiving Day

Thanksgiving Day is celebrated on the fourth Thursday in November. This formula calculates Thanksgiving Day for the year in cell A1:

```
=DATE(A1,11,1)+IF(5<WEEKDAY(DATE(A1,11,1)),7-WEEKDAY
(DATE(A1,11,1))+5,5-WEEKDAY(DATE(A1,11,1)))+((4-1)*7)
```

Christmas Day

This holiday always falls on December 25:

```
=DATE(A1,12,25)
```

Determining the last day of a month

To determine the date that corresponds to the last day of a month, you can use the `DATE` function. However, you need to increment the month by 1 and use a day value of 0. In other words, the "0th" day of the next month is the last day of the current month.

The following formula assumes that a date is stored in cell A1. The formula returns the date that corresponds to the last day of the month:

```
=DATE(YEAR(A1),MONTH(A1)+1,0)
```

You can use a variation of this formula to determine how many days comprise a specified month. The formula that follows returns an integer that corresponds to the number of days in the month for the date in cell A1:

```
=DAY(DATE(YEAR(A1),MONTH(A1)+1,0))
```

Determining whether a year is a leap year

To determine whether a particular year is a leap year, you can write a formula that determines whether the twenty-ninth day of February occurs in February or March. You can take advantage of the fact that Excel's `DATE` function adjusts the result when you supply an invalid argument — for example, a day of 29 when February contains only 28 days.

The following formula returns TRUE if the year of the date in cell A1 is a leap year. Otherwise, it returns FALSE.

```
=IF(MONTH(DATE(YEAR(A1),2,29))=2,TRUE,FALSE)
```

This function returns the wrong result (TRUE) if the year is 1900. See the section "Excel's leap year bug," earlier in this chapter.

Determining a date's quarter

For financial reports, you may find it useful to present information in terms of quarters. The following formula returns an integer between 1 and 4 that corresponds to the calendar quarter for the date in cell A1:

```
=ROUNDUP(MONTH(A1)/3,0)
```

This formula divides the month number by 3 and then rounds up the result.

Time-Related Functions

Excel also includes a number of functions that enable you to work with time values in your formulas. This section contains examples that demonstrate the use of these functions.

Table 16-5 summarizes the time-related functions available in Excel. When you use the Insert Function dialog box, these functions appear in the Date & Time function category.

TABLE 16-5

Time-Related Functions

Function	Description
HOUR	Converts a serial number to an hour
MINUTE	Converts a serial number to a minute
MONTH	Converts a serial number to a month
NOW	Returns the serial number of the current date and time
SECOND	Converts a serial number to a second
TIME	Returns the serial number of a particular time
TIMEVALUE	Converts a time in the form of text to a serial number

Displaying the current time

This formula displays the current time as a time serial number (or as a serial number without an associated date):

```
=NOW()-TODAY()
```

You need to format the cell with a time format to view the result as a recognizable time. The quickest way is to choose Home ➪ Number ➪ Format Number and select Time from the drop-down list.

This formula is updated only when the worksheet is calculated.

To enter a time stamp (that doesn't change) into a cell, press Ctrl+Shift+: (colon).

Displaying any time

One way to enter a time value into a cell is to just type it, making sure that you include at least one colon (:). You can also create a time by using the `TIME` function. For example, the following formula returns a time comprised of the hour in cell A1, the minute in cell B1, and the second in cell C1:

```
=TIME(A1,B1,C1)
```

Like the `DATE` function, the `TIME` function accepts invalid arguments and adjusts the result accordingly. For example, the following formula uses 80 as the minute argument and returns 10:20:15 AM. The 80 minutes are simply added to the hour, with 20 minutes remaining.

```
=TIME(9,80,15)
```

CAUTION **If you enter a value greater than 24 as the first argument for the `TIME` function, the result may not be what you expect. Logically, a formula such as the one that follows should produce a date/time serial number of 1.041667 (that is, one day and one hour).**

```
=TIME(25,0,0)
```

In fact, this formula is equivalent to the following:

```
=TIME(1,0,0)
```

You can also use the `DATE` function along with the `TIME` function in a single cell. The formula that follows generates a date and time with a serial number of 39420.7708333333—which represents 6:30 PM on December 4, 2007:

```
=DATE(2007,12,4)+TIME(18,30,0)
```

The `TIMEVALUE` function converts a text string that looks like a time into a time serial number. This formula returns 0.2395833333, the time serial number for 5:45 AM:

```
=TIMEVALUE("5:45 am")
```

To view the result of this formula as a time, you need to apply number formatting to the cell. The `TIMEVALUE` function doesn't recognize all common time formats. For example, the following formula returns an error because Excel doesn't like the periods in "a.m."

```
=TIMEVALUE("5:45 a.m.")
```

Calculating the difference between two times

Because times are represented as serial numbers, you can subtract the earlier time from the later time to get the difference. For example, if cell A2 contains 5:30:00 and cell B2 contains 14:00:00, the following formula returns 08:30:00 (a difference of eight hours and 30 minutes):

```
=B2-A2
```

If the subtraction results in a negative value, however, it becomes an invalid time; Excel displays a series of pound signs (#######) because a time without a date has a date serial number of 0. A negative time results in a negative serial number, which is not permitted.

If the direction of the time difference doesn't matter, you can use the `ABS` function to return the absolute value of the difference:

```
=ABS(B2-A2)
```

This "negative time" problem often occurs when calculating an elapsed time — for example, calculating the number of hours worked given a start time and an end time. This presents no problem if the two times fall in the same day. But if the work shift spans midnight, the result is an invalid negative time. For example, you may start work at 10:00 PM and end work at 6:00 AM the next day. Figure 16-6 shows a worksheet that calculates the hours worked. As you can see, the shift that spans midnight presents a problem (cell C3).

FIGURE 16-6

Calculating the number of hours worked returns an error if the shift spans midnight.

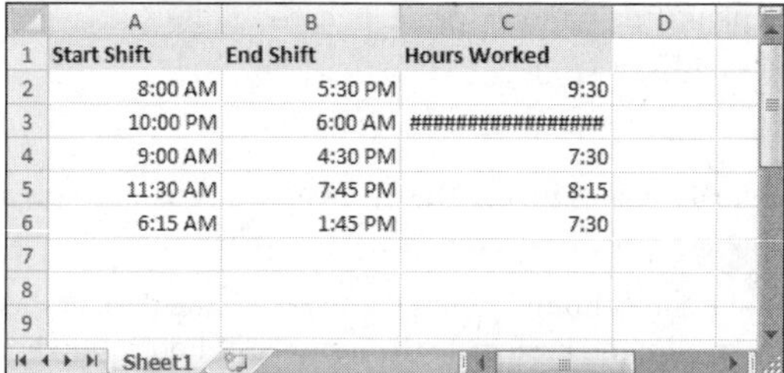

	A	B	C	D
1	Start Shift	End Shift	Hours Worked	
2	8:00 AM	5:30 PM	9:30	
3	10:00 PM	6:00 AM	################	
4	9:00 AM	4:30 PM	7:30	
5	11:30 AM	7:45 PM	8:15	
6	6:15 AM	1:45 PM	7:30	
7				
8				
9				

Sheet1

Using the `ABS` function (to calculate the absolute value) isn't an option in this case because it returns the wrong result (16 hours). The following formula, however, *does* work:

```
=IF(B2<A2,B2+1,B2)-A2
```

TIP **Negative times *are* permitted if the workbook uses the 1904 date system. To switch to the 1904 date system, use the Advanced section of the Excel Options dialog box. Place a check mark next to the Use 1904 Date System option. But beware! When changing the workbook's date system, if the workbook uses dates, the dates will be off by four years For more information about the 1904 date system, see the sidebar titled "Choose Your Date System: 1900 or 1904," earlier in this chapter.**

Summing times that exceed 24 hours

Many people are surprised to discover that when you sum a series of times that exceed 24 hours, Excel doesn't display the correct total. Figure 16-7 shows an example. The range B2:B8 contains times that represent the hours and minutes worked each day. The formula in cell B9 is:

```
=SUM(B2:B8)
```

As you can see, the formula returns a seemingly incorrect total (17 hours, 45 minutes). The total should read 41 hours, 45 minutes. The problem is that the formula is displaying the total as a date/time serial number of 1.7395833, but the cell formatting is not displaying the *date* part of the date/time. The answer is incorrect because cell B9 has the wrong number format.

FIGURE 16-7

Incorrect cell formatting makes the total appear incorrectly.

	A	B	C	D
1	Day	Hours Worked		
2	Sunday	0		
3	Monday	8:30		
4	Tuesday	8:00		
5	Wednesday	9:00		
6	Thursday	9:30		
7	Friday	4:15		
8	Saturday	2:30		
9	Total Hours	17:45		
10				
11				
12				

Sheet1 Sheet2

To view a time that exceeds 24 hours, you need to apply a custom number format for the cell so that square brackets surround the *hour* part of the format string. Applying the number format here to cell B9 displays the sum correctly:

```
[h]:mm
```

Figure 16-8 shows another example of a worksheet that manipulates times. This worksheet keeps track of hours worked during a week (regular hours and overtime hours).

The week's starting date appears in cell D5, and the formulas in column B fill in the dates for the days of the week. Times appear in the range D8:G14, and formulas in column H calculate the number of hours worked each day. For example, the formula in cell H8 is:

```
=IF(E8<D8,E8+1-D8,E8-D8)+IF(G8<F8,G8+1-G8,G8-F8)
```

FIGURE 16-8

An employee timesheet workbook.

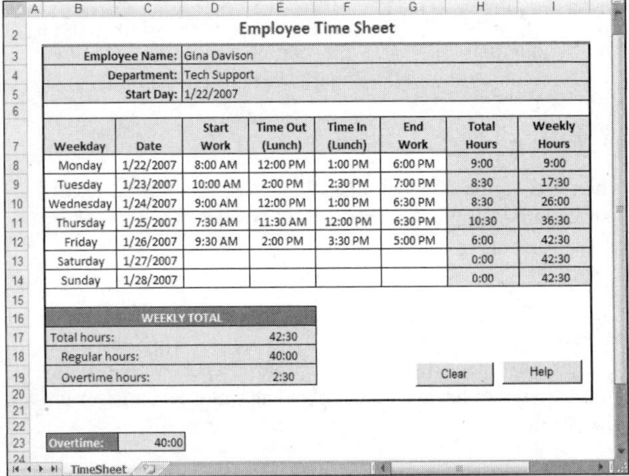

Employee Time Sheet

Employee Name: Gina Davison
Department: Tech Support
Start Day: 1/22/2007

Weekday	Date	Start Work	Time Out (Lunch)	Time In (Lunch)	End Work	Total Hours	Weekly Hours
Monday	1/22/2007	8:00 AM	12:00 PM	1:00 PM	6:00 PM	9:00	9:00
Tuesday	1/23/2007	10:00 AM	2:00 PM	2:30 PM	7:00 PM	8:30	17:30
Wednesday	1/24/2007	9:00 AM	12:00 PM	1:00 PM	6:30 PM	8:30	26:00
Thursday	1/25/2007	7:30 AM	11:30 AM	12:00 PM	6:30 PM	10:30	36:30
Friday	1/26/2007	9:30 AM	2:00 PM	3:30 PM	5:00 PM	6:00	42:30
Saturday	1/27/2007					0:00	42:30
Sunday	1/28/2007					0:00	42:30

WEEKLY TOTAL	
Total hours:	42:30
Regular hours:	40:00
Overtime hours:	2:30

Clear Help

Overtime: 40:00

TimeSheet

The first part of this formula subtracts the time in column D from the time in column E to get the total hours worked before lunch. The second part subtracts the time in column F from the time in column G to get the total hours worked after lunch. I use `IF` functions to accommodate graveyard shift cases that span midnight — for example, an employee may start work at 10:00 PM and begin lunch at 2:00 AM. Without the `IF` function, the formula returns a negative result.

The following formula in cell H17 calculates the weekly total by summing the daily totals in column H:

```
=SUM(H8:H14)
```

This worksheet assumes that hours in excess of 40 hours in a week are considered overtime hours. The worksheet contains a cell named *Overtime*, in cell C23. This cell contains 40:00. If your standard workweek consists of something other than 40 hours, you can change this formula.

The following formula (in cell H18) calculates regular (nonovertime) hours. This formula returns the smaller of two values: the total hours or the overtime hours:

```
=MIN(E17,Overtime)
```

The final formula, in cell H19, simply subtracts the regular hours from the total hours to yield the overtime hours.

```
=E17-E18
```

The times in H17:H19 may display time values that exceed 24 hours, so these cells use a custom number format:

```
[h]:mm
```

Converting from military time

Military time is expressed as a four-digit number from 0000 to 2359. For example, 1:00 AM is expressed as 0100 hours, and 3:30 PM is expressed as 1530 hours. The following formula converts such a number (assumed to be in cell A1) to a standard time:

```
=TIMEVALUE(LEFT(A1,2)&":"&RIGHT(A1,2))
```

The formula returns an incorrect result if the contents of cell A1 do not contain four digits. The following formula corrects the problem, and it returns a valid time for any military time value from 0 to 2359:

```
=TIMEVALUE(LEFT(TEXT(A1,"0000"),2)&":"&RIGHT(A1,2))
```

Following is a simpler formula that uses the `TEXT` function to return a formatted string, and then it uses the `TIMEVALUE` function to express the result in terms of a time.

```
=TIMEVALUE(TEXT(A1,"00\:00"))
```

Converting decimal hours, minutes, or seconds to a time

To convert decimal hours to a time, divide the decimal hours by 24. For example, if cell A1 contains 9.25 (representing hours), this formula returns 09:15:00 (9 hours, 15 minutes):

```
=A1/24
```

To convert decimal minutes to a time, divide the decimal hours by 1,440 (the number of minutes in a day). For example, if cell A1 contains 500 (representing minutes), the following formula returns 08:20:00 (8 hours, 20 minutes):

```
=A1/1440
```

To convert decimal seconds to a time, divide the decimal hours by 86,400 (the number of seconds in a day). For example, if cell A1 contains 65,000 (representing seconds), the following formula returns 18:03:20 (18 hours, 3 minutes, and 20 seconds):

```
=A1/86400
```

Adding hours, minutes, or seconds to a time

You can use the `TIME` function to add any number of hours, minutes, or seconds to a time. For example, assume that cell A1 contains a time. The following formula adds 2 hours and 30 minutes to that time and displays the result:

```
=A1+TIME(2,30,0)
```

You can use the `TIME` function to fill a range of cells with incremental times. Figure 16-9 shows a worksheet with a series of times in 10-minute increments. Cell A1 contains a time that was entered directly. Cell A2 contains the following formula, which copied down the column:

```
=A1+TIME(0,10,0)
```

FIGURE 16-9

Using a formula to create a series of incremental times.

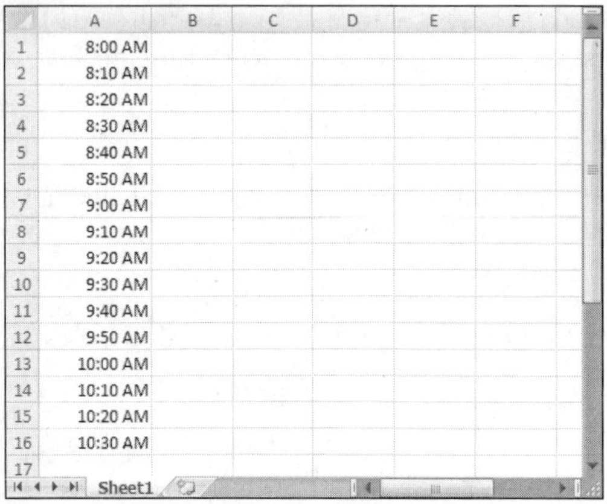

	A	B	C	D	E	F
1	8:00 AM					
2	8:10 AM					
3	8:20 AM					
4	8:30 AM					
5	8:40 AM					
6	8:50 AM					
7	9:00 AM					
8	9:10 AM					
9	9:20 AM					
10	9:30 AM					
11	9:40 AM					
12	9:50 AM					
13	10:00 AM					
14	10:10 AM					
15	10:20 AM					
16	10:30 AM					
17						

Sheet1

Rounding time values

You may need to create a formula that rounds a time to a particular value. For example, you may need to enter your company's time records rounded to the nearest 15 minutes. This section presents examples of various ways to round a time value.

The following formula rounds the time in cell A1 to the nearest minute:

```
=ROUND(A1*1440,0)/1440
```

The formula works by multiplying the time by 1440 (to get total minutes). This value is passed to the ROUND function, and the result is divided by 1440. For example, if cell A1 contains 11:52:34, the formula returns 11:53:00.

The following formula resembles this example, except that it rounds the time in cell A1 to the nearest hour:

```
=ROUND(A1*24,0)/24
```

If cell A1 contains 5:21:31, the formula returns 5:00:00.

The following formula rounds the time in cell A1 to the nearest 15 minutes (a quarter of an hour):

```
=ROUND(A1*24/0.25,0)*(0.25/24)
```

In this formula, 0.25 represents the fractional hour. To round a time to the nearest 30 minutes, change 0.25 to 0.5, as in the following formula:

```
=ROUND(A1*24/0.5,0)*(0.5/24)
```

Working with non–time-of-day values

Sometimes, you may want to work with time values that don't represent an actual time of day. For example, you may want to create a list of the finish times for a race or record the time you spend jogging each day. Such times don't represent a time of day. Rather, a value represents the time for an event (in hours, minutes, and seconds). The time to complete a test, for example, may be 35 minutes and 45 seconds. You can enter that value into a cell as:

```
00:35:45
```

Excel interprets such an entry as 12:35:45 AM, which works fine. (Just make sure that you format the cell so that it appears as you like.) When you enter such times that do not have an hour component, you must include at least one zero for the hour. If you omit a leading zero for a missing hour, Excel interprets your entry as 35 hours and 45 minutes.

Figure 16-10 shows an example of a worksheet set up to keep track of a person's jogging activity. Column A contains simple dates. Column B contains the distance in miles. Column C contains the time it took to run the distance. Column D contains formulas to calculate the speed in miles per hour. For example, the formula in cell D2 is:

```
=B2/(C2*24)
```

Column E contains formulas to calculate the pace, in minutes per mile. For example, the formula in cell E2 is:

```
=(C2*60*24)/B2
```

Columns F and G contain formulas that calculate the year-to-date distance (using column B) and the cumulative time (using column C). The cells in column G are formatted using the following number format (which permits time displays that exceed 24 hours):

```
[hh]:mm:ss
```

FIGURE 16-10

This worksheet uses times not associated with a time of day.

	A	B	C	D	E	F	G	H
1	Date	Distance	Time	Speed (mph)	Pace (min/mile)	YTD Distance	Cumulative Time	
2	1/1/2007	1.50	00:18:45	4.80	12.50	1.50	00:18:45	
3	1/2/2007	1.50	00:17:40	5.09	11.78	3.00	00:36:25	
4	1/3/2007	2.00	00:21:30	5.58	10.75	5.00	00:57:55	
5	1/4/2007	1.50	00:15:20	5.87	10.22	6.50	01:13:15	
6	1/5/2007	2.40	00:25:05	5.74	10.45	8.90	01:38:20	
7	1/6/2007	3.00	00:31:06	5.79	10.37	11.90	02:09:26	
8	1/7/2007	3.80	00:41:06	5.55	10.82	15.70	02:50:32	
9	1/8/2007	5.00	01:09:00	4.35	13.80	20.70	03:59:32	
10	1/9/2007	4.00	00:45:10	5.31	11.29	24.70	04:44:42	
11	1/10/2007	3.00	00:29:06	6.19	9.70	27.70	05:13:48	
12	1/11/2007	5.50	01:08:30	4.82	12.45	33.20	06:22:18	
13								
14								

Sheet1

Summary

In this chapter, you learned how Excel treats dates and times as serial numbers. You can use dates and times in formulas, so long as you understand how the serial numbers work. This chapter also introduced you to some Excel functions that work with dates and times, and showed you specific, handy examples of formulas you can build to tackle certain date and time calculation tasks.

Chapter 17

Creating Formulas That Count and Sum

IN THIS CHAPTER

Information on counting and summing cells

Basic counting formulas

Advanced counting formulas

Formulas for performing common summing tasks

Conditional summing formulas using a single criterion

Conditional summing formulas using multiple criteria

Many of the most common spreadsheet questions involve counting and summing values and other worksheet elements. It seems that people are always looking for formulas to count or to sum various items in a worksheet. If I've done my job, this chapter answers the vast majority of such questions. It contains many examples that you can easily adapt to your own situation.

Counting and Summing Worksheet Cells

Generally, a *counting formula* returns the number of cells in a specified range that meet certain criteria. A *summing formula* returns the sum of the values of the cells in a range that meet certain criteria. The range you want counted or summed may or may not consist of a worksheet database.

Table 17-1 lists the Excel worksheet functions that come into play when creating counting and summing formulas. Not all these functions are covered in this chapter. If none of the functions in Table 17-1 can solve your problem, it's likely that an array formula can come to the rescue.

NOTE **If your data is in the form of a table, you can use autofiltering to accomplish many counting and summing operations. Just set the AutoFilter criteria, and the table displays only the rows that match your criteria (the nonqualifying rows in the table are hidden). Then you can select formulas to display counts or sums in the table's total row. Refer to Chapter 19 for more information on using tables.**

TABLE 17-1

Excel's Counting and Summing Functions

Function	Description
COUNT	Returns the number of cells that contain a numeric value.
COUNTA	Returns the number of nonblank cells.
COUNTBLANK	Returns the number of blank cells.
COUNTIF	Returns the number of cells that meet a specified criterion.
COUNTIFS*	Returns the number of cells that meet multiple criteria.
DCOUNT	Counts the number of records that meet specified criteria; used with a worksheet database.
DCOUNTA	Counts the number of nonblank records that meet specified criteria; used with a worksheet database.
DEVSQ	Returns the sum of squares of deviations of data points from the sample mean; used primarily in statistical formulas.
DSUM	Returns the sum of a column of values that meet specified criteria; used with a worksheet database
FREQUENCY	Calculates how often values occur within a range of values and returns a vertical array of numbers. Used only in a multicell array formula.
SUBTOTAL	When used with a first argument of 2, 3, 102, or 103, returns *a count* of cells that comprise a subtotal; when used with a first argument of 9 or 109, returns *the sum* of cells that comprise a subtotal.
SUM	Returns the sum of its arguments.
SUMIF	Returns the sum of cells that meet a specified criterion.
SUMIFS*	Returns the sum of cells that meet multiple criteria.
SUMPRODUCT	Multiplies corresponding cells in two or more ranges and returns the sum of those products.
SUMSQ	Returns the sum of the squares of its arguments; used primarily in statistical formulas.
SUMX2PY2	Returns the sum of the sum of squares of corresponding values in two ranges; used primarily in statistical formulas.
SUMXMY2	Returns the sum of squares of the differences of corresponding values in two ranges; used primarily in statistical formulas.
SUMX2MY2	Returns the sum of the differences of squares of corresponding values in two ranges; used primarily in statistical formulas.

* These are new functions, available only in Excel 2007.

Getting a Quick Count or Sum

Excel's status bar can display useful information about the currently selected cells — no formulas required. Normally, the status bar displays the sum and count of the values in the selected range. You can, however, right-click to bring up a menu with other options. You can choose any or all of the following: Average, Count, Numerical Count, Minimum, Maximum, and Sum.

Basic Counting Formulas

The basic counting formulas presented here are all straightforward and relatively simple. They demonstrate the capability of the Excel counting functions to count the number of cells in a range that meet specific criteria. Figure 17-1 shows a worksheet that uses formulas (in column E) to summarize the contents of range A1:B10 — a 20-cell range named *Data*. This range contains a variety of information, including values, text, logical values, errors, and empty cells.

FIGURE 17-1

Formulas in column E display various counts of the data in A1:B10.

	A	B	C	D	E	F
1	Jan	Feb		Total cells:	20	
2	525	718		Blank cells:	6	
3				Nonblank cells:	14	
4	3			Numeric values:	7	
5	552	911		Non-text cells:	17	
6	250	98		Text cells:	3	
7				Logical values:	2	
8	TRUE	FALSE		Error values:	2	
9		#DIV/0!		#N/A errors:	0	
10	Total	#NAME?		#NULL! errors:	0	
11				#DIV/0! errors:	1	
12				#VALUE! errors:	0	
13				#REF! errors:	0	
14				#NAME? errors:	1	
15				#NUM! errors:	0	
16						

Sheet1

Counting the total number of cells

To get a count of the total number of cells in a range (empty and nonempty cells), use the following formula. This formula returns the number of cells in a range named *Data*. It simply multiplies the number of rows (returned by the `ROWS` function) by the number of columns (returned by the `COLUMNS` function).

```
=ROWS(Data)*COLUMNS(Data)
```

This formula will not work if the Data range consists of noncontiguous cells. In other words, Data must be a rectangular range of cells.

Counting blank cells

The following formula returns the number of blank (empty) cells in a range named *Data*:

```
=COUNTBLANK(Data)
```

The `COUNTBLANK` function also counts cells containing a formula that returns an empty string. For example, the formula that follows returns an empty string if the value in cell A1 is greater than 5. If the cell meets this condition, the `COUNTBLANK` function counts that cell.

```
=IF(A1>5,"",A1)
```

About This Chapter's Examples

Most of the examples in this chapter use named ranges for function arguments. When you adapt these formulas for your own use, you'll need to substitute either the actual range address or a range name defined in your workbook.

Also, some examples consist of array formulas. An *array formula* is a special type of formula that enables you to perform calculations that would not otherwise be possible. You can spot an array formula because it's enclosed in curly brackets when it's displayed in the Formula bar. In addition, I use this syntax for the array formula examples presented in this book. For example:

```
{=Data*2}
```

When you enter an array formula, press Ctrl+Shift+Enter (not just Enter) and *don't* type the brackets. (Excel inserts the brackets for you.) If you need to edit an array formula, don't forget to use Ctrl+Shift+Enter when you've finished editing (otherwise, the array formula will revert to a normal formula and it will return an incorrect result).

You can use the `COUNTBLANK` function with an argument that consists of entire rows or columns. For example, this next formula returns the number of blank cells in column A:

```
=COUNTBLANK(A:A)
```

The following formula returns the number of empty cells on the entire worksheet named Sheet1. You must enter this formula on a sheet other than Sheet1, or it will create a circular reference.

```
=COUNTBLANK(Sheet1!1:1048576)
```

Counting nonblank cells

To count nonblank cells, use the `COUNTA` function. The following formula uses the `COUNTA` function to return the number of nonblank cells in a range named *Data*:

```
=COUNTA(Data)
```

The `COUNTA` function counts cells that contain values, text, or logical values (`TRUE` or `FALSE`).

If a cell contains a formula that returns an empty string, that cell is included in the count returned by `COUNTA`, even though the cell appears to be blank.

Counting numeric cells

To count only the numeric cells in a range, use the following formula (which assumes the range is named *Data*):

```
=COUNT(Data)
```

Cells that contain a date or a time are considered to be numeric cells. Cells that contain a logical value (TRUE or FALSE) aren't considered to be numeric cells.

Counting text cells

To count the number of text cells in a range, you need to use an array formula. The array formula that follows returns the number of text cells in a range named *Data*:

```
{=SUM(IF(ISTEXT(Data),1))}
```

Counting nontext cells

The following array formula uses Excel's `ISNONTEXT` function, which returns `TRUE` if its argument refers to any nontext cell (including a blank cell). This formula returns the count of the number of cells not containing text (including blank cells):

```
{=SUM(IF(ISNONTEXT(Data),1))}
```

Counting logical values

The following array formula returns the number of logical values (TRUE or FALSE) in a range named *Data*:

```
{=SUM(IF(ISLOGICAL(Data),1))}
```

Counting error values in a range

Excel has three functions that help you determine whether a cell contains an error value:

- `ISERROR`: Returns `TRUE` if the cell contains any error value (#N/A, #VALUE!, #REF!, #DIV/0!, #NUM!, #NAME?, or #NULL!)
- `ISERR`: Returns `TRUE` if the cell contains any error value except #N/A
- `ISNA`: Returns `TRUE` if the cell contains the #N/A error value

You can use these functions in an array formula to count the number of error values in a range. The following array formula, for example, returns the total number of error values in a range named *Data*:

```
{=SUM(IF(ISERROR(data),1))}
```

Depending on your needs, you can use the `ISERR` or `ISNA` function in place of `ISERROR`.

If you would like to count specific types of errors, you can use the `COUNTIF` function. The following formula, for example, returns the number of #DIV/0! error values in the range named *Data*:

```
=COUNTIF(Data,"#DIV/0!")
```

Advanced Counting Formulas

Most of the basic examples I presented earlier in this chapter use functions or formulas that perform conditional counting. The advanced counting formulas that I present here represent more complex examples for counting worksheet cells, based on various types of criteria.

Some of these examples are array formulas.

Counting cells by using the COUNTIF function

Excel's COUNTIF function is useful for single-criterion counting formulas. The COUNTIF function takes two arguments:

- *range*: The range that contains the values that determine whether to include a particular cell in the count
- *criteria*: The logical criteria that determine whether to include a particular cell in the count

Table 17-2 lists several examples of formulas that use the COUNTIF function. These formulas all work with a range named *Data*. As you can see, the *criteria* argument proves quite flexible. You can use constants, expressions, functions, cell references, and even wildcard characters (* and ?).

TABLE 17-2

Examples of Formulas Using the COUNTIF Function

=COUNTIF(Data,12)	Returns the number of cells containing the value 12
=COUNTIF(Data,"<0")	Returns the number of cells containing a negative value
=COUNTIF(Data,"<>0")	Returns the number of cells not equal to 0
=COUNTIF(Data,">5")	Returns the number of cells greater than 5
=COUNTIF(Data,A1)	Returns the number of cells equal to the contents of cell A1
=COUNTIF(Data,">"&A1)	Returns the number of cells greater than the value in cell A1
=COUNTIF(Data,"*")	Returns the number of cells containing text
=COUNTIF(Data,"???")	Returns the number of text cells containing exactly three characters
=COUNTIF(Data,"budget")	Returns the number of cells containing the single word *budget* (not case sensitive)
=COUNTIF(Data,"*budget*")	Returns the number of cells containing the text *budget* anywhere within the text
=COUNTIF(Data,"A*")	Returns the number of cells containing text that begins with the letter *A* (not case sensitive)
=COUNTIF(Data,TODAY())	Returns the number of cells containing the current date
=COUNTIF(Data, ">"&AVERAGE(Data))	Returns the number of cells with a value greater than the average
=COUNTIF(Data,">"&AVERAGE (Data)+STDEV(Data)*3)	Returns the number of values exceeding three standard deviations above the mean
=COUNTIF(Data,3)+COUNTIF (Data,-3)	Returns the number of cells containing the value 3 or –3
=COUNTIF(Data,TRUE)	Returns the number of cells containing logical TRUE
=COUNTIF(Data,TRUE) +COUNTIF(Data,FALSE)	Returns the number of cells containing a logical value (TRUE or FALSE)
=COUNTIF(Data,"#N/A")	Returns the number of cells containing the #N/A error value

Counting cells by using multiple criteria

In many cases, your counting formula will need to count cells only if two or more criteria are met. These criteria can be based on the cells that are being counted or based on a range of corresponding cells.

Figure 17-2 shows a simple worksheet that I use for the examples in this section. This sheet shows sales data categorized by Month, SalesRep, and Type. The worksheet contains named ranges that correspond to the labels in row 1.

NEW FEATURE **Several of the examples in this section use the `COUNTIFS` function, which is new to Excel 2007. I also present alternative versions of the formulas, which should be used if you plan to share your workbook with others who don't use Excel 2007.**

FIGURE 17-2

This worksheet demonstrates various counting techniques that use multiple criteria.

	A	B	C	D
1	Month	SalesRep	Type	Amount
2	January	Albert	New	85
3	January	Albert	New	675
4	January	Brooks	New	130
5	January	Cook	New	1350
6	January	Cook	Existing	685
7	January	Brooks	New	1350
8	January	Cook	New	475
9	January	Brooks	New	1205
10	February	Brooks	Existing	450
11	February	Albert	New	495
12	February	Cook	New	210
13	February	Cook	Existing	1050
14	February	Albert	New	140
15	February	Brooks	New	900
16	February	Brooks	New	900
17	February	Cook	New	95
18	February	Cook	New	780

Sheet1

Using And criteria

An And criterion counts cells if all specified conditions are met. A common example is a formula that counts the number of values that fall within a numerical range. For example, you may want to count cells that contain a value greater than 100 *and* less than or equal to 200. For this example, the new `COUNTIFS` function will do the job:

```
=COUNTIFS(Amount,">100",Amount,"<=200")
```

NOTE **If the data is contained in a table, you can use the new Excel 2007 method of referencing data within a table. For example, if the table is named Table1, you can rewrite the preceding formula as:**

```
=COUNTIFS(Table1[Amount],">100",Table1[Amount],"<=200")
```

This method of writing formulas does not require named ranges.

The COUNTIFS function accepts any number of paired arguments. The first member of the pair is the range to be counted (in this case, the range named Amount); the second member of the pair is the criterion. The preceding example contains two sets of paired arguments and returns the number of cells in which Amount is greater than 100 and less than or equal to 200.

Prior to Excel 2007, you would need to use a formula like this:

```
=COUNTIF(Amount,">100")-COUNTIF(Amount,">200")
```

The formula counts the number of values that are great than 100 and then subtracts the number of values that are greater than or equal to 200. The result is the number of cells that contain a value greater than 100 and less than or equal to 200. This formula can be confusing because the formula refers to a condition ">200" even though the goal is to count values that are less than or equal to 200. Yet another alternate technique is to use an array formula, like the one that follows. You may find it easier to create this type of formula:

```
{=SUM((Amount>100)*(Amount<=200))}
```

When you enter an array formula, remember to use Ctrl+Shift+Enter and don't type the brackets.

Sometimes, the counting criteria will be based on cells other than the cells being counted. You may, for example, want to count the number of sales that meet the following criteria:

- Month is January, *and*
- SalesRep is Brooks, *and*
- Amount is greater than 1000

The following formula (for Excel 2007 only) returns the number of items that meets all three criteria. Note that the COUNTIFS function uses three sets of pairs of arguments.

```
=COUNTIFS(Month,"January",SalesRep,"Brooks",Amount,">1000")
```

An alternative formula, which works with all versions of Excel, uses the SUMPRODUCT function. The following formula returns the same result as the previous formula:

```
=SUMPRODUCT((Month="January")*(SalesRep="Brooks")*(Amount>1000))
```

Yet another way to perform this count is to use an array formula:

```
{=SUM((Month="January")*(SalesRep="Brooks")*(Amount>1000))}
```

Using Or criteria

To count cells by using an Or criterion, you can sometimes use multiple COUNTIF functions. The following formula, for example, counts the number of sales made in January or February:

```
=COUNTIF(Month,"January")+COUNTIF(Month,"February")
```

You can also use the COUNTIF function in an array formula. The following array formula, for example, returns the same result as the previous formula:

```
{=SUM(COUNTIF(Month,{"January","February"}))}
```

But if you base your Or criteria on cells other than the cells being counted, the `COUNTIF` function won't work. (Refer to Figure 17-2.) Suppose that you want to count the number of sales that meet the following criteria:

- Month is January, *or*
- SalesRep is Brooks, *or*
- Amount is greater than 1000

If you attempt to create a formula that uses `COUNTIF`, some double counting will occur. The solution is to use an array formula like this:

```
{=SUM(IF((Month="January")+(SalesRep="Brooks")+(Amount>1000),1))}
```

Combining And and Or criteria

In some cases, you may need to combine And and Or criteria when counting. For example, perhaps you want to count sales that meet the following criteria:

- Month is January, *and*
- SalesRep is Brooks, *or* SalesRep is Cook

This array formula returns the number of sales that meet the criteria:

```
{=SUM((Month="January")*IF((SalesRep="Brooks")+
(SalesRep="Cook"),1))}
```

Counting the most frequently occurring entry

The `MODE` function returns the most frequently occurring value in a range. Figure 17-3 shows a worksheet with values in range A1:A10 (named *Data*). The formula that follows returns 10 because that value appears most frequently in the *Data* range:

```
=MODE(Data)
```

FIGURE 17-3

The `MODE` function returns the most frequently occurring value in a range.

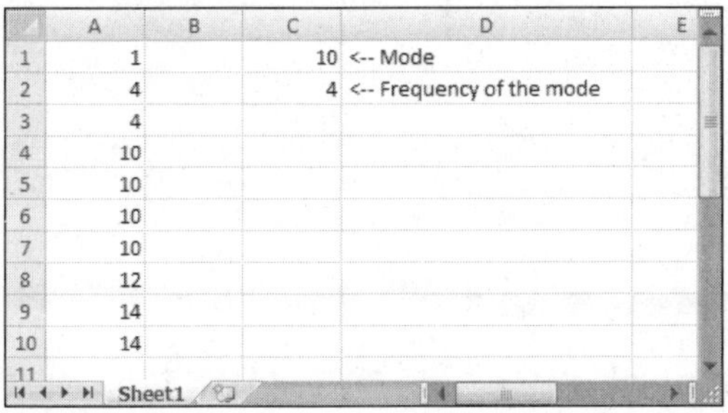

	A	B	C	D	E
1	1		10	<-- Mode	
2	4		4	<-- Frequency of the mode	
3	4				
4	10				
5	10				
6	10				
7	10				
8	12				
9	14				
10	14				
11					

Sheet1

To count the number of times the most frequently occurring value appears in the range (in other words, the frequency of the mode), use the following formula:

```
=COUNTIF(Data,MODE(Data))
```

This formula returns 4, because the modal value (10) appears four times in the *Data* range.

The `MODE` function works only for numeric values. It simply ignores cells that contain text. To find the most frequently occurring text entry in a range, you need to use an array formula.

To count the number of times the most frequently occurring item (text or values) appears in a range named *Data*, use the following array formula:

```
{=MAX(COUNTIF(Data,Data))}
```

This next array formula operates like the `MODE` function, except that it works with both text and values:

```
{=INDEX(Data,MATCH(MAX(COUNTIF(Data,Data)),COUNTIF(Data,Data),0))}
```

Counting the occurrences of specific text

The examples in this section demonstrate various ways to count the occurrences of a character or text string in a range of cells. Figure 17-4 shows a worksheet used for these examples. Various text strings appear in the range A1:A10 (named *Data*); cell B1 is named *Text*.

FIGURE 17-4

This worksheet demonstrates various ways to count characters in a range.

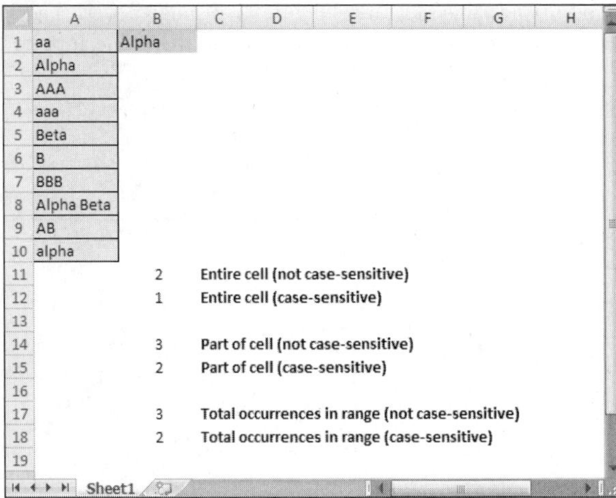

Entire cell contents

To count the number of cells containing the contents of the *Text* cell (and nothing else), you can use the `COUNTIF` function as the following formula demonstrates.

```
=COUNTIF(Data,Text)
```

For example, if the *Text* cell contains the string "Alpha" the formula returns 2 because two cells in the *Data* range contain this text. This formula is not case sensitive, so it counts both "Alpha" (cell A2) and "alpha" (cell A10). Note, however, that it does not count the cell that contains "Alpha Beta" (cell A8).

The following array formula is similar to the preceding formula, but this one is case sensitive:

```
{=SUM(IF(EXACT(Data,Text),1))}
```

Partial cell contents

To count the number of cells that contain a string that includes the contents of the *Text* cell, use this formula:

```
=COUNTIF(Data,"*"&Text&"*")
```

For example, if the *Text* cell contains the text "Alpha" the formula returns 3 because three cells in the *Data* range contain the text "alpha" (cells A2, A8, and A10). Note that the comparison is not case sensitive.

If you need a case-sensitive count, you can use the following array formula:

```
{=SUM(IF(LEN(Data)-LEN(SUBSTITUTE(Data,Text,""))>0,1))}
```

If the *Text* cells contain the text "Alpha" the preceding formula returns 2 because the string appears in two cells (A2 and A8).

Total occurrences in a range

To count the total number of occurrences of a string within a range of cells, use the following array formula:

```
{=(SUM(LEN(Data))-SUM(LEN(SUBSTITUTE(Data,Text,""))))/
LEN(Text)}
```

If the *Text* cell contains the character "B" the formula returns 7 because the range contains seven instances of the string. This formula is case sensitive.

The following array formula is a modified version that is not case sensitive:

```
{=(SUM(LEN(Data))-SUM(LEN(SUBSTITUTE(UPPER(Data),
UPPER(Text),""))))/LEN(Text)}
```

Counting the number of unique values

The following array formula returns the number of unique values in a range named *Data*:

```
{=SUM(1/COUNTIF(Data,Data))}
```

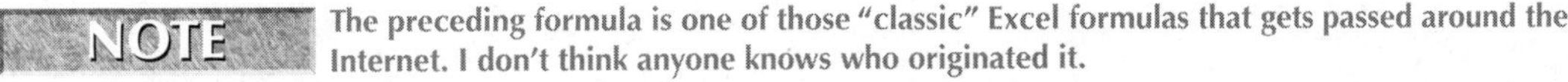

The preceding formula is one of those "classic" Excel formulas that gets passed around the Internet. I don't think anyone knows who originated it.

Useful as it is, this formula does have a serious limitation: If the range contains any blank cells it returns an error. The following array formula solves this problem:

```
{=SUM(IF(COUNTIF(Data,Data)=0,"",1/COUNTIF(Data,Data)))}
```

Creating a frequency distribution

A *frequency distribution* basically comprises a summary table that shows the frequency of each value in a range. For example, an instructor may create a frequency distribution of test scores. The table would show the count of A's, B's, C's, and so on. Excel provides a number of ways to create frequency distributions. You can

- Use the FREQUENCY function
- Use the Analysis ToolPak add-in
- Create your own formulas
- Use a pivot table

The FREQUENCY function

Using the FREQUENCY function to create a frequency distribution can be a bit tricky. This function always returns an array, so you must use it in an array formula that's entered into a multicell range.

Figure 17-5 shows some data in range A1:E25 (named *Data*). These values range from 1 to 500. The range G2:G11 contains the bins used for the frequency distribution. Each cell in this bin range contains the upper limit for the bin. In this case, the bins consist of <=50, 51–100, 101–150, and so on.

FIGURE 17-5

Creating a frequency distribution for the data in A1:E25.

	A	B	C	D	E	F	G	H
1	55	316	223	185	124		Bins	
2	124	93	163	213	314		50	
3	211	41	231	241	212		100	
4	118	113	400	205	254		150	
5	262	1	201	12	101		200	
6	167	479	205	337	118		250	
7	489	15	89	362	148		300	
8	179	248	125	197	177		350	
9	456	153	269	49	127		400	
10	289	500	198	317	300		450	
11	126	114	303	314	270		500	
12	151	279	347	314	170			
13	250	175	93	209	61			
14	166	113	356	124	242			
15	152	384	157	233	99			
16	277	195	436	6	240			
17	147	80	173	211	244			
18	386	93	330	400	141			
19	332	173	129	323	188			
20	338	263	444	84	220			
21	221	402	498	98	2			
22	201	400	3	190	105			
23	35	225	12	265	329			
24	43	302	125	301	444			
25	56	9	135	500	398			
26								

FREQUE

To create the frequency distribution, select a range of cells that corresponds to the number of cells in the bin range (in this example, H2:H11). Then enter the following array formula (press Ctrl+Shift+Enter to enter it):

```
{=FREQUENCY(Data,G2:G11)}
```

The array formula returns the count of values in the *Data* range that fall into each bin. To create a frequency distribution that consists of percentages, use the following array formula:

```
{=FREQUENCY(Data,G2:G11)/COUNT(Data)}
```

Figure 17-6 shows two frequency distributions — one in terms of counts and one in terms of percentages. The figure also shows a chart (histogram) created from the frequency distribution.

FIGURE 17-6

Frequency distributions created by using the FREQUENCY function.

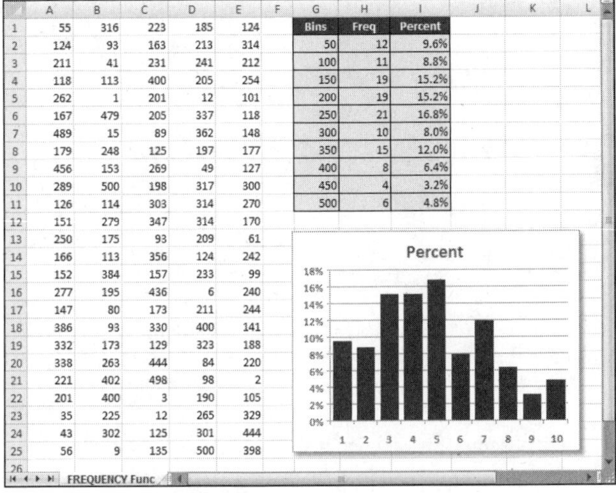

	A	B	C	D	E
1	55	316	223	185	124
2	124	93	163	213	314
3	211	41	231	241	212
4	118	113	400	205	254
5	262	1	201	12	101
6	167	479	205	337	118
7	489	15	89	362	148
8	179	248	125	197	177
9	456	153	269	49	127
10	289	500	198	317	300
11	126	114	303	314	270
12	151	279	347	314	170
13	250	175	93	209	61
14	166	113	356	124	242
15	152	384	157	233	99
16	277	195	436	6	240
17	147	80	173	211	244
18	386	93	330	400	141
19	332	173	129	323	188
20	338	263	444	84	220
21	221	402	498	98	2
22	201	400	3	190	105
23	35	225	12	265	329
24	43	302	125	301	444
25	56	9	135	500	398

Bins	Freq	Percent
50	12	9.6%
100	11	8.8%
150	19	15.2%
200	19	15.2%
250	21	16.8%
300	10	8.0%
350	15	12.0%
400	8	6.4%
450	4	3.2%
500	6	4.8%

Using formulas to create a frequency distribution

Figure 17-7 shows a worksheet that contains test scores for 50 students in column B (the range is named *Grades*). Formulas in columns G and H calculate a frequency distribution for letter grades. The minimum and maximum values for each letter grade appear in columns D and E. For example, a test score between 80 and 89 (inclusive) earns a B. In addition, a chart displays the distribution of the test scores.

The formula in cell G2 that follows is an array formula that counts the number of scores that qualify for an A:

```
=COUNTIFS(Grades,">="&D2,Grades,"<="&E2)
```

You may recognize this formula from a previous section in this chapter (see "Counting cells by using multiple criteria"). This formula was copied to the four cells below G2.

FIGURE 17-7

Creating a frequency distribution of test scores.

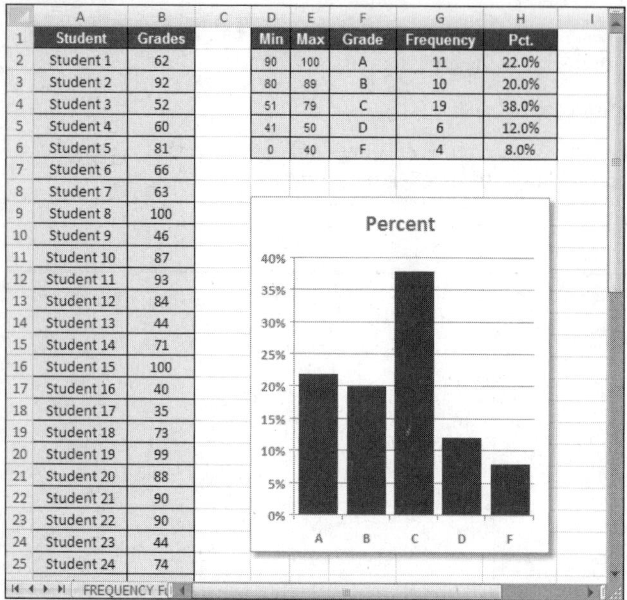

Student	Grades
Student 1	62
Student 2	92
Student 3	52
Student 4	60
Student 5	81
Student 6	66
Student 7	63
Student 8	100
Student 9	46
Student 10	87
Student 11	93
Student 12	84
Student 13	44
Student 14	71
Student 15	100
Student 16	40
Student 17	35
Student 18	73
Student 19	99
Student 20	88
Student 21	90
Student 22	90
Student 23	44
Student 24	74

Min	Max	Grade	Frequency	Pct.
90	100	A	11	22.0%
80	89	B	10	20.0%
51	79	C	19	38.0%
41	50	D	6	12.0%
0	40	F	4	8.0%

NOTE The preceding formula uses the `COUNTIFS` function, which is new to Excel 2007. For compatibility with previous Excel versions, use this array formula:

```
{=SUM((Grades>=D2)*(Grades<=E2))}
```

The formulas in column H calculate the percentage of scores for each letter grade. The formula in H2, which was copied to the four cells below H2, is

```
=G2/SUM($G$2:$G$6)
```

Using the Analysis ToolPak to create a frequency distribution

The Analysis ToolPak add-in, distributed with Excel, provides another way to calculate a frequency distribution. Start by entering your bin values in a range. Then choose Data ➪ Analysis ➪ Analysis to display the Data Analysis dialog box. If this command is not available, see the sidebar, "Is the Analysis Toolpak Installed?".

In the Data Analysis dialog box, select Histogram and click OK. You should see the Histogram dialog box shown in Figure 17-8.

Specify the ranges for your data (Input Range), bins (Bin Range), and results (Output Range), and then select any options. Figure 17-9 shows a frequency distribution (and chart) created with the Histogram option.

CAUTION Note that the frequency distribution consists of values, not formulas. Therefore, if you make any changes to your input data, you need to rerun the Histogram procedure to update the results.

FIGURE 17-8

The Analysis ToolPak's Histogram dialog box.

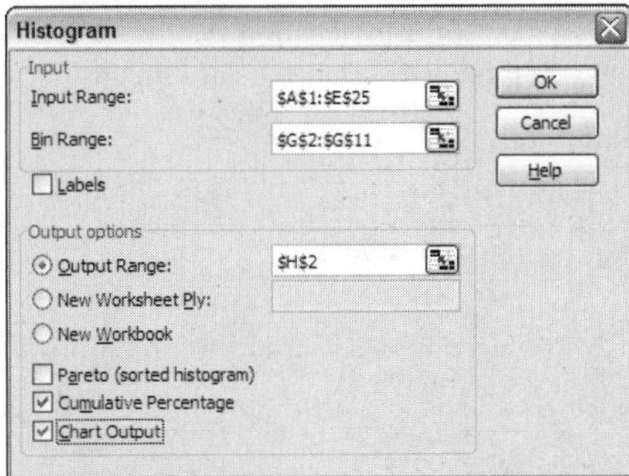

FIGURE 17-9

A frequency distribution and chart generated by the Analysis ToolPak's Histogram option.

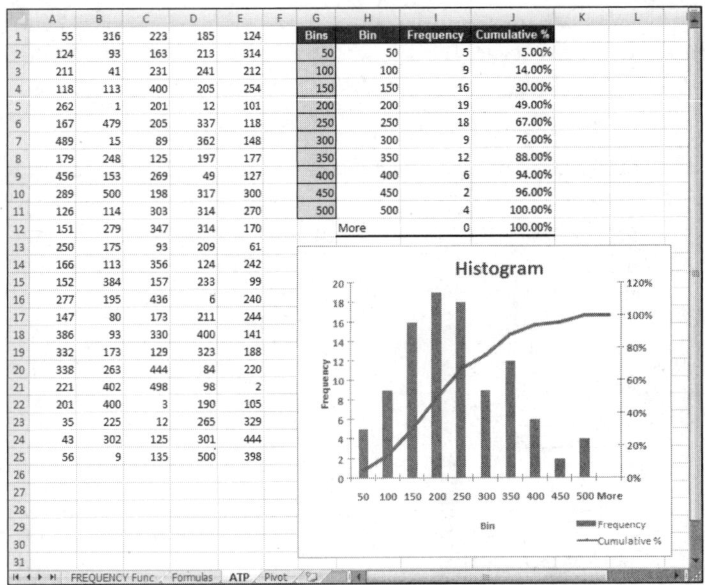

	A	B	C	D	E	F	G	H	I	J
1	55	316	223	185	124		Bins	Bin	Frequency	Cumulative %
2	124	93	163	213	314		50	50	5	5.00%
3	211	41	231	241	212		100	100	9	14.00%
4	118	113	400	205	254		150	150	16	30.00%
5	262	1	201	12	101		200	200	19	49.00%
6	167	479	205	337	118		250	250	18	67.00%
7	489	15	89	362	148		300	300	9	76.00%
8	179	248	125	197	177		350	350	12	88.00%
9	456	153	269	49	127		400	400	6	94.00%
10	289	500	198	317	300		450	450	2	96.00%
11	126	114	303	314	270		500	500	4	100.00%
12	151	279	347	314	170			More	0	100.00%
13	250	175	93	209	61					
14	166	113	356	124	242					
15	152	384	157	233	99					
16	277	195	436	6	240					
17	147	80	173	211	244					
18	386	93	330	400	141					
19	332	173	129	323	188					
20	338	263	444	84	220					
21	221	402	498	98	2					
22	201	400	3	190	105					
23	35	225	12	265	329					
24	43	302	125	301	444					
25	56	9	135	500	398					

Is the Analysis Toolpak Installed?

To make sure that the Analysis Toolpak add-in is installed, Click the Data tab. If the Ribbon displays the Data Analysis command in the Analysis group, you're all set. If not, you'll need to install the add-in:

1. **Choose Office Button ⇨ Excel Options to display the Excel Options dialog box.**
2. **Click the Add-ins choice at the left.**
3. **Select Excel Add-Ins from the drop-down labeled Manage.**
4. **Click Go to display the Add-Ins dialog box.**
5. **Place a check mark next to Analysis ToolPak.**
6. **Click OK.**

Note: In the Add-Ins dialog box, you see an additional add-in, Analysis ToolPak - VBA. This add-in is for programmers, and you don't need to install it.

Using a pivot table to create a frequency distribution

If your data is in the form of a table, you may prefer to use a pivot table to create a histogram. Figure 17-10 shows the student grade data summarized in a pivot table. The data bars were added using the new conditional formatting features in Excel 2007.

FIGURE 17-10

Using data bars within a pivot table to display a histogram.

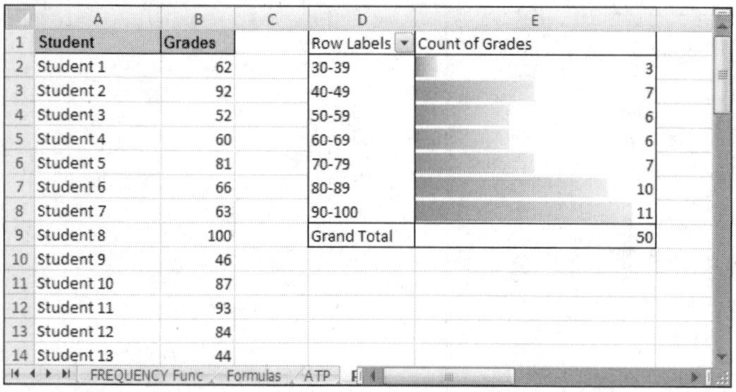

	A	B	C	D	E
1	Student	Grades		Row Labels	Count of Grades
2	Student 1	62		30-39	3
3	Student 2	92		40-49	7
4	Student 3	52		50-59	6
5	Student 4	60		60-69	6
6	Student 5	81		70-79	7
7	Student 6	66		80-89	10
8	Student 7	63		90-100	11
9	Student 8	100		Grand Total	50
10	Student 9	46			
11	Student 10	87			
12	Student 11	93			
13	Student 12	84			
14	Student 13	44			

FREQUENCY Func / Formulas / ATP

Summing Formulas

The examples in this section demonstrate how to perform common summing tasks by using formulas. The formulas range from very simple to relatively complex array formulas that compute sums by using multiple criteria.

Summing all cells in a range

It doesn't get much simpler than this. The following formula returns the sum of all values in a range named *Data*:

```
=SUM(Data)
```

The SUM function can take up to 255 arguments. The following formula, for example, returns the sum of the values in five noncontiguous ranges:

```
=SUM(A1:A9,C1:C9,E1:E9,G1:G9,I1:I9)
```

You can use complete rows or columns as an argument for the `SUM` function. The formula that follows, for example, returns the sum of all values in column A. If this formula appears in a cell in column A, it generates a circular reference error.

```
=SUM(A:A)
```

The following formula returns the sum of all values on Sheet1 by using a range reference that consists of all rows. To avoid a circular reference error, this formula must appear on a sheet other than Sheet1.

```
=SUM(Sheet1!1:1048576)
```

The `SUM` function is very versatile. The arguments can be numerical values, cells, ranges, text representations of numbers (which are interpreted as values), logical values, and even embedded functions. For example, consider the following formula:

```
=SUM(B1,5,"6",,SQRT(4),A1:A5,TRUE)
```

This odd formula, which is perfectly valid, contains all of the following types of arguments, listed here in the order of their presentation:

- A single cell reference
- A literal value
- A string that looks like a value
- A missing argument
- An expression that uses another function
- A range reference
- A logical `TRUE` value

CAUTION **The `SUM` function is versatile, but it's also inconsistent when you use logical values (`TRUE` or `FALSE`). Logical values stored in cells are always treated as 0. But logical `TRUE`, when used as an argument in the `SUM` function, is treated as 1.**

Computing a cumulative sum

You may want to display a cumulative sum of values in a range — sometimes known as a "running total." Figure 17-11 illustrates a cumulative sum. Column B shows the monthly amounts, and column C displays the cumulative (year-to-date) totals.

The formula in cell C2 is:

```
=SUM(B$2:B2)
```

Notice that this formula uses a *mixed reference*—that is, the first cell in the range reference always refers to the same row (in this case, row 2). When this formula is copied down the column, the range argument adjusts such that the sum always starts with row 2 and ends with the current row. For example, after copying this formula down column C, the formula in cell C8 is:

```
=SUM(B$2:B8)
```

FIGURE 17-11

Simple formulas in column C display a cumulative sum of the values in column B.

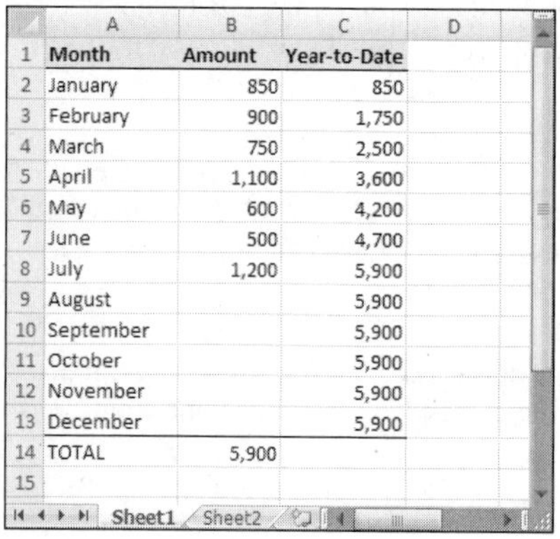

	A	B	C	D
1	Month	Amount	Year-to-Date	
2	January	850	850	
3	February	900	1,750	
4	March	750	2,500	
5	April	1,100	3,600	
6	May	600	4,200	
7	June	500	4,700	
8	July	1,200	5,900	
9	August		5,900	
10	September		5,900	
11	October		5,900	
12	November		5,900	
13	December		5,900	
14	TOTAL	5,900		
15				

Sheet1 Sheet2

You can use an `IF` function to hide the cumulative sums for rows in which data hasn't been entered. The following formula, entered in cell C2 and copied down the column, is:

```
=IF(B2<>"",SUM(B$2:B2),"")
```

Figure 17-12 shows this formula at work.

FIGURE 17-12

Using an IF function to hide cumulative sums for missing data.

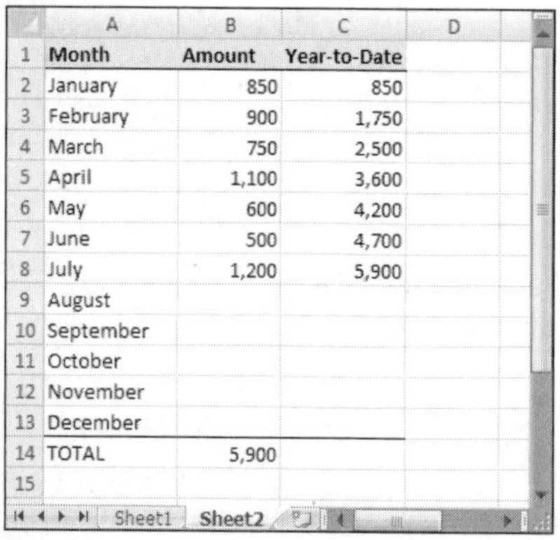

	A	B	C	D
1	Month	Amount	Year-to-Date	
2	January	850	850	
3	February	900	1,750	
4	March	750	2,500	
5	April	1,100	3,600	
6	May	600	4,200	
7	June	500	4,700	
8	July	1,200	5,900	
9	August			
10	September			
11	October			
12	November			
13	December			
14	TOTAL	5,900		
15				

Sheet1 Sheet2

Summing the "top n" values

In some situations, you may need to sum the *n* largest values in a range — for example, the top 10 values. If your data resides in a table, you can use autofiltering to hide all but the top *n* rows and then display the sum of the visible data in the table's total row.

Another approach is to sort the range in descending order and then use the `SUM` function with an argument consisting of the first *n* values in the sorted range.

A better solution — which doesn't require a table or sorting — uses an array formula like this one:

```
{=SUM(LARGE(Data,{1,2,3,4,5,6,7,8,9,10}))}
```

This formula sums the ten largest values in a range named *Data*. To sum the 10 smallest values, use the `SMALL` function instead of the `LARGE` function:

```
{=SUM(SMALL(Data,{1,2,3,4,5,6,7,8,9,10}))}
```

These formulas use an array constant comprised of the arguments for the `LARGE` or `SMALL` function. If the value of *n* for your top-*n* calculation is large, you may prefer to use the following variation. This formula returns the sum of the top 30 values in the *Data* range. You can, of course, substitute a different value for 30.

```
{=SUM(LARGE(Data,ROW(INDIRECT("1:30"))))}
```

Conditional Sums Using a Single Criterion

Often, you need to calculate a *conditional sum*. With a conditional sum, values in a range that meet one or more conditions are included in the sum. This section presents examples of conditional summing by using a single criterion.

The `SUMIF` function is very useful for single-criterion sum formulas. The `SUMIF` function takes three arguments:

- ***range***: The range containing the values that determine whether to include a particular cell in the sum.
- ***criteria***: An expression that determines whether to include a particular cell in the sum.
- ***sum_range***: Optional. The range that contains the cells you want to sum. If you omit this argument, the function uses the range specified in the first argument.

The examples that follow demonstrate the use of the `SUMIF` function. These formulas are based on the worksheet shown in Figure 17-13, set up to track invoices. Column F contains a formula that subtracts the date in column E from the date in column D. A negative number in column F indicates a past-due payment. The worksheet uses named ranges that correspond to the labels in row 1.

Let a Wizard Create Your Formula

Excel ships with an add-in called Conditional Sum wizard. After you install this add-in, you can invoke the wizard by choosing Formulas ➪ Solutions ➪ Conditional Sum.

You can specify various conditions for your summing, and the add-in creates the formula for you (always an array formula). The Conditional Sum wizard add-in, although a handy tool, is not all that versatile. For example, you can combine multiple criteria by using an And condition but not an Or condition.

To install the Conditional Sum wizard add-in:

1. **Choose Office Button ➪ Excel Options to display the Excel Options dialog box.**
2. **Click the Add-ins choice on the left.**
3. **Select Excel Add-Ins from the drop-down list labeled Manage.**
4. **Click Go to display the Add-Ins dialog box.**
5. **Place a check mark next to Conditional Sum wizard.**
6. **Click OK.**

FIGURE 17-13

A negative value in column F indicates a past-due payment.

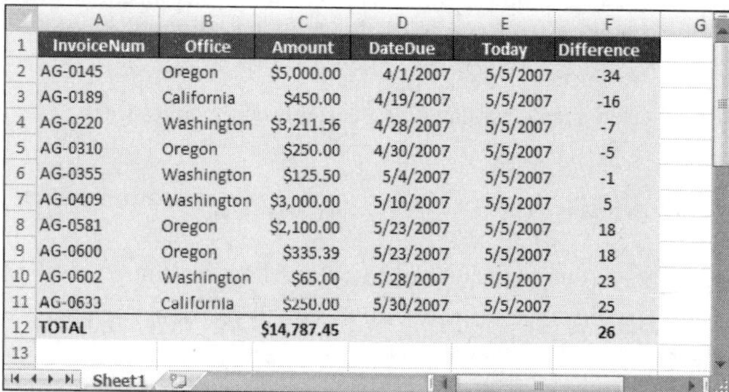

	A	B	C	D	E	F	G
1	InvoiceNum	Office	Amount	DateDue	Today	Difference	
2	AG-0145	Oregon	$5,000.00	4/1/2007	5/5/2007	-34	
3	AG-0189	California	$450.00	4/19/2007	5/5/2007	-16	
4	AG-0220	Washington	$3,211.56	4/28/2007	5/5/2007	-7	
5	AG-0310	Oregon	$250.00	4/30/2007	5/5/2007	-5	
6	AG-0355	Washington	$125.50	5/4/2007	5/5/2007	-1	
7	AG-0409	Washington	$3,000.00	5/10/2007	5/5/2007	5	
8	AG-0581	Oregon	$2,100.00	5/23/2007	5/5/2007	18	
9	AG-0600	Oregon	$335.39	5/23/2007	5/5/2007	18	
10	AG-0602	Washington	$65.00	5/28/2007	5/5/2007	23	
11	AG-0633	California	$250.00	5/30/2007	5/5/2007	25	
12	TOTAL		$14,787.45			26	
13							

Sheet1

Summing only negative values

The following formula returns the sum of the negative values in column F. In other words, it returns the total number of past-due days for all invoices. For this worksheet, the formula returns –63.

```
=SUMIF(Difference,"<0")
```

Because you omit the third argument, the second argument ("<0") applies to the values in the *Difference* range.

You don't need to hard-code the arguments for the SUMIF function into your formula. For example, you can create a formula, such as the following, which gets the criteria argument from the contents of cell G2:

```
=SUMIF(Difference,G2)
```

This formula returns a new result if you change the criteria in cell G2.

Summing values based on a different range

The following formula returns the sum of the past-due invoice amounts (in column C):

```
=SUMIF(Difference,"<0",Amount)
```

This formula uses the values in the *Difference* range to determine if the corresponding values in the *Amount* range contribute to the sum.

Summing values based on a text comparison

The following formula returns the total invoice amounts for the Oregon office:

```
=SUMIF(Office,"=Oregon",Amount)
```

Using the equal sign is optional. The following formula has the same result:

```
=SUMIF(Office,"Oregon",Amount)
```

To sum the invoice amounts for all offices *except* Oregon, use this formula:

```
=SUMIF(Office,"<>Oregon",Amount)
```

Summing values based on a date comparison

The following formula returns the total invoice amounts that have a due date after May 1, 2007:

```
=SUMIF(DateDue,">="&DATE(2007,5,1),Amount)
```

Notice that the second argument for the SUMIF function is an expression. The *expression* uses the DATE function, which returns a date. Also, the comparison operator, enclosed in quotes, is concatenated (using the & operator) with the result of the DATE function.

The formula that follows returns the total invoice amounts that have a future due date (including today):

```
=SUMIF(DateDue,">="&TODAY(),Amount)
```

Conditional Sums Using Multiple Criteria

The examples in the preceding section all used a single comparison criterion. The examples in this section involve summing cells based on multiple criteria.

Figure 17-14 shows the sample worksheet again, for your reference. The worksheet also shows the result of several formulas that demonstrate summing by using multiple criteria.

FIGURE 17-14

This worksheet demonstrates summing based on multiple criteria.

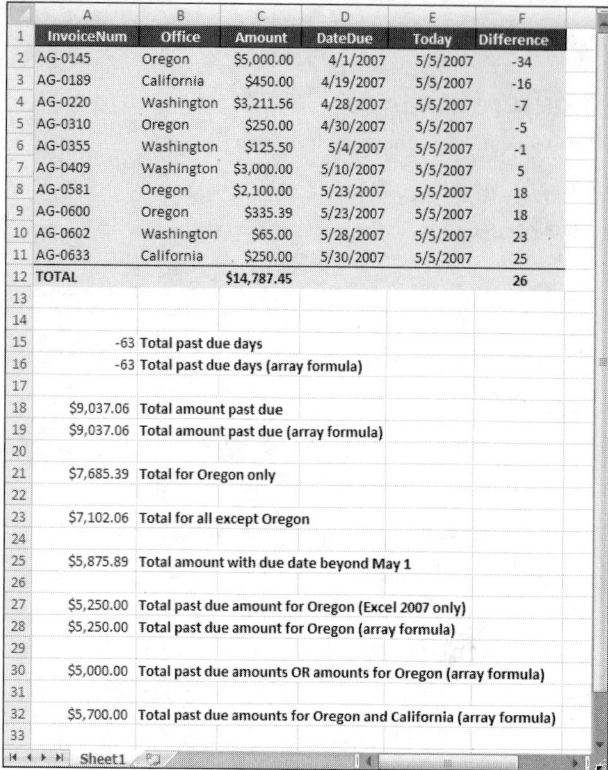

	A	B	C	D	E	F
1	InvoiceNum	Office	Amount	DateDue	Today	Difference
2	AG-0145	Oregon	$5,000.00	4/1/2007	5/5/2007	-34
3	AG-0189	California	$450.00	4/19/2007	5/5/2007	-16
4	AG-0220	Washington	$3,211.56	4/28/2007	5/5/2007	-7
5	AG-0310	Oregon	$250.00	4/30/2007	5/5/2007	-5
6	AG-0355	Washington	$125.50	5/4/2007	5/5/2007	-1
7	AG-0409	Washington	$3,000.00	5/10/2007	5/5/2007	5
8	AG-0581	Oregon	$2,100.00	5/23/2007	5/5/2007	18
9	AG-0600	Oregon	$335.39	5/23/2007	5/5/2007	18
10	AG-0602	Washington	$65.00	5/28/2007	5/5/2007	23
11	AG-0633	California	$250.00	5/30/2007	5/5/2007	25
12	TOTAL		$14,787.45			26
13						
14						
15	-63	Total past due days				
16	-63	Total past due days (array formula)				
17						
18	$9,037.06	Total amount past due				
19	$9,037.06	Total amount past due (array formula)				
20						
21	$7,685.39	Total for Oregon only				
22						
23	$7,102.06	Total for all except Oregon				
24						
25	$5,875.89	Total amount with due date beyond May 1				
26						
27	$5,250.00	Total past due amount for Oregon (Excel 2007 only)				
28	$5,250.00	Total past due amount for Oregon (array formula)				
29						
30	$5,000.00	Total past due amounts OR amounts for Oregon (array formula)				
31						
32	$5,700.00	Total past due amounts for Oregon and California (array formula)				
33						

Sheet1

Using And criteria

Suppose that you want to get a sum of the invoice amounts that are past due *and* associated with the Oregon office. In other words, the value in the Amount range will be summed only if both of the following criteria are met:

- The corresponding value in the Difference range is negative.
- The corresponding text in the Office range is "Oregon."

If you're using Excel 2007, the following formula does the job:

```
=SUMIFS(Amount,Difference,"<0",Office,"Oregon")
```

The array formula that follows returns the same result and will work in all versions of Excel.

```
{=SUM((Difference<0)*(Office="Oregon")*Amount)}
```

Using Or criteria

Suppose that you want to get a sum of past-due invoice amounts *or* ones associated with the Oregon office. In other words, the value in the Amount range will be summed if either of the following criteria is met:

- The corresponding value in the Difference range is negative.
- The corresponding text in the Office range is "Oregon".

This example requires an array formula:

```
{=SUM(IF((Office="Oregon")+(Difference<0),1,0)*Amount)}
```

A plus sign (+) joins the conditions; you can include more than two conditions.

Using And and Or criteria

As you may expect, things get a bit tricky when your criteria consists of both And and Or operations. For example, you may want to sum the values in the Amount range when both of the following conditions are met:

- The corresponding value in the Difference range is negative.
- The corresponding text in the Office range is "Oregon" or "California".

Notice that the second condition actually consists of two conditions joined with Or. The following array formula does the trick:

```
{=SUM((Difference<0)*IF((Office="Oregon")+
(Office="California"),1)*Amount)}
```

Summary

This chapter provided valuable tutelage in creating formulas that handle particular counting and summing operations in a worksheet. Applying any of the numerous examples covered here will save you significant time while making your worksheets into more powerful business tools.

Chapter 18

Getting Started Making Charts

When most people think of Excel, they think of crunching rows and columns of numbers. But as you probably know already, Excel is no slouch when it comes to presenting data visually in the form of a chart. In fact, it's a safe bet that Excel is the most commonly used software for creating charts.

This chapter presents an introductory overview of the Excel program's charting ability.

IN THIS CHAPTER

What Is a Chart?

A *chart* is a visual representation of numeric values. Charts (also known as *graphs*) have been an integral part of spreadsheets since the early days of Lotus 1-2-3. Charts generated by early spreadsheet products were quite crude but have improved significantly over the years. Excel provides you with the tools to create a wide variety of highly customizable charts.

NEW FEATURE **Excel 2007 charting is a good news/bad news situation. The good news is that Excel 2007 charts have a great new look. The bad news is that Microsoft did not provide any new chart types or any significant new features.**

Displaying data in a well-conceived chart can make your numbers more understandable. Because a chart presents a picture, charts are particularly useful for summarizing a series of numbers and their interrelationships. Making a chart can often help you spot trends and patterns that may otherwise go unnoticed.

Figure 18-1 shows a worksheet that contains a simple column chart that depicts a company's sales volume by month. Viewing the chart makes it very apparent that sales were down in the summer months (June through August), but they increased steadily during the final four months of the year. You could, of course, arrive at this same conclusion simply by studying the numbers. But viewing the chart makes the point much more quickly.

FIGURE 18-1

A simple column chart depicts the monthly sales volume.

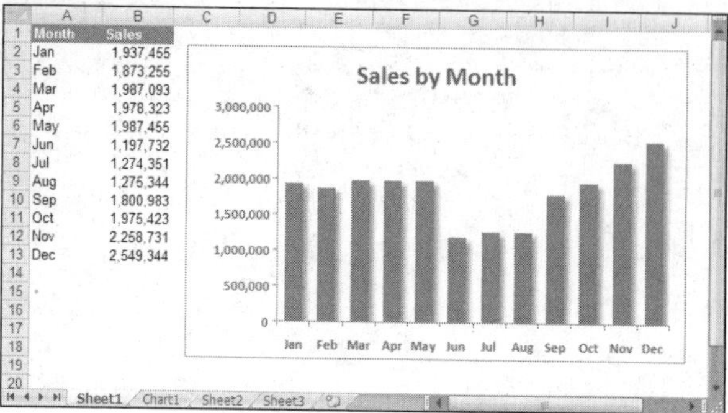

A column chart is just one of many different types of charts that you can create with Excel.

Understanding How Excel Handles Charts

Before you can create a chart, you must have some numbers — sometimes known as *data.* The data, of course, is stored in the cells in a worksheet. Normally, the data that a chart uses resides in a single worksheet, but that's not a strict requirement. A chart can use data that's stored in any number of worksheets, and the worksheets can even be in different workbooks.

A chart is essentially an *object* that Excel creates upon request. This object consists of one or more *data series,* displayed graphically. The appearance of the data series depends on the selected *chart type.* For example, if you create a line chart that uses two data series, the chart contains two lines, each representing one data series. The data for each series is stored in a separate row or column. Each point on the line is determined by the value in a single cell and is represented by a marker. You can distinguish each of the lines by its thickness, line style, color, or data markers (squares, circles, and so on).

Figure 18-2 shows a line chart that plots two data series across a 12-month period. I used different data markers (squares versus circles) to identify the two series, as shown in the *legend* at the bottom of the chart. The chart clearly shows the sales in the Eastern Region are declining steadily, while Western Region sales are increasing at a slower rate.

A key point to keep in mind is that charts are *dynamic.* In other words, a chart series is linked to the data in your worksheet. If the data changes, the chart is updated automatically to reflect those changes.

After you've created a chart, you can always change its type, change the formatting, add new data series to it, or change an existing data series so that it uses data in a different range.

Before you create a chart, you need to determine whether you want it to be an embedded chart or one that resides on a chart sheet. However, you can change your mind later on because it's very easy to move an embedded chart to a chart sheet (and vice versa).

FIGURE 18-2

This line chart displays two data series.

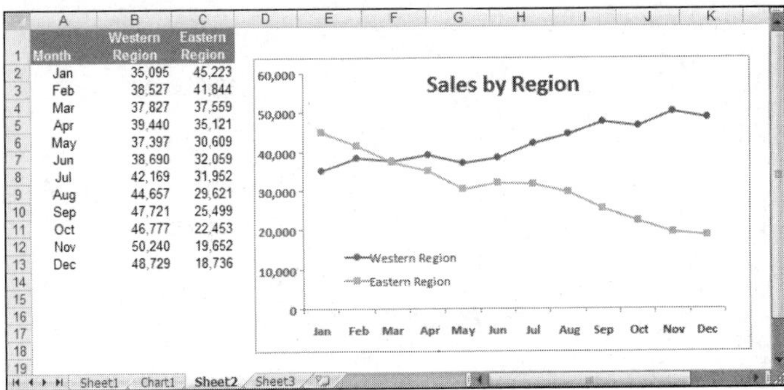

Embedded charts

An *embedded chart* basically floats on top of a worksheet, on the worksheet's draw layer. The charts shown previously in this chapter are both embedded charts.

As with other drawing objects (such as Shapes or SmartArt), you can move an embedded chart, resize it, change its proportions, adjust its borders, and perform other operations. Using embedded charts enables you to print the chart next to the data that it uses.

To make any changes to the actual chart in an embedded chart object, you must click it to *activate* the chart. When a chart is activated, Excel displays the Chart Tools context tab. The Ribbon provides many tools for working with charts.

Chart sheets

When you create a chart on a chart sheet, the chart occupies the entire sheet. If you plan to print a chart on a page by itself, using a chart sheet is often your better choice. If you have many charts to create, you may want to create each one on a separate chart sheet to avoid cluttering your worksheet. This technique also makes locating a particular chart easier because you can change the names of the chart sheets' tabs to provide a description of the chart that it contains.

The Excel Ribbon changes when a chart sheet is active, similar to the way it changes when you select an embedded chart.

Excel displays a chart in a chart sheet in WYSIWYG (What You See Is What You Get) mode: The printed chart looks just like the image on the chart sheet. If the chart doesn't fit in the window, you can use the scroll bars to scroll it or adjust the zoom factor. You also can change its orientation (tall or wide) by using Page Layout ➪ Page Setup ➪ Orientation.

If you create a chart on a chart sheet, you can easily convert it to an embedded chart. Choose Chart Tools ➪ Design ➪ Location ➪ Move Chart to display the Move Chart dialog box. Select the worksheet that will hold the embedded chart from the As Object In drop-down box. Excel deletes the chart sheet and moves the chart to the sheet that you specify. This operation also works in the opposite direction: You can select an embedded chart and relocate it to a new chart sheet.

Parts of a Chart

Refer to the accompanying chart as you read the following description of the chart's elements.

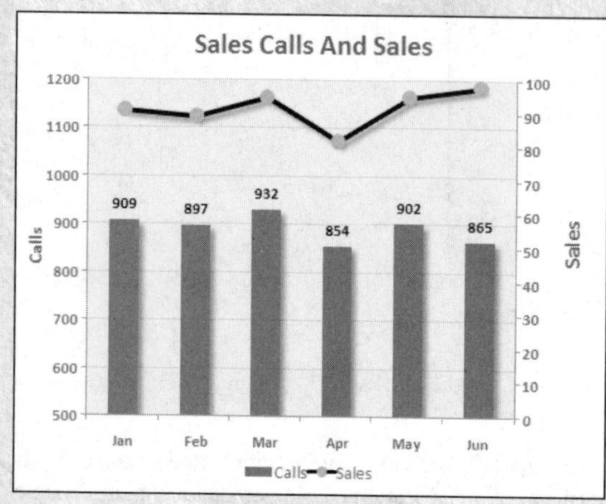

This particular chart is a *combination chart* that displays two *data series:* Calls and Sales. Calls are plotted as vertical columns, and the Sales are plotted as a line with round markers. Each column (or marker on the line) represents a single *data point* (the value in a cell).

The chart has a horizontal axis, known as the *category axis.* This axis represents the category for each data point (January, February, and so on).

Notice that this chart has two vertical axes, known as *value axes,* and each one has a different scale. The axis on the left is for the columns (Calls), and the axis on the right is for the line (Sales).

The value axes also display scale values. The axis on the left displays scale values from 500 to 1,200, in *major unit* increments of 100. The value axis on the right uses a different scale: 0 to 100, in increments of 10.

A chart with two value axes is appropriate because the two data series vary dramatically in scale. If the Sales data were plotted using the left axis, the line wouldn't even be visible.

Most charts provide some method of identifying the data series or data points. A *legend,* for example, is often used to identify the various series in a chart. In this example, the legend appears on the bottom of the chart. Some charts also display *data labels* to identify specific data points. The example chart displays data labels for the Calls series, but not for the Sales series. In addition, most charts (including the example chart) contain a *chart title* and additional labels to identify the axes or categories.

The example chart also contains horizontal *grid lines* (which correspond to the left value axis). Grid lines are basically extensions of the value axis scale, which makes it easier for the viewer to determine the magnitude of the data points.

In addition, all charts have a *chart area* (the entire background area of the chart) and a *plot area*. The plot area shows the actual chart, and in this example, the plot area has a different background color (a light gray instead of white).

Charts can have additional parts or fewer parts, depending on the chart type. For example, a pie chart has *slices* and no axes. A 3-D chart may have *walls* and a *floor*. You can also add many other types of items to a chart. For example, you can add a *trend line* or display *error bars*. In other words, after you create a chart, you have a great deal of flexibility in customizing the chart.

Creating a Chart

Creating a chart is fairly simple:

1. **Make sure that your data is appropriate for a chart.**
2. **Select the range that contains your data.**
3. **Select a chart type by clicking a chart icon in the Insert ➪ Charts.** These icons display drop-down lists that display subtypes.
4. **(Optional) Use the commands in the Chart Tools context menu to change the look or layout of the chart or add or delete chart elements.**

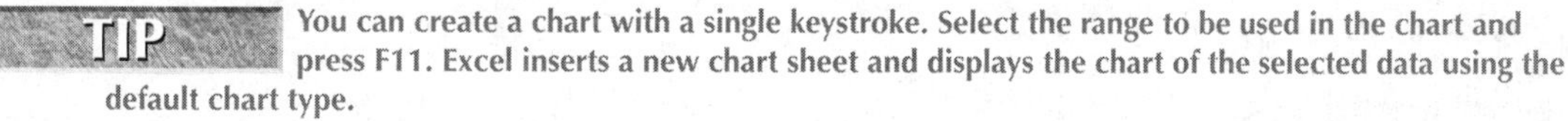

TIP **You can create a chart with a single keystroke. Select the range to be used in the chart and press F11. Excel inserts a new chart sheet and displays the chart of the selected data using the default chart type.**

Hands On: Creating and Customizing a Chart

This section contains a step-by-step example of creating a chart and applying some customizations. If you've never created a chart, this is a good opportunity to get a feel for how it works.

Figure 18-3 shows a worksheet with a range of data. This data is customer survey results by month, broken down by customers in three age groups. In this case, the data resides in a table (created by choosing Insert ➪ Tables ➪ Table), but that's not a requirement to create a chart.

FIGURE 18-3

The source data for the hands-on chart example.

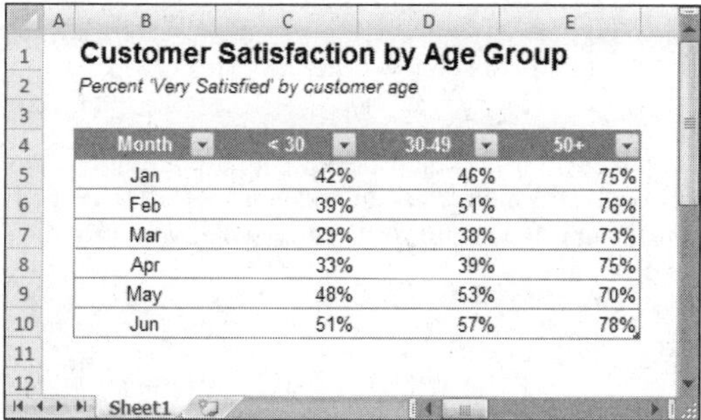

Customer Satisfaction by Age Group

Percent 'Very Satisfied' by customer age

Month	< 30	30-49	50+
Jan	42%	46%	75%
Feb	39%	51%	76%
Mar	29%	38%	73%
Apr	33%	39%	75%
May	48%	53%	70%
Jun	51%	57%	78%

Selecting the data

The first step is to select the data for the chart. Your selection should include such items as labels and series identifiers (row and column headings).

For this example, select the range B4:E10. This range includes the category labels but not the title (which is in B1).

NOTE **The data that you use in a chart need not be in contiguous cells. You can press Ctrl and make a multiple selection. The initial data, however, must be on a single worksheet. If you need to plot data that exists on more than one worksheet, you can add more series after the chart is created. In all cases, however, data for a single chart series must reside on one sheet.**

Choosing a chart type

After you've selected the data, select a chart type from Insert ➪ Charts. Each control in this group is a drop-down list, which lets you further refine your choice by selecting a subtype.

For this example, choose Insert ➪ Charts ➪ Column ➪ Clustered Column. In other words, you're creating a column chart, using the clustered column subtype. Excel displays the chart shown in Figure 18-4.

FIGURE 18-4

A clustered columns chart.

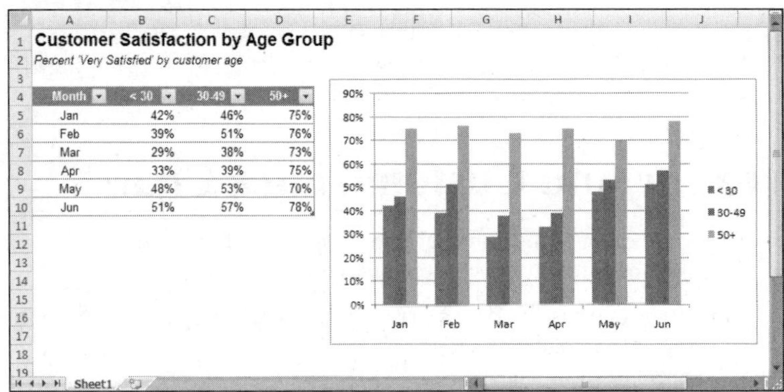

Experimenting with different layouts

The chart shown in Figure 18-4 looks pretty good, but it's just one of several predefined layouts for a clustered column chart.

To see some other configurations for the chart, select the chart and apply a few other layouts in the Chart Tools ➪ Design ➪ Chart Layouts group.

NOTE **Every chart type has a set of layouts that you can choose from. A layout contains additional chart elements, such as a title, data labels, axes, and so on. You can add your own elements to your chart, but often using a predefined layout saves time. Even if the layout isn't exactly what you want, it may be close enough that you need to make only a few adjustments.**

Figure 18-5 shows the chart after selecting a layout that adds a chart title and moves the legend to the bottom.

FIGURE 18-5

The chart, after selecting a different layout.

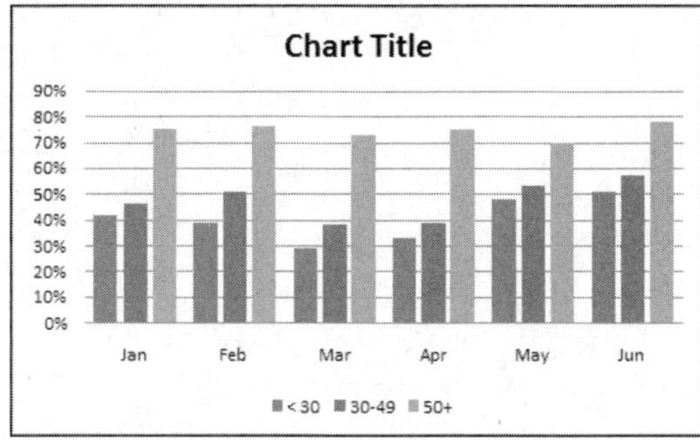

The chart title is a text element that you can select and edit. Alternatively, you can link the chart title to a cell so the title always displays the contents of a particular cell. To create a link to a cell, click the chart title, type an equal sign (=), and click the cell. Excel displays the link in the Formula bar. In the example, the contents of cell A1 is perfect for the chart title.

Experiment with the Chart Tools ➪ Layout tab to make other changes to the chart. For example, you can remove the grid lines, add axis titles, relocate the legend, and so on. Making these changes is easy and intuitive.

Trying another view of the data

The chart, at this point, shows six clusters (months) of three data points in each (age groups). Would the data be easier to understand if we plotted the information in the opposite way?

Try it. Select the chart and then choose Chart Tools ➪ Design ➪ Data ➪ Switch Row/Column. Figure 18-6 shows the result of this change. I also selected a different layout, which provides more separation between the three clusters.

NOTE **The orientation of the data has a drastic effect on the look of your chart. Excel has its own rules that it uses to determine the initial data orientation when you create a chart. If Excel's orientation doesn't match your expectation, it's easy enough to change.**

The chart, with this new orientation, reveals information that wasn't so apparent in the original version. The <30 and 30–49 age groups both show a decline in satisfaction for March and April. The 50+ age group didn't have this problem, however.

FIGURE 18-6

The chart, after changing the row and column orientation.

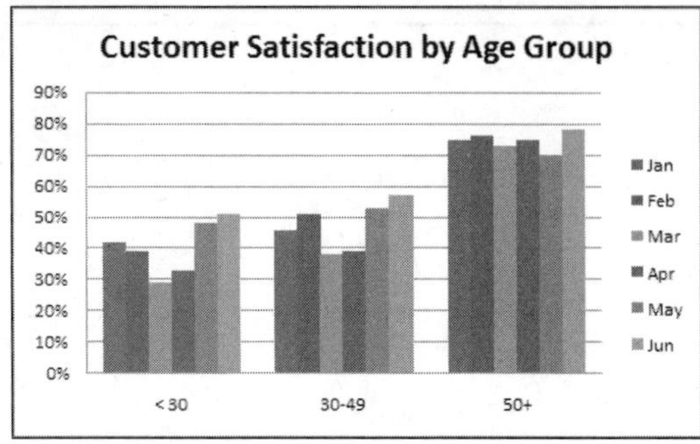

Trying other chart types

Although a clustered column chart seems to work well for this data, there's no harm in checking out some other chart types. Choose Design ➪ Type ➪ Change Chart Type to experiment with other chart types. This command displays the Change Chart Type dialog box, shown in Figure 18-7. The main categories are listed on the left, and the subtypes are shown as icons. Select an icon, click OK, and Excel displays the chart using the new chart type. If you don't like the result, select Undo.

Figure 18-8 shows a few different chart type options.

FIGURE 18-7

Use this dialog box to change the chart type.

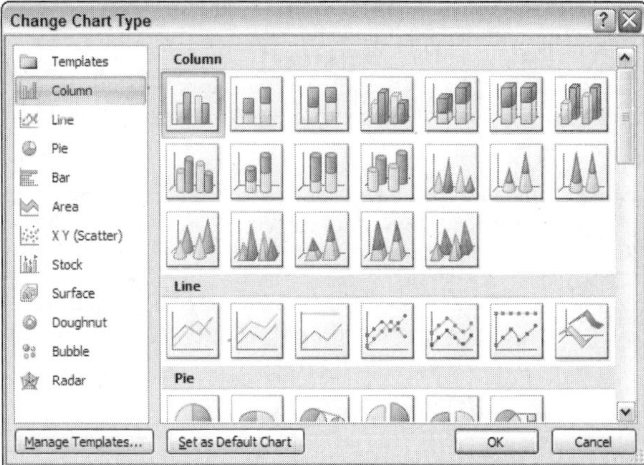

FIGURE 18-8

The customer satisfaction chart, using four different chart types.

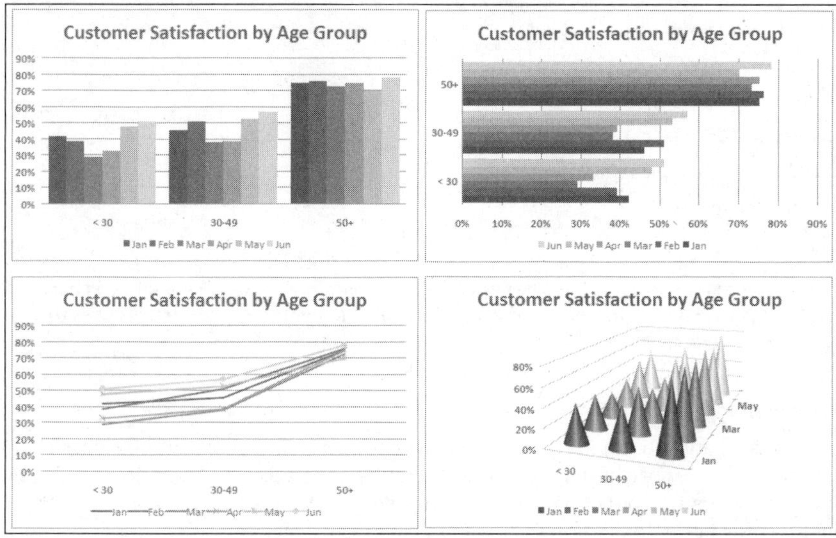

Trying other chart styles

If you'd like to try some of the prebuilt chart styles, select the chart and choose Chart Tools ➪ Design ➪ Chart Styles gallery. You'll find an amazing selection of different colors and effects, all available with a single mouse click.

TIP **The styles displayed in the gallery depend on the workbook's theme. When you choose Page Layout ➪ Themes to apply a different theme, you'll have a new selection of chart styles designed for the selected theme.**

Figure 18-9 shows the chart after drastically changing its appearance by applying a new chart style, which adds a three-dimensional look to the columns.

FIGURE 18-9

A single click applies a new style and dramatically changes the chart's look.

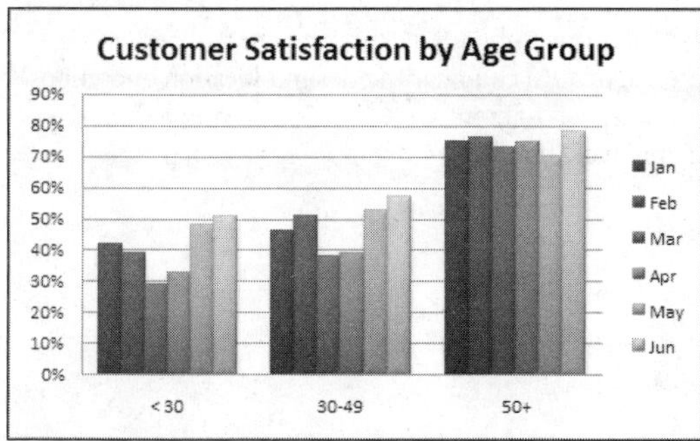

Working with Charts

This section covers some common chart modifications:

- Moving and resizing charts
- Copying a chart
- Deleting a chart
- Adding chart elements
- Moving and deleting chart elements
- Formatting chart elements
- Printing charts

NOTE **Before you can modify a chart, the chart must be activated. To activate an embedded chart, click it. Doing so activates the chart and also selects the element that you click. To activate a chart on a chart sheet, just click its sheet tab.**

Moving and resizing a chart

If your chart is an embedded chart, you can freely move and resize it with your mouse. Click the chart's border and then drag the border to move the chart. Drag any of the eight "handles" to resize the chart. The handles are the black dots that appear on the chart's corners and edges when you click the chart's border. When the mouse pointer turns into a double arrow, click and drag to resize the chart.

When a chart is selected, you can use the Format ➪ Size controls to adjust the height and width of the chart. Use the spinners, or type the dimensions directly into the Height and Width controls.

You also can use standard cut and paste techniques to move an embedded chart. In fact, this is the only way move a chart from one worksheet to another. Select the chart and choose Home ➪ Clipboard ➪ Cut (or press Ctrl+X). Then activate a cell near the desired location and choose Home ➪ Clipboard ➪ Paste (or press Ctrl+V). The new location can be in a different worksheet or even in a different workbook. If you paste the chart to a different workbook, it will be linked to the data in the original workbook.

To move an embedded chart to a chart sheet (or vice versa), select the chart and choose Chart Tools ➪ Location ➪ Move Chart to display the Move Chart dialog box.

Copying a chart

To make an exact copy of an embedded chart, press and hold down the Ctrl key. Click the chart and then drag the mouse pointer to a new location. To make a copy of a chart sheet, use the same procedure, but drag the chart sheet's tab.

Standard copy and paste techniques also work. Select the chart (an embedded chart or a chart sheet) and choose Home ➪ Clipboard ➪ Copy (or press Ctrl+C). Then activate a cell near the desired location and choose Home ➪ Clipboard ➪ Paste (or press Ctrl+V). Whether pasted to a different worksheet or even in a different workbook, the chart will be linked to the data in the original workbook.

Deleting a chart

To delete an embedded chart, press Ctrl and click the chart (this selects the chart as an object). Then press Delete. When the Ctrl key is pressed, you can select multiple charts, and then delete them all with a single press of the Del key.

To delete a chart sheet, right-click its sheet tab and choose Delete from the shortcut menu. To delete multiple chart sheets, select them by pressing Ctrl while you click the sheet tabs.

Adding chart elements

To add new elements to a chart (such as a title, legend, data labels, or gridlines), use the controls in the Chart Tools ➪ Layout group. These controls are arranged into logical groups, and they all display a drop-down list of options.

Moving and deleting chart elements

Some of the elements within a chart can be moved. The movable chart elements include the titles, the legend, and data labels. To move a chart element, simply click it to select it. Then drag its border. The easiest way to delete a chart element is to select it and then press Delete. You can also use the controls in the Chart Tools ➪ Layout group to turn off the display of a particular chart element. For example, to delete data labels, choose Chart Tools ➪ Layout ➪ Labels ➪ Data Labels ➪ None.

A few chart elements consist of multiple objects. For example, the data labels element consists of one label for each data point. To move or delete one data label, click once to select the entire element and then click a second time to select the specific data label. You can then move or delete the single data label.

Formatting chart elements

Many users are content to stick with the predefined chart layouts and chart styles. For more precise customizations, Excel allows you to work with individual chart elements and apply additional formatting. You can use the Ribbon commands for some modifications, but the easiest way to format chart elements is to right-click the element and choose Format from the shortcut menu. The exact command depends on the element you select. For example, if you right-click the chart's title, the shortcut menu command is Format Chart Title.

The Format command displays a stay-on-top tabbed dialog box with options for the selected element.

Figure 18-10 shows the Format Axis dialog box, which I displayed by right-clicking the vertical axis and selecting Format Axis from the shortcut menu.

TIP **If you've applied formatting to a chart element and decide that it wasn't such a good idea, you can revert to the original formatting for the particular chart style. Right-click the chart element and choose Reset To Match Style from the shortcut menu. To reset the entire chart, select the chart area when you issue the command.**

NEW FEATURE **In previous versions of Excel, double-clicking a chart element displayed its Format dialog box. That mouse action no longer works in Excel 2007.**

FIGURE 18-10

Each chart element has a formatting dialog box. This one is used to format a chart axis.

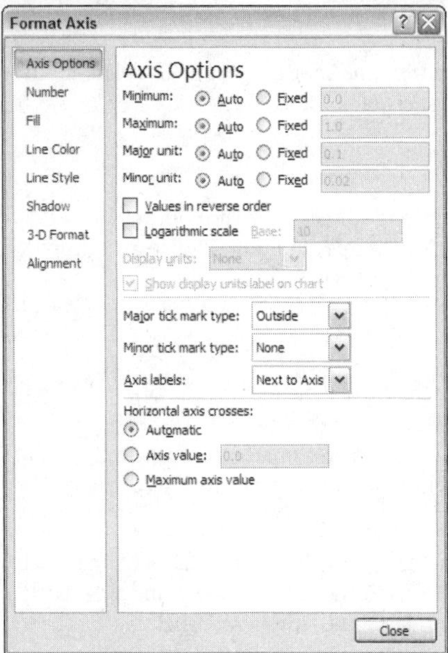

Printing charts

Printing embedded charts is nothing special; you print them the same way that you print a worksheet. As long as you include the embedded chart in the range that you want to print, Excel prints the chart as it appears onscreen. When printing a sheet that contains embedded charts, it's a good idea to preview first (or use Page Layout View) to ensure that your charts do not span multiple pages. If you created the chart on a chart sheet, Excel always prints the chart on a page by itself.

If you select an embedded chart and use Office ➪ Print, Excel prints the chart on a page by itself and does *not* print the worksheet.

If you don't want a particular embedded chart to appear on your printout, select the chart and display the Size And Properties dialog box. Choose Chart Tools ➪ Format, and then click the dialog box launcher in the Size group. In the Size And Properties dialog box, click the Properties tab and remove the check mark from the Print Object checkbox.

Understanding Chart Types

People who create charts usually do so to make a point or to communicate a specific message. Often, the message is explicitly stated in the chart's title or in a text box within the chart. The chart itself provides visual support.

Choosing the correct chart type is often a key factor in the effectiveness of the message. Therefore, it's often well worth your time to experiment with various chart types to determine which one conveys your message best.

In almost every case, the underlying message in a chart is some type of *comparison*. Examples of some general types of comparisons include:

- **Compare item to other items:** For example, a chart may compare sales in each of a company's sales regions.
- **Compare data over time:** For example, a chart may display sales by month and indicate trends over time.
- **Make relative comparisons:** An example is a common pie chart that depicts relative values in terms of pie "slices."
- **Compare data relationships:** An XY chart is ideal for this comparison. For example, you might show the relationship between marketing expenditures and sales.
- **Frequency comparison:** You can use a common histogram, for example, to display the number (or percentage) of students who scored within a particular grade range.
- **Identify "outliers" or unusual situations:** If you have thousands of data points, creating a scatter chart may help identify data that is not representative.

Choosing a chart type

A common question among Excel users is "How do I know which chart type to use for my data?" Unfortunately, this question has no cut-and-dried answer to. Perhaps the best answer is a vague one: Use the chart type that gets your message across in the simplest way.

Figure 18-11 shows the same set of data plotted by using six different chart types. Although all six charts represent the same information (monthly Web site visitors), they look quite different from one another.

The column chart (upper left) is probably the best choice for this particular set of data because it clearly shows the information for each month in discrete units. The bar chart (upper right) is similar to a column chart, but the axes are swapped. Most people are more accustomed to seeing time-based information extend from left to right rather than from top to bottom.

The line chart (middle left) may not be the best choice because it seems to imply that the data is continuous— that points exist in between the 12 actual data points. This same argument may be made against using an area chart (middle right).

The pie chart (lower left) is simply too confusing and does nothing to convey the time-based nature of the data. Pie charts are most appropriate for a data series in which you want to emphasize proportions among a relatively small number of data points. If you have too many data points, a pie chart can be impossible to interpret.

The radar chart (lower right) is clearly inappropriate for this data. People aren't accustomed to viewing time-based information in a circular direction!

Fortunately, changing a chart's type is an easy procedure, so you can experiment with various chart types until you find the one that represents your data accurately, clearly, and as simply as possible.

FIGURE 18-11

The same data, plotted by using six chart types.

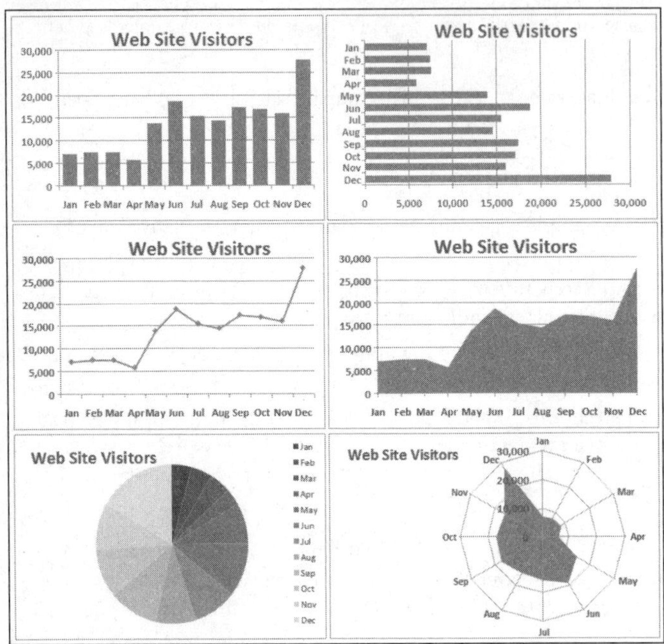

Summary

This chapter introduced Excel charts, including the differences between embedded charts and separate chart sheets, and parts of a chart. You learned how to create a chart; move, resize, and copy a chart; and how to work with chart elements. For many uses, the information in this chapter is sufficient to create a wide variety of charts.

Chapter 19

Working with Database Tables in Excel

Dictionaries are databases. Encyclopedias are databases. So are phone books, almanacs, tide tables, and the like. Most of these static databases are organized in some sort of simple ascending alphabetical or chronological sequence. Computerized databases, though, are capable of much greater flexibility. The order in which items exist in an Excel database is not important, as various operations (such as sorting and filtering by a number of factors) can be performed on the data.

NOTE Although Excel is a great tool to use for simple tables and databases, you should be aware that Microsoft Office includes an application that is specialized for databases. If your database needs are large or complex, or if your database needs to be accessed by many people at once, you should use Access. For more information about Access, refer to Part VII, "Tracking Detailed Data with Access."

IN THIS CHAPTER

- Understanding tables and databases
- Working with a table or database
- Entering and editing records
- Sorting and filtering data
- Subtotaling data
- Using Excel data in a mail merge

Understanding Tables (Lists) and Databases

Databases are organized collections of information. In that sense, practically every list of data you've ever used has been a database.

Defining databases and tables

Databases and tables are the same thing in Excel. Although Microsoft defines a table in Excel as "a series of rows and columns that contains related data," that's a pretty good thumbnail description of a basic database, and many worksheets that people create fit that definition.

Previous versions of Excel called a database on a worksheet a list. Excel 2007 now uses the term *table*, and you can designate any range on a worksheet as a table. After you do so, you will be able to take advantage of tools for quickly sorting, filling, using formulas, and so on in the table.

CROSS-REF **The section called "Using Formulas in Tables" in Chapter 15 already presented basic information about using formulas in tables. This chapter focuses on the database-type capabilities for tables, instead.**

Records and fields

Although you're used to thinking in terms of rows and columns in Excel worksheets, when you're using Excel to track lists of information as in a database program, the proper database parlance is to call the rows "records" and the columns "fields." Thus, every database record (a row of cells) is composed of the data in each cell in that row (the individual field entries).

Whereas a row (or "record") can contain many types of data, the data that goes into a particular column (or "field") is always the same kind. For instance, you might have a database that consists of annual mean temperatures for a range of years. The first column would be the year, the second the mean temperature for a city, the third the temperature for another city, and so on. For the database to make sense, in each row the year would always have to be entered in the first column. If you entered it in the third column, it would be impossible for you to properly utilize the information because the database would be looking for a temperature and find the year instead.

Working with a Database or Table

The first row of a database or table has to contain the labels for the columns (fields). Microsoft advises you to format these cells as text before you type any of the labels, but there doesn't seem to be any real need for this action. Generally speaking, a column label that isn't text is pretty rare, and the General format, which is the default when you type text, seems to work just fine with all the database operations.

NOTE **Formatting the cells as text after the fact works without a hitch, so there's even less reason to do it beforehand. The only possible exception would be if you were using some sort of unusual label (like a date) for your fields.**

Creating a database and formatting it as a table

Here's the database and table creation process, step by step:

1. **Type the field labels in the first row.**
2. **Type the list data starting in the second row, entering one record of data in each row (see Figure 19-1).**

FIGURE 19-1

Entering a list of information that will be formatted as a table.

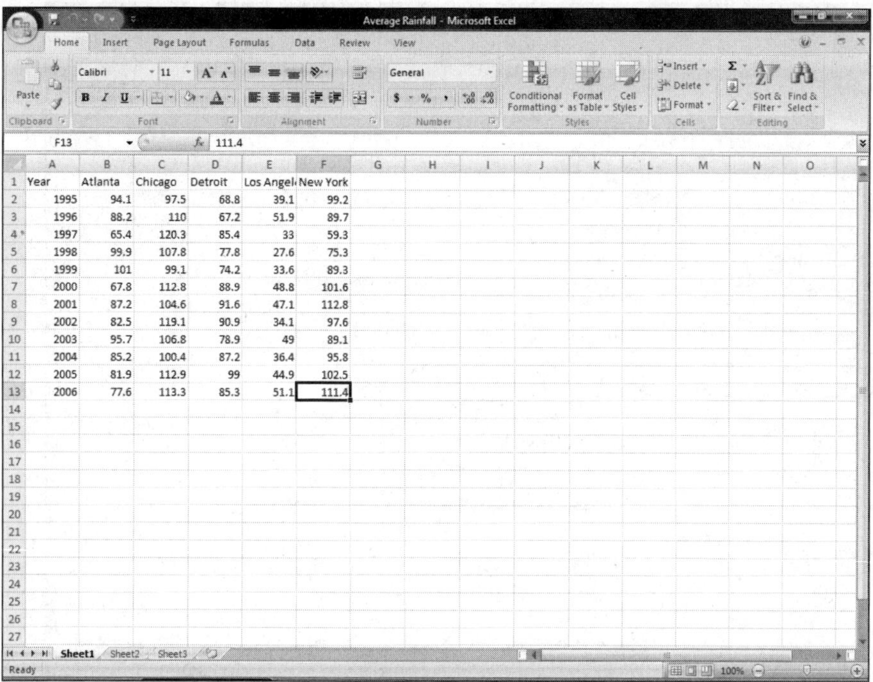

Year	Atlanta	Chicago	Detroit	Los Angel	New York
1995	94.1	97.5	68.8	39.1	99.2
1996	88.2	110	67.2	51.9	89.7
1997	65.4	120.3	85.4	33	59.3
1998	99.9	107.8	77.8	27.6	75.3
1999	101	99.1	74.2	33.6	89.3
2000	67.8	112.8	88.9	48.8	101.6
2001	87.2	104.6	91.6	47.1	112.8
2002	82.5	119.1	90.9	34.1	97.6
2003	95.7	106.8	78.9	49	89.1
2004	85.2	100.4	87.2	36.4	95.8
2005	81.9	112.9	99	44.9	102.5
2006	77.6	113.3	85.3	51.1	111.4

3. **Select the range that holds the list of data you entered.**
4. **Select Insert ⇨ Tables ⇨ Table.**
5. **Leave the My Table Has Headers checkbox checked in the Create Table dialog box that appears (Figure 19-2), and then click OK.** Excel converts the list to a table, displaying an AutoFilter arrow at the top of each column and displaying the Table Tools, as shown in Figure 19-3.

FIGURE 19-2

Telling Excel where to find the table.

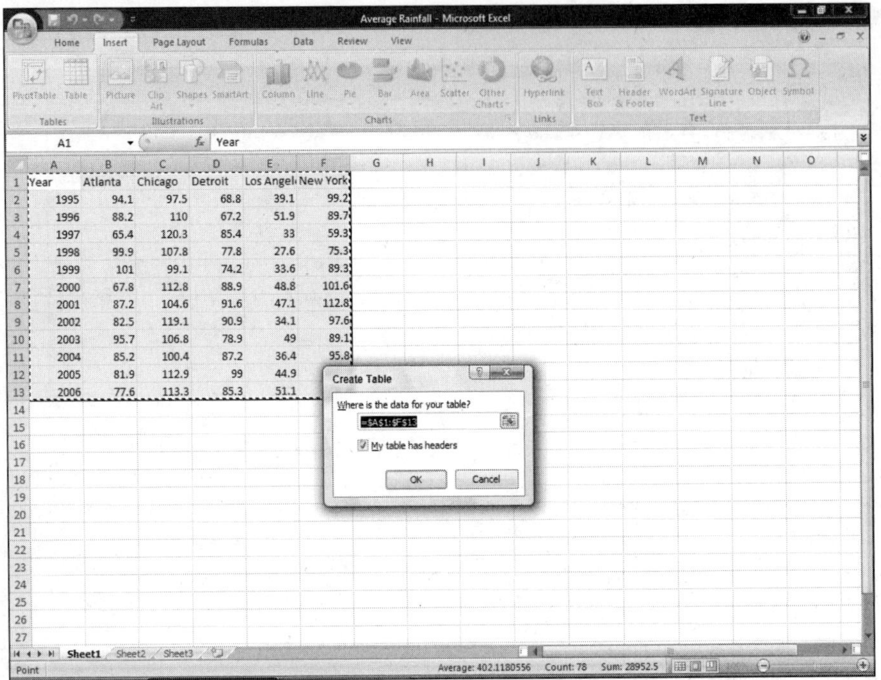

CAUTION You should have only a single database or table on a worksheet. Even though it's physically possible to have more than one, you run a risk of confusing Excel when it comes to manipulating the data or performing other operations like a mail merge. Because you can have multiple worksheets in a workbook, this requirement doesn't pose any kind of practical problem.

NOTE If you stop after Step 2 above, you can still perform operations like sorting the list of data. However, defining the data as a table enables you to take advantage of extra data features in Excel.

FIGURE 19-3

Tools appear for the newly formatted table.

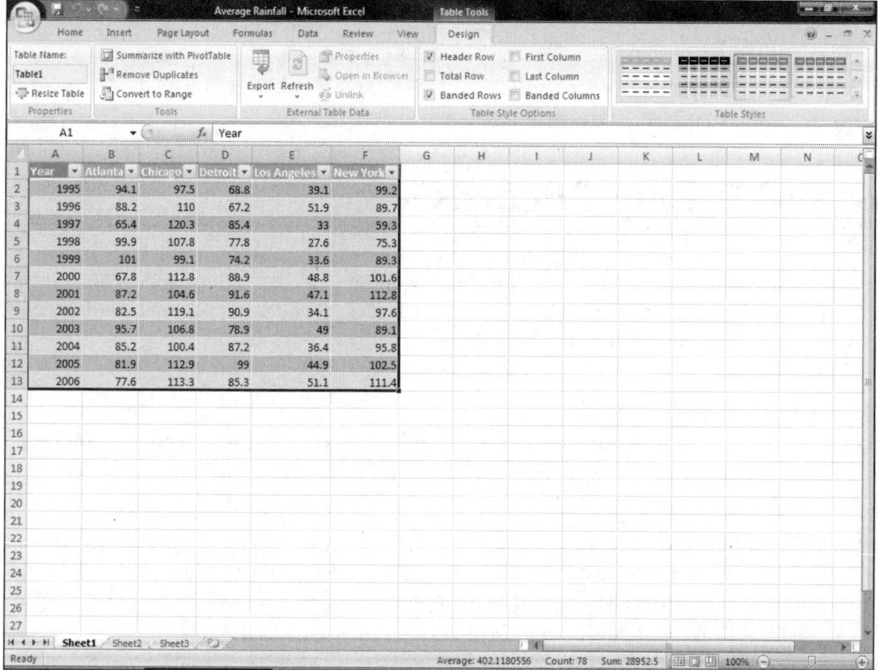

Applying a table format

Excel applies a colorful table style to each new table you define in a workbook file. When you click in any cell in the table and then click the Design tab, the tab offers contextual Table Tools (refer to Figure 19-4) for working with the table. For example, you can click one of the Table Styles choices at the far right to apply new formatting to all the cells in the table.

You can work with the choices in the Table Style Options group, for example, to specify whether the rows in the table are banded (formatted with different colors and rules or not).

The Tools and External Table Data groups offer useful choices such as Convert to Range, which converts a table back to a regular range of text, and Remove Duplicates, for finding duplicate records (rows) and removing the extras.

FIGURE 19-4

You can apply new formatting and more using these Ribbon choices.

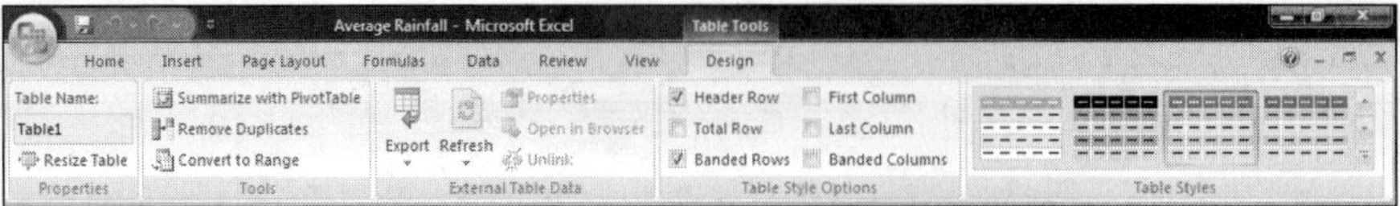

Entering and Editing Records

Over time, any list of data requires changes. Most often, the list of items that you're working with grows over time as you acquire more customers, offer more products, work with more vendors, and so on. Fortunately, the list of data on a worksheet can grow as your needs dictate, and Excel provides a variety of methods for updating and controlling the data in any table.

Using keyboard entry

Plain old keyboard entry, just the same as entering any other worksheet cell data, seems a bit unglamorous and tedious. Still, typing in new records is just part of the bargain when you're maintaining any list of information.

Whenever you type data into the next blank row below a table that you've defined on a worksheet, Excel automatically assumes that you want to add to the table, and so it adjusts the range defined as the table and formats the new record or row using the style applied to the rest of the table. For example, Figure 19-5 shows a new row of data being entered into the table from Figure 19-3.

If you add new row(s) or column(s) of data that aren't automatically included by Excel, you can expand or resize the table. To do so:

1. **Select Design ⇨ Properties ⇨ Resize Table.**
2. **Specify the range that holds the old and new table contents using the Select the New Data Range for Your Table text box of the Resize Table dialog box.**
3. **Click OK.** Excel expands the table to encompass the new range.

FIGURE 19-5

Excel automatically expands the table to encompass any new row you type.

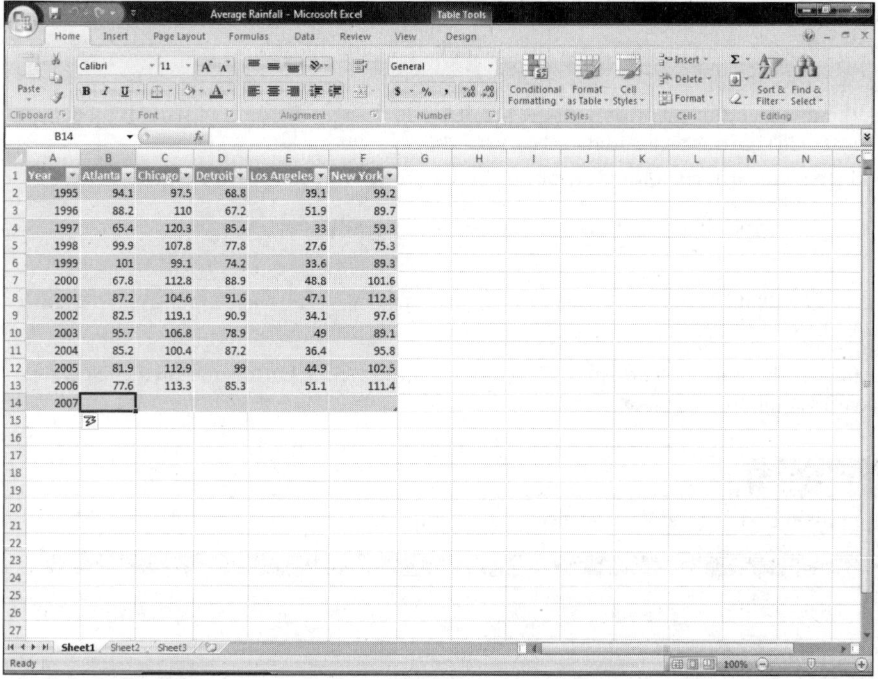

Year	Atlanta	Chicago	Detroit	Los Angeles	New York
1995	94.1	97.5	68.8	39.1	99.2
1996	88.2	110	67.2	51.9	89.7
1997	65.4	120.3	85.4	33	59.3
1998	99.9	107.8	77.8	27.6	75.3
1999	101	99.1	74.2	33.6	89.3
2000	67.8	112.8	88.9	48.8	101.6
2001	87.2	104.6	91.6	47.1	112.8
2002	82.5	119.1	90.9	34.1	97.6
2003	95.7	106.8	78.9	49	89.1
2004	85.2	100.4	87.2	36.4	95.8
2005	81.9	112.9	99	44.9	102.5
2006	77.6	113.3	85.3	51.1	111.4
2007					

Using the data form

Once you've established your basic database or table, you can use the data form to delete or edit data in any field of any record. You also can use it to input entirely new records.

As Chapter 13 explained, you have to add a button for the data form to the Quick Access toolbar in order to use the form. You add the button by customizing the Quick Access toolbar. To do so, right-click the toolbar and then click Customize Quick Access toolbar. Select Commands Not in the Ribbon from the Choose Commands from drop-down list, scroll down, click Form, click Add, and then click OK.

To use the data form, follow these steps:

1. **Select any cell within the list or table.** (The list need not be defined as a table. It need only have a header row to identify the name of each field.) This cell can be within a record or within the field labels on the top row, just as long as it's not outside the list or table.
2. **Click the Form button on the Quick Access toolbar.** Figure 19-6 shows this button, and the resulting form that appears.
3. **Click the down and/or up arrows on the scroll bar to display the desired record, then edit text box (field) entries as desired.**
4. **To add a new record, click the New button and then type the new field entries.**

Pressing the Esc key when no changes have been made will close the form.

You can walk through the entire database by repeatedly pressing Enter without entering any new data.

5. **To permanently remove the displayed record, click the Delete button and then click OK in the confirmation message box (Figure 19-7).**

FIGURE 19-6

You can use this form to add information to a list or table.

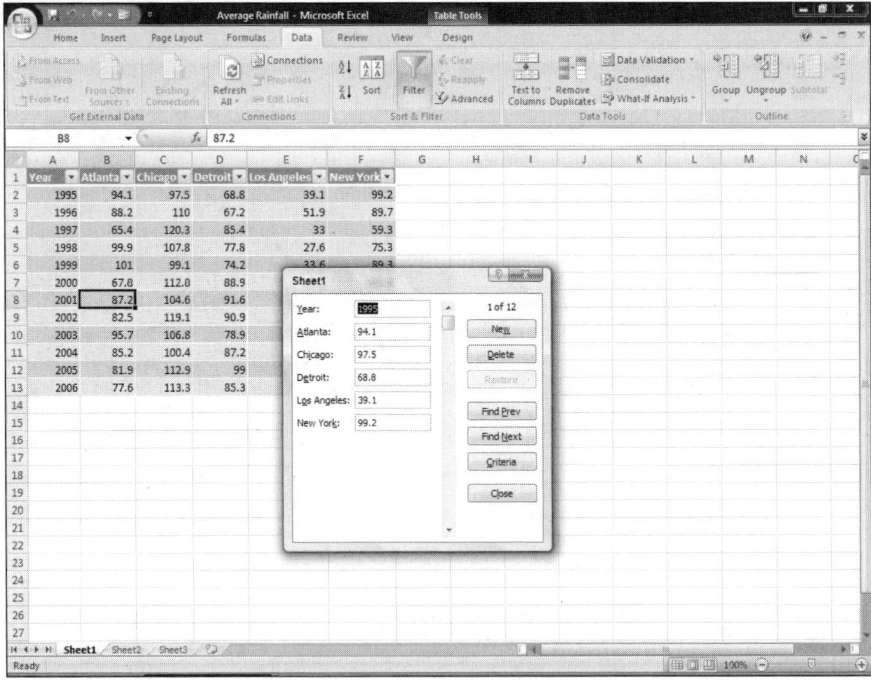

FIGURE 19-7

Confirm that you want to delete the record, when prompted.

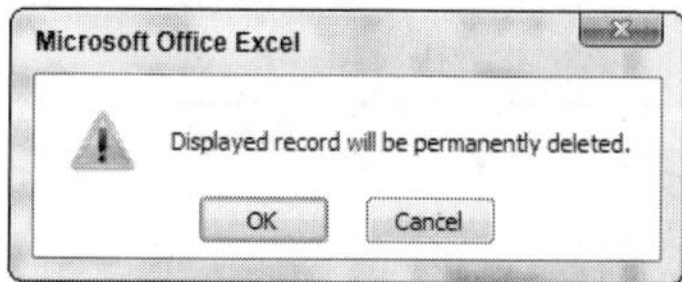

6. **Click Close to close the form dialog box when you finish.**

CAUTION **When you delete a record from the database with the form's Delete button, the warning message isn't kidding about its being permanently gone. You can't even use Undo to reverse the action the way you can with other actions.**

Data validation parameters

As in prior versions, Excel 2007 enables you to set up data validation that you can use to ensure that accurate values are entered in a list or table. For example, you can specify that a field can only hold a whole number between two other values, or a date after a particular point in time.

To set values and parameters for data validation, follow these steps:

1. **Click the column heading (column letter) for the field you want to apply the data validation to.**
2. Select Data ➪ Data Tools ➪ Data Validation from the Ribbon.
3. Click the Settings tab in the Data Validation dialog box (see Figure 19-8).

FIGURE 19-8

This dialog box enables you to specify what entries are "legal" for a table field.

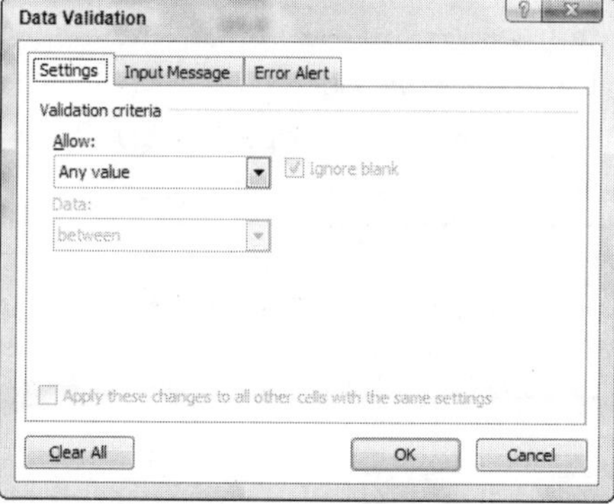

4. **Choose from one of the values under Allow (for a description of these values, see Table 19-1).**

TABLE 19-1

Value Settings for Data Validation

Allowed Value	Meaning
Any Value	No restrictions
Whole Number	Restricted to numbers without decimals
Decimal	Restricted to numbers, but allows decimals
List	Restricted to a preset list of options
Date	Restricted to calendar data
Time	Restricted to clock data
Text Length	Restricted to specified length
Custom	Restricted to custom formula

5. **Choose from one of the options under Data (described in Table 19-2).** The Data field is disabled for some of the Allow options.

TABLE 19-2

Options for Data Validation Values

Option	Meaning
Between	The value must fall between minimum and maximum values.
Not between	The value must not be between the specified values.
Equal to	The value must be the same as the specified value.
Not equal to	The value must not be the specified value.
Greater than	The value must be more than the specified value.
Less than	The value must be less than the specified value.
Greater than or equal to	The value must be the same as or more than the specified value.
Less than or equal to	The value must be the same as or less than the specified value.

6. **The parameters displayed depend on the options chosen under Allow and Data.** Enter the parameters for the restrictions. In many cases, these are simply minimum and/or maximum values, such as the lowest and highest numbers or the earliest and latest dates allowed.
7. **Click the OK button to finish.**

CAUTION **The Clear All button on the bottom of the Data Validation dialog box doesn't just clear the entries on the currently selected tab. It clears all the entries on all three tabs. Don't use it unless you mean to do that. If you click Clear All by mistake, clicking Cancel will restore the cleared values if they were previously entered and accepted.**

List, text length, and custom values

Three of the value options listed in Table 19-1 require further explanation. The List option draws from a predefined list of values. You can type them in directly under Source (separated by commas), or you can specify a range of cells in that space that contain the list of acceptable entries. Text length, despite the name, does not require that it be applied to text. You can also specify the length of a number with it. (In other words, you can specify the number of digits in a number.) The Custom setting limits the entry to anything that fits a formula you've designed. As with the List parameters, you can either type it in directly (under Formula), or specify a cell reference that contains the formula.

Error messages

Any time you set validation parameters (anything other than All Values), an error message will be generated if inappropriate values are entered. The default error message has a title of simply "Microsoft Excel" and is so general as to be virtually meaningless — "The value you entered is not valid. A user has restricted values that can be entered into this cell." To change this, follow these steps:

1. **Select the column heading for the field you want to create an error message for.**
2. **Select Data ➪ Data Tools ➪ Data Validation from the Ribbon.**
3. **Click the Error Alert tab (see Figure 19-9).**

FIGURE 19-9

Set up validation error messages on this tab.

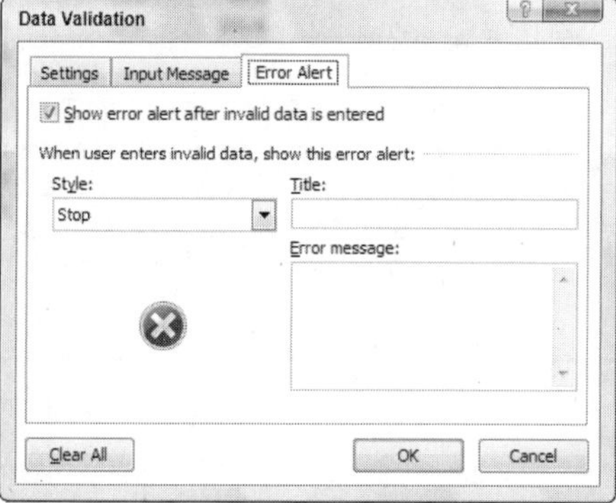

4. **Choose the desired type of warning from the Style drop-down list: Stop, Warning, and Information.** Stop is the default, and presents a red circle with a white X in the middle of it when an error occurs. Warning shows a yellow triangle with a black exclamation point in the middle, and Information shows a dialog balloon with a blue "i" in the middle. Each of the three gives you the option to enter the title and text of the error message, or both. If you do not specify one of them, it will remain at the default setting. The three differ as follows:
   - The Stop error message presents Retry and Cancel buttons (see Figure 19-10). The effect of both is identical, with only a small technical difference. The Retry button highlights the erroneous entry, meaning that anything you type will replace it. The Cancel button deletes the erroneous entry, also leaving you free to type a new one.

FIGURE 19-10

The Stop error message.

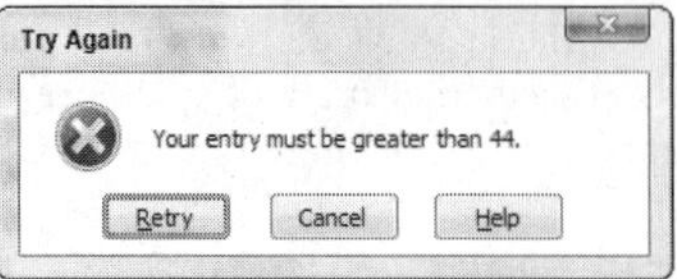

- The Warning error message presents three options: Yes, No, and Cancel buttons (see Figure 19-11). Clicking the Yes button enters the erroneous value even though it's supposed to be excluded. Clicking the No button is identical to clicking the Retry button for the Stop error message — it highlights the erroneous entry so you can type a new one. The Cancel button, once again, simply deletes the erroneous entry and leaves the cell selected, so you can type a new entry if you want to or move on.

FIGURE 19-11

The Warning error message.

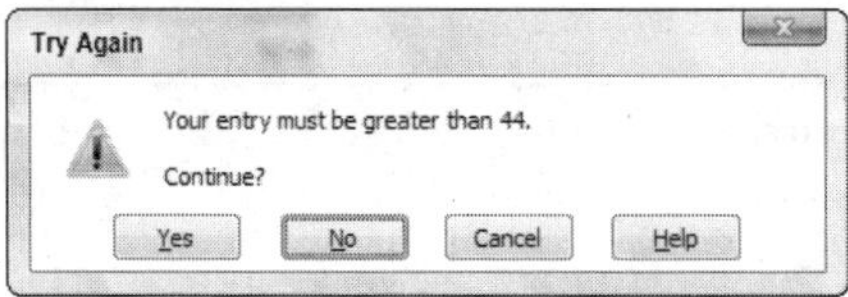

- The Information error message presents only OK and Cancel buttons (see Figure 19-12). Clicking the OK button enters the erroneous value, whereas clicking the Cancel button deletes the erroneous entry and leaves the cell selected.

FIGURE 19-12

The Information error message.

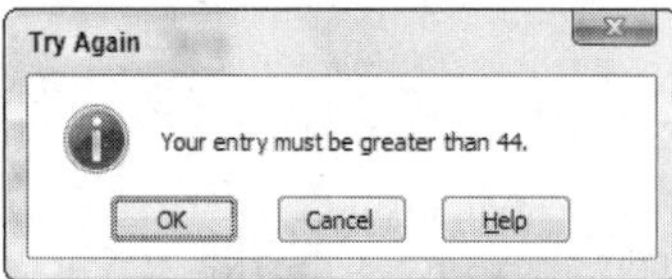

5. **Click the OK button to complete the process.**

Cell input messages

Cell input messages are not an integral part of the data-validation process but a fairly frivolous add-on. These messages are displayed whenever a cell containing them is selected. Although they can be used to say things like, "Enter such and such a value in this cell," the purpose of the cell should already be obvious from the field label. If it isn't, give some serious thought to rewriting your field labels.

In actual practice, cell input messages have limited utility and tend mainly to simply obscure part of the database from view. If you must use them, use them sparingly, or you will find that they make the database totally unworkable. However, in some cases they can serve to help bullet-proof your worksheets, as in the example in Figure 19-13.

To create a cell input message, follow these steps:

1. **Select either the column heading for the field or the individual cell you want to apply the data validation to.**
2. **Select Data ➪ Data Tools ➪ Data Validation from the Ribbon.**
3. **Click the Input Message tab.**
4. **Enter the Title and Input Message text for the error message.** If you do not specify the text, no message will appear, even if you do specify a title. If you do specify a title, the title will show in the first line of the message in bold print.
5. **Click the OK button to complete the process.**

FIGURE 19-13

A cell input message.

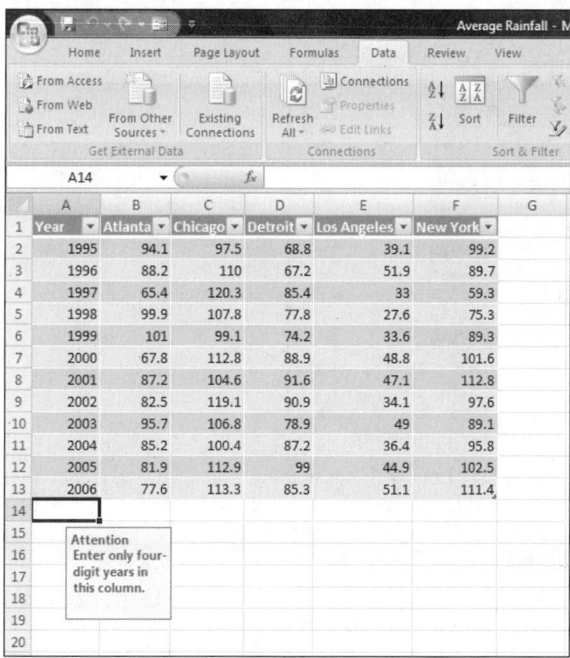

Sorting and Filtering Data

The order in which you enter the records in your database doesn't ultimately matter, because you can sort and filter the table after the fact. Sorting simply changes the order in which the rows or records are displayed, whereas filtering creates a display of only those rows or records that fit criteria you have specified.

Sorting data

The easiest way to sort is to simply select any cell in the column you want to sort by and then click either the Sort Ascending or Sort Descending buttons in the Sort * Filter group of the Data tab on the Ribbon. The Sort Ascending button sorts from A to Z (it's the one with A on top and Z on the bottom). Technically speaking, it sorts from zero to Z, but that wouldn't make as good an icon. The Sort Descending button sorts from Z to A (okay, Z to zero), and it's the one with Z on top and A on the bottom. Figure 19-14 shows data sorted in descending order by year.

FIGURE 19-14

Sort the list or table to change its order.

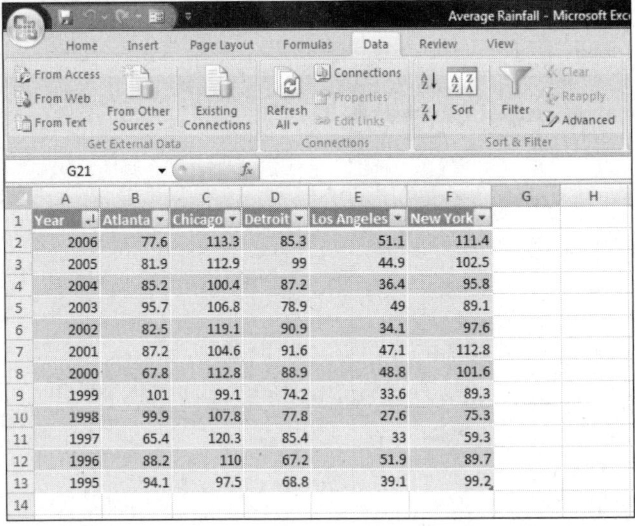

Year	Atlanta	Chicago	Detroit	Los Angeles	New York
2006	77.6	113.3	85.3	51.1	111.4
2005	81.9	112.9	99	44.9	102.5
2004	85.2	100.4	87.2	36.4	95.8
2003	95.7	106.8	78.9	49	89.1
2002	82.5	119.1	90.9	34.1	97.6
2001	87.2	104.6	91.6	47.1	112.8
2000	67.8	112.8	88.9	48.8	101.6
1999	101	99.1	74.2	33.6	89.3
1998	99.9	107.8	77.8	27.6	75.3
1997	65.4	120.3	85.4	33	59.3
1996	88.2	110	67.2	51.9	89.7
1995	94.1	97.5	68.8	39.1	99.2

The drawback to this method, as with so many things that are simple to use, is that it lacks real power. Often, you'll find that you need to sort by more than one column. For instance, you might need to sort a customer database by both state and product ordered so you can determine which products are selling best in which states. Or you might want to sort the weather database by year and temperature.

To sort by multiple columns, follow these steps:

1. **Select any cell in the list or table.**
2. **Select Data ➪ Sort & Filter ➪ Sort in the Ribbon.** If you failed to select a cell in the database, Excel will tell you it can't find it. In that case, go back to Step 1.
3. **Specify sort levels in the Sort dialog box (see Figure 19-15).** Click the Add Level button to specify each new sort level, then use the Column, Sort On, and Order drop-down lists to specify the field, type of cell information, and sort order for the sort.

FIGURE 19-15

Use this dialog box to set up a more advanced sort.

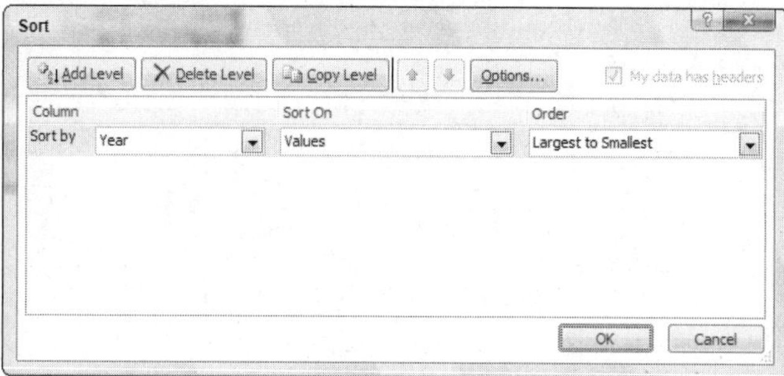

4. **Click the OK button to apply the sort.**

Filtering data

Filtering your data is much more powerful than simply sorting it. Instead of being limited to three columns as you are for a sort, you can filter on any or all columns in your table. Filtering removes from view any record that doesn't match your criteria (but not from the database or worksheet). When you're done, you can restore all the records to view. The AutoFilter feature in Excel enables you to apply the filtering. To filter your data, follow these steps:

1. **Select any cell in the database.**
2. **Select Data ➪ Sort & Filter ➪ Filter from the Ribbon.** By default, the field (column) names for any table that you've designated already include AutoFilter buttons for filtering the data, so you can skip this step.
3. **To filter by an entry in a field, click the column's AutoFilter drop-down arrow, and then click the to check the entry to match.** Figure 19-16 shows an AutoFilter drop-down menu. If needed, you can click the Select All choice to clear all the checks, and then click a single check box to filter by that value.

FIGURE 19-16

AutoFiltering.

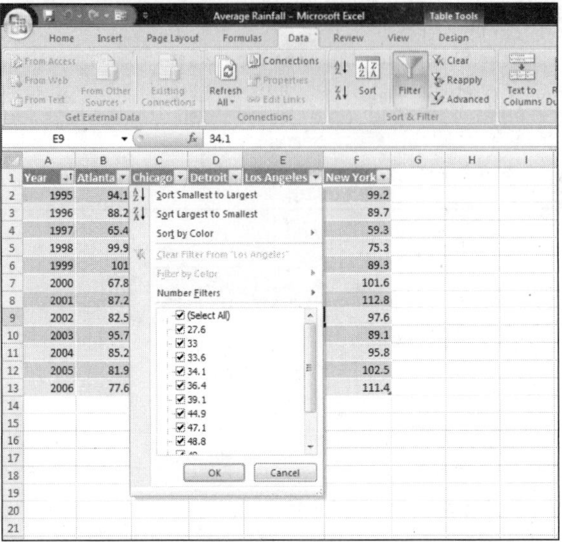

4. **To create a more general filter, click the Number Filters choice, click one of the choices in the submenu that appears (Figure 19-17), specify the filter criteria in the Custom AutoFilter dialog box that appears (Figure 19-18), and then click OK to apply the filter.** The field name appears in the dialog box, with the comparison operator you selected from the submenu already specified, as well. You can either select a value from the drop-down list on the right or type in a value of your own.
5. **Specify another criterion if desired.** When you add a second criterion for filtering, you have the option of using either a logical And or logical Or. With And, both criteria must be true; with Or, either criterion can be true. Click either the And or the Or radio button to select it.
6. **Click OK to implement the filtering.**

FIGURE 19-17

This submenu offers choices for creating a custom AutoFilter.

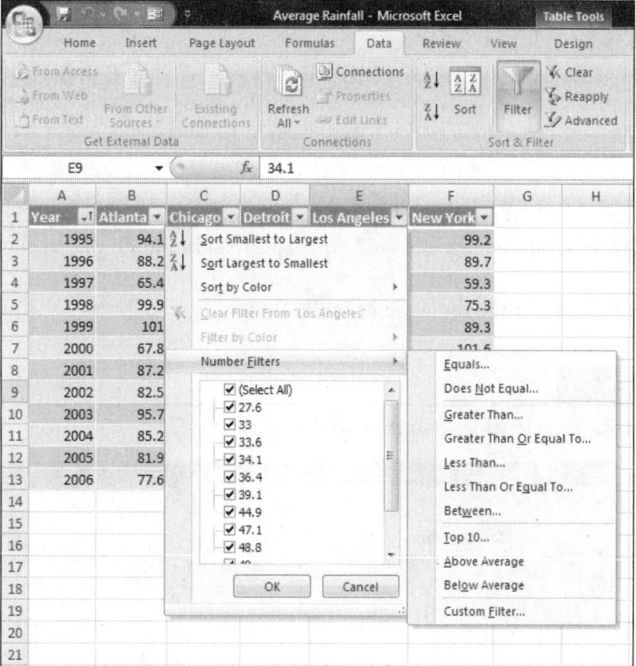

FIGURE 19-18

Specify the Custom AutoFilter criteria here.

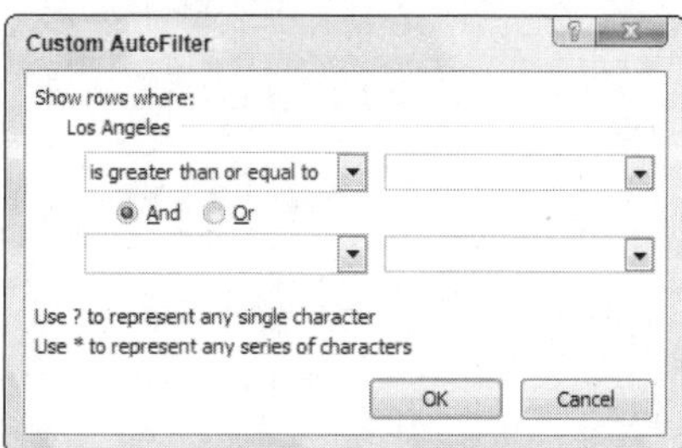

To remove the filtering so that all the rows are visible, either select Clear Filters From from the drop-down-menus of each filtered field or select Data ➪ Sort & Filter ➪ Clear in the Ribbon. To turn off AutoFilter, select Data ➪ Sort & Filter ➪ Filter from the Ribbon.

Subtotaling data

Excel's subtotal feature is accessed via the Data tab of the Ribbon and is used with a sorted list. It's not useful for every single type of database you can create, but only for those in which values can be kept track of for specific, repeated factors. Figure 19-19, for example, shows a database of sales people, which includes their monthly sales totals.

To subtotal a database, such as subtotaling the sales totals in this example by salesperson, follow these steps:

1. **Sort the database or table by the field you want to subtotal.** In this case, that would be the Salesperson field.
2. **Select any cell within the database or table.**

FIGURE 19-19

A sales database list to which subtotals will be applied.

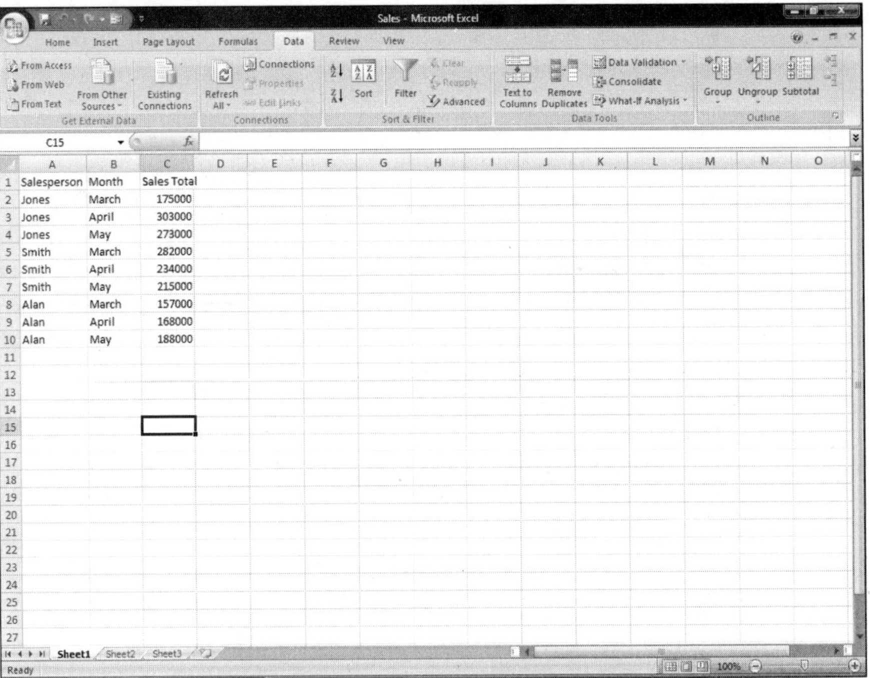

3. **Select Data ➪ Outline ➪ Subtotal from the Ribbon.**
4. **In the Subtotal dialog box, click the drop-down list labeled At Each Change In and select the field that you want to subtotal, as shown in the example in Figure 19-20.**

FIGURE 19-20

Set up the subtotaling here.

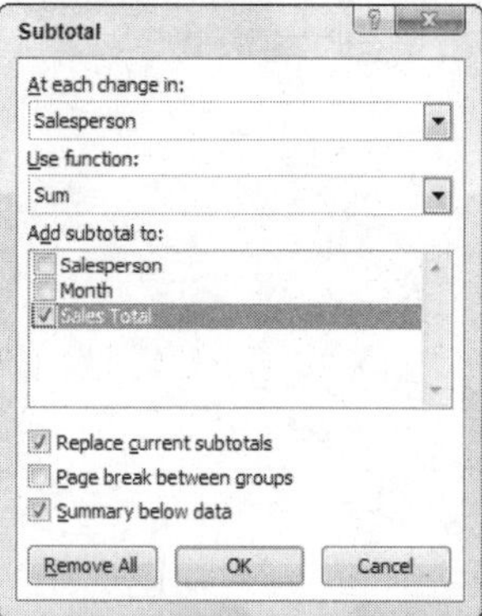

5. **Select a function from the Use Function drop-down list.** The functions listed in the drop-down list are the names of worksheet functions, some of which you learned about in earlier chapters. The available functions are as follows:
   - Sum
   - Count
   - Average
   - Max
   - Min
   - Product
   - Count Numbers
   - StdDev
   - StdDevp
   - Var
   - Varp
6. **Select the fields for which you want to show subtotals in the Add Subtotal To area.**
7. **Click the OK button.** The subtotals appear in the list or table, as in the example shown in Figure 19-21.

FIGURE 19-21

Database with subtotals added.

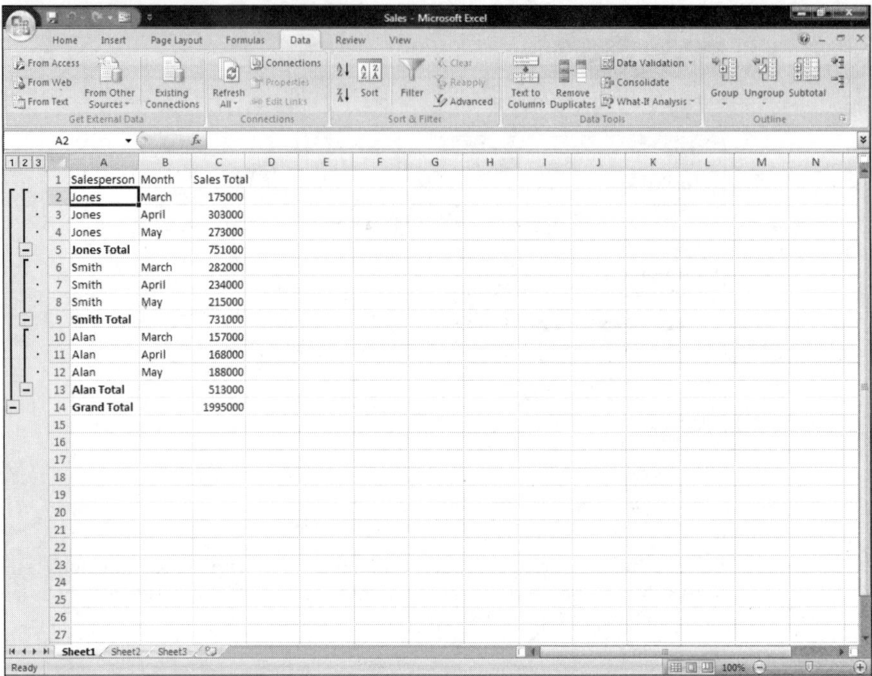

	Salesperson	Month	Sales Total
2	Jones	March	175000
3	Jones	April	303000
4	Jones	May	273000
5	**Jones Total**		751000
6	Smith	March	282000
7	Smith	April	234000
8	Smith	May	215000
9	**Smith Total**		731000
10	Alan	March	157000
11	Alan	April	168000
12	Alan	May	188000
13	**Alan Total**		513000
14	**Grand Total**		1995000

You can shrink the database so that only the subtotals show by clicking the minus signs to the left of the records.

To remove the subtotals, you can either click the Undo button immediately after adding the subtotals or select Data ➪ Outline ➪ Subtotal from the Ribbon, and then click the Remove All button.

Using Excel Data in a Mail Merge

To use Excel data in a mail merge in Microsoft Word, you select the Excel file holding the database or table as the recipient list (use the Select Recipients button in the Start Mail Merge group on the Mailings tab in Word) during the merge process. The Select Table dialog box, shown in Figure 19-22, prompts you to specify which worksheet in the file holds the database list or table. Click the sheet, and then click OK.

You can then use the choices in the Write & Insert Fields group (Figure 19-23) on the Mailings tab in Word to insert fields from the database.

FIGURE 19-22

Click the sheet that holds the database or table.

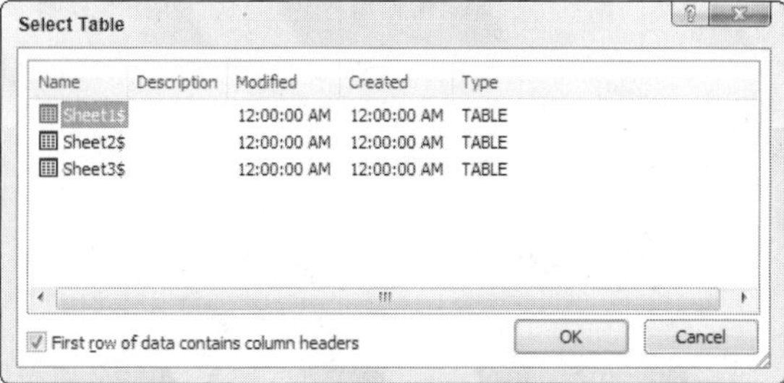

FIGURE 19-23

Inserting fields from the Excel database for a merge.

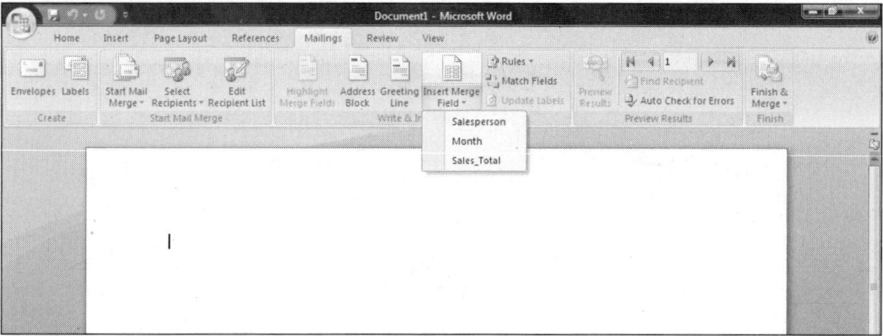

CROSS-REF For more information on mail merge, see Chapter 10.

Summary

In this chapter, you learned how to create and manipulate databases (lists) and tables in Excel. The chapter showed you how to enter information the right way so that you can use it as a database or table, how to set up a table, and how to change table formatting. You also learned how to sort, filter, and subtotal a database or table, as well as how to use the database table in a Word mail merge.

Part IV

Persuading and Informing with PowerPoint

IN THIS PART

Chapter 20

A First Look at PowerPoint 2007

IN THIS CHAPTER

A *presentation* is any kind of interaction between a speaker and audience, but it usually involves one or more of the following visual aids: 35mm slides, overhead transparencies, computer-based slides (either local or at a Web site or other network location), hard-copy handouts, and speaker notes. PowerPoint 2007 can create all of these types of visual aids, plus many other types that you learn about as we go along.

In this chapter you'll get a big-picture introduction to PowerPoint 2007, and then we'll fire up the program and poke around a bit to help you get familiar with the interface.

What's New in PowerPoint 2007?

Like other programs in the Office 2007 suite, PowerPoint 2007 takes a radical and innovative new approach to its user interface. Although it's very convenient to use once you master it, even experienced users of earlier versions might need some help getting started. Here's a quick summary of the new features you'll encounter.

Tabs and the Ribbon

Instead of using a complex menu system, PowerPoint 2007 relies on a graphical *Ribbon* with multiple tabbed pages (referred to as *tabs*). Each tab is like a toolbar, with buttons and lists you can select or open.

Tabs are not easily customizable as toolbars were in earlier versions, but the *Quick Access Toolbar* provides a home for any custom buttons or shortcuts you would like to keep readily available. You can add almost any button or command to the Quick Access Toolbar by right-clicking it and choosing Add to Quick Access Toolbar.

Office (File) menu

One menu remains: the Microsoft Office menu (abbreviated in this book as *Office menu*). You can access it by clicking the Microsoft Office Button (again, abbreviated in this book as *Office Button*), the big round button in the top-left corner of the screen.

The commands on the Office menu are for working with the file itself: saving, printing, opening, closing, and so on. These commands were on the File menu in earlier PowerPoint versions (and in fact, some people actually still call the Office menu the "File menu").

Styles for graphics and text

If you've worked with Microsoft Word, you are probably familiar with the concept of styles. A *style* is a saved formatting specification that you can apply to multiple blocks of text in Word, to ensure consistency. For example, to ensure that all of your headings are formatted the same way, apply a Heading style to each one.

PowerPoint 2007 extends the concept of styles to cover graphic objects such as pictures, drawn lines, and shapes as well as text. For example, suppose you want each photo to have a beveled edge effect; you can simply apply a picture style that contains the desired edge type to each picture. No more manual formatting of multiple graphic objects!

Styles are found in various parts of PowerPoint, depending on the object type. For example, Figure 20-1 shows the Picture Styles section of the Format tab, available when a picture is selected. Shape Styles (for drawn lines and shapes) and WordArt Styles (for text) are also available.

FIGURE 20-1

You can apply styles to easily and consistently format graphic objects.

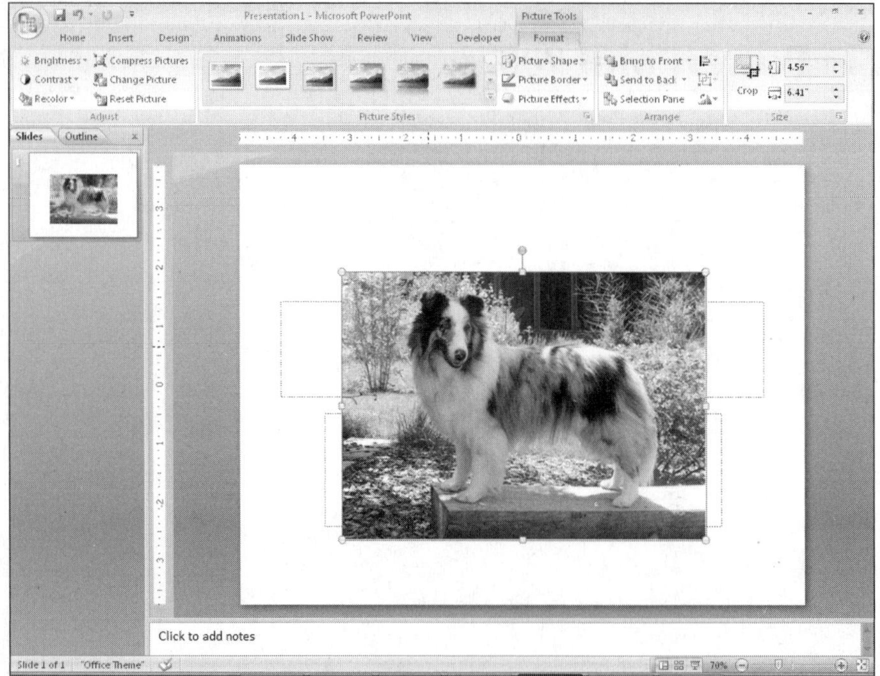

More drawing and photo formatting choices

Drawn objects (formerly called AutoShapes, now called Office Art graphics) are much improved in PowerPoint 2007. You can not only apply basic colors and fills to them, but you can add shadows, glows, surfaces, and 3-D tilt and rotation. In earlier versions, the 3-D option simply enabled you to extend perspective to create "sides" on a flat object. In PowerPoint 2007, the 3-D option now enables you to tilt the entire object. Figure 20-2 shows examples of some of the new effects.

All of the new effects for drawn objects can also be applied to the borders of other graphics, such as imported pictures. There are also some new tools for working with photos, including applying a tint to a picture and changing the shape of the photo frame.

More text formatting options

PowerPoint 2007 adds several new text formatting capabilities to help users further polish their work. For example, you can now control character spacing and kerning, use different underline styles and colors, and make all characters in a line equal height.

Perhaps the most significant improvement in text formatting, however, is the ability to format any text using the full range of WordArt formatting tools. WordArt (a.k.a. shaped text) has been around in Office programs for years, but there has always been a strict differentiation between regular text and WordArt. Regular text (that is, text appearing in the presentation outline) could not receive WordArt formatting such as reshaping, stretching, and distortion.

FIGURE 20-2

Many more effects are available for drawn lines and shapes.

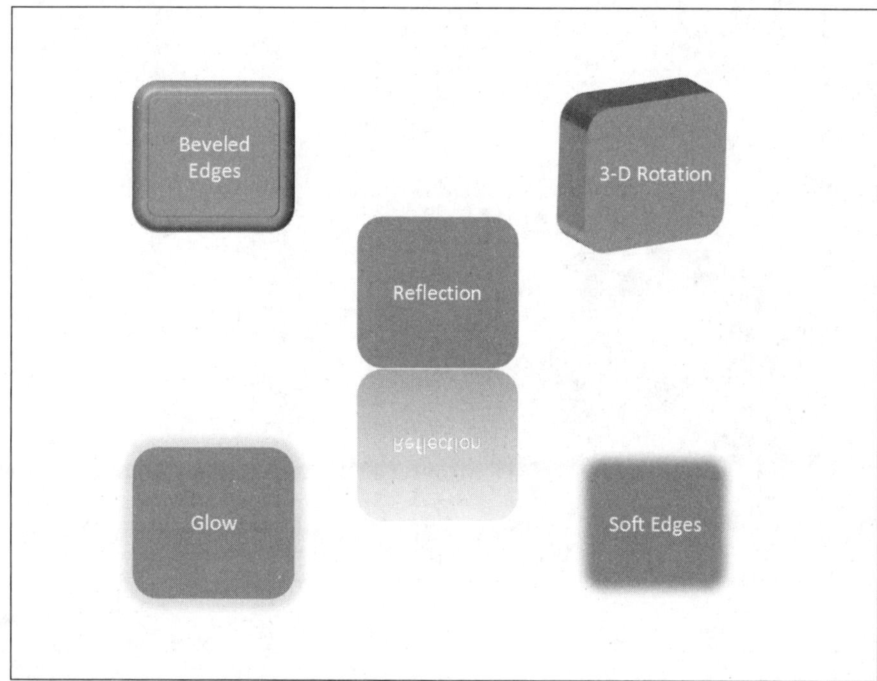

PowerPoint 2007 loses the differentiation between WordArt text and regular text, so the full gamut of formatting features are available to all text, regardless of position or usage. You can format individual words as separate pieces of WordArt, or entire text boxes by using a common WordArt style. In Figure 20-3, the slide title "Green Hill Shelties" is regular text, and appears on the presentation outline, but it also benefits from WordArt formatting effects.

Color, font, and effect themes

Styles can automate the formatting of individual objects, but you can also apply overall themes to the entire presentation to change all of the formatting at once. A *theme* is a set of formatting specifications that are applied to objects and text consistently throughout the presentation (except in cases where an object has manual formatting applied that overrides the theme).

There are three elements to a theme: the colors, the fonts, and the effects. Colors are applied via a set of placeholders, as they were in PowerPoint 2003, but now you can apply tints or shades of a color much more easily. Whenever you open a list or menu that contains a color picker, you select from a palette like the one in Figure 20-4. The top row contains swatches for the colors in the current theme, and beneath them are various tints (lighter versions) and shades (darker versions) of the colors. By applying theme colors instead of fixed colors, you enable objects to change color automatically when you switch to a different theme.

FIGURE 20-3

WordArt can now be applied to regular text, including slide titles.

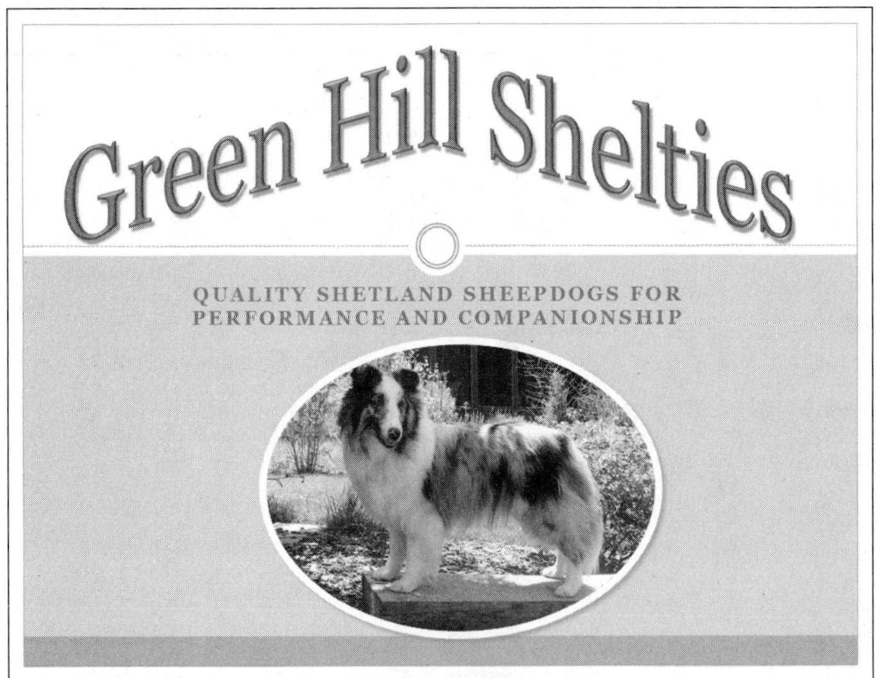

FIGURE 20-4

Choose colors for text and graphic objects from a color picker that focuses on theme-based color choices.

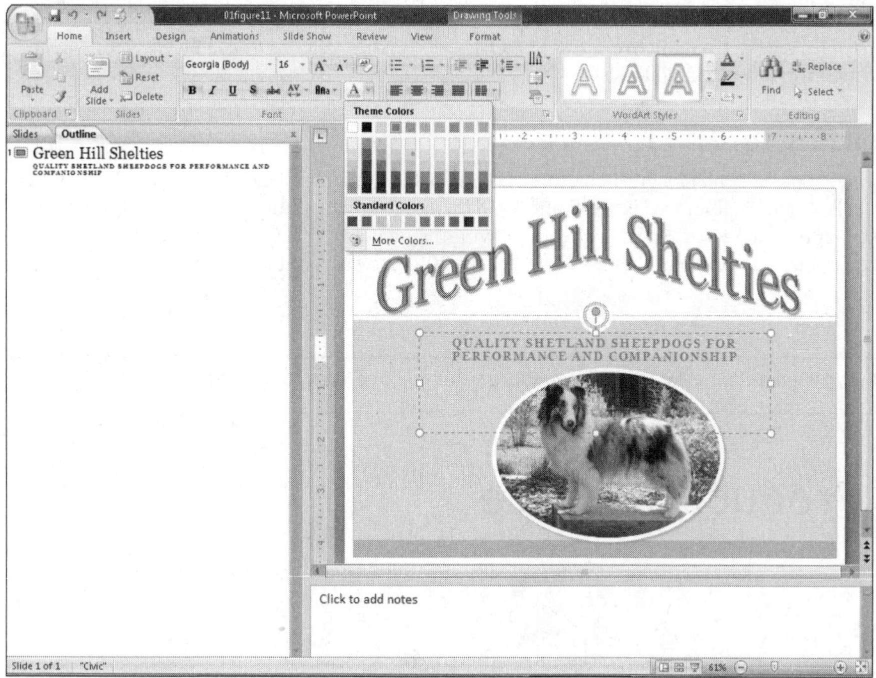

Font themes apply one font for headings and another for body text. In PowerPoint 2007 it is usually best not to apply a specific font to any text, but instead to apply either (Body) or (Heading) to it. Then you can let the font theme dictate the font choices, so that they will update automatically when you chose a different theme. On the Font drop-down list, the top choices are now (Body) and (Heading). The font listed next to them is the font that happens to be applied with the current theme.

Effect themes apply shadows and 3-D effects to graphic objects. PowerPoint 2007's new gallery of effects are impressive, and can make plain lines and shapes appear to pop off the screen with textures that simulate glass, metal, or other surfaces.

CROSS-REF For more on font themes, see Chapter 22.

SmartArt

SmartArt uses groups of lines and shapes to present text information in a graphical, conceptually meaningful way. Experts have been saying for years that people respond better to information when it is presented graphically, but the difficulty in constructing attractive diagrams has meant that most people used plain bulleted lists for everything. SmartArt can convert a bulleted list into a conceptual diagram in just a few clicks.

Figure 20-5 shows a plain bulleted list (left) and a SmartArt diagram constructed from it. The SmartArt is not only more interesting to look at, but it also conveys additional information — it shows that the product life cycle repeats continuously.

NOTE **SmartArt is similar to the Diagrams feature found in PowerPoint 2003, but is based on a new graphics engine from Microsoft called Escher 2.0. (Charts also use this same graphics engine, and share the same formatting capabilities.)**

Better charting tools

In earlier Office versions, Excel had a great charting feature, but the other applications suffered along with an inferior tool called Microsoft Graph. PowerPoint 2007 includes a great, all-new charting tool, the same one that's in Excel 2007. Like SmartArt, it is integrated with the new Escher 2.0 graphics engine, and you can format the charts with a variety of theme effects. Figure 20-6 shows a typical chart.

FIGURE 20-5

SmartArt diagrams are easy to create and make information more palatable and easy to understand.

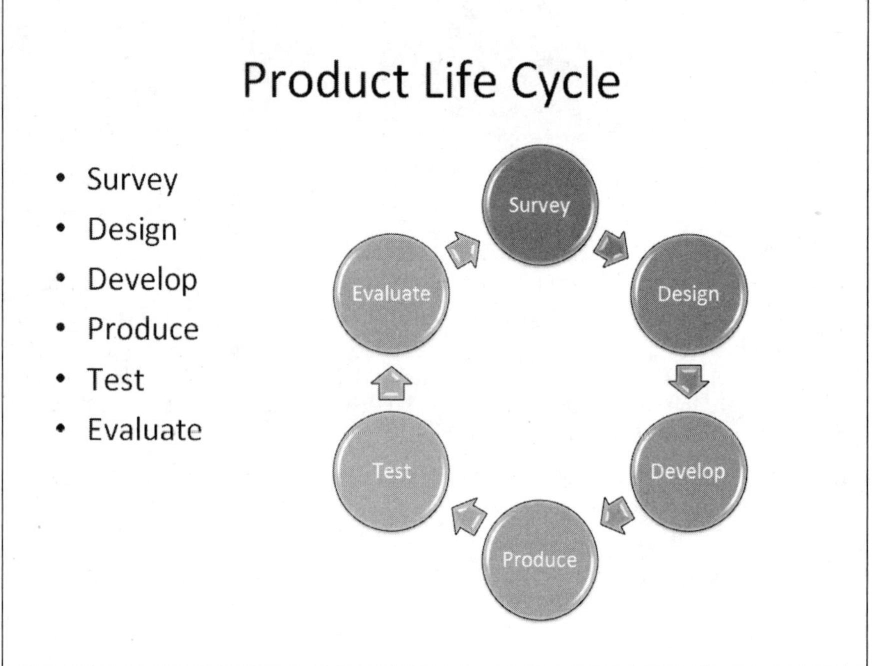

FIGURE 20-6

You can construct charts more easily with better formatting and layout options in PowerPoint 2007.

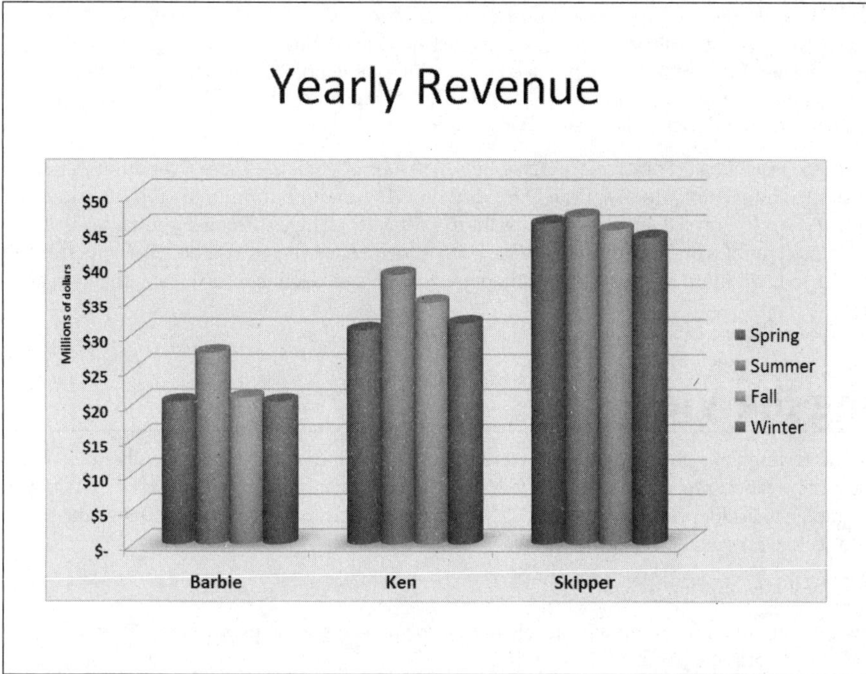

Custom slide layouts

In earlier versions of PowerPoint, you were stuck with the slide layouts that came with PowerPoint. In PowerPoint 2007, you can create your own slide layouts, complete with content placeholders, and apply them as easily as you can apply the built-in ones. This makes it easy to reuse complex layouts without having to resort to manually created text frames each time. Custom layouts are configured from within the expanded and improved Slide Master view.

Starting and Exiting PowerPoint

You can start PowerPoint just like any other program in Windows: from the Start menu. Follow these steps:

1. Click the Start button. The Start menu opens.
2. Click All Programs.
3. Click Microsoft Office.
4. Click Microsoft Office PowerPoint 2007. The program starts.

If you have opened PowerPoint before, a shortcut to it might appear in the Recently Used Programs list, which is directly above the All Programs command on the Start menu. If you use other applications more frequently than PowerPoint, PowerPoint may scroll off this list and you therefore have to access it via the All Programs menu.

TIP **If you don't want to worry about PowerPoint scrolling off the list of the most frequently used programs on the Start menu, right-click PowerPoint's name on the Start menu and choose Pin to Start Menu. PowerPoint will then appear on the list at the top of the left column of the Start menu. To remove it from there later, right-click it and choose Unpin from Start Menu.**

When you are ready to leave PowerPoint, select Office Button ➪ Exit or click the Close (X) button in the top-right corner of the PowerPoint window. (The Office button is the round button in the top left corner.) If you have any unsaved work, PowerPoint asks if you want to save your changes. Because you have just been playing around in this chapter, you probably do not have anything to save yet. (If you do have something to save, see Chapter 21 to learn more about saving.) Otherwise, click No to decline to save your changes, and you're outta there.

Changing the View

A *view* is a way of displaying your presentation on-screen. PowerPoint comes with several views because at different times during the creation process, it is helpful to look at the presentation in different ways. For example, when you add a graphic to a slide, you need to work closely with that slide, but when you rearrange the slide order, you need to see the presentation as a whole.

PowerPoint offers the following views:

- **Normal:** A combination of several resizable panes, so you can see the presentation in multiple ways at once. Normal is the default view.
- **Slide Sorter:** A light-table-type overhead view of all the slides in your presentation, laid out in rows, suitable for big-picture rearranging.
- **Notes Page:** A view with the slide at the top of the page and a text box below it for typed notes. (You can print these notes pages to use during your speech.)
- **Slide Show:** The view you use to show the presentation on-screen. Each slide fills the entire screen in its turn.

There are two ways to change a view: click a button on the View tab, or click one of the view buttons in the bottom-right corner of the screen. See Figure 20-7. All of the views are available in both places except Notes Page, which you can access only from the View tab.

TIP **When you save, close, and reopen a file, PowerPoint opens the same view in which you left the file. To have the files always open in a particular view, choose Office Button ➪ PowerPoint Options ➪ Advanced, and open the Open All Documents Using This View list and select the desired view. The options on this list include some custom versions of Normal view that have certain panes turned off. For example, you can open all documents in Normal – Outline and Slide view to always start with the Notes pane turned off.**

FIGURE 20-7

Select a view from the View tab or from the viewing controls in the bottom-right corner of the screen.

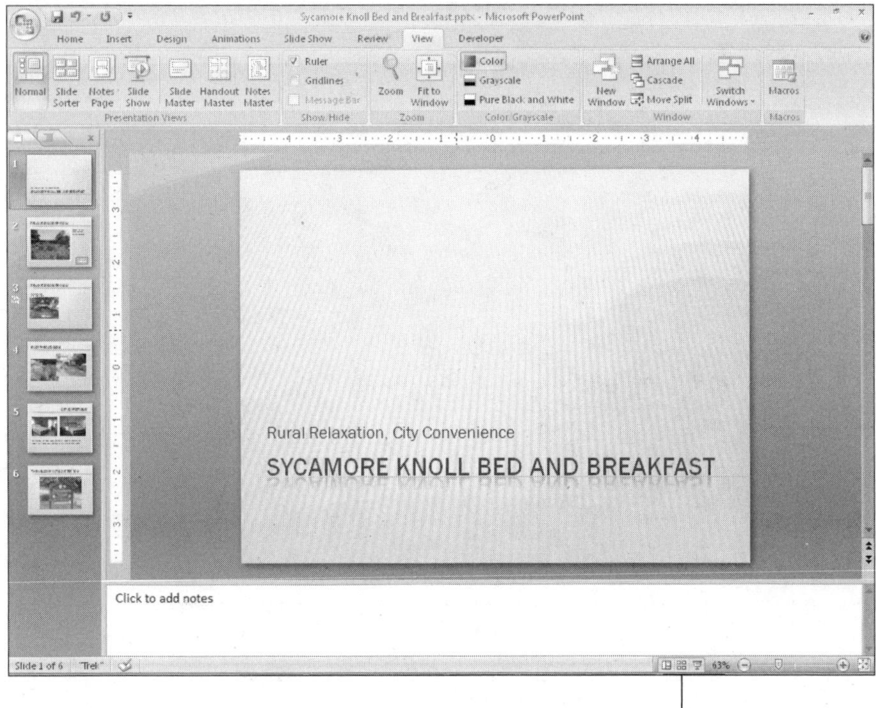

Normal view

Normal view, shown in Figure 20-8, is a very flexible view that contains a little of everything. In the center is the active slide, below it is a Notes pane, and to its left is a dual-use pane with two tabs: Outline and Slides. (Figure 20-7 shows Slides, and Figure 20-8 shows Outline.) When the Outline tab is selected, the text from the slides appears in an outline form. When the Slides tab is selected, thumbnail images of all the slides appear (somewhat like Slide Sorter view, which you will see later in this chapter).

Each of the panes in Normal view has its own scroll bar, so you can move around in the outline, the slide, and the notes independently of the other panes. You can resize the panes by dragging the dividers between the panes. For example, to give the notes area more room, point the mouse pointer at the divider line between it and the slide area so that the mouse pointer becomes a double-headed arrow, and then hold down the left mouse button as you drag the line up to a new spot.

FIGURE 20-8

Normal view, the default, offers access to the outline, the slide, and the notes all at once.

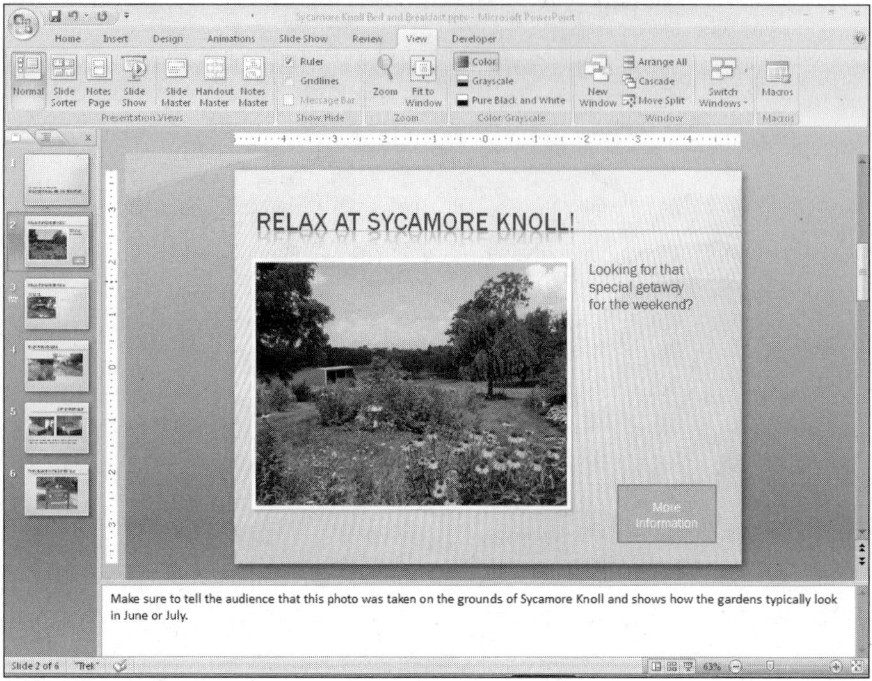

The Slides/Outline pane is useful because it lets you jump quickly to a specific slide by clicking on it. For example, in Figure 20-7 you can click on any of the slide thumbnails on the Slides tab to display it in the Slide pane. Or in Figure 20-8 you can click some text anywhere in the outline to jump to the slide containing that text.

TIP **In earlier versions of PowerPoint, an Outlining toolbar was available when working with the Outline tab. In PowerPoint 2007, you can right-click anywhere in the outline to access some of those same tools on a context menu.**

You can turn the Slides/Outline pane off completely by clicking the X button in its top-right corner. This gives maximum room to the Slides pane. When you turn it off, the Notes pane disappears too; they cannot be turned on/off separately. To get the extra panes back, reapply Normal view.

Slide Sorter view

If you have ever worked with 35mm slides, you know that it can be helpful to lay the slides out on a big table and plan the order in which to show them. You rearrange them, moving this one here, that one there, until the order is perfect. You might even start a pile of backups that you will not show in the main presentation, but will hold back in case someone asks a pertinent question. That's exactly what you can do with Slide Sorter view, shown in Figure 20-9. It lays out the slides in miniature, so you can see the big picture. You can drag the slides around and place them in the perfect order. You can also return to Normal view to work on a slide by double-clicking the slide.

FIGURE 20-9

Use Slide Sorter view for a birds-eye view of the presentation.

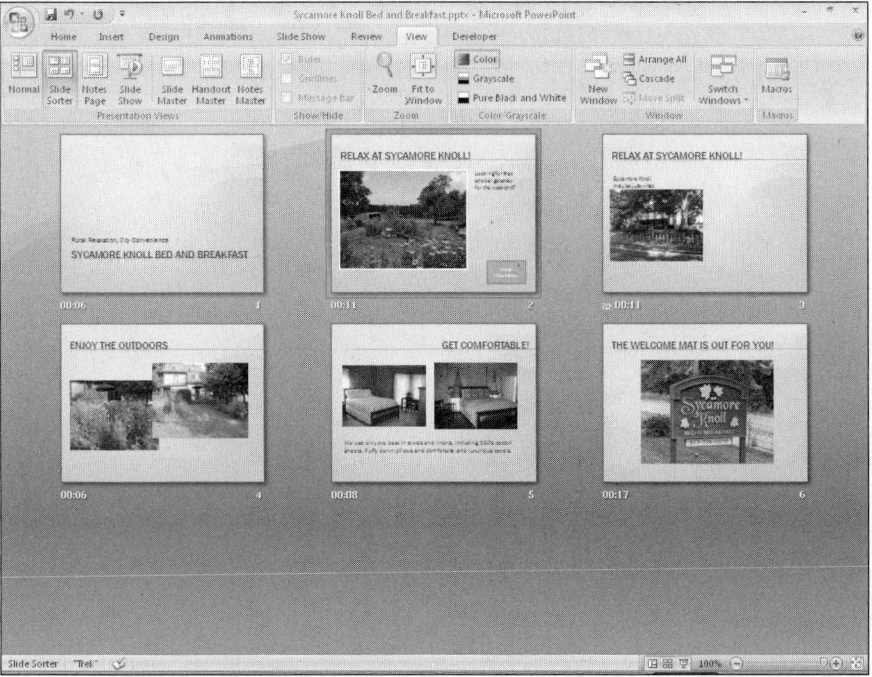

Slide Show view

When it's time to rehearse the presentation, nothing shows you the finished product quite as clearly as Slide Show view does. In Slide Show view (Figure 20-10), the slide fills the entire screen. You can move from slide to slide by pressing the Page Up or Page Down keys, or by using one of the other movement methods available.

CROSS-REF **You learn about these other movement methods in Chapter 26.**

You can right-click in Slide Show view to display a menu that enables you to control the show without leaving it. To leave the slide show, choose End Show from the menu or just press the Esc key.

TIP **When entering Slide Show view, the method you use determines which slide you start on. If you use the Slide Show View button in the bottom-right corner of the screen, the presentation will start with whatever slide you have selected. (You can also press Shift+F5 to do this, or choose Slide Show ⇨ From Current Slide.) If you use the View ⇨ Slide Show or Slide Show ⇨ From Beginning command, or press F5, the presentation will start at the beginning.**

FIGURE 20-10

Slide Show view lets you practice the presentation in real life.

Notes Page view

When you give a presentation, your props usually include more than just your brain and your slides. You typically have all kinds of notes and backup material for each slide — figures on last quarter's sales, sources to cite if someone questions your data, and so on. In the old days of framed overhead transparencies, people used to attach sticky notes to the slide frames for this purpose, and hope that nobody asked any questions that required diving into the four-inch-thick stack of statistics they brought.

Today, you can type your notes and supporting facts directly in PowerPoint. As you saw earlier, you can type them directly into the Notes pane below the slide in Normal view. However, if you have a lot of notes to type, you might find it easier to work with Notes Page view instead.

Notes Page view is accessible only from the View tab. In this view, you see a single slide (uneditable) with a text area, called the *notes placeholder*, below it for your notes. See Figure 20-11. You can refer to these notes as you give an on-screen presentation, or you can print notes pages to stack neatly on the lectern next to you during the big event. If you have trouble seeing the text you're typing, zoom in on it, as described in the next section.

FIGURE 20-11

Notes Page view offers a special text area for your notes, separate from the slides.

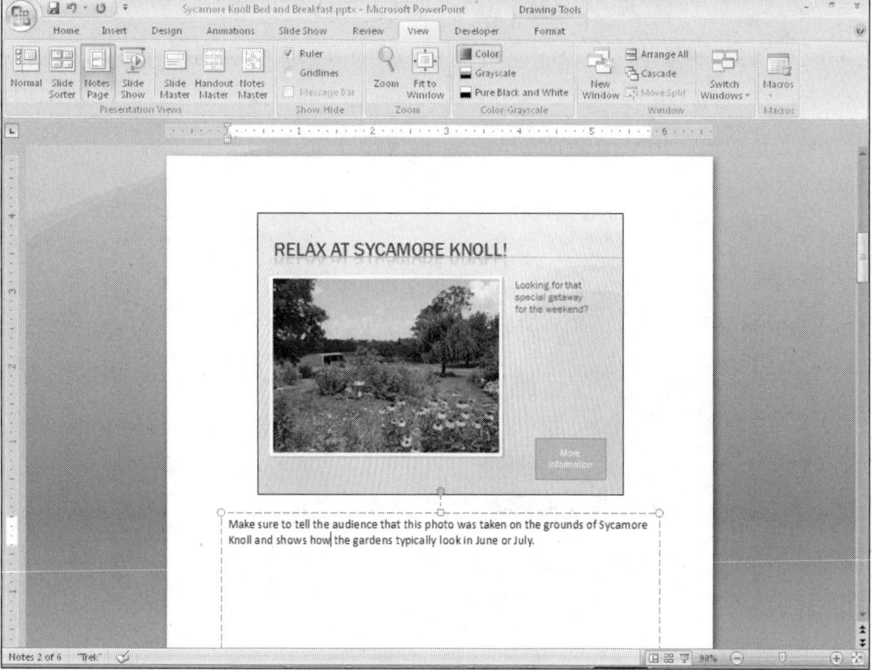

Zooming In and Out

If you need a closer look at your presentation, you can zoom the view in or out to accommodate almost any situation. For example, if you have trouble placing a graphic exactly at the same vertical level as some text in a box next to it, you can zoom in for more precision. You can view your work at various magnifications on-screen without changing the size of the surrounding tools or the size of the print on the printout.

In Normal view, each of the panes has its own individual zoom. To set the zoom for the Slides/Outline pane only, for example, select it first; then choose a zoom level. Or to zoom only in the Slide pane, click it first. In a single-pane view like Notes Page or Slide Sorter, a single zoom setting affects the entire work area.

The larger the zoom number, the larger the details on the display. A zoom of 10% would make a slide so tiny that you couldn't read it. A zoom of 400% would make a few letters on a slide so big they would fill the entire pane.

The easiest way to set the zoom level is to drag the Zoom slider in the bottom-right corner of the PowerPoint window, or click its plus or minus buttons in increment the zoom level. See Figure 20-12.

To resize the current slide so that it is as large as possible while still fitting completely in the Slides pane, click the Fit Slide to Current Window button, or click the Fit to Window button in the Zoom group on the View tab.

FIGURE 20-12

Zoom in or out to see more or less of the slide(s) at once.

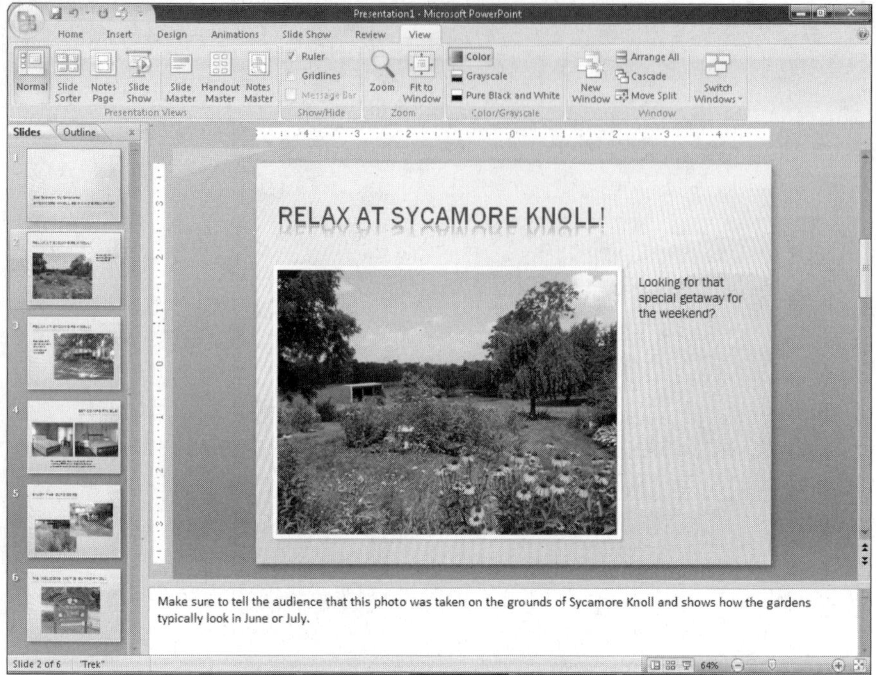

Another way to control the zoom is with the Zoom dialog box. On the View tab, in the Zoom group, click the Zoom button. (You can also open that dialog box by clicking the % next to the Zoom slider.) Make your selection, as shown in Figure 20-13, by clicking the appropriate button, and then click OK. Notice that you can type a precise zoom percentage in the Percent text box. You can specify any percentage you like, but some panes and views will not go higher than 100%.

FIGURE 20-13

You can zoom with this Zoom dialog box rather than the slider if you prefer.

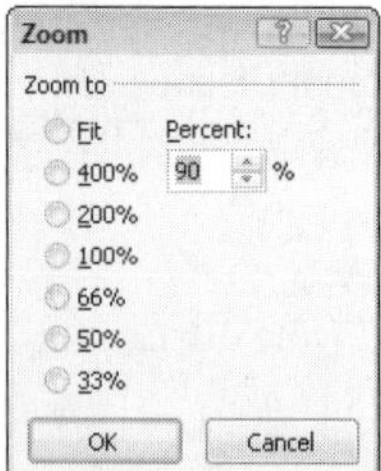

Enabling Optional Display Elements

PowerPoint has a lot of optional screen elements that you may (or may not) find useful, depending on what you're up to at the moment. The following sections describe them.

Ruler

Vertical and horizontal rulers around the slide pane can help you place objects more precisely. To toggle them on or off, mark or clear the Ruler check box on the View tab. Rulers are available only in Normal and Notes Page views.

The rulers help with positioning no matter what content type you are working with, but when you are editing text in a text frame they have an additional purpose as well. The horizontal ruler shows the frame's paragraph indents and any custom tab stops, and you can drag the indent markers on the ruler just like you can in Word.

The ruler's unit of measure is controlled from the Regional Settings in the Control Panel in Windows.

TIP

The vertical ruler is optional. To disable it while retaining the horizontal ruler, choose Office Button ➪ PowerPoint Options, click Advanced, and in the Display section, clear the Show Vertical Ruler check box.

Gridlines

Gridlines are non-printing dotted lines at regularly spaced intervals that can help you line up objects on a slide. Figure 20-14 shows gridlines (and the ruler) enabled.

To turn gridlines on or off, use any of these methods:

- Press Shift+F9.
- On the View tab, in the Show/Hide group, mark or clear the Gridlines check box.
- On the Design tab, in the Arrange group, choose Align ➪ Show Gridlines.

There are many options you can set for the gridlines, including whether objects snap to it, whether the grid is visible, and what the spacing should be between the gridlines. To set grid options, follow these steps:

1. **On the Home tab, in the Drawing group, choose Arrange ➪ Align ➪ Grid Settings, or right-click the slide background and choose Grid and Guides.** The Grid and Guides dialog box opens (see Figure 20-15).
2. **In the Snap To section, mark or clear these check boxes.**
   - Snap Objects to Grid: Specifies whether or not objects will shift automatically align with the grid.
   - Snap Object to Other Objects: Specifies whether or not objects will automatically align with other objects.
3. **In the Grid Settings section, enter the amount of space between gridlines desired.**
4. **Mark or clear the Display Grid On Screen check box to display or hide the grid.** (Note that you can make objects snap to the grid without the grid being displayed.)
5. **Click OK.**

FIGURE 20-14

Gridlines and the ruler help align objects on a slide.

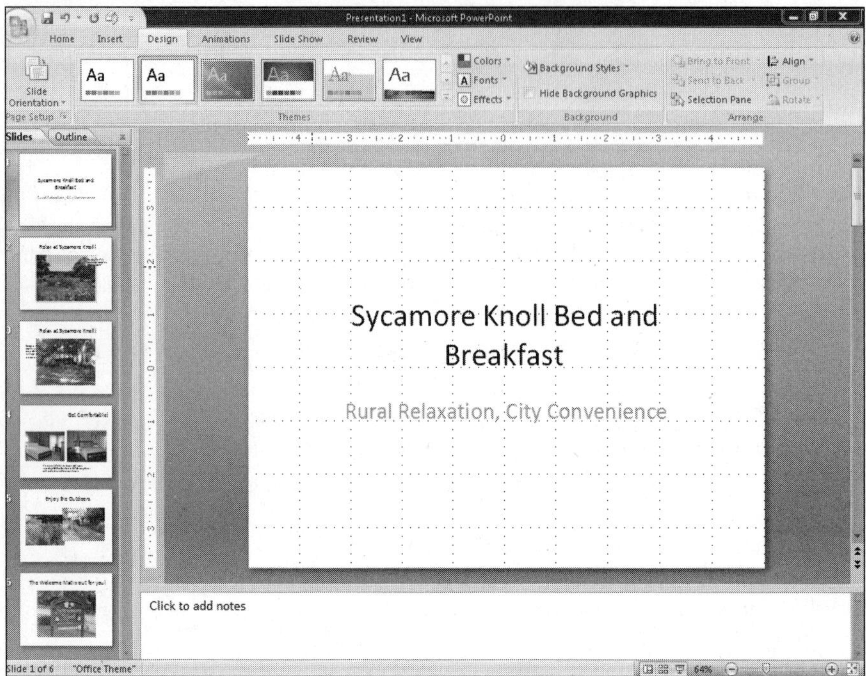

FIGURE 20-15

Set grid options and spacing.

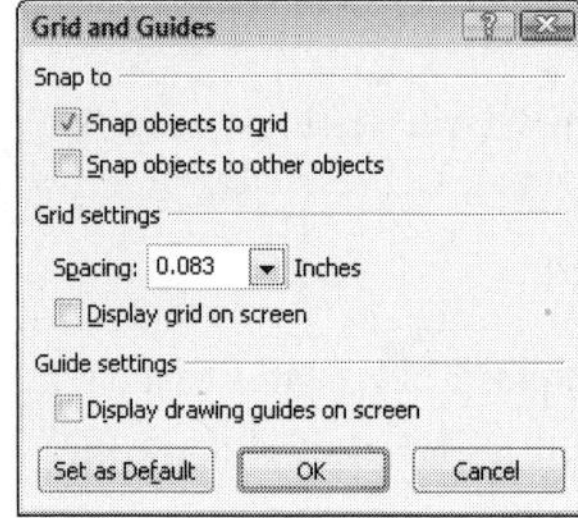

Guides

Guides are like gridlines except they are individual lines, rather than a grid of lines, and you can drag them to different positions on the slide. As you drag a guide, a numeric indicator appears to let you know the ruler position. See Figure 20-16. Use the Grid and Guides dialog box to turn guides on/off, or press Alt+F9.

FIGURE 20-16

Guides are movable, non-printing lines that help with alignment.

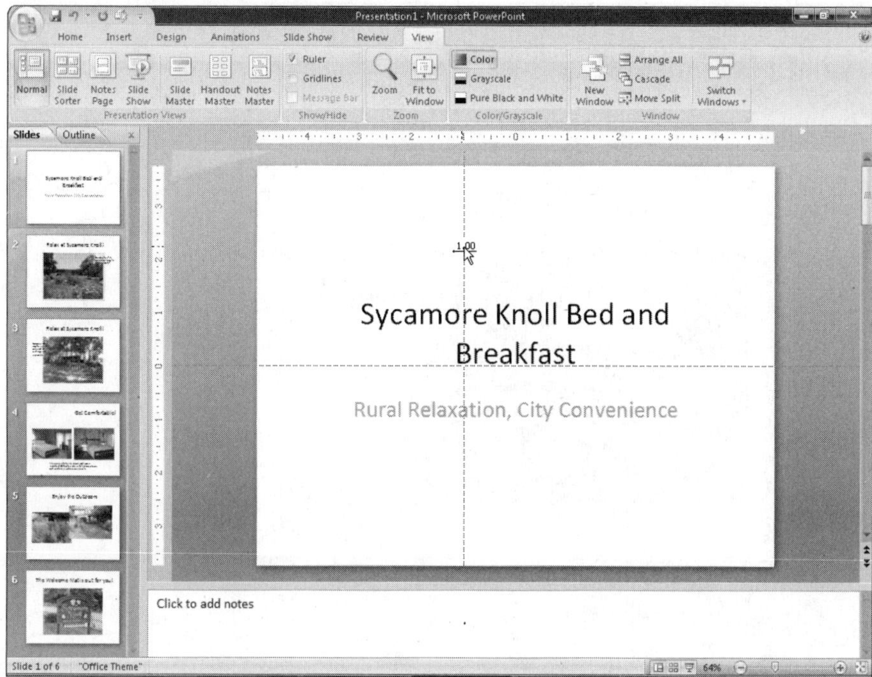

You can create additional sets of guide lines by holding down the Ctrl key while dragging a guide (to copy it). You can have up to eight horizontal and vertical guides, all at positions you specify.

Color/grayscale/pure black and white views

Most of the time you will work with your presentation in color. However, if you plan to print the presentation in black and white or grayscale (for example, on overhead transparencies or black-and-white handouts), you should check to see what it will look like without color.

TIP **This Color/Grayscale/Pure Black and White option is especially useful when you are preparing slides that will eventually be faxed, because a fax is pure black and white in most cases. Something that looks great on a color screen could look like a shapeless blob on a black-and-white fax. It doesn't hurt to check.**

Click the Grayscale or the Pure Black and White button on the View tab to switch to one of those views. When you do so, a Grayscale or Black and White tab becomes available, as shown in Figure 20-17. From its Setting group, you can fine-tune the grayscale or black-and-white preview. Choose one that shows the object to best advantage; PowerPoint will remember that setting when printing or outputting the presentation to a grayscale or black-and-white source.

FIGURE 20-17

Select a grayscale or a black-and-white preview type.

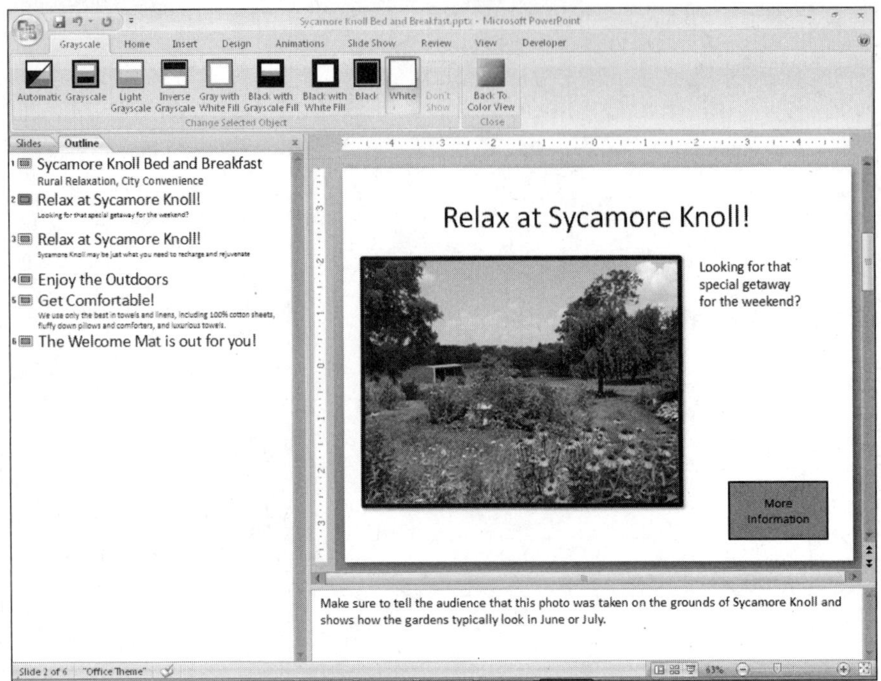

When you are finished, click the Back to Color View button on the Grayscale tab. Changing the Black and White or Grayscale settings doesn't affect the colors on the slides; it only affects how the slides will look and print in black and white or grayscale.

Opening a New Display Window

Have you ever wished you could be in two places at once? Well, in PowerPoint, you actually can. PowerPoint provides a way to view two spots in the presentation at the same time by opening a new window.

To display a new window, display the View tab and click New Window in the Window group. Then use Arrange All or Cascade to view both windows at once.

You can use any view with any window, so you can have two slides in Normal view at once, or Slide Sorter and Notes Pages view, or any other combination. Both windows contain the same presentation, so any changes you make in one window are reflected in the other window.

Arranging windows

When you have two or more windows open, whether they are for the same presentation or different ones, you need to arrange them for optimal viewing. You saw earlier in this chapter how to resize a window, but did you know that PowerPoint can do some of the arranging for you?

When you want to arrange the open windows, do one of the following:

- **Tile:** On the View tab, click Arrange All to tile the open windows so there is no overlap.
- **Cascade:** On the View tab, click Cascade to arrange the open windows so the title bars cascade from upper-left to lower-right on the screen. Click a title bar to activate a window.

These commands do not apply to minimized windows. If you want to include a window in the arrangement, make sure you restore it from its minimized state first.

Switching among windows

If you have more than one window open and can see at least a corner of the window you want, click it to bring it to the front. If you have one of the windows maximized, on the other hand, or if another window is obscuring the one you want, click Switch Windows (on the View tab) and select the window you want to view.

Summary

This chapter provided an introduction to PowerPoint. You learned about PowerPoint 2007's new features and how to control the view of the PowerPoint window.

Chapter 21

Creating a Presentation, Slides, and Text

If you're an experienced Windows and PowerPoint user, starting new presentations and saving files may be second nature to you. If so — great! You may not need this chapter. On the other hand, if you aren't entirely certain about some of the finer points, such as saving in different formats or locations, stick around.

In this chapter, you'll learn how to create, save, and reopen presentations file, and how to build a simple text-based presentation by creating new slides and entering text on them. You'll learn how to import content from other programs and how to create, size, and position text boxes to hold the text for your presentation.

IN THIS CHAPTER

Starting a New Presentation

You can start a blank presentation from scratch, or you can base the new presentation on a template or on another presentation. Using a template or existing presentation can save you some time. However, if you have a specific vision you're going for, starting a presentation from scratch gives you a clean canvas to work from.

Starting a blank presentation from scratch

When you start PowerPoint, a new blank presentation begins automatically with one slide. Just add your content to it, add more slides if needed, change the formatting (as you'll learn in upcoming chapters), and go for it.

If you need to start another blank presentation, follow these steps:

1. **Choose Office Button ⇨ New.** The New Presentation dialog box opens. See Figure 21-1.

2. **Blank Presentation is already** selected. Click Create.

FIGURE 21-1

Select Blank Presentation from the New Presentation dialog box.

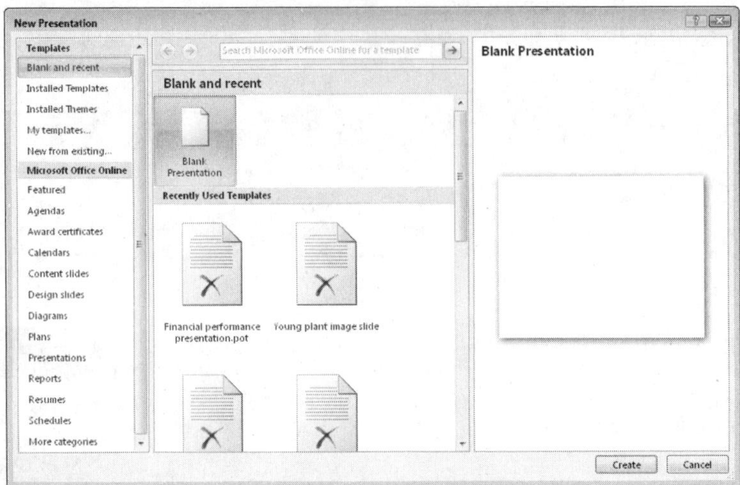

Press the Ctrl+N shortcut key to start a new presentation.

Starting a presentation from a template

A *template* is a file that contains starter settings — and sometimes starter content — on which you can base new presentations. Templates vary in their exact offerings, but can include sample slides, a background graphic, custom color and font themes, and custom positioning for object placeholders.

When selecting a template, you can choose from these categories:

- **Installed Templates:** Microsoft-provided templates that come preinstalled with PowerPoint
- **My Templates:** Templates that you have created and saved yourself and templates that you previously downloaded from Microsoft Office Online
- **Microsoft Office Online templates:** Microsoft-provided templates that you download from Microsoft on an as-needed basis

NOTE **Also under Templates in Figure 21-1 is *Installed Themes.* Themes are not exactly templates, but they are similar. Chapter 1 explained the difference. You can start a new presentation based on a theme as an alternative to using a template. Such a presentation starts with defined color, font, and effect settings.**

Using an installed template

There are only a few installed templates because Microsoft assumes that most people have an always-on Internet connection these days. Each installed template demonstrates a special-purpose type of presentation, such as a photo album, pitchbook, or quiz show. There is one Corporate Presentation template as well, but if you are interested in standard corporate presentation templates, you might prefer to look at the online offerings instead.

Follow these steps to start a presentation based on an installed template:

1. **Choose Office Button ➪ New.** The New Presentation dialog box opens.
2. **In the Templates list, click Installed Templates.** A list of the installed templates appears.
3. **Click a template to see a preview of it.**
4. **Select the template you want and click Create.** A new presentation opens based on that template.

Using a saved template

When you start a new presentation with an online template, as in the preceding section, PowerPoint copies that template to your hard disk so you can reuse it in the future without connecting to the Internet. It is stored, along with any custom template you have created, in the My Templates folder.

To access these downloaded and custom templates, follow these steps:

1. **Choose Office Button ➪ New.** The New Presentation dialog box opens (see Figure 21-1).
2. **Click My Templates.** A different New Presentation dialog box appears containing templates that you have downloaded or created. See Figure 21-2.
3. **Click OK.** A new presentation opens based on that template.

FIGURE 21-2

Choose a previously used or custom template.

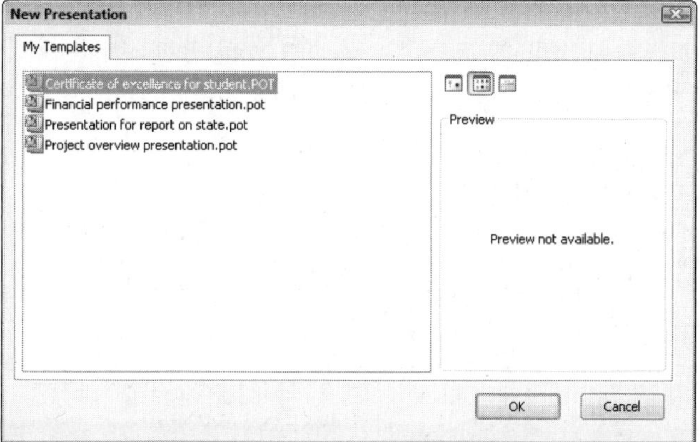

TIP **Recently used template names appear on the right side of the New Presentation dialog box when it opens initially. You can select a template from there and click Create. To remove an item from the Recently Used Templates, right-click the item and choose Remove Item from List. To clear the whole list at once, right-click any entry and choose Remove All Items from List.**

Using an online template

The bulk of the templates for presentations are available online. You can access the library of online templates without leaving PowerPoint. Follow these steps:

1. **Choose Office Button ⇨ New.** The New Presentation dialog box opens.
2. **In the Templates list, in the Microsoft Office Online section, click the category of template you want. If you want standard business presentations, click Presentations; most of the other categories have special purposes.**
3. **Depending on the category you choose, a subcategory list might appear in the center pane.** If it does, click the subcategory that you want.
4. **Click a template to see a preview of it.**
5. **Select the template that you want and click Download.** A new presentation opens based on that template.

TIP **Spend some time exploring the templates available on Microsoft Office Online. There's a lot here! For example, Design Slides has templates that don't contain any sample content — just design elements. This category has subcategories for earlier versions of PowerPoint, so if there was a particular design template you loved in, say, PowerPoint 2000, you can find it again here.**

Basing a new presentation on an existing one

If you already have a presentation that's similar to the new one you need to create, you can base the new presentation on the existing one.

Follow these steps to use an existing presentation as a template:

1. **Choose Office Button ⇨ New.** The New Presentation dialog box opens.
2. **Click New from Existing.** The New from Existing Presentation dialog box opens. See Figure 21-3.
3. **Navigate to the location containing the existing presentation and select it.** When you select a presentation, the Open button changes to a Create New button.
4. **Click Create New.**

Basing a new presentation on content from another application

PowerPoint can open files in several formats other than its own, so you can start a new presentation based on some work you have done elsewhere. For example, you can open a Word outline in PowerPoint. The results might not be very attractive — but you can fix that later with some text editing, slide layouts, and design changes.

To open a file from another application, do the following:

1. **Choose Office Button ⇨ Open.** The Open dialog box appears.
2. **Click the File Type button (or Files of Type in Windows XP) and choose the file type.** For example, to open a text file, choose All Outlines. See Figure 21-4.
3. **Select the desired file, and then click Open.**
4. **Save your work as a PowerPoint file by choosing Office Button ⇨ Save As.**

CROSS-REF **See the section "Saving Your Work" for more details on saving. You can also import a Word outline into an existing presentation.**

FIGURE 21-3

Select an existing presentation to use as a template.

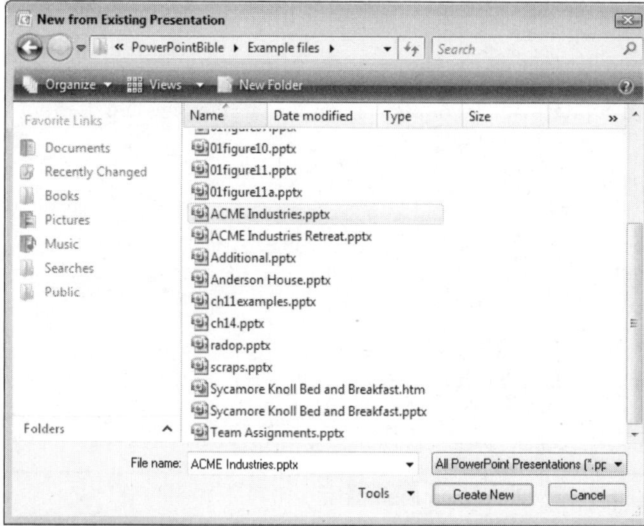

FIGURE 21-4

Select a data file from some other program as the basis of a new presentation.

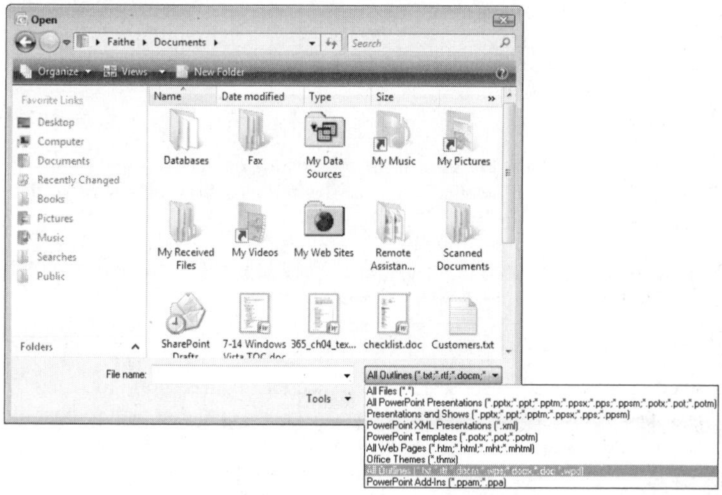

Saving Your Work

PowerPoint is typical of most Windows programs in the way it saves and opens files. The entire PowerPoint presentation is saved in a single file, and any graphics, charts, or other elements are incorporated into that single file.

The first time you save a presentation, PowerPoint opens the Save As dialog box, prompting you for a name and location. Thereafter, when you save that presentation, PowerPoint uses the same settings and does not prompt you for them again.

Saving for the first time

If you haven't previously saved the presentation you are working on, Save and Save As do the same thing: They open the Save As dialog box. From there, you can specify a name, file type, and file location. Follow these steps:

1. **Choose Office Button ➪ Save.** The Save As dialog box appears.
2. **Enter a filename in the File name box.** See Figure 21-5.

FIGURE 21-5

Save your work by specifying a name for the presentation file.

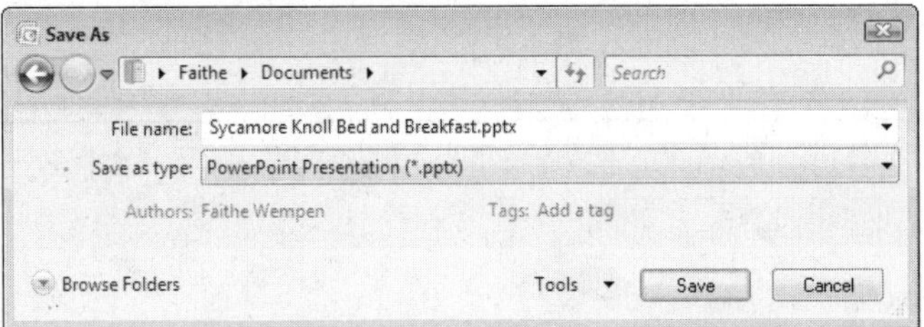

In Windows Vista, the Save As dialog box does not show the existing content of the current location by default. To view it, click the Browse Folders arrow in the bottom-left corner of the dialog box.

CROSS-REF To save in a different location, see the section "Changing drives and folders." To save in a different format, see the section "Saving in a different format."

3. **Click Save.** Your work is saved.

Filenames can be up to 255 characters. For practical purposes, however, keep the names short. You can include spaces in the filenames and most symbols except <, >, ?, *, /, and \. However, if you plan to post the file on a network or the Internet at some point, you should avoid using spaces; use the underscore character instead to simulate a space if needed. There have also been problems reported with files that use exclamation points in their names, so beware of that. Generally it is best to avoid punctuation marks in names.

TIP If you want to transfer your presentation file to a different computer and show it from there, and that other computer does not have the same fonts as your PC, you should embed the fonts in your presentation so the desired fonts are available on the other PC. To embed fonts from the Save As dialog box, click the Tools button, choose Save Options, and mark the Embed Fonts in the File checkbox. This option makes the saved file larger than normal, so choose it only when necessary. For more information on advanced saving features, see the section "Specifying Save Options."

Saving Subsequent Times

After you have once saved a presentation, you can resave it with the same settings (same file type, name, and location) in any of the following ways:

- Choose Office Button ➪ Save.
- Press Ctrl+S.
- Click the Save button on the Quick Access toolbar.

If you need to save your presentation under a different name, as a different file type, or in a different location, use the Save As command instead. This reopens the Save As dialog box, as in the preceding steps, so that you can save differently. The originally saved copy will remain under the original name, type, and location.

TIP If you frequently use Save As, you may want to place a button for it on the Quick Access Toolbar. To do this, right-click the Save As command and choose Add to Quick Access Toolbar.

Changing drives and folders

By default, all files in PowerPoint (and all of the Office applications) are saved to the Documents folder (or My Documents under Windows XP) for the current user. Each user has his or her own version of this folder, so that each person's documents are kept separate depending on who is logged in to the PC.

The Documents folder is a convenient save location for beginners, because they never have to worry about changing the drive or folder. However, more advanced users will sometimes want to save files to other locations. These other locations can include floppy disks, other hard disks in the same PC, hard disks on other PCs in a network, hard disks on Web servers on the Internet, or writeable CDs.

TIP Each user has a Documents or My Documents folder in his or her own profile. The actual location of that folder depends on the Windows version. For example, if Mary is logged in, the path would be C:\Users\Mary\Documents. In Windows XP, the path would be C:\Documents and Settings\Mary\My Documents. If your usual PowerPoint files seem to be missing at some point, make sure you are logged in under your usual user name.

Throughout all of the Office programs, the dialog boxes that save and open files are different depending on the operating system you are using.

Changing the save location (Windows Vista)

Windows Vista's Save As dialog box offers several alternatives for navigating between locations. Here's a summary:

- **Browse Folders:** By default a compact version of the Save As dialog box appears, as in Figure 21-5. To see the full version, as in Figure 21-6, click the Browse Folders arrow.

- **Favorite Links list:** This area displays shortcuts for popular locations such as Documents and Desktop. Double-click a shortcut here to jump to the desired location. This area does not appear unless Browse Folders is turned on.

Add your own favorite locations to the Favorite Links list by dragging their icons into the Favorite Links pane.

- **Folders list:** This area displays a folder tree of locations, similar to the folder list in a Windows Explorer window. See Figure 21-6. To display the Folders list if it does not already appear, click the up arrow to the right of Folders (below the Favorite Links list). To hide the Folders list, click the down arrow (which replaces the up arrow).

FIGURE 21-6

Jump to a desired location using the Favorite Links and/or Folders lists.

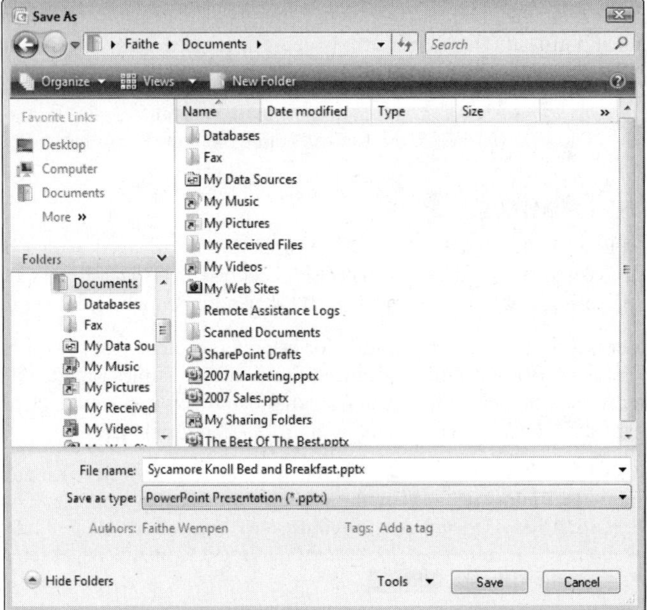

TIP

Drag the divider line between the Favorite Links and Folders lists to adjust their relative sizes. Drag the vertical divider line between them and the file listing to make the Favorite Links and Folders panes wider or narrower. You can also enlarge the whole Save As dialog box if needed by dragging its border.

- **Address bar:** This area shows the path to the currently displayed location. You can jump directly to any of those levels by clicking the name there. This is similar to the "Up One Level" feature from Windows XP style dialog boxes except you are not limited to going up a single level at a time — you can go directly up to any level. You can also click the right-pointing arrow to the right of any level to see a menu of other folders within that location, and jump to any of them from the menu. See Figure 21-7.

FIGURE 21-7

Click an arrow on the Address bar to see a menu of locations at the chosen level within the current path.

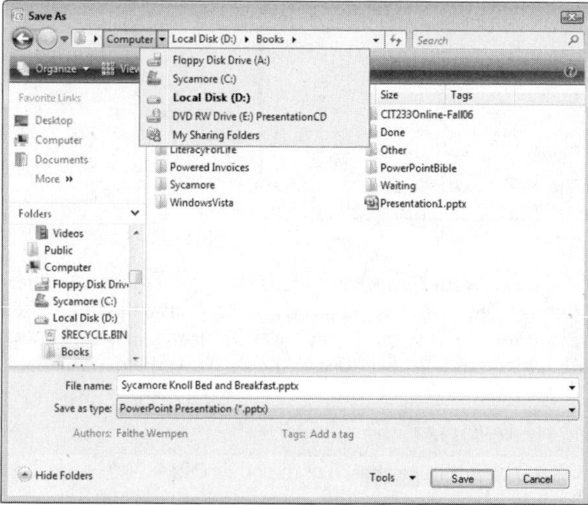

Changing the save location (Windows XP)

Under Windows XP, the Save In list shows the top-level locations on the system, including each drive, My Documents, and My Network Places. Open the list, as shown in Figure 21-8, and select the location in which you want to start. Then double-click folder icons in the file listing to drill down to the location in which you want to save. To go back up one level, click the Up One Level button. See Figure 21-8.

Along the left side of the Save As dialog box is the *Places Bar.* It's roughly equivalent to the Favorite Links list in Windows Vista. You can click a folder to jump to the desired location to save a file.

FIGURE 21-8

Select a top-level location from the Save In list and then double-click folders to work your way through to the desired location.

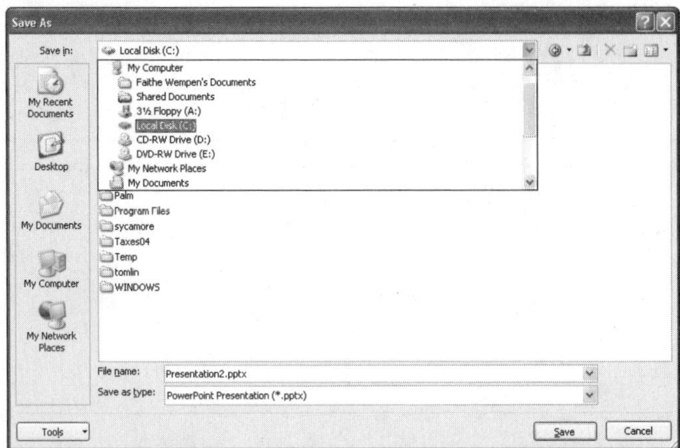

TIP **If you consistently want your PowerPoint files saved into a different folder, change the default file location. Choose Office Button ➪ PowerPoint Options and click Save. Then type a new file location in the Default File Location text box. You cannot browse for it; you must know the full path name. Separate the parts of the path with \ symbols, like this: C:\Books\PowerPoint\PPBible.**

Saving in a different format

PowerPoint 2007 has a new XML-based file format, like the other Office 2007 applications. XML stands for eXtensible Markup Language; it is a text-based coding system similar to HTML that describes formatting by using inline bracketed codes and style sheets. XML-based data files are smaller than the data files from earlier PowerPoint versions, and they support all of the latest PowerPoint 2007 features. For best results, use this format whenever possible.

There are also several variants of this format for specialty uses. For example, there's a macro-enable version with a .pptm extension. There are also "show" variants (.ppsx and .ppsm) that open in Slide Show view by default, and template variants (.potx and .potm) that function as templates.

TIP **PowerPoint 2007 does not include macro recording functionality, so why is there a macro-enabled file format? It's because of Visual Basic for Applications (VBA). From the Developer tab, you can access a VBA editor, which lets you embed VBA code inside a PowerPoint presentation file (provided it is in a macro-enabled format).**

However, not everyone has PowerPoint 2007, and only PowerPoint 2007 can open files with these new formats. (You can download a compatibility pack for earlier PowerPoint versions that will allow them to accept the new files, but you can't assume that everyone who has an earlier version of PowerPoint will download it.) Therefore you might need to save presentations in other file formats in order to share files with other people.

The available formats are shown in Table 21-1. In the Save As dialog box, open the Save as Type drop-down list and select the desired format. See Figure 21-9.

FIGURE 21-9

Choose a different format, if needed, from the Save As Type drop-down list.

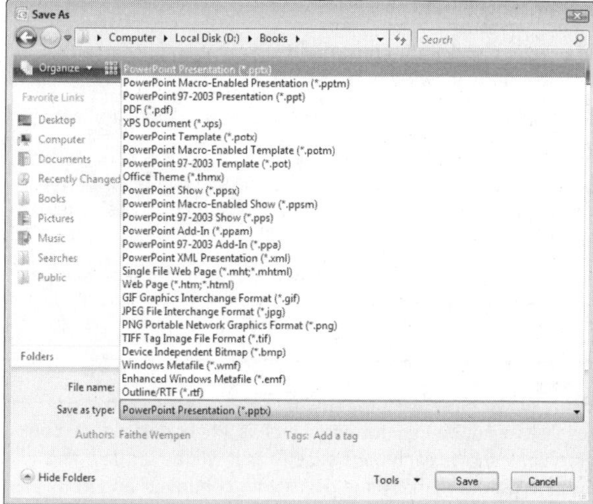

TABLE 21-1

PowerPoint Save As Formats

Presentations

Format	Extension	Usage Notes
PowerPoint Presentation	.pptx	The default; use in most cases. Can open only in PowerPoint 2007 (or on an earlier version with a conversion add-on installed).
PowerPoint Macro-Enabled Presentation	.pptm	Same as above except it supports the storage of VBA or macro code.
PowerPoint 97-2003 Presentation	.ppt	A backward-compatible format for sharing files with users of PowerPoint 97, 2000, 2002 (XP), or 2003.
PowerPoint Template	.potx	A 2007-format template file.
PowerPoint Macro-Enabled Template	.potm	A 2007-format template file that supports the storage of VBA or macro code.
PowerPoint 97-2003 Template	.pot	A backward-compatible template file, also usable with PowerPoint 97, 2000, 2002 (XP), or 2003.
PowerPoint Show	.ppsx	Just like a regular PowerPoint file except it opens in Slide Show view by default; useful for distributing presentations to the audience on disk.
PowerPoint Macro-Enabled Show	.ppsm	Same as above except it supports the storage of VBA or macro code.

continued

TABLE 21-1 *(continued)*

Presentations

Format	Extension	Usage Notes
PowerPoint 97-2003 Show	.pps	Same as a regular backward-compatible presentation file except it opens in Slide Show view by default.
PowerPoint XML Presentation	.xml	A presentation in XML format, suitable for integrating into an XML information storage system.
Single File Web Page	.mht, .mhtml	A complete presentation stored in a single file that can be displayed in most modern Web browsers. Suitable for posting on a Web site or sending via e-mail.
Web Page	.htm, .html	A typical text HTML file with each graphic element in a separate file. Suitable for posting on a Web site.

Graphics/Other

Format	Extension	Usage Notes
PDF	.pdf	Produces files in Adobe PDF format, which is a hybrid of a document and a graphic. It shows each page exactly as it will be printed, and yet allows the user to mark up the pages with comments and to search the document text. Available only after downloading PDF and XPS support from Office Online. You must have a PDF reader such as Adobe Acrobat to view PDF files.
XPS	.xps	Much the same as PDF except it's a Microsoft format. Windows Vista comes with an XPS viewer application.
Office Theme	.thmx	Somewhat like a template, but it contains only theme settings (fonts, colors, and effects). Use this if you want to apply the colors, fonts, and effects from the current presentation to other presentations but you don't want to save any of the content or layout.
PowerPoint Add-In	.ppam	A file containing executable code (usually VBA) that extends PowerPoint's capabilities.
PowerPoint 97-2003 Add-In	.ppa	Same as above except the add-in is backward-compatible.
GIF Graphics Interchange Format	.gif	Static graphic. GIFs are limited to 256 colors.
PNG Portable Network Graphics Format	.png	Static graphic. Similar to GIF except without the color depth limitation. Uses lossless compression; takes advantage of the best features of both GIF and JPG.
JPEG File Interchange Format	.jpg	Static graphic. JPG files can be very small, making them good for Web use. A lossy format, so picture quality may not be as good as with a lossless format.
TIFF Tagged Image File Format	.tif	Static graphic. TIF is a high-quality file format suitable for slides with high-resolution photos. A lossless compression format.
Device Independent Bitmap	.bmp	Static graphic. BMP is the native format for Windows graphics, including Windows background wallpaper.

Graphics/Other

Format	Extension	Usage Notes
Windows Metafile	.wmf	Static graphic. A vector-based format, so it can later be resized without distortion. Not Mac-compatible.
Enhanced Windows Metafile	.emf	Enhanced version of WMF; not compatible with 16-bit applications. Also vector-based and non-Mac-compatible.
Outline/RTF	.rtf	Text and text formatting only; excludes all non-text elements. Only text in slide placeholders will be converted to the outline. Text in the Notes area is not included.

TIP If you consistently want to save in a different format from PowerPoint 2007, choose Office Button ⇨ PowerPoint Options and click Save. Then, choose a different format from the Save Files in this Format drop-down list. This makes your choice the default in the Save As Type drop-down list in the Save As dialog box. Not all of the formats are available here; your choices are PowerPoint Presentation (the default), PowerPoint Macro-Enabled Presentation, and PowerPoint 97-2003.

Table 21-1 lists a lot of choices, but don't let that overwhelm you. You have three main decisions to make:

- **PowerPoint 2007 format or backward-compatible with PowerPoint 97-2003.** Unless compatibility is essential, go with the 2007 format because you get access to all of the new features. (See Table 21-2 to learn what you'll lose with backward-compatibility.) If you use a backward-compatible format, some of the features described in this book work differently or aren't available at all.
- **Macro-enabled or not.** Most people will never need to create a macro-enabled presentation. PowerPoint 2007 does not support macro recording, so the only macros you would have would be written in VBA, and most PowerPoint users aren't fluent in VBA programming.
- **Regular presentation or PowerPoint Show.** The "show" variant starts the presentation in Slide Show view when it is loaded in PowerPoint; that's the only difference between it and a regular presentation. You can build your presentation in a regular format, and then save in show format right before distribution.

Most of the other choices from Table 21-2 are special-purpose, and not suitable for everyday use. The following sections explain some of those special types.

TABLE 21-2

PowerPoint 2007 Features Not Supported in Previous PowerPoint Versions

Feature	Issues
SmartArt Graphics	Converted to uneditable pictures
Charts (except Microsoft Graph charts)	Converted to editable OLE objects, but the chart might appear different
Custom Slide Layouts	Converted to multiple masters
Drop Shadows	Soft shadows converted to hard shadows

continued

TABLE 21-2 *(continued)*

Feature	Issues
Equations	Converted to uneditable pictures
Heading and body fonts	Converted to static formatting
New effects: ■ 2-D or 21-D text ■ Gradient outlines for shapes or text ■ Strikethrough and double-strikethrough ■ Gradient, picture, and texture fills on text ■ Shadows, soft edges, reflections ■ Most 21-D effects	Converted to uneditable pictures
Themes	Converted to styles
Theme colors	Converted to styles
Theme effects	Converted to styles
Theme fonts	Converted to regular font usage

Saving for use on the Web

To share your presentation on the Web with people who don't have PowerPoint, you can save in one of the Web Page formats.

You have two choices for Web format: Web Page or Single File Web Page. Web Page creates an HTML document that has links to the slides, and then the slides and their graphics are stored in a separate folder. This would be suitable for posting on a Web site. Single File Web Page creates a single .mht document that contains all of the HTML codes and all of the slides. This would be suitable for e-mailing, for example. (In fact, the "M" in the name format is short for "mail," because this format was originally designed for e-mail use.) However, with both of these Web formats, you lose some of the special effects, so you might prefer to distribute the presentation in a different way on the Web. If keeping the full effect of all the effects is important, consider saving in one of the PowerPoint Show formats and then make the PowerPoint Viewer utility available for free download from the same Web page.

Saving slides as graphics

If you save your presentation in one of the graphic formats shown in the Graphics/Other section of Table 21-1, the file ceases to be a presentation and becomes a series of unrelated graphic files, one per slide. If you choose one of these formats, you're asked whether you want to export the current slide only or all slides. If you choose all slides, PowerPoint creates a new folder in the selected folder with the same name as the original presentation file and places the graphics files in it.

Saving slide text only

If you want to export the text of the slides to some other application, consider the Outline/RTF format, which creates an outline similar to what you see in the Outline pane in PowerPoint. This file can then be opened in Word or any other application that supports RTF text files. Only text in placeholders is exported, though, not text in manually inserted text boxes.

Specifying Save Options

The Save Options enable you to fine-tune the saving process for special needs. For example, you can employ Save Options to embed fonts, to change the interval at which PowerPoint saves AutoRecover information, and more.

There are two ways to access the Save options:

- Choose Office Button ➪ PowerPoint Options and click Save.
- From the Save As dialog box, click Tools ➪ Save Options.

The PowerPoint Options dialog box appears, as in Figure 21-10.

FIGURE 21-10

Set Save Options to match the way you want PowerPoint to save your work.

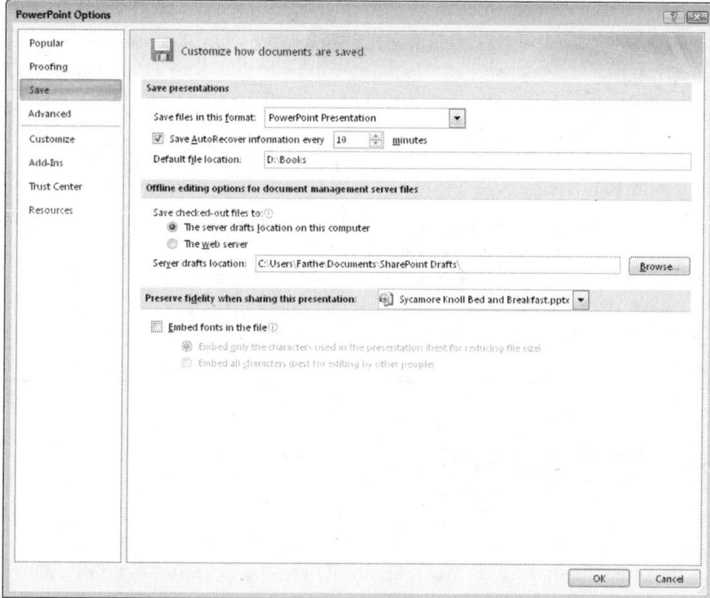

Then set any of the options desired. They are summarized in Table 21-3. Click OK when you are finished.

One of the most important features described in Table 21-3 is AutoRecover, which is turned on by default. This means if a system error or power outage causes PowerPoint to terminate unexpectedly, you do not lose all of the work you have done. The next time you start PowerPoint, it opens the recovered file and asks if you want to save it.

CAUTION **AutoRecover is *not* a substitute for saving your work the regular way. It does not save in the same sense that the Save command does; it only saves a backup version as PowerPoint is running. If you quit PowerPoint normally, that backup version is erased. The backup version is available for recovery only if PowerPoint terminates abnormally (because a system lockup or a power outage, for example).**

TABLE 21-3

Save Options

Feature	Purpose
Save Files in This Format	Sets the default file format to appear in the Save As dialog box. Your choices are a regular presentation, a macro-enabled presentation, or a 97-2003 backward-compatible presentation.
Save AutoRecover info every ___ minutes	PowerPoint saves your work every few minutes so that if the computer has problems and causes PowerPoint to terminate abnormally, you do not lose much work. Lower this number to save more often (for less potential data loss) or raise it to save less often (for less slowdown/delay related to repeated saving).
Default file location	Specify the location that you want to start from when saving with the Save As dialog box. By default it is your Documents (or My Documents) folder.
Save Checked-Out Files To	Sets the location in which any drafts will be saved that you have checked out of a Web server library such as SharePoint. If you choose The Server Drafts Location on This Computer, then you must specify what that location will be in the Server Drafts Location box. If you choose to save to The Web Server, it's not an issue because every save goes immediately back to the server.
Preserve Fidelity When Sharing This Presentation	This drop-down list enables you to select from among all the open presentation files for the following setting to affect.
Embed Fonts in the File	Turn this on if you are saving a presentation for use on a different PC that might not have the fonts installed that the presentation requires. You can choose to embed the characters in use only (which minimizes the file size, but if someone tries to edit the presentation they might not have all of the characters out of the font that they need), or to embed all characters in the font set. Unlike the others, this setting applies only to the current presentation file.

Closing and Reopening Presentations

You can have several presentation files open at once and switch freely between them, but this can bog down your computer's performance somewhat. Unless you are doing some cut-and-paste work, it's best to have only one presentation file open — the one you are actively working on. It's easy to close and open presentations as needed.

Closing a presentation

When you exit PowerPoint, the open presentation file automatically closes, and you're prompted to save your changes if you have made any. If you want to close a presentation file without exiting PowerPoint, follow these steps:

1. **Choose Office Button ⇨ Close.** (Figure 21-11 shows the Close command.)

   If you have not made any changes to the presentation since the last time you saved, you're done.

2. **If you have made any changes to the presentation, you're prompted to save them.** If you don't want to save your changes, click No, and you're done.

FIGURE 21-11

Close the presentation via the Office menu.

3. **If you want to save your changes, click Yes.** If the presentation has already been saved once, you're done.
4. **If the presentation has not been saved before, the Save As dialog box appears.** Type a name in the File Name text box and click Save.

Opening a presentation

To open a recently used presentation, select it from the right side of the Office menu. Although only one file appears in Figure 21-11, up to nine can appear by default.

TIP **To pin a certain file to the Office menu's list so that it never scrolls off, click the pushpin icon to the right of the file's name on the menu. You can increase or decrease the number of recently used files that appear on the Office menu. Choose Office Button ➪ Office Button ➪ PowerPoint Options, click Advanced, and in the Display section, set the Number of Documents in the Recent Documents List.**

If the presentation you want to open does not appear on the Office menu, follow these steps to find and open it:

1. **Choose Office Button ➪ Open.** The Open dialog box appears.
2. **Choose the file you want.** If necessary, change the location to find the file.

CROSS-REF **See the section "Changing drives and folders" earlier in this chapter if you need help.**

3. **Click Open.** The presentation opens.

To open more than one presentation at once, hold down the Ctrl key as you click each file you want to open. Then, click the Open button and they all open in their own windows.

The Open button in the Open dialog box has its own drop-down list from which you can select commands that open the file in different ways. See Figure 21-12, and refer to Table 21-4 for an explanation of the available options.

FIGURE 21-12

The Open button's menu contains several special options for opening a file.

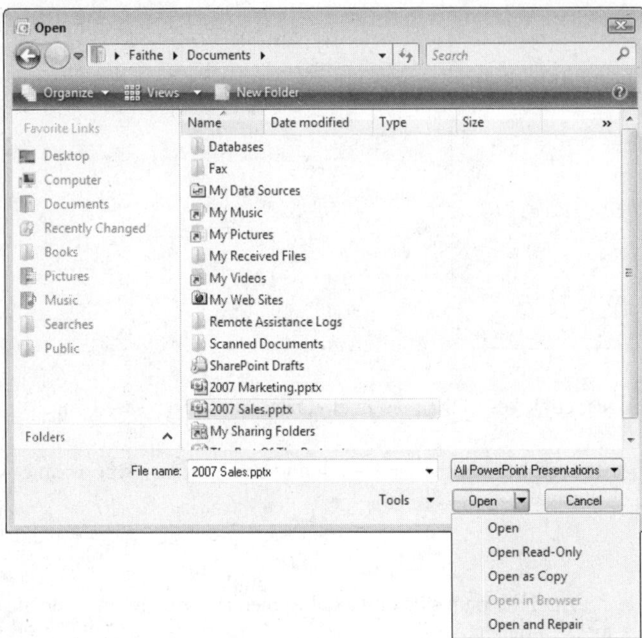

TABLE 21-4

Open Options

Open Button Setting	Purpose
Open	The default simply opens the file for editing.
Open Read-Only	Allows changes but prevents those changes from being saved under the same name.
Open Copy	Opens a copy of the file, leaving the original untouched.
Open in Browser	Applicable only for Web-based presentations, opens it for viewing in a Web browser.
Open and Repair	Opens the file, and identifies and repairs any errors it finds in it.
Show Previous Versions	Applicable only if the presentation file is stored on an NTFS volume under Windows Vista. See the next section for details.

Opening a file from a different program

Just as you can save files in various program formats, you can also open files from various programs. PowerPoint can detect the type of file and convert it automatically as you open it, so you do not have to know the exact file type. (For example, if you have an old PowerPoint file with a .ppt extension, you don't have to know what version it came from.) The only problem is with files that don't have extensions that PowerPoint automatically recognizes. In that case, you must change the File Type setting in the Open dialog box to All Files so that the file to be opened becomes available on the file list. See Figure 21-13. This change is valid for only this one use of the Open dialog box; the file type reverts to All PowerPoint Presentations, the default, the next time you open it.

FIGURE 21-13

To open files from different programs, change the File Type setting to All Files.

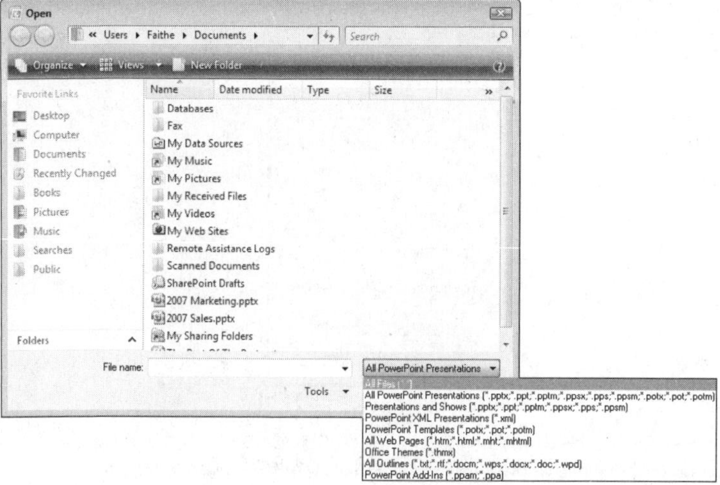

CAUTION **PowerPoint opens only presentation files and text-based files such as Word outlines. If you want to include graphics from another program in a PowerPoint presentation, copy-and-paste them into PowerPoint or insert them using the Picture command on the Insert tab. Do not attempt to open them with the Open dialog box.**

Finding a presentation file to open

If you have forgotten where you saved a particular presentation file, you're not out of luck. The Open dialog box (under Windows Vista) includes a Search box that can help you locate it. See Figure 21-14.

To search for a file, follow these steps:

1. **Choose Office Button ⇨ Open to display the Open dialog box.**
2. **Navigate to a location that you know the file is in.** For example, if you know it is on the C: drive, click Computer in the Favorite Links list and then double-click the C: drive.

3. **Click in the Search box and type part of the filename (if you know it) or a word or phrase used in the file.** See Figure 21-14.
4. **Press Enter.** A list of files appears that match that specification.
5. **Open the file as you normally would.**

FIGURE 21-14

Use the Search box in the Open dialog box (Windows Vista only) to look for a file.

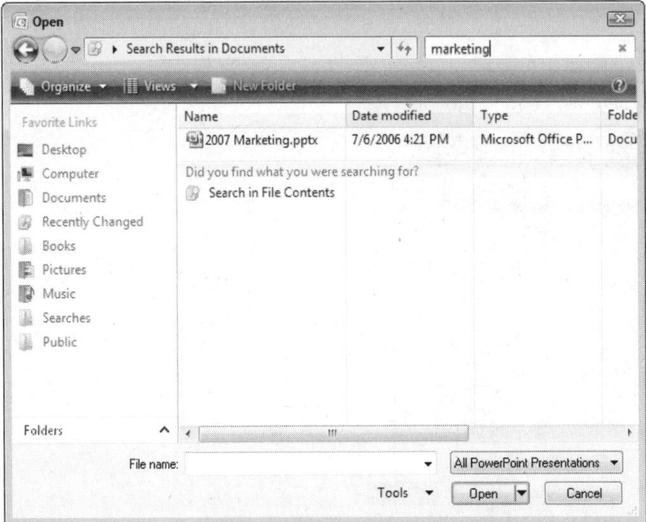

NOTE You can also use the Search utility from outside of PowerPoint. In Windows, click Start and choose Search. Although the Search utility in Windows Vista is different from the one in Windows XP, both can find a file by name, content, author, date, or many other properties.

Creating New Slides

Different templates start a presentation with different numbers and types of slides. A blank presentation has only a single slide, and you must create any others that you want.

There are several ways to create new slides. For example, you can type new text in the outline and then promote it to slide status, or you can add slides with the New Slide button that is on the Insert tab. You can also copy existing slides, either within the same presentation or from other sources. The following sections outline these procedures in more detail.

Creating new slides from the Outline pane

As discussed in Chapter 20, the Outline pane shows the text from the presentation's slides in a hierarchical tree, with the slide titles at the top level (the slide level) and the various levels of bulleted lists on the slides displaying as subordinate levels. Text that you type in the Outline pane appears on the slide, and vice versa, as shown in Figure 21-15.

FIGURE 21-15

When you type text into the Outline pane, it automatically appears on the current slide.

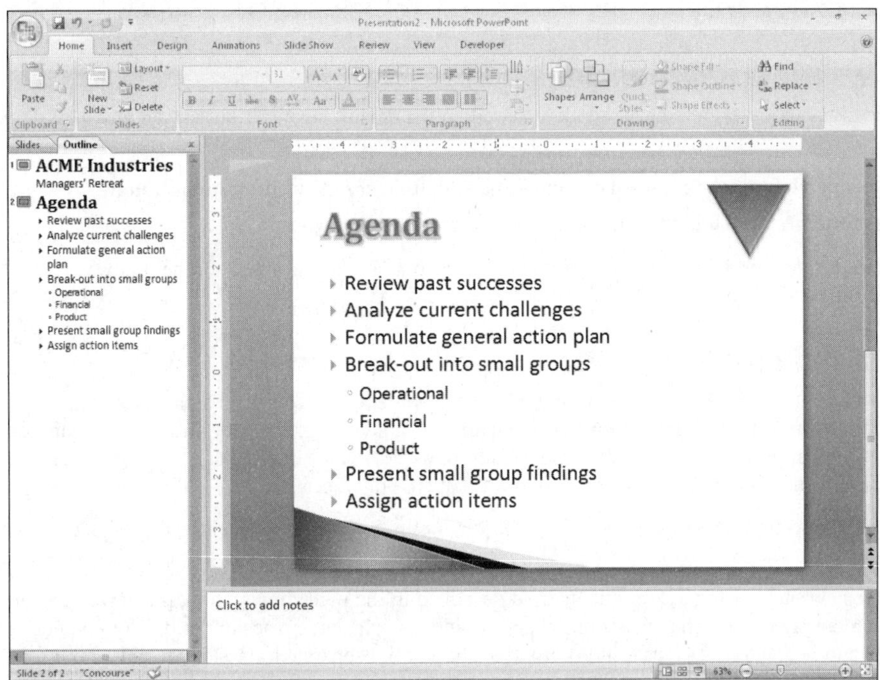

NOTE The Outline pane doesn't actually show all of the text in all cases; see the section "Creating Text Boxes Manually" later in this chapter to find out why text in some text boxes does not appear in the Outline pane.

Follow these steps to create a new slide from the Outline pane:

1. **Switch to Normal view.**
2. **Right-click the existing line on the Outline pane that the new slide should follow.**
3. **Click New Slide.** A new line appears in the Outline pane, with a slide symbol to its left.
4. **Type the title for the new slide.** The title appears both in the Outline pane and on the slide.

You can also create a new slide by starting a new line in the Outline pane and then promoting it to slide level by pressing Shift+Tab. Follow these steps to insert a new slide in this way:

1. **Position the insertion point at the end of the last line of the slide that the new slide should follow, and press Enter to start a new line.**
2. **Press Shift+Tab to promote the new line to the highest level (press it multiple times if needed), so that a slide icon appears to its left.**
3. **Type the title for the new slide.** The title appears both in the Outline pane and on the slide.

After creating the slide, you can continue creating its content directly in the Outline pane. Press Enter to start a new line, and then use Tab to demote, or Shift+Tab to promote, the line to the desired level. You can also right-click the text and choose Promote or Demote. Promoting a line all the way to the top level changes the line to a new slide title.

Creating a slide from the Slides pane

Here's a very quick method for creating a new slide, based on the default layout. It doesn't get much easier than this:

1. **In Normal view, in the Slides pane, click the slide that the new slide should follow.**
2. **Press Enter.** A new slide appears using the Title and Content layout.

The drawback to this method is that you cannot specify the layout. To choose a layout other than the default one, see the next section.

Creating a slide from a layout

A *slide layout* is a layout guide that tells PowerPoint what placeholder boxes to use on a particular slide and where to position them. Although slide layouts can contain placeholders for text, they also contain graphics, charts, tables, and other useful elements. After you create a new slide with placeholders, you can click a placeholder to open whatever controls you need to insert that type of object.

CROSS-REF **See the section, "Using Content Placeholders" for more information on inserting objects.**

When you create new slides using the outline method described in the preceding section, the new slides use the Title and Content layout, which consists of a slide title and a single, large placeholder box for content. If you want to use another layout, such as a slide with two adjacent but separate frames of content, you must either switch the slide to a different layout after its creation (using the Layout menu on the Home tab), or you must specify a different layout when you initially create the slide.

To specify a certain layout as you are creating a slide, follow these steps:

1. **In Normal or Slide Sorter view, select or display the slide that the new one should follow.**

   You can select a slide by clicking its thumbnail image in Slide Sorter view or on the Slides pane in Normal view. You can also move the insertion point to the slide's text in the Outline pane.

2. **On either the Home tab, do one of the following:**
   - To add a new slide using the default Title and Content layout, click the top (graphical) portion of the New Slide button.
   - To add a new slide using another layout, click the bottom (text) portion of the New Slide button and then select the desired layout from the menu, as shown in Figure 21-16.

TIP **The layouts that appear on the menu come from the slide master. To customize these layouts, click Slide Master on the View tab. You will learn more about the slide master and about changing layouts in Chapter 22.**

FIGURE 21-16

Create a new slide, based on the layout of your choice.

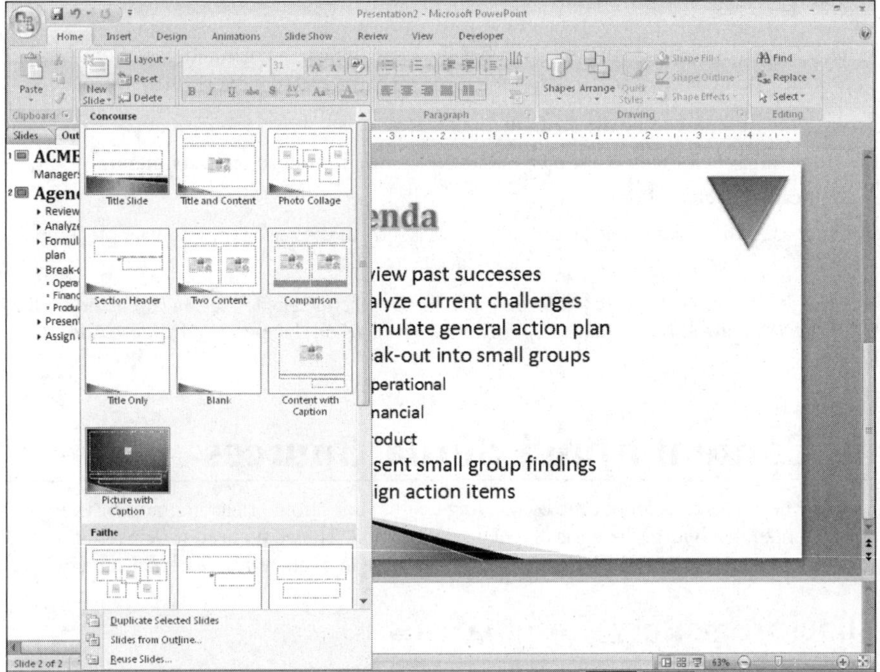

Copying slides

Another way to create a new slide is to copy an existing one in the same presentation. This is especially useful when you are using multiple slides to create a progression because one slide is typically identical to the next slide in a sequence, except for a small change.

There are several ways to copy one or more slides. One way is to use the Windows Clipboard, as in the following steps:

1. **Select the slide or slides that you want to copy.** See "Selecting slides" later in this chapter for more information about selecting slides.

CAUTION **If you select from the Outline pane, make sure that you click the icon to the left of the slide's title so that the entire slide is selected; if you select only part of the text on the slide, then only the selected part is copied.**

2. **Press Ctrl+C.** You can also click the Copy button on the Home tab, or right-click the selection and click Copy.

3. **Select the slide that the pasted slide or slides should follow.** Alternately, in the Outline pane, click to place the insertion point where you want the insertion.
4. **Press Ctrl+V.** You can also click the Paste button on the Home tab, or right-click the destination and click Paste.

PowerPoint also has a Duplicate Slides command that does the same thing as a copy-and-paste command. Although it may be a little faster, it gives you less control as to where the pasted copies will appear:

1. **Select the slide or slides to be duplicated.**
2. **On the Home tab, click the bottom part of the New Slide button to open its menu.**
3. **Click Duplicate Selected Slides.**

   PowerPoint pastes the slides immediately after the last slide in the selection. For example, if you selected slides 1, 3, and 6, then the copies are placed after slide 6.

TIP To make duplication even faster, you can place the Duplicate Selected Slides command on the Quick Access toolbar. To do that, right-click the command on the menu and choose Add to Quick Access toolbar.

Inserting Content from External Sources

Many people find that they can save a lot of time by copying text or slides from other programs or from other PowerPoint presentations to form the basis of a new presentation. There's no need to reinvent the wheel each time! The following sections look at various ways to bring in content from external sources.

Copying slides from other presentations

There are several ways to copy slides from other presentations. You can:

- Open the presentation, save it under a different name, and then delete the slides that you *don't* want, leaving a new presentation with the desired slides ready for customization.
- Open two PowerPoint windows side-by-side and drag-and-drop slides between them.
- Open two PowerPoint presentations, copy slides from one of them to the Clipboard (Ctrl+C), and then paste them into the other presentation (Ctrl+V).
- Use the Reuse Slides feature in PowerPoint, as described next.

To reuse slides from other presentations with the Reuse Slides feature, follow these steps:

1. **On the Home tab, click the lower portion of the New Slide button to open its menu.**
2. **Click Reuse Slides.** The Reuse Slides pane appears.
3. **Click Open a PowerPoint File**

   OR

   Click the Browse button and then click Browse File.
4. **In the Browse dialog box, select the presentation from which you want to copy slides, and click Open.** Thumbnail images of the slides in the presentation appear in the Reuse Slides pane, as shown in Figure 21-17.

FIGURE 21-17

Choose individual slides to copy to the current presentation.

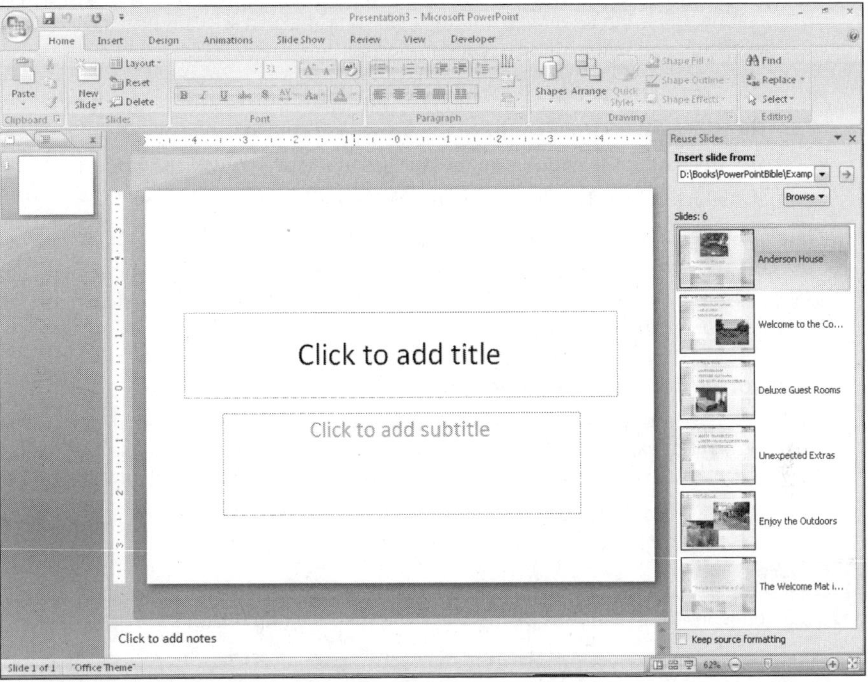

5. **(Optional) If you want to keep the source formatting when copying slides, select the Keep Source Formatting check box at the bottom of the task pane.**
6. **(Optional) You can move the cursor over a slide to see an enlarged image of it.**
7. **Do any of the following:**
   - To insert a single slide, click it.
   - To insert all slides at once, right-click any slide and choose Insert All Slides.
   - To copy only the theme (not the content), right-click any slide and choose Apply Theme to All Slides, or Apply Theme to Selected Slides.

CAUTION **Copying the theme with the Apply Theme to All Slides or Apply Theme to Selected Slides command does not copy the background graphics, layouts, or anything else other than the three elements that are included in a theme: font choices, color choices, and effect choices. If you want to copy all of the formatting, select the Keep Source Formatting checkbox (Step 5) and insert one or more slides.**

Inserting new slides from an Outline

All of the Microsoft Office applications work well together, and so it's easy to move content between them. For example, you can create an outline for a presentation in Microsoft Word and then import it into

PowerPoint. PowerPoint uses the heading styles that you assigned in Word to decide which items are slide titles and which items are slide content. The top-level headings (Heading 1) form the slide titles.

To try this out, open Word, switch to Outline view (from the View tab), and then type a short outline of a presentation. Press Tab to demote, or Shift+Tab to promote, a selected line. Then save your work, go back to PowerPoint, and follow these steps to import it:

1. **On the Home tab, click the lower portion of the New Slide button to open its menu.**
2. **Click Slides from Outline.** The Insert Outline dialog box opens.
3. **Select the file containing the outline text that you want to import.**
4. **Click Insert.** PowerPoint imports the outline.

If there were already existing slides in the presentation, they remain untouched. (This includes any blank slides, and so you might need to delete the blank slide at the beginning of the presentation after importing.) All of the Heading 1 lines from the outline become separate slide titles, and all of the subordinate headings become bullet points in the slides.

Tips for better Outline importing

Although PowerPoint can import any text from any Word document, you may not always get the results that you want or expect. For example, you may have a document that consists of a series of paragraphs with no heading styles applied. When you import this document into PowerPoint, it might look something like Figure 21-18.

FIGURE 21-18

A Word document consisting mainly of plain paragraphs makes for an unattractive presentation.

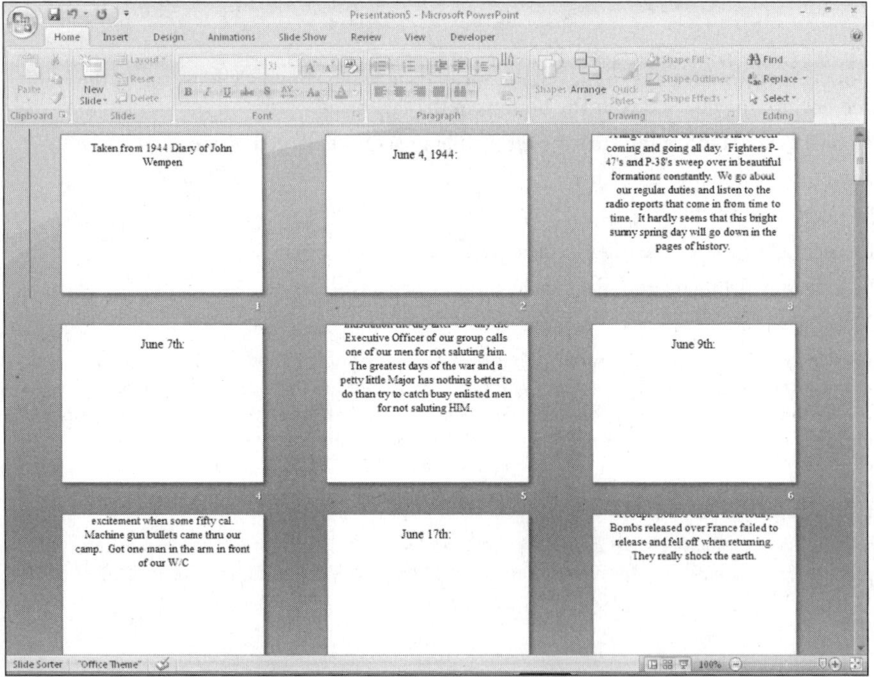

Figure 21-18 is a prime example of what happens if you don't prepare a document before you import it into PowerPoint. PowerPoint makes each paragraph its own slide. It can't tell which ones are actual headings and which ones aren't because there are no heading styles in use. The paragraphs are too long to fit on slides, and so they are truncated off the tops of the slides. Extra blank lines are interpreted as blank slides. Quite a train wreck, isn't it? Figure 21-18 also illustrates an important point to remember: regular paragraph text does not work very well in PowerPoint. PowerPoint text is all about short, snappy bulleted lists and headings. The better that you prepare the outline before importing it, the less cleanup you will need to do after importing. Here are some tips:

- Non-headings in Word do not import into PowerPoint unless you use no heading styles at all in the document (as in Figure 21-18). Apply heading styles to the text that you want to import.
- Stick with basic styles only in the outline: for example, just Heading 1, Heading 2, and so on.
- Delete all blank lines above the first heading. If you don't, you will have blank slides at the beginning of your presentation.
- Strip off as much manual formatting as possible from the Word text, so that the text picks up its formatting from PowerPoint. To strip off formatting in Word, select the text and press Ctrl+spacebar.
- Do not leave blank lines between paragraphs. These will translate into blank slides or blank bulleted items in PowerPoint.
- Delete any graphic elements, such as clip art, pictures, charts, and so on. They will not transfer to PowerPoint anyway and may confuse the import utility.

Importing from other text-based formats

In addition to Word, PowerPoint also imports from plain-text files, from WordPerfect (5.x or 6.x), from Microsoft Works, and from Web pages. The procedure is the same as in the preceding steps. If the file does not appear in the Insert Outline dialog box, change the file type to the desired file type.

If you are setting up a plain-text file for import, you obviously won't have the outlining tools from Word at your disposal. Instead, you must rely on tabs. Each line that should be a title slide should start at the left margin; first-level bullet paragraphs should be preceded by a single tab; second-level bullets should be preceded by two tabs, and so on.

Post-import cleanup

After importing text from an outline, there will probably be a few minor corrections that you need to make. Run through this checklist:

- The first slide in the presentation might be blank. If it is, then delete it.
- The Title Slide layout may not be applied to the first slide; apply that layout, if necessary. (You can use the Layout list on the Home tab.)
- A theme may not be applied; choose one from the Design tab, if necessary.

CROSS-REF **See Chapter 22 for more information on working with themes.**

- Some of the text might contain manual formatting that interferes with the theme formatting and creates inconsistency. Remove any manual formatting that you notice. (One way to do this is to select all of the text in the Outline pane by pressing Ctrl+A and then stripping off the manual formatting by pressing Ctrl+spacebar.)

- If some of the text is too long to fit comfortably on a slide, change to a different slide layout, such as a two-column list, if necessary. You might also need to split the content into two or more slides.
- There might be some blank bullet points on some slides (if you missed deleting all of the extra paragraph breaks before the import). Delete these bullet points.

Opening a Word document as a new presentation

Instead of importing slides from a Word document or other text-based document, as described in the preceding section, you can simply open the Word document in PowerPoint. PowerPoint starts a new presentation file to hold the imported text. This saves some time if you are starting a new presentation anyway, and you don't have any existing slides to merge with the incoming content.

To open a Word document in PowerPoint, follow these steps:

1. **Choose Office Button ➪ Open.** The Open dialog box appears.
2. **Change the file type to All Outlines.**
3. **Select the document.**
4. **Click Open.** The document outline becomes a PowerPoint presentation, with all Heading 1 paragraphs becoming title slides.

You can't open or insert a Word outline in PowerPoint if it is currently open in Word. This limitation is an issue only for Word files, not plain text or other formats.

Importing text from Web pages

PowerPoint accepts imported text from several Web-page formats, including HTML and MHTML (Single File Web Page). It is helpful if the data is in an orderly outline format, or if it was originally created from a PowerPoint file, because there will be less cleanup needed.

There are several ways to import from a Web page:

- Open a Web-page file as you would an outline (see the preceding section), but set the file type to All Web Pages.
- Insert the text from the Web page as you would a Word outline (In the Home tab, click New Slide ➪ Slides from Outline).
- Reuse slides from a Web presentation as you would from any other presentation (In the Home tab, click New Slide ➪ Reuse Slides).

CAUTION **You should use one of the above methods rather than pasting HTML text directly into PowerPoint. This is because when you paste HTML text, you might get additional HTML tags that you don't want, including cross-references that might cause your presentation to try to log onto a Web server every time you open it.**

When importing from a Web page, don't expect the content to appear formatted the same way that it was on the Web page. We're talking strictly about text import here. The formatting on the Web page comes from HTML tags or from a style sheet, neither of which you can import. If you want an exact duplicate of the Web page's appearance, take a picture of the page with the Shift+PrintScreen command, and then paste it into PowerPoint (Ctrl+V) as a graphic.

If you are importing an outline from an MHTML-format Web page that contains pictures, the pictures are also imported into PowerPoint. If importing from a regular HTML file, you cannot import the pictures.

If you need to show a live Web page from within PowerPoint, try Shyam Pillai's free Live Web add-in, found at `www.mvps.org/skp/liveweb.htm`**.**

Managing Slides

After inserting a few slides into a presentation, and perhaps building some content on them, you might decide to make some changes, such as rearranging, deleting, and so on. The following sections explain how to manage and manipulate the slides in a presentation.

Selecting slides

Before you can issue a command that acts upon a slide or a group of slides, you must select the slides that you want to affect. You can do this from either Normal or Slide Sorter view, but Slide Sorter view makes it easier because you can see more slides at once. From Slide Sorter view, or from the Slides pane in Normal view, you can use any of these techniques to select slides:

- To select a single slide, click it.
- To select multiple slides, hold down the Ctrl key as you click each one. Figure 21-19 shows slides 1, 3, and 6 selected, as indicated by the shaded border around the slides.

FIGURE 21-19

Select slides in Slide Sorter view by holding down the Ctrl key and clicking each slide.

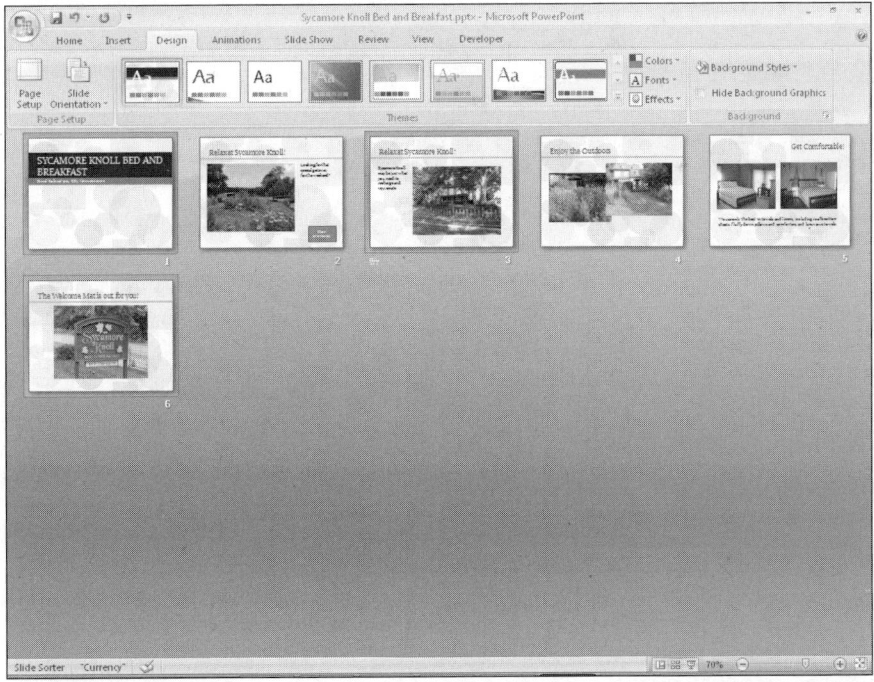

- To select a contiguous group of slides (for example, slides 1, 2, and 3), click the first slide, and then hold down the Shift key as you click the last one. All of the slides in between are selected as well.

To cancel the selection of multiple slides, click anywhere outside of the selected slides.

To select slides from the Outline pane in Normal view, click the slide icon to the left of the slide's title; this selects the entire slide, as shown in Figure 21-20. It's important to select the entire slide and not just part of its content before issuing a command such as Delete, because otherwise, the command only affects the portion that you selected.

Deleting slides

You may want to get rid of some of the slides, especially if you created your presentation using a template that contained a lot of sample content. For example, the sample presentation may be longer than you need, or you may have inserted your own slides instead.

Select the slide or slides that you want to delete, and then do any of the following:

- On the Home tab, click Delete.
- Right-click the selection and choose Delete Slide.
- Press the Delete key on the keyboard.

FIGURE 21-20

Select slides in the Outline pane by clicking the slide icon to the left of the slide title.

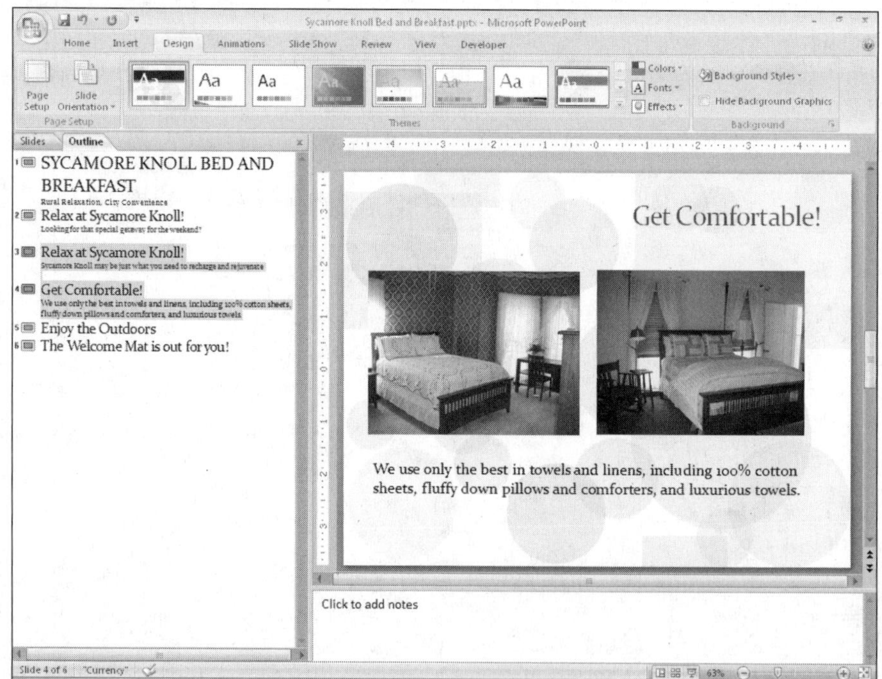

Undoing mistakes

Here's a command that can help you in almost all of the other chapters in this book: undoing. The Undo command allows you to reverse past actions. For example, you can use it to reverse all of the deletions that you made to your presentation in the preceding section. The easiest way to undo a single action is to click the Undo button on the Quick Access toolbar or press Ctrl+Z. You can click it as many times as you like; each time you click it, you undo one action.

TIP **By default, the maximum number of Undo operations is 20, but you can change this. Choose Office Button ⇨ PowerPoint Options, then click Advanced, and in the Editing Options section, change the Maximum Number of Undos setting. Keep in mind that if you set the number of undos too high, it can cause performance problems in PowerPoint.**

You can undo multiple actions at once by opening the Undo button's drop-down list, as shown in Figure 21-21. Just drag the mouse across the actions that you want to undo (you don't need to hold down the mouse button). Click when the desired actions are selected, and presto, they are all reversed. You can select multiple actions to undo, but you can't skip around. For example, to undo the fourth item, you must undo the first, second, and third ones, as well.

The Redo command is the opposite of Undo. If you make a mistake with the Undo button, you can fix the problem by clicking the Redo button. Like the Undo button, it has a drop-down list, and so you can redo multiple actions at once.

FIGURE 21-21

Use the Undo button to undo your mistakes and the Redo button to reverse an Undo operation.

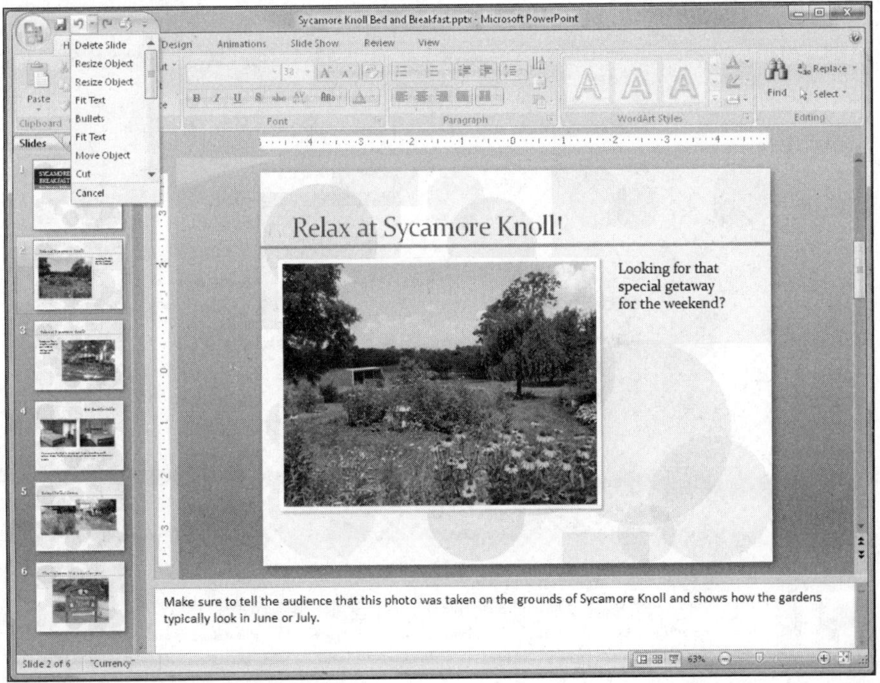

The Redo command is available only immediately after you use the Undo command. If Redo isn't available, a Repeat button appears in its place. The Repeat command enables you to repeat the last action that you performed (and it doesn't have to be an Undo operation). For example, you can repeat some typing, or some formatting. Figure 21-22 shows the Repeat button.

Rearranging slides

The best way to rearrange slides is to do so in Slide Sorter view. In this view, the slides in your presentation appear in thumbnail view, and you can move them around on the screen to different positions, just as you would manually rearrange pasted-up artwork on a table. Although you can also do this from the Slides pane in Normal view, you are able to see fewer slides at once. As a result, it can be more challenging to move slides around, for example, from one end of the presentation to another. To rearrange slides, use the following steps:

1. **Switch to Slide Sorter view.**
2. **Select the slide that you want to move.** You can move multiple slides at once if you like.
3. **Drag the selected slide to the new location.** The mouse pointer changes to a little rectangle next to the pointer arrow as you drag. A vertical line also appears where the slide will go if you release the mouse button at that point, as shown in Figure 21-23.
4. **Release the mouse button.** The slide moves to the new location.

FIGURE 21-22

The Repeat button appears when Redo is not available, and enables you to repeat actions.

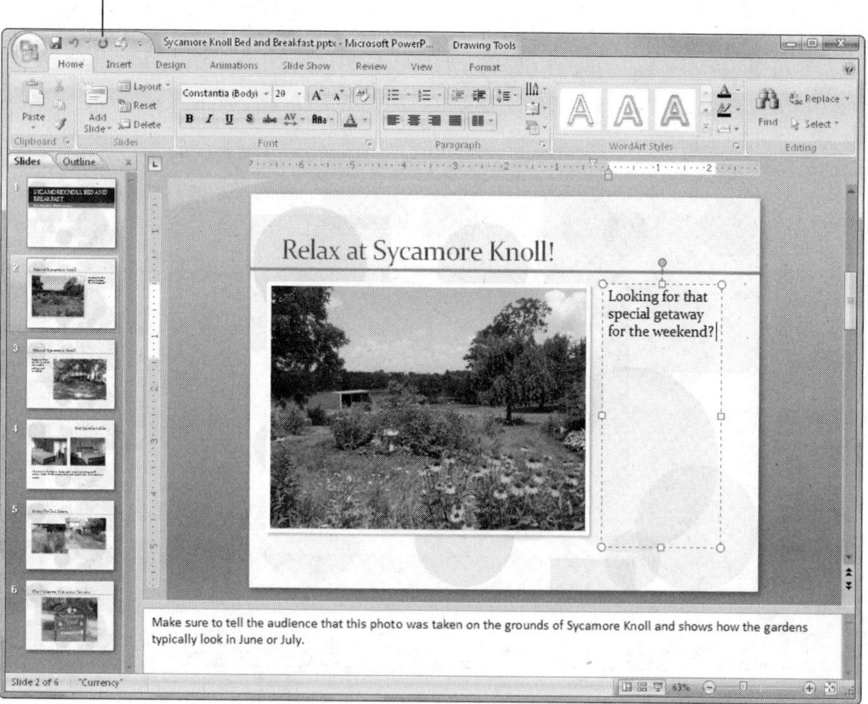

FIGURE 21-23

As you drag a slide, its new position is indicated by a vertical line.

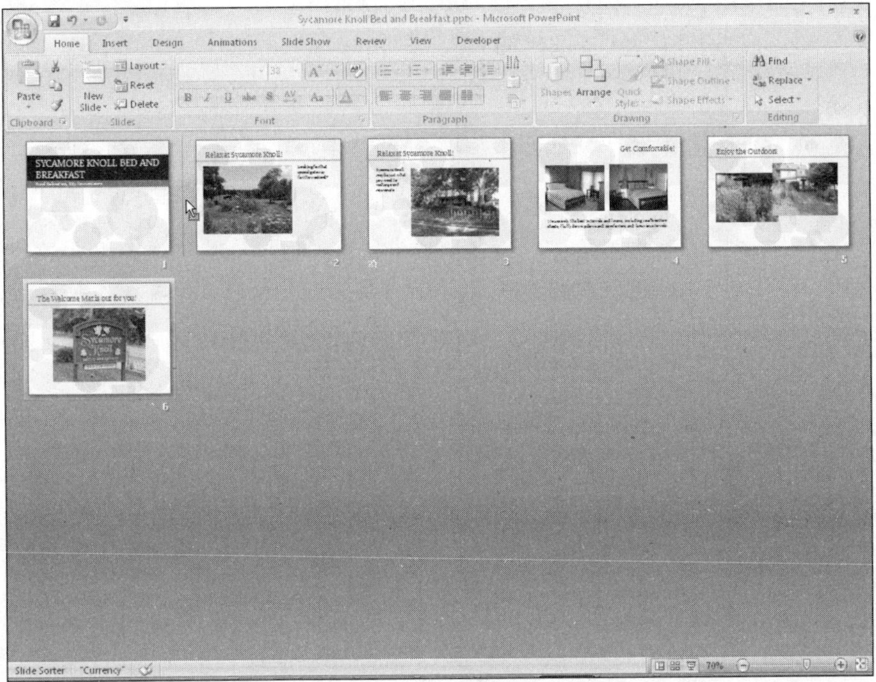

You can also rearrange slides in the Outline pane in Normal view. This is not quite as easy as using Slide Sorter view, but it's more versatile. Not only can you drag entire slides from place to place, but you can also move individual bullets from one slide to another.

Follow these steps to move content in the Outline pane:

1. **Switch to Normal view and display the Outline pane.**
2. **Position the mouse pointer over the slide's icon.** The mouse pointer changes to a four-headed arrow.
3. **Click on the icon.** PowerPoint selects all of the text in that slide.
4. **Drag the slide's icon to a new position in the outline.** As you drag, a horizontal line appears to indicate where the slide will go, as shown in Figure 21-24.
5. **Release the mouse button when the horizontal line is in the right place.** All of the slide's text moves with it to the new location.

FIGURE 21-24

Drag a slide's icon to move it up or down in the Outline pane.

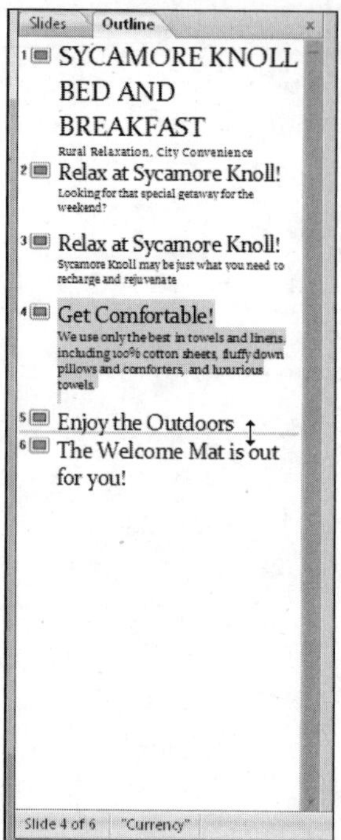

There are also keyboard shortcuts for moving a slide up or down in the Outline pane that may be faster than clicking the toolbar buttons. You can press the Alt+Shift+Up arrow keys to move a slide up and the Alt+Shift+Down arrow keys to move the slide down.

These shortcuts work equally well with single bullets from a slide. Just click to the left of a single line to select it, instead of clicking the Slide icon in Step 3.

Using Content Placeholders

Now that you know something about inserting and managing entire slides, let's take a closer look at the content within a slide. The default placeholder type is a multipurpose content placeholder, as shown in Figure 21-25.

FIGURE 21-25

A content placeholder can contain a variety of different elements.

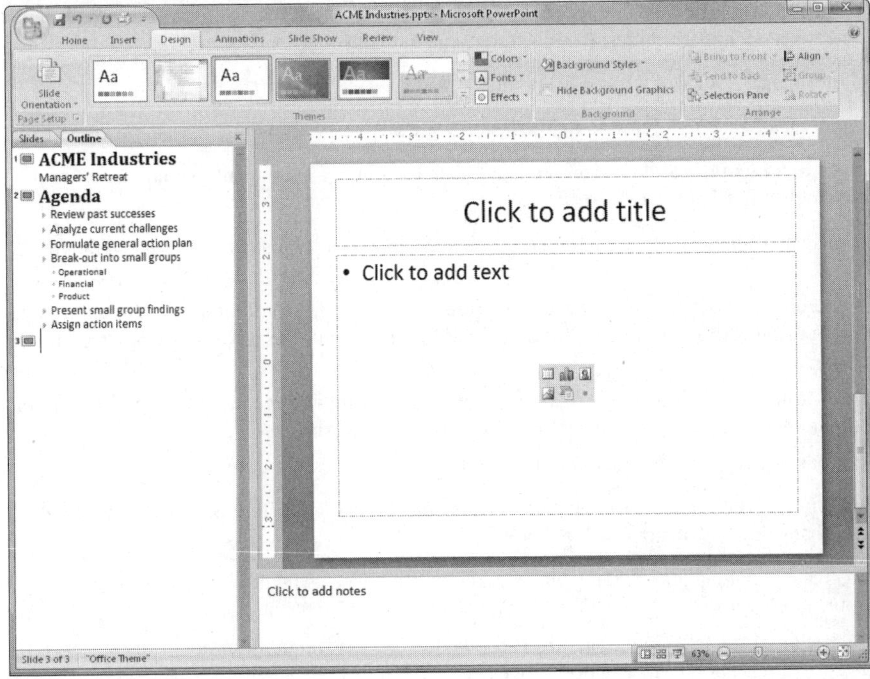

Inserting content into a placeholder

To type text into a content placeholder, click inside the placeholder box and start typing. You can enter and edit text as you would in any word-processing program. To insert any other type of content into a placeholder, click one of the icons shown in Figure 21-26. A dialog box opens to help you select and insert that content type.

A content placeholder can hold only one type of content at a time. If you click in the placeholder and type some text, the icons for the other content types disappear. To access them again, you must delete all of the text from the placeholder.

Placeholders versus manually inserted objects

You can insert content on a slide independently of a placeholder by using the Insert tab's buttons and menus. This technique allows you to insert an item in its own separate frame on any slide, to coexist with any placeholder content. You can learn how to insert each content type in the chapters in which they are covered (see the preceding list).

Creating Text Boxes Manually

The difference between a placeholder-inserted object and a manually inserted one is most significant with text boxes. Although you might think that a text box would create consistent results, there are actually some significant differences between placeholder text boxes and manually inserted ones.

Here are some of the characteristics of a text placeholder:

- You cannot create new text placeholder boxes on your own, except in Slide Master view.

CROSS-REF **You learn how to use Slide Master view to create your own layouts that contain custom text placeholders in Chapter 22.**

- If you delete all of the text from a text placeholder, the placeholder instructions return (in Normal view).
- A text placeholder box has a fixed size on the slide, regardless of the amount or size of text that it contains. You can resize it manually, but if you reapply the layout, the placeholder box snaps back to the original size.
- AutoFit is turned on by default in a text placeholder, so that if you type more text than will fit, or resize the frame so that the existing text no longer fits, the text shrinks in size.
- The text that you type in a text placeholder box appears in the Outline pane.

A manual text box, on the other hand, is one that you create yourself using the Text Box tool on the Insert tab. Here are some characteristics of a manual text box:

- You can create a manual text box anywhere, and you can create as many as you like, regardless of the layout.
- If you delete all of the text from a manual text box, the text box remains empty or disappears completely. No placeholder instructions appear.
- A manual text box starts out small vertically, and expands as you type more text into it.
- A manual text box does not use AutoFit by default; the text box simply becomes larger to make room for more text.
- You cannot resize a manual text box so that the text that it contains no longer fits; PowerPoint refuses to make the text box shorter vertically until you delete some text from it. (However, you can decrease its horizontal width.)
- Text typed in a manual text box does not appear in the Outline pane.

Figure 21-26 shows two text placeholders (one empty) and a text box. Notice that the empty placeholder contains filler text to help you remember that it is there. Notice also that only the text from the placeholder appears in the Outline pane; the text-box text does not. Empty text boxes and placeholders do not show up in Slide Show view, so you do not have to worry about deleting any unneeded ones.

FIGURE 21-26

Two text placeholders and a text box.

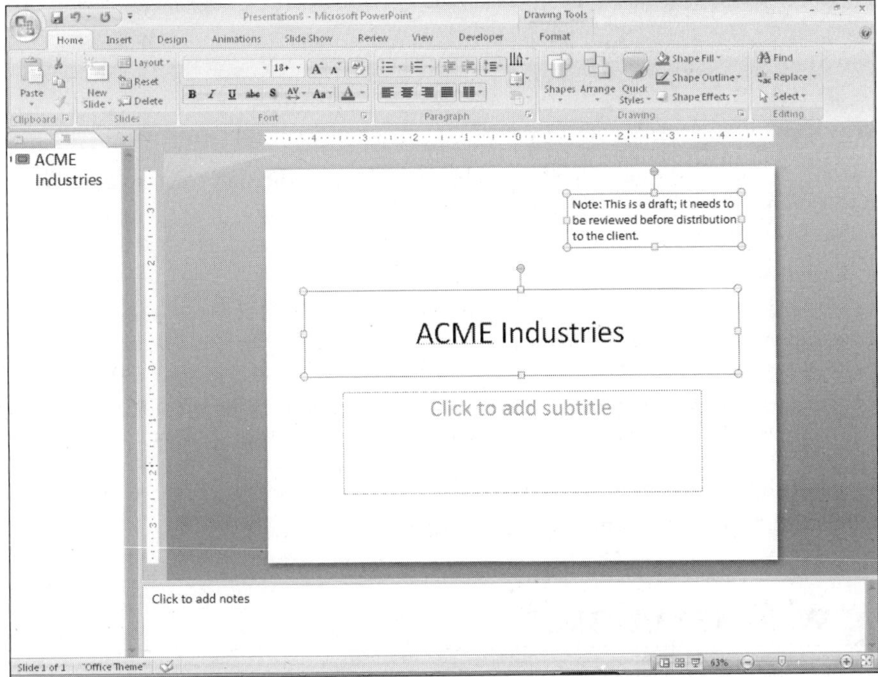

When should you use a manual text box?

Graphical content such as photos and charts can work well either in placeholders or as manually inserted objects. However, when it comes to text, you should stick with placeholders as often as possible. Placeholder text appears in the Outline pane, whereas text in a manually inserted text box does not. When the bulk of a presentation's text is in manually created text boxes, the outline becomes less useful because it doesn't contain the presentation text. In addition, when you change to a different formatting theme that includes different positioning for placeholders — for example, to accommodate a graphic on one side — the manual text boxes do not shift. As a result, they might end up overlapping the new background graphic with unattractive results. In a case such as this, you would need to manually go through each slide and adjust the positioning of each text box.

However, there are times when a manually created text box is preferable or even necessary. For example, suppose that you have a schematic diagram of a machine and you need to label some of the parts. Manually placed text boxes are perfect for these little snippets of text that are scattered over the surface of the picture. Manual text boxes are also useful for warnings, tips, and any other information that is tangential to the main discussion. Finally, if you want to vary the placement of the text on each slide (consciously circumventing the consistency provided by layouts), and you want to precisely position each box, then manual text boxes work well because they do not shift their position when you apply different themes or templates to the presentation.

TIP If you insert text in a placeholder and then change the slide's layout so that the slide no longer contains that placeholder (for example, if you switch to Title Only or Blank layout), the text remains on the slide, but it becomes an *orphan*. If you delete the text box, then it simply disappears; a placeholder does not reappear. However, it does not become a manual text box, because its content still appears in the Outline pane, while a manual text box's content does not.

Creating a manual text box

To manually place a text box on a slide, follow these steps:

1. **If necessary, reposition the existing placeholders or objects on the slide to make room for the new text box.**
2. **On the Insert tab, click Text Box.** The mouse pointer turns into a vertical line.
3. **Do either of the following:**
   - To create a text box that automatically enlarges itself horizontally as you type more text, but does not automatically wrap text to the next line, click once where you want the text to start, and begin typing.
   - To create a text box with a width that you specify, and that automatically wraps text to the next line and grows in height as needed, click and drag to draw a box where you want the text box to be. Its height will initially snap back to a single line's height, regardless of the height that you initially draw; however, it will grow in height as you type text into it.
4. **Type the text that you want to appear in the text box.**

Working with Text Boxes

Text boxes (either placeholder or manual) form the basis of most presentations. Now that you know how to create them, and how to place text in them, let's take a look at how to manipulate the boxes themselves.

CROSS-REF Are you looking for information about formatting text boxes—perhaps to apply a background color or a border to one? See the formatting text boxes discussion in Chapter 7.

Selecting text boxes

On the surface, this topic might seem like a no-brainer. Just click it, right? Well, almost. A text box has two possible "selected" states. One state is that the box itself is selected, and the other is that the insertion point is within the box. The difference is subtle, but it becomes clearer when you issue certain commands. For example, if the insertion point is in the text box and you press Delete, PowerPoint deletes the single character to the right of the insertion point. However, if you select the entire text box and press Delete, PowerPoint deletes the entire text box and everything in it.

To select the entire text box, click its border. You can tell that it is selected because the border appears as a solid line. To move the insertion point within the text box, click inside the text box. You can tell that the insertion point is there because you can see it flashing inside, and also because the box's border now consists of a dashed line. Figure 21-27 shows the difference between the two borders.

FIGURE 21-27

The border of a text box is different when the box itself is selected (left) and when the insertion point is in the box (right).

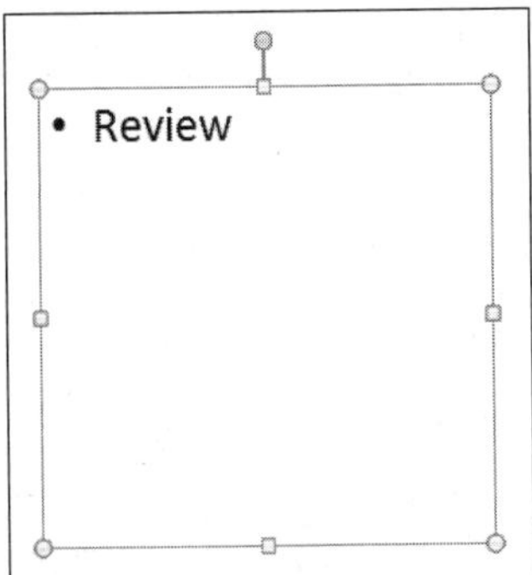

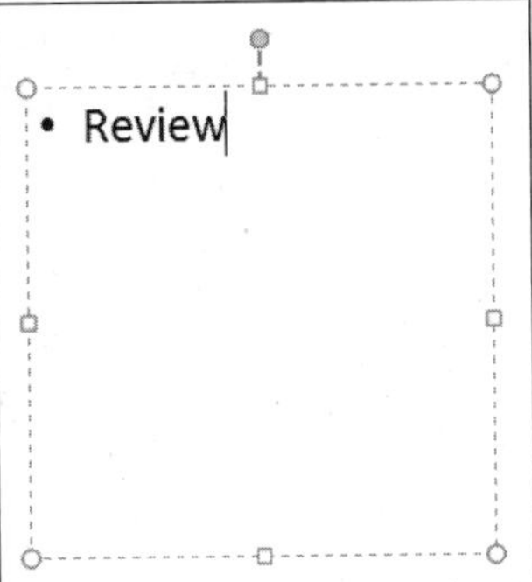

In the rest of this book, when you see the phrase "select the text box," it means in the first way; the box itself should be selected, and the insertion point should *not* appear in it. For most of the upcoming sections it does not make any difference, although in a few cases it does.

When the insertion point is flashing in a text box, you can press Esc to select the text box itself.

You can select more than one text box at once by holding down the Shift key as you click additional text boxes. This technique is useful when you want to select more than one text box, for example, so that you can format them in the same way, or so that you can resize them by the same amount.

Sizing a text box

The basic techniques for sizing text boxes in PowerPoint are the same for every object type (for that matter, they are also the same as in other Office applications). To resize a text box, or any object, follow these steps:

1. **Position the mouse pointer over a selection handle for the object.** The mouse pointer changes to a double-headed arrow.

   If you want to resize proportionally, make sure that you use a corner selection handle, and hold down the Shift key as you drag.
2. **(Optional) To resize proportionally, hold down the Shift key.**
3. **Click and drag the selection handle to resize the object's border.**

CAUTION **Allowing PowerPoint to manage placeholder size and position through layouts ensures consistency among your slides. When you start changing the sizes and positions of placeholders on individual slides, you can end up creating consistency problems, such as headings that aren't in the same spot from slide to slide, or company logos that shift between slides.**

You can also set a text box's size from the Size group on the Drawing Tools Format tab. When the text box is selected, its current dimensions appear in the Height and Width boxes, as shown in Figure 21-28. You can change the dimensions within these boxes.

FIGURE 21-28

You can set an exact size for a text box from the Format tab's Size group.

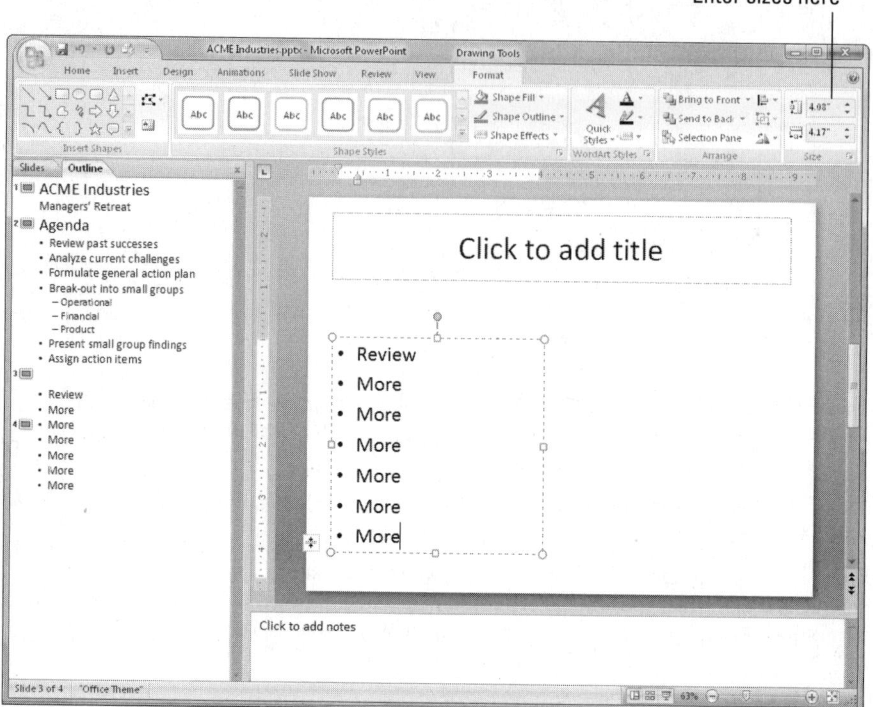

You can also set the size of a text box from the Size and Position dialog box:

1. **Click the Dialog Box Launcher in the Size group on the Drawing Tools Format tab, as shown in Figure 21-28.** The Size and Position dialog box opens.
2. **On the Size tab, set the height and width for the text box, as shown in Figure 21-29.**

   To keep the size proportional, select the Lock Aspect Ratio checkbox in the Scale section before you start adjusting the height or width.
3. **Click Close to close the dialog box.**

FIGURE 21-29

You can adjust the size of the text box from the Size and Position dialog box.

TIP The Size and Position dialog box is *non-modal.* This means that you can leave it open and continue to work on your presentation. It also means that any changes that you make in this dialog box are applied immediately; there is no Cancel button in the dialog box to cancel your changes. To reverse a change, you can use the Undo command (Ctrl+Z).

Positioning a text box

To move an object, simply drag it by any part of its border other than a selection handle. Select the object, and then position the mouse pointer over a border so that the pointer turns into a four-headed arrow. Then drag the object to a new position. With a text box, you must position the mouse pointer over a border and not over the inside of the frame; with all other object types, you don't have to be that precise; you can move an object by dragging anywhere within it.

To set an exact position, use the Size and Position dialog box:

1. **Click the Dialog Box Launcher in the Size group on the Drawing Tools Format tab, as shown in Figure 21-28.** The Size and Position dialog box opens.
2. **On the Position tab, shown in Figure 21-30, set the horizontal and vertical position, and the point from which it is measured.** By default, measurements are from the top-left corner of the slide.
3. **Click Close to close the dialog box.**

FIGURE 21-30

You can adjust the position from the Size and Position dialog box.

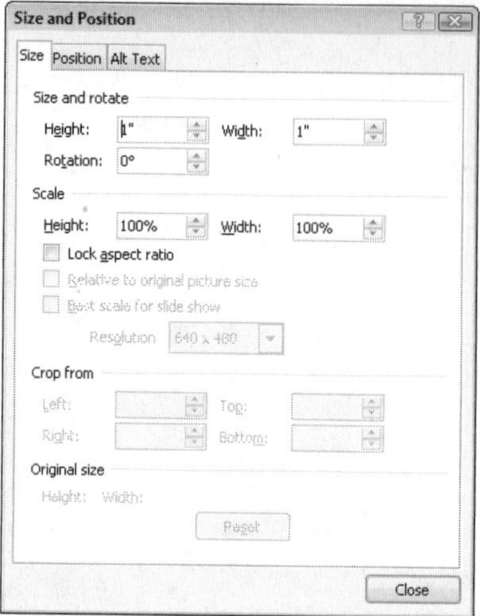

Changing a text box's AutoFit behavior

When there is too much text to fit in a text box, there are three things that may happen:

- **Do Not AutoFit:** The text and the box can continue at their default sizes, and the text can overflow out of the box or be truncated.
- **Shrink Text on Overflow:** The text can shrink its font size to fit in the text box. This is the default setting for placeholder text boxes.
- **Resize Shape to Fit Text:** The text box can enlarge to the size needed to contain the text. This is the default setting for manual text boxes.

Whenever there is too much text in a placeholder box, the AutoFit icon appears in the bottom-left corner. Click that icon to display a menu, as shown in Figure 21-31. From that menu, you can turn AutoFit on or off.

With a manual text box, the AutoFit icon does not appear, and so you must adjust the AutoFit behavior in the text box's properties. The following method works for both manual and placeholder boxes:

1. **Right-click the border of the text box and choose Format Shape.**
2. **Click Text Box.**
3. **In the Autofit section, choose one of the AutoFit options, as shown in Figure 21-32.**
4. **Click Close.**

FIGURE 21-31

You can use the AutoFit icon's menu to change the AutoFit setting for a text box.

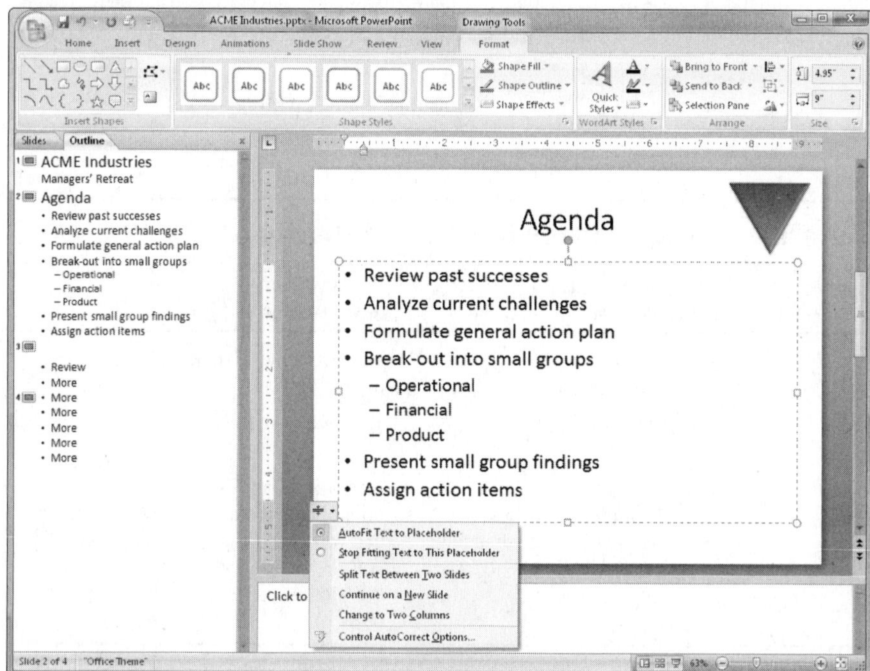

FIGURE 21-32

You can set AutoFit properties in the Format Shape dialog box.

One other setting that also affects AutoFit behavior is the Wrap Text in Shape option. This on/off toggle enables text to automatically wrap to the next line when it reaches the right edge of the text box. By default, this setting is On for placeholder text boxes and for manual text boxes that you create by dragging. However, it is Off by default for manual text boxes that you create by clicking. You can change the setting by displaying the text box's properties, as shown in Figure 21-18, and selecting or deselecting the Wrap Text in Shape checkbox.

Table 21-5 summarizes the various AutoFit behaviors and how they interact with one another.

TABLE 21-5

AutoFit and Resize Shape to Fit Text Behaviors

Setting	Default For	When Wrap Text in Shape is on	When Wrap Text in Shape is off
Do Not Autofit	n/a	Text overflows at bottom of text box only	Text overflows at right and bottom of text box
Shrink Text on Overflow	Placeholders	Text shrinks to fit	Text shrinks to fit
Resize Shape to Fit Text	Manual text boxes	Text box expands vertically only (default for manual text box that you create by dragging)	Text box expands vertically and horizontally (default for manual text box that you create by clicking). However, if you clicked to create the text box initially, the width keeps expanding until you press Enter.

Formatting text in a text box

As in Word 2007, the primary buttons for formatting text are found on the Home tab in PowerPoint, as shown in Figure 21-33. To format text, either select the text box or specific text within the box (see the earlier section, "Selecting Text Boxes," and then use the desired formatting choice in either the Font or Paragraph group on the Home tab. (These tools work nearly identical to those described for Word in Chapters 5 and 6.)

FIGURE 21-33

Use the choices in the Font and Paragraph groups to format text.

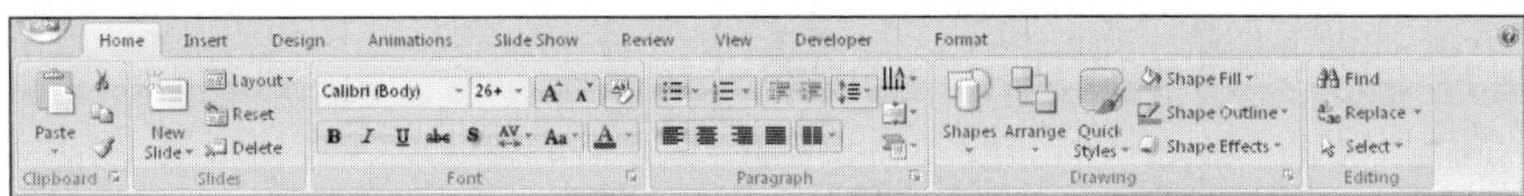

Summary

This chapter made you a master of files. You can now confidently create new presentations, and save, open, close, and delete PowerPoint presentation files. You can also save files in different formats, search for missing presentations, and lots more. This is rather utilitarian knowledge and not very much fun to practice, but later you will be glad you took the time to learn it, when you have important files you need to keep safe.

In this chapter, you learned how to create new slides, either from scratch or from outside sources. You learned how to select, rearrange, and delete slides, and how to place content on a slide. Along the way, you learned the difference between a content placeholder and a manually inserted object, and you how to create your own text boxes, move and resize objects, and find or replace text. These are all very basic skills, and perhaps not as interesting as some of the more exciting topics to come, but mastering them will serve you well as you build your presentation.

In the next chapter, you'll learn about themes and layouts, two of the innovative features in PowerPoint 2007 that make it such an improvement over earlier versions. You'll find out how a theme differs from a template and how it applies font, color, and effect formatting to a presentation. You will then apply layouts and create your own custom layouts and themes.

Chapter 22

Working with Layouts, Themes, and Masters

IN THIS CHAPTER

Most presentations consist of multiple slides, so you'll need a way of ensuring consistency among them. Not only will you want each slide (in most cases) to have the same background, fonts, and text positioning, but you will also want a way of ensuring that any changes you make to those settings later automatically populate across all your slides.

To accomplish these goals, PowerPoint offers layouts, themes, and masters. *Layouts* determine the positioning of placeholders, *themes* assign color, font, and background choices, and *masters* transfer theme settings to the slides and provide an opportunity for repeated content, such as a logo, on each slide. In this chapter you learn how to use layouts, themes, and masters to create a presentation that is attractive, consistent, and easy to manage.

Understanding Layouts and Themes

As you learned in Chapter 21, a *layout* is a positioning template. The layout used for a slide determines what content placeholders will appear and how they will be arranged. For example, the default layout, called Title and Content, contains a placeholder for a title across the top of the slide and a multipurpose placeholder for body content in the center.

A *theme* is a group of design settings. It includes color settings, font choices, object effect settings, and in some cases also a background graphic. In Figure 22-1 later in the chapter, the theme applied is called Concourse, and it is responsible for the colored swoop in the corner, the color of that swoop, and the fonts used on the slide. A theme is applied to a *slide master*, which is a sample slide and not part of the regular presentation, existing only behind the scenes to provide its settings to the real slides. It holds the formatting that you want to be consistent among all the slides in the presentation (or at least a group of them, because a presentation can have multiple slide masters). Technically, you do not apply a theme to a slide; you apply a theme to a slide master, and then you apply a slide master to a slide. That's because a slide master can actually contain some additional elements besides the formatting of the theme such as extra graphics, dates, footer text, and so on.

Themes versus templates

PowerPoint 2007 handles themes, layouts, and slide masters very differently from earlier versions, and this can take some getting used to if you're upgrading.

In PowerPoint 2003, you applied a *design template* (not a theme) to the slide master. A design template was a regular PowerPoint template file (.pot extension) with color choices, font choices, and background graphics. You could have multiple slide masters in a single presentation, so you could base some slides on a different design template than others. PowerPoint 2007 still uses templates, but its primary means of changing the presentation's look and feel is to apply different *themes* to the slide master rather than different templates to the presentation as a whole.

A PowerPoint 2007 template contains at least one slide master, and that slide master has a theme applied to it, so technically every template contains at least one theme. A template with multiple slide masters can therefore carry multiple themes. However, when you apply a template to an existing presentation, only the theme associated with its default (first) slide master is applied. If you start a new presentation based on that template, though, and the template contains more than one theme, you have access to all the stored themes within it.

A theme is both simpler than and more complex than a template. It is simpler in that it cannot hold some of the things a real template can hold. A theme can provide only font, color, effect, and background settings to the presentation. (It can in some cases also provide slide layouts, but let's postpone that discussion for a bit.) And a theme can contain only one set of settings, whereas a template that has multiple slide masters can contain multiple sets of settings. On the other hand, a theme can also do *more* than a PowerPoint template; you can apply a theme saved as a separate file to other Office applications, so you can share its color, font, and effect settings with Word or Excel, for example.

Where themes are stored

A theme is an XML file (or a snippet of XML code embedded in a presentation or template file). A theme can come from any of these sources:

- **Built-in:** Some themes are embedded in PowerPoint itself, and are available from the Themes gallery on the Design tab regardless of the template in use.
- **Custom (automatically loaded):** The default storage location for theme files in Windows Vista is C:\Users*username*\AppData\Roaming\Microsoft\Templates\Document Themes. For Windows XP, it is C:\Documents and Settings\username\Application Data\Microsoft\Templates\Document Themes. All themes (and templates containing themes) stored here are automatically displayed among the gallery of theme choices on the Design tab, in a Custom category.
- **Inherited from starting template:** If you start a presentation using a template other than the default blank one, that template might have one or more themes included in it.
- **Stored in current presentation:** If you modify a theme in Slide Master view while you are working on a presentation, the modified code for the theme is embedded in that presentation file.
- **Stored in a separate file:** If you save a theme (using any of a variety of methods you'll learn later in this chapter), you create a separate theme file with a .thmx extension. These files can be shared among other Office applications, so you can standardize settings such as font and color choices across applications. (Some of the unique PowerPoint portions of the theme are ignored when you use the theme in other applications.)

Themes, layouts, and Slide Master view

In PowerPoint 2003, slide layouts were almost completely separate from slide masters, and were completely separate from design templates. PowerPoint 2003 provided noncustomizable layouts you could apply to change the placeholder types and positions, and these layouts were largely unaffected by the design applied to the slider master. The slide master consisted of a single slide defining generic placement for all the title and content placeholders, with an optional second slide to separately define the placement for title slides.

In PowerPoint 2007, the slide master has separate layout masters for each layout, and you can customize and create new layouts. For example, Figure 22-1 shows Slide Master view (View ➪ Slide Master). Notice along the left side that there is a different, separately customizable layout master for each available layout, all grouped beneath the slide master. Any changes you make to the slide master trickle down to the individual layout masters, but you can also customize each of the individual layout masters to override a trickle-down setting. For example, on a particular layout you can choose to omit the background graphic to free up its space on the slide for extra content.

FIGURE 22-1

In Slide Master view, notice that each layout has its own customizable layout master.

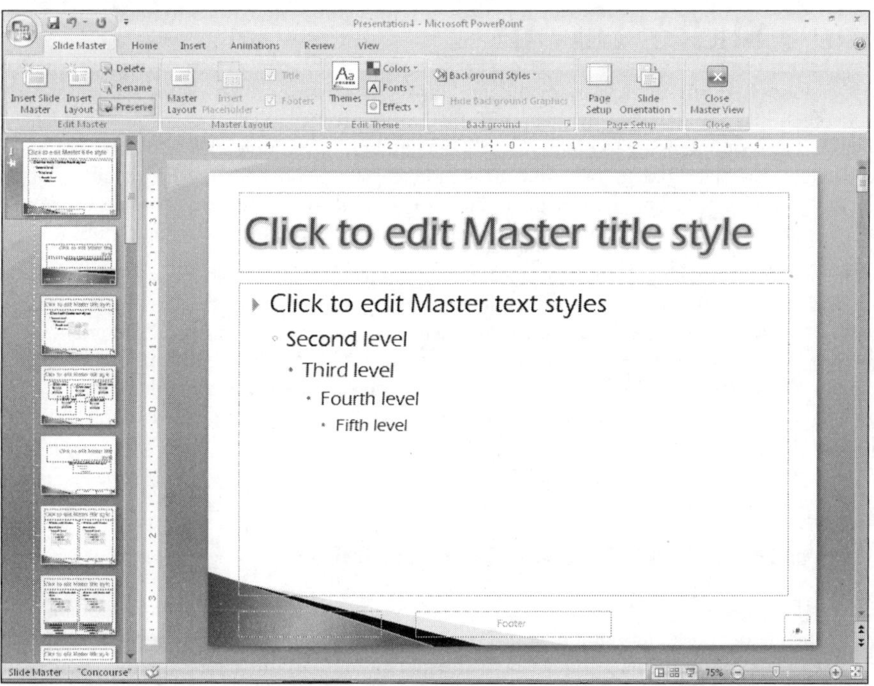

A *master* is a set of specifications that govern formatting and appearance. PowerPoint actually has three masters: the Slide Master (for slides), the Handout Master (for handouts), and the Notes Master (for speaker notes). This chapter deals only with the Slide Master.

CROSS-REF For more on the Handout and Notes Masters, see Chapter 25.

The *slide master* holds the settings from a theme and applies them to one or more slides in your presentation. A slide master is not exactly the same thing as a theme because the theme can also be external to PowerPoint and used in other programs, but there's a rough equivalency there. A slide master is the representation of a particular theme applied to a particular presentation.

NOTE Which themes appear in Slide Master view? The ones you have applied to at least one slide in the presentation, plus any custom themes copied from another presentation (see the section "Copying a theme from another presentation" for more details) and any themes inherited from the template used to create the presentation. The built-in themes do not show up here unless they are in use.

When you make changes to a slide master, those changes trickle down to the individual layout masters associated with it. When you make changes to an individual layout master, those changes are confined to that layout in that master only.

To enter Slide Master view, choose View ➪ Slide Master. When you do so, a Slide Master tab appears. To exit from Slide Master view, choose Slide Master ➪ Close or select a different view from the View tab.

Changing a Slide's Layout

Although earlier versions of PowerPoint had many different layouts, they were all mostly the same, but with different types of content placeholders. In PowerPoint 2007, there are fewer layouts, but the placeholders on them are much more accommodating to different types of content. For example, the default layout, called Title and Content, has placeholders for a slide title plus a single type of content — text, a table, a chart, a picture, a piece of clip art, a SmartArt diagram, or a movie. That's a big improvement because now you can choose based on the layout you want, and not the type of content you might decide to put into it.

When you change the layout, you change the type and/or positioning of the placeholders on it. If the previous placeholders had content in them, that content shifts to a new location on the slide to reflect the different positioning for that placeholder type. If the new layout does not contain a placeholder appropriate for that content, the content remains on the slide, but becomes *orphaned*. That means it is a free-floating object, outside of the layout. You need to manually position an orphaned object if it's not in the right spot. However, if you later apply a different layout that does contain a placeholder for the orphaned object, it snaps back into that placeholder.

Are Layouts Stored in Themes?

Yes and no. Yes, custom layouts are stored with theme files, but they are not always immediately available when you apply that theme to a presentation. It depends on how you apply the theme. If you start a new presentation based on a template that contains a certain theme, then whatever custom layouts are defined for that theme in the template are automatically made available. However, if you apply the theme to the presentation later, then the custom layouts don't carry over — you only get the colors, fonts, effects, and backgrounds. We'll look at some ways to get around this later in the chapter, in "Customizing and Creating Layouts."

To switch a slide to a different layout, follow these steps:

1. **Select the slide(s) to affect.**
2. **On the Home tab, click Layout.** A menu of layouts appears. See Figure 22-2.
3. **Click the desired layout.**

FIGURE 22-2

Switch to a different layout for the selected slide(s).

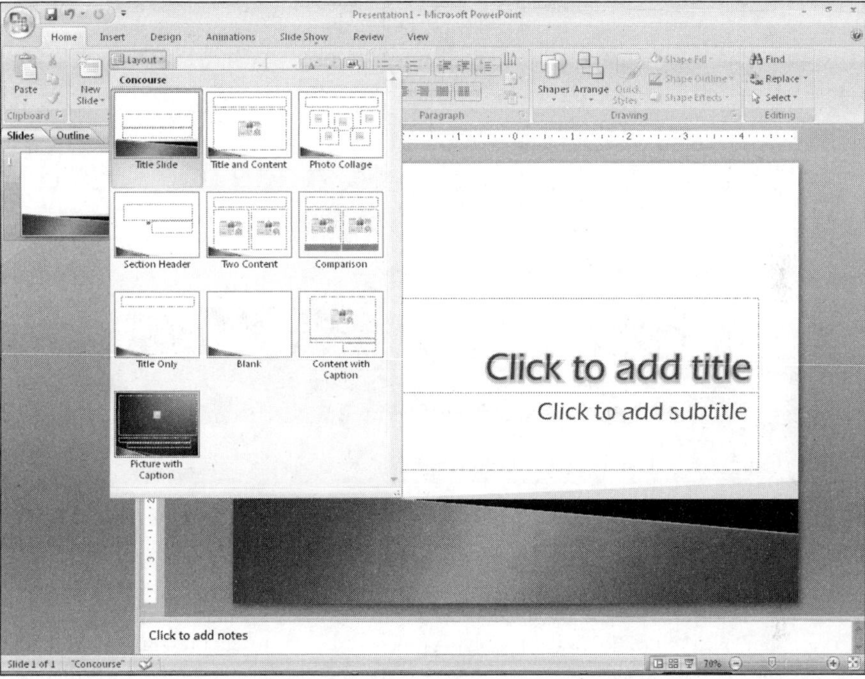

CROSS-REF **If you want to modify a built-in layout, or create your own layouts, see the section "Customizing and Creating Layouts" later in this chapter.**

When a presentation has more than one slide master defined, separate layouts appear for each of the slide master themes. Figure 22-3 shows the Layout menu for a presentation that has two slide masters.

FIGURE 22-3

When there are multiple slide masters, each one's layout is separate.

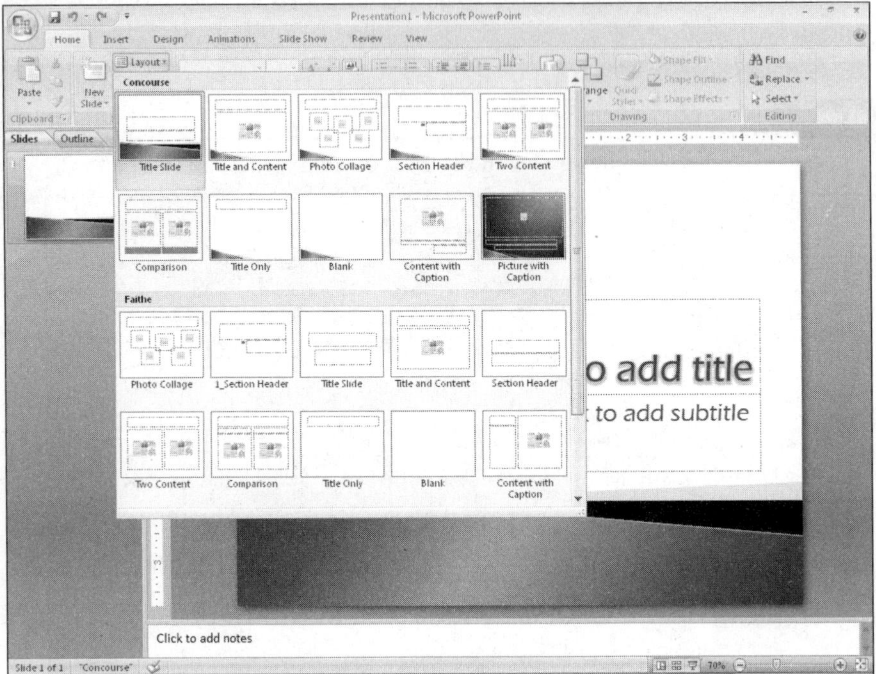

Applying a Theme

As you learned in the section "Understanding Layouts and Themes" at the beginning of this chapter, themes are the PowerPoint 2007 way of applying different designs to the presentation. A theme includes a background graphic (usually), color and font choices, and graphic effect settings. A theme can also include custom layouts, although these are not available when you apply the theme to an existing presentation. (More on that quandary later in the chapter.)

The method for applying a theme depends on whether that theme is already available in the current presentation or not. Some themes are built into PowerPoint so that they are always available; other themes are available only when you use certain templates, or when you specifically apply them from an external file. The following sections explain each of those possibilities.

NOTE **_Themes_, also called _design themes_, contain a combination of colors, fonts, effects, backgrounds, and layouts. There are also more specialized themes: color themes, font themes, and effect themes. When this book uses the term "theme" alone, it's referring to a design theme. Where there is potential for confusion, the book calls it a design theme to help differentiate it from the lesser types of themes.**

Applying a theme from the gallery

A *gallery* in PowerPoint is a menu of samples from which you can choose. The Themes gallery is a menu of all of the built-in themes plus any additional themes available from the current template or presentation file.

To select a theme from the gallery, follow these steps:

1. **(Optional) If you want to affect only certain slides, select them. (Slide Sorter view works well for this.)**
2. **On the Design tab, in the Themes group, if the theme you want appears, click it, and skip the rest of these steps.** If the theme you want does not appear, you will need to open the gallery. To do so, click the More button (down arrow with the line over it), as shown in Figure 22-4.

FIGURE 22-4

Open the Themes gallery by clicking the down arrow with the line above it.

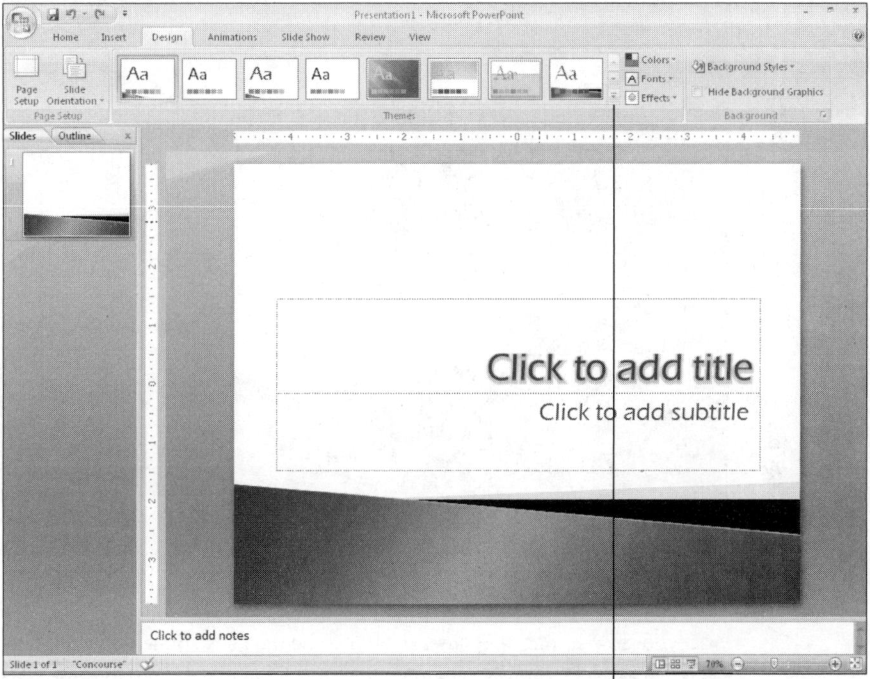

The Themes gallery opens, as you see in Figure 22-5. The gallery is divided into sections based upon the source of the theme. Themes stored in the current presentation appear at the top; custom themes you have added appear next. Built-in themes appear at the bottom.

TIP You can drag the bottom-right corner of the menu to resize the gallery. To filter the gallery so that only a certain category of theme appears, click the down arrow to the right of All Themes at the top and select a category from the menu that appears.

FIGURE 22-5

Select the desired theme from the menu.

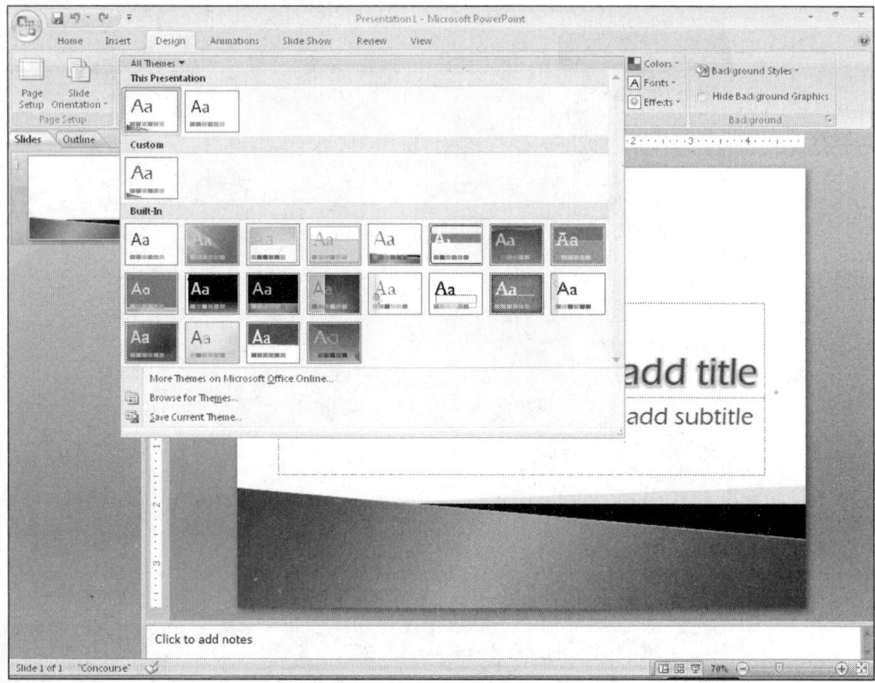

3. **Click the theme you want to apply.**
   - If you selected multiple slides in Step 1, the theme is applied only to them.
   - If you selected a single slide in Step 1, the theme is applied to the entire presentation.

TIP To override the default behavior in Step 3, so that you can apply a different theme to a single slide, right-click instead of clicking in Step 3 and choose Apply to Selected Slide(s) from the shortcut menu.

Applying a theme from a theme or template file

You can open and use externally saved theme files in any Office application. This makes it possible to share color, font, and other settings between applications to create consistency between documents of various types. You can also save and load themes from templates.

CROSS-REF To create your own theme files, see the section "Creating a new theme" later in this chapter.

To apply a theme to the presentation from a theme or template file, follow these steps:

1. **On the Design tab, open the Themes gallery (see Figure 22-4) and click Browse for Themes.** The Choose Theme or Themed Document dialog box opens.
2. **Navigate to the folder containing the file and select it (Figure 22-6).**
3. **Click Apply.**

FIGURE 22-6

Select the desired theme in the dialog box.

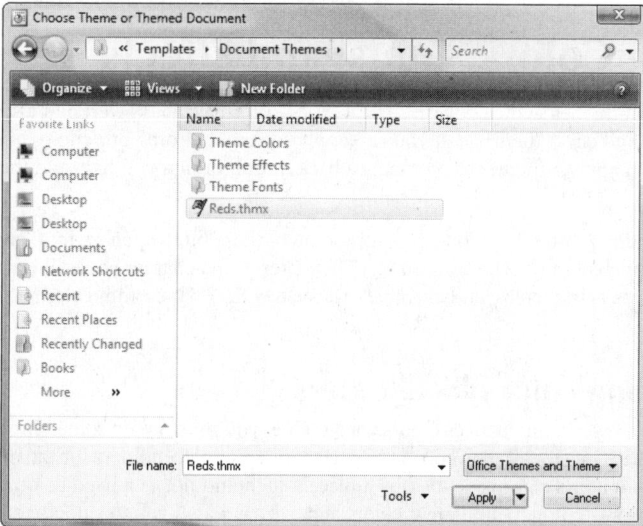

NOTE **Any custom themes you might have previously saved are located by default in C:\Users\username\AppData\Roaming\Microsoft\Templates\Document Themes (in Windows Vista) or C:\Documents and Settings\username\Application Data\Microsoft\Templates\Document Themes (in Windows XP). However, you don't need to navigate to that location to open a theme file because all themes stored here are automatically included in the gallery already.**

A theme file contains only one theme, but a template file can potentially contain multiple themes. So how does PowerPoint know which one you want to apply if you apply from a template? If the template file contains any slides, the theme that the first slide uses is applied. Otherwise the first theme in the template (as determined by the order in Slide Master view) is applied.

Applying a theme to a new presentation

Applying a theme from a theme or template file to an existing presentation, as in the preceding section, applies only the formatting; it does not copy any custom slide layouts you might have created. To copy the custom layouts, you must start a new presentation based on the theme.

To start a new presentation based on the theme, follow these steps:

1. **Choose Office Button ➪ Open. The Open dialog box appears.**
2. **Open the File Type list and choose Office Themes.**
3. **Navigate to the location containing the theme and select it. Custom themes are stored by default in C:\Users*username*\AppData\Roaming\Microsoft\Templates\Document Themes for Windows Vista or C:\Documents and Settings\username\Application Data\Microsoft\Templates\Document Themes for Windows XP.**
4. **Click Open.** PowerPoint starts a new presentation based on that theme and any custom layouts that the theme includes.

To copy a theme from one presentation to another — including all its custom layouts, if any — see the section "Managing themes" later in this chapter.

Changing Colors, Fonts, and Effects

In addition to overall themes, which govern several types of formatting, PowerPoint also provides many built-in color, font, and effect themes that you can apply separately from your choice of overall theme. So, for example, you can apply a theme that contains a background design you like, and then change the colors and fonts for it.

In the following sections, you'll learn how to apply some of these built-in color, font, and effect settings to a presentation without changing the overall theme. Then later in the chapter you will learn how to save these customized settings as new themes, and even how to create your own custom color and font settings in a theme.

Understanding color placeholders

To understand how PowerPoint changes colors via a theme, you must know something about how it handles color placeholders in general. PowerPoint uses a set of color placeholders for the bulk of its color formatting. Because each item's color is defined by a placeholder, and not as a fixed color, you can easily change the colors by switching to a different color theme. That way if you decide, for example, that you want all the slide titles to be blue rather than green, you make the change once and it is applied to all slides automatically.

A group of colors assigned to preset placeholders is a *color theme*. PowerPoint contains 20+ built-in color themes that are available regardless of the overall theme applied to the presentation. Because most design themes use placeholders to define their colors, you can apply the desired design theme to the presentation and then fine-tune the colors afterward by experimenting with the built-in color themes.

How many color placeholders are there in a color theme? There are actually 12, but sometimes not all of them are available to be applied to individual objects. When you choose a color theme (Design ➪ Colors), the gallery of themes from which you choose shows only the first 8 colors of each color theme. It doesn't matter so much here because you can't apply individual colors from there anyway. When selecting colors from a color picker (used for applying fill and border color to specific objects), as in Figure 22-7, there are 10 theme swatches. And when you define a new custom color scheme, there are 12 placeholders to set up. The final two are for visited and unvisited hyperlinks; these colors aren't included in a color picker.

FIGURE 22-7

PowerPoint uses color pickers such as this one to enable you to easily apply color placeholders to objects.

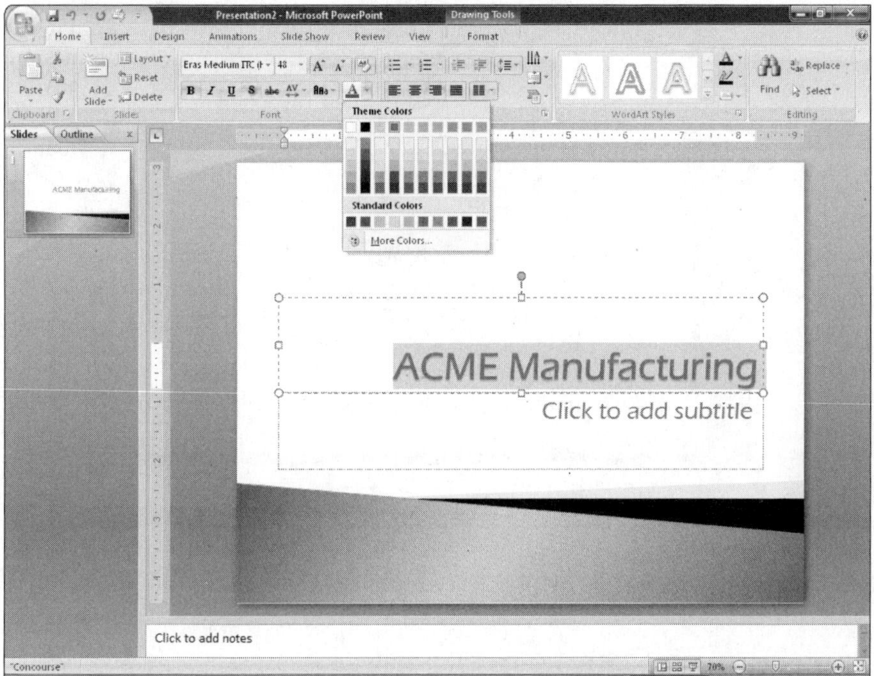

Switching color themes

After applying the overall theme you want, you might want to apply different colors. To switch to a different color theme, follow these steps:

1. **(Optional) To apply a different color theme to a slide master other than the default one, open Slide Master view (View ➪ Slide Master) and click the desired slide master.** Otherwise, the color change will apply to all slides that use the default slide master. The default slide master is the first one listed in Slide Master view.
2. **On the Design tab (or the Slide Master tab if in Slide Master view), click Colors.** A gallery of color themes opens.
3. **(Optional) Point to a color theme and observe the preview on the slide behind the list.**
4. **Click the desired color theme.** See Figure 22-8.

FIGURE 22-8

Select the desired theme from the dialog box.

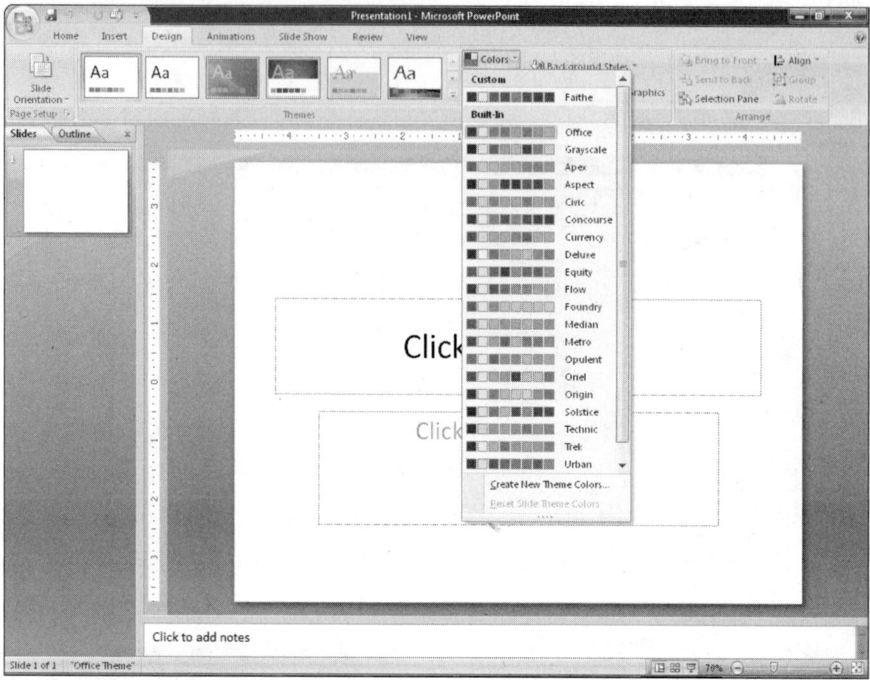

CROSS-REF **You can also create custom color themes; see "Creating a custom color theme" later in this chapter for details.**

Understanding font placeholders

By default in most themes and templates, text box fonts are not set to a specific font, but to one of two designations: Heading or Body. Then a *font theme* defines what specific fonts to use. To change the fonts across the entire presentation, all you have to do is apply a different font theme.

A *font theme* is an XML-based specification that defines a pair of fonts: one for headings and one for body text. Then that font is applied to the text boxes in the presentation based on their statuses of Heading or Body. For example, all of the slide titles are usually set to Heading, and all of the content placeholders and manual text boxes are usually set to Body.

In a blank presentation (default blank template), when you click inside a slide title placeholder box, you see Calibri (Headings) in the Font group on the Home tab. Figure 22-9 shows that the current font is Calibri, but that it is being used only because the font theme specifies it. You could change the font theme to Verdana/Verdana, for example, and then the font designation for that box would appear as Verdana (Headings).

FIGURE 22-9

When some text is using a font placeholder rather than a fixed font, (Headings) or (Body) appears after its name in the Font group on the Home tab.

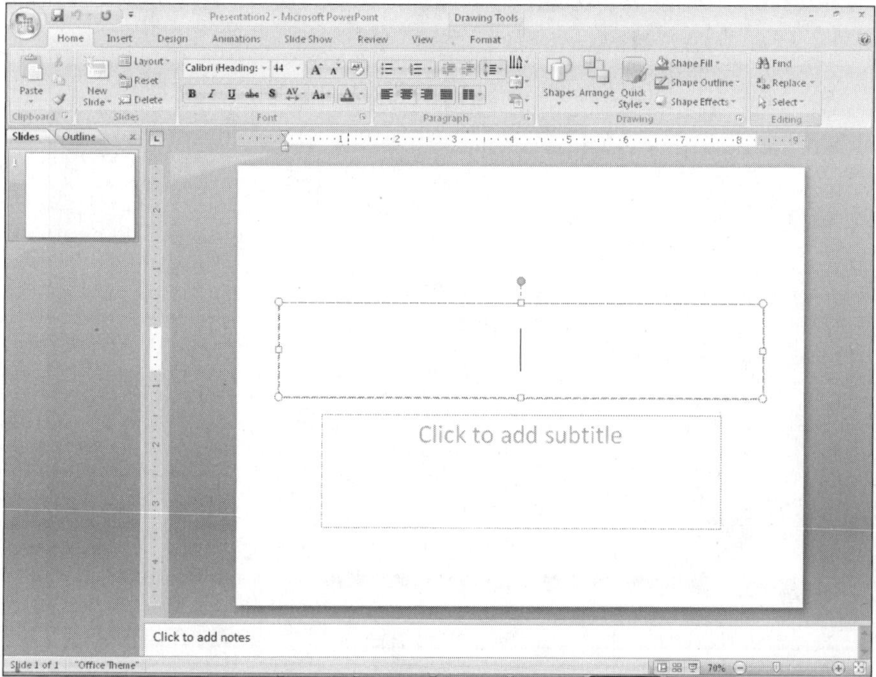

In some font themes, the same font is used for both headings and body. In a default blank presentation both fonts are Calibri, for example, and the Verdana/Verdana set is an additional example. In many other font themes, though, the heading and body fonts are different.

Switching font themes

After applying an overall theme, you might decide you want to use different fonts in the presentation. To switch to a different font theme, follow these steps:

1. **(Optional) To apply a different font theme to a slide master other than the default one, open Slide Master view (View ➪ Slide Master) and click the desired slide master.** Otherwise, the font change will apply to all slides that use the default slide master. The default slide master is the first one listed in Slide Master view.
2. **On the Design tab (or Slide Master tab, if in Slide Master view), click Fonts.** A gallery of font themes opens.
3. **(Optional) Point to a font theme and observe the change on the slide behind the list.**
4. **Click the desired font theme.** See Figure 22-10.

FIGURE 22-10

Select the desired font theme.

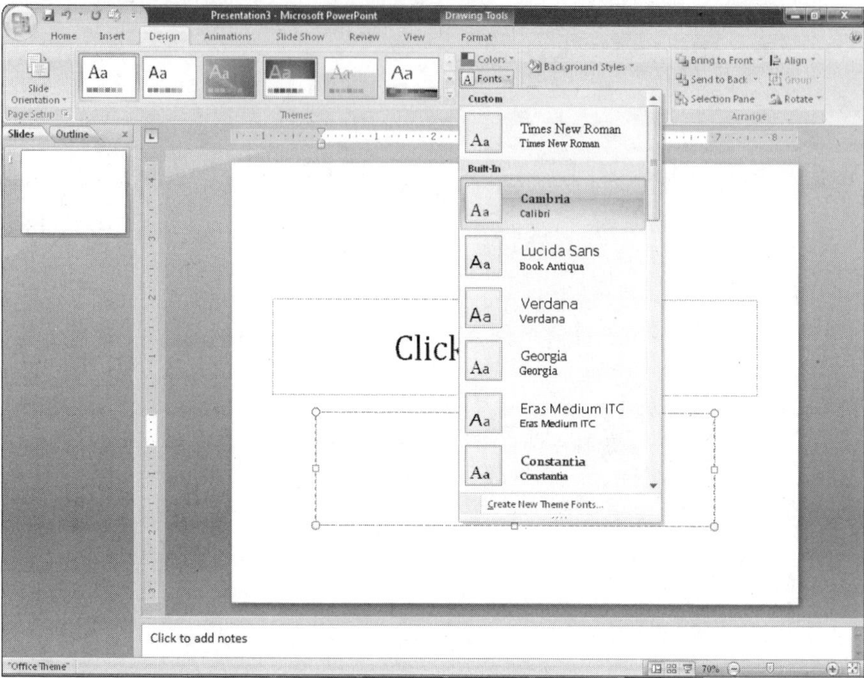

Changing the effect theme

Effect themes apply to several types of drawings that PowerPoint can construct, including SmartArt, charts, and drawn lines and shapes. They make the surfaces of objects formatted with 3-D attributes look like different textures (more or less shiny-looking, colors more or less deep, and so on).

Setting Up a Graphic on Which to Test Effect Themes

Because you haven't worked with any of these graphics yet in this book, you haven't had an opportunity to try them out yet. Effect themes are most evident when there are colorful 3-D graphics in use, so do the following to construct a dummy diagram that you can use to try out effect themes:

1. **On the Insert tab, click SmartArt.**
2. **Click Cycle, click the top left diagram, and click OK.**
3. **On the SmartArt Tools Design tab, click Change Colors, and click the first sample under Colorful.**
4. **On the Smart Art Tools Design tab, open the SmartArt Styles gallery and click the first sample under 3-D.**

Now you have a diagram on which you can see the effect themes applied.

To change the effect theme, follow these steps:

1. **On the Design tab, click Effects.** A gallery of effect themes opens.
2. **(Optional) Point to a theme and observe the change on the slide behind the list.** (This works only if you have an object on that slide that is affected by the effect theme; see the sidebar "Setting Up a Graphic on Which to Test Effect Themes" to set up such an object.)
3. **Click the desired effect theme.** See Figure 22-11.

FIGURE 22-11

Select the desired effect theme.

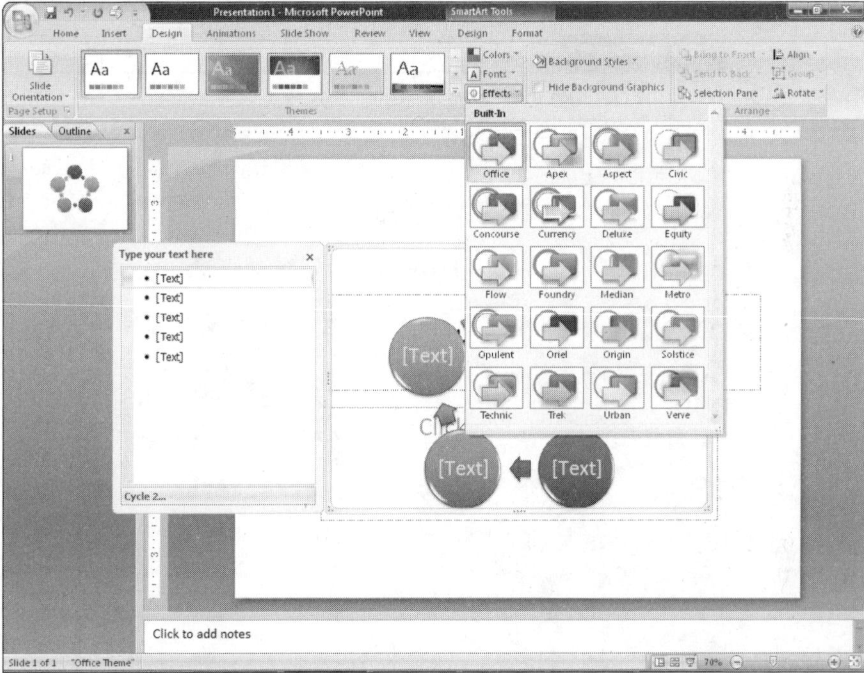

Creating and Managing Custom Color and Font Themes

You can define your own custom color themes and font themes, and save them for reuse in other presentations. By default these are saved in the personal folders for the logged-in user on the local PC, and they remain available to that user regardless of the theme or template in use.

These custom color and font themes are also included if you save the overall theme as a separate theme file (.thmx), as you will learn to do later in this chapter, so that you can take those settings to another PC or send them to some other user.

Creating a custom color theme

A custom color theme defines specific colors for each of the 12 color placeholders (including the two that you can't directly use — the ones for hyperlinks). To create a custom color theme, first apply a theme to the current presentation that is as close as possible to the theme you want. This makes it easier because you have to redefine fewer placeholders. Then follow these steps:

1. **On the Design tab, open the Colors list and choose Create New Theme Colors.** The Create New Theme Colors dialog box opens.
2. **Type a name for the new color theme in the Name box, replacing the default name (Custom 1, or other number if there is already a Custom 1).**
3. **Click a color placeholder and open its menu.** See Figure 22-12.

FIGURE 22-12

Select the color for the chosen placeholder.

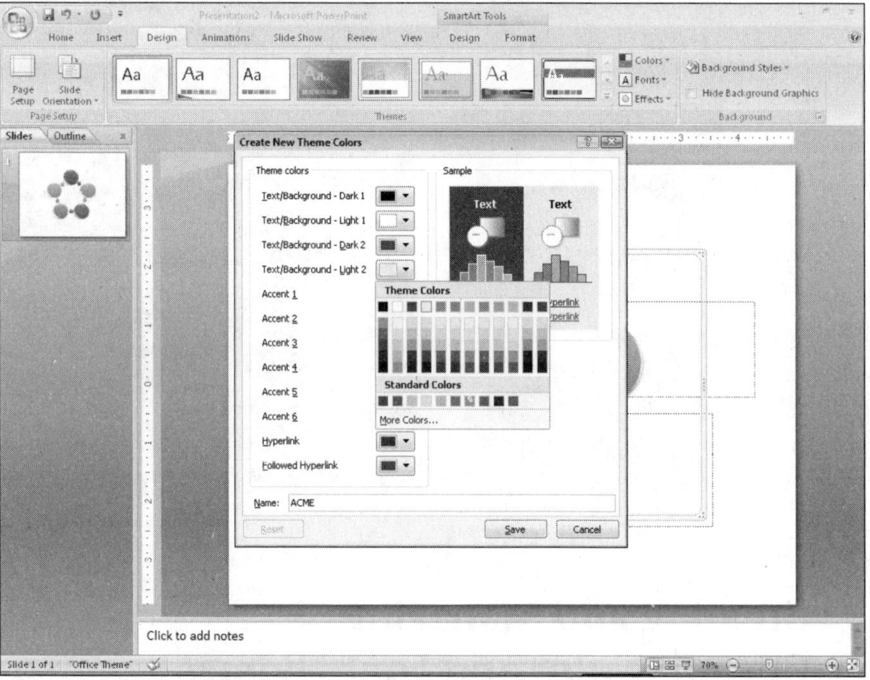

4. **Click a color.** Alternatively, you can click More Colors, select a color from the Colors dialog box (Figure 22-13), and click OK. The Colors dialog box has two tabs: The Standard tab has color swatches, and the Custom tab enables you to define a color numerically by its RGB (Red Green Blue) or HSL (Hue Saturation Lightness).

FIGURE 22-13

Choose a custom color if none of the standard colors is appropriate.

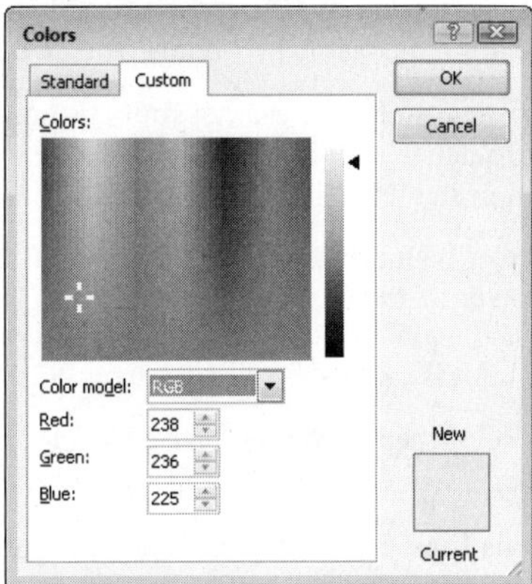

5. **(Optional) Click the Preview button to see the effect of the change on the current slide.**
6. **Redefine any other colors as needed.**
7. **Click Save.** The color scheme is saved, and now appears at the top of the Colors gallery, in the Custom area.

Sharing a custom color theme with others

A custom color scheme is available only to the currently logged-in user on the PC on which it is created. If you want to share it with another user on the same PC, you can copy it into his or her user folder:

- In Windows Vista:

  C:\Users*username*\AppData\Roaming\Microsoft\Templates\Document Themes\Theme Colors

  where *username* is that user's login name.
- In Windows XP:

  C:\Documents and Settings*username*\Application Data\Microsoft\Templates\Document Themes\Theme Colors.
- The default color themes are located in:

  C:\Program Files\Microsoft\Office\Document Themes 12\Theme Colors regardless of the operating system version.

Another way to share a custom color theme is to create the new color theme and then save the (overall) theme to a theme file (.thmx). See the section "Creating a new theme" later in this chapter. The resulting theme file will contain the custom colors, as well as the usual theme content.

Deleting a custom color theme

A custom color theme remains until you delete it from the Theme Colors folder for your user profile. To delete a theme color, use Windows Explorer to navigate to this folder:

C:\Users*username*\AppData\Roaming\Microsoft\Templates\Document Themes\Theme Colors

where *username* is your login name, and you'll find an .xml file for each of your custom color themes. Delete the files for the color themes that you want to delete. You can also right-click the color theme in the Gallery, click Edit, and then click the Delete button in the Edit Theme Colors dialog box.

TIP **If you don't want to delete a custom color theme, but you also don't want it showing up on your Colors menu in PowerPoint all the time, move the file to a folder outside of the Document Themes folder hierarchy. For example, create an Unused Themes folder on your hard disk and move it there until you need it. When you want to use the custom color theme again, move the file back to its original location.**

If you don't want to leave PowerPoint to delete the color theme, you can take advantage of the fact that you can use most dialog boxes in PowerPoint that save or open files to manage files in general. Follow these steps:

1. **Open any dialog box that saves or opens files.** For example, on the Design tab, open the Themes gallery and choose Browse for Themes.
2. **Navigate to the location of the color themes:**
   C:\Users*username*\AppData\Roaming\Microsoft\Templates\Document Themes\Theme Colors
3. **Open the File Type list and choose All Files so that all of the files appear.**
4. **Select the file for the color theme that you want to delete and press the Delete key on the keyboard.**
5. **Click Cancel to close the dialog box.**

Creating a custom font theme

You can create your own custom font themes, which are then available in all presentations. A custom font theme defines two fonts: one for headings and one for body text. To create a custom font theme, follow these steps:

1. **On the Design tab, open the Fonts list and choose Create New Theme Fonts.** The Create New Theme Fonts dialog box opens, as shown in Figure 22-14.
2. **Type a name for the new font theme in the Name box, replacing the default text there.**
3. **Open the Heading Font drop-down list and select the desired font for headings.**
4. **Open the Body Font drop-down list and select the desired font for body text.**
5. **Click Save.** The font theme is saved and now appears at the top of the Fonts list, in the Custom area.

FIGURE 22-14

Create a new custom font theme by specifying the fonts to use.

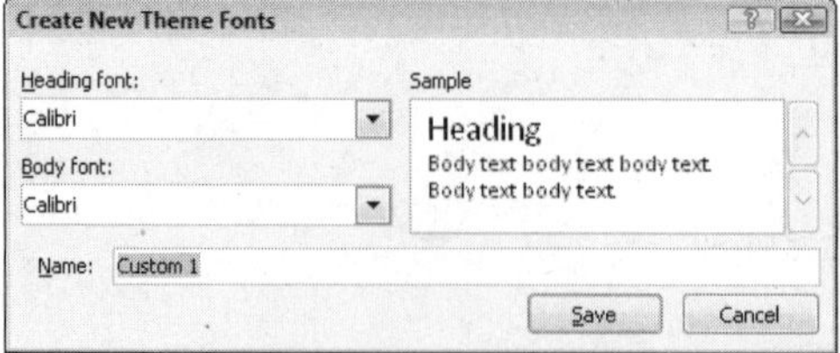

Sharing a custom font theme with others

A custom font theme is available only to the currently logged-in user on the PC on which it is created. If you want to share it with another user on the same PC, you can copy it into his or her user folder:

- In Windows Vista:

  C:\Users*username*\AppData\Roaming\Microsoft\Templates\Document Themes\Theme Fonts

  where *username* is that user's login name.
- In Windows XP:

  C:\Documents and Settings*username*\Application Data\Microsoft\Templates\Document Themes\Theme Fonts

You can also share a custom font theme by creating it and then saving the (overall) theme as a new theme (.thmx) file. Then you can share that theme file with others via e-mail, disk, or other distribution methods.

To save your theme as a new theme, see the section "Creating a new theme."

Deleting a custom font theme

A custom font theme remains until you delete it from the Theme Fonts folder for your user profile. To delete a font theme, use Windows Explorer to navigate to this folder:

- In Windows Vista:

  C:\Users*username*\AppData\Roaming\Microsoft\Templates\Document Themes\Theme Fonts
- In Windows XP:

  C:\Documents and Settings*username*\Application Data\Microsoft\Templates\Document Themes\Theme Fonts

  where *username* is your login name, and you'll find an .xml file for each of your custom font themes. Delete the files for the font themes that you want to delete.

You can also delete it from within PowerPoint by browsing for the file with any dialog box that saves or opens files, or by right-clicking the font theme in the Gallery, clicking Edit, and then clicking Delete in the Edit Theme Fonts dialog box.

Deleting a custom font theme from a dialog box is essentially the same as deleting a custom color theme. See the section "Deleting a custom color theme" for more details.

Changing the Background

The *background* is the color, texture, pattern, or image that is applied to the entire slide (or slide master), on which everything else sits. By its very definition, it applies to the entire surface of the slide; you cannot have a partial background. However, you can have a *background graphic* overlaid on top of the background. A background graphic is a graphic image placed on the slide master that complements and works with the background.

It's important to understand the distinction between a background and a background graphic because even though most themes contain both, they are set up differently, and making the change you want to the overall appearance of your slides often involves changing both. For example, Figure 22-15 shows the Concourse theme applied to a slide master. The slide background is pure white, and a blue and black background graphic is overlaid on it.

Most themes consist of both background formatting (even if it is just a solid color) and a background graphic. The background graphics included in the built-in themes in PowerPoint are unique to those themes, and not available as separate graphics outside of them. So, for example, if you want the colored swoop shown in Figure 22-15, the only way to get it is to apply the Concourse theme. Because the decorative background graphics are unique to each theme, many people choose a theme based on the desired background graphic, and then customize the slide master's appearance to modify the theme as needed.

FIGURE 22-15

A slide's background is separate from its background graphic(s) if any are present.

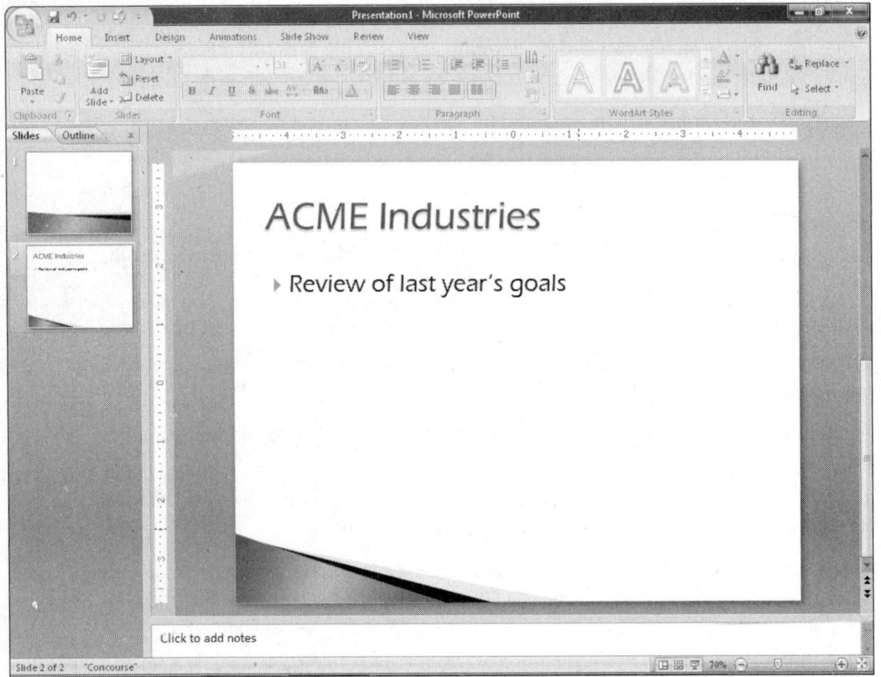

TIP **To use a background graphic from one template with the look-and-feel of another, apply the first theme to a slide, and then in Slide Master view, copy the background graphic to the Clipboard. Then apply the second theme and paste the graphic from the clipboard into the slide master.**

Applying a background style

Background styles are preset background formats that come with the built-in themes in PowerPoint. Depending on the theme you apply, different background styles are available. These background styles all use the color placeholders from the theme, so their color offerings change depending on the color theme applied.

To apply a background style, follow these steps:

1. **(Optional) To affect only certain slides, select them.**
2. **On the Design tab, click Background Styles.** A gallery of styles appears. See Figure 22-16.
3. **Click the desired style to apply it to the entire presentation.** Alternatively, you can right-click the desired style and choose Apply to Selected Slides.

FIGURE 22-16

Apply a preset background style.

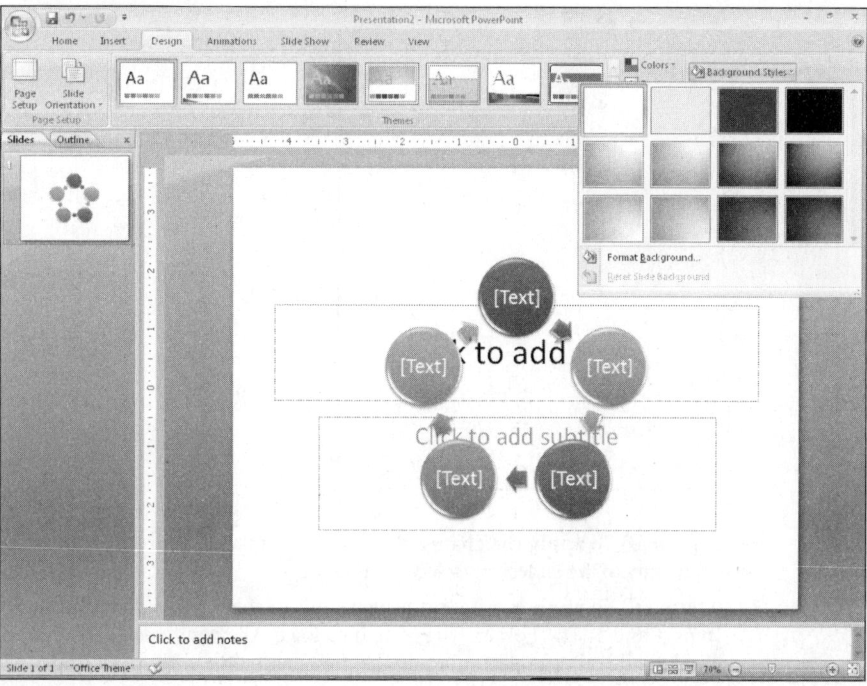

You cannot customize background styles or add your own custom background styles; there are always 12 of them, and they are always determined by the theme. If you need a different background, you can choose Format Backgrounds and then customize the background settings as described in the following sections.

Applying a background fill

A custom background fill can include solid colors, gradients, textures, or graphics. This section covers how to specify your own background fill, which involves the following steps:

1. **(Optional) To affect only certain slides, select them.**
2. **On the Design tab, click Background Styles.** The Background Styles gallery opens.
3. **Click Format Background.** The Format Background dialog box opens.
4. **Choose the option button that best describes the type of fill you want.** See Figure 22-17.
5. **Set the options for the fill type that you chose.** For example, in Figure 22-17, click the Color button and choose a solid color. The changes you make apply immediately.

FIGURE 22-17

Select a background fill type, and configure the options for the type you chose.

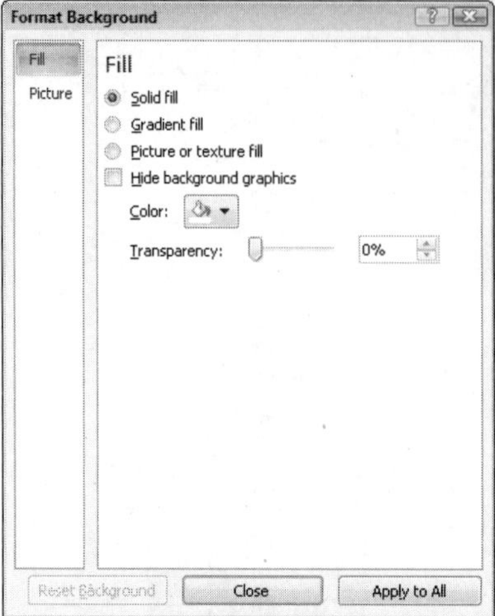

6. **(Optional) To apply the change to all slides, click Apply to All.** Otherwise the change will apply only to the slides you selected in Step 1.
7. **(Optional) To apply a different background to some other slides, select them and repeat steps 4 and 5.** The Format Background dialog box is nonmodal, so its changes are applied immediately, and you can select things in the presentation file without closing it.
8. **Click Close to exit the dialog box.**

Working with background graphics

In the preceding steps, one of the fill types you could choose was Picture or Texture Fill. This type of fill covers the entire background with the picture or texture that you specify.

This is not a background graphic, however. A *background graphic* is an object or a picture overlaid on top of the background on the slide master. It complements the background, and it might or might not cover the entire background.

NOTE **Some theme-provided background graphics actually consist of multiple shapes grouped together. You can ungroup them so that you can modify or remove only a portion of the background graphic.**

Displaying and hiding background graphics

Sometimes a background graphic can get in the way of the slide's content. For example, on a slide that contains a large chart or diagram, a background graphic around the border of the slide can overlap the content. You don't have to delete the background graphic entirely to solve this problem; you can turn it off for individual slides. To hide the background graphics on one or more slides, follow these steps:

1. **Select the slide(s) to affect.**
2. **On the Design tab, mark the Hide Background Graphics checkbox.**

Clear the check box to redisplay the background graphics later as needed.

Deleting background graphics

The background graphics reside on the slide master, so to remove one, you must use Slide Master view. Follow these steps:

1. **On the View tab, click Slide Master.** Slide Master view opens.
2. **Select the slide master or layout master that contains the graphic to delete.**
3. **Click the background graphic to select it.**
4. **Press the Delete key on the keyboard.**

TIP Some background graphics are on the slide master itself, and others are on individual layout masters. The background graphics on the slide master trickle down to each of its layout masters, but can't be selected/deleted from the individual layout masters.

To use a background graphic only on certain layouts, cut it from the slide master to the Clipboard (Ctrl+X), and then paste it individually onto each layout master desired (Ctrl+V). Alternatively, turn on the background graphic for the slide master and then use Hide Background Graphics on individual layout masters that should not contain it.

Adding your own background graphics

You can add your own background graphics, either to the slide master or to individual layout masters. This works just like adding any other graphic to a slide (see Chapter 24) except you add it to the master instead of to an individual slide.

Inserting pictures is covered in greater detail in Chapter 24, but here are the basic steps for adding a background graphic:

1. **Display the slide master or layout master on which you want to place the background graphic.**
2. **Do any of the following:**
   - On the Insert tab, click Picture. Select a picture to insert and click Open.
   - On the Insert tab, click Clip Art. Search for a piece of clip art to use, and insert it on the master.
   - In any application (including PowerPoint), copy any graphic to the Clipboard by pressing Ctrl+C; then display the master and paste the graphic by pressing Ctrl+V.

TIP Most of the background graphics that come with the built-in themes are either semi-transparent or use one of the placeholder colors for their fill. Therefore changing the color theme also changes the color of the background graphic. Keep that in mind if you are creating your own background graphics; it's better to use theme colors or transparency than to use fixed colors that might clash with a color theme that you later apply.

Working with Preset Placeholders

As a review, to enter Slide Master view, display the View tab and click Slide Master. One or more slide masters appear in the left pane, with its own subordinate layout masters. A slide master has five preset placeholders that you can individually remove or move around. Figure 22-18 points them out on a slide master with the Concourse theme applied, but they might be in different locations in other themes:

- **Title:** The placeholder for the title on each slide
- **Text:** The main content placeholder on each slide
- **Date:** The box that displays the current date on each slide

- **Slide number:** The box that displays the slide number on each slide
- **Footer:** A box that displays repeated text at the bottom of each slide

These elements are all enabled by default, but the Footer is empty by default so it is not visible on individual slides unless you type some text into it in Slide Master view or add text to it using Insert Header and Footer. Each of these elements trickles down to the layout masters beneath it, so formatting, moving, or deleting one of these elements from the slide master also changes it on each of the layouts. See Figure 22-18 for an example of the various placeholders.

FIGURE 22-18

Each slide master contains these placeholders (or can contain them)

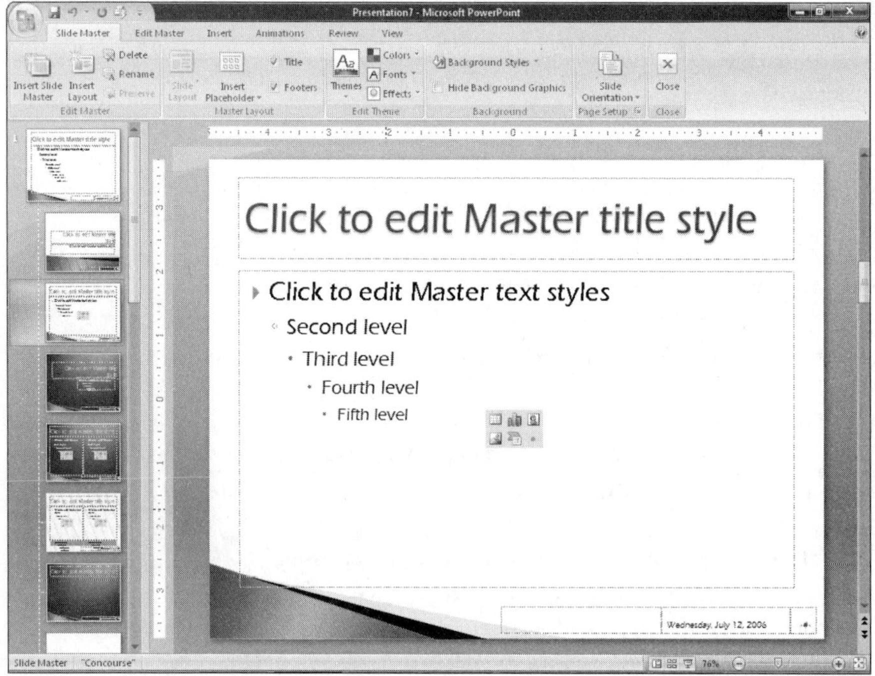

Formatting a preset placeholder

You can format the text in each of the placeholders on the slide master just like any regular text, and that formatting carries over to all slides and layouts based on it. For example, if you format the code in the Slide Number box with a certain font and size, it will appear that way on every slide that uses that slide master. You can also format the placeholder boxes just like any other text boxes. For example, you can add a border around the page number's box, and/or fill its background with color.

TIP If you want to make all the text in a heading all caps or small caps, use the Font dialog box. From the Home tab, click the dialog box launcher in the Font group and mark the Small Caps or All Caps checkbox there.

Moving, deleting, or restoring preset placeholders

You can move each of the placeholders on the slide master or an individual layout master. For example, you might decide you want the Footer box at the top of the slide rather than the bottom, or that you want to center the slide number at the bottom of the slide. To move a placeholder, click it to select it and then drag its border.

To delete one of the placeholders on the slide master, select its box and press the Delete key on the keyboard. Deleting it from the slide master deletes it from all of the associated layouts as well.

To restore deleted placeholders on the slide master, follow these steps:

1. **In Slide Master view, select the slide master (not a layout).**
2. **On the Slide Master tab, click Slide Layout.** The Master Layout dialog box opens. Check boxes for already displayed elements are marked and unavailable. Checkboxes for previously deleted elements are available as shown in Figure 22-19.
3. **Mark the checkboxes for the elements that you want to restore.**
4. **Click OK.**

FIGURE 22-19

Restore deleted placeholders from the slide master.

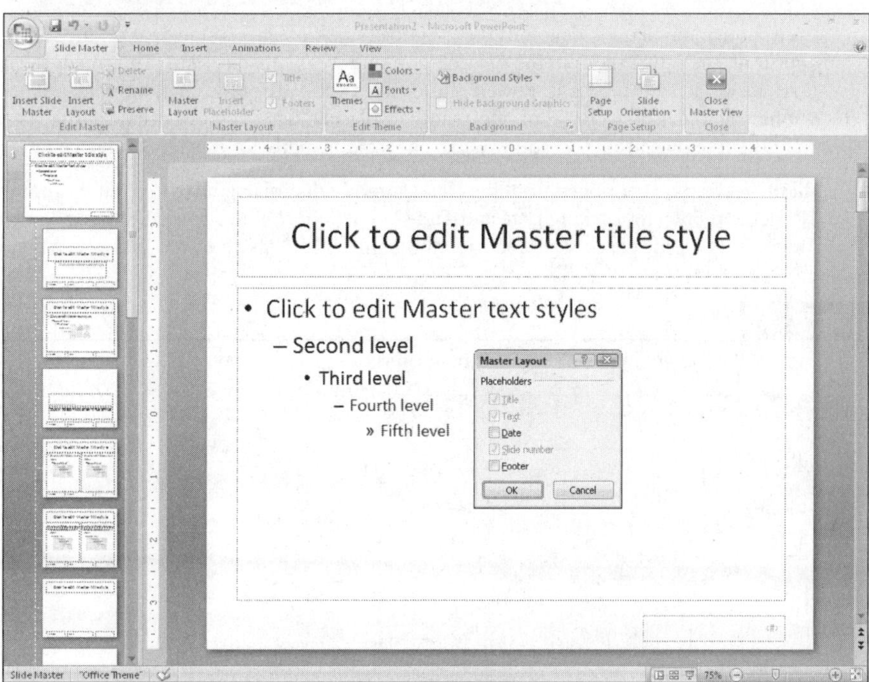

CAUTION Restored placeholders might not appear in the same spots as they did originally; you might need to move them. To put the placeholders back to their original locations, reapply the theme from the Themes button on the Slide Master tab.

Here are some more details you should remember about deleting and restoring:

- On an individual layout master, you can quickly delete and restore the Title and Footer placeholders by marking or clearing the Title and Footers check boxes on the Slide Master tab. The "footer" that this checkbox refers to is actually all three of the bottom-of-the-slide elements: the actual footer, the date box, and the slide number box.
- You can also individually delete the placeholders from a layout master, the same as on a slide master. Just select a placeholder box and press the Delete key.
- You can restore all of the placeholders, except Text, by marking the aforementioned checkboxes on the Slide Master tab. Whenever any of the three footer boxes are missing, the Footers checkbox becomes cleared, and you can restore the missing box(es) by re-selecting the checkbox.
- You cannot restore the Text placeholder, however, on an individual layout master. You must recreate it with the Insert Placeholder command.

CROSS-REF For more on the Insert Placeholder command, see the section "Customizing and Creating Layouts."

Displaying the date, number, and footer on slides

Even though the placeholders for Date, Number, and Footer might appear on the slide master, they do not appear on the actual slides in the presentation unless you enable them. This might seem counterintuitive at first, but it's actually a benefit. PowerPoint enables you to turn the date, number, and footer on and off without having to delete, recreate, or reformat their placeholders. You can decide at the last minute whether you want them to display or not, and you can choose differently for different audiences and situations.

All three areas are controlled from the Header and Footer dialog box. To open it, from the Insert tab click Header and Footer. (Clicking Date and Time or clicking Number opens the same dialog box.) Then on the Slide tab, mark the checkboxes for each of the three elements you want to use. See Figure 22-20.

FIGURE 22-20

Choose which of the footer elements should appear on slides.

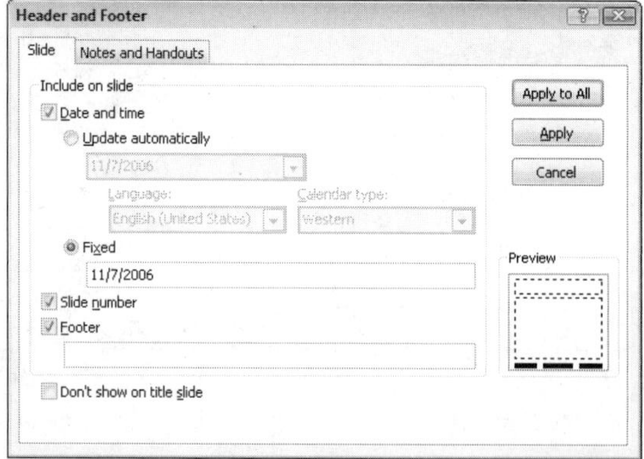

Date and Time

You can set Date and Time either to Update Automatically or to Fixed:

- Update Automatically pulls the current date from the computer's clock and formats it in whatever format you choose from the drop-down list. You can also select a language and a Calendar Type (although unless you are presenting in some other country than the one for which your version of PowerPoint was developed, this is probably not an issue).
- Fixed prints whatever you enter in the Fixed text box. When Fixed is enabled, it defaults to today's date in the m/dd/yyyy format.

TIP **In addition to (or instead of) placing the date on each slide, you can insert an individual instance of the current date or time on a slide, perhaps as part of a sentence. To do so, position the insertion point inside a text box or placeholder and then on the Insert tab, click Date and Time. Select the format you want from the dialog box that appears and click OK.**

Slide Number

This option shows the slide number on each slide, wherever the Number placeholder is positioned. You can format the Number placeholder on the master slide with the desired font, size, and other text attributes.

By default, slide numbering starts with 1. You can start with some other number if you like by following these steps:

1. **Close Slide Master view if it is open. To do so, click the Close button on the Slide Master tab.**
2. **On the Design tab, click the dialog box launcher in the Page Setup group.** The Page Setup dialog box opens.
3. **In the Number Slides From box, increment the number to the desired starting number.**
4. **Click OK.**

TIP **You can insert the slide number on an individual slide, either instead of or in addition to the numbering on the Slide Master. Position the insertion point, and then on the Insert tab, click Slide Number. If you are in Slide master view, this places a code on the Slide Master for the slide number that looks like this: <#>. If you are on an individual slide, it inserts the same code but the code itself is hidden and the actual number appears.**

Footer

The footer is blank by default. Mark the Footer check box, and then enter the desired text in the Footer box. You can then format the footer text from the slide master as you would any other text. You can also enter the footer text in the Header and Footer dialog box's Footer text box.

Don't Show on Title Slide

This checkbox in the Header and Footer dialog box suppresses the date/time, page number, and footer on slides that use the Title Slide layout. Many people like to hide those elements on title slides for a cleaner look and to avoid repeated information (for example, if the current date appears in the subtitle box on the title slide).

Customizing and Creating Layouts

In addition to customizing the slide master (including working with its preset placeholder boxes, as you just learned), you can fully customize the individual layout masters. This very useful capability is brand new in PowerPoint 2007.

A layout master takes some of its settings from the slide master with which it is associated. For example, by default it takes its background, fonts, color scheme, and preset placeholder positioning from the slide master. But it also can be individually customized; you can override the slide master's choices for background, colors, and fonts, and you can create, modify, and delete various types of content placeholders.

Understanding Content placeholders

There are seven basic types of content you can insert on a PowerPoint slide: Text, Picture, Chart, Table, Diagram, Media (video or sound), and Clip Art. A placeholder on a slide master or layout master can specify one of these types of content that it will accept, or you can designate it as a Content placeholder, such that it will accept any of the seven types. Most of the layouts that PowerPoint generates automatically for its themes use the Content placeholder type because it offers the most flexibility. By making all placeholders Content, PowerPoint can get by with fewer separate layout masters because users will choose the desired layout based on the positioning of the placeholders, not their types.

A Content placeholder appears as a text placeholder with a small palette of icons in the center, one for each of the content types. Each content placeholder can hold only one type of content at a time, so as soon as the user types some text into the content placeholder or clicks one of the icons in the palette and inserts some content, the placeholder becomes locked into that one type of content until the content is deleted from it.

NOTE **On a slide that contains a placeholder that contains some content (any type), selecting the placeholder and pressing Delete removes the content. To remove the placeholder itself from the layout, select the empty placeholder and press Delete. If you then want to restore the placeholder, reapply the slide layout to the slide.**

You can move and resize a placeholder on a layout master as you would any other object. Drag a selection handle on the frame to resize it, or drag the border of the frame (not on a selection handle) to move it.

CROSS-REF **The Content placeholders were identified back in Chapter 21. You can also see Chapter 21 for more on moving and resizing an object.**

Adding a custom placeholder

You can add a placeholder to either the slide master or to an individual layout master. If you add it to the slide master, it will repeat on every layout master, it's more common to add placeholders to individual layouts.

To add a placeholder, follow these steps:

1. **In Slide Master view, select the layout master (or slide master) to affect.**
2. **On the Slide Master tab, click the bottom part of the Insert Placeholder button to open its menu.**
3. **Click Content to insert a generic placeholder, or click one of the specific content types. See Figure 22-21.** The mouse pointer becomes a cross-hair.
4. **Drag on the slide to draw the placeholder box of the size and position desired.** A blue box appears showing where the placeholder box will go. When you release the mouse button, the new placeholder appears on the slide.

FIGURE 22-21

Create a new placeholder on a slide.

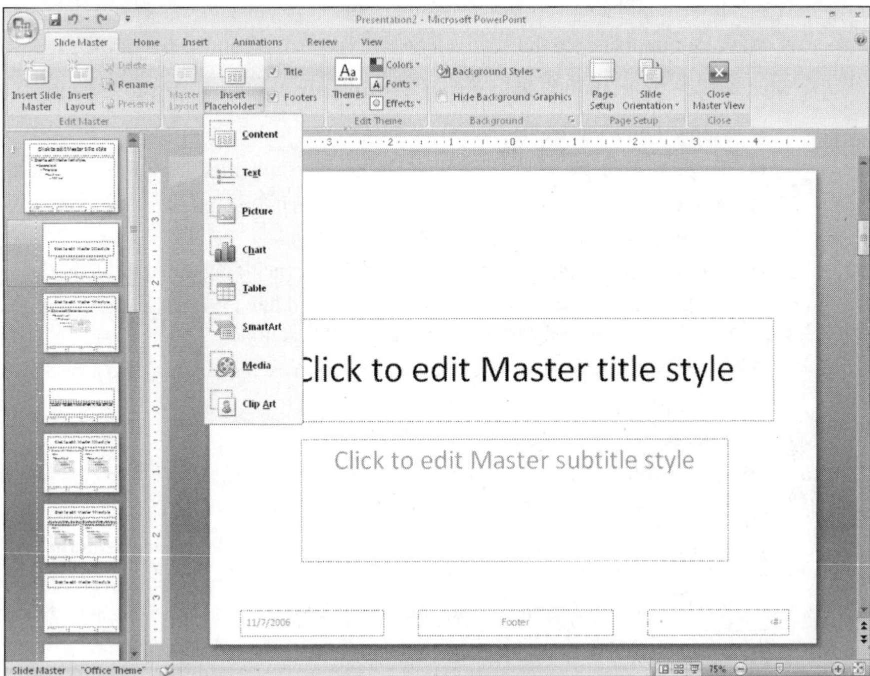

Deleting and restoring a custom placeholder

To delete a custom placeholder, select it and press the Delete key, just as you learned to do earlier with the preset placeholders.

The difference between custom and preset placeholders is not in the deleting, but rather in the restoring. You can immediately undo a deletion with Ctrl+Z, but you cannot otherwise restore a deleted custom placeholder from a layout master. PowerPoint retains no memory of the content placeholders on individual layouts. Therefore, you must recreate any content placeholders that you have accidentally deleted.

To restore one of the built-in layouts, copy it from another slide master. See the sections "Duplicating and Deleting layouts" and "Copying layouts between slide masters" later in this chapter.

Overriding the slide master formatting for a layout

You can apply formatting to a layout in almost exactly the same ways as you apply formatting to a regular slide or to a slide master. Only a few things are off-limits:

- You cannot apply a different theme to one layout. To use a different theme for some slides, create a whole new slide master (covered later in this chapter).
- You cannot apply a different font, color, or effect theme, because these are related to the main theme and the slide master. If you need different fonts or colors on a certain layout, specify fixed font formatting for the text placeholders in that layout, or specify fixed color choices for objects.

- You cannot delete a background graphic that is inherited from the slide master; if you want it only on certain layouts, delete it from the slide master, and then paste it individually onto each layout desired, or select Hide Background Graphics from the Slide Master tab and then deselect Hide Background Graphics from certain layouts.
- You cannot change the slide orientation (portrait or landscape) or the slide size.

So what *can* you do to an individual layout, then? Plenty. You can do the following:

- Apply a different background.
- Reposition, resize, or delete preset placeholders inherited from the slide master.
- Apply fixed formatting to text placeholders, including different fonts, sizes, colors, attributes, indents, and alignment.
- Apply fixed formatting to any placeholder box, including different fill and border styles and colors.
- Create manual text boxes and type any text you like into them. You might do this to include an explanatory note on certain slide layouts, for example.
- Insert pictures or clip art that should repeat on each slide that uses a certain layout.

Creating a new layout

In addition to modifying the existing layouts, you can create your own brand-new layouts, defining the exact placeholders you want. To create a new layout, follow these steps:

1. From Slide Master view, click the slide master with which to associate the new layout.
2. Click Insert Layout. A new layout appears. Each new layout you create starts with preset placeholders inherited from the slide master for Title, Footer, Date, and Slide Number.
3. (Optional) Delete any of the preset placeholders that you don't want.
4. Insert new placeholders as needed.
5. (Optional) Name the layout.

CROSS-REF **To insert a placeholder, see the section "Adding a custom placeholder" earlier in the chapter. To name the layout, see the next section, "Renaming a layout."**

NOTE **The new layout is part of the slide master, but not part of the theme. The theme is applied to the slide master, but at this point their relationship ends; and changes that you make to the slide master do not affect the theme. To save your custom layout(s), you have two choices: You can save the presentation as a template, or you can save the theme as a separate file. You learn more about saving themes in "Managing themes" later in this chapter.**

Renaming a layout

Layout names can help you determine the purpose of a layout if it is not obvious from viewing its thumbnail image.

To change the name of a layout, or to assign a name to a new layout you've created, follow these steps:

1. **In Slide Master view, right-click the layout and choose Rename Layout.** The Rename Layout dialog box opens.
2. **Type a new name for the layout, replacing the existing name.** See Figure 22-22.
3. **Click Rename.**

FIGURE 22-22

Change the name of a layout to clarify its purpose.

Duplicating and deleting layouts

You might want to copy a layout to get a head start on creating a new one. To copy a layout, right-click the layout in Slide Master view and choose Duplicate Layout. A copy of the layout appears below the original.

If you are never going to use a certain layout, you might as well delete it; every layout you can delete makes the file a little bit smaller. To delete a layout, right-click the layout in Slide Master view and choose Delete Layout.

Copying layouts between slide masters

When you create additional slide masters in the presentation, any custom layouts you've created for the existing slide masters do not carry over. You must manually copy them to the new slide master.

To copy a layout from one slide master to another, follow these steps:

1. **In Slide Master view, select the layout to be copied.**
2. **Press Ctrl+C.**
3. **Select the slide master under which you want to place the copy.**
4. **Press Ctrl+V.**

You can also copy layouts between slide masters in different presentations. To do so, open both presentation files, and then perform the above steps. The only difference is that after Step 2, you must switch to the other presentation's Slide Master view.

Managing Slide Masters

Let's review the relationship one more time between slide masters and themes. A theme is a set of formatting specs. Themes are not applied directly to slides — they are applied to slide masters, which are then in turn applied to slides. The slide masters exist within the presentation file itself. You can change them by applying different themes, but they are essentially "built in" to the presentation file.

When you change to a different theme for all of the slides in the presentation, your slide master changes its appearance. You can tweak that appearance in Slide Master view. As long as all of the slides in the presentation use the same theme, you need only one slide master. However, if you apply a different theme to some of your slides, you need another master, because a master can have only one theme applied to it at a time. PowerPoint automatically creates the additional master(s) for you, and they are all available for editing in Slide Master view.

If you later reapply a single theme to all of the slides in the presentation, you do not need multiple masters anymore, so the unused one is automatically deleted. In addition to all this automatic creation and deletion of slide masters, you can also manually create and delete slide masters on your own. Any slide masters that you create manually are automatically preserved, even if they aren't always in use. You must manually delete them if you don't want them anymore.

In the following sections, you learn how to create and delete slide masters manually, and how to rename them. You also learn how to lock one of the automatically created slide masters so that PowerPoint does not delete it if it falls out of use.

Creating and deleting slide masters

To create another slide master, click Insert Slide Master on the Slide Master tab. It appears below the existing slide master(s) in the left pane of Slide Master view. From there, just start customizing it. You can apply a theme to it, modify its layouts and placeholders, and all the usual things you can do to a slide master. Another way to create a new slide master is to duplicate an existing one. To do this, right-click the slide master and choose Duplicate Master.

To delete a slide master, select it in Slide Master view (make sure you select the slide master itself, not just one of its layouts) and press the Delete key. If any of that slide master's layouts were applied to any slides in the presentation, those slides automatically convert to the default slide master's equivalent layout. If no exact layout match is found, PowerPoint does its best: It uses its default Title and Content layout, and includes any extra content as orphaned items.

Renaming a slide master

Slide master names appear as category headings on the Layout list as you are selecting layouts. For example, in Figure 22-23, the slide master names are Faithe and Concourse.

FIGURE 22-23

Slide master names form the category titles on the Layout list.

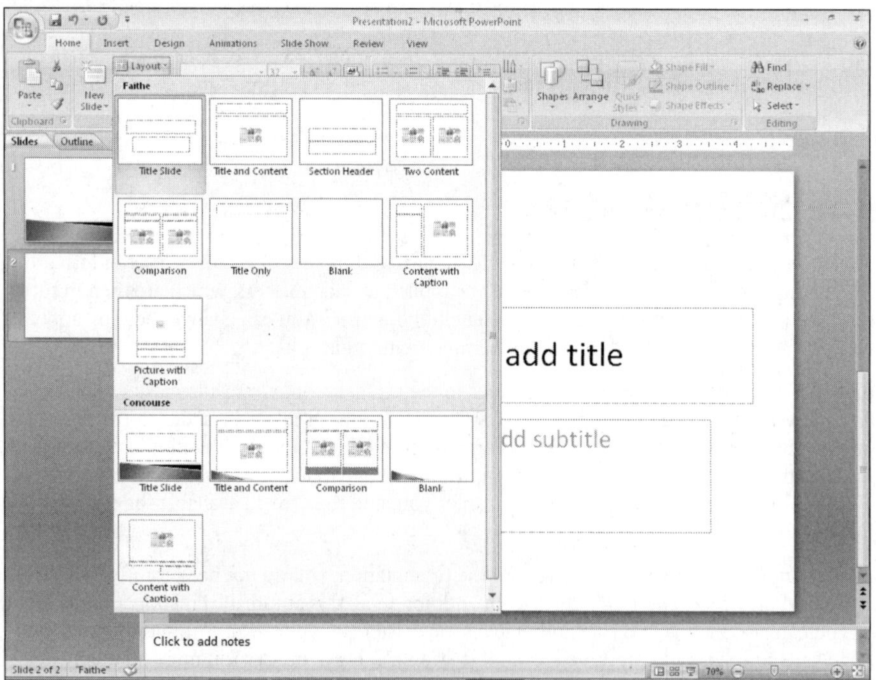

To rename a slide master, follow these steps:

1. **In Slide Master view, right-click the slide master and choose Rename Master. The Rename Master dialog box opens.**
2. **Type a new name for the master, replacing the existing name.**
3. **Click Rename.**

Preserving a slide master

Unless you have created the slide master yourself, it is temporary. Slide masters come and go as needed, as you format slides with various themes. To lock a slide master so that it doesn't disappear when no slides are using it, right-click the slide master and choose Preserve Master. A check mark appears next to Preserve Master on its right-click menu, indicating it is saved. To unpreserve it, select the command again to toggle the check mark off. See Figure 22-24.

FIGURE 22-24

The Preserve Master command saves a slide master so that PowerPoint cannot automatically delete it.

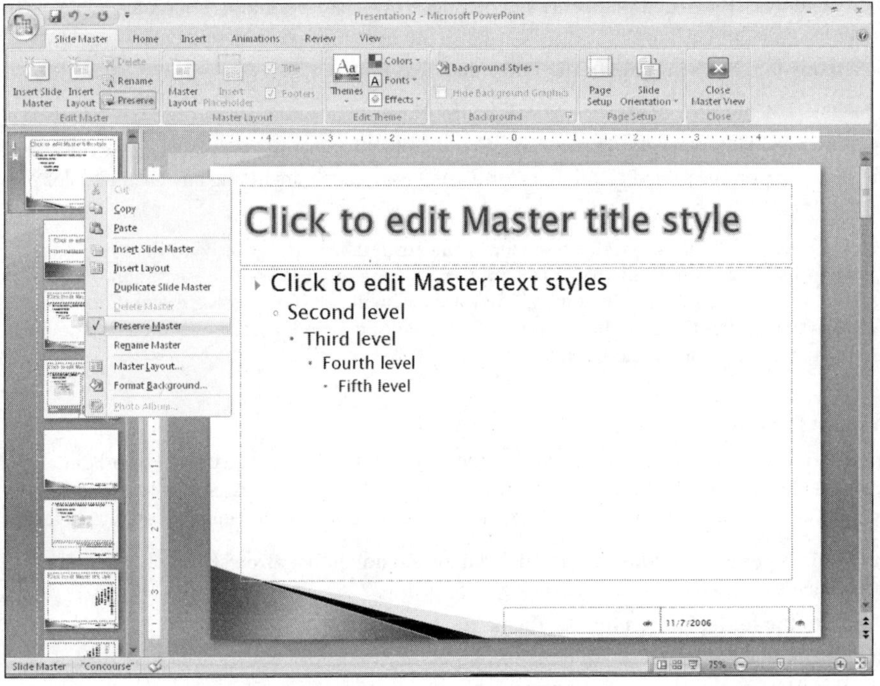

Managing Themes

As you learned earlier in the chapter, themes are applied to slide masters to create the background, color, font, and effect formatting for a presentation. Some themes are built into PowerPoint, and you can also create and save your own themes as separate files and apply them to other presentations or even to other Office documents, such as in Word and Excel. In this section you learn how to create new themes, manage theme files, and apply themes across multiple presentations.

Creating a new theme

To create a new theme, first format a slide master exactly the way you want, including any custom layouts, backgrounds, colors, and font themes. Then save the slide master's formatting as a new theme by following these steps:

1. **On the Slide Master or the Design tab, click Themes, and click Save Current Theme.** The Save Current Theme dialog box opens.
   - The default location shown in the Save Current Theme dialog box under Windows Vista is C:\Users*username*\AppData\Roaming\Microsoft\Templates\Document Themes.
   - For Windows XP, it is C:\Documents and Settings*username*\Application Data\Microsoft\Templates\Document Themes.
2. **Type a name for the theme file in the File Name text box.**
3. **Click Save.** The new theme is saved to your hard disk.

The new theme is now available from the Themes button's menu in all presentations you create while logged in as the same user on the same PC. All of its formatting is available, including any custom color or font themes it includes.

TIP **As noted earlier, if the saved theme includes any custom layouts, PowerPoint does not make them available automatically when you apply the theme to an existing presentation. If you start a new presentation based on the theme, though, they are available. To start a new presentation based on a theme, open the theme file (Office Button ⇨ Open). PowerPoint does not actually open the theme file, but instead it starts a new presentation based on it.**

Renaming a theme

You can rename a theme file by renaming the .thmx file from Windows Explorer, outside of PowerPoint. You can also rename a theme file from inside PowerPoint by using any dialog box that saves or opens files. For example, to use the Choose Theme or Themed Document dialog box to rename a theme, follow these steps:

1. **From the Design or Slide Master tab, click Themes, and choose Browse for Themes.** The Choose Theme or Themed Document dialog box opens.
2. **Navigate to the folder containing the theme file to rename.**
   - By default, theme files are stored under Windows Vista in C:\Users*username*\AppData\Roaming\Microsoft\Templates\Document Themes.
   - For Windows XP, it is C:\Documents and Settings*username*\Application Data\Microsoft\Templates\Document Themes.

3. **Right-click the theme file and choose Rename.**
4. **Type the new name for the theme and press Enter.**
5. **Click Cancel to close the dialog box.**

Deleting a theme

A custom theme file continues appearing on the Themes button's menu indefinitely. If you want to remove it from there, you must delete it from the Document Themes folder, or move it to some other location for storage. To delete a theme, follow these steps:

1. **From the Design or Slide Master tab, click Themes, and choose Browse for Themes.** The Choose Theme or Themed Document dialog box opens.
2. **Navigate to the folder containing the theme files:**
   - In Windows Vista: C:\Users*username*\AppData\Roaming\Microsoft\Templates\Document Themes.
   - In Windows XP: C:\Documents and Settings*username*\Application Data\Microsoft\Templates\Document Themes.
3. **Right-click the theme file and choose Delete.**
4. **At the Delete File confirmation box, click Yes.**
5. **Click Cancel to close the dialog box.**

Copying a theme from another presentation

A presentation file "contains" themes in that the themes are applied to its slide masters. (That's how a template contains themes too.) As you learned earlier, you can preserve a slide master in Slide Master view so that it doesn't get deleted automatically when there are no slides based on it; by creating new slide masters, applying themes to them, and then preserving them, you can create a whole library of themes in a single presentation or template file. Then to make this library of themes available in another presentation, you simply base the new presentation on that existing presentation (or template).

However, if you did not initially base the new presentation on the template or presentation that contains the theme you want, you can apply the theme from it after the fact. One way to do this is to copy and paste (or drag and drop) the slide master from one file's Slide Master view to the other's.

Follow these steps to copy a slide master (and thereby copy its theme) to another presentation:

1. **Open both presentations.**
2. **In the presentation that contains the theme, enter Slide Master view (View ⇨ Slide Master).**
3. **Select the slide master (top slide in the left pane) and press Ctrl+C to copy it.**
4. **Switch to the other presentation (View ⇨ Switch Windows)**
5. **Enter Slide Master view (View ⇨ Slide Master).**
6. **Press Ctrl+V to paste the slide master (and its associated theme and layouts).**

Summary

In this chapter you learned how themes and slide masters make it easy to apply consistent formatting in a presentation, and how layout masters are associated with slide masters and provide consistent layouts for the slides based on them. You learned how to create, edit, rename, and delete themes and layouts, and how to copy themes between presentations.

Now that you know how to format entire presentations using themes, you're ready to start learning how to make exceptions to the formatting rules that the themes impose. In the next chapter you will learn how to format text in PowerPoint, and apply different fonts, sizes, attributes, and special effects. You can use this knowledge to make strategic changes to the text placeholders on slide masters to further customize your themes, or you can make changes to text on individual slides on a case-by-case basis to make certain slides stand out from the rest.

Chapter 23

Working with Tables and Charts

IN THIS CHAPTER

You can type tabular data — in other words, data in a grid of rows and columns — directly into a table. You also can apply formatting that makes tabular data easier to read and more attractive.

When you need to present data in a graphical format that's easy to understand, PowerPoint's charting tool is perfect for this purpose. The new PowerPoint 2007 charting interface is based upon the one in Excel, and so you don't have to leave PowerPoint to create, modify, and format professional-looking charts.

In this chapter, you'll learn how to create and manage PowerPoint tables and how to create charts that present numeric data in a visual format.

NOTE What's the difference between a chart and a graph? Some purists will tell you that a chart is either a table or a pie chart, whereas a graph is a chart that plots data points on two axes, such as a bar chart. However, Microsoft does not make this distinction, and neither do I in this chapter. I use the term "chart" in this chapter for either kind.

Creating a New Table

A table is a great way to organize little bits of data into a meaningful order. For example, you might use a table to show sales results for several salespeople or to contain a multicolumn list of team member names.

NOTE Text from a table does not appear in the presentation's outline.

There are several ways to insert a table, and each method has its purpose. The following sections explain each of the table creation methods.

A table can be part of a content placeholder, or it can be a separate, free-floating item. If the active slide has an available placeholder that can accommodate a table, and there is not already content in that placeholder, the table is placed in it. Otherwise the table is placed as an independent object on the slide, and is not part of the layout.

TIP Depending on what you want to do with the table, it could be advantageous in some cases to *not* have the table be part of the layout. For example, perhaps you want the table to be a certain size and to not change when you apply a different theme. To ensure that the table is not part of the layout, start with a slide that uses a layout that contains no table-compatible placeholder, such as Title Only.

NOTE In earlier versions of PowerPoint, an AutoLayout feature changed the layout to one that contained a table placeholder if none were available. A lot of people found that annoying, though, and PowerPoint 2007 does not do it.

Creating a table with the Insert Table dialog box

To create a basic table with a specified number of rows and columns, you can use the Insert Table dialog box. You can open it in either of two ways (see Figure 23-1):

- In a content placeholder, click the Table icon.
- On the Insert tab, choose Table ➪ Insert Table.

FIGURE 23-1

Open the Insert Table dialog box from either the Table button's menu or a content placeholder.

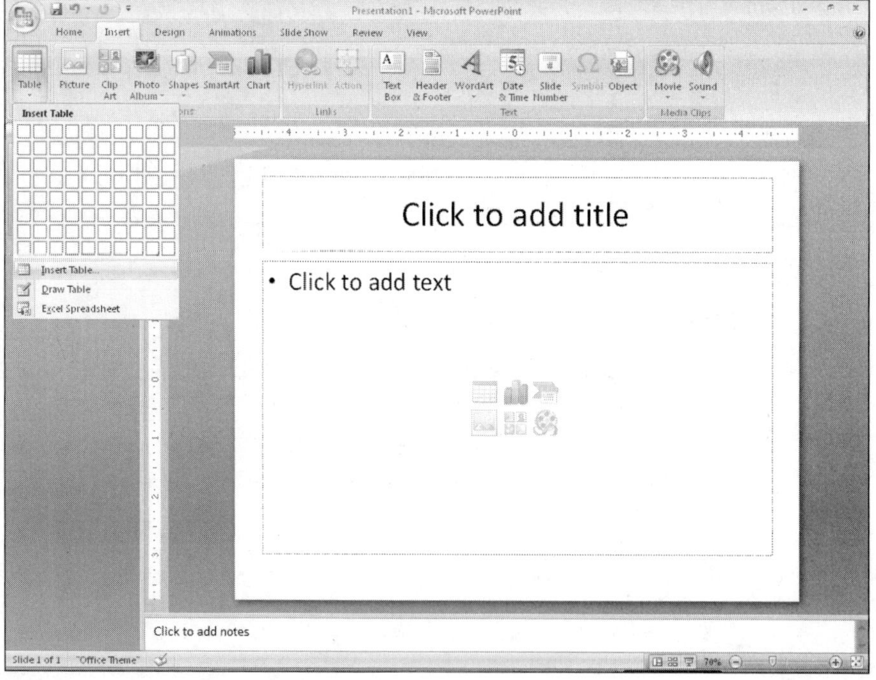

In the Insert Table dialog box shown in Figure 23-2, specify a number of rows and columns and click OK. The table then appears on the slide.

FIGURE 23-2

Enter the number of rows and columns to specify the size of the table that you want to create.

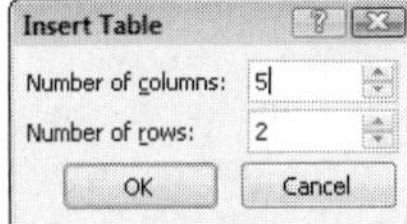

Creating a table from the Table button

When you opened the Table button's menu (see Figure 23-1) in the preceding section, you probably couldn't help but notice the grid of white squares. Another way to create a table is to drag across this grid until you select the desired number of rows and columns. The table appears immediately on the slide as you drag, so you can see how it will look, as shown in Figure 23-3.

FIGURE 23-3

Drag across the grid in the Table button's menu to specify the size of the table that you want to create.

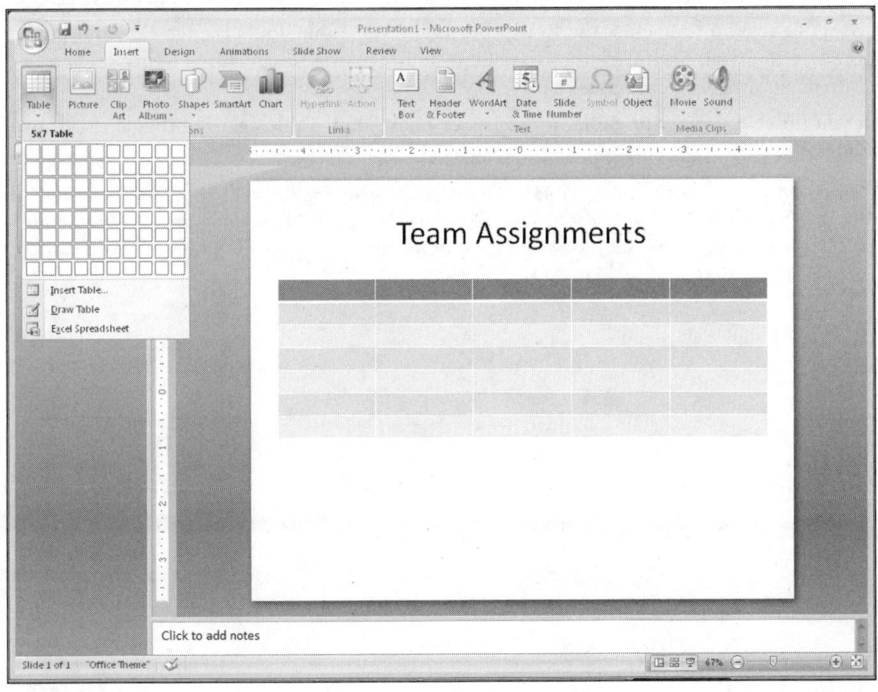

Other than the method of specifying rows and columns, this method is identical to creating a table via the dialog box, because the same issues apply regarding placeholders versus free-floating tables. If a placeholder is available, PowerPoint uses it.

When you create a table with this method and the preceding one, the table is automatically formatted with one of the preset table styles. You learn how to change this later in the chapter.

Drawing a table

I've saved the most fun method for last. Drawing a table enables you to use your mouse pointer like a pencil to create every row and column in the table in exactly the positions you want. You can even create unequal numbers of rows and columns. This method is a good one to use whenever you want a table that is non-standard in some way—different row heights, different column widths, different numbers of columns in some rows, and so on. To draw a table, follow these steps:

1. **From the Insert tab, click Table, and choose Draw Table. The mouse pointer turns into a pencil.**
2. **Drag to draw a rectangle representing the outer frame of the table.** Then release the mouse button to create the outer frame and to display the Design tab.
3. **The mouse pointer remains a pencil; drag to draw the rows and columns you want.** You can draw a row or column that runs all the way across or down the table's frame, or you can stop at any point to make a partial row or column. See Figure 23-4. When you begin to drag vertically or horizontally, PowerPoint locks into that mode and keeps the line exactly vertical or horizontal and straight. (Exception: It allows you to draw a diagonal line between two corners of existing cells.)
4. **(Optional) To erase a line, click the Eraser button on the Table Tools Design tab, and then click the line to erase.** Then click the Draw Table button on the Design tab to return the mouse pointer to its drawing (pencil) mode.
5. **When you finish drawing the table, press Esc or click Draw Table again to toggle the drawing mode off.**

TIP

If you need a table that is mostly uniform but has a few anomalies, such as a few combined cells or a few extra divisions, create the table using the Insert Table dialog box or the grid on the Table button, and then use the Draw Table and/or Eraser buttons on the Design tab to modify it.

FIGURE 23-4

You can create a unique table with the Draw Table tool.

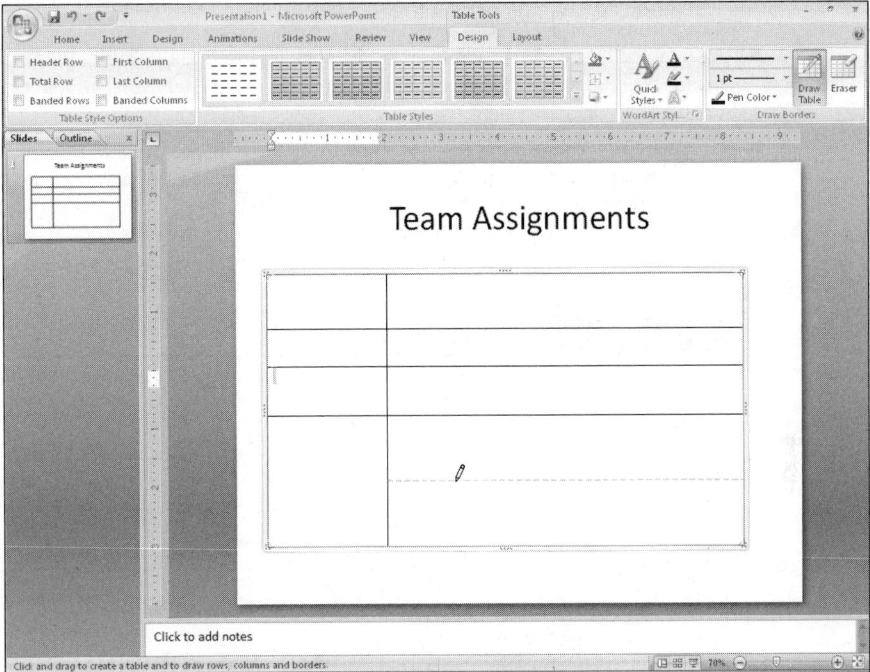

Moving Around in a Table

Each cell is like a little text box. To type in a cell, click in it and type. It's pretty simple! You can also move between cells with the keyboard. Table 23-1 lists the keyboard shortcuts for moving the insertion point in a table.

TABLE 23-1

Moving the Insertion Point in a Table

To Move to:	Press This:
Next cell	Tab
Previous cell	Shift+Tab
Next row	Down arrow
Previous row	Up arrow
Tab stop within a cell	Ctrl+Tab
New paragraph within the same cell	Enter

Selecting Rows, Columns, and Cells

If you want to apply formatting to one or more cells, or issue a command that acts upon them such as Copy or Delete, you must first select the cells to be affected:

- **A single cell:** Move the insertion point by clicking inside the desired cell. At this point, any command acts on that individual cell and its contents, not the whole table, row, or column. Drag across multiple cells to select them.
- **An entire row or column:** Click any cell in that row or column and then open the Select button's menu on the Layout tab and choose Select Column or Select Row (Figure 23-5). Alternatively, position the mouse pointer above the column or to the left of the row, so that the mouse pointer turns into a black arrow, and then click to select the column or row. (You can drag to extend the selection to additional columns or rows when you see the black arrow.)

FIGURE 23-5

Select a row or column with the Select button's menu, or click above or to the left of the column or row.

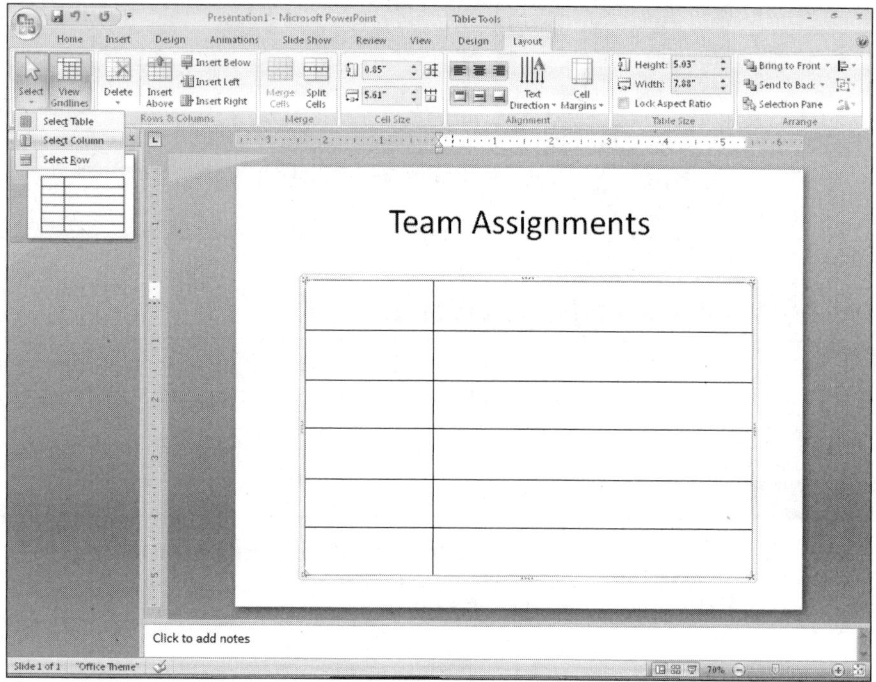

There are two ways to select the entire table — or rather, two senses in which the entire table can be "selected."

- **Select all table cells:** When you select all of the cells, they all appear with shaded backgrounds, and any text formatting command that you apply at that point affects all of the text in the table. To select all cells, do any of the following:
  - Choose Select Table from the Select button's menu, shown in Figure 23-5.
  - Drag across all of the cells in the entire table.
  - Click inside the table, and then press Ctrl+A.
- **Select the entire table:** When you do this, the table's frame is selected, but the insertion point is not anywhere within the table and cells do not appear with a shaded background. You do this kind of selection before moving or resizing the table, for example. To select the entire table, do any of the following:
  - Click the frame of the table.
  - Click inside the table, and then press Esc once.
  - Right-click the table and choose Select Table.
- **Drag a marquee around the table:** You can use the mouse to drag a marquee (a box) around the table. This is also called *lassoing*. When you release the mouse button, everything inside the area is selected.

Editing a Table's Structure

Now that you've created a table, let's look at some ways to modify the table's structure, including resizing the entire table, adding and deleting rows and columns, and merging and splitting cells.

Resizing the overall table

As with any other framed object in PowerPoint, dragging the table's outer frame resizes it. Position the mouse pointer over one of the selection handles (the dots on the sides and corners) so that the mouse pointer becomes a double-headed arrow, and drag to resize the table. See Figure 23-6.

If you drag when the mouse pointer is over any other part of the frame, so that the mouse pointer becomes a four-headed arrow, you move the table rather than resize it.

To maintain the aspect ratio (height to width ratio) for the table as you resize it, hold down the Shift key as you drag a corner of the frame. If maintaining the aspect ratio is not critical, you can drag either a corner or a side.

FIGURE 23-6

To resize a table, drag a selection handle on its frame.

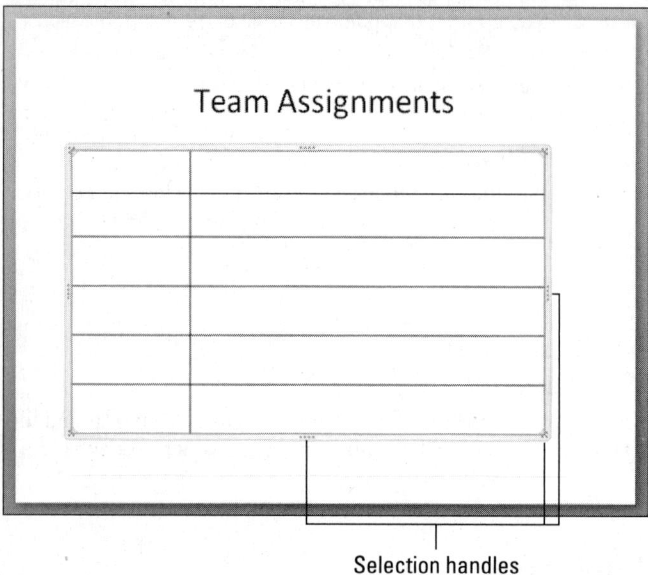

All of the rows and columns maintain their spacing proportionally to one another as you resize them. However, when a table contains text that would no longer fit if its row and column were shrunken proportionally with the rest of the table, the row height does not shrink fully; it shrinks as much as it can while still displaying the text. The column width does shrink proportionally, regardless of cell content.

You can also specify an exact size for the overall table frame by using the Table Size group on the Layout tab. From there you can enter Height and Width values (Figure 23-7). To maintain the aspect ratio, mark the Lock Aspect Ratio checkbox *before* you change either the Height or Width settings.

FIGURE 23-7

Set a precise height and width for the table from the Table Size group.

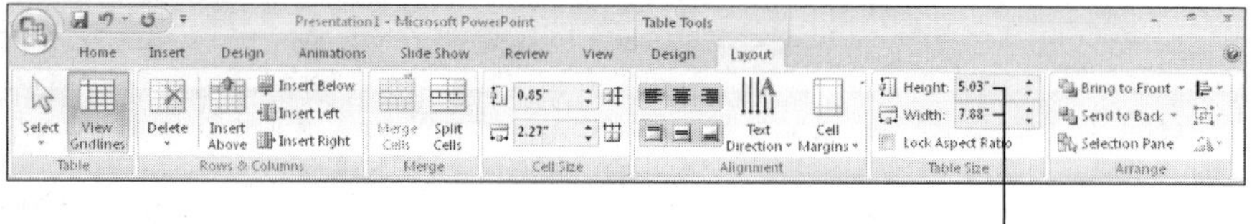

Inserting or deleting rows and columns

Here's an easy way to create a new row at the bottom of the table: Position the insertion point in the bottom-right cell and press Tab. Need something more complicated than that? The Layout tab contains buttons in the Rows & Columns group for inserting rows or columns above, below, to the left, or to the right of the selected cell(s), as shown in Figure 23-8. By default, each button inserts a single row or column at a time, but if you select multiple existing ones beforehand, these commands insert as many as you've selected. For example, to insert three new rows, select three existing rows and then click Insert Above or Insert Below.

FIGURE 23-8

Insert rows or columns by using these buttons on the Layout tab.

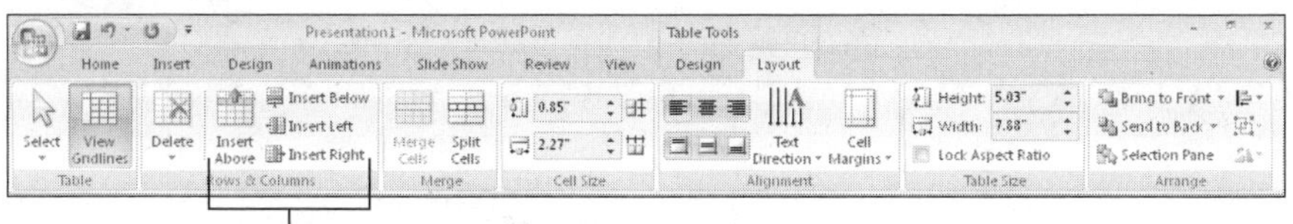

Use to add rows or columns

Alternatively, you can right-click any existing row or column, point to Insert, and choose one of the commands on the submenu. These commands are the same as the names of the buttons in Figure 23-8.

CAUTION **Adding new rows increases the overall vertical size of the table frame, even to the point where it runs off the bottom of the slide. You might need to adjust the overall frame size after adding rows. On the other hand, inserting columns does not change the overall frame size; it simply resizes the existing columns so that they all fit and are all a uniform size (unless you have manually adjusted any of them to be a custom size).**

To delete a row or column (or more than one of each), select the row(s) or column(s) that you want to delete, and then open the Delete button's menu on the Layout tab and choose Delete Rows or Delete Columns.

You cannot insert or delete individual cells in a PowerPoint table. (This is unlike in Excel, where you can remove individual cells and then shift the remaining ones up or to the left.)

Merging and splitting cells

If you need more rows or columns in some spots than others, you can use the Merge Cells and Split Cells commands. Here are some ways to merge cells:

- Click the Eraser button on the Design tab, and then click the line you want to erase. The cells on either side of the deleted line are merged.
- Select the cells that you want to merge and click Merge Cells on the Layout tab.
- Select the cells to merge, right-click them, and choose Merge Cells.

Here are some ways to split cells:

- Click the Draw Table button on the Design tab, and then drag to draw a line in the middle of a cell to split it.
- Select the cell that you want to split, right-click it, and choose Split Cells. In the Split Cells dialog box (see Figure 23-9), select the number of pieces in which to split in each direction, and click OK.
- Select the cell to split, and then click Split Cells on the Layout tab. In the Split Cells dialog box (see Figure 23-9), select the number of pieces in which to split in each direction, and click OK.

FIGURE 23-9

Specify how the split should occur.

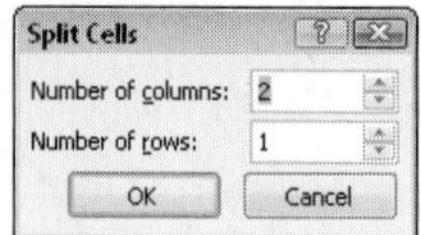

Applying Table Styles

The quickest way to format a table attractively is to apply a table style to it. When you insert a table using any method except drawing it, a table style is applied to it by default; you can change to some other style if desired, or you can remove all styles from the table, leaving it plain black and white.

When you hover the mouse pointer over a table style, a preview of it appears in the active table. The style is not actually applied to the table until you click the style to select it, however.

If the style you want appears on the Table Tools Design tab without opening the gallery, you can click it from there. If not, you can scroll row by row through the gallery by clicking the up/down arrow buttons, or you can open the gallery's full menu as shown in Figure 23-10.

To remove all styles from the table, choose Clear Table from the bottom of the gallery menu. This reverts the table to default settings: no fill, and plain black 1-point borders on all sides of all cells.

The table styles use theme-based colors, so if you change to a different presentation theme or color theme, the table formatting might change. (Colors, in particular, are prone to shift.)

By default, the first row of the table (a.k.a. the *header row)* is formatted differently from the others, and every other row is shaded differently. (This is called *banding*.) You can control how different rows are treated differently (or not) from the Table Style Options group on the Table Tools Design tab. There is a checkbox for each of six settings:

- Header row: The first row
- Total row: The last row
- First column: The leftmost column
- Last column: The rightmost column
- Banded rows: Every other row formatted differently
- Banded columns: Every other column formatted differently

FIGURE 23-10

Apply a table style from the gallery.

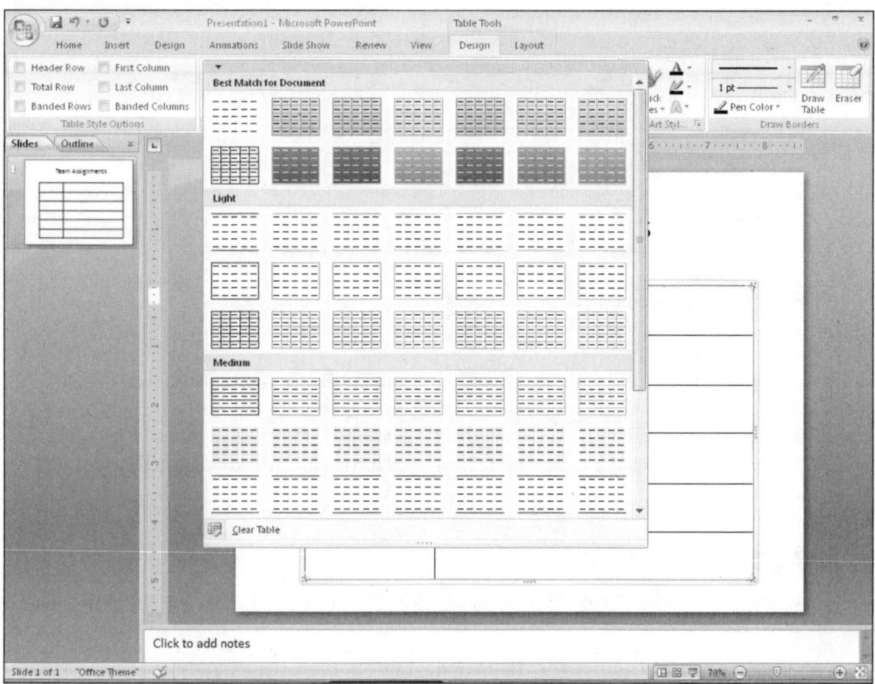

CAUTION With some of the styles, there is not a whole lot of difference between some of the settings. For example, you might have to look very closely to see the difference between First Column being turned on or off; ditto with Last Column and Total Row.

Formatting Table Cells

Although table styles provide a rough cut on the formatting, you might like to fine-tune your table formatting as well. In the following sections you learn how to adjust various aspects of the table's appearance.

Changing row height and column width

You might want a row to be a different height or a column a different width than others in the table. To resize a row or column, follow these steps:

1. **Position the mouse pointer on the border below the row or to the right of the column that you want to resize.** The mouse pointer turns into a line with arrows on each side of it.
2. **Hold down the mouse button as you drag the row or column to a new height or width.** A dotted line appears showing where it will go.
3. **Release the mouse button.**

You can also specify an exact height or width measurement using the Height and Width boxes in the Cell Size group on the Layout tab. Select the row(s) or column(s) to affect, and then enter sizes in inches or use the increment buttons, as shown in Figure 23-11.

FIGURE 23-11

Set a precise size for a row or column.

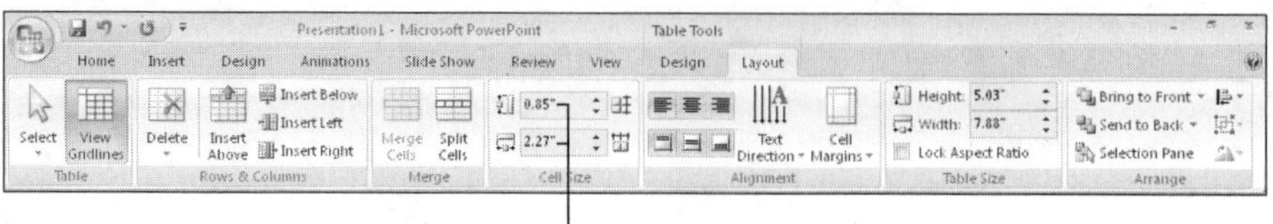

The Distribute Rows Evenly and Distribute Columns Evenly buttons in the Cell Size group (see Figure 23-11) adjust each row or column in the selected range so that the available space is occupied evenly among them. This is handy especially if you have drawn the table yourself rather than allowed PowerPoint to create it initially. If PowerPoint creates the table, the rows and columns are already of equal height and width by default.

Table margins and alignment

Remember, PowerPoint slides do not have any margins per se; everything is in a frame. An individual cell does have *internal* margins, however.

You can specify the internal margins for cells using the Margins button on the Layout tab, as follows:

1. **Select the cells to which the setting should apply.** To apply settings to the entire table, select the entire table.
2. **On the Layout tab, click the Margins button.** A menu of margin presets opens.
3. **Click one of the presets or choose Custom Margins, and then follow these steps:**
   a. In the Cell Text Layout dialog box, set the Left, Right, Top, and Bottom margin settings, as shown in Figure 23-12.
   b. Click OK.

FIGURE 23-12

You can set the internal margins on an individual cell basis for each side of the cell.

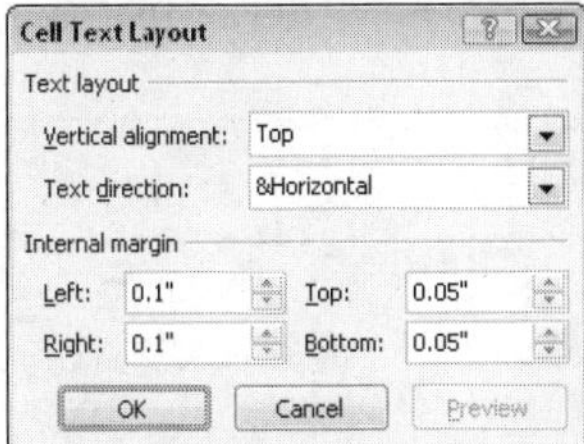

Applying borders

The border lines around each cell are very important because they separate the data in each cell. By default (without a table style) there's a 1-point border around each side of each cell, but you can make some or all borders thicker, a different line style (dashed, for example), a different color, or remove them altogether to create your own effects. Here are some ideas:

- To make items appear to "float" in multiple columns on the slide (that is, to make it look as if they are not really in a table at all — just lined up extremely well), remove all table borders.
- To create a header row at the top without using the Quick Style Options, make the border beneath the first row of cells darker or thicker than the others.
- To make certain rows or columns appear as if they are outside of the table, turn off their borders on all sides except the side that faces the other cells.
- To make certain items appear as if they have been crossed off a list, format those cells with diagonal borders. This creates the effect of an X running through each cell. These diagonal lines are not really borders in the sense that they don't go around the edge of the cell, but they're treated as borders in PowerPoint.

When you apply a top, bottom, left, or right border, those positions refer to the entire selected block of cells if you have more than one cell selected. For example, suppose you select two adjacent cells in a row and apply a left border. The border applies only to the leftmost of the two cells. If you want the same border applied to the line between the cells too, you must apply an inside vertical border.

To apply a border, follow these steps:

1. **Select the cell(s) that you want to affect.**
2. **In the Draw Borders group on the Table Tools Design tab, select a line style, width, and color from the Pen Style, Pen Weight, and Pen Color drop-down lists.** See Figure 23-13.

FIGURE 23-13

Use the Draw Borders group's lists to set the border's style, thickness, and color.

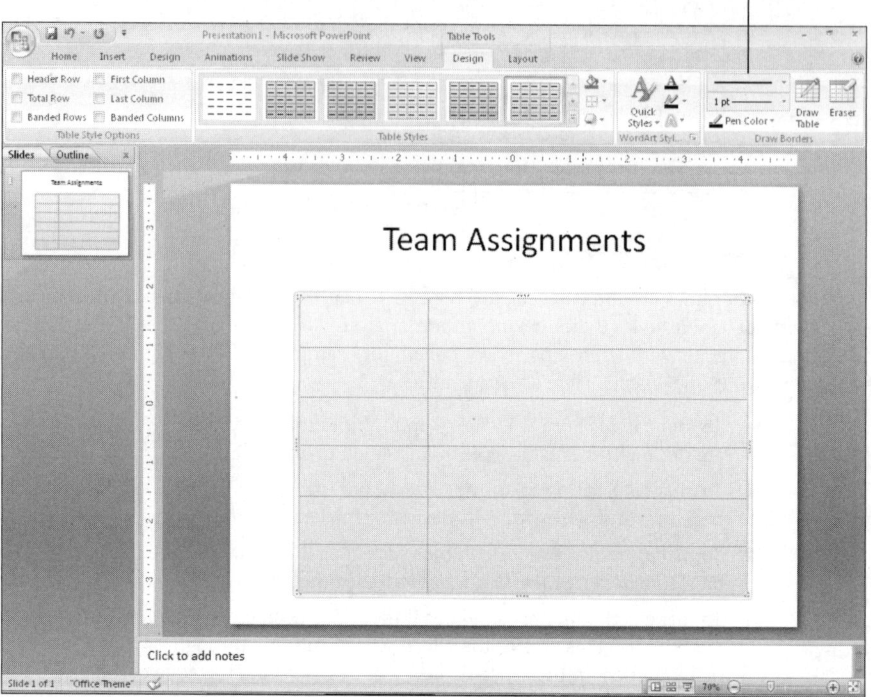

Try to use theme colors rather than fixed colors whenever possible, so that if you change to a different color theme later, the colors you choose now won't clash.

3. **Open the Borders button's menu in the Table Styles group and choose the sides of the selected area to which the new settings should apply. See Figure 23-14.** For example, to apply the border the bottom of the selected area, click Bottom Border.

   If you want to remove all borders from all sides, choose No Border from the menu.

4. **If necessary, repeat Step 3 to apply the border to other sides of the selection.** Some of the choices on the Borders button's menu apply to only one side; others apply to two or more at once.

FIGURE 23-14

Select the side(s) to apply borders to the chosen cells.

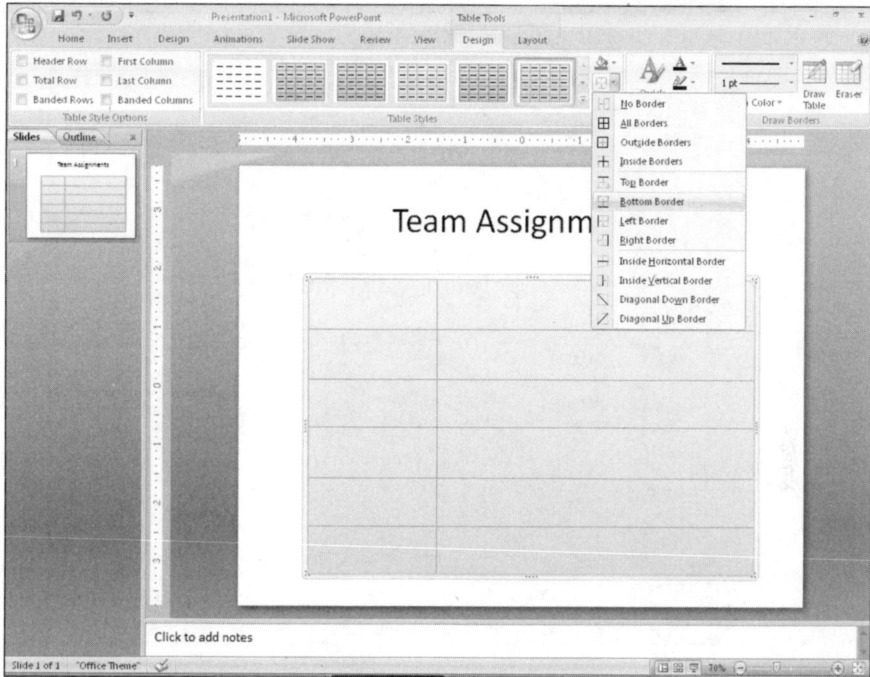

Applying fills

By default, table cells have a transparent background so that the color of the slide beneath shows through. When you apply a table style, as you learned earlier in the chapter, the style specifies a background color — or in some cases, multiple background colors depending on the Quick Style Options you choose for special treatment of certain rows or columns.

You can also manually change the fill for a table to make it either a solid color or a special fill effect. You can apply this fill to individual cells, or you can apply a background fill for the entire table.

Filling individual cells

Each individual cell has its own fill setting; in this way a table is like a collection of individual object frames, rather than a single object. To set the fill color for one or more cells, follow these steps:

1. **Select the cell(s) to affect, or to apply the same fill color to all cells, select the table's outer frame.**
2. **On the Table Tools Design tab, click the down arrow next to the Shading button to open its palette.**

3. **Select the desired color or fill effect. See Figure 23-15.**

FIGURE 23-15

Apply a fill effect to the selected cell(s).

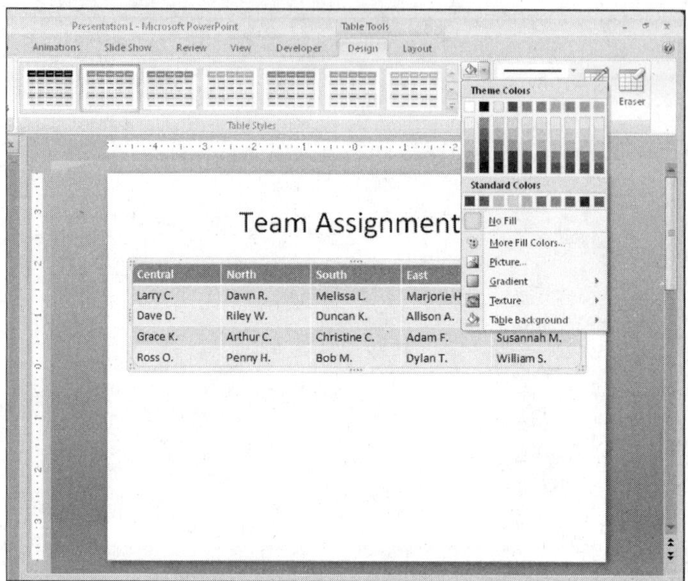

CROSS-REF **Also see the section "Filling a table with a picture" later in this chapter for some issues involving picture fills specific to tables.**

TIP **For a semitransparent, solid-color fill, first apply the fill and then right-click the cell and choose Format Shape. In the Format Shape dialog box, drag the Transparency slider. For some types of fills, you can also set the transparency when you initially apply the fill.**

Applying an Overall Table Fill

New in PowerPoint 2007, you can apply a solid color fill to the entire table that is different from the fill applied to the individual cells. The table's fill color is visible only in cells in which the individual fill is set to No Fill (or a semitransparent fill, in which case it blends).

To apply a fill for the entire table, open the Shading button's menu and point to Table Background, and then choose a color, as shown in Figure 23-16.

FIGURE 23-16

Apply a fill to the table's background.

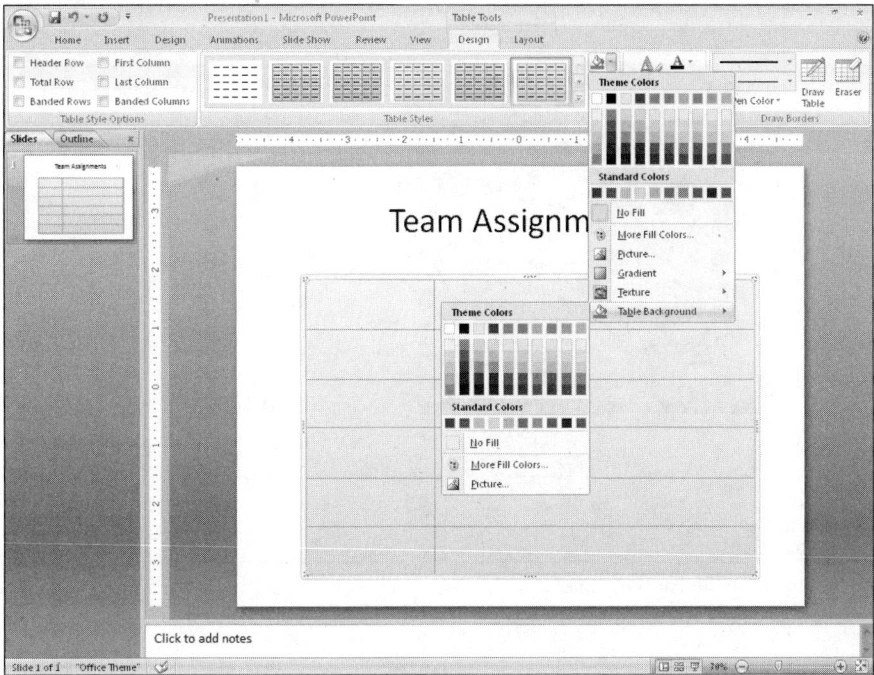

To test the new background, select some cells and choose No Fill for their fill color. The background color appears in those cells. If you want to experiment further, try applying a semi-transparent fill to some cells, and see how the color of the background blends with the color of the fill.

Filling a table with a picture

When you fill one or more cells with a picture, each cell gets its own individual copy of it. For example, if you fill a table with a picture of a dog, and the table has six cells, you get six dogs as shown in Figure 23-17).

If you want a single copy of the picture to fill the entire area behind the table, there are two ways you can do this. One is to set the picture to be tiled like a texture. Follow these steps:

1. **Apply the picture to all of the cells in the table, or to the range of cells in which you want it to appear.** To do this:
   - **a.** Select the cells, and then right-click the selection and choose Format Shape.
   - **b.** Click Fill, and then click Picture or Texture Fill.
   - **c.** Click the File button, select the picture file, and click Insert.
2. **Mark the Tile Picture as Texture checkbox.** See Figure 23-18.

FIGURE 23-17

When you apply a picture fill to a table, each cell gets its own copy.

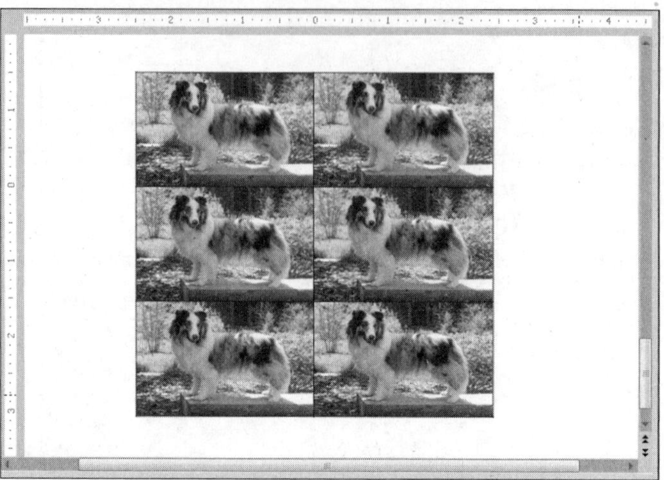

FIGURE 23-18

Set the picture to be tiled as a texture.

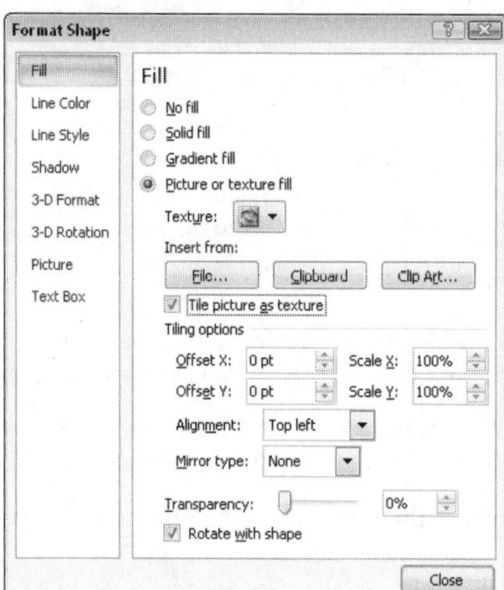

At this point, the picture fills the table without regard for cell borders, but it probably doesn't fill it exactly. Depending on the original size of the graphic and the size of the table, you probably either see a truncated version of the picture or a tiled version that does not match up with the cell borders. Figure 23-19 shows some examples.

FIGURE 23-19

The picture is too large (left) or too small (right) for the table fill.

To adjust the picture, use the Tiling Options in the Format Shape dialog box, shown in Figure 23-18:

- Adjust the position of the picture within the table by changing the Offset X and Offset Y values. These are measured in points, and move the picture to the right (X) and down (Y).
- Change the sizing of the picture by adjusting the Scale X and Scale Y values. The smaller the number, the smaller the picture — but don't go too small or the picture will start to tile (unless that's what you want, of course).
- Change the way the picture aligns in the table by changing the Alignment.
- (Optional) Set a mirror type if desired so that if you do have multiple copies tiled within the frame, each copy is flipped horizontally and/or vertically. (This is not common.)

It can take some time to get the picture optimally adjusted so that it exactly fits in the allotted space. If all of that seems like more than you want to mess with, there is an alternative method: make the table transparent and place the picture behind it on the slide. Here's how:

1. **Place the picture on the slide by choosing Insert ➪ Picture.**
2. **Select the picture and choose Format ➪ Send to Back.** (If the picture is the only object on the slide, this command is unavailable, but the command is unnecessary in that case.)
3. **Create a plain unformatted table on top of the picture.**
4. **Set the table's fill to No Fill if it is not already transparent.**
5. **Resize the table and the picture as needed so they are both the same size.** You might need to crop the picture to keep the right aspect ratio.

FIGURE 23-20

A picture placed behind a transparent table appears to fill its background.

Applying a shadow to a table

New in PowerPoint 2007, you can apply a shadow effect to a table. You can make it any color you like, and adjust a variety of settings for it.

If the cells have no fill, the shadow will apply to the gridlines, not to the table as a whole object.

To apply a shadow to a table, follow these steps:

1. **Select the table's outer frame, and then right-click the frame and choose Format Shape.**
2. **Click Shadow, and then choose a preset and a color.** See Figure 23-21.
3. **(Optional) If desired, drag any of the sliders to fine-tune the shadow.**
4. **Click Close to close the Format Shape dialog box when you are finished.**

Applying a 3-D effect to a table

PowerPoint does not enable you to apply 3-D effects to tables, so you have to fudge that by creating the 3-D effect with rectangles and then overlaying a transparent table on top of the shapes. As you can see in Figure 23-22, it's a pretty convincing facsimile.

FIGURE 23-21

Apply a shadow to a table.

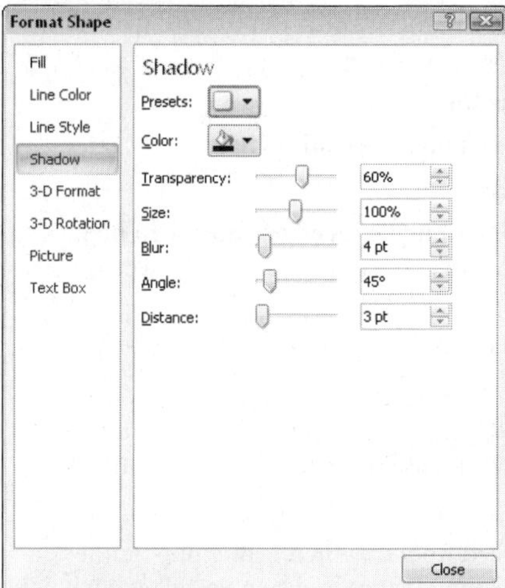

FIGURE 23-22

This 3-D table is actually a plain table with a 3-D rectangle behind it.

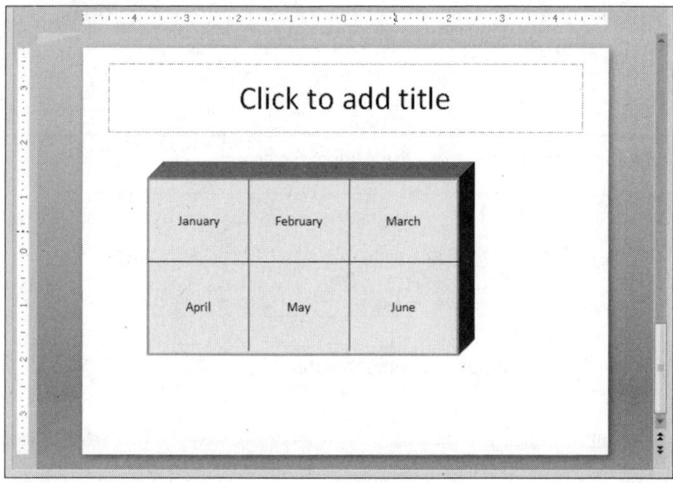

Here's the basic procedure:

1. **Create a rectangle from the Shapes group on the Insert tab, and apply a 3-D effect to it.** Use any effect you like. To create the traditional "box" appearance as in Figure 23-22, apply the second Oblique preset and then in the 3-D Format options, increase the Depth setting to about 100 points.
2. **Size the rectangle so that its face is the same size as the table.**
3. **On the Format tab, click Send to Back to send the rectangle behind the table.**
4. **Set the table's fill to No Fill if it is not already transparent.**
5. **(Optional) Set the table's outer frame border to None to make its edges appear to blend with the edges of the rectangle.** To do that, open the Borders button's menu and select Outside Border to toggle that off.

Changing text alignment

If you followed the preceding steps to create the effect shown in Figure 23-22, you probably ran into a problem: Your text probably didn't center itself in the cells. That's because by default each cell's vertical alignment is set to Top, and horizontal alignment is set to Left.

Although the vertical and horizontal alignments are both controlled from the Alignment group on the Layout tab, they actually have two different scopes. Vertical alignment applies to the entire cell as a whole, whereas horizontal alignment can apply differently to individual paragraphs within the cell. To set vertical alignment for a cell, follow these steps:

1. **Select one or more cells to affect.** To affect only one cell, you do not have to select it; just click inside it.
2. **On the Layout tab, in the Alignment group, click one of the vertical alignment buttons: Align Top, Center Vertically, or Align Bottom.** See Figure 23-23.

FIGURE 23-23

Set the vertical and horizontal alignment of text from the Alignment group.

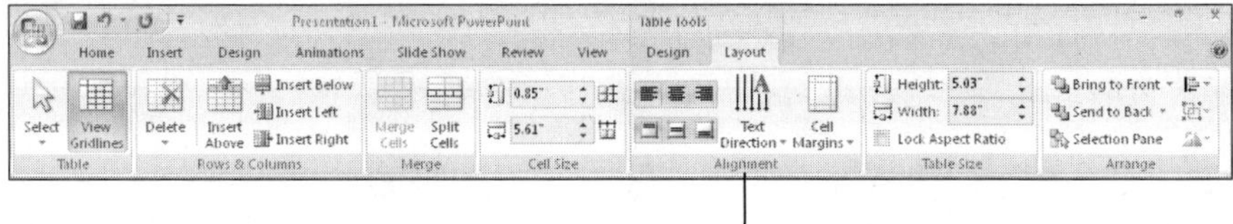

To set the horizontal alignment for a paragraph, follow these steps:

1. **Select one or more paragraphs to affect.** If you select multiple cells, all paragraphs within those cells are affected. If you click in a cell without selecting anything, the change only affects the paragraph in which you clicked.
2. **On the Layout tab, in the Alignment group, click one of the horizontal alignment buttons: Align Left, Center, or Align Right.** See Figure 23-23. You can also use the paragraph alignment buttons on the Home tab for horizontal alignment, or the buttons on the mini toolbar.

The horizontal alignments all have keyboard shortcuts: Ctrl+L for left, Ctrl+E for center, and Ctrl+R for right.

Changing text direction

The default text direction for table cells is Horizontal, which reads from left to right (at least in countries where that's how text is read). Figure 23-24 shows the alternatives.

FIGURE 23-24

You can set types of text direction

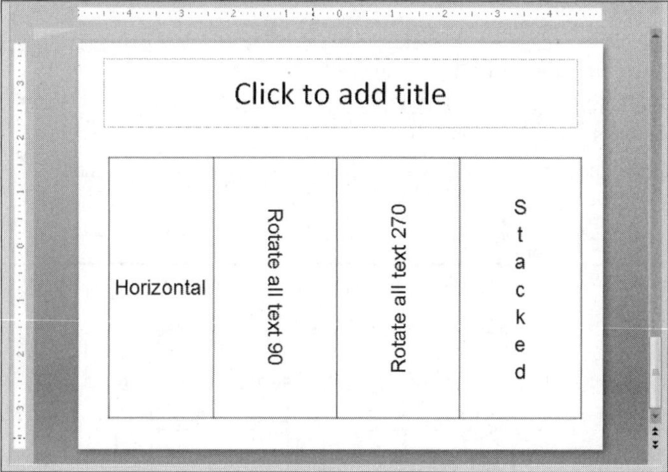

To change the text direction for a cell, follow these steps:

1. **Select the cell(s) to affect. To affect only a single cell, move the insertion point into it.**
2. **On the Layout tab, click Text Direction.**
3. **Select a text direction from the menu that appears.**

You cannot set text direction for individual paragraphs; the setting applies to the entire cell.

Understanding Charts

PowerPoint 2007's charting feature is based upon the same Escher 2.0 graphics engine as is used for drawn objects. Consequently, most of what you have learned about formatting objects in earlier chapters (about Word) also applies to charts. For example, you can apply shape styles to the individual elements of a chart, and apply WordArt styles to chart text. However, there are also many chart-specific formatting and layout options, as you will see throughout this chapter.

Parts of a chart

The sample chart shown in Figure 23-25 contains these elements:

- **Data series:** Each different bar color represents a different series: Q1, Q2, and Q3.
- **Legend:** Colored squares in the Legend box describe the correlation of each color to a data series.
- **Categories:** The North, South, East, and West labels along the bottom of the chart are the categories.
- **Category axis:** The horizontal line running across the bottom of the chart is the category axis, also called the horizontal axis.
- **Value axis:** The vertical line running up the left side of the chart, with the numbers on it, is the value axis, also called the vertical axis.
- **Data points:** Each individual bar is a data point. The numeric value for that data point corresponds to the height of the bar, measured against the value axis.
- **Walls:** The walls are the areas behind the data points. On a 3-D chart, as shown in Figure 23-25, there are both back and side walls. On a 2-D chart, there is only a back wall.
- **Floor:** The floor is the area on which the data points sit. A floor appears only in a 3-D chart.

FIGURE 23-25

Parts of a chart

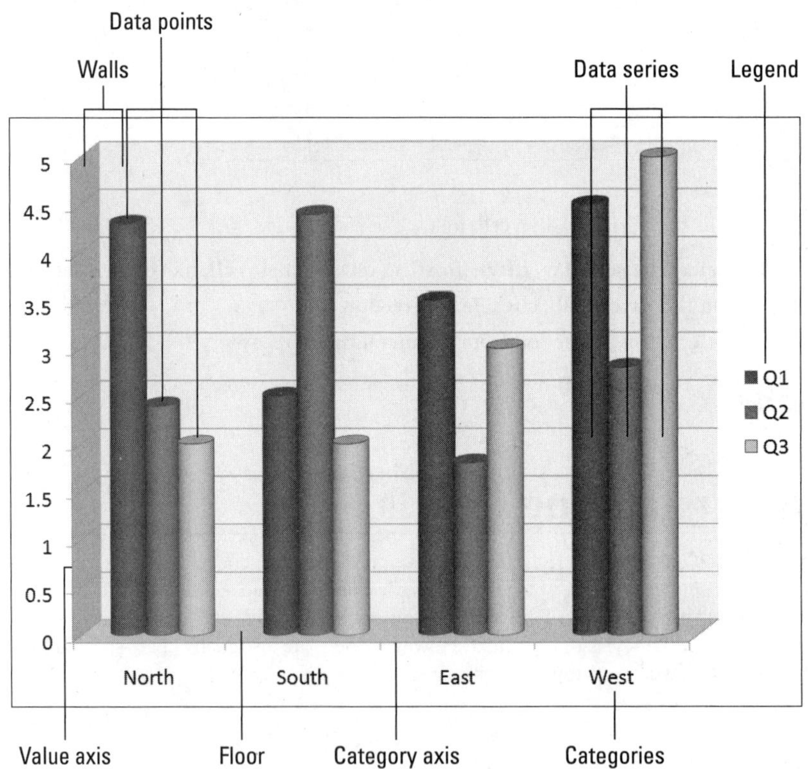

PowerPoint 2007 versus legacy charts

When you are working with a chart in PowerPoint 2007 format, you have access to three Chart Tools tabs—Design, Layout, and Format—and also to a separate Excel window for entering and editing your data. Because the PowerPoint 2007 charting engine uses Excel as its basis, there is no longer a big advantage to creating charts in Excel and then copying them over to PowerPoint. Figure 23-26 shows the PowerPoint 2007 charting interface, along with the Layout tab.

If you later save the file as a PowerPoint 97-2003 presentation, it does not take away your ability to access the PowerPoint 2007 charting interface when working in PowerPoint 2007. The chart is still saved as a PowerPoint 2007 object in the 2003 file, but it also contains a 2003 version of itself, for backward compatibility. When you open the presentation in PowerPoint 2003, it initially looks like a PowerPoint 2007 style chart, but if you double-click it to edit it (or enter editing mode for it in some other way), it switches to a 97-to-2003-style chart and loses its 2007-style appearance.

FIGURE 23-26

The PowerPoint 2007 charting interface

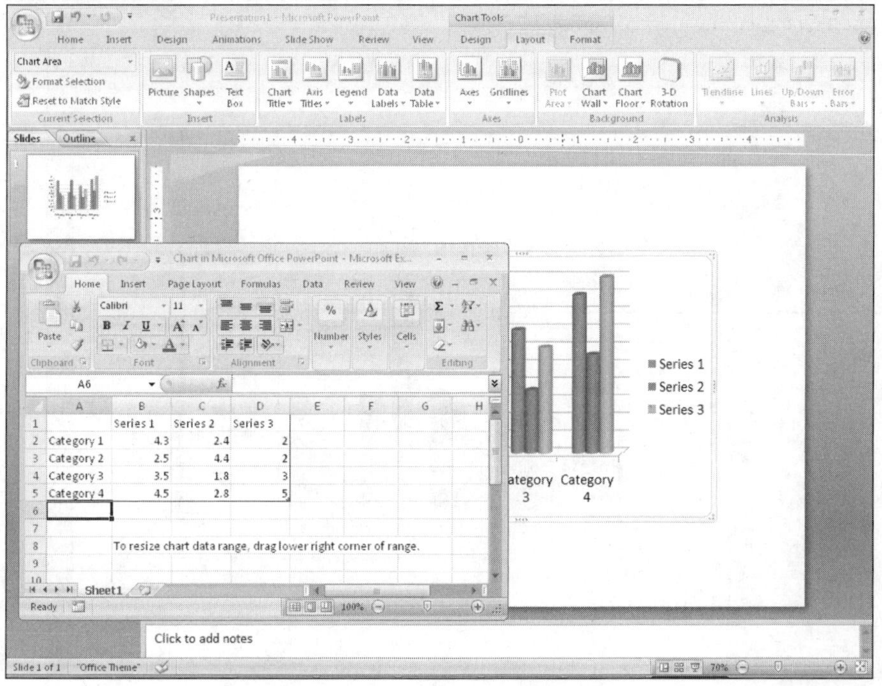

If you want to make sure that the chart appears exactly as you created it in PowerPoint 2003, even if it is edited there, then you should insert the chart initially using Microsoft Graph, rather than the PowerPoint 2007 charting tools. To do this, insert a Microsoft Graph object by following these steps:

1. **On the Insert tab, click Object.** The Object dialog box opens.
2. **Click Create New.**
3. **On the Object Type list, click Microsoft Graph Chart.**
4. **Click OK.** The Microsoft Graph window opens within PowerPoint, complete with a 2003-style menu bar from which you can access all of the same controls that were available in PowerPoint 2003's charting interface. The Microsoft Graph window is shown in Figure 23-27.

TIP **When you double-click to edit a Microsoft Graph chart within a PowerPoint 2007 presentation file, a message appears asking whether you want to Convert, Convert All, or Edit Existing. If you choose to convert (this chart or all charts) to 2007 format, you can use the new charting tools. If you choose Edit Exiting, MS Graph opens.**

FIGURE 23-27

Microsoft Graph from within PowerPoint 2007.

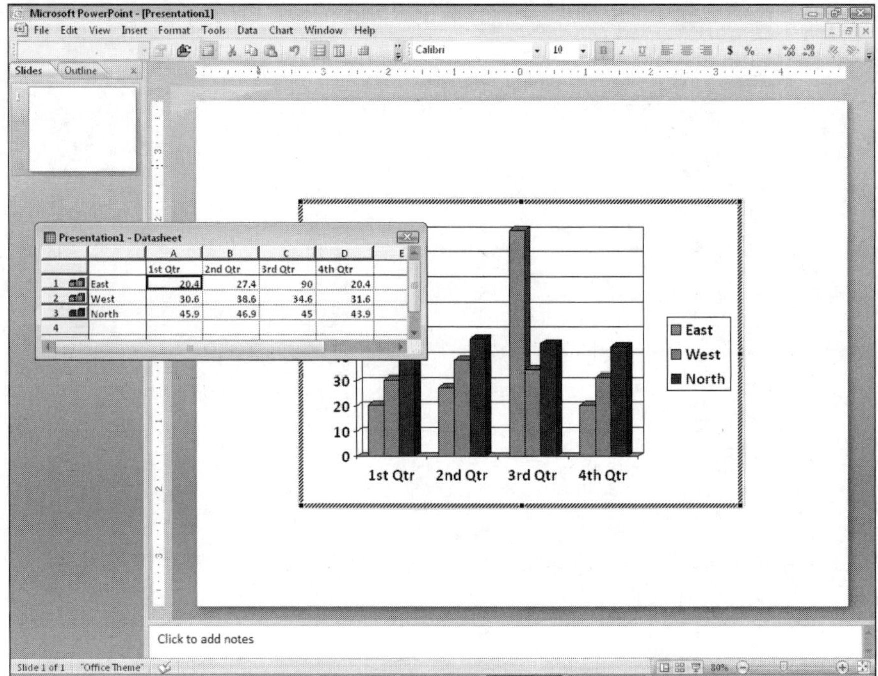

Starting a New Chart

The main difficulty with creating a chart in a non-spreadsheet application such as PowerPoint is that there is no data table from which to pull the numbers. Therefore, PowerPoint creates charts using data that you have entered in an Excel window. By default, it contains sample data, which you can replace with your own data.

You can place a new chart on a slide in two ways: you can either use a chart placeholder from a layout, or you can place one manually.

If you are using a placeholder, click the Insert Chart icon. If you are placing a chart manually, follow these steps:

1. **On the Insert tab, click Chart.** The Insert Chart dialog box opens, as shown in Figure 23-28.

FIGURE 23-28

Select the desired chart type.

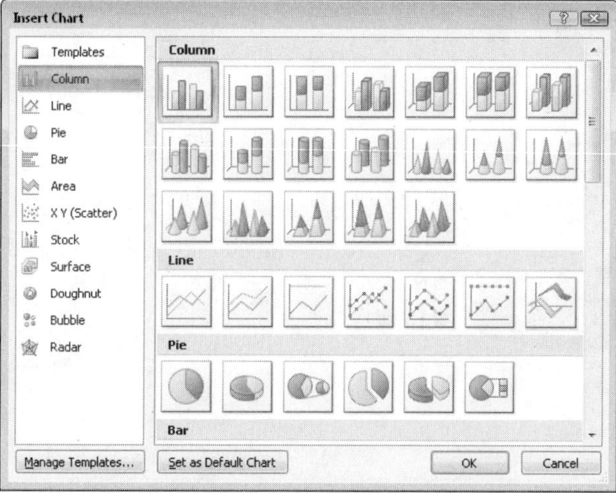

2. **Click the desired chart type.** See Table 23-2 for an explanation of the chart types. Figures 23-29 and 23-30 show examples of some of the chart types.
3. **Click OK.** The chart appears on the slide, and an Excel datasheet opens with sample data.

4. **Modify the sample data as needed.** To change the range of cells that appear in the chart, see the section, "Redefining the data range," later in this chapter. If you want, you can then close the Excel window to move it out of the way.

NOTE **After you have closed the Excel window, you can open it again by clicking Edit Data on the Chart Tools Design tab.**

FIGURE 23-29

Examples of chart types, from top left, clockwise: column, line, bar, and pie.

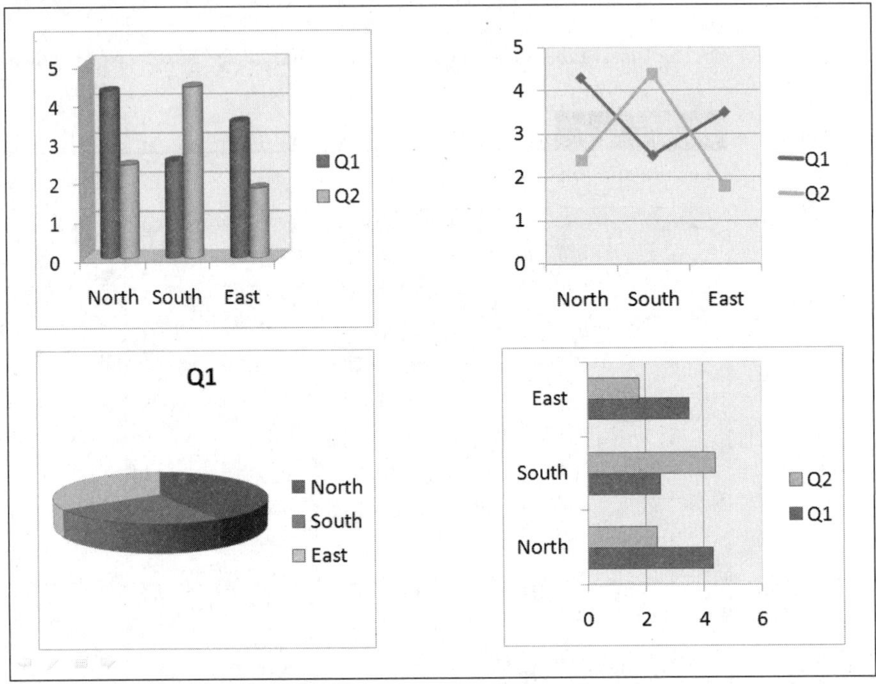

FIGURE 23-30

Examples of chart types, from top left, clockwise: area, scatter, doughnut, and surface.

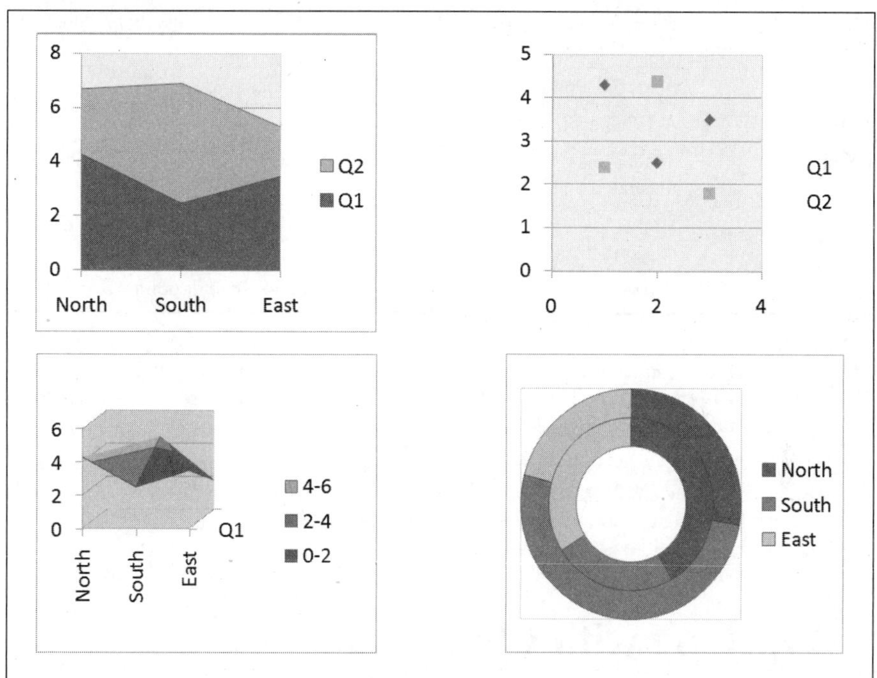

TABLE 23-2

Chart Types in PowerPoint 2007's Charting Tool

Type	Description
Column	Vertical bars, optionally with multiple data series. Bars can be clustered, stacked, or based on a percentage, and either 2-D or 3-D.
Line	Shows values as points, and connects the points with a line. Different series use different colors and/or line styles.
Pie	A circle broken into wedges to show how parts contribute to a whole. This de-emphasizes the actual numeric values. In most cases, this type is a single-series only.
Bar	Just like a column chart, but horizontal.
Area	Just like a column chart, but with the spaces filled in between the bars.

continued

TABLE 23-2 *(continued)*

Type	Description
XY (Scatter)	Shows values as points on both axes, but does not connect them with a line. However, you can add trend lines.
Stock	A special type of chart that is used to show stock prices.
Surface	A 3-D sheet that is used to illustrate the highest and lowest points of the data set.
Doughnut	Similar to a pie chart, but with multiple concentric rings, so that multiple series can be illustrated.
Bubble	Similar to a scatter chart, but instead of fixed-size data points, bubbles of varying sizes are used to represent a third data variable.
Radar	Shows changes of data frequency in relation to a center point.

At any point, you can return to your PowerPoint presentation by clicking anywhere outside of the chart on the slide. To edit the chart again, you can click the chart to redisplay the chart-specific tabs.

TIP

If you delete a column or row by selecting individual cells and pressing Delete to clear them, the empty space that these cells occupied remains in the chart. To completely remove a row or column from the data range, select the row or column by clicking its header (letter for column; number for row) and click Delete on the Home tab in Excel.

Working with Chart Data

After you create a chart, you might want to change the data range on which it is based, or how this data is plotted. The following sections explain how you can do this.

Plotting by rows versus by columns

By default, the columns of the datasheet form the data series. However, if you want, you can switch the data around so that the rows form the series. Figures 23-31 and 23-32 show the same chart plotted both ways so that you can see the difference.

NOTE

What does the term *data series* mean? Take a look at Figures 23-31 and 23-32. Notice that there is a legend next to each chart that shows what each color (or shade of gray) represents. Each of these colors, and the label associated with it, is a series. The other variable (the one that is not the series) is plotted on the chart's horizontal axis.

FIGURE 23-31

A chart with the columns representing the series.

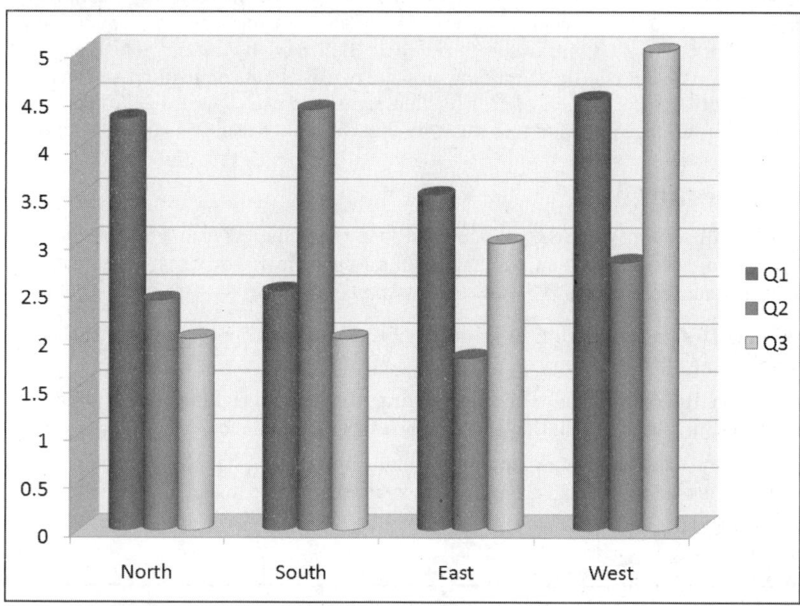

FIGURE 23-32

A chart with the rows representing the series.

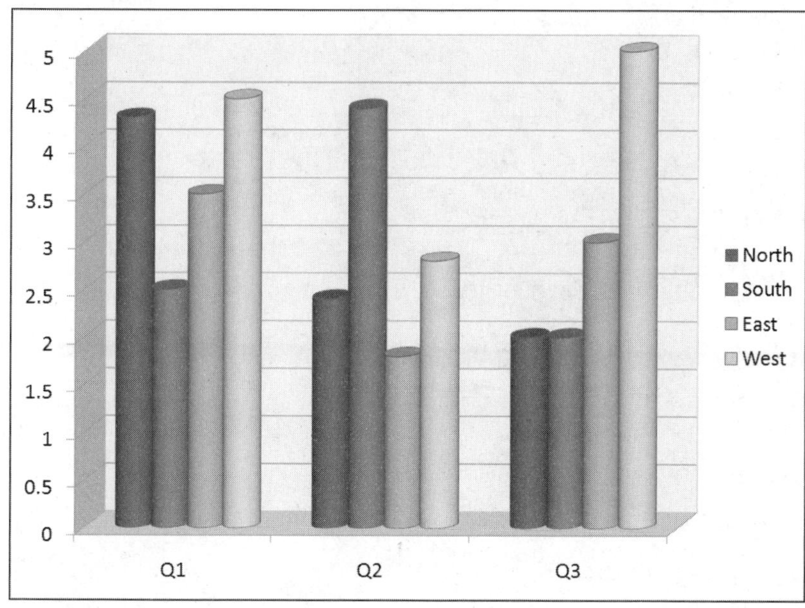

To switch back and forth between plotting by rows and by columns, click the Switch Row/Column button on the Chart Tools Design tab.

TIP A chart can carry a very different message when you arrange it by rows versus by columns. For example, in Figure 23-31, the chart compares the quarters. The message here is about improvement — or lack thereof — over time. Contrast this to Figure 23-32, where the series are the regions. Here, you can compare one region to another. The overriding message here is about competition — which division performed the best in each quarter? It's easy to see how the same data can convey very different messages; make sure that you pick the arrangement that tells the story that you want to tell in your presentation.

Redefining the data range

After you have created your chart, you may decide that you need to use more or less data. Perhaps you want to exclude a month or quarter of data, or to add another region or salesperson. To add or remove a data series, you can simply edit the datasheet. To do so, follow these steps:

1. **On the Chart Tools Design tab, click Edit Data.** The Excel datasheet appears. A blue outline appears around the range that is to be plotted.
2. **(Optional) To change the data range to be plotted, drag the bottom-right corner of the blue outline.** For example, in Figure 23-33, the West division is being excluded.

   You can also enlarge the data range by expanding the blue outline. For example, you could enter another series in column E in Figure 23-33 and then extend the outline to encompass column E.

FIGURE 23-33

You can redefine the range for the chart by dragging the blue outline on the datasheet.

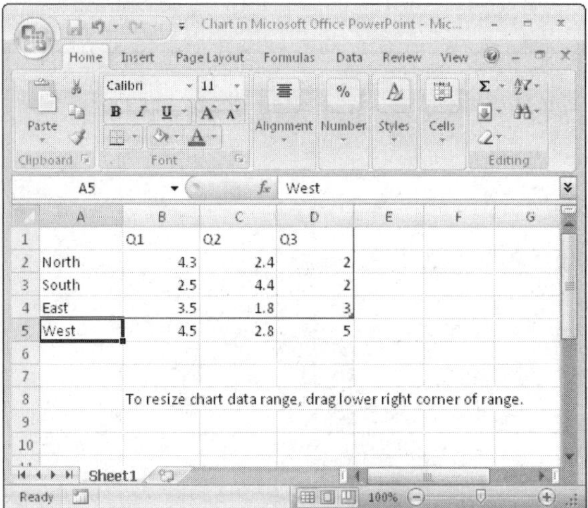

	A	B	C	D
1		Q1	Q2	Q3
2	North	4.3	2.4	2
3	South	2.5	4.4	2
4	East	3.5	1.8	3
5	West	4.5	2.8	5

The preceding steps work well if the range that you want to include is contiguous, but what if you wanted to exclude a row or column that is in the middle of the range? To define the range more precisely, follow these steps:

1. **On the Chart Tools Design tab, click Select Data. The Select Data Source dialog box opens, along with the Excel datasheet, as shown in Figure 23-34.**
2. **Do any of the following:**
   - To remove a series, select it from the Legend Entries (Series) list and click Remove.
   - To add a series, click Add, and then drag across the range on the datasheet to enter it into the Edit Series dialog box; then click OK to accept it.
   - To edit a series, select it in the Legend Entries (Series) list and click Edit. Then drag across the range or make a change in the Edit Series dialog box, and click OK.

FIGURE 23-34

To fine-tune the data ranges, you can use the Select Data Source dialog box.

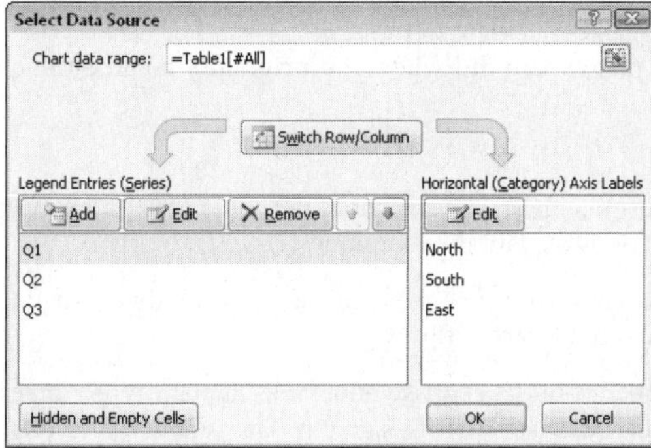

3. **(Optional) To redefine the range from which to pull the horizontal axis labels, click the Edit button in the Horizontal (Category) Axis Labels section.** A dotted outline appears around the current range; drag to redefine that range and click OK.
4. **(Optional) To redefine how empty or hidden cells should be treated, click the Hidden and Empty Cells button. In the Hidden and Empty Cell Settings dialog box that appears, choose whether to show data in hidden rows and columns, and whether to define empty cells as gaps in the chart or as zero values.** Then click OK. The Hidden and Empty Cells Settings dialog box is shown in Figure 23-35.

FIGURE 23-35

Specify what should happen when the data range contains blank or hidden cells.

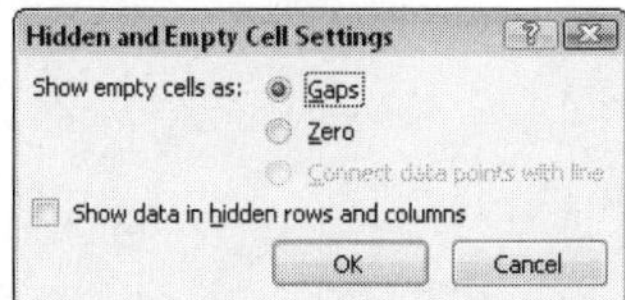

5. **When you are finished editing the settings for the data ranges, click OK to close the Select Data Source dialog box.**
6. **(Optional) Close the Excel datasheet window, or leave it open for later reference.**

Chart Types and Chart Layout Presets

The default chart is a column chart. However, there are a lot of alternative chart types to choose from. Not all of them will be appropriate for your data, of course, but you may be surprised at the different spin on the message that a different chart type presents.

CAUTION Many chart types come in both 2-D and 3-D models, and you can choose which chart type looks most appropriate for your presentation. However, try to be consistent. For example, it looks nicer to stay with all 2-D or all 3-D charts rather than mixing the types in a presentation.

You can revisit your choice of chart type at any time by following these steps:

1. **Select the chart, if needed, so that the Chart Tools Design tab becomes available.**
2. **On the Design tab, click Change Chart Type.**
3. **Select the desired type, just as you did when you originally created the chart.** Figure 23-28 shows the chart types.
4. **Click OK.**

This is the basic procedure for the overall chart type selection, but there are also many options for fine-tuning the layout. The following sections explain these options.

TIP To change the default chart type, after selecting a chart from the Change Chart Type dialog box, click the Set as Default Chart button.

PowerPoint provides a limited number of preset chart layouts for each chart type. You can choose these presets from the Chart Layouts group in the Chart Tools Design tab. They are good starting points for creating your own layouts, which you will learn about in this chapter.

To choose a layout, click the down arrow in the Chart Layouts group and select one from the gallery, as shown in Figure 23-36. Although you cannot add your own layouts to these presets, you can create chart templates, which are basically the same thing with additional formatting settings. This chapter also covers chart template creation.

FIGURE 23-36

You can choose one of the preset layouts that fits your needs.

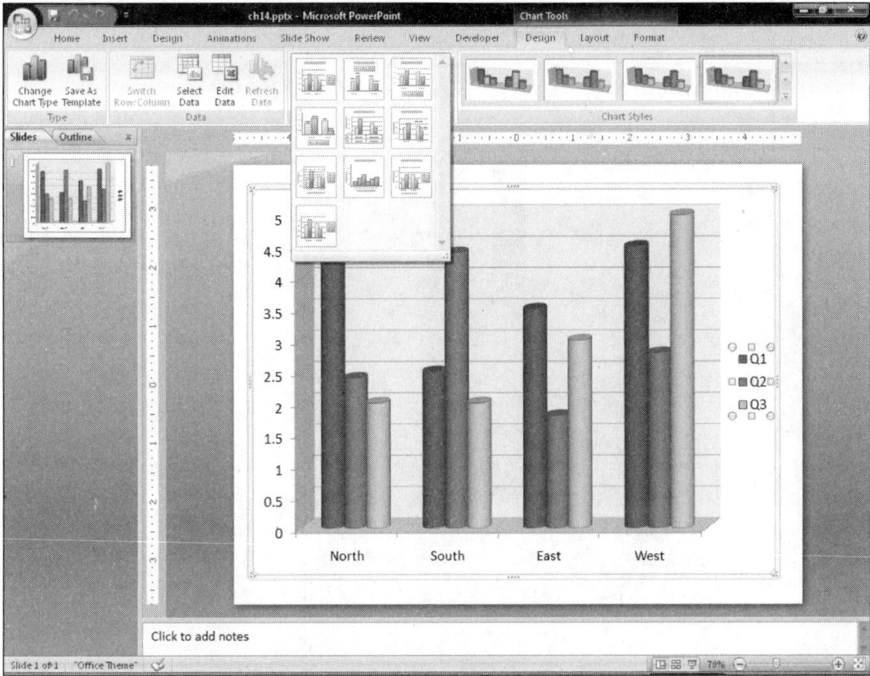

Working with Labels

On the Chart Tools Layout tab, the Labels group provides buttons for controlling which labels appear on the chart. Figure 23-37 points out the various labels that you can use.

FIGURE 23-37

Labels help to make it clear to the audience what the chart represents.

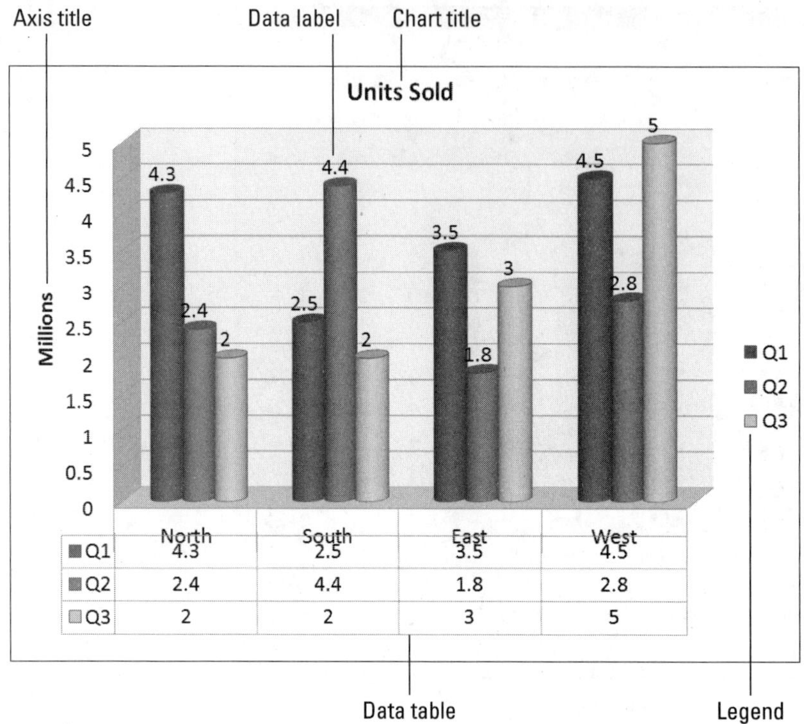

Each of these label types has a button on the Layout tab that opens a drop-down list that contains some presets. The drop-down list also contains a "More" command for opening a dialog box that contains additional options. For example, the drop-down list for the Chart Title button contains a "More Title Options" command, as shown in Figure 23-38.

TIP **New in PowerPoint 2007, you can add data labels by right-clicking a series and choosing Add Data Labels. You can also format label text from the mini bar, which may be easier than using the Home tab's controls.**

You can format the label text, just as you can format any other text. To do this, select the text and then use the Font group on the Home tab. This allows you to choose a font, size, color, alignment, and so on.

You can also format the label box by right-clicking it and choosing Format *name*, where *name* is the type of label that the box contains. In some cases, the dialog box that appears contains only standard formatting controls that you would find for any object, such as Fill, Border Color, Border Styles, Shadow, 3-D Format, and Alignment. These controls should already be very familiar to you from earlier in this chapter. In other cases, in addition to the standard formatting types, there is also a unique section that contains extra options that are specific to the content type. For example, for the Legend, there is a Legend Options section in which you can set the position of a legend.

FIGURE 23-38

Each type of label has its own button that displays a drop-down list.

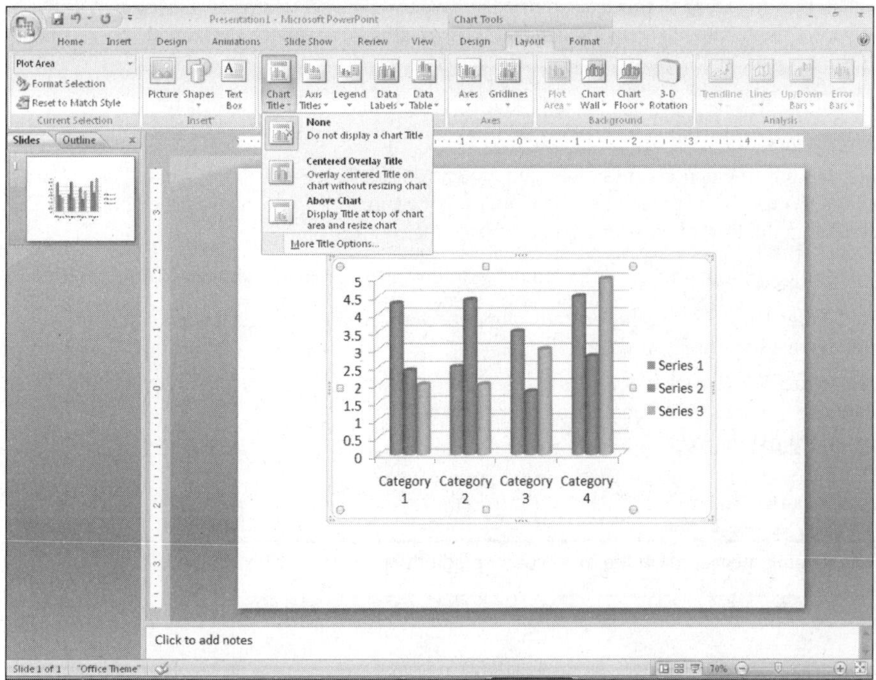

The following sections look at each of the label types more closely. These sections will not dwell on the formatting that you can apply to them (fonts, sizes, borders, fills, and so on) because this formatting is the same for all of them, as it is with any other object. Instead, they concentrate on the options that make each label different.

Working with chart titles

A chart title is text that typically appears above the chart — and sometimes overlapping it — that indicates what the chart represents. Although you would usually want either a chart title *or* a slide title, but not both, this could vary if you have multiple charts or different content on the same slide.

You can select a basic chart title, either above the chart or overlapping it, from the Chart Title drop-down list, as shown in Figure 23-28. You can also drag the chart title around after placing it. For more options, you can choose More Title Options to open the Format Chart Title dialog box. However, in this dialog box there is nothing that specifically relates to chart titles; the available options are for formatting (Fill, Border Color, and so on), as for any text box.

Working with axis titles

An axis title is text that defines the category or the unit of measurement on an axis. For example, in Figure 23-27, the vertical axis title is Millions.

Axis titles are defined separately for the vertical and the horizontal axes. Click the Axis Titles button on the Layout tab, and then select either Primary Horizontal Axis Title or Primary Vertical Axis Title to display a submenu that is specific to that axis. When you turn on an axis title, a text box appears containing default placeholder text, "Axis Title." Click in this text box and type your own label to replace it, as shown in Figure 23-39. If you've plotted any data on a secondary axis, you'll see Secondary Horizontal and Secondary Vertical Axis Title options as well.

You can easily select all of the placeholder text by clicking in the text box and pressing Ctrl+A.

For the horizontal axis title, the options are simple: either None or Title Below Axis, as shown in Figure 23-39. You can choose More Primary Horizontal Axis Title Options, but again, as with the regular title options, there are no unique settings in the dialog box—just general formatting controls.

For the vertical axis title, you can choose from among the following options, as shown in Figure 23-40.

- **Rotated Title:** The title appears vertically along the vertical axis, with the letters rotated 90 degrees (so that their bases run along the axis).
- **Vertical Title:** The title appears vertically along the vertical axis, but each letter remains unrotated, so that the letters are stacked one on top of the other.
- **Horizontal Title:** The title appears horizontally, like regular text, to the left of the vertical axis.

FIGURE 23-39

An axis title describes what is being measured on the axis; you can edit the placeholder text in the title.

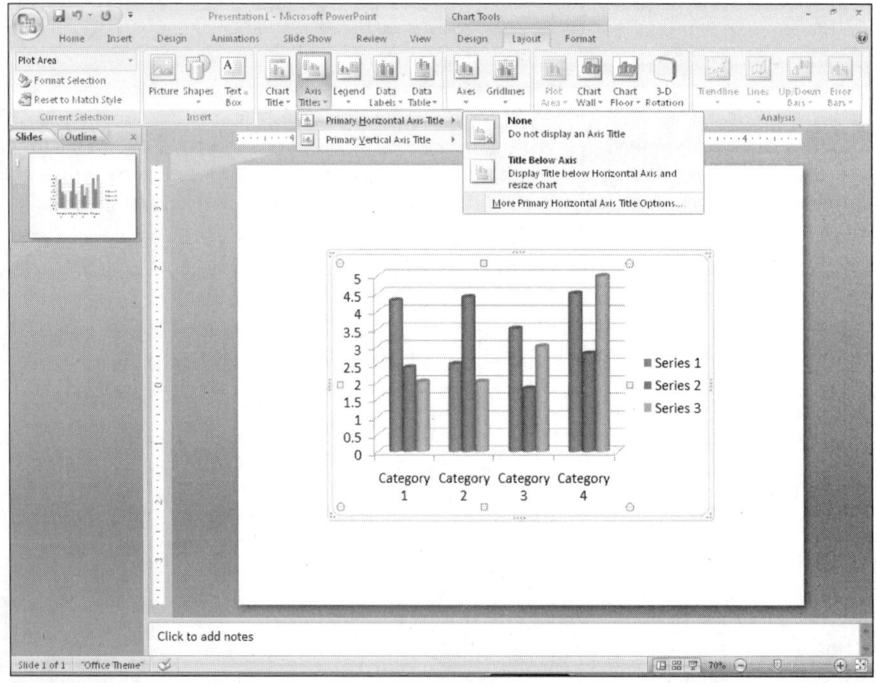

FIGURE 23-40

You can select these vertical axis titles, from left to right: Rotated Title, Vertical Title, and Horizontal Title.

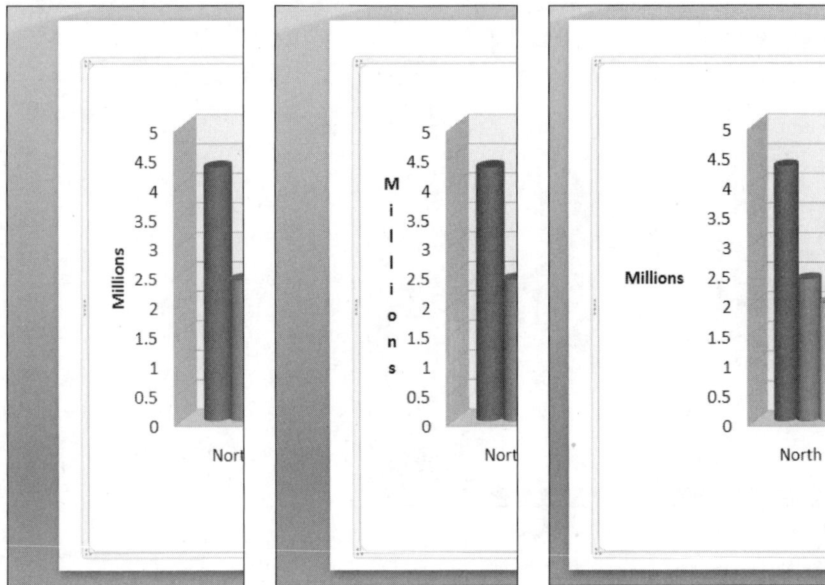

Each type of vertical axis shrinks the chart somewhat when you activate it, but the Horizontal Title format shrinks the chart more than the others because it requires more space to the left of the chart.

CAUTION **If you turn off an axis title by setting it to None and then turn it back on again, you will need to retype the axis title; it returns to the generic placeholder text.**

If the chart does not resize itself automatically when you turn on the vertical axis title, you might need to adjust the chart size manually. Click the chart, so that selection handles appear around the inner part of the chart (the *plot area)*, as shown in Figure 23-41. Then drag the left side-selection handle inward to decrease the width of the chart to make room for the vertical axis label.

FIGURE 23-41

You can adjust the size of the plot area to make more room for the vertical axis title.

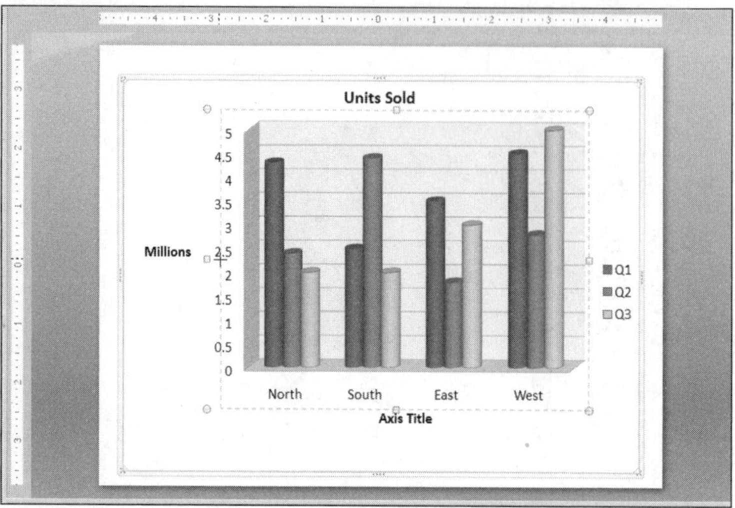

Working with legends

The *legend* is the little box that appears next to the chart (or sometimes above or below it). It provides the key that describes what the different colors or patterns mean. For some chart types and labels, you may not find the legend to be useful. If it is not useful for the chart that you are working on, you can turn it off by clicking the Legend button on the Layout tab and then clicking None. You can also just click it and press Delete. Turning off the legend makes more room for the chart, which grows to fill the available space. To turn the legend back on, click the Legend button again and select the position that you want for it, as shown in Figure 23-42.

FIGURE 23-42

You can select a legend position, or turn the legend off altogether.

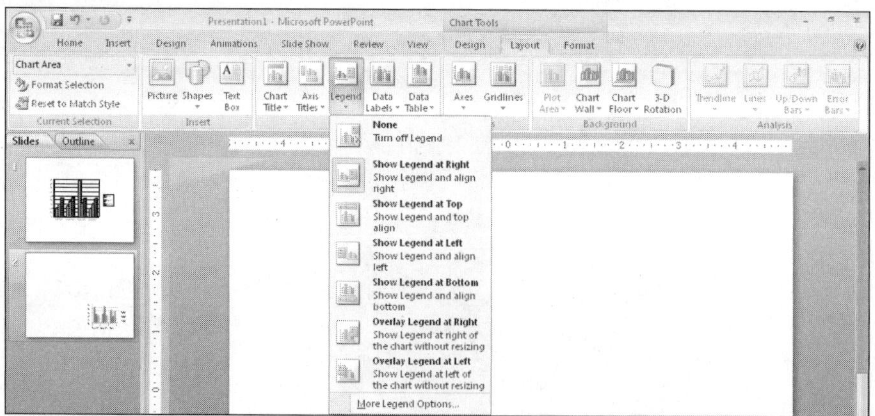

CAUTION Hiding the legend is not a good idea if you have more than one series in your chart, because the legend helps people to distinguish which series is which. However, if you have only one series, a legend might not be useful.

To resize a legend box, you can drag one of its selection handles. The text and keys inside the box do not change in size.

When you right-click the legend and choose Format Legend, or when you choose More Legend Options from the Legend drop-down list on the Layout tab, the Format Legend dialog box opens with the Legend Options displayed, as shown in Figure 23-43. From here, you can choose the legend's position in relation to the chart and whether or not it should overlap the chart. If it does not overlap the chart, the plot area will be automatically reduced to accommodate the legend.

NOTE The controls on the Legend Options tab refer to the legend's position in relation to the chart, not to the position of the legend text within the legend box. You can drag the legend wherever you want it on the chart after placing it.

Adding data labels

Data labels show the numeric values (or other information) that are represented by each bar or other shape on the chart. These labels are useful when the exact numbers are important or where the chart is so small that it is not clear from the axes what the data points represent.

To turn on data labels for the chart, click the Data Labels button on the Layout tab. The options available depend on whether it's a 2-D or 3-D chart. Figure 23-44 shows the options for 2-D charting; for a 3-D chart your only choices are Show and None.

FIGURE 23-43

You can set legend options in the Format Legend dialog box.

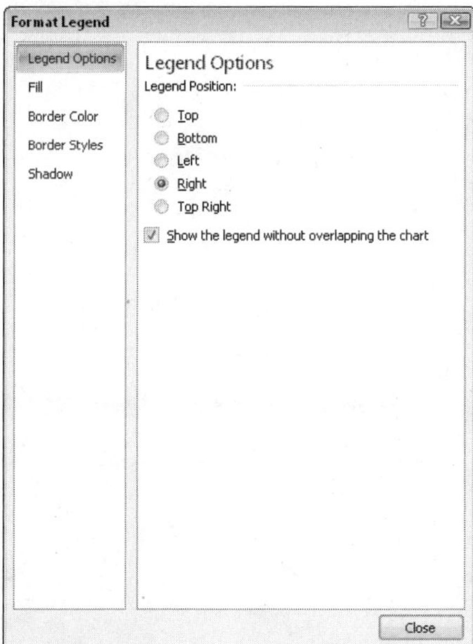

FIGURE 23-44

You can display or hide data labels using the Data labels button.

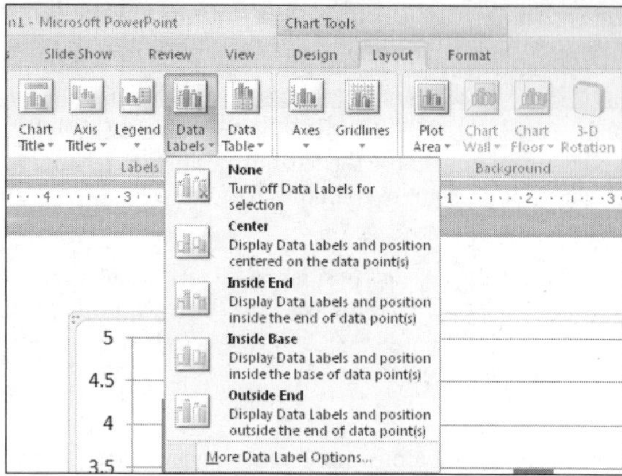

Data labels show the values by default, but you can also set them to display the series name and the category name, or any combination of the three. The data labels can also include the legend key, which is a colored square. To set these options, choose More Data Label Options from the Data Labels drop-down menu, to access the Format Data Labels dialog box, as shown in Figure 23-45. For a 3-D chart, the Label Position section does not appear.

FIGURE 23-45

You can set data label options using the Format Data Labels dialog box.

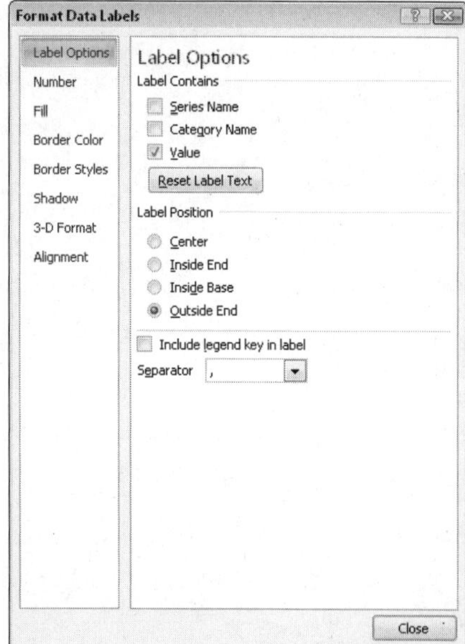

TIP To turn the data labels on or off for a particular data point or data series, select it and then select the None or Show option in the Data Labels drop-down menu. This is useful when you want to highlight a particular value or set of values.

Adding a data table

Sometimes the chart tells the full story that you want to tell, but other times the audience may benefit from seeing the actual numbers on which you have built the chart. In these cases, it is a good idea to include the data table with the chart. A data table contains the same information that appears on the datasheet.

To display the data table with a chart, click the Data Table button on the Layout tab, as shown in Figure 23-46, and choose to include a data table either with or without a legend key.

FIGURE 23-46

Use a data table to show the audience the numbers on which the chart is based.

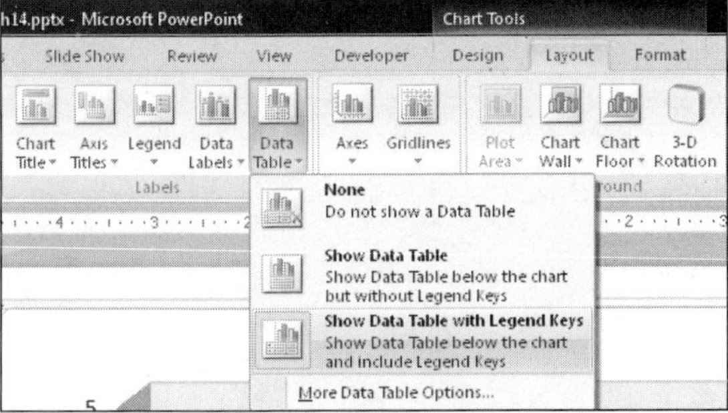

To format the data table, choose More Data Table Options from the Data Table drop-down menu. From the Format Data Table dialog box that appears, you can set data table border options, as shown in Figure 23-47. For example, you can display or hide the horizontal, vertical, and outline borders for the table from here.

FIGURE 23-47

Use the Data Table Options to specify which borders should appear in the data table.

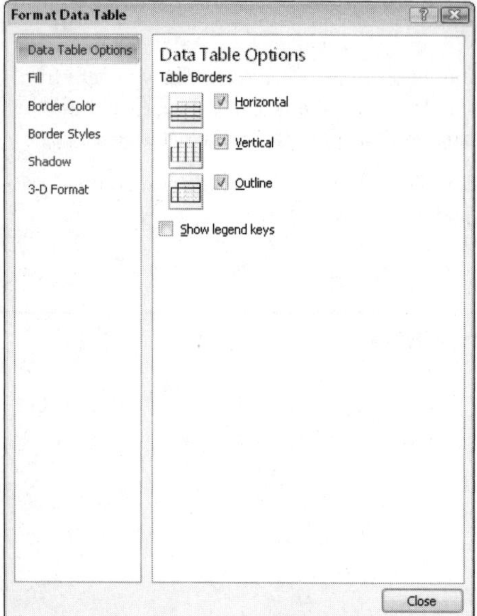

Controlling the Axes

No, axes are not the tools that chop down trees. *Axes* is the plural of *axis*, and an axis is the side of the chart containing the measurements against which your data is plotted. For example, in Figure 23-48, the horizontal axis contains the names of the divisions, and the vertical axis contains million-unit amounts (0 through 5).

You can change the various axes in a chart in several ways. For example, you can make an axis run in a different direction (such as from top-to-bottom instead of bottom-to-top for a vertical axis), and you can turn the text on or off for the axis and change the axis scale.

Using axis presets

You can select some of the most popular axis presets using the Axes button on the Layout tab. As with the axis titles that you learned about earlier in this chapter, there are separate submenus for horizontal and vertical axes. Figure 23-48 shows the options for horizontal axes, and Figure 23-49 shows those for vertical axes.

FIGURE 23-48

Presets for horizontal axes.

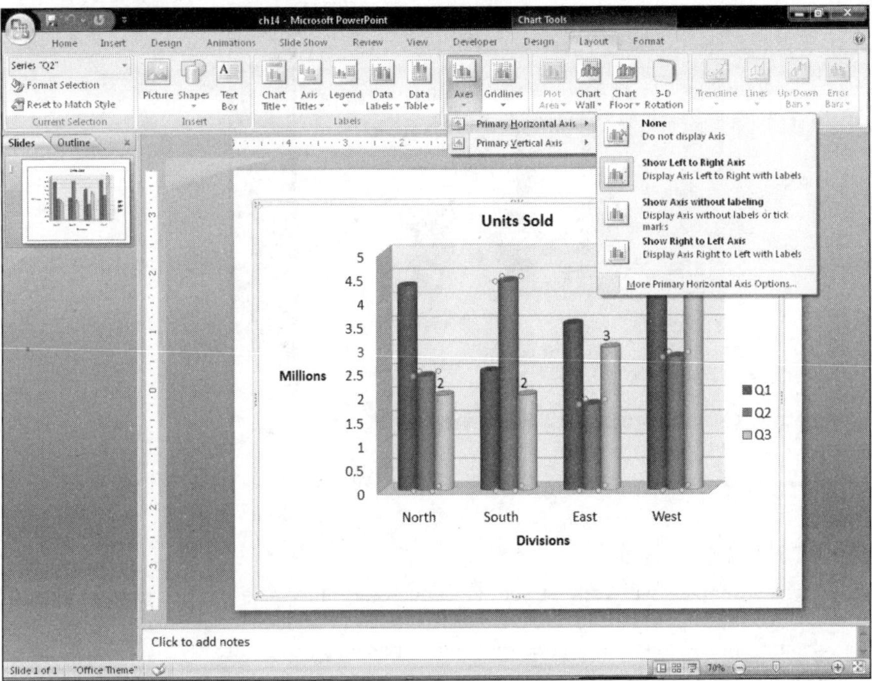

FIGURE 23-49

Presets for vertical axes.

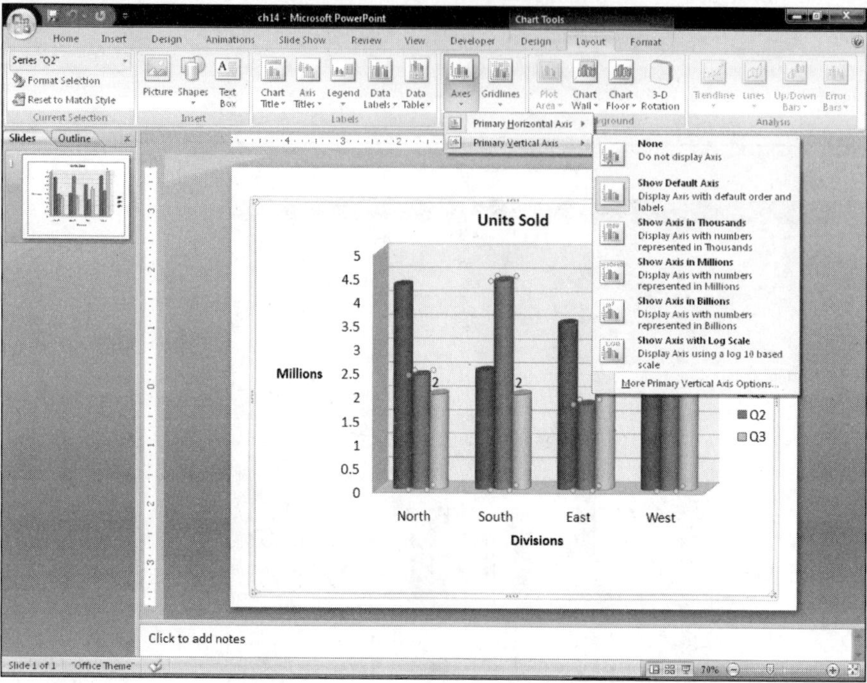

Setting axis scale options

The *scale* determines which numbers will form the start and end points of the axis line. For example, take a look at the chart in Figure 23-50. The bars are so close to one another in value that it is difficult to see the difference between them. Compare this chart to one showing the same data in Figure 23-51, but with an adjusted scale. Because the scale is smaller, the differences now appear more dramatic.

FIGURE 23-50

This chart does not show the differences between the values very well.

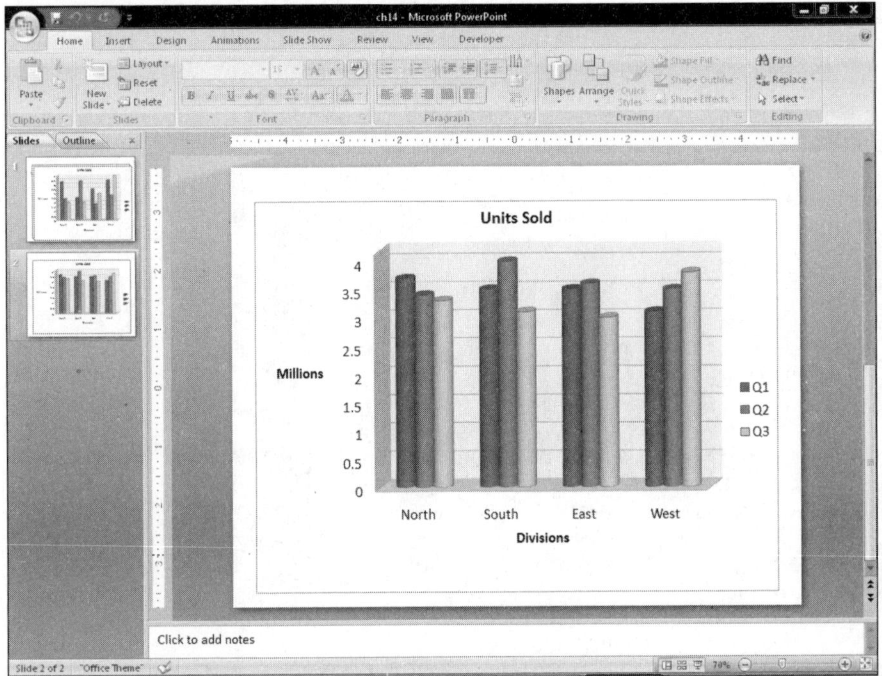

TIP You will probably never run into a case as dramatic as the difference between Figures 23-50 and 23-51 because PowerPoint's charting feature has an automatic setting for the scale that is turned on by default. However, you may sometimes want to override this setting for a different effect, such as to minimize or enhance the difference between data series. This is a good example of "making the data say what you want." For example, if you wanted to make the point that the differences between three months were insignificant, then you would use a larger scale. If you wanted to highlight the importance of the differences, then you would use a smaller scale.

FIGURE 23-51

A change to the values of the axis scale makes it easier to see the differences between values.

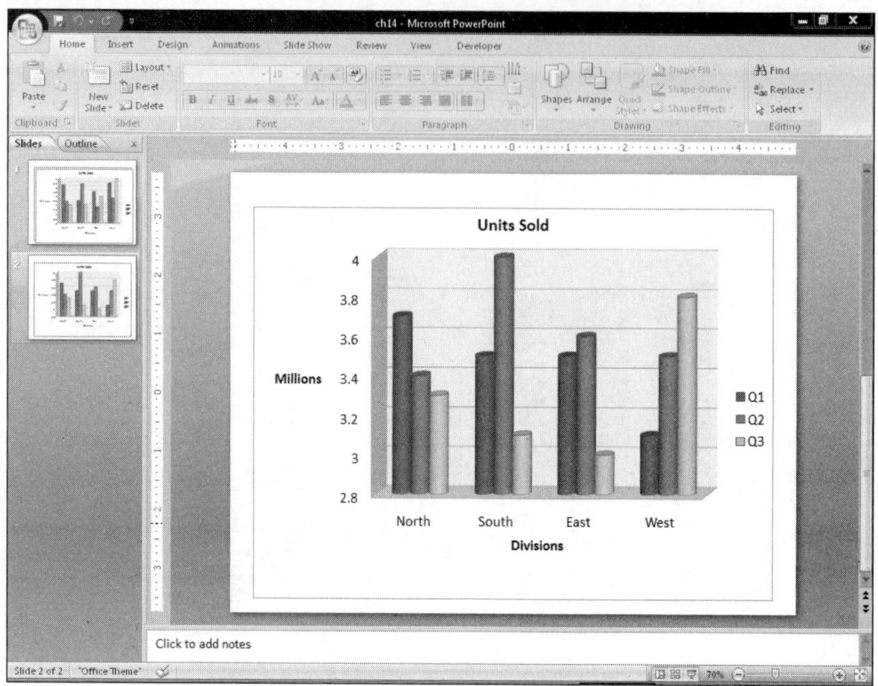

To set the scale for an axis, follow these steps:

1. **On the Layout tab, choose Axes ➪ Primary Vertical Axis ➪ More Primary Vertical Axis Options.** The Format Axis dialog box opens, displaying the Axis Options, as shown in Figure 23-52.
2. **Drag the Format Axis dialog box to the side so that you can see the results on the chart.**
3. **If you do not want the automatic value for one of the measurements, click Fixed and enter a different number in its text box.**
   - **Minimum** is the starting number. The usual setting is 0, as shown in Figure 23-50, although in Figure 23-51, it is set to 2.8.
   - **Maximum** is the top number. This number is 4 in both Figure 23-50 and Figure 23-51.
   - **Major unit** determines the axis text. It is also the unit by which gridlines stretch out across the back wall of the chart. In Figure 23-50, gridlines appear at increments of 0.5 million units; in Figure 23-51, they appear by 0.2 million units.
   - **Minor unit** is the interval of smaller gridlines between the major ones. Most charts look better without minor units, because these units can make a chart look cluttered. You should leave this setting at Auto. You can also use this feature to place tick marks on the axes between the labels of the major units.

FIGURE 23-52

You can set axis options in the Format Axis dialog box, including the axis scale.

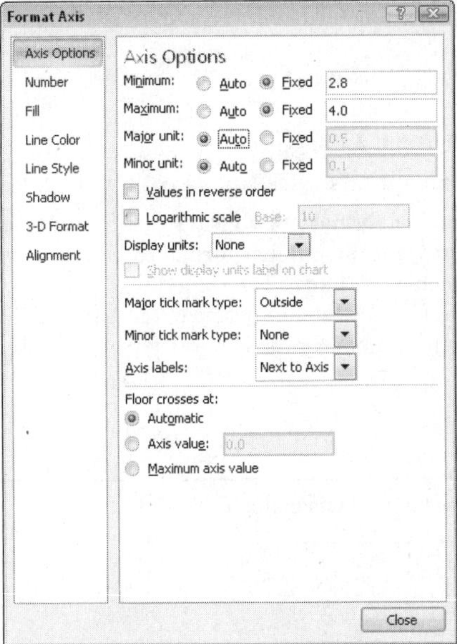

4. ***(Optional)* If you want to activate any of these special features, select their checkboxes.** Each of these checkboxes recalculates the numbers in the Minimum, Maximum, Major Unit, and Minor Unit text boxes.
   - **Values in reverse order.** This checkbox turns the scale backwards so that the greater values appear at the bottom or left.
   - **Logarithmic scale.** Rarely used by ordinary folks, this checkbox recalculates the Minimum, Maximum, Major Unit, and Minor Unit according to a power of 10 for the value axis, based on the range of data. (If this explanation doesn't make any sense to you, then you're not the target audience for this feature.)
   - **Floor crosses at.** When you select this feature, you can enter a value indicating where the axes should cross. You can specify an axis value of a particular number, or use Maximum axis value.
5. **(Optional) You can set a display unit to simplify large numbers.** For example, if you set display units to Thousands, then the number 1000 appears as "1" on the chart. If you then select the Show Display Units Label on Chart checkbox, an axis label will appear as "Thousands."
6. **(Optional) You can set tick-mark types for major and minor marks.** These marks appear as little lines on the axis to indicate the units. You can use tick marks either with or without gridlines. (To set gridlines, use the Gridlines button's menu on the Chart Tools Layout tab.)
7. **If you are happy with the results, click Close.**

Setting a number format

You can apply a number format to axes and data labels that show numeric data. This is similar to the number format that is used for Excel cells; you can choose a category, such as Currency or Percentage, and then fine-tune this format by choosing a number of decimal places, a method of handling negative numbers, and so on.

To set a number format, follow these steps:

1. **Right-click the axis and choose Format Axis.**
2. **In the Format Axis dialog box that appears, click Number.** A list of number formats appears.
3. **(Optional) You can select the number format in two ways: the first way is to select the Linked to Source checkbox if you want the number format to be taken from the number format that is applied to the datasheet in Excel.** The second way is to click the desired number format in the Category list. Options appear that are specific to the format that you selected. For example, Figure 23-53 shows the options for the Number type of format, which is a generic format.

FIGURE 23-53

You can set a number format in the Format Axis dialog box.

4. **(Optional) You can fine-tune the numbering format by changing the code in the Format Code text box.** The number signs (#) represent optional digits, while the zeroes represent required digits.
5. **Click Close to close the dialog box.**

To see some examples of custom number formats that you might use in the Format Code text box, choose Custom as the number format.

Formatting a Chart

In the following sections, you learn about chart formatting. There is so much that you can do to a chart that this subject could easily take up its own chapter! For example, just like any other object, you can resize a chart. You can also change the fonts, change the colors and shading of bars, lines, or pie slices, use different background colors, change the 3-D angle, and much more.

TIP The Format dialog box can remain open while you format various parts of the chart. Just click a different part of the chart behind the open dialog box (drag it off to the side if needed); the controls in the dialog box change to reflect the part that you have selected.

Clearing manually applied formatting

PowerPoint uses Format dialog boxes that are related to the various parts of the chart. These dialog boxes are *nonmodal*, which means that they can stay open indefinitely, that their changes are applied immediately, and that you don't have to close the dialog box to continue working on the document. Although this is handy, it is all too easy to make an unintended formatting change.

To clear the formatting that is applied to a chart element, select it and then, on the Format tab, click Reset to Match Style. This strips off the manually applied formatting from that element, returning it to whatever appearance is specified by the chart style that you have applied.

Formatting titles and labels

Once you add a title or label to your chart, you can change its size, attributes, colors, and font. Just right-click the title that you want to format and choose Format Chart Title (or whatever kind of title it is; for example, an axis label is called Axis Title). The Format Chart Title (or Format Axis Title) dialog box appears.

NOTE The formatting covered in this section applies to the text box, not to the text within it. If you need to format the fill, outline, or typeface, use the mini toolbar (right-click to open it) or use the font tools on the Home tab.

The categories in this dialog box vary, depending on the type of text that you are formatting, but the following categories are generally available:

- **Fill:** You can choose No Fill, Solid Fill, Gradient Fill, Picture or Text Fill, or Automatic. When you select Automatic, the color changes to contrast with the background color specified by the theme.
- **Border Color:** You can choose No Line, Solid Line, or Automatic. When you select Automatic, the color changes to contrast with the background color specified by the theme.
- **Border Styles:** You can set a width, a compound type (that is, a line made up of multiple lines), and a dash type.
- **Shadow:** You can apply a preset shadow in any color you want, or you can fine-tune the shadow in terms of transparency, size, angle, and so on. You might need to apply a fill to the box in order for the shadow to appear. This shadow is for the text box, not for the text within it; use the Font group on the Home tab to apply the text shadow, or the shadows available for WordArt.

- **3-D Format:** You can define 3-D settings for the text box, such as Bevel, Depth, Contour, and Surface.
- **Alignment:** You can set vertical and horizontal alignment, angle, and text direction, as well as control AutoFit settings for some types of text.

NOTE **Alignment is usually not relevant in a short label or title text box. The text box is usually exactly the right size to hold the text, and so there is no other way for the text to be aligned. Therefore, no matter what alignment you choose, the text looks very much the same.**

From the Home tab or the mini toolbar, you can also choose all of the text effects that you learned about earlier in this book, such as font, size, font style, underline, color, alignment, and so on.

Applying chart styles

Chart styles are presets that you can apply to charts in order to add colors, backgrounds, and fill styles. The Chart Styles gallery, shown in Figure 23-54, is located on the Chart Tools Design tab, which appears when you select a chart.

FIGURE 23-54

You can apply a chart style using the Chart Styles gallery.

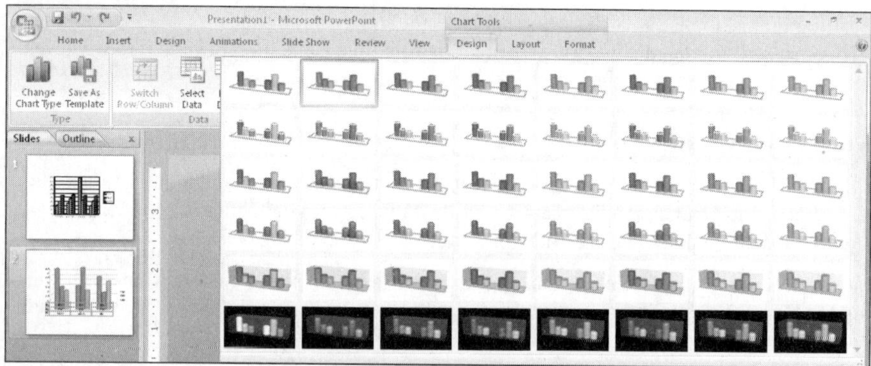

Chart styles are based on the themes and color schemes in the PowerPoint Design tab. When you change the theme or the colors, the chart style choices also change.

NOTE **You cannot add to the presets in the Chart Styles gallery, but you can save a group of settings as a template. To do this, use the Save As Template command on the Chart Tools Design tab.**

Formatting the chart area

Your next task is to format the big picture: the *chart area*. The chart area is the big frame that contains the chart and all of its elements: the legend, the data series, the data table, the titles, and so on.

The Format Chart Area dialog box has many of the same categories as for text boxes — such as fill, border color, border styles, shadow, and 3-D format — and it also adds 3-D rotation if you are working with a 3-D chart. You can choose to rotate and tilt the entire chart, just as you did with drawn shapes earlier in this book.

Formatting the legend

When you use a multi-series chart, the value of the legend is obvious — it tells you which colors represent which series. Without the legend, your audience will not know what the various bars or lines mean. You can do all of the same formatting for a legend that you can for other chart elements. Just right-click the legend, choose Format Legend from the shortcut menu, and then use the tabs in the Format Legend dialog box to make your modifications. The available categories are Fill, Border Color, Border Styles, and Shadow, as well as the Legend options mentioned earlier in this chapter.

TIP **If you select one of the individual keys in the legend and change its color, the color on the data series in the chart changes to match. This is especially useful with stacked charts, where it is sometimes difficult to select the data series that you want.**

Formatting gridlines and walls

Gridlines help the reader's eyes move across the chart. Gridlines are related to the axes, which you learned about earlier in this chapter. Although both vertical and horizontal gridlines are available, most people use only horizontal ones. *Walls* are nothing more than the space between the gridlines, formatted in a different color than the plot area. You can set the Walls fill to None to hide them. (Don't you wish tearing down walls was always that easy?) You can also use the Chart Wall and Chart Floor buttons on the Layout tab.

NOTE **You can only format walls on 3-D charts; 2-D charts do not have them. To change the background behind a 2-D chart, you must format the plot area.**

In most cases, the default gridlines that PowerPoint adds work well. However, you may want to make the lines thicker or a different color, or turn them off altogether.

Gridline presets are available from the Gridlines drop-down menu on the Layout tab. There are separate submenus for vertical and horizontal gridlines, as shown in Figure 23-55. You can also choose the More command for either of the gridlines submenus for additional options.

FIGURE 23-55

You can apply gridline presets from the Gridlines drop-down menu.

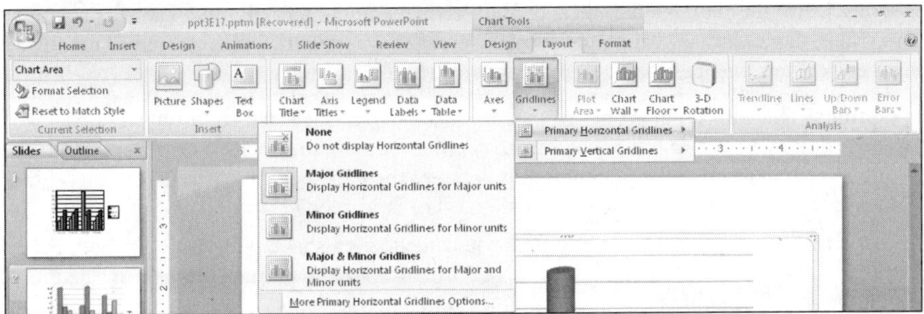

To change the gridline formatting, right-click a gridline and choose Format Major Gridlines. You can then adjust the line color, line style, and shadow from the Format Major Gridlines dialog box, as shown in Figure 23-56.

FIGURE 23-56

You can set gridline colors, styles, and shadows in the Format Major Gridlines dialog box.

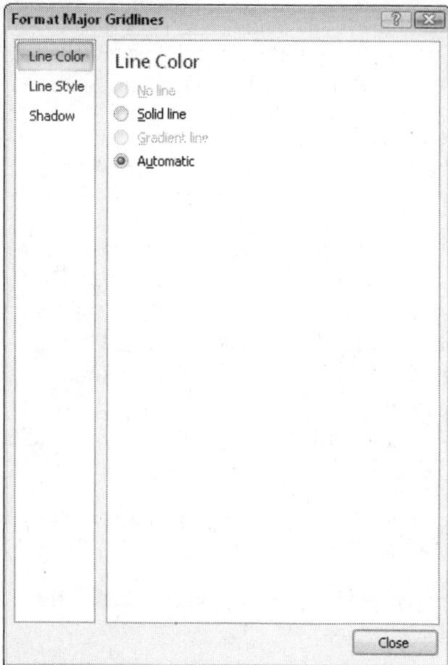

NOTE Gridline spacing is based on the major and minor units that you have set in the Format Axis dialog box (vertical or horizontal). To set this spacing, see the section "Setting axis scale options," earlier in this chapter.

Formatting the data series

To format a data series, just right-click the bar, slice, or chart element, and choose Format Data Series from the shortcut menu. Then, depending on your chart type, different tabs appear that you can use to modify the series appearance. Here are the ones for bar and column charts, for example:

- **Series Options:** This tab contains options that are specific to the selected chart type. For example, when working with a 3-D bar or column chart, the series options include Gap Depth and Gap Width, which determine the thickness and depth of the bars. For a pie chart, you can set the rotation angle for the first slice, as well as whether a slice is "exploded" or not.
- **Shape:** For charts involving bars and columns, you can choose a shape option such as Box, Full Pyramid, Partial Pyramid, Cylinder, Full Cone, or Partial Cone. The partial options truncate the top part of the shape when it is less than the largest value in the chart.
- **Fill:** You can choose a fill, including solid, gradient, or picture/texture.
- **Border Color:** The border is the line around the shape. You can set it to a solid line, no line, or Automatic (that is, based on the theme).

- **Border Styles:** The only option available on this tab for most chart types is Width, which controls the thickness of the border. For line charts, you can set arrow options and other line attributes.
- **Shadow:** You can add shadows to the data series bars or other shapes, just as you would add shadows to anything else.
- **3-D Format:** These settings control the contours, surfaces, and beveling for 3-D data series.

Other chart types have very different categories available. For example, a line chart has Marker Options, Marker Fill, Line Color, Line Style, Marker Line Color, and Marker Line Style, in addition to the generic Series Options, Shadow, and 3-D Format categories.

Rotating a 3-D Chart

Three-dimensional charts have a 3-D Rotation option in the Format Chart Area dialog box. This feature works just the same as with other 3-D objects, where you can rotate the chart on the X-, Y-, and Z-axis. In addition, there are some extra chart-specific options, as shown in Figure 23-57. For example, you can set the chart to AutoScale, control its depth, and reset it to the default rotation.

FIGURE 23-57

You can adjust the 3-D rotation of a chart.

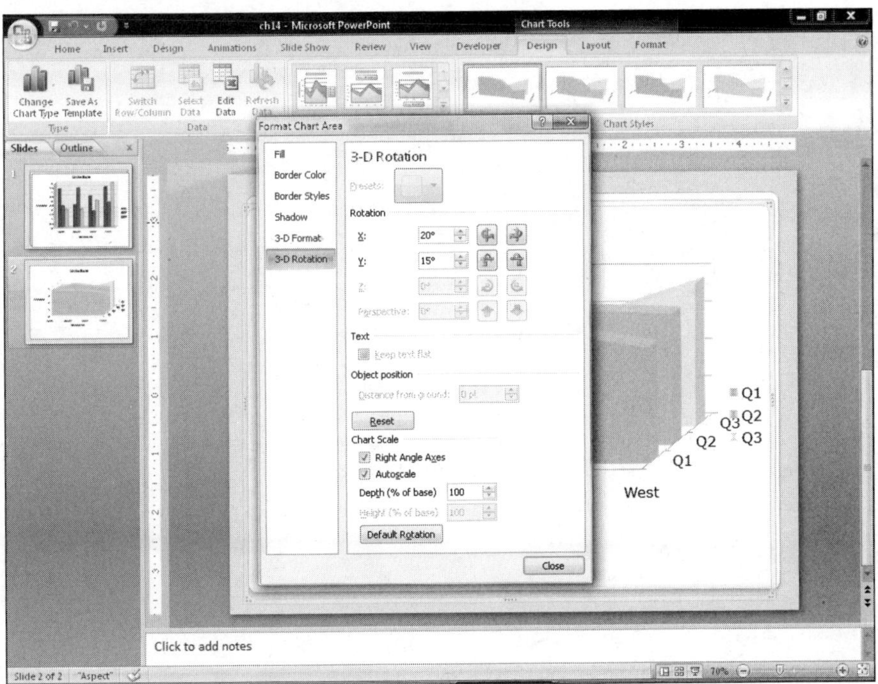

Summary

In this chapter, you learned the ins and outs of creating and formatting tables in PowerPoint including how to insert, draw, move and resize the various cells of a table as well as how to add fills, styles and effects. You also learned now to create and format charts using PowerPoint. You learned how to create charts, change their type and their data range, and use optional text elements on them such as titles, data labels, and so on. You also learned how to format charts. In the next chapter, you learn how to work with clip art, pictures, and diagrams.

Chapter 24

Using SmartArt Diagrams, Clip Art, and Pictures

IN THIS CHAPTER

- Understanding SmartArt types and their uses
- Inserting, editing, and modifying a diagram
- Modifying an organization chart structure
- Resizing and restructuring a diagram
- Choosing and inserting appropriate clip art
- Clip art search methods
- Working with clip art collections
- Understanding raster graphics
- Importing image files into PowerPoint
- Sizing and cropping photos
- Compressing images

Just as charts and graphs can enliven a boring table of numbers, a SmartArt diagram can enliven a conceptual discussion. SmartArt helps the audience understand the interdependencies of objects or processes in a visual way, so they don't have to juggle that information mentally as you speak. Some potential uses include organizational charts, hierarchy diagrams, and flow charts. Similarly, the right clip art image or photo can highlight a concept or present a product with clarity that words cannot achieve.

In this chapter you will learn how to create and fine-tune SmartArt diagrams, and how to select and insert clip art in your presentations. You'll also learn how to integrate photos and images from other sources, including how to compress them so they take up less disk space.

Understanding SmartArt Types and Their Uses

SmartArt replaces the old Diagrams and Organization Chart features in earlier PowerPoint versions. SmartArt is a special class of vector graphic object that combines shapes, lines, and text placeholders. SmartArt is most often used to illustrate relationships between bits of text.

The SmartArt interface is similar regardless of the type of diagram you are creating. You can type directly into the placeholders on the diagram, or you can display a text pane to the side of the diagram and type into that, much as you would type into an outline pane to have text appear in a slide's text placeholder boxes. See Figure 24-1. You can also select some text, right-click it, and choose Convert to SmartArt.

FIGURE 24-1

A typical SmartArt diagram being constructed.

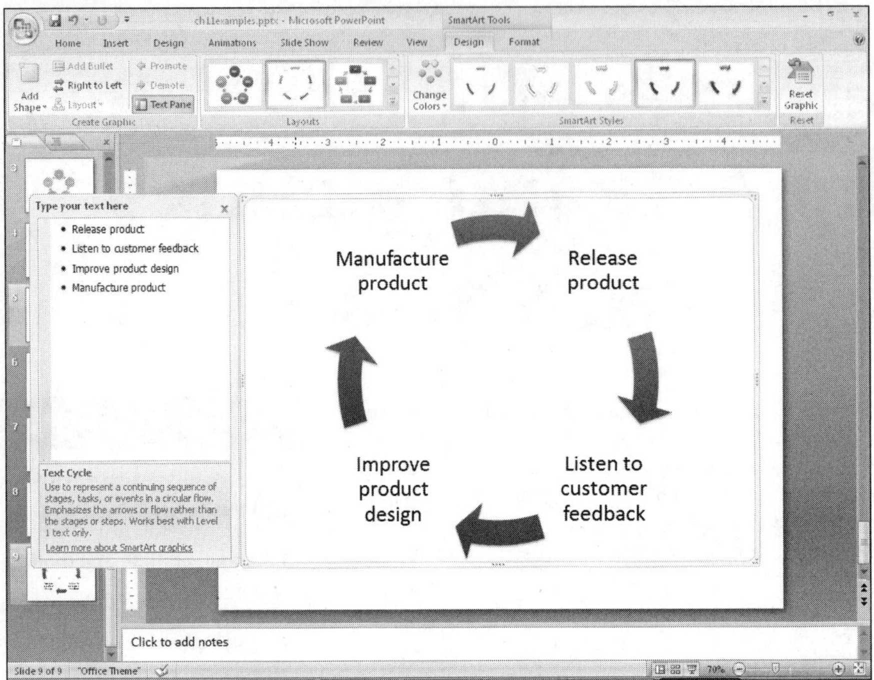

There are seven types of SmartArt diagrams in PowerPoint 2007, and each is uniquely suited for a certain type of data delivery.

List

A list diagram presents information in a fairly straightforward, text-based way, somewhat like a fancy outline. List diagrams are useful when information is not in any particular order, or when the process or progression between items is not important. The list can have multiple levels, and you can enclose each level in a shape or not. Figure 24-2 shows an example.

Process

A process diagram is similar to a list, but it has directional arrows or other connectors that represent the flow of one item to another. This adds an extra aspect of meaning to the diagram. For example, in Figure 24-3, the way the boxes are staggered and connected with arrows implies that the next step begins before the previous one ends.

FIGURE 24-2

A list diagram deemphasizes any progression between items.

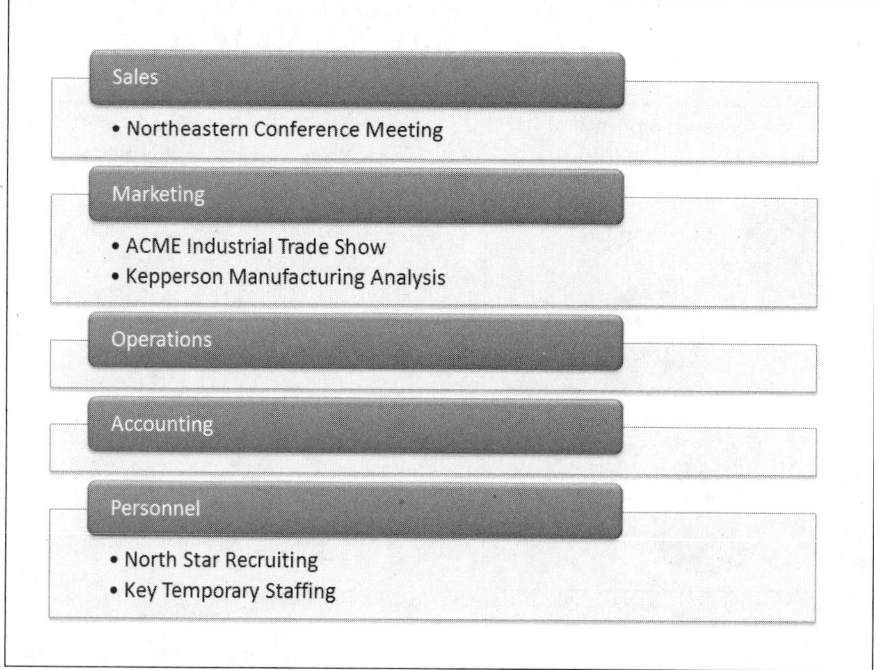

FIGURE 24-3

A process diagram shows a flow from point A to point B.

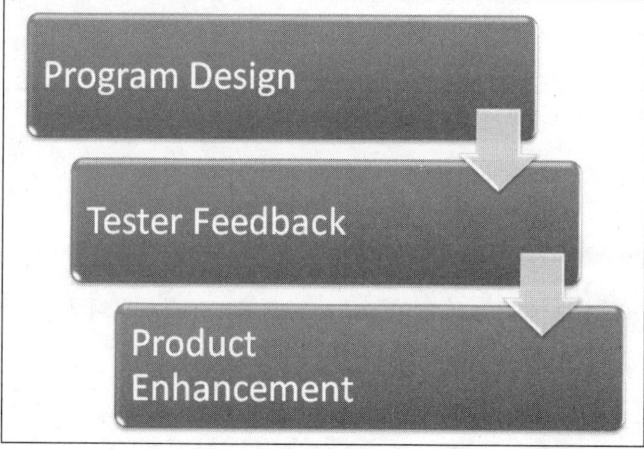

Cycle

A cycle diagram also illustrates a process, but a repeating or recursive one — usually a process in which there is no fixed beginning or end point. You can jump into the cycle at any point. In Figure 24-4, for example, the ongoing process of product development and improvement is illustrated.

FIGURE 24-4

A cycle diagram traces the steps of a repeating process.

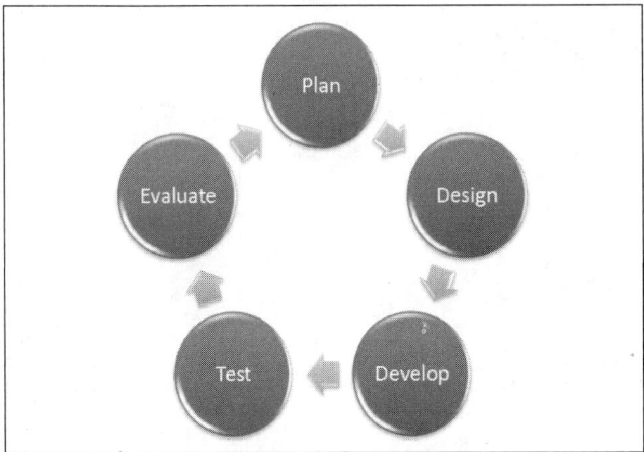

Hierarchy

A hierarchy chart is an organization chart. It shows structure and relationships between people or things in standardized levels. For example, it can show who reports to whom in a company's employment system. It is useful when describing how the organization functions and who is responsible for what. In Figure 24-5, for example, three organization levels are represented, with lines of reporting drawn between each level. Hierarchy diagrams can also run horizontally, for use in tournament rosters.

FIGURE 24-5

A hierarchy diagram, also called an organization chart, explains the structure of an organization.

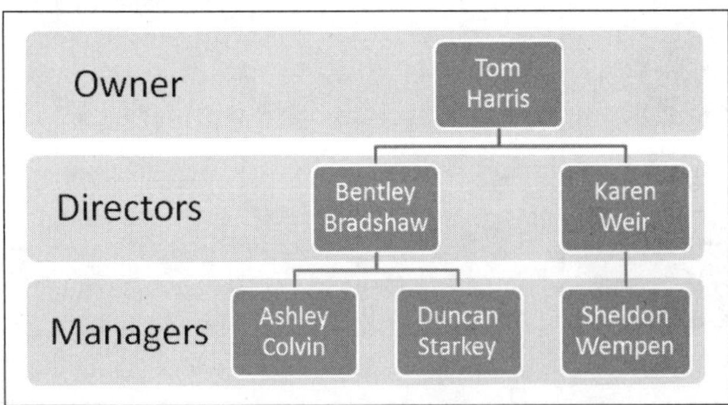

TIP Should you include your company's organization chart in your presentation? That's a question that depends on your main message. If your speech is about the organization, you should. If not, show the organization structure only if it serves a purpose to advance your speech. Many presenters have found that an organization chart makes an excellent backup slide. You can prepare it and have it ready in case a question arises about the organization. Another useful strategy is to include a printed organization chart as part of the handouts you distribute to the audience, without including the slide in your main presentation.

Relationship

Relationship diagrams graphically illustrate how parts relate to a whole. One common type of relationship diagram is a Venn diagram, as in Figure 24-6, showing how categories of people or things overlap. Relationship diagrams can also break things into categories or show how parts contribute to a whole, as with a pie chart.

FIGURE 24-6

A relationship diagram shows how parts relate to a whole.

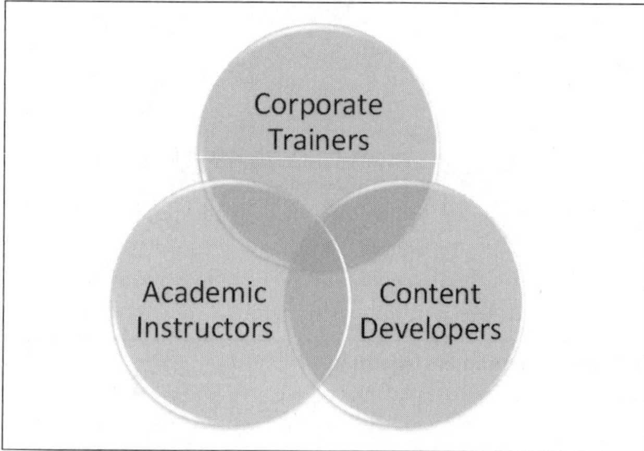

Matrix

A matrix also shows the relationship of parts to a whole, but it does so with the parts in orderly looking quadrants. You can use matrix diagrams when you do not need to show any particular relationship between items, but you want to make it clear that they make up a single unit. See Figure 24-7.

FIGURE 24-7

A matrix diagram uses a grid to represent the contributions of parts to a whole.

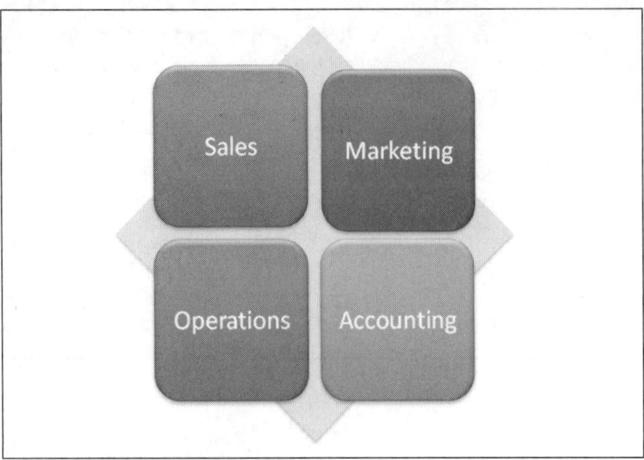

Pyramid

A pyramid diagram is just what the name sounds like — it's a striated triangle with text at various levels, representing not only the relationship between the items, but also that the items at the smaller part of the triangle are less numerous or more important. For example, in Figure 24-8, the diagram shows that there are many more workers than there are executives.

FIGURE 24-8

A pyramid diagram represents the progression between less and more of something.

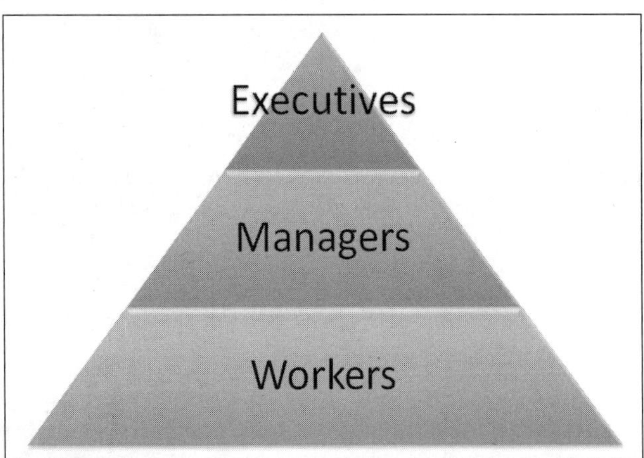

TIP **Notice in Figure 24-8 that the labels do not confine themselves to within the associated shape. If this is a problem, you might be able to make the labels fit with a combination of line breaks (Shift+Enter) and font changes.**

Inserting a Diagram

All SmartArt diagrams start out the same way — you insert them on the slide as you can any other slide object. That means you can either use a diagram placeholder on a slide layout or you can insert the diagram manually.

To use a placeholder, start with a slide that contains a layout with a diagram placeholder in it, or change the current slide's layout to one that does. Then click the Insert SmartArt Graphic icon in the placeholder, as shown in Figure 24-9. To insert from scratch, click the SmartArt button on the Insert tab.

FIGURE 24-9

Click the SmartArt icon in the placeholder on a slide.

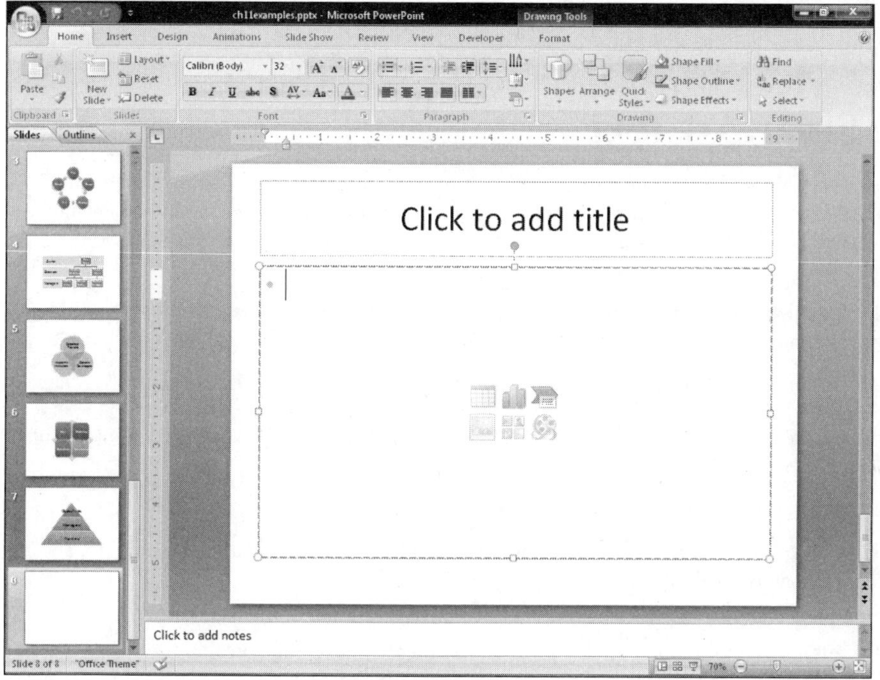

Another way to start a new diagram is to select some text and then right-click the selection and choose Convert to SmartArt.

Any way you start it, the Choose a SmartArt Graphic dialog box opens, as shown in Figure 24-10. Select one of the seven SmartArt categories, click the desired SmartArt object, and click OK, and the diagram appears. From there it's just a matter of customizing.

NOTE **Some diagrams appear in more than one category. To browse all of the categories at once, click All in Figure 24-10.**

When you select a diagram, SmartArt Tools tabs become available (Design and Format). You will learn what each of the buttons on them does as this chapter progresses. The buttons change depending on the type of diagram.

FIGURE 24-10

Select the diagram type you want to insert.

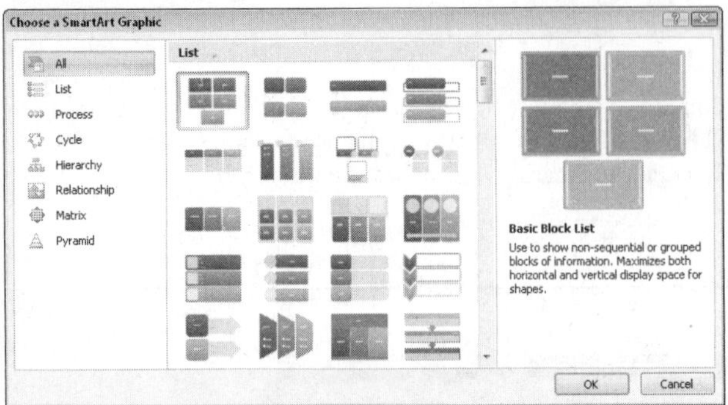

Editing SmartArt Text

All SmartArt has text placeholders, which are basically text boxes. You simply click in one of them and type. Then use the normal text-formatting controls (Font, Font Size, Bold, Italic, and so on) on the Home tab to change the appearance of the text, or use the WordArt Styles group on the Format tab to apply WordArt formatting.

You can also display a text pane, as you saw in Figure 24-1, and type or edit the diagram's text there. The text pane serves the same purpose for a diagram that the Outline pane serves for the slide as a whole.

CAUTION **The text in the outline pane is not always in the order you would expect it to be for the diagram because it forces text to appear in linear form from a diagram that is not necessarily linear. It does not matter how the text appears in the text pane because only you see that. What matters is how it looks in the actual diagram.**

Here are some tips for working with diagram text:

- To leave a text box empty, just don't type anything in it. The *Click to add text* words do not show up in a printout or in Slide Show view.
- To promote a line of text, press Shift+Tab; to demote it, press Tab in the text pane.
- Text wraps automatically, but you can press Shift+Enter to insert a line break if needed.
- In most cases, the text size shrinks to fit the graphic in which it is located. There are some exceptions to that, though; for example, at the top of a pyramid, the text can overflow the tip of the pyramid.
- All of the text is the same size, so if you enter a really long string of text in one box, the text size in all of the related boxes shrinks too. You can manually format parts of the diagram to change this behavior, as you will learn later in the chapter.
- If you resize the diagram, its text resizes automatically.

NOTE **In PowerPoint 2003, you could not move shapes around in a diagram by default because AutoLayout was enabled. You don't have that problem in PowerPoint 2007 with SmartArt, though; you can select and move individual parts of the diagram freely, as you would any shapes.**

Modifying SmartArt Structure

The structure of the diagram includes how many boxes it has and where they are placed. Even though the diagram types are all very different, the way you add, remove, and reposition shapes in them is surprisingly similar across all types.

NOTE **When you add a shape, you add both a graphical element (a circle, a bar, or other) and an associated text placeholder. The same applies to deletion; removing a shape also removes its associated text placeholder from the diagram.**

Inserting and deleting shapes

To insert a shape in a diagram, follow these steps:

1. **Click a shape that is adjacent to where you want the new shape to appear.**
2. **On the SmartArt Tools Design tab, click Add Shape.**

You can either click the top part of the Add Shape button to add a shape of the same level and type as the selected one, or you can click the bottom part of the button to open a menu from which you can choose other variants. The choices on the menu depend on the diagram type and the type of shape selected. For example, in Figure 24-11, you can insert a shape into a diagram either before or after the current one (same outline level), or you can insert a shape that is subordinate (below) or superior to (above) the current one.

FIGURE 24-11

Add a shape to the diagram.

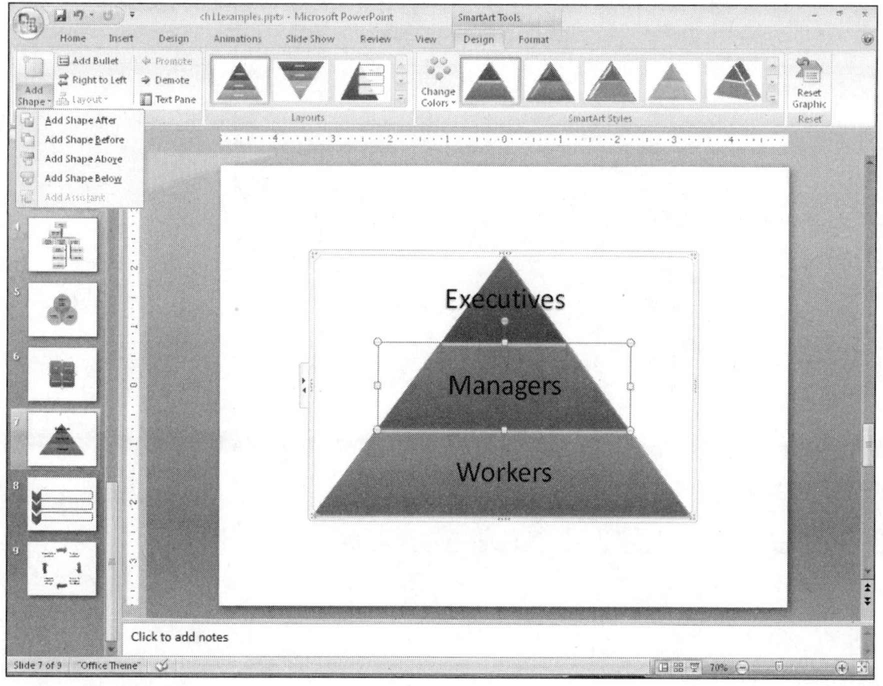

To delete a shape, click it to select it in the diagram, and then press the Delete key on the keyboard. You might need to delete subordinate shapes before you can delete the main shape.

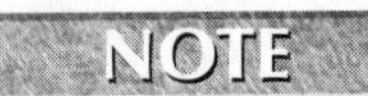

Not all diagram types can accept different numbers of shapes. For example the four-square matrix diagram is fixed at four squares.

Adding bullets

In addition to adding shapes to the diagram, you can add bullets — that is, subordinate text to a shape. To do so, click the Add Bullet button. Bullets appear indented under the shape's text in the text pane, as shown in Figure 24-12.

Promoting and demoting text

The difference between a shape and a bullet is primarily a matter of promotion and demotion in the Text Pane's outline. The text pane works just as the regular Outline pane does in this regard; you can promote with Shift+Tab or demote with Tab. You can also use the Promote and Demote buttons on the SmartArt Tools Design tab.

FIGURE 24-12

Create subordinate bullet points under a shape.

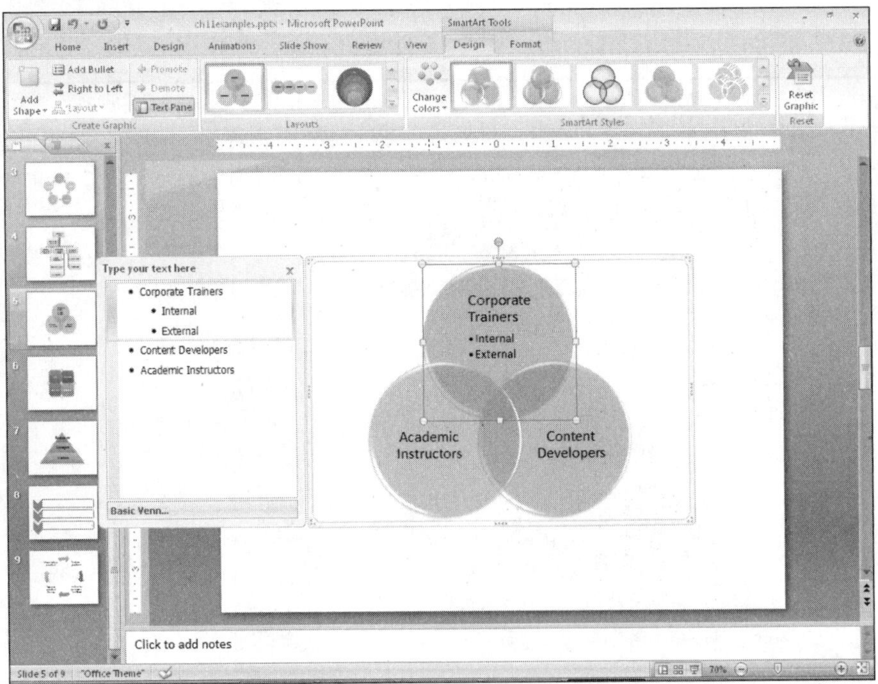

Changing the flow direction

Each diagram flows in a certain direction. A cycle diagram flows either clockwise or counterclockwise. A pyramid flows either up or down.

If you realize after typing all of the text that you should have made the SmartArt diagram flow in the other direction, you can change it by clicking the Right to Left button on the Design tab. It is a toggle; you can switch back and forth freely.

Reordering shapes

Not only can you reverse the overall flow of the diagram, but you can also move around individual shapes. For example, suppose you have a diagram that illustrates five steps in a process and you realize that steps 3 and 4 are out of order. You can move one of them without having to retype all of the labels.

The best way to move a shape is to reorder the text in the text pane. Follow these steps:

1. **Display the text pane if it does not already appear.** You can either click the arrow button to the left of the diagram or click the Text Pane button on the SmartArt Tools Design tab.
2. **Select some text to be moved in the text pane.**
3. **Press Ctrl+X to cut it to the Clipboard.**
4. **Click in the text pane at the beginning of the line above which it should appear.**
5. **Press Ctrl+V to paste.**

PowerPoint 2003 diagrams had a Shape Forward and Shape Backward button for moving shapes, but SmartArt does not have that. The text pane's editing capabilities make up for it, though.

Repositioning shapes

You can individually select and drag each shape to reposition it on the diagram. Any connectors between it and the other shapes are automatically resized and extended as needed. For example, in Figure 24-13, notice how the arrows that connect the circles in the cycle diagram have elongated as one of the circles has moved out.

Resetting a graphic

After making changes to a SmartArt diagram, you can return it to its default settings with the Reset Graphic button on the SmartArt Tools Design tab. This strips off everything, including any SmartArt styles and manual positioning, and makes it exactly as it was when you inserted it except it keeps the text that you've typed.

Changing to a different diagram layout

The layouts are the diagram types. When you insert a SmartArt diagram you choose a type, and you can change that type at any time later.

To change the layout type, use the Layouts gallery on the Design tab, as shown in Figure 24-14. You can open the gallery and click the desired type, or click More Layouts at the bottom of its menu to redisplay the same dialog box as in Figure 24-10, from which you can choose any layout.

FIGURE 24-13

When you move pieces of a diagram, connectors move and stretch as needed.

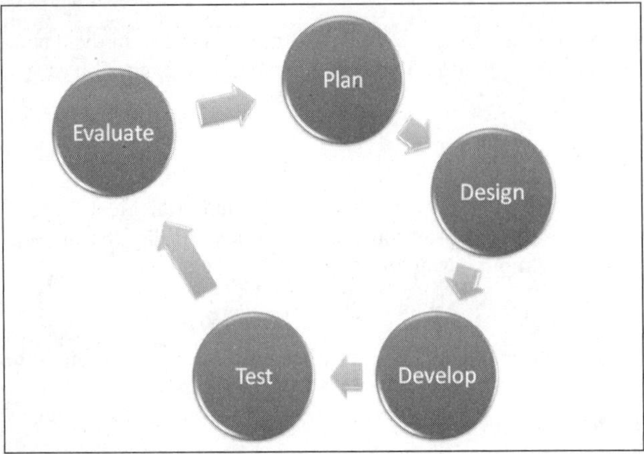

FIGURE 24-14

Switch to a different diagram layout.

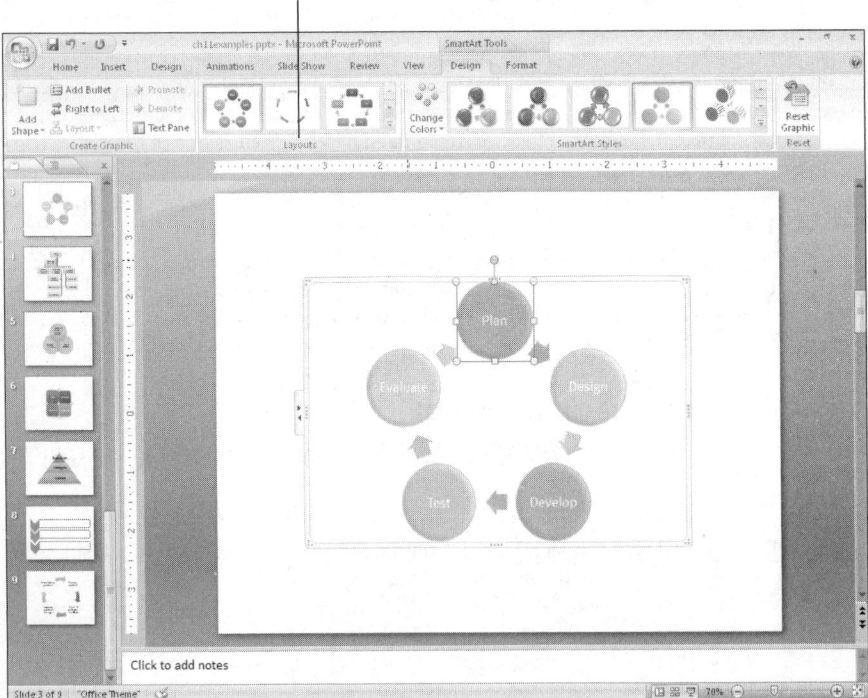

Modifying a Hierarchy Diagram Structure

Hierarchy diagrams (organization charts) show the structure of an organization. They have some different controls for changing their structure compared to other diagrams, so this chapter looks at them separately.

Inserting and deleting shapes

The main difference when inserting an organization chart shape (that is, a box into which you will type a name) is that you must specify which existing box the new one is related to and how it is related.

For example, suppose you have a supervisor already in the chart and you want to add some people to the chart who report to him. You would first select his box on the chart, and then insert the new shapes with the Add Shape button. For a box of the same level, or of the previously inserted level, click the top part of the button; for a subordinate or other relationship, open the button's menu. See Figure 24-15. The chart can have only one box at the top level, however, just as a company can have only one CEO.

FIGURE 24-15

Add more shapes to a hierarchy diagram.

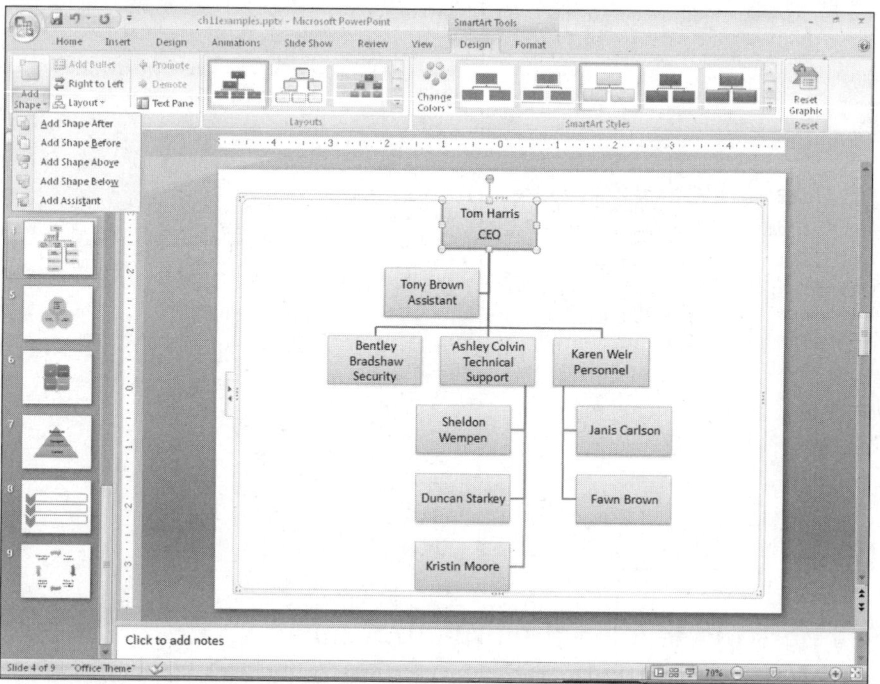

When you insert a new shape in a hierarchy diagram, four of the options are the same as with any other diagram, and one is new: Add Shape After and Add Shape Before insert shapes of the same level as the selected one, and Add Shape Above and Add Shape Below insert a superior and subordinate level respectively. The new option, Add Assistant, adds a box that is neither subordinate nor superior, but a separate line of reporting, as shown in Figure 24-16.

NOTE **An *assistant* is a person whose job is to provide support to a certain person or office. An executive secretary is one example. In contrast, a *subordinate* is an employee who may report to a manager but whose job does not consist entirely of supporting that manager. Confused? Don't worry about it. You don't have to make a distinction in your organization chart. Everyone can be a subordinate (except the person at the top of the heap, of course).**

To delete a shape, select it and press the Delete key, as with all of the other diagram types.

FIGURE 24-16

An Assistant box in a hierarchy chart.

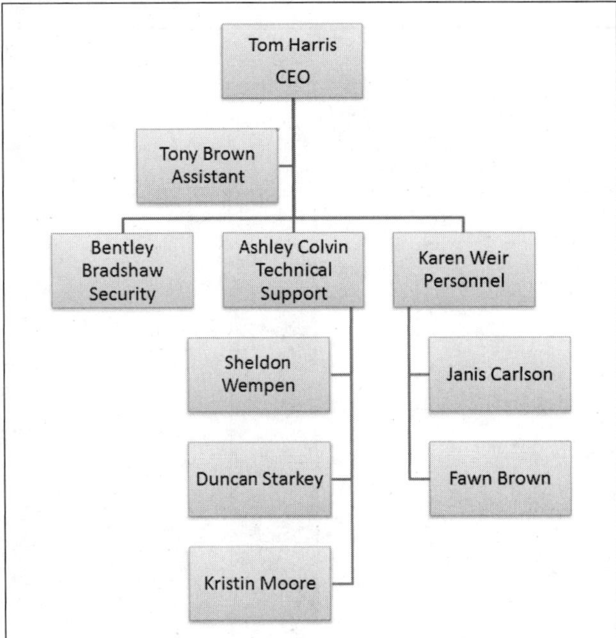

Changing a person's level in the organization

As the organization changes, you might need to change your chart to show that people report to different supervisors. The easiest way to do that is to move the text in the text pane, the same way as you learned in the section "Reordering shapes" earlier in this chapter.

For example, in Figure 24-16, suppose you want to promote Ashley Colvin to be at the same level as Karen Weir and Bentley Bradshaw. You could click Ashley Colvin in the text pane and press Shift+Tab to promote her. Furthermore, suppose you want Sheldon Wempen to report to her. You could select his name, press Ctrl+X to cut, click under Ashley Colvin, and then press Ctrl+V to paste.

Controlling subordinate layout options

When subordinates report to a supervisor, you can list the subordinates beneath that supervisor in a variety of ways. In Standard layout, each subordinate appears horizontally beneath the supervisor. See Figure 24-17.

FIGURE 24-17

This is the standard layout for a branch of an organization chart.

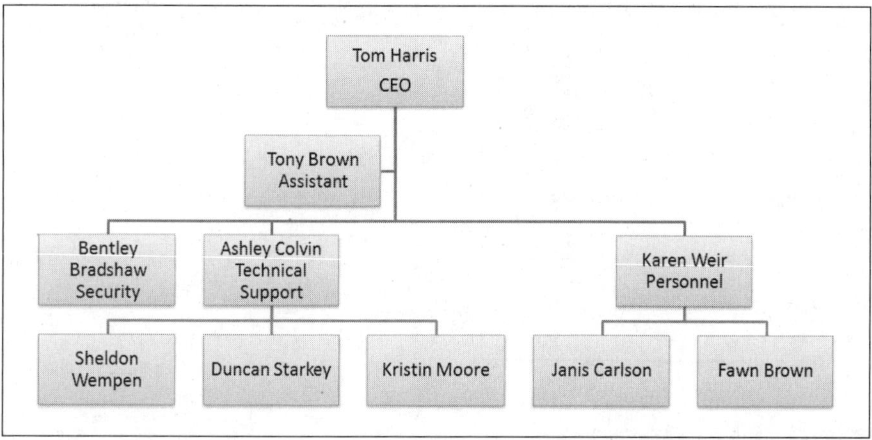

However, in a large or complex organization chart, the diagram can quickly become too wide with the Standard layout. Therefore, there are "hanging" alternatives that make the chart more vertically oriented. The alternatives are Both, Left Hanging, and Right Hanging. They are just what their names sound like. Figure 24-18 shows examples of Left Hanging (the people reporting to Ashley Colvin) and Right Hanging (the people reporting to Karen Weir).

The layout is chosen for individual branches of the organization chart, so before selecting an alternative layout, you must click on the supervisor box whose subordinates you want to change. To change a layout, follow these steps:

1. **Click the box for the supervisor whose layout you want to change.**
2. **On the Design tab, click Layouts. A menu of layout options appears.**
3. **Choose one of the layouts (Standard, Both, Left Hanging, or Right Hanging).**

NOTE If the Layout button's menu does not open, you do not have a box selected in a hierarchy diagram.

FIGURE 24-18

Hanging layouts make the chart more vertically oriented.

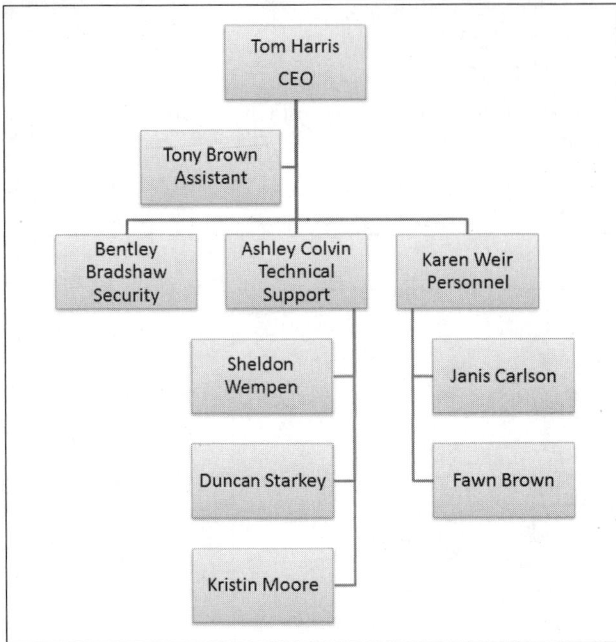

Formatting a Diagram

You can format a diagram either automatically or manually. Automatically is the default, and many PowerPoint users don't even realize that manual formatting is a possibility. The following sections cover both.

Applying a SmartArt style

SmartArt Styles are preset formatting specs (border, fill, effects, shadows, and so on) that you can apply to an entire SmartArt diagram. They make it easy to apply surface texture effects that make the shapes look reflective or appear to have 3-D depth or perspective.

SmartArt Styles do not include color changes. Those are separately controlled with the Change Colors button on the SmartArt Tools Design tab.

To apply a SmartArt style, follow these steps:

1. **Select the diagram so that the SmartArt Tools Design tab becomes available.**
2. **On the SmartArt Tools Design tab, click one of the SmartArt Styles samples (see Figure 24-19), or open the gallery and select from a larger list (see Figure 24-20).**

FIGURE 24-19

Select a SmartArt Style.

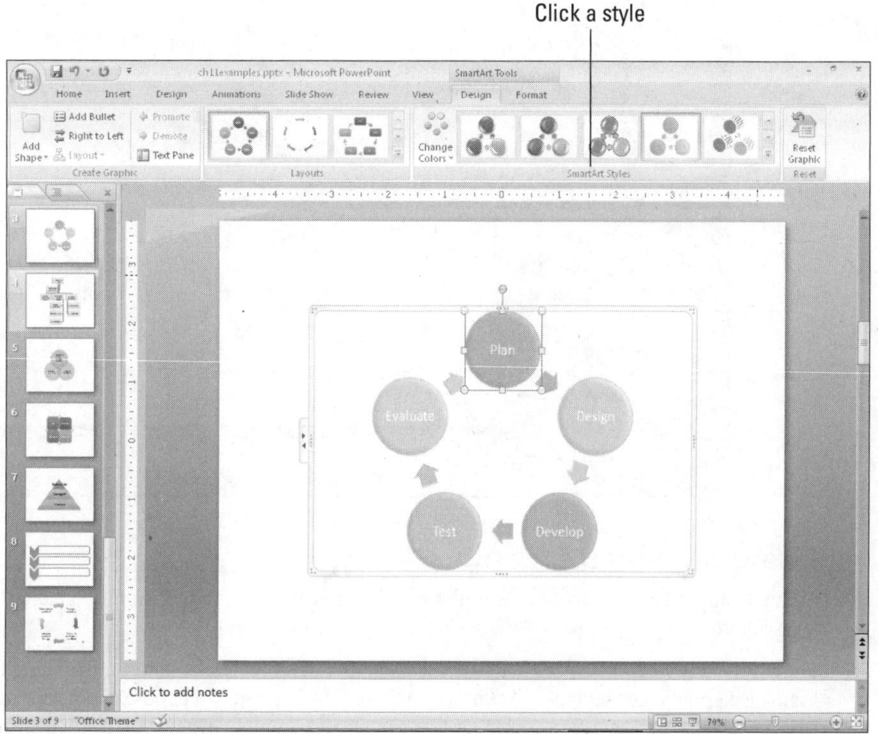

FIGURE 24-20

Open the SmartArt Style gallery for more choices.

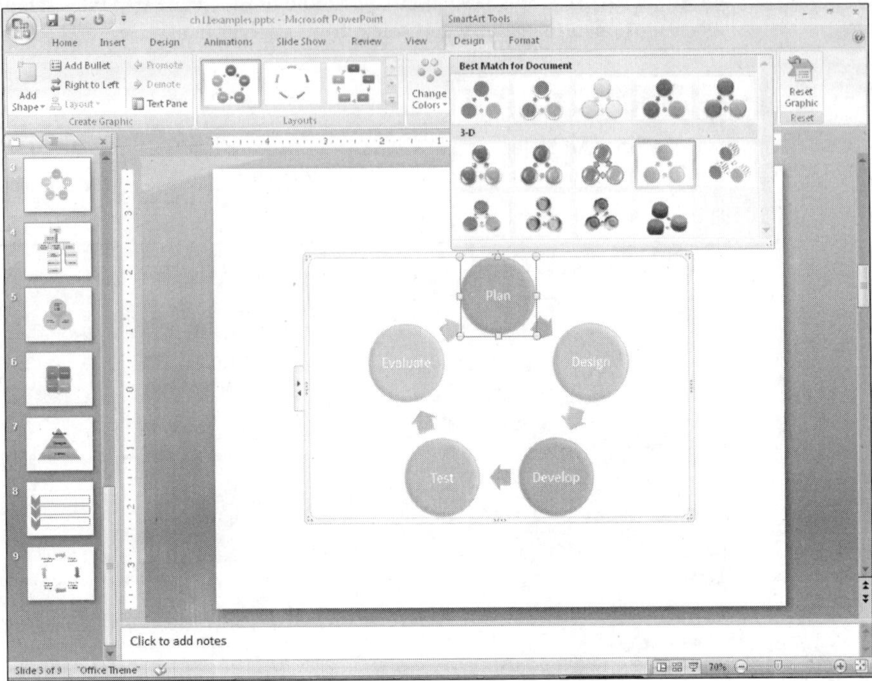

Changing SmartArt colors

After you apply a SmartArt style, as in the preceding section, you might want to change the colors used in the diagram.

The easiest way to apply colors is to use the Change Colors button's menu on the Design tab. You can select from a gallery of color schemes. As shown in Figure 24-21, you can choose a Colorful scheme (one in which each shape has its own color), or you can choose a monochrome color scheme based on any of the current presentation color theme's color swatches.

Manually applying colors and effects to individual shapes

In addition to formatting the entire diagram with a SmartArt Style, you can also format individual shapes using Shape Styles. Here are the steps:

1. **Select a shape in a SmartArt diagram.**
2. **On the SmartArt Tools Format tab, select a shape style from the Shape Styles gallery.**
3. **(Optional) Fine-tune the style by using the Shape Fill, Shape Outline, and/or Shape Effects buttons, and their associated menus.**

FIGURE 24-21

Select a color scheme from the Change Colors button's menu.

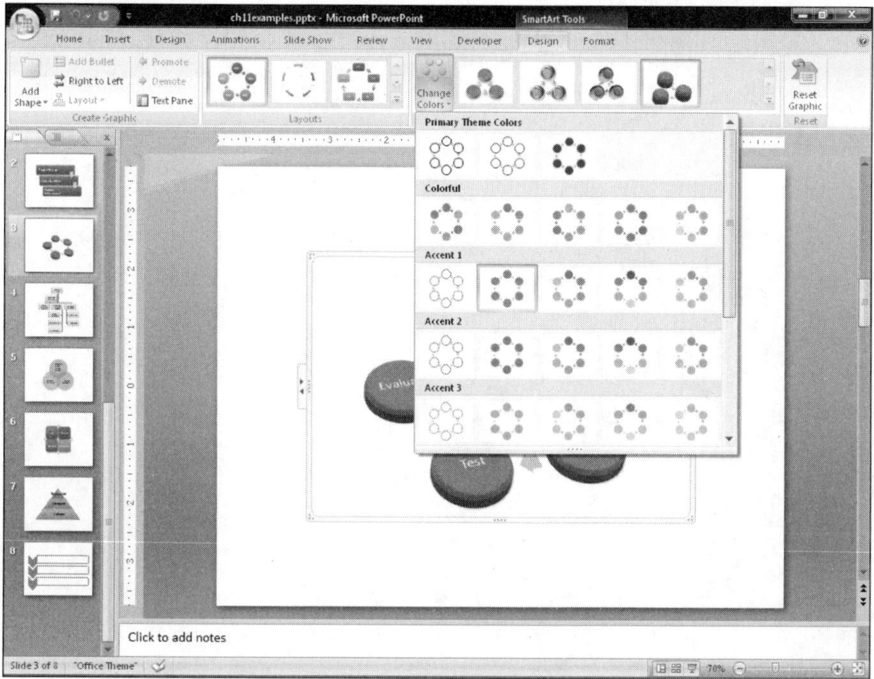

Manually formatting the diagram text

WordArt formatting works the same in a SmartArt diagram as it does everywhere else in PowerPoint. Use the WordArt Styles gallery and controls on the SmartArt Tools Format tab to apply text formatting to individual shapes, or select the entire diagram to apply the changes to all shapes at once.

Making a shape larger or smaller

In some diagram types, it is advantageous to make certain shapes larger or smaller than the others. For example, if you want to emphasize a certain step in a process, you can create a diagram where that step's shape is larger. Then you can repeat that same diagram on a series of slides, but with a different step in the process enlarged on each copy, to step through the process. There are several options for this:

- You can manually resize a shape by dragging its selection handles, the same as with any other object. However, this is imprecise, and can be a problem if you want multiple shapes to be enlarged because they won't be consistently so.
- You can set a precise size for the entire diagram using the Size group on the Format tab, a height and width measurement, as shown in Figure 24-22. However, if different shapes are already different sizes, and you want to resize them in proportion, this won't help.
- You can use the Larger or Smaller buttons on the Format tab to bump up or down the sizes of one or more shapes slightly with each successive click.

FIGURE 24-22

Use Format tab choices to adjust shape size and appearance.

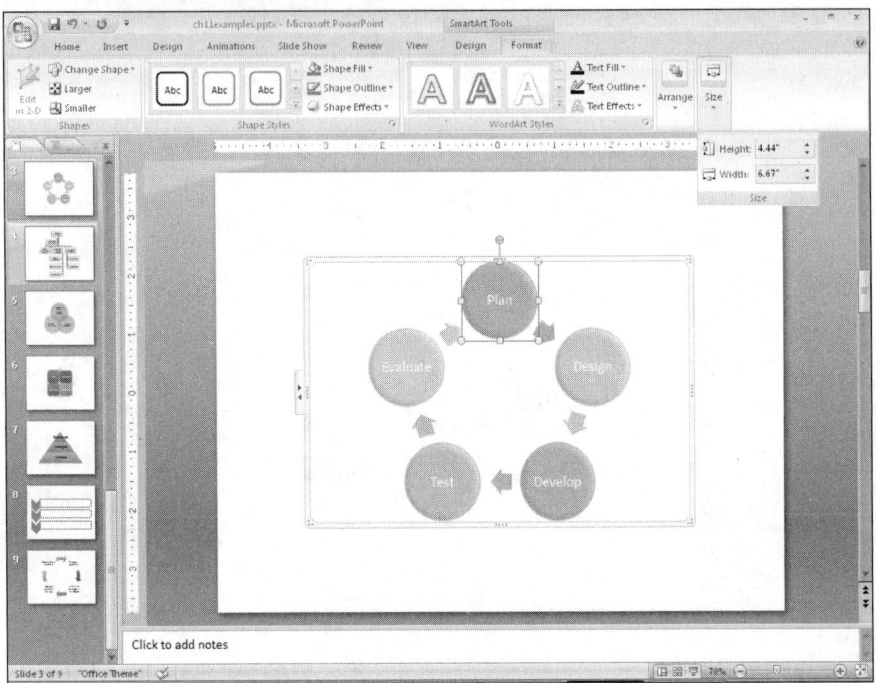

Resizing the entire SmartArt graphic object

When you resize the entire SmartArt object as a whole, everything within its frame changes size proportionally. There are several ways to do this:

- Drag and drop a corner selection handle on the SmartArt graphic's outer frame.
- Use the Size controls on the SmartArt Tools Format tab to enter a precise height and width.
- Right-click the outer frame of the SmartArt and choose Size and Position. The Size and Position dialog box opens, as shown in Figure 24-23; on the Size tab, enter a height and width in inches, or scale it by a percentage in the Scale box. Mark the Lock Aspect Ratio checkbox if you want to maintain the proportions.

FIGURE 24-23

Right-click the graphic and choose Size and Position to open this dialog box.

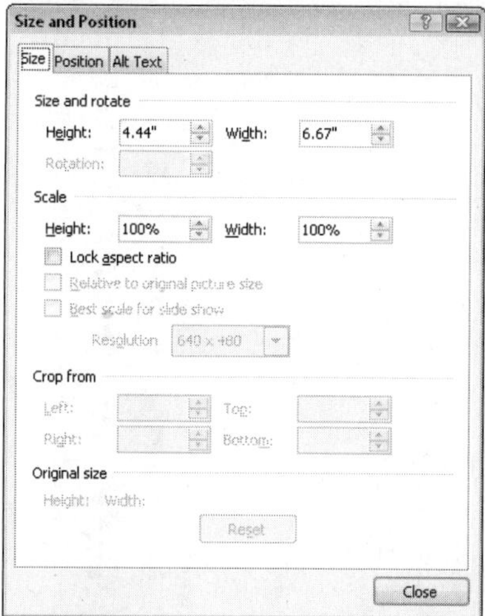

Editing in 2-D

If you choose one of the 3-D selections from the SmartArt Style gallery, the text might become a bit hard to read and edit when you are working with the diagram at a small zoom percentage. There are a couple of ways around this:

- Right-click a shape and choose Edit Text. The face of the shape appears in 2-D temporarily, making it easier to edit the text.
- Click the Edit in 2-D button on the SmartArt Tools Format tab. The entire diagram appears in 2-D temporarily.

CAUTION **Even though the face of the shape appears in 2-D, which you think would make it easier to read, in some diagram types and styles the text might still be fuzzy and hard to read. You might be better off editing it in the text pane.**

Changing the shapes used in the diagram

Each SmartArt layout has its own defaults that it uses for the shapes, but you can change these manually. On the SmartArt Tools Format tab, click Change Shape to open a palette of shapes. Then click the desired shape to apply to the selected shape, as shown in Figure 24-24. You can also access this from the right-click menu.

Each shape is individually configurable. If you simply select the entire diagram, the Change Shape button is not available; you must select each shape you want to change. Hold down the Shift key as you click on each one to be selected.

FIGURE 24-24

Apply a different shape to a part of the diagram.

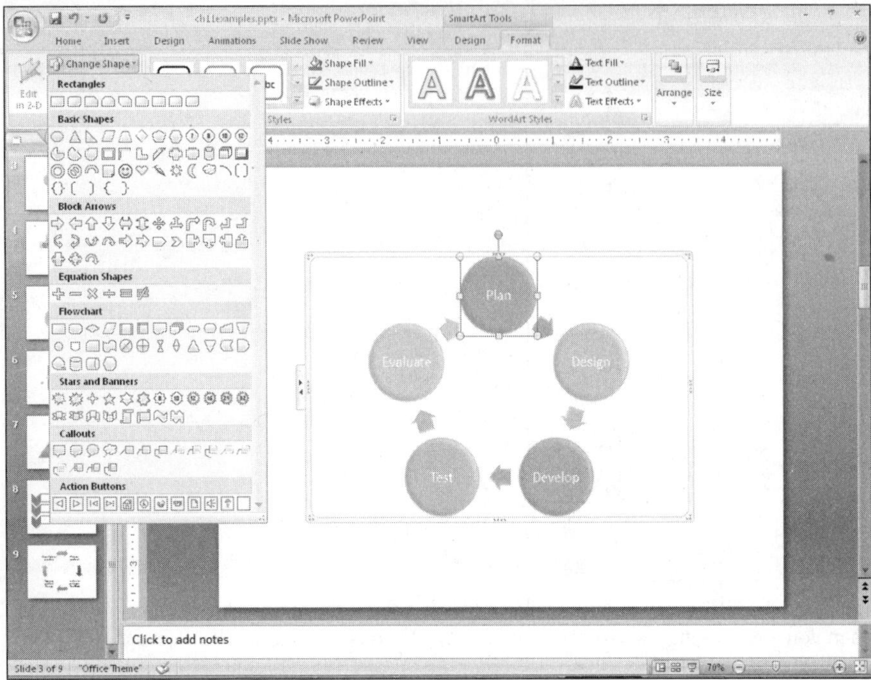

Choosing Appropriate Clip Art

Clip art is pre-drawn art that comes with PowerPoint or that is available from other sources (such as through the Internet). There are thousands of images that you can use royalty-free in your work, without having to draw your own. For example, suppose you are creating a presentation about snow skiing equipment. Rather than hiring an artist to draw a picture of a skier, you can use one of PowerPoint's stock drawings of skiers and save yourself a bundle.

Being an owner of a Microsoft Office product entitles you to the use of the huge clip art collection that Microsoft maintains on its Web site, and if you are connected to the Internet while you are using PowerPoint, PowerPoint can automatically pull clips from that collection as easily as it can from your own hard drive. You can also use the Clip Organizer to catalog and organize artwork in a variety of other formats, including photos that you scan, photos that you take with your digital camera, and drawings and pictures that you acquire from the Internet and from other people.

Don't just use any old image! You must never use clip art simply because you can; it must be a well-thought-out decision. Here are some reasons for using clip art, and ways to make it look good:

- If your message is very serious, or you are conveying bad news, don't use clip art. It looks frivolous in these situations.

- Use cartoonish images only if you specifically want to impart a lighthearted, fun feel to your presentation.
- The clip art included with Office has many styles of drawings, ranging from simple black-and-white shapes to very complex, shaded color drawings and photographs. Try to stick with one type of image rather than bouncing among several drawing styles.
- Use only one piece of clip art on each slide. Also, do not use clip art on every slide, or it becomes overpowering.
- Don't repeat the same clip art on more than one slide in the presentation unless you have a specific reason to do so.
- If you can't find clip art that is exactly right for the slide, then don't use any. It is better to have none than to have an inappropriate image.
- If clip art is important, and Office doesn't have what you want, you can buy more. Don't try to struggle along with the clips that come with Office if it isn't meeting your needs; impressive clip art collections are available at reasonable prices at your local computer store, as well as online.

About the Clip Organizer

The Clip Organizer is a Microsoft utility that you access from within an Office application such as PowerPoint. It organizes and catalogs artwork of various types. The primary type is clip art, but it can also hold sounds, videos, and photos. All of the Microsoft-provided clip art is automatically included in the Clip Organizer, including links to online Microsoft clip art; you can also add your own clips from your hard disk. Most of the Microsoft clip art is online, rather than stored locally, so you will need Internet access to use it.

The Clip Organizer has two main interfaces. When you use the Clip Art command on the Insert tab, you work with the Clip Art task pane, and clips that you select are inserted onto the active slide, as shown in the section "Inserting Clip Art on a Slide." When you use the Clip Organizer utility separately, you must copy and paste the clip art into the presentation using the Clipboard.

Depending on what you are inserting, you might also encounter other interfaces that access the Clip Organizer, such as interfaces for choosing custom bullet characters, which are also stored as clip art.

Inserting Clip Art on a Slide

You can insert clip art on a slide either with or without a content placeholder. If you use a content placeholder, PowerPoint inserts the clip art wherever the placeholder is; if you don't, PowerPoint inserts the clip art at the center of the slide. (You can move it afterwards, of course.)

TIP **Most clip art files in Microsoft Office applications have a .wmf extension, which stands for Windows Metafile. WMF is a *vector* graphic format, which means that it is composed of mathematical formulas rather than individual pixels. This allows you to resize it without distortion, and keeps the file size very small. Some other clip art files are Enhanced Metafile (.emf) files, which are like WMF files but with some improvements. The Clip Organizer can also organize *bitmap* graphic files (that is, graphics composed of individual pixels of color), as you see later in this chapter. However, there are some editing activities through PowerPoint that you can perform only on WMF and EMF files.**

To find and insert a piece of clip art, follow these steps:

1. ***(Recommended)* If you want to include Web collections when searching for clip art, make sure that you are connected to the Internet. Otherwise, you are limited to the clip art on your local hard disk.**
2. **On the Insert tab, click Clip Art.** The Clip Art pane appears. Alternatively, you can click the Clip Art icon in a content placeholder.
3. **In the Search For text box, type the subject keyword that you want to search for.**
4. ***(Optional)* Narrow down where you want to search, using the Search In list, and the types of results that you want, using the Results Should Be list.**
5. **Click Go.** The matching clip art appears, as shown in Figure 24-25.

FIGURE 24-25

The clip art that matches your search specifications appears in the task pane.

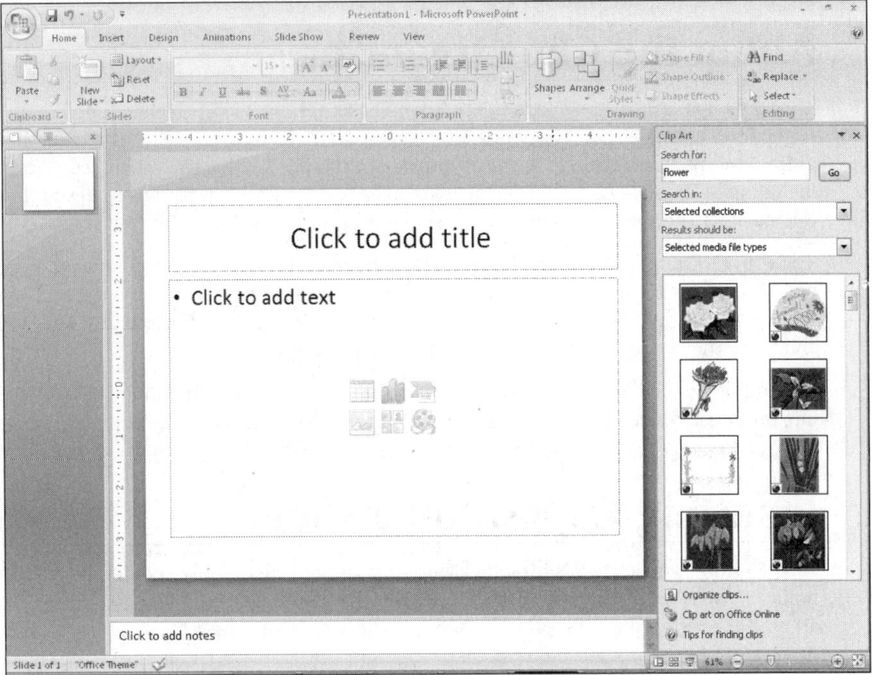

6. **Click the clip art that you want to insert.** It appears on the slide.
7. **Edit the image, for example, by resizing or moving it, as needed.**

Clip Art Search Methods

Now that you've seen the basic process for searching for a clip by keyword, let's look at some ways to fine-tune those results so that you can more easily find what you want.

Using multiple keywords

If you enter multiple keywords in the Search For text box of the Clip Art pane, only clips that contain all of the entered keywords appear in the search results. You can simply type the words separated by spaces; you do not have to use any special symbols or punctuation in order to use multiple keywords.

Specify which collections to search

Clip art is stored in *collections*, which are logical groupings of artwork arranged by subject or location. There are three main collections:

- **Office Collections:** These are the clips that came with Microsoft Office 2007.
- **My Collections:** These include any clips that you have marked as favorites, as well as any uncategorized clips. They also include any clips that you have added through the Clip Organizer, any downloaded clips, and any clips shared from a network drive.
- **Web Collections:** These are clip collections that are available online via Microsoft. This is by far the largest collection, but you must be connected to the Internet in order to access it. All of the clips from this collection appear with a little globe icon in the corner when you preview them in the task pane.

Within each of these large collections are multiple smaller collections (like subfolders within folders) that are based on subject. For example, Office Collections has sub-collections for Academic, Agriculture, Animals, and so on.

NOTE **The physical location of the Office Collections clips is** `Program Files\Microsoft Office\MEDIA\CAGCAT10`**. However, users don't normally need to know this because PowerPoint manages the locations of the clip art automatically.**

When you search for clips that contain certain keywords using the Clip Art pane, you have the option to specify which collections you want to look in. If you are working on a PC that uses a dial-up connection, or that has sporadic or no Web access, you might want to exclude the Web Collections from the search to avoid the delay while PowerPoint looks for and fails to find the Internet connection. You can also exclude certain categories to avoid having too many results to wade through.

To narrow the list of collections in which to search, follow these steps:

1. **From the Clip Art pane, open the Search In drop-down list.** A list of collections appears.
2. **Deselect the checkbox for any collection that you want to exclude.** You can also click the plus sign next to the collection to see its individual sub-collections, and then deselect the checkbox for one or more of these sub-collections, as shown in Figure 24-26.
3. **Continue the clip search as you normally would.**

FIGURE 24-26

Narrow the search for a clip to certain collections by deselecting the checkboxes for unwanted collections.

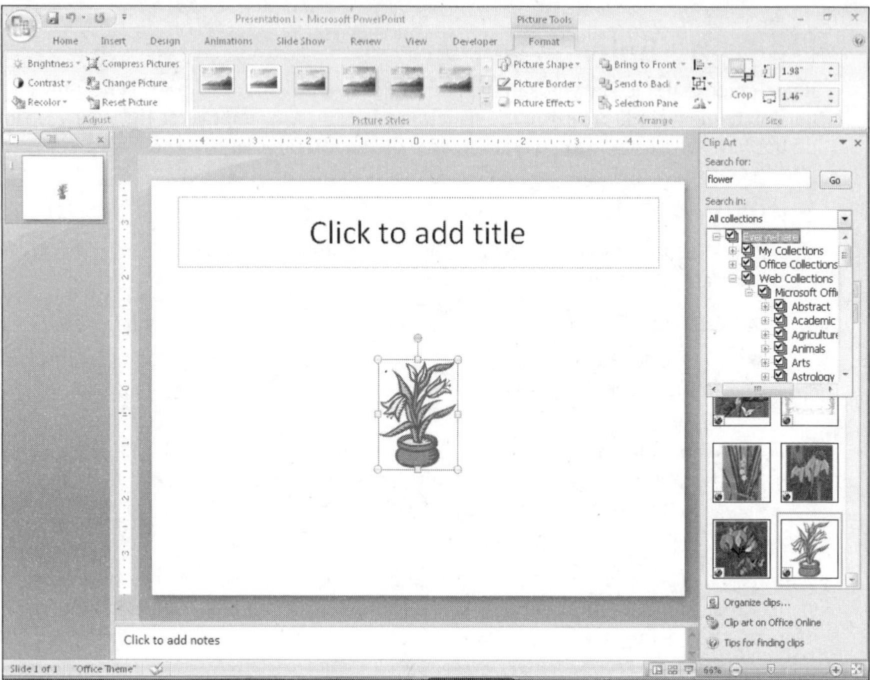

Specify which media file types to find

Besides true clip art (WMF and EMF files), you can also find movies, sounds, and pictures using the Clip Art pane. You can learn more about each of these media types in later chapters, but let's take a quick look here at how to include them in searches. To filter results by media type (or to enable additional media types), follow these steps:

1. **From the Clip Art pane, open the Results Should Be drop-down list.** A list of media types appears.
2. **Select or deselect checkboxes for media types that you want to include or exclude, respectively.** You can also click the plus sign next to a media type to see its individual subtypes, and then deselect the checkbox for one or more of these subtypes, as shown in Figure 24-27.

NOTE Notice in Figure 24-27 that the Clip Art pane is wider than in Figure 24-26. It is widened to show that you can view more of the descriptions of each file type. To widen this pane, click-and-drag its left edge to the left.

FIGURE 24-27

Narrow the search for a clip to certain file types by only selecting checkboxes for the media types that you want.

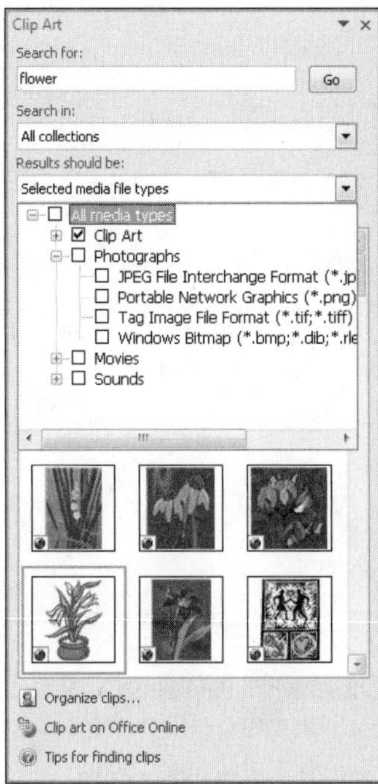

Working with Clip Art Collections

The Clip Organizer is a utility that manages the clips from various collections. You can use the Clip Organizer to browse entire clip collections by subject, regardless of keyword. It also manages clips of other types, including bitmap images (such as scanned photos), sounds, and video clips. In the following sections, you learn how to browse, categorize, and organize clips in the Clip Organizer, as well as how to add clips to it.

Opening and browsing the clip organizer

To open the Clip Organizer, click the Organize Clips link at the bottom of the Clip Art pane. The Collection List pane lists the three default groups: My Collections, Office Collections, and Web Collections. Within each of these collections are nested folders, or sub-collections, containing clips. To expand or collapse a folder, double-click it, or click the plus or minus sign to its left, as shown in Figure 24-28.

FIGURE 24-28

You can browse clip art by collection, as well as by category within a collection.

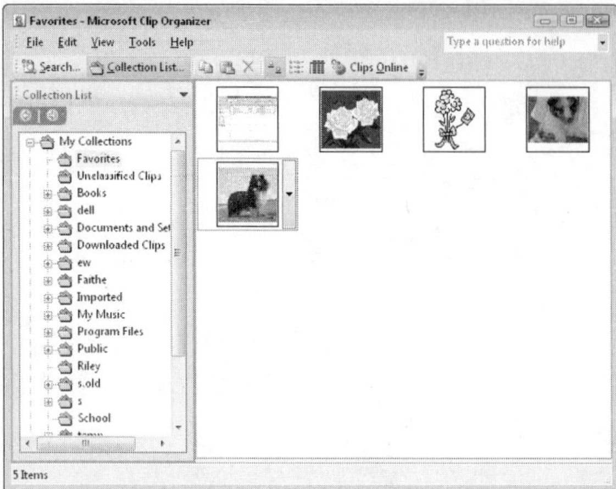

The My Collections group contains two collections by default:

- **Favorites:** This is where clips are placed when you make them available offline. (This is covered in the section "Making clips available offline.")
- **Unclassified Clips:** This is where clips are placed when they are manually added to the Clip Organizer. (This is covered in the section "Working with clip keywords and information.")

You can add more collections to the My Collections group, as well as more clips. It is the only group that you can modify. The Office Collections group contains collections that Microsoft provides and stores on your hard disk. The Web Collections group contains collections that you access through the Internet.

Using the clip organizer to insert clip art

As you saw at the beginning of this chapter, when you insert clip art from the Clip Art pane, you cannot browse for it. You can only search based on keywords. If you would rather peruse the available clip art in a more leisurely fashion, you can open the Clip Organizer to do so.

The Clip Organizer is not really designed for easy insertion of clips into a presentation, but it is possible to do this using the Clipboard. To select a clip from the Clip Organizer for insertion in your presentation, do the following:

1. **From the Clip Art pane, click Organize Clips.** The Clip Organizer window opens.
2. **Make sure that Collection List, and not Search, is selected on the toolbar.** Click Collection List, if necessary.
3. **Click the collection that you want to browse.** The Clip Organizer displays the available clips. When you find the clip that you want to insert, right-click it and choose Copy.
4. **Close or minimize the Clip Organizer.** Display the slide in PowerPoint on which you want to place the clip, and then right-click and choose Paste. Alternatively, you can drag-and-drop clips from the Clip Organizer window onto a PowerPoint slide.

Creating and deleting folders

Each folder in the Clip Organizer represents a collection (or a sub-collection within a collection). The folders that you create are placed in the My Collections group, and you can place clips into a collection or sub-collection by dragging and dropping them into the desired folder. To create a folder in the Clip Organizer, follow these steps:

1. **In the Clip Organizer, choose File ➪ New Collection.** The New Collection dialog box opens, as shown in Figure 24-29.

FIGURE 24-29

You can create new collection folders.

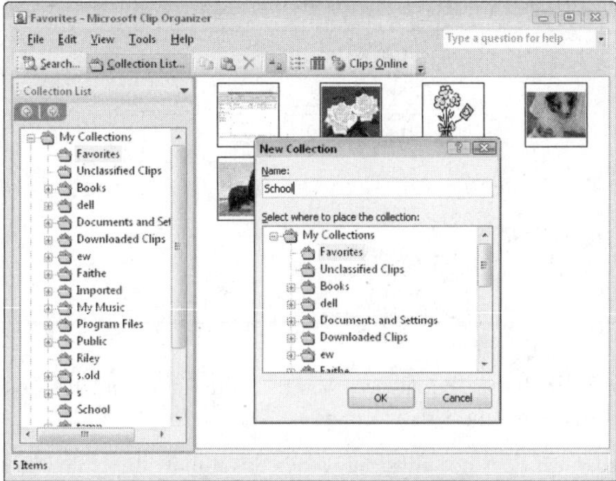

2. **In the Name text box, type a name for the new collection.**
3. **To create a top-level collection, click My Collections.** To create a folder within a collection, click that collection within My Collections.
4. **Click OK.** The Clip Organizer creates the new folder.

To delete a folder, right-click it and choose Delete *foldername*, where *foldername* is the name of the folder.

Moving clips between collections

A clip can exist in multiple collections simultaneously; only one copy actually exists on your hard disk, but pointers to it can appear in multiple places. When you drag a clip from one collection to another, you are actually making a copy of its pointer to the new location. The shortcut to the clip is not removed from the original collection. You can delete a clip from a collection by right-clicking it and choosing Delete, or pressing the Delete key.

Cataloging clips

There are probably images elsewhere on your PC that you would like to use in PowerPoint besides the Microsoft Office clip art collection. For example, perhaps you have some scanned photos or some clip art that you have downloaded from a Web site that offers free clips. If you need to use this downloaded clip art only once or twice, you can simply insert it with the Picture button on the Insert tab. However, if you want to use the clip art more often, you can add it to your Clip Organizer.

You can include images in all image formats in the Clip Organizer, not just the default format that PowerPoint's clip art uses. The image formats that PowerPoint supports are shown in Table 24-1.

TABLE 24-1

PowerPoint Image Formats

BMP	EPS	PCX
CDR	FPX	PNG
CGM	GIF	RLE
DIB	JPG/JPEG/JPE/JFIF	TGA
DRW	MIX	TIF/TIFF
DXF	PCD	WMF
EMF	PCT/PICT	WPG

The Clip Organizer is not only for clip art, but also for scanned and digital camera photos, video clips, and sound clips. It can accept many sound and video formats.

Adding a clip to the Clip Organizer does not physically move the clip; it simply creates a link to it in the Clip Organizer so that the clip is included when you search or browse for clips.

NOTE **Any clips that you add are placed in My Collections; you cannot add clips to the Office Collections or Web Collections categories. This is the case whether you add them automatically or manually.**

Adding clips automatically to the Clip Organizer

The quickest way to catalog the clips on your hard disk is to allow the Clip Organizer to import the clips automatically. To automatically catalog your clips, follow these steps:

1. **From the Clip Organizer, choose File ➪ Add Clips to Organizer ➪ Automatically.**
2. ***(Optional)* In the dialog box that appears, click the Options button to open the Auto Import Settings dialog box.** You can then select or deselect checkboxes for various locations that you want to include in the automatic cataloging, as shown in Figure 24-30. The first time you open this dialog box, the utility scans the hard disk for clips, and you must wait for a minute or so while it does this.

FIGURE 24-30

You can specify the locations that you want the Clip Organizer to catalog.

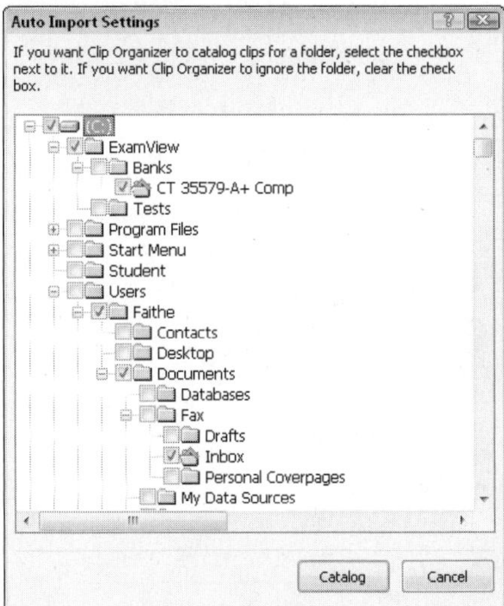

3. **If you performed Step 2, click Catalog to perform the search for clips.** If you did not perform step 2, click OK to perform the search.
4. **Wait for the Clip Organizer to catalog the clips.** This process takes several minutes and includes several steps, including creating the collections, adding the clips, and adding keywords to them.

Adding clips manually to the Clip Organizer

Not all clips are picked up automatically during the cataloging process, and so you might need to manually add some clips. For example, the automatic cataloging process only looks for clips on your local hard disks, and you might want to catalog some clips in a network location.

CAUTION **Some earlier versions of Office stored the local collection of clip art in a different place. For example, Office XP stored this collection in** `Program Files\Common Files\Microsoft Shared\Clipart\Catcat50`**. By default, the clip art in this old location does not appear in the collections for Office 2003 or 2007 applications. In addition, it is not detected by the automatic cataloging process. The only way to import it into the Clip Organizer is by manually cataloging it, as described here.**

To manually add one or more clips, do the following:

1. **From the Clip Organizer window, choose File ➪ Add Clips to Organizer ➪ On My Own.** The Add Clips to Organizer window appears.
2. **Navigate to the clips that you want to add.** They can be in a local, network, or Internet location.

3. **Select the clips.** To select more than one clip, hold down the Shift key to select a contiguous group or the Ctrl key to select a non-contiguous group.
4. **Click the Add To button.** A list of the existing collections in the Clip Organizer appears, as shown in Figure 24-31.

FIGURE 24-31

You can specify the location to which you want to add the clips.

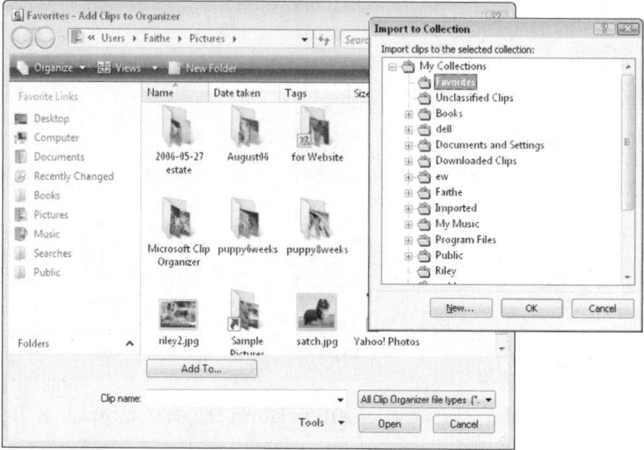

5. **Select the collection in which you want to place the new clips, and click OK.** If you would rather create a new clip collection, click My Collections and then click New. Type a name for the new collection and click OK. Then select the new folder on the list and click OK.
6. **Click the Add button.** The Clip Organizer adds the clips to the specified collection.

Working with CIL or MPF files

Occasionally, you might encounter a file that claims to be clip art but that has a .cil or .mpf extension. Both of these are clip art "package" formats that Microsoft has used to bundle and transfer clip art at one time or another. MPF is the newer format, for Office XP and higher; CIL is the older format, for Office 97 and 2000.

These packages are executable, which means that executing them copies the art to the Clip Organizer. When you find one of these files, you can choose to run it rather than save it to immediately extract its clips, or you can download the file and then double-click it to extract the clip art from it later.

Deleting clips from the Clip Organizer

After the automatic cataloging process (and possibly after the manual one), you might end up with some clip collections within My Collections that you don't want. The automatic cataloging process sometimes identifies files that are not really useful as clip art — for example, little graphics that are part of some other application's operation.

To remove a graphic — or even an entire folder — from your Clip Organizer, right-click it and choose Delete. Figure 24-32 shows a situation where the Clip Organizer has cataloged the clips from of a folder labeled i386; this folder is actually used for installing Windows. In the example, you can right-click the i386 folder in the folder tree and choose Delete "i386" to get rid of it. This does not delete the pictures or the folder from the hard disk; it simply removes its reference from the Clip Organizer. You can also delete individual clips in the same way.

FIGURE 24-32

You can remove a clip or a category from the Clip Organizer by right-clicking it and choosing Delete.

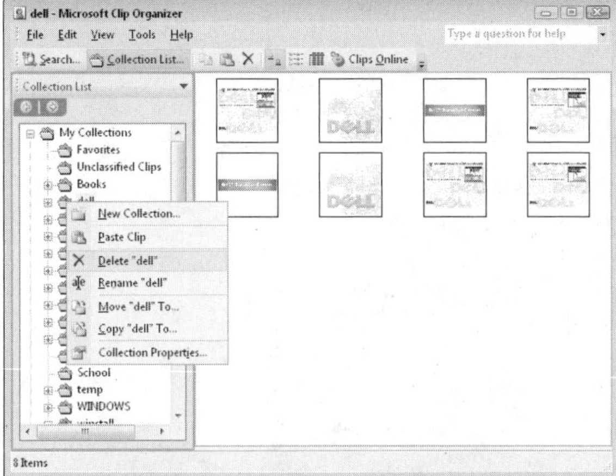

Making clips available offline

Most of the clips that appear in the Clip Organizer are not on your local hard disk; they are online. This means that you do not have access to them when you are not connected to the Internet. If you find some clip art in the Clip Organizer that you want to have available offline, you can add the clip to your local hard disk, as follows:

1. **In the Clip Organizer or the Clip Art pane, open the menu of the clip that you want (the arrow to its right) and choose Make Available Offline.** The Copy to Collection dialog box opens.

   If the Make Available Offline command is not present, it means that this clip is already on your local hard disk.

2. **Select the collection in which you want to place the clip.** (You can also click New to create a new collection.) Then click OK.

Browsing for more clips on Office Online

When you browse for clip art while connected to the Internet, the Office Online clip art automatically appears. However, you can also visit the Office Online Web site to browse the clip art directly.

To open a Web browser window for the Office Online clip art gallery, do one of the following:

- From the Clip Art pane, click the Clip art on Office Online link.
- From the Clip Organizer window, click the Clips Online toolbar button.

Either way, the same Web page displays (provided you have Internet access). It contains information about clip art, links to art collections, featured clips, and more. It is constantly changing, but Figure 24-33 shows how it looked on the day I visited.

If you have a full-time Internet connection, there is little reason to download clips to your hard disk from the Office Online Web site because your clip art search by keyword will always include this Web site. However, if your Internet connection is not always active, you might want to download the clips you need in advance so that they will be available when you need them.

FIGURE 24-33

Visit the Office Online clip art Web page for more information and more clip art.

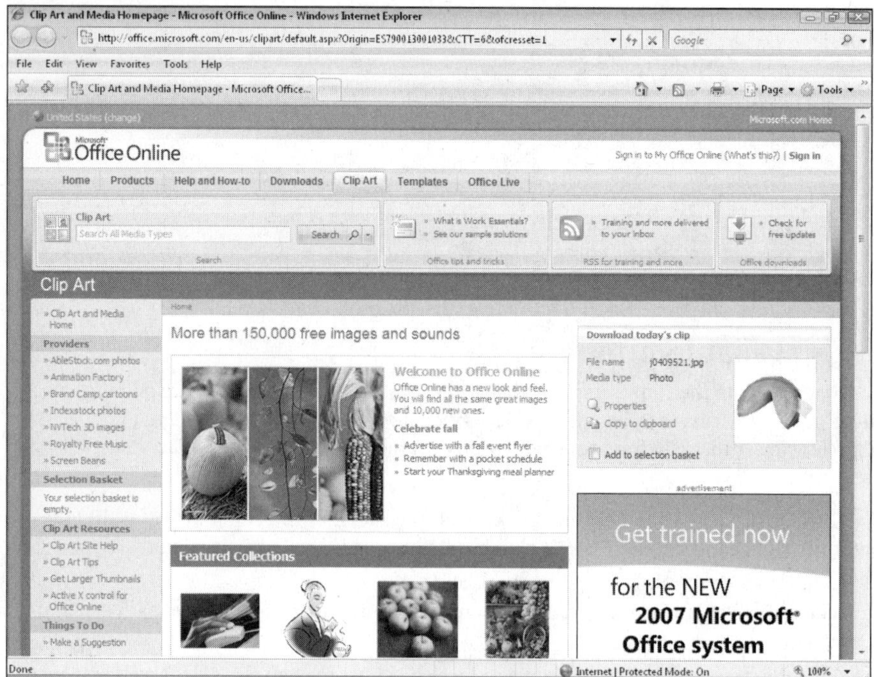

To copy clips from the Office Online Web site to your hard disk for later use, follow these steps:

1. **From the Office Online clip art Web page, scroll down to the Browse Clip Art and Media Categories list and click a category to display it. The available clips in the category appear, as in the example in Figure 24-34.**
2. **In the list of clips, select the checkboxes for the clips that you want.** You may find multiple pages of clips in that category; click the Next arrow to go to the next page.

FIGURE 24-34

You can download clips from Office Online for future use.

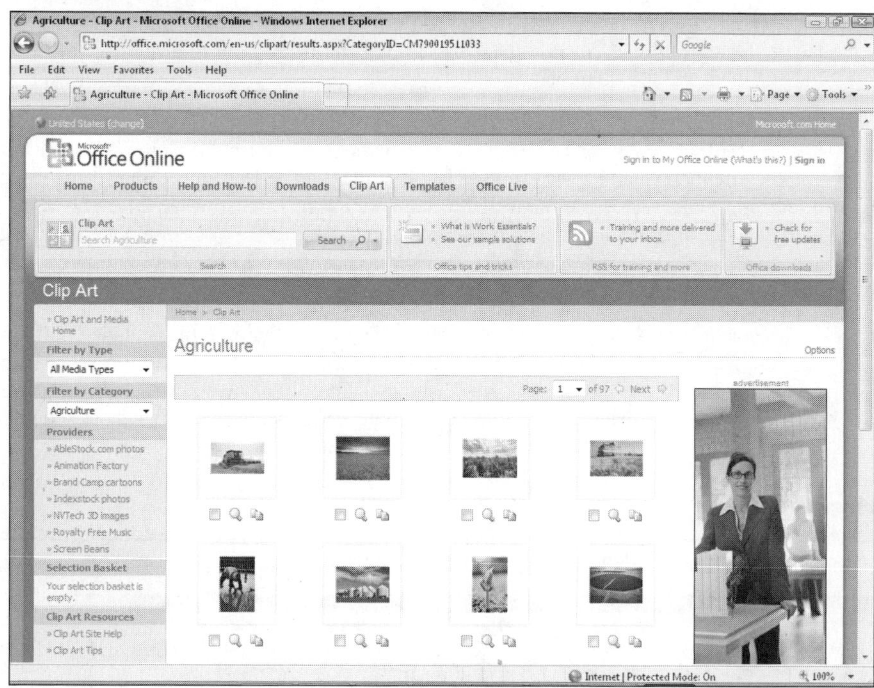

3. **When you finish making selections, click the Download hyperlink at the left.** For example, if you select five items, the link is labeled "Download 5 items."
4. **If this is the first time that you have used the service, a Terms of Use screen appears. Scroll down to the bottom and click Accept to continue.**
5. **Click Download Now.**
6. **A dialog box appears, saying that it is downloading the file Clipart.mpf, and asking whether you want to save or open it. Choose Open.**

NOTE MPF stands for Media Package File. When downloading one of these files, you should choose to open it rather than save it, because opening it integrates its content automatically with the Clip Organizer. Saving the file stores it somewhere on your hard disk without adding the clips to the Clip Organizer. However, you might need to do this if you download clips that you want to use on another PC; in this case, you can transfer the MPF file to the other PC before double-clicking to open it.

CAUTION When an MPF file unpacks, it uses the Temporary Internet File folder to do so. If this folder is too full (indicating that there is insufficient space remaining on the hard disk), the clips may not import into Clip Organizer.

The selected clips appear in the Clip Organizer, in the Downloaded Clips folder under My Collections. They are now ready for you to use.

Understanding Raster Graphics

Whether you're putting together a slide show to display your vacation photos or adding photos of industrial products to a business presentation, PowerPoint has the tools and capabilities you need. And with the new Picture Styles feature in PowerPoint 2007, it has never been easier to give those photos professional-looking frames, shadows, and other effects.

There are two kinds of graphics in the computer world: *vector* and *raster*. Vector graphics (clip art, drawn lines and shapes, and so on) are created with mathematical formulas. Some of the advantages of vector graphics are their small file size and the fact that they can be resized without losing any quality. The main disadvantage of a vector graphic is that it doesn't look "real." Even when an expert artist draws a vector graphic, you can still tell that it's a drawing, not a photograph. For example, perhaps you've seen the game *The Sims*? Those characters and objects are 3-D vector graphics. They look pretty good but there's no way you would mistake them for real people and objects.

In this chapter, you'll be working with raster graphics. A raster graphic is made up of a very fine grid of individual colored *pixels* (dots). The grid is sometimes called a *bitmap*. Each pixel has a unique numeric value representing its color. Figure 24-35 shows a close-up of a raster image. You can create raster graphics from scratch with a "paint" program on a computer, but a more common way to acquire a raster graphic is by using a scanner or digital camera as an input device.

FIGURE 24-35

A raster graphic, normal size (right) and zoomed in to show individual pixels (left).

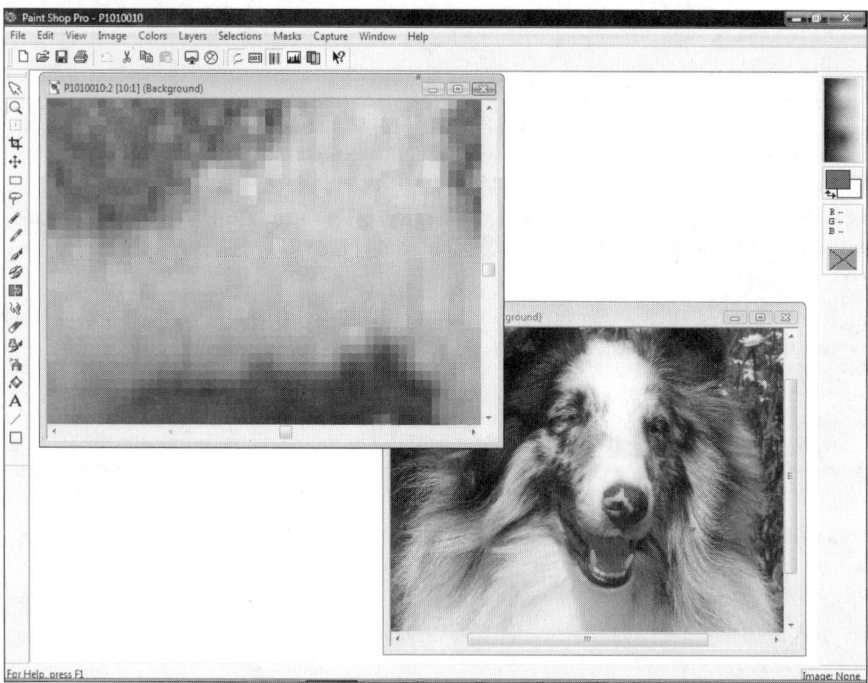

NOTE The term *bitmap* is sometimes used to refer generically to any raster graphic, but it is also a specific file format for raster graphics, with a BMP extension. This is the default format for the Paint program that comes with Windows XP and Windows XP desktop wallpaper.

Because there are so many individual pixels and each one must be represented numerically, raster graphics are much larger than vector graphics. They take longer to load into the PC's memory, take up more space when you store them as separate files on disk, and make your PowerPoint presentation file much larger. You can compress a raster graphic so that it takes up less space on disk, but the quality may suffer. Therefore, it's best to use vector graphics when you want simple lines, shapes, or cartoons and reserve raster graphics for situations where you need photographic quality.

The following sections explain some of the technical specifications behind raster graphics; you'll need this information to make the right decisions about the way you capture the images with your scanner or digital camera, and the way you use them in PowerPoint.

Resolution

The term *resolution* has two subtly different meanings. One is the size of an image, expressed in the number of pixels of width and height, such as 800x600. The other meaning is the number of pixels per inch when the image is printed, such as 100 dots per inch (dpi). The former meaning is used mostly when referring to images of fixed physical size, such as the display resolution of a monitor. In this book, the later meaning is mostly used.

If you know the resolution of the picture (that is, the number of pixels in it), and the resolution of the printer on which you will print it (for example, 300 dpi), you can figure out how large the picture will be in inches when you print it at its native size. Suppose you have a picture that is 900 pixels square, and you print it on a 300 dpi printer. This makes it 3 inches square on the printout.

Resolution on pre-existing graphics files

When you acquire an image file from an outside source, such as downloading it from a Web site or getting it from a CD of artwork, its resolution has already been determined. Whoever created the file originally made that decision. For example, if the image was originally scanned on a scanner, whoever scanned it chose the scan resolution—that is, the dpi setting. That determined how many individual pixels each inch of the original picture would be carved up into. At a 100 dpi scan, each inch of the picture is represented by 100 pixels vertically and horizontally. At 300 dpi, each inch of the picture is broken down into three times that many.

If you want to make a graphic take up less disk space, you can use an image-editing program to change the image size, and/or you can crop off one or more sides of the image.

CAUTION If you crop or decrease the size of an image in an image-editing program, save the changes under a different filename. Maintain the original image in case you ever need it for some other purpose. Decreasing the image resolution decreases its dpi setting, which decreases its quality. You might not notice any quality degradation onscreen, but you will probably notice a difference when you are printing the image at a large size. That's because the average monitor displays only 96 dpi, but the average printer prints at 600 dpi or higher.

PowerPoint slides do not usually need to be printed at a professional-quality resolution, so image quality on a PowerPoint printout is not usually an issue. However, if you use the picture for something else later, such as printing it as a full-page color image on photo paper, then a high dpi file can make a difference.

Resolution on graphics you scan yourself

When you create an image file yourself by using a scanner, *you* choose the resolution, expressed in dpi, through the scanner software. For example, suppose you scan a 4-inch by 6-inch photo at 100 dpi. The scanner will break down each 1-inch section of the photo horizontally and vertically into 100 separate pieces and decide on a numeric value that best represents the color of each piece. The result is a total number of pixels of 4 x 100 x 6 x 100, or 240,000 pixels. Assuming each pixel requires 3 bytes of storage, the fill becomes approximately 720KB in size. The actual size varies slightly depending on the file format.

Now, suppose you scan the same photo at 200 dpi. The scanner breaks down each 1-inch section of the photo into 200 pieces, so that the result is 4 x 200 x 6x 200, or 960,000 pixels. Assuming again that one pixel required 3 bytes for storage (24 bits), the file will be approximately 2.9MB in size. That's a big difference.

The higher the resolution in which you scan, the larger the file becomes, but the details of the scan also become finer. However, unless you are zooming in on the photo, you cannot tell a difference between 100 dpi and a higher resolution. That's because most computer monitors display at 96 dpi, so any resolution higher than that does not improve the output.

Let's look at an example. In Figure 24-36 you can see two copies of an image open in a graphics program. The same photo was scanned at 75 dpi (left) and 150 dpi (right). However, the difference between them is not significant when the two images are placed on a PowerPoint slide, as shown in Figure 24-37. The lower resolution image is at the top left, but there is no observable difference in the size at which they are being used.

FIGURE 24-36

At high magnification, the difference in dpi for a scan is apparent.

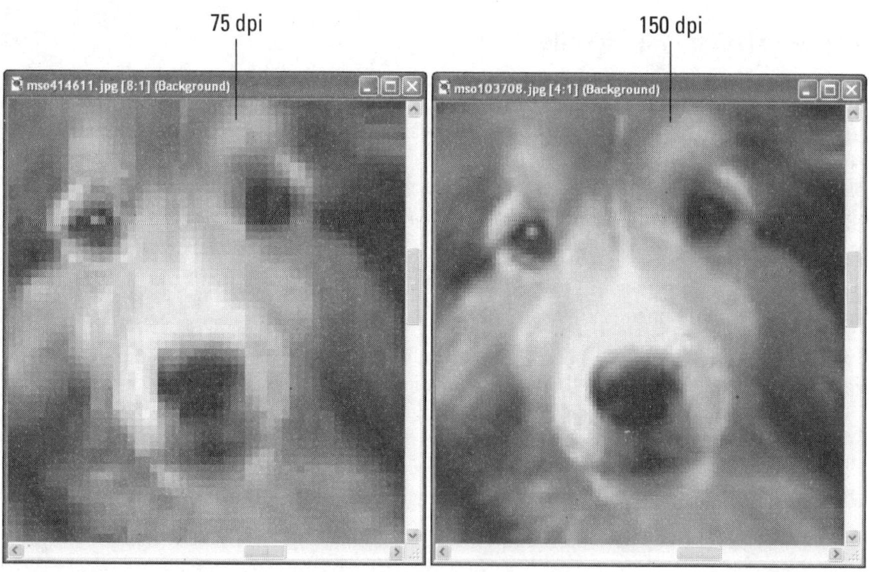

FIGURE 24-37

When the image is used at a normal size, there is virtually no difference between a high-dpi and low-dpi scan.

Resolution on digital camera photos

Top-quality digital cameras today take very high-resolution pictures, and are much higher than you will need for an onscreen PowerPoint presentation. At a typical size and magnification, a high-resolution graphic file is overkill; it wastes disk space needlessly. Therefore, you may want to adjust the camera's image size so that it takes lower-resolution pictures for your PowerPoint show.

If you think you might want to use those same pictures for some other purpose in the future, such as printing them in a magazine or newsletter, then go ahead and take them with the camera's highest setting, but you should compress them in PowerPoint or resize them in a third-party image editing program. See the section "Compressing Images" later in this chapter to learn how.

Color depth

Color depth is the number of bits required to describe the color of a single pixel in the image. For example, in 1-bit color, a single binary digit represents each pixel. Each pixel is either black (1) or white (0). In 4-bit color, there are 16 possible colors because there are 16 combinations of 1s and 0s in a four-digit binary number. In 8-bit color there are 256 combinations.

Scanners and color depth

If you are shopping for a scanner, you will probably notice that they're advertised with higher numbers of bits than the graphics formats support. This is for error correction. If there are extra bits, it can throw out the bad bits to account for "noise" and still end up with a full set of good bits. Error correction in a scan is a rather complicated process, but fortunately your scanner driver software takes care of it for you.

For most file formats, the highest number of colors you can have in an image is 16.7 million colors, which is 24-bit color (also called *true color*). It uses 8 bits each for Red, Green, and Blue.

There is also 32-bit color, which has the same number of colors as 24-bit, but adds 8 more bits for an Alpha channel. The Alpha channel describes the amount of transparency for each pixel. This is not so much an issue for single-layer graphics, but in multi-layer graphics, such as the ones you can create in high-end graphics programs like Photoshop, the extent to which a lower layer shows through an upper one is important.

TIP **For a great article on alpha channel usage in PowerPoint by Geetesh Bajaj, go to** `www.indezine.com/products/powerpoint/ppalpha.html`.

A color depth of 48-bit is fairly new, and it's just like 24-bit color except it uses 16 rather than 8 bits to define each of the three channels: Red, Green, and Blue. It does not have an Alpha channel bit. Forty-eight-bit color depth is not really necessary, because the human eye cannot detect the small differences it introduces. Of the graphics formats that PowerPoint supports, only PNG and TIFF support 48-bit color depth.

Normally, you should not decrease the color depth of a photo to less than 24-bit unless there is a major issue with lack of disk space that you cannot resolve any other way. To decrease the color depth, you would need to open the graphic file in a third-party image-editing program, and use the command in that program for decreasing the number of colors. Before going through that, try compressing the images in the presentation (see the section "Compressing Images" later in the chapter) to see if that solves the problem.

File format

Many scanners scan in JPEG format by default, but most also support TIF, and some also support other formats. Images you acquire from a digital camera are almost always JPEG. Images from other sources may be any of dozens of graphics formats, including PCX, BMP, GIF, or PNG.

Different graphic formats can vary tremendously in the size and quality of the image they produce. The main differentiators between formats are the color depth they support and the type of compression they use (which determines the file size).

Remember earlier how I explained that each pixel in a 24-bit image requires 3 bytes? (That's derived by dividing 24 by 8 because there are 8 bits in a byte.) Then you multiply that by the height, and then by the width, to determine the image size? Well, that formula was not completely accurate because it does not include compression. *Compression* is an algorithm (basically a math formula) that decreases the amount of space that the file takes up on the disk by storing the data about the pixels more compactly. A file format will have one of these three states in regard to compression:

- **No compression:** The image is not compressed.
- **Lossless compression:** The image is compressed, but the algorithm for doing so does not throw out any pixels so there is no loss of image quality when you resize the image.
- **Lossy compression:** The image is compressed by recording less data about the pixels, so that when you resize the image there may be a loss of image quality.

Table 24-2 provides a brief guide to some of the most common graphics formats. Generally speaking, for most onscreen presentations JPEG should be your preferred choice for graphics because it is compact and Web-accessible (although PNG is also a good choice and uses lossless compression).

TABLE 24-2

Popular Graphics Formats

Extension	Pronunciation	Compression	Notes
JPEG or JPG	"Jay-peg"	Yes	Stands for Joint Photographic Experts Group. Very small image size. Uses lossy compression. Common on the Web. Up to 24-bit.
GIF	"gif" or "jif"	Yes	Stands for Graphic Interchange Format. Limited to 8-bit (256 color). Uses proprietary compression algorithm. Allows animated graphics, which are useful on the Web. Color depth limitation makes this format unsuitable for photos.
PNG	"ping"	Yes	Stands for Portable Network Graphic. An improvement on GIF. Up to 48-bit color depth. Lossless compression, but smaller file sizes than TIF. Public domain format.
BMP	"B-M-P" or "bump" or "bitmap"	No	Default image type for Windows XP. Up to 24-bit color. Used for some Windows wallpaper and other Windows graphics.
PCX	"P-C-X"	Yes	There are three versions: 0, 2, and 5. Use version 5 for 24-bit support. Originally introduced by a company called ZSoft; sometimes called ZSoft Paintbrush format.
TIF or TIFF	"tiff"	Optional	Stands for Tagged Image Format. Supported by most scanners and some digital cameras. Up to 48-bit color. Uses lossless compression. Large file size but high quality.

TIP **If you are not sure what format you will eventually use for an image, scan it in TIF format and keep the TIF copy on your hard disk. You can always save a copy in JPEG or other formats when you need them for specific projects. The TIF format's compression is lossless, so it results in a high-quality image.**

Importing Image Files into PowerPoint

Most of the choices you make regarding a raster image's resolution, color depth, and file type are done outside of PowerPoint. Consequently, by the time you're ready to put them into PowerPoint, the hard part is over.

Assuming you have already acquired the image, use the following steps to insert it into PowerPoint.

1. **Display the slide on which you want to place the image.**
2. **If the slide has a content placeholder for Insert Picture from File, as in Figure 24-38, click it.** Otherwise, click Picture on the Insert tab. The Insert Picture dialog box opens.

FIGURE 24-38

You can insert a picture by using the Insert Picture from File content placeholder icon.

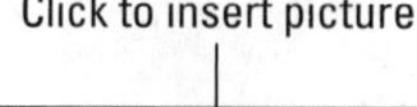

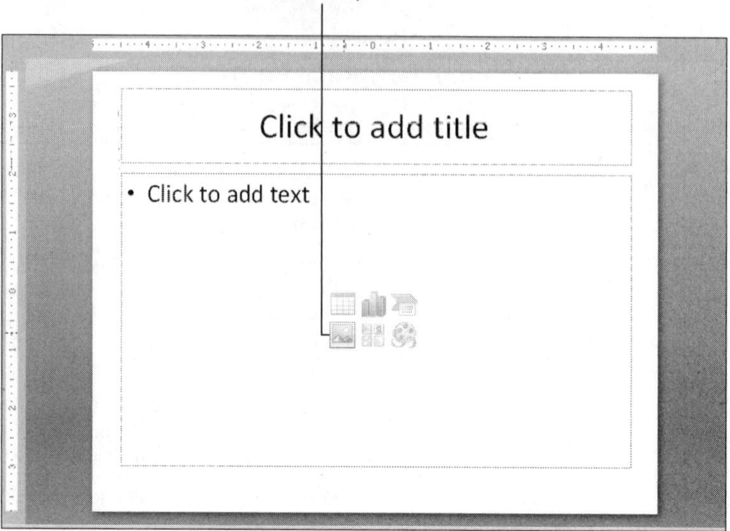

3. **Select the picture to import.** See Figure 24-39. You can switch the view by using the View (or Views) button in the dialog box to see thumbnails or details if either is effective in helping you determine which file is which.
4. **Click Insert.** The picture is inserted.

FIGURE 24-39

Select the picture to be inserted.

TIP If you have a lot of graphics in different formats, consider narrowing down the list that appears by selecting a specific file type from the file type list. By default it is set to All Pictures, as in Figure 24-39.

Linking to a graphic file

If you have a sharp eye, you may have noticed that the Insert button in Figure 24-5 has a drop-down list associated with it. That list has these choices:

- **Insert:** The default, inserts the graphic but maintains no connection.
- **Link to File:** Creates an OLE link to the file, but does not maintain a local copy of it in PowerPoint.
- **Insert and Link:** Creates a link to the file, and also inserts a local copy of its current state, so if the linked copy is not available in the future, the local copy will still appear.

Use Link to File whenever you want to insert a pointer rather than the original. When the presentation opens, it pulls in the graphic from the disk. If the graphic is not available, it displays an empty frame with a red X in the corner in the graphic's place. Using Link to File keeps the size of the original PowerPoint file very small because it doesn't actually contain the graphics — only links to them. However, if you move or delete the graphic, PowerPoint won't be able to find it anymore.

The important thing to know about this link in the Link to File feature is that it is not the same thing as an OLE link. This is not a dynamic link that you can manage. It is a much simpler link and much less flexible. You can't change the file location to which it is linked, for example; if the location of the graphic changes, you must delete it from PowerPoint and reinsert it.

TIP If you are building a graphic-heavy presentation on an older computer, you might find that it takes a long time to move between slides and for each graphic to appear. You can take some of the hassle away by using Link to File instead of inserting the graphics. Then temporarily move the graphic files to a subfolder so PowerPoint can't find them. It displays the placeholders for the graphics on the appropriate slides, and the presentation file is much faster to page through and edit. Then when you are ready to finish up, close PowerPoint and move the graphics files back to their original locations so PowerPoint can find them again when you reopen the presentation file.

Acquiring images from a scanner

If you have a compatible scanner attached to your PC, you can scan a picture directly into the Clip Organizer (which you learned about earlier in this chapter), and from there import it into PowerPoint. You can also use the scanner's interface from outside of PowerPoint (and outside of the Clip Organizer).

NOTE Earlier versions of PowerPoint had direct access to the Scanner and Camera Wizard in Windows from the Insert menu, but PowerPoint 2007 does not have this. The only way to access the Scanner and Camera Wizard in Office 2007 applications is via the Clip Organizer.

To scan an image from the Clip Organizer, follow these steps:

1. **On the Insert tab, click Clip Art.** The Clip Art task pane opens.
2. **Click Organize Clips.** The Clip Organizer window opens.
3. **Choose File ⇨ Add Clips to Organizer ⇨ From Scanner or Camera.** The Insert Picture from Scanner or Camera dialog box opens.
4. **Choose the scanner from the Device list, as shown in Figure 24-40.**

FIGURE 24-40

Select the device and the basic properties.

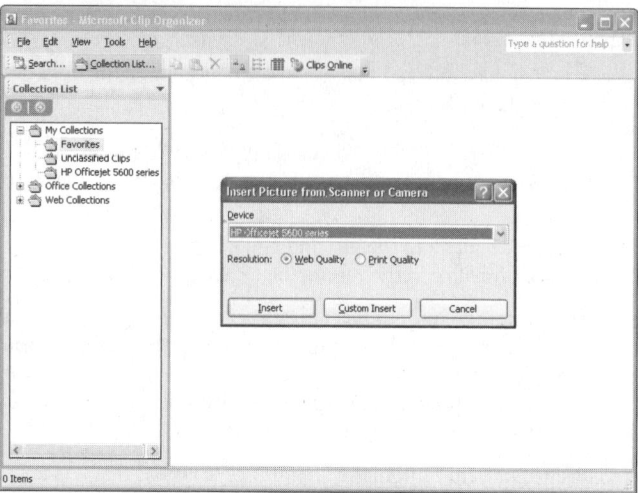

5. **Choose a resolution: Web (low) or Print (high).** Lower resolution means smaller file size and fewer pixels overall comprising the image. Low resolution is the best choice for onscreen presentations.
6. **Click Insert to scan with the default settings, or click Custom Insert, make changes to the settings, and click Scan.**

The Custom Insert option opens the full controls for the scanner. They vary a bit depending on the model; the box for an HP scanner is shown in Figure 24-41.

FIGURE 24-41

Custom insert options are available when scanning into the Clip Organizer.

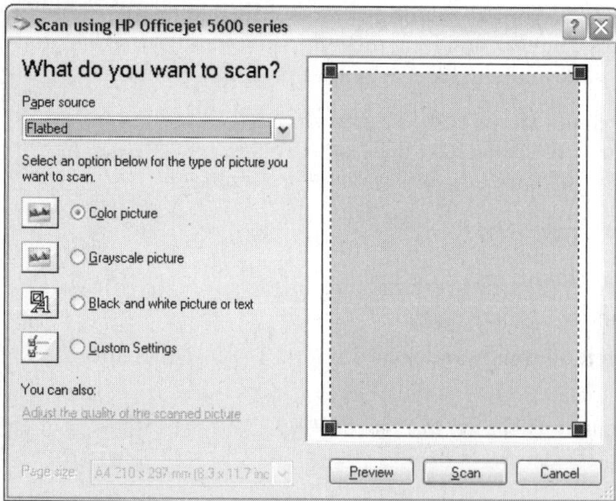

Here are some of the things you can do here:

- **Choose a scanning mode:** Color Picture, Grayscale Picture, or Black and White Picture or Text. This option determines the color depth. Color is full 24-bit color. Grayscale is 256 shades of gray (8-bit, single color). Black and white is single-bit scanning that produces an extremely small file similar to a fax.
- **Preview the scan:** Click the Preview button to do a test scan and then drag the black squares in the preview area to adjust what portion of the image is saved when you do the "real scan" by clicking the Scan button.
- **Choose a paper source:** If your scanner has a document feeder, you have that choice on the Paper Source drop-down list in addition to Flatbed (the default).
- **Adjust the resolution, brightness, and contrast:** Click the Adjust the Quality of the Scanned Picture hyperlink to open an Advanced Properties dialog box. From there you can drag the Brightness and Contrast sliders and choose a resolution setting (dots per inch). The default is 150 dpi.

TIP **The default setting of 150 dpi is appropriate in most cases where you are using the image at approximately the same size as the original, but if you are concerned about file size, you can reduce this to 100 dpi without a noticeable loss of image quality onscreen. If you plan on using the image at a large size, like full screen, and the image was originally a very small hard copy, then scan at a higher resolution.**

Acquiring images from a digital camera

There are a lot of ways to transfer images from a digital camera in Windows XP or Windows Vista. You can connect most cameras to the PC via a USB port and treat them as a removable drive, from which you can drag and drop pictures into a folder on your hard disk. You can also remove the memory card from the camera and use a card reader, and in some cases you can even insert a memory card into a printer and print the images directly.

With all of these methods available, inserting directly from the camera into the Clip Organizer is probably not your first choice. However, if you want to try it, use the same method as with the scanner. Then just follow the prompts to select and insert the picture.

NOTE **When you hear digital cameras referred to in *megapixel*, it means a million pixels in total — the height multiplied by the width. For example, a 1,152 by 864-pixel image is approximately 1 megapixel (995,328 pixels, to be exact). High-end cameras are in the 8-megapixel or more range these days, which is overkill for use in a PowerPoint show. Such cameras have settings you can change that control the image size, though, so you can reduce the image size on the camera itself.**

Sizing and Cropping Photos

After placing a photo on a slide, you will probably need to adjust its size, and/or crop it, to make it fit in the allotted space the way you want it. The following sections explain these techniques.

Sizing a photo

Sizing a photo is just like sizing any other object. Drag its selection handles. Drag a corner to maintain the aspect ratio, or drag a side to distort it. (Distorting a photo is seldom a good idea, though, unless you're after some weird funhouse effect.)

You can also specify an exact size for a photo the same as with drawn objects. Right-click the photo and choose Size and Position to set a size in the Size and Position dialog box (see Figure 24-42). Alternatively, you can display the Format tab, and then use the Height and Width boxes in the Size group.

FIGURE 24-42

Size a photo via either the dialog box or the Format tab.

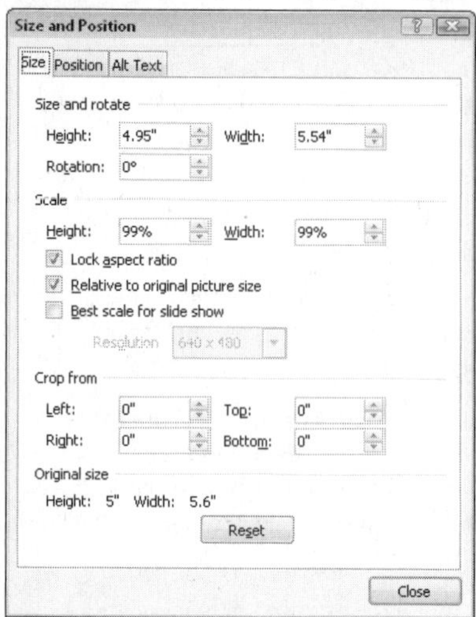

The most straightforward way to specify the size is in inches in the Height and Width boxes, either in the dialog box or on the tab. These measurements correspond to the markers on the onscreen ruler in Normal view. The size of a slide varies depending on how you have it set up (by using the Page Setup tab), but an average slide size is 10 inches wide by 7.5 inches tall. You can also size the photo using the Scale controls in the Size and Position dialog box, in which you adjust the size based on a percentage of the original size.

NOTE **The Scale is based on the original size, not the current size. So, for example, if you set the Height and Width to 50%, close the dialog box, and then reopen it and set them each to 75%, the net result will be 75% of the original, not 75% of the 50%. You can override this by deselecting the Relative to Original Picture Size checkbox, however (see Figure 24-8).**

If you are setting up a presentation for the primary purpose of showing full-screen graphics, you can use the Best Scale for Slide Show checkbox (see Figure 24-8). This enables you to choose a screen resolution, such as 640x480 or 800x600, and size the pictures so that they will show to the best advantage in that resolution. Choose the resolution that corresponds to the display setting on the PC on which you will show the presentation. To determine what the resolution is on the PC, right-click the Windows desktop, choose Properties, and then look up the resolution under Settings.

TIP **When possible, develop your presentation at the same Windows screen resolution as the PC on which you present the show. Many digital projectors display at 1024 x 768.**

Cropping a photo

Cropping is for those times when you want only a part of the image. For example, you might have a great photo of a person or animal, but there is extraneous detail around it, as shown in Figure 24-43. You can crop away all but the important object in the image with a cropping tool.

FIGURE 24-43

This picture can benefit from cropping

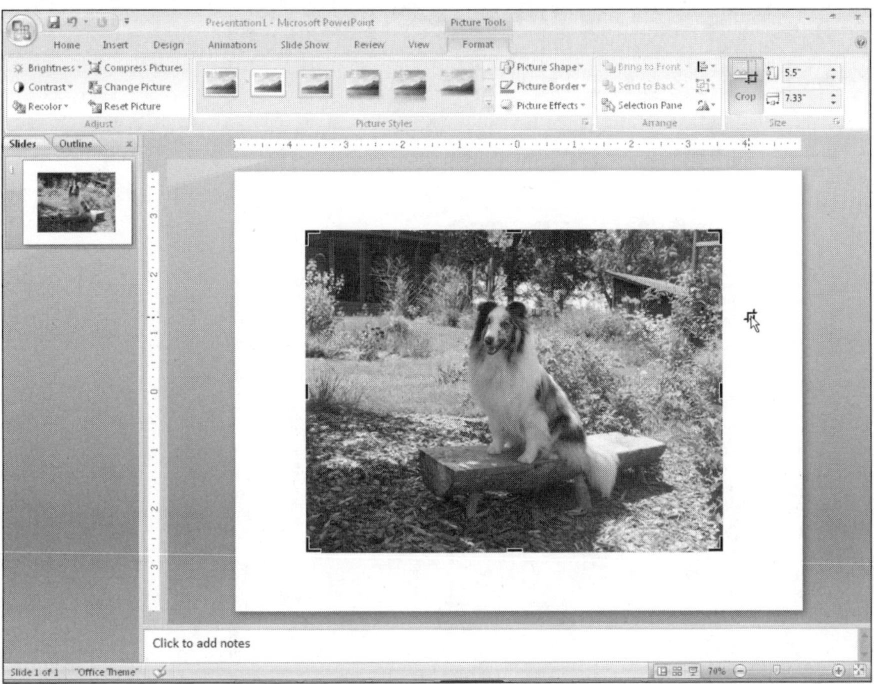

TIP Here's something important to know: Cropping and sizing a picture in PowerPoint does not reduce the overall size of the PowerPoint presentation file. When you insert a picture, PowerPoint stores the whole thing at its original size and continues to store it that way regardless of any manipulations you perform on it within PowerPoint. That's why it's recommended throughout this chapter that you do any editing of the photo in a third-party image program before you import it into PowerPoint. However, there's a work-around. If you use the Compress Pictures option (covered later in this chapter), it discards any cropped portions of the images. That means the file size decreases with the cropping, and that you can't reverse the cropping later.

You can crop two sides at once by cropping at the corner of the image, or crop each side individually by cropping at the sides. To crop an image, do the following:

1. **Select the image, so the Picture Tools Format tab becomes available.**
2. **Click the Crop button on the Picture Tools Format tab.** Your mouse pointer changes to a cropping tool and crop marks appear on the picture (see Figure 24-43).
3. **Position the pointer over a side handle of the image frame, on a side where you want to cut some of the image off.**
4. **Drag the handle inward toward the center of the image until only the part of the image you want to keep is inside the thin line.**
5. **Repeat Steps 3 and 4 for each side.** Then click the Crop button again, or press Esc, to turn cropping off.

Figure 24-44 shows the result of cropping the image from Figure 24-43.

FIGURE 24-44

The picture has been improved by cropping and resizing it.

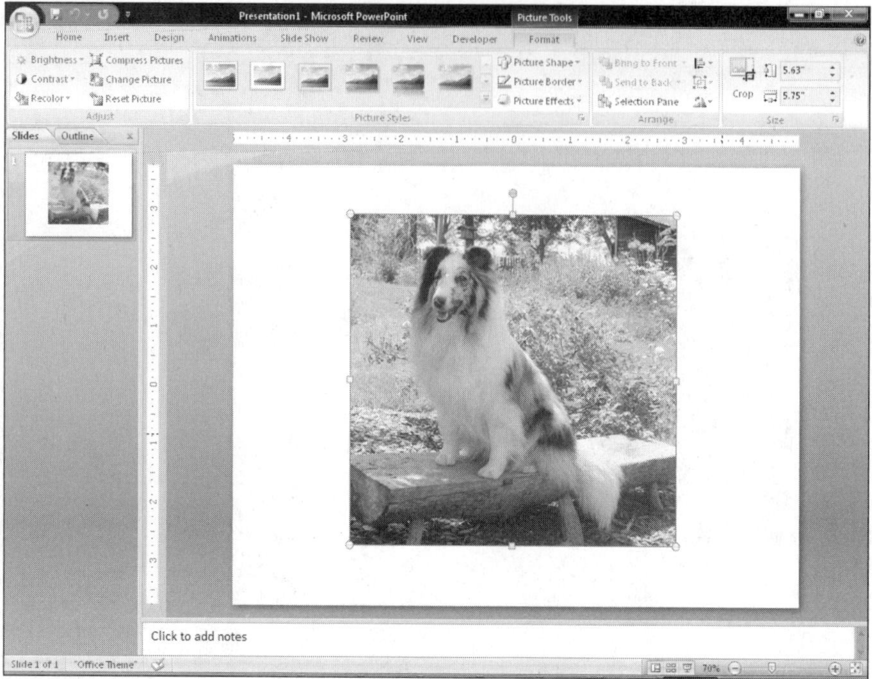

To undo a crop, reenter cropping mode by clicking the Crop button again, and then drag the side(s) back outward again. Or you can simply reset the photo, as described in the following section.

You can also crop "by the numbers" with the Crop settings in the Size and Position dialog box (see Figure 24-42).

CAUTION **You cannot uncrop after compressing the picture (assuming you use the default compression options that include deleting cropped areas of pictures). By default, saving compresses and makes crops permanent, so be sure to undo any unwanted cropping before you save.**

Resetting a photo

Once the picture is in PowerPoint, any manipulations you do to it are strictly on the surface. It changes how the picture appears on the slide, but it doesn't change how the picture is stored in PowerPoint. Consequently you can reset the picture back to its original settings at any time (provided you have not compressed the picture). This resetting also clears any changes you make to the image's size, contrast, and brightness (which are discussed in the next section).

Resetting a photo is different depending on what aspects of it you want to reset:

- If you want to reset its cropping and sizing, on the Picture Tools Format tab, click the dialog box launcher in the Size group and click the Reset button in the Size and Position dialog box.
- If you want to reset its formatting, on the Picture Tools Format tab, click the Reset Picture button in the Adjust group.

Compressing Images

Having an image that is too large (that is, too high a dpi) is not a problem quality-wise. You can resize it in PowerPoint to make it as small as you like; just drag its selection handles. There will be no loss of quality as it gets smaller. However, as mentioned earlier in the chapter, having a picture that is much larger than necessary can increase the overall size of the PowerPoint file, which can become problematic if you plan to distribute the presentation on floppy disk or over the Internet.

To avoid problems with overly large graphic files, you can compress the images to reduce their resolution and remove any cropped portions. You can do this from within PowerPoint or with a third-party utility.

Reducing resolution and compressing images in PowerPoint

PowerPoint offers an image compression utility that compresses all of the pictures in the presentation in a single step and reduces their resolution to the amount needed for the type of output you specify (e-mail, Screen, or Print). To reduce resolution and compress images, do the following:

1. **Click a picture, so that the Format tab appears.**
2. **Click the Compress Pictures button.** The Compress Pictures dialog box appears, as shown in Figure 24-45).

FIGURE 24-45

Click OK to compress with the default settings or click Options to fine-tune.

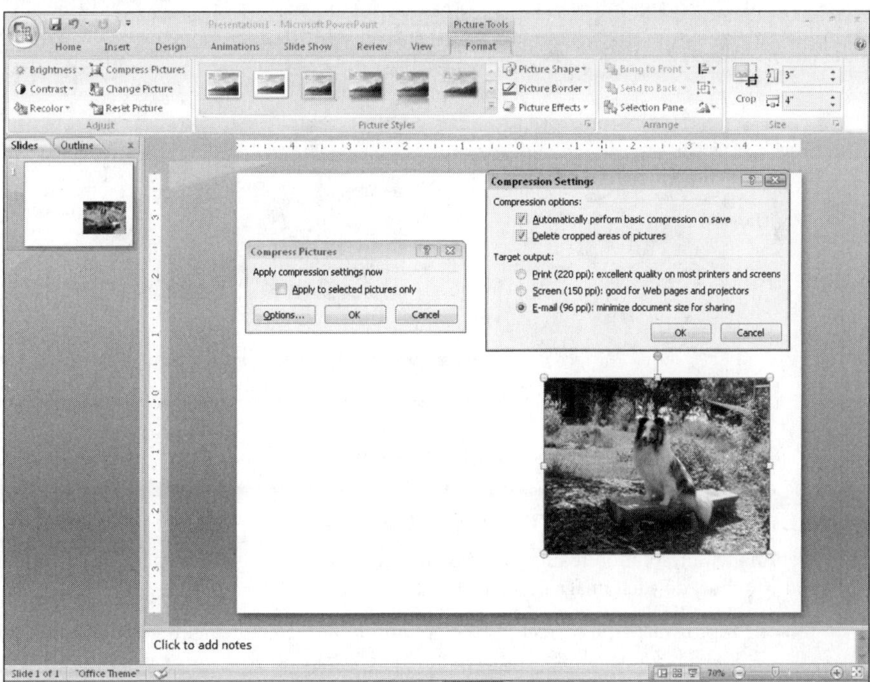

3. **(Optional) If you do not want to compress all of the pictures, mark the Apply to Selected Pictures Only checkbox.**
4. **(Optional) Click the Options button to display the Compression Settings dialog box, as shown in Figure 24-46, and then change any of these options and click OK.**
   - **Automatically Perform Basic Compression on Save:** This automatically compresses any images in your file when you save the file.
   - **Delete Cropped Areas of Pictures:** This makes any cropping you've done permanent.
   - **Target Output:** Choose a resolution to which you want to reduce the picture(s): Print, Screen, or E-mail.

FIGURE 24-46

Adjust compression settings here.

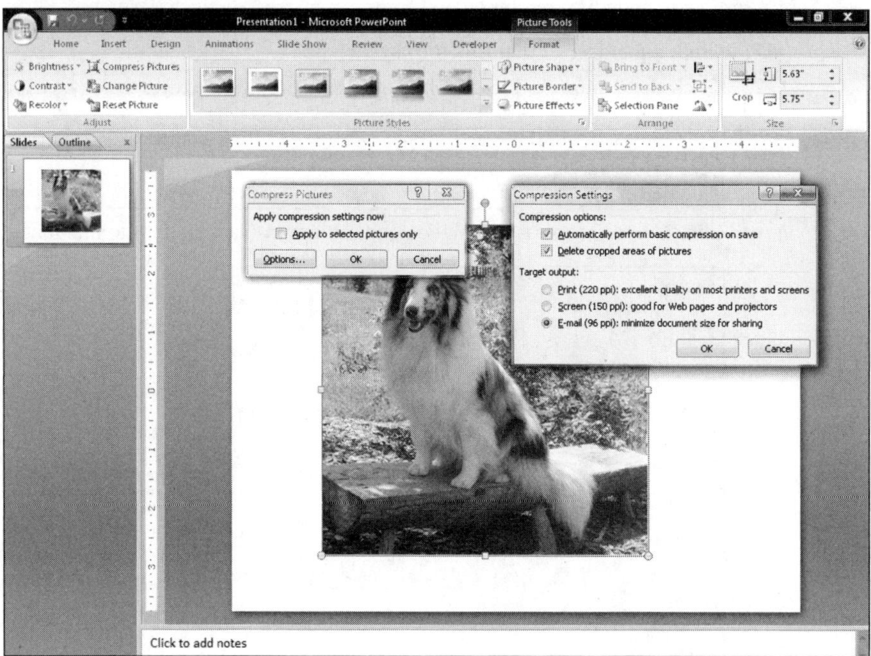

5. **Click OK to perform the compression.**

Reducing resolution with a third-party utility

Working with resolution reduction from an image-editing program is somewhat of a trial-and-error process, and you must do each image separately.

You can approximate the correct resolution by simply "doing the math." For example, suppose you have a 10" x 7.5" slide. Your desktop display is set to 800x600. So your image needs to be 800 pixels wide to fill the slide. Your image is a 5" x 3" image, so if you set it to 200 dpi, that gives you 1,000 pixels, which is a little larger than you need but in the ballpark.

Summary

In this chapter, you learned how to create SmartArt diagrams, and use clip art and pictures into your presentation. You learned how to select a diagram type, how to rearrange shapes in a diagram, and how to apply formatting. You learned how to insert and manage clip art, how to organize your clips in the Clip Organizer, and how to find more clips online. The chapter taught you about the technical specs for graphics that determine their file size, quality, and flexibility, and you learned how to insert them into your presentations. You will probably find lots of creative uses for diagrams, clip art, and pictures now that you know how you can make the most of them!

In the next chapter, you'll learn how to make your presentation even more lively and useful by adding animations and transitions, and by creating the support materials that you'll use for presenting.

Chapter 25

Building Animation Effects, Transitions, and Support Materials

You invest hard work in creating presentation content so that you can deliver your important message to an audience. When you are delivering a live presentation — also called a slide show — you need to make sure that your speaking manner and the presentation have enough zip to hold the audience members' interest. This chapter teaches you how to add that zip with animation effects and transitions, and how to print the support materials you'll need to ensure you can give a great presentation.

IN THIS CHAPTER

Understanding Animation and Transitions

In PowerPoint, *animation* is the way that individual objects enter or exit a slide. On a slide with no animation, all of the objects on the slide simply appear at the same time when you display it. (Boring, eh?) However, you can apply animation to the slide so that the bullet points fly in from the left, one at a time, and the graphic drops down from the top afterward.

A *transition* is another kind of animation. A transition refers to the entry or exit of the entire slide, rather than of an individual object on the slide.

Here are some ideas for using animation effectively in your presentations:

- Animate parts of a chart so that the data appears one series at a time. This technique works well if you want to talk about each series separately.
- Set up questions and answers on a slide so that the question appears first, and then, when you click the question, the answer appears.
- Dim each bullet point when the next one comes into view, so that you are, in effect, highlighting the current one.

- Make an object appear and then disappear. For example, you might have an image of a lightning bolt that flashes on the slide for one second and then disappears, or a picture of a racecar that drives onto the slide from the left and then immediately drives out of sight to the right.
- Rearrange the order in which objects appear on the slide. For example, you could make numbered points appear from the bottom up for a Top Ten list.

Assigning Transitions to Slides

Transitions determine how you get from slide A to slide B. Back in the old slide projector days, there was only one transition: the old slide was pushed out, and the new slide dropped into place. However, with a computerized presentation, you can choose from all kinds of fun transitions, including wipes, blinds, fly-ins, and much more. These transitions are almost exactly like the animations, except that they apply to the whole slide (or at least the background — the base part of the slide — if the slide's objects are separately animated).

NOTE **The transition effect for a slide refers to how the slide enters, and not how it exits. As a result, if you want to assign a particular transition while moving from slide 1 to slide 2, you would assign the transition effect to slide 2.**

The individual transitions are hard to describe in words; it is best if you just view them onscreen to understand what each one does. You should try out several transitions before making your final selection.

Automatic versus manual transitions

Generally speaking, if there is a live person controlling and presenting the show, transitions should be manual. With manual transitions, the presenter must click the mouse to move to the next slide, just like clicking the advance button on a 35mm slide projector. This might sound distracting, but it helps the speaker to maintain control of the show. If someone in the audience asks a question or wants to make a comment, the show does not continue on blindly, but pauses to accommodate the delay.

However, if you are preparing a self-running presentation, such as for a kiosk, automatic transitions are a virtual necessity. You can also set automatic timings for slides without recording any narration.

Setting up automatic transition timings

By default, PowerPoint uses manual transitions, and so you must specifically set up automatic timings if you want them. For automatic timings, you can either assign the same transition time to all slides, or individual times for each slide. The most effective method of assigning individual times for each slide is to rehearse the timings. This is covered in the next section.

CAUTION **You will probably want to assign automatic transitions to either all or none of the slides in the presentation, but not a mixture of the two. This is because mixed transition times can cause confusion, when some of the slides automatically advance and others do not. However, there may be situations where you need to assign different timings and effects to the various slides' transitions.**

To assign an automatic transition to an individual slide, follow these steps:

1. **View or select the slide in Normal or Slide Sorter view.** If you use Slide Sorter view, you can more easily select multiple slides to which you can apply the transition.
2. **On the Animations tab, in the Transition to This Slide group, select the Automatically After checkbox.**
3. **In the Automatically After text box, type a transition time, in seconds, to replace the default time, as shown in Figure 25-1.**

FIGURE 25-1

You can specify automatic transition times on the Animations tab.

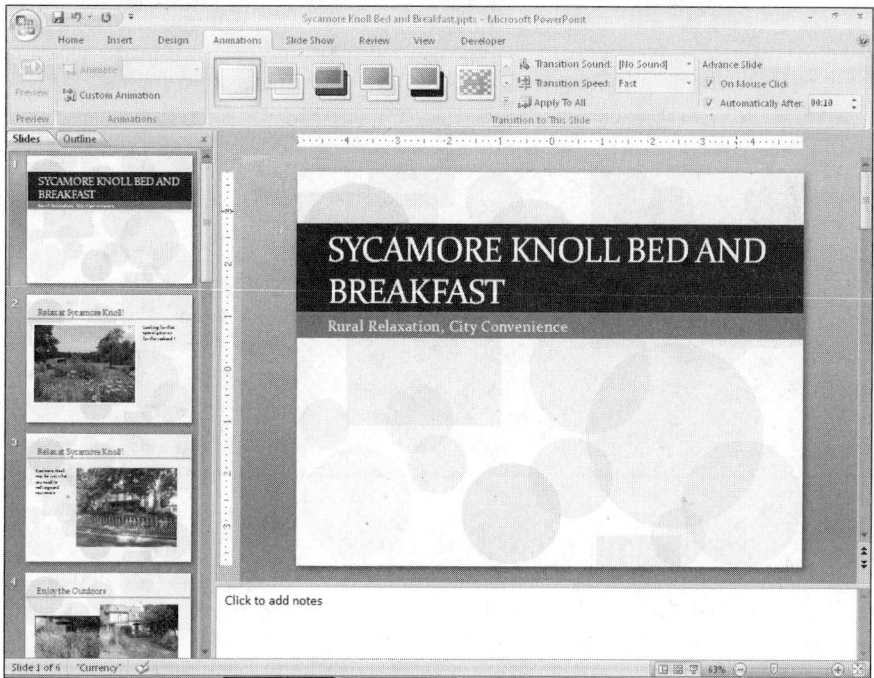

4. **(Optional) To apply this setting to all slides in the presentation, click Apply to All.**

It is perfectly okay to leave the On Mouse Click checkbox selected, even if you choose automatic transitions — in fact, this is a good idea. There may be times when you want to manually advance to the next slide before the automatic transition time has elapsed, and leaving this option selected allows you to do so.

It does not matter what transition you select. Even if you select No Transition, transitions will still occur — that is, one slide will change to another. There will simply be no special effect.

Transition timings appear beneath each slide in Slide Sorter view, as shown in Figure 25-2.

FIGURE 25-2

You can view slide timings in Slide Sorter view.

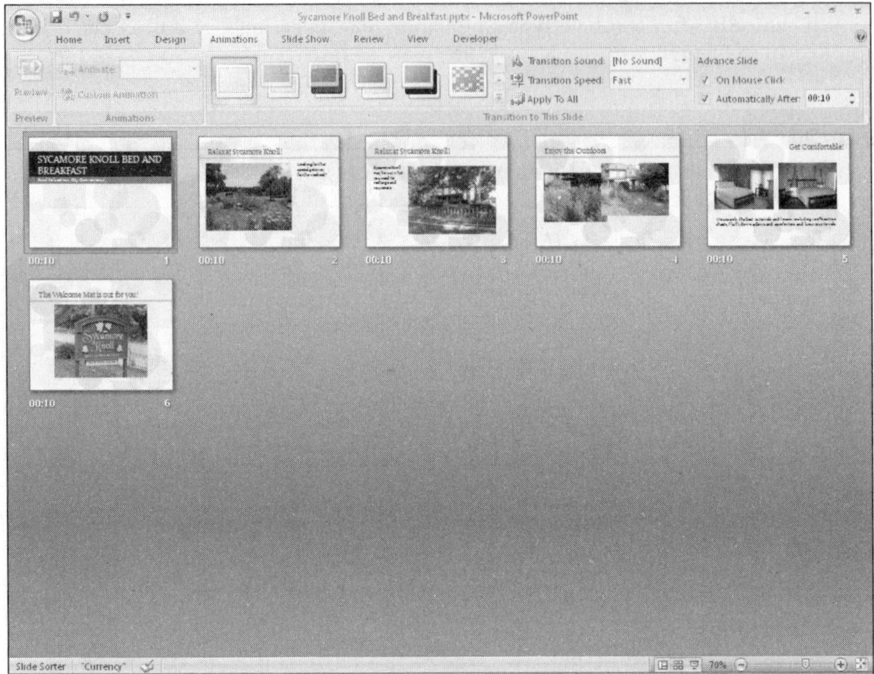

Rehearsing and recording timings

The trouble with setting the same automatic timings for all slides is that not all slides deserve or need equal time onscreen. For example, some slides may have more text than others, or more complex concepts to grasp. To allow for the differences, you can manually set the timings for each slide, as described in the preceding section. However, another way is to use the Rehearse Timings feature to run through your presentation in real time, and then to allow PowerPoint to set the timings for you, based on that rehearsal.

NOTE **When you set timings with the Rehearse Timings feature, PowerPoint ignores any hidden slides. If you later unhide these slides, they are set to advance automatically. You need to individually assign them an Automatically After transition time, as described in the preceding section.**

To set transition timings with the Rehearse Timings feature, follow these steps:

1. **On the Slide Show tab, click Rehearse Timings.** The slide show starts with the Rehearsal toolbar in the upper-left corner, as shown in Figure 25-3.

FIGURE 25-3

Use the Rehearsal toolbar to set timings for automatic transitions.

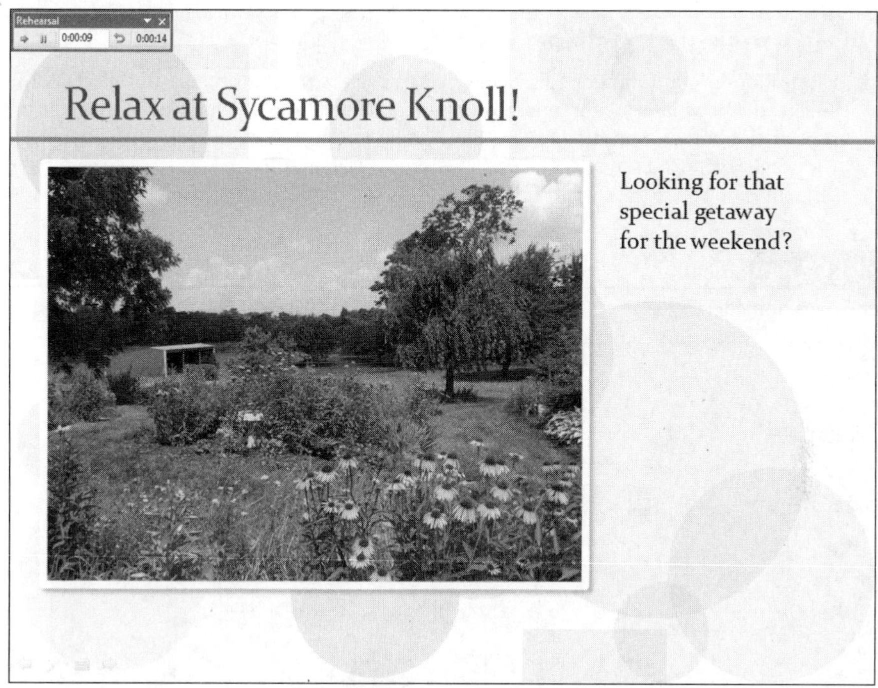

2. **Click through the presentation, displaying each slide for as long as you want it to appear in the actual show.** To move to the next slide, you can click the slide, click the Next button in the Rehearsal toolbar (right-pointing arrow), or press Page Down.

   When setting timings, it may help to read the text on the slide, slowly and out loud, to simulate how an audience member who reads slowly would proceed. When you have read all of the text on the slide, pause for one or two more seconds and then advance. If you need to pause the rehearsal at any time, click the Pause button. When you are ready to resume, click the Pause button again.

   If you make a mistake on the timing for a slide, click the Repeat button to begin timing this slide again from 00:00.

TIP If you want a slide to display for a fairly long time, such as 30 seconds or more, you might find it faster to enter the desired time in the Current Slide Timing text box on the Rehearsal toolbar, rather than waiting the full amount of time before advancing. To do this, click in the text box, type the desired time, and press Tab. You must press the Tab key after entering the time — do not click the Next button — or PowerPoint will not apply your change.

3. **When you reach the final slide, a dialog box appears, asking whether you want to keep the new slide timings. Click Yes.**

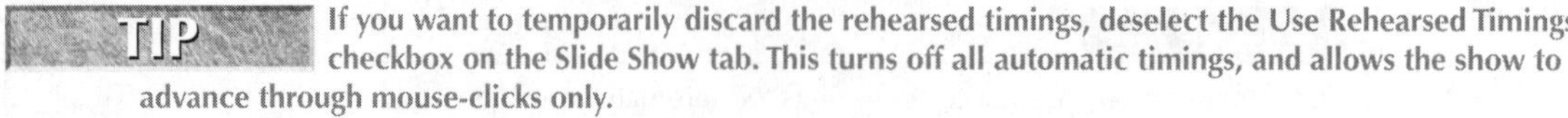

If you want to temporarily discard the rehearsed timings, deselect the Use Rehearsed Timings checkbox on the Slide Show tab. This turns off all automatic timings, and allows the show to advance through mouse-clicks only.

Choosing transition effects

Transitions occur from slide to slide, even if you select No Transition as the effect. With the No Transition effect, the previous slide disappears and the next one appears. If you want a different transition, you must specify it from the Transition to This Slide group in the Animations tab. A gallery of transition effects appears, where you can select an effect, as shown in Figure 25-4. You can also select a sound and change the transition speed.

FIGURE 25-4

Select a transition effect.

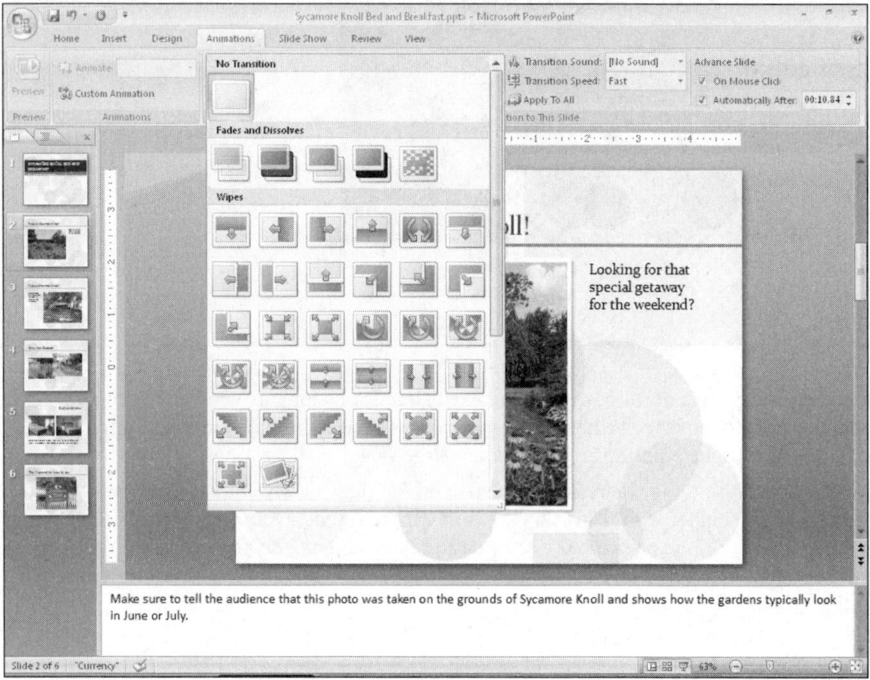

To apply a transition effect to a slide, follow these steps:

1. **Select and display the slide or slides that you want to affect.**
2. **On the Animations tab, open the gallery of effects in the Transition to This Slide group and click the one that you want, or click No Transition to turn off any existing transition effect.** The gallery of effects is shown in Figure 25-4.
3. **(Optional) Open the Transition Speed drop-down list and select a transition speed.**

4. **(Optional) Open the Transition Sound drop-down list and select a transition sound.**
5. **(Optional) Click Apply to All to make the same transition apply to all slides in the presentation, and not just the selected slides.**

In the Transition Sound menu, shown in Figure 25-5, you can choose from among PowerPoint's default sound collection for the slide transition, or you can choose any of the following:

- **No Sound:** Does not assign a sound to the transition.
- **Stop Previous Sound:** Stops any sound that is already playing. This usually applies where the previous sound was very long and was not finished when you moved on to the next slide, or in cases where you used the Loop Until Next Sound transition (see below).
- **Other Sound:** Opens a dialog box from which you can select another sound file stored on your system.
- **Loop Until Next Sound:** An on/off toggle that sets whatever sound you select to loop continuously either until another sound is triggered or until a slide appears that has Stop Previous Sound set for its transition.

FIGURE 25-5

You can select a transition sound.

Using an Animation Preset

PowerPoint 2007 has very few animation presets compared to earlier versions. In fact, there are just three: Fade, Wipe, and Fly In. Each preset has two options: for the text to enter the slide all at once or by paragraphs. These presets provide quick and convenient shortcuts to common effects. To apply an animation preset, follow these steps:

1. **Select the text box or other object to which you want the animation preset to apply.**
2. **On the Animations tab, open the Animate drop-down list and select a preset, as shown in Figure 25-6.**

FIGURE 25-6

You can select an animation preset.

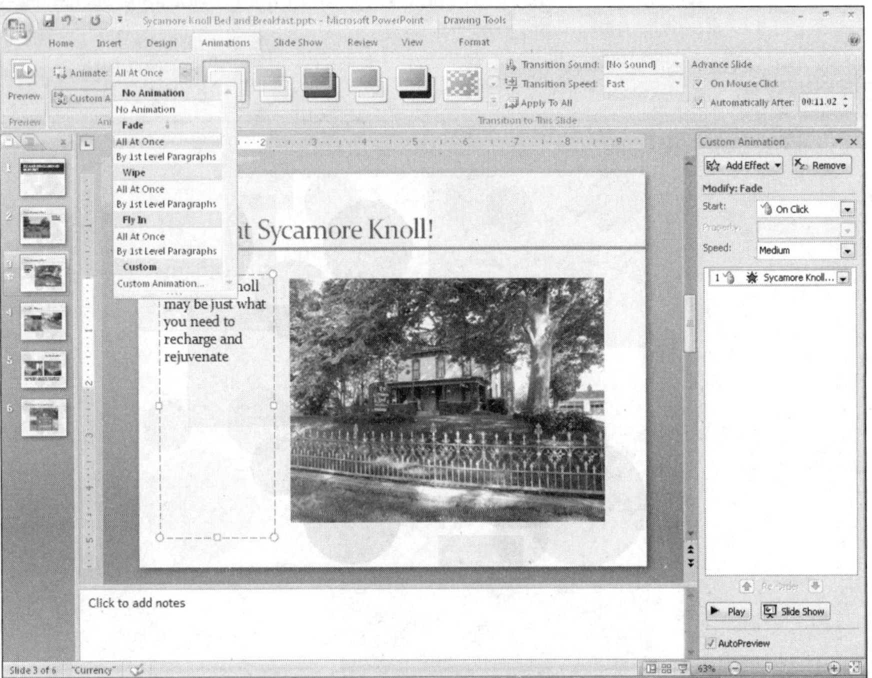

The When and How of Handouts

If you are presenting a live show, the centerpiece of your presentation is your slides. Whether you show them using a computer screen, a slide projector, or an overhead projector, the slides — combined with your own dazzling personality — make the biggest impact. But if you rely on your audience to remember everything you say, you may be disappointed. With handouts, the audience members can follow along with you during the show and even take their own notes. They can then take the handouts home with them to review the information again later.

You probably want a different set of support materials for yourself than you want for the audience. Support materials designed for the speaker's use are called speaker notes. In addition to small printouts of the slides, the speaker notes contain any extra notes or background information that you think you may need to jog your memory as you speak. Some people get very nervous when they speak in front of a crowd; speaker notes can remind you of the joke you wanted to open with or the exact figures behind a particular pie chart.

Presentation professionals are divided about how and when to use handouts most effectively. Here are some of the many conflicting viewpoints. I can't say who is right or wrong, but each of these statements brings up issues that you should consider. The bottom line is that each of them is an opinion on how much power and credit to give to the audience; your answer may vary depending on the audience you are addressing.

- **You should give handouts at the beginning of the presentation. The audience can absorb the information better if they can follow along on paper.**

  This approach makes a lot of sense. Research has proven that people absorb more facts if presented with them in more than one medium. This approach also gives your audience free will; they can listen to you or not, and they still have the information. It's their choice, and this can be extremely scary for less-confident speakers. It's not just a speaker confidence issue in some cases, however. If you plan to give a lot of extra information in your speech that's not on the handouts, people might miss it if you distribute the handouts at the beginning because they're reading ahead.

- **You shouldn't give the audience handouts because they won't pay as close attention to your speech if they know that the information is already written down for them.**

  This philosophy falls at the other end of the spectrum. It gives the audience the least power and shows the least confidence in their ability to pay attention to you in the presence of a distraction (handouts). If you truly don't trust your audience to be professional and listen, this approach may be your best option. However, don't let insecurity as a speaker drive you prematurely to this conclusion. The fact is that people won't take away as much knowledge about the topic without handouts as they would if you provide handouts. So, ask yourself if your ultimate goal is to fill the audience with knowledge or to make them pay attention to you.

- **You should give handouts at the end of the presentation so that people will have the information to take home but not be distracted during the speech.**

  This approach attempts to solve the dilemma with compromise. The trouble with it, as with all compromises, is that it does an incomplete job from both angles. Because audience members can't follow along on the handouts during the presentation, they miss the opportunity to jot notes on the handouts. And because the audience knows that handouts are coming, they might nod off and miss something important. The other problem is that if you don't clearly tell people that handouts are coming later, some people spend the entire presentation frantically copying down each slide on their own notepaper.

Creating Handouts

To create handouts, you simply decide on a layout (a number of slides per page) and then choose that layout from the Print dialog box as you print. No muss, no fuss! If you want to get more involved, you can edit the layout in Handout Master view before printing.

Choosing a layout

Assuming you have decided that handouts are appropriate for your speech, you must decide on the format for them. You have a choice of one, two, three, four, six, or nine slides per page.

- 1: Places a single slide vertically and horizontally "centered" on the page.
- 2: Prints two big slides on each page. This layout is good for slides that have a lot of fine print and small details or for situations where you are not confident that the reproduction quality will be good. There is nothing more frustrating for an audience than not being able to read the handouts!
- 3: Makes the slides much smaller — less than one-half the size of the ones in the two-slide layout. But you get a nice bonus with this layout: lines to the side of each slide for note-taking. This layout works well for presentations where the slides are big and simple, and the speaker is providing a lot of extra information that isn't on the slides. The audience members can write the extra information in the note-taking space provided.
- 4: Uses the same size slides as the three-slide layout, but they are spaced out two-by-two without note-taking lines. However, there is still plenty of room above and below each slide, so the audience members still have lots of room to take notes.
- 6: Uses slides the same size as the three-slide and four-slide layouts, but crams more slides on the page at the expense of note-taking space. This layout is good for presentation with big, simple slides where the audience does not need to take notes. If you are not sure if the audience will benefit at all from handouts being distributed, consider whether this layout would be a good compromise. This format also saves paper, which might be an issue if you need to make hundreds of copies.
- 9: Makes the slides very tiny, almost like a Slide Sorter view, so that you can see nine at a time. This layout makes them very hard to read unless the slide text is extremely simple. I don't recommend this layout in most cases, because the audience really won't get much out of such handouts.

TIP **One good use for the nine-slides model is as an index or table of contents for a large presentation. You can include a nine-slides-per-page version of the handouts at the beginning of the packet that you give to the audience members, and then follow it up with a two-slides-per-page version that they can refer to if they want a closer look at one of the slides.**

Finally, there is an Outline handout layout, which prints an outline of all of the text in your presentation — that is, all of the text that is part of placeholders in slide layouts; any text in extra text boxes you have added manually is excluded. It is not considered a handout when you are printing, but it is included with the handout layouts in the Handout Master. More on this type of handout later in the chapter.

Printing handouts

When you have decided which layout is appropriate for your needs, print your handouts as follows:

1. **(Optional) If you want to print only one particular slide, or a group of slides, select the ones you want in either Slide Sorter view or in the slide thumbnails task pane on the left.**
2. **Select Office Button ⇨ Print.** The Print dialog box appears.
3. **Set options for your printer or choose a different printer.** See the "Setting Printer-Specific Options" section later in this chapter for help with this.
4. **In the Print Range area, choose one of the following:**
   - **All** to print the entire presentation.
   - **Current Slide** to print whatever slide you selected before you issued the Print command.

- **Selection** to print multiple slides you selected before you issued the Print command. It is not available if you did not select any slides beforehand.
- **Custom Show** to print a certain custom show you have set up. It is not available if you do not have any custom shows.
- **Slides** to print the slide numbers that you type in the accompanying text box. Indicate a contiguous range with a dash. For example, to print slides 1 through 9, type **1-9**. Indicate non-contiguous slides with commas. For example, to print slides, 2, 4, and 6, type **2, 4, 6**. Or to print slides 2 plus 6 through 10, type **2, 6-10**. To print them in reverse order, type the order that way, such as **10-6, 2**.

5. **Enter a number of copies in the Number of Copies text box.** The default is 1. If you want the copies collated (applicable to multipage printouts only), make sure you mark the Collate checkbox.
6. **Open the Print What drop-down list and choose Handouts.** The Handouts section of the box becomes available, as shown in Figure 25-7.

FIGURE 25-7

Choose Handouts to print and specify which handout layout you want.

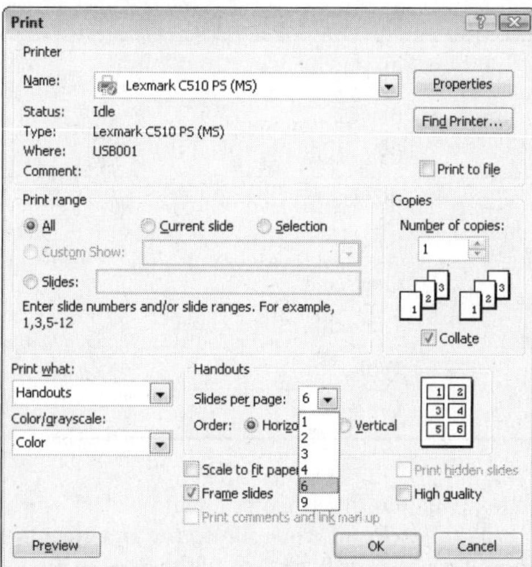

NOTE: If you want to print an outline, choose Outline View instead of Handouts in Step 6, and then skip Steps 7–9. An outline can be a useful handout for an audience in certain situations.

7. **Open the Slides Per Page drop-down list and choose the number of slides per page you want.**
8. **If available, choose an Order: Horizontal or Vertical. Not all number-of-slide choices (from Step 7) support an Order choice.**

NOTE: Order in Step 8 refers to the order in which the slides are placed on the page. Horizontal places them by rows, and Vertical places them by columns. This ordering has nothing to do with the orientation of the paper (Portrait or Landscape). You set the paper orientation in the Page Setup dialog box (Design ⇨ Page Setup).

9. **Open the Color/Grayscale drop-down list and select the color setting for the printouts:**
   - **Color:** Sends the data to the printer assuming that color will be used. When you use this setting with a black-and-white printer, it results in slides with grayscale or black backgrounds. Use this setting if you want the handouts to look as much as possible like the onscreen slides.
   - **Grayscale:** Sends the data to the printer assuming that color will not be used. Colored backgrounds are removed, and if text is normally a light color on a dark background, that is reversed. Use this setting if you want PowerPoint to optimize the printout for viewing on white paper.
   - **Pure Black and White:** This format hides most shadows and patterns, as described in Table 25-1. It's good for faxes and overhead transparencies.

TABLE 25-1

Differences Between Grayscale and Pure Black and White

Object	Grayscale	Pure Black and White
Text	Black	Black
Text Shadows	Grayscale	Black
Fill	Grayscale	Grayscale
Lines	Black	Black
Object Shadows	Grayscale	Black
Bitmaps	Grayscale	Grayscale
Clip Art	Grayscale	Grayscale
Slide Backgrounds	White	White
Charts	Grayscale	White

TIP To see what your presentation will look like when printed to a black-and-white printer, on the View tab click Grayscale or Pure Black and White. If you see an object that is not displaying the way you want, right-click it and choose Grayscale or Black and White. One of the options there may help you achieve the look you're after.

10. **Mark any desired checkboxes at the bottom of the dialog box:**
    - **Scale to Fit Paper:** Enlarges the slides to the maximum size they can be and still fit on the layout (as defined in the Handout Master, covered later in this chapter).
    - **Frame Slides:** Draws a black border around each slide image. Useful for slides being printed with white backgrounds.
    - **Print Comments:** Prints any comments that you have inserted with the Comments feature in PowerPoint.
    - **Print Hidden Slides:** Includes hidden slides in the printout. This option is not available if you don't have any hidden slides in your presentation.
    - **High Quality:** Optimizes the appearance of the printout in small ways, such as allowing text shadows to print.

11. (Optional) Click the Preview button to see a preview of your handouts; then click the Print button to return to the Print dialog box.
12. Click OK. The handouts print, and you're ready to roll!

CAUTION **Beware of the cost of printer supplies. If you are planning to distribute copies of the presentation to a lot of people, it may be tempting to print all of the copies on your printer. But the cost per page of printing is fairly high, especially if you have an inkjet printer. You will quickly run out of ink in your ink cartridge and have to spend $20 or more for a replacement. Consider whether it might be cheaper to print one original and take it to a copy shop.**

Setting printer-specific options

In addition to the controls in the Print dialog box in PowerPoint, there are controls you can set that affect the printer you have chosen. In the Printer section of the Print dialog box, you can open the Name drop-down list and choose the printer you want to use to print the job, as shown in Figure 25-8. Most home users have only one printer, but business users may have more than one to choose from, especially on a network.

FIGURE 25-8

Select a printer if you have more than one.

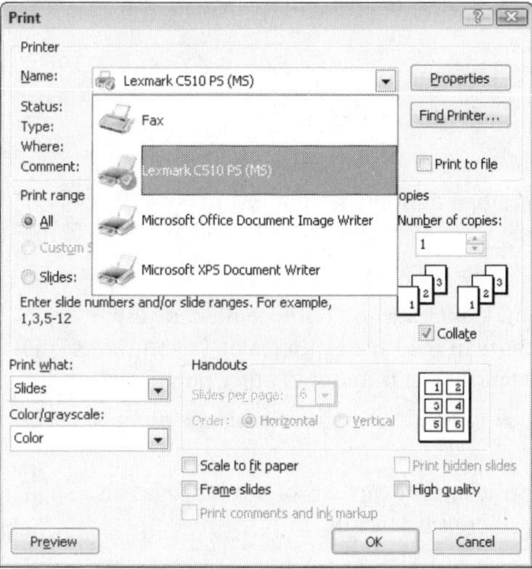

NOTE **Some of the "printers" listed are not really physical printers but drivers that create other types of files. For example, Microsoft XPS Document Writer saves a file in XPS format, which is Microsoft's version of a PostScript-type format.**

After choosing a printer, you can click the Properties button to display its Properties dialog box. The properties shown are different for different kinds of printers. Figure 25-9 shows the box for my Lexmark Optra S 1855 printer, a color laser printer. Notice that there are six tabs: Layout, Paper/Quality, Output Options, Watermark, Profiles, and About. The tabs may be different for your printer.

FIGURE 25-9

Each printer's options are slightly different, but the same types of settings are available on most printers.

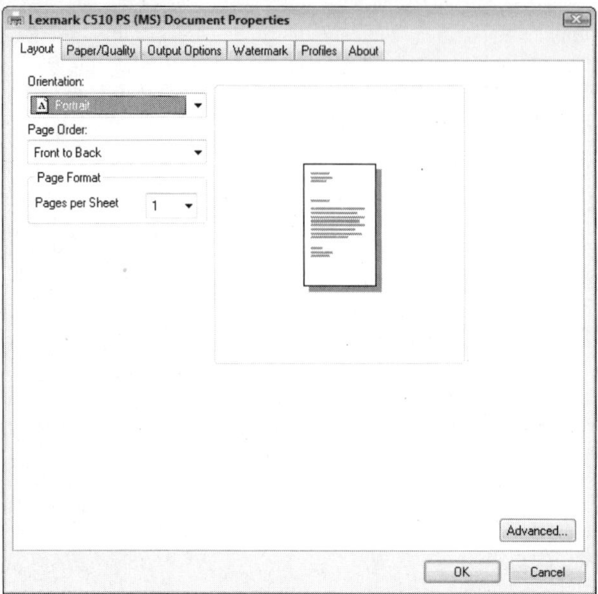

These settings affect how the printer behaves in all Windows-based programs, not just in PowerPoint, so you need to be careful not to change anything that you don't want globally changed. Here are some of the settings you may be able to change on your printer:

- **Orientation:** You can choose between Portrait and Landscape. It's not recommended that you change this setting here, though; make such changes in the Page Setup dialog box in PowerPoint instead. Otherwise, you may get the wrong orientation on a printout in other programs.
- **Page Order:** You can choose Front to Back or Back to Front. This determines the order the pages print.
- **Pages Per Sheet:** The default is 1, but you can print smaller versions of several pages on a single sheet. This option is usually only available on PostScript printers.
- **Paper Size:** The default is Letter, but you can change to Legal, A4, or any of several other sizes.
- **Paper Source:** If your printer has more than one paper tray, you may be able to select Upper or Lower.
- **Copies:** This sets the default number of copies that should print. Be careful; this number is a multiplier. If you set two copies here, and then set two copies in the Print dialog box in PowerPoint, you end up with four copies.
- **Graphics Resolution:** If your printer has a range of resolutions available, you may be able to choose the resolution you want. My printer lets me choose between 300 and 600 dots per inch (dpi); on an inkjet printer, choices are usually 360, 720, and 1,440 dpi. Achieving a resolution of 1,440 on an inkjet printer usually requires special glossy paper.

- **Graphic Dithering:** On some printers, you can set the type of dithering that makes up images. *Dithering* is a method of creating shadows (shades of gray) from black ink by using tiny cross-hatch patterns. You may be able to choose between Coarse, Fine, and None.
- **Image Intensity:** On some printers, you can control the image appearance with a light/dark slide bar.

Some printers, notably inkjets, come with their own print-management software. If that's the case, you may have to run that print-management software separately from outside of PowerPoint for full control over the printer's settings. You can usually access such software from the Windows Start menu.

Using the Handout Master

Just as the Slide Master controls your slide layout, the Handout Master controls your handout layout. To view the Handout Master, on the View tab click Handout Master, as shown in Figure 25-10. Unlike the Slide Master and Title Master, you can have only one Handout Master layout per presentation.

FIGURE 25-10

The Handout Master lets you define the handout layout to be printed.

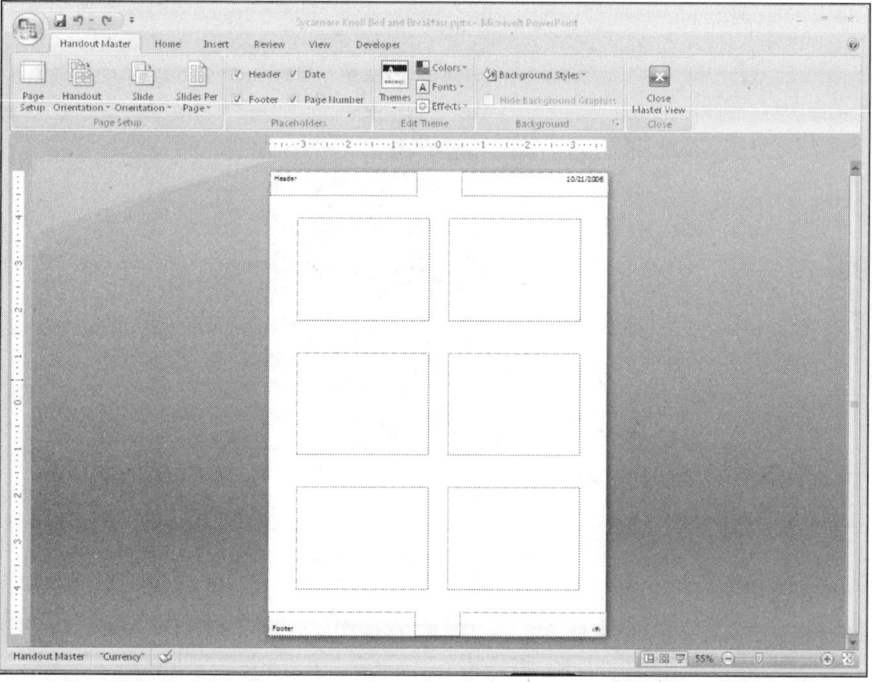

You can do almost exactly the same things with the Handout Master that you can with the Slide Master. The following sections describe some of the common activities.

Setting the number of slides per page

You can view the Handout Master with various numbers of slides per page to help you see how the layout will look when you print it. However, the settings are not different for each number of slides per page; for example, if you apply a header or footer, or page background, for a three-slides-per-page layout, it also applies to all the others as well. To choose the number of slides per page to display as you work with the Handout Master, click the Slides Per Page button and then make your selection from its menu. See Figure 25-11.

FIGURE 25-11

Choose a number of slides per page.

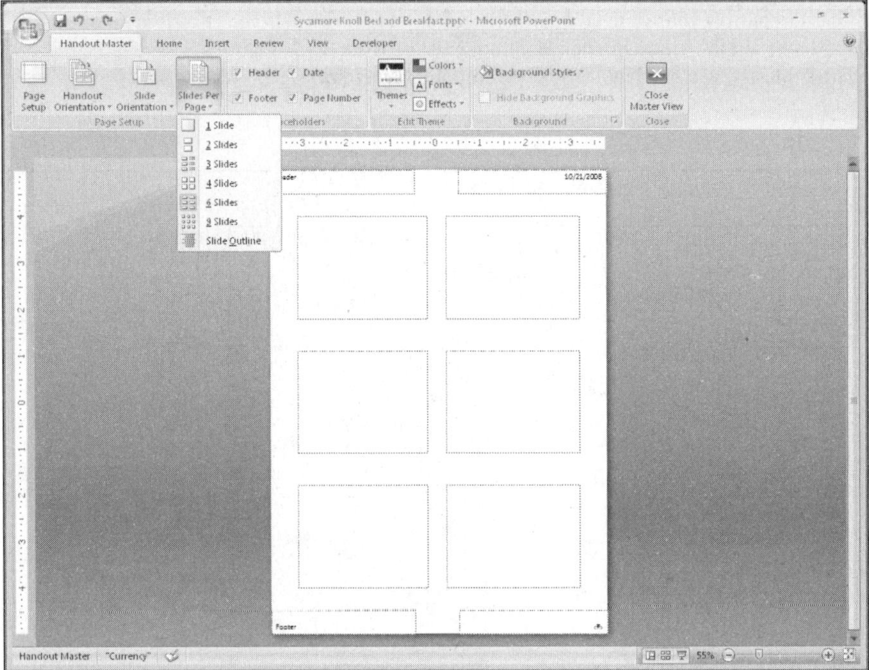

Using and positioning placeholders

The Handout Master has four placeholders by default: Header, Footer, Date, and Page Number, in the four corners of the handout respectively:

- **Header:** Appears in the upper-left corner, and is a blank box into which you can type fixed text that will appear on each page of the printout.
- **Footer:** Same thing as Header but appears in the lower-left corner.
- **Date:** Appears in the upper-right corner, and shows today's date by default.
- **Page Number:** Appears in lower-right corner and shows a code for a page number <#>. This will be replaced by an actual page number when you print.

In each placeholder box, you can type text (replacing, if desired, the Date and Page codes already there in those). You can also drag the placeholder boxes around on the layout.

There are two ways to remove the default placeholders from the layout. You select the placeholder box and press Delete, or you can clear the checkbox for that element on the Handout Master tab as shown in Figure 25-12.

FIGURE 25-12

Turn on/off placeholder elements from the Handout Master tab.

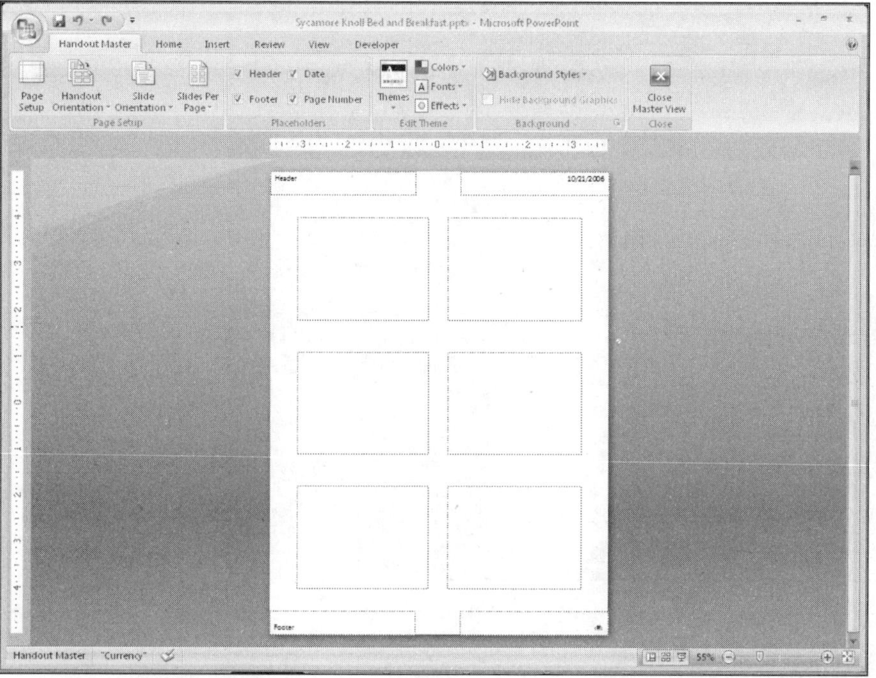

NOTE Because the header and footer are blank by default, there is no advantage to deleting these placeholders unless they have something in them you want to dispose of; having a blank box and having no box at all have the same result.

TIP You can't move or resize the *slide* placeholder boxes on the Handout Master, nor can you change its margins. If you want to change the size of the slide boxes on the handout or change the margins of the page, consider exporting the handouts to Word and working on them there.

Setting handout and slide orientation

Orientation refers to the direction on the page the material runs. If the top of the paper is one of the narrow edges, it's called Portrait; if the top of the paper is a wide edge, it's Landscape. Figure 25-13 shows the difference in handout orientation.

You can also set an orientation for the slides themselves on the handouts. This is a separate setting that does not affect the handout page in terms of the placement of the header, footer, and other repeated elements. Figure 25-14 shows the difference between portrait and landscape slide orientation on a portrait handout.

FIGURE 25-13

Portrait (top) and Landscape (bottom) handout orientation

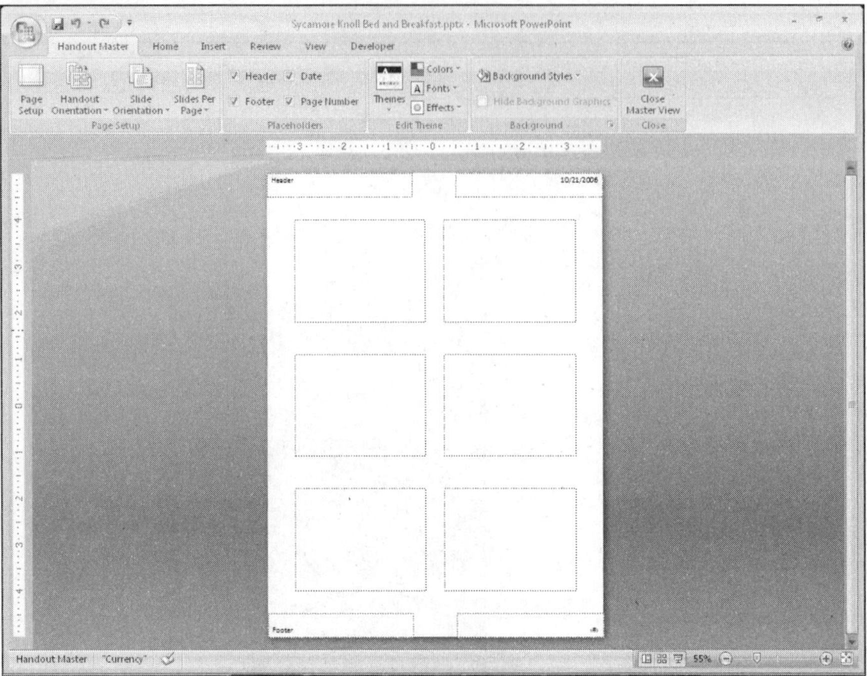

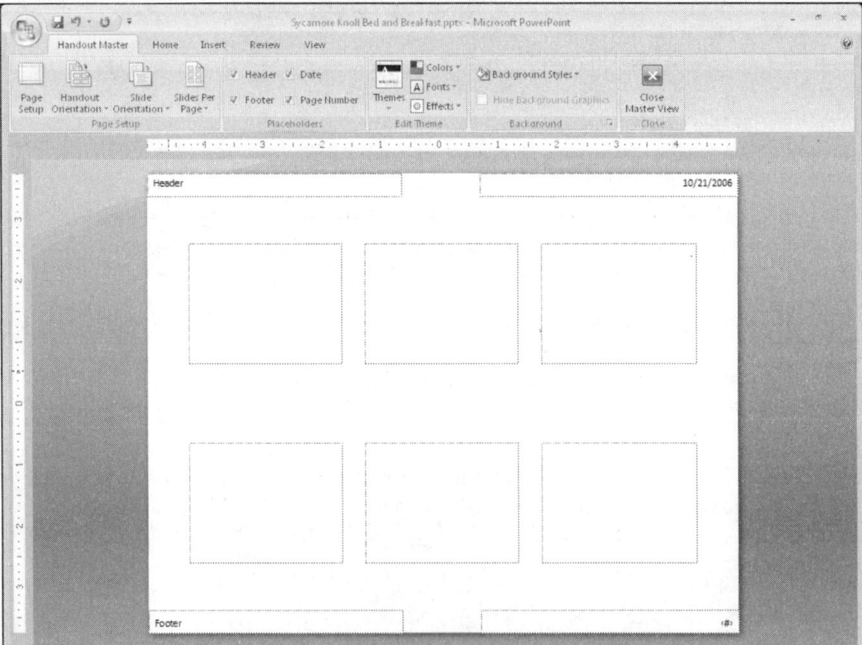

FIGURE 25-14

Landscape (top) and Portrait (bottom) slide orientation.

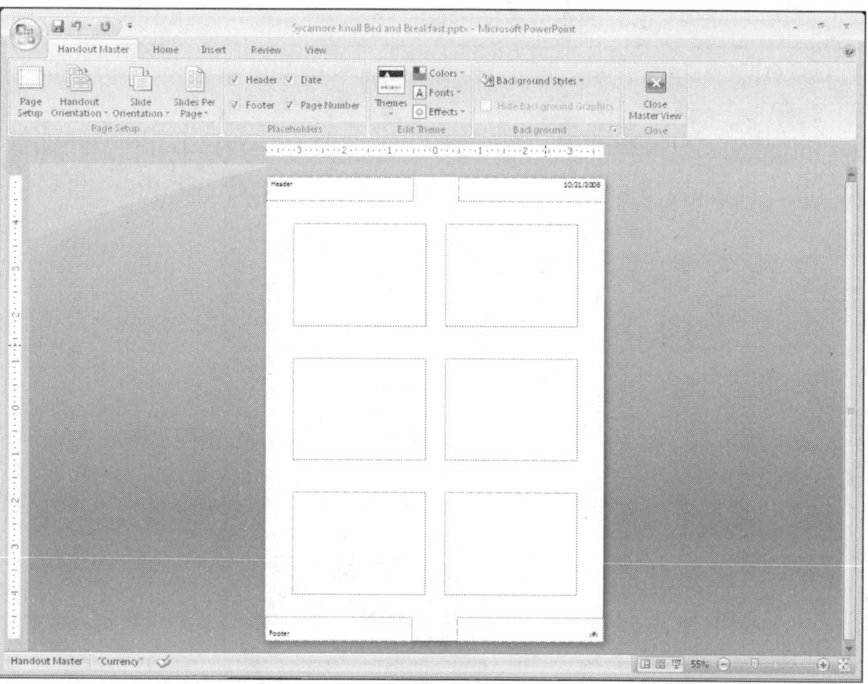

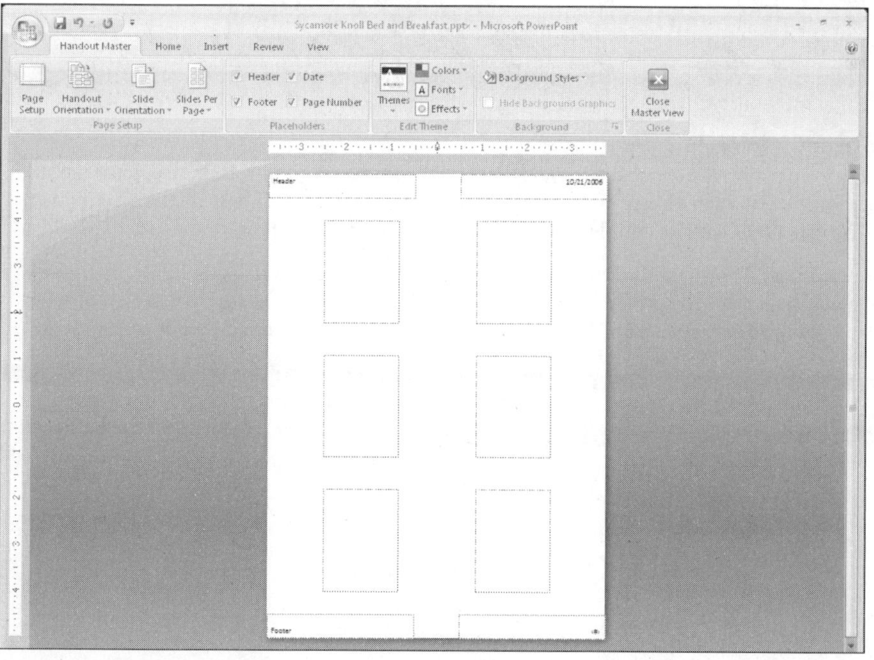

To set either of these orientations, use their respective drop-down lists on the Handout Master tab, in the Page Setup group. See Figure 25-15.

FIGURE 25-15

Set orientation from the Page Setup group.

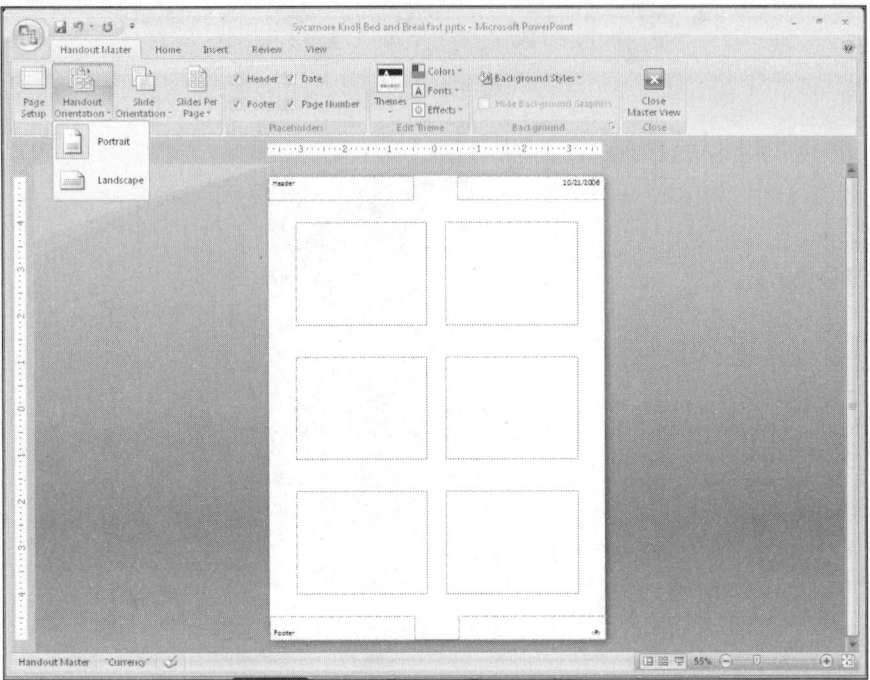

Formatting handouts

You can manually format any text on a handout layout using the formatting controls on the Home tab, the same as with any other text. Such formatting affects only the text you select, and only on the layout you're working with. You can also select the entire placeholder box and apply formatting.

You can also apply Colors, Fonts, and/or Effects themes from the Edit Theme group, as shown in Figure 25-16 much like you can do for the presentation as a whole. The main difference is that you cannot select an overall theme from the Themes button; all the themes are unavailable from the list while in Handout Master view. The settings you apply here affect only the handouts, not the presentation as a whole.

NOTE **You probably won't have much occasion to apply an Effects theme to a handout layout because handouts do not usually have objects that use effects (i.e., drawn shapes, charts, or SmartArt diagrams).**

FIGURE 25-16

Apply color, font, and/or effect themes from the Edit Theme group.

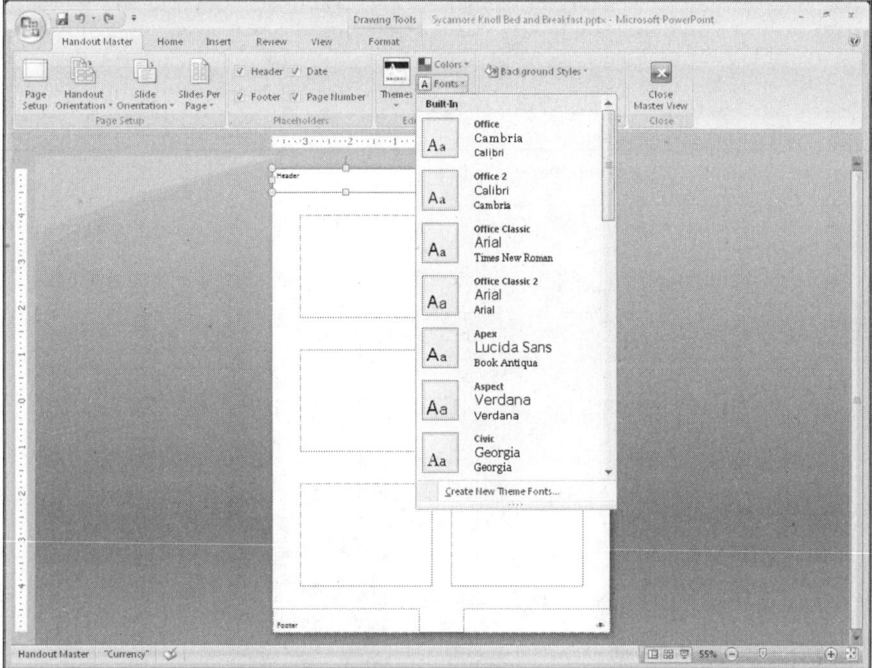

Creating Speaker Notes

Speaker notes are like handouts, but for you. Only one printout format is available for them: the Notes Pages layout. It consists of the slide on the top half (the same size as in the two-slides-per-page handout) with the blank space below it for your notes to yourself.

Speaker notes printed in PowerPoint are better than traditional note cards for several reasons. For one thing, you can type your notes right into the computer and print them out on regular paper. There's no need to jam a note card into a typewriter and use messy correction fluid or erasers to make changes. The other benefit is that each note page contains a picture of the slide, so it's not as easy to lose your place while speaking.

Typing speaker notes

You can type your notes for a slide in Normal view (in the notes pane), or in Notes Page view. The latter shows the page more or less as it will look when you print your notes pages; this can help if you need to gauge how much text will fit on the printed page.

To switch to Notes Page view, on the View tab click Notes Page as shown in Figure 25-17. Unlike some of the other views, there is no shortcut button for this view in the bottom-right corner of the PowerPoint window. Once you're in Notes Page view, you can zoom and scroll just like in any other view to see more or less of the page at once. You can scroll further to move from slide to slide, or you can move from slide to slide in the traditional ways (the Page Up and Page Down keys on the keyboard or the Next Slide or Previous Slide buttons onscreen).

FIGURE 25-17

Notes Page view is one of the best ways to work with your speaker notes.

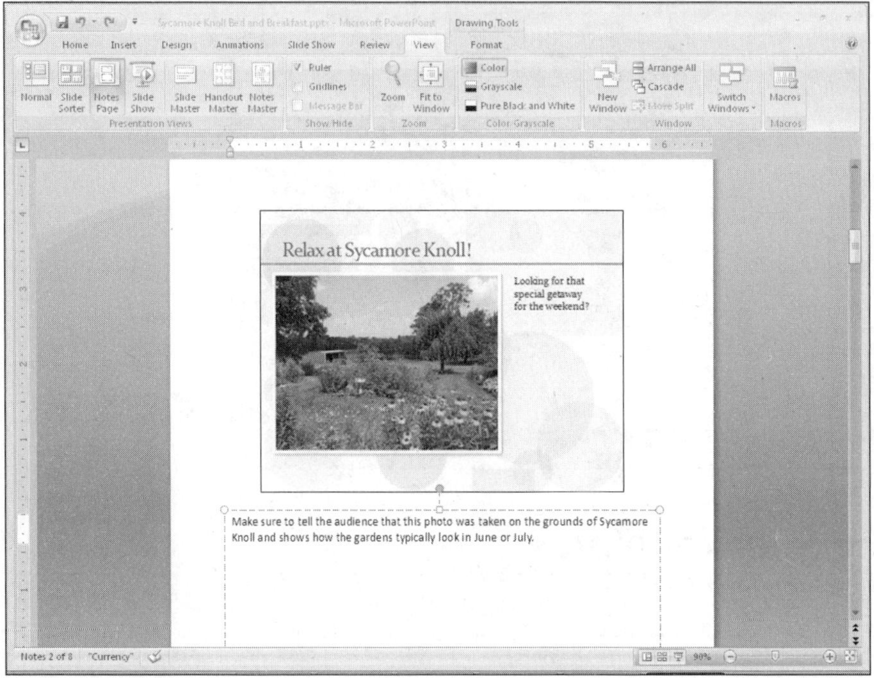

NOTE **Use the Zoom control to zoom in or out until you find the optimal view so that the text you type is large enough to be clear, but small enough so that you can see across the entire width of the note area. I find that 66 to 85 percent works well on my screen at 800x600 resolution, but yours may vary.**

Just type your notes in the Notes area, the same as you would type any text box in PowerPoint. The lines in the paragraph wrap automatically. Press Enter to start a new paragraph. When you're done, move to the next slide.

Changing the notes page layout

Just as you can edit your handout layouts, you can also edit your notes page layout. Just switch to its Master and make your changes. Follow these steps:

1. **On the View tab, click Notes Master.**
2. **Edit the layout, as you have learned to edit other masters.** See Figure 25-18. This can include:
   - Moving placeholders for the slide, the notes, or any of the header or footer elements.
   - Changing the font used for the text in any of those areas.
   - Resizing the placeholder for the slide graphic.
   - Resizing the Notes pane.
   - Adding clip art or other graphics to the background.
   - Adding a colored, textured, or patterned background to the notes page.
3. **When you are finished, click the Close Master View button to return to Normal view.**

FIGURE 25-18

You can edit the layout of the notes pages in Notes Master view.

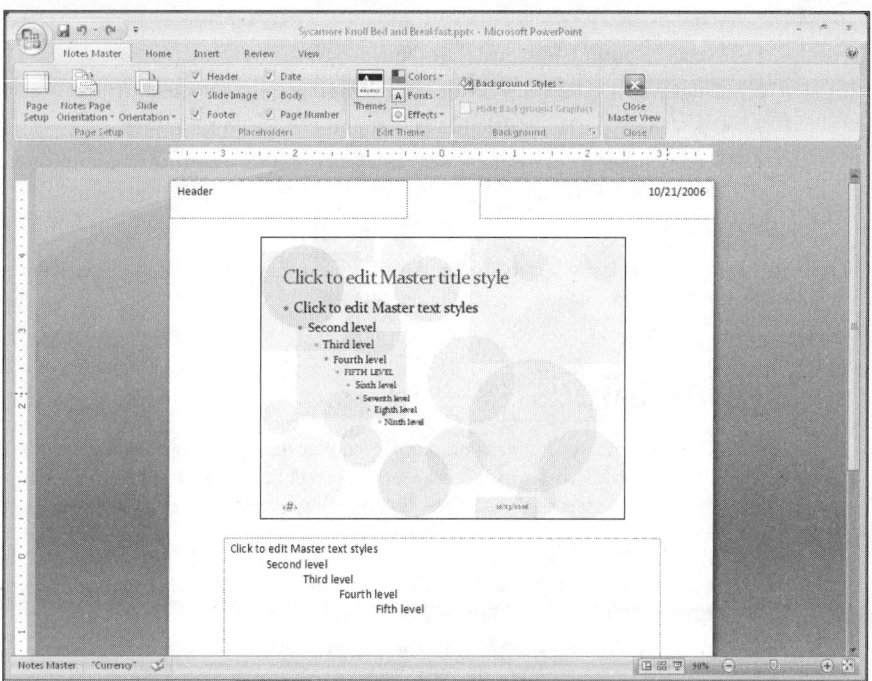

Printing notes pages

When you're ready to print your notes pages, follow these steps:

1. **Choose Office Button ➪ Print.** The Print dialog box opens.
2. **Open the Print What drop-down list and choose Notes Pages.**
3. **Set any other options, just as you did when printing handouts earlier in the chapter.** (If you need to choose which printer to use or to set the options for that printer, see the "Setting printer-specific options" section earlier in this chapter.) There are no special options for notes pages.
4. **Click OK.** The notes pages print.

CAUTION If you print notes pages for hidden slides, you may want to arrange your stack after they're printed so that the hidden slides are at the bottom. That way you won't get confused when giving the presentation.

Printing an Outline

If text is the main part of your presentation, you might prefer to print an outline instead of mini-slides. You can use the outline for speaker notes, audience handouts, or both. To print the text from Outline view, follow these steps:

1. **View the outline in Normal or Outline view.**
2. **Choose Office Button ➪ Print. The Print dialog box opens.**
3. **Open the Print What drop-down list and choose Outline View.**
4. **Set any other print options, as you learned in the "Printing handouts" section earlier in the chapter.**
5. **Click OK.**

Be aware, however, that the outline will not contain text that you've typed in manually placed text boxes or any other non-text information, such as tables, charts, and so on.

Printing Slides

Of course, you can print your slides one per page rather than printing handouts or notes pages. You may print slides, for example, when you need to send a presentation to a client rather than presenting it in person. Printing presentation slides works just like printing a document from any other application:

1. **Click Office Button ➪ Print or press Ctrl+P.** The Print dialog box appears.
2. **Select the printer to use from the Name drop-down list.** The printer becomes the current or active printer.
3. **Specify what slides to print in the Page Range area of the dialog box.**
4. **Specify how many copies to print in the Copies area of the dialog box.** In some cases, you also can choose to collate the printed pages.
5. **Leave Slides selected from the Print What drop-down list.**

6. **If you're using a color printer, make a choice from the Color/Grayscale drop-down list to determine whether to print in color.**
7. **Choose other print settings as desired.** Here are the other available settings and how they behave, when checked:
   - **Scale to Fit Paper.** Sizes each slide to fit the selected paper size, so slides don't print off the edges of the pages.
   - **Frame Slides.** Adds a printed border around each slide.
   - **Print Comments and Ink Markup.** If the file contains revision comments or ink markups added during a live slide show, they will print.
   - **Print Hidden Slides.** Also prints any hidden slides in the presentation.
   - **High Quality.** Sends slides to the printer using the highest quality settings, but may slow down the print job.
8. Click OK.

FIGURE 25-19

Choose printout settings in the Print dialog box.

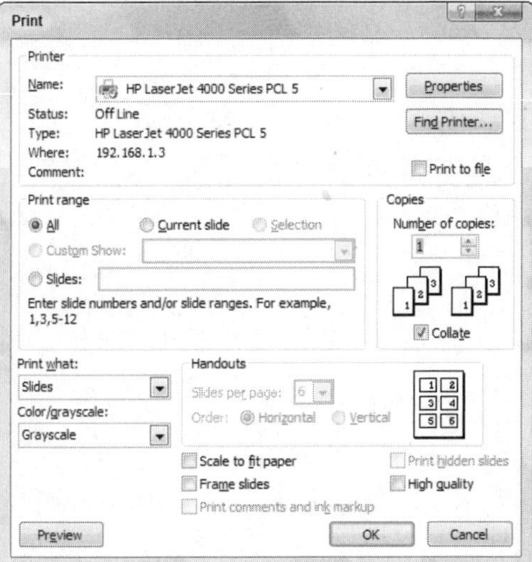

Summary

In this chapter, you learned how to animate the objects on your slides to create some great special effects, and how to create animated transitions from slide to slide. You also learned how to create support materials for a presentation, such as handouts and speaker notes, and how to format and fine-tune their formatting. Finally, you learned how to print notes pages and slides.

Chapter 26

Delivering a Live Presentation

IN THIS CHAPTER

- Starting and ending a show
- Using the on-screen show controls
- Using the on-screen pen
- Hiding slides for backup use
- Giving a presentation on a different computer
- Working with audio-visual equipment

It's show time! Well, actually I hope for your sake that it is *not* time for the show this very instant, because things will go much more smoothly if you can practice using PowerPoint's slide show controls before you have to go live.

Presenting the show can be as simple or as complex as you make it. At the most basic level, you can start the show, move through it slide-by-slide with simple mouse-clicks or key presses, and then end the show. However, to take advantage of PowerPoint's extra slide show features, you should spend a little time studying the following sections.

NOTE The first part of this chapter assumes that you are showing your presentation on a PC that has PowerPoint 2007 installed; sections later in this chapter discuss other situations.

Starting and Ending a Show

To start a show, do any of the following:

- Click the Slide Show View button in the bottom-right corner of the screen.
- On the View tab, click Slide Show.
- Press F5.
- Press Shift+F5.

These methods are not all exactly alike. For example, if you click the Slide Show View button in the bottom-right corner, or press Shift+F5, the first slide to appear is the currently selected one in PowerPoint. If you click the Slide Show button on the View tab or press F5, it starts with the first slide in the presentation, regardless of which slide was selected.

Once the show is underway, you can control the movement from slide to slide as described in the section, "Moving from slide to slide."

To end the show, do any of the following:

- Right-click and choose End Show.
- Press Esc, - (minus), or Ctrl+Break.

If you want to temporarily pause the show while you have a discussion, you can blank the screen by pressing W or , (comma) for a white screen, or B or . (period) for a black screen. To resume the show, press any key.

TIP If you set up the slide transitions to occur automatically at a certain time, you can stop or restart the show by pressing S or + (plus sign). However, this is more of an issue for self-running shows, which are discussed in Chapter 21.

Using the On-screen Show Controls

When you display a slide show, the mouse pointer and show controls are hidden. To make them appear, you can move the mouse. When you do this, very faint buttons appear in the bottom-left corner of the slide show, as shown in Figure 26-1, and the mouse pointer also appears. You can toggle the pointer and these buttons on and off by pressing A or = (equals). Ctrl+H hides the pointer and buttons. When you toggle this feature on, the following buttons appear:

FIGURE 26-1

Buttons appear in the bottom-left corner of a slide in Slide Show view. The third button opens a menu that controls navigation between slides.

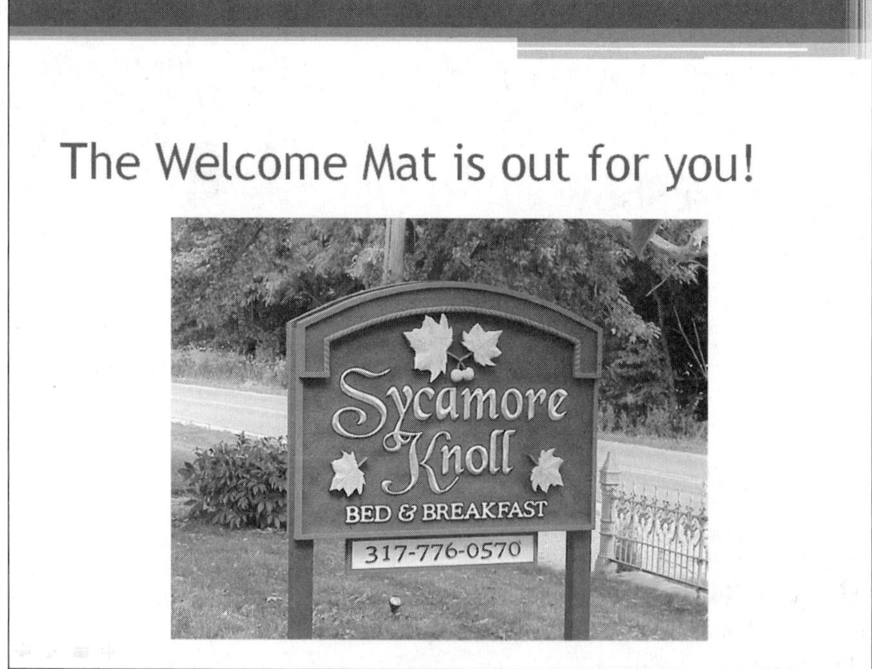

- **Back,** the leftmost button, takes you back to the previous slide, or to the previous animation event if the present slide contains animation.
- **Pen,** next to Back, opens a menu for controlling the appearance of the pen or pointer. (I discuss this feature later in this chapter.)
- **Slide,** which displays a box icon, opens a menu for navigating between slides. You can also open the navigation menu, shown in Figure 26-2, by right-clicking anywhere on the slide.

TIP **You can set up your show to move backwards when you click the right-mouse button. Choose Office Button ➪ PowerPoint Options, click Advanced, and in the Slide Show section, deselect the Show Menu on Right Mouse Click check box. If you do that, you can't right-click to open the navigation menu, though.**

- **Forward,** the rightmost button, moves you to the next slide. Normally, you can just click to go to the next slide, but if you are using the pen (covered later in this chapter), then clicking it causes it to draw, rather than advance the presentation. In this situation, you can use the Forward button.

NOTE **Because the slide navigation menu that appears is identical whether you click the Slide button or right-click anywhere on the slide, this chapter only mentions the right-click method whenever you need to choose something from this menu. However, keep in mind that you can also click the Slide button if you prefer.**

FIGURE 26-2

Click the Slide button or right-click on the slide to open this menu.

There are a lot of shortcut keys to remember when working in Slide Show view, and so PowerPoint provides a handy summary of these keys. To see them, right-click and choose Help, or press F1. The Slide Show Help dialog box appears, as shown in Figure 26-3. Click OK to close this dialog box when you are done.

Moving from Slide to Slide

The simplest way to move through a presentation is to move to the next slide. To do so, you can use any of these methods:

- Press any of these keys: N, Spacebar, right arrow, down arrow, Enter, or Page Down.
- Click the left-mouse button.
- Right-click and then choose Next.
- Click the right-pointing arrow button in the bottom-left corner of the slide.

If you have animated any elements on a slide, these methods advance the animation, and do not necessarily move to the next slide. For example, if you have animated your bulleted list so that the bullets appear one at a time, then any of the actions in this list make the next bullet appear, rather than making the next slide appear. Only after all of the objects on the current slide have displayed does PowerPoint advance to the next slide. If you need to immediately advance to the next slide, you can use the instructions in the section, "Jumping to specific slides," later in this chapter.

FIGURE 26-3

The Slide Show Help dialog box provides a quick summary of the shortcut keys that are available during a presentation.

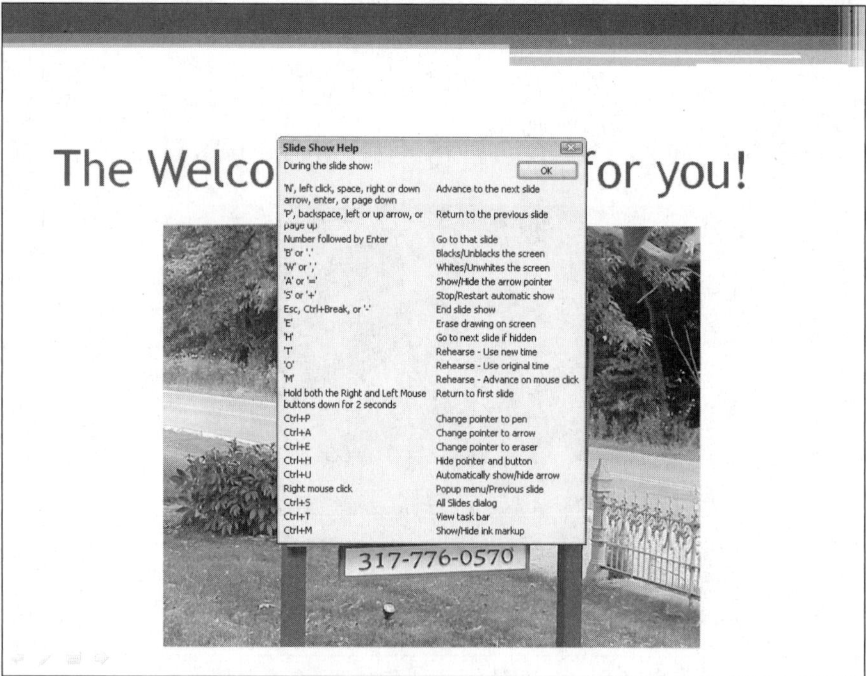

To back up to the previous slide, use any of these methods:

- Press any of these keys: P, Backspace, left arrow, up arrow, or Page Up.
- Click the left-pointing arrow button on the bottom-left corner of the slide.
- Right-click and then choose Previous.

You can also go back to the last slide that you viewed. To do this, right-click and choose Last Viewed. Although you would think that the last slide viewed would be the same as the previous slide, this is not always the case. For example, if you jump around in the slide show — such as to a hidden slide — then the last slide viewed is not the previous slide in the show, but the hidden slide that you have just viewed.

Jumping to Specific Slides

There are several ways to jump to a particular slide. One of the easiest ways is to select the slide by its title. To do so, follow these steps:

1. **During the slide show, right-click to display the shortcut menu.**
2. **Select Go to Slide.** A submenu appears, listing the titles of all of the slides in the presentation, as shown in Figure 26-4. Parentheses around the slide numbers indicate hidden slides.
3. **Click the slide title to which you want to jump.**

FIGURE 26-4

You can go to a specific slide using the Go to Slide command on the menu.

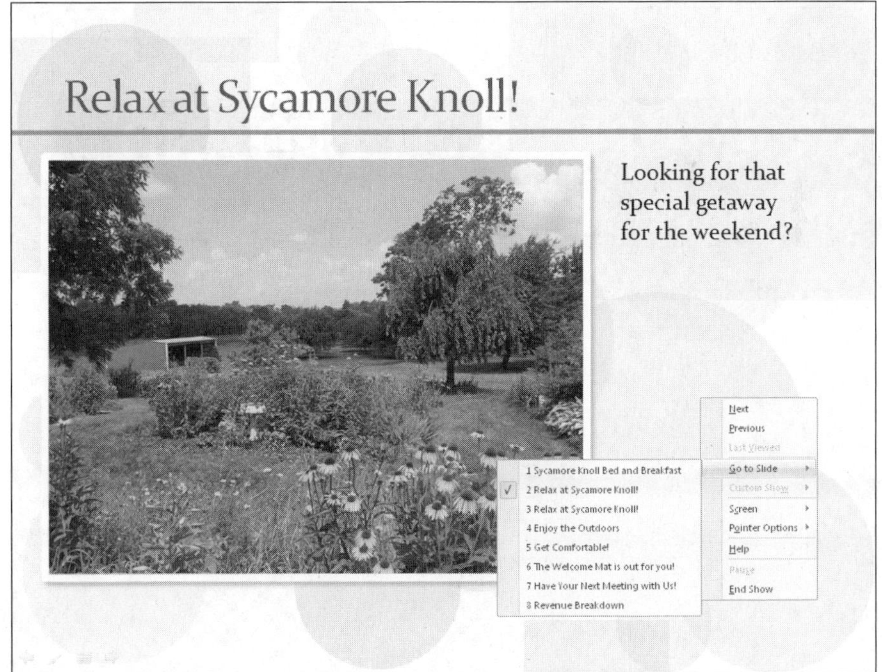

TIP The slide titles in this list come from title placeholders. If you want to show text on the list here but you don't want it to appear on the slide, type it in a title placeholder and then drag the placeholder off the edge of the slide, so it doesn't show in Slide Show view.

You can also jump to a certain slide number by typing this number and pressing Enter. For example, to go to the third slide, you would type **3** and then press Enter. Another way is to press Ctrl+S to open an All Slides dialog box listing the titles of all of the slides in the presentation. You can click a slide to select it and then click Go To, as shown in Figure 26-5.

To jump back to the first slide in the presentation, hold down both the left- and right-mouse buttons for two seconds (or type **1** and press Enter).

Blanking the Screen

Sometimes during a live presentation there may be a delay. Whether it is a chatty audience member with a complicated question, a fire drill, or just an intermission, you will want to pause the show.

If you have the slides set for manual transition, then whichever slide you stopped on remains on the screen until you resume. However, you may not want this. For example, it may be distracting to the audience, especially if the pause is to allow someone to get up and speak in front of the screen. A solution is to turn the screen into a blank expanse of black or white. To do so, type W or a comma (for white), or B or a period (for black). To return to the presentation, you can press the same key, or press any key on the keyboard.

FIGURE 26-5

The All Slides dialog box lists the titles of all of the slides so that you can select the one that you want to go to.

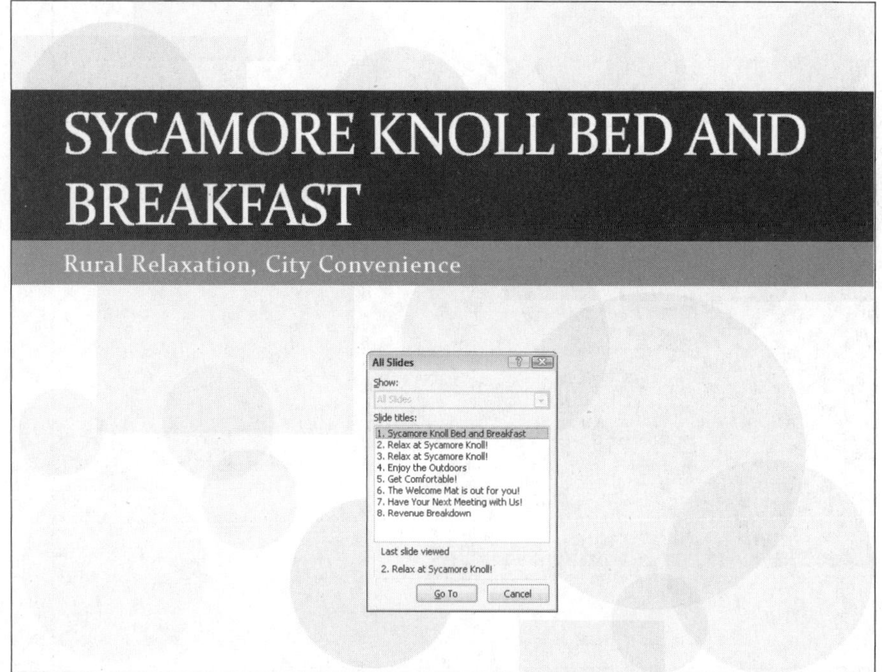

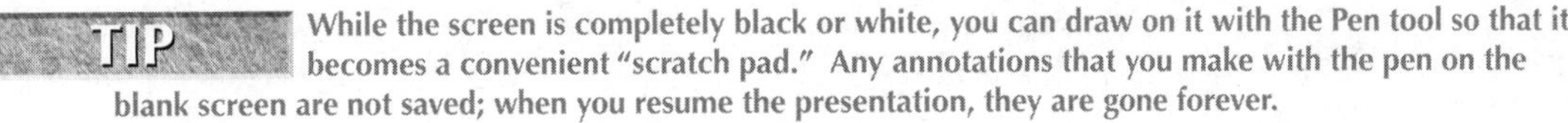

While the screen is completely black or white, you can draw on it with the Pen tool so that it becomes a convenient "scratch pad." Any annotations that you make with the pen on the blank screen are not saved; when you resume the presentation, they are gone forever.

Using the On-screen Pen

Have you ever seen a coach in a locker room, drawing out football plays on a chalkboard? Well, you can do the same thing in PowerPoint. You can have impromptu discussions of concepts that are illustrated on slides, and punctuate the discussion with your own circles, arrows, and lines. Perhaps during the discussion portion of your presentation, you may decide that one point on the slide is not important. In this case, you can use the pen to cross it out. Conversely, a certain point may become really important during a discussion so that you want to emphasize it. In this case, you can circle it or underline it with the pen cursor.

You can choose your pen color as follows:

1. **Move the mouse or press A to make the buttons appear.**
2. **Click the Pointers button (the one that looks like a pen).** A menu appears.
3. **Select Ink Color and then click the color you want, as shown in Figure 26-6.**

FIGURE 26-6

You can select a pen type and an ink color for it.

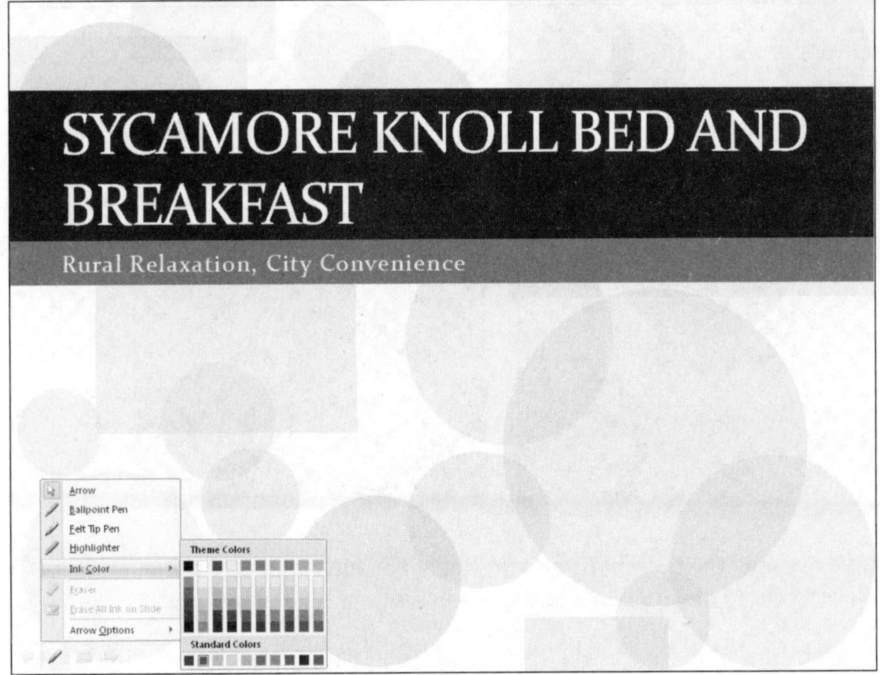

EXPERT TIP To change the default pen color for the show, so that you do not always have to manually select the color you want, click Set Up Show on the Slide Show tab. Then, in the Pen Color drop-down list, choose the color you want.

You can turn on the type of pen that you want, as follows:

1. **Click the Pointers button again.**
2. **Click the type of pen that you want:**

   Ballpoint: A thin line

   Felt Tip Pen: A thicker line

   Highlighter: A thick, semi-transparent line

NOTE The on-screen buttons in the slide show continue to work while you have a pen enabled, but you have to click them twice to activate them — once to tell PowerPoint to temporarily switch out of the Pen mode, and then again to open the menu.

You can also turn on the default pen type (Felt Tip) by pressing Ctrl+P, and then return to the arrow again by pressing Ctrl+A or Esc.

After enabling a pen, just drag-and-draw on the slide to make your mark. You should practice drawing lines, arrows, and other shapes because it takes a while to master. Figure 26-7 shows an example of using the pen.

FIGURE 26-7

You can draw on the slide with the pen tools.

Get Comfortable!

We use only the best in towels and linens, including 100% cotton sheets, fluffy down pillows and comforters, and luxurious towels.

CAUTION As you can see from Figure 26-7, the on-screen pen is not very attractive. If you know in advance that you are going to emphasize certain points, then you may prefer to build the emphasis into the presentation by making these points larger, bolder, or in different colors. You can also circle the points using an oval shape with a 1-spoke wheel animation.

To erase your lines and try again, press E (for Erase), or open the Pointer menu and choose Erase All Ink On Slide. To erase just a part of the ink, open the Pointer menu, choose Eraser, and then use the mouse pointer to erase individual lines.

NOTE Unlike in some earlier versions of PowerPoint, drawings stay with a slide, even when you move to another slide.

When you exit Slide Show view after drawing on slides, a dialog box appears, asking whether you want to keep or discard your annotations. If you choose Keep, the annotations become drawn objects on the slides, which you can then move or delete, similar to an AutoShape.

To change the pen back to a pointer again, open the Pointer menu and choose Arrow, press Ctrl+A, or press Esc. The pen remains a pen when you advance from slide to slide. In earlier versions of PowerPoint, it reverted back to an arrow automatically when you changed slides.

Hiding Slides for Backup Use

You may not always want to show every slide that you have prepared. Sometimes it pays to prepare extra data in anticipation of a question that you think someone might ask, or to hold back certain data unless someone specifically requests it.

By hiding a slide, you keep it filed in reserve, without making it a part of the main slide show. Then, at any time during the presentation when (or if) it becomes appropriate, you can display that slide. Hiding refers only to whether the slide is a part of the main presentation's flow; it has no effect in any other view.

TIP If you have only a handful of slides to hide, go ahead and hide them. However, if you have a large group of related slides to hide, consider creating a custom show for them instead.

Hiding and Unhiding Slides

A good way to hide and unhide slides is in Slide Sorter view because an indicator appears below each slide to show whether it is hidden. This way, you can easily determine which slides are part of the main presentation. In the slide thumbnail pane in Normal view, hidden slides appear ghosted out.

Follow these steps to hide a slide:

1. **Switch to Slide Sorter view.**
2. **Select the slide or slides that you want to hide.** Remember, to select more than one slide, hold down the Ctrl key as you click the ones that you want.
3. **Click the Hide Slide button on the Slide Show toolbar.** A gray box appears around the slide number and a diagonal line crosses through it, indicating that it is hidden.

To unhide a slide, select the slide and click the Hide Slide button again. The slide's number returns to normal. You can also right-click a slide and choose Hide Slide or Unhide Slide to toggle the hidden attribute on and off.

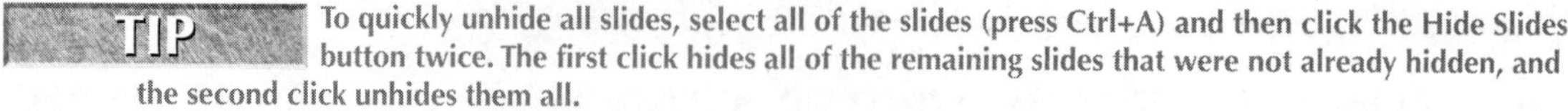

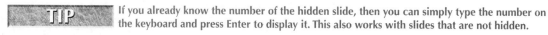

TIP To quickly unhide all slides, select all of the slides (press Ctrl+A) and then click the Hide Slides button twice. The first click hides all of the remaining slides that were not already hidden, and the second click unhides them all.

Showing a Hidden Slide During a Presentation

When you advance from one slide to the next during a show, hidden slides do not appear. (This is what being hidden is about, after all.) If you need to display one of the hidden slides, follow these steps:

1. **In Slide Show view, open the Screen menu, either by clicking the Screen icon or by right-clicking anywhere in the screen.**
2. Choose **Go to Slide, and then choose the slide to which you want to jump.** Hidden slides show their slide numbers in parentheses, but you can access them like any other slide, as shown in Figure 26-8.

TIP If you already know the number of the hidden slide, then you can simply type the number on the keyboard and press Enter to display it. This also works with slides that are not hidden.

FIGURE 26-8

You can jump to a hidden slide just as you would to any other slide.

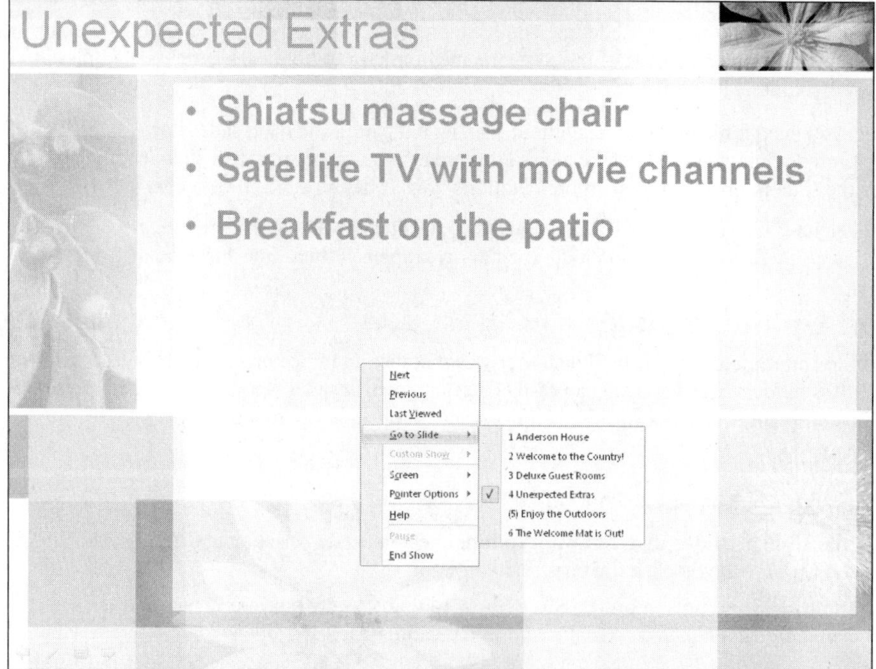

Once you display a hidden slide, you can easily return to it later. When you move backwards through the presentation (using the Backspace key, the left- or up-arrow key, or the on-screen Back button), any hidden slides that you displayed previously are included in the slides that PowerPoint scrolls back through. However, when you move forward through the presentation, the hidden slide does not reappear, regardless of when you viewed it previously. You can always jump back to it again using the preceding steps.

Giving a Presentation on a Different Computer

The computer on which you create a presentation is usually not the same computer that you will use to show it. For example, you may be doing the bulk of your work on your desktop computer in your office in Los Angeles, but you need to use your laptop computer to give the presentation in Phoenix.

One way to transfer a presentation to another computer is simply to copy the PowerPoint file (the file with the .pptx extension) using a floppy disk or other removable media. However, this method is imperfect because it assumes that the other computer has all of the fonts, sounds, and other elements that you need for every part of the show. This can be a dangerous assumption. For example, suppose that your presentation contains a link to some Excel data. If you do not also copy the Excel file, then you cannot update the data when you are on the road.

A better way to ensure that you are taking everything you need while traveling is to use the Package for CD feature in PowerPoint. This feature reads all of the linked files and associated objects and ensures that they are transferred along with the main presentation. You do not actually need to copy the presentation to a writeable CD, and you do not need a CD-R or CD-RW drive to use this feature. You can copy the presentation to anywhere you want, such as to a ZIP drive or a network location.

Copying a Presentation to CD

If you have a CD-R or CD-RW drive, then copying the presentation to CD is an attractive choice. It produces a self-running disc that contains a PowerPoint Viewer application, the presentation file, and any linked files.

By default, a packaged CD includes the PowerPoint Viewer, and the presentation file is in PowerPoint 2003 format. PowerPoint automatically saves 2007-version files back to 2003 format before it burns them to CD. However, you can override this behavior, as you will see later in this chapter in "Setting Copy Options".

TIP **You can copy many presentation files onto a single CD, not just the currently active one. The only limit is the size of the disc (usually 650MB to 700MB). By default, the currently active presentation is included, although the following steps show you how to add other presentations. You can also set up these presentations to run automatically one after another, or you can specify that a menu appears so that the user can choose the presentation that they want to view.**

Here is the basic procedure, which is elaborated on in the following sections:

1. **Place a blank CD-R or CD-RW disc in your writeable CD drive.**
2. **Finalize the presentation in PowerPoint.** If you are using a CD-R disc, keep in mind that this disc type is not rewriteable, and so you should ensure that the presentation is exactly as you want it.
3. **Choose Office Button ➪ Publish ➪ Package for CD.**
4. **A warning appears about updating file formats; click OK.** The Package for CD dialog box opens, as shown in Figure 26-9.

FIGURE 26-9

Use the Package for CD feature to place all of the necessary files for the presentation on a CD.

5. **Type a name for the CD; this is similar to adding a volume label for the disc.**
6. ***(Optional)* Add more files to the CD if you want.** See the next section, "Creating a CD containing multiple presentation files," for more details.
7. ***(Optional)* Set any options that you want.** See the section, "Setting Copy options," later in this chapter, for more details.
8. **Click Copy to CD.** The CD-writing process may take several minutes, depending on the writing speed of your CD drive and the size of the presentation files that you are placing on it.
9. **A message appears when the files are successfully copied to the CD, asking whether you want to copy the same files to another CD.** Click Yes or No. If you choose No, then you must also click Close to close the Package for CD dialog box.

The resulting CD automatically plays the presentations when you insert it in any computer. You can also browse the CD's contents to open the PowerPoint Viewer separately and use it to play specific presentations.

CAUTION **File corruption can occur on a CD drive during the writing process. After burning a CD, test it thoroughly by running the complete presentation from CD before you rely on the CD copy as the version that you take with you while traveling.**

Creating a CD Containing Multiple Presentation Files

By default, the active presentation is included on the CD, but you can also add others, up to the capacity of your disc. For example, if you have several versions of the same presentation for different audiences, then a single CD can contain all of them. As you are preparing to copy the files using the Package for CD dialog box, shown in Figure 26-9, follow these steps to add more files:

1. **Click Add Files.** An Add dialog box opens, similar to the Open dialog box that you use to open PowerPoint files.
2. **Select the additional files that you want to include, and click Add to return to the Package for CD dialog box.** The list of files now appears as shown in Figure 26-10, with extra controls.

NOTE **You can select multiple files from the same location by holding down the Ctrl key as you click the ones you want. To include multiple files from different locations, repeat steps 1 and 2 for each location.**

FIGURE 26-10

When you specify multiple files for a CD, you can specify the order in which they should play.

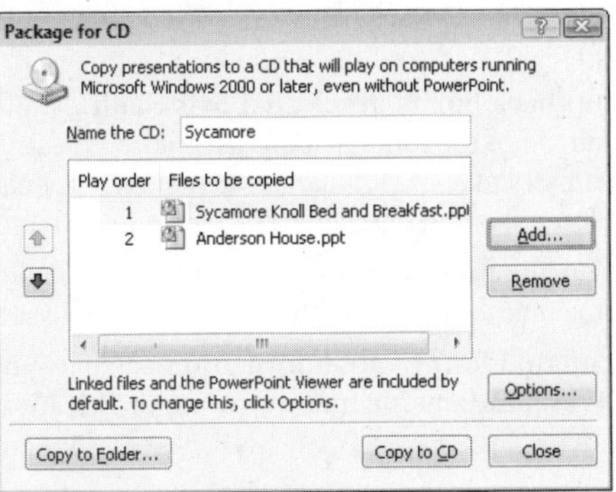

3. **If you set up the CD to play the presentations automatically (as shown in the next section), the order in which they appear on the list becomes significant.** You can rearrange the list by clicking a presentation and then clicking the Up- or Down-arrow buttons to the left of the list.
4. **If you need to remove a presentation from the list, click it and then click Remove.**
5. **Continue making the CD as you normally would.**

Setting Copy Options

The default copy options are suitable in most situations. However, you may sometimes want to modify them. To do this, open the Package for CD dialog box, and follow these steps:

1. **Click Options.** The Options dialog box open, as shown in Figure 26-11.
2. **Select a package type.** You can choose Viewer Package, which includes the PowerPoint Viewer and saves the file in 2003 format, or you can choose Archive Package, which does not update the file format and does not include the viewer on the CD.

FIGURE 26-11

You can set options for copying the presentations to CD.

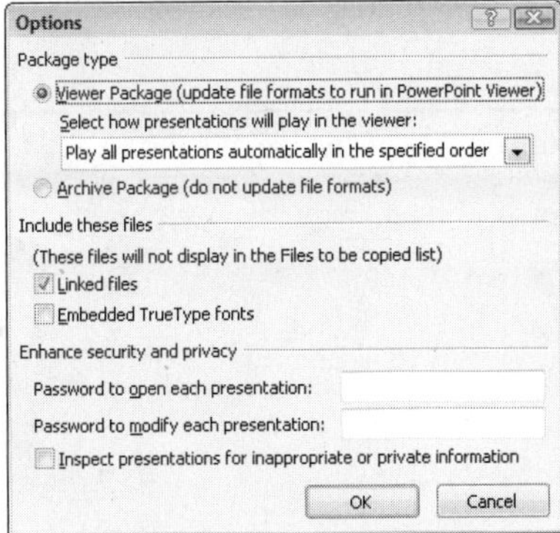

3. **The Linked Files check box is selected by default; this option tells PowerPoint to include the full copies of all linked files.** You can deselect this option if you want; a static copy of the linked data will remain in the presentation, but the link will not work. You should leave this option selected if you have sounds or multimedia files in your presentation, because these files are always linked (with the exception of some WAV files).
4. **The Embedded TrueType Fonts check box is deselected by default.** If you think that the destination computer may not contain all of the fonts that are used in the presentation, then select this option. This makes the presentation file slightly larger. Remember, not all fonts can be embedded; this depends on the level of embedding allowed by the font's manufacturer.
5. **If you want to add passwords for the presentations, do so in the Enhance Security and Privacy section.** There are separate text boxes for open and modify passwords.
6. **If you want to check the presentation for private information, such as your name or any comments, select the Inspect Presentations for Inappropriate or Private Information check box.**
7. **Click OK, and then write the CD as you normally would.**

NOTE If you select the check box in step 6, as part of the process, the Document Inspector window opens, and you can use it to check the document for selected types of content.

Copying a Presentation to Other Locations

Although it is not well known, you can also use the Package for CD feature to copy presentation files and their associated support files to any location you want. For example, you can transfer files to another computer on a network, or place them on a floppy or ZIP disc. To do so, follow these steps:

1. **In the Package for CD dialog box, set up the package exactly the way you want it, including all of the presentation files and options.** See the preceding sections for more information.
2. **Click Copy to Folder.** A Copy to Folder dialog box appears.
3. **Type a name for the new folder to be created in the Name the Folder text box.**
4. **Type a path for the folder in the Choose Location text box, as shown in Figure 26-12.**
5. **Click OK.**
6. **If a warning appears about linked files, then click Yes or No as appropriate.** PowerPoint copies the files to that location.
7. **If a warning appears about comments or ink annotations, click Continue.**
8. **Click Close to close the Package for CD dialog box.**

FIGURE 26-12

You can copy presentation files and support files anywhere, not just to a CD.

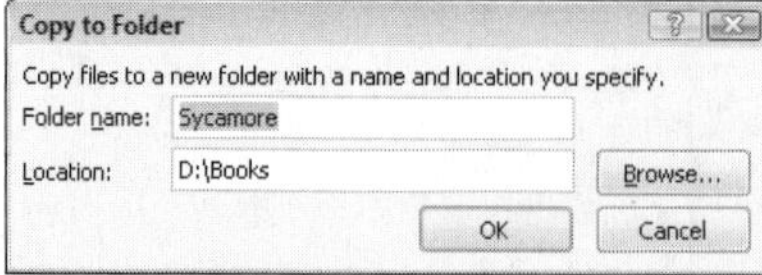

Using a presentation CD with the PowerPoint Viewer

To use a self-running presentation CD, just insert it in the CD drive. The presentation starts automatically. You can then move through the presentation as described later in this chapter.

If you have placed multiple presentations on the CD and have specified that a menu should appear for them, then this menu appears when you insert the CD. Select the presentation that you want, and click Open to start it. When the presentation has finished, this menu will reappear.

Working with Audio-visual Equipment

The first part of this chapter assumed that you were using a computer with a single monitor to show your presentation, but this may not always be the case. This section looks at the entire range of audio-visual options from which you can choose. There are many models of projection equipment in conference rooms all across the world, but most of them fall into one of these categories:

- **Noncomputerized equipment:** This can include an overhead transparency viewer, a 35mm slide projector, or other older technology. You face two challenges if you need to work with this category of equipment: one is figuring out how the equipment works because every model is different, and the other is producing attractive versions of your slides to work with them. There are companies that can produce 35mm slides from your PowerPoint files, or you can invest in a slide-making machine yourself. For transparencies, you simply print your slides on transparency film that is designed for your type of printer.
- **Single computer with a single monitor:** If there is a computer with a monitor in the meeting room, then you can run your presentation on that computer. You can do this with the Publish to CD feature that is discussed in the preceding sections, and then run the presentation directly from the CD.
- **Single computer with a dual-monitor system:** On systems with dual monitors, one monitor is shown to the audience and the other is for your own use. This is useful when you want to display your speaker notes on the monitor that the audience does not see. However, you might need to set up multi-monitor support in Windows so that you can view different displays on each monitor.
- **Projection system (LCD) or large monitor without a computer:** If the meeting room has a large monitor but no computer, you will need to bring your own laptop computer and connect it to the monitor. Most of these systems use a standard VGA plug and cable.

The following sections look at some of these options in more detail.

Presenting with Two Screens

If you have two monitors — either your laptop computer screen and an external monitor, or two external monitors hooked up to the same computer — you can display the presentation on one of them and your own notes on the other one. This is a very handy setup!

CAUTION **To use two screens, you need the full version of PowerPoint on your laptop, not just the PowerPoint Viewer. You also need compatible hardware. For example, your laptop must have an external VGA port and a built-in video card that supports DualView in your version of Windows. If you have a desktop computer, you must have two separate video cards or a video card with two separate video ports.**

Configuring Display Hardware for Multi-Screen Viewing

First, you need to prepare your hardware. On a laptop computer, this means enabling both the built-in and the external monitor ports and connecting an external monitor. Some laptops toggle between internal, external, and dual monitors with a Fn key combination; refer to your laptop's documentation.

On a desktop computer, install a second video card and monitor, and then do the following to set them up in Windows:

1. **When Windows restarts after you install the second video card, right-click the desktop and choose Personalize (Windows Vista) or Properties (Windows XP).**
2. **Click Display Settings (Windows Vista), or click the Settings tab (Windows XP).**
3. **A sample area displays two monitors, as shown in Figure 26-13.**

FIGURE 26-13

You must set up the second monitor in Windows before setting it up in PowerPoint.

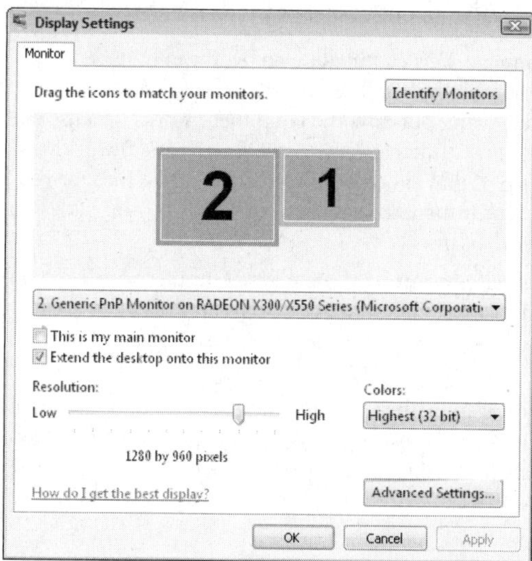

4. **The monitor that you use most of the time should be monitor 1, and the other one should be monitor 2.** To determine which is which, click Identify Monitors (or the Identify button if you are using Windows XP); large numbers appear briefly on each screen.
5. **If you need to swap the numbering of the monitors, click the one that should be the primary monitor and then select the This is My Main Monitor check box (Windows Vista) or the Use This Device as the Primary Monitor check box (Windows XP).** This option will be unavailable if the currently selected monitor is already set to be the primary one.
6. **Select the secondary monitor, and then select the Extend my Desktop onto This Monitor check box (Windows Vista) or Extend the Desktop Onto This Monitor check box (Windows XP).**

7. *(Optional)* **If the monitors are not arranged in the sample area in the way that they are physically positioned on your desk, you can drag the icons for the monitors to where you want them.**
8. *(Optional)* **You can click a monitor in the sample area to adjust its display settings.**

TIP You can also adjust the refresh rate for each monitor. To do this, make sure that you have selected the video card to which the monitor is attached, and then click the Advanced Settings button (Windows Vista) or the Advanced button (Windows XP). On the Monitor tab in the dialog box that appears, change the refresh rate. A higher refresh rate reduces screen flicker, but if you exceed the monitor's maximum supported rate, the display may appear distorted and the screen may be damaged.

9. **Click OK.** You are now ready to work with the two monitors in PowerPoint.

You can now drag items from your primary monitor to your secondary one! This can also be useful outside of PowerPoint as well. For example, you can have two applications open at once, each in its own monitor window.

Setting Up a Presentation for Two Screens

If you have two monitors available, and configured as described in the preceding section, you can use the following steps to help PowerPoint recognize and take advantage of these monitors:

1. **Open the presentation in PowerPoint.**
2. **On the Slide Show tab, click Set Up Slide Show.** The Set Up Show dialog box opens, as shown in Figure 26-14.

FIGURE 26-14

You can set up the show for multiple monitors in the Set Up Show dialog box.

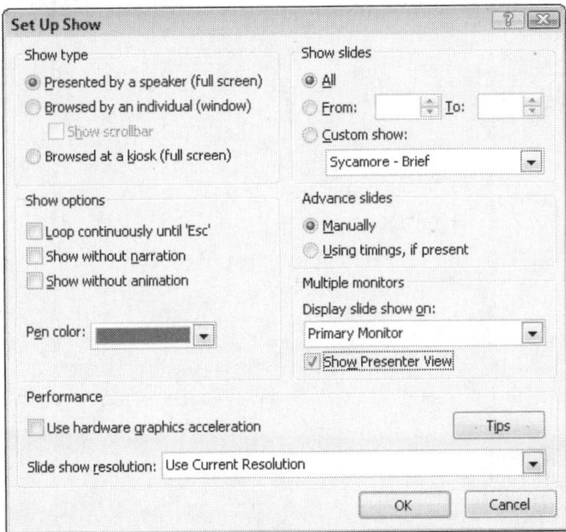

3. **In the Multiple Monitors section, open the Display Slide Show On drop-down list and choose the monitor that the audience will see.**
4. **Select the Show Presenter View check box.** This will give you a separate, very useful control panel on the other monitor during the show, as described in the next section.

5. **Click OK.** You are now ready to show the presentation using two separate displays — one for you and one for the audience.

Presenting with Two Screens Using Presenter View

Presenter View is a special view of the presentation that is available only on systems with more than one monitor, and only where you have selected the Show Presenter View check box in the Set Up Show dialog box, as described in the preceding section. This view provides many useful tools for managing the show behind-the-scenes, as shown in Figure 26-15. It appears automatically on the non-audience monitor when you enter Slide Show view, and includes the following features:

- At the bottom of the screen is a pane containing thumbnail images of each slide. You can jump to a slide by selecting it here. You can also move between slides by using the large left- and right-arrow buttons.
- The speaker notes for each slide appear in the right pane. You cannot edit them from here, however. Zoom buttons appear below the speaker notes pane, so you can zoom in and out on the notes.
- A Time and Duration display appears below the current slide. It tells you the current time and how long you have been talking.
- The panes are adjustable by dragging the dividers between them, so you can have larger thumbnails, a smaller slide display, more or less room for notes, and so on.

FIGURE 26-15

Presenter View provides tools for helping you manage your slideshow from a second monitor.

Presenter View does not have all of the features that you have learned about so far in Slide Show view. However, keep in mind that the audience's monitor is still active and available for your use! Because you extended the desktop onto the second monitor, you can simply move the mouse pointer onto the audience's display and then use the buttons in the corner (or the right-click menu) as you normally would.

Summary

In this chapter, you learned how to prepare for a big presentation. You now know how to package a presentation and move it to another computer, how to set up single and multi-screen audio-visual equipment to work with your laptop, and how to control a presentation on-screen using your computer. You also know how to jump to different slides, and how to take notes during a meeting. You're all set! All you need now is a nice starched shirt and a shoeshine.

Part V

Organizing Messages, Contacts, and Time with Outlook

IN THIS PART

Chapter 27

Fundamentals of E-Mail

Before you can send and receive e-mail using Outlook, you must set up at least one e-mail account, providing Outlook with the information it needs to connect to your online e-mail account. From there, you can compose, send, and receive messages. Outlook provides great tools for creating and organizing your messages, as well as options for customizing how it works with your messages. This chapter helps you learn the basics for all of those actions in Outlook.

Setting Up Your E-Mail Accounts

Before you can use Outlook to send and receive e-mail, you must set up your e-mail account. You can have more than one account — you'll follow the same steps for each one. There are two parts to this.

First, your account must be set up on the server or at your ISP. This is not done in Outlook. If your account is at your workplace, it will likely have been set up by an IT person and he or she will have provided you with the required information such as your e-mail address and password. If you are setting up a home or small business account, you may be doing this yourself. The details depend on your ISP, so I cannot provide instructions, but as part of the process you will either specify or be given your e-mail address and password.

Second, you must set up your account in Outlook. This process provides Outlook with the information, such as your e-mail address and password, that it needs to connect to your e-mail server and send and receive messages. If you are at work, you may be lucky enough to have your IT guru set up Outlook for you, in which case you can skip this section. If you must do it yourself, the minimum information you need is your e-mail address and your password. You may also need to know the addresses for your organization's or ISP's e-mail server. The URL looks much like a Web page address and will be something like `mail.hosting.com`. Some mail accounts require two addresses, one for incoming mail and another for outgoing mail.

Free Hotmail Accounts and Outlook

As of this writing, you cannot use Outlook to connect to a free Hotmail account — you must have one of its subscription accounts. You will have to access your free Hotmail account using your Web browser, as usual.

Outlook supports several different kinds of e-mail accounts including a Microsoft Exchange Server account. The account setup process differs depending on whether you have an Exchange account, an HTTP account such as Hotmail or MSN, or one of the other supported account types (POP and IMAP). All these procedures are covered in the following sections.

Automatic e-mail account setup

Outlook can automatically configure some e-mail accounts. This works for some but not all POP, IMAP, Exchange Server, or HTTP accounts. To use the automated e-mail account setup feature, you need to have your e-mail address and your password. Then, here are the steps to follow:

1. **From the menu, choose Tools ➪ Account Settings to display the Account Settings dialog box.** Make sure that the E-Mail tab is selected, as shown in Figure 27-1. If any e-mail accounts are already set up, they will be listed here. If you're just getting started, the list will be blank.
2. **Click the New button to display the Add New E-Mail Account dialog box (Figure 27-2).** Make sure that the Microsoft Exchange Server, POP3, IMAP, or HTTP option is selected; then click Next.

FIGURE 27-1

The Account Settings dialog box.

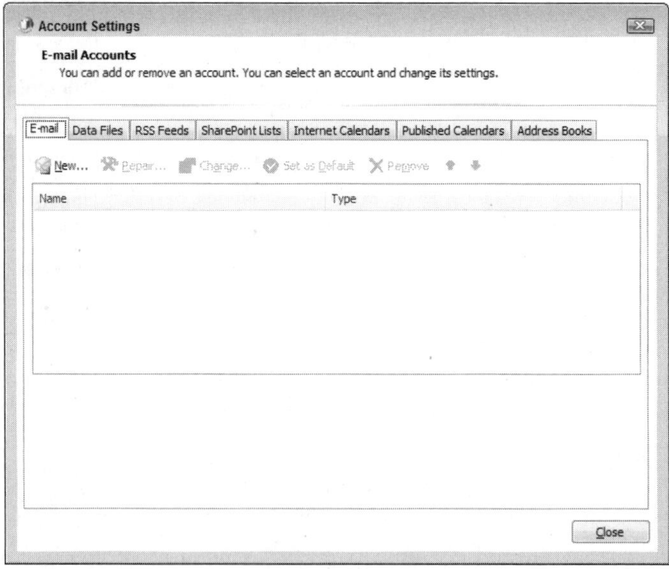

FIGURE 27-2

The Add New E-Mail Account dialog box.

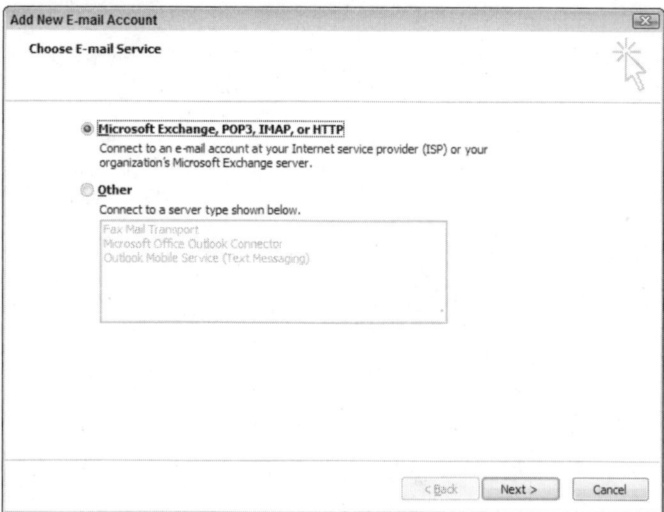

3. **The next dialog box, shown in Figure 27-3, asks for three pieces of information:**
   - Your name
   - Your e-mail address
   - Your password
4. **After you enter the information, click Next.** Outlook will try to connect to your e-mail server and set up the account.

In Step 3 in the preceding list, you have the option of proceeding with manual account setup by selecting the Manually Configure Server Settings or Additional Server Types option and clicking Next. Manual e-mail account setup is described for the various account types later in this chapter.

E-Mail Terminology

All these acronyms can be confusing! POP stands for Post Office Protocol, a technology for receiving e-mail. You'll also see POP3 used; they mean the same thing. IMAP is Internet Mail Access Protocol, another incoming mail technology. HTTP stands for Hypertext Transfer Protocol, which in addition to being a central technology for the Web is also used by some mail systems. SMTP is Simple Mail Transfer Protocol, the almost universally used technology for sending e-mail.

FIGURE 27-3

Entering your name, e-mail address, and password during e-mail account setup.

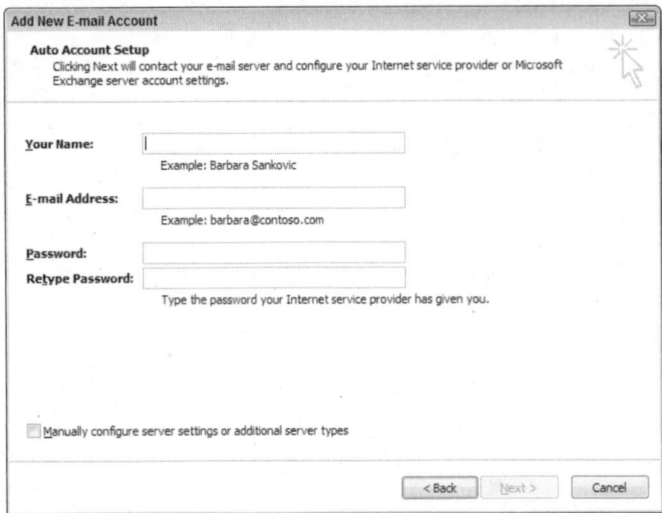

If you are continuing with automatic account setup, Outlook will attempt to connect to your e-mail server and set up the account. In most cases this will work just as it is supposed to. The setup process will finish, the new account will be listed in the e-mail accounts list, and you'll be able to start sending and receiving messages. However, this automated process does not always work. You may encounter one of the following situations:

- Outlook tells you that it cannot establish an encrypted connection to the server and offers to try again using an unencrypted connection. Click next to proceed. The process will either complete properly or you'll encounter one of the other conditions in this list.
- Outlook cannot establish a connection to your account and asks you to verify the spelling of your e-mail address. Make any needed corrections and click Next to try again. The process will either complete properly or you'll encounter the final condition in this list.
- If the preceding steps fail, Outlook will require that you manually configure the server settings. This option will be automatically selected in the Add New E-Mail Account dialog box. Click Next to continue. The manual account setup steps differ for the various account types and are covered in the following sections.

Manual e-mail account setup (POP and IMAP)

If automatic account setup does not work for your POP or IMAP account, you will have to perform the setup it manually. It's a bit more involved but nothing to be afraid of. You need some information in addition to your e-mail address and password. This information should be available from your ISP or your IT person:

- The addresses of your incoming mail server and outgoing mail server. These may be the same but are usually different. For POP incoming mail servers, the address usually looks something like pop.example.com. For outgoing mail servers, it may look like mail.example.com or smtp.example.com. Your ISP will provide the correct information to enter.
- The username and password for your account login.

When you have this information, you are ready to begin. The first dialog box in the manual account setup process is shown in Figure 27-4. You will arrive at this dialog box if automatic setup failed or if you explicitly selected manual account setup. Both of these are explained in the previous section, "Automatic e-mail account setup."

FIGURE 27-4

The first step for manual e-mail account setup.

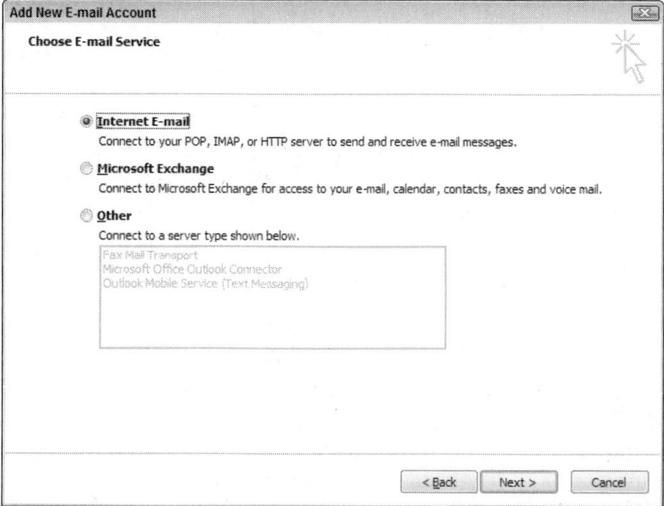

Here are the steps to follow:

1. **Select the Internet E-Mail option.**
2. **Click Next to display the dialog box shown in Figure 27-5.** Enter all the requested information in the corresponding boxes and be sure to select the type of e-mail server from the Account Type list. The Remember Password option and Require Logon using Secure Password Authentication option are explained later in this chapter. Most people should leave these at their default settings. The More Settings button is also explained later in this chapter.
3. **After you have entered all the information, click the Test Account Settings button.** If the test works, click Next and then Finish to complete the account setup. If the test does not work, please refer to the next section ("If your account settings don't work") for steps to resolve the problem.

Two options are available in the Add New E-Mail Account dialog box. If you select the Remember Password option, Outlook will be able to automatically log on to your e-mail account as needed. Otherwise, you will be prompted for the password each time.

Secure Password Authentication, or SPA, is an additional level of security that some mail servers have implemented. If your server requires this, you should have been told and given any additional credentials required for login.

FIGURE 27-5

Entering required information for manual POP or IMAP e-mail account setup.

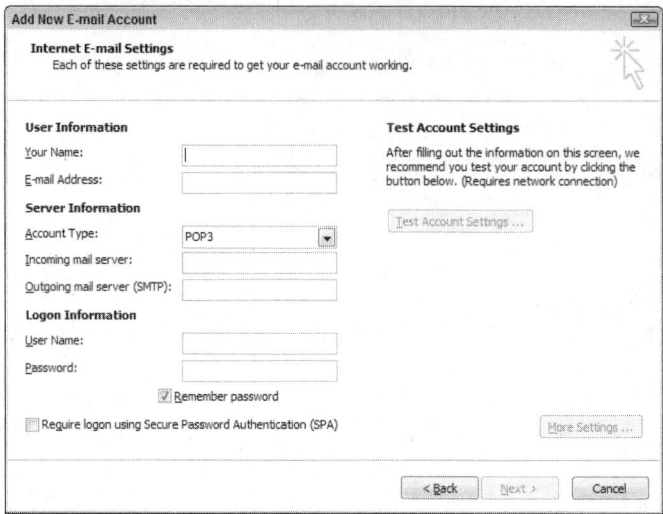

If your account settings don't work

It's not uncommon for e-mail account settings to not work at first. When you click the test Account Settings button, Outlook tries to log onto your incoming mail server and send a test message via your outgoing mail server. One or both of these tests may fail, and the results shown in the Test Account Settings dialog box (shown in Figure 27-6, which depicts a failed test) will tell you the results. Note also that this dialog box has an Errors tab, shown in Figure 27-7. The information on this tab may give you a clue as to where the problem lies. For example, if the problem is reported as The Server Rejected Your Login, the problem almost surely lies with the username or password that you entered.

FIGURE 27-6

This dialog box displays the results of testing your e-mail account settings.

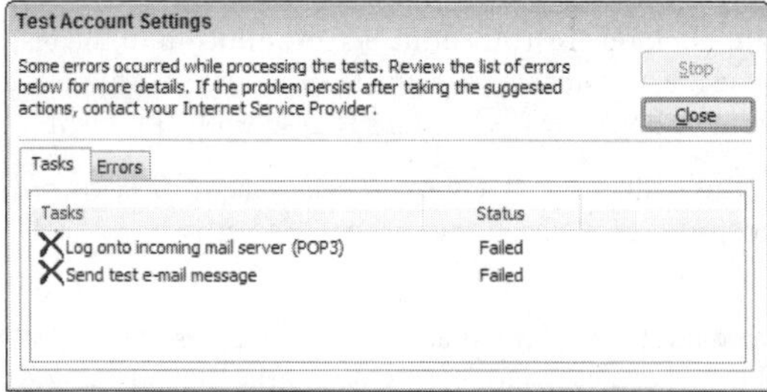

FIGURE 27-7

The Errors tab provides details on why the account settings test failed.

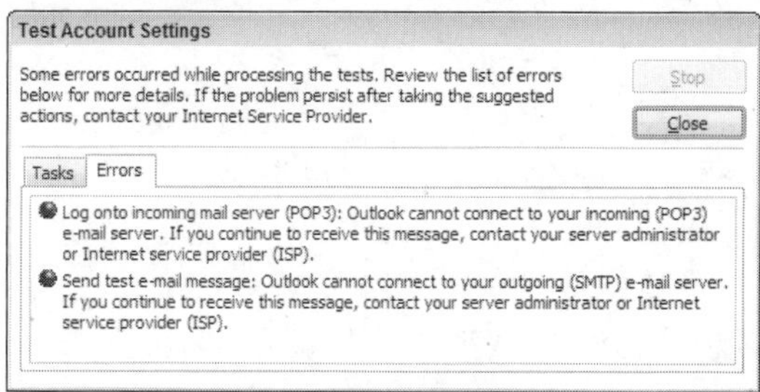
Test Account Settings

Some errors occurred while processing the tests. Review the list of errors below for more details. If the problem persist after taking the suggested actions, contact your Internet Service Provider.

Stop

Close

Tasks | Errors

Log onto incoming mail server (POP3): Outlook cannot connect to your incoming (POP3) e-mail server. If you continue to receive this message, contact your server administrator or Internet service provider (ISP).

Send test e-mail message: Outlook cannot connect to your outgoing (SMTP) e-mail server. If you continue to receive this message, contact your server administrator or Internet service provider (ISP).

The most common cause of problems is simply mistyping some of the information required in the account setup dialog box. Everything must be 100 percent correct!

If the test failed in the outgoing mail server part, it most likely means that your outgoing mail server requires authentication. Setting this option is examined in the following section.

More account settings

The E-Mail Account Setup Dialog box, shown in Figure 27-5, has a button labeled More Settings. You may not need to make any changes here, but if you do, you can refer to this section for the details.

Clicking the More Settings button brings up the Internet E-Mail Settings dialog box. This dialog box has four tabs for POP and IMAP accounts and a fifth for IMAP accounts only. The next sections look at these in turn.

General

The General Tab, shown in Figure 27-8, has these three entries:

- **Mail Account:** This is the name Outlook uses to refer to the account, for example in the account list. The default is your e-mail address but you can change it to anything you like, such as Work E-Mail or Yahoo Account.
- **Organization:** If you enter your organization name here, it will be included in the headers of all e-mail messages you send. Recipients normally do not see these headers, and Outlook does not make use of this information in any way. Other e-mail programs may, however.
- **Reply E-Mail:** When recipients receive an e-mail from you and reply by clicking the Reply button in their e-mail program, their reply message is sent to this address. By default, it is the e-mail address associated with the current e-mail account, but if you have more than one e-mail account, you can enter another address here.

FIGURE 27-8

The General tab in the Internet E-Mail Settings dialog box.

Outgoing Server

The Outgoing Server tab, shown in Figure 27-9, lets you specify authentication — that is, logon — settings for your outgoing mail server. By default, this option is turned off because most outgoing mail servers do not require authentication. If yours does, select the My Outgoing Server (SMTP) Requires Authentication box and then select other options and enter information as follows:

- **Use Same Settings As My Incoming Mail server:** Outlook will log on to your outgoing mail server using the same username and password that you specified for your incoming mail server. This is the most commonly used setting.
- **Log On Using:** Select this option if your outgoing server requires its own logon. Then enter your username and password in the corresponding fields. The Remember password option and the Require Secure Password Authentication (SPA) options work the same as was described for them in the previous section, "Manual e-mail account setup."
- **Log On to Incoming Mail Server before Sending Mail:** Select this option only if your incoming mail server is the same as your outgoing mail server. You will know that this is the case when you are given the same address for both servers and enter this address for both during account setup.

Connection

The Connection tab, shown in Figure 27-10, lets you specify details of how Outlook connects to your e-mail server. To set these options, you need to know how your computer is connected to the Internet. If you are at work, you almost surely connect via a local area network (LAN). If you are at home and have a cable modem or DSL connection, including wireless connections, this is also a LAN. A dial-up or phone line connection is an older connection technology that is still in use by many people.

If you are connected via a LAN, select the Connect Using My Local Area Network (LAN) option. If you select this option, you can also select the Connect Via Modem When Outlook Is Offline option. Doing so causes Outlook to use a dialup connection (assuming that one is available) to connect when the LAN is not available.

FIGURE 27-9

The Outgoing Server tab in the Internet E-Mail Settings dialog box.

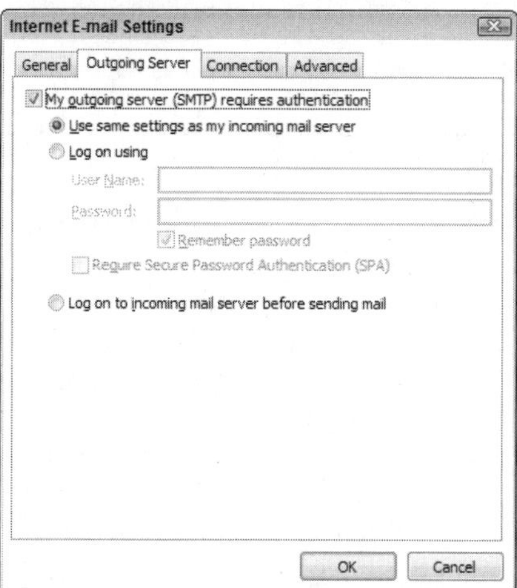

If you connect via a modem (phone line), select the Connect Using My Phone Line option. You may already have a dial-up connection defined in Windows. If not, you must define one before you can use Outlook for e-mail. Defining a dial-up network connection is a process that is part of the Windows operating system, not Outlook, and is beyond the scope of this book. Please refer to Windows online help for more information. If you select this option, you then must select the defined dial-up connection that you want to use in the Modem section of the dialog box. You can use the Add button to add a new dial-up connection and the Properties button to examine and modify the properties of an existing connection.

FIGURE 27-10

The Connection tab in the Internet E-Mail Settings dialog box.

Advanced

The Advanced tab contains options that most people will never need to change. You may not be "most people," however, so I explain these settings here. Note that the options available on this tab differ slightly for POP and IMAP accounts, as shown in Figures 27-11 and 27-12, respectively.

FIGURE 27-11

The Advanced tab for POP accounts tab in the Internet E-Mail Settings dialog box.

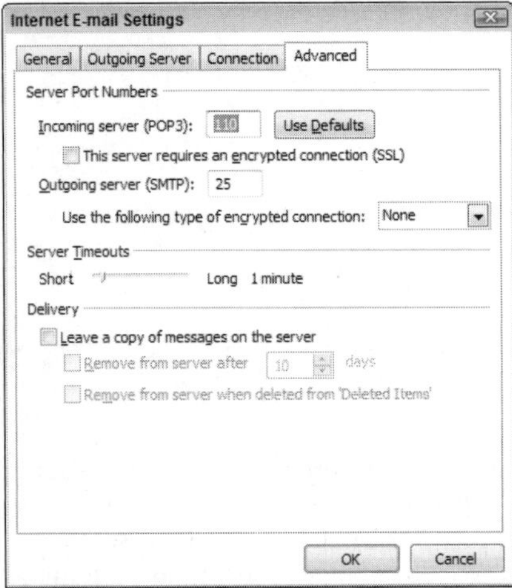

FIGURE 27-12

The Advanced tab for IMAP accounts in the Internet E-Mail Settings dialog box.

The advanced settings that are common to both POP and IMAP accounts are the following:

- **Server Port Numbers, Incoming server:** The default values are 110 for POP servers and 143 for IMAP servers. It's rare for a server to be set up on different ports, but if yours is, you can enter the correct port numbers here.
- **Server Port Numbers, Outgoing Server:** Regardless of whether your incoming server is POP or IMAP, your outgoing server is SMTP and the default port number is 25. Do not change this unless you know that your outgoing mail server uses a different port — a rare occurrence.
- **This Server Requires an Encrypted Connection (SSL):** Turn this option on for the incoming or outgoing mail server, or both, if required.
- **Server Timeouts:** This is the amount of time that Outlook will wait for the mail server to respond when retrieving or sending e-mail. The default setting of 1 minute works fine in most cases. If you find Outlook timing out, it probably means that you are working over a slow connection or that your server is often busy. Try a longer timeout setting to resolve this problem.

If you are working with a POP account, you have several settings available that control how Outlook handles messages on the server:

- **Leave a Copy of Messages on the Server:** By default, messages that you have received are removed from the server as soon as they are downloaded to Outlook. Turn this option on if you want Outlook to leave the messages on the server after download. This can be useful if you want to later retrieve your messages from another computer.
- **Remove from Server after . . . Days:** Specifies how long messages are to be retained on the server after they have been downloaded.
- **Remove from Server when Deleted from "Deleted Items":** A message is retained on the server until you permanently delete it in Outlook.

If you are working with an IMAP account, there is one unique option, Root Folder Path, that specifies the root folder of the mailbox. Normally you leave this blank and Outlook uses the default root folder on the server. If you need to specify a different root folder, enter it here.

Folders

The Folders tab is available in the Internet E-Mail Settings dialog box only for IMAP accounts. It lets you specify whether copies of sent mail should be stored in the default Sent Items folder or somewhere else. If you choose the latter option, you can select the folder to use or create a new folder.

Manual e-mail account setup (Exchange server)

If automatic account setup does not work for your Exchange account, you must exit Outlook and set up the account through the Windows Control Panel. Although some of the dialog boxes look the same, you cannot set up an Exchange account manually while Outlook is running. To complete this setup, you need to know the address of your Exchange server (or its NETBIOS name), the username that has been set up for you, and your password.

Downloading an Exchange Profile

Some Exchange account providers give you the option of downloading an Exchange profile file to your computer. When you run this file, it sets up the Exchange profile for you. If available, this is an easy and error-free way to set up an Exchange profile.

These are the steps to set up an Exchange account:

1. **Make sure that Outlook is not running.**
2. **Select Control Panel from the Windows Start menu.**
3. **Double-click the Mail icon to display the Mail Setup dialog box.**
4. **Click the E-Mail Accounts button to open the Account Settings dialog box.** This is the same dialog box that you see when setting up accounts from within Outlook (shown earlier in Figure 27-2).
5. **On the E-Mail tab, click the New button to display the Add New E-Mail Account dialog box.**
6. **Make sure that the Microsoft Exchange, POP3, IMAP, or HTTP option is selected and then click Next.**
7. **In the next dialog box, select the Manually Configure Server Settings option and then click Next.**
8. **In the next dialog box, select the Microsoft Exchange option and then click Next.**
9. **In the next dialog box, shown in Figure 27-13, enter your Exchange server address and username.**
10. **If a dialog box appears asking whether you want to continue, click OK.**
11. **Click Finish.**

After setting up your account, you can start Outlook. You will be prompted for the Exchange account password. If the connection is established, Outlook displays `Connected to Microsoft Exchange` at the right end of the status bar (which is at the bottom of the Outlook window).

FIGURE 27-13

Entering information about your Exchange server and username.

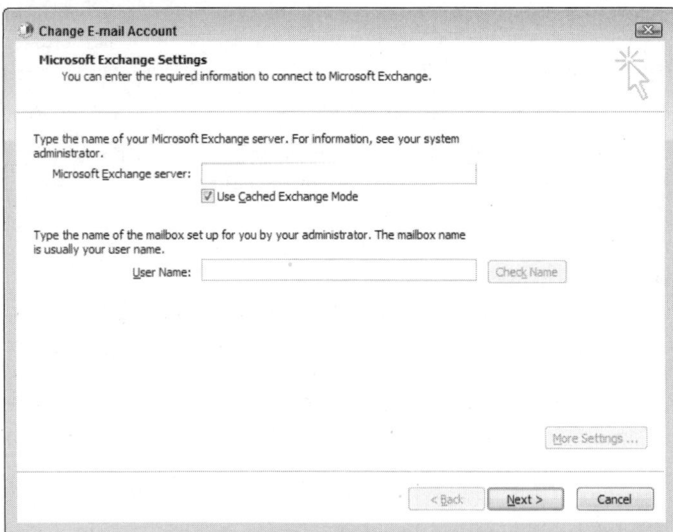

Manual e-mail account setup (HTTP)

You have an HTTP mail account if you have signed up for e-mail with the MSN Premium, MSN Hotmail Plus, and Microsoft Office Outlook Live subscription service. Other e-mail providers may also have HTTP

Only One Exchange Account

Although Outlook can support multiple e-mail accounts, you can have only one Exchange account set up.

accounts that are compatible with Outlook. If so, they will have provided you with the information you need to set up the account when you signed up.

HTTP mail accounts are designed primarily for Web use — that is, you will use a browser such as Internet Explorer to log on to your e-mail account and read and send messages. However, it can be useful to set up an Outlook account, too, so that you can download and read mail in Outlook and use the program's various features to organize your messages. Be aware that not all HTTP e-mail accounts are compatible with Outlook.

To set up your HTTP e-mail account in Outlook, you need your e-mail address and password. If you are setting up an HTTP account that is not Hotmail or MSN, you will also need to know the address (URL) of the mail server and your username. Then, follow these steps:

1. **Select the Manually Configure Server Settings option in the dialog box (refer to Figure 27-3) and then click Next.**
2. **In the next dialog box that appears, make sure that the Internet E-Mail option is selected; then click Next.**
3. **In the next dialog box that appears, which is shown in Figure 27-14, enter your name, e-mail address, username, and password.** Make sure that HTTP is selected in the Account Type list.
4. **Select Hotmail, MSN, or Other in the HTTP Service Provider list.**

FIGURE 27-14

Entering information for manual HTTP mail account setup.

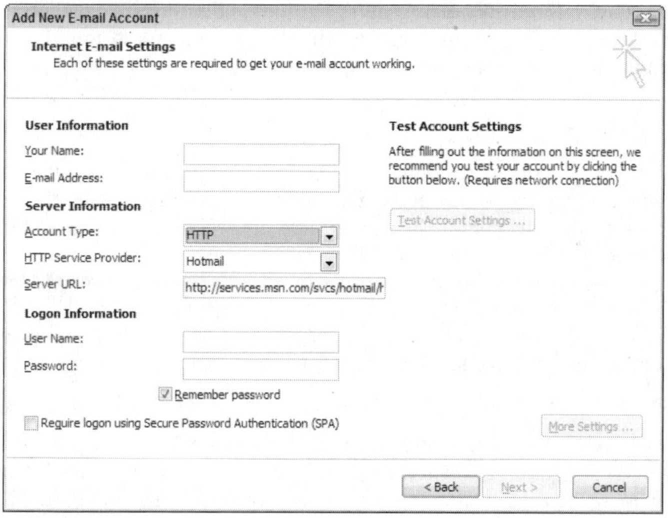

5. **If you selected Other in the previous step, enter the URL of your HTTP e-mail server in the provided box.**
6. **Click Next to complete account setup.**

Modifying Account Settings

If you should need to change your account settings, the procedure is similar to setting up the account in the first place. Choose Tools ➪ Account Settings to display the Account Settings dialog box, and make sure that the E-Mail tab is displayed. Select the account of interest (necessary only if you have more than one) and then click the Change button. You are taken through one or more dialog boxes where you can view and change the settings for this account. The settings depend on the type of account and are explained earlier in this chapter in the section on setting up e-mail accounts.

You can take several other actions with e-mail accounts in the Account Settings dialog box, as follows:

- **Repair:** Outlook tries to connect to your e-mail provider and refresh your account settings. This is the first step to try if an e-mail account has suddenly stopped working.
- **Remove:** Deletes the account.
- **Set as Default:** If you have two or more e-mail accounts, this option makes the selected account the default.

What exactly is the default e-mail account? It's the account that is used to send e-mail messages that you create from scratch. When you create an e-mail message by replying to a message you have received, it is sent using the account that the "reply to" message was received through. Note, however, that when you are composing an e-mail message, you can always change the account that the message is to be sent through. This feature is explained in the next chapter.

Using Outlook Profiles

An Outlook profile stores information about a user's accounts and settings. All Outlook users have a single profile, and for most people that is all that is needed. In some circumstances, multiple profiles can be useful. This section explains how to create and use profiles in Outlook.

Understanding profiles

In the first part of this chapter, you learned how to set up your e-mail accounts. Later chapters in this part of the book deal with configuring other aspects of Outlook such as RSS feeds and the screen appearance. All this information constitutes your profile. The vast majority of users never need more than one profile, but in some situations they can be useful, such as the following:

- If you want to completely segregate two or more types of information, such as work and personal, you can create a profile for each.
- If you want to keep your regular POP and IMAP e-mail accounts separate from an Exchange account.
- If more than one person uses the same computer, each person can have his or her own profile.

The third reason is usually a moot point because modern versions of Windows provide for different user accounts for logging onto Windows, which automatically gives each user his or her own Outlook profile. If, however, you want more than one person to use the same Windows logon and have separate Outlook data, you can use profiles.

Please note that creating an Outlook profile is not the same as creating a separate personal folders file. Although a given Outlook profile can have one or more personal folder files, each profile's folders are kept separate from other profiles.

Creating a new profile

When you first install Outlook, a wizard walks you through the steps of creating a profile. To create a new profile, you use not Outlook but rather the Windows Control Panel, as follows:

1. **Select Control Panel from the Windows Start menu.**
2. **Open Mail to display the Mail Setup - Outlook dialog box.**
3. **Click the Show Profiles button to open the Mail dialog box.** This dialog box lists the existing profiles; the default profile is named Outlook.
4. **Click the Add button to open the New Profile dialog box.**
5. **Enter a name for the new profile and click OK.**
6. **Follow the onscreen prompts to set up your e-mail account.** This procedure is covered earlier in this chapter.

Other actions you can take in the Mail dialog box are the following:

- **Remove:** Removes the selected profile from the system.
- **Properties:** Lets you view and edit the properties of the profile including the e-mail account settings and data files.
- **Copy:** Makes a copy of the selected profile under a new name. This is useful if you want a new profile that has some of the same settings as an existing one. Create a copy, then edit it as needed.
- **Prompt for a Profile:** If this option is selected and you have more than one profile, Outlook will prompt you to select the profile you want to use each time the program starts.
- **Always use the Profile:** Select the profile that you want Outlook to use from the list.

Switching profiles

You cannot switch from one profile to another while Outlook is running. If you selected the Prompt for a Profile option (as explained in the preceding section), quit Outlook and restart it; then select the desired profile when prompted.

If you selected the Always Use This Profile Option (also explained in the preceding section), you must perform the following steps:

1. **Quit Outlook.**
2. **Select Control Panel from the Windows Start menu.**
3. **From Control Panel, open Mail.**
4. **Click the Show Profiles button.**
5. **Select the Prompt for a Profile option.**
6. **Close all dialog boxes.**
7. **Start Outlook.**

Composing and Sending Messages

Outlook's e-mail features are sophisticated and comprehensive. Underneath all that power, however, are the fundamental tasks of composing, sending, and reading messages. This section explains the basics of composing and sending e-mail messages.

Quick compose and send

Outlook provides much flexibility when it comes to creating and formatting e-mail messages. Often, however, all you want to do is to quickly create and send a basic message. Here's how:

1. **If the Mail pane is displayed, click the New button on the toolbar or press Ctrl+N to create a new, blank e-mail message.** If another pane is displayed, click the down arrow to the right of the New button and select Mail Message from the list. The new message appears, as shown in Figure 27-15.

FIGURE 27-15

A blank e-mail message ready to be composed and sent.

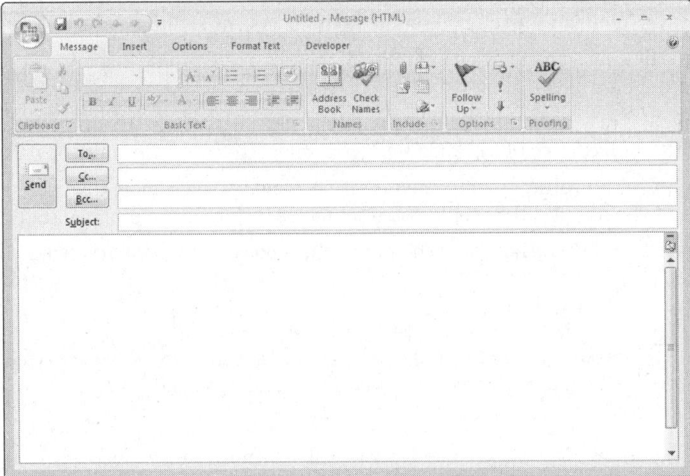

2. **Type the recipient's address in the To field, or click the To button and select a recipient from your address book.**
3. **Type the message subject in the Subject field.**
4. **Type the body of the message in the main section of the message window.**
5. **Click the Send button.**

That's all there is to it. Depending on Outlook's Send and Receive options, your message is sent immediately or placed in the Outbox to be sent the next time a Send or Receive is performed. If you want to be sure that the message is sent immediately, press F9.

Sending a Message

When you click the Send button to send an e-mail message, Outlook places the message in the Outbox. This is one of the mail folders displayed in the navigation pane. Depending on your connection status and Outlook option settings, the message may be transmitted to your e-mail provider immediately or it may wait until your are online or until a timed send/receive occurs. In either case, once the message is sent it is removed from the Outbox folder and a copy is saved in the Sent Items folder.

You can also create a new e-mail message using settings other than the defaults by selecting New Mail Message Using from the Actions menu. Then, from the submenu, do one of the following:

- To create a message based on stationery, select one of the recently used stationeries that are listed (if any) or select More Stationery to select from all available stationery.
- To create a message in a format (HTML, Rich Text, or plain text) other than the default, select the desired format.

Message addressing options

An e-mail message can have multiple recipients, and each recipient can be one of three types:

- To: The main message recipient(s). Every message must have at least one recipient in the To field.
- CC (Carbon Copy): Generally you use CC when a person needs to be aware of the content of the message but is not a primary recipient — that is, does not need to respond or take action. All recipients of a message can see who is in the CC list.
- BCC (Blind Carbon Copy): Like CC but the names and e-mail addresses of BCC recipients are not visible to any other recipients of the message.

Changing the reply to address

By default, the reply to address that is part of every e-mail message you sent is the reply address that you specified when you set up the e-mail account. There may be situations when you want replies to a message that you send directed to a different e-mail address. To do so, follow these steps:

1. **Click the Direct Replies To button in the More Options group of the Options tab on the Ribbon.** Outlook will open the Message Options dialog box.
2. **Under Delivery Options, make sure the Have Replies Sent To option is checked.**
3. **Enter the desired reply address in the adjacent box, or click the Select Names button to choose from your address book.**
4. **Click OK.**

Entering recipients manually

You can type recipients directly into the To, CC, and BCC fields. To enter more than one recipient in a field, use a semicolon as a separator between addresses.

Outlook's AutoComplete feature is by default turned on for all recipient fields. As you start entering an address or name, Outlook displays suggestions based on what you have entered in the past. The suggestions come from a list of names and e-mail addresses that you have entered previously. Outlook will narrow the

Where's the BCC Field?

By default, an e-mail form does not display the BCC field in its header; it displays just the To and CC fields. You can still add BCC recipients using the Contacts list, however. If you want the BCC field displayed, click the Options tab at the top of the message window and click the Show BCC button.

list as you enter more of the name or address. If the recipient you want is displayed, select it by clicking. You can also highlight it with the up and down arrow keys and press Enter. Otherwise, just continue typing in the full name or address.

When Outlook is first installed, the AutoComplete list is empty, so it may seem to not be working. As you continue to use Outlook, however, it will become a useful tool. Names that you use less frequently move to the bottom of the list and eventually disappear.

Entering recipients from your Contacts (Address Book)

Any recipients you have added as Contacts (see Chapter 30) are listed in your Address Book and can be added to an e-mail message with a few clicks. If you refer back to Figure 27-15, you can see that the e-mail window has To and CC buttons next to the corresponding fields. If the BCC field is visible, it will have an adjacent BCC button. Click any of these buttons to open the Select Names dialog box, shown in Figure 27-16.

FIGURE 27-16

Selecting e-mail recipients from your Address Book.

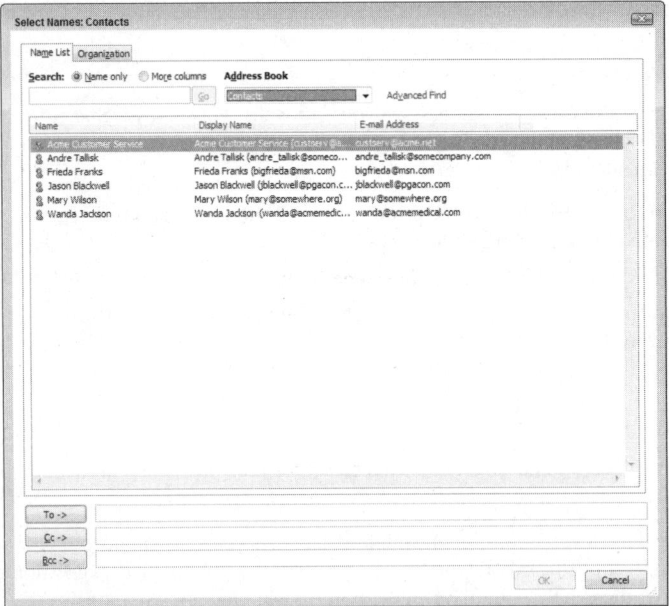

Deleting AutoComplete Items

If someone changes his or her e-mail address, you may find that old, invalid address still appearing on the AutoComplete list. When the list is displayed and you see an address you no longer want, use the down-arrow key to highlight it; then press Del.

If you have more than one address book, you should select it from the Address Book drop-down list. The default address book, which is adequate for many Outlook users, is called Contacts. The entries in the selected address book are displayed in an alphabetized list. Then, add recipients to your message as follows:

- Select a single recipient by clicking it. Select multiple recipients by holding down Ctrl while clicking.
- Add the selected recipient(s) to the To, CC, or BCC field by clicking the corresponding button.
- Add the selected recipients to the active field by pressing Enter. The active field is the one corresponding to the button you clicked — To, CC, or BCC — to display the Select Names dialog box.
- Add a single recipient to the active field by double-clicking the recipient in the list.
- To remove a recipient from the To, CC, or BCC field, click it — the entire name will become highlighted — and press Del.

When you are finished adding recipients, click the OK button to return to the message.

Searching for recipients

The Select Names dialog box lets you search for recipients by name or other information. Look at the upper-left corner of the Select Names dialog box (refer to Figure 27-2). If you select the Name option and start typing in the box, Outlook automatically highlights the first contact in the list that matches what you have typed so far. If Outlook finds no matches, the highlight moves to the end of the list.

If you select the All Fields option, enter the desired search text in the box and click the Go button. Outlook displays any contacts that have a match in any of their fields, such as Company or Mailing Address. See Chapter 29 to learn about Outlook contacts and the various kinds of information that can be stored.

Sending attachments

An attachment is a file that you send along with an e-mail message. When the recipient receives the message, he or she can save the file to disk and open it. Attachments can be a very useful way to pass documents around — whether you're sending photos of the kids to other family members or distributing a Word document to your colleagues for review.

You should be aware of some concerns with attachments. One has to do with file size. Most e-mail accounts limit the size of attachments that can accompany an e-mail message. The limit varies between different accounts, but 10MB is a common figure. Even if your account allows you to send large attachments, the recipient's account may prohibit receiving them.

Another concern about attachments relates to security. Certain types of files can harm your computer by introducing a virus or by other means. Outlook and other e-mail client programs block potentially harmful attachments based on the filename extension, which indicates the type of file. For example, executable program files use the `.exe` extension and are blocked by Outlook.

One approach to dealing with both of these concerns is to use a file archiving utility to compress your files into a zip or other kind of archive. Compression not only reduces the file size but also hides the extensions of files that might be blocked on the receiving end.

What kinds of files can you send and receive as attachments? Any image file is okay, including those with the `.jpg`, `.gif`, `.png`, and `.tif` extensions. So are text files (`.txt` extension), XML files (`.xml` extension), and most Microsoft Office documents: Word (`.doc` and `.docx` extensions), Excel (`.xls` and `.xlsx` extensions), and PowerPoint (`.ppt` and `.pptx` extensions). ZIP archives (`.zip` extension) are okay, too.

You may want to review the section on attachment security in Chapter 20 if you will be sending or receiving many attachments. The remainder of this section shows you how to add attachments to a message.

When you are composing an e-mail message, you attach a file as follows:

1. **If necessary, click the Message tab on the Ribbon.**
2. **Click the Attach File button (with a paper clip icon).** Outlook opens the Insert File dialog box, as shown in Figure 27-17. The initial display is of the files in your My Documents (Windows XP) or Documents (Windows Vista) folder.

FIGURE 27-17

Selecting files to attach to a message.

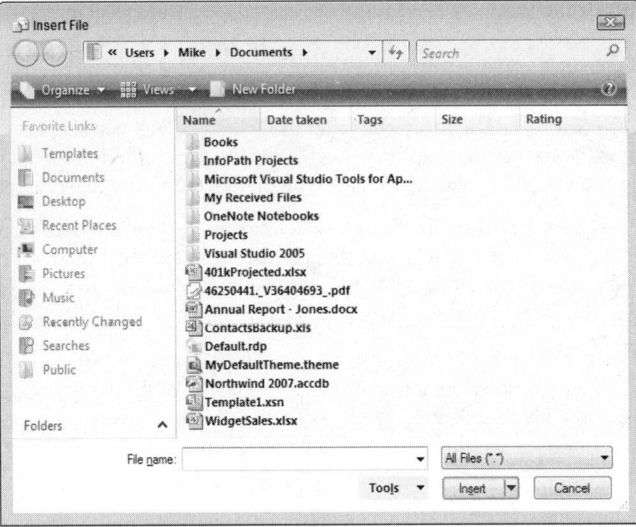

3. **If necessary, use the dialog box to navigate to the folder containing the file.**
4. **Click the name of the file to attach. To attach multiple files from the same folder, hold down the Ctrl key while clicking.**
5. **Click the Insert button.**

After you have attached one or more files, the message displays an Attached line in the header, as shown in Figure 27-18. The attached files are listed here along with the file size. If you change your mind and want to remove a file, click its name in the Attached box and press Del.

FIGURE 27-18

The names of attached files are displayed in the message header.

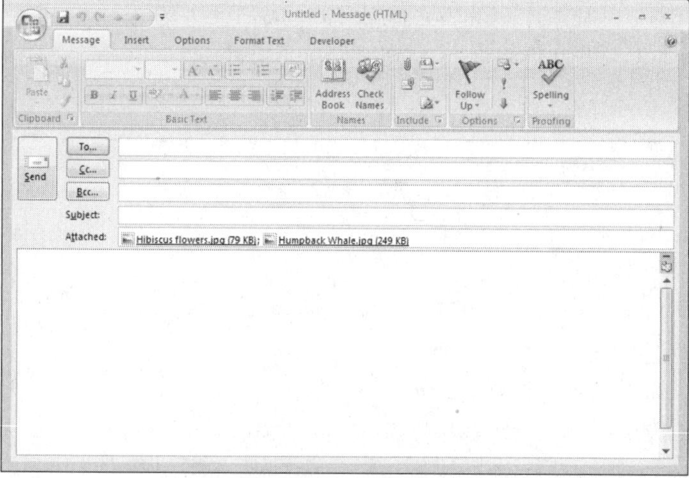

Saving message drafts

If you have started to compose a message and decide to complete it later, you can save a copy in the Drafts folder by clicking the Save icon — it looks like a diskette — on the Quick Access Toolbar at the top left of the message window. You can also select Save from the menu that is displayed by clicking the Office Button (the round icon in the top-left corner of the message window).

When you are ready to continue working on the message, open the Drafts folder by clicking it in the navigation pane; then, double-click the message to open it. You can now complete and send the message as usual.

By default, Outlook saves copies of open items, including messages you are composing, every three minutes.

Sending and Receiving

Outlook's default is to send and receive messages on all accounts when the program first starts and then every 30 minutes. If you want to send or receive manually, click the Send/Receive button on the toolbar or press F9.

Reading and Replying to Messages

When Outlook receives an e-mail message, it places it in your Inbox folder, as shown in Figure 27-19. By default, messages are sorted by the time and date they were received. You can see that the sender, the subject, the time and date received, and the message size are displayed. Please also note the following:

- A message that you have not yet read is displayed in bold type with a closed envelope icon; see, for example, the top message in the figure. A message that has been read is displayed in normal type with an open envelope icon; see the bottom message in the figure.
- If the message includes one or more attachments, a paper clip icon is displayed.

FIGURE 27-19

Messages that you receive are placed in your Inbox folder.

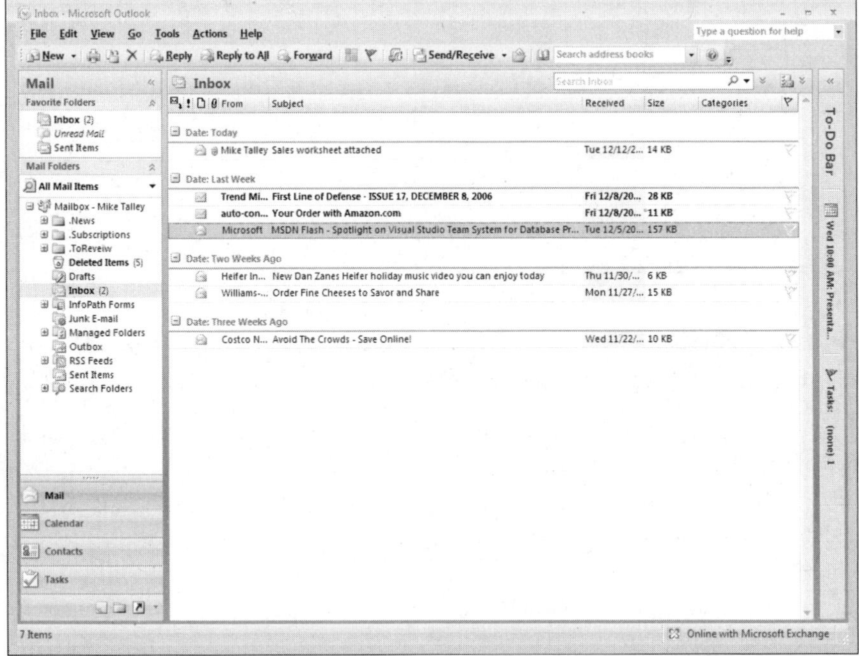

Reading a message

To read a message, double-click it in the Inbox. The message opens in its own window, as shown in Figure 27-20.

While you have an e-mail message open, you can carry out the following actions:

- Print the message by clicking the Print button on the Quick Access toolbar.
- Close the message and delete it by clicking the Delete button on the ribbon. Outlook moves the message to the Deleted Items folder.
- Close the message without deleting it by clicking the X icon at the right end of the title bar.

Other actions that you can take with an e-mail message are covered later in this chapter.

FIGURE 27-20

Reading an e-mail message.

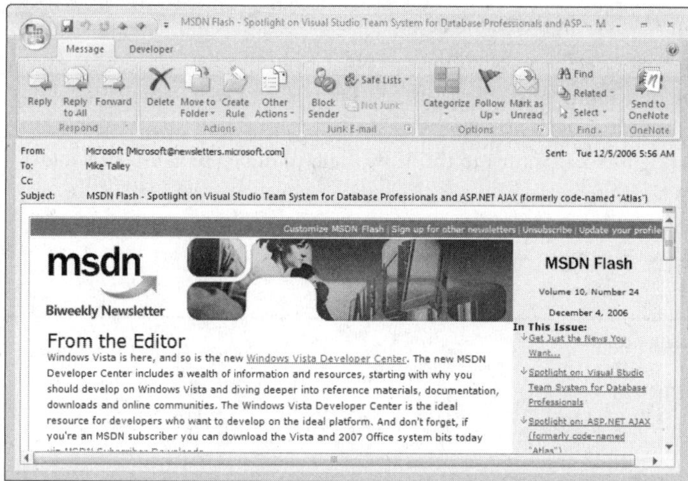

You can also move the message from the Inbox to another folder. Doing so is useful when you want to organize received e-mail messages. You learn more about working with Outlook folders later in the chapter. The basic steps for moving an open message are the following:

1. **Click the Move to Folder button on the Message tab of the Ribbon.**
2. **Select Other Folder from the menu.** Outlook displays the Move Item to dialog box, as shown in Figure 27-21.

FIGURE 27-21

Moving an e-mail message to another folder.

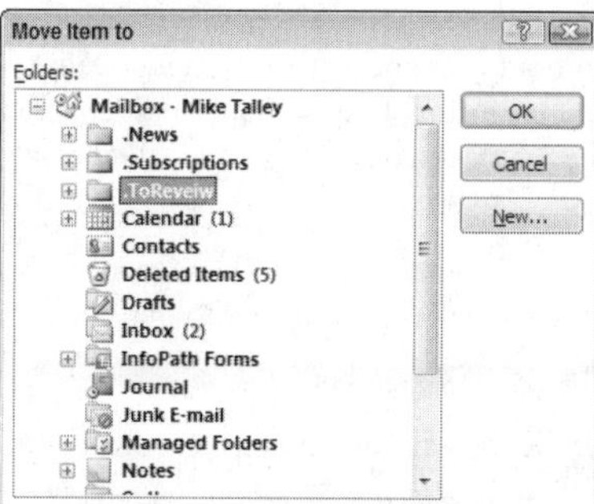

3. **Click the destination folder.** Or, to create a new folder, click the New button. Details on creating a new folder are presented later in the chapter.
4. **Click OK.** The message is closed and moved to the specified folder.

When you are moving an e-mail message to another folder, you are given the opportunity to create a new folder. When you click the New button in the Move Item to dialog box, Outlook opens the Create New Folder dialog box, shown in Figure 27-22. Then, follow these steps:

1. **Enter the name for the new folder in the Name box.**
2. **Make sure that Mail and Post Items is selected in the Folder Contains list.**
3. **Click the location for the new folder in the list.** The new folder is created as a subfolder to the item you select here.
4. **Click OK to close the dialog box and return to the Move Item to dialog box.** The new folder is selected in the list.
5. **Click OK to complete moving the mail message.**

FIGURE 27-22

Creating a new folder to move an e-mail message to.

Marking messages as read or unread

Messages that have not been read are displayed in bold font and with a closed envelope icon. When you open a message, it is marked as read and displayed in normal font with an open envelope icon. You can control how a message is flagged. Perhaps you open a message and then are called away; you might want to mark it as unread so that you will be sure to look at it again later.

If the message is open, simply click the Mark as Unread button on the Message tab of the Ribbon. If no message is open, you can select a message in the Inbox (or whatever mail folder you are in) and then:

- Choose Edit ➪ Mark as Read to mark the message as read.
- Choose Edit ➪ Mark as Unread to mark the message as unread.
- Choose Edit ➪ Mark All as Read to mark all messages in the folder as read.

Using the Reading Pane

Outlook's Reading Pane lets you view the contents of a message without opening it. When the Reading Pane is displayed, it shows the contents of whatever message is selected in the Inbox (or whatever other mail folder you are working in). This is shown in Figure 27-23.

FIGURE 27-23

Using the Reading Pane to view a message.

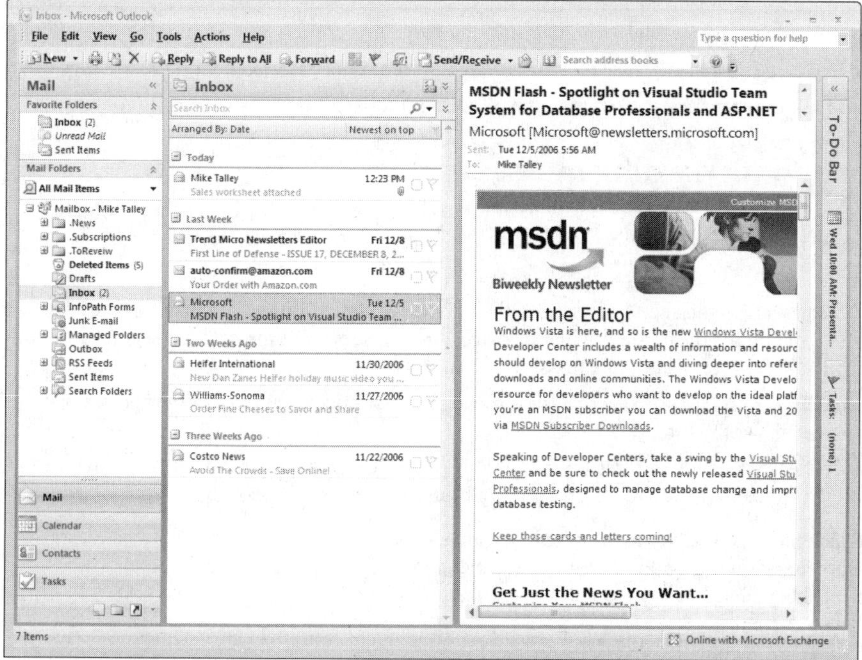

The Reading Pane can be displayed at the bottom of the screen or along the right edge. To control the display of the Reading Pane, choose View ➪ Reading Pane and then select Right, Bottom, or Off.

Normally, viewing a message in the Reading Pane does not mark it as read; this requires opening the message. However, you can tell Outlook to mark messages as read when they are viewed in the reading pane as follows:

1. **Choose Tools ➪ Options to open the Options dialog box.**
2. **Click the Other tab.**
3. **Click the Reading Pane button to open the Reading Pane dialog box.**
4. **Select the box next to the Mark Items as Read When Viewed in Reading Pane option.**
5. **Click OK twice to close all dialog boxes.**

Other actions for received messages

When you are viewing a message that you have received, you can take several other actions besides those already described with the message. Each of these actions corresponds to a button on the Message ribbon:

- **Create Rule:** Lets you create a rule for handling similar messages. Rules are covered in Chapter 28.
- **Block Sender:** Adds the message sender to your Blocked Senders list and moves the message to the junk e-mail folder. You find more details on dealing with junk e-mail in Chapter 28.
- **Safe Lists:** Adds the sender or the sender's domain to your safe list. See Chapter 28 for more details.
- **Categorize:** Assign the message to an Outlook category.
- **Follow Up:** Flag the message for follow-up or create a reminder associated with the message.
- **Related:** Find other messages from the same sender or that are related by subject or content.

Replying to and forwarding messages

Replying to and forwarding messages are two very useful things you can do with e-mail using Outlook. When a mail message is open, you have three buttons in the Respond group of the Message tab of the Ribbon:

- **Reply:** Creates a new message addressed to the person who sent you the original message. The new message contains the entire original message, and the subject of the new message is "Re:" followed by the subject of the original message.
- **Reply to All:** Same as Reply except the new message is also addressed to any other people the original message was sent to.
- **Forward:** Creates a new, unaddressed message. The new message quotes the entire original message and the subject is "FW:" followed by the subject of the original message.

At this point, the new message is ready for editing. You can add your own text to the body of the message, add or remove recipients (you must add at least one recipient when forwarding), add attachments, and so on. When you're finished, click Send.

Another message forwarding option is to select Forward As Attachment from the Actions menu. A new e-mail message is created with the original message attached as a separate file rather than being inserted into the body of the new message.

Working with received attachments

Outlook lets you save attachments to disk and also lets you view attachments without opening them in their native application. The viewing option is available for many attachment types including most image files, Word documents, and Excel workbooks.

Saving attachments

When a received message includes one or more attachments, it will have a small, paper clip icon displayed in the Inbox. There are two ways to save attachments. The first method lets you save attachments without opening the message:

1. **Select the message in the Inbox (or whatever mail folder you are working in).**
2. **Choose File ➪ Save Attachments from the menu.**
3. **On the next menu, select the attachment to save.** Outlook opens the Save Attachment dialog box.

What About Attachments?

When you reply (or reply all) to a message, any attachments that came with the original message are not included. When you forward a message, however, attachments are included.

4. **Navigate to the folder where you want the attachment saved.**
5. **Edit the attachment filename, if desired.** Warning: Do not change the extension!
6. **Click Save.**

Repeat these steps, if necessary, for other attachments.

If the message has more than one attachment, the menu that Outlook displays in the preceding Step 3 also has a Save All Attachments command. Selecting this command opens the Save All Attachments dialog box, as shown in Figure 27-24. Note that all attachments are listed and selected. Then:

1. **If you want to save just some of the attachments, select them by clicking and Ctrl+clicking (to select more than one individual attachment) or Shift+clicking (to select a group of adjacent attachments).**
2. **Click OK.** Outlook displays the Save All Attachments dialog box.
3. **Select the folder to save the attachments in.** You cannot edit attachment names; they are saved under their original names.
4. **Click OK.**

FIGURE 27-24

Saving all message attachments simultaneously.

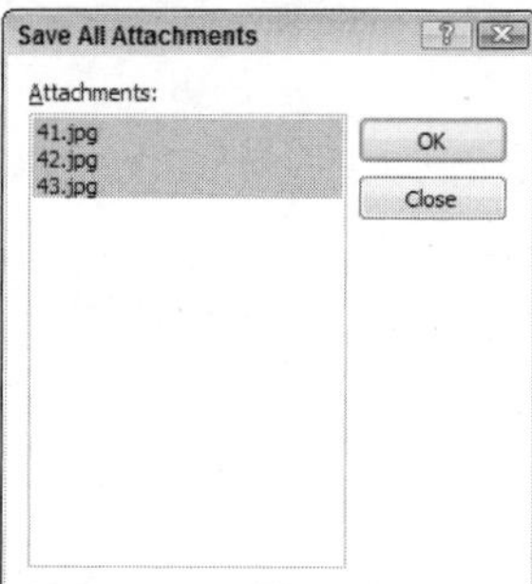

You can use the other way to save attachments when the message is open or displayed in the reading pane:

1. **In the message header, right-click an attachment name.**
2. **Choose Save As from the shortcut menu.**
3. **In the next dialog box, select a folder for the attachment and the attachment name, if desired.**
4. **Click Save.**

Viewing attachments

When a message that you receive includes one or more attachments, they are listed below the message head (both in the reading pane and when the message is open). You also see a Message button next to the attachment names. You can take the following actions:

- Click an attachment name to view the attachment.
- Click the Message button to return to the message.

Figure 27-25 shows these elements along with an attachment that is being viewed.

FIGURE 27-25

Viewing an attachment.

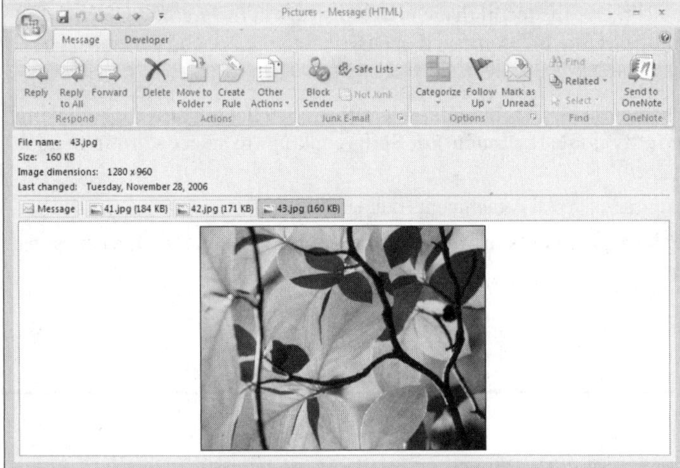

Opening attachments

You usually open an attachment in its native application by saving the attachment to disk, as described previously, and then starting the application and opening the file as usual. You can, however, open an attachment directly from Outlook by following these steps:

1. **Open the message or display it in the Reading Pane.**
2. **Right-click the attachment name.**
3. **Select Open from the context menu.**

   Depending on the file type, Outlook may display a warning dialog box asking whether you want to open or save the file. Click Open, and the attachment is opened in its native application.

The reason for the cautionary dialog box in Step 3 is security. Some kinds of files, such as Word documents and Excel workbooks, have the potential to contain malicious macro code that can harm your system. This code is harmless unless the file is opened, so you may want to save it to disk first and run a virus scan before opening it.

If you do open an attachment this way, you can work with it in the application as you normally would, including saving to disk.

Native Applications

A native, or default, application is an application that is registered on your system for working with a particular kind of file. For some kinds of files, only one application can be "native," such as Microsoft Word for Word files and Excel for Excel files. For other kinds of files, such as image files, there are many possibilities and it will depend on what's installed on your system. For example, on my system, PhotoShop is registered as the native application for most image files, but on your system it might be Paint Shop Pro or Corel Draw.

Understanding the Inbox Display

The Inbox, or any other Outlook folder that contains e-mail messages, provides you with a lot of information about the messages it contains. The display is arranged in columns, or fields, with each field identified at the top of the display. You can customize this display by adding, removing, and rearranging columns. It's important for you to understand the meaning of the fields in the default Inbox display. They are, from left to right in the default display (see Figure 27-26):

FIGURE 27-26

The field headings in the default Inbox display.

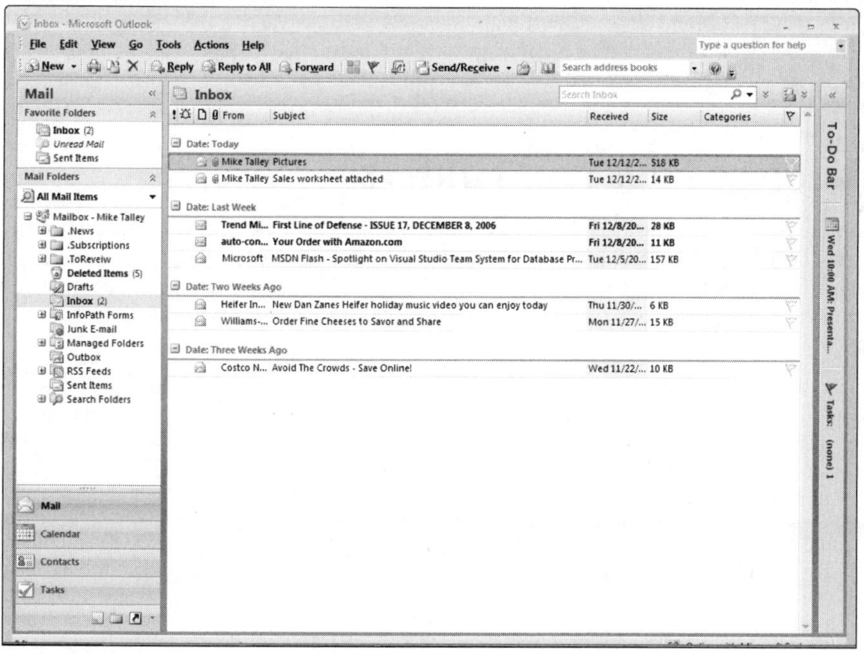

- **Importance (exclamation point icon):** A red exclamation point is displayed in this field if the sender marked the message as having high importance. Nothing is displayed for normal importance.
- **Reminder (bell icon):** A bell is displayed in this field if the message has been associated with a reminder.
- **Read (page icon):** Displays a closed or open envelope for unread and read messages, respectively. Also displays various icons for special messages such as alerts and meeting requests.
- **Attachment (paper clip icon):** Displays a paper clip icon if the message includes one or more attachments.
- **From:** The name or e-mail address of the message sender.
- **Subject:** The message subject.
- **Received:** The time and date the message was received.
- **Size:** The size of the message and any attachments.
- **Categories:** If the message has been assigned to a category, the category name and icon are displayed here.
- **Follow-up (flag icon):** Displays a flag indicating the follow-up status of the message. A clear flag indicates no follow-up status. Various colored flags indicate other follow-up statuses, such as due tomorrow or due next week. A checkmark indicates complete.

You can sort the messages in the Inbox by any of the fields that are displayed. Simply click the field heading to sort by that field in ascending order; click a second time to sort in descending order. If the field heading is wide enough, it displays an upward or downward pointing arrow to show you that the messages are sorted by that field in ascending or descending order, respectively. For example, in Figure 27-26, you can see that the messages are sorted by the Received field in descending order.

Understanding Files and Folders

All computer users are familiar with the idea of a *file*. It's a unit of storage on a disk that contains data, such as a word processing document, a spreadsheet, or a digital photograph. Outlook uses files to store all its information, ranging from e-mail account settings and user options to all its e-mail messages, appointments, tasks, and other items. In fact, Outlook uses a single file called an *Outlook Personal Folders file* to store just about everything.

Most computer users are also familiar with the concept of a *folder* (sometimes called a *directory*). Folders are used to divide a hard disk into discrete storage areas; can you imagine the confusion if all your files were stored in the same location? Outlook uses folders, too, but they are not the same as disk folders. They serve the same purpose — to help organize the items that are stored — but they exist within the Outlook Personal Folder file and not as separate folders on your hard disk.

Outlook folders come in different types based on the kind of item they are designed to hold. For example, your Inbox is a folder and it is intended to hold e-mail messages, but you cannot store a contact there.

Outlook Data Files

For most Outlook users, program data and items are stored in an Outlook Personal Folders file. This is true if you are using a POP, an IMAP, or an HTML e-mail account. The file has the `.pst` extension and is by default named Outlook.pst. The folder on your hard disk where this file is normally kept is as follows:

- **Windows XP and Windows Server 2003:** X:\Documents and Settings*user*\Local Settings\Application Data\Microsoft\Outlook
- **Windows Vista:** X:\ *user*\Local Settings\AppData\Microsoft\Outlook

Here, X is the drive letter, usually C, where the operating system stores user settings, and *user* is the name you have used to log onto Windows. If the computer is configured for more than one user, each will have his or her own separate and independent Outlook Personal Folders file.

You can have more than one Personal Folders file, but only one is designated as the default, which means that Outlook uses it to store account settings, messages, and other items. Additional PST files are used for special purposes such as archiving old items. You cannot change the storage location of the default PST file.

Outlook data file compatibility

Beginning with Outlook 2003 and continuing with the current version, Microsoft changed the internal format of PST files to allow for storage of more items and folders and to support multilingual Unicode data. This format is not compatible with Outlook versions 97 through 2002. If you install a new Outlook over one of these older versions, the old format PST file is automatically converted to the new format. If, however, you want your PST file to be compatible with Outlook 2002 and earlier, you must create a PST file in the older format.

Offline folders file

If you use a Microsoft Exchange e-mail account rather than, or in addition to, an IMAP, a POP, or an HTML account, you may have an Offline Folders file (which has the `.ost` extension). Normally, Exchange keeps copies of your messages and other items on the server, but you can configure Outlook to keep a local copy of the items on your system, in the Offline Folders file. Doing so allows you to work with your Outlook items when a connection to the Exchange server is not available.

Hidden Folders?

The folder where the Outlook data file is kept may be *hidden*, which means that it normally does not show up in Windows Explorer or My Computer. To see hidden folders and files, you must change a view option by choosing Options from the Tools menu (in My Computer or Explorer, not Outlook) in Windows XP, or by choosing Organize ⇨ Folder and Search Options from the Command Bar in Windows Vista. Then, on the View tab, select the Show Hidden Files and Folders option.

Working with Outlook Folders

Outlook folders let you organize all the myriad items that you work with in Outlook. Outlook comes with a default set of folders that is a good starting point, but many users find these folders insufficient. This section shows you how to create new folders and work with folders and folder items.

As mentioned earlier, Outlook folders are designed to hold a specific type of item. The choices are as follows:

- **Calendar folders** hold appointments and other scheduling items.
- **Mail folders** hold e-mail messages.
- **Contacts folders** hold contact information.
- **Journal folders** hold journal entries.
- **Task folders** hold task items.
- **Notes folders** hold notes.

You cannot move an item into a folder of the wrong type, such as moving an e-mail message into a Contacts folder. The one exception to this rule is the Deleted Items folder, which can hold any type of item.

Note that RSS feed items are treated like e-mail messages by Outlook when it comes to folder types.

Outlook's default folders

When installed, Outlook has a set of default folders that are located at the top level in your Personal Folders file. You cannot rename, move, or delete these default folders. They are as follows:

- **Calendar:** Holds calendar items (appointments, and so on.).
- **Contacts:** Holds your contacts.
- **Deleted Items:** Holds any and all items you have deleted before they are permanently deleted. See the section "Deleting Items and Using the Deleted Items Folder," later in this chapter.
- **Drafts:** Holds e-mail messages you have started composing but not yet sent.
- **Inbox:** Holds received e-mails.
- **Journal:** Holds your journal items.
- **Junk E-Mail:** Holds e-mail that has been flagged as junk (spam).
- **Notes:** Holds your notes.
- **Outbox:** Holds e-mails that you have sent but that have not yet been transferred to your e-mail server.
- **Quarantine:** Holds e-mails that have been flagged as containing a virus, worm, or other malicious element.
- **RSS Feeds:** Holds content from your subscribed RSS feeds.
- **Sent Items:** Holds copies of e-mail messages that you have sent.

Creating a new e-mail folder

E-mail folders get their own section because Outlook treats them a bit differently from other folders. To be more specific, you cannot organize e-mail folders into groups but rather have to organize them hierarchically when you create them.

When you create a new e-mail folder, you can place it at the top level under Personal Folders — the same level as Outlook's default folders. You can also put it in an existing folder. You can put folders within folders to essentially any level and thereby organize your e-mail messages in the way that best suits you.

Look at the example in Figure 27-27, which shows Outlook's default e-mail folders. You can see that they are all at the same level within Personal Folders.

FIGURE 27-27

The organization of Outlook's default e-mail folders.

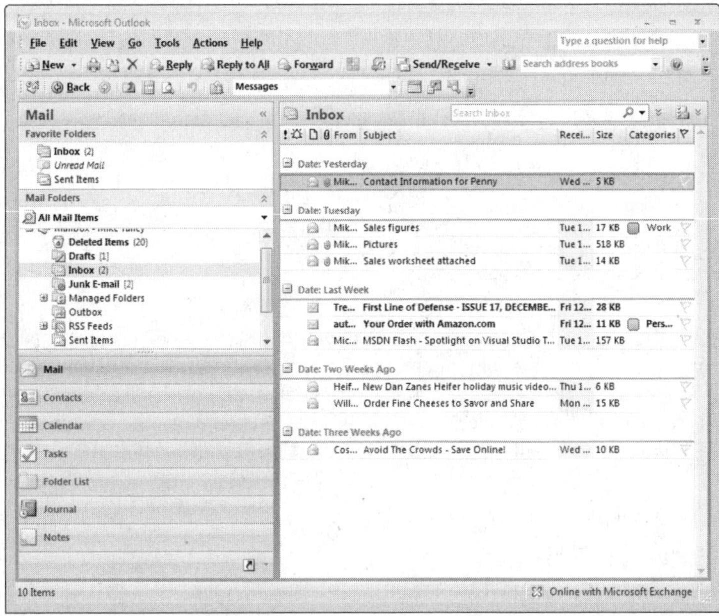

Suppose that you want to organize e-mails from your clients by creating an e-mail folder for each client. For this example, I assume that you have three clients: Acme, Consolidated, and National. One approach is to create three new folders at the top level. The resulting structure is shown in Figure 27-28.

FIGURE 27-28

New e-mail folders can be created at the top level of the folder hierarchy.

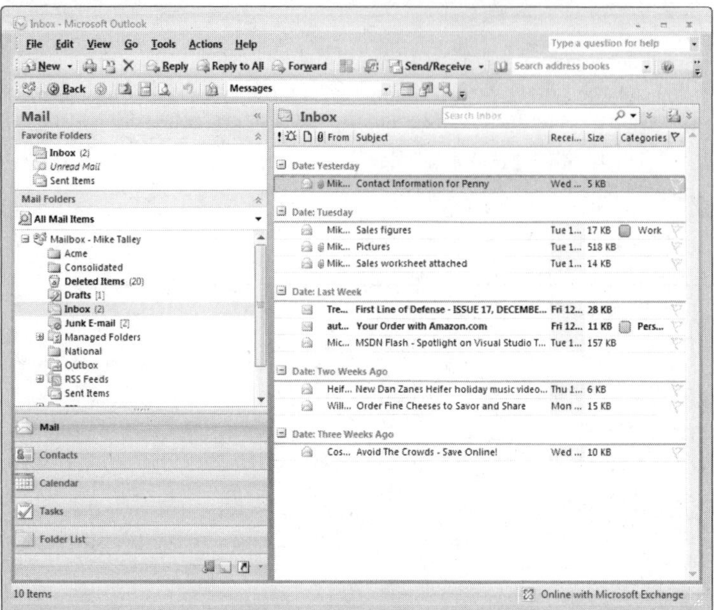

Another approach, one that I prefer, is to use the ability to create folders within other folders, resulting in a hierarchy of folders that is structured according to the folder contents. This approach can be implemented by creating a Clients folder at the top level and then creating Acme, Consolidated, and National folders in the Clients folder. This structure is shown in Figure 27-29. Note that a folder that contains other folders — Clients, in this case — displays an adjacent plus or minus icon that you can click to show or hide the subfolders.

In any event, you do not have to decide all the details of your e-mail folder structure ahead of time because you can always move the folders around if needed.

Now you can get to the details of creating a new e-mail folder. Here are the steps to follow:

1. **If necessary, click the Mail button on the Navigation Pane to display the mail folders.**
2. **If you want the new folder at the top level, right-click Personal Folders (or whatever name you have assigned to the top level).** Otherwise, right-click the folder that you want the new folder in.
3. **Select New Folder from the shortcut menu.** Outlook displays the New Folder dialog box (Figure 27-30). The location for the new folder is shaded in the folder display — Inbox, for example, in the figure. You can, if necessary, change the location at this point.
4. **Type the name of the new folder in the Name box.**
5. **Make sure that Mail and Post Items is selected in the Folder Contains list.**
6. Click OK.

The new folder is created and you can start using it to store mail items.

FIGURE 27-29

New e-mail folders can also be created in a hierarchical structure by placing folders within other folders.

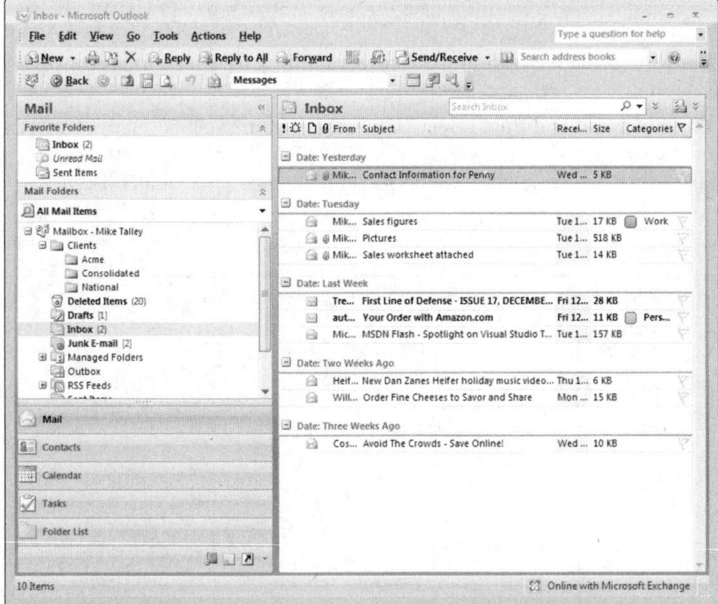

FIGURE 27-30

Creating a new folder to hold e-mail items.

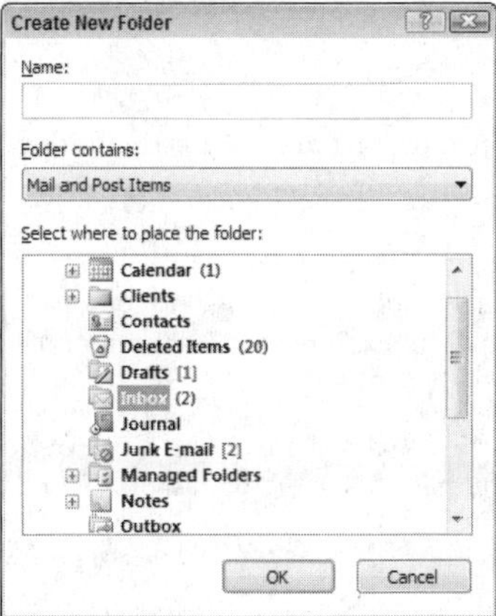

Creating a new non-e-mail folder

Non-mail folders — those for tasks, calendar, journal, and contacts — are handled a bit differently than mail folders. Rather than organize folders by placing them in other folders, as you do with mail folders, you use *groups*. First, the following steps show how to create a non-mail folder:

1. **Click the appropriate button in the navigation pane corresponding to where you want to add a new folder — Calendar, Contacts, and so on.**
2. **Choose Folder from the File menu and then select New Folder from the next menu.** Outlook displays the Create New Folder dialog box (Figure 27-31). The folder for the type of item you selected in Step 1 — Calendar in the figure, for example — is highlighted in the folder list.

FIGURE 27-31

Creating a new folder, Tasks, in this case, to hold non-e-mail items.

3. **Enter the name of the new folder in the Name box.**
4. **Make sure that the Folder Contains list displays the appropriate type of item for the folder you are creating.**
5. **Click OK.**

After you create a non-e-mail folder, it is displayed near the top of the Navigation Pane along with other folders, including the default one, for that type of item. Figure 27-32 shows an example for Tasks after creating two new task folders called Work-related and Personal.

WARNING You can create new Task folders if you want, but be forewarned that task items you move from the default task folder to a new folder are not updated if you have assigned the task to someone else and receive accept, decline, or progress update messages.

FIGURE 27-32

User-created folders for non-e-mail items are displayed along with the default folder in the Navigation Pane.

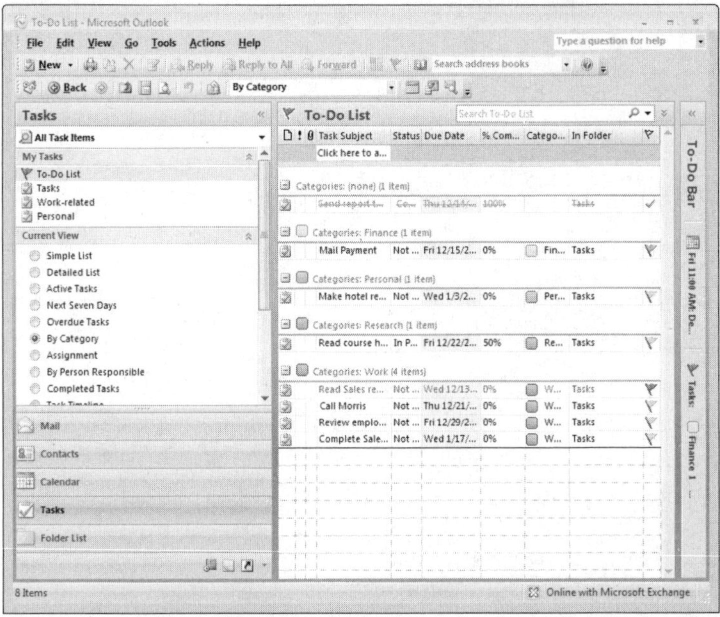

Organizing folders in groups

Outlook folders that are not e-mail folders can be organized into groups. This is similar in concept to organizing e-mail folders by their location in the folder hierarchy, but the procedures are a bit different.

By default, every category of non-e-mail item has a single group with a name such as My Contacts, My Tasks, and so on. If you create new folders, they are displayed as part of this default group. For example, Figure 27-33 shows the Contact folders after adding four new folders to the default Contacts folder. They are all part of the default My Contacts group (which can be expanded or collapsed using the adjacent arrow).

By creating new groups, you can organize these folders as desired. In this example, there are five Contacts folders, and you might want to arrange them as follows:

- The Contacts folder, for miscellaneous contacts, remains in the My Contacts group.
- The Personal Contacts and Family Contacts go into a new group named Personal.
- The Work Contacts and Freelance Contacts folders go into a new group called Work.

The result of this reorganization (which I show you how to do in a moment) is shown in Figure 27-34. Now you can expand and contract individual groups to find just the items you need.

FIGURE 27-33

All folders for non-e-mail items are initially part of the default group, which is My Contacts in this figure.

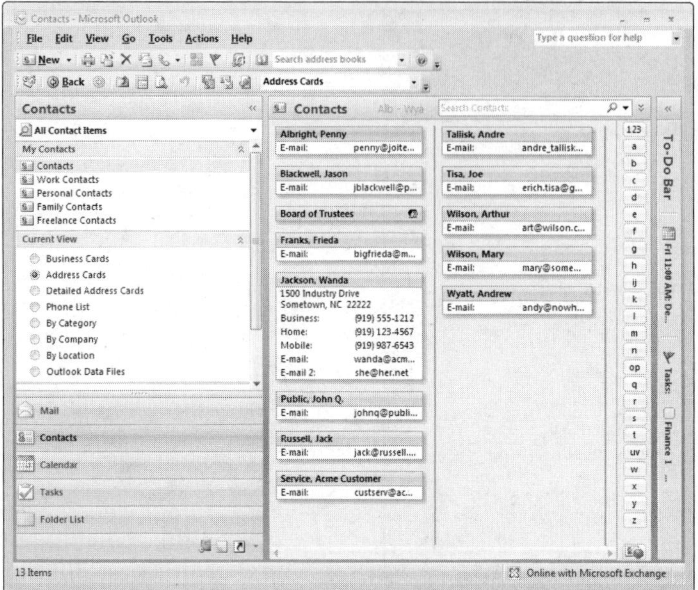

FIGURE 27-34

You can organize folders into separate groups.

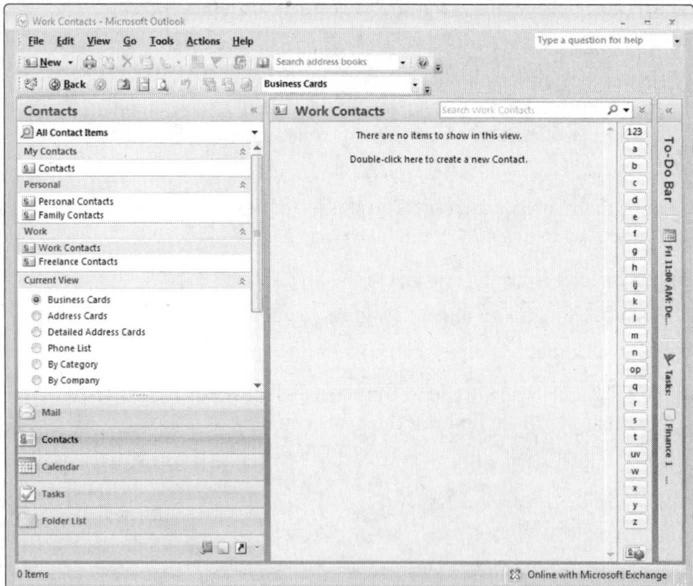

Creating a new group

To create a new group, right-click an existing group (for example, My Contacts in Figure 27-34) and select New Group from the context menu. Then, type in the name for the group and press Enter.

A newly created group is empty, as you might well expect. To move a folder to it, point at the folder, press and hold the left mouse button, and drag it to the destination folder. Figure 27-35 shows how you would move the Personal Contacts folder to the My Contacts group.

FIGURE 27-35

Moving a folder to a different group.

Folder being moved

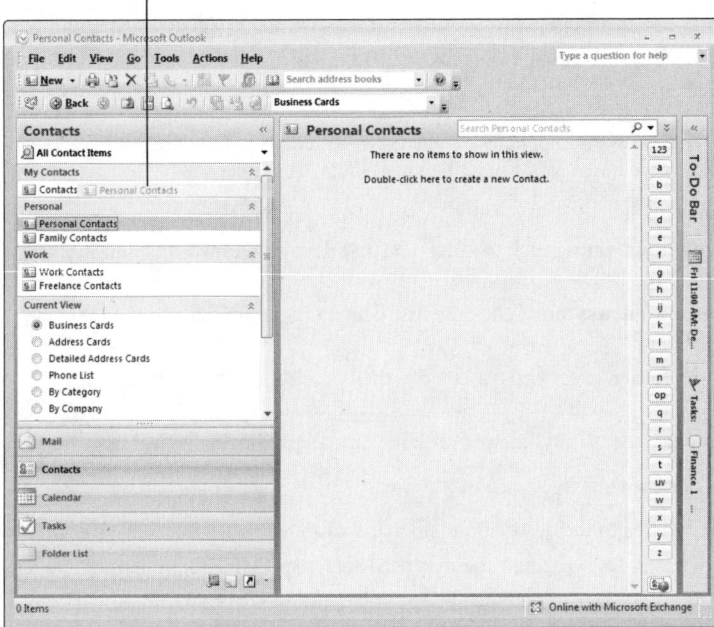

To create a new folder within a group, follow the procedures earlier in this chapter for creating a new folder; then move it to the desired group.

Working with groups

You can take the following actions with a group by right-clicking it and selecting one of the following options from the context menu:

- Rename (the group)
- Remove (the group and any folders it contains)
- Arrange by Name — order the folders in the group alphabetically.
- Move Up/Down in List — change the position of the group in the list.

Additional actions you can take with groups are covered in the next section.

Working with folders, groups, and items

This section covers the everyday tasks that you need to perform with your folders, groups, and Outlook items to keep them organized.

Viewing folder contents

When you switch from one type of item to another — for example, from viewing mail items to viewing contact items — Outlook automatically displays the contents of one folder, usually the default one, in the main Outlook window. To view the contents of another folder (also called opening the folder):

- Click the folder to display its contents in the main window.
- Right-click the folder and select Open in New Window to view the folder's contents in a new window.

You can open as many new windows as you want. When you close a window, Outlook continues running as long as at least one window is open.

Moving or copying items

Outlook lets you move or copy items between folders. For some types of items, only moving, not copying, is allowed. To move or copy one or more items, you must first select them, as follows:

- **To select a single item**, click it.
- **To select multiple contiguous items**, click the first item and then hold down the Shift key and click the last item.
- **To select multiple noncontiguous items**, click the first item and then hold down the Ctrl key and click each additional item.
- **To select all items in the folder**, press Ctrl+A. You can then deselect individual items with Shift+click.
- **To deselect multiple items**, release any key and click any nonselected item.

Now you can move or copy the selected items in one of several ways:

- Drag the item or group of items to the destination folder and drop.
- Choose Cut (to move) or Copy from the Edit menu. Then, open the destination folder and choose Paste from the Edit menu.
- Choose Move to Folder from the Edit menu. Outlook opens the Move Items dialog box, shown in Figure 27-36. Select the destination folder from the list and then click OK. You can also click the New button in this dialog box to create a new folder.

Moving, copying, deleting, and renaming folders

As you fine-tune your Outlook organization, you may want to move folders to new locations. Depending on the type of folder, you may be able to copy a folder as well. E-mail folders can be moved to a new location in the folder hierarchy, whereas other folders can be moved from one group to another.

To move an e-mail folder, point at it and drag it to the new location. For example, Figure 27-37 shows how you move the National folder from its location in the Clients folder to a new location in the Work Stuff folder.

FIGURE 27-36

Use this dialog box to move an item or items to a different folder.

FIGURE 27-37

Moving an e-mail folder to a new location.

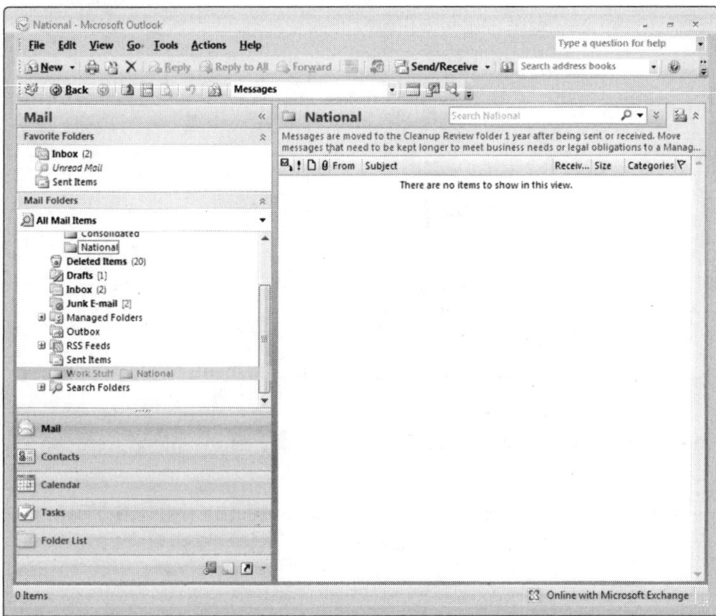

Shortcut Keys for Copy, Cut, and Paste

The standard Windows shortcut keys work in Outlook: Ctrl+C for copy, Ctrl+X for cut, and Ctrl+V for paste.

To move a non-e-mail folder, point at it and drag it from the current group to the new group. Figure 27-38 shows how you move the Freelance Contacts folder from the Work group to the My Contacts group.

FIGURE 27-38

Moving a contacts folder to a new location.

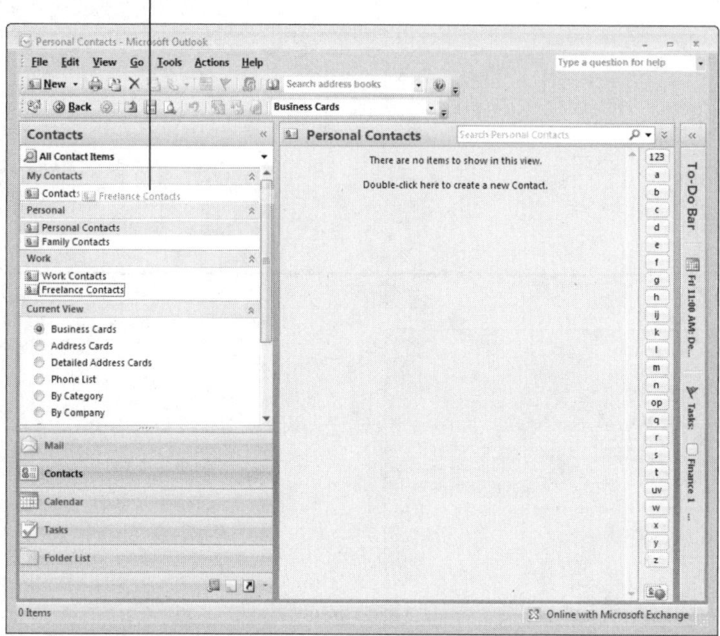

You can also use the Copy (when allowed), Cut, and Paste commands on the Edit menu to copy and move folders.

To delete a folder, right-click it and select Delete *XXXX* (where *XXXX* is the name of the folder) from the context menu.

To rename a folder, right-click it and select Rename *XXXX* (where *XXXX* is the name of the folder) from the context menu; then type in the new name and press Enter.

Deleting Items and Using the Deleted Items Folder

When you delete a folder or an Outlook item, it does not vanish permanently — at least not immediately. Rather, it goes to the Deleted Items folder. This is a safety feature that allows users to recover from accidental deletions. You can "delete" items in the usual way (select them and press Del) or you can drag them to the Deleted items folder.

"Undeleting" Items

If an item has not been permanently deleted — that is, if it is still in the Deleted Items folder — you can "undelete" it by moving it back to its original folder (or another folder of the same type).

When you delete an item from the Deleted Items folder, it is truly gone. Most people prefer to delete items from this folder manually by selecting one or more items and pressing Del. To delete all items from the Deleted Items folder, choose Empty "Deleted Items" Folder from the Tools menu. You can also tell Outlook to automatically empty the Deleted Items folder whenever the program exits, as follows:

1. **Choose Tools ➪ Options to open the Options dialog box.**
2. **Click the Other tab (shown in Figure 27-39).**

FIGURE 27-39

Setting options for emptying the Deleted Items folder.

3. **Select the Empty Deleted Items Folder Upon Exiting option.**
4. **Click OK.**

Setting Options for an Individual E-Mail Message

Although you can create and send e-mail messages using all of Outlook's default settings, you would be missing a lot of flexibility and convenience if you did so. The various e-mail options that Outlook offers let you use e-mail in the way that is most convenient and productive for you. These options fall into two categories: those that apply to a single message and those that apply globally. This section explains a variety of options available for individual e-mail messages that you create.

Changing the send account

This topic is relevant only if you have two or more e-mail accounts. By default, messages are sent as follows:

- Messages you create from scratch are sent using the default e-mail account.
- Messages that are replies to a message you received are sent using the account through which the original message was received.
- Messages you forward are sent using the account through which the original message was received.

To change the send account for a message:

1. **Click the Account button on the Message tab of the Ribbon.** A menu is displayed with the current send account checked.
2. **Select the desired account from the menu.**

Saving sent items

By default, e-mail messages that you send are saved in the Sent Items folder. You can change this location for an individual message as follows:

1. **Click the Save Sent Item button on the Options tab of the Ribbon.**
2. **To save the item to a folder other than the default, click Other Folder and then select the folder.**
3. **To not save the item at all, click Do Not Save.**

Changing the Default E-Mail Account

To change the default e-mail account:

1. **Choose Tools ➪ Account Settings from the main Outlook menu to display the Account Settings dialog box.**
2. **If necessary, click the E-Mail tab.** The current default account is indicated in the account list by "(send from this account by default)."
3. **Click another account in the list.**
4. **Click the Set as Default button.**
5. **Click Close.**

Sending items with a message

You learned earlier how you can attach a file to a message. Outlook also lets you attach certain items, specifically calendars and business cards, to a message.

Sending a calendar

Sending calendar information with a message can be useful to let colleagues know when you are and are not available for a meeting. To send calendar information with an e-mail message, click the Calendar button in the Include section of the Message tab on the Ribbon. Outlook displays the Send a Calendar via E-Mail dialog box, shown in Figure 27-40. You make entries in this dialog box to specify the calendar information that will be sent, as follows:

1. **If you have more than one calendar, select the calendar to use from the Calendar list.**
2. **Select the date range from the Date range list. Predefined ranges include today, tomorrow, and the next 7 days.** Select Specify Dates from the list to enter a custom date range.
3. **From the Detail list, select the level of calendar detail that you want included in the message.** The choices are the following:
   - **Availability Only:** Time is shown as Free, Busy, Tentative, or Out of Office.
   - **Limited Details:** In addition to availability, this option includes the subjects of calendar items.
   - **Full Details:** In addition to availability, this option includes the full detail of calendar items.
4. **Select the Show Time Within My Working Hours Only option to limit the sent calendar information to these hours.** By default, they are 8:00 a.m. to 5:00 p.m. Monday–Friday. Click the Set Working Hours link to change this setting.
5. **Click the Show button to display three additional options.** Two of them relate to what information is included in the message. These options are relevant only if you selected Limited Details or Full Details. The third option determines the format of the sent calendar: Daily Schedule or List of Events. See the main text for information on these two layouts.
6. **Click OK to close the dialog box and insert the calendar information in the message.**

FIGURE 27-40

Sending calendar information in an e-mail message.

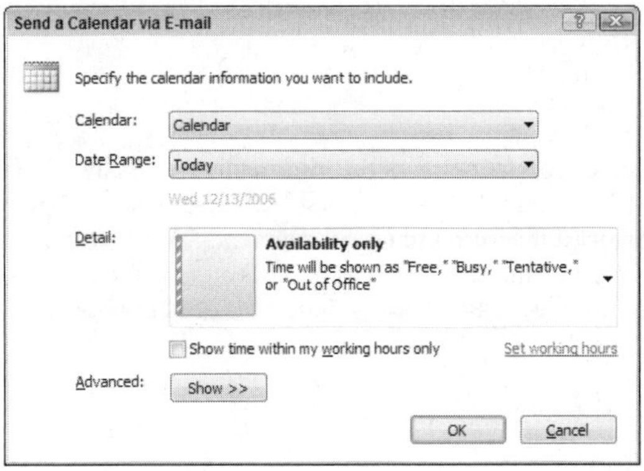

When calendar information is inserted in an e-mail message, at the top is a calendar of the month or months involved with the relevant days highlighted and underlined, as shown for July 13–19 in Figure 27-41. The recipient can click these days to go to the detail section for that day.

FIGURE 27-41

This part of the calendar information includes links to individual days.

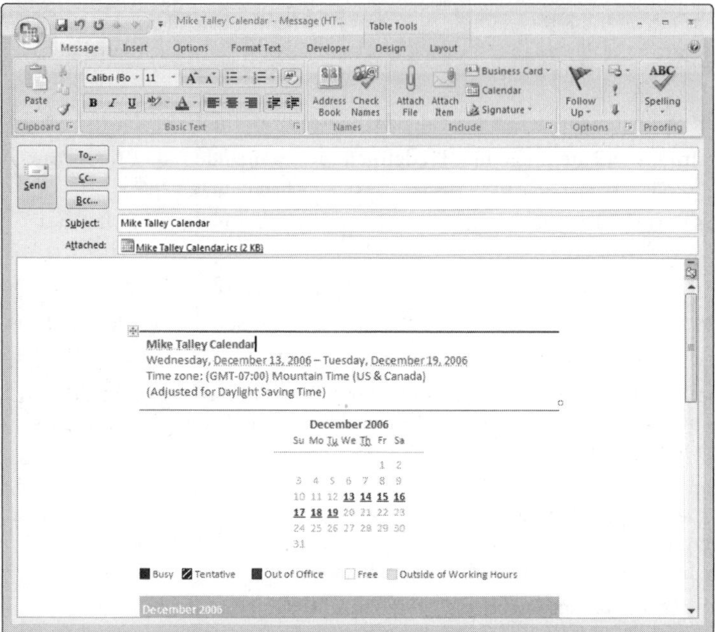

If the calendar information was sent using the Daily Schedule option, the details appear as shown in Figure 27-42. You can see that blocks of time during each day are marked as free, busy, and so on.

If the calendar information was sent using the List of Events option, the message lists specific calendar events only — free time is not explicitly marked.

Sending a business card

A business card is just what it sounds like — an electronic representation of the information normally found on a paper business card. Every entry in a contacts list automatically has a business card created for it. You can insert these cards into e-mail messages to send contact information to e-mail recipients. When you do so, a visual representation of the business card is added to the message and a VCF file is attached to the message. The recipient can use the VCF file to quickly add the contact information to his or her own Contacts list.

FIGURE 27-42

Display of calendar details when the Daily Schedule option is used to send the calendar.

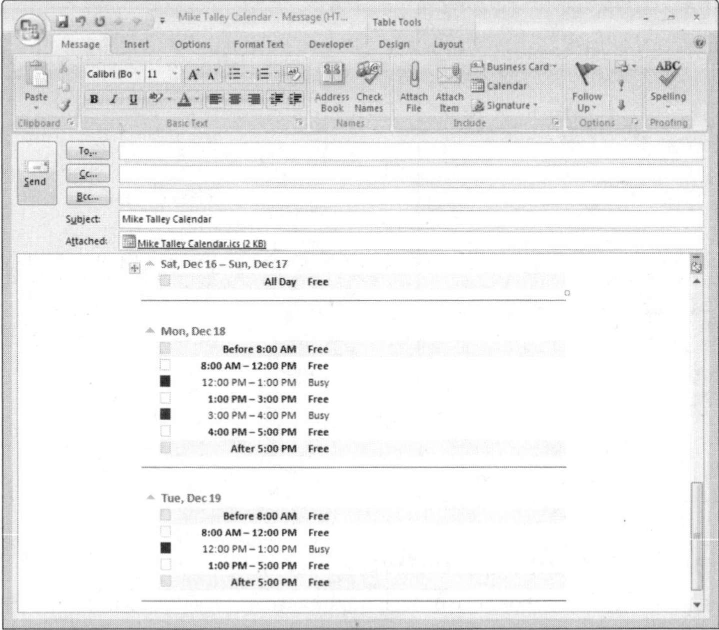

To send a business card with an e-mail message:

1. **Click the Business Card button in the Include group of the Message tab on the Ribbon.** The menu that is displayed lists recently sent business cards.
2. **Select the card you want to send, or select Other Business Cards to select from your Contacts list.**
3. **If you selected Other Business Cards, Outlook displays the Insert Business Card dialog box, as shown in Figure 27-43.**
4. **If you have more than one address book, select the desired one from the Look In list.**
5. **Click the contact whose business card you want to include. The card is previewed in the lower part of the dialog box.**
6. **If you want to include more than one card, hold down Ctrl while clicking.**
7. **Click OK.**

Your Own Business Card

If you create an entry for yourself in your Contacts list, you can send your own business card with e-mail messages.

FIGURE 27-43

Selecting a business card to include in an e-mail message.

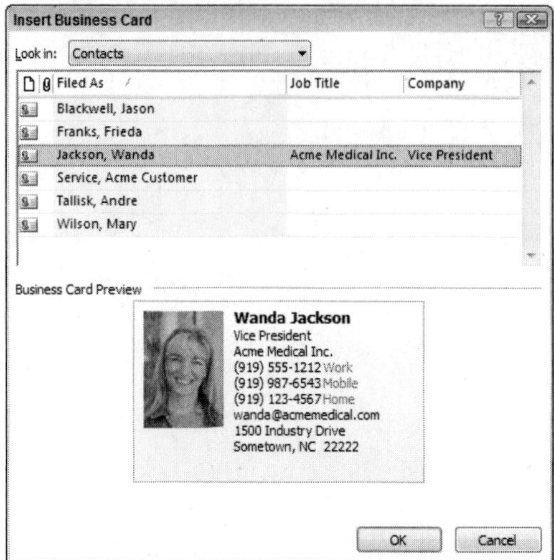

Setting message importance and sensitivity

An e-mail message can be flagged as having low importance or high importance. Low is the default. The recipient's e-mail program may indicate the importance of a message in some way. For example, Outlook displays an exclamation point next to the message in the Inbox if it is marked as having high importance. Many e-mail clients, including Outlook, also allow recipients to sort their received messages by importance.

To mark a message with high importance, click the High Importance button (a red exclamation point) in the Options section of the Message ribbon. To return a message to the default setting of low importance, click the Low Importance button (a downward-pointing arrow).

Setting message restrictions

Message restrictions, or permissions, let you restrict who can view your e-mail messages and what they can do with them (for example, can the message be forwarded?). This feature, which is applicable to all Office documents as well as e-mail messages, is part of Information Rights Management, or IRM.

IRM is based on the concept of *credentials*. To create rights-restricted content, such as an e-mail message, you must possess appropriate credentials to associate with the message. The recipient must also possess the appropriate credentials to view or take other actions with the content.

IRM requires that both the creator and the recipient of restricted content be subscribed to an IRM server. Many people use the Windows Right Management (WRM) service, which at present is free (but with no guarantee that Microsoft will continue the service indefinitely). WRM uses .Net Passport as a means of verifying identities and validating credentials. Some companies use their own IRM server or one provided by a third party.

The steps described in this section assume that you have a rights management client installed on your computer and have set up the necessary credentials.

By default, e-mail messages are created with no restrictions. You can add a Do Not Forward restriction by clicking the Permissions button on the Message ribbon and selecting Do Not Forward from the menu. This button is displayed only if you are set up for IRM. This restriction permits recipients to view the message if they have the required credentials, but not to forward, print, or copy the message.

You may be asked which credentials to use for this message (an individual can possess multiple credentials). When a message you are composing is restricted, it displays a banner below the Ribbon describing the restrictions, as shown in Figure 27-44.

If you attach a document, workbook, or presentation to a message, the restricted permissions of the message are applied to the attachments as well. If the attachment has already had restrictions set in the originating program (Word, Excel, or PowerPoint), those restrictions also remain in effect.

FIGURE 27-44

A message that has restrictions applied displays a notification of that fact below the Ribbon.

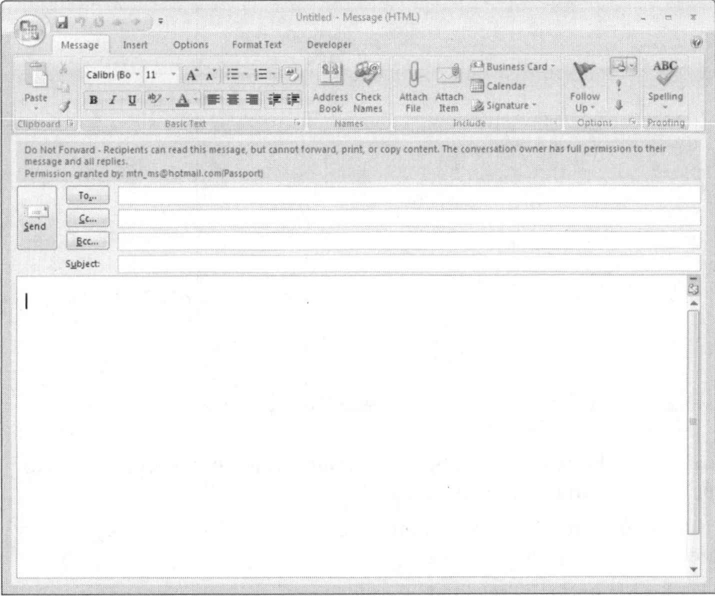

You may also have custom restrictions available to you. In a company, the IT department may have defined a restriction level that restricts contents to people on the company network. Your IT person can provide you with information on custom restrictions if they are in use in your organization.

Flagging a message for follow-up

Sometimes, when you send a message, you would like to be reminded to follow up on the message — for example, to make sure that you have received a reply. You can flag a message for follow up and, optionally, have Outlook remind you. Here's how:

1. **Click the Follow Up button on the Message tab of the Ribbon.** Outlook displays the menu shown in Figure 27-45.

FIGURE 27-45

Flagging a message for follow-up.

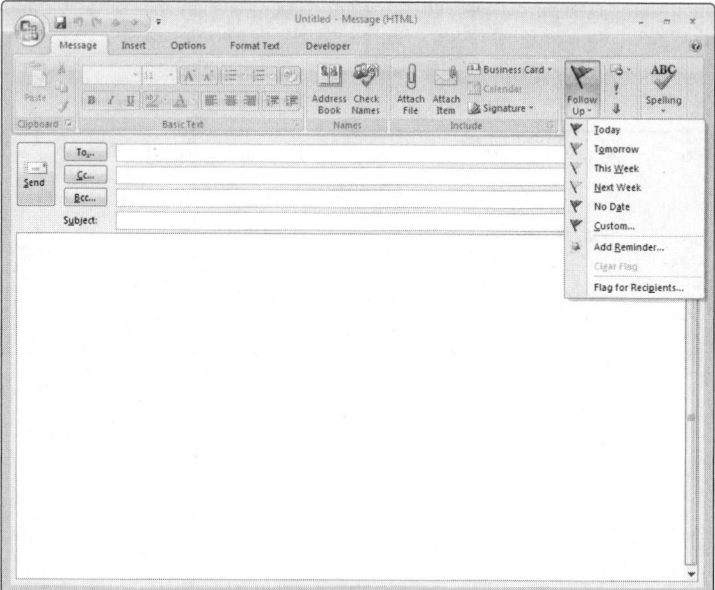

2. **To flag for follow up at one of the predefined times (for example, tomorrow or next week), choose the corresponding command on the menu.**
3. **To specify a custom time, choose the Custom command.** Outlook displays the Custom dialog box, as shown in Figure 27-46.
4. **Make sure that the Flag for Me option is selected.**
5. **From the Flag To list, select the type of follow up (for example, Follow Up, Reply, and so on).**
6. **Enter the desired start and due dates in the corresponding fields.** Click the down arrow next to each field to select from a calendar.
7. **If you want Outlook to remind you of this item, select the Reminder option and then enter the date and time in the adjacent fields.**
8. Click OK.

FIGURE 27-46

Specifying a custom follow-up interval.

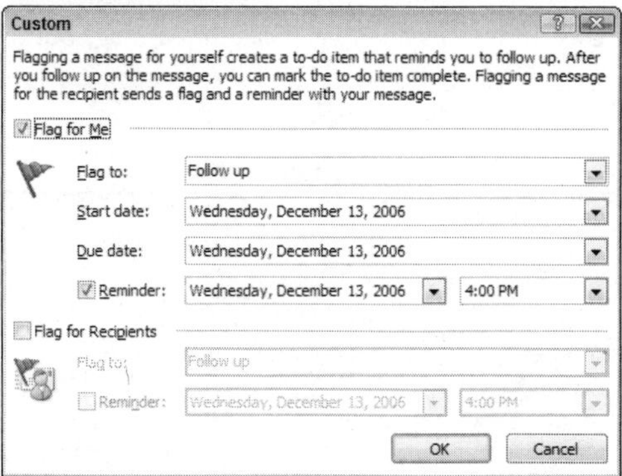

You can also flag a message for the recipient. All you need to do is select Flag for Recipients from the Follow Up menu (Figure 27-45) and then enter the relevant information in the lower part of the Custom dialog box (Figure 27-46).

When an Outlook user receives a message with such a flag, the flag status column in the Inbox displays a special icon indicating that follow up information is included with the message. The user can right-click this icon to add the message to his or her to-do list. E-mail programs other than Outlook may ignore this information or handle it differently.

Assigning a message to a category

Outlook's categories are a powerful tool for organizing all kinds of information. When you create a message, you can assign it to a category. Then you can find the message — the saved copy of the sent message, that is — based on this category. To assign a category to a message:

1. **Click the Dialog Box Launcher in the More Options group of the Options tab on the Ribbon to display the Message Options dialog box.**
2. **At the lower left of the dialog box, click the Categories button.**
3. **Select the desired category from the menu.** Or, click Clear All Categories to remove any category assignment from the message.

Requesting delivery and read receipts

When you send a message, you can request delivery or read receipts (or both) by selecting the corresponding option in the Tracking group of the Options tab of the Ribbon. A delivery receipt is generated when the message is delivered to the recipient, and a read receipt is generated when the message is opened by the recipient. The receipt consists of an e-mail message back to you that contains the date and time that the original message was delivered or read.

Delivery and read receipts sound like a great idea but their usefulness in practice is limited. The delivery receipt must be generated by the e-mail server software, and sometimes this feature is turned off by the server administrator to reduce the load on the server. Even if you do receive a delivery receipt, there is no guarantee that the recipient has read the message. Likewise, the read receipt is sent by Outlook (or whatever other e-mail program the recipient is using), and the user may have this feature turned off.

When you have sent a message and requested a receipt, Outlook automatically processes the receipt when and if it arrives (unless you have turned this feature off under Tracking Options, as explained later in this chapter). When you open the message in the Sent Items folder, the Message tab of the Ribbon displays a Show group with Message and Tracking buttons (Figure 27-47). Click the Tracking button to view the details of any receipts that have been received for this message. Click the Message button to return to the message text.

FIGURE 27-47

Viewing the tracking status of a message.

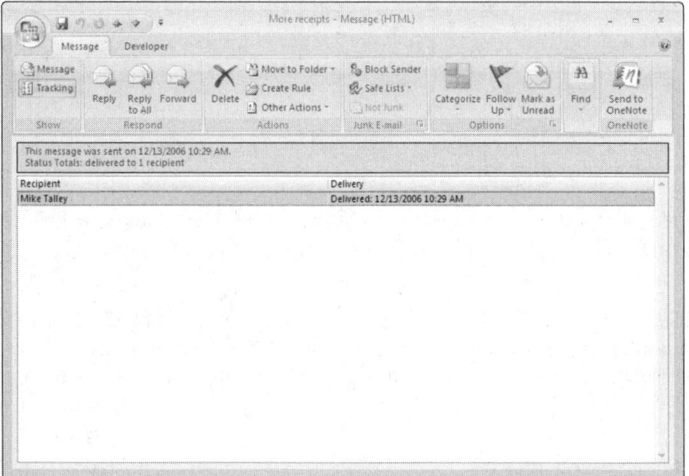

Be aware that if Outlook has not yet received and processed any receipt for a message, the Tracking button is not available on the Message tab of the Ribbon.

Delaying delivery

If you do not want a message delivered right away, you can specify a "do not deliver before" date, as follows:

1. **Click the Delay Delivery button in the More Options group of the Options tab of the Ribbon.** Outlook displays the Message Options dialog box (Figure 27-48).
2. **In the Delivery Options section, select the Do Not Deliver Before option.**
3. **Enter the desired date and time in the adjacent fields.**
4. **Click the Close button.**

If you are using a Microsoft Exchange e-mail account, the message is sent to the server and held there until the specified date and time. If you are using another kind of e-mail account, the message is held in Outlook's outbox until the first send operation that occurs after the specified date and time.

FIGURE 27-48

Delaying the delivery of a message.

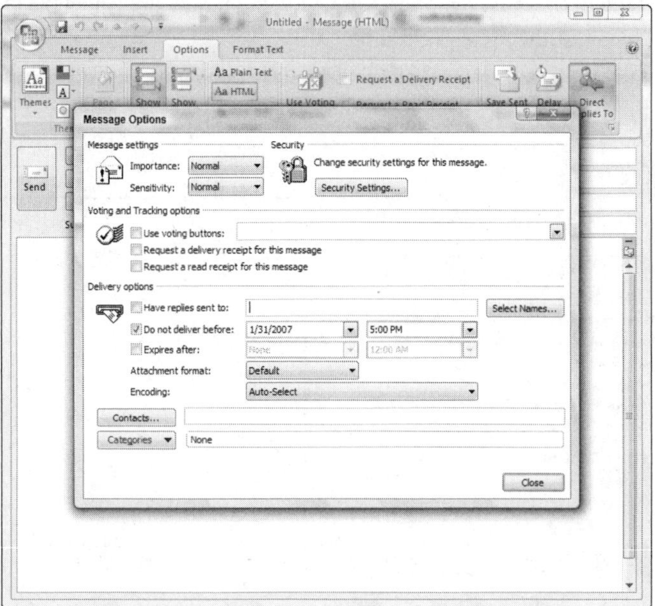

Setting a message expiration date

If you are sending a message that is relevant for only a limited period, you can set an expiration date for the message. When the recipient receives the message, that message will behave normally until the expiration date, after which it will display in the Inbox (or whatever folder it is in) with a line through the header. The recipient can still open the message, but the strikethrough provides a visual indication that the message has expired. Other e-mail programs may handle message expiration differently.

To set an expiration date:

1. **Click the Dialog Box Launcher in the Options group of the Message tab of the Ribbon.** Outlook displays the Message Options dialog box (shown previously in Figure 27-48).
2. **In the Delivery Options section of the dialog box, select the Expires After option.**
3. **Enter the desired expiration date and time in the adjacent fields.**
4. **Click Close.**

Setting Global E-Mail Options

A number of Outlook's options apply globally to all messages and to e-mail in general. You select these options using several dialog boxes that display the options in related groups. This section follows the same organization.

Mail preferences

To view and change e-mail preferences:

1. **Choose Tools ➪ Options from the main Outlook window to display the Options dialog box.**
2. **If necessary, click the Preferences tab.**
3. **At the top of this dialog box, click the E-Mail Options button.** Outlook displays the E-Mail Options dialog box (Figure 27-49).

FIGURE 27-49

Setting global e-mail preferences.

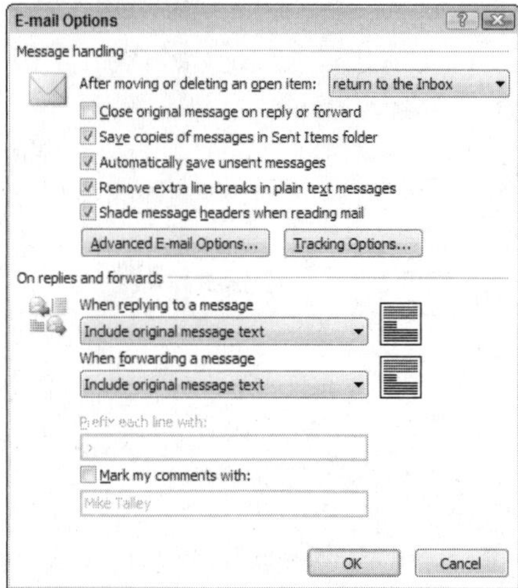

4. **Set options in this dialog box as explained in the following list.**
5. **Click OK.**

The options in the Message Handling section of the E-Mail Options dialog box are as follows:

- **Close Original Message on Reply or Forward:** When you select Forward or Reply in a message that you received, the original message is closed.
- **Save Copies of Messages in Sent Items Folder:** When you send a message, a copy is saved in the Sent Items folder (recommended!).
- **Automatically Save Unsent Messages:** Messages you have started composing but not sent are saved in the Drafts folder.
- **Remove Extra Line Breaks in Plain Text Messages:** Unneeded line breaks are stripped from plain-text messages.
- **Shade Message Headers when Reading Mail:** When you are reading a message that contains quoted components, Outlook uses subtle shading to mark the quoted section. (This feature does not always work properly, I have found.)

- **Advanced E-Mail Options:** Click this button to view and set advanced e-mail options (explained in the next section).
- **Tracking Options:** Click this button to view and set tracking options (explained in a following section).

The On Replies and Forwards section of this dialog box determines what Outlook does when you reply to a message or forward a message. You set each independently but the options are essentially the same, as follows:

- **Do Not Include Original Message:** Replies are sent without the original message. Not applicable to forwarded messages.
- **Attach Original Message:** Replies and forwards are sent with the original message included as an attachment.
- **Include Original Message Text:** Replies and forwards are sent with the original message included as part of the new message.
- **Include and Indent Original Message Text:** Replies and forwards are sent with the original message included as part of the new message, indented with respect to the other parts of the message.
- **Prefix Each Line of the Original Message:** Replies and forwards are sent with the original message included as part of the new message, with each line of the original message prefixed by what is entered in the Prefix Each Line With field (by default, this is the > sign).

The final option in this dialog box is Mark My Comments With. You use this option when you prefer to reply to or forward messages with your comments included along with the original message text. When this option is selected, your comments are each preceded by your name (or whatever you specify) in brackets.

Advanced e-mail options

When you click the Advanced E-Mail Options button in the E-Mail options dialog box, Outlook displays the dialog box shown in Figure 27-50.

FIGURE 27-50

Setting advanced e-mail options.

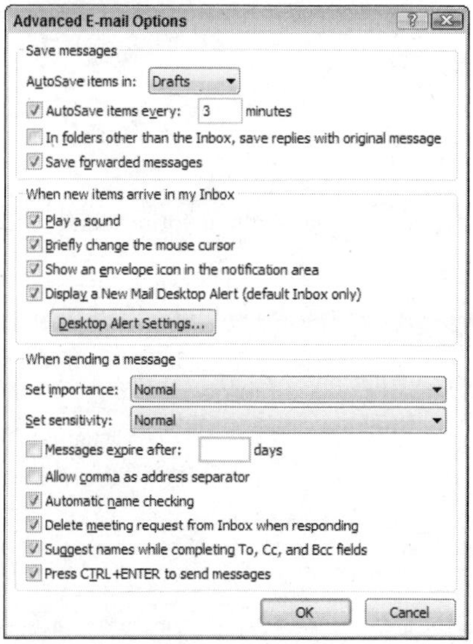

Most of these options are self-explanatory, so I do not go into details with those. The few that may require explanation are the following:

- **AutoSave Items In:** Specifies the folder when Outlook automatically saves items (for example, messages you have started composing but not yet sent).
- **In Folders Other Than the Inbox:** When you reply to a message that is located in any folder other than the Inbox, your reply is saved in that folder rather than in the Sent Items folder. This feature can help to keep related messages together.
- **Display a New Mail Desktop Alert:** When a new message arrives, Outlook displays a small, semitransparent preview of the message in the lower-right corner of your screen. Click the Desktop Alert Settings button to specify the details of how this alert appears.
- **Set Importance/Sensitivity:** Specifies the default importance and sensitivity levels for new messages that you create.

Tracking Options

If you click the Tracking Options button in the E-Mail options dialog box, Outlook displays the dialog box shown in Figure 27-51.

FIGURE 27-51

Setting e-mail tracking options.

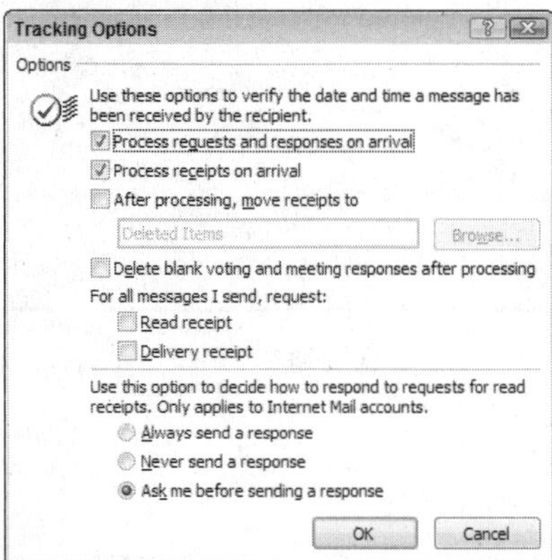

The options in the top portion of this dialog box determine how Outlook handles requests for read and delivery receipts and receipts that have been returned to you, as follows.

- **Process Requests and Responses on Arrival:** When a read or delivery receipt is received, Outlook records the receipt as part of the original item (the sent message).
- **Process Receipts on Arrival:** Receipts are deleted on arrival (after processing).
- **After Processing, Move Receipts To:** Specify a folder for saving processed receipts.

In the middle of this dialog box are options that you can set if you want every message you send to include a request for a delivery, read receipt, or both.

At the bottom of the dialog box, you can specify how Outlook handles requests for receipts that you receive.

Mail Setup

To access the Mail Setup dialog box, choose Tools ➪ Options from the main Outlook window and then click the Mail Setup tab in the Options dialog box. This tab is shown in Figure 27-52.

FIGURE 27-52

The Mail Setup tab in the Options dialog box.

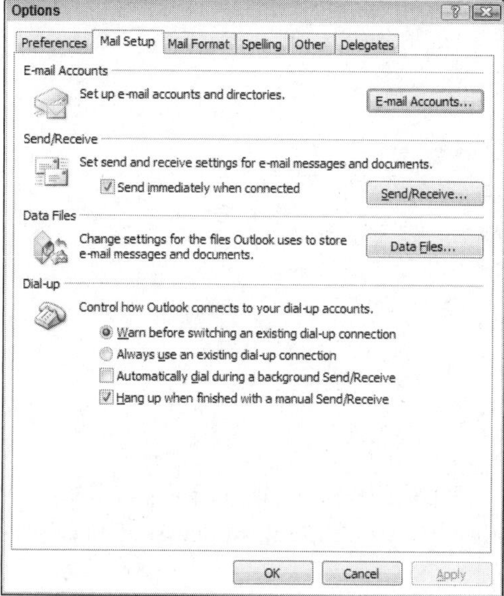

The E-Mail Accounts button lets you access Outlook's e-mail accounts to add, delete, or modify accounts. Working with e-mail accounts is covered earlier in the chapter.

The Send Immediately When Connected option specifies that a message you create and send is sent immediately rather than put in the Outbox and sent the next time a send/receive operation takes place. If you click the adjacent Send/Receive button, Outlook opens a dialog box in which you can specify how often Outlook performs an automatic send/receive. The default is 30 minutes.

If you click the Data Files button on the Mail Setup tab, Outlook opens a dialog box in which you can change settings related to the data files that Outlook uses to store information (messages, calendar, and so on).

The final group of options on the Mail Setup tab are relevant only if you are using a dial-up (modem) connection to the network. For most users, the default settings are fine and need not be changed.

Mail Format

To access the Mail Format dialog box, choose Tools ➪ Options from the main Outlook menu and then click the Mail Format tab in the Options dialog box. This tab is shown in Figure 27-53.

FIGURE 27-53

The Mail Format tab in the Options dialog box.

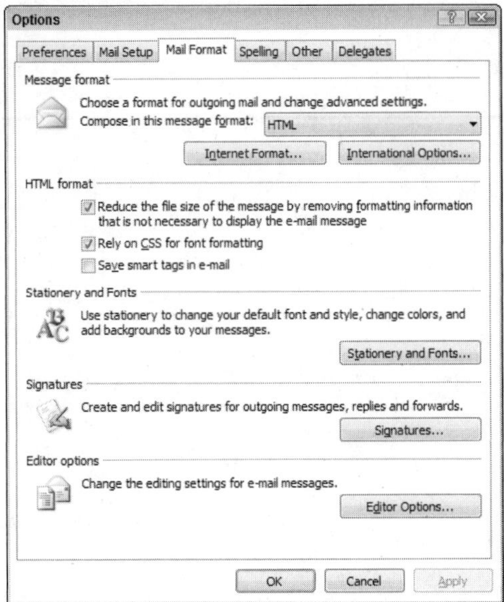

The Message Format section of this dialog box has the following elements:

- **Compose in this Format:** Select the default format (HTML, Rich Text, or plain text) for new messages.
- **Internet Format:** Click this button to specify that messages you create in rich-text format (RTF) are converted to HTML or plain text when being sent to Internet mail accounts (which generally cannot read RTF messages).
- **International Options:** Click this button to set language options for new messages.

The HTML Format section has these options:

- **Reduce the File Size:** Make HTML messages as small as possible by removing unneeded formatting information.
- **Rely on CSS for Font Formatting:** Select this option if you want to use Cascading Style Sheets for font formatting.
- **Save Smart Tags in E-Mail:** Smart Tags are sent as part of a message rather than being present only while you are composing the message.

The Stationery and Fonts button and the Signatures button give you access to the tools for creating and modifying these items, specifying the defaults to use with new messages, and so on.

Click the Editor Options button and then click Advanced to display the window that is shown in Figure 27-54. You use this window to set a variety of options that control how the e-mail editor works. Note the list of three categories on the left: Popular, Proofing, and Advanced. Click each one to display a different set of related options.

FIGURE 27-54

Setting options for the e-mail editor.

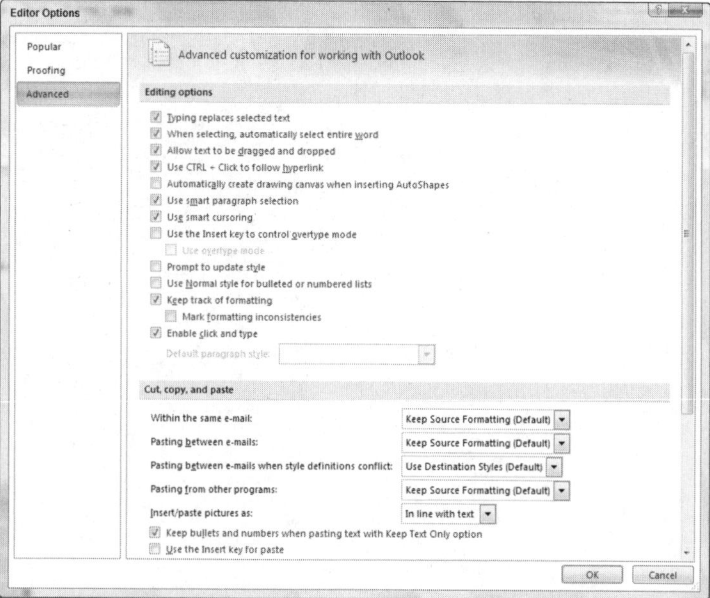

Many people use Outlook without ever making changes to any of these options, but they are available if you want to make the editor better suit your working style. If you have used the Microsoft Word word processing program, you may recognize a good deal of overlap between Outlook's editor options and the options available in Word. There is a good reason for this overlap — Outlook's editor is in fact based on Word.

Summary

This chapter explained the fundamentals of setting up your e-mail account and sending and receiving e-mail messages. It also covered sending attachments, dealing with attachments that you receive, and using the Inbox. Outlook data consists of items such as e-mail messages, appointments, and contacts. These items are organized into folders that are, in most cases, specialized to hold a single type of item. Folders in turn are stored in a Personal Folders file that also contains your account information and other Outlook settings. This chapter showed you how to work with items, folders, and data files to keep your Outlook information organized, accessible, and backed up. It seems that Outlook has an overwhelming number of e-mail options. Fortunately, most options can be left with their default settings and changed only when you have a specific reason to do so. As you become more familiar with Outlook, you gain a better understanding of how to set options to maximize your convenience and productivity.

Chapter 28

Processing and Securing E-Mail

IN THIS CHAPTER

Understanding junk e-mail filtering

Setting junk e-mail options

Defining blocked and allowed lists

Understanding e-mail rules

Defining a new rule

Looking at some rule examples

Managing e-mail rules

Protecting against viruses

Understanding Outlook's attachment blocking

Implementing macro security

Using certificates and digital signatures

Encrypting and digitally signing messages

Junk e-mail, often called spam, is a problem for most e-mail users. It can range from a minor annoyance for a home user to a major problem for a large organization, clogging mail servers and reducing the efficiency of employees. Fortunately, Outlook provides you with tools that greatly reduce the spam problem. You also can use message rules to process incoming e-mail, cutting down on the amount of time you spend moving messages around or deleting them. Computer security has unfortunately become a very important topic. With the almost universal use of the Internet and e-mail, it's easier than ever for various kinds of malicious software such as viruses to spread. Security issues also include message privacy and verification of people's identities. Because e-mail is the favored means of spreading such malware, Outlook users have to be particularly vigilant. This chapter explains the various tools that Outlook provides to make you more efficient in dealing with spam and managing messages, and to enhance your security.

Understanding Junk E-Mail Filtering

Junk e-mail filtering works on two principles. The first is the content of the message; certain keywords and phrases are considered likely to be spam. The other is the identity of the sender. You can define a safe list — people whose messages are never treated as spam regardless of content. Likewise, you can define a blocked list — people whose messages are always treated as spam regardless of content. In either case, messages that Outlook flags as spam are placed in the Junk E-Mail folder rather than the Inbox.

Why doesn't Outlook just delete spam messages? The fact is that content-based spam filtering is not perfect, and legitimate messages are sometimes caught as spam. Some people like to quickly scan their Junk E-Mail folder before permanently deleting the messages just to make sure that a legitimate message has not been caught. However, if you want spam to be deleted automatically, you can tell Outlook to do this. See the next section, "Setting Junk E-Mail Options," for details.

Third-Party Anti-Spam Software

Several anti-spam programs are on the market that work in conjunction with Outlook to catch spam. These programs may provide more sophisticated filtering options and other features. If you are using one of these programs, you may want to turn Outlook's spam filtering off. You do not have to, however; leaving it on does no harm and may in fact catch spam that the other program misses.

Setting Junk E-Mail Options

You set Outlook's filtering and handling of junk e-mail in the Junk E-Mail Options dialog box, as follows:

1. **Choose Tools ⇨ Options from the main Outlook window to display the Options dialog box.**
2. **On the Preferences tab, click the Junk E-Mail button.** Outlook displays the Junk E-Mail dialog box.
3. **If necessary, click the Options tab (shown in Figure 28-1).**

FIGURE 28-1

Setting options for junk e-mail filtering.

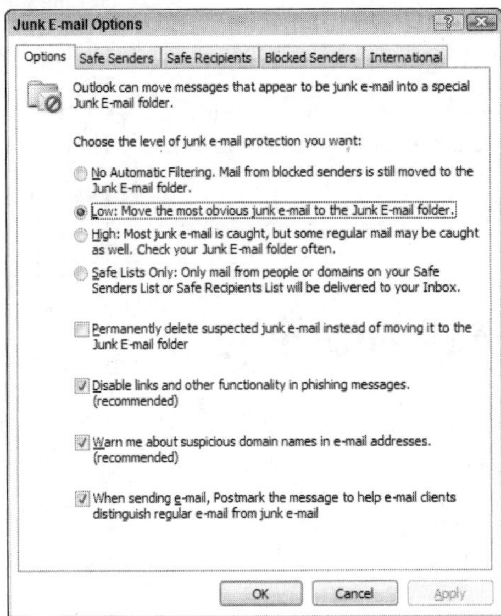

4. **Choose option settings as described in the following list.**
5. **Click OK.**

The first option in this dialog box determines the level of filtering based on message content. You have four levels to choose from:

- **No Automatic Filtering:** Messages are not filtered based on their content.
- **Low:** Only obvious spam is treated as such. Some spam will get through to your Inbox.
- **High:** More stringent spam rules are applied when message content is scanned. Some legitimate messages may be treated as spam.
- **Safe Lists Only:** Only messages from senders on your safe lists (explained later in this chapter) are allowed through; all other messages are treated as spam regardless of their content.

The other options in this dialog box are as follows:

- **Permanently Delete:** Messages that Outlook considers to be spam are deleted rather than moved to the Junk E-Mail folder. You may not want to use this option unless you are sure that legitimate messages are not mistakenly being tagged as spam.
- **Disable Links:** Phishing messages (see the "Phishing" sidebar) usually contain links to Web pages where you are asked for confidential information such as passwords. If this option is selected, Outlook disables these links.
- **Warn Me About:** A spoofed domain name is one that is not what it appears to be. For example, a link might display `www.microsoft.com` but actually be a link to another domain. If this option is selected, Outlook warns you about possible spoofed domain names in a message.
- **When Sending E-mail, Postmark:** If this option is selected, all messages you send are postmarked as an anti-spam measure. See the following section for more information on postmarking.

Understanding postmarking

Postmarking is a new technique that is designed to help in the fight against spam. Postmarking a message adds to the time required to process and send it. For normal users who send dozens or even hundreds of e-mails a day, the extra time required is insignificant. For spammers who rely on being able to send millions of e-mails, however, the extra time results in an increase in costs. Therefore, a postmarked message is less likely to be spam than one that is not postmarked. Postmarks are just one of many factors that an e-mail client can take into account when filtering spam.

Phishing

Phishing is a particularly dangerous kind of junk e-mail. A phishing message pretends to be from a company you do business with, for example, PayPal or eBay. The message asks you to take some seemingly legitimate action, such as resetting your password. When you follow the link to a Web site, the site looks just like the real thing, but it is not — it's a fake Web site set up by the phisher. The result is that some unscrupulous person now has your password, and you can imagine the possible consequences.

Spam and Viruses

Is spam related to viruses? Not directly, although viruses often arrive as part of a spam message (but can come with a legitimate message, too). Virus protection in Outlook is covered in Chapter 27.

Blocking and Allowing Specific Addresses

A very useful tool in the fight against spam is Outlook's ability to define lists of e-mail addresses and domains that are always blocked or always allowed through.

Defining safe senders

A *safe sender* is a person, or more precisely an e-mail address, whose e-mail messages are always considered to be okay — not spam — regardless of the content. Sometimes a safe senders list is called a *white list*. You can create a safe senders list based on your contacts and by entering individual addresses. You can also specify entire domains as safe — for example, all messages from Microsoft.com would be considered to be safe. Here are the steps to follow:

1. **Choose Tools ➪ Options from the main Outlook window to display the Options dialog box.**
2. **On the Preferences tab, click the Junk E-Mail button.** Outlook displays the Junk E-Mail dialog box.
3. **If necessary, click the Safe Senders tab (shown in Figure 28-2).**

FIGURE 28-2

Defining your Safe Senders list.

Blocking/Allowing Individual Senders

The context menu is a fast way to add addresses to your safe and blocked lists. All you have to do is right-click the message in the Inbox (or whatever folder it is in), choose Junk E-Mail from the context menu, and then choose the desired action from the next menu. If you have opened a message, you can use the commands in the Junk E-Mail section of the ribbon to perform related commands:

- **Block Sender**: Adds the message sender to your Blocked Senders list.
- **Safe Lists**: Choose from the menu to add the sender to your Safe Senders or Safe Recipients list or to add the sender's domain to your Safe Senders list.
- **Not Junk**: This command is available only if the message is in your Junk E-Mail folder. Click to move the message to the Inbox and add the sender to your Safe Senders list.

4. **To add an address or domain to the list, click the Add button.**
5. **Enter the address (for example, `someone@microsoft.com`) or the domain (for example, `microsoft.com` or `@microsoft.com`).**
6. **Click OK to add the address or domain to the safe list.**
7. **To edit or remove a safe list entry, highlight it in the list and then click the Edit or Remove button.**
8. **Click OK.**

The other two options in this dialog box are self-explanatory. It is recommended to have the Also Trust E-Mail from My Contacts option selected, because this saves you the effort of entering these addresses manually.

The Import and Export tools are useful if you want to transfer a safe list between Outlook and another e-mail program, or pass your safe list to a friend or colleague. The import/export format is a plain-text file with one address per line.

Defining safe recipients

The safe recipients list, located on another tab in the Junk E-Mail Options dialog box, is similar to the safe senders list but it marks messages as okay based on their recipients rather than their sender. This is useful when you are on a distribution list or in another situation in which you receive e-mails that are sent to a list of recipients, including you. When an e-mail address is on the safe recipients list, any message sent to you *and* to that address will never be treated as spam, regardless of the message sender and content. The Safe Recipients tab works exactly the same as the Safe Senders tab, described in the previous section.

Defining blocked senders

A blocked sender is an e-mail address or domain whose messages are always treated as spam. The Blocked Senders tab in the Junk E-Mail Options dialog box works exactly like the Safe Senders tab as described earlier.

International junk e-mail options

You may receive some e-mails that appear to be gibberish — random, meaningless characters. These messages occur when a sender's e-mail program uses a different character encoding than the one you are using.

For example, a person in China likely uses Chinese encoding to create a message in Chinese characters. If your e-mail reader is set to use, say, English encoding, the message displays as gibberish. Outlook lets you block messages that use specified character encodings. It also lets you block e-mails from certain countries based on the top-level domain of the sender's address. Here are the steps to follow:

1. **Choose Tools ➪ Options from the main Outlook window to display the Options dialog box.**
2. **On the Preferences tab, click the Junk E-Mail button.** Outlook displays the Junk E-Mail dialog box.
3. **If necessary, click the International tab.**
4. **To block top-level domains, click the Blocked Top-Level Domains button to display a list of domains (Figure 28-3).**

FIGURE 28-3

Specifying top-level domains to block.

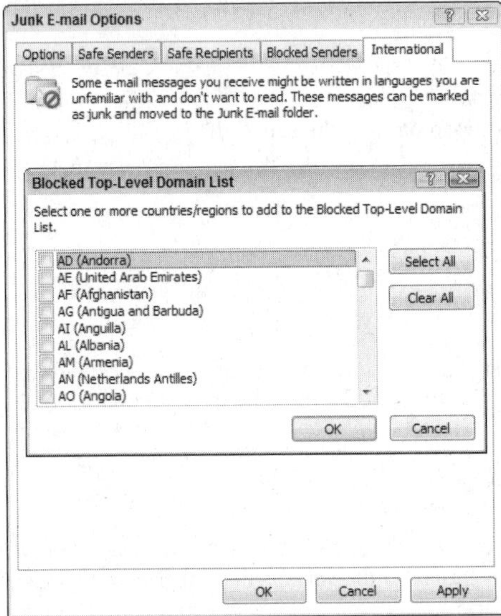

5. **Select the domains you want to block and then click OK.**
6. **To block character encodings, click the Blocked Encodings List to display a list of encodings (Figure 28-4).**
7. **Select the character encodings you want to block and then click OK.**
8. **Click OK to close the Junk E-Mail Options dialog box.**

What's a Top-Level Domain?

The top-level domain of an e-mail address is the part after the last period. People in the United States are used to seeing top-level domains such as `.com`, `.org`, and `.edu` that indicate the type or organization. In the rest of the world, however, the top-level domain usually identifies the country of origin — for example, `.ca` for Canada, `.cn` for China, and `.fr` for France. For the United States, `.us` is used, although rarely.

FIGURE 28-4

Specifying character encodings to block.

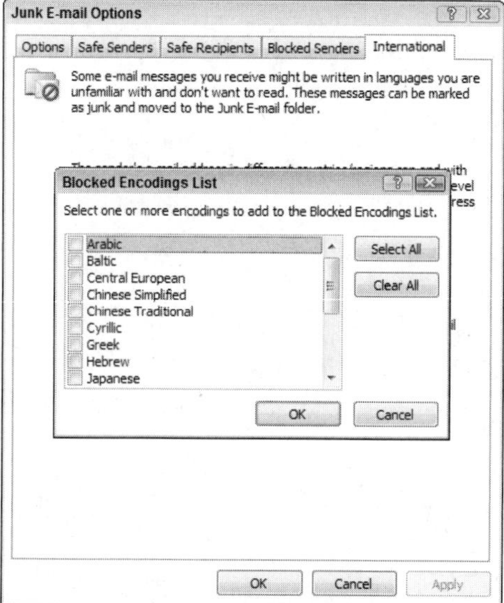

Understanding E-Mail Rule Basics

Outlook lets you automate the handling of e-mail messages with *rules*. A rule can perform actions such as move messages from a specific person to a designated folder or delete messages with certain words in the subject. Rules can also display alerts, play sounds, and move InfoPath forms and RSS feed items. Rules can help you save time and stay organized.

Outlook e-mail rules are all similar in that they specify a *condition* and an *action*. A rule can be defined to apply to e-mail messages when they arrive, which is most common, and to messages as you send them. The Rules Wizard, through which you create rules, provides a set of partially defined rules for commonly needed actions — all you need to do is fill in the details. This wizard also provides the capability to define a rule completely from scratch, a feature you'll use if one of the existing rule templates does not meet your needs.

Creating a New Rule

To create a new e-mail rule, select Rules and Alerts from the Tools menu. Outlook displays the Rules and Alerts dialog box, in which you should select the E-Mail Rules tab. If you have any rules already defined, they are listed here. You can work with existing rules as described later in this chapter. To create a new rule, click the New Rule button to display the Rules Wizard, as shown in Figure 28-5.

FIGURE 28-5

The first step in defining a new rule.

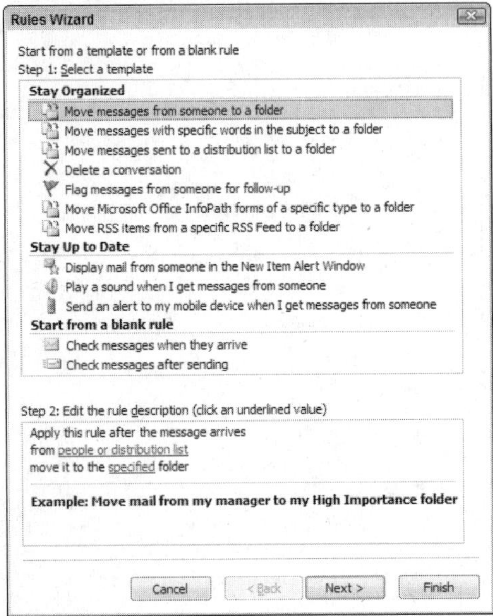

You can see that this dialog box has two parts, Select a Template at the top and Edit the Rule Description at the bottom. The following sections look at these in turn.

Selecting a rule template

The Select a Template portion of this dialog box is divided into three sections, each containing two or more templates:

- **Stay Organized:** Templates that move, delete, or flag messages or other items
- **Stay Up to Date:** Templates for alerting you when messages arrive
- **Start From a Blank Rule:** Templates that are empty and let you define a rule from scratch

The remainder of this section deals with the first two of these categories. Starting from a blank rule is covered separately later in this chapter.

When you click an item in the Select a Template section, the Edit the Rule Description section displays the rule definition along with an example. Editing the definition is covered in the next section.

Editing a rule description

A rule definition contains underlined elements that represent the parts of the rule that you can edit. Figure 28-5, for example, shows a definition with two editable elements: People or Distribution List and Specified. When you click such an underlined element, Outlook opens a dialog box in which you can specify the details. In this example:

- Click People or Distribution List to open a dialog box in which you can select the people, distribution lists, or both from your address book. The rule will be applied to messages from the selected people.
- Click Specified to select a folder to which matching messages will be moved.

After you have made selections for the editable rule items, the rule displays the selected information. An example is shown in Figure 28-6, in which the rule is defined to move messages from "Andre Tallisk" to the "Clients" folder. Note that these elements of the rule are still underlined and can be clicked to make changes as needed.

FIGURE 28-6

A completed rule definition displays the details that you have specified.

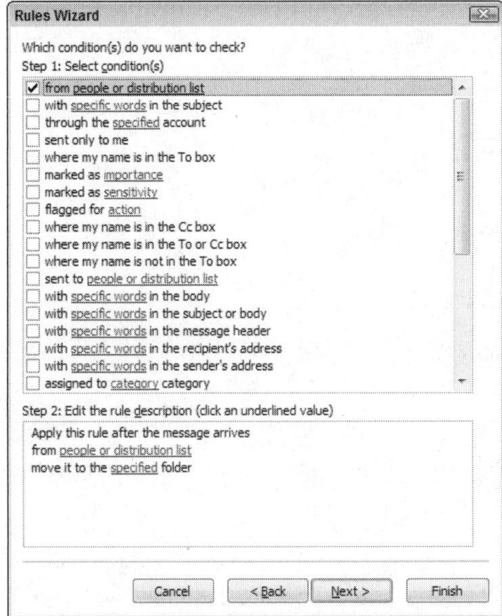

Finishing the rule

At this point, the rule is ready to use. You can click Finish in the Rules Wizard dialog box to save the rule. In some cases, you may want to fine-tune the rule; if so, click the Next button. Fine-tuning a rule is essentially the same as creating a rule from a blank template, covered in the next section.

Creating a rule from a blank template

If the rule templates that Outlook provides do not suit your needs, you can create a rule from a blank template. In the first step of the Rules Wizard, shown earlier in Figure 28-5, you must select one of the following from the Start From a Blank Rule section:

- **Check Messages When They Arrive:** Creates a rule that works with messages you receive
- **Check Messages After Sending:** Creates a rule that works with messages you send

After making your selection, click the Next button. Outlook displays the next wizard step as shown in Figure 28-7. You use this dialog box to specify the conditions for the rule. You can have more than one condition for a rule. When you do, all conditions must be met for a message to be processed. The steps to follow are:

FIGURE 28-7

Selecting conditions for a rule.

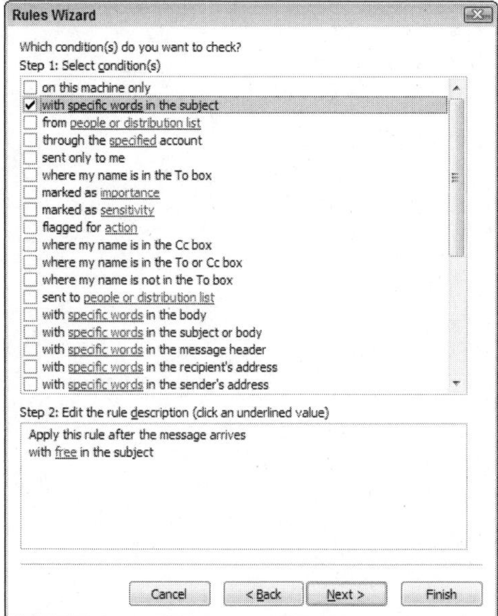

1. **Click the box next to a description to place a checkmark in the box and add the condition to the rule description.**
2. **If the condition requires it, click the underlined element in the description to specify the details.**
3. **Repeat Steps 1 and 2 if needed to add conditions to the rule.**
4. **Click the Next button to proceed to the next wizard step, where you will define the rule's action. This dialog box is shown in Figure 28-8.**

FIGURE 28-8

Selecting an action for a rule.

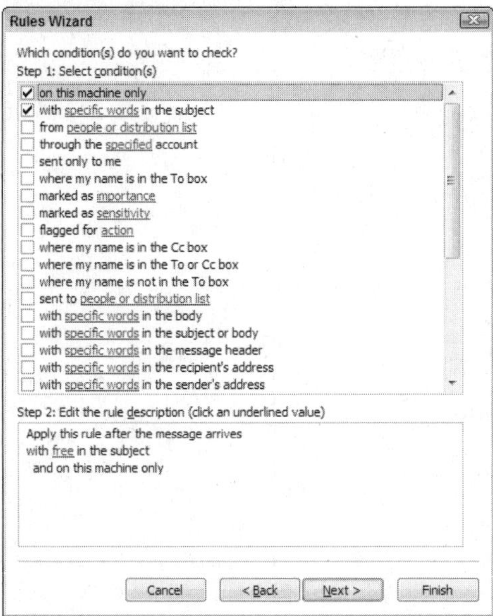

5. **Select the action that you want to be part of the rule.**
6. **If necessary, click any underlined element in the action to specify the details.**
7. **Click Next to display the next wizard step, where you specify any exceptions to the rule (Figure 28-9).** An exception lets you modify a rule, as in this example: If the message subject contains the word *free*, delete it unless the sender is in my Contacts list. Exceptions are optional, and they are added the same way as conditions and actions.
8. **Click Next to go to the final step of the wizard (Figure 28-10).** In this dialog box, you specify a name for the rule and have the opportunity to edit the rule by clicking underlined elements in the rule description. You can also set the following options:
   - **Run This Rule Now:** Apply the rule to messages already in your mailbox.
   - **Turn on this Rule:** Enable the rule for newly received or sent messages.
   - **Create This Rule on All Accounts:** Apply the rule for all your e-mail accounts (relevant only if you have multiple accounts).
9. **Click Finish to complete the rule definition and return to the Rules and Alerts dialog box.**

FIGURE 28-9

Specifying exceptions for a rule.

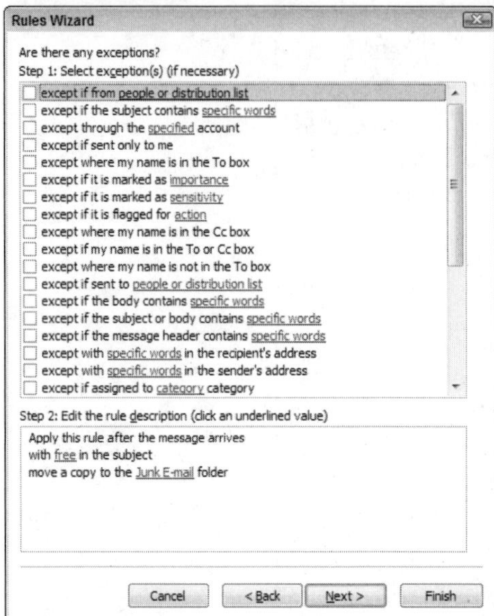

FIGURE 28-10

The final step of the Rules Wizard.

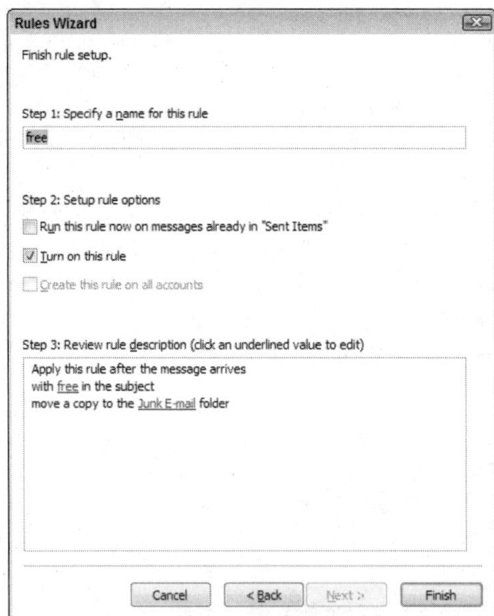

Some Rule Examples

Outlook e-mail rules are admittedly rather complex. It may help you to understand them if you follow the steps required to define a few different kinds of rules.

Rule example 1

This first rule example shows you how to define a rule that moves all messages from a certain domain to a specified folder. It would be useful if, for example, you are doing some contracting work for a company and are interacting with several people there. This rule moves all e-mail that you receive from anyone at that company into one folder, helping you to stay organized.

The first step is to create the folder:

1. **In the mail Navigation Pane, click the location where you want to place the new folder.** You can click a mailbox if you want the new folder to be at the top level in that mailbox. You can also click an existing folder to create the new folder within that folder.
2. **Click the arrow next to the New button on the toolbar and select Folder from the menu.** Outlook displays the Create New Folder dialog box.
3. **Enter the new folder name in the Name box.**
4. **Make sure that Mail and Post Items is selected in the Folder Contains list.**
5. **Click OK.**

Now that you have created the folder, you can proceed to defining the rule:

1. **Choose Tools ➪ Rules and Alerts from the Outlook menu to display the Rules and Alerts dialog box.**
2. **On the E-Mail Rules tab, click the New Rule button.** Outlook displays the Rules Wizard dialog box.
3. **In the Stay Organized section, click the Move Messages from Someone to a Folder template.**
4. **In the Edit the Rule Description section, click the People or Distribution List link.** Outlook displays the Rule Address dialog box (Figure 28-11).
5. **If you wanted to move messages from a single individual who is in your Contacts list, you could click that person's entry in the list and then click the From button.** Because we want to move all messages from a domain, enter **acme.com** in the From box.
6. **Click OK.**

   Outlook may display a dialog box claiming not to recognize "acme.com" because it is not a complete e-mail address. This is okay—just click Cancel to close this dialog box and return to the Rules Wizard.
7. **In the Edit the Rule Description section, click the Specified link.** Outlook displays the Rules and Alerts dialog box.
8. **Select the desired destination folder and then click OK.** Note that if you had not created the new folder earlier, you could do it now by clicking the New button in this dialog box.
9. **Back in the Rules Wizard dialog box, click the Finish button to close the Rules Wizard and return to the Rules and Alerts dialog box.**

After you create a rule, you will see it listed in the Rules and Alerts dialog box. It is assigned a default name based on the information in the rule. You can, if desired, change the rule name as explained later in this chapter in the section on managing rules.

FIGURE 28-11

Specifying an address to be part of a new e-mail rule.

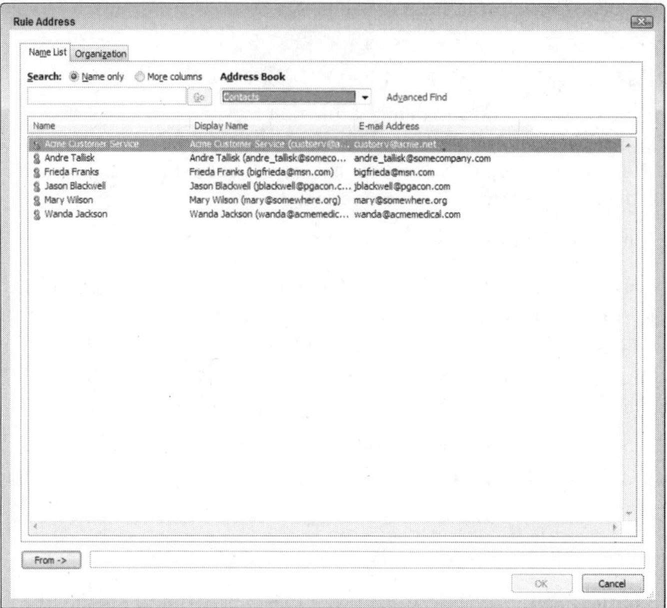

Rule example 2

This rule example shows you how you can use a rule to help guard against spam. Let's say that you receive a many junk e-mails offering to sell you prescription medication online. However, the subject of the message is often disguised, so you want to define a rule that looks for the word *prescription* in both the subject and the body of the message, and if the word is found, Outlook deletes the message.

But there's a wrinkle — you do in fact get some meds from a legitimate online drug store, and you do not want e-mails from that store to be caught — so the rule will have to include an exception. Here are the steps for creating this rule:

1. **Choose Tools ➪ Rules and Alerts from the Outlook menu to display the Rules and Alerts dialog box.**
2. **On the E-Mail Rules tab, click the New Rule button.** Outlook displays the Rules Wizard dialog box.
3. **In the Start From a Blank Rule section, select the Check Messages When They Arrive template.**
4. **Click Next to display a list of conditions.**
5. **Select With Specific Words in the Subject or Body.**
6. **In the lower part of this dialog box, click the Specific Words link to open the Search Text dialog box (Figure 28-12).**

FIGURE 28-12

Use this dialog box to specify words that will be searched for in a message.

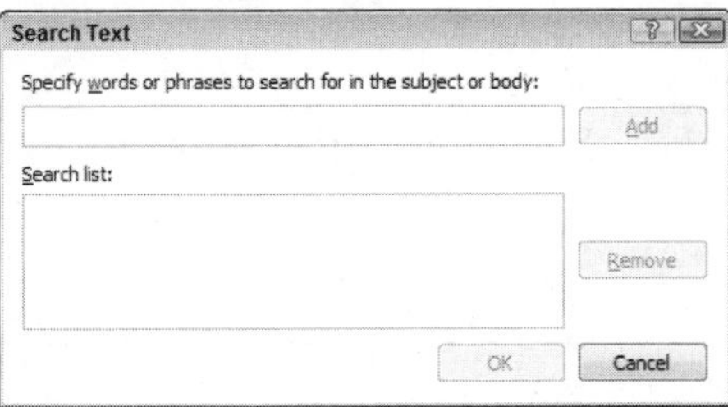

7. **Enter** prescription **in the upper box and then click Add to add the word to the list.** If you wanted to search for more than one word, you would repeat this step as needed.
8. **Click OK to return to the Rules Wizard dialog box.**
9. **Click Next to display a list of actions.**
10. **Select the Delete It action.** Doing so tells Outlook to move matching messages to the Deleted Items folder. You can also select the Permanently Delete It action, which does precisely what it says.
11. **Click Next to display a list of exceptions.**
12. **Select the Except If from People or Distribution List exception.**
13. **In the lower part of the dialog box, click the People or Distribution List link to display the Rule Address dialog box.**
14. **If the legitimate online pharmacy's address is in your Contacts list, you can add it using the From button.** Otherwise, just type it in the From box and then click OK.
15. **Back in the Rules Wizard dialog box, click Finish to complete your rule definition.**

Rule example 3

Our final rule example shows you how to process messages that you send. Suppose that your major client is Acme Corporation and you have created an Outlook category specifically for items that are related to Acme. You want all messages you send to Acme to be placed in this category automatically. Here's how:

1. **Choose Tools ➪ Rules and Alerts from the Outlook menu to display the Rules and Alerts dialog box.**
2. **On the E-Mail Rules tab, click the New Rule button.** Outlook displays the Rules Wizard dialog box.
3. **In the Start From a Blank Rule section, select the Check Messages After Sending template.**
4. **Click Next to display a list of conditions.**
5. **Select Sent to People or Distribution List.**
6. **In the lower part of the dialog box, click the People or Distribution List link to open the Rule Address dialog box.**
7. **Enter** acme.com **in the To box and then click OK.**

8. **Outlook may display a dialog box claiming not to recognize "acme.com" because it is not a complete e-mail address.** This is okay — just click Cancel to close this dialog box and return to the Rules Wizard.
9. **Click Next to display a list of actions.**
10. **Select the Assign it to the Category option.**
11. **In the lower part of the dialog box, click the Category link to open the Color Categories dialog box (Figure 28-13).**

FIGURE 28-13

Selecting a category to assign sent messages to.

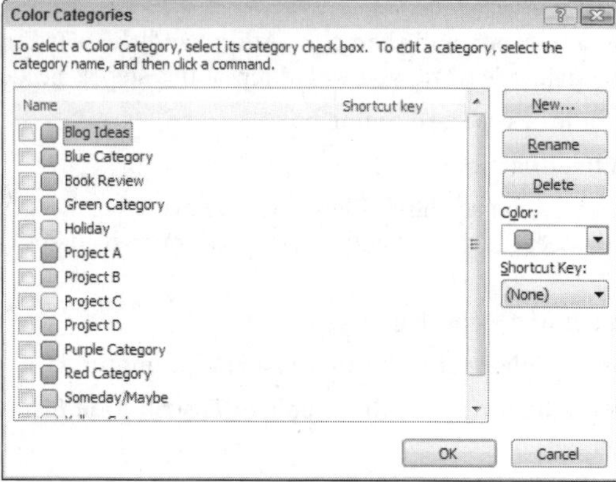

12. **Select the desired category — in this case, it would be Acme — then click OK to return to the Rules Wizard dialog box.**
13. **Back in the Rules Wizard dialog box, click Finish to complete your rule definition.**

Managing Rules

When you select Rules and Alerts from the Tools menu, the E-Mail Rules tab in the Rules and Alerts dialog box lists all the rules that are defined (Figure 28-14). If you have more than one rule, they are applied in top-down order. The actions you can take in this dialog box are the following:

- To edit a rule, click it and then click the Change Rule button. Then select Edit Rule Settings or Rename Rule from the menu.
- To change a rule's position in the list, click it and then click the up or down arrow button.
- To copy a rule, click it and then click the Copy button. Outlook will make a copy of the rule, which you can then rename and modify as desired.
- To delete a rule, click it and then click the Delete button.

- To run rules, click the Run Rules Now button. Then, in the dialog box that is displayed, select the rules to run and the folder(s) and messages to apply the rules to (Figure 28-15).
- To inactivate a rule, click the adjacent box to remove the checkmark.
- To import or export your rules from or to other versions of Outlook, or for use by a friend or colleague, click the Options button.

FIGURE 28-14

You manage your e-mail rules in the Rules and Alerts dialog box.

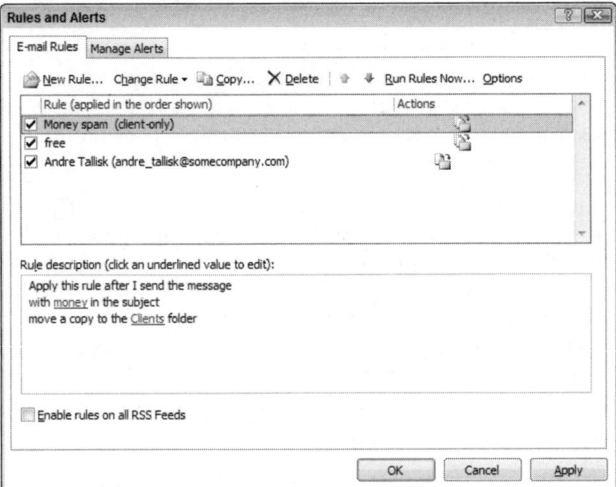

FIGURE 28-15

Running rules manually.

A Virus by Any Other Name

Technically, a *virus* is a piece of software that not only infects a computer system but also actively spreads itself to other systems by means of a host file, similarly to biological viruses that cause colds and other human illnesses. The term is often used more broadly to include other kinds of "malware" — a generic term for harmful software — that do not fit the strict definition of a virus, such as worms and Trojan horses.

Protecting Against Viruses

Everyone has heard about *viruses*, those malicious software elements that infect and harm computer systems. Viruses range from the merely annoying to the truly disastrous, but they all have one thing in common — you do not want them on your system! Because viruses often spread by means of e-mail, Outlook provides you with some defenses against them.

It's important to understand that Outlook itself does not have any anti-virus capabilities. An *anti-virus program* is specialized to detect and remove viruses and will have a way to automatically download the latest virus definitions so that it can stay up-to-date. Symantec, Zone Alarm, and McAfee are three of the better-known publishers of anti-virus software. Most systems have anti-virus software installed, and part of protecting yourself against viruses that come with e-mail is to make sure that your anti-virus program is configured properly. Specifically, you should set the anti-virus program's options so that it always scans incoming e-mail and attachments for viruses before they get to Outlook. It's also advisable to set the program to scan outgoing e-mail and attachments in order to prevent you from inadvertently spreading a virus that you have been infected with through other means (such as a floppy disk).

On-demand e-mail scan

If you have an Outlook-compatible anti-virus program installed, you will find two virus-related commands on Outlook's Tools menu:

- **Scan for Viruses:** Opens your anti-virus program and performs an immediate virus scan of e-mail items according to the program options. Use this command when you are not sure that the anti-virus program's automatic scanning is enough.
- **E-Mail Scan Properties:** Opens your anti-virus program's Options dialog box, in which you can specify the details of how the program scans e-mail items for viruses.

The details of how the virus scan works and how you set options depend on the specific anti-virus program that you have installed. Please refer to that program's documentation for more information.

Reassuring E-Mail Recipients

People worry about getting viruses via e-mail, and I think it's a good idea to reassure them that messages from you are safe. I include a brief note at the bottom of every e-mail that I send that states, "This e-mail message and any attachments have been scanned for viruses by XXX" (where XXX is the name of the anti-virus program that I use).

Protection Against Phishing Attacks

Phishing is a technique where you receive an e-mail that appears to be from a legitimate company that you do business with, perhaps an online payment service such as PayPal. The message asks you to click a link to go to the company's Web site to renew your password or some such thing. Although the site looks legitimate, it is in fact a cleverly designed front that lets unscrupulous people get hold of your password. Outlook provides anti-phishing protections.

Dealing with Attachments

One of the most common ways for viruses to spread is by means of e-mail attachments. However, all attachments are not equal in their ability to spread a virus. Certain file types are potentially very dangerous, such as executable programs, batch files, and installation files. Others, such as image and music files, are generally safe.

Automatically blocked attachments

Because of the potential danger posed by some file types, Outlook blocks certain kinds of attachments that are sent to you; you receive the message with a notification that an unsafe attachment has been blocked. This blocking is built into Outlook and cannot be turned off or changed. The blocked file types are listed in Table 28-1.

Outlook also catches these file types on the way out — that is, if you try to send them as an attachment. They aren't necessarily blocked, but Outlook reminds you that the recipient may not be able to receive them — and definitely won't if he or she uses Outlook — and asks you if you want to proceed.

TABLE 28-1

File Types That Are Blocked by Outlook

Extension	File Type
ADE	Access Project Extension (Microsoft)
ADP	Access project (Microsoft)
APP	Executable application
ASP	Active Server Page
BAS	BASIC source code
BAT	Batch processing
CER	Internet Security Certificate file
CHM	Compiled HTML jelp
CMD	DOS CP/M command file, or a command file for Windows NT
COM	Command
CPL	Windows Control Panel Extension (Microsoft)
CRT	Certificate file

continued

TABLE 28-1 *(continued)*

Extension	File Type
CSH	csh script
DER	DER-encoded X509 certificate file
EXE	Executable file
FXP	FoxPro compiled source (Microsoft)
HLP	Windows Help file
HTA	Hypertext application
INF	Information or Setup file
INS	IIS Internet Communications settings (Microsoft)
ISP	IIS Internet Service Provider settings (Microsoft)
ITS	Internet Document Set, Internet Translation
JS	JavaScript source code
JSE	JScript encoded script file
KSH	UNIX shell script
LNK	Windows Shortcut file
MAD	Access Module shortcut (Microsoft)
MAF	Access (Microsoft)
MAG	Access diagram shortcut (Microsoft)
MAM	Access macro shortcut (Microsoft)
MAQ	Access query shortcut (Microsoft)
MAR	Access report shortcut (Microsoft)
MAS	Access Stored Procedures (Microsoft)
MAT	Access table shortcut (Microsoft)
MAU	Media Attachment Unit
MAV	Access view shortcut (Microsoft)
MAW	Access Data Access Page (Microsoft)
MDA	Access Add-in (Microsoft), MDA Access 2 Workgroup (Microsoft)
MDB	Access Application (Microsoft), MDB Access Database (Microsoft)
MDE	Access MDE database file (Microsoft)
MDT	Access Add-in Data (Microsoft)
MDW	Access Workgroup Information (Microsoft)
MDZ	Access Wizard Template (Microsoft)
MSC	Microsoft Management Console Snap-in control file (Microsoft)
MSH	Microsoft Shell
MSH1	Microsoft Shell
MSH2	Microsoft Shell

Extension	File Type
MSHXML	Microsoft Shell
MSH1XML	Microsoft Shell
MSH2XML	Microsoft Shell
MSI	Windows Installer File (Microsoft)
MSP	Windows Installer Update
MST	Windows SDK Setup Transform Script
OPS	Office Profile settings file
PCD	Visual Test (Microsoft)
PIF	Windows Program Information file (Microsoft)
PLG	Developer Studio Build Log
PRF	Windows System file
PRG	Program file
PST	Exchange Address Book file, Outlook Personal Folder File (Microsoft)
REG	Registration Information/Key for Registry Data File
SCF	Windows Explorer command
SCR	Windows screen saver
SCT	Windows Script component, FoxPro screen (Microsoft)
SHB	Windows Shortcut into a document
SHS	Shell Scrap Object file
TMP	Temporary file/folder
URL	Internet location
VB	VBScript file or any VisualBasic source
VBE	VBScript encoded script file
VBS	VBScript script file, Visual Basic for Applications script
VSMACROS	Visual Studio .NET binary-based macro project (Microsoft)
VSW	Visio workspace file (Microsoft)
WS	Windows script file
WSC	Windows script component
WSF	Windows script file
WSH	Windows Script Host settings file

Blocked File Types and Exchange

If you use an Exchange account for e-mail, these same file types are blocked by default. However, the Exchange administrator can modify the list if needed.

Sending ZIP Files as Attachments

When you create a ZIP file, you have the option of protecting it with a password. Although doing so can provide security against unauthorized access to the ZIP file's contents, it can prevent anti-virus software from checking the ZIP file's contents for viruses.

Other attachment types

Some other file types are not on the blocked list even though they have the potential to carry viruses. These file types are not blocked because they are very commonly sent as attachments. They include Microsoft Word documents (`.doc`), Excel workbooks (`.xls`), and PowerPoint files (`.ppt`). When you receive this kind of file as an attachment, it's important for you to be aware of the potential for harm. Even if you have anti-virus software, you cannot be sure that it will catch every virus, particularly because new ones are created regularly.

The general rule is to not open any such file unless you trust the source. It is also wise to have macro security set to a safe level, as described elsewhere in this chapter.

Sending blocked file types

Many people have perfectly legitimate reasons for sending blocked file types as attachments. You have two ways to get around Outlook's restrictions to do this:

- **Change the file's extension.** For example, if you want to forward a compiled HTML help file named MyHelp.CHM, change the file extension to something that Outlook won't block, such as MyHelp.TXT. In your message, instruct the file recipient to change the file extension back before using the file.
- **Put the file in a ZIP or other kind of archive.** This kind of file is permitted by Outlook. You need to instruct the recipient as to how the file can be extracted, of course.

Macro Security

A *macro* is a sequence of program commands that have been recorded and saved and can be executed with a single command. Outlook has its own macro capabilities_More germane to the topic of security, however, are the macros in programs such as Microsoft Word and Excel. Such macros are part of the document file and as such are included when the file is sent as an e-mail attachment. A malicious macro can be set to execute automatically when the file is opened and can potentially wreak havoc on your system and data files. Such viruses are called *macro viruses*.

Anti-virus programs catch most macro viruses, and the precaution of not opening attachments from unknown sources is another layer of protection. The final layer of protection against macro viruses is the macro security level in your programs.

Macro security applies to all Office programs, and it is set in the Trust Center. The *Trust Center* is an Office component, not specifically part of Outlook or any other any program. On Outlook, you access the Trust Center by selecting Trust Center from the Tools menu. Then, in the list on the left, click Macro Security. The Macro Security screen is shown in Figure 28-16.

FIGURE 28-16

Setting macro security in the Trust Center.

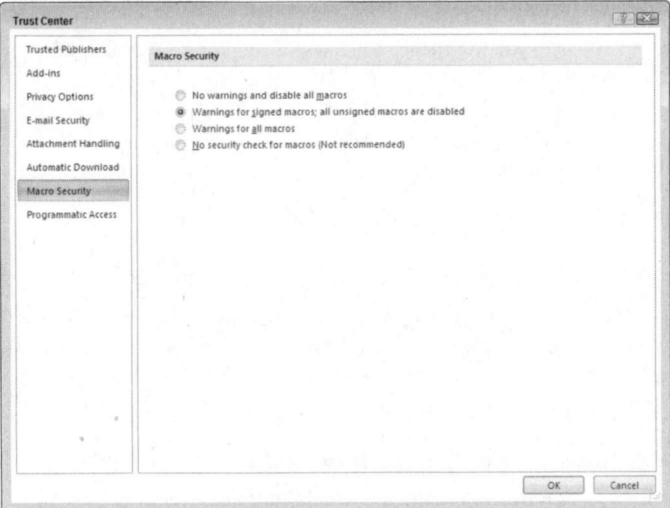

You can see that the options mention signed macros. *Digital signing* is a way that the person who creates a macro can "sign" it so that the recipient can be assured that it comes from a trusted source. You'll learn more about digital signatures later in this chapter. You can choose from four levels of macro security, described here from the strictest to the least strict:

- **No Warnings and Disable All Macros:** No macros, whether signed or not, are ever run.
- **Warnings for Signed Macros; Unsigned Macros are Disabled:** For a signed macro, the program displays a warning and asks you whether it should be run. Unsigned macros are never run. This is the default macro security level.
- **Warnings for All Macros:** The program displays a warning for any macro, signed or unsigned, and asks you whether it should be run.
- **No Security Check for Macros:** All macros are run without a warning. For reasons that are probably obvious, this level is not recommended.

The default level of macro security for all Office programs is recommended. You can always set a lower level temporarily if you want to run some unsigned macros from a trusted source.

Using Certificates and Digital Signatures

A *certificate*, also known as a *digital ID*, provides a higher level of security with Outlook. You can use a certificate to send encrypted e-mails so that only the intended recipient can view the contents. You can also use them to sign messages to prevent tampering and prove your identity. Finally, you can use a digital ID in lieu of a username and password to access certain restricted Web sites, although this use is not relevant to Outlook.

Digital IDs are based on the technique of a *public/private key pair*. These are two long numbers that are related to each other. You can use either key of the pair to encrypt data, and only people who have the other key of the pair are able to unencrypt the data. When you have a digital signature, you keep your private key secret and make your public key freely available. Here's how it works:

- To send an encrypted message to people, you use their public key to encrypt it. Only they can unencrypt the message because no one else has their private key.
- To prove your identity, encrypt some data using your private key. When recipients of a message decrypt the data using your public key, if the data is intact they will know that you must have encrypted it because nobody else has your private key.

Digital certificates have expiration dates, typically one year after they are issued.

Obtaining a digital ID

If you are using Outlook at work, your employer may provide a digital ID to you that you'll import as described in the next section. Otherwise, you can get your own. Digital IDs are provided by independent companies for a small fee. A digital ID is linked to a specific e-mail address and cannot be used with other addresses.

To get your own digital ID:

1. **Choose Trust Center from the Tools menu to open the Trust Center.**
2. **Select E-mail Security from the list on the left to display the E-Mail Security page (Figure 28-17).**

FIGURE 28-17

Using the Trust Center to get a digital ID.

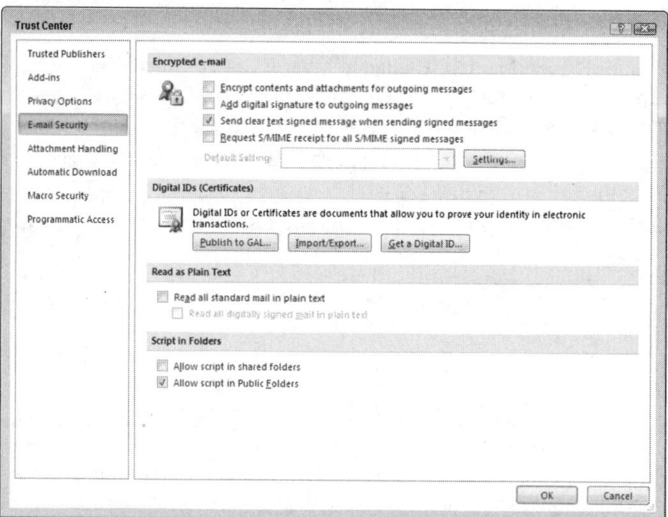

3. **Click the Get a Digital ID button.** Your Web browser opens and displays a Microsoft page that lists companies that sell digital IDs.
4. **Select the company you want and follow the prompts to register for and pay for your digital ID.**

After you complete the ordering process, the issuing company will send you an e-mail containing instructions for installing the digital ID.

Importing/exporting digital IDs

Digital IDs can be provided to you in a file as well as obtained over the Web, as described in the previous section. Your employer may provide you with an ID in a file; you can also export an existing ID to a file for backup purposes. These files are password protected for security reasons.

To import a digital ID:

1. **Choose Trust Center from the Tools menu to open the Trust Center.**
2. **Select E-mail Security from the list on the left.**
3. **Under Digital IDs, click the Import/Export button to display the Import/Export Digital ID dialog box (Figure 28-18).**

FIGURE 28-18

The Import/Export Digital ID dialog box.

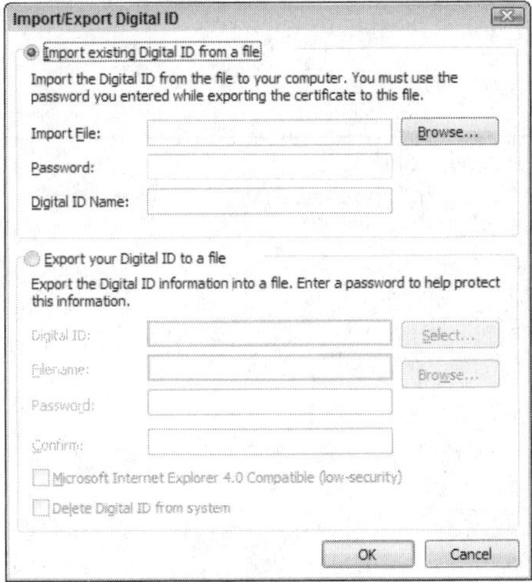

4. **Select the Import Existing Digital ID option.**
5. **Enter the name of the file in the Import File box, or use the Browse button to locate it.** Digital ID files have the `.epf`, `.pfx`, or `.p12` extension.
6. **Enter the file password in the Password box.**
7. **Enter a name of your choosing for the certificate in the Digital ID Name box.**
8. **Click OK.**

Exporting a digital ID uses the same dialog box as shown in Figure 28-18 except that you must select the Export option. Then, follow these steps:

1. **If you have more than one digital ID, use the Select button to choose the ID to export.**
2. **Enter the export filename in the File name box, or use the Browse button to select an export location.**
3. **Enter and confirm the password in the boxes provided.**
4. **Select the Microsoft Internet Explorer 4.0 Compatible option only if you will use the exported ID with older versions of Internet Explorer.**
5. **Select Delete Digital ID From System if you want to completely delete the ID rather than export it.**
6. **Click OK.**

Receiving digitally signed messages

When you receive a digitally signed message, the only difference is that the message says `Signed By XXXX` (where *XXXX* is the sender's e-mail address) in the header, just below the subject line. You can use such a message to add the sender's public key to your Contacts list, as explained in the next section.

Just because a message is signed does not mean that the signature is legitimate. On the same line that `Signed By XXXX` is displayed, Outlook displays a red ribbon icon, as shown in Figure 28-19, to indicate that the signature is valid. If the signature is not valid, the message `There are problems with the signature` is displayed, and you can click a button to view the details. A digital signature could be invalid because it has expired, the issuing authority has revoked it, or the server that verifies the certificate is invalid.

FIGURE 28-19

This icon indicates that the digital signature in a message is valid.

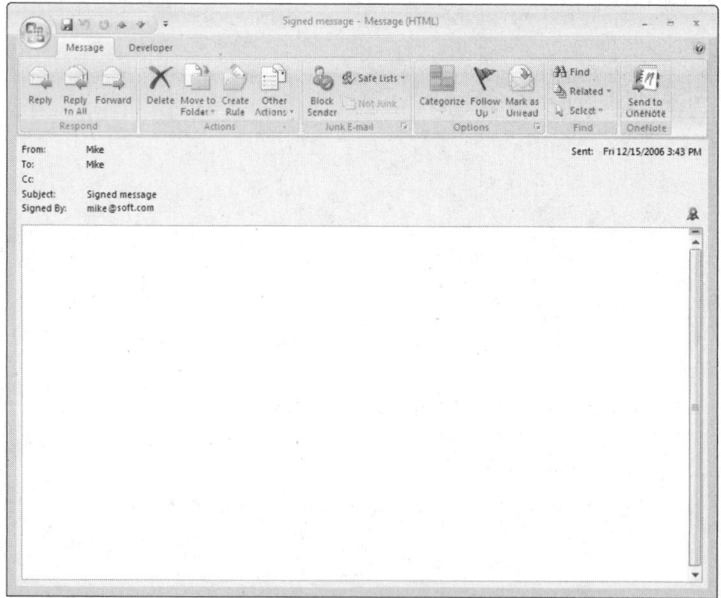

Obtaining other people's public keys

To send an encrypted message to people, you must have their public key. You can get this from a signed message that an intended recipient sent you. That recipient's certificate will be added to his or her entry in Contacts, and it will be available for you to use to send encrypted e-mail. Follow these steps to send an encrypted e-mail message:

1. **Open the digitally signed message.**
2. **Right-click the sender's name or address in the From box.**
3. **Choose Add to Outlook Contacts from the shortcut menu.**
4. **If the contact already exists in your Contacts folder, Outlook notifies you.** Select Update Information of Selected Contact.

You can view a contact's certificates by opening the contact and clicking the Certificates button in the Show section of the Ribbon. Outlook displays a list of the contact's certificates, if there are any, as shown in Figure 28-20. You can take the following actions by clicking the buttons at the right side of this window:

- **Properties:** View the certificate details, including the name of the issuing company and its expiration date.
- **Set as Default:** If the contact has more than one certificate, this command sets the one that will be used as the default for encrypting messages to the contact.
- **Import:** This option lets you import a person's certificate from a file. Certificate files have the `.p7c` or `.cer` extension.
- **Export:** This option lets you export the certificate to a file. Doing so can be useful when you want to transfer a contact's certificate to another computer.
- **Remove:** This option deletes the certificate from the contact information.

FIGURE 28-20

Viewing a contact's digital certificates.

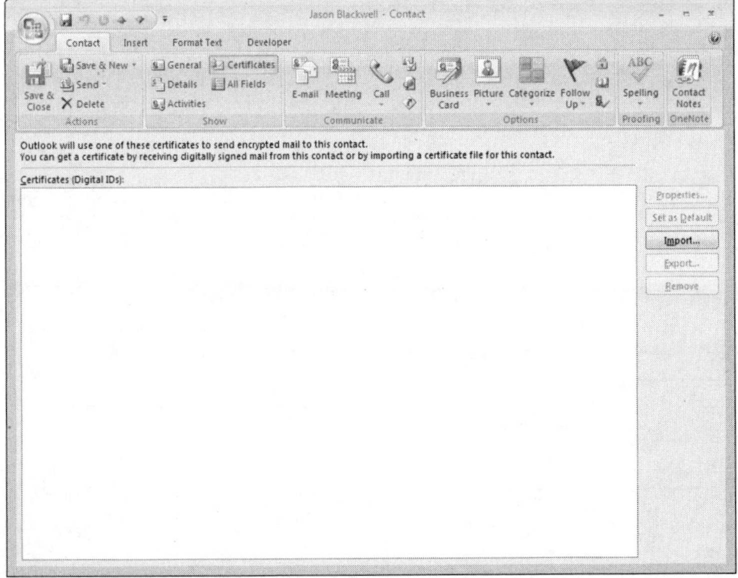

Encrypting and digitally signing messages

It's important to understand that encrypting a message and signing a message are two different things, as follows:

- **Encrypting** uses the recipient's public key to encrypt the message and attachments so that only the recipient can read them.
- **Signing** uses your digital ID to mark a message so that recipients can verify that it really came from you.

A message can be signed, encrypted, or both.

Encrypting messages

You can send an encrypted message to anyone for whom you have the public key — in other words, you have that recipient's certificate as part of his or her contact information. You can encrypt single messages or specify that all messages be encrypted (when possible).

To encrypt a single message:

1. **Create the new message.**
2. **Click the arrow in the Options section of the Message ribbon to display the Message Options dialog box.**
3. **Click the Security Settings button to open the Security Properties dialog box (Figure 28-21).**

FIGURE 28-21

The Security Properties dialog box.

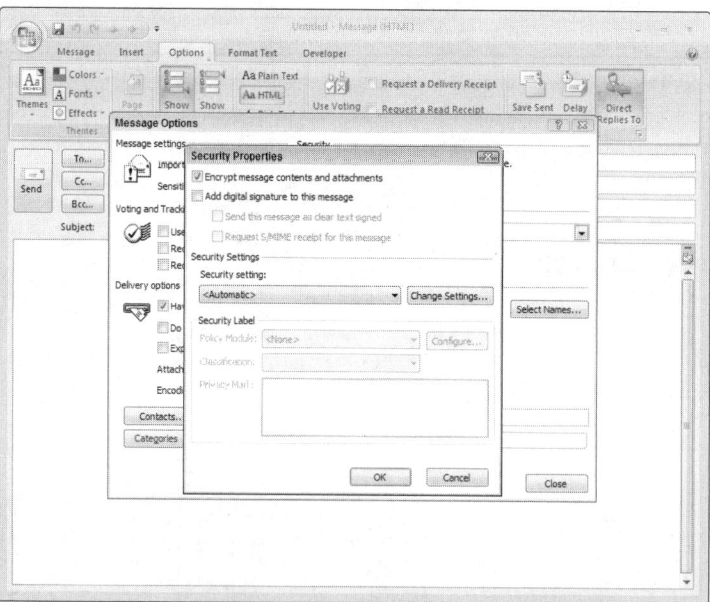

4. **Select the Encrypt Message Contents and Attachments option.**
5. **Click OK; then, click Close to return to the message.**
6. **Compose and send the message as usual.**

Of course, messages can be encrypted only when they are going to one or more recipients for whom you have a certificate. If you request encryption for a message going to people for whom you do not have a certificate, Outlook displays a message and gives you the option of sending the message without encryption.

You can also tell Outlook to encrypt all outgoing messages and attachments. Of course, this capability affects only messages that you send to people whose public key you have. To tell Outlook to encrypt all outgoing messages and attachments, follow these steps:

1. **Choose Trust Center from the Tools menu to open the Trust Center window.**
2. **Select E-Mail Security from the list on the left.**
3. **Select the Encrypt Contents and Attachments for Outgoing Messages option.**

Digitally signing messages

As with encryption, you can apply digital signatures to individual outgoing messages or to all of them.

To add a digital signature to an individual message:

1. **Create, compose, and address a new e-mail message as usual.**
2. **Click the arrow in the Options section of the Message ribbon to display the Message Options dialog box.**
3. **Click the Security Settings button to open the Security Properties dialog box (shown previously in Figure 28-21).**
4. **Select the Add Digital Signature to the Message option.**
5. **Click OK; then, click Close to return to the message.**

To add a digital signature to all outgoing messages:

1. **Choose Trust Center from the Tools menu.**
2. **Click E-mail Security.**
3. **In the Encrypted E-Mail section, select the Add Digital Signature to Outgoing Messages option.**
4. **Click OK.**

HTML Message Dangers

Because HTML messages can contain script and ActiveX controls, they are a potential source of virus attacks. To guard against and HTML viruses that make it past your anti-virus software, you can tell Outlook to display HTML messages as plain text. Because scripts and ActiveX controls are not activated until the HTML is displayed, this prevents them from doing harm.

Switching from Plain Text to HTML Display

If you have set your options to read HTML messages as plain text, you can switch an individual open message to HTML display by clicking the Info bar and selecting Display as HTML.

To guard against malicious HTML messages:

1. **Select Trust Center from the Tools menu.**
2. **Click E-mail Security.**
3. **Under Read as Plain Text, select Read All Standard Mail in Plain Text (this means unsigned messages).**
4. **If you want to include digitally signed messages, select Read All Digitally Signed Mail in Plain Text.**
5. **Click OK.**

Summary

Spam, or junk e-mail, is a serious problem for most e-mail users. Outlook provides you with some powerful tools to detect and filter spam. By understanding these tools and using them efficiently, you can greatly reduce the negative impact that spam has on your productivity. E-mail rules are another way that Outlook helps you save time and stay organized. You may be hesitant to spend the time to define a rule, but in the long run they will be well worth the effort. Of course, rules are probably not warranted for situations that arise only occasionally, but most people who rely on e-mail in their work — and who doesn't these days? — will find plenty of good uses for them. You ignore e-mail security at your own peril. In today's interconnected world, it is all too easy for viruses and other malicious software to spread. Fortunately, Outlook provides you with a number of tools that help you to protect yourself against these threats.

Chapter 29

Working with Contacts

Outlook's Contacts feature is much more than a simple address book. It provides you with powerful tools not only to store but also find and use information about your business and personal contacts.

IN THIS CHAPTER

Understanding Outlook Contacts

Outlook's Contacts feature is one of its most powerful features. At heart, the Contacts feature is just an address book, but what an address book! Of course, it covers the basics of organizing names, addresses, and phone numbers, but it can do so much more. Many people use Contacts primarily as a way to store people's e-mail addresses for ease of sending e-mails. This is important, but if that's all you use Contacts for, you are really missing out. For example, you should know that you can use Outlook Contacts to

- Create electronic business cards so that you can send your or other people's contact information by e-mail
- Store multiple phone numbers, e-mail addresses, and postal address for an individual
- Perform an automated mail merge, creating a mailing to some or all of your contacts
- Automatically dial a contact's phone number (if your computer is equipped with a modem)
- Store a photograph as part of a contact's information
- Define custom fields to store whatever information you need as part of a contact
- View a map of the location of a contact's address

After you understand all the power of Outlook contacts, you can use as many or as few of its features as you like.

Note that Personal Address Books, a feature available in earlier versions of Outlook, is no longer supported.

The Contacts Window

When you select Contacts in the Navigation pane, the top part of the pane displays the name of your address book. Usually, this name is Contacts. If you have more than one address book, they are all displayed here. Using multiple address books is covered later in this chapter; most people have and need only one.

Below the address book name is a section titled Current View (see Figure 29-1). Here you can select how information will be displayed in the Contacts window. You have several options, including through business cards, by phone list, by company, and by location. Simply click the view you want and the Contacts window changes immediately.

FIGURE 29-1

Outlook offers several different ways to view contacts.

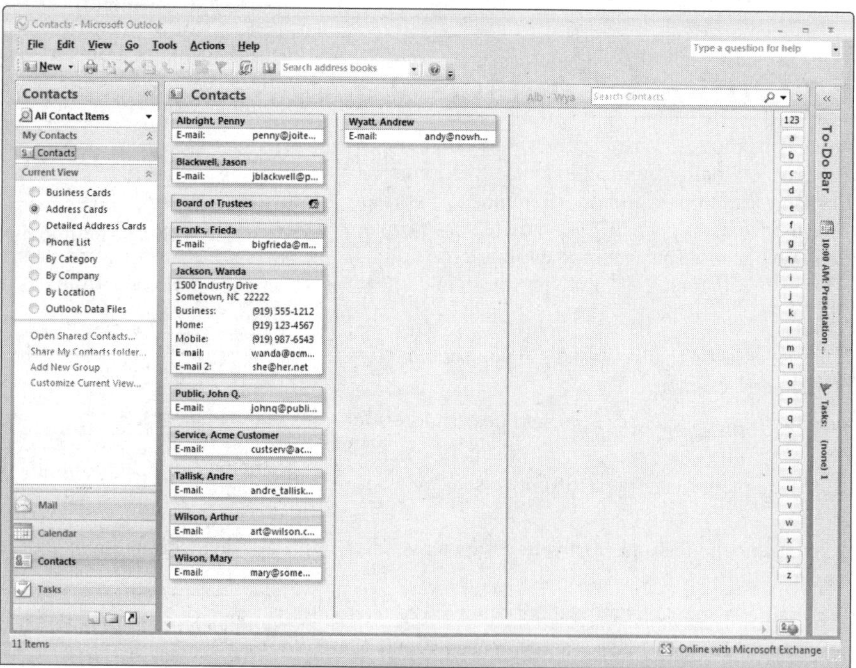

At the bottom of the Current View section (you may need to scroll to bring these into view) are two commands: Add New Group and Customize Current View. The next sections look at these in turn.

Adding a new contact group

By default, an address book is not subdivided. As the number of contacts grows, you may find it useful to define groups to organize contacts in a way that makes them easier to find and use. You might have Work, Personal, and Family groups, for example. To define a group, follow these steps:

1. **Make sure that Contacts is selected in the Navigation pane.**
2. **At the bottom of the Current View list, click the Add New Group link.** Outlook adds a group called New Group under My Contacts (Figure 29-2).

FIGURE 29-2

After adding a new group to your contacts.

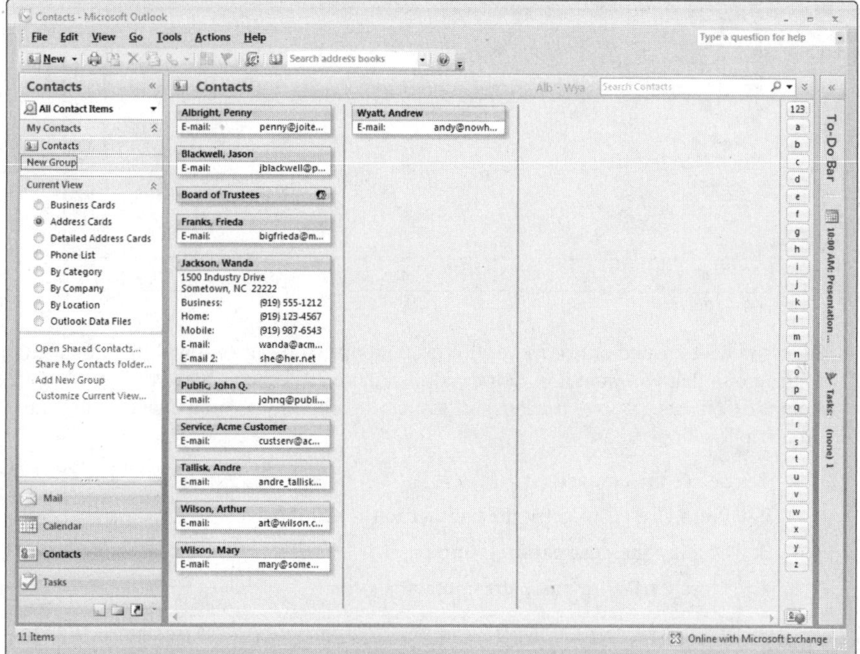

3. **Type in the group name and press Enter.**
4. **Repeat Steps 2–3 as needed to create more groups.**

Figure 29-3 shows how the Navigation pane looks after you create three new groups.

FIGURE 29-3

After creating and renaming three new groups.

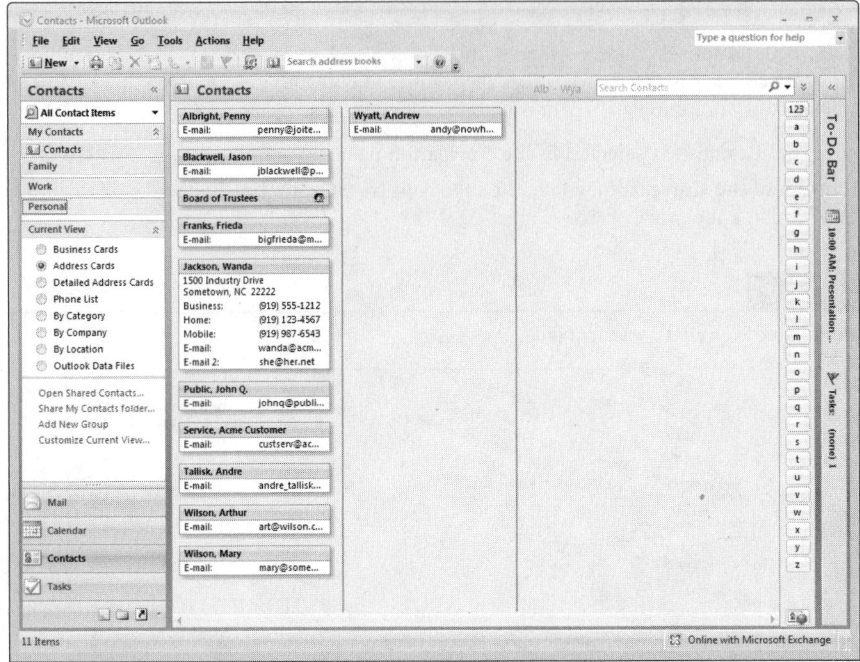

After you have created one or more additional groups, you can simply drag a contact from its current group to the group that you want it in. For example, Figure 29-4 shows how you would move Wanda Jackson from the Contacts group to the Personal Contacts group. If you want a given contact to be in more than one group, follow these steps:

1. **Select the contact.**
2. **Press Ctrl+C to copy the contact to the Clipboard.**
3. **Display the destination group.**
4. **Press Ctrl+V to paste the contact.**

Enabling Instant Search

The Instant Search feature is available by default in the Windows Vista operating system, but not in Windows XP. You may be prompted to download and install the search components when you start Outlook or another Office program. If you do not do so and then try to use Instant Search in Outlook, you will be prompted again. If you do not enable Instant Search, your search capabilities in Outlook will be limited compared to what is described here.

FIGURE 29-4

Moving a contact from one group to another.

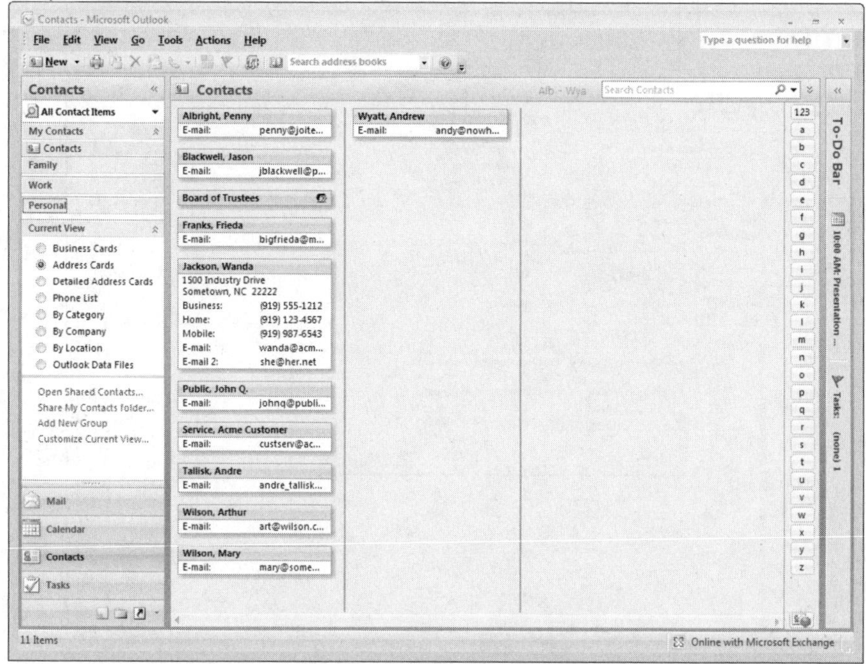

Customizing a Contacts view

The different views that Outlook provides for contacts can be customized to suit your need. You cannot, however, create a new view from scratch. To customize a view:

1. **Select the view that you want to customize in the Current View list.**
2. **At the bottom of the Current View list, click the Customize Current View link.** Outlook displays the Customize View dialog box (Figure 29-5).
3. **Click one of the buttons to change related view settings (explained in more detail in the text).** The text next to each button describes the purpose of each.
4. **If necessary, click Reset Current View to return the view to its original default settings.**
5. **Click OK to save your changes and close the dialog box.**

Depending on the view you are customizing, you may have only some of the buttons in the Customize View dialog box available. This is because certain aspects of a view are not relevant to some views. The aspects of the view that you change with the different buttons are described in Table 29-1.

FIGURE 29-5

Customizing a Contacts view.

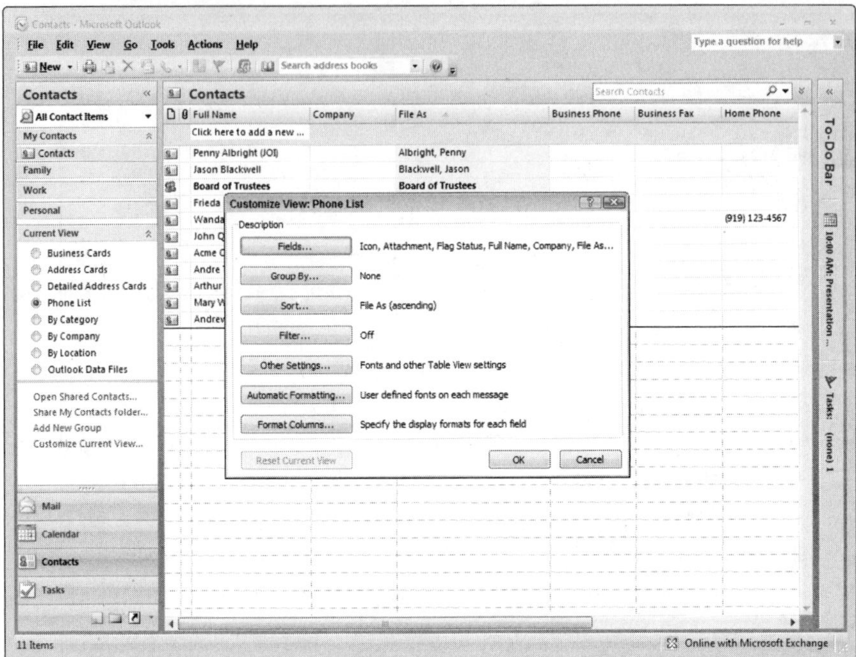

TABLE 29-1

Components of Customizing a Contacts View

Button	Action
Fields	Specify which fields (items of information) are included in the view.
Group By	Define grouping for the displayed contacts based on one or more fields. For example, you can group contacts by company or state.
Sort	Define how contacts are sorted. You can sort by last name, for example.
Filter	Display only those contacts that meet your defined criteria.
Other Settings	Specify fonts, grid lines, and other details of Contact View layout.
Automatic Formatting	Define special formatting for contacts that meet certain conditions, such as for a contact associated with an overdue task or that one that has been flagged.
Format Columns	Define formatting for columns in the view.

Finding contacts

As your Contacts list grows, you may find it helpful to search for contacts rather than simply look through the list hoping to find what you are looking for. At the top right of the Contacts window is a search field in which you type the text you are looking for. Outlook automatically filters the contacts to show only those that match what you have entered. An example is shown in Figure 29-6. If no matches occur, a message to that effect is displayed.

FIGURE 29-6

Searching for contacts.

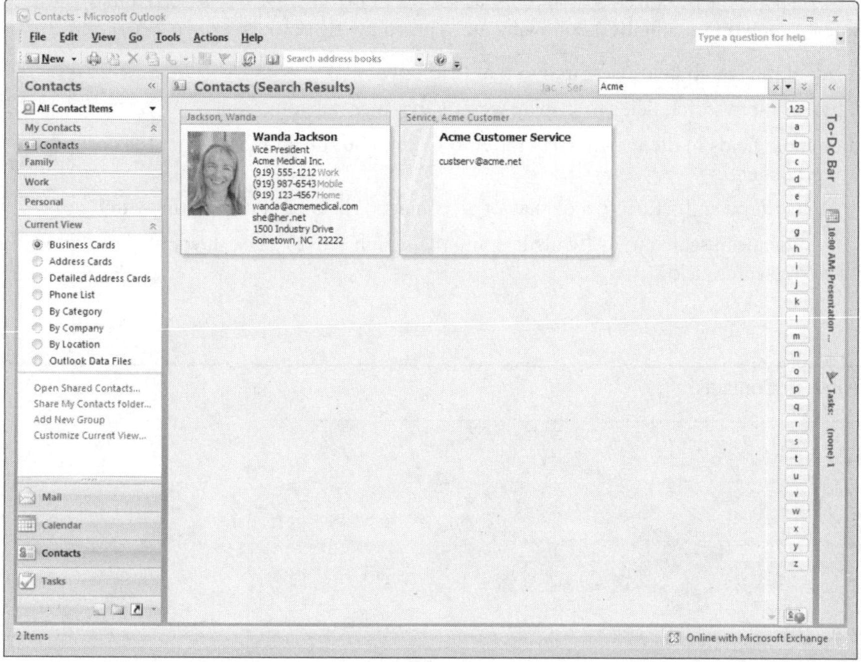

After conducting a search, click the X next to the search box to clear the search and return to displaying all contacts.

Searching by Category

Assigning your contacts to categories, as is explained later in this chapter, can make the advanced search tool even more useful. When you add criteria to the search, one of your choices is Categories. You can use this criterion to find all contacts that fall into a certain category. Searching by category can be particularly useful when you want to perform a mail merge, as described later in this chapter.

Finding Contacts Alphabetically

In some Contacts views, Outlook displays a column of index buttons at the right side of the Contacts window; the first of these buttons is labeled 123, followed by buttons labeled A through Z. Click one of these buttons to scroll the Contacts display to entries that begin with the specified letter.

The search I have just described searches all the contact fields for the text you entered. If you want to search in specific fields, you can perform an advanced search by clicking the double down arrow to the right of the search box. Outlook displays the advanced search tools, as shown in Figure 29-7. (Your screen may show different fields than are shown in the figure.) Following are ways to use these tools:

- Type in any of the search fields to search in that field only.
- Type in two or more search fields to display records that meet all your criteria.
- To include more fields in the search, click the Add Criteria button and then select the desired fields from the menu.
- To clear each criteria and return to a display of all contacts, click the X next to the search box.
- To close the advanced search tools (while keeping the search active), click the double up arrow to the right of the search field.

FIGURE 29-7

Performing an advanced search in Contacts.

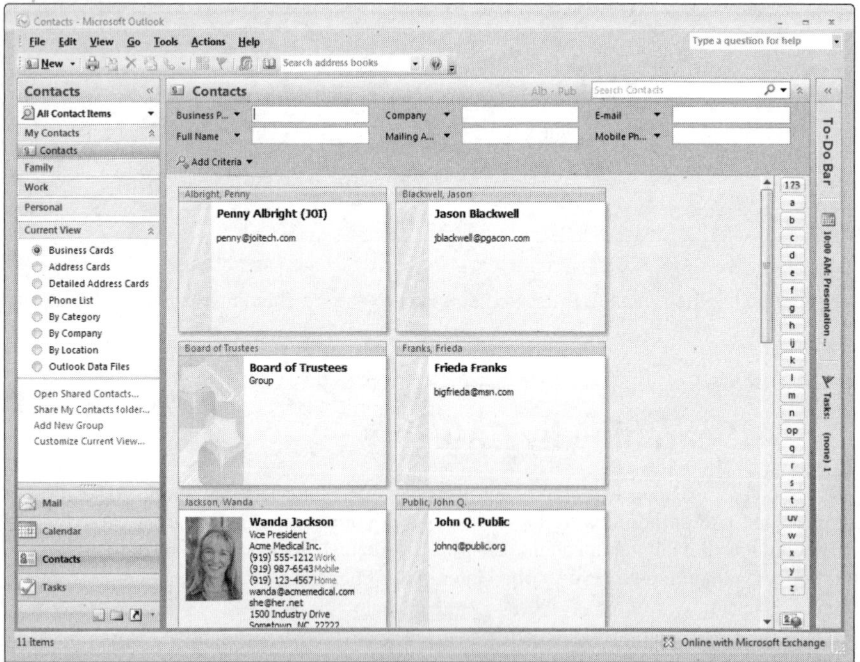

Adding Contacts to the Address Book

Outlook provides you with several ways to add information to an address book.

Adding a contact manually

To add a new contact to the address book:

- If Contacts are active in Outlook, click the New button on the toolbar or press Ctrl+N.
- If Contacts are not active in Outlook, click the arrow next to the New button on the toolbar and select Contact from the menu.

In either case, Outlook displays a new, blank contact form, as shown in Figure 29-8. Type in the information—only a name is required, and you can use or not use the other fields as you desire—and then click Save and Close on the Ribbon. If you want to save this contact and enter another, click Save and New. Most of the fields on the contact form are self-explanatory, but I provide full details about the form later in this chapter.

FIGURE 29-8

A blank contact form.

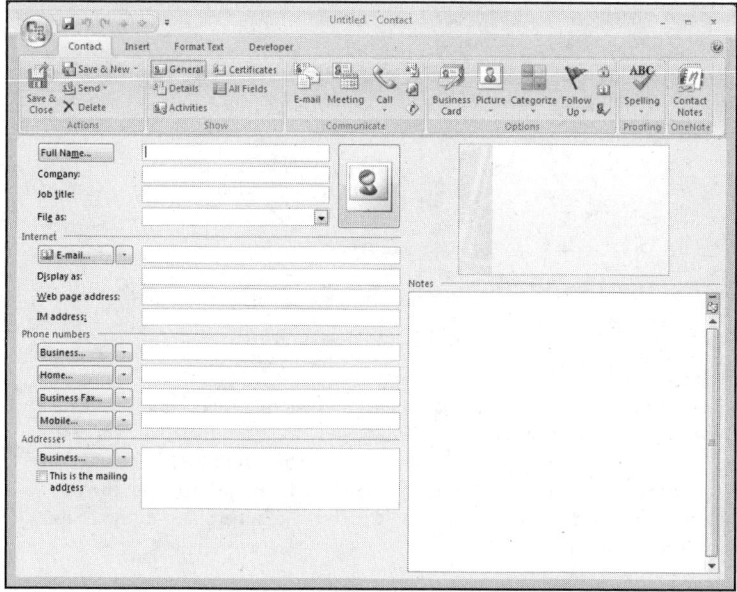

Adding a contact from a received e-mail

When you have opened a received e-mail, the From field displays the name or the e-mail address (or both) of the sender. It also displays any other recipients—other than you, that is—in the To and Cc fields. You can add the From person or any of the other To or Cc people to your Contacts list by right-clicking it and choosing Add to Outlook Contacts from the context menu. Outlook opens a new contact form with the available information filled in. This information includes only the person's e-mail address and perhaps name. You can add additional information to the contact form, if desired, and then click Save and Close.

Adding a contact from an Outlook contact

The heading of this section may seem confusing but it makes more sense when you understand that an Outlook user can send a contact as an attachment to an e-mail message. The technique for doing this is covered later in this chapter, in the section "Sending contact information by e-mail."

If you receive a contact in an e-mail message, it appears as an attachment identified by a small business card icon and the contact's name, as shown in Figure 29-9. If you double-click the attachment, Outlook opens a new contact form with the contact's information entered. You can edit the information if needed and then save it to your address book.

FIGURE 29-9

When you receive an Outlook contact attached to an e-mail message, it is identified by a small business card icon.

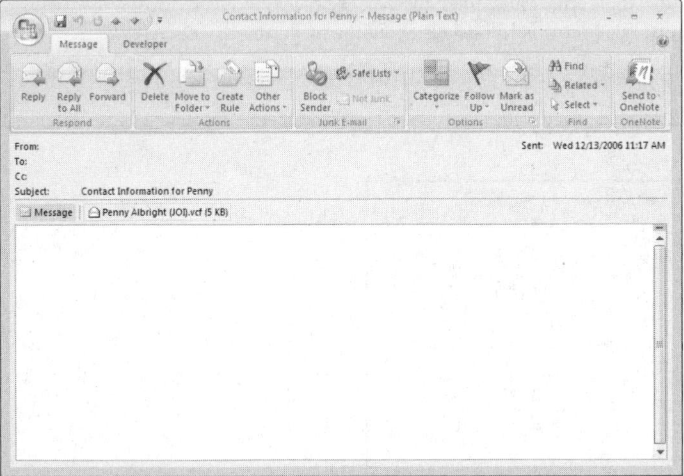

Adding a contact from a vCard file

A vCard file is a special file format designed to send contact information. Although this is not Outlook's native format for sending and receiving contact information, Outlook can read vCard files that you may receive from people using other e-mail software. vCard files work the same way as Outlook contacts that were described in the previous section: You double-click the attachment to add the information to your address book. Outlook users can also send vCards to other people, which is explained later in the chapter in the section "Sending contact information by e-mail."

Working with Distribution Lists

A distribution list is a collection of two or more contacts. You can easily send an e-mail message to everyone on the list simply by selecting the list from your address book when addressing the message; you don't need to add each person individually to the message's To field.

Creating a Distribution list

To create a Distribution list, click the down arrow next to the New button on the toolbar and choose Distribution List from the menu. Outlook opens a Distribution List form, as shown in Figure 29-10. The form initially is empty, of course; this example shows some names that have been added.

FIGURE 29-10

A Distribution list can contain two or more contacts.

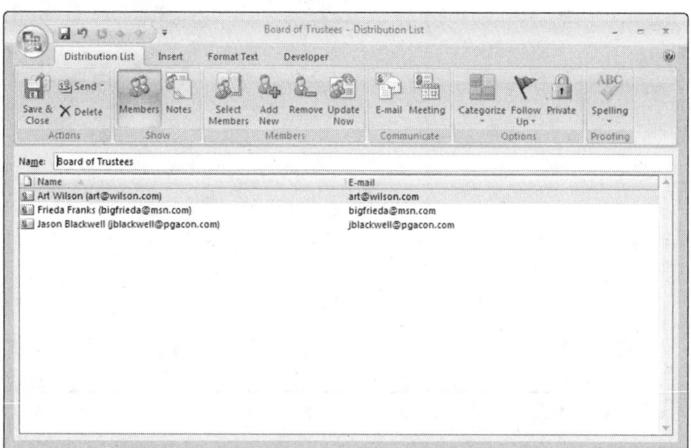

To add contacts that are already in your address book, click the Select members button. Outlook displays the Select Members dialog box, as shown in Figure 29-11. If you have more than one address book, you must select the desired one in the Address Book list. Then select individual contacts by clicking (Ctrl+click to select more than one) each one and then clicking the Members button followed by the OK button. You can also select existing distribution lists to add to the new list.

To add a contact that is not in your address book to the list, click the Add New button. Outlook displays the Add New Member dialog box (Figure 29-12). Enter the new contact's name and e-mail address and select the Add to Contacts option if you want the person added as an individual entry to your Contacts list as well as to this Distribution list. Then, click OK.

Updating a Distribution List

Suppose that one of your contacts changes his or her e-mail address and you make the necessary edit in that contact's entry in your address book. This change will *not* be reflected automatically in any Distribution lists that you have this person in. You must manually update each list by opening it and clicking the Update Now button on the ribbon.

FIGURE 29-11

Selecting contacts from your address book to add to a distribution list.

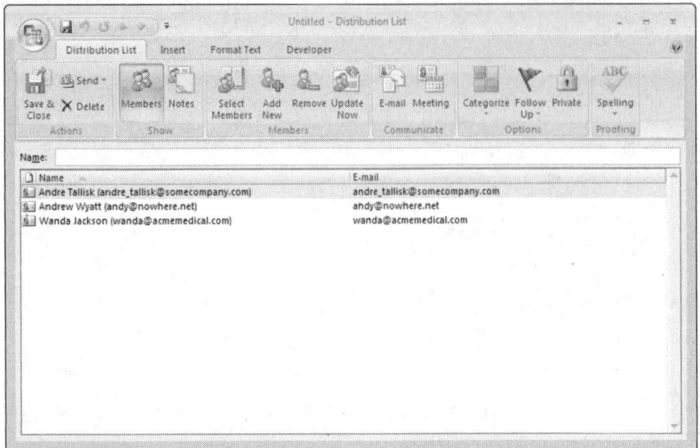

FIGURE 29-12

Adding a contact who is not in your address book to a distribution list.

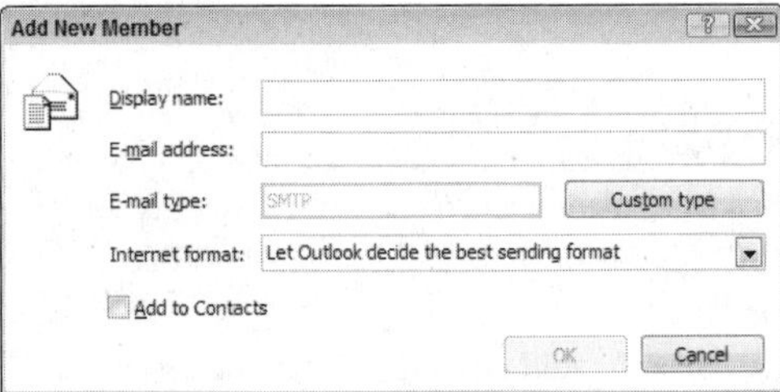

Using Distribution lists

In many ways, a Distribution list is like an individual entry in your address book. When a Distribution list is open, you can use the various buttons on the Ribbon (E-Mail, Meeting, Categorize, and so on) just as you do for an individual contact (as described elsewhere in this chapter). You can also send a Distribution list as an attachment to an e-mail message, as described in the section "Sending contact information by e-mail."

When you address an e-mail message to a distribution list, the list name is displayed in the To or Cc field of the message with an adjacent + sign, as shown in Figure 29-13. If you click this + sign, the list is expanded to display its individual members just as though you had added them individually to the To or Cc field. This feature can be useful if you want to send a message to everyone on the list except one or two people; you can expand the Distribution list and delete those few individuals from the To or Cc field of the message.

FIGURE 29-13

A distribution list in the To field of an e-mail message.

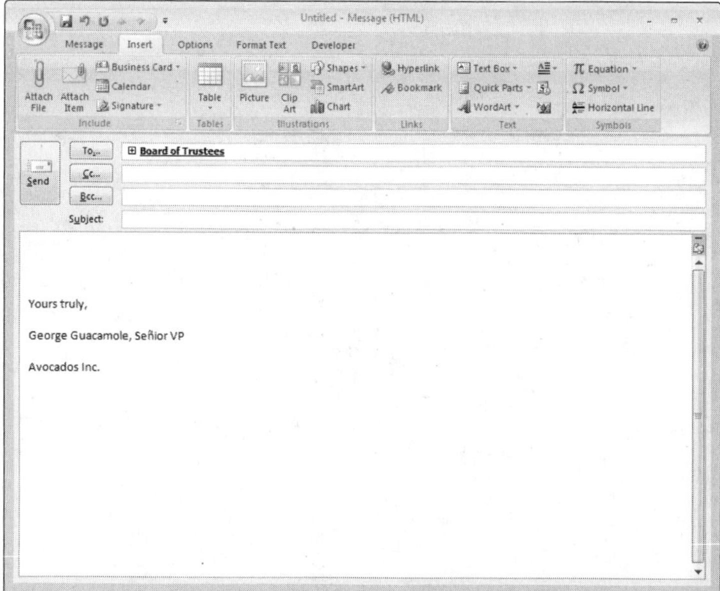

More about Contacts

Outlook contacts function as much more than as the contents of a simple address book. This section covers additional details and capabilities of Outlook contacts.

The Contact form

The Contact form, shown in Figure 29-14, provides places for you to enter many different kinds of information about a contact. The only field that is required is the name; you can use all, some, or none of the other fields, as you like. Some of the elements on the Contacts form may deserve an explanation, as provided in the following sections.

Full Name

You can simply enter a contact's name in the Full Name field in the usual way, for example John. Q. Public. You can also click the adjacent Full Name button to bring up the Check Full Name dialog box, shown in Figure 29-15. Here you can specify a title such as Dr. or Mrs. and a suffix such as Jr. or Sr.

Note the option in this dialog box: Show This Again When Name Is Incomplete or Unclear. When this option is on (the default), Outlook opens this dialog box automatically when you enter an incomplete name such as "Fred" in the Full Name field.

The File As field determines how a contact will be filed in the address book. The default is last name first (Public, John Q.) but you can also choose to file a contact first name first.

FIGURE 29-14

The Contact form provides fields for a wide variety of information about the contact.

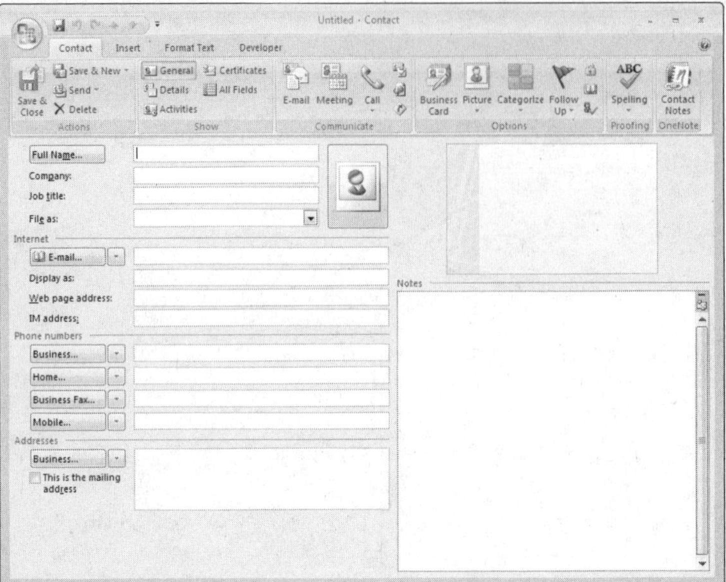

FIGURE 29-15

The Check Full Name dialog box lets you enter more details for a contact's name.

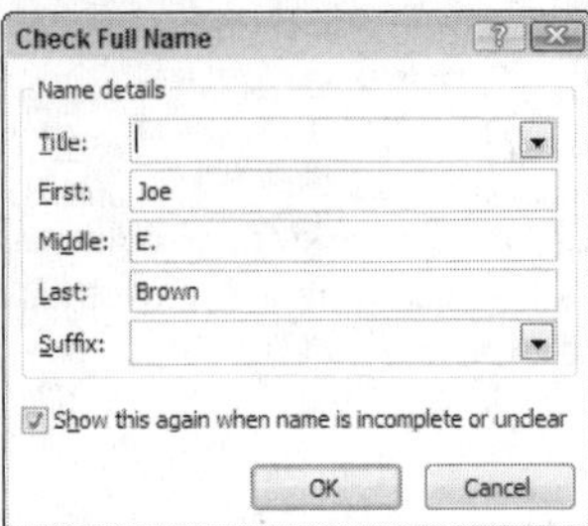

Phone Numbers

The Phone Numbers section of the contacts form provides spaces for four numbers. By default, these are labeled as Business, Home, Business Fax, and Mobile, but you can change which numbers are displayed in a particular Phone Number field by clicking the adjacent down arrow and selecting from the list. Some of the choices available are Home Fax, Pager, and Assistant. Outlook saves a phone number for each designation, but only four numbers are displayed on the Contacts form at one time. When you open the list of designations, those for which you have entered a phone number are checked.

Quick E-Mail

When a contact is open, click the E-Mail button on the Ribbon to create a new e-mail message addressed to the contact.

Next to each Phone Number field is a button with the field's designation on it. If you click one of these buttons, Outlook opens the Check Phone Number dialog box, shown in Figure 29-16. Here you can enter additional details for the phone number if desired.

FIGURE 29-16

The Check Phone Number dialog box lets you enter more details for a contact's phone number.

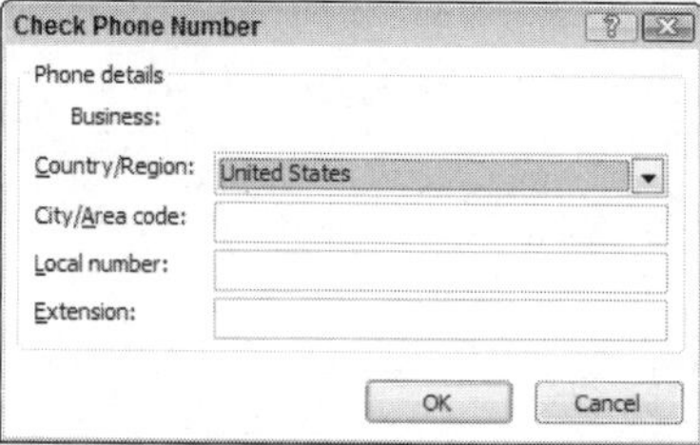

Addresses

The Addresses section of the contacts form can store up to three addresses designated as Home, Business, and Other. Select the one to display by clicking the down arrow adjacent to the address box. Click the adjacent button to open the Check Address dialog box (Figure 29-17), in which you can enter or edit address details. By default, Outlook displays this dialog box automatically if you enter an address that appears to be incomplete or unclear.

One of the addresses for a contact can be designated as the mailing address by selecting the corresponding option. Outlook uses this address when you are doing a mail merge using Outlook contact data. Mail merge is discussed later in this chapter.

FIGURE 29-17

The Check Address dialog box lets you enter more details for a contact's address.

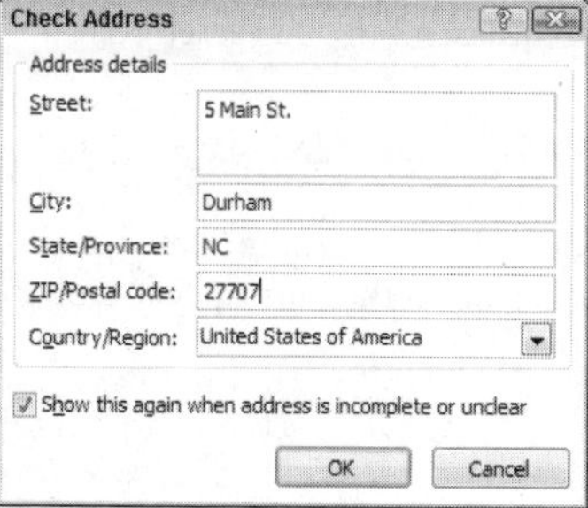

Picture

You can associate a picture with a contact by clicking the Picture button on the contacts form. Outlook displays a dialog box that lets you browse for the picture file. When you have associated a picture with a contact, it displays on the picture button and on the contact's business card, as shown in Figure 29-18. To remove or change the picture, right-click it and choose from the context menu.

FIGURE 29-18

You can associate a picture with a contact.

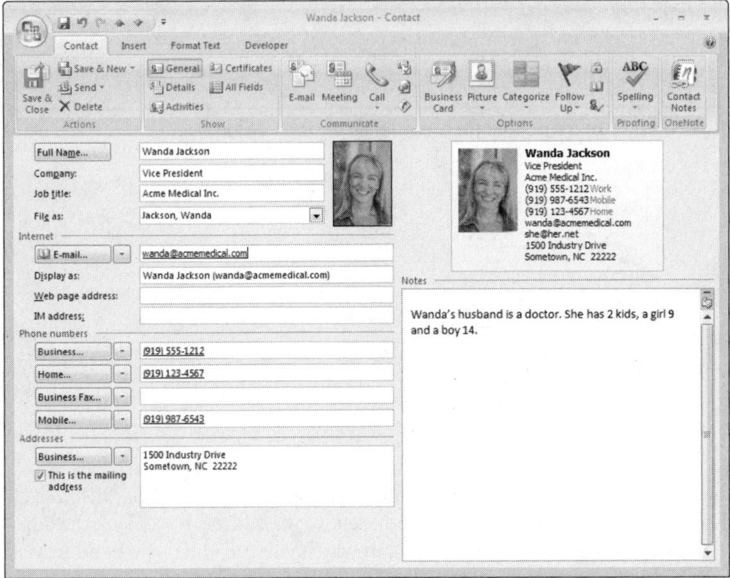

E-mail addresses

Outlook can store as many as three e-mail addresses for a contact, designated as E-Mail, E-Mail 2, and E-Mail 3. You select which one to display on the contacts form using the arrow adjacent to the E-Mail field.

If you create an e-mail message to a contact by clicking the E-mail button on the Ribbon on a contact form, Outlook creates a message addressed to all the e-mail addresses for that contact. If you click the To button on an e-mail message, the list of contacts displays each e-mail separately, and you can choose the one to use.

The Display As field determines how the contact is displayed in a message's To or Cc field. By default, Outlook displays the contact's name followed by the e-mail address in parentheses, but you can edit this to display as desired — for example, just the person's name.

Notes

The Notes section on a contact form is for entry of any arbitrary information that you want to save with the contact. Simply click in the box and enter or edit as usual. You can use the tools on the Format Text Ribbon to apply formatting to the Notes text, if desired.

Other contact displays

The default contact display, called General, has been shown in the figures throughout this chapter so far. This is the display that you will probably use most often. Several other displays, or views, are available; you select the display to view from the Show section of the Contact Ribbon.

Details

The Details view gives you access to secondary information about a contact. This view is shown in Figure 29-19. This information includes fields such as Department, Office, Nickname, and Spouse/Partner as well as details for the person's NetMeeting settings. You may never use this view, but it's available if you need it.

FIGURE 29-19

The Details view for a contact.

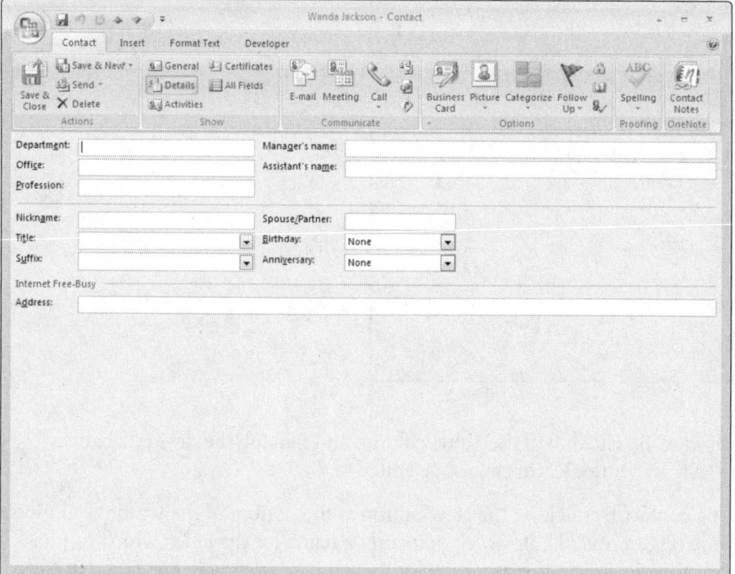

Certificates

One of the security features available in Outlook is digital certificates. A contact can send you a certificate, and you can then use this certificate to send encrypted mail to that person. The Certificates display lets you view and work with the certificate(s) that you have for a contact. Digital certificates are covered in Chapter 28.

All Fields

The All Fields display lets you view all or selected subsets of the data associated with a contact. The amount of information — number of fields — that an individual contact can hold is quite impressive and is way too much to display fully in any other contact view. The All Fields display also lets you define your own custom fields for a contact and to change the properties of some fields.

The All Fields display is shown in Figure 29-20. Near the top is the Select From list, in which you choose which fields to display in the window. You can display all fields as well as one of several defined subsets, such as All Contact Fields or All Mail Fields.

FIGURE 29-20

The All Fields view for a contact.

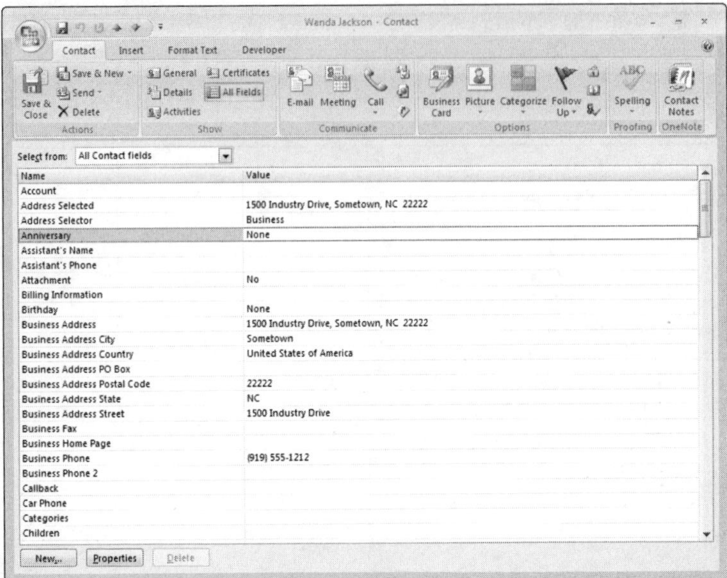

Some fields can be edited in this view by clicking in the Value column and making the desired changes. Other fields are generated internally by Outlook and cannot be edited.

You can add a custom field to the contact by clicking the New button at the bottom of the window. Outlook displays the New Field dialog box (Figure 29-21), in which you enter a name for the field (which cannot duplicate an existing field name). You also select the data type for the field. Your choices are Text, Number, Percent, Currency, Yes/No, and Date/Time. For certain data types, you can also select a format from the Format list. When you are finished, click OK and the custom field will be added to the All Fields display.

FIGURE 29-21

Defining a new field for a contact.

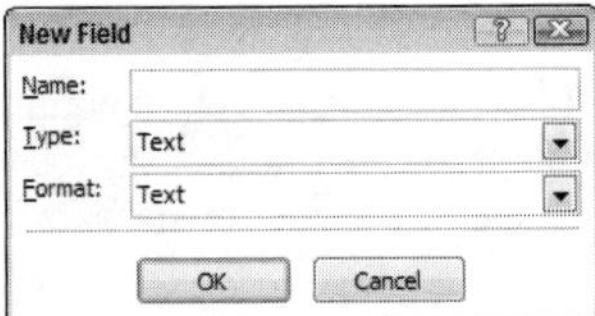

You can change the properties of a field by clicking it in the list and then clicking the Properties button. This is relevant only for user-defined fields; the properties of Outlook's built-in fields are locked.

Editing the business card

Outlook creates a business card for each contact based on a default template. As you can see in Figure 29-22, this template includes name, company, title, phone numbers, e-mail and postal addresses, and a photo (assuming that these elements are part of the contact).

FIGURE 29-22

The default business card template includes the information needed most often.

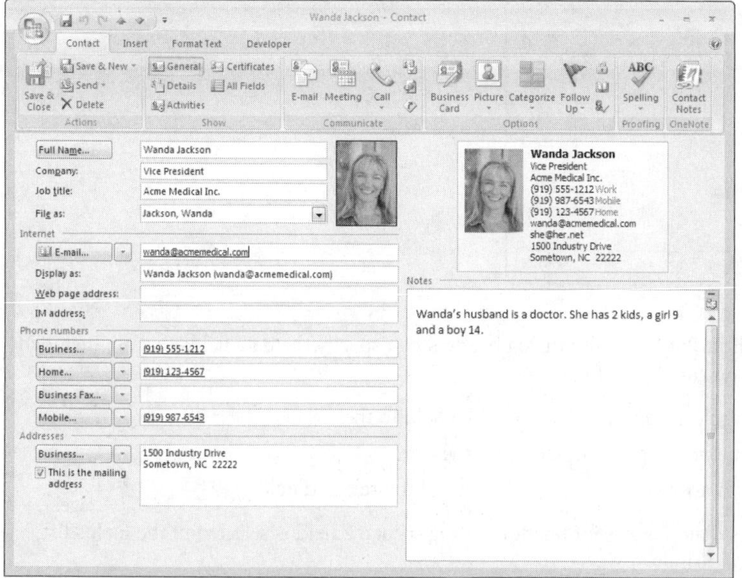

To edit the business card for a contact, click the Business Card button on the Contact tab of the Ribbon. Outlook opens the Edit Business Card dialog box, shown in Figure 29-23.

The top-left section of this dialog box previews how the business card will look with your edits. The top-right section defines the overall layout of the card:

- **Layout:** Specifies the image location. You can also omit the image or use it as the card background.
- **Background:** Lets you select a background color for the card.
- **Image:** Lets you specify a different image when you click the Change button.
- **Image Area:** Determines how much of the card is occupied by the image. The maximum is 50 percent.
- **Image Align:** Determines how the image is positioned within the image area.

FIGURE 29-23

Editing the business card for an individual contact.

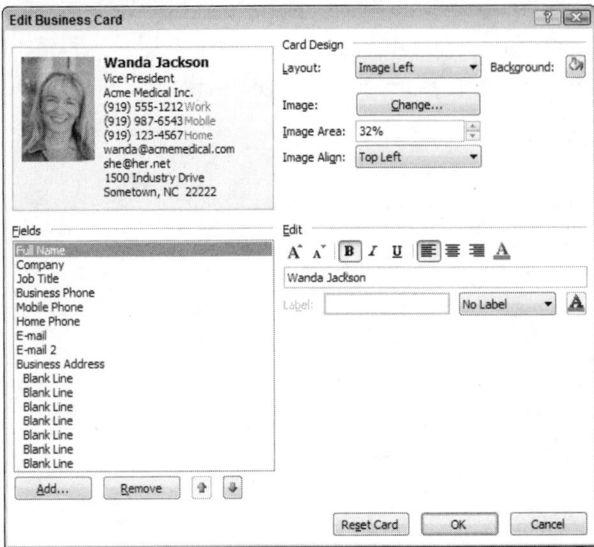

The lower-left section of the Edit Business Card dialog box lets you specify the data fields that are included on the card and their order. You can do the following:

- Click Add and then select from the menu to add a field to the card.
- Click Remove to remove the selected field from the card.
- Click the up or down arrow to change the position of the selected field.

The lower-right section of this dialog box is for text formatting. When a field is selected in the Fields list, use the tools here to do the following:

- Increase or decrease font size
- Make font bold, italic, or underlined
- Align text left, center, or right
- Change font color

Oddly enough, you cannot change the font used on a business card; you can change only its size.

The Label section lets you add a label to any data field. You can specify the text of the label, its color, and whether it is displayed to the left or right of the item.

Click the Reset Card button to undo any edits you have made and return the card to the default appearance. Click OK to save your changes and close the dialog box.

Dialing the phone

If your computer is equipped with a modem, you can have Outlook dial the phone for you based on the number associated with a contact. Then you can pick up your handset and complete the call as usual. You must have the modem and handset on the same line, which can be inconvenient if you use the modem to access the Internet. If your Internet connection is via cable modem or DSL, or via a second telephone line, you may want to dedicate an old modem as a dedicated dialer on your voice line. The speed of the modem is not relevant in this application.

When a contact is open, click the arrow on the Call button on the Contact tab to display the menu shown in Figure 29-24. This menu lists all the phone numbers for the current contact. Select the one to dial, and Outlook opens the New Call dialog box (Figure 29-25) with the selected phone number entered. The settings and commands in this dialog box are as follows:

- **Dialing Properties:** Opens the Dialing Properties dialog box, in which you define rules for dialing from your computer. You should not have to change these because they will have been set up when you installed and configured your modem.
- **Create Journal Entry:** Creates an Outlook Journal entry for the call, noting the number called and the time and date of the call.
- **Dialing Options:** Lets you set speed dialer options and add names and numbers to the Speed Dial list.
- **Start Call:** Dials the number.
- **End Call:** Hangs up.

The Call menu has several other commands, as follows:

- **Redial:** Dials a recently called number
- **Speed Dial:** Dials a number on your speed dial list
- **New Call:** Opens the New Call dialog box without any phone number entered

Outlook can also make Instant Messenger calls. If you have specified an Instant Messenger address for the contact, this option appears on the Call menu.

FIGURE 29-24

Using Outlook to dial the phone.

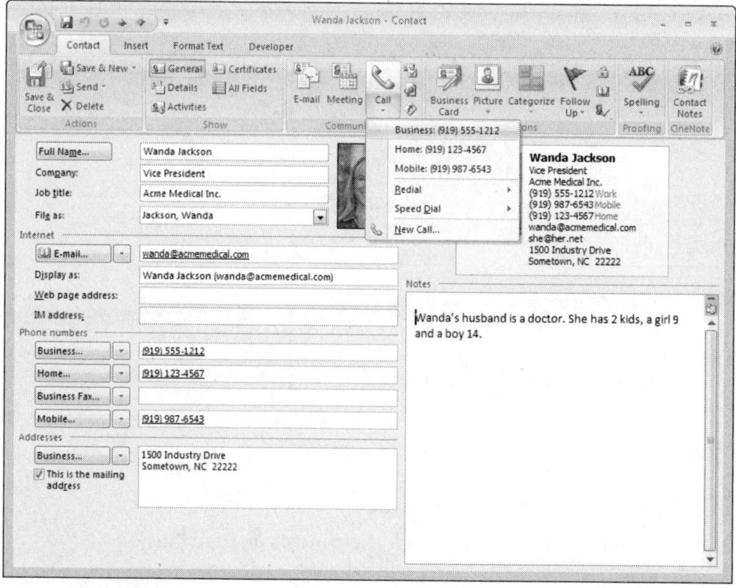

FIGURE 29-25

The New Call dialog box.

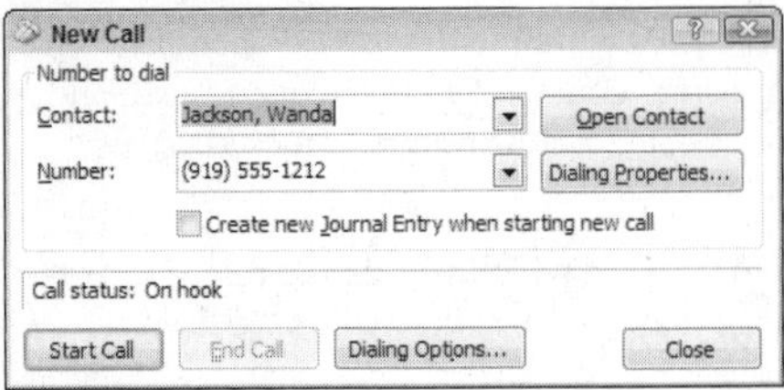

Sending contact information by e-mail

Sending contact information attached to an e-mail message can be very useful. Doing so lets recipients enter the information in their address book quickly and without errors. If you keep an entry for yourself in your address book, you can easily send your own information as well.

Sending contact information in Outlook format

Outlook offers two formats for sending contact information. Outlook's native format is to send the information as an Outlook item. You can send individual contacts and distribution lists this way. Information sent this way can be used by other Outlook users and possibly by users of other e-mail programs that support this format. To send contact information as an Outlook item, follow these steps:

1. **Create and address the e-mail message as usual.**
2. **On the Insert tab of the Ribbon, click the Insert Item button.** Outlook displays the Insert Item dialog box (Figure 29-26).

FIGURE 29-26

Inserting an item into an e-mail message.

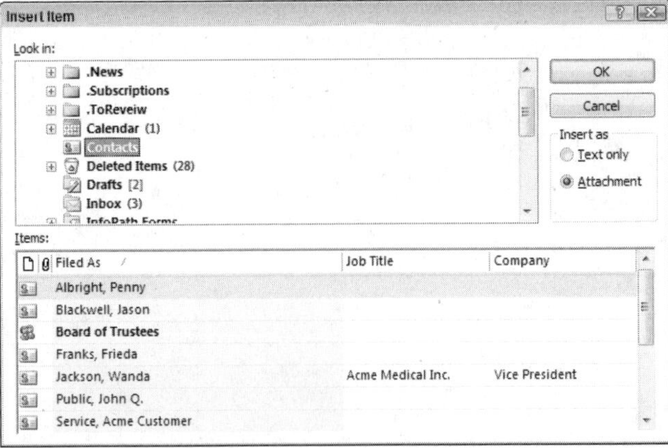

3. **In the Look In list at the top of the dialog box, click the Contacts folder.**
4. **In the Items list at the bottom of the dialog box, click the contact or Distribution List to send.** Hold down the Ctrl key while clicking to select more than one contact.

5. **Make sure that the Attachment option is selected. If you select the Text Only option, the information is added to the body of the message but the recipient will not be able to automatically add it to his or her address book.**
6. **Click OK.** The item, with a small business card icon, is added to the message's attachment list.

Sending contact information in vCard Format

The second format for sending contact information is vCard, a widely supported format for contact information. Most e-mail programs support this format, and you may want to use it when you are not sure that all the intended recipients use an e-mail program that supports Outlook items. You can send only individual contacts, not Distribution lists, using a vCard,. To send a vCard, follow these steps:

1. **Open the contact that you want to send.**
2. **In the Contact window, click the File button and choose Save As from the File menu.** Outlook displays the Save As dialog box (Figure 29-27).

FIGURE 29-27

Saving a contact as a vCard file.

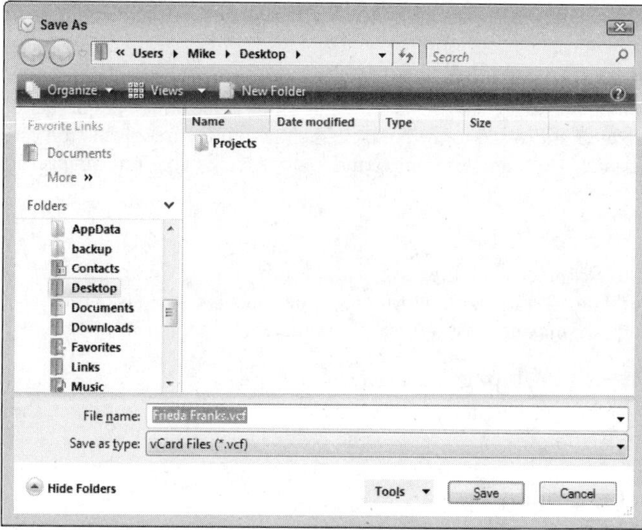

3. **Use the dialog box tools to navigate to the location where you want to save the vCard file.**
4. **In the Save as Type list, select vCard Files (`*.vcf`).**
5. **The default name for the file is the contact name.** You can edit this name if desired.
6. **Click Save.**
7. **Create an e-mail message and attach the vCard file that you just saved.**

Sending contact information from the Contact form

When you have a contact open, the Actions group of the Contact tab of the Ribbon includes a Send button. You can use this button to send the open contact in one of three ways by selecting the desired command from the associated menu:

- **Send as Business Card:** Outlook creates a new message with the contact inserted in the message body as a business card and attached to the message as a vCard file.
- **In Internet Format (vCard):** Outlook creates a new message with the contact attached to the message as a vCard file.
- **In Outlook Format:** Outlook creates a new message with the contact attached to the message as an Outlook item.

Other contact actions

This section describes some of the other actions you can perform with contacts.

Viewing a map of the contact's address

If a contact has a valid address entered, you can click the Map button on the Contact tab of the Ribbon to open a Web browser and view a map of the specified location. This feature is powered by the Windows Live Local Web site, which provides other services such as driving directions and business search.

Inviting the contact to a meeting

To invite the contact to a meeting, click the Meeting button on the Contact tab of the Ribbon. Outlook creates a new meeting request addressed to the contact, as shown in Figure 29-28. You can specify the subject and location, enter the date, start and end times, and include a message. You can also add other recipients to the request.

Assigning a task to a contact

To assign a new task to a contact, click the Assign Task button on the Contact ribbon. Outlook opens a task window, as shown in Figure 29-29, in which you can enter details of the task and save it. You learn more about tasks, including assigning an existing task to a contact, in Chapter 30.

Viewing the contact's Web page

If you have entered a Web page URL for a contact, clicking the Web Page button on the Contact ribbon launches your default Web browser and displays the Web page.

Tagging a contact for follow up

To tag a contact for follow up, click the Follow Up button in the Options section of the Contact ribbon and select the desired follow-up interval from the menu.

Use the Context Menus

Many of the actions that you can take with contacts that are described in this section can be accessed without opening the contact. In the Contacts window, simply right-click the contact and choose from the context menu. You can use this technique to send a contact, call a contact, or assign a follow-up of category to a contact.

FIGURE 29-28

Sending a meeting request to a contact.

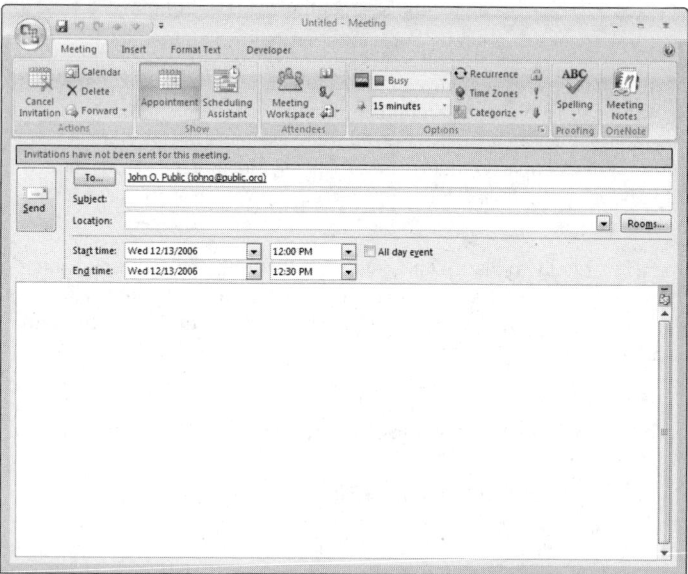

FIGURE 29-29

Assigning a task to a contact.

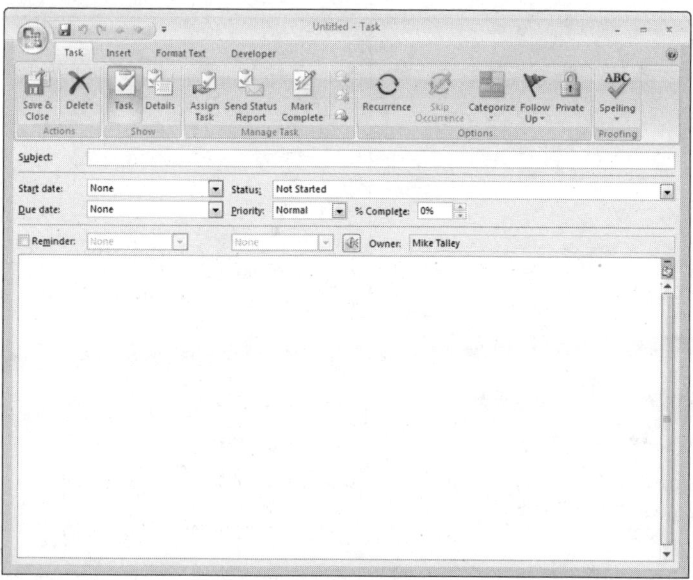

Performing a Mail Merge from Your Contacts

Mail merge is a technique that lets a form letter be addressed and sent to many different individuals. It can also be used to create mailing labels, envelopes, and catalogs such as a mailing list. Microsoft Office has merge tools built into several of its applications, most notably Word, and Outlook is included in this list.

When would you use Outlook to perform a mail merge? Only when the names and addresses that you want to use are in your Outlook address book. In this situation, using Outlook is often the simplest approach. Even so, some factors may mitigate against using Outlook for a merge and instead using the more advanced mail merge tools available in other Office applications. For example, Outlook cannot separate documents by ZIP code to get reduced mailing rates, and it would not be a good choice for a large merge that will create thousands of documents. You need to have Microsoft Word installed on your system to perform a mail merge.

The first step in performing a mail merge is usually to filter your contacts so that only the ones you want included are shown. You can do this by using Outlook's search capability or by customizing the Contacts view, both of which are covered earlier in this chapter. However, you can skip this step and select the contacts to include later. Then, follow these steps:

1. **Make sure that Contacts are active.**
2. **Choose Mail Merge from the Tools menu.** Outlook displays the Mail Merge dialog box, as shown in Figure 29-30.
3. **Make entries in this dialog box as described in the list that follows these steps.**

FIGURE 29-30

Performing a mail merge with Outlook contacts.

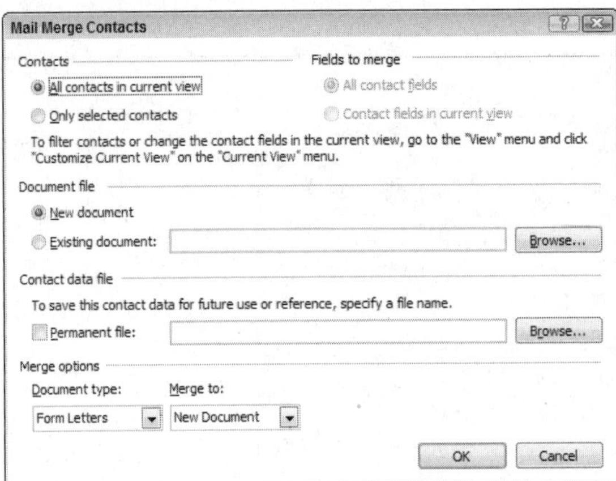

4. **Click OK to open Word to complete the merge.**

The options in the Mail Merge dialog box are as follows:

- **Contacts:** Select All Contacts in Current View to include all displayed contacts in the merge. Select Only Selected Contacts to select contacts to include later.

- **Field to Merge:** Specifies whether only visible contact fields or all contact fields will be available for the merge. These options may or may not be available depending on the current Contacts view.
- **Document File:** Specifies whether the merge will use a new or an existing Word document. If you choose the latter option, use the Browse button to locate the document to use.
- **Contact Data File:** You can select this option to save the merge contact data in a separate Word document. Typically, this option is used to create a record of the people who were included in the mailing.
- **Document Type:** You can merge to form letters, mailing labels, envelopes, or a catalog.
- **Merge To:** Specify whether the merge output goes to a Word document, to the printer, or to e-mail, as follows:
  - **New Document:** Merge creates a Word document that you can edit as needed before creating the final output.
  - **Printer:** The merged document is created and sent directly to the default printer.
  - **E-mail:** The merged documents are created as e-mail messages and placed in your Outbox.

In most situations, the remainder of the merge process is carried out in Word. Please consult your Word documentation for more information.

Working with Multiple Address Books

The majority of Outlook users have only a single address book. This is all that most people need, in fact. In some situations, you may have two or more address books. This can happen if you create more than one Outlook data file. Each data file will have its own address book, and you will have access to the one in whichever Outlook data file is open. You might want to use more than one Outlook data file if you want to keep your personal e-mail completely separate from your work e-mail. You learned more about working with Outlook data files in Chapter 27.

Another situation in which you will have more than one address book is when you have both a regular (that is, SMTP/POP) e-mail account and a Microsoft Exchange account set up in Outlook. The regular account will have its own address book and the Exchange account will have another, separate one. You will have both available to you at the same time in Outlook; they are listed at the top of the Navigation pane when Contacts are active, and you can choose to view one or the other. When you add a contact, it is added to whichever address book is active.

Setting Contact Options

Outlook has some global options that affect the way contacts work. To view and change these options:

1. **Choose Options from the Tools menu to display the Options dialog box.**
2. **If necessary, click the Preferences tab.**
3. **Click the Contact Options button to display the Contact Options dialog box (Figure 29-31).**
4. **Set options as described in the list that follows these steps.**
5. **Click OK twice to exit all dialog boxes.**

FIGURE 29-31

Setting global options for contacts.

The options that are available for contacts are as follows:

- **Default Full Name Order:** Specifies how contacts are sorted when you order them based on full name. You can choose First Middle Last, Last First, or First Last1 Last2.
- **Default File As Order:** Specifies how contacts are sorted when you order them based on the File As field. Your choices are Last First, First Last, Company, Last First (Company), Company (Last, First).
- **Check for Duplicate Contacts:** Outlook warns you if you try to enter a new contact with the same name as an existing contact.
- **Show Contact Linking on All Forms:** Controls whether all information linked to a contact (tasks, for example) is displayed.
- **Show an Additional Contacts Index:** Outlook displays a second set of index buttons at the right edge of the Contacts window using the language you select from the list.

Summary

The Outlook Contacts feature is a powerful tool for managing and using information about people. It goes way beyond the basic address book to store just about any kind of information about a person you can imagine. What's more, it makes it easy to find and use that information in various ways. Many people find contacts to be one of Outlook's most useful tools.

Chapter 30

Working with Appointments and Tasks

A calendar is something you hang on the wall, right? It has a page for each month and a picture of a puppy, lighthouse, or famous painting. If that's what you think, then you haven't used the Outlook Calendar! Outlook provides a sophisticated calendar that helps you manage your time efficiently. In today's busy world, few of us have any shortage of things to do. A list of tasks always seems to be waiting for our attention, particularly in a high-pressure business or professional environment. This chapter covers the Outlook Calendar and task (To-Do list) features that can help you stay on time and on track with whatever you do.

IN THIS CHAPTER

Understanding the Outlook Calendar

At its heart, the Outlook Calendar stores and displays appointments. An *appointment* is just what it sounds like — a scheduled event with a title and a time and date specified for the beginning and end of the event. Outlook distinguishes between two types of appointments:

- A regular appointment has a specific start time and stop time. It is usually on the same day but does not have to be.
- An all-day event does not have specific start and stop times but rather takes up all of one or more days.

Scheduling appointments may not sound so special, and in fact it's not. But it's the way that Outlook lets you organize, use, and share your appointments that makes the Calendar so useful.

Using the Calendar

To show the Calendar, click the Calendar button in the Navigation pane. The view window shows the Calendar itself, and we'll get to that in a moment. The top section of the Navigation pane shows a small calendar of the current month, called the *Date Navigator*, which has several useful features, as shown in Figure 30-1 and described in the following list:

- Today's date is enclosed in a box — the 22nd in Figure 30-1.
- The days that are displayed in the larger Calendar view are highlighted in the small calendar. In Figure 30-1, these encompass the 21st through the 25th.
- Days on which there is at least one appointment are in bold.
- The arrows to the left and right of the month and year can be clicked to move to the previous or next month, updating the Calendar view as well.
- You can click any day number to change the Calendar view accordingly.

FIGURE 30-1

In Calendar view, the Navigation pane displays the Date Navigator.

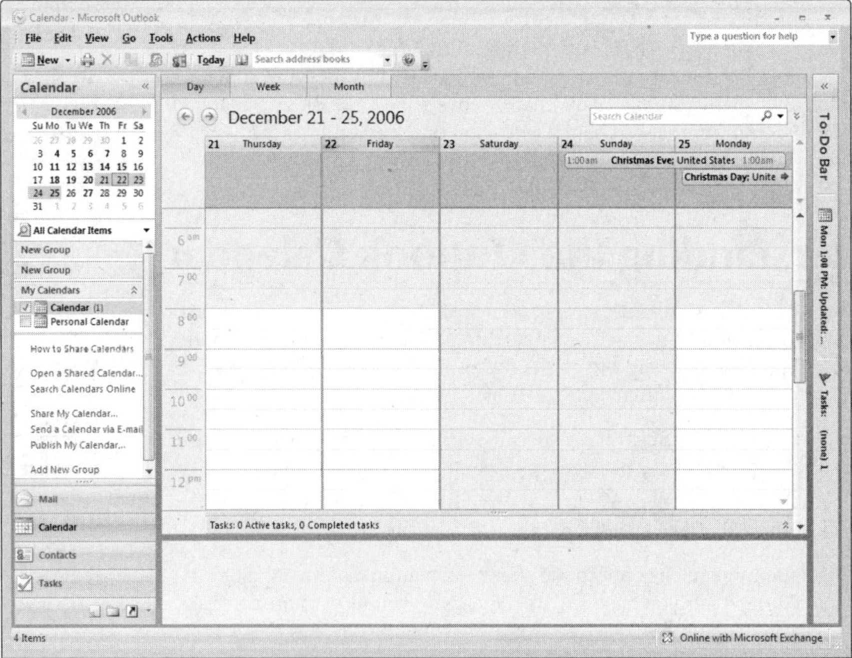

No Date Navigator?

If the Date Navigator is not displayed in the Navigation pane, it is probably because it is displayed in the To-Do bar. The Date Navigator is displayed in one place or the other, not both. You learn about the To-Do bar later in this chapter.

Working with Calendar views

When the Calendar is displayed, you can choose between viewing a single day, a week, or an entire month. In Week view, you can also choose to view the entire week or just the work week (Monday–Friday), and in Month view you can set the level of detail display to low, medium, or high. You select your view using the buttons at the top of the Calendar. In this area, Outlook also displays the date or date range displayed as well as buttons that move the calendar forward or back by one of whatever unit (day, week, or month) is displayed (see Figure 30-2).

FIGURE 30-2

The Outlook Calendar can display a day, a week, or a month at a time.

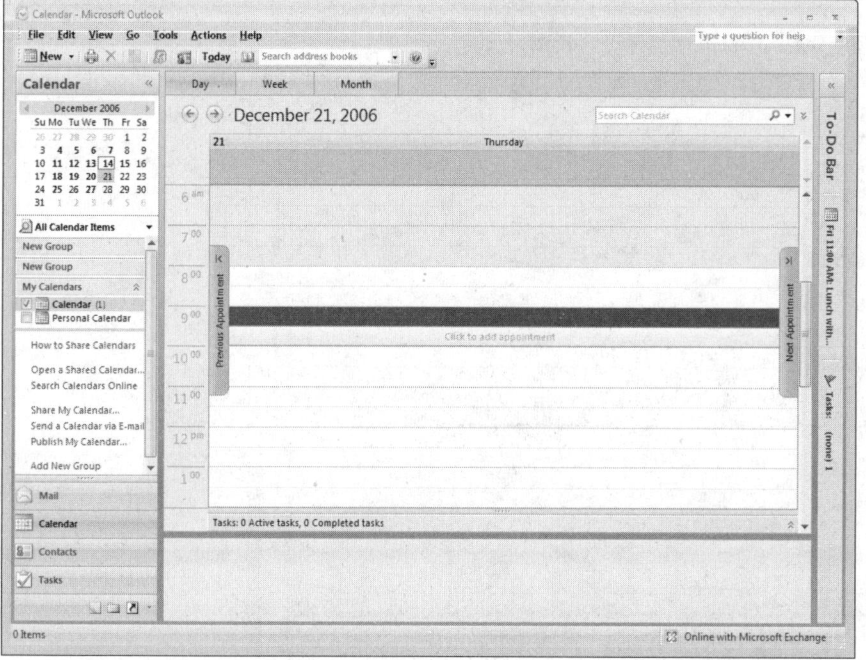

Finding Today

No matter what day, week, or month you are viewing in the Calendar, you can always go directly to the current day by clicking the Today button on the toolbar.

Using the Calendar Day view

When the Calendar is displaying a single day, it looks as shown in Figure 30-3. Times of the day are listed at the left edge of the window, and each appointment is displayed in its assigned time slot. Use the scroll bar to bring different times into view. Any all-day events for the day are displayed at the top of the window.

Click an appointment to select it; it displays with a black border and small handles (boxes) on the top and bottom border. You can:

- Point at the appointment and drag to move it to a different time slot.
- Point at one of the handles and drag it to change either the start or stop time.

If you double-click an appointment, it opens for editing, as explained later in this chapter.

FIGURE 30-3

The Outlook Calendar displaying a single day's appointments.

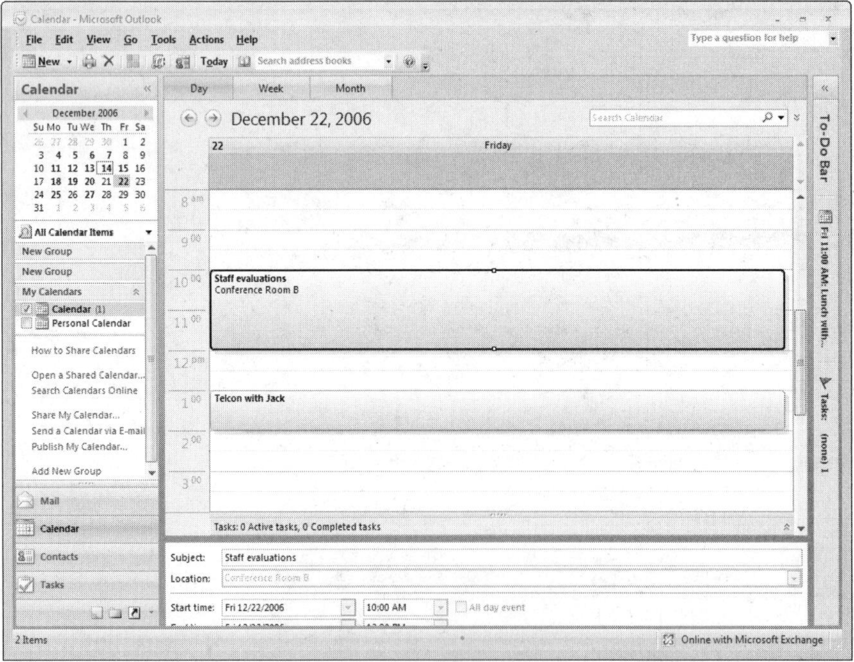

Displaying the Reading Pane

If the Reading pane is not displayed, you can turn it on by selecting Reading Pane from the View menu and then selecting the desired position — bottom or right. You can also toggle the Reading pane display with the Reading Pane button on the toolbar.

Using the Calendar Week view

The Calendar Week view is shown in Figure 30-4. This example shows only the work week; you can display the full seven-day week by selecting the Show Full Week option at the top of the window.

In essence, the Week view consists of five or seven single-day views side-by-side, and you can perform the same actions as described for the Day view. You can also drag an appointment to a different day.

NOTE **When an appointment is selected, its details are displayed at the bottom of the window in the Reading pane (refer to Figure 30-3). This feature can be useful when the Calendar itself is too crowded to show these details for each appointment.**

FIGURE 30-4

The Outlook Calendar displaying an entire week's appointments.

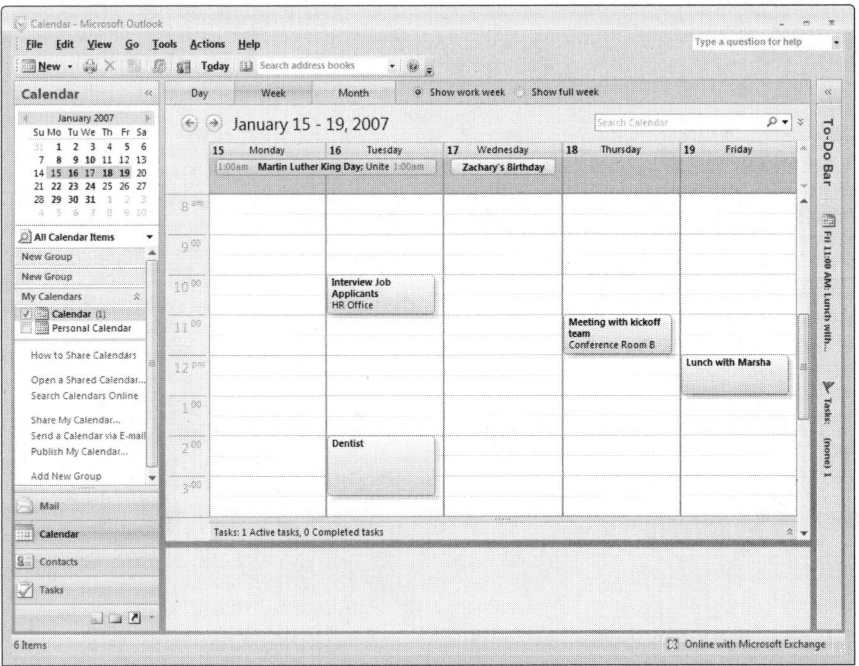

Using the Calendar Month view

The Month view shows an entire month of appointments, as shown in Figure 30-5. Appointments for each day are displayed in order but without time details. If an all-day event exists for the day, it is displayed at the top with a line around it — for example, the "Meeting with Sales Staff" appointment on the 13th and 14th, shown in the Figure 30-5. If a day has more appointments than can be shown, a small down arrow is displayed. Click the arrow to open the single day display where you can view all appointments for that date.

Figure 30-5 shows the month display with the High option selected for details. You can also select Low or Medium details, as follows:

- **Low:** Shows only all-day events. Appointments with specific start and stop times are not displayed.
- **Medium:** All-day events are displayed as usual. Appointments with specific start and stop times are displayed as shaded lines or rectangles with the position and thickness of the line or rectangle indicating the approximate time and duration of the appointment.

FIGURE 30-5

The Outlook Calendar displaying a month's appointments.

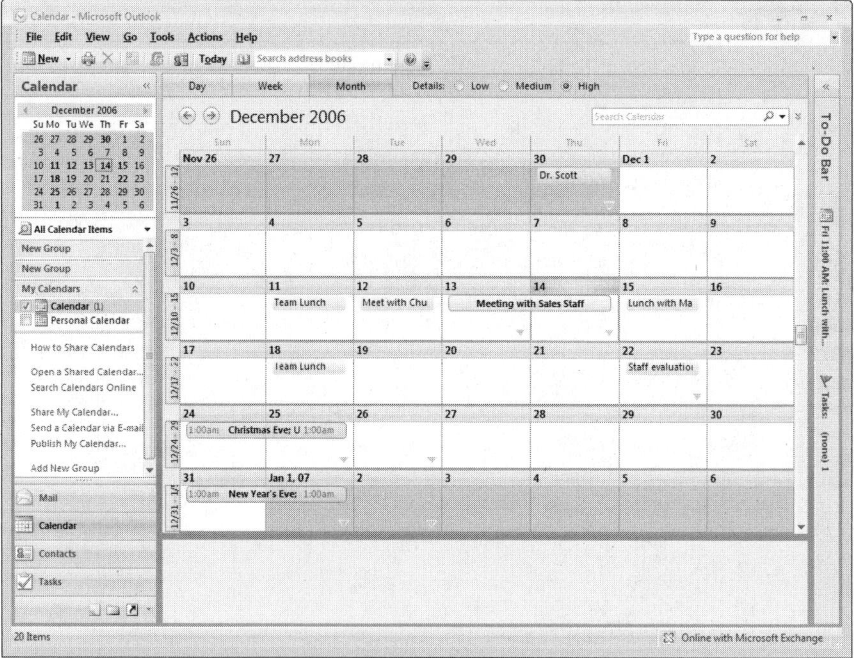

Customizing the Calendar View

If you open the Current View list on the toolbar, you see an item called *Define Views*. This command lets you define a custom view for the Calendar.

Using the To-Do bar with appointments

Outlook's To-Do bar can be useful for working with Calendar items. To display the To-Do bar, choose To-Do Bar from the View menu and then choose Normal. The To-Do Bar is shown in Figure 30-6.

The To-Do bar can display three items:

- The Date Navigator, a small monthly calendar whose features are explained earlier in this chapter. If the Date Navigator is displayed in the To-Do bar, it will not be displayed in the Navigation pane.
- A list of appointments for the current week.
- A list of tasks. Tasks are not directly related to the Calendar and will be explained later in the chapter.

FIGURE 30-6

The To-Do bar can display the Date Navigator and upcoming appointments.

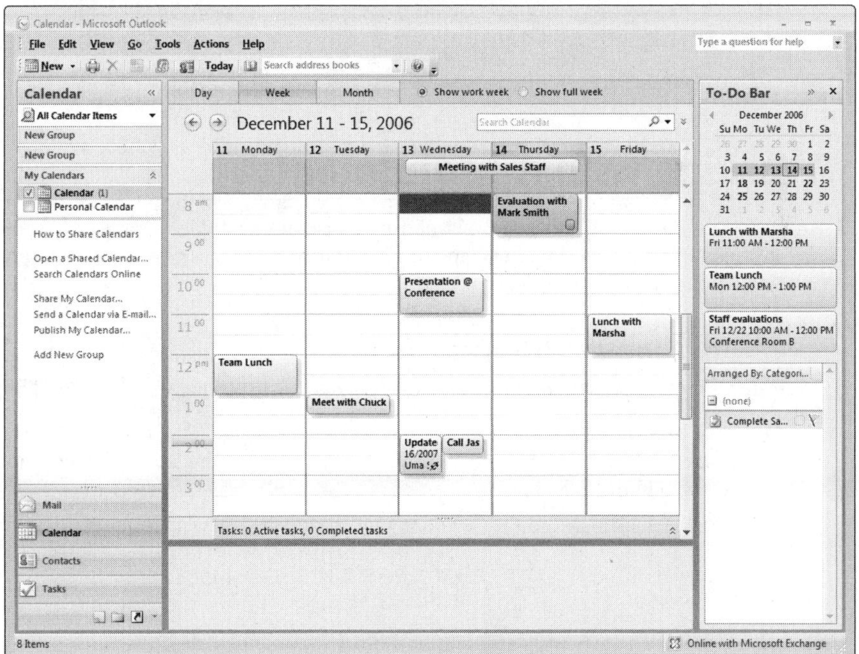

To-Do Bar Appointment Display

You can specify how many appointments are displayed in the To-Do bar; the default is three. However many you choose to display, the To-Do bar always displays the appointments that are coming up the soonest.

You can control what is displayed on the To-Do bar. You can display all, two, or one of the items in the preceding list. To change the To-Do bar display, choose To-Do Bar from the View menu and then select or deselect the individual items — Date Navigator, Appointments, and Task List — on the next menu. You can also select Options from this menu to display the To-Do Bar Options dialog box, shown in Figure 30-7. Here you can turn the display of individual items on or off as well as specify how many months are displayed in the Date Navigator and how many appointments are displayed.

FIGURE 30-7

Setting To-Do bar display options.

To-Do Bar Options

Show Date Navigator

Number of month rows: 1

Show Appointments

Number of appointments: 3

Show Task List

OK Cancel

Working with Appointments

An Outlook appointment can be very simple, or you can use Outlook's tools to add various features and options to an appointment. The following sections start with the basics of creating a simple appointment and then look at the various options.

Creating a simple appointment

To create a simple appointment, make sure that Outlook is displaying the Calendar. Then do either of the following:

- Click the New button on the toolbar. Outlook opens a new appointment form for whatever day is selected in the Calendar.
- Double-click a day on the Calendar. Outlook opens a new appointment form for that day.

The appointment form is shown in Figure 30-8 before any information has been entered. Then, follow these steps:

FIGURE 30-8

An Outlook appointment form.

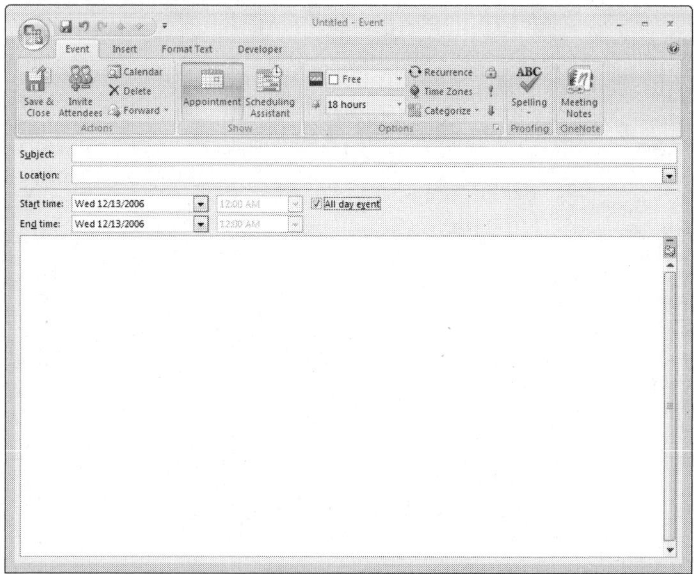

1. **At a minimum, you must enter a subject for the appointment.** The subject is the title of the appointment and is displayed in the Calendar — or at least part of it will be, depending on the length.
2. **Optionally, enter a location for the appointment.** If you click the arrow adjacent to the Location fields, Outlook displays a list of previously used locations from which you can select. Otherwise, just type the location into the field. If space allows, the location displays along with the appointment subject in the Calendar.
3. **If necessary, adjust the start or stop date (or both) by clicking the arrow next to the displayed date and selecting from the calendar that Outlook displays.** An appointment can span two or more days, if needed.
4. **If the appointment is an all-day event, make sure that the All Day Event option is selected.** An all-day event marks one or more entire days as busy, with no specific start and stop times.
5. **If the appointment is not an all-day event, make sure that the All Day Event option is not selected.** Outlook displays fields for the start and stop times.

6. **To select a start or stop time, click the adjacent arrow and select from the list that is displayed (Figure 30-9).**

FIGURE 30-9

Selecting the stop time for an appointment.

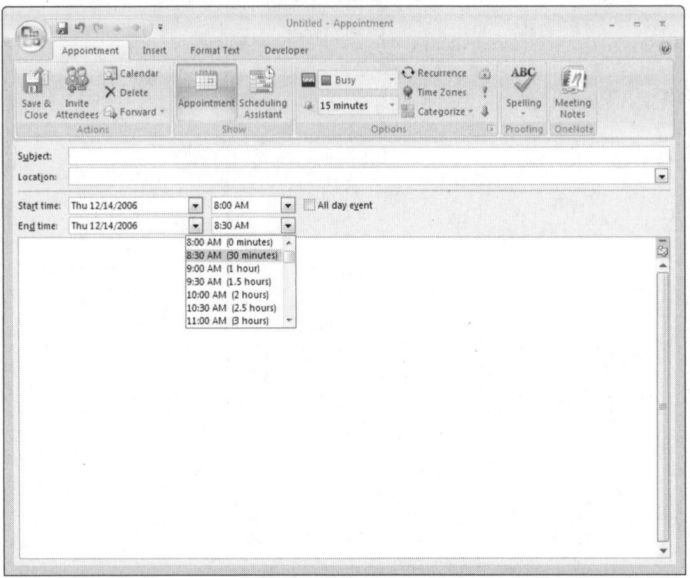

7. **Optionally, enter any desired notes in the field provided.**
8. **Click the Save & Close button on the Event or Appointment tab of the Ribbon.**

NOTE If you've marked an appointment to be an all-day event, the first Ribbon tab in the appointment form window is the Event tab. When you have not marked an appointment as an all-day event, the first tab is the Appointment tab.

WARNING When you create an appointment that is an all-day event, Outlook does not mark the time as "busy" but rather keeps it marked as "free." If you want an all-day event to display on the Scheduling page as either "tentative" or "busy," you must explicitly select this option in the Options section of the Event tab of the Ribbon.

Dealing with Conflicts

Outlook does not specifically warn you of potential conflicts; you are free to schedule overlapping appointments if you want. When an overlap exists, Outlook displays a striped bar between the appointments in Week view and Day view.

Editing and deleting appointments

To edit an appointment, double-click it in Calendar view to open the Appointment form. Make any needed changes and click the Save & Close button on the Event or Appointment tab of the Ribbon.

To delete an appointment, click it in Calendar view to select it; then, press Del.

If you simply want to change the duration of an appointment, you can do so without opening the appointment form. When you select the appointment in the Calendar by clicking it, it displays small, square handles on its border, as shown in Figure 30-10. For a regular appointment, the handles will be at the top and bottom, as shown in the figure. Drag the top or bottom handle to change the appointment's start or stop time, respectively. For an all-day event, the handles are on the left and right edges and can be dragged to change the start or stop time.

You can also change an appointment's time, date, or both without changing its duration; do so by pointing at the appointment and dragging it to the new position on the Calendar.

FIGURE 30-10

Drag a selected appointment's handles to change its duration.

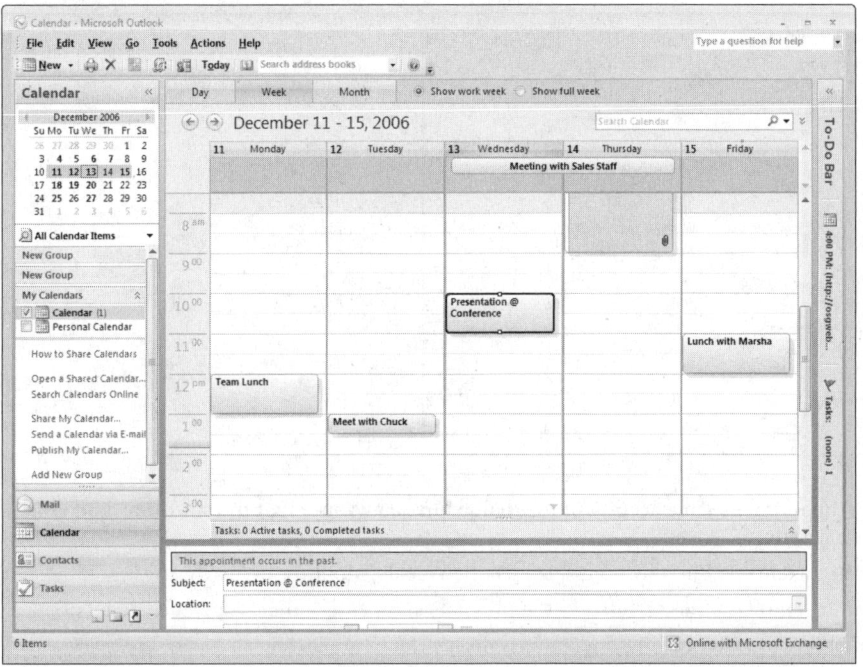

Appointment options

When you create an appointment, there are several optional features you may want to use. They are described in the following sections.

Scheduling recurring events

Some events occur on a regular basis. Perhaps you have a chiropractor appointment at 10:00 a.m. every Monday, or a company strategy meeting on the first Tuesday of each month. You can enter such appointments only once and have Outlook create all the recurrences automatically. Here's how:

1. **Use the techniques described earlier in this chapter to create an appointment for the first instance, but do not save and close it.**
2. **In the Appointment form, click the Recurrence button in the Options group of the Event or Appointment tab of the Ribbon.** Outlook displays the Appointment Recurrence dialog box, as shown in Figure 30-11.

FIGURE 30-11

Defining a recurring appointment.

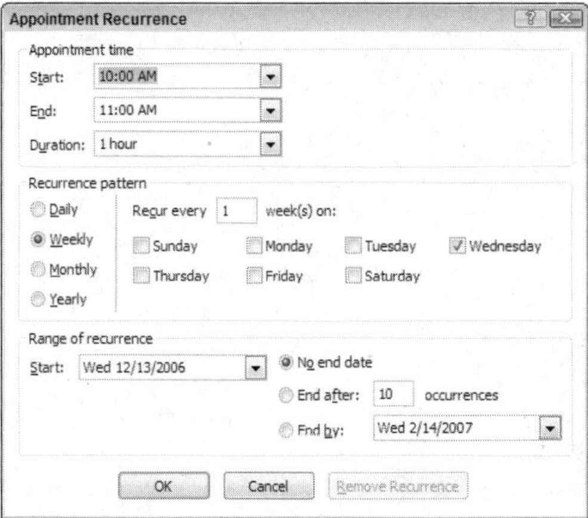

3. **In the Appointment Time section of the dialog box, make sure that the start time and stop time are correct.**
4. **In the Recurrence Pattern section, select Daily, Weekly, Monthly, or Yearly.**
5. **Depending on the option selected in the previous step, enter other recurrence details:**
   - **Daily:** Specify how often the appointment recurs (for example, every two days) or that it occurs every weekday.
   - **Weekly:** Specify how often the appointment recurs (for example, every week) and then on which day or days.
   - **Monthly:** Specify how often the appointment recurs (for example, every three months) and on which day. You can select a day by number, such as the 15th of every month. You can also select a day by day of week, such as the second Tuesday of the month.

6. **Under Range of Recurrence, enter the starting date and then specify when the recurrences end.** Your choices are the following:
   - No end date
   - End after a certain number of occurrences
   - End by a specified date
7. **Click OK to return to the Appointment form.**
8. **Complete any additional appointment details as needed.**
9. **Click Save & Close.**

When you open an existing recurring appointment for editing, you can click the Recurrence button to open the Appointment Recurrence dialog box to modify the recurrence pattern. You can also remove the recurrence by clicking the Remove Recurrent button in this dialog box. Outlook removes all instances of the appointment from the Calendar except the next one.

If you try to delete a recurring appointment, Outlook gives you the option of deleting all occurrences of the appointment or just the current one.

Using appointment reminders

Outlook can remind you of an appointment by displaying a dialog box and playing a sound. You can specify how much advance notice you get and change the sound that is played. You can also turn reminders off. To set a reminder, follow these steps:

1. **Create the appointment, or open an existing one for editing.**
2. **Click the Reminder list in the Options group of the Event or Appointment tab of the Ribbon (Figure 30-12).**
3. **Select the desired duration of the advance warning, from 0 minutes to 2 weeks.** The default is 15 minutes before the start time, although you can change this in Calendar Options (covered later in this chapter). Select None for no reminder.
4. **Select Sound to specify the sound that is played when a reminder is displayed.** Deselect the Play This Sound option if you do not want a sound played (a dialog box is displayed).
5. **Click OK to return to the appointment form.**

When a reminder comes due, Outlook plays the sound (if one was specified for the appointment) and displays the dialog box shown in Figure 30-13. If more than one reminder is due, they will all be listed. The actions you can take are the following:

- Click Dismiss to dismiss the selected reminder.
- If more than one reminder is listed, click Dismiss All to dismiss all listed reminders.
- Click Open Item to open the corresponding appointment.
- Click Snooze to be reminded again in the specified time, selected from the adjacent list. You can, for example, choose to be reminded 5 minutes before the appointment start time, or 10 minutes from the current time.

FIGURE 30-12

Specifying the reminder interval for an appointment.

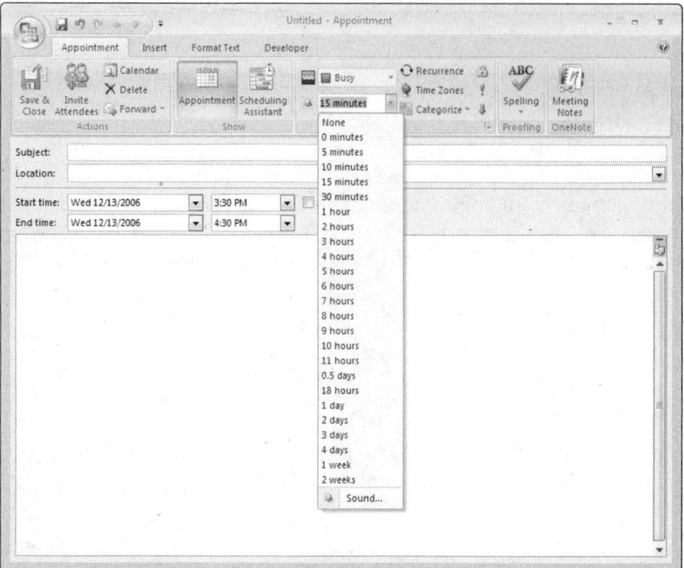

FIGURE 30-13

The Appointment Reminder dialog box.

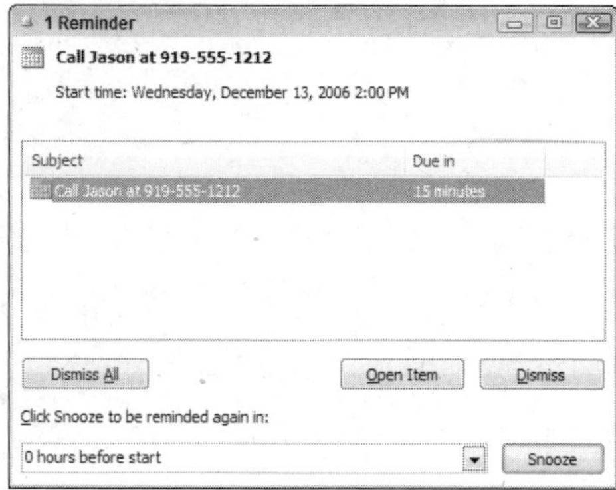

Dismissing a reminder does not affect the appointment itself, which remains in your calendar.

Using other time zones

By default, Outlook appointments use the time zone that your system is set up to use. At times, you may want to use another time zone — for example, if you are in New York and your client says, "Call me at 8:00 a.m. my time." You may not know the number of hours difference, but as long as you know his time zone you are all set.

When you have the Appointment form open, click the Time Zones button in the Options group of the Event or Appointment tab of the Ribbon to display time zone selectors next to the start and stop time fields (Figure 30-14). Change either the start or stop time zone to the desired setting; the other will change to the same thing. Now the start and stop times you enter will be interpreted as being in the selected time zone, and the appointment will be displayed in the correct local time slot. For example, if you are in the Eastern time zone and enter an appointment from 8:00 a.m. to 9:00 a.m. in the Pacific time zone, the appointment will display between 11:00 and 12:00 a.m. on your Calendar because the Pacific zone is three hours behind the Eastern zone.

FIGURE 30-14

Basing an appointment on a different time zone than the one you are in.

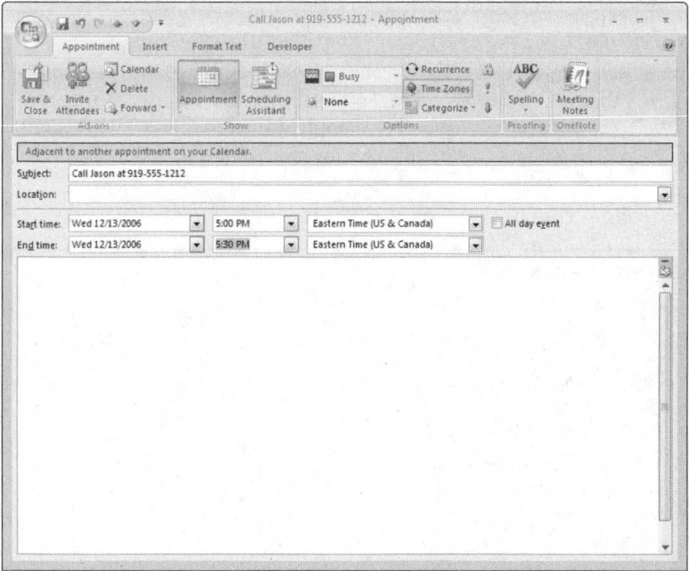

Forwarding an appointment

Outlook lets you forward an appointment to an e-mail recipient. Forwarding is different from inviting an attendee to a meeting (covered elsewhere in the next chapter). You have two ways to forward an Outlook appointment:

- Open the appointment and click the Forward button in the Actions group of the Event or Appointment tab of the Ribbon.
- Right-click the appointment in the Calendar and select Forward from the shortcut menu.

In either case, Outlook creates a new e-mail message with the appointment attached as an Outlook item and the title of the appointment inserted in the Subject field. You then address and complete the e-mail message as usual. If you are using Outlook with an Exchange Server account, the appointment itself is forwarded without being attached to an e-mail message.

When the recipients receive a forwarded appointment, they can double-click the attachment to open it. It opens in an appointment window, and users can save it to their calendar or discard it as desired. Of course, recipients must be using Outlook or another program that supports the Outlook appointment format.

Another forwarding option for appointments is the iCalendar format. This is a widely supported format for calendar information and is supported by Outlook as well as many other scheduling programs. If you are not sure that all your recipients are using Outlook, using this format may be a good idea when forwarding an appointment. To do so, follow these steps:

1. **In an open appointment, click the arrow next to the Forward button in the Actions group of the Event or Appointment tab.**
2. **Choose Forward as iCalendar from the menu. Outlook creates a new e-mail message with the iCalendar attached.**
3. **Complete and send the message as usual.**

Assigning appointments to categories

As with most Outlook items, an appointment can be assigned to a category. Outlook comes with six predefined and color-coded categories. Initially they are named according to their color, but you can change this to more meaningful names such as "Work" and "Personal," as in the example shown in Figure 30-15. The first time you apply a category color, you are prompted to enter a name for the category.

FIGURE 30-15

The color-coded categories appear in the Appointment window.

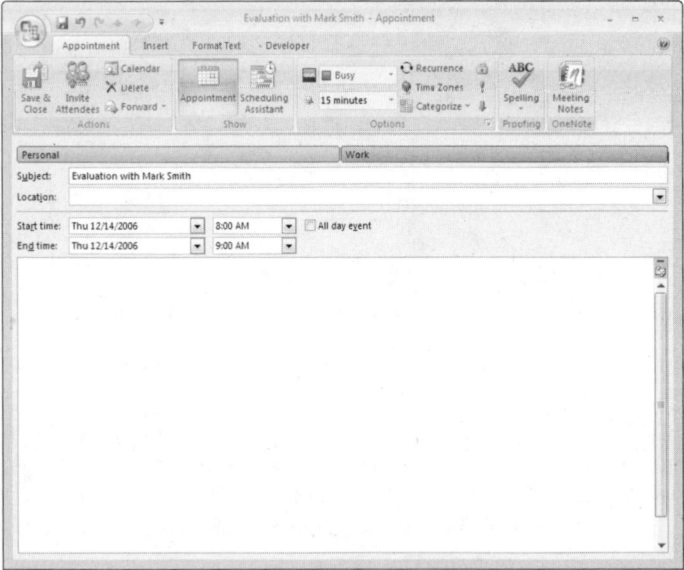

You have two ways to assign an appointment to a category:

- With the appointment open, click the Categorize button in the Options group of the Event or Appointment tab of the Ribbon and select the desired category from the list that is displayed. Select Clear All Categories to remove any assigned categories from the appointment.
- In the Calendar, right-click the appointment and select Categorize from the shortcut menu. Then, select the desired category.

An appointment, as is true of other Outlook items, can be assigned to more than one category. In the Calendar, a categorized appointment is displayed in the color of the assigned category.

Setting appointment importance

By default, all appointments that you create are assigned normal importance. You can assign either low or high importance to an open appointment by clicking the corresponding button in the Options group of the Event or Appointment tab of the Ribbon. Then you can use this importance level as a criterion when using the Search feature in your Calendar, as discussed elsewhere in this chapter.

Marking an appointment as private

Outlook gives you the ability to publish your calendar so that other people can view your schedule. This topic is covered elsewhere in this chapter. You may at times want to mark an appointment as private so that other people viewing your calendar cannot see the details. They can still see that you are busy during the period of the appointment but will not have access to details about the appointment.

To mark an open appointment as private, click the Private (padlock) button in the Options group of the Event or Appointment tab of the Ribbon.

Determining how an appointment displays on the Scheduling page

Outlook's Scheduling page provides a view of your schedule and the schedules of other people whose calendars you have imported. It is a very useful tool for finding time that is free for all the people you want to attend a meeting.

An appointment in your calendar can display in one of several ways on the Scheduling page: Busy, Tentative, Out of Office, or Free. This display affects your own Scheduling page as well as that of other people with whom you are sharing your calendar. When you create an appointment, you can specify how it will display. (The default is Busy except for all-day events, as mentioned earlier in this chapter.) To do so, click the Show As list on the Options group of the Event or Appointment tab on the Ribbon and select from the list (Figure 30-16).

Why Display an Appointment as "Free"?

It may seem strange that Outlook gives you the option of displaying an appointment as Free on the Scheduling page. It makes sense, however, when you realize that some appointments are not critical and can easily be changed. For example, you can just as well get that haircut tomorrow as today. By displaying such appointments as free, you do not prevent other people from scheduling a meeting at that time when they view your schedule.

FIGURE 30-16

Specifying how an appointment displays on the Scheduling page.

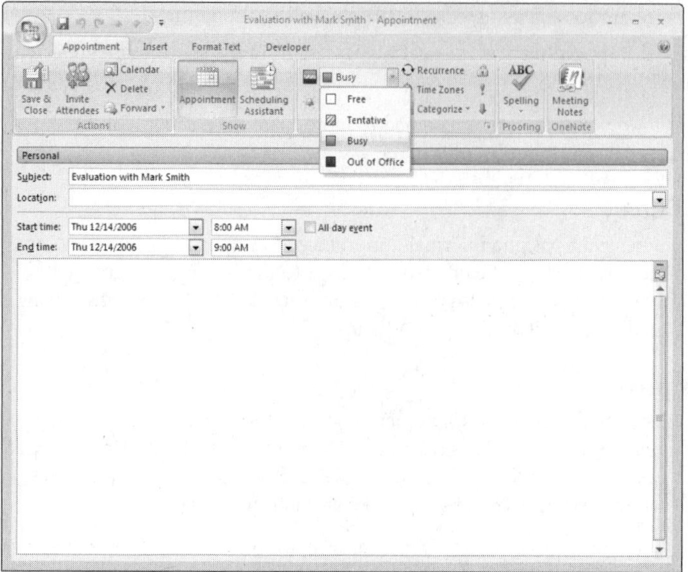

Searching the Calendar

As your Calendar becomes filled with appointments past and future, it will become difficult if not impossible to find information by simply scrolling through the Calendar. You can use the Search feature to filter the Calendar to show just the information you want. For example, you can filter to show only appointments within a certain month assigned to a specific category.

For a basic search, enter your search term in the Search Calendar box at the top right of the Calendar display (Figure 30-17). You can also click the down arrow to select from previously used search terms. Outlook automatically searches as you enter the term and displays only matching appointments (or a message, if it finds no matching entries). Click the X that is adjacent to the Search box to cancel the search and return to displaying all Calendar items.

FIGURE 30-17

Performing a basic search of the Calendar.

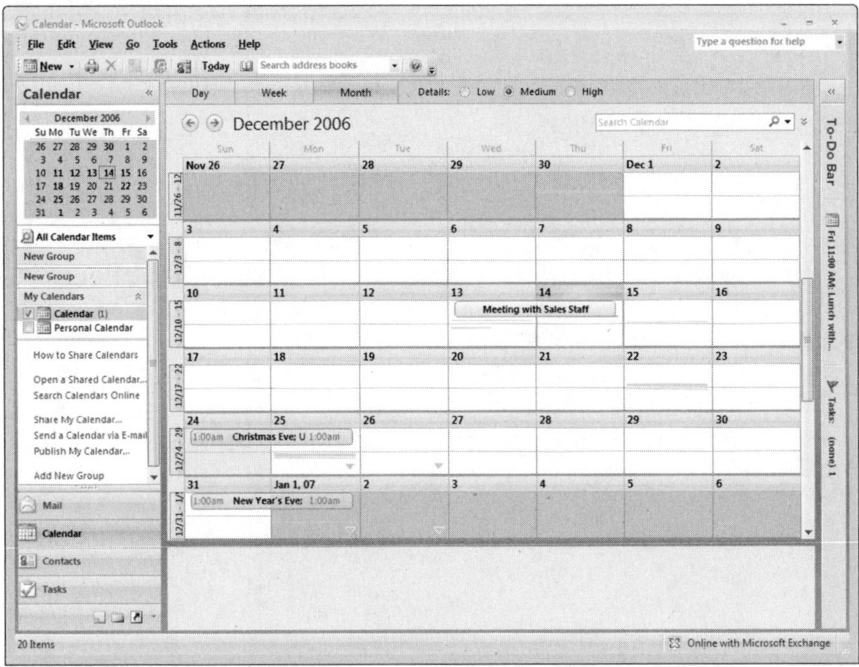

If you need more control over the search, click the double down arrow at the top-right corner of the Calendar display. Outlook displays addition criterion fields, as shown in Figure 30-18. Each field lets you enter a search term or select from a drop-down list. As you make entries, the Calendar display is automatically filtered to show only matching entries. You can also take the following actions:

- To change a displayed criterion field — for example, from Categories to Sensitivity — click the arrow adjacent to the field name and select from the list that is displayed.
- To remove a criterion field, click the arrow adjacent to the field name and select Remove.
- To add a new criterion field, click Add Criteria and select from the list.
- To cancel the search and display all Calendar entries, click the X to the right of the Search Calendar box.
- To hide the additional criterion fields, click the double up arrow at the top-right corner of the Calendar display.

FIGURE 30-18

Fields for performing an advanced search of the Calendar.

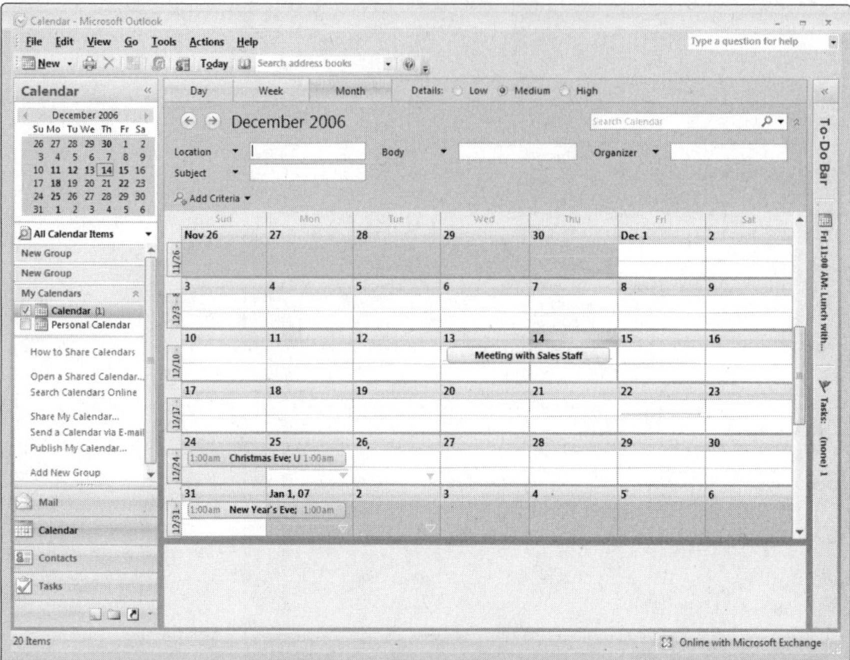

Setting Calendar Options

The Outlook Calendar comes with default settings for many aspects of its operation. As you become familiar with the Calendar, you may want to make changes to these settings to customize the Calendar for the way you work. You access Calendar options by choosing Options from the Tools menu and then, in the Options dialog box, clicking the Preferences tab. The Calendar section of this tab is shown in Figure 30-19.

The one option that is shown here relates to reminders for appointments. By default, Outlook reminds you of appointments 15 minutes before the start time (you can change this for individual appointments, of course). To change the default lead time, select it from the drop-down list. You can select any time from 0 minutes to two weeks. If you do not want a default reminder for messages, deselect the Default Reminder option.

FIGURE 30-19

The Calendar section of the Preferences tab in the Options dialog box.

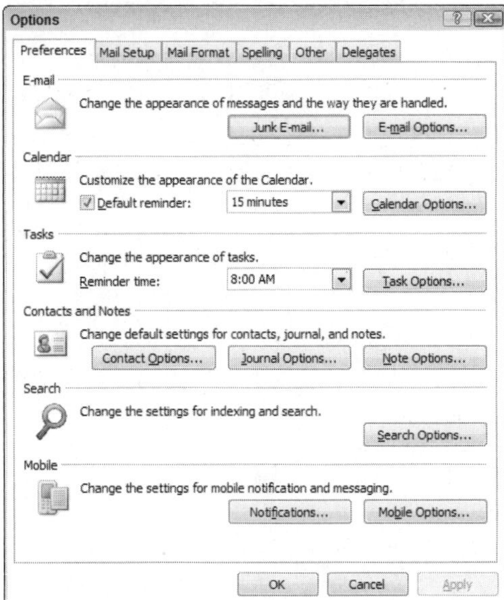

Other Calendar options are accessed by clicking the Calendar Options button to display the Calendar Options dialog box, shown in Figure 30-20. The various options available here are divided into several sections. The first section has to do with how Outlook defines the work week, as follows:

- **Calendar work week:** Select days that you want to be considered part of the work week, and deselect those that you do not.
- **First day of week:** Select the day that Outlook uses as the first day of the week for Calendar displays.
- **Start time/end time:** Select the times of day that Outlook uses for the start and stop of the work day.
- **First week of year:** Select how Outlook determines the first week of the year. The options are Starts on Jan 1 (the week that contains Jan 1), the first week with four days in the new year, and the first week that is entirely in the new year.

The next section of the Calendar Options dialog box includes options for a variety of features:

- **Show "Click to Add" Prompts on the Calendar:** Outlook displays prompts on the calendar where you can click to add an appointment.
- **Show Week Numbers:** Outlook displays week numbers (the week of the year) where indicated. An example is shown in Figure 30-21.

FIGURE 30-20

The Calendar Options dialog box.

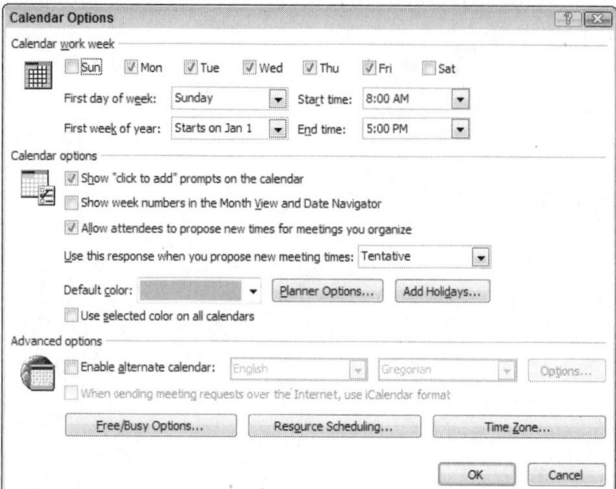

FIGURE 30-21

Outlook can display week numbers in the Date Navigator, shown here, and also in the Month view.

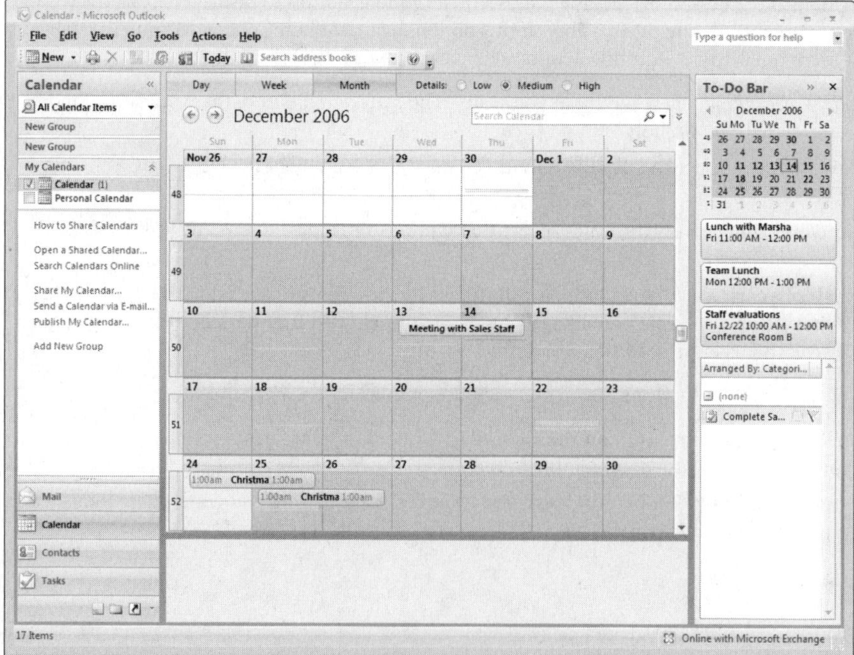

- **Allow Attendees to Propose:** People whom you invite to meetings are allowed to respond by proposing a new time for the meeting.
- **Use This Response:** Select from the list to specify whether new meeting times that you propose are marked as Tentative, Accept, or Decline.
- **Default Color:** Select the color to use for the calendar display.
- **Use Selected Color:** The color you choose is used for all calendars you view, not just your own calendar.
- **Planner Options:** Click this button to display the Planner Options dialog box, in which you can set options for the Meeting Planner and Group Schedule features.
- **Add Holidays:** Lets you copy holidays for one or more specific countries onto your calendar. You select the country or countries from a list.

Finally, this dialog box has a few advanced options, as follows:

- **Enable Alternate Calendar:** Lets you display an alternate calendar in parallel with the default one using the language and calendar structure you select.
- **When Sending Meeting Requests:** Sends meeting requests in the more widely supported iCalendar format instead of Outlook's proprietary format.
- **Free/Busy Options:** Sets options for publishing your calendar. These options are covered earlier in the chapter.
- **Resource Scheduling:** Sets options for working with meeting requests. These options are covered earlier in the chapter.
- **Time Zone:** Sets the default time zone for your calendar and also permits you to display a second, alternate time zone in the Calendar.

Understanding Tasks

A *task* is similar to an appointment in that it is something you must attend to. It is different in that it does not have a specific date or time associated with it, although it may well have a due date by which it is supposed to be completed. In this sense, Outlook tasks are pretty much like a paper to-do list that you stick on the fridge. When you look a little deeper, however, you'll find that they can do so much more:

- You can be reminded of a task at a specified time and date.
- You can specify different priorities for different tasks.
- You can assign a task to someone else and send that person a message with the required information.
- You can assign a status to a task (not started, in progress, and so on) as well as a percent completed value.
- You can send a status report on a task to other people.

I find that Outlook's Task feature is something I use all the time.

Using the Task View

To switch to Task view in Outlook, click the Tasks button in the Navigation pane or choose Tasks from the Go menu. The default Tasks view, shown in Figure 30-22, displays active tasks — those not yet completed. They are arranged by due date initially, although you can change the sort order by clicking the column headings (To-Do Title, Status, and so on) at the top of the list.

Strictly speaking, the display shown in Figure 30-22 is the *To-Do list* — that is, uncompleted tasks. If you want to display all tasks, including completed ones, click the Tasks item under My Tasks in the Navigation pane (Figure 30-23). This view shows all tasks, with completed ones displayed and crossed out.

FIGURE 30-22

The default Tasks view displays a list of all your active tasks.

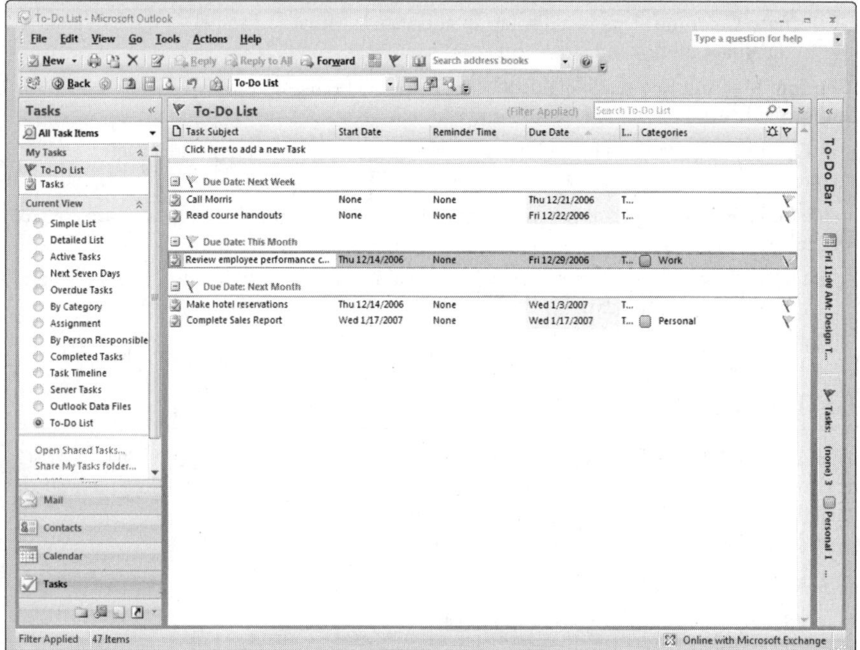

No Due Date?

Although most tasks have a due date, it is not required. Tasks that do not have a due date are displayed in their own section, No Due Date, when tasks are organized by due date.

FIGURE 30-23

You can also display all tasks, including completed ones.

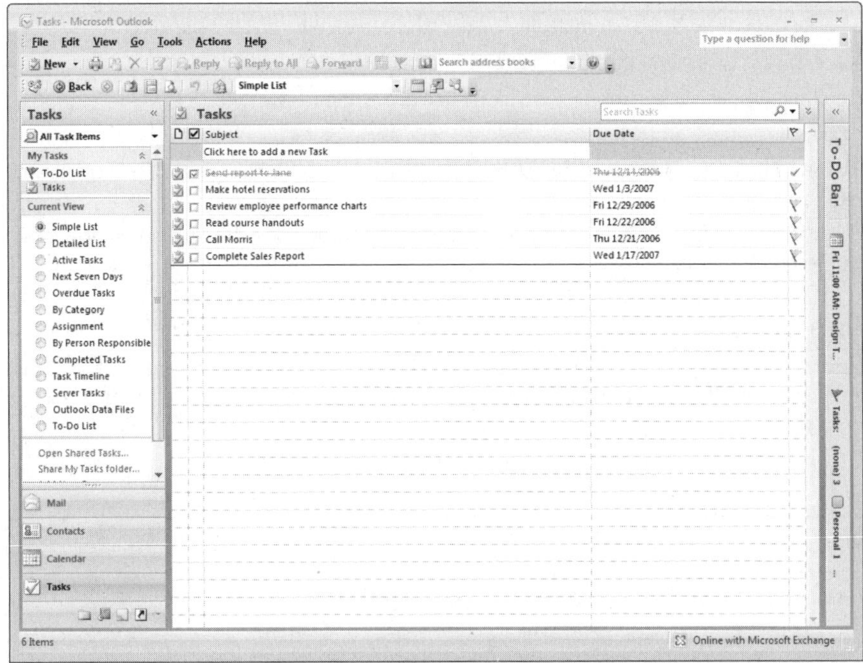

While you are viewing tasks, you can open a single task by double-clicking it. You can also perform certain actions with the task by right-clicking it and selecting from the context menu. These actions are the following:

- Mark a task as complete
- Assign the task to someone
- Add a follow-up to the task
- Assign a category to the task

You learn more about these actions later in the chapter when I show you how to create a new task.

Outlook provides you with several other ways to view your tasks. You can switch to a different view by selecting the desired view in the Navigation pane. The views are as follows:

- **Simple List:** A list of all tasks including completed ones (same as clicking Tasks, as described earlier).
- **Detailed List:** Similar to Simple List but with more details about each task.
- **Active Tasks:** Tasks not marked as completed.
- **Next Seven Days:** Tasks due within the next seven days.

- **Overdue Tasks:** Tasks whose due date has passed but are not marked as completed.
- **By Category:** All tasks organized by assigned category.
- **Assignment:** Tasks organized by the person they are assigned to.
- **By Person Responsible:** Tasks organized by owner (the person who created the task).
- **Completed Tasks:** Tasks that have been marked as completed.
- **Task Timeline:** Displays tasks arranged on a timeline according to due date.
- **Server Tasks:** Lists tasks and whom each task has been assigned to.
- **Outlook Data Files:** Displays tasks organized by the Outlook data file they are in. This is relevant only if you have more than one Personal Folders File.
- **To-Do List:** Displays active tasks in a simplified, easy-to-use format. See the upcoming "To-Do List view" section for more details.

Task Timeline view

Task Timeline view arranges tasks on a timeline according to their due date, as shown in Figure 30-24. This visual representation can be useful for finding time periods when many tasks are due, or for locating relatively free periods on your schedule.

FIGURE 30-24

Tasks displayed on a timeline.

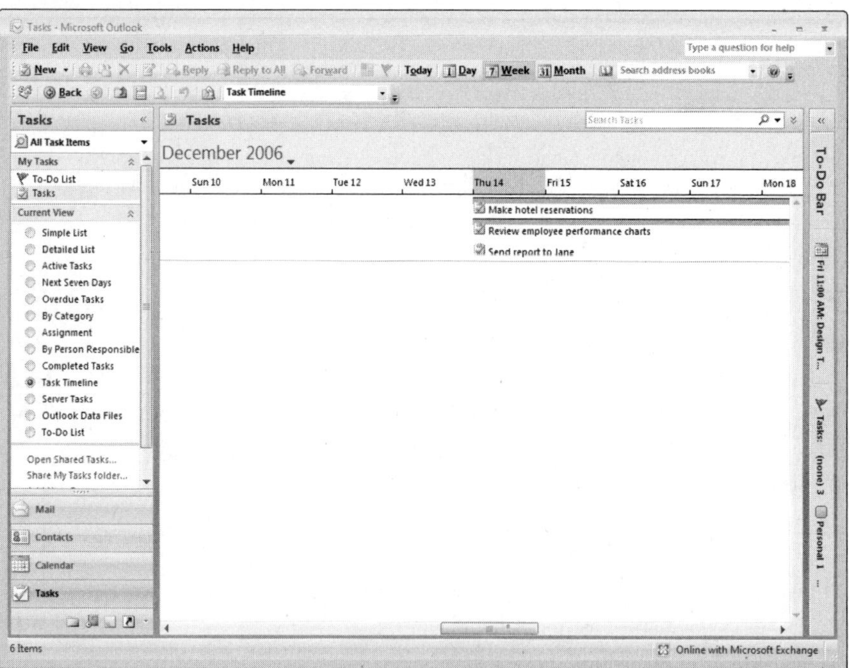

What about Start Dates?

A task can have a start date assigned to it as well as a due date. A start date can be useful when you have a reason that you cannot start a task before that date. When displayed in Timeline view, a task with a start date is displayed at the start date with a line extending to the due date.

In Figure 30-24, the Task Timeline view is displaying a week, with the days listed across the top of the display. You can switch between Day, Week, and Month views by clicking the corresponding button on the toolbar. You can also quickly scroll to today by clicking the Today button. To scroll forward and backward in time, use the horizontal scrollbar at the bottom of the window.

To-Do List view

The To-Do List view displays a simplified list of active tasks. It is not the same thing as the To-Do bar, which is explained later in the chapter. The To-Do list is shown in Figure 30-25. In the figure, the tasks are arranged by due date, as indicated by the heading at the top of the list. Click this heading to arrange the tasks by other fields, such as Category or Importance.

FIGURE 30-25

Viewing the To-Do list.

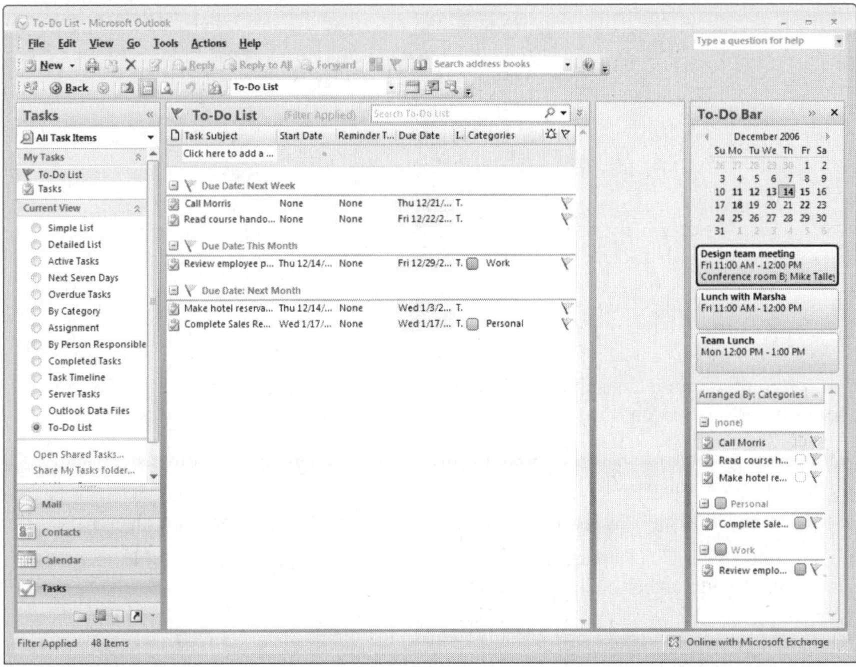

At the top of the To-Do list is a box labeled Type a New Task. You can click here and type a new task title. When you press Enter, the task is automatically created with a due date of today and default settings for other task data such as importance. Double-click the newly created task to change the due date or any other aspects of the task.

Creating a New Task

To create a new task, click the New button when you are in Task view, or select Task from the New menu when in any other view. (You can also press Ctrl+Shift+K.) Outlook creates a new task and displays it as shown in Figure 30-26.

FIGURE 30-26

Creating a new task.

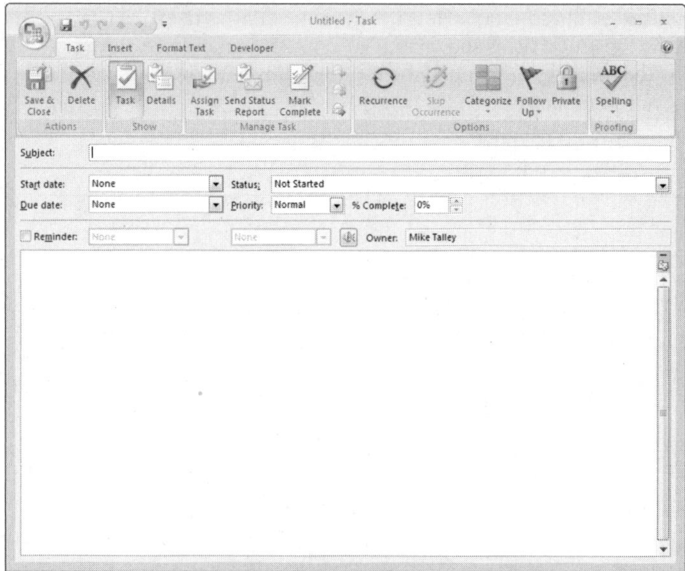

The only required entry on this form is the subject, which will be the title of the task that is displayed in Task view. The other task information on this form is explained here and in the following sections:

- **Start Date:** If you want to specify a start date for the task, click the adjacent down arrow and select the date from the calendar.
- **Due Date:** Click the adjacent down arrow and select the task's due date from the calendar.
- **Status:** By default, this is Not Started. If necessary, you can open this list and select In Progress, Completed, Waiting on Someone Else, or Deferred.
- **Priority:** The default is Normal; you can also select Low or High.

- **% Complete:** If the task is already partially complete, use the up and down arrows to specify the correct value in this field.
- **Categorize:** Click this button to assign the task to an Outlook category.
- **Follow-up:** Click this button to assign a follow-up to the task.
- **Private:** Click this button to make the task private so that it will not be viewable by other people when you share your calendar.
- **Reminder:** Select this option if you want to be reminded of the task; then, use the adjacent fields to specify the date and time of the reminder. Click the speaker icon to change the sound that will be played at the reminder time.
- **Contacts:** Click this button to associate the task with one or more of your contacts.
- **Save & Close:** Click this button on the Task tab of the Ribbon when you are finished defining the task.

Other aspects of creating a new task are explained in the following sections.

Entering task details

If you click the Details button in the Show group of the Task tab of the Ribbon, Outlook displays the Details window for the task. This window is shown in Figure 30-27.

FIGURE 30-27

Entering details for a new task.

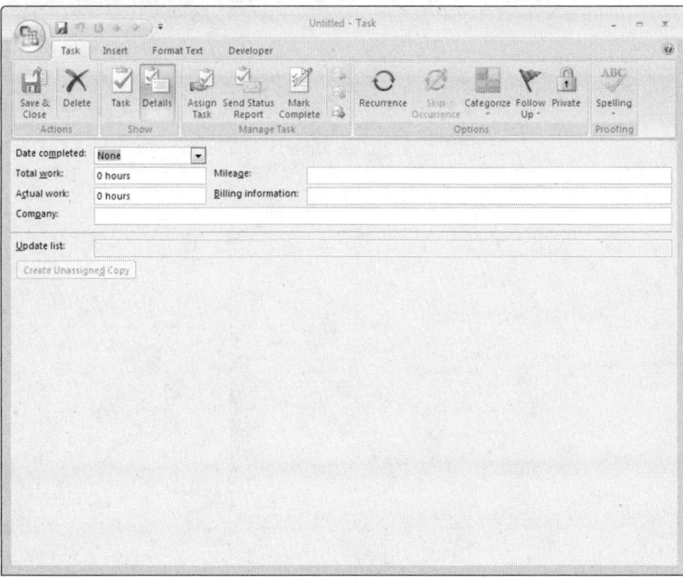

The fields available in the Details window let you keep track of additional information related to a task. You can specify the completion date, enter information about the time spent on the task, identify a company associated with the task, track mileage, and enter billing information. Outlook does not track this information for you but just provides these detail fields for you to enter it in.

The lower section of the Details window is relevant only if the task has been assigned to someone; this window is explained in the next section.

When you have finished entering details for the task, click the Task button in the Show group of the Task tab on the Ribbon to return to the regular Task window. You can also click Save & Close if you have finished defining the task.

Assigning a task

Outlook lets you assign a task to someone else. Doing so can be useful in a variety of situations, such as when you are heading a committee and need to delegate various jobs to the committee members. By using Outlook's Assign Task command, you can track progress and be notified when each task has been completed.

To assign a task, create the task as described earlier in this chapter. You can also open an existing task and, as long as you are the owner of the task, assign it to someone else. Here's how:

1. **Click the Assign Task button in the Manage Task group of the Task tab of the Ribbon.** Outlook displays the form shown in Figure 30-28. This is actually just the regular task form with a few extra elements.

FIGURE 30-28

Assigning a task to someone.

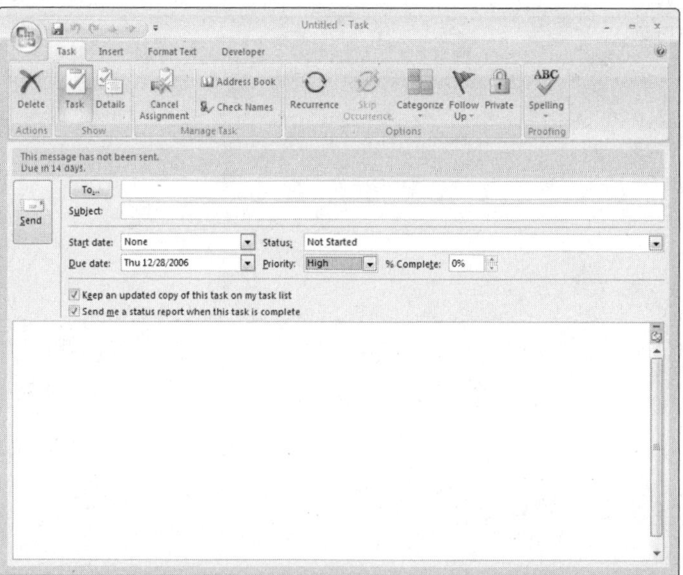

2. **In the To field, enter the e-mail address of the person you are assigning the task.** You can also click the To button and select from your contacts.
3. **Enter additional information about the task, such as subject and due date, if it has not already been entered.**
4. **Select or deselect the two available options (explained next).**
5. **Click the Send button.**

Two options are available when you assign a task to someone, as follows:

- **Keep an Updated Copy of This Task on My Task List:** You receive automatic updates when the person whom you assign the task to updates its status.
- **Send Me a Status Report When This Task Is Complete:** You receive an automatic notification when the person whom you assign the task to marks it as completed.

When you send a task assignment, the recipient receives an e-mail message containing information about the assignment and permitting the recipient to either accept or decline the assignment. You learn more about this and other aspects of task assignments later in this chapter, in the section "Working with Assigned Tasks."

Specifying task recurrence

As do appointments, tasks can have a defined recurrence. For example, you may have to review each month's sales figures by the end of the next month. Rather than enter a new task each month, you can define a task that recurs each month.

To define a recurring task, create the task as usual, and before saving and closing it, click the Recurrence button in the Options group of the Task tab of the Ribbon. Outlook opens the Task Recurrence dialog box, as shown in Figure 30-29.

FIGURE 30-29

Defining a recurring task.

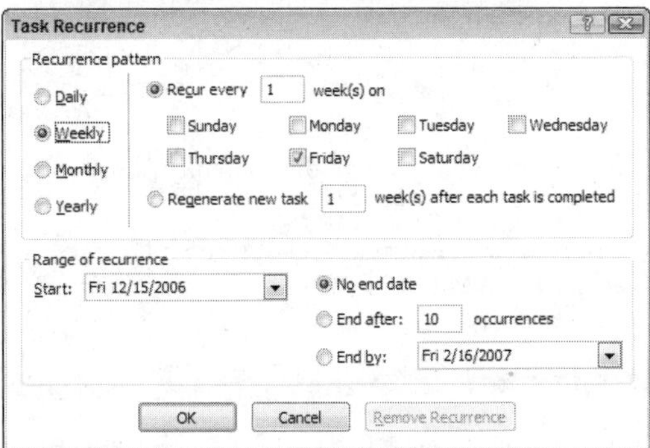

Assigning Recurring Tasks

When you assign a recurring task, a copy of the task remains in your Task list but cannot be updated automatically. However, if you requested a status report when the task is complete, you receive a status report for each occurrence of the task that is completed.

The four basic patterns of recurrence are Daily, Weekly, Monthly, and Yearly. When you choose the basic pattern in the top left of the dialog box, the remainder of the options change to reflect what's available:

- **Daily:** You can choose every so many days or every weekday.
- **Weekly:** You specify how often (every week, every two weeks, and so on) and the day or days of the week.
- **Monthly:** You specify which day of the month, either as a number (the 25th of each month, for example) or a day of the week (the first Thursday, for example).
- **Yearly:** You specify a specific date (June 12, for example) or a day of a month (the first Monday in June, for example).

In all cases, you also specify a start date and when the recurring task ends.

Working with Assigned Tasks

Working with assigned tasks, whether you are the person doing the assigning or the person accepting the assignment, can be a bit confusing. After you understand it, however, I think you'll find the tool very useful.

Receiving a task assignment

When someone sends you a task assignment, you receive an e-mail message that looks as shown in Figure 30-30. There are three buttons of importance on the Task tab of the Ribbon in the message window:

- **Accept:** Accepts the assignment, adds it to your Task list, and notifies the person who sent you the assignment that you have accepted.
- **Decline:** Declines the assignment and notifies the person who sent you the assignment that you have declined.
- **Assign Task:** Lets you assign the task to a third person, who will receive the same notification and can accept, decline, or assign the task to yet another person. The person who originally assigned the task to you will be notified of the reassignment.

Receiving accept/decline notifications

When you send a task assignment to someone, one of three things will happen (assuming that the assignment is not simply ignored!):

- First, the person may accept the task. You receive a message to that effect, and the task is automatically updated to reflect that the task was accepted and is now owned by that person.

About Task Ownership

A task has, at any given moment, one and only one owner. Owning a task means that you can assign it to someone else. Here's how ownership works:

- When you create a task, you are the original owner.
- When you assign the task to someone, that person becomes the temporary owner.
- The person who receives the assignment can do one of three things: (1) accept the task and become the owner; (2) decline the task and return ownership to you; or (3) assign the task to a third person, who then becomes the temporary owner.

If you assign a task to someone and that person declines, ownership passes back to you only when you reclaim ownership by returning the task to your task list. It does not happen automatically.

- Second, the person may decline the task. You receive an e-mail notification. When you open this e-mail, you can take one of the following two actions by clicking the corresponding button on the toolbar:
  - **Return the Task to Your Task List:** You regain ownership of the task.
  - **Assign Task:** Assign the task to someone else.
- Finally, the person you assigned the task to may assign it to someone else. That person can accept, decline, or reassign the task.

FIGURE 30-30

Receiving a task assignment from someone else.

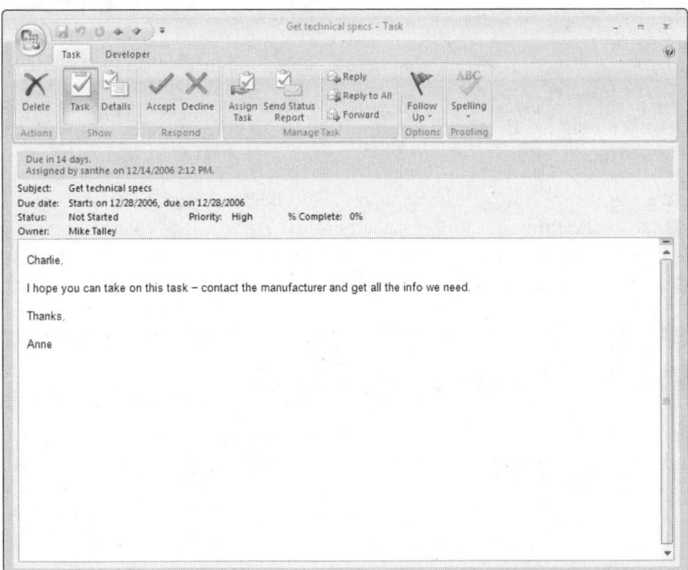

Assigning a Task to Multiple People

Although Outlook does not prevent you from assigning a task to two or more people, you cannot keep an updated copy of the task in your task list. For this reason, it is better to divide a multi-person task into parts and assign each part, as a separate task, to an individual person.

Task status reports

When you have accepted a task assignment, you own that task, and no one but you can change the task even though it may be on someone else's task list. You can then, as you work on the task, open it and update the status and percentage completed of the task; you can also mark it as completed. When you do so and save the modified task, an update is sent to the person who assigned you the task (assuming that the Keep an Updated Copy of This Task on My Task List option was selected when you were sent the assignment). By default, this update does not appear in the task assigner's Inbox but is processed automatically, and the updated information is available the next time the task assigner views the task.

Likewise, if the Send Me a Status Report When This Task Is Complete option was selected when you were sent the assignment, the person who assigned the task receives an automatic update when you mark the task as complete. Although Task Complete updates are processed automatically, they appear in the person's Inbox.

A task can have more than one prior owner. Suppose, for example, that person A created the task and sent a task request to person B. Then, person B sent a task request to person C, who accepted the task. C is the owner of the task and both A and B are prior owners and will receive status updates.

Sending a status report manually

Sometimes you may want to manually send a status report or comments about a task. Here are two situations in which doing so might be desirable:

- The original task request (when you were assigned the task) did not include a request for automatic status updates.
- You were not assigned the task; it is simply a task that you created but want to keep other people updated about.

To manually send a status report, open the task and click the Send Status Report button in the Manage Task group of the Task tab of the Ribbon. Outlook creates an e-mail message with information about the task status in the body of the message. You can add text as needed. If the task was assigned to you, the To field already contains the addresses of the task's prior owners. You can add additional recipients if desired.

Other Ways of Viewing Tasks

The most flexible way to view your tasks is by using Task view, as explained earlier in this chapter. You can also have Outlook display tasks on the To-Do bar and in Calendar view.

Viewing tasks on the To-Do bar

You can display active tasks on the To-Do bar along with the Date Navigator and upcoming appointments. They are displayed at the bottom, as shown in Figure 30-31.

If you do not see your tasks on the To-Do bar, you may need to change the To-Do bar display by right-clicking it and then selecting Task List from the shortcut menu.

Viewing tasks on the Calendar

The Outlook Calendar can display the daily Task list along with your appointments. The daily Task list is displayed below the appointment section of the calendar, as shown in Figure 30-32. You have three options as to how the daily Task list is displayed:

- **Normal,** as shown in the figure, with task subjects, categories, and follow-up flags
- **Minimized,** which displays the number of active tasks for the displayed time period without any details
- **Off,** which does not display the list

To switch between daily Task list views, display the Outlook Calendar and then choose Daily Task List from the View menu. Then, select the desired view from the next menu. This menu also lets you specify whether to display tasks by due date (the default) or start date, and whether to show completed tasks.

FIGURE 30-31

Viewing the daily Task list on the To-Do bar.

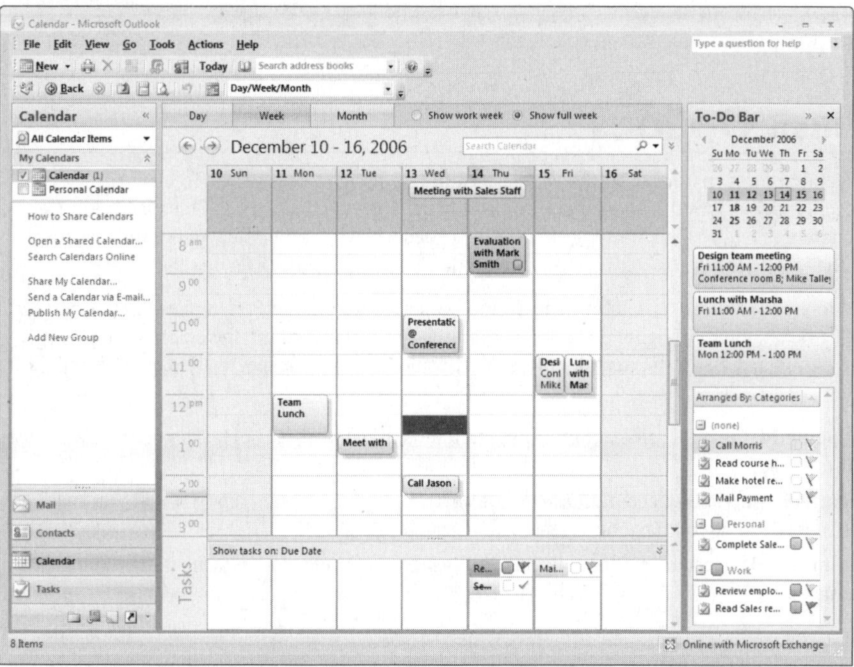

FIGURE 30-32

Viewing the daily task list on the Outlook Calendar.

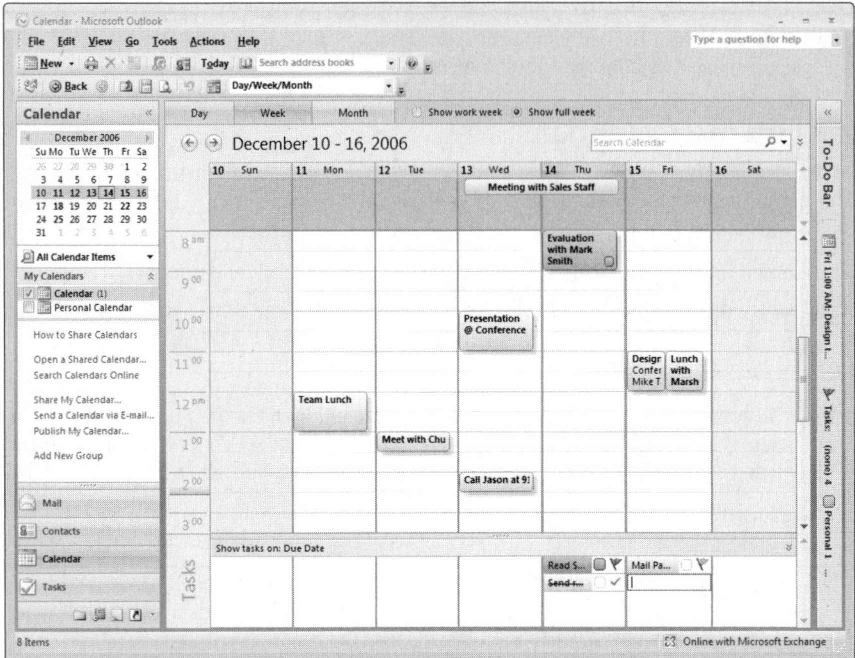

Setting Task Options

Outlook offers several options that relate to the way tasks and task assignments work. To view and change these options, select Options from the Tools menu to display the Options dialog box. One task option is located on the Preferences tab, as shown in Figure 30-33. It specifies what time of day a reminder is displayed for a task that is due today (only for tasks with a reminder set, of course).

The other task options are accessed by clicking the Task Options button on the Preferences tab to open the Task Options dialog box, shown in Figure 30-34. The first two options determine the colors used to display overdue tasks and completed tasks; the default colors are red and dark gray, respectively. The other options are as follows:

- **Keep Updated Copies:** If selected, Outlook maintains updated copies of tasks you have assigned on your task list.
- **Send Status Reports:** If selected, Outlook automatically sends a status report when you mark as completed a task that you have been assigned.
- **Set Reminders:** If selected, Outlook automatically sets a reminder for all tasks that you create with a due date.

FIGURE 30-33

The Task Options section of the Preferences tab in the Options dialog box.

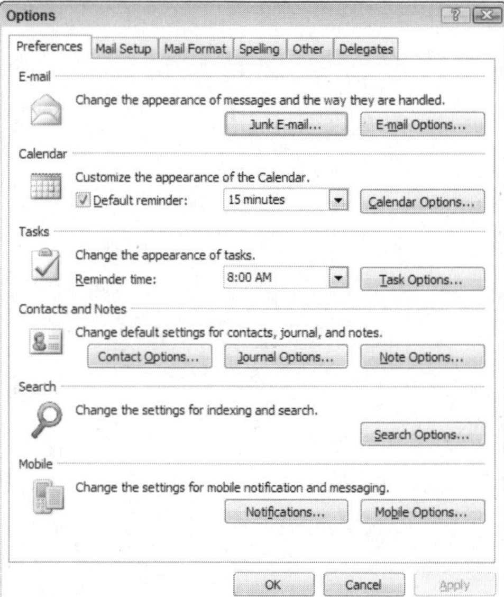

FIGURE 30-34

The Task Options dialog box.

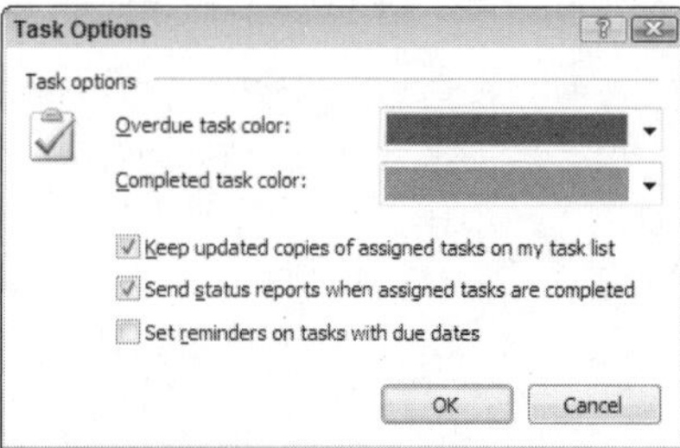

Summary

Outlook's Calendar is a powerful and flexible tool for keeping track of your appointments and other time commitments. Much more than a simple date book, the Outlook Calendar can do things such as remind you of an upcoming appointment.

Outlook provides some powerful tools for keeping track of your tasks. Although a task does not have a specific period of time associated with it (unlike an appointment), it can have a due date. By listing your tasks and optionally reminding you of when they are due, Outlook can greatly reduce the chance that you'll forget to do something important. Outlook even lets you assign tasks to other people and track their progress, a truly valuable tool for a manager or team leader.

Part VI

Designing Publications with Publisher

IN THIS PART

Chapter 31

Introducing Publisher

IN THIS CHAPTER

- Learning how to get around in Publisher
- Choosing and using a publication design
- Typing text or inserting it from a file
- Working with text autoflow and flowing text between frames
- Formatting text
- Inserting and formatting pictures
- Drawing your own shapes and lines
- Adding and editing a table

Desktop publishing made creating printed publications easier and faster but for years remained the bailiwick of graphic art and design superheroes. The software was expensive and difficult to master and provided little in the way of design help for mere mortals.

Microsoft Office Publisher was one of the first programs to make publication design affordable and doable for Joe Blow (and Jill Blow) computer users. From its first version, Publisher offered easy tools, a variety of styles and graphics, and attractive publication designs. This chapter shows you how to use Microsoft Office Publisher 2007 to choose a publication template and add text and graphics to complete a publication.

The Publisher Workspace

Each time you start Publisher, the program prompts you to create a new *publication* file by selecting a template. You can either create a new publication as described in the next section, or click the template window Close (X) button and then use the File ➪ Open command to open a publication you created previously. In either case, Publisher displays a publication and tools in its workspace (Figure 31-1) so that you can get to work.

You will design the publication by adding text, graphic objects, and other elements to the white *page* area. When the publication has multiple pages, you can move between pages by pressing Ctrl+Page Up and Ctrl+Page Down, or by clicking the icon for a page in the *status bar* at the bottom of the workspace. The gray area that appears around the page is called the *scratch area*. This area serves as a holding space for any object that you want to pull off the page and reuse elsewhere. For example, you can drag a graphic off one page to the scratch area, display another page, and then drag the graphic onto that page.

FIGURE 31-1

The Publisher workspace offers a variety of tools for creating publications.

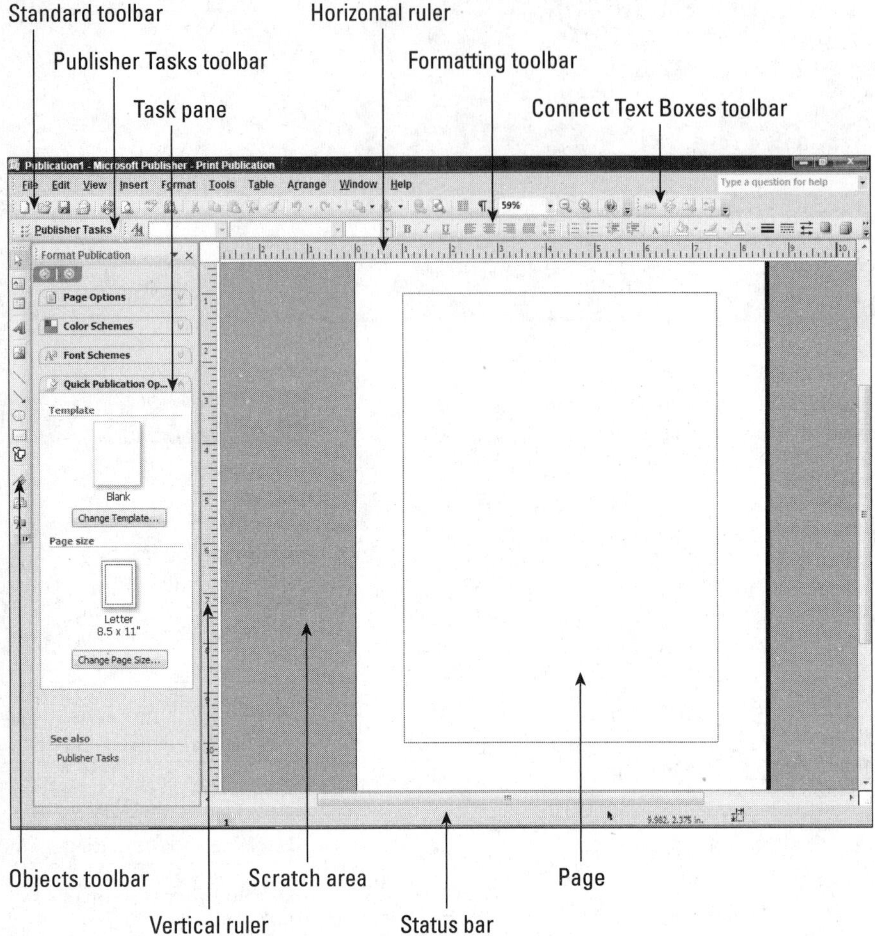

The *vertical* and *horizontal rulers* enable you to align objects on a page with precision. As you drag an object, a moving marker appears on each ruler to indicate the mouse position, and the position measurements appear in the status bar. By default, when you drag an object and release the mouse, the object will snap into alignment with ruler marks. You can turn this snap feature on and off using the Arrange ➪ Snap ➪ To Ruler Marks command. You can create custom green *guide* lines for arranging objects by dragging them out from either ruler, as shown in the example in Figure 31-2. Then, drag objects to align with your guides.

NOTE **You also can use the Measurement toolbar, described later in the chapter, to size and position objects.**

FIGURE 31-2

Drag from either ruler to create a guide.

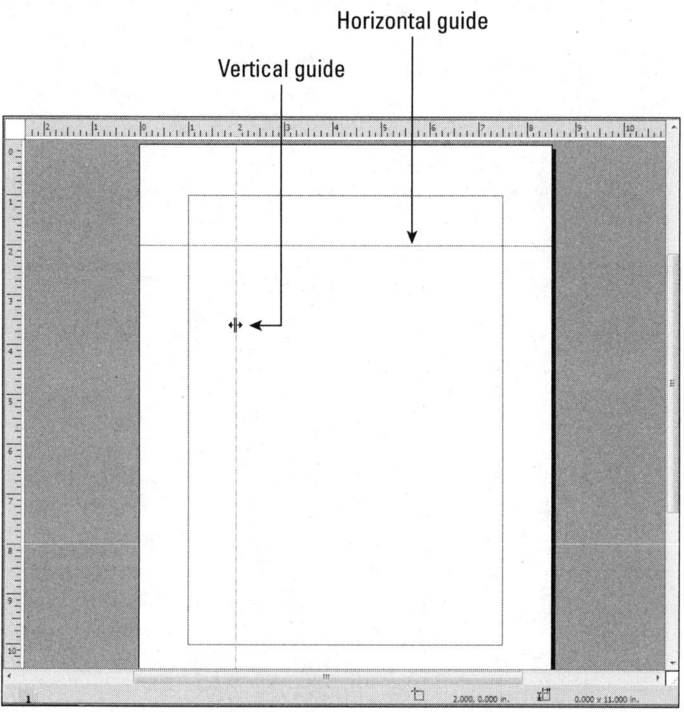

The *task pane* near the left side of the screen presents choices for the current operation that you're performing on the publication. For example, Figure 31-1 shows the Format Publication task pane. Different task panes display as you work and choose commands, but you also can jump directly to a particular task pane by clicking the name of the current task pane at the top of the pane and then clicking the name of the task pane to display in the menu.

Publisher's toolbars offer a variety of buttons and lists that you can use to add and work with publication content and publication files. You can right-click any toolbar to see the shortcut menu and then click a toolbar name to toggle the named toolbar off and on. This feature provides you the flexibility to display only the tools you need onscreen at any given time. Publisher displays these five toolbars onscreen by default:

- **Standard:** This toolbar includes buttons for saving and opening files, printing, copying and pasting, undoing and redoing, and changing the *zoom* for the publication.
- **Connect Text Boxes:** This toolbar, which becomes active when you select a text box, enables you to link, unlink, and move between text boxes.
- **Publisher Tasks:** Clicking the one button on this toolbar displays the Publisher Tasks task pane, shown in Figure 31-3. Click links in this task pane to get help or tips about performing certain activities in Publisher. You can use the Back and Forward buttons near the top of the task pane to navigate through the information or to move all the way back to the task pane that appeared before you clicked the Publisher Tasks button.

FIGURE 31-3

Use this task pane to get tips and instructions for selected activities.

- **Formatting:** As its name suggests, the Formatting toolbar supplies settings for formatting objects, especially text. Clicking the first button on the toolbar displays the Styles text pane. The next several lists and buttons enable you to apply formatting settings such as the font, attributes, and alignment to text, whereas additional buttons enable you to choose fill and line colors and weights, shadow, and 3-D effects.
- **Objects:** This toolbar offers buttons for adding all types of content into a publication, including text boxes, tables, and WordArt; graphics, lines, and shapes; and specialized content from the Design Gallery or Content Library. Clicking the first button on the toolbar disables any other selected button, so you can once again click with the mouse to select objects.

Remember, to see the function of any toolbar button or list, point to it with the mouse to display a pop-up tip identifying what the button or list does.

Using a Template to Create a Publication

Any time you start Publisher or select the File ➪ New command (Ctrl+N), Publisher displays the window (Figure 31-4) in which you can navigate to and select a template to use to create a new publication file.

TIP **To skip the template selection process and create a new, blank publication, click the New button at the far left end of the Standard toolbar.**

Click a category in the Publication Types list in the left pane or one of the icons in the Popular Publication Types area in the center of the window. Publisher displays the templates in that category. Click the desired template to see a preview in the upper-right corner, as shown in Figure 31-5. If you want to see more template choices, you can typically scroll down or click the View Templates from Microsoft Office Online list above the template thumbnails to find and select additional templates.

When you've found the template you'd like to use, you can set up the template by making choices in the Customize and Options areas below the template preview. After you've made the desired choices, click the Create button in the lower-right corner to create the new publication. It will appear in the workspace, as in the example in Figure 31-6, so that you can begin replacing placeholder information with the unique information for your publication.

FIGURE 31-4

Publisher enables you to select a template from any of a number of categories (Publication Types).

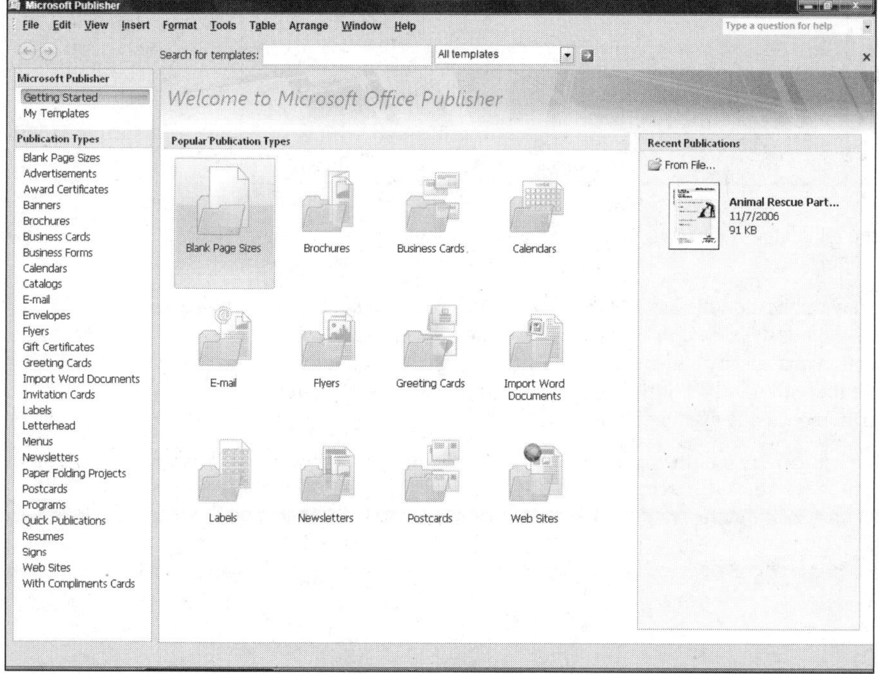

FIGURE 31-5

Browse, preview, and select a template.

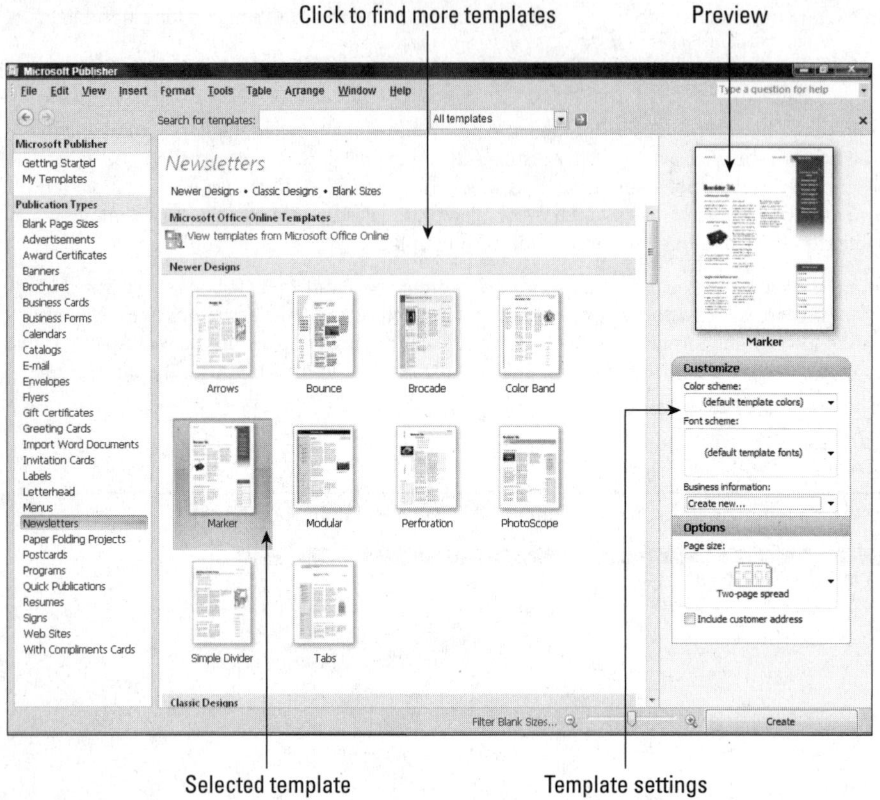

Notice that the new publication file has a placeholder name, *Publication1*, in the example in Figure 31-6. Remember to use the File ➪ Save command (Ctrl+S) or click the Save button on the Standard toolbar to name the publication and specify a save location for it. Press Ctrl+S periodically to save changes as you make them in the file, and use the File ➪ Open command (Ctrl+O) or click the Open button on the Standard toolbar to reopen any existing publication.

NOTE **You can click one of the publications listed in the Recent Publications list as shown at the far right in Figure 31-4 to reopen a recently used file. Clicking the From File link at the far right enables you to open a Publisher or Word file to use as the basis for a new publication file.**

FIGURE 31-6

The new document based on the template appears.

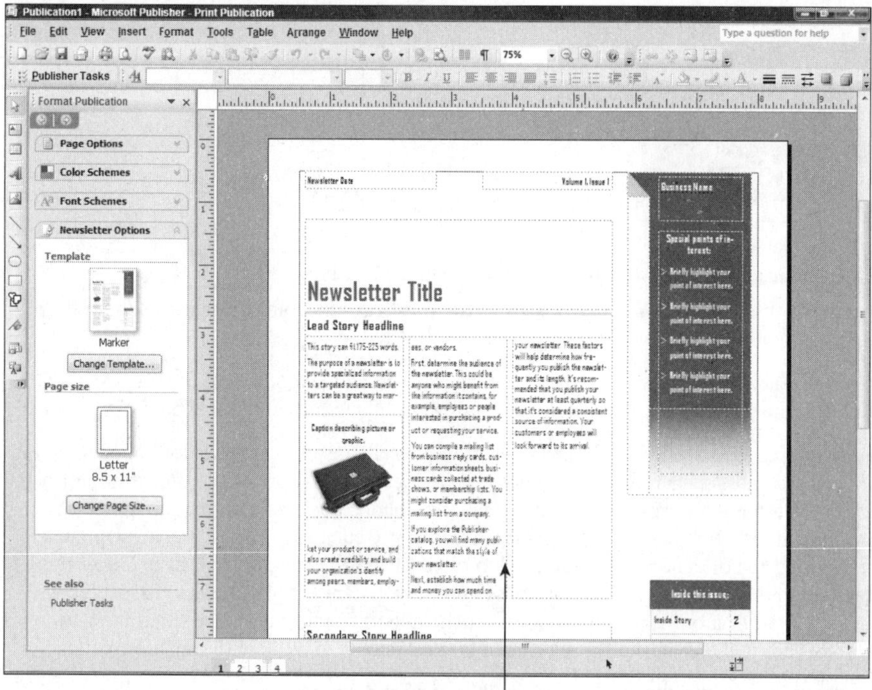

Text boxes with instructions

Working with Text

In Publisher, you add text into a *text box*. A text box has a dashed boundary that defines where the text will appear. If you created your publication from a template, the template design provided placeholder text boxes within the publication, as in the example shown in Figure 31-6. In that case, you can simply use an existing text box to add the text. You also can create your own text boxes as required for your publication design.

Typing text in a placeholder

Adding text into a placeholder text box requires that you select the placeholder and the text within the placeholder to replace the example text. Use these steps to add text into a placeholder text box in a file based on a template:

1. **Click the text within the placeholder.** In most cases, this action selects both the text box and all the placeholder text within it, as shown in Figure 31-7. Selection handles appear around the text box, and the placeholder text is highlighted.

FIGURE 31-7

Click the text in a template text box to select both the text box and the example text.

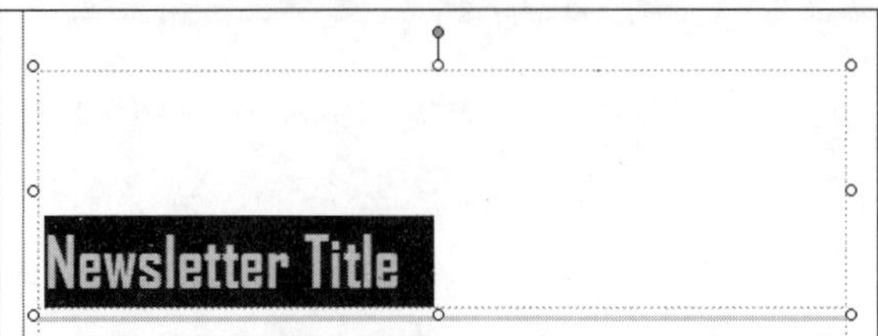

2. **Type the replacement text.** Your new text appears in the text box.
3. **Click outside the text box on a blank area of the publication.** Doing so deselects the text box, finishing your entry.

Text boxes do not resize automatically in Publisher, so if the text you add is too long to fit within the text box, you need to resize the text, as described later in "Resizing, autoflow, and linked text boxes."

Many of the templates have automated placeholders that automatically insert business information stored in the *business information set* in Publisher. If you have not yet specified information for the business information set, choose Edit ➪ Business Information and then click the Change Business Information link at the bottom of the Business Information task pane. Enter the information, click Save, and then click Update Publication. You can drag any of the components listed in the Business Information task pane onto a publication to add that item to the publication. Each business information item (or placeholder) has a blue dashed underline in the publication. When you point to such an item, you can click the smart tag button that appears and then click a choice in the shortcut menu to decide how to work with the information.

After you click in a text box, you can press the Del key to delete it from the publication.

Creating a placeholder and adding text

Whether you used a template as the basis for your publication or created the publication from scratch, you can add a new text box to place text in any location that you like in the publication. To add the text box, use the Text Box button, which is the second button on the Objects toolbar at the left side of the Publisher window.

1. **Click the Text Box button on the Objects toolbar.**
2. **Drag diagonally on the publication page to create the text box in the desired size and shape (Figure 31.8).** When you release the mouse button, the blinking insertion point appears within the text box.
3. **Type the text.** Your new text appears in the text box.
4. **Click outside the text box on a blank area of the publication.** Doing so deselects the text box, finishing your entry.

Text you add into a text box is also called a *story*.

FIGURE 31-8

Drag to define the size and shape for the text box.

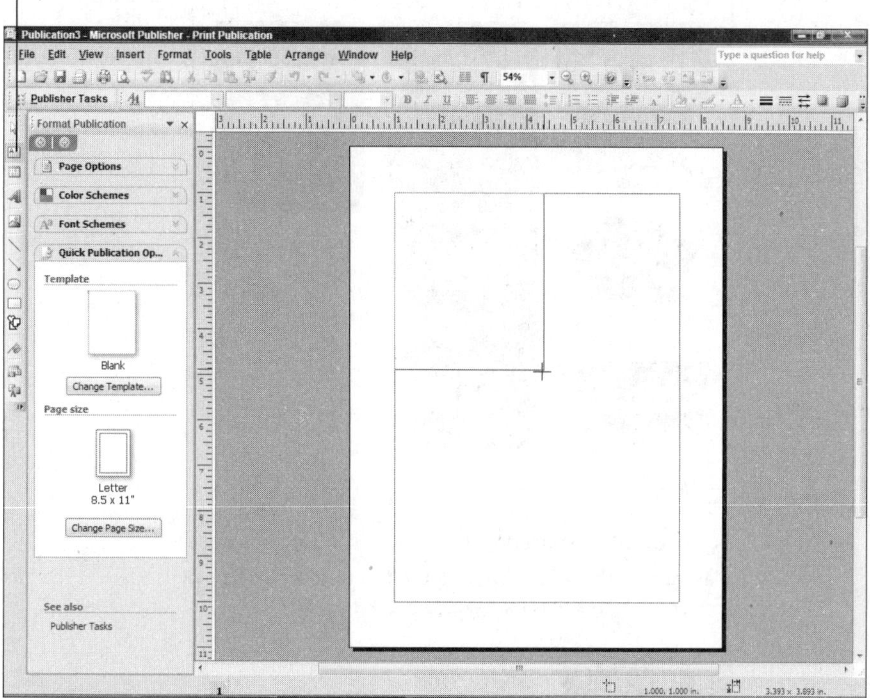

Inserting a text file

Often, writing text and designing a publication are two separate activities assigned to two different people within an organization or group, especially for a publication that requires a lot of text, such as a newsletter or catalog. The person handling the writing assignment typically uses Word, WordPad, or another word processing program to write and edit the text, because a word processing program is the better tool for that purpose.

You need not worry about retyping text supplied by a colleague. Instead, you can insert word processing files in popular formats including Word, WordPerfect, plain text (`.txt`), or Rich Text Format (`.rtf`) directly into a text placeholder. The steps for doing so, which follow, basically combine the process for adding text into a text box and opening a file:

1. **Click the text within the placeholder.** If the text box is a template placeholder, this action selects both the text box and all the text within it. In the case of a placeholder for a newsletter story or other situation with *linked* text boxes, Publisher selects the entire placeholder story within all the linked boxes, as in the example in Figure 31-9.

FIGURE 31-9

Publisher selects the entire story in linked text boxes.

2. **Select Insert ➪ Text File.** The Insert Text dialog box appears.
3. **Navigate to the folder holding the file to insert.** The dialog box lists the files with readable text formats stored in that folder, as in Figure 31-10.

FIGURE 31-10

Insert a text file from a word processing program to avoid retyping the information.

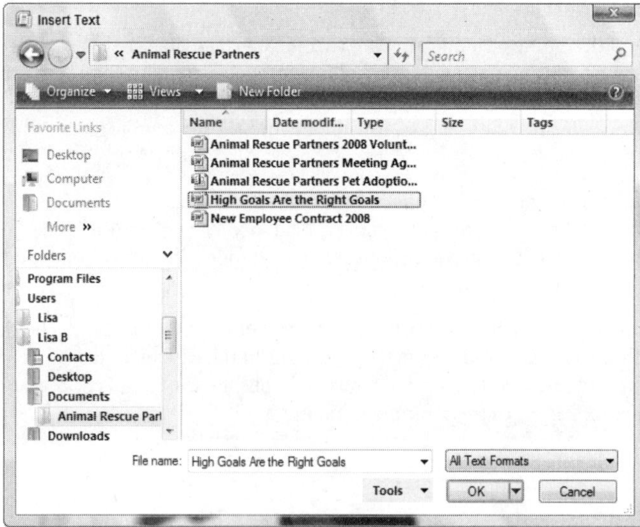

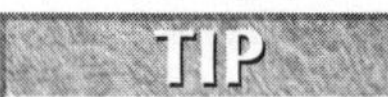

Click All Text Formats and then select Recover Text from Any File to list all the folder's files in the dialog box.

4. **Click the name of the text file to insert and then click OK.** The text from the inserted file appears in the placeholder you selected in Step 1.

Depending on the file format of the inserted file and whether any text and style formatting was applied in the original document, you may need to change the formatting of the text after inserting the file. The later section titled "Formatting text" delves into some of the formatting methods you can use.

NOTE **If the writer for a publication that you're creating uses an old or rare word processing program, have the writer use the Save As or Export command in the program to save the file that you need to use as a plain-text or Rich Text Format file. Even PowerPoint can save files in Outline/RTF format.**

Resizing, autoflow, and linked text boxes

Publisher does not resize a text box if the text you type or a file you insert is too lengthy. When the number of words you've typed into a text box exceeds the number the box can hold, a Text in Overflow button like the one shown near the lower-right corner of the text box in Figure 31-11 appears. When you see that button, you can drag one of the handles on the text box to enlarge the box to display the text in its entirety. You also can flow the text into another text box, as described later in this section.

FIGURE 31-11

The Text in Overflow button cues you that the text doesn't fit in the text box.

If you insert a file into a text box and the file's contents are too large for the text box, Publisher displays a message box like the one shown in Figure 31-12. If you click Yes, Publisher automatically flows the extra text into subsequent frames in the publication until all the text has been placed, a feature called *autoflow*. If you click No, you can instead handle the extra text by resizing the text box manually. Or, you can link the text box to another of your choice, thus choosing exactly which text box will receive the flowed text. Linking text boxes enables you to control how a story flows from one text box to another.

FIGURE 31-12

Publisher enables you to autoflow extra text from an inserted file into other text boxes in the publication.

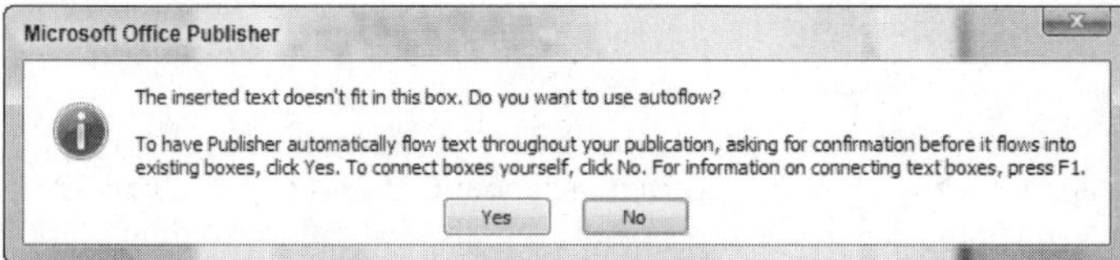

TIP **You can set up Publisher to resize text so that it can to some degree fit itself within the existing boundary of a text box. To toggle this AutoFit Text feature on and off, select Format ➪ AutoFit Text ➪ Best Fit or Format ➪ AutoFit Text ➪ Shrink Text On Overflow.**

To link two text boxes so that the overflow text flows from one to the other:

1. **Click the text box that holds the overflow text.** The Text in Overflow button appears below the text box.
2. **Click the Create Text Box Link button on the Connect Text Boxes toolbar.** The mouse pointer changes to a pitcher appearance.
3. **Move the mouse pointer over the text box into which you want to flow the overflow text.** As shown in Figure 31-13, the mouse pointer changes to a "pouring" appearance to indicate that it is in position to add the overflow text into the text box.

FIGURE 31-13

Linking text boxes flows text between them.

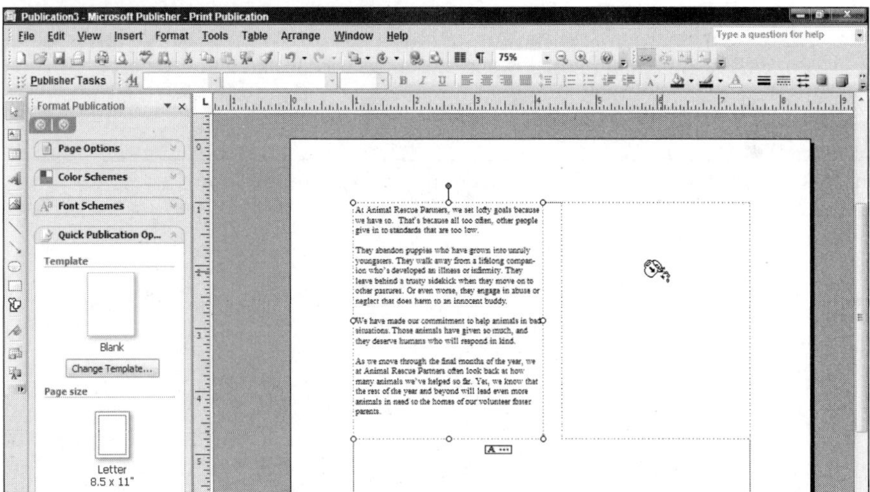

4. **Click the text box to link.** The overflow text appears in the box. If a Text in Overflow button appears below the newly linked text box, it holds still more overflow text that you can display by resizing or linking to another text box.

Other special buttons appear when you click a linked text box. You may see the Go To Previous Text Box button above a linked text box. Clicking that button selects the previous text box. When a Go To Next Text Box button appears below a linked text box, you can click the button to select the later text box.

Formatting text

Some text formatting in Microsoft Publisher works similarly to the prior editions of Word and PowerPoint, and you can refer to earlier chapters about those programs to learn more about fonts, font sizes, alignments, and the type of text formats that you can apply. Click in the text box that has the text to format, drag over text within the text box to make a more specific selection to format or press Ctrl+A to select the entire story, and then use the choices on the Formatting toolbar or the Format menu to apply the desired changes. For example, you can click the Bold button on the Formatting toolbar to apply boldface, or click the Bullets button to convert the text to a bulleted list.

Often, text that you've imported from another file will have its own formatting applied rather than adhere to the formatting established by the publication template. In this case, you can work with the Styles task pane to apply template formatting to the text:

1. **Click in the text box that holds the text to format.**
2. **Drag over text within the text box or press Ctrl+A to select the entire story.** The Ctrl+A shortcut even selects text in linked text boxes, making this a convenient shortcut when you need to reformat a larger volume of text distributed across multiple frames.
3. **Click the drop-down list at the top of the task pane and then click Styles.** The Styles task pane appears.
4. **Click the desired style (Figure 31-14).** Publisher applies the style to the selected text.

FIGURE 31-14

Applying a template style saves formatting legwork.

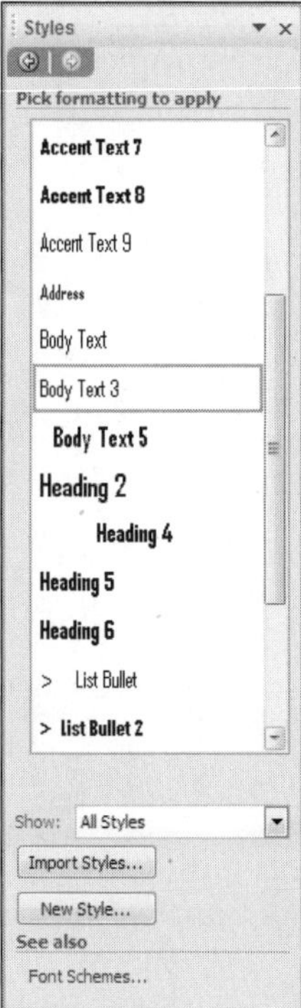

NOTE Many of the body text styles automatically include spacing between paragraphs, so if you've pressed Enter to add space between paragraphs when creating your text — either in Publisher or in a word processing program — you may want to remove those extra hard returns after applying body text styles in Publisher.

One new feature that Publisher 2007 shares with some other Microsoft Office 2007 applications is the ability to apply a new *font scheme* to the publication. Changing the font scheme changes the entire set of styles in the publication to styles that use different fonts, sizes, and so on. By making one choice in a task pane, you can update the look of all the text in the publication. Here's how to choose a new font scheme via the Format Publication task pane:

1. **Click the drop-down list at the top of the task pane and then click Format Publication.** Note that if you've just created the publication, this task pane should already appear by default.
2. **Click Font Schemes in the task pane.** The task pane changes to display the available font schemes.
3. **Scroll the list of schemes (Figure 31-15) and click the new scheme to apply.** Publisher updates the fonts throughout the document for any text to which you've previously applied styles. If you want to return to the default font scheme for the template, choose the top font scheme choice.

FIGURE 31-15

Applying a font scheme updates all the document styles to use new formatting.

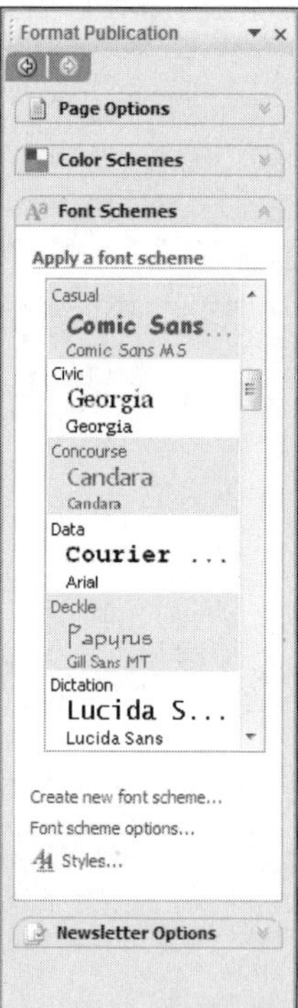

The Measurement toolbar

One nice benefit about Publisher's templates is that they have already been set up with great precision. All the text boxes, graphics, and other elements have been sized and aligned to exact dimensions. If you want to be as precise with your own publication — such as making sure that text boxes have the same width or sizing of a graphic to fit exactly within a column, you can use the Measurement toolbar (Figure 31-16).

FIGURE 31-16

View and change numerous dimensions for a selected object or text using the Measurement toolbar.

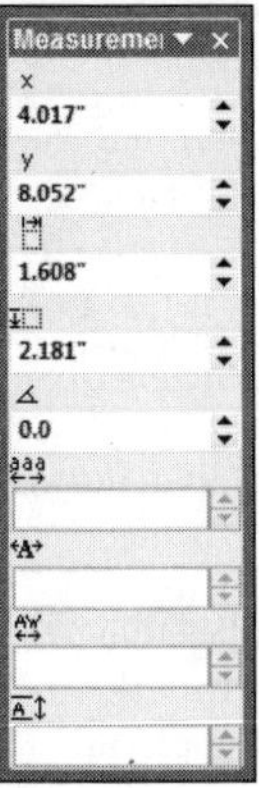

The Measurement toolbar displays the exact x (horizontal) and y (vertical) position of the upper-left corner of the selected text box or object. It also lists the object's width, height, and rotation angle (if any). If you've selected text within a text box, the Measurement toolbar also displays text settings including Tracking, Text Scaling, Kerning, and Line Spacing.

To change any of the settings for the selected object or text, you can enter a new value in the applicable text box on the Measurement toolbar and press Enter, or you can use the spinner arrow buttons to change the entry. In this way, if you want three different text boxes in a publication to be exactly 2.205" wide, you can use the Measurement toolbar to set that width dimension.

To display and hide the Measurement toolbar, you can right-click any toolbar and click Measurement. You also can select View ➪ Toolbars ➪ Measurement or double-click either the Object Position or Object Size icons on the status bar to open the Measurement toolbar.

Working with Graphics

Graphics bring publication stories to life. If you're a Realtor creating a flyer to describe a terrific house that you have for sale, anyone who sees your flyer will *really* know how fabulous the house is if you include pictures of the granite countertops in the kitchen, the luxurious bathroom, and the gorgeous patio and landscaping in the back yard. Publisher makes it easy to add pictures and other graphic elements to punch up a story and really sell your message.

Inserting a picture file

Digital cameras and scanners are virtually as cheap as film cameras once were. Even the typical home or small business generally has a digital camera and users who take and transfer dozens of digital pictures to the computer's hard disk. Microsoft Publisher enables you to place pictures in formats commonly captured by digital cameras, such as JPEG and TIFF, as well as numerous other graphics formats created with drawing and painting programs, directly into a publication.

This process does not require a picture placeholder, so when you're ready to insert a digital picture file into a publication, follow this process:

1. **Display the page in the publication on which you'd like to insert the picture.** Clicking a page icon in the status bar takes you there.
2. **Select Insert ➪ Picture ➪ From File.** The Insert Picture dialog box appears.
3. **Navigate to the folder holding the file to insert.** The dialog box lists the files with readable graphics formats stored in that folder.

Click All Pictures and then select a particular format to list only picture files using that format.

4. **Click the name of the text file to insert and then click Insert.** The inserted picture file appears on the page.

After you insert the picture, you need to resize and position it as needed. You can drag the handles that appear on the corners and sides of the picture (Figure 31-17) to resize it, or move the mouse within the picture and drag to move it. You also can use the Measurement toolbar as described earlier to set the picture's size and position. When you finish sizing the picture, click outside it to deselect it.

FIGURE 31-17

Resize and move the inserted picture as needed.

NOTE **You can insert an image directly from a scanner or digital camera connected with your system. For the process to work, the device must be installed under Windows, connected to the system, and then powered on (or for a camera, to the mode for playing back or transferring pictures). Then use the Insert ➪ Picture ➪ From Scanner or Camera command to start the transfer process. Refer to Chapter 9,**

"Tables and Graphics," for more details about working with a scanner or digital camera to bring an image into an Office application.

CAUTION If you plan to have your publication professionally printed, you need to use high-resolution pictures to get good results. If you crop a portion of a digital camera shot and then size it at a large size in the publication, those changes might result in a low-resolution graphic that prints with a fuzzy or blocky appearance. If you have any doubts about how an image might print, ask the print shop to inspect your publication file for such problems *before* proceeding with your print order.

Inserting a Clip Art image

If you don't have your own digital pictures but want to flesh out your publication with some images, you can take advantage of the Clip Art available in Office and via Microsoft Office Online. The Clip Art task pane enables you to search for the type of picture you want, such as a flower, boat, or person. You enter a word or phrase describing the type of clip art you want, and Publisher by default searches for matches both in installed clip art and online. Follow these steps when you want to insert a clip art graphic into a publication:

1. **Display the page in the publication on which you'd like to insert the clip art.** Clicking a page icon in the status bar takes you there.
2. **Select Insert ➪ Picture ➪ Clip Art.** The Clip Art task pane appears.
3. **Type the descriptive word or phrase in the Search For text box at the top of the pane; then, click Go.** Thumbnail images of matching clip art appear in the task pane, as shown in Figure 31-18.

FIGURE 31-18

Find and insert clip art using the Clip Art task pane.

The first time you search for clip art, a Microsoft Clip Organizer prompt asks whether you want to search online clips by default. Click Yes to do so.

4. **Scroll down to review all the available choices.**
5. **Click the clip art media object to place on the publication.** It appears on the page you specified in Step 1. You can then resize the picture as needed to fit with the other contents in your publication, and click outside the picture to deselect it.

Changing a placeholder picture

Many publication templates include placeholder graphics that provide suggested sizes and locations where you can insert your own pictures or alternate clip art images. When you insert the replacement picture or clip art graphic, Publisher automatically resizes the replacement image to fit within the frame for the existing image.

To replace a placeholder image, right-click it to display a shortcut menu. (If the picture frame is grouped with a text frame for a caption, click the group first and then right-click the image.) Select Change Picture in the shortcut menu that appears and then select Clip Art or From File in the submenu that appears. From there, the process works just like the steps you've already learned for inserting a picture or clip art object.

Formatting pictures

You can adjust numerous settings to fine-tune a picture and its placement, including settings such as an added fill color or outline, size and rotation, layout and text wrapping, and brightness and contrast. The available settings vary somewhat depending on whether the selected picture is a digital image file or clip art graphic, and whether the picture is inserted on its own or is within a frame that's grouped with other objects.

The settings for formatting a picture appear in the Format Picture dialog box. To display the dialog box, right-click the picture (click the grouped object first, if needed), and then select Format Picture. Change settings on the tabs in the Format Picture dialog box (Figure 31-19) as needed, and then click OK to apply your choices to the picture.

The green handle that appears at the top center of a selected picture, clip art object, or other drawn object is the rotation handle. Drag it to rotate the selected object.

Drawing lines and shapes

You also can enhance a publication by drawing shapes using the Line, Arrow, Oval, Rectangle, and AutoShapes buttons on the Objects toolbar. For example, you might draw an arrow to point to an important piece of information or draw a banner AutoShape to layer behind headline text.

To draw the shape, click the desired button on the Objects toolbar. If you click the AutoShapes button, a menu appears. Click a shape category in the menu and then click the specific AutoShape you want to draw in the submenu that appears, as shown in Figure 31-20.

FIGURE 31-19

The tabs in this dialog box offer numerous settings for fine-tuning the appearance of a clip art object.

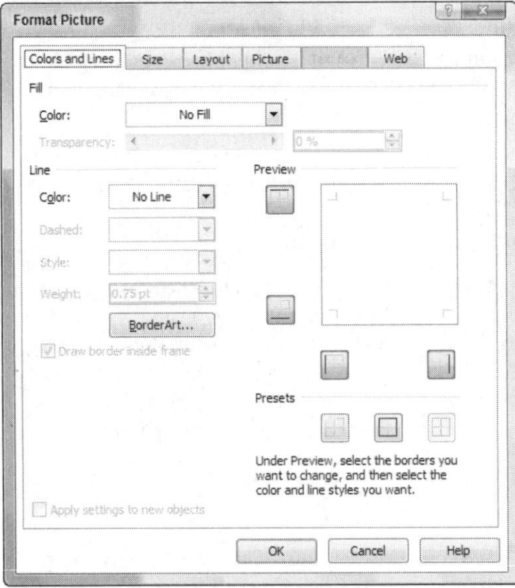

FIGURE 31-20

You can select an AutoShape to draw from the AutoShapes tool.

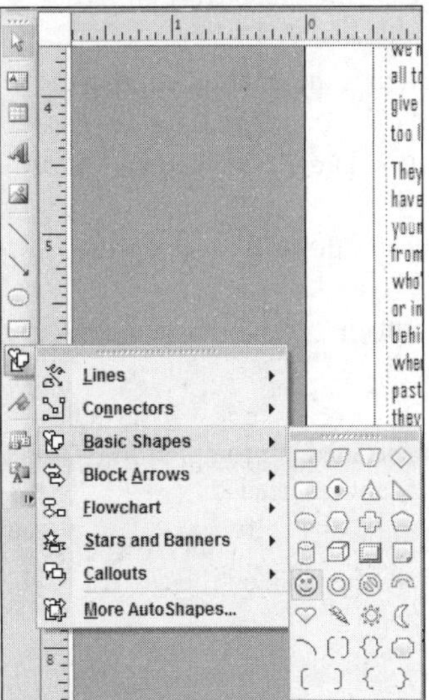

After you've selected the desired line or shape, drag on the publication page to draw the object. Keep these hints in mind when you draw and work with shapes:

- Drag in the desired direction to create a line or arrow. If you want to help the line snap to vertical, horizontal, or a 45-degreee angle, press the Shift key when your line is close to the desired angle.
- Drag diagonally to draw an oval, rectangle, or AutoShape. Press and hold Shift as you drag to constrain the shape to proportional dimensions; doing so results in a perfect circle or square, or an AutoShape that fits within a perfect circle or square.
- After you draw an AutoShape, you can change it to another AutoShape by selecting Arrange ➪ Change AutoShape and then selecting the desired shape using the submenus that appear.
- Some AutoShapes include a special yellow handle when selected. You can use this handle to reshape the object, such as dragging to increase the 3-D angle of the shape.
- Right-click a shape and then select Format AutoShape to display the Format AutoShape dialog box, where you can change shape settings, as for a picture. One cool thing you can do is insert a picture within a shape or AutoShape. To do so, open the Color drop-down list in the Fill area of the Colors and Lines tab and then select Fill Effects. Click the Picture tab in the Fill Effects dialog box that appears and then use the Select Picture button to open the Select Picture dialog box. Navigate to and select the desired picture file, click Insert, and then click OK twice to fill the shape.

Working with Tables

When you need to organize information in a series of rows and columns, you don't have to draw and arrange a text box for each bit of data. You can instead create a *table*, which has cells formed by the intersections of rows and columns. When you create a table using these steps, you specify the number of rows and columns and pick the initial table design:

1. **Display the page in the publication on which you'd like to insert the table.** Clicking a page icon in the status bar takes you there.
2. **Click the Insert Table button on the Objects toolbar.** This button is the third down from the top and looks as though it has a grid on it.
3. **Drag diagonally on the publication to specify the table's location and size.** When you release the mouse button, the Create Table dialog box appears.
4. **Change the Number of Rows and Number of Columns settings as desired to set up the table.**
5. **Select a format to apply in the Table Format list.** As shown in Figure 31-21, the Sample area in the dialog box displays the appearance of the selected formatting.
6. **Click OK.** The table will appear in the specified location. If Publisher needs to resize the table frame to accommodate the number of rows and/or columns you specified, a prompt appears to ask you to confirm the resize. Click Yes to have Publisher size the table as needed.

TIP **You also can open the Create Table dialog box by selecting Table ➪ Insert ➪ Table. After you make your choices and click OK, Publisher automatically places the table on the current publication page, on which you can move and resize it as needed.**

FIGURE 31-21

Create a table by specifying rows, columns, and format.

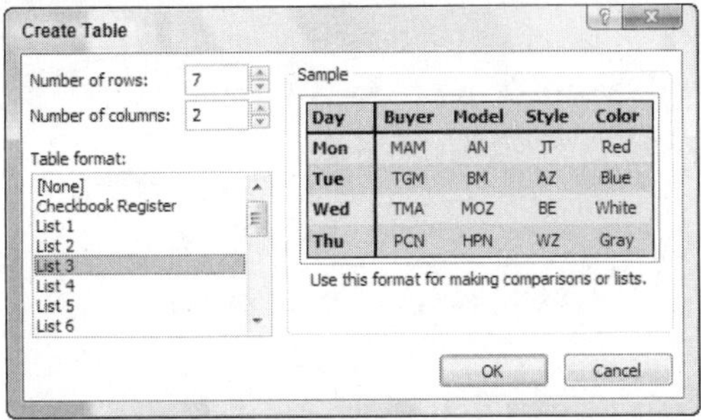

Entering and editing table data

When the new table appears, the insertion point appears in the upper-left cell. Simply type the entry for each cell and press Tab to move on to the next cell. If you type more text than the cell can initially handle, Publisher wraps the text to the next line and increases the row height as needed. You can press Shift+Tab to back up to a previous cell as needed.

To edit the entry in any particular table cell, click the cell and then make the desired changes by selecting and replacing text or using editing keys such as Backspace. When you finish entering and editing table text, click outside the table to deselect it.

Click a table at any time to reselect it.

Working with the table format

As with other objects you've seen in this chapter, you can right-click on a table and then click Format Table to open the Format Table dialog box. Note that the settings on the Colors and Lines tab apply only to the selected cell — the cell on which you right-clicked to open the dialog box. If you want to work with colors and fills for more than one cell, you have to select those cells before right-clicking and selecting Format Table. To select cells, first click the table. Then drag over the cells to select. You also can move the mouse pointer outside the table boundary above a column or to the left of a row that you want to select. When the mouse pointer changes to a black arrow pointing to the row or column, clicking the mouse selects the entire row or column. Also note that the Format Table dialog box includes a Cell Properties tab, on which you can change the vertical text alignment, margins, and text rotation for the selected cells.

One last table skill that's handy to know is how to resize the width of a table column. To do so, point to the right border of the column until you see the resizing pointer, which appears at the far right of the Monday row in Figure 31-22. Then drag left or right to fix the column width as desired.

FIGURE 31-22

Drag to adjust table column width.

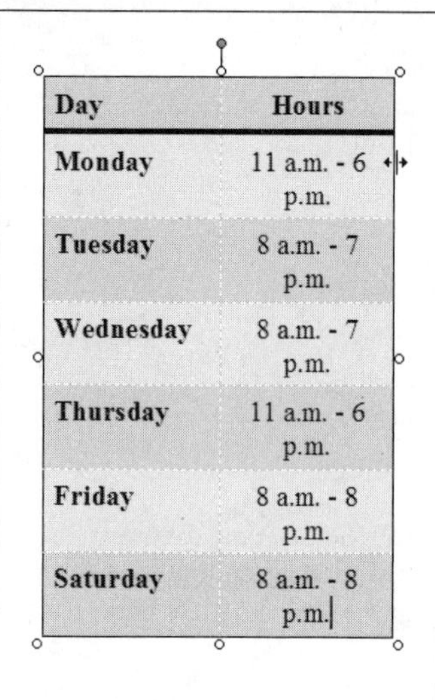

Day	Hours
Monday	11 a.m. - 6 p.m.
Tuesday	8 a.m. - 7 p.m.
Wednesday	8 a.m. - 7 p.m.
Thursday	11 a.m. - 6 p.m.
Friday	8 a.m. - 8 p.m.
Saturday	8 a.m. - 8 p.m.

Summary

Making it through this chapter provided you with the basic know-how for creating a publication in Microsoft Publisher. You learned to work with the main toolbars and other features of the Publisher workspace, as well as how to create a blank file or a file based on a template supplied with Publisher or Microsoft Office Online. You learned how to add text into a text box supplied by a template, how to create a text box and type in text, how to insert text from a word processing file, and how to format your text with formatting tools, styles, and a font scheme. You learned how to use the Measurement toolbar to format objects, as well as how to insert, create, and change graphics and tables to enhance the publication's appearance and supplement the message delivered in the text.

Chapter 32

Design Dazzling Publications with Publisher

Starting your design with one of Publisher's templates virtually guarantees that you will create a nice-looking publication. You know your message and your audience best, so you can improve on a template by adding graphics and changing aspects of the overall document design. You can use special graphic features that emphasize or decorate text, add predesigned objects such as coupons, and work with page options such as the color scheme for the publication. From there, you can fine-tune objects and page settings and then wrap up and print the publication. This chapter shows you how to do all that to add your own razzle-dazzle to a publication.

IN THIS CHAPTER

- Adding eye appeal with BorderArt, drop caps, and WordArt
- Inserting an object from the Design Gallery
- Updating the publication background, page, and color settings
- Aligning and grouping objects
- Working with text wrapping and hyphenation
- Adding and numbering pages
- Checking and printing the publication
- Prepping for a professional print job

Adding Special Effects

One of the advantages of using Publisher to design your publications is that Publisher makes laying out and designing document text easier. Linked text boxes give you much control over where information appears in a document. Beyond dealing with that aspect of text design, Publisher also provides you with tools to dress up text to catch your reader's eye: BorderArt, drop caps, and WordArt.

BorderArt

You learned in Chapter 31 that you can right-click an inserted picture, clip art, or table object and select a format command that opens a formatting dialog box. Similarly, you can right-click any text box in a publication and click Format Text Box to open the Format Text box dialog box (Figure 32-1). You can use the tabs in this dialog box to add fills and outlines to the text box, and more. In addition, you can click the BorderArt button on the Colors and Lines tab to open the BorderArt dialog box.

FIGURE 32-1

Overall text box formatting settings appear in the Format Text Box dialog box.

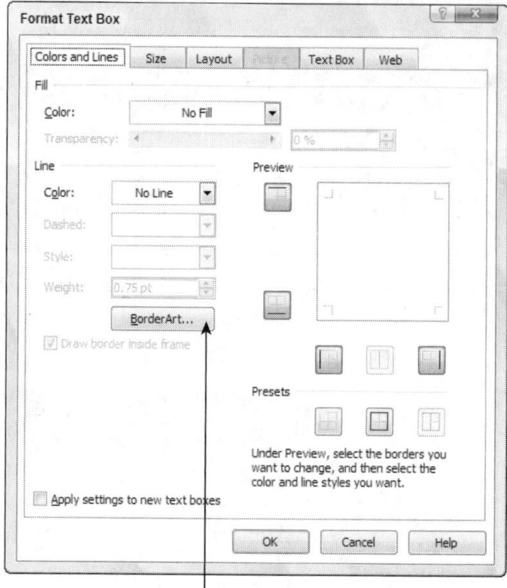

Rather than use a plain colored line around your text box, BorderArt applies a border made up of small graphics. The graphics range from geometric forms that apply a formal, decorative feel to items that set a fun mood or tone, such as ladybugs or candy corn. The available BorderArt designs fit any number of occasions, making them ideal to use in almost any of your publications, including invitations and greeting cards, for example.

As shown in Figure 32-2, you can preview any border by selecting it in the Available Borders list at the left side of the dialog box. The border design appears in the Preview area at the right, using its default settings. By default, Publisher stretches the border graphics to fill the border area a little more completely. If you prefer to turn off this feature, click the Don't Stretch Pictures option button near the lower-left corner of the dialog box. Each border has an automatic size, shown in the Preview. If you want to control the border width yourself, click the Always Apply at Default Size checkbox to uncheck it before continuing.

When you've selected the BorderArt and changed any settings as needed, click OK to close the BorderArt dialog box and return to the Format Text Box dialog box. Change the Weight entry on the Colors and Lines tab to set the border width if needed. You also can modify the border color in the Line area, but you may not want to do so if the BorderArt graphics already include great colors. Click OK to close the dialog box and finish applying the BorderArt. As shown in the party invitation in Figure 32-3, the BorderArt can make even simple text pop from the page.

FIGURE 32-2

You can preview a border in the BorderArt dialog box.

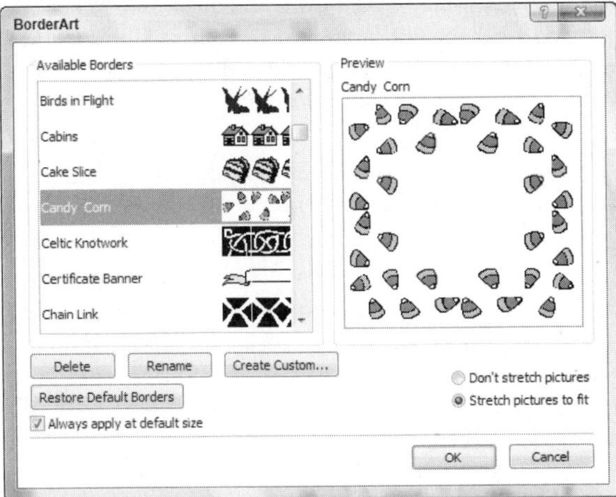

FIGURE 32-3

Party time! Seasonal or theme-oriented BorderArt works well for greeting cards and invitations.

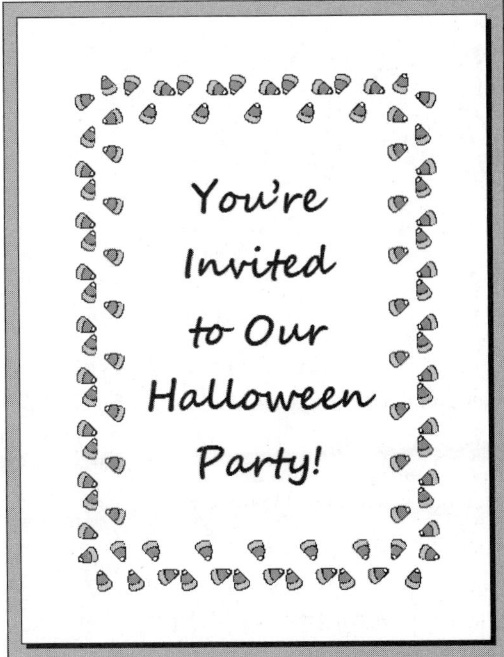

You can create your own BorderArt using any graphic image stored on your hard disk or listed in the Microsoft Office Clip Organizer. Click Create Custom in the BorderArt dialog box. To open a file from the hard disk rather than Clip Organizer, click the Use Clip Organizer to Select the Picture checkbox in the Create Custom Border dialog box to clear the checkbox. Then click Select Picture. Use the Insert Picture dialog box that appears to select a picture or clip art image; then click Insert or OK. Publisher converts the picture into a border. Type a name for the new border into the Name Custom Border dialog box and click OK. The new border appears in the Available Borders list in the BorderArt dialog box until you select the border and click Delete.

Choose small, simple pictures to convert to custom border art. For example, you might want to crop a single flower out of a larger picture and use that smaller flower as your BorderArt graphic.

Drop caps

Formatting the first letter of a story or paragraph as *drop cap* draws the eye to that spot in your publication. Setting up a letter as a drop cap increases its size, causing it to stand above the first line of text or have the first few lines wrap around it, or both. The drop cap style you choose might also use a contrasting color or other text formatting to give it a fancy appearance. Figure 32-4 shows a story with a drop cap applied.

FIGURE 32-4

Attract readers to a story by setting the first paragraph off with a drop cap.

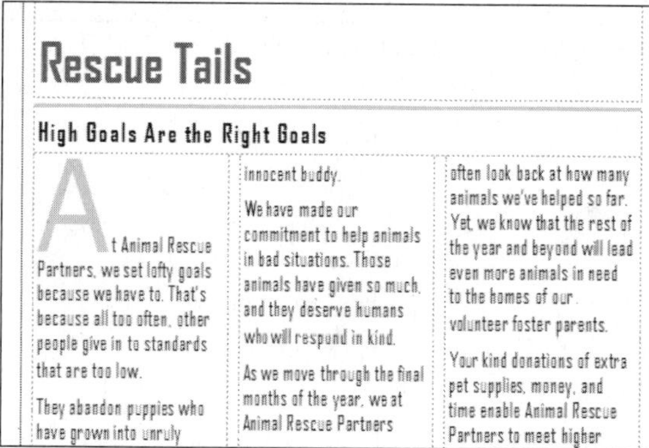

Follow these steps to create a drop cap in a story:

1. **Select the text box and then click in the paragraph where you want to add the drop cap.**
2. **Select Format ➪ Drop Cap.** The Drop Cap dialog box appears.
3. **Scroll the Available Drop Caps choices as needed and then click a drop cap style.** The Preview at the right shows how the drop cap will look when applied to the paragraph, as in the example in Figure 32-5.
4. **Click OK to apply the drop cap.**

Clicking the Remove button in the Drop Cap dialog box removes the drop cap from the paragraph.

FIGURE 32-5

Make sure that the drop cap fits your text by checking the Preview.

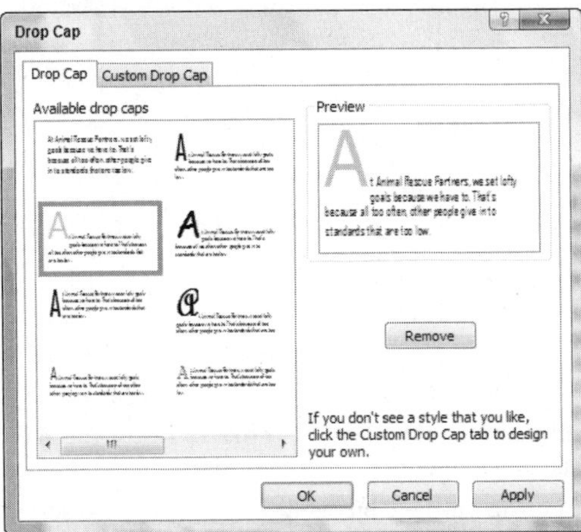

If none of the available drop cap styles is quite what you're looking for, you can click the Custom Drop Cap tab in the Drop Cap dialog box to display the settings for creating your own custom drop cap, as shown in Figure 32-6. You can work with the drop cap position, size, and text appearance. As you try on various setting combinations, the Preview at the right shows you how your paragraph will look with the custom drop cap. Click OK to apply the custom drop cap and close the dialog box.

WordArt

The last several versions of some Office applications have all included WordArt, a feature that enables you to convert a word or phrase to a colorful graphic object. For example, rather than have "just" a title for your newsletter, you can create a WordArt object that really pops, like the example shown in Figure 32-7.

FIGURE 32-6

For a truly custom drop cap, work with the settings here.

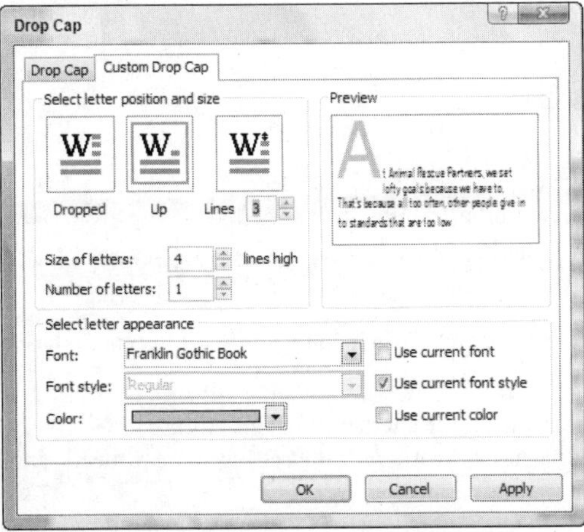

FIGURE 32-7

No mere text attracts attention the way that WordArt can.

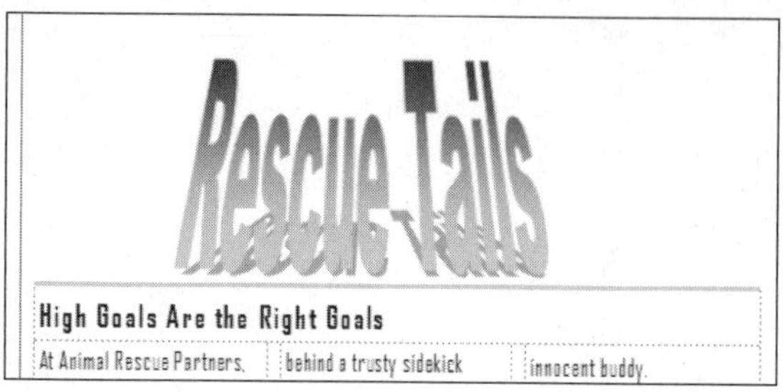

To create a WordArt object in a publication, follow these steps:

1. **Display the page in the publication on which you'd like to insert the WordArt.** Clicking a page icon in the status bar takes you there.
2. **Click the Insert WordArt button on the Objects toolbar, or select Insert ➪ Picture ➪ WordArt.** The WordArt Gallery dialog box (Figure 32-8) appears.

FIGURE 32-8

Give some text WordArt style — simple, wavy, shadowed, vertical, or 3-D.

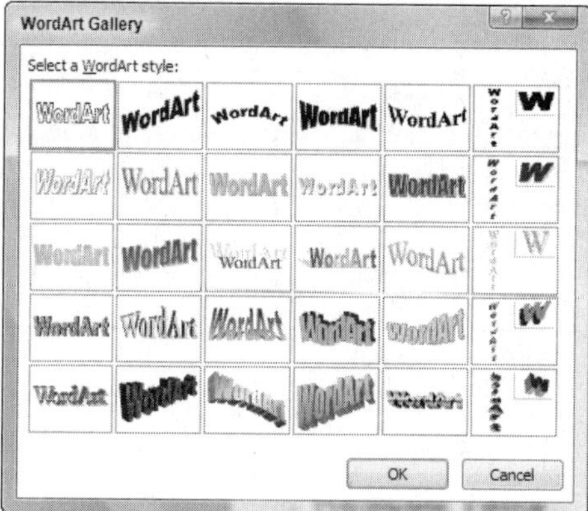

3. **Click a WordArt style and then click OK.** The Edit WordArt Text dialog box appears.
4. **Type the WordArt text and adjust its font, size, and attributes as needed.**
5. **Click OK.** The WordArt object appears on the publication, where you can size and position it as desired.

Keep WordArt text brief. Decorative text created with WordArt can be difficult to read in large quantities.

When you select any WordArt object, the WordArt toolbar appears. It offers buttons for editing the WordArt's text, changing the WordArt's style and shape, and more. Work with the settings here as needed to finish designing and positioning the WordArt object.

Using the Design Gallery

Publications often include special elements not typically found in ordinary business documents. For example, a new product brochure might include a coupon. A flyer might need phone number tear-off tabs along the bottom. A newsletter might need a masthead with certain information or a volunteer sign-up form. Building these types of elements from scratch by layering graphics, text boxes, and borders could be time consuming, but you don't have to bother. Instead, you can add any of a number of predesigned items from the Design Gallery to your publication and then customize the item with your own text.

Follow these steps to add a Design Gallery object to a publication:

1. **Display the page in the publication on which you'd like to insert the Design Gallery object.** Clicking a page icon in the status bar takes you there.
2. **Click the Design Gallery Object button on the Objects toolbar, or select Insert ➪ Design Gallery Object.** The Design Gallery window opens.
3. **Click a choice in the list of categories at the left.** The available objects in that category appear in the preview area in the center of the dialog box, as shown in Figure 32-9. If needed, drag the zoom slider at the bottom of the window to increase the preview size so that you can see more object details.

FIGURE 32-9

The Design Gallery has done the design work for you, offering dozens of objects you can insert into your publications.

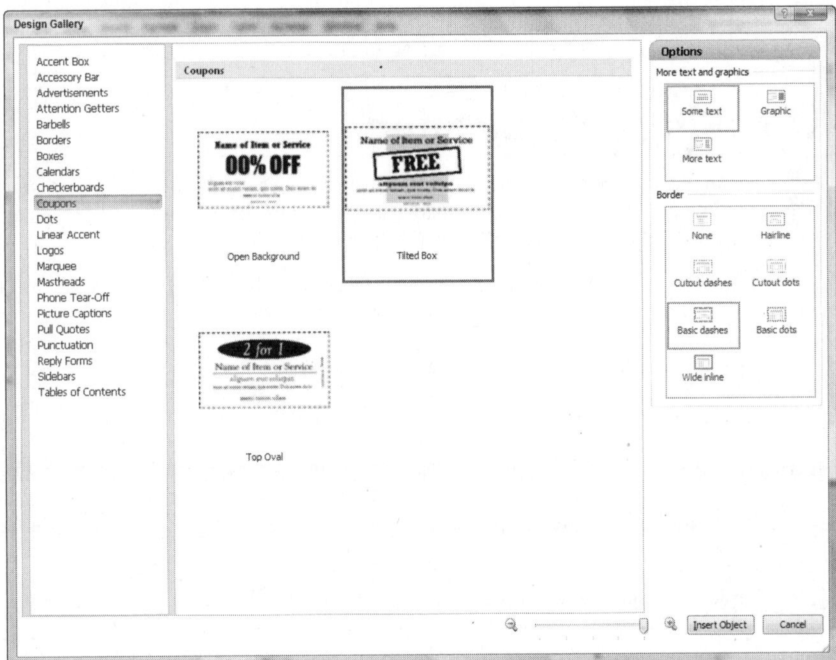

4. **Click the desired object.**
5. **Choose any Options to adjust the object from the Options pane at the right if it appears.** For example, Figure 32-9 shows that you can change the amount of text and graphics as well as the border style for a coupon Design Gallery object.
6. **Click Insert Object.** The object appears on the publication page, where you can move and resize it, and update it with your own text if required. Figure 32-10 shows an example coupon Design Gallery Object.

FIGURE 32-10

Inspire your readers to action with Design Gallery objects.

Updating a Publication

Not only can you change settings for the text and objects in a publication, you also can make a number of changes to upgrade the publication itself. You can change the background fill for the pages, change how the page information is arranged, and choose another color scheme.

To make some publication-wide design changes, work with the Format Publication task pane. To make other publication-wide changes, use Format menu commands.

Changing the background

Many publication designs purposely do not have a background color. That's because for years few computer printers could print *bleeds* — in which color prints all the way to the edge of the page. Some color printers now can handle bleeds. If that applies in your case or if you're sending the publication for commercial printing (or you don't really care if your background doesn't print all the way to the edges of the page), you can apply a background to your publication.

CAUTION **Printing a bleed can add significantly to your costs because the printer may have to trim away more paper stock around the edges of each page. Be sure you know whether your print shop charges more for bleeds.**

To apply or remove a background, select Format ➪ Background. The Background task pane appears. You can display choices in a particular color range by clicking a color in the Apply a Background choices at the top of the task pane (Figure 32-11). Then click a specific background choice to apply in the More Colors list below. The publication immediately previews the background choice. To remove any applied background, click the white box with the X in it in the upper-left corner of the More Colors list.

Changing Page Options

The Page Options available in the Format Publication task pane vary depending on the selected publication. For a newsletter, for example, you might be able to specify the number of Columns per page or add one of the Suggested Objects to the page.

To change the options for a publication page, first display the page to change. Then display the Format Publication task pane by clicking the name at the top of the task pane and then clicking Format Publication in the menu or by selecting Format ➪ Format Publication. Click the Pages Options choice at the top of the task pane and then use the choices that appear (Figure 32-12) to make the desired changes to the page.

FIGURE 32-11

Pump up your pages with a background color or pattern.

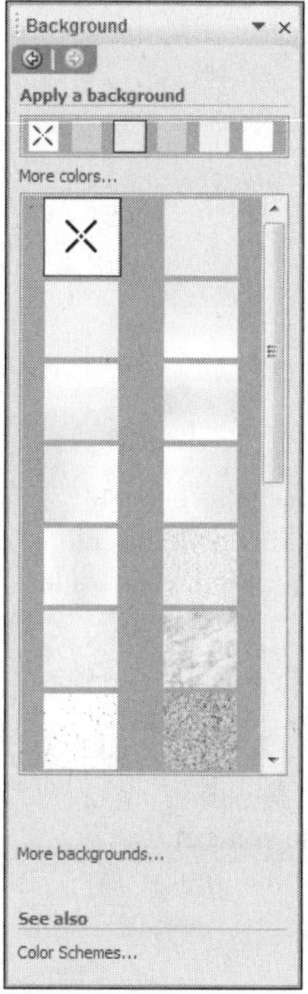

FIGURE 32-12

Click Page Options in the Format Publication task pane to see your choices for working with page elements.

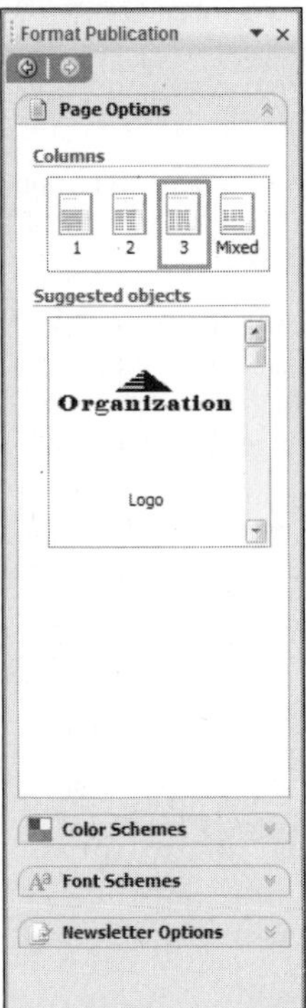

Changing colors

In addition to an overall font scheme, every publication has an overall *color scheme*. The color scheme defines a main color and several accent colors for use throughout the publication. Sticking with the color scheme's colors for the text and objects in the publication helps to ensure that the publication retains coherence in its design.

To choose another color scheme for your publication, go to the Format Publication task pane by clicking the name at the top of the task pane and then clicking Format Publication in the menu or by selecting Format ➪ Format Publication. Click the Color Schemes choice in the task pane to display the available color schemes, as shown in Figure 32-13. Click the desired color scheme. When you do so, Publisher automatically replaces the previous main and accent colors with those from the new scheme, so you can see the impact of the change on your publication. You can continue applying other color schemes until you've found one that suits your needs.

FIGURE 32-13

Bring new colors into your publication by choosing another color scheme here.

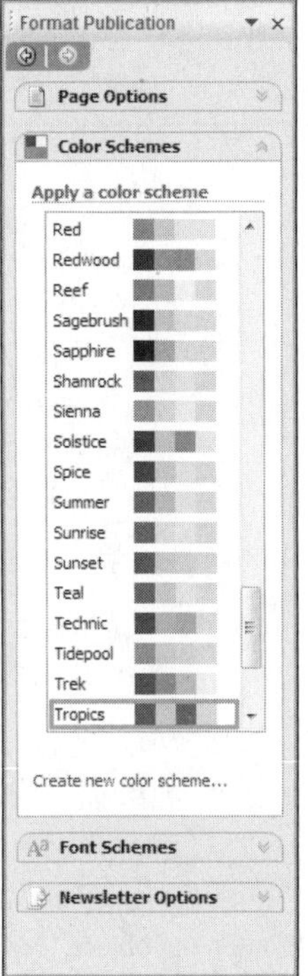

Fine-Tuning Objects

If you can't find just the right Design Gallery object or other object settings to meet your needs, or if you just like noodling around with design possibilities in your publications, you may find yourself creating and positioning many objects. Although you can drag with the mouse and use tools such as the Measurement toolbar to help you size and position objects, other shortcuts might be more appropriate in some cases. This section shows you some more tricks — aligning and grouping objects, and wrapping and hyphenating text.

Aligning objects

Aligning objects can be a little frustrating, especially if you have a finicky mouse or are working with a notebook touchpad to drag objects. You can use the arrow keys to move a selected object, but each press of a key merely *nudges* the object a very small distance in the indicated direction. Plus, if you're trying to do something trickier such as align multiple selected objects, you have no precise way to do it with the mouse.

Use the commands on the Arrange ➪ Align or Distribute submenu instead of the mouse to align multiple selected objects. After you Shift+click to select the desired objects, select one of the commands on that submenu to align the objects' left, center, and right horizontal dimensions or top, middle, or bottom vertical dimensions. You also can use the Distribute Horizontally or Distribute Vertically choice to space the objects equally.

Figure 32-14 shows an example of how you can use the Arrange ➪ Align or Distribute submenu commands to work with publication objects. After selecting both objects, both the Arrange ➪ Align or Distribute ➪ Align Center and Arrange ➪ Align or Distribute ➪ Align Middle commands were selected. These commands placed the center point of the puppy clip art image right over the center point of the heart AutoShape.

FIGURE 32-14

Snap objects into position using alignment commands.

TIP To control how an object layers when positioned with other objects, right-click the object, point to the Order command, and click one of the choices in the submenu that appears. For example, the Bring to Front command positions the selected object in front of (on top of) other stacked objects.

Grouping objects

After you've placed multiple objects into the position you want, such as in the example in Figure 32-14, you should group the objects so that you can move them around as a unit without accidentally misaligning one or more of them. When you use Shift+click to select multiple objects, the Group Objects button shown in Figure 32-15 appears. Click that button to group the objects, or select Arrange ➪ Group (Ctrl+Shift+G). To ungroup a selected group, click the Ungroup Objects button that appears, or select Arrange ➪ Ungroup (Ctrl+Shift+G).

Note that you can still select an individual object within a group, such as to work with the object's formatting settings. First click the group and then click the individual object. Selection handles with x marks in them appear around the selected object within the group.

FIGURE 32-15

Click the Group Objects button to make the selected objects stick together as a single unit.

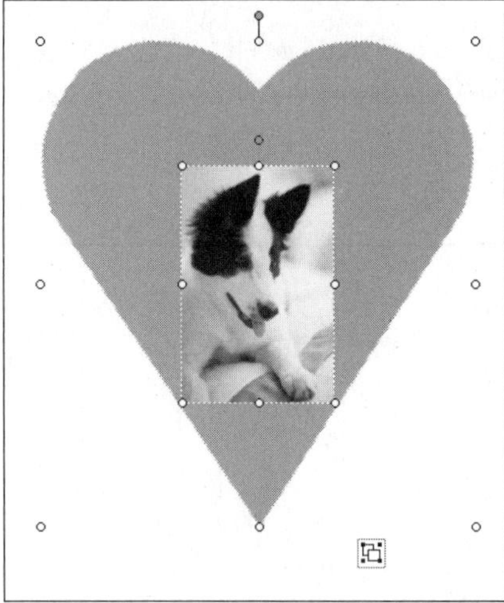

Wrapping and hyphenating text

Your text will read much better if you make sure that you've chosen the right text-wrapping settings for objects and have chosen whether to use hyphenation in a story.

You can apply one of several text-wrapping styles to objects, typically shapes or picture objects that you want to appear within the text. Wrapping style options include Square, Tight, Through, Top and Bottom, and None. For example, Figure 32-16 illustrates the Tight wrapping style used for a grouped object. To choose a wrapping setting, right-click the picture or object and then click Format Picture or Format Object. Click the Layout tab in the dialog box that appears, click a choice in the Wrapping Style area, and then click OK.

FIGURE 32-16

The right wrapping setting makes sure that text remains readable when it flows around the object.

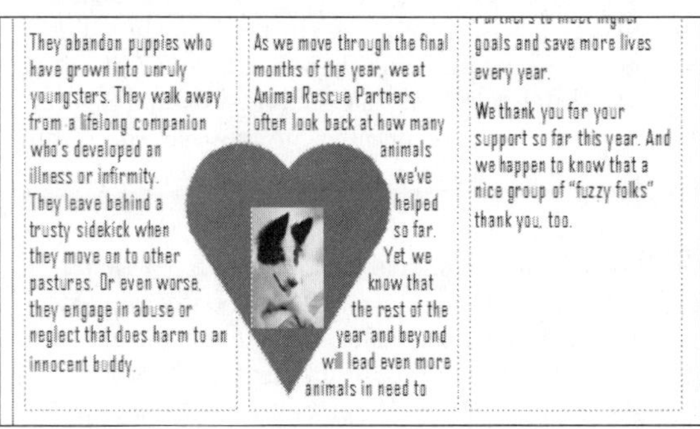

If you're wrapping text tightly around an object or have a narrow textbox with large text, Publisher may by default hyphenate words to try to fill the space as well as possible. Many readers prefer not to see hyphens because they become tiring to see in longer stories. You can use these steps to turn the automatic hyphenation off in any story:

1. **Click in the story for which you'd like to change hyphenation settings.**
2. **Select Tools ⇨ Language ⇨ Hyphenation (Ctrl+Shift+H).** The Hyphenation dialog box shown in Figure 32-17 opens.

FIGURE 32-17

Control hyphenation in any story by using this dialog box.

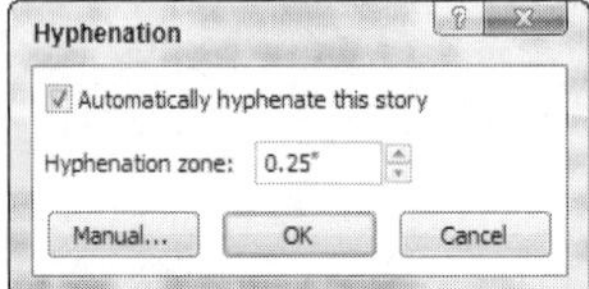

3. **Click the Automatically Hyphenate This Story checkbox to clear the check.**
4. **Click OK.** Publisher removes the hyphenation from the story you selected in Step 1.

Working with Pages

Many publications you create will be multipage documents, either to hold all the information that you want to present, as for a newsletter, or to come out in the proper format when folded, as for a greeting card. You can add any number of pages as needed to any publication.

Adding pages

The status area at the bottom of Publisher shows a numbered icon for each page in the publication. To go to another page, just click the icon for that page at the bottom. You can insert more pages as needed to expand the contents of the publication.

If you want to insert a new page before or after a particular page that's already in the publication, click the icon for that page in the status area. Then select Insert ⇨ Page (Ctrl+Shift+N). The Insert dialog box that appears varies depending on the type of publication you're working in. For example, when you're inserting a page in a file that was created as a blank publication, the dialog box looks like the one shown in Figure 32-18. Specify how many pages to insert and whether to insert before or after the current page; choose any other options you want and then click OK. Publisher will choose the appropriate left-hand or right-hand layout for the inserted page.

If you are inserting a page in a file that was based on a more complicated template, such as a newsletter, Publisher assumes that you want to insert pages consistent with the layout of the existing pages and may even assume that you want to insert a pair of facing pages, so it displays a dialog box like the one in Figure 32-19. You can use either drop-down list at the top of the dialog box to choose another type of page, as shown for Right-Hand Page at the top of Figure 32-19, or you can click the More button to display the Insert Page dialog box shown in Figure 32-18. After you make your choice, click OK to insert the page(s).

FIGURE 32-18

If you started with a blank publication, Publisher assumes that you want to insert more blank pages.

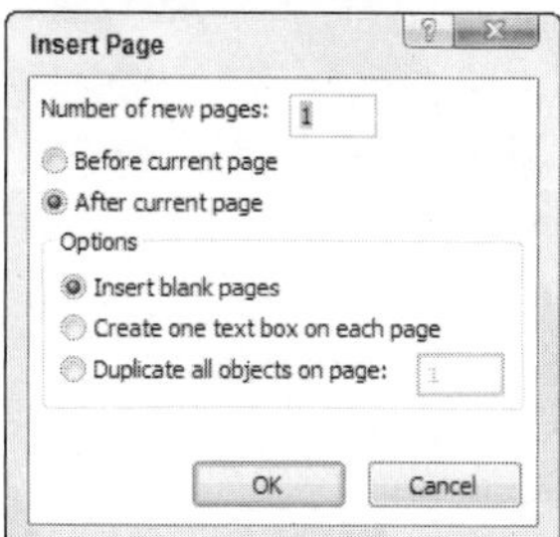

FIGURE 32-19

In other types of publications, Publisher assumes that you want to insert pages that follow the template design.

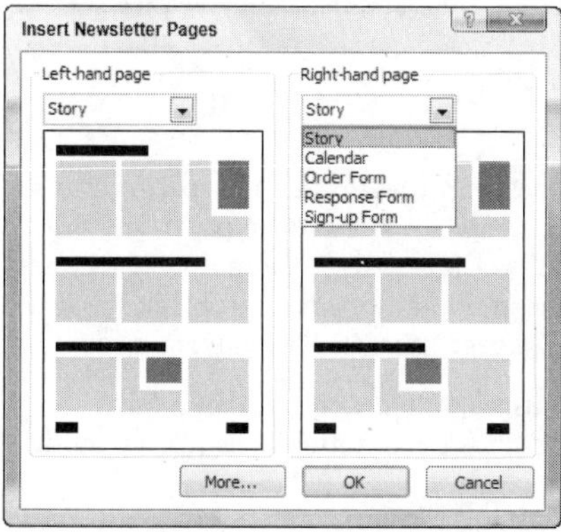

To create an exact duplicate of the current page, use the Insert ➪ Duplicate Page command (Ctrl+Shift+U).

To delete a page, right-click its icon in the status bar and then click Delete Page in the shortcut menu.

Numbering pages

As a courtesy to your readers, you should always include page numbers for multipage documents. Including page numbers has the added benefit of giving anyone printing the document a heads-up about the order in which to place the pages. The process for adding page numbers places them in the header or footer area (above or below the rest of the text) in the position that you specify.

Select Insert ➪ Page Numbers to open the Page Numbers dialog box (Figure 32-20). Make a choice from the Position drop-down list to determine whether to place the page numbers in the header or footer. Choose the horizontal position you want for the page numbers from the Alignment drop-down list, and check or clear the Show Page Number on First Page checkbox as needed to determine whether a page number appears for Page 1. Then click OK to finish adding the page numbers.

FIGURE 32-20

You can add page numbers in the header or footer and choose their alignment.

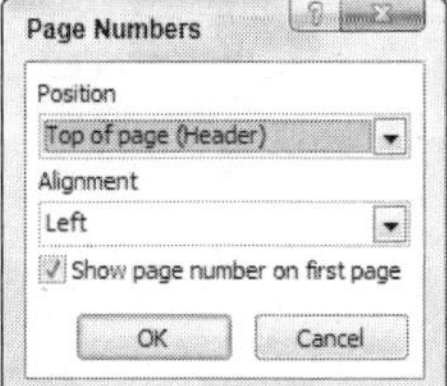

Checking and Printing

Printing your publication can be a thrilling moment — or an absolute dud if you discover that you've missed something and have to go back and fix it. So before you print, take the time to use the Design Checker. After that, it's off to the printer!

Always remember to save your final changes to the publication before printing by pressing Ctrl+S or selecting File ➪ Save.

Using the Design Checker

Publisher's Design Checker checks a publication for boo-boos such as empty text boxes and spacing errors. Running the Design Checker so that you can uncover and fix these errors saves you toner, paper, and printing time. Among the problems Design Checker looks for are text in overflow areas, disproportional pictures, empty frames, covered objects, objects partially off the page, objects in nonprinting regions, blank space at the top of the page, spacing between sentences, and (for Web sites) a page unreachable by hyperlinks.

Select Tools ➪ Design Checker to run the design check. When it finishes, results appear in the Design Checker task pane, as shown in Figure 32-21. To correct each error, click the error in the list. Publisher displays the location where the error occurs so that you can correct it.

It's also not a bad idea to run a Spelling check before printing. Publisher's Spelling check works just like the ones in other Office applications, so just press F7 to start the process.

If you plan to have the document commercially printed, click the Run Commercial Printing Checks checkbox at the top of the Design Checker task pane to check that option. The Design Checker then immediately displays any errors that might cause a problem at a commercial printer, such as the publication's being in the wrong color mode. When you click this type of error, a drop-down arrow appears beside it. Click that error to display a drop-down menu with options for correcting or learning more about the error.

Printing

When you're satisfied that your publication is as near to perfect as you can make it, you're ready to print. Printing is pretty much the same as in any Office application — choose File ➪ Print and then select a printer, a range of pages to print, and the number of copies you want.

FIGURE 32-21

D'oh! Design Checker caught a number of errors in this publication.

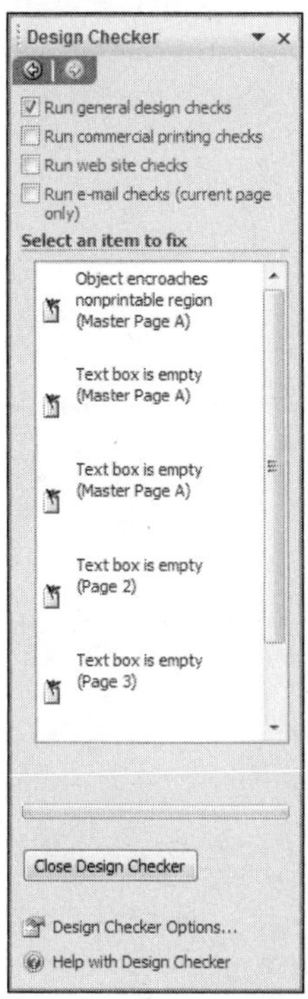

The Printer Details tab of the Print dialog box contains an important button, Advanced Printer Setup, which you need to know about. Clicking it opens a dialog box (Figure 32-22) with specialized printing settings, including the following:

- What resolution to use when printing linked graphics.
- Whether to allow the printer to substitute its own fonts for those used in the publication.
- Whether to allow bleeds (images that extend to the edge of the paper). Because most printers won't print right to the edge, you have to make your page size slightly smaller than your paper size and then trim the paper to achieve this effect.
- Options for creating a publication that can be turned into the separations needed for color printing on a printing press at a commercial printer. You can choose the output (such as Composite Grayscale, Composite CMYK, Composite RGB, or Separations), the resolution, and more. You'll probably want to consult with your printer before selecting any options here.

After you've chosen all the Advanced Printer Setup choices, click OK and then Print to send the publication to your printer.

WARNING **Publisher's Standard toolbar does offer a Print button for printing the publication. However, that button acts more like a quick print button; clicking the button sends the print job directly to the last-used printer without giving you the opportunity to change print settings.**

FIGURE 32-22

The settings here are important for commercial printing and advanced print jobs of your own.

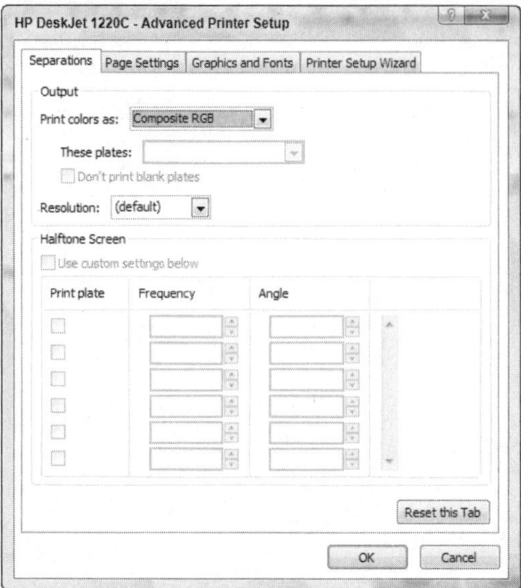

Preparing for Outside Printing

Sometimes you want to be able to send your publication to a print shop for printing on a professional press rather than on your own printer. Publisher can help you prepare your files for that purpose.

Give Your Printer and Yourself a Break

Small print shops labor every day to deal with errors in Publisher files, from wrong output colors to unneeded spot colors to other poor document design and setup problems. If you're unwilling or unable to take the time to learn about and fix these types of issues, please be willing to pay your service bureau a fair fee for fixing them. The following are always good practices for working with a print shop to get your publication file printed right:

- Know and adhere to the print shop's requirements.
- If you have questions but want to do the work yourself, consult Publisher's extensive help on this subject and ask the printer for tips.
- Most print shops will review a file for problems before printing it. Sending your file for such an advanced check-up provides time to fix problems.
- Be professional. A professional admits to errors and is willing to learn and change. If you keep submitting bad files to the print shop, you'll keep getting poorly printed materials.

Choose File ➪ Pack and Go ➪ Take to a Commercial Printing Service. (The other option here, Take to Another Computer, can split your file over multiple disks, embed necessary fonts, and include linked graphics, making it easy for you or someone else to work on your publication on another computer.) Choosing File ➪ Pack and Go ➪ Take to a Commercial Printing Service opens a wizard that takes you step by step through the process of preparing your files for outside printing, including embedding TrueType fonts, including linked graphics, creating links for embedded graphics, compressing your publication, and adding an unpacking a utility for uncompressing it when it gets to its destination.

NOTE **Some printers now prefer that you submit your publication as a PDF file. Microsoft offers a free add-in that you can download and install to enable Publisher to create PDF files. Search Publisher help for "PDF" to learn more about PDF files and getting the PDF add-in.**

Summary

This final *Office 2007 Bible* chapter about Microsoft Publisher gave you the information you need to improve the contents and design for the publication, add missing elements, and finalize and print the publication. The chapter showed you how to use special effects such as BorderArt, drop caps, and WordArt, how to add a Design Gallery object, and how to change overall page and publication design settings such as the color scheme. You learned how to better align objects and wrap text around them, as well as how to group them. You worked with pages and page numbering before seeing how to check the design and print. Finally, the chapter introduced you to good practices for preparing a publication for commercial printing.

Part VII

Tracking Detailed Data with Access

IN THIS PART

Chapter 33

An Introduction to Database Development

In this chapter, you learn the concepts and terminology of databases and how to design the tables that your forms and reports will use. Finally, you build the actual tables used by this book's Access Auto Auctions example database.

The fundamental concept underlying Access databases is that data is stored in tables. Tables are comprised of rows and columns of data, much like an Excel worksheet. Each table represents a single entity, such as a person or product.

As you work with Access, you'll spend considerable time designing and refining the tables in your Access applications. Table design and implementation are two characteristics that distinguish database development from most other activities you may pursue.

After you understand the basic concepts and terminology, the next important lesson to learn is good database design. Without a good design, you constantly rework your tables, and you may not be able to extract the information you want from your database. Throughout this section, you learn how to use the basic components of Access applications, including queries, forms, and reports. You also learn how to design and implement each of these objects. The Access Auto Auctions case study provides invented examples, but the concepts are not fictitious.

This chapter is not easy to understand; some of its concepts are complex. If your goal is to get right into Access, you may want to skip to Chapter 36 and read about the process of building tables. If you're fairly familiar with Access but new to designing and creating tables, you may want to read this chapter before starting to create tables.

CROSS-REF To jump right into using Access, skip to Chapter 36.

IN THIS CHAPTER

- **Understanding what a database is**
- **Examining the differences between databases, tables, records, fields, and values**
- **Learning why multiple tables are used in a database**
- **Looking at database objects**
- **Learning a five-step design method**
- **Creating the overall design of a database system**
- **Designing database tables and relationships**
- **Designing input forms**
- **Designing menus**

The Database Terminology of Access

Before examining the actual table examples in this section, it's a good idea to have a firm understanding of the terminology that is used when working with databases — especially Access databases. Microsoft Access follows traditional database terminology. The terms *database, table, record, field,* and *value* indicate a hierarchy from largest to smallest.

Databases

Generally, the word *database* is a computer term for a collection of information concerning a certain topic or business application. Databases help you organize this related information in a logical fashion for easy access and retrieval.

Databases aren't only for computers. There are also manual databases; we simply refer to these as *manual filing systems* or *manual database systems.* These filing systems usually consist of people's names, papers, folders, and filing cabinets — paper is the key to a manual database system. In a real manual database system, you probably have in/out baskets and some type of formal filing method. You access information manually by opening a file cabinet, taking out a file folder, and finding the correct piece of paper. You use paper forms for input, perhaps by using a typewriter. You find information by manually sorting the papers or by copying information from many papers to another piece of paper (or even into an Excel spreadsheet). You may use a spreadsheet or calculator to analyze the data or display it in new and interesting ways.

An Access database is nothing more than an automated version of the filing and retrieval functions of a paper filing system. Access databases store information in a carefully defined structure. Access tables store data in a variety of forms, from simple lines of text (such as name and address) to complex data such as pictures, sounds, or video images. Storing data in a precise, known format enables a database management system (DBMS) like Access to turn data into useful information.

Tables serve as the primary data repository in an Access database. Queries, forms, and reports provide access to the data, enabling a user to add or extract data, and presenting the data in useful ways. Most developers add macros or Visual Basic for Applications (VBA) code to forms and reports to make their applications easier to use.

A relational database management system (RDBMS), such as Access, stores data in related tables. For instance, a table containing employee data (names and addresses) may be related to a table containing payroll data (pay date, pay amount, and check number). Queries allow the user to ask complex questions (such as "What is the sum of all paychecks issued to Jane Doe in 2007?") from these related tables, with the answers displayed as onscreen forms and printed reports.

In Access, a *database* is the overall container for the data and associated objects. It is more than the collection of tables, however — a database includes many types of objects, including queries, forms, reports, macros, and code modules.

Access works a single database at a time. As you open Access, a single database is presented for you to use. You may open several copies of Access at the same time and simultaneously work with more than one database.

Many Access databases contain hundreds, or even thousands, of tables, forms, queries, reports, macros, and modules. With a few exceptions, all of the objects in an Access 2007 database reside within a single file with an extension of `accdb`, `.accde`, or `.adp`.

The `.adp` file format is a special database format used by Access to act as a front end to work with SQL Server data.

Tables

A table is just a container for raw information (called *data*), similar to a folder in a manual filing system. Each table in an Access database contains information about a single entity, such as a person or product, and the data is organized into rows and columns.

In the section titled "A Five-Step Design Method," later in this chapter, you learn a successful technique for planning Access tables. In Chapter 36, you learn some of the very important rules governing relational table design and how to incorporate those rules into your Access databases. These rules and guidelines ensure your applications perform with the very best performance while protecting the integrity of the data contained within your tables.

In fact, it is very important that you begin to think of the objects managed by your applications in abstract terms. Because each Access table defines an entity, you must learn to think of the table *as* the entity. As you design and build Access databases, or even when working with an existing application, you must think of how the tables and other database objects represent the physical entities managed by your database.

After you create a table, you view the table in a spreadsheet-like form, called a *datasheet,* comprising rows and columns (known as *records* and *fields,* respectively — see the following section, "Records and fields"). Figure 33-1 shows the datasheet view of the Contacts table in the Access Auto Auction application.

FIGURE 33-1

A table displayed as a datasheet.

tblContacts : Table

Contact ID	Contact Type	First Name	Last Name	Company	Address	City	
1	Buyer	John	Jones	Nopa Auto Par	11253 Main St	Springfield	MA
2	Seller	Hank	Masters	Jiffy Auto Sale	623 Field Road	Springfield	MO
3	Both	Larry	Minkler	All Start Autos	971 E Main St	Detroit	MI
11	Both	Joe	Hammerman	Columbia Chev	105 Main Stree	Columbia	MA
12	Buyer	Cary	James	James Auto Pa	59 South Stree	Portland	CT
13	Buyer	Mark	Uno	Fillion Sales Ar	8908 North Pa	South Windsor	CT
14	Buyer	Brandon	Aley	Tip Top Chevy	1916 Erickson	Fairbanks	MA
15	Both	Michael	Dennis	Newbury Auto	75 Main Street	Bedford	NY
16	Both	Mark	Martin	Peekskill Sales	51 Tolland Tnp	Lake Peekskill	NY
17	Both	Karl	Johnson	KJ Auto Repair	350 Broadway	Rye	NY
18	Both	William	Gleason	R & G Monda Ir	196 East Street	Derby	CT
19	Both	Alex	Tomaso	Tires National	46 School Stre	Oneco	CT
20	Both	Karla	Hayes	Hayes Auction	54 E Center Str	Granby	CT
21	Seller	Teresa	Aikins	Middletown A	100 Northfield	Middletown	CT
22	Both	John	Marino	Bill Thomas Sal	986 Buckingha	Brewster	NY
23	Both	Donald	Peterson	Yantic Auto Pa	8 Oak Street	Yantic	CT
24	Seller	Dennie	Parkson	ACC Car Sales	963 New Engla	Peekskill	NY
25	Buyer	Ann	Bond	A-1 Auto Sales	54 South Main	Colchester	CT
26	Seller	Joe	Crook	Main Street Us	61 North Main	Windsor	CT
27	Both	Jeffrey	Lan	LAN Trucking	108 Thomas Rd	North Branch	NJ
28	Buyer	Matt	Smith	ABC Trucking	7 Depot Rd	Stratford	CT
29	Both	David	Smith	Fordman Color	123 Federal St	Quincy	MA
30	Both	Cindy	Casey	Circle Auto Sal	123 South Stre	Newington	NH
31	Both	Karen	Bailey	Sammy Fordm	59 West Churc	Westbourgh	MA
32	Both	Alvin	Schindler	Pine Plains RM	Rt 9	Pine Plains	NY

Record: 5 of 58 No Filter Search

The Contacts table represents people who work with the Auto Auction. Notice how the table is divided into horizontal (left-to-right) rows, and vertical (top-to-bottom) columns of data. Each row (or record) defines a single contact, while each column (or field) represents one type of information known about a contact entity.

For instance, the top row in tblContacts contains data describing John Jones, including his first name and last name, his address, and the company he works for. Each bit of information describing Mr. Jones is a field (`FirstName`, `LastName`, `Address`, `Company`, and so on). Fields are combined to form a record, and records are grouped to build the table.

Each field in an Access table includes many properties that specify the type of data contained within the field, and how Access should handle the field's data. These properties include the name of the field (`LastName`) and the type of data in the field (`Text`). A field may include other properties as well. For instance, the Size property tells Access how many characters to allow for a person's last name. (You learn much more about fields and field properties in Chapter 36.)

Records and fields

As Figure 33-1 shows, the datasheet is divided into rows (called *records*) and columns (called *fields*), with the first row (the heading on top of each column) containing the names of the fields in the database. Each row is a single record containing fields that are related to that record. In a manual system, the rows are individual forms (sheets of paper), and the fields are equivalent to the blank areas on a printed form that you fill in.

Values

At the intersection of a row (record) and a column (field) is a *value* — the actual data element. For example, John, the name in the first record, represents one data value. You may have a couple questions, such as: What makes this row different from other rows in the table? Is it possible to have another John Jones in the same table? If there is more than one John Jones, how does the database tell them apart?

Relational Databases

Microsoft Access is a relational database development system. Access data is stored in related tables, where data in one table (such as customers) is related to data in another table (such as orders). Access maintains the relationships between related tables, making it easy to extract a customer and all of the customer's orders, without losing any data or pulling order records not owned by the customer.

Working with multiple tables

Multiple tables simplify data entry and reporting by decreasing the input of redundant data. By defining two tables for an application that uses customer information, for example, you don't need to store the customer's name and address every time the customer purchases an item.

After you've created the tables, they need to be related to each other. For example, if you have a Contacts table and a Sales table, you must relate the Contacts table to the Sales table in order to see all the sales records for a Contact. If you had only one table, you would have to repeat the Contact name and address for each sale record. Two tables let you look up information in the Contact table for each sale by using the related fields Contact ID (in Contacts) and Buyer ID (in Sales). This way, when a customer changes address, for example, the address changes only in one record in the Contact table; when the Sales information is on-screen, the correct contact address is always visible.

Separating data into multiple tables within a database makes the system easier to maintain because all records of a given type are within the same table. By taking the time to segment data properly into multiple tables, you experience a significant reduction in design and work time. This process is known as *normalization*. (You can read about normalization in Chapter 36.)

Later in this chapter in the section titled "A Five-Step Design Method," you have the opportunity to work through a case study for the Access Auto Auctions that consists of five tables.

Knowing why you should create multiple tables

The prospect of creating multiple tables always intimidates beginning database users. Most often, they want to create one huge table that contains all of the information they need — in this case, a Customer table with all the sales performed by the customer and all the items sold or bought for each customer.

So, they create a single table containing a lot of fields, including fields for customer information (contact), sales information (date of sale, salesperson, amount paid, discounts, and so on), and the product information (quantity sold, product description, individual prices, and so on) for each sale. Such a table quickly grows to an unmanageable number of fields and continues growing as new items are added.

As you can see, the table design begins to take on a life of its own. After you've created the single table, it becomes even more difficult to maintain. You begin to realize that you have to input the customer information for every sale a customer makes (repeating the information over and over). The same is true for the items purchased for each sale, which is multiple items for each sale (thus, duplicating information again). This makes the system more inefficient and prone to data-entry mistakes. The information stored in the table becomes inefficiently maintained — many fields may not be appropriate for each record, and the table ends up with a lot of empty fields.

It's important to create tables that hold the minimum of information while still making the system easy to use and flexible enough to grow. To accomplish this, you need to consider making more than one table, with each table containing records with fields that are related only to the focus of that table. Then, after you create the tables, you link them so that you're able to glean useful information from them. Although this process sounds extremely complex, the actual implementation is relatively easy. Again, this process of creating multiple tables from a single table is known as *normalization* (or normalizing your tables).

Access Database Objects and Views

If you're new to databases (or even if you're an experienced database user), you need to understand some key concepts before starting to build Access databases. The Access database contains seven types of top-level objects, which consist of the data and tools that you need to use Access:

- **Table:** Holds the actual data
- **Query:** Searches for, sorts, and retrieves specific data
- **Form:** Lets you enter and display data in a customized format
- **Report:** Displays and prints formatted data
- **Pages:** Publishes data to a corporate intranet
- **Macro:** Automates tasks without programming
- **Module:** Contains programs written in the Visual Basic for Applications (VBA) programming language

Datasheets

Datasheets are one of the many ways by which you can view data in Access. Although not a database object, a datasheet displays a list of records from a table in a format similar to an accounting spreadsheet or Excel worksheet. A datasheet displays data as a series of rows and columns (comparable to an Excel spreadsheet). A datasheet displays a table's information in its raw form. The datasheet view is the default mode for displaying all fields for all records.

You scroll through the datasheet using the directional keys on your keyboard. You can also display related records in other tables while in a datasheet. In addition, you can make changes to the displayed data.

Use caution when making changes or allowing a user to modify data in datasheet format. When a datasheet record is updated, the data in the underlying table is permanently changed.

Queries

Queries extract information from a database. A query selects and defines a group of records that fulfill a certain condition. Many forms and most reports are based on queries that pre-filter data before it is displayed. Queries are often called from VBA procedures to change, add, or delete database records.

An example of a query is when a person at the Auto Sales office tells the database, "Show me all customers, in alphabetical order by name, who live in Massachusetts and bought something over the past six months, and display them sorted by Customer name," or "Show me all customers who bought cars for a value of $35,000 or more for the past six months and display them sorted by customer name and then by value of the car."

Instead of asking the question in English words, the person uses the query by example (QBE) method. When you enter instructions into the QBE Design window, the query translates the instructions into Structured Query Language (SQL) and retrieves the desired data. Chapter 38 discusses the QBE Design window and building queries.

In the first example, the query first combines data from both the Sales and Contact tables, using the related field Contact ID (the common link between the tables). Next, it retrieves the first name, last name, and any other data you want to see. Access then filters the records, selecting only those in which the value of the sales date is within six months of the current date. The query sorts the resulting records first by contact's last and first names. Finally, the records appear onscreen in a datasheet.

A similar action takes place for the second example — using sales, contacts, invoice items, and products and the criteria applied to the search is where the `Description` field has a car bought whose value in the `Price` field is greater than or equal to $35,000.

After you run a query, the resulting set of records may be used in a form that is displayed onscreen or printed in a report. In this way, user access is limited to the data that meets the criteria in the returned records.

Data-entry and display forms

Data-entry forms help users get information into a database table quickly, easily, and accurately. Data-entry and display forms provide a more structured view of the data than what a datasheet provides. From this structured view, database records can be viewed, added, changed, or deleted. Entering data through the data-entry forms is the most common way to get the data into the database table.

Data-entry forms restrict access to certain fields within the table. Forms also check the validity of your data before it is added to the database table.

Most users prefer to enter information into data-entry forms rather than datasheet views of tables. Data-entry forms often resemble familiar paper documents and can aid the user with data-entry tasks. Forms make data entry self-explanatory by guiding the user through the fields of the table being updated.

Display-only screens and forms are solely for inquiry purposes. These forms allow for the selective display of certain fields within a given table. Displaying some fields and not others means that you can limit a user's access to sensitive data while allowing inquiry into other fields.

Reports

Reports present your data in printed format. Access supports several different types of reports. A report may list all records in a given table (such as a customer table) or may list only the records meeting a certain criterion, such as all customers living in the State of Washington. You do this by basing the report on a query that selects only the records needed by the report.

Your reports can combine multiple tables to present complex relationships among different sets of data. An example is printing an invoice. You access the customer table to obtain the customer's name and address (and other relevant data) and related records in the sales table to print the individual line-item information for the products ordered. You then instruct Access to calculate the totals and print them in a specific format on the form. Additionally, you can have Access output records into an *invoice report,* a printed document that summarizes the invoice.

TIP **When you design your database tables, keep in mind all the types of information that you want to print. Doing so ensures that the information you require in your various reports is available from within your database tables.**

Designing the system's objects

To create database objects, such as tables, forms, and reports, you first complete a series of tasks known as *design.* The better your design is, the better your application will be. The more you think through your design, the faster you can complete any system. The design process is not some necessary evil, nor is its intent to produce voluminous amounts of documentation. The sole intent of designing an object is to produce a clear-cut path to follow as you implement it.

A Five-Step Design Method

Figure 33-2 is a version of the design method that is modified especially for use with Access. This is a top-down approach, starting with the overall system design and ending with the forms design, and it consists of five steps.

These five design steps, along with the database system illustrated by the examples in this book, teach a great deal about Access and provide a great foundation for creating database applications — including tables, queries, forms, data pages, reports, macros, and simple VBA (Visual Basic for Applications) modules.

The time you spend on each step depends entirely on the circumstances of the database you're building. For example, sometimes the users give you an example of a report they want printed from their Access database, and the sources of data on the report are so obvious that designing the report takes a few minutes. Other times, particularly when the users' requirements are complex, or the business processes supported by the application require a great deal of research, you may spend many days on Step 1.

As you read through each step of the design process, *always* look at the design in terms of outputs and inputs. Although you see actual components of the system (cars, buyers, sellers, and transactions), remember that the focus of this chapter is how to design each step. As you watch the Access Auto Auctions system being designed, pay attention to the design process, not the actual system.

FIGURE 33-2

The five-step design flowchart. This design methodology is particularly well-suited for Access databases.

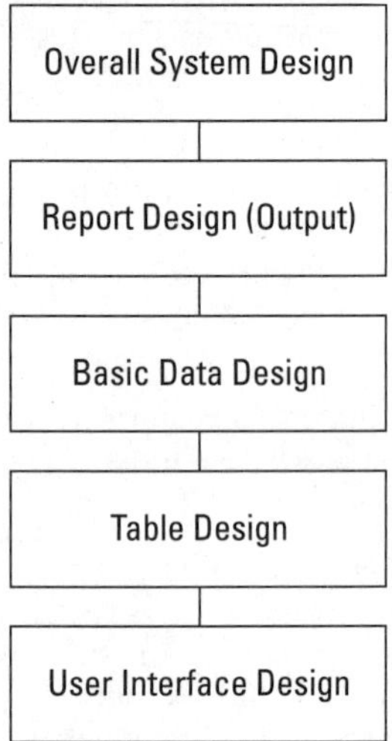

Step 1: The overall design — from concept to reality

All software developers face similar problems, the first of which is determining how to meet the needs of the end user. It's important to understand the overall requirements before zeroing in on the details.

The five-step design method shown in Figure 33-2 helps you to create the system that you need, at an affordable price (measured in time or dollars). The Access Auto Auctions database, for example, allows the client to sell items (vehicles and parts) to customers. The Access Auto Auctions database automates the following tasks:

- Entering and maintaining contact information for customers and sellers (name, address, and financial history)
- Entering and maintaining sales information (sales date; payment method; total amount, including tax; buyer ID; and other fields)
- Entering and maintaining sales line item information (details of items actually purchased)
- Viewing information from all the tables (sales, contacts, sales line items purchased, and payment information)
- Asking all types of questions about the information in the database
- Producing a current contacts directory
- Producing a monthly invoice report
- Producing a customer sales history
- Producing mailing labels and mail-merge reports

These nine tasks that the Access Auto Auctions automates have been expressed by the client. You may need to consider other tasks as you start the design process.

Most of the information that is necessary to build the system comes from the eventual users. This means that you need to sit down with them and learn how the existing process works. To accomplish this you need to do a thorough *needs analysis* of the existing system and how you might automate it.

One way to accomplish this is to prepare a series of questions that give insight to the client's business and how the client uses his data. For example, when considering automating an auto auction business, you may consider asking these questions:

- What reports and forms are currently used?
- How are sales, customer, contacts, and other records currently stored?
- How are billings processed?

As you ask these questions and others, the client will probably remember other things about his business that you should know.

A walkthrough of the existing process is also necessary to get a "feel" for the business. Most likely, you'll have to go back several times to observe the existing process and how the employees work.

When you prepare to follow the remaining steps, keep the client involved — let him know what you're doing and ask for his input as to what you want to accomplish, making sure it is within the scope of his needs.

Step 2: Report design

Although it may seem odd to start with reports, in many cases users are more interested in the printed output from a database than they are in any other aspect of the application. Reports often include virtually every bit of data managed by an application. Because reports tend to be comprehensive, reports are often the best way to gather important information about a database's requirements. In the case of the Access Auto Auctions database, the printed reports contain detailed and summarized versions of most all the data in the database.

After you've defined the Access Auto Auctions' overall systems in terms of what must be accomplished, you can begin report design.

When you see the reports that you will create in this section, you may wonder, "Which comes first — the chicken or the egg?" Does the report layout come first, or do you first determine the data items and text that make up the report? Actually, these items are considered at the same time.

It isn't important how you lay out the fields in a report. The more time you take now, however, the easier it will be to construct the report. Some people go so far as to place gridlines on the report so that they will know the exact location they want each bit of data to occupy. In this example, you can just do it visually.

The reports in Figures 33-3 and 33-4 were created with two different purposes. The report in Figure 33-3 displays information about an individual contact (buyer, seller, or both). In contrast, the report in Figure 33-4 is an invoice with billing and customer information. Both of these reports were based on the type of information they use. The design and layout of each report is driven by the report's purpose and the data it contains.

CROSS-REF **You can read more about the reports for the Access Auto Auctions system in Chapter 39.**

FIGURE 33-3

A contact information report.

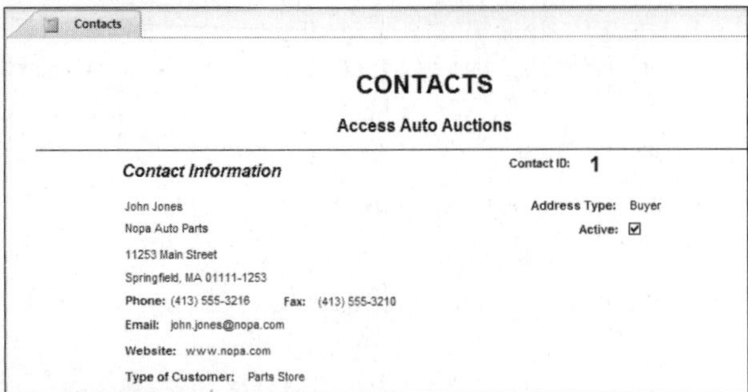

Contacts

CONTACTS

Access Auto Auctions

Contact Information

Contact ID: 1

John Jones
Nopa Auto Parts
11253 Main Street
Springfield, MA 01111-1253

Address Type: Buyer
Active: ☑

Phone: (413) 555-3216 Fax: (413) 555-3210
Email: john.jones@nopa.com
Website: www.nopa.com
Type of Customer: Parts Store

FIGURE 33-4

A sales invoice report containing sales information.

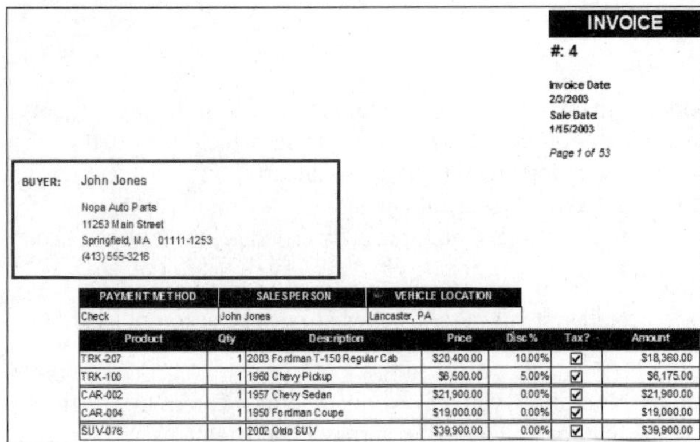

INVOICE

#: 4

Invoice Date
2/3/2003
Sale Date
1/15/2003

Page 1 of 53

BUYER: John Jones
Nopa Auto Parts
11253 Main Street
Springfield, MA 01111-1253
(413) 555-3216

PAYMENT METHOD	SALESPERSON	VEHICLE LOCATION
Check	John Jones	Lancaster, PA

Product	Qty	Description	Price	Disc %	Tax?	Amount
TRK-207	1	2003 Fordman T-150 Regular Cab	$20,400.00	10.00%	☑	$18,360.00
TRK-100	1	1960 Chevy Pickup	$6,500.00	5.00%	☑	$6,175.00
CAR-002	1	1957 Chevy Sedan	$21,900.00	0.00%	☑	$21,900.00
CAR-004	1	1950 Fordman Coupe	$19,000.00	0.00%	☑	$19,000.00
SUV-076	1	2002 Oldo SUV	$39,900.00	0.00%	☑	$39,900.00

Step 3: Data design: What fields are required?

The next step in the design phase is to take an inventory of all the information or data fields that are needed by the reports. One of the best methods is to list the data items in each report. As you do so, take careful note of items that are included in more than one report. Make sure that you keep the same name for a data item that is in more than one report because the data item is really the same item.

Another method is to see whether you can separate the data items into some logical arrangement. Later, these data items are grouped into table structures and then mapped onto data-entry screens (forms). You should enter customer data (buyers and sellers), for example, as part of a contact table process, not as part of a sales entry.

Determining contact information

First, look at each report you have reviewed or attempted to make for the Access Auto Auctions system. For this system, start with the customer data and list the data items, as shown in Table 33-1.

TABLE 33-1

Customer-Related Data Items Found in the Reports

Contacts Report	Invoice Report
Customer Name	Customer Name
Street	Street
City	City
State	State
ZIP Code	ZIP Code
Phone Number	Phone Number
Type of Customer	
E-Mail Address	
Web Site Information	
Contact Log Information (four fields)	
Discount Rate	
Customer Since	
Last Sales Date	
Sales Tax Rate	
Credit Information (four fields)	

As you can see by comparing the type of contact (customer) information needed for each report, there are many common fields. Most of the data fields pertaining to the customer are found in both reports. Table 33-1 shows only some of the fields that are used in each reportthose related to customer information. Fields appearing on both reports appear on the same rows in the table, which allows you to see more easily which items are in which reports. You can look across a row instead of looking for the same names in both reports. Because the related row and the field names are the same, you can easily make sure that you have all the data items. Although locating items easily is not critical for this small database, it becomes very important when you have to deal with large tables containing many fields.

Determining sales information

After extracting the customer data, you can move on to the sales data. In this case, you need to analyze only the Invoice report for data items that are specific to the sales. Table 33-2 lists the fields in the report that contain information about the sales.

As you can see when you examine the type of sales information needed for the report, a couple of items (fields) are repeating (for example, the `Product Purchased`, `Number of Items Purchased`, and `Price of Item` fields). Each invoice can have multiple items, and each of these items needs the same type of information — number ordered and price per item. Each sales invoice will probably have more than one item that is sold and being invoiced. Also, each invoice may include partial payments, and it is possible that this payment information will have multiple lines of payment information, so these repeating items can be put into their own grouping.

TABLE 33-2

Sales Data Items Found in the Reports

Individual Invoice Report	Line Item Data
Invoice Number	
Sales Date	
Invoice Date	
Payment Method	
Payment Salesperson	
Discount (overall for sale)	
Tax Location	
Tax Rate	
Product Purchased (multiple lines)	Product Purchased
Quantity Purchased (multiple lines)	Quantity Purchased
Description of Item Purchased (multiple lines)	Description of Item Purchased
Price of Item (multiple lines)	Price of Item
Discount for each item (multiple lines)	Discount for Each Item
Taxable? (multiple lines)	Taxable?
Payment Type (multiple lines)	
Payment Date (multiple lines)	
Payment Amount (multiple lines)	
Credit Card Number (multiple lines)	
Expiration Date (multiple lines)	

Determining line item information

You can take all the individual items that you found in the sales information group in the preceding section and extract them to their own group for the invoice report. Table 33-2 shows the information related to each line item.

Looking back at the report in Figure 33-4, you can see that the data from Table 33-2 doesn't list the calculated field amount, but you can re-create it easily in the report.

TIP **Unless a numeric field needs to be specifically stored in a table, simply recalculate it when you run the report (or form). You should avoid creating fields in your tables that can be created based on other fields — these calculation fields can be easily created and displayed in a form or report. As you'll read in Chapter 36, storing calculated values in database tables leads to data maintenance problems.**

Step 4: Table design

Now for the difficult part: You must determine what fields are needed for the tables that make up the reports. When you examine the multitude of fields and calculations that make up the many documents you have, you begin to see which fields belong to the various tables in the database. (You already did much of the preliminary work by arranging the fields into logical groups.) For now, include every field you extracted. You will need to add others later (for various reasons), although certain fields won't appear in any table.

It is important to understand that it isn't necessary to add every little bit of data into the database's tables. For instance, users may express a desire to add vacation and other out-of-office days to the database to make it easy to know which employees are available on a particular day. However, it is very easy to burden an application's initial design by incorporating too many ideas during the initial development phases. Because Access tables are so easy to modify later on, it is probably best to put aside noncritical items until the initial design is complete. Generally speaking, it's not difficult to accommodate user requests after the database development project is under way.

After you've used each report to display all the data, it's time to consolidate the data by purpose (for example, grouped into logical groups) and then compare the data across those functions. To do this step, first you look at the contact information and combine all of its different fields to create one set of data items. Then you do the same thing for the sales information and the line item information. Table 33-3 compares data items from these three groups of information.

TABLE 33-3

Comparing the Data Items from the Contact Information, Sales Information, and Line Item Information

Contacts Data	Invoice Data	Line Items
Customer Name	Invoice Number	Product Purchased
Street	Sales Date	Quantity Purchased
City	Invoice Date	Description of Item Purchased
State	Payment Method	Price of Item
ZIP Code	Payment Salesperson	Discount for Each Item
Phone Numbers (two fields)	Discount (overall for this sale)	Taxable?
Type of Customer	Tax Location	
E-Mail Address	Tax Rate	
Web Site Information	Payment Type (multiple lines)	
Contact Log Information (four fields)	Payment Date (multiple lines)	
Discount Rate	Payment Amount (multiple lines)	
Customer Since	Credit Card Number (multiple lines)	
Last Sales Date	Expiration Date (multiple lines)	
Sales Tax Rate		
Credit Information (four fields)		

Consolidating and comparing data is a good way to start creating the individual table definitions for Access Auto Auctions, but you have much more to do.

As you learn more about how to perform a data design, you also learn that the contacts data must be split into two groups. Some of these items are used only once for a contact, while other items may have multiple entries. An example is the Contact Log information. Each contact may have multiple log items recorded in the database. This is also true for the Sales column — the payment information can have multiple lines of information.

It is necessary to further break these types of information into their own columns, thus separating all related types of items into their own columns — an example of the *normalization* part of the design process. For example, one customer can have multiple contacts with the company. One customer may make multiple payments toward a single sale. Of course, we've already broken the data into three categories above: contacts, invoices, and sales line items.

Keep in mind that one customer may have multiple invoices, and each invoice may have multiple line items on it. The contact category represents customer (buyer or seller) information, the invoice category contains information about individual sales, and the line items category contains information about each invoice. Notice that these three columns are all related; for example, one customer can have multiple invoices and each invoice may require multiple detail lines (line items).

The relationships between tables can be different. For example, each sales invoice has one and only one customer, while each customer may have multiple sales. A similar relationship exists between the sales invoice and the line items of the invoice.

CROSS-REF **We cover creating and understanding relationships and the normalization process in Chapter 36.**

Assuming that the three groupings represent the main three tables of your system, less additional fields, you need to link tables together. This step, of course, means adding table relationships to the database design.

Database table relationships require a unique field in both tables involved in a relationship. Without a unique identifier in each table, the database engine is unable to properly join and extract related data.

None of the tables in our design has a unique identifier, which means that you need to add at least one more field to each table to serve as the anchor for a relationship to other tables. For example, you could add a `ContactID` field to the Contacts table, then add the same field to the Invoice table, and establish a relationship between the tables through the `ContactID` field in each table. The database engine uses the relationship between the Contacts and Invoices table to link customers with their invoices. Linking tables is done through special fields, known as *key* fields.

With an understanding of the need for linking one group of fields to another group, you can add the required key fields to each group. Table 33-4 shows two new groups and link fields created for each group of fields. These linking fields, known as *primary keys* and *foreign keys,* are used to link these tables together.

The field that uniquely identifies each row in a table is called the *primary key.* The corresponding field in a related table is called the *foreign key.* In our example, the `ContactID` field in the Contacts table is a primary key, while the `ContactID` field in the Invoices table is a foreign key.

Let's assume a certain record in the Contacts table has 12 in its `ContactID` field. Any records in the Invoices table with 12 in its `ContactID` field is "owned" by contact number 12. As you'll see in Chapters 2 and 3, special rules apply to choosing and managing primary and foreign keys. The notion of primary and foreign keys is the single most important concept behind relational databases. You can read much more about this important concept in Chapters 2 and 3.

With the key fields added to each table, you can now find a field in each table that links it to other tables in the database. For example, Table 33-4 shows a `ContactID` field in both the Contacts table (where it is the table's primary key) and the Invoice table (where it is a foreign key).

TABLE 33-4

Main Tables with Keys

Contacts Data	Invoice Data	Line Items Data	Contact Log Data	Sales Payment Data
ContactID	InvoiceID	InvoiceID	ContactLogID	InvoiceID
Customer Name	ContactID	Line Number	ContactID	Payment Type
Street	Invoice Number	Product Purchased	Contact Date	Payment Date
City	Sales Date	Quantity Purchased	Contact Notes	Payment Amount
State	Invoice Date	Description of Item Purchased	Follow Up?	Credit Card Number
ZIP Code	Payment Method	Price of Item	Follow-Up Date	Expiration Date
Phone Numbers (two fields)	Payment Salesperson	Discount for Each Item		
Type of Customer	Discount (overall for this sale)	Taxable?		
E-Mail Address	Tax Location			
Web Site Information	Tax Rate			
Discount Rate				
Customer Since				
Last Sales Date				
Sales Tax Rate				

You have identified the core of the three primary tables for your system, as reflected by the first three columns in Table 33-4. This is the general, or first, cut toward the final table designs. You have also created two additional tables (columns) from fields shown in Table 33-3.

Taking time to properly design your database and the tables contained within it is arguably the most important step in developing a database-oriented application. By designing your database efficiently, you maintain control of the data — eliminating costly data-entry mistakes and limiting your data entry to essential fields.

Although these chapters are not geared toward teaching database theory and all of its nuances, this is a good point to briefly describe the art of database normalization. Normalization is the process of breaking data down into constituent tables. Earlier in this chapter you read about how many Access developers add dissimilar information, such as contacts, invoice data, and invoice line items, into one large table. A large table containing dissimilar data quickly becomes unwieldy and hard to keep updated. Because a contact's phone number appears in every row containing that customer's data, multiple updates must be made when the contact's phone number changes.

Normalization is the process of breaking data into smaller, more manageable tables. Each table defines one and only one *entity*, such as a contact or an invoice, but not both. The contact and invoice tables are related through a primary key (`ContactID` in the customers table) and a foreign key (also named `ContactID`) in the invoices table.

Step 5: Form design: Input

After you've created the data and established table relationships, it's time to design your forms. *Forms* are made up of the fields that can be entered or viewed in Edit mode. If at all possible, your screens should look much like the forms that you use in a manual system. This setup makes for the most user-friendly system.

When you're designing forms, you need to place three types of objects onscreen:

- Labels and text box data-entry fields (the fields on Access forms and reports are usually called *controls*)
- Special controls (multiple-line text boxes, option buttons, list boxes, checkboxes, business graphs, and pictures)
- Graphical objects to visually enhance them (colors, lines, rectangles, and three-dimensional effects)

When designing a form, place your fields (text boxes, checkboxes, list boxes, and radio buttons) just where you want them on the form. Ideally, if the form is being developed from an existing printed form, the Access data-entry form should resemble the printed form. The fields should be in the same relative place on the screen as they are in the printed counterpart.

Labels display messages, titles, or captions. Text boxes provide an area where you can type or display text or numbers that are contained in your database. Checkboxes indicate a condition and are either unchecked or checked (selected). Other types of controls available with Access include list boxes, combo boxes, option buttons, toggle buttons, and option groups.

Chapter 37 covers the various types of controls available in Access.

Summary

This chapter introduces the concepts and considerations driving database development. There is no question that data is important to users. Most companies simply cannot operate without their customer and product lists, accounts receivable and accounts payable, and payroll information. Even very small companies must efficiently manage their business data.

Good database design means much more than sitting down and knocking together a few tables. Very often, poor database design habits come back to haunt developers and users in the form of missing or erroneous information on screens and printed reports. Users quickly tire of re-entering the same information over and over again, and business managers and owners expect database applications to *save* time and money, not contribute to a business's overhead.

Chapter 34

Creating Access Tables

In this chapter, you learn how to create a new Access database and its tables. You establish the database container to hold your tables, forms, queries, reports, and code that you build as you learn Access. Finally, you create the actual tables used by the Access Auto Auctions database.

IN THIS CHAPTER

- Creating a new Access database
- Creating a table
- Navigating in the Table window
- Entering field names and descriptions
- Selecting a field data type
- Entering field properties
- Creating a primary key
- Saving a table's design
- Renaming, copying, and deleting tables

Getting Started with Access 2007

As you open Access 2007, the default environment (see Figure 34-1) is revealed. We'll examine the Access environment in more detail later in this chapter, but you should understand the major components of the user interface as you get started using Access 2007. Even experienced Access developers are surprised at how different Access 2007 looks from previous versions.

Each time you open Access, the welcome screen may or may not look different, depending on whether you have elected to have Office Online periodically updated. In an effort to provide a high level of support for Microsoft Office users, Microsoft has equipped each of the Office applications with the ability to communicate directly with Microsoft's Web servers and download new content to the user's desktop. Notice the Automatically Update This Content from Office Online button in the Office Online box near the bottom-center of this main screen. This button configures Microsoft Access to look for new Office Online content each time you open Access. In fact, your Access Welcome Screen will likely look quite different from Figure 34-1 because of the content continuously released by Microsoft Office Online.

The center of the screen is dominated by the Microsoft Office Online "templates," which are described in the next section. The right side of the screen contains a list of recently opened databases, while the left side of the screen contains a navigation bar for templates.

FIGURE 34-1

The Access 2007 welcome screen provides a wealth of information.

The Templates section

When you start Microsoft Access, you see the initial welcome screen (refer to Figure 34-1). For online users of Microsoft Access 2007, the content of the welcome screen changes from time to time as Microsoft updates the online templates available on the Microsoft Web site.

We'll take a look at creating a new database in the "Creating a Database" section of this chapter. In the meantime, let's take a look at the purpose of online templates. Microsoft has long been concerned that building Access databases is too difficult for most people. Not everyone takes the time to understand the rules governing database design, or to learn the intricacies of building tables, queries, forms, and reports.

Microsoft established the online templates repository as a way to provide beginners and other busy people the opportunity to download partially or completely built Access applications. The template databases cover many common business requirements such as inventory control and sales management. You may want to take a moment to explore the online templates, but they aren't covered in these chapters about Access.

The File menu

Our main interest at the moment is the large round button in the upper-left corner of the main Access screen. This button, called the Office Button, opens the File menu (see Figure 34-2), which is the gateway to a large number of options for creating, opening, or configuring Access databases. Notice that a list of recently opened databases appears to the right of the buttons in the File menu.

FIGURE 34-2

The File menu contains many important commands.

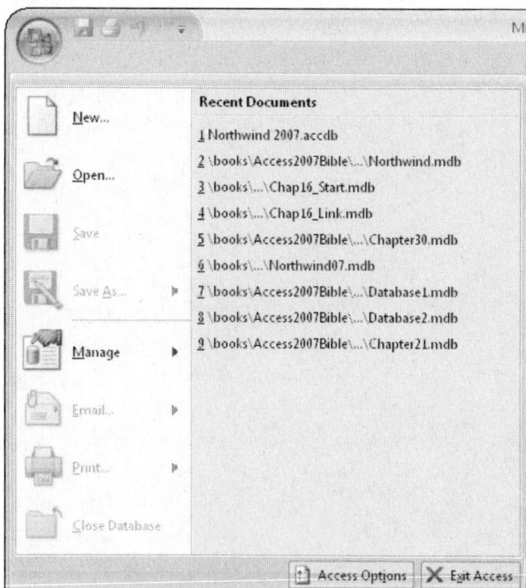

Rather than discuss each of these commands at the moment, we'll cover each command in detail as we work through the Access user interface. For the moment, notice the `New` command at the very top of the File menu. We'll use this button to create a new Access database in the next section.

NOTE **Some confusion exists over the name of the large, round button you see in the upper-left corner of the main Access window. Most users call this button the File button and the drop-down that appears as this button is clicked the File menu. However, Microsoft refers to the round button as the Microsoft Office Button and its drop-down as the Office menu. You'll see both expressions used in this book, but in all cases we're referring to the large, round button in the upper-left corner of the main Access 2007 screen.**

Creating a Database

There are many ways to create a new database file. You may have noticed the Blank Database button in the upper-left corner of the Office Online area in the main Access screen. This button and the Office Button ➪ `New` choice both reveal the Blank Database area in the right section of the main screen. Clicking either of these buttons transforms the main screen, as shown in Figure 34-3. The Blank Database area replaces the list of recently opened databases on the main screen.

Enter the name of the new database in the `File Name` box in the Blank Database area. By default, Access creates the new database file in whichever Windows folder you most recently opened from within Access. If you want to use a different folder, use the folder icon to the right of the File Name box to browse to the location you want to use.

FIGURE 34-3

Enter the name of the new database in the File Name box in the Blank Database area.

Access provides a default name of `Database1.accdb` for new databases. Be sure to provide a name that you'll recognize. In Figure 34-4, the new database is named `MyAccessAutoAuctions.accdb`. (Entering the extension `.accdb` is optional because Access automatically supplies it if you do not.)

When the new database is created, Access automatically opens it for you.

NOTE **Access 2007 recognizes all previous versions of Access database files. By default, the 2007 format (with the `.accdb` extension) is used, but you can specify either Access 2000, 2002–2003, or Access 2007 as the default format. Choose Office Button ➪ Access Options ➪ Personalize, select the Default File Format option, and choose whichever format you prefer. For instance, if much of your Access 2007 work is performed on Access 2000 databases, you should choose the 2000 format to preserve backward compatibility. Users still working with Access 2000 are not able to open Access files created in the `.accdb` format.**

This book uses a mix of Access file formats for its examples. All of the Access Auto Auctions for these chapters in Access 2007 format, but other examples may be in Access 2000 or 2002–2003 formats.

Access 2007 works directly with Access 2000, 2002–2003, and 2007 databases. Earlier Access database files (such as Access 97 or 95) must be converted to 2000, 2002–2003, or 2007 before they can be used in Access 2007. Access examines the database file you're opening and, if it determines the file must be converted, presents you with the Database Enhancement dialog box shown in Figure 34-5.

Responding Yes to the Database Enhancement dialog box opens a second dialog box (not shown) asking for the name of the converted database. Selecting No opens the obsolete database in read-only mode, enabling you to view, but not modify, objects in the database. This process is sometimes referred to as *enabling* the obsolete database.

FIGURE 34-4

The new MyAccessAutoAuctions database is created.

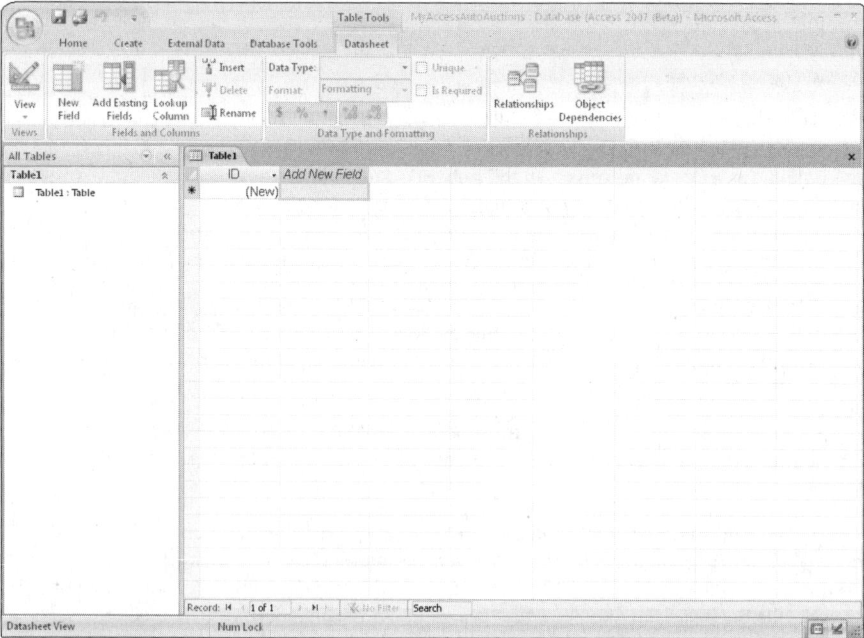

FIGURE 34-5

Opening an obsolete Access data file invokes the Database Enhancement dialog box.

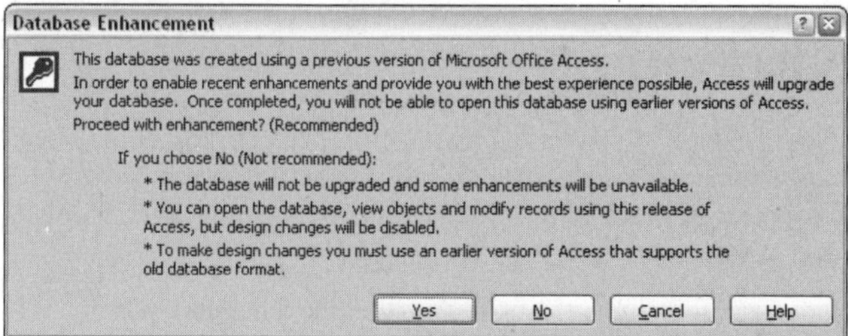

Choosing to enable an obsolete database is sometimes necessary when you must understand the design of an old database, but if users are still working with the old database and it cannot be upgraded to Access 2007 format.

If you're following the examples in this book, note that we have chosen `MyAccessAutoAuctions.accdb` as the name of the database file you create as you complete this chapter. This database is for our hypothetical business, Access Auto Auctions. After you enter the filename, Access creates the empty database.

Understanding How Access Works with Data

There are many ways that Microsoft Access works with data. For simplicity, most of the examples in this book use data stored in local tables. A *local table* is contained within the Access `.accdb` file that is open in front of you. This is how you've seen examples so far.

In many professionally developed Microsoft Access applications, the actual tables are kept in a database (usually called the *back end*) separate from the other interface objects (forms, reports, queries, pages, macros, and modules). The back-end data file stays on a file server on the network, and each user has a copy of the front-end database (containing the forms and reports) on his computer. This is done to make the application more maintainable. By separating the data and their tables into another database, maintenance work (building new indexes, repairing the tables, and so on) is more easily done without affecting the remainder of the system.

For example, you may be working with a multiuser system and find a problem with a form or report in the database. If all the data and interface objects are in the same database, you have to shut down the system while repairing the broken form or report — other users could not work with the application while you repair the form or report.

By separating data from other objects, you can fix the erring object while others are still working with the data. After you've fixed the problem, you deliver the new changes to the others, and they import the form or report into their local databases.

In addition, there is a more critical reason to separate your data from the interface objects: security. By maintaining the data in its own database, you maintain better control over the information. The back-end database is physically separated from users, and it is unlikely a user can accidentally or intentionally delete or modify the back-end database files. Also, the back-end database is easily backed up and maintained without affecting users.

While you may want to first develop your application with the tables within the `.accdb` database, later you can use the Database Splitter wizard to automatically move the tables in your `.accdb` file to a separate Access `.accdb` file.

The Access 2007 Environment

The initial Access screen, after creating a new database, is shown in Figure 34-6. Along the top of the screen is the Access *ribbon*, which replaces the toolbars and menus seen in previous versions of Access. The ribbon is divided into a number of groups. We'll be looking at each of the groups and the controls in each group as we work our way through the next several chapters.

At the left side of the screen is the *Navigation Pane* containing the names of all of the different types of objects in the Access database. In Figure 34-6, the Navigation Pane displays the names of tables in the database, but could just as easily show queries, forms, reports, and other Access object types. The Navigation Pane can even display a combination of different types of objects.

The right side of the screen shows a blank table, ready to be filled in with the details necessary for the table to be used in the new Access database.

FIGURE 34-6

The main Access interface when working with a new database.

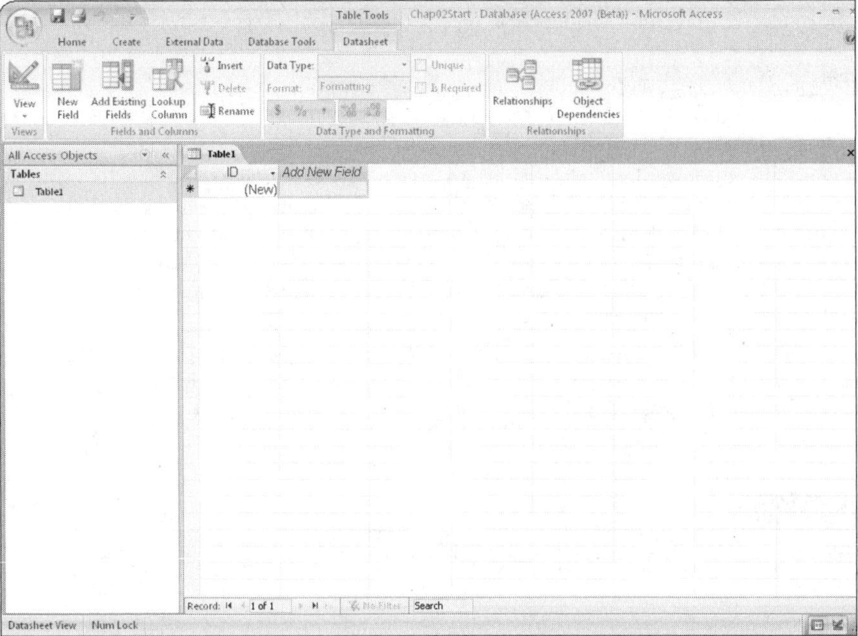

The Navigation Pane

The Navigation Pane, at the left of the screen, is your primary navigation aid when working with Access. By default, the list is filled with the names of tables in the current database but can also display other types of objects by clicking on the drop-down list in the Navigation Pane's title bar to reveal the navigation options (see Figure 34-7).

FIGURE 34-7

Choosing an alternate display for the Navigation pane.

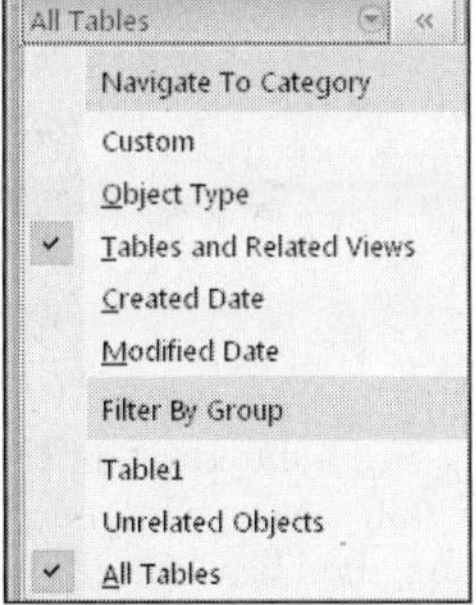

The navigation options are:

- **Custom:** The Custom option creates a new tab in the Navigation pane. This new tab is titled Custom Group 1 by default and contains objects that you drag and drop into the tab's area. Items added to a custom group still appear in their respective "object type" view, as described next.
- **Object Type:** The Object Type setting is most similar to previous versions of Access. When selected, Object Type transforms the selection list to display the usual Access object types: tables, queries, forms, reports, and so on.
- **Tables and Related Views:** The Tables and Related Views setting requires a bit of explanation. Access 2007 tries very hard to keep the developer informed of the hidden connections between objects in the database. For instance, a particular table may be used in a number of queries, or referenced from a form or report. In previous versions of Access, these relationships were very difficult to determine, and, before Access 2007, no effective tool was built into Access to help you understand these relationships.

  Figure 34-8 shows how the Tables and Related Views works. The Shippers table has been expanded to show that it is related to six other objects in the Northwind Traders database. This information helps a developer to understand that changing the Shippers table affects a number of other objects in the database.

FIGURE 34-8

The Tables and Related Views setting is a powerful tool for analyzing an Access database.

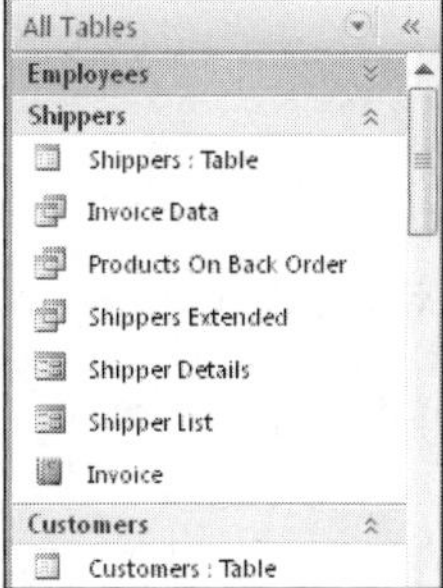

- **Created Date, Modified Date:** These options group the database objects by either the created date or the modified date. These settings are useful when you need to know when an object was either created or last modified.
- **Filter By Group:** The Filter By Group option filters the selected object type (tables, forms, and so on) by a number of grouping options. The grouping option is determined by the navigation category chosen in Navigate To Category selected at the top of the Navigation pane. For instance, selecting Created Date changes the options under the Filter By Group to the following options: Today, Yesterday, Last Week, Two Weeks Ago, and so on.

  The Filter By Group option is really only helpful when you have a fairly large number of objects in your Access database. If you have an Access database containing several hundred different forms, you'll find it very useful to filter by forms that were modified within the last week or so. But when there are only a few objects in a database, the Filter By Group option has little effect.

- **Unrelated Objects, All Tables:** These options appear in Figure 34-7 because the `Tables and Related Views` is selected as the primary navigation option. The `Unrelated Objects` is the opposite of the `Tables and Related Views`. When selected, the `Unrelated Objects` option shows you all of the objects that are not related to the selected table, query, or other Access object.

The `All Tables` setting is the default when choosing to view tables in the database.

The Ribbon

The Access Ribbon occupies the top portion of the main access screen. The Ribbon replaces the menus and toolbars seen in previous versions of Access. The Ribbon's appearance changes depending on what task you're working on in the Access environment. Figure 34-9 shows the Datasheet Ribbon seen when you're working with Access tables. A very different Ribbon appears when working with forms or reports.

FIGURE 34-9

The Access 2007 Ribbon.

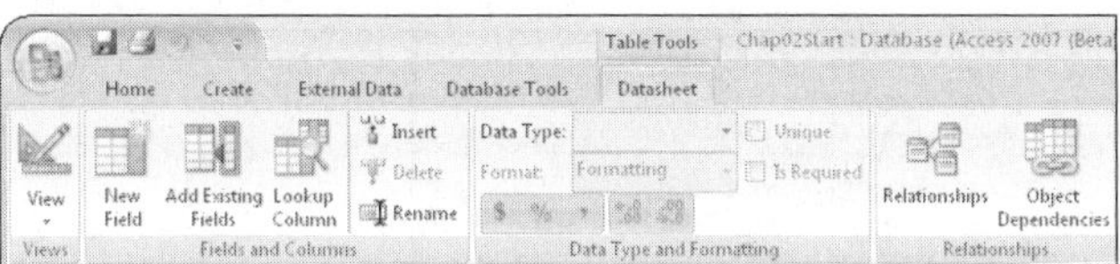

The Ribbon is divided into a number of groups, each containing any number of controls. In Figure 34-9, the `Data Type and Formatting` group is selected. The `Data Type and Formatting group` includes options for selecting how a datasheet appears on the screen, while the `Fields and Columns` group contains commands for modifying and specifying the fields within the table.

The other groups on the Datasheet tab (`Views`, `Fields and Columns`, and `Relationships`) contain controls that perform other tasks commonly associated with Access datasheets. For instance, the `View` control in the `Views` group changes the datasheet view of the table to design view, making it easy to update the table's design.

Instead of explaining each of the groups and controls within groups on the Ribbon, we will study each relevant Ribbon command in the proper context in this chapter and chapters that follow.

Other relevant features of the Access environment

The Access environment includes a number of other important features. In the far-right lower corner are two buttons that enable you to quickly change the selected objects in the middle of the screen from Design view to the object's Normal view. For instance, in the case of an Access table, the Normal view is to display the table as a datasheet, while a report's Normal view is to display the report in Print Preview.

Figure 34-10 illustrates one of the more interesting changes for Access 2007. A common complaint among some developers with earlier versions of Access was the fact that, when multiple objects were simultaneously opened in the Access environment, the objects would often overlap and obscure each other, making it more difficult to navigate between the objects. For instance, in Access 2000 you might have a form open in Design view and a table open in Datasheet view at the same time. Invariably, one of these objects would overlap the other and, depending on how large the object was, might completely obscure the other object.

FIGURE 34-10

The tabbed interface is a welcome addition to Access 2007.

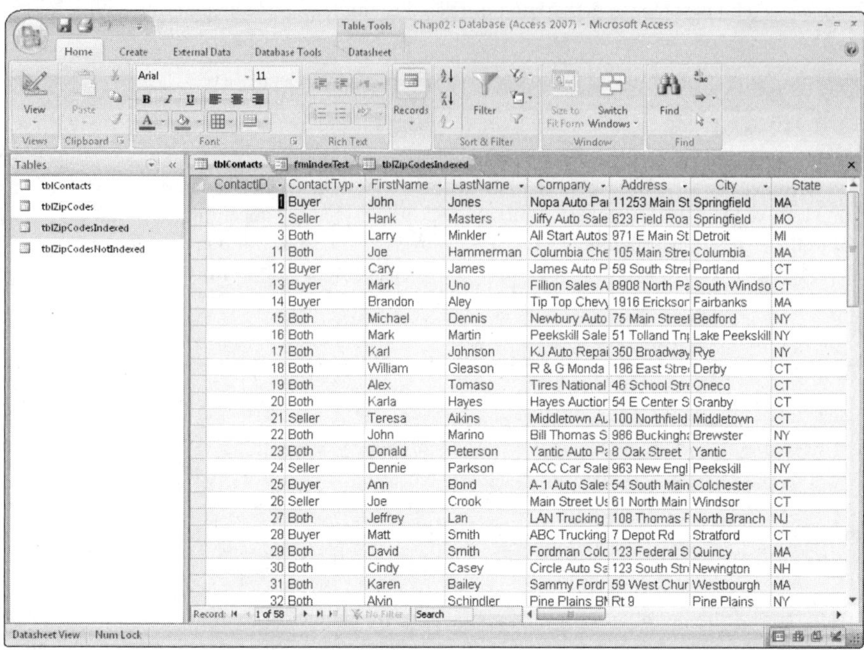

Microsoft has added a tabbed user interface to Access, preventing objects from obscuring other objects that are open at the same time. In Figure 34-10, the contacts (tblContacts) table is currently in use. Two other database objects (frmIndexTest and tblZipCodesIndexed) are also opened in the Access work area. Clicking on a tab associated with an object, such as `frmIndexTest`, instantly brings that object to the top.

When an object such as `tblContacts` is put into Design view (by clicking to the last word, right-clicking the tab, and selecting `Design View`) the data sheet is replaced with the Table Designer (see Figure 34-11). The Access 2007 environment is highly adaptable to whichever tasks you are currently performing in your database.

TIP **If you decide you don't care for the tabbed interface, select the Office Button, and click the Access Options button in the lower-right corner of the Office menu. Then, select the Current Database tab, and change the Document Window Options from Tabbed Documents to Overlapping Windows. You then need to close and reopen the database file for the change to take effect.**

FIGURE 34-11

The Access environment adapts to your workflow.

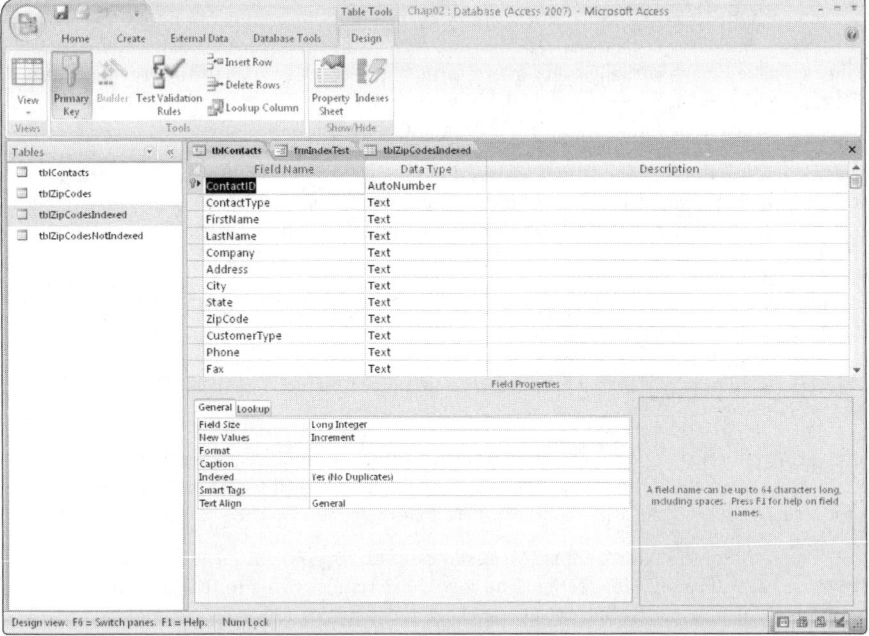

Creating a New Table

Creating database tables is as much art as it is science. A good working knowledge of the user's requirements is a primary requirement for any new database project. Let's take a look at the steps required to create basic Access tables. In the following sections, you'll study the process of adding tables to an Access database, including the relatively complex subject of choosing the proper data type to assign to each field in a table.

It is always a good idea to plan tables on paper first, before sitting down at Access and using the Access tools to add tables to the database. Many tables, especially small ones, really don't require a lot of forethought before adding them to the database. After all, not much planning is required to design a table holding lookup information such as the names of cities and states. However, more complex entities such as customers and products usually require considerable thought and effort to properly implement.

Although you can create the table interactively without any forethought, carefully planning a database system is a good idea. You can make any changes later, but doing so wastes time; generally, the result is a system that is harder to maintain than one that is well planned from the beginning. Before you get started, you should understand the table design process.

In the following sections, we'll be exploring the new, blank table added by Access as the new database was created. It's important to understand the steps required to add new tables to an Access database. Because the steps required to add tables have changed so dramatically from earlier versions of Access, even experienced Access developers will want to read the following sections.

The importance of naming conventions

As your databases grow in size and complexity, the need to establish a naming convention for the objects in your databases increases. As you already know, changes to the name of an object are not propagated throughout the database. Even with the `Name AutoCorrect` option turned on (Office Button ➪ Access Options ➪ Current Database ➪ Name AutoCorrect Options), Access only corrects the most obvious name changes. Changing the name of a table breaks virtually every query, form, and report that uses the information from that table. Your best defense is to adopt reasonable object names and use a naming convention early on as you begin building Access databases and to stick with the naming convention throughout the project.

Access imposes very few restrictions on the names assigned to database objects. Therefore, it is entirely possible to have two distinctly different objects (for instance, a form and a report, or a table and a macro) with the same name. (You can't, however, have a table and a query with the same name, because tables and queries occupy the same namespace in the database.)

Although simple names like Contacts and Orders are adequate, as a database grows in size and complexity you may become confused about which object a particular name refers to. When working with Visual Basic for Applications (VBA), the programming language built into Access 2007, there must be no ambiguity or confusion between referenced objects. Having both a form and a report named Contacts might be confusing to you *or* your code.

The simplest naming convention is to prefix object names with a three- or four-character string indicating the type of object carrying the name. Using this convention, tables are prefixed with `tbl` and queries with `qry`. The prefix for forms, reports, macros, and modules are `frm`, `rpt`, `mcr`, and `bas` or `mod`, respectively.

In this book, most compound object names appear in mixed case: `tblBookOrders`, `tblBookOrderDetails`, and so on. Most people find mixed-case names easier to read and remember than names that appear in all-uppercase or all-lowercase characters (such as `TBLBOOKORDERS` or `tblbookorderdetails`).

Also, at times, we'll use informal references for database objects. For instance, the formal name of the table containing contact information in the previous examples is `tblContacts`. An informal reference to this table might be "the contacts table."

In most instances, your users never see the formal names of database objects. One of your challenges as an application developer is to provide a seamless user interface that hides all data-management and data-storage entities that support the user interface. You can easily control the text that appears in the title bars and surfaces of the forms, reports, and other user interface components to hide the actual names of the data structures and interface constituents.

Take advantage of the long object names that Access permits to give your tables, queries, forms, and reports descriptive, informative names. There is no reason why you should confine a table name to `ConInfo` when `ContactInformation` is handled just as easily and is much easier to understand.

Descriptive names can be carried to an extreme, of course. There's no point in naming a form `frmUpdateContactInformation` if `frmUpdateInfo` does just as well. Long names are more easily misspelled or misread than shorter names, so use your judgment.

Finally, although Access lets you use spaces in database object names, you should avoid spaces at all costs. Spaces do not add to readability and can cause major headaches, particularly when upsizing to client-server environments or using OLE automation with other applications. Even if you don't anticipate extending your Access applications to client-server or incorporating OLE or DDE automation into your applications, get into the habit of not using spaces in object names.

The table design process

Creating a table design is a multistep process. By following the steps in order, your table design can be created readily and with minimal effort:

1. **Create a new table.**
2. **Enter field names, data types, and (optionally) descriptions.**
3. **Enter properties for the fields.**
4. **Set the table's primary key.**
5. **Create indexes for necessary fields.**
6. **Save the table's design.**

Generally speaking, some tables are never really finished. As users' needs change, or the business rules governing the application change, you may find it necessary to open an existing table in Design view. This part of the book, like most texts on Access, describes the process of creating tables as if every table you ever work on is brand new. The truth is, however, that most of the work that you do on an Access application is performed on existing objects in the database. Some of those objects you have added yourself, while other objects may have been added by another developer at some time in the past. However, the process of maintaining an existing database component is exactly the same as creating the same object from scratch.

TIP **Just a quick note about modifying tables once they're built: Adding a *new* field to a table almost never causes problems. Existing queries, forms, and reports, and even VBA code, will continue using the table as before. After all, these objects won't reference the new field because the field was added after their creation. Therefore, you can add a new field and incorporate the field where needed in your application, and everything works as expected.**

The trouble comes from removing or renaming a field in a table. Even with AutoCorrect turned on, Access will not update field name references in VBA code, in control properties, and in expressions throughout the database. *Changing* an existing field (or any other database object, for that matter) is always a bad idea. You should always strive to provide your tables, fields, and other database objects with good, strong, descriptive names at the time you add them to the database, rather than planning to go back later and fix them.

Adding a new table to the database

Begin by selecting the Create tab on the Ribbon at the top of the Access screen. The Create tab (see Figure 34-12) contains all of the tools necessary to create not only tables, but also forms, reports, and other database objects.

FIGURE 34-12

The Create tab contains tools necessary for adding new objects to your Access database.

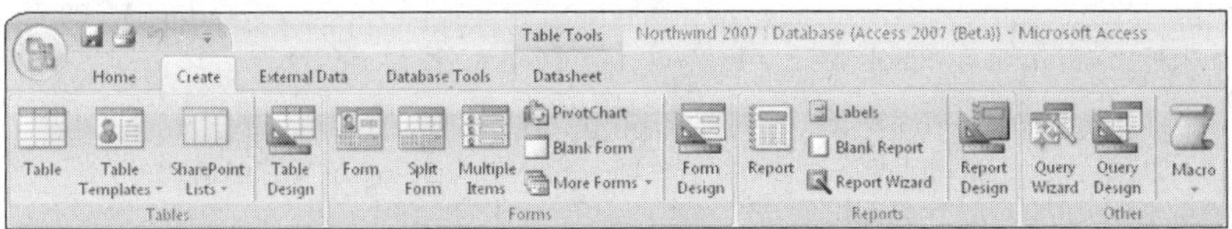

There are two main ways to add new tables to an Access database, both of which are invoked from the Tables group on the Create tab:

- **Clicking on the Table button:** Adds a complete new table to the database.
- **Clicking on the Table Design button:** Adds a table in Design view to the database.

For our example, we'll be using the Table Design button, but first, let's take a look at the Table button.

Clicking on the `Table` button adds a new table to the Access environment. The new table appears in Datasheet view in the tabbed region of the Access screen. A portion of the new table is shown in Figure 34-13. Notice that the new table appears in Datasheet view, with an ID column already inserted, and an Add New Field column to the right of the ID field.

FIGURE 34-13

A portion of the new table in Datasheet view in the Access environment.

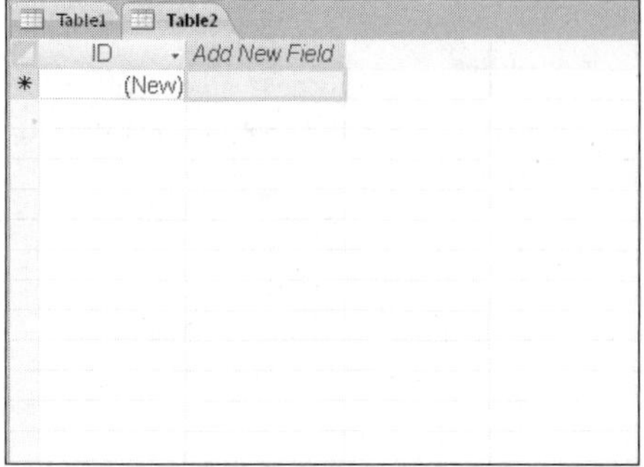

The `Add New Field` column is intended to permit users to quickly add tables to an Access database. All that is needed is to simply begin entering data into the `Add New Field` column. You assign the field a name by right-clicking the field's heading, selecting Rename Column, and entering a name for the field. In other words, building an Access table can be very much like creating a spreadsheet in Microsoft Excel. This approach was usually referred to as "creating a table in Datasheet view" in previous versions of Microsoft Access.

Although it is entirely possible to build an access table without ever switching to Design view, we believe that this is a terrible idea. Building tables by entering data and casually providing names for the table's fields circumvents one of the most critical steps in building a serious database system.

Relational database systems such as Access are constructed by breaking data into constituent entities, and then building a table for each entity. The tables in an Access database should carefully and accurately reflect the entities they describe. Seemingly small issues, such as deciding which data type to assign to a field, has a dramatic impact on the utility, performance, and integrity of the database and its data.

Each table added to an Access database, and each field added to every table, should have a purpose in the overall database design. Even when adding tables using the Table button, it is far too easy to add tables that do not conform to good design rules, and which do not fit well into the database's design.

The second approach to add new tables is to use the Table Design button, located on the right side of the Tables grouping on the Create tab. Access opens a new table in Design view, as shown in Figure 34-14.

The table designer is quite easy to understand, and each column is clearly labeled. At the far left is the `Field Name` column, where you input the names of fields you add to the table. You assign a data type to each field in the table and (optionally) provide a description for the field.

FIGURE 34-14

A new table added in Design view.

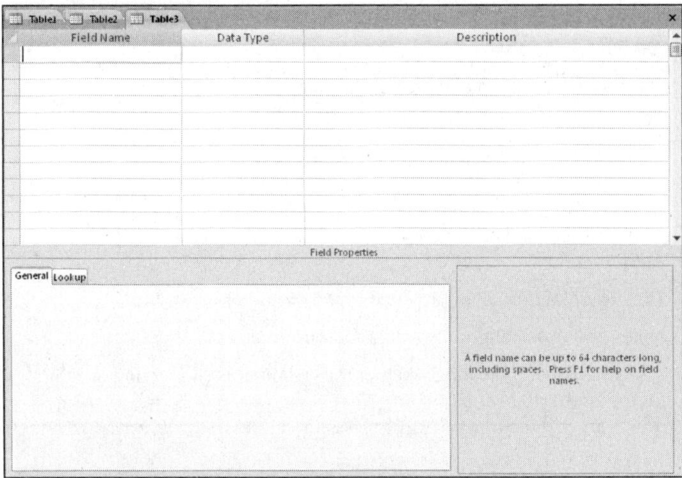

For this chapter's example, we'll create the Contacts table for the Access Auto Auctions application. The basic design of this table is outlined in Table 34-1.

TABLE 34-1

The Access Auto Auctions Contacts Table Design

Field Name	Data Type	Description
ContactID	AutoNumber	Primary key
ContactType	Text 50	Type of contact (Wholesaler, dealer, parts store, other)
FirstName	Text 50	Contact's first name
LastName	Text 50	Contact's last name
Company	Text 50	The Contact's employer or other affiliation
Address	Text 50	Contact's address
City	Text 50	Contact's city
State	Text 50	Contact's state
ZipCode	Text 50	Contact's zip code
Phone	Text 50	Contact's phone
Fax	Text 50	Contact's fax
E-Mail	Text 100	Contact's e-mail address
WebSite	Text 100	Contact's Web address

continued

TABLE 34-1 *(continued)*

Field Name	Data Type	Description
`OrigCustDate`	DateTime	The date the contact first purchased something from Access Auto Auctions
`TaxLocation`	Text 50	Used to determine the applicable sales tax
`CreditLimit`	Currency	Customer's credit limit in dollars
`CurrentBalance`	Currency	Customer's current balance in dollars
`CreditStatus`	Text	A description of the customer's credit status
`LastSalesDate`	DateTime	The most recent date the customer purchased something from Access Auto Auctions
`DiscountPercent`	Double	The customary discount provided to the customer
`Notes`	Memo	Notes and observations regarding this customer
`Active`	Yes/No	A yes/no value, indicating whether the customer is still buying or selling to Access Auto Auctions

Some of the fields in the preceding table are rather generous in the amount of space allocated for the field's data. For instance, it is unlikely that anyone's name occupies 50 characters, but there is no harm in providing for very long names. Access only stores as many characters as are actually entered into a text field. Therefore, allocating 50 characters does not actually use 50 characters for every name in the database.

The design spelled out in Table 34-1 is a good starting point for the Contacts table.

Looking once again at Figure 34-14, you see that the Table Design window consists of two areas:

- **The field entry area (top):** Use the field entry area to enter each field's name and data type. You can also enter an optional description.
- **The field properties area (bottom):** The property area at the bottom of the window is for entering more different specifications, called *properties,* for each field. These properties include field size, format, input mask, and default value, among others. The actual properties displayed in the properties area depend upon the data type of the field. You learn much more about these properties later in this book.

You can switch between the upper and lower areas of the table designer by clicking the mouse when the pointer is in the desired pane or by pressing F6.

Using the Design Ribbon tab

The Design tab on the Access Ribbon, shown in Figure 34-15, contains many controls that assist in creating a new table definition.

We will only mention a few of these buttons at this time. You'll learn much more about the other buttons later as needed.

Primary Key

Use this button to designate which of the fields in the table you want to use as the table's primary key. By tradition, the primary key appears at the top of the list of fields in the table. Moving a field is easy: Simply left-click on the gray selector to the left of the field's name to highlight the field in the Table Designer, and drag the field to its new position.

FIGURE 34-15

The Design tab of the Ribbon.

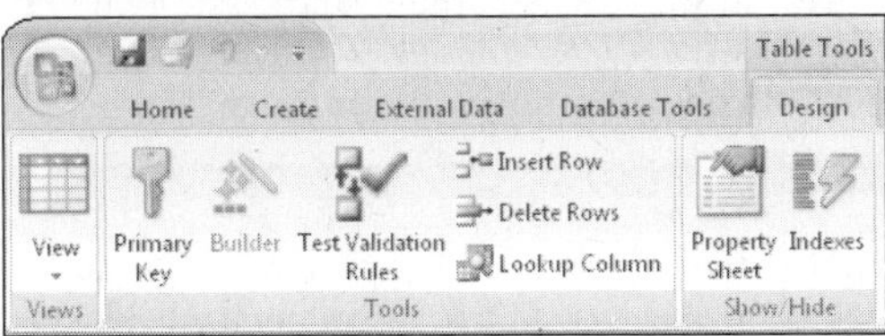

Insert Rows

Although it makes very little difference to the database engine, many developers are fussy about the sequence of fields in a table. Also, particularly when assigning an index or composite index to a table, you want the fields to be next to each other in the table's field list (composite keys consist of multiple fields combined as a single key). The `Insert Row` button inserts a blank row just above the position occupied by the mouse cursor. For instance, if the cursor is currently in the second row of the Table Designer, clicking the `Insert Row` button inserts an empty row in the second position, moving the existing second row to the third position.

Delete Rows

Conversely, the `Delete Rows` button removes a row from the table's design. Be careful, however, because Access does not ask you to confirm the deletion before actually removing the row.

Property Sheet

The `Property Sheet` button opens the Properties window (see Figure 34-16) for the table. These properties enable you to specify important table characteristics such as a validation rule to apply to the entire table, or an alternate sort order for the table's data.

FIGURE 34-16

The Table properties window.

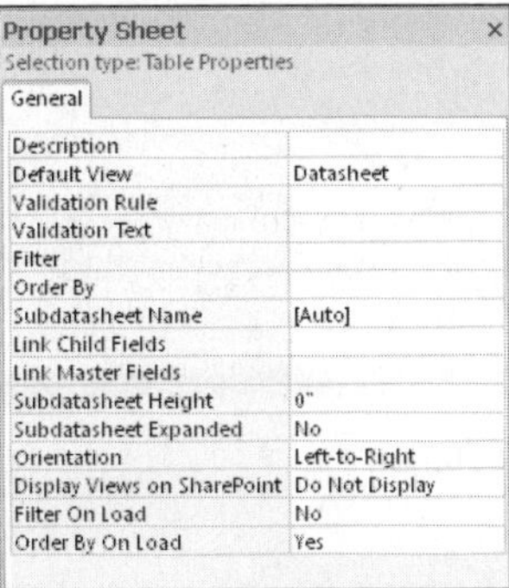

Indexes

Indexes are discussed in much more detail later in this chapter. Clicking the Indexes button opens the Indexes dialog box, enabling you to specify the details of indexes on the fields in your table.

Working with fields

Fields are created by entering a field name and a field data type in each row of the field entry area of the Table Design window. The field description is an option to identify the field's purpose. The description appears in the status bar at the bottom of the screen during data entry. After entering each field's name and data type, you can further specify how each field is used by entering properties in the property area.

Naming a field

A field name should be descriptive enough to identify the field to you as the developer, to the user of the system, and to Access. Field names should be long enough to quickly identify the purpose of the field, but not overly long. (Later, as you enter validation rules or use the field name in a calculation, you'll want to save yourself from typing long field names.)

To enter a field name, position the pointer in the first row of the Table Design window under the `Field Name` column. Then type a valid field name, observing these rules:

- Field names can be from 1 to 64 characters.
- Field names can include letters, numbers, and many special characters.
- Field names cannot include a period (.), exclamation point (!), brackets ([ ]), or accent grave (`).
- You can't use low-order ASCII characters, for example Ctrl+J or Ctrl+L (ASCII values 0 to 31).
- You can't start with a blank space.
- You can't use a double quotation mark (") in the name of a Microsoft Access project file.

You can enter field names in upper-, lower-, or mixed case. If you make a mistake while typing the field name, position the cursor where you want to make a correction and type the change. You can change a field name at any time — even if it's in a table and the field contains data — for any reason.

NOTE **Access is not case sensitive, so the database itself doesn't care whether you name a table `tblContacts` or `TblContacts`. The selection of upper-, lower-, or mixed case is entirely your decision and should be aimed at making your table names descriptive and easy to read.**

CAUTION **After your table is saved, if you change a field name that is also used in queries, forms, or reports, you have to change it in those objects as well. One of the leading causes of errors in Access applications stems from changing the names of fundamental database objects such as tables and fields, but neglecting to make all of the changes required throughout the database. Overlooking a field name reference in the control source of a control on the form or report, or deeply embedded in VBA code somewhere in the application, is far too easy.**

Specifying a data type

The next step is to actually create your tables and define your fields for those tables. You must also decide what type of data each of your fields will hold. In Access, you can choose any of several data types (these data types are detailed later in this chapter):

- **Text:** Alphanumeric characters, up to 255 characters
- **Memo:** Alphanumeric characters, very long strings up to 65,538 (64K) characters
- **Number:** Numeric values of many types and formats
- **Date/Time:** Date and time data
- **Currency:** Monetary data
- **AutoNumber:** Automatically incremented numeric counter

- **Yes/No:** Logical values, Yes/No, True/False
- **OLE Object:** Pictures, graphs, sound, video, word processing, and spreadsheet files
- **Hyperlink:** A field that links to a picture, graph, sound, video, and word processing and spreadsheet files

One of these data types must be assigned to each of your fields. You must also specify the length of the Text fields, or accept the default of 50 characters for Text fields.

Designing data-entry rules

The last major design decision concerns data validation, which becomes important as users enter data. You want to make sure that only good data (data that passes certain defined tests) gets into your system. You have to deal with several types of data validation. You can test for known individual items, stipulating that the `Gender` field can accept only the values `Male`, `Female`, or `Unknown`, for example. Or you can test for ranges, specifying that the value of `Weight` must be between `0` and `1,500` pounds.

Designing lookup tables

Sometimes you need to design entire tables to perform data validation or just to make it easier to create your system; these are called *lookup tables*. For example, because Access Auto Auctions needs a field to determine the customer's tax rate, you may decide to use a lookup table that contains the tax location, and tax rate. Another example is when a customer pays an invoice using some specific method — cash, credit card, money order, and on and on.

Because the tax rate can change, storing tax rates makes much more sense than hard-coding tax rates into the application. Using lookup tables, Access looks up the current tax rate in `tblTaxRates` whenever an invoice is created. The tax rate applied to an invoice is stored along with the other invoice data in the Invoice/Sales table because it is time-dependent data, and the value stored in `tblTaxRates` may be different in the future.

Another purpose of a lookup table is to limit data entry in a field to a specific value. For example, you can use a table containing payment types (cash, check, MasterCard, and so on). The payment types table (`tblPaymentTypes`) can be used as a lookup table to ensure only approved payment methods can be entered in the Invoice table.

TIP **When you create a field in a table, you can use the data type Lookup Wizard. It is not an actual data type but is instead a way of storing a field one way and displaying it another way.**

Although you can create a field on a data-entry form that limits the entry of valid contact types to seller, buyer, or both, you create a table with only one field — ContactType — and use the ContactType field in tblContacts to link to this field in the ContactType lookup table.

NOTE **You create a lookup table in exactly the same way as you create any other table, and it behaves in the same way. The only difference is in the way you use the table's data.**

Several lookup tables are included in the Access Auto Auctions application: `tblPaymentType`, `tblTaxRates`, and `tblCategories`.

Assigning field data types

After you name a field, you must decide what type of data the field holds. Before you begin entering data, you should have a good grasp of the data types that your system will use. Ten basic types of data are shown in Table 34-2; some data types (such as numbers) have several options.

TABLE 34-2

Data Types Available in Microsoft Access

Data Type	Type of Data Stored	Storage Size
Text	Alphanumeric characters	0–255 characters
Memo	Alphanumeric characters	0–65,536 characters
Number	Numeric values	1, 2, 4, or 8 bytes, 16 bytes for Replication ID (GUID)
Date/Time	Date and time data	8 bytes
Currency	Monetary data	8 bytes
AutoNumber	Automatic number increments	4 bytes, 16 bytes for Replication ID (GUID)
Yes/No	Logical values: Yes/No, True/False	1 bit (0 or –1)
OLE Object	Pictures, graphs, sound, video	Up to 1GB (disk space limitation)
Hyperlink	Link to an Internet resource	0–64,000 characters
Attachment	A special field (new in Access 2007) that enables you to attach external files to an Access database	Varies by attachment
Lookup Wizard	Displays data from another table	Generally 4 bytes

Figure 34-17 shows the Data Type drop-down list used to select the data type for any field you just created.

FIGURE 34-17

The Data Type drop-down list.

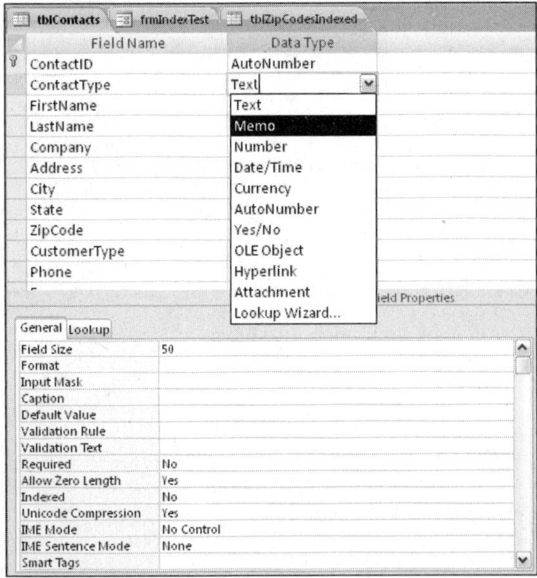

Here are the basic rules to consider when choosing the data type for new fields in your tables:

- **The data type should reflect the data stored in the field.** For instance, you should select one of the numeric data types to store numbers like quantities and prices. Do not store data like phone numbers or Social Security numbers in numeric fields, however. Your application will not be performing numeric operations like addition or multiplication on phone numbers, so this data should not be stored in numeric fields. Instead, use text fields for common data such as Social Security numbers and phone numbers.

  Also, numeric fields never store leading zeros. Putting a zip code such as 02173 into a numeric field means only the last four digits (2173) are actually stored.
- **Consider the storage requirements of the data type you've selected.** Although you can use a long integer data type in place of a simple integer or byte value, the storage requirements of a long integer (4 bytes) is twice that of a simple integer. This means that twice as much memory is required to use and manipulate the number and twice as much disk space is required to store its value. Whenever possible, use byte or integer data types for simple numeric data.
- **Will you want to sort or index the field?** Because of their binary nature, memo and OLE object fields cannot be sorted or indexed. Use memo fields sparingly. The overhead required to store and work with memo fields is considerable.
- **Consider the impact of data type on sorting requirements.** Numeric data sort differently than text data. Using the numeric data type, a sequence of numbers will sort as expected: 1, 2, 3, 4, 5, 10, 100. The same sequence stored as text data will sort like this: 1, 10, 100, 2, 3, 4, 5. If it's important to sort text data in a numeric sequence, you'll have to first apply a conversion function to the data before sorting.

NOTE **If it's important to have text data representing numbers to sort in the proper order, you may want to prefix the numerals with zeros (001, 002, and so on). Then the text values will sort in the expected order: 001, 002, 003, 004, 005, 010, 100.**

- **Is the data text or date data?** When working with dates, you're almost always better off storing the data in a `Date/Time` field than as a `Text` field. Text values sort differently than date data (dates are stored internally as numeric values), which can upset reports and other output that rely on chronological order.
- **Keep in mind the reports that will be needed.** You won't be able to sort or group memo or OLE data on a report. If it's important to prepare a report based on memo or OLE data, add a Tag field like a date or sequence number, which can be used to provide a sorting key, to the table.

Text data type

Any type of data that is simply characters (letters, numbers, punctuation). Names, addresses, and descriptions are all text data, as are numeric data that are not used in a calculation (such as telephone numbers, Social Security numbers, and zip codes).

Although you specify the size of each `Text` field in the property area, you can enter no more than 255 characters of data in any `Text` field. Access uses variable length fields to store text data. If you designate a field to be 25 characters wide and you use only 5 characters for each record, then only enough room to store 5 characters is used in your database.

You will find that the `.accdb` database file may quickly grow quite large, but text fields are not the usual cause. However, it is good practice to limit text field widths to the maximum you believe they will be used for. Names are tricky because some cultures have long names. However, it is a safe bet that a postal code might be less than 12 characters wide while a U.S. state abbreviation is always 2 characters wide. By limiting the size of the text width, you also limit the number of characters that users can enter when the field is used in a form.

Memo data type

The Memo data type holds a variable amount of data from 0 to 65,536 characters for each record. Therefore, if one record uses 100 characters, another requires only 10, and yet another needs 3,000, you use only as much space as each record requires.

Notice that you did not specify a field size for the Memo data type. Access allocates as much space is necessary for the memo data.

Number data type

The Number data type enables you to enter *numeric* data; that is, numbers that will be used in mathematical calculations. (If you have data that will be used in monetary calculations, you should use the Currency data type, which performs calculations without rounding errors.)

The exact type of numeric data stored in a number field is determined by the Field Size property. Table 34-3 lists the various numeric data types, their maximum and minimum ranges, the decimal points supported by each numeric data type, and the storage (bytes) required by each numeric data type.

TABLE 34-3

Numeric Field Settings

Field Size Setting	Range	Decimal Places	Storage Size
Byte	0 to 255	None	1 byte
Integer	–32,768 to 32,767	None	2 bytes
Long Integer	–2,147,483,648 to 2,147,483,647	None	4 bytes
Double	-1.797×10^{308} to 1.797×10^{308}	15	8 bytes
Single	-3.4×10^{38} to 3.4×10^{38}	7	4 bytes
Replication ID	N/A	N/A	16 bytes
Decimal	1–28 precision	15	8 bytes

Many errors are caused by choosing the wrong numeric type for number fields. For instance, notice that the maximum value for the Integer data type is 32,767. We once saw a database that ran perfectly for several years and then started crashing with overflow errors. It turned out that the overflow was caused by a particular field being set to the Integer data type, and when the company occasionally processed very large orders, the 32,767 maximum was exceeded.

It is best to design your tables very conservatively and allow for larger values than you ever expect to see in your database. This is not to say that it is a good idea to use the Double data type for all numeric fields. The Double data type is very large (8 bytes) and is quite slow when used in calculations for another numeric operation. Instead, the Single data type is probably best for most floating-point calculations, and the Long Integer is best for most data where decimal points are irrelevant.

Date/Time data type

The Date/Time data type is a specialized number field for holding dates or times (or dates *and* times). When dates are stored in a Date/Time field, it is easy to calculate days between dates and other calendar operations. Date data stored in Date/Time fields sort and filter properly as well.

Currency

The `Currency` data type is another specialized number field. `Currency` numbers are not rounded during calculations and preserve 15 digits of precision to the left of the decimal point and 4 digits to the right. Because the `Currency` data type uses a fixed-decimal-point position, it is faster in numeric calculations than doubles.

AutoNumber

The `AutoNumber` field is another specialized `Number` data type. When an `AutoNumber` field is added to a table, Access automatically assigns an integer value to the field (beginning at 1) and increments the value each time a record is added to the table. Alternatively (determined by the `New Values` property), the value of the `AutoNumber` field is a random integer that is automatically inserted into new records.

Only one `AutoNumber` field can appear in a table. Once assigned to a record, the value of an `AutoNumber` field cannot be changed programmatically or by the user. `AutoNumber` fields are equivalent to the `Long Integer` data type and occupy 4 bytes, but display only positive values. The range of possible values for `AutoNumber` fields range from 1 to 4,294,967,296 — more than adequate to use as the primary key for most tables.

Yes/No

`Yes/No` fields accept only one of two possible values. Internally stored as a 1 or 0 bit, the `Yes/No` field is used to indicate yes/no, on/off, or true/false. A `Yes/No` field occupies a single bit of storage.

OLE Object

The `OLE Object` field stores OLE data, highly specialized binary objects such as Microsoft Word documents, Excel worksheets, sound or video clips, and images. The OLE object is created by an OLE server application and can be linked to the parent application or embedded in the Access table. OLE objects can only be displayed in bound object frames in Access forms and reports. OLE objects can be as large as 1GB or more in size. OLE fields cannot be indexed.

Attachment

The `Attachment` data type is new for Access 2007. In fact, the `Attachment` data type is one of the reasons Microsoft changed the format of the Access data file. The older MDB format is unable to accommodate attachments.

The Attachment data type is relatively complex, compared to the other type of Access fields.

Hyperlink data type

The `Hyperlink` data type field holds combinations of text and numbers stored as text and used as a hyperlink address. It can have up to three parts:

- The visual text that appears in a field (usually underlined).
- The Internet address — the path to a file (UNC, or Universal Naming Convention, path) or page (URL or Uniform Resource Locator).
- Any sub-address within the file or page. An example of a sub-address is the name of an Access 2000 form or report. Each part is separated by the pound symbol (#).

Lookup Wizard

The `Lookup Wizard` data type inserts a field that enables the end user to choose a value from another table or from the results of an SQL statement. The values may also be presented as a combo box or list box. At design time, the `Lookup Wizard` leads the developer through the process of defining the lookup characteristics when this data is assigned to a field.

Dragging a field created by the `Lookup Wizard` from the field list as you design a form, a combo box or list box is automatically created on the form. The list box or combo box also appears on a query datasheet that contains the field.

Entering a field description

The field description is completely optional; you use it only to help you remember a field's uses or to let another developer understand the field's purpose. Often you don't use the description column at all, or you use it only for fields whose purpose is not obvious. If you enter a field description, it appears in the status bar whenever you use that field in Access — in the datasheet or in a form. The field description can help clarify a field whose purpose is ambiguous or give the user a fuller explanation of the values valid for the field during data entry.

Creating tblContacts

Working with the different data types (plus the Lookup Wizard), you should be ready to create the final working copy of our example, `tblContacts`. When creating the table, you must add a field that is used to link this table to two other tables (`tblSales` and `tblContactLog`) in the Access Auto Auctions application.

AutoNumber fields and Access

Access gives special considerations to AutoNumber fields and assigning values to AutoNumber fields. You cannot change a previously defined field from another type to AutoNumber. If you try to change an existing field in a table to the AutoNumber field type, Access displays a `Control can't be edited: It's bound to AutoNumber field "ContactID"` error in the status bar (the exact error you see will differ, of course, depending on which field is designated as the AutoNumber).

Completing tblContacts

With tblContacts in Design view, you're now ready to create or modify all the fields of `tblContacts`. Table 34-1, earlier in this chapter, shows the completed field definitions for `tblContacts`. If you're following the examples, you should be able to complete the table design. Enter the field names and data types exactly as shown. You may also need to rearrange some of the fields. The next few pages explain how to change existing fields (which includes rearranging the field order, changing a field name, and deleting a field).

Here are the steps for adding fields to a table structure:

1. **Place the cursor in the Field Name column in the row where you want the field to appear.**
2. **Enter the field name and press Enter or Tab.**
3. **In the Data Type column, click the down arrow and select the data type.**
4. **Place the pointer in the Description column and type a description (optional).**

Repeat each of these steps to create each of the data entry fields for `tblContacts`. You can press the down-arrow (↓) key to move between rows, or simply use the mouse and click on any row. Remember that F6 moves you from the top to the bottom of the Table Design window and back.

Setting the Primary Key

Every table should have a *primary key* — one or more fields with a unique value for each record. (This principle is called *entity integrity* in the world of database management.) In `tblContacts`, the `ContactID` field is the primary key. Each contact has a different `ContactID` value so that you can identify one from the other. `ContactID 17` refers to one and only one record in the Contacts table. If you don't specify a primary key (unique value field), Access can create one for you.

Understanding unique values

Without the `ContactID` field, you'd have to rely on another field or combination of fields for uniqueness. You couldn't use the `LastName` field because two customers could easily have the same last name. In fact, you couldn't even use the `FirstName` and `LastName` fields together (multi-field key), for the same reason — two people could be named James Smith. You need to come up with a field that makes every record unique. Looking at the table, you may think that you could use a combination of the `LastName`, `FirstName`, and `Company` fields, but theoretically, it's possible that two people working at the same company have the same name.

The easiest way to solve this problem is to add an `AutoNumber` field for the express purpose of using it as the table's primary key. This is exactly the situation with the `Contacts` table. The primary key of this table is `ContactID`, an `AutoNumber` field.

If you don't designate a field as a primary key, Access can add an `AutoNumber` field and designate it as the table's primary key. This field contains a unique number for each record in the table, and Access maintains it automatically.

Generally speaking, you may want to create and maintain your own primary key, even if you always use AutoNumber fields as primary keys:

- A primary key is always an index.
- An index maintains a presorted order of one or more fields that greatly speeds up queries, searches, and sort requests.
- When you add new records to your table, Access checks for duplicate data and doesn't allow any duplicates for the primary key field.
- By default, Access displays a table's data in the order of its primary key.

By designating a field such as `ContactID` as the unique primary key, you can see your data in a meaningful order. In our example, because the `ContactID` field is an AutoNumber, its value is assigned automatically by Access in the order that a record is put into the system.

Choosing a primary key

Although all of the tables in the Access Auto Auctions application use `AutoNumber` fields as their primary keys, you should be aware of the reasons why `AutoNumbers` make such excellent primary keys. The characteristics of primary keys include the following:

- The primary key must uniquely identify each record.
- The primary key cannot be null.
- The primary key must exist when the record is created.
- The primary key definition must remain stable — you should never change a primary key value once it is established.
- The primary key must be compact and contain as few attributes as possible.

The ideal primary key is, then, a single field that is immutable and guaranteed to be unique within the table. For these reasons, the Access Auto Auctions database uses the `AutoNumber` field exclusively as the primary key for all tables.

Creating the primary key

The primary key can be created in any of three ways. With a table open in Design View:

- Select the field to be used as the primary key and select the Primary Key button (the key icon) in the Tools group in the ribbon's Design tab.
- Right-click on the field to display the shortcut menu and select Primary Key.
- Save the table without creating a primary key, and allow Access to automatically create an `AutoNumber` field.

After you designate the primary key, a key icon appears in the gray selector area to the left of the field's name to indicate that the primary key has been created.

Creating composite primary keys

Although rarely done these days, it is possible to designate a combination of fields to be used as a table's primary key. Such keys are often referred to as *composite* primary keys. As indicated in Figure 34-18, select the fields that you want to include in the composite primary key, then click the key icon in the Tools Ribbon tab. It helps, of course, if the fields lie right next to each other in the table's design.

FIGURE 34-18

Creating a composite primary key.

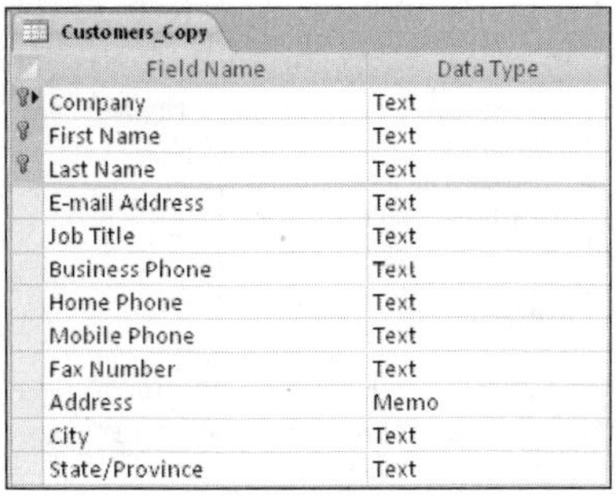

Customers_Copy

Field Name	Data Type
Company	Text
First Name	Text
Last Name	Text
E-mail Address	Text
Job Title	Text
Business Phone	Text
Home Phone	Text
Mobile Phone	Text
Fax Number	Text
Address	Memo
City	Text
State/Province	Text

Composite primary keys are primarily used when the developer strongly feels that a primary key should be comprised of data that occurs naturally in the database. There was a time when all developers were taught that every table should have a *natural* primary key.

The reason that composite primary keys are seldom used these days is because developers have come to realize that data is highly unpredictable. Even if your users promise that a combination of certain fields will never be duplicated in the table, things have a way of turning out differently than planned. Using a *surrogate* primary key, such as an AutoNumber, separates the table's design from the table's data. The problem with *natural primary keys* (meaning, data that occurs naturally in the table) is that, eventually, given a large enough data set, the values of fields chosen as the table's primary key are likely to be duplicated.

Furthermore, when using composite keys, maintaining relationships between tables becomes more complicated because the fields must be duplicated in all the tables containing related data. Using composite keys simply adds to the complexity of the database without adding stability, integrity, or other desirable features.

Printing a Table Design

You can print a table design by choosing the Analyze Table button in the Analyze group on the ribbon's Database Tools tab. The Analyze group contains a number of tools that makes it easy to document your database objects. When you select the Analyze Table button, Access shows you a dialog box that lets you select objects to print. In Figure 34-19, there is only one object (`tblContacts`) under the Tables tab. Select it by clicking the checkbox next to the table name.

FIGURE 34-19

The Access Documenter dialog box.

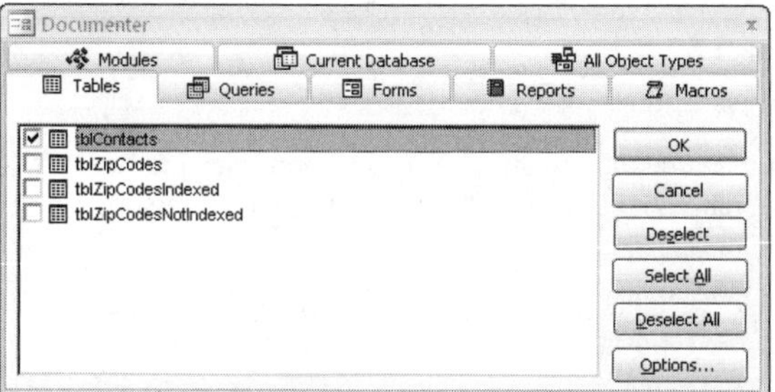

You can also set various options for printing. When you click the Options button, a dialog box appears that enables you to select which information from the Table Design to print. You can print the various field names, all of their properties, the indexes, and even network permissions.

After you select which data you want to view, Access generates a report; you can view it in a Print Preview window or send the output to a printer.

The Database Documenter creates a table of all the objects and object properties you specify. You can use this utility to document such database objects as forms, queries, reports, macros, and modules.

Saving the Completed Table

You can save the completed table design by choosing Office Button ➪ Save or by clicking the Save button in the upper-left corner of the Access environment. If you are saving the table for the first time, Access asks for the name of the table. Table names can be up to 64 characters long and follow standard Access object-naming conventions.

If you have saved this table before and want to save it with a different name, choose Office Button ➪ Save As and enter a different table name. This action creates a new table design and leaves the original table with its original name untouched. If you want to delete the old table, select it in the Navigation pane and press the `Delete` key. You can also save the table when you close it.

Manipulating Tables in a Database Window

As you create many tables in your database, you may want to use them in other databases or copy them for use as a history file. You may want to copy only the table structure. You can perform many operations on tables in the Navigation pane, including

- Renaming tables
- Deleting tables
- Copying tables in a database
- Copying a table from another database

You perform these tasks by direct manipulation or by using menu items.

Renaming tables

Rename a table with these steps:

1. **Select the table name in the Database window.**
2. **Click once on the table name, and press F2.**
3. **Type the new name of the table and press Enter.**

You can also rename the table by right-clicking on its name in the Navigation pane, and selecting Rename from the shortcut menu. After you change the table name, it appears in the Tables list, which re-sorts the tables in alphabetical order.

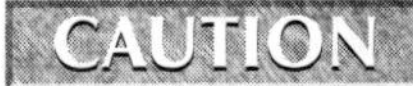

If you rename a table, you must change the table name in any objects where it was previously referenced, including queries, forms, and reports.

Deleting tables

Delete a table by selecting the table in the Navigation pane and pressing the Delete key. Another method is by right-clicking a table and selecting Delete from the shortcut menu. Like most delete operations, you have to confirm the delete by selecting Yes in a confirmation dialog box.

Copying tables in a database

The copy and paste options in the Clipboard group on the Home tab allow you to copy any table in the database. When you paste the table back into the database, you choose from three option buttons:

- Structure Only
- Structure and Data
- Append Data to Existing Table

Selecting the `Structure Only` button creates a new table, empty table with the same design as the copied table. This option is typically used to create a temporary table or an archive table to which you can copy old records.

When you select `Structure and Data`, a complete copy of the table design and all of its data is created.

Selecting the `Append Data to Existing Table` button adds the data of the selected table to the bottom of another. This option is useful for combining tables, such as when you want to add data from a monthly transaction table to a yearly history table.

Follow these steps to copy a table:

1. **Right-click the table name in the Navigation pane.**
2. **Choose Copy from the shortcut menu, or choose the Copy button in the Clipboard group on the Home tab.**
3. **Choose Paste from the shortcut menu, or choose the Paste button in the Clipboard group on the Home tab.**
4. **Provide the name of the new table.**
5. **Choose one of the Paste options (`Structure Only`, `Structure and Data`, or `Append Data to Existing Table`).**
6. **Click OK to complete the operation.**

Figure 34-20 shows the `Paste Table As` dialog box, where you make these decisions. To paste the data, you have to select the type of paste operation and type the name of the new table. When you are appending data to an existing table, you must type the name of an existing table.

FIGURE 34-20

Pasting a table activates this dialog box. You can paste only the structure, the data and structure, or the data to an existing table.

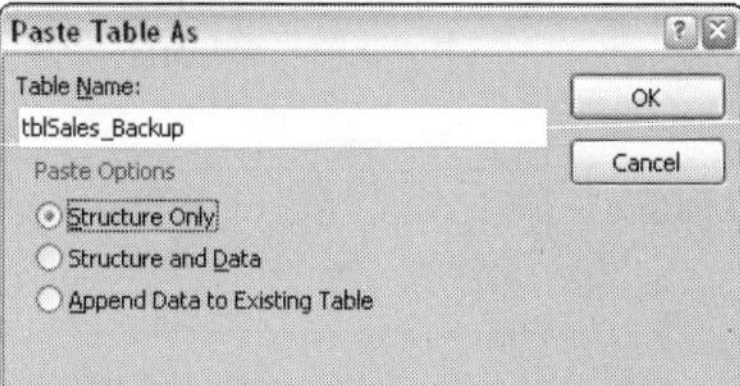

Copying a table to another database

Just as you can copy a table within a database, you can copy a table to another database. There are many reasons why you may want to do this. Possibly you share a common table among multiple systems, or you may need to create a backup copy of your important tables within the system.

When you copy tables to another database, the relationships between tables are not copied; Access copies only the table design and the data. The method for copying a table to another database is essentially the same as for copying a table within a database. To copy a table to another database, follow these steps:

1. **Right-click the table name in the Navigation pane.**
2. **Choose Copy from the shortcut menu, or choose the Copy button in the Clipboard group on the Home tab.**
3. **Open the other Access database.**
4. **Choose Edit Paste from the shortcut menu, or choose the Copy button in the Clipboard group on the Home tab.**
5. **Provide the name of the new table.**
6. **Choose one of the Paste options (`Structure Only`, `Structure and Data`, or `Append Data to Existing Table`).**
7. **Click OK to complete the operation.**

Adding Records to a Database Table

So far you have only created one table in the MyAccessAutoAuctions database: `tblContacts`.

Adding records is as simple as selecting the table name in the database container and clicking on its name to bring up the table in Datasheet view. Once opened, you can type in values for each field. Figure 34-21 shows adding records in datasheet mode to the table.

You can enter information into all fields except the Contact ID field (`ContactID`). `AutoNumber` fields automatically provide a number for you.

FIGURE 34-21

Adding records to a table using Datasheet view.

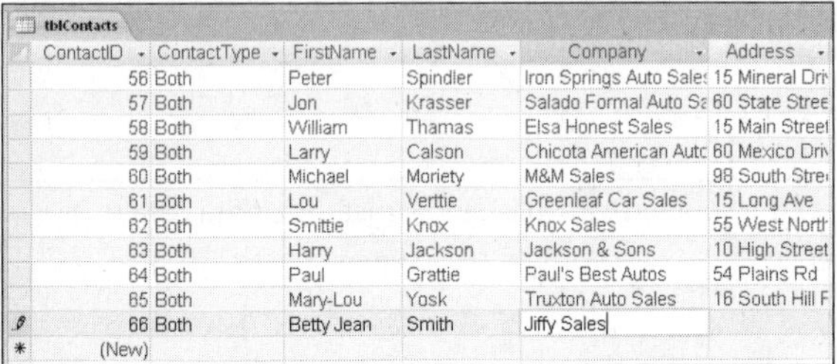

tblContacts

	ContactID	ContactType	FirstName	LastName	Company	Address
	56	Both	Peter	Spindler	Iron Springs Auto Sale	15 Mineral Dri
	57	Both	Jon	Krasser	Salado Formal Auto Sa	60 State Stree
	58	Both	William	Thamas	Elsa Honest Sales	15 Main Street
	59	Both	Larry	Calson	Chicota American Autc	60 Mexico Driv
	60	Both	Michael	Moriety	M&M Sales	98 South Stre
	61	Both	Lou	Verttie	Greenleaf Car Sales	15 Long Ave
	62	Both	Smittie	Knox	Knox Sales	55 West North
	63	Both	Harry	Jackson	Jackson & Sons	10 High Street
	64	Both	Paul	Grattie	Paul's Best Autos	54 Plains Rd
	65	Both	Mary-Lou	Yosk	Truxton Auto Sales	16 South Hill F
	66	Both	Betty Jean	Smith	Jiffy Sales	
*	(New)					

Although you can add records directly into the table through the Datasheet view, it is not the most efficient way. Adding records using forms is better.

Opening a datasheet

To open a datasheet from the Database window, click Tables in the Navigation Pane. Then, double-click the name of the table you want to open, for example, `tblProducts`.

An alternative method for opening the datasheet is to right-click on the table name and select Open from the pop-up menu.

If you are in any of the design windows, click on the Datasheet View command in the ribbon's View group to view your data in a datasheet.

Moving within a datasheet

You easily move within the Datasheet window using the mouse to indicate where you want to change or add to your data — just click a field and record location. In addition, the ribbons, scroll bars, and Navigation buttons make it easy to move among fields and records. Think of a datasheet as a spreadsheet without the row numbers and column letters. Instead, columns have field names, and rows are unique records that have identifiable values in each cell.

Table 34-4 lists the navigational keys that you can use for moving within a datasheet.

TABLE 34-4

Navigating in a Datasheet

Navigational Direction	Keystrokes
Next field	Tab
Previous field	Shift+Tab
First field of current record	Home
Last field of current record	End
Next record	Down arrow (↓)
Previous record	Up arrow (↑)
First field of first record	Ctrl+Home
Last field of last record	Ctrl+End
Scroll up one page	PgUp
Scroll down one page	PgDn

The Navigation buttons

The *Navigation buttons* (shown in Figure 34-22) are the six controls located at the bottom of the Datasheet window, which you click to move between records. The two leftmost controls move you to the first record or the previous record in the datasheet. The three rightmost controls position you on the next record, last record, or new record in the datasheet. If you know the record number (the row number of a specific record), you can click the record number box, enter a record number, and press Enter.

FIGURE 34-22

The Navigation buttons of a datasheet.

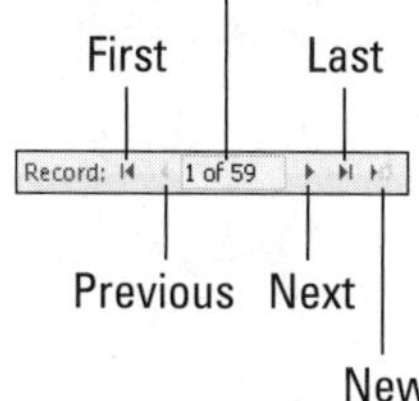

If you enter a record number greater than the number of records in the table, an error message appears stating that you can't go to the specified record.

Entering new data

All the records in your table are visible when you first open it in Datasheet View. If you just created your table, the new datasheet doesn't contain any data. Figure 34-32 shows an empty datasheet. When the datasheet is empty, the first row contains an asterisk (*) in the record selector — indicating it's a new record.

FIGURE 34-23

An empty datasheet. Notice that the first record is blank and has an asterisk in the record selector.

New Record Indicator

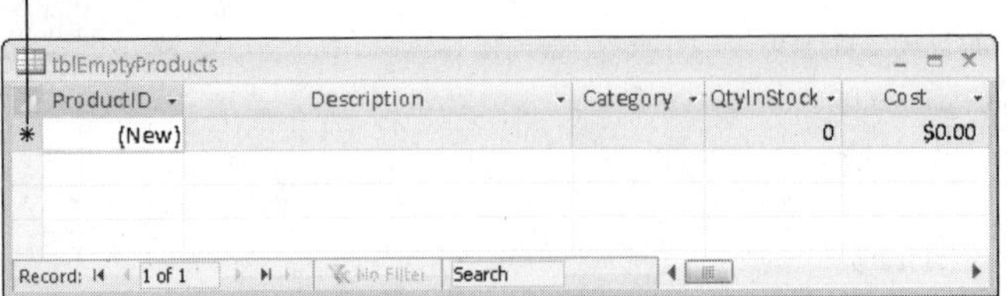

tblEmptyProducts

	ProductID	Description	Category	QtyInStock	Cost
*	(New)			0	$0.00

Record: 1 of 1 No Filter Search

The new record appears at the bottom of the datasheet when the datasheet already contains records. Click the New Record command in the ribbon's Record group, or click the new record navigation button to move the cursor to the new row — or simply click on the last row, which contains the asterisk. The asterisk turns into a pencil when you begin entering data, indicating that the record is being edited. A new row — containing an asterisk — appears below the one you're entering data into. The new-record pointer always appears in the last row of the datasheet. Figure 34-24 shows adding a new record into `tblProducts`.

FIGURE 34-24

Entering a new record into the datasheet of tblProducts.

Record Selectors

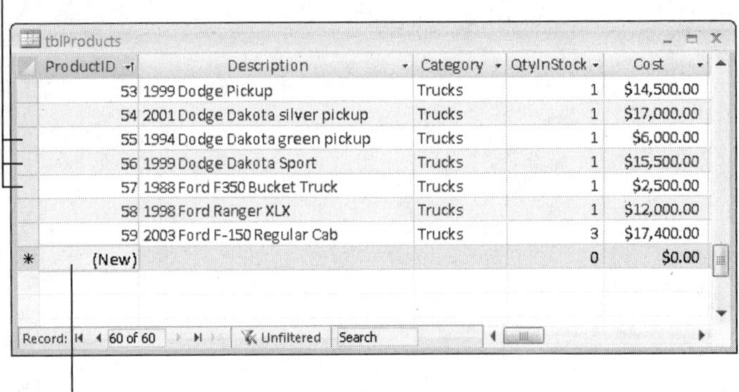

tblProducts

	ProductID	Description	Category	QtyInStock	Cost
	53	1999 Dodge Pickup	Trucks	1	$14,500.00
	54	2001 Dodge Dakota silver pickup	Trucks	1	$17,000.00
	55	1994 Dodge Dakota green pickup	Trucks	1	$6,000.00
	56	1999 Dodge Dakota Sport	Trucks	1	$15,500.00
	57	1988 Ford F350 Bucket Truck	Trucks	1	$2,500.00
	58	1998 Ford Ranger XLX	Trucks	1	$12,000.00
	59	2003 Ford F-150 Regular Cab	Trucks	3	$17,400.00
*	(New)			0	$0.00

Record: 60 of 60 Unfiltered Search

New Row

To add a new record to the open Datasheet View of the `tblProducts`, follow these steps:

1. **Click the New Record button.**
2. **Type in values for all fields of the table, moving between fields by pressing the Enter key or the Tab key.**

When adding or editing records, you may see three different record pointers:

- Record being edited
- Record is locked (multiuser systems)
- New record

CAUTION **If the record contains an `AutoNumber` field, Access shows the name (New) in the field. You cannot enter a value in this type of field; rather, simply press the Tab or Enter key to skip this field. Access automatically puts the number in when you begin entering data.**

Saving the record

Moving to a different record saves the record you're editing. Tabbing through all the fields, clicking on the Navigation buttons, clicking Save in the ribbon's Record group, and closing the table all write the edited record to the database. You'll know the record is saved when the pencil disappears from the record selector.

To save a record, you must enter valid values into each field. The fields are validated for data type, uniqueness (if indexed for unique values), and any validation rules that you have entered into the `Validation Rule` property. If your table has a primary key that's not an `AutoNumber` field, you'll have to make sure you enter a unique value in the primary key field to avoid an error message. Using an `AutoNumber` field as a table's primary key ensures you won't get this error message when entering data.

The Undo button in the Quick Access toolbar reverses changes to the current record and to the last saved record. After you change a second record, you cannot undo the saved record.

You can save the record to disk without leaving the record by pressing Shift+Enter.

Now you know how to enter, edit, and save data in a new or existing record. Next you learn how Access validates your data as you make entries into the fields.

Understanding automatic data type validation

Access validates certain types of data automatically. Therefore, you don't have to enter any data-validation rules for these data types when you specify table properties. The data types that Access validates automatically include

- Number/Currency
- Date/Time
- Yes/No

Access validates the data type when you move off the field. When you enter a letter into a Number or Currency field, you don't initially see a warning not to enter these characters. However, when you tab out of or click on a different field, you get a warning like the one shown in Figure 34-25. This particular warning lets you choose to enter a new value or change the column's data type to Text. You'll see this message if you enter other inappropriate characters (symbols, letters, and so on), enter more than one decimal point, or enter a number too large for a certain Number data type.

FIGURE 34-25

The warning Access displays when entering data that doesn't match the field's data type. Access gives you a few choices to correct the problem.

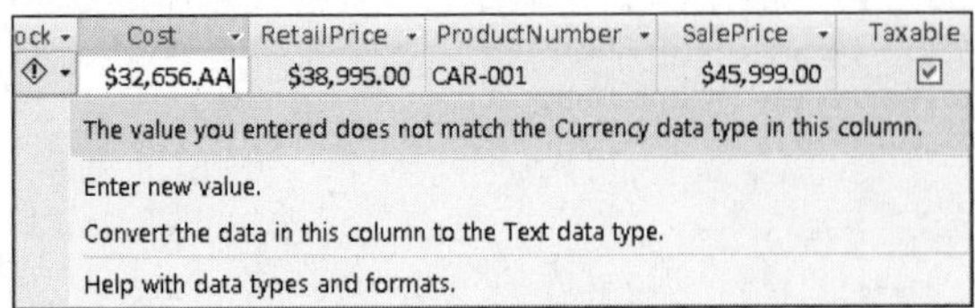

Access validates Date/Time fields for valid date or time values. You'll see a warning similar to the one shown in Figure 34-34 if you try to enter a date such as 14/45/05, a time such as 37:39:12, or an invalid character in a Date/Time field.

Yes/No fields require that you enter one of these defined values: Yes, True, -1, or a number other than 0 (it displays as a -1) for Yes; or No, False, Off, or 0 for No. Of course, you can define your own acceptable values in the Format property for the field, but generally these are the only acceptable values. If you enter an invalid value, the warning appears with the message to indicate an inappropriate value.

Display a checkbox in Yes/No fields to prevent users from entering invalid data.

Navigating Records in a Datasheet

Wanting to make changes to records after you've entered them is not unusual. You may want to change records for several reasons:

- You receive new information that changes existing values.
- You discover errors in existing values.
- You need to add new records.

When you decide to edit data in a table, the first step is to open the table — if it isn't already open. From the list of tables in the Navigation pane, double-click on `tblProducts` to open it in Datasheet View. If you're already in Design View for this table, click the Datasheet View button to switch views.

When you open a datasheet in Access that has related tables, a column with a plus sign (+) is added to access the related records, or sub-datasheets.

Moving between records

You can move to any record by scrolling through the records and positioning your cursor on the desired one. With a large table, scrolling through all the records might take a while, so you'll want to use other methods to get to specific records quickly.

Use the vertical scroll bar to move between records. The scroll-bar arrows move one record at a time. To move through many records at a time, drag the scroll box or click the areas between the scroll box and the scroll-bar arrows.

Watch the ScrollTips when you use scroll bars to move to another area of the datasheet. Access does not update the record number box until you click a field.

Use the five Navigation buttons to move between records. You simply click these buttons to move to the desired record. If you know the record number (row number of a specific record), click the record number box, enter a record number, and press Enter.

Also use the Go To command in the ribbon's Find group to navigate to the First, Previous, Next, Last, and New records.

Finding a specific value

Although you can move to a specific record (if you know the record number) or to a specific field in the current record, usually you'll want to find a certain value in a record. You can use one of these methods for locating a value in a field:

- Select the Find command (a pair of binoculars) from the ribbon's Find group.
- Press Ctrl+F.
- Use the Search box at the bottom of the datasheet window.

The first two methods display the Find and Replace dialog box. To limit the search to a specific field, place your cursor in the field you want to search before you open the dialog box. Change the Look In combo box to the table name to search the entire table for the value.

TIP **If you highlight the entire record by clicking the record selector (the small gray box next to the record), Access automatically searches through all fields.**

The Find and Replace dialog box lets you control many aspects of the search. Enter the value you want to search for in the Find What combo box — which contains a list of recently used searches. You can enter a specific value or choose to use three types of wildcards:

* (any number of characters)

? (any one character)

(any one number)

To look at how these wildcards work, first suppose that you want to find any value in the `Description` field of `tblProducts` beginning with 2001; for this, you type **2001***. Then suppose that you want to search for values ending with Sedan, so you type ***Sedan**. If you want to search for any value that begins with 2001, ends with Sedan, and contains any number of characters in between, you type **2001*Sedan**.

The Match drop-down list contains three choices that eliminate the need for wildcards:

- Any Part of Field
- Whole Field
- Start of Field

The default is Whole Field, which finds only the whole value you enter. For example, the Whole Field option finds the value FORD only if the value in the field being searched is exactly FORD. If you select Any Part of Field, Access searches to see whether the value is contained anywhere in the field; this search finds the value FORD in the field values FORDMAN, 2001 FORD F-150, and FORD. A search for FORD using the Start of Field option searches from the beginning of the field, and returns no values because the `Description` field always begins with a year (1999, 2003, and so on).

In addition to these combo boxes, you can use two checkboxes at the bottom of the Find and Replace dialog box:

- **Match Case:** Match Case determines whether the search is case-sensitive. The default is not case-sensitive (not checked). A search for SMITH finds smith, SMITH, or Smith. If you check the Match Case checkbox, you must then enter the search string in the exact case of the field value. (The data types Number, Currency, and Date/Time do not have any case attributes.)

  If you have checked Match Case, Access does not use the value Search Fields As Formatted (the second checkbox), which limits the search to the actual values displayed in the table. (If you format a field for display in the datasheet, you should check the box.)
- **Search Fields As Formatted:** The Search Fields As Formatted checkbox, the selected default, finds only text that has the same pattern of characters as the text specified in the Find What box. Clear this box to find text regardless of the formatting. For example, if you're searching the `Cost` field for a value of $16,500, you must enter the comma if Search Fields as Formatted is checked. Uncheck this box to search for an unformatted value (16500).

CAUTION **Checking Search Fields As Formatted may slow the search process.**

The search begins when you click the Find Next button. If Access finds the value, the cursor highlights it in the datasheet. To find the next occurrence of the value, click the Find Next button again. The dialog box remains open so that you can find multiple occurrences. Choose one of three search direction choices (Up, Down, All) in the Search drop-down list to change the search direction. When you find the value that you want, click Close to close the dialog box.

Use the search box at the bottom of the Datasheet window (refer to Figure 6-1) to quickly search for the first instance of a value. When using the search box, Access searches the entire datasheet for the value in any part of the field. If you type FORD in the search box, the datasheet moves as you type each letter. First, it finds an *F*; then it finds *FO* and so on. Once it finds the value, it stops searching. To find more than one instance, use the Find and Replace dialog box.

Changing Values in a Datasheet

If the field that you are in has no value, you can type a new value into the field. When you enter new values into a field, follow the same rules as for a new-record entry.

Generally, you enter a field with either no characters selected or the entire value selected. If you use the keyboard (Tab or Arrow keys) to enter a field, you select the entire value. (You know that the entire value is selected when it is displayed in reverse video.) When you begin to type, the new content replaces the selected value automatically.

When you click in a field, the value is not selected. To select the entire value with the mouse, use any of these methods:

- Click just to the left of the value when the cursor is shown as a large plus sign.
- Double-click in the field. (This only works if the field doesn't contain spaces.)
- Click to the left of the value, hold down the left mouse button, and drag the mouse to select the whole value.
- Click in the field and press F2.

TIP You may want to replace an existing value with the value from the field's Default Value property. To do so, select the value and press Ctrl+Alt+Spacebar. To replace an existing value with that of the same field from the preceding record, press Ctrl+' (single quote mark). Press Ctrl+; (semicolon) to place the current date in a field.

CAUTION Pressing Ctrl+- (minus sign) deletes the current record.

If you want to change an existing value instead of replacing the entire value, use the mouse and click in front of any character in the field to activate Insert mode; the existing value moves to the right as you type the new value. If you press the Insert key, your entry changes to Overstrike mode; you replace one character at a time as you type. Use the arrow keys to move between characters without disturbing them. Erase characters to the left by pressing Backspace, or to the right of the cursor by pressing Delete.

Table 34-5 lists editing techniques.

TABLE 34-5

Editing Techniques

Editing Operation	Keystrokes
Move the insertion point within a field	Press the right-arrow (→) and left-arrow (←) keys
Insert a value within a field	Select the insertion point and type new data
Select the entire field	Press F2
Replace an existing value with a new value	Select the entire field and type a new value
Replace a value with the value of the previous field	Press Ctrl+' (single quote mark)
Replace the current value with the default value	Press Ctrl+Alt+Spacebar
Insert a line break in a Text or Memo field	Press Ctrl+Enter
Save the current record	Press Shift+Enter or move to another record
Insert the current date	Ctrl+; (semicolon)
Insert the current time	Ctrl+: (colon)
Add a new record	Ctrl++ (plus sign)
Delete the current record	Ctrl+- (minus sign)
Toggle values in a checkbox or option button	Spacebar
Undo a change to the current field	Press Esc or click the Undo button
Undo a change to the current record	Press Esc or click the Undo button a second time after you undo the current field

Fields that you can't edit

Some fields can't be edited, such as:

- **AutoNumber fields:** Access maintains AutoNumber fields automatically, calculating the values as you create each new record. AutoNumber fields can be used as the primary key.
- **Calculated fields:** Access uses calculated fields in forms or queries; these values are not actually stored in your table.

- **Locked or disabled fields:** You can set certain properties in a form to prevent editing for a specific field.
- **Fields in multiuser locked records:** If another user locks the record, you can't edit any fields in that record.

Summary

This chapter has covered the important topics of creating new Access databases, and adding tables to Access databases. Although this chapter covered these topics from the perspective of creating brand-new databases and tables, the operations you performed in this chapter are identical to the maintenance procedures you perform on existing databases and tables.

The next chapter drills into very important topics about creating and using forms.

Chapter 35

Creating and Entering Data with Basic Access Forms

Forms provide the most flexible way of viewing, adding, editing, and deleting your data. They are also used for *switchboards* (forms with buttons that provide navigation), dialog boxes that control the flow of the system, and displaying messages. Controls are the objects on forms such as labels, text boxes, buttons, and many others. In this chapter, you learn how to create different types of forms and get an understanding about the types of controls that are used on a form. You also learn how to enter data with a form and print a form.

IN THIS CHAPTER

- Creating different types of forms
- Understanding controls
- Adding controls to a form
- Using the Field List
- Using the Ribbon's Controls group
- Selecting controls
- Manipulating controls
- Understanding control properties
- Using the Property Sheet
- Control naming conventions
- Using Form View
- Navigating in a form
- Editing data in a form
- Entering pictures and data into OLE fields and Memo fields
- Using the date picker
- Switching views
- Printing a form

ON the WEB In this chapter, you use `tblProducts` in the `Chapter35.accdb` database to provide the data necessary to create the examples used in this chapter. That example database is available for download from `http://www.wiley.com/TOCOME`. When you open the file, you can click Options in the Security Warning bar, click Enable This Content in the Microsoft Office Security Options dialog box, and then click OK.

Adding Forms Using the Ribbon

Use the Form group in the Create tab on the Ribbon to add forms to your database. The commands in the Form group — shown in Figure 35-1 — let you create the following different types of forms:

- **Form:** Creates a new form that lets you enter information for one record at a time. You must have a table, query, form, or report open or selected to use this command.
- **Split Form:** Creates a split form that shows a datasheet in the lower section and a form in the upper section for entering information about the record selected in the datasheet.
- **Multiple Items:** Creates a form that shows multiple records in a datasheet, with one record per row.
- **PivotChart:** Instantly creates a PivotChart form.

- **Blank Form:** Instantly creates a blank form with no controls.
- **More Forms:** This drop-down list lets you start the Form Wizard or instantly create a Datasheet, Modal Dialog, or PivotTable.
- **Form Design:** Creates a new blank form and displays it in Design View.

FIGURE 35-1

The Ribbon's Create tab. Use the Form group to add new forms to your database.

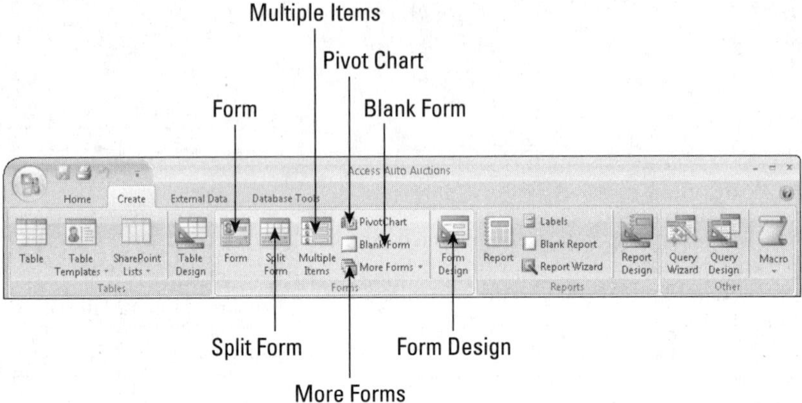

Creating a new form

Use the Form command in the Form group of the Ribbon's Create tab to create a new form based on a table or query selected in the Navigation Pane. To create a form based on the example `tblProducts` table you created in the last chapter, follow these steps:

1. **Select `tblProducts` in the Navigation Pane.**
2. **Click the Create tab on the Ribbon, and then click on the Form command in the Form group.**

   Access creates a new form containing all the fields from `tblProducts` displayed in Layout View, shown in Figure 35-2. Layout View lets you see the forms data while changing the layout of controls on the form.

NOTE You may notice that Figures showing forms and other objects in this chapter and the next two no longer show the objects in the new tabbed format that is the default in Access 2007. That's because in some objects, like a form, you might not be able to see the fields completely in a tab rather than a window. The example files that you download for this chapter and the next two have already been set up to use windows rather than tabs for objects. To change between the tab and window display methods, select Office Button ➪ Access Options. Click Current Database in the list at the left. Under Document Window options (in the Application Options section), click Overlapping Windows to display objects in windows, or Tabbed Documents to show tabs (make sure that Display Document Tabs is also checked). When you click OK, a message box tells you that you must close and reopen the database for the change to take effect. Click OK. Select Office Button ➪ Close Database to close the file, and then reopen it. Also note that depending on the screen resolution that you're using, some fields may appear cut off, even in a window. You can change your screen resolution or resize the Navigation Pane as needed to show more information in the windows in Access, as needed.

FIGURE 35-2

Creating a new form. Use the Form command to quickly create a new form with all the fields from a table or query.

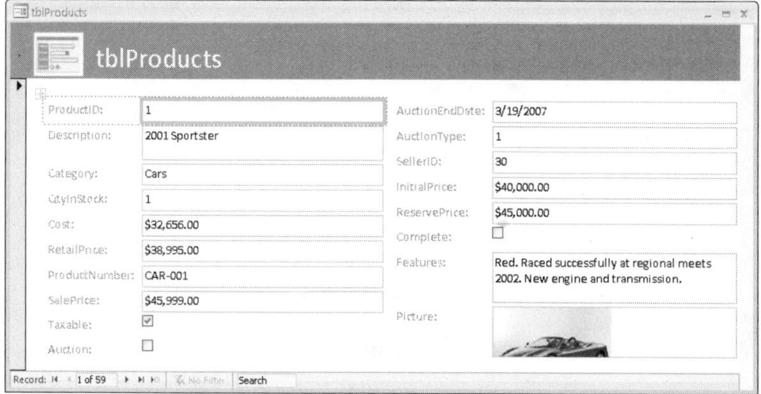

Creating a split form

Use the Split Form command in the Form group on the Create tab of the Ribbon to create a split form based on a table or query selected in the Navigation Pane. This new feature gives you two views of the data at the same time, letting you select a record from a datasheet in the upper section and edit the information in a form in the lower section. To create a split form based on `tblProducts`, follow these steps:

1. **Select `tblProducts` in the Navigation Pane.**
2. **Click the Create tab on the Ribbon, and then click on the Split Form command in the Form group.**

   Access creates a new split form based on `tblProducts` displayed in Layout View, shown in Figure 35-3. Resize the form and use the splitter bar in the middle to make the lower section completely visible.

Creating a multiple-items form

Use the Multiple Items command in the Form group of the Ribbon's Create tab to create a multiple-items form based on a table or query selected in the Navigation Pane. This new feature creates a form that looks like a datasheet, but it lets you add graphical elements, buttons, and other controls. To create a multiple-items form based on `tblProducts`, follow these steps:

1. **Select `tblProducts` in the Navigation Pane.**
2. **Click the Create tab on the Ribbon, and then click on the Multiple Items command in the Form group.**

   Access creates a new multiple items form based on `tblProducts` displayed in Layout View, shown in Figure 35-4. Although the form looks similar to a datasheet, you can only resize the rows and columns in Design View and Layout View.

FIGURE 35-3

Create a split form when you want to select records from a list and edit them in a form. Use the splitter bar to resize the upper and lower sections of the form.

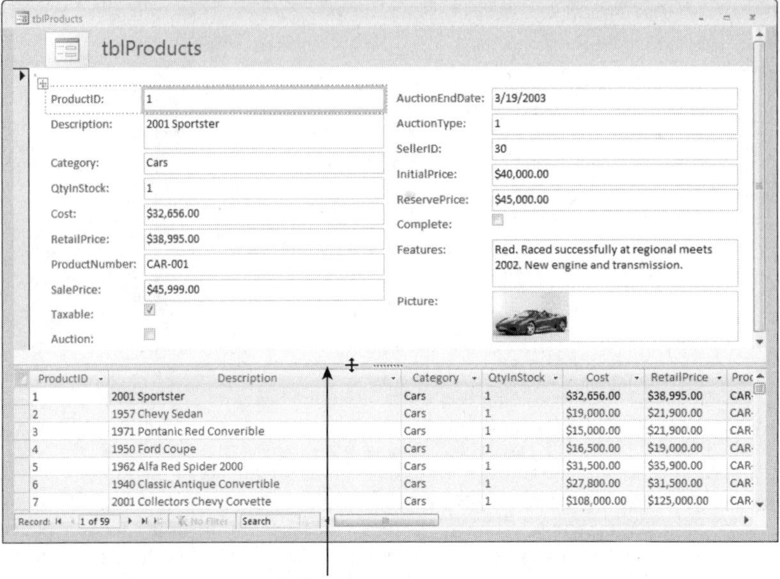

FIGURE 35-4

Create a multiple items form when you want to see data similar to Datasheet View but also want to add form controls such as buttons and graphical elements.

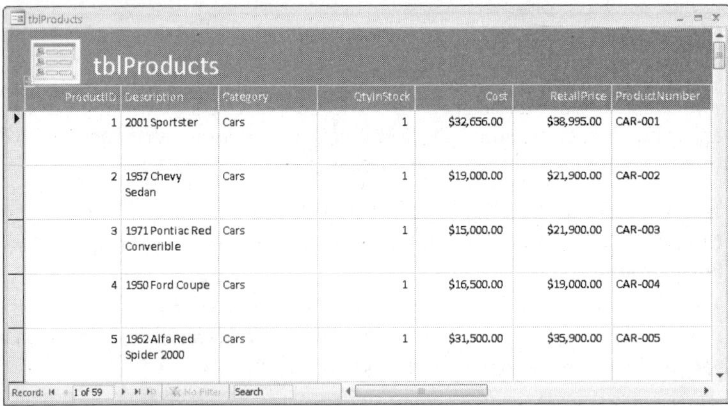

Creating a form using the Form Wizard

Use the Form Wizard command in the Form group's More Forms drop-down list to create a form using a wizard. The Form Wizard visually walks you through a series of questions about the form that you want to create and then creates it for you automatically. The Form Wizard lets you select which fields you want on the form, the layout (Columnar, Tabular, Datasheet, Justified) of the form, the style (Access 2003, Access 2007, Apex, and so on), and the title on the form.

To start the Form Wizard based on `tblProducts`, follow these steps:

1. **Select `tblProducts` in the Navigation Pane.**
2. **Click the Create tab on the Ribbon, and then click on the Form group's More Forms drop-down and select Form Wizard.**

   Access starts the Form Wizard shown in Figure 35-5. Choose which table or query you want the form based on using the Tables/Queries drop-down list. Use the buttons in the middle of the form to add and remove fields to the Available Fields and Selected Fields list boxes.

FIGURE 35-5

Use the Form Wizard to create a form with the fields you choose, as well as the layout and styles you want.

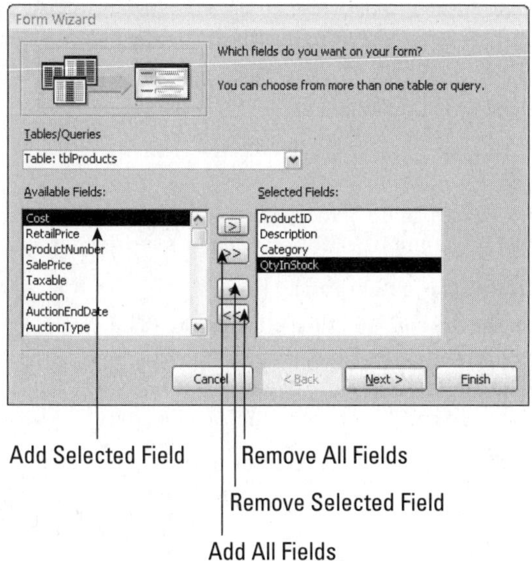

You can also double-click any field in the Available Fields list box to add it to the Selected Fields list box.

The series of buttons at the bottom of the form let you navigate through the other steps of the wizard. The types of buttons available here are common to most wizard dialog boxes:

- **Cancel:** Cancel the wizard without creating a form
- **Back:** Return to the preceding step of the wizard
- **Next:** Go to the next step of the wizard
- **Finish:** End the wizard using the current selections

If you click Next or Finish without selecting any fields, Access tells you that you must select fields for the form before you can continue.

Creating a datasheet form

Use the Datasheet command in the Form group's More Forms drop-down list to create a form that looks like a table or query's datasheet. A datasheet form is useful when you want to see the data in a row and column format but want to limit which fields are displayed and editable. To create a datasheet form based on `tblProducts`, follow these steps:

1. **Select `tblProducts` in the Navigation Pane.**
2. **Click the Create tab on the Ribbon, and then click on the Form group's More Forms drop-down and select Datasheet.**

   You can view any form you create as a datasheet by selecting Datasheet View from the Home tab's View drop-down. A datasheet form appears in Datasheet View by default when you open it.

You can prevent users from viewing a form as a datasheet by setting the form's properties. You'll learn more about form properties later in this chapter.

Creating a blank form

Use the Blank Form command in the Form group of the Create tab on the Ribbon to create a form without any controls. To create a blank form based on `tblProducts`, follow these steps:

1. **Select `tblProducts` in the Navigation Pane.**
2. **Click the Create tab on the Ribbon, and then click on the Blank Form command in the Form group.**

   Access creates a new blank form based on `tblProducts` displayed in Layout View. In the next section, you'll learn how to add and customize controls on the form.

Use the Form Design command in the Form group of the Create tab on the Ribbon to create a blank form and display it in Design View.

Adding Controls

In this section, you'll learn how to change a form's design using Design View. You'll add, move, and resize different controls, as well as customize other aspects of a form.

Click on Design View from the View drop-down in the Home tab's Views group to switch a form to Design View. The Design tab on the Form Design Tools contextual tab — shown in Figure 35-6 — lets you add and customize controls on your form.

FIGURE 35-6

The Design tab lets you add and customize controls in a form's Design View.

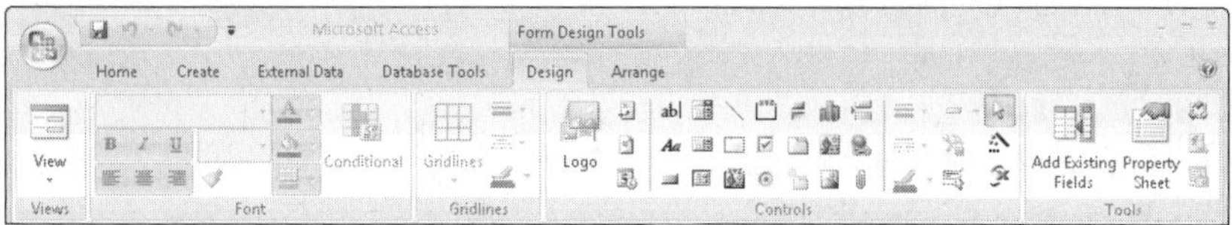

NEW FEATURE The Controls group on the Ribbon's Design tab replaces the Toolbox from previous versions of Access.

Resizing the form area

The white area of the form is where you work. This is the size of the form when it is displayed. Resize the white area of the form by placing the cursor on any of the area borders and dragging the border of the area to make it larger or smaller. Figure 35-7 shows a blank form in Design View being resized.

FIGURE 35-7

Design View of a blank form. Resize the form area by dragging the bottom-right corner.

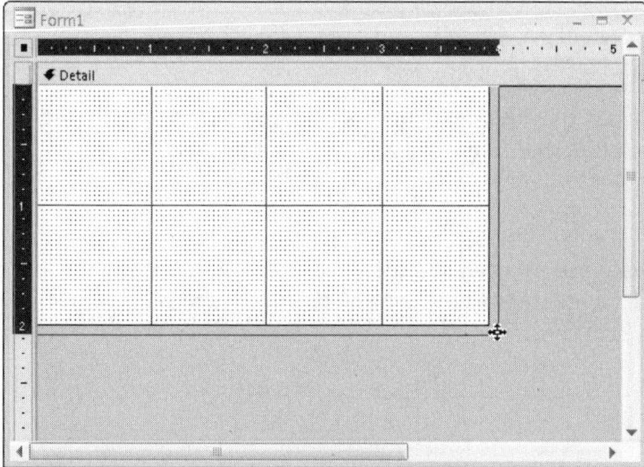

Saving the form

You can save the form at any time by clicking on Save in the Quick Access toolbar. When you're asked for a name for the form, give it a meaningful name (for example, `frmProducts`, `frmCustomers`, `frmProductList`). If you've already given the form a name, you won't be prompted for a name when you click Save.

When you close a form, Access asks you to save it. If you don't save a form, all changes since you opened the form (or the last time you pressed Save) are lost. You should frequently save the form while you work if you're satisfied with the results.

TIP **If you are going to make extensive changes to a form, you might want to make a copy of the form. If you want to work on the form `frmProducts`, you can copy and then paste the form in the database window, giving it a name like `frmProductsOriginal`. Later, when you have completed your changes and tested them, you can delete the original copy.**

Understanding controls

Controls and properties form the basis of forms and reports. It is critical to understand the fundamental concepts of controls and properties before you begin to apply them to custom forms and reports.

NOTE **Although this chapter is about forms, you will learn that forms and reports share many common characteristics including controls and what you can do with them. As you learn about controls in this chapter, you will be able to apply nearly everything you learn when you create reports.**

The term *control* has many definitions in Access. Generally, a control is any object on a form or report, such as a label or text box. These are the same controls that you use in any Windows application, such as Access, Excel, or Web-based HTML forms, or those that are used in any language, such as .Net, Visual Basic, C++, or even C#. Although each language or product has different file formats and different properties, a text box in Access is the same as a text box in any other Windows product.

You enter data into controls and display data using controls. A control can be bound to a field in a table (when the value is entered in the control it is also saved in some underlying table field), or it can be unbound and displayed in the form but not saved when the form is closed. A control can also be an object, such as a line or rectangle. Calculated fields are also controls, as are pictures, graphs, option buttons, checkboxes, and objects. Some controls that aren't part of Access are developed separately — these are ActiveX controls. ActiveX controls extend the base feature set of Access 2007 and are available from a variety of vendors. Many ActiveX controls are shipped with Access 2007.

Whether you're working with forms or reports, essentially the same process is followed to create and use controls. In this chapter, we explain controls from the perspective of a form.

The different control types

Forms and reports contain many different control types. You can add these controls to forms using the Controls group shown in Figure 35-6. Hovering the mouse over the control displays a ScreenTip telling you what the control is. Table 35-1 briefly describes each control.

TABLE 35-1

Controls in Access Forms and Reports

Control	What It Does
Text Box	Displays and allows users to edit data.
Label	Displays static text that typically doesn't change.
Button	Also called a command button. Calls macros or runs VBA code when clicked.
Combo Box	A drop-down list of values.
List Box	A list of values that is always displayed on the form or report.
Subform/Subreport	Displays another form or report within the main form or report.
Line	A graphical line of variable thickness and color, which is used for separation.

Control	What It Does
Rectangle	A rectangle can be any color or size or can be filled in or blank; the rectangle is used for emphasis.
Image	Displays a bitmap picture with very little overhead.
Option Group	Holds multiple option buttons, checkboxes, or toggle buttons.
Check Box	A two-state control, shown as a square that contains a check mark if it's on and an empty square if it's off.
Option Button	Also called a radio button, this button is displayed as a circle with a dot when the option is on.
Toggle Button	This is a two-state button — up or down — which usually uses pictures or icons instead of text to display different states.
Tab Control	Displays multiple pages in a file folder type interface.
Page	Adds a "page" on the form or report. Additional controls are added to the page, and multiple pages may exist on the same form.
Chart	This chart displays data in a graphical format.
Unbound Object Frame	This frame holds an OLE object or embedded picture that is not tied to a table field and can include graphs, pictures, sound files, and video.
Bound Object Frame	This frame holds an OLE object or embedded picture that is tied to a table field.
Page Break	This is usually used for reports and indicates a physical page break.
Hyperlink	This control creates a link to a Web page, a picture, an e-mail address, or a program.
Attachment	This control manages attachments for the Attachment data type.

The Use Control Wizards command, located on the right side of the Controls group, doesn't add a control to a form; instead, it determines whether a wizard is automatically activated when you add certain controls. The Option Group, Combo Box, List Box, Subform/Subreport, Bound and Unbound Object Frame, and Command Button controls all have wizards that Access starts when you add a new control. You can also use the ActiveX Controls command (found in the bottom-right corner of the Controls group) to display a list of ActiveX controls, which you can add to Access 2007.

Understanding bound, unbound, and calculated controls

These are the three basic categories of controls:

- **Bound controls:** These are controls that are bound to a table field. When you enter a value into a bound control, Access automatically updates the table field in the current record. Most of the controls that let you enter information can be bound; these include OLE (Object Linking and Embedding) fields. Controls can be bound to most data types, including text, dates, numbers, Yes/No, pictures, and memo fields.
- **Unbound controls:** Unbound controls retain the entered value, but they don't update any table fields. You can use these controls for text label display, for controls such as lines and rectangles, or for holding unbound OLE objects (such as bitmap pictures or your logo) that aren't stored in a table but on the form itself. Unbound controls are also known as *variables* or *memory variables*.
- **Calculated controls:** Calculated controls are based on expressions, such as functions or calculations. Calculated controls are also unbound because they don't update table fields. An example of a calculated control is `=[SalePrice] - [Cost]`. This control calculates the total of two table fields for display on a form but is not bound to any table field.

The two ways to add a control

You add a control to a form in either of two ways:

- Click a button in the Design tab's Controls group on the Ribbon and draw a new unbound control on the form.
- Drag a field from the Field List to add a bound control to the form.

A bound control is one that is linked to a table field, while an unbound control is one that is not bound to a table field. A control bound to a table places the data directly into the table by using the form.

Using the Controls group to add a control

By using the buttons in the Controls group to add a control, you decide which type of control to use for each field. The control you add is unbound (or not attached to the data in a table field) and has a default name such as Text21 or Combo11. After you create the control, you decide what table field to bind the control to, enter text for the label, and set any properties. You'll learn more about setting properties later in this chapter.

You can add one control at a time using the Controls group. To create three different unbound controls, perform these steps:

1. **Click the Create tab on the Ribbon, and then click on the Form Design command in the Form group to create a new form in Design View.**
2. **Click the Design tab on the Ribbon, and then click the Text Box button (ab|) in the Controls group.**

   The selected button appears with a colored background.
3. **Move the mouse pointer to the Form Design window.**

   The cursor changes to the Text Box icon.
4. **Click and hold down the mouse button where you want the control to begin, and drag the mouse to size the control.**
5. **Click the Option Button in the Controls group.**
6. **Move the mouse pointer in the Form Design window.**

   The cursor changes to the Option Button icon.
7. **Click and hold down the mouse button where you want the control to begin, and drag the mouse to size the control.**
8. **Click the Check Box button in the Controls group.**
9. **Move the mouse pointer in the Form Design window.**

   The cursor changes to the Check Box icon.
10. **Click and hold down the mouse button where you want the control to begin, and drag the mouse to size the control.**

    When you're done, your screen should resemble the one shown in Figure 35-8.

TIP Clicking the Form Design window with a control selected creates a default-sized control. If you want to add multiple controls of the same type, double-click on the icon in the Controls group, and then draw as many controls as you want on the form.

FIGURE 35-8

Unbound controls added from the Controls group.

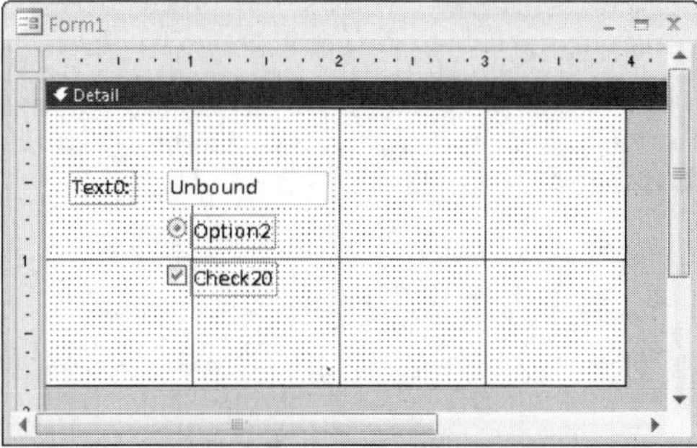

Using the Field List to add a control

The Field List displays a list of fields from the table or query the form is based on. You add bound controls to the form by dragging fields from the Field List onto the form. Select and drag them one at a time, or select multiple fields by using the Ctrl key or Shift key.

- Select multiple contiguous fields by holding down the Shift key and clicking the first and last fields that you want.
- Select multiple noncontiguous fields by holding down the Ctrl key and clicking each field that you want.

Click the Add Existing Fields command in the Design tab's Tools group to display the Field List. By default, the Field List appears docked on the right of the Access window, shown in Figure 35-9. This window is movable and resizable and displays a vertical scroll bar if it contains more fields than can fit in the window.

FIGURE 35-9

Click Add Existing Fields in the Tools group to show the Field List, docked on the right of the Access window.

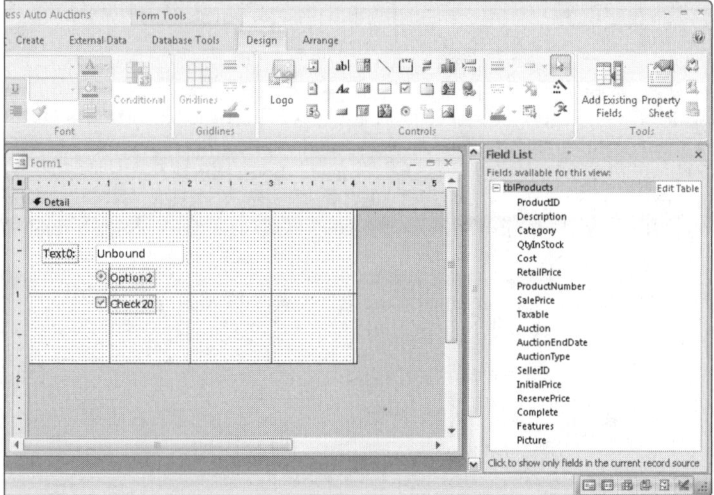

Generally, dragging a field from the Field List window adds a bound text box to the Form Design window. If you drag a Yes/No field from the Field List window, you add a checkbox. If you drag a field that has a Lookup property, you add a List Box control or Combo Box control. If you drag an OLE field from the Field List window, you create a bound object frame. Optionally, you can select the type of control by selecting a control from the Controls group and dragging the field to the Form Design window.

CAUTION **When you drag fields from the Field List window, the first control is placed where you release the mouse button. Make sure that you have enough space to the left of the control for the labels. If you don't have sufficient space, the labels slide under the controls.**

You gain several distinct advantages by dragging a field from the Field List window:

- The control is bound automatically to the field that you dragged it from.
- Field properties inherit table-level formats, status-bar text, and data-validation rules and messages.
- The label control and label text are created with the field name as the caption.
- The label control is attached to the field control, so they move together.

Select and drag the `Description`, `Category`, `RetailPrice`, and `AuctionEndDate` fields from the Field List window to the form, as shown in Figure 35-10. Double-clicking a field also adds it to the form.

FIGURE 35-10

Drag fields from the Field List to add bound controls to the form.

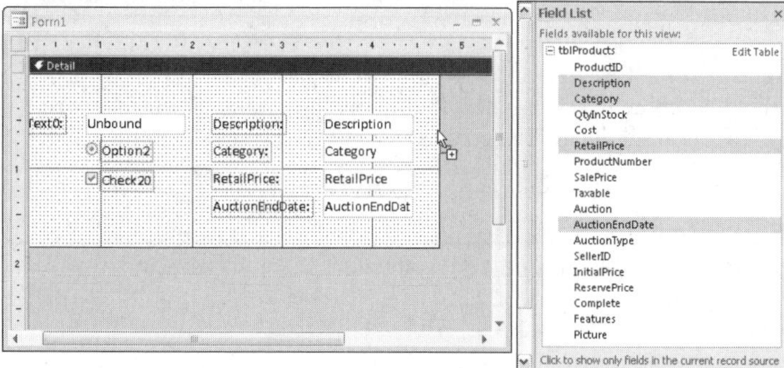

You can see four new controls in the form's Design View — each one consists of a Label control and a Text Box control (Access attaches the Label control to the text box automatically). You can work with these controls as a group or independently, and you can select, move, resize, or delete them. Notice that each control has a label with a caption matching the field name, and the Text Box control displays the bound field name used in the text box. If you want to resize just the control and not the label, you must work with the two controls separately.

Close the Field List by clicking the Add Existing Fields command in the Design tab's Tools group or the Close button on the Field List.

TIP In Access, you can change the type of control after you create it; then you can set all the properties for the control. For example, suppose that you add a field as a Text Box control and you want to change it to a List Box. You can right-click the control and select Change To from the pop-up menu to change the control type. However, you can change only from some types of controls to others. You can change anything to a Text Box control; option buttons, toggle buttons, and checkboxes are interchangeable, as are List Boxes and Combo Boxes.

In Figure 35-10, notice the difference between the controls that were dragged from the Field List window and the controls that were created from the Controls group. The Field List window controls are bound to a field in `tblProducts` and are appropriately labeled and named. The controls created from the Controls group are unbound and have default names. The default names are automatically assigned a number according to the type of control.

Later, you learn how to change the control names, captions, and other properties. Using properties speeds the process of naming controls and binding them to specific fields. If you want to see the differences between bound and unbound controls, switch to Form View using the View command in the Home tab's Views group. The `Description`, `Category`, `RetailPrice`, and `AuctionEndDate` controls display data since they're bound to `tblProducts`. The other three controls don't display data because they aren't bound to any data source.

NOTE If a form's Record Source property isn't set, you will not see a Field List window.

TIP If you first select a control type in the Controls group and then drag a field from the Field List, a control is created (using the selected control type) that is automatically bound to the data field in the Field List.

Which method to use

The deciding factor of whether to use the field list or the Controls group is this: Does the field exist in the table/query or do you want to create an unbound or calculated expression? By using the Field List window and the Controls group together, you can create bound controls of nearly any type. You will find, however, that some data types don't allow all the control types found in the Controls group. For example, if you select the Chart control type from the Controls group and drag a single field to the form, a text box control is added instead of a chart control.

The following properties always inherit their settings from the field's table definition:

- Format
- Decimal Places
- Status Bar Text (from the field Description)
- Input Mask
- Default Value
- Validation Rule
- Validation Text

Changes made to a control's properties don't affect the field properties in the source table.

Each type of control has a different set of properties, as do objects such as forms, reports, and sections within forms or reports. In the next few chapters, you learn about many of these properties as you use each of the control types to create more complex forms and reports.

Selecting Controls

After you add a control to the form, you can resize, move, or copy it. The first step is to select one or more controls. Depending on its size, a selected control may show from four to eight *handles* (small squares called *moving and sizing handles*) around the control — at the corners and midway along the sides. The Move handle in the upper-left corner is larger than the other handles and you use it to move the control. You use the other handles to size the control. Figure 35-11 displays some selected controls and their moving and sizing handles.

FIGURE 35-11

A conceptual view of selecting controls and their moving and sizing handles.

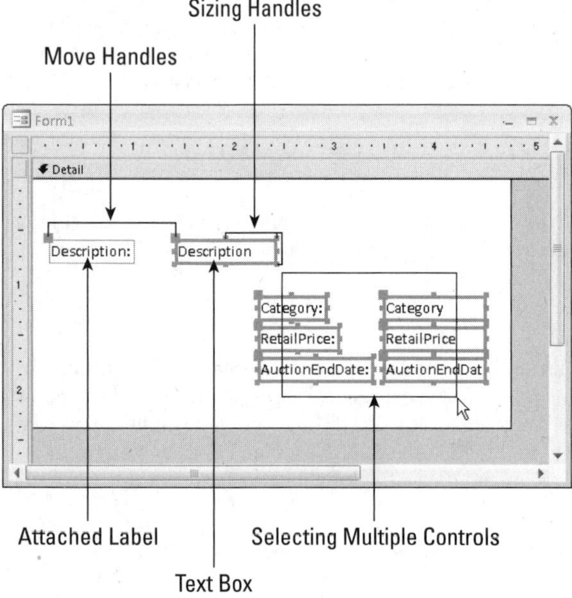

The Select command (top leftmost command) in the Controls group must be on for you to select a control. The pointer appears as an arrow pointing diagonally toward the upper-left corner. If you use the Controls group to create a single control, Access automatically reselects the pointer as the default.

Selecting a single control

Select any single control by clicking anywhere on the control. When you click a control, the handles appear. If the control has an attached label, the Move handle for the label also appears. If you select a label control that is part of an attached control, all the handles for the label control are displayed, and only the Move handle appears in the attached control.

Selecting multiple controls

You can select multiple controls in these ways:

- Click each desired control while holding down the Shift key.
- Drag the pointer through or around the controls that you want to select.
- Drag in the ruler to select a range of controls.

Figure 35-11 shows selecting the multiple bound controls graphically. When you select multiple controls by dragging the mouse, a rectangle appears as you drag the mouse. Be careful to only drag the rectangle through the controls you want to select. Any control you touch with the rectangle or enclose within it is selected. If you want to select labels only, make sure that the selection rectangle only encloses the labels.

TIP

If you find that controls are not selected when the rectangle passes through the control, you may have the Selection behavior global property set to fully enclosed. This means that a control is selected only if the selection rectangle completely encloses the entire control. The normal default for this option is partially enclosed. Change this option by clicking the Microsoft Office Button and selecting Access Options. Then select Object Designers and set the Forms/Reports Selection behavior to Partially Enclosed.

By holding down the Shift key, you can select several noncontiguous controls. This lets you select controls on totally different parts of the screen. Using Shift to select controls is different from using Shift to select files in Windows Explorer and fields in the Field List. You have to Shift+click on each control to add it to the selection.

Click on the form in Design View and then press Ctrl+A to select all the controls on the form. Press Shift and click on any selected control to remove it from the selection.

Deselecting controls

Deselect a control by clicking an unselected area of the form that doesn't contain a control. When you do so, the handles disappear from any selected control. Selecting another control also deselects a selected control.

Manipulating Controls

Creating a form is a multistep process. The next step is to make sure that your controls are properly sized and moved to their correct positions. The Arrange tab of the Ribbon — shown in Figure 35-12 — contains commands used to assist you in manipulating controls.

FIGURE 35-12

The Arrange tab lets you work with moving and sizing controls, as well as manage the overall layout of the form.

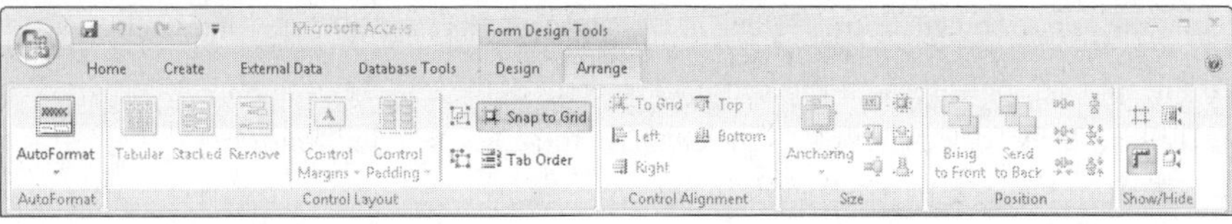

Resizing a control

You can *resize* controls by using any of the smaller handles on the control. The handles in the control corners let you make the field larger or smaller in both width and height — and at the same time. Use the handles in the middle of the control sides to size the control larger or smaller in one direction only. The top and bottom handles change the height of the control; the left and right handles change the control's width.

When the mouse pointer touches a corner handle of a selected control, the pointer becomes a diagonal double arrow. You can then drag the sizing handle until the control is the desired size. If the mouse pointer touches a side handle in a selected control, the pointer changes to a horizontal or vertical double-headed arrow. Figure 35-13 shows the Description control after being resized. Notice the double-headed arrow in the corner of the Description control.

FIGURE 35-13

Resizing a control.

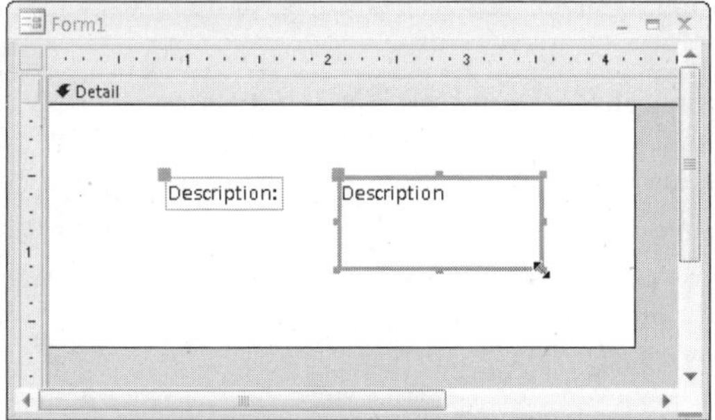

TIP You can resize a control in very small increments by holding the Shift key and pressing the arrow keys. This technique also works with multiple controls selected. Using this technique, a control changes by only 1 pixel at a time (or moves to the nearest grid line if Snap to Grid is selected in the Arrange tab's Control Layout group).

When you double-click on any of the sizing handles, Access resizes a control to a best fit for the text in the control. This is especially handy if you increase the font size and then notice that the text is cut off either at the bottom or to the right. For label controls, note that this *best-fit sizing* adjusts the size vertically and horizontally, though text controls are resized only vertically. This is because when Access is in form-design mode, it can't predict how much of a field to display — the field name and field contents can be radically different. Sometimes, Access doesn't correctly resize the label.

Sizing controls automatically

The Size group on the Arrange tab on the Ribbon has several commands that help size controls based on the value of the data, the grid, or other controls, while in Design View. Here are the Size commands:

- **Size To Fit:** Adjusts control height and width for the font of the text they contain
- **Size To Tallest:** Makes selected controls the height of the tallest selected control
- **Size To Shortest:** Makes selected controls the height of the shortest selected control
- **Size To Grid:** Moves all sides of selected controls in or out to meet the nearest points on the grid

- **Size To Widest:** Makes selected controls the width of the widest selected control
- **Size To Narrowest:** Makes selected controls the height of the narrowest selected control

You can access many commands by right-clicking after selecting multiple controls. When you right-click on multiple controls, a shortcut menu displays choices to size and align controls.

Moving a control

After you select a control, you can easily move it, using either one of these methods:

- Click on the control and hold the mouse button down; the cursor changes to a four-directional arrow. Drag the mouse to move the control to a new location.
- Click once to select the control and move the mouse over any of the highlighted edges; the cursor changes to a four-directional arrow. Drag the mouse to move the control to a new location.
- Select the control and use the arrow keys on the keyboard to move the control. Using this technique, a control changes by only 1 pixel at a time (or moves to the nearest grid line if Snap to Grid is selected in the Arrange tab's Control Layout group).

When an attached label is created automatically with another control, it is called a *compound control.* If a control has an attached label, the label and control move together; it doesn't matter whether you click the control or the label.

You can move a control separately from an attached label by pointing to the Move handle of the control and then dragging it. Move the label control separately from the other control by pointing to the Move handle of the label control and dragging it separately.

Figure 35-14 shows a Label control that has been separately moved to the top of the Text Box control. The four-directional arrow cursor indicates that the controls are ready to be moved together. To see this cursor, the control(s) must already be selected.

FIGURE 35-14

Moving a control.

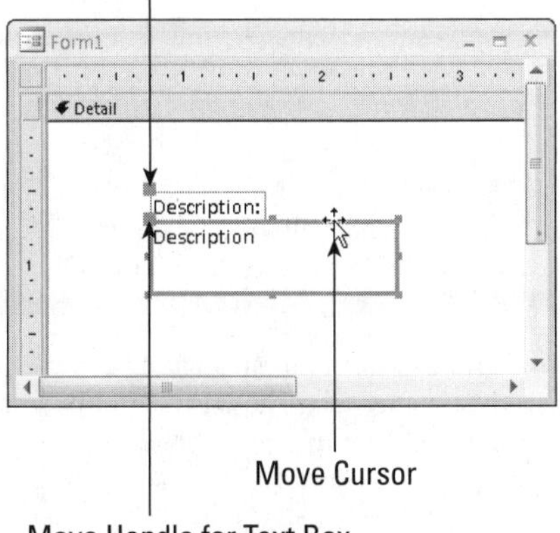

Press Esc before you release the mouse button to cancel a moving or a resizing operation. After a move or resizing operation is complete, click the Undo button on the Quick Access toolbar to undo the changes, if necessary.

Aligning controls

You may want to move several controls so that they are all *aligned* (lined up). The Arrange tab's Control Alignment group has several options described in the following list:

- **Left:** Aligns the left edge of the selected controls with that of the leftmost selected control
- **Right:** Aligns the right edge of the selected controls with that of the rightmost selected control
- **Top:** Aligns the top edge of the selected controls with that of the topmost selected control
- **Bottom:** Aligns the bottom edge of the selected controls with that of the bottommost selected control
- **To Grid:** Aligns the top-left corners of the selected controls to the nearest grid point

You can align any number of selected controls by selecting a command from the Control Alignment group. When you choose one of the commands, Access uses the control that is the closest to the desired selection as the model for the alignment. For example, suppose that you have three controls and you want to left-align them. They are aligned on the basis of the control farthest to the left in the group of the three controls.

Figure 35-15 shows several sets of controls. The first set of controls is not aligned. The Label controls in the second set of controls have been left-aligned. The Text Box controls in the second set have been right-aligned. Each label, along with its attached text box, has been bottom-aligned.

FIGURE 35-15

An example of unaligned and aligned controls on the grid.

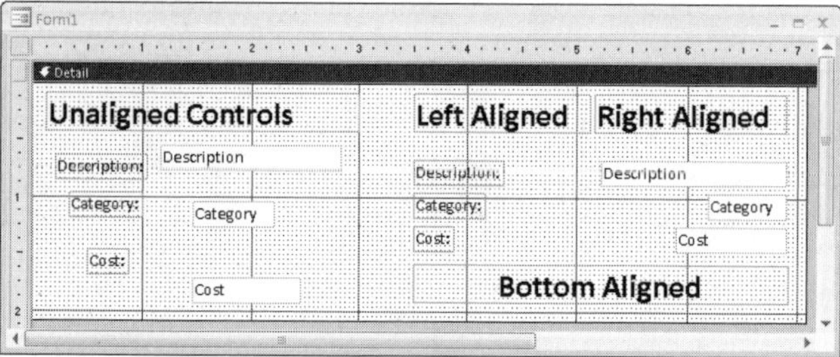

Each type of alignment must be done separately. In this example, you can left-align all the labels or right-align all the text boxes at once. However, you must bottom-align each label and its text control separately (three separate alignments).

The series of dots in the background of Figure 35-15 is the *grid*. The grid can assist you in aligning controls. Hide or display the grid by selecting the Show Grid command from the Arrange tab's Show/Hide group. You can also hide or display the ruler using the Ruler command in the Show/Hide group.

Use the Snap to Grid command in the Arrange tab's Control Layout group to align new controls to the grid as you draw or place them on a form. It also aligns existing controls to the grid when you move or resize them. Snap to Grid is on when it appears selected in the Ribbon.

When Snap to Grid is on and you draw a new control by clicking on the form and dragging to size the control, Access aligns the four corners of the control to points on the grid. When you place a new control by clicking the control in the Field List and then dragging it to the form, only the upper-left corner is aligned.

As you move or resize existing controls, Access 2007 lets you move only from grid point to grid point. When Snap to Grid is off, Access 2007 ignores the grid and lets you place a control anywhere on the form or report.

TIP **You can temporarily turn Snap to Grid off by pressing the Ctrl key before you create a control (or while sizing or moving it). You can change the grid's *fineness* (number of dots) from form to form by using the Grid X and Grid Y Form properties. (Higher numbers indicate greater fineness.)**

The Arrange tab's Position group contains commands to adjust the space between multiple controls. These commands change the space between controls on the basis of the space between the first two selected controls. If the controls are across the screen, use horizontal spacing. If they are down the screen, use vertical spacing. These commands are as follows:

- **Make Horizontal Spacing Equal:** Makes the horizontal space between selected controls equal. You must select three or more controls for this command to work.
- **Increase Horizontal Spacing:** Increases the horizontal space between selected controls by one grid unit.
- **Decrease Horizontal Spacing:** Decreases the horizontal space between selected controls by one grid unit.
- **Make Vertical Spacing Equal:** Makes the vertical space between selected controls equal. You must select three or more controls for this command to work.
- **Increase Vertical Spacing:** Increases the vertical space between selected controls by one grid unit.
- **Decrease Vertical Spacing:** Decreases the vertical space between selected controls by one grid unit.

TIP **Aligning controls aligns the control boxes only. If you want to align the text within the controls (also known as *justifying the text*), you must use the Design tab's Font group and select the Left, Right, or Center commands.**

Modifying the appearance of a control

To modify the appearance of a control, select the control and click on commands that modify that control, such as commands in the Font group or Controls group. To change the text color and font of the `Description` label, follow these steps:

1. **Click `Description` label on the form.**
2. **In the Design tab's Font group, change the Font Size to 14, click the Bold command, and change the Font Color to blue.**
3. **Resize the `Description` label so the larger text fits (remember, you can double-click any of the sizing handles to autosize the label).**

Modifying the appearance of multiple controls

To modify the appearance of multiple controls at once, select the controls and click on commands to modify the controls, such as commands in the Font group or Controls group. To change the text color and font of the `Description`, `Category`, and `Cost` labels and text boxes, follow these steps:

1. **Select the three labels and three text boxes by dragging a selection box through them (refer to Figure 35-11).**
2. **In the Design tab's Font group, change the Font Size to 14, click the Bold command, and change the Font Color to blue.**
3. **Resize the labels and text boxes so the larger text fits (remember, you can double-click any of the sizing handles to autosize the controls).**

   As you click the commands, the controls' appearances change to reflect the new selections (shown in Figure 35-16). The fonts in each control increase in size, become bold, and turn blue. Any changes you make apply to all selected controls.

FIGURE 35-16

Changing the appearance of multiple controls at the same time.

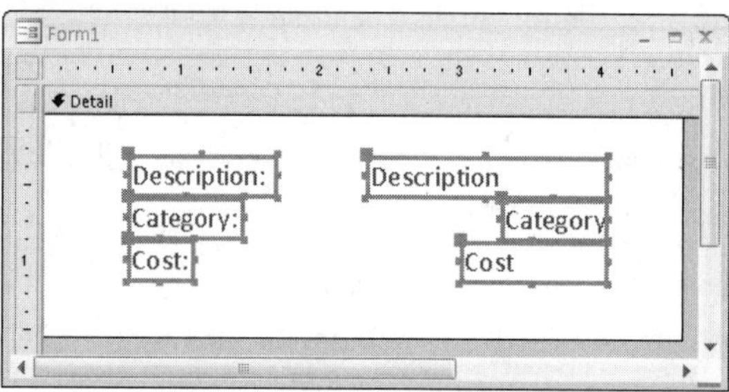

When multiple controls are selected, you can also move the selected controls together. When the cursor changes to the four-directional arrow, click and drag to move the selected controls. You can also change the size of all the controls at once by resizing one of the controls in the selection. All the selected controls increase or decrease by the same number of units.

Grouping controls

If you routinely change properties of multiple controls, you may want to group them together. To group controls together, select the controls by holding down the Shift key and clicking them or dragging the selection box through them. After the desired controls are selected, select the Group command from the Arrange tab's Control Layout group; the Group button appears to the left of the Snap to Grid button. A box appears around the selected controls, as shown in Figure 35-17, indicating they're grouped together.

After you've grouped the controls together, whenever you click any of the controls inside the group, the entire group is selected. Double-click on a control to select just that one control. After a single control in the group is selected, you can click on any other control to select it.

FIGURE 35-17

Grouping multiple controls together.

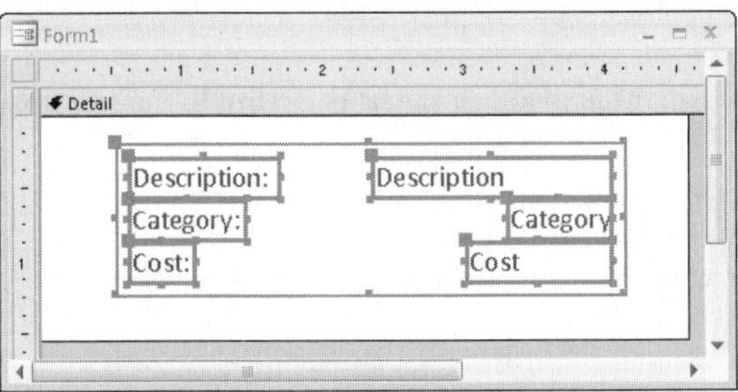

To resize the entire group, put your mouse on the side you want to resize. After the double arrow appears, click and drag until you reach the desired size. Every control in the group changes in size. To move the entire group, click and drag the group to its new location. With grouped controls, you don't have to select all the controls every time you change something about them.

To remove a group, select the group by clicking any field inside the group, then select the Ungroup command from the Arrange tab's Control Layout group.

Deleting a control

You can delete a control by simply selecting it in the form's Design View and pressing the Delete key on your keyboard. The control and any attached labels will disappear. You can bring them back by immediately selecting Undo from the Quick Access toolbar. You can also select Cut from the Home tab's Clipboard group or Delete from the Home tab's Records group.

You can delete more than one control at a time by selecting multiple controls and pressing Delete. You can delete an entire group of controls by selecting the group and pressing Delete. If you have a control with an attached label, you can delete only the label by clicking the label itself and then selecting one of the delete methods. If you select the control, both the control and the label are deleted. To delete only the label of the Description control, follow the next set of steps (this example assumes that you have the Description text box control in your Form Design window):

1. **Select the `Description` label control only.**
2. **Press Delete to remove the label from the form.**

Attaching a label to a control

If you accidentally delete a label from a control, you can reattach it. To create and then reattach a label to a control, follow these steps:

1. **Click the Label button on the Controls group.**
2. **Place the mouse pointer in the Form Design window.**

   The mouse pointer becomes the Text Box button.
3. **Click and hold down the mouse button where you want the control to begin; drag the mouse to size the control.**

4. **Type** Description: **and click outside the control.**
5. **Select the `Description` label control.**
6. **Select Cut from the Home tab's Clipboard group.**
7. **Select the `Description` text box control.**
8. **Select Paste from the Home tab's Clipboard group to attach the label control to the text box control.**

Another way to attach a label to a control is to click the informational icon next to the label, shown in Figure 35-18. This informational icon lets you know that this label is unassociated with a control. Click the Associate Label with a Control command from the menu, and then select the control you want to associate the label with.

FIGURE 35-18

Associating a label with a control.

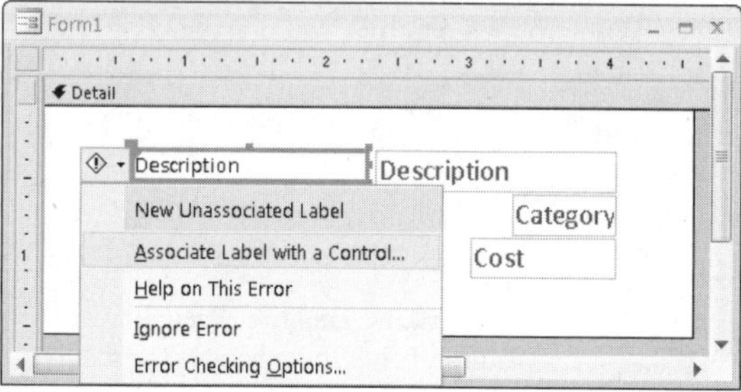

Copying a control

You can create copies of any control by copying it to the Clipboard and then pasting the copies where you want them. If you have a control for which you have entered many properties or specified a certain format, you can copy it and revise only the properties (such as the control name and bound field name) to make it a different control. This capability is useful with a multiple-page form when you want to display the same values on different pages and in different locations, or when copying a control from one form to another.

Changing the control type

In Figure 35-19, the Complete control is a checkbox. Although there are times you may want to use a checkbox to display a Boolean (Yes/No) data type, there are other ways to display the value, such as a toggle button. A toggle button is raised if it's true and depressed (or at least very unhappy) if it's false.

Use these steps to turn the checkbox into a toggle button:

1. **Select the Complete label control (just the label control, not the checkbox).**
2. **Press the Delete key to delete the label control because it is not needed.**
3. **Right-click the `Complete` checkbox, and choose Change To ⇨ Toggle Button from the pop-up menu.**
4. **Resize the toggle button and click inside it to get the blinking cursor; then type** Complete **on the button as its caption (shown on the right of Figure 35-19).**

FIGURE 35-19

Become a magician and turn a checkbox into a toggle button.

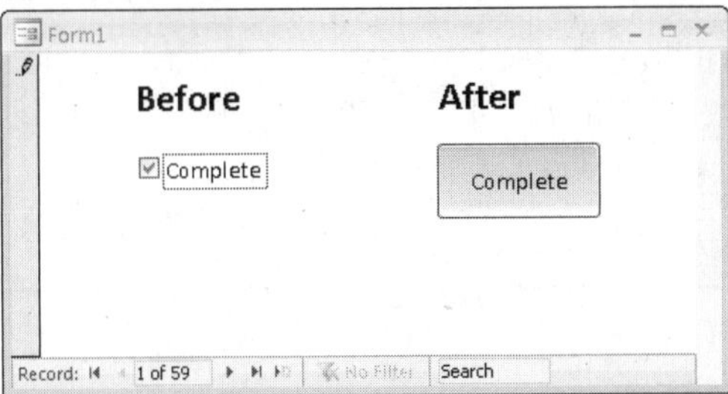

Understanding Properties

Properties are named attributes of controls, fields, or database objects that are used to modify the characteristics of a control, field, or object. Examples of these attributes are the size, color, appearance, or name of an object. A property can also modify the behavior of a control, determining, for example, whether the control is read-only or editable and visible or not visible.

Properties are used extensively in forms and reports to change the characteristics of controls. Each control on the form has properties. The form itself also has properties, as does each of its sections. The same is true for reports; the report itself has properties, as does each report section and individual control. The label control also has its own properties, even if it is attached to another control.

Everything from moving and resizing controls to changing fonts and colors that you do with the Ribbon commands can be done by setting properties. In fact, all these commands do is change properties of the selected controls.

Displaying the Property Sheet

Properties are displayed in a Property Sheet (sometimes called a Property window). To display the Property Sheet for the Description text box, follow the steps below. You will be creating a new blank form.

1. **Drag the first five fields, `ProductID` through `Cost`, from the Field List window to the form's Design View.**
2. **Click the Description text box control to select it.**
3. **Click the Property Sheet command in the Design tab's Tools group to display the Property Sheet — which appears docked to the right side of the Access window, taking the place of the Field List.**

   The screen should look like the one shown in Figure 35-20.

Because the Property Sheet is a window, it can be undocked, moved, and resized. It does not, however, have Maximize or Minimize buttons. There are several ways to display a control's Property Sheet if it's not visible:

- Select a control and click the Property Sheet command in the Design tab's Tools group.
- Double-click any control.
- Right-click any control and select Properties from the pop-up menu.

Understanding the Property Sheet

With the Property Sheet displayed, click on any control in Design View to display the properties for that control. Select multiple controls to display similar properties for the selected controls.

In Figure 35-20, the Property Sheet has been sized to fit the screen. By widening the Property Sheet, you can see more of its values; by increasing the length, you can see more controls at one time. The vertical scroll bar lets you move between various properties.

FIGURE 35-20

Change an object's properties with the Property Sheet.

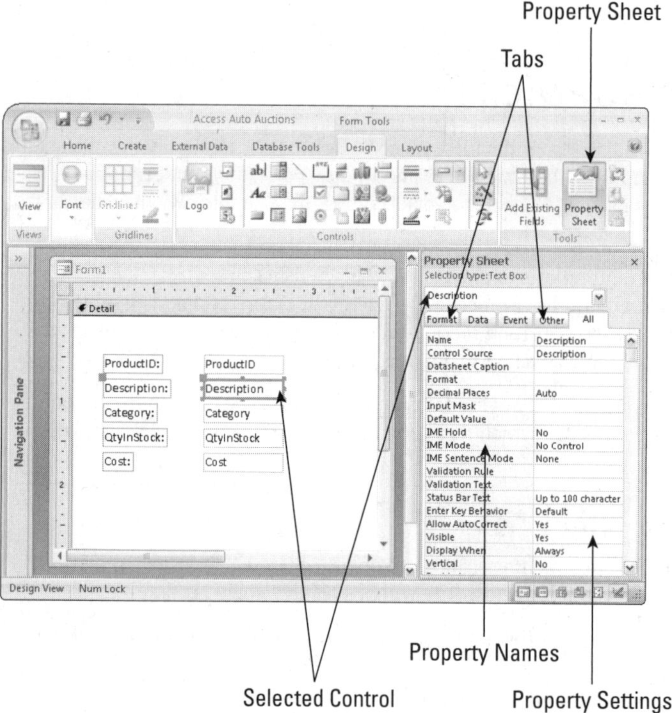

The Property Sheet has an All tab that lets you see all the properties for a control. Or you can choose another tab to limit the view to a specific group of properties. The specific tabs and groups of properties are as follows:

- **Format:** These properties determine how a label or value looks: font, size, color, special effects, borders, and scroll bars.
- **Data:** These properties affect how a value is displayed and the data source it is bound to: control source, input masks, validation, default value, and other data type properties.

- **Event:** Event properties are named events, such as clicking a mouse button, adding a record, pressing a key for which you can define a response (in the form of a call to a macro or a VBA procedure), and so on.
- **Other:** Other properties show additional characteristics of the control, such as the name of the control or the description that displays in the status bar.

Figure 35-20 shows the Property Sheet for the Description text box. The first column lists the property names; the second column is where you enter or select property settings or options.

Changing a control's property setting

There are many different methods for changing property settings, including the following:

- Entering or selecting the desired value in a Property window
- Changing a property directly by changing the control itself, such as changing its size
- Using inherited properties from the bound field or the control's default properties
- Entering color selections for the control by using the Ribbon commands
- Changing label text style, size, color, and alignment by using the Ribbon commands

You can change a control's properties by clicking a property and typing the desired value.

In Figure 35-21, you can see a down arrow and a button with three dots to the right of the `Control Source` property-entry area. Some properties display a drop-down arrow in the property-entry area when you click in the area. The drop-down arrow tells you that Access has a list of values from which you can choose. If you click the down arrow in the `Control Source` property, you find that the drop-down list displays a list of all fields in the data source — `tblProducts`. Setting the `Control Source` property to a field in a table creates a bound control.

FIGURE 35-21

The Property Sheet undocked

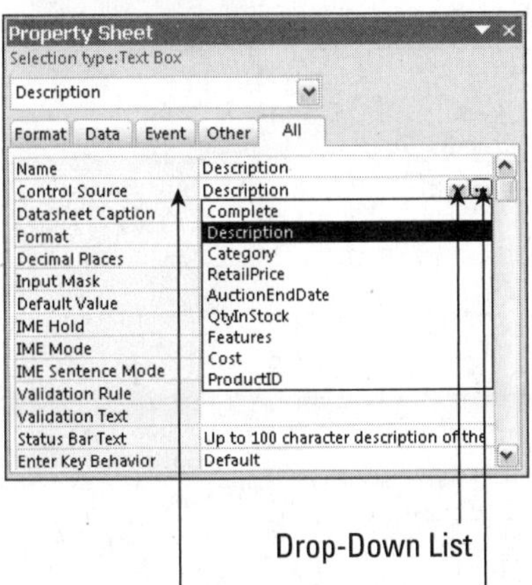

Some properties have a list of standard values such as Yes or No; others display varying lists of fields, forms, reports, or macros. The properties of each object are determined by the object itself and what the object is used for.

A nice feature in Access 2007 is the capability to cycle through property choices by repeatedly double-clicking on the choice. For example, double-clicking on the `Display When` property alternately selects Always, Print Only, and Screen Only.

The Builder button contains an ellipsis (three dots) and opens one of the many builders in Access — including the Macro Builder, the Expression Builder, and the Module Builder. When you open a builder and make some selections, the property is filled in for you.

Each type of object has its own property window and properties. These include the form itself, each of the form sections, and each of the form's controls. You display each of the property windows by clicking on the object first. The property window will instantly change to show the properties for the selected object.

Naming control labels and their captions

You might notice that each of the data fields has a Label control and a Text Box control. Normally, the label's `Caption` property is the same as the text box's `Name` property. The text box's `Name` property is usually the same as the table's field name — shown in the `Control Source` property. Sometimes, the label's `Caption` is different because a value was entered into the `Caption` property for each field in the table.

When creating controls on a form, it's a good idea to use standard naming conventions when setting the control's `Name` property. Name each control with a prefix followed by a meaningful name that you'll recognize later (for example, `txtTotalCost`, `cboState`, `lblTitle`). Table 35-2 shows the naming conventions for form and report controls. You can find a very complete, well-established naming convention online by searching for "Reddick Naming Convention."

TABLE 35-2

Form/Report Control Naming Conventions

Prefix	Object
`frb`	Bound Object frame
`cht`	Chart (Graph)
`chk`	Check Box
`cbo`	Combo Box
`cmd`	Command Button
`ocx`	ActiveX Custom Control
`det`	Detail (section)
`gft[n]`	Footer (group section)
`fft`	Form Footer section
`fhd`	Form Header section
`ghd[n]`	Header (group section)
`hlk`	Hyperlink
`img`	Image

Prefix	Object
`lbl`	Label
`lin`	Line
`lst`	List Box
`opt`	Option Button
`grp`	Option Group
`pge`	Page (tab)
`brk`	Page break
`pft`	Page Footer (section)
`phd`	Page Header (section)
`shp`	Rectangle
`rft`	Report Footer (section)
`rhd`	Report Header (section)
`sec`	Section
`sub`	Subform/Subreport
`tab`	Tab Control
`txt`	Text Box
`tgl`	Toggle Button
`fru`	Unbound Object Frame

The properties displayed in Figure 35-21 are the specific properties for the Description text box. The first two properties, `Name` and `Control Source`, are set to Description.

The `Name` is simply the name of the field itself. When a control is bound to a field, Access automatically assigns the `Name` property to the bound field's name. Unbound controls are given names such as Field11 or Button13. However, you can give the control any name you want.

With bound controls, the `Control Source` property is the name of the table field to which the control is bound. In this example, Description refers to the field with the same name in `tblProducts`. An unbound control has no control source, whereas the control source of a calculated control is the actual expression for the calculation, as in the example `=[SalePrice] - [Cost]`.

Using Form View

Form View is where you actually view and modify data. Form View enables you to enter and review the data in a user-friendly format.

You can use the form to add records into the database. Click the New navigation button to start a new record, if needed (see below), and then type or select data in the fields, pressing Tab to move between fields.

To demonstrate the use of the Form View, follow these steps to create a new form based on `tblProducts`:

1. **Select `tblProducts` in the Navigation Pane.**
2. **Click the Create tab on the Ribbon.**
3. **Click on the Form command in the Forms group.**
4. **Click the Form View button on the Home tab's Views group to switch from Layout View to Form View.**

Figure 35-22 shows the Access window with the newly created form displayed in Form View. This view has many of the same elements as Datasheet View. At the top of the screen, you see the Access title bar, Quick Access toolbar, and the Ribbon. The form in the center of the screen displays your data, one record at a time.

FIGURE 35-22

A form in Form View.

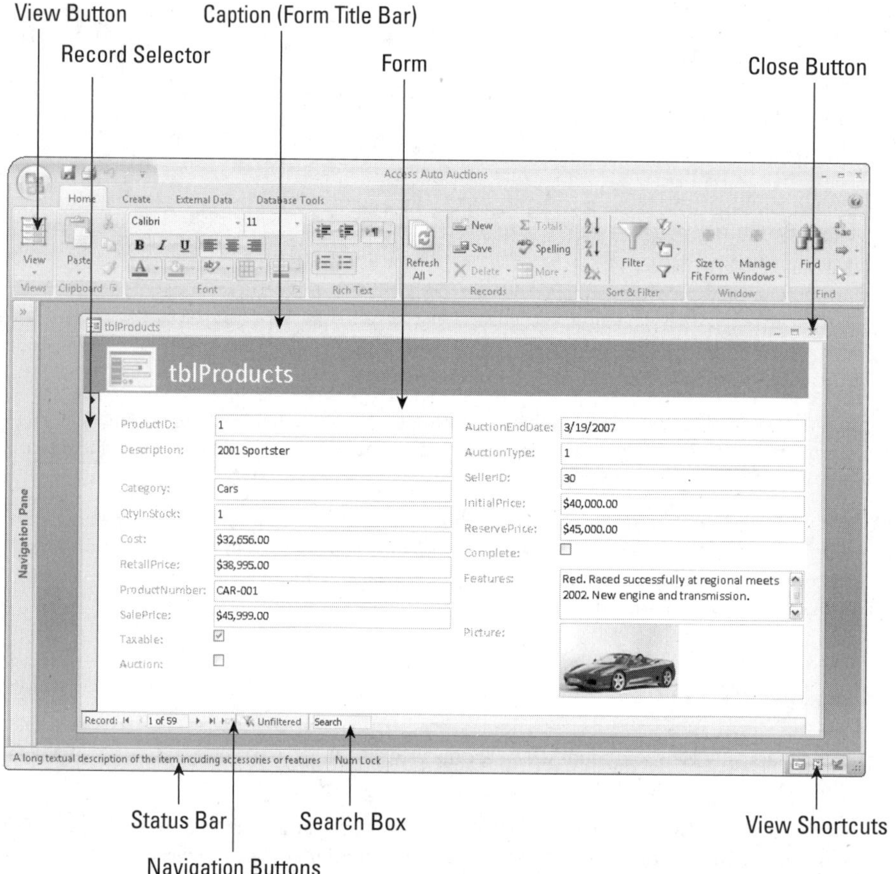

If the form contains more fields than can fit onscreen at one time, Access 2007 automatically displays a horizontal and/or vertical scroll bar that can be used to see the remainder of the data. You can also see the rest of the data by pressing the PgDn key. If you're at the bottom of a form, or the entire form fits on the screen, and press PgDn, you'll move to the next record.

The status bar at the bottom of the window displays the active field's Field Description that you defined when you created the table (or form). If no Field Description exists for a specific field, Access displays the words Form View. Generally, error messages and warnings appear in dialog boxes in the center of the screen (rather than in the status bar). The navigation buttons, search box, and view shortcuts are found at the bottom of the screen. These features let you move quickly from record to record, find data quickly, or switch views.

The Form view Ribbon appearance

In the Form view, the Ribbon (shown in Figure 35-23) provides commands for working with the data. The Home tab has some familiar objects on it, as well as some new ones. This section provides an overview of the Home tab in the Form view; the individual commands will be described in more detail later in this chapter.

FIGURE 35-23

The Ribbon's Home tab in Form view.

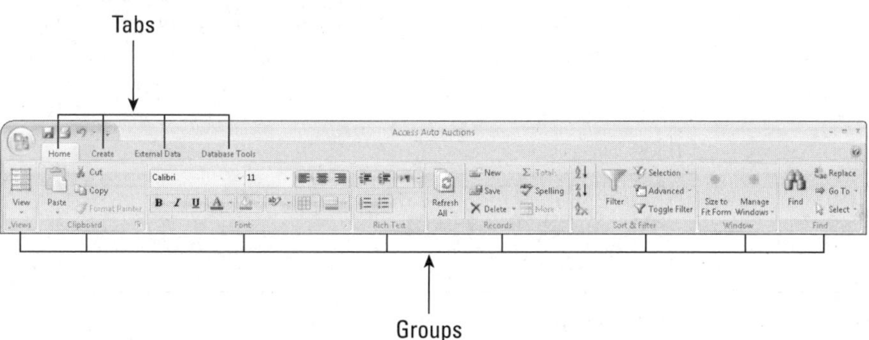

The first group is the View group, which allows you to switch between Form View, Datasheet View, PivotTable View, PivotChart View, Layout View, and Design View. You can see all six choices by clicking the command's down-arrow. Clicking Form View lets you manipulate data on the form. Datasheet View shows the data in a row-and-column format. Design View permits you to make changes to the form's design. Layout View lets you change the form's design while viewing data. PivotTable View and PivotChart View let you create PivotTables and PivotCharts based on the form's data. All these commands may not be available on all forms. By setting the form's properties, you can limit which views are available. You'll learn more about form properties later in this chapter.

The Clipboard group contains the Cut, Copy, and Paste commands. These commands work like the commands in other applications (Word, Excel, and so on). The Paste command's down arrow gives you three choices: Paste, Paste Special, and Paste Append. Paste Special gives you the option of pasting the contents of the Clipboard in different formats (Text, CSV, Records, etc.) Paste Append pastes the contents of the Clipboard as a new record — provided a record with a similar structure was copied.

The Font group lets you change the look of the datasheet in Datasheet View. Use these commands to change the font, size, bold, italic, color, and so on. Use the Align Left, Align Right, and Align Center commands to justify the data in the selected column. Click the Gridlines command to toggle gridlines on and off. Use the Alternate Fill/Back Color command to change the colors of alternating rows, or make them all the same. When modifying text in a memo field with the `Text Format` property set to `Rich Text`, you can use these commands to change the fonts, colors, and so on.

The Rich Text group lets you change a memo field's data if the field's `Text Format` property is set to `Rich Text`. Use these commands to add bullets or numbered lists and change the indentation levels.

The Records group lets you save, delete, or add a new record to the form. It also contains commands to show totals, check spelling, freeze and hide columns, and change the row height and cell width in Datasheet View.

The Sort & Filter group lets you change the order of the records, as well as limit the records being displayed— based on criteria you want.

The Find group lets you find and replace data and go to specific records in the datasheet. Use the select command to select a record or all records.

Navigating between fields

Navigating a form is nearly identical to navigating a datasheet. You can easily move around the form window by clicking the field that you want and making changes or additions to your data. Because the form window displays only as many fields as can fit onscreen, you need to use various navigational aids to move within your form or between records.

Table 35-3 displays the navigational keys used to move between fields within a form.

TABLE 35-3

Navigating in a Form

Navigational Direction	Keystrokes
Next field	Tab, right-arrow (→) or down-arrow (↓) key, or Enter
Previous field	Shift+Tab, left-arrow (←), or up arrow (↑)
First field of current record	Home or Ctrl+Home
Last field of current record	End or Ctrl+End
Next page	PgDn or Next Record
Previous page	PgUp or Previous Record

If you have a form with more than one page, a vertical scroll bar displays. You can use the scroll bar to move to different pages on the form. You can also use the PgUp and PgDn keys to move between form pages. You can move up or down one field at a time by clicking the scroll-bar arrows. With the scroll-bar button, you can move past many fields at once.

Moving between records in a form

Although you generally use a form to display one record at a time, you still need to move between records. The easiest way to do this is to use the Navigation buttons, as shown in Figure 35-24. The Navigation buttons let you move to the desired record.

The Navigation buttons (shown in Figure 35-24) are the six controls located at the bottom of the Form window, which you click to move between records. The two leftmost controls move you to the first record or the previous record in the form. The three rightmost controls position you on the next record, last record, or new record in the form. If you know the record number (the row number of a specific record), you can click the Record Number box, enter a record number, and press Enter.

The record number between the Navigation buttons is a virtual record number. The number is not attached to any specific record—it's just an indicator as to the record number you're on given the current filter or sort. It will change with each time you filter or sort the records. The number to the right of the record number displays the number of records in the current view. The number of records displayed might not be the total number of records in the underlying table or query; this number changes when you filter the data on the form.

FIGURE 35-24

The Navigation buttons of a form.

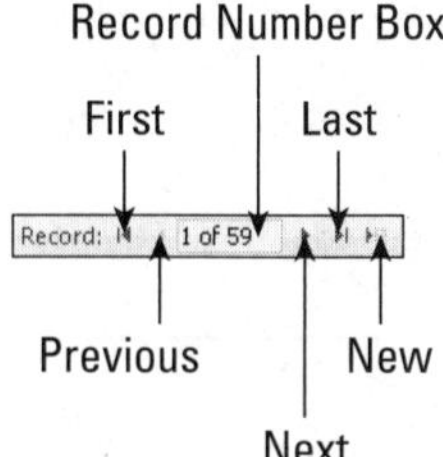

You can also press PgDn to move to the current field in the next record, or PgUp to move to the current field in the preceding record.

Changing Values in a Form

You can add, change, and delete data within a table by using a form. Table 35-4 summarizes these techniques.

Controls that you can't edit

Some controls can't be edited, such as:

- **Controls displaying AutoNumber fields:** Access maintains AutoNumber fields automatically, calculating the values as you create each new record.
- **Calculated controls:** Access uses calculated controls in forms or queries; these values are not actually stored in your table.
- **Locked or disabled fields:** You can set certain properties to prevent editing for specific controls.
- **Controls in multiuser locked records:** If another user locks the record, you can't edit any controls in that record.

TABLE 35-4

Editing Techniques

Editing Technique	Keystrokes
Move insertion point within a control	Press the right-arrow (→) and left-arrow (←) keys
Insert a value within a control	Select the insertion point and type new data
Select the entire text in a control	Press F2
Replace an existing value with a new value	Select the entire field and type a new value
Replace value with value of preceding field	Press Ctrl+' (single quotation mark)
Replace current value with default value	Press Ctrl+Alt+Spacebar
Insert current date into a control	Press Ctrl+; (semicolon)
Insert current time into a control	Press Ctrl+: (colon)
Insert a line break in a Text or Memo control	Press Ctrl+Enter
Insert new record	Press Ctrl++ (plus sign)
Delete current record	Press Ctrl+- (minus sign)
Save current record	Press Shift+Enter or move to another record
Toggle values in a checkbox or option button	Spacebar
Undo a change to the current control	Press Esc or click the Undo button
Undo a change to the current record	Press Esc or click the Undo button a second time after you Undo the current control

Working with pictures and OLE objects

OLE (Object Linking and Embedding) objects are objects not part of an Access database. These commonly include pictures but an OLE field can also contain links to objects such as Word documents, Excel spreadsheets, and audio files such as `.mp3`, `.wav`, or `.wmv` files. You can also include video files such as `.mpg` or `.avi` files.

In Datasheet View, you can't view a picture or any OLE object without accessing the OLE server (such as Word, Excel, or the Microsoft Media Player). In Form View, however, you can size the OLE control area to be large enough to display a picture, business graph, or any visual OLE object. You can also size text-box controls on forms so that you can see the data within the field — you don't have to zoom in on the value, as you do with a datasheet field.

Any object supported by an OLE server can be stored in an Access OLE field. OLE objects are entered into a form so that you can see, hear, or use the value. As with a datasheet, you have two ways to enter OLE fields into a form:

- Paste them in from the commands in the Home tab's Clipboard group.
- Right-click on the OLE field and click Insert Object from the pop-up menu to display the Insert Object dialog box, shown in Figure 35-25.

FIGURE 35-25

The Insert Object dialog box.

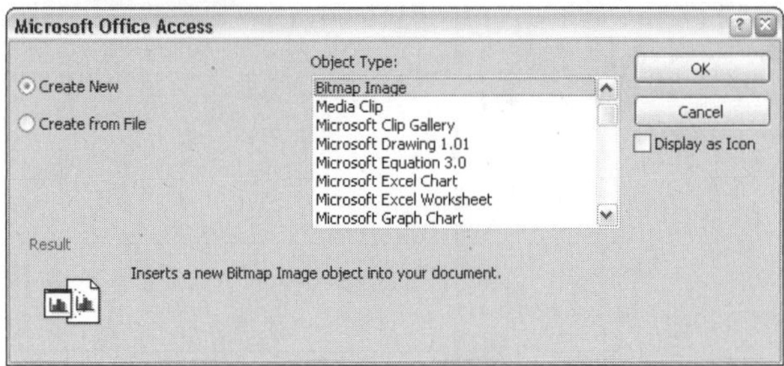

Use the Insert Object dialog box to add a new object to the OLE field, or add an object from an existing file. Choose the Create from File option button to add a picture or other OLE object from a file that already exists.

When displaying a picture in an OLE control, set the `Size Mode` property to control how the picture is displayed. The settings for this property are:

- **Clip:** Keeps the picture at its original size and truncates any portion of the picture that doesn't fit in the control.
- **Zoom:** Fits the picture in the control and keeps it in its original proportion, which may result in extra white space.
- **Stretch:** Sizes picture to fit exactly between the frame borders; this setting may distort the picture.

Memo field data entry

The `Features` field in the form shown in Figure 35-22 is a Memo data type. This type of field allows up to 65,535 bytes of text for each field. The first two sentences of data appear in the text box. When you click in this text box, a vertical scroll bar appears. Using this scrollbar, you can view the rest of the data in the control.

Better yet, you can resize the Memo control in the form's Design View if you want to make it larger to see more data. You can also press Shift+F2 and display a Zoom dialog box, as shown in Figure 35-26, which lets you see more data.

Date field data entry

The `AuctionEndDate` field in the form shown in Figure 35-26 is a Date/Time data type. This field is formatted to accept and show date values. When you click in this text box, a Date Picker icon appears next to it, as shown in Figure 35-27. Click the Date Picker to display a calendar from which you can choose a date.

If the Date Picker doesn't appear, switch to Design View and change the control's `Show Date Picker` property to `For dates`. Set the `Show Date Picker` property to `Never` if you don't want to use the Date Picker.

FIGURE 35-26

The Zoom dialog box.

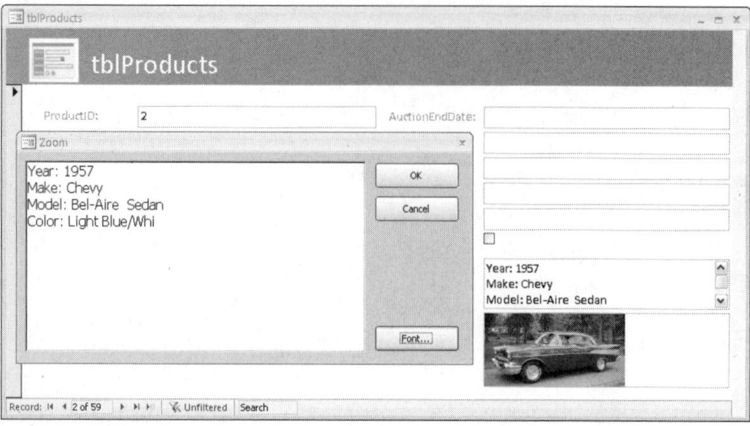

FIGURE 35-27

Using the Date Picker, new to Access 2007.

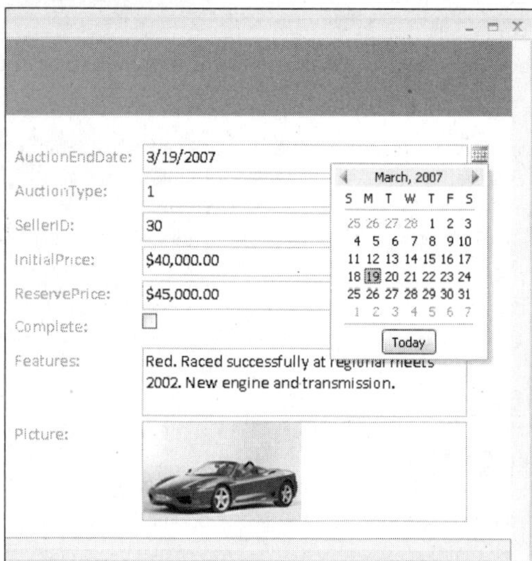

Using option groups

Option groups let you choose values from option buttons (sometimes called radio buttons). Option buttons let you select one value while deselecting the previous value. Option groups work best when you have a small number of choices to select from. Figure 35-28 shows an option group next to the `Auction` check-box; both controls perform the same operation.

FIGURE 35-28

Using an option group to select a numeric value.

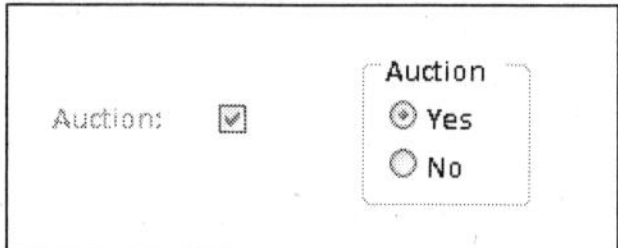

The easiest and most efficient way to create option groups is with the Option Group Wizard. You can use it to create option groups with multiple option buttons, toggle buttons, or checkboxes. When you're through, all your control's property settings are correctly set. This wizard greatly simplifies the process and enables you to create an option group quickly. To create an option group, switch to Design View and select the Option Group command from the Design tab's Controls group. Make sure the Use Control Wizards command is selected.

Option groups can only be bound to numeric fields. When creating an option group for a Yes/No field (which is numeric), set the Yes value to –1 and the No value to 0.

Using combo boxes and list boxes

Access has two types of controls — *list boxes* and *combo boxes* — that enable you to show lists of data from which a user can select. The list box is always open and ready for selection, whereas the combo box has to be clicked to open the list for selection. Also the combo box enables you to enter a value that is not on the list and takes up less room on the form.

You may want to replace the Category text box with a combo box containing values from `tblCategories`, as shown in Figure 35-29. The easiest way to do this is with the Combo Box Wizard. This wizard walks you through the steps of creating a combo box that looks up values in another table. To create a combo box, switch to Design View and select the Combo Box command from the Design tab's Controls group. Make sure the Use Control Wizards command is selected.

FIGURE 35-29

Using a combo box to select value from a list.

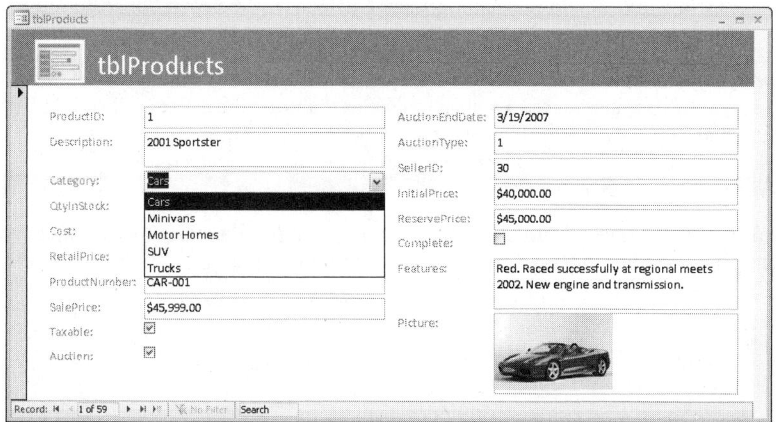

After you create the combo box, examine the `Row Source Type`, `Row Source`, `Column Count`, `Column Heads`, `Column Widths`, `Bound Column`, `List Rows`, and `List Width` properties. Once you become familiar with setting these properties, you can right-click a text box, select Change To ➪ Combo Box, and set the combo box's properties manually.

Switching to Datasheet View

While in the form, you can display a Datasheet View of your data by using one of the following methods:

- Click the Datasheet View command in the Home tab's Views group.
- Click the Datasheet View button in the View Shortcuts section at the bottom-right of the Access window.
- Right-click on the form's title bar — or any blank area of the form — and choose Datasheet View from the pop-up menu.

The datasheet is displayed with the cursor on the same field and record that it occupied in the form. If you move to another record and field and then redisplay the form, the form appears with the cursor on the field and with the record it last occupied in the datasheet.

To return to Form View — or any other view — select the desired view from the Views group, the View Shortcuts, or the pop-up menu.

Note that you can enter records in the Datasheet View by making the desired entries in cells, much as you would make entries in an Excel spreadsheet. You can use the techniques covered in Table 35-4 to add and edit field entries in the Datasheet View, as well as Form View.

Saving a record

Access saves each record when you move off it. Pressing Shift+Enter or selecting Save in the Home tab's Records group saves a record without moving off it. Closing the form also saves a record.

Printing a Form

You can print one or more records in your form exactly as they appear on-screen. (You learn how to produce formatted reports in Chapter 39.) The simplest way to print is to click the Print icon in the Quick Access toolbar. This prints the form to the Windows default printer. Click on the Microsoft Office Button to view other print options.

Printing a form is like printing anything else; you're in a WYSIWYG ("What You See Is What You Get") environment, so what you see on the form is essentially what you get in the printed hard copy. If you added page headers or page footers, they're printed at the top or bottom of the page. The printout contains any formatting that you specified in the form (including lines, boxes, and shading) and converts colors to grayscale if you're using a monochrome printer.

The printout includes as many pages as necessary to print all the data. If your form is wider than a single printer page, you need multiple pages to print your form. Access breaks up the printout as necessary to fit on each page.

You can also control printing from the Print dialog box, which you open by clicking the Microsoft Office Button, and then clicking on Print. From this dialog box, customize your printout by selecting from several options:

- **Print Range:** Prints the entire form or only selected pages or records
- **Copies:** Determines the number of copies to be printed
- **Collate:** Determines whether multiple copies are collated

You can also click the Properties button and set options for the selected printer or select the printer itself to change the type of printer. The Setup button allows you to set margins and print headings.

Using the Print Preview window

Although you may have all the information in the form ready to print, but you aren't sure whether that information will print on multiple pages or fit on one printed page. To preview your print job, click the Print Preview command under the Print menu to display the Print Preview window. The default view is the first page in single-page preview. Use the Ribbon commands to select different views and zoom in and out. Click Print to print the form to the printer. Click the Close Print Preview command on the right side of the Print Preview tab of the Ribbon to return to Form View.

Summary

In this chapter, you learned how to add different types of forms to your database using the Create tab's Form group. You learned about the different types of controls and how to add them to the form. Then you learned how to move and resize these controls.

You also learned how properties are the building blocks of an object. The Property Sheet contains every attribute of the control, from where it's located on the form to what data it displays to what font it's displayed in. You learned how to display the Property Sheet and how to change a few properties, including the `Name` property using naming conventions.

You also learned that you can enter database data in Form View. You learned how to navigate between fields and records and how to use controls such as option groups and combo boxes to facilitate data entry. Finally, you learned how to print the form.

Chapter 36

Selecting Data with Queries

Queries are an essential part of any database application. Queries are the tools that enable you and your users to extract data from multiple tables, combine it in useful ways, and present it to the user as a datasheet, on a form, or as a printed report.

You may have heard the old cliché, "Queries convert data to information." To a certain extent, this statement is true (that's why it's a cliché). The data contained within tables is not particularly useful because, for the most part, the data in tables appears in no particular order. Also, in a properly normalized database, important information is spread out among a number of different tables. Queries are what draw these various data sources together and present the combined information in such a way that users can actually work with the data.

In this chapter, you learn what a query is and how to create them. Using the Sales (`tblSales`), Contacts (`tblContacts`), Sales Line Items (`tblSalesLineItems`), and Products (`tblProducts`) tables, you create several types of queries for the Access Auto Auctions database.

IN THIS CHAPTER

- Understanding the different types of Access queries
- Creating queries
- Selecting tables and fields for queries
- Displaying information in queries
- Sorting information in queries
- Selecting specific records in queries
- Printing the results of queries
- Adding more than one table to a query
- Working around query limitations

ON the WEB **This chapter will use the database named `Chapter36.accdb`. That example database is available for download from `http://www.wiley.com/TOCOME`. When you open the file, you can click Options in the Security Warning bar, click Enable This Content in the Microsoft Office Security Options dialog box, and then click OK.**

Understanding Queries

A database's primary purpose is to store and extract information. Information can be obtained from a database immediately after you enter the data or days, weeks, or even years later. Of course, retrieving information from database tables requires knowledge of how the database is set up.

For example, printed reports are often filed in a cabinet, arranged by date and by a sequence number that indicates when the report was produced. To obtain a specific report, you must know its year and sequence number. In a good filing system, you may have a cross-reference book to help you find a specific report. This book may have all reports categorized alphabetically by type of report and, perhaps, by date. Such a book can be helpful, but if you know only the report's topic and approximate date, you still have to search through all sections of the book to find out where to get the report.

Unlike manual databases, computer databases like Microsoft Access easily obtain information to meet virtually any criteria you specify.

This is the real power of a database — the capacity to examine the data in more ways than you can imagine. Queries, by definition, ask questions about the data stored in the database. Most queries are used to drive forms, reports, and graphical representations of the data contained in a database.

What is a query?

The word *query* comes from the Latin word *quærere*, which means "to ask or inquire." Over the years, the word *query* has become synonymous with *quiz, challenge, inquire,* or *question*. So, think of a query as a question or inquiry posed to the database about information contained in its tables.

A Microsoft Access query is a question that you ask about the information stored in your Access tables. You build queries with the Access query tools, and then save it as a new object in your Access database. Your query can be a simple question about data within a single table, or it can be a more complex question about information stored in several tables. After you submit the question, Microsoft Access returns only the information you requested.

Using queries this way, you ask the Access Auto Auctions database to show you only trucks that were sold in the year 2007. To see the *types* of trucks sold for the year 2007, you need information from three tables: `tblSales`, `tblSalesLineItems`, and `tblProducts`. Figure 36-1 is a typical Query Design window. Although it may look complex, it's actually very simple and easy to understand.

After you create and run a query, Microsoft Access retrieves and displays the requested records as a datasheet. This set of records is called a *recordset,* which is the set of records selected by a query. As you've seen, a datasheet looks just like a spreadsheet, with its rows of records and columns of fields. The datasheet (of the recordset) can display many records simultaneously.

You can easily filter information from a single table using the Search and Filter capabilities of a table's datasheet view (Filter by Selection and Filter by Form). Queries allow you to view information from a single table, or from multiple tables at the same time (as in Figure 36-1). Many database queries extract information from several tables.

Clicking the bottom portion of the View button on the Home tab of the Ribbon allows you to switch to the Datasheet view where you will now see the six records that match the query shown in Figure 36-1. This is a relatively easy-to-design query when you understand how to use the Access query designer. This simple query has many elements that demonstrate the power of the Access query engine: sorting a result set of records, specifying multiple criteria, and even using a complex `Or` condition in one of those fields.

You can build very complex queries using the same query designer. Suppose, for instance, that you want to send a notice to all previous buyers of more than one car in the past year that several new cars are available for auction. This type of query requires getting information from four tables: `tblContacts`, `tblSales`, `tblSalesLineItems`, and `tblProducts`. The majority of the information you need is in `tblContacts` and `tblProducts`.

FIGURE 36-1

A typical three-table select query. This query displays the sales date, number of trucks, and type of truck for all trucks sold in the year 2007.

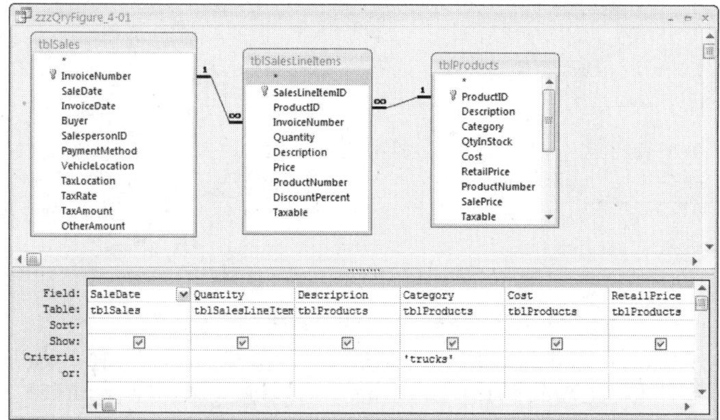

In this case, you want Access to show you a datasheet of all Contact names and addresses where they have met your specified criteria (two or more cars purchased in 2007). In this case, Access retrieves customer names and cities from the `tblContacts` table and then obtains the number of cars from the `tblProducts` table, and the year of sale from the `tblSales` table. Figure 36-2 shows this relatively complex query. Access then takes the information that's common to your criteria, combines it, and displays all the information in a single datasheet. This datasheet is the result of a query that draws from the `tblContacts`, `tblSales`, `tblSalesLineItems`, and `tblProducts` tables. The database query performed the work of assembling all the information for you. Figure 36-3 shows the resulting datasheet.

FIGURE 36-2

A more complex query returning customers that purchased more than one car in 2007.

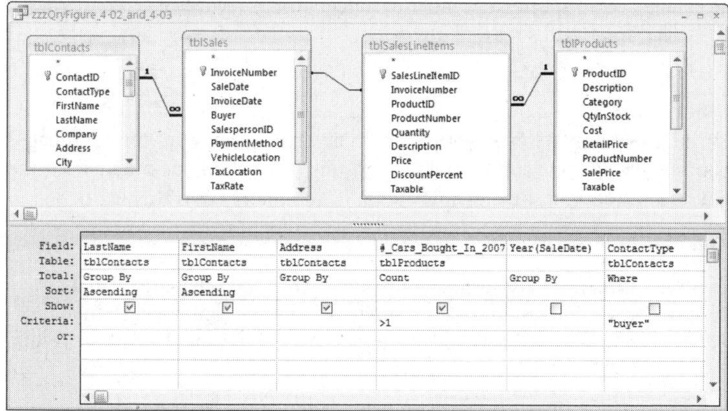

FIGURE 36-3

The resulting datasheet of the query shown in Figure 36-2.

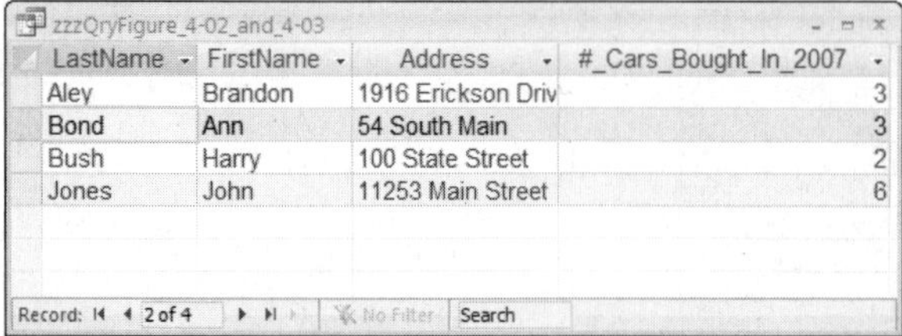

zzzQryFigure_4-02_and_4-03

LastName	FirstName	Address	#_Cars_Bought_In_2007
Aley	Brandon	1916 Erickson Driv	3
Bond	Ann	54 South Main	3
Bush	Harry	100 State Street	2
Jones	John	11253 Main Street	6

Record: 2 of 4 No Filter Search

Types of queries

Access supports many different types of queries, grouped into six basic categories:

- **Select:** These are the most common types of queries. As its name implies, the select query selects information from one or more tables, creating a recordset. Generally speaking, the data returned by a select query is updatable and is often used to populate forms and reports.
- **Total:** These are special type of select queries. Total queries provide sums or other calculations (such as count) from the records returned by a select query. Selecting this type of query adds a Total row in the QBE (Query by Example) grid.
- **Action:** These queries enable you to create new tables (Make Tables) or change data (delete, update, and append) in existing tables. Action queries affect many records as a single operation.
- **Crosstab:** These queries can display summary data in cross-tabular form like a spreadsheet, with row and column headings based on fields in the table. The individual cells of the recordset are computed or calculated from data in the underlying tables.
- **SQL:** There are three SQL (Structured Query Language) query types — Union, Pass-Through, and Data Definition. These queries are used for advanced database manipulation, such as working with client/server SQL databases like SQL Server or Oracle. You create these queries by writing specific SQL statements.
- **Top(n):** Top(n) queries enable you to specify a number or percentage of records you want returned from any type (select, total, and so on) of query.

Query capabilities

Queries are flexible. They provide the capability of looking at your data in virtually any way you can imagine. Most database systems are continually evolving and changing over time. Very often, the original purpose of a database is very different from its current use.

Here is a sampling of what you can do with Access queries:

- **Choose tables:** Obtain information from a single table or from many tables that are related by some common data. Suppose you're interested in seeing the customer name along with the items purchased by each type of customer. When using several tables, Access returns the data as a combined single datasheet.
- **Choose fields:** Specify which fields from each table you want to see in the recordset. For example, you can select the customer name, zip code, sales date, and invoice number from `tblContacts` and `tblSales`.

- **Choose records:** Select records based on selection criteria. For example, you may want to see records for only sellers in `tblContacts`.
- **Sort records:** You may want to sort records in a specific order. For example, you may need to see customers sorted by last name and first name.
- **Perform calculations:** Use queries to perform calculations on data. Perform calculations such as averaging, totaling, or counting fields and records.
- **Create tables:** Create a new table based on data returned by a query.
- **Base forms and reports on queries:** The recordset you create from a query may have just the right fields and data needed for a report or form. Basing a form or report on a query means that every time you print the report or open the form, you will see the most current information in the tables.
- **Create graphs based on queries:** Create graphs from data returned by a query.
- **Use a query as a source of data for other queries (subquery):** Create additional queries based on records returned by another query. This is very useful for performing ad hoc queries, where you may repeatedly make small changes to the criteria. In this case, the second query is used to change the criteria while the first query and its data remain intact.
- **Make changes to tables:** Access queries can obtain information from a wide range of sources. You can retrieve data stored in dBASE, Paradox, Btrieve, and Microsoft SQL Server databases, as well as Excel spreadsheets, text files, and other data sources.

How recordsets work

Access takes the records that result from a query and displays them in a datasheet. The set of records is commonly called (oddly enough) a *recordset.* Physically, a recordset looks much like a table. A recordset is, in fact, a *dynamic* set of records. The set of records returned by a query is not stored within the database, unless you have directed access to build a table from those records.

When you close a query, the query's recordset is gone; it no longer exists. Even though the recordset itself no longer exists, the data that formed the recordset remains stored in the underlying tables.

When you run a query, Access places the returned records into a recordset. When you save the query, only the structure of the query is saved, and not the returned records. Consider these benefits of *not* saving the recordset to a physical table:

- A smaller amount of space on a storage device (usually a hard drive) is needed.
- The query uses updated versions of records.

Every time the query is executed, it reads the underlying tables and re-creates the recordset. Because recordsets themselves are not stored, a query automatically reflects any changes to the underlying tables made since the last time the query was executed — even in a real-time, multiuser environment.

Creating a Query

After you create your tables and place data in them, you're ready to work with queries. To begin a query, choose the Create tab of the Ribbon, and click on the Query Design button in the Other group. Access opens the query designer in response.

Figure 36-4 shows two windows. The underlying window is the Query Designer. Floating on top of the designer is the Show Table dialog box. The Show Table window is *modal*, which means that you must do something in the dialog box before continuing with the query. Before you continue, you add the tables required for the query. In this case, `tblProducts` is highlighted to be added.

FIGURE 36-4

The Show Table dialog box in the Query Design window.

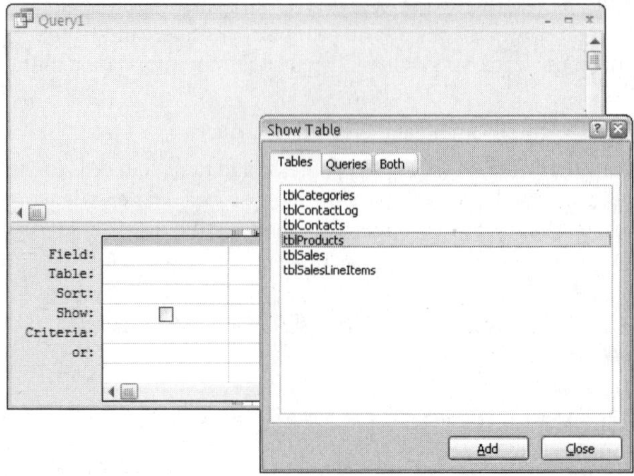

The Show Table dialog box shown in Figure 36-5 displays all tables and queries in your database. Double-click on `tblProducts` to add it to the query design. Close the Show Table dialog box after adding `tblProducts`. Figure 36-5 shows `tblProducts` added to the query.

FIGURE 36-5

The Query Design window with `tblProducts` added to the Query Designer.

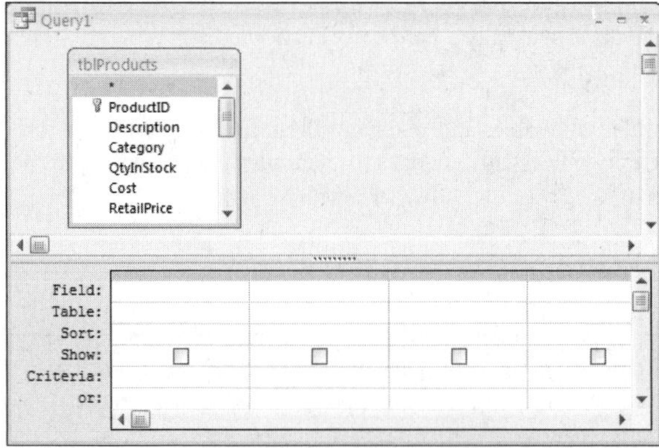

To add additional tables to the query, right-click on the query's design surface and select Show Table from the shortcut menu that appears. Alternatively, drag tables from the Navigation pane on to the Query Designer's surface.

Removing a table from the Query Designer is easy. Just right-click on the table in the Query Designer and select Remove Table from the shortcut menu.

Using the Query window

The Query window has two main views: Design view and Datasheet view. The difference between them is self-explanatory: The Design view is where you create the query, and the Datasheet view displays the records returned by the query.

The Query Design window should now look like Figure 36-5, with `tblProducts` displayed in the top half of the Query Design window.

The Query Design window consists of two sections:

- The table/query entry pane (top)
- The Query by Example (QBE) design grid (bottom)

The upper pane is where tables or queries and their fields are displayed. Tables and queries are displayed as small windows inside the top pane (the proper name of this window is Field List). The Field List window can be resized by clicking on the edges and dragging it to a different size.

The Query by Example (QBE) grid holds the field names involved in the query and any criteria used to select records. Each column in the QBE grid contains information about a single field from a table or query contained within the upper pane.

Navigating the Query Design window

The two window panes are separated horizontally by a pane-resizing bar (see Figure 36-5). Move the bar up or down to change the relative sizes of the upper and lower panes.

Switch between the upper and lower panes by clicking the desired pane or by pressing F6 to switch panes. Each pane has horizontal and vertical scrollbars to help you move around.

You actually build the query by dragging fields from the upper pane to the QBE grid.

Using the Design tab in Query Design view

The Design tab that appears on the Ribbon (shown in Figure 36-6) when you've displayed the Query Design view contains many different buttons specific to building and working with queries.

FIGURE 36-6

The Design tab in Query Design view.

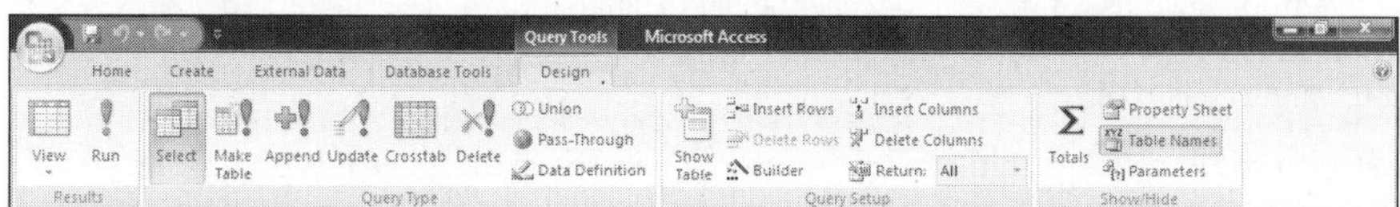

This Design tab has many buttons that can be helpful when designing your queries. Although each button is explained as it is used in these chapters about Access, here are the main buttons:

- **View:** Switches between the Datasheet view and Design view. The View drop-down control also enables you to display the underlying SQL statement behind the query (more on this later).
- **Save (in the Quick Access Toolbar):** Saves the query. It is a good idea to save your work often, especially when creating complex queries.
- **Make Table, Append, Update, and Crosstab:** Specify the type of query you are building.
- **Run:** Runs the query. Displays a select query's datasheet, serving the same function as the View button. However, when working with action queries, it actually performs the operations specified by the query.
- **Show Table:** Opens the Show Table dialog box.

The remaining buttons are used for creating more advanced queries, printing the contents of the query, and displaying a query's property sheet.

Using the QBE grid of the Query Design window

As you saw earlier, Figure 36-5 displays an empty QBE grid, which has six labeled rows:

- **Field:** Where field names are entered or added
- **Table:** Shows the table the field is from (useful in queries with multiple tables)
- **Sort:** Enables sorting instructions for the query
- **Show:** Determines whether to display the field in the returned recordset
- **Criteria:** Criteria that filter the returned records
- **or:** This row is the first of a number of rows to which you can add multiple query criteria.

You learn more about these rows as you create queries in this chapter.

Selecting Fields

There are several ways to add fields to a query. You can add fields one at a time, select and add multiple fields, or select and add all fields. You use your keyboard or mouse to add fields.

Adding a single field

You add a single field in several ways. One method is to double-click the field name in the Field List (also called a Table window); the field name immediately appears in the first available column in the QEB pane. Alternatively, drag a field from a table in the top portion of the query designer, and drop it on a column in the QBE grid. Dropping a field between two other fields in the QBE grid pushes other fields to the right.

Another way to add fields to the QBE grid is to click an empty Field cell in the QBE grid, and select the field name from the drop-down list in the cell, or type the field's name into the cell. Figure 36-7 shows selecting the Cost field from the drop-down list. Once selected, simply move to the next field cell and select the next field you want to see in the query.

You'll find a similar list of all the tables in the query in a drop-down list in the Table row of the QBE grid.

After selecting the fields, run the query by clicking the Datasheet button or the Run button on the Design tab of the Ribbon. Click the Design View button on the Design tab to return to the design window.

FIGURE 36-7

Adding fields in the QBE grid. Clicking the down arrow reveals a drop-down list from which you select a field.

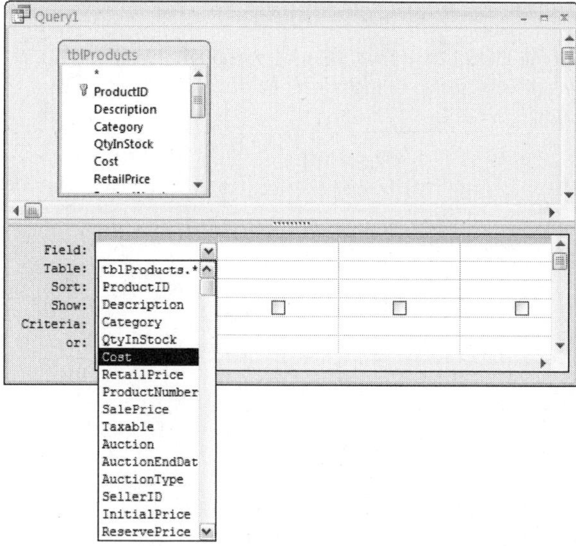

Adding multiple fields

You add multiple fields in a single action by selecting the fields from the Field List and dragging them to the QBE grid. The selected fields do not have to be contiguous (one after the other). Hold down the Shift key while selecting multiple fields. Figure 36-8 illustrates the process of adding multiple fields.

FIGURE 36-8

Selecting several fields to move to the QBE grid.

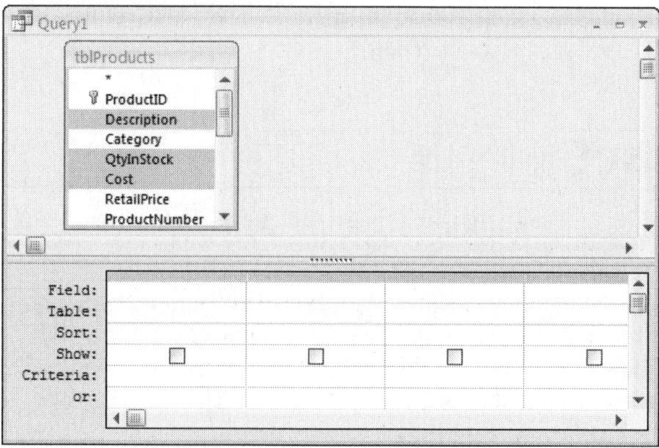

The fields are added to the QBE grid in the order in which they occur in the table.

You can also add all the fields in the table by clicking on the Field List's header (where it says `tblProducts` in Figure 36-9) to highlight all the fields in the table. Then drag the highlighted fields to the QBE grid.

Alternatively, click and drag the asterisk (*) from the Field List to the QBE grid. Although this action does not add all the fields to the QBE grid, the asterisk directs Access to include all fields in the table in the query.

FIGURE 36-9

Adding the asterisk to the QBE grid selects all fields in the table.

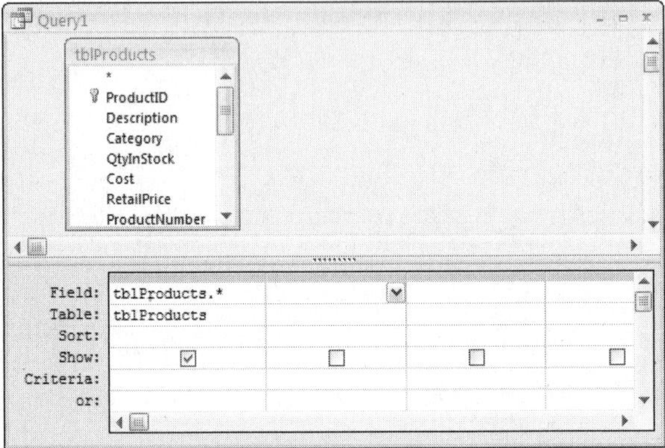

Unlike selecting all the fields, the asterisk places a reference to all the fields in a single column. When you drag multiple columns, as in the preceding example, you drag names to the QBE grid. If you later change the design of the table, you also have to change the design of the query. The advantage of using the asterisk for selecting all fields is that changes to the underlying tables don't require changes to the query. The asterisk means to select all fields in the table, regardless of the field names or changes in the number of fields in the table.

The downside of using the asterisk to specify all fields in a table is that the query, as instructed, returns all the fields in a table, whether or not every field is used on a form or report.

Displaying the Recordset

Click the Run button or the Datasheet View button on the Design tab to view the query's results (see Figure 36-10).

Working with records in Datasheet view is covered in detail in Chapter 36. As you can see in that chapter, filtering, sorting, rearranging, and searching within a datasheet is quite easy. Our simple select query did not transform the data in any way, so the data shown in Figure 36-10 is completely editable. We can modify existing data, delete rows, and even add new records to this data set, if we want.

When you're working with data in the datasheet, all the table and field properties defined at the table level are in effect. Therefore, validation rules, default values, and other properties assert themselves even though the datasheet is the result of a query.

FIGURE 36-10

The datasheet view of the query.

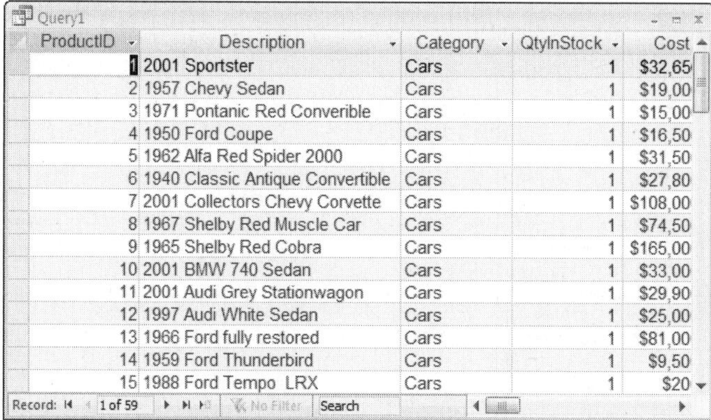

Query1

ProductID	Description	Category	QtyInStock	Cost
1	2001 Sportster	Cars	1	$32,65
2	1957 Chevy Sedan	Cars	1	$19,00
3	1971 Pontanic Red Converible	Cars	1	$15,00
4	1950 Ford Coupe	Cars	1	$16,50
5	1962 Alfa Red Spider 2000	Cars	1	$31,50
6	1940 Classic Antique Convertible	Cars	1	$27,80
7	2001 Collectors Chevy Corvette	Cars	1	$108,00
8	1967 Shelby Red Muscle Car	Cars	1	$74,50
9	1965 Shelby Red Cobra	Cars	1	$165,00
10	2001 BMW 740 Sedan	Cars	1	$33,00
11	2001 Audi Grey Stationwagon	Cars	1	$29,90
12	1997 Audi White Sedan	Cars	1	$25,00
13	1966 Ford fully restored	Cars	1	$81,00
14	1959 Ford Thunderbird	Cars	1	$9,50
15	1988 Ford Tempo LRX	Cars	1	$20

Record: 1 of 59 No Filter Search

Earlier versions of Access referred to an updatable datasheet as a *Dynaset*. This expression emphasized the fact that the datasheet was dynamically linked to its underlying data sources. However, this expression has fallen by the wayside because very often the data in a query's datasheet is not updatable. For instance, transforming the data in any way, such as combining first and last names as a single field, makes the datasheet non-updatable. You'll see data transformations later in this chapter.

At any time, clicking the Design View button on the Home tab of the Ribbon returns you to Query Design mode.

Working with Fields

There are times when you want to work with the fields you've already selected — rearranging their order, inserting a new field, or deleting an existing field. You may even want to add a field to the QBE grid without showing it in the datasheet. Adding a field without showing it enables you to sort on the hidden field, or to use the hidden field as criteria.

Selecting a field in the QBE grid

Before you can move a field's position, you must first select it. To select it, you will work with the field selector row.

The *field selector row* is the narrow gray area at the top of each column in the QBE grid at the bottom of the Query Designer. Recall that each column represents a field. To select the Category field, move the mouse pointer until a small selection arrow (in this case, a dark downward arrow) is visible in the selector row and then click the column. Figure 36-11 shows the selection arrow above the Category column just before it is selected.

Select multiple contiguous fields by clicking the first field you wish to select and then dragging across the field selector bars of the other fields.

FIGURE 36-11

Selecting a column in the QBE grid. The pointer changes to a downward-pointing arrow when you move over the selection row.

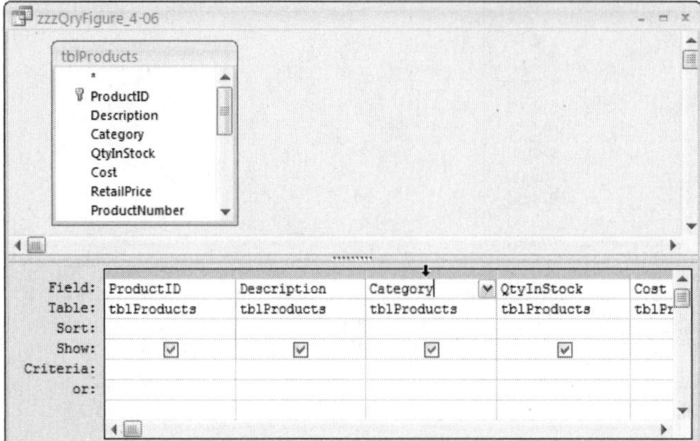

Changing field order

The left-to-right order in which fields appear in the QBE grid determines the order in which they appear in Datasheet view. You may want to move the fields in the QBE grid to achieve a new sequence of fields in the query's results. With the fields selected, you can move the fields on the QBE design by simply dragging them to a new position.

Left-click on a field's selector bar, and, while holding down the left mouse button, drag the field into a new position in the QBE grid.

Figure 36-12 shows the `Category` field highlighted. As you move the selector field to the left, the column separator between the fields `ProductID` and `Description` changes (gets wider) to show you where `Category` will go.

Resizing columns in the QBE grid

The QBE grid generally shows five or six fields in the viewable area of your screen. The remaining fields are viewed by moving the horizontal scroll bar at the bottom of the window.

There are times that you may want to shrink some fields to be able to see more columns in the QBE grid. You adjust the column width to make them smaller (or larger) by moving the mouse pointer to the margin between two fields, and dragging the column resizer left or right (see Figure 36-13). An easier way to resize columns in the QBE grid is to double-click on the line dividing two columns in the grid. Access "auto-sizes" the column to fit the data displayed in the column.

Removing a field

Remove a field from the QBE grid by selecting the field (or fields) and pressing the Delete key. You can also right-click on a field's selector and choose Cut from the shortcut menu.

FIGURE 36-12

Moving the Category field to between ProductID and Description. Notice the QBE field icon below the arrow near the Description column.

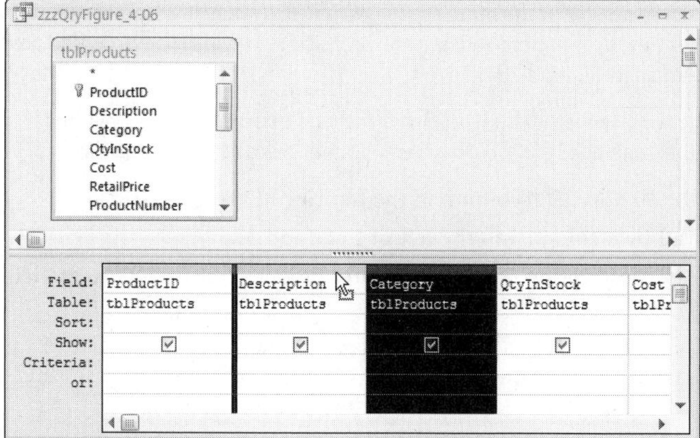

FIGURE 36-13

Resizing columns in the QBE grid.

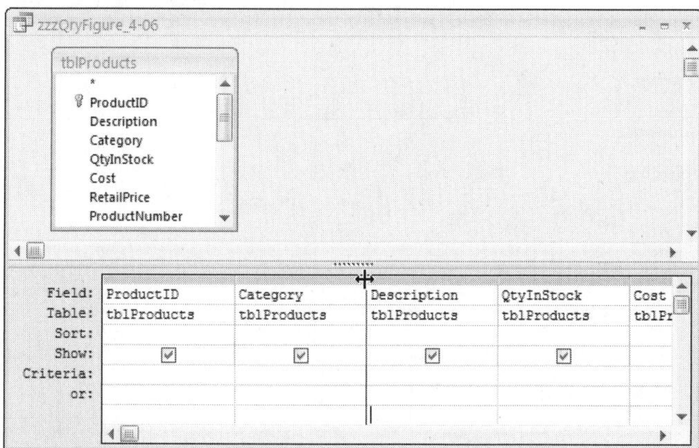

Inserting a field

Insert new fields in the QBE grid by dragging a field from a Field List above the QBE grid and dropping it onto a column in the QBE grid. The new column is inserted to the left of the column you dropped the field on. Double-clicking a field in a Field List adds the new column at the far right position in the QBE grid.

Providing an alias for the field name

To make the query datasheet easier to read, you can provide aliases for the fields in your query. An alias becomes the field's heading in the query's datasheet, but does not affect the field's name or how the data is stored and used by Access. Aliases are sometimes useful to help users better understand the data returned by a query. Data in queries are often transformed by performing simple operations such as combining a person's first and last name as a single field. In these situations, aliases are very useful because they provide an easily recognizable reference to the transformed data.

To follow along with this example, create a query using the fields from the `tblProducts` as shown in Figure 36-12. Follow these steps to establish an alias for the `ProductID` and `Description` fields:

1. **Click to the left of the *P* of the `ProductID` column in the top row of the QBE grid.**
2. **Type** Product-Number **followed by a colon (:) to the left of `ProductID`.**
3. **Click to the left of the *D* in the Description column and enter** Product Description: **to the left of the field name.**

   When you run the query, the aliases you created appear as the column headings. Figure 36-14 shows both the query in Design view and the query's datasheet. Notice that the `ProductID` and `Description` column sport their new aliases instead of their respective field names.

FIGURE 36-14

Aliases can be useful to help users understand data.

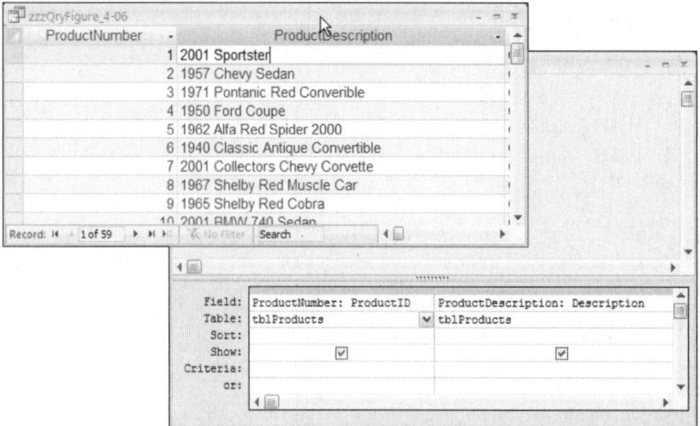

Aliases should be used with caution, however. Because an alias masks the name of the field underlying a datasheet, it's easy to become confused which column headings are aliases and which are field names. It is a complete waste of time looking for a field named `ProductDescription`, based on a datasheet column heading. It would be nice if Access somehow distinguished between aliases and field names in Datasheet view, but the only way to know for sure is to examine the query's design.

Showing a field

While performing queries, you may want to show only some of the fields in the QBE grid. Suppose, for example, you've chosen `ContactType`, `FirstName`, `LastName`, `Address`, `City`, and `State`. Then you decide that you want to temporarily look at the same data, without the `ContactType` and `Address` fields. You could start a new query adding all of the fields except `Address` and `ContactType`, or you can simply "turn off" the `Address` and `ContactType` fields by unchecking the checkbox in the Show row of each of these columns (see Figure 36-15).

FIGURE 36-15

The Show checkbox is unchecked for the Address and ContactType fields.

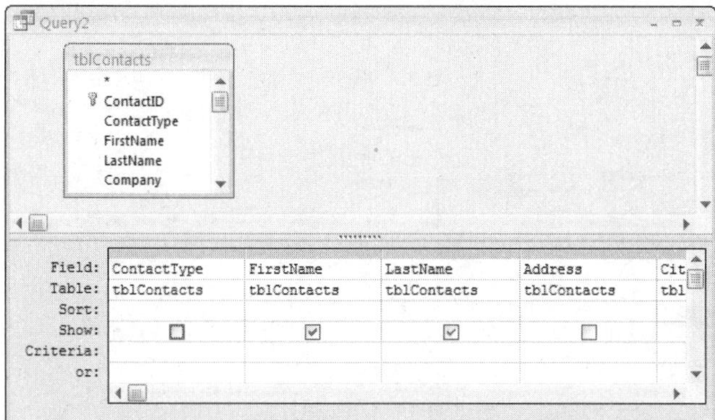

By default, every field you add to the QBE grid has its Show checkbox selected.

Another common reason to hide a field in the query is because the field is used for searching or sorting, but its value is not needed in the query. For instance, consider a query involving the invoices from the Access Auto Auctions database. For a number of reasons, the users may want to see the invoices sorted by the order date, even though the actual order date is irrelevant for this particular purpose. Simply include the `OrderDate` field in the QBE grid, set the sort order for the `OrderDate` field, and uncheck its Show box. Access sorts the data by the `OrderDate` field even though the field is not shown in the query's results.

CAUTION **If you save a query that has an unused field (its Show box is unchecked and no criteria or sort order is applied to the field), Access eliminates the field from the query. The next time you open the query, the field will not be included in the query's design.**

Changing the Sort Order

When viewing a recordset, you often want to display the data in a sorted order. You may want to sort the recordset to make it easier to analyze the data (for example, to look at all the `tblProducts` sorted by `category`).

Sorting places the records in alphabetical or numeric order. The sort order can be ascending (0 to 9 and A to Z) or descending (9 to 0 and Z to A). You can sort on a single field or multiple fields.

You input sorting directions in the Sort row in the QBE grid. To specify a sort order on a particular field (such as `LastName`), perform these steps:

1. **Position the cursor in the Sort cell in the `LastName` column.**
2. **Click the drop-down list that appears in the cell, and select the sort order (Ascending or Descending) you want to apply.**

Figure 36-16 shows the QBE grid with ascending sorts specified for the `LastName` and `FirstName` fields. Notice that the `LastName` field is still showing the sort options available. Also notice that the word *Ascending* is being selected in the field's Sort: cell.

FIGURE 36-16

An ascending sort has been specified for the LastName and FirstName fields.

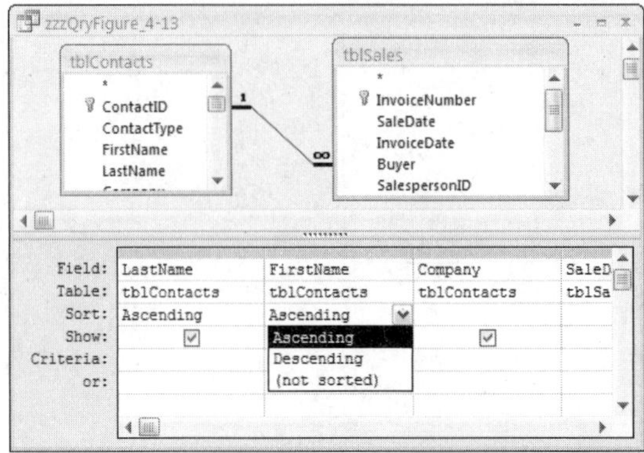

You *cannot* sort on a Memo or an OLE object field.

The left-to-right order in which fields appear in the QBE grid is important when sorting on more than one field. Not only do the fields appear in the datasheet in left-to-right order, they are sorted in the same order (this is known as *sort order precedence*). The leftmost field containing sort criteria is sorted first, the first field to the right containing sort criteria is sorted next, and so on. In the example shown in Figure 36-16, the `LastName` field is sorted first, and then the `FirstName` field.

Figure 36-17 shows the results of the query shown in Figure 36-16. Notice that the data is sorted by the values in the `LastName` column, and the values in the `FirstName` column are sorted within each name in the `LastName` column. This is why Ann Bond appears before John Bond in the query's data.

FIGURE 36-17

The order of the fields is critical when sorting on multiple fields.

qryFigure_4-16 and_4-17

LastName	FirstName	City	State
Aikins	Teresa	Middletown	CT
Aley	Brandon	Fairbanks	MA
Bailey	Karen	Westbourgh	MA
Bond	Ann	Colchester	CT
Bond	John	West Bridgewater	MA
Bush	Harry	Mohegan Lake	NY
Calson	Larry	Chicota	TX
Casey	Cindy	Newington	NH
Casey	Debbie	Jackhorn	KY
Crook	Joe	Windsor	CT
Davis	Larry	Sherman Oaks	CA
Dennis	Michael	Bedford	NY
Gleason	William	Derby	CT

Record: 4 of 58 No Filter Search

Displaying Only Selected Records

So far, you've been working with all the records of the `tblContacts` and `tblProducts` tables. Most often users want to work only with records conforming to some criteria. Otherwise, too many records may be returned by a query, causing serious performance issues. For example, you may want to look only at contacts that are buyers and not sellers. Access makes it easy for you to specify a query's criteria.

Understanding selection criteria

Selection criteria are simply filtering rules applied to data as it is extracted from the database. Selection criteria instruct Access which records you want to look at in the recordset. A typical criterion might be "all sellers," or "only those vehicles that are not trucks," or "cars with retail prices greater than $45,000."

Selection criteria limit the records returned by a query. Selection criteria aid the user by selecting only the records a user wants to see, and ignoring all the others.

You specify criteria in the Criteria row of the QBE grid. You designate criteria as an expression. The expression can be as a simple example (like "Trucks" or "Not Trucks") or can take the form of complex expressions using built-in Access functions.

Entering simple string criteria

Character-type criteria are applied to Text-type fields. Most often, you will enter an example of the text you want to retrieve. Here is a small example that returns only product records where the product type is "Cars":

1. **Add `tblProducts` and choose the `Description`, `Category`, and `Cost` fields.**
2. **Type** CARS **into the Criteria cell under the Category column.**
3. **Run the query.**

   Only cars are displayed — in this case, 25 records (see Figure 36-18). Observe that you did not enter an equal sign or place quotes around the sample text, yet Access added double quotes around the value. Access, unlike many other database systems, automatically makes assumptions about what you want.

Figure 36-18 shows both the query design and the datasheet resulting from the query. This figure also illustrates one reason you may wish to hide a column in a query. There's no point in displaying "Cars" and every row in the third column. In fact, because this query only returns information about cars, the user can very well assume that every record references a car and there's no need to display a product category in the query. Unchecking the Category's Show box in the queries design would remove the Category column from the datasheet, making the data easier to understand.

You could enter the criteria expression in any of these other ways:

- CARS
- = CARS
- "CARS"
- = "Cars"

By default, Access is *not* case sensitive, so any form of the word *cars* works just as well as this query's criteria.

Figure 36-18 is an excellent example for demonstrating the options for various types of simple character criteria. You could just as well enter "Not Cars" in the criteria column, to return all products that are not cars (trucks, vans, and so on).

FIGURE 36-18

Specifying character criteria. In this case, because you want to see only cars, you enter "CARS" as the criteria.

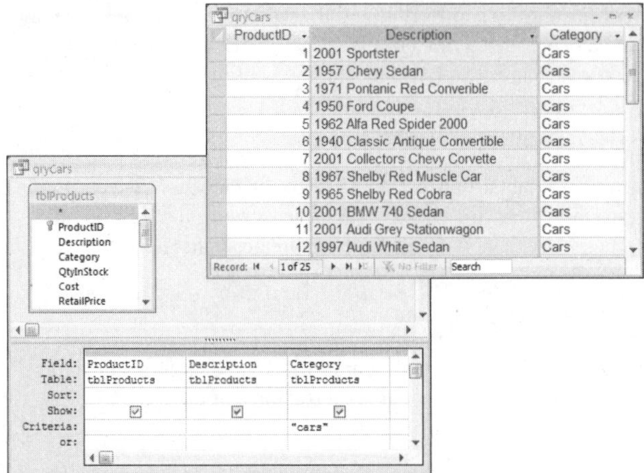

Generally, when dealing with character data, you enter equalities, inequalities, or a list of values that are acceptable.

This capability is a powerful tool. Consider that you have only to supply an example and Access not only interprets it but also uses it to create the query recordset. This is exactly what *Query by Example* means: You enter an example and let the database build a query based on the example.

To erase the criteria in the cell, select the contents and press Delete, or select the contents and Right Click Cut from the shortcut menu that appears. You can also right-click Paste to revert to the previous content (in this case, a blank cell).

Entering other simple criteria

You can also specify criteria for `Numeric`, `Date`, and `Yes/No` fields. Simply enter the example data in the criteria field.

It is also possible to add more than one criteria to a query. For example, suppose that you want to look only at contacts who are both sellers *and* buyers ("BOTH" type in the `ContactType` field), and those contacts have been customers since January 1, 2007 (where `OrigCustDate` is greater or equal to January 1, 2007). This query requires criteria in both the `ContactType` and `OrigCustDate` fields. To do this, it is critical that you place both examples on the same Criteria row. Follow these steps to create this query:

1. **Create a new query starting with** `tblContacts`**.**
2. **Add** `ContactType`, `FirstName`, `LastName`, `State`, **and** `OrigCustDate` **to the QBE grid.**
3. **Enter** BOTH **in the Criteria cell in the** `ContactType` **column.**
4. **Enter** >= 01/01/07 **in the Criteria cell in the** `OrigCustDate` **column.**
5. **Run the query.**

   Figure 36-19 shows how the query should look.

Access displays records of contacts that are both sellers and buyers that became customers after January 1, 2007 — in this example, two contact records.

FIGURE 36-19

Specifying character and date criteria in the same query.

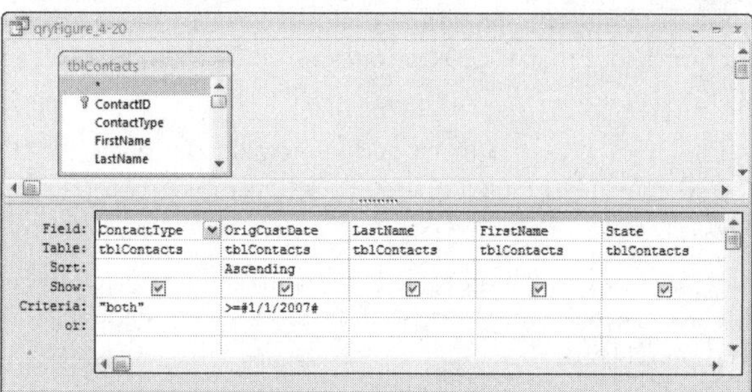

Access uses comparison operators to compare `Date` fields to a value. These operators include less than (<), greater than (>), equal to (=), or a combination of these operators. Notice that Access automatically adds pound sign (#) delimiters around the date value. Access uses these delimiters to distinguish between date and text data. The pound signs are just like the quote marks Access added to the "Cars" criteria. Because the `OrigCustDate` is a `DateTime` field, Access understands what you want and inserts the proper delimiters for you.

Printing a Query's Recordset

After you create your query, you can easily print all the records in the recordset. Although you can't specify a type of report, you can print a simple matrix-type report (rows and columns) of the recordset created by your query.

You do have some flexibility when printing a recordset. If you know that the datasheet is set up just as you want, you can specify some options as you follow these steps:

1. **Use the datasheet you just created for both sellers and buyers that have been customers since 01/01/2007.**
2. **If you are not in the Datasheet view, switch to the Query Datasheet mode by clicking the Datasheet button on the Design tab of the Ribbon.**
3. **Choose Office Button ⇨ Print.**
4. **Specify the print options that you want in the Print dialog box and click OK.**

The printout reflects all layout options in effect when you print the dataset. Hidden columns do not print, and gridlines print only if the Gridlines option is on. The printout reflects the specified row height and column width.

Saving a Query

Click the Save button at the top of the Access screen to save your query. Access asks you for the name of the query if this is the first time the query has been saved.

After saving the query, Access returns you to the mode you were working in. Occasionally, you will want to save and exit the query in a single operation. To do this, click the Close Window button in the upper-right corner of the Query Designer. Access always asks you to confirm saving the changes before it actually saves the query.

Adding More Than One Table to a Query

Using a query to obtain information from a single table is common; often, however, you need information from several related tables. For example, you may want to obtain a buyer's name and vehicle type purchased by the contact. This query requires four tables: `tblContacts`, `tblSales`, `tblSalesLineItems`, and `tblProducts`.

In Chapter 34, you learned the importance of primary and foreign keys and how they link tables together. You learned how to use the Relationships window to create relationships between tables. Finally, you learned how referential integrity affects data in tables.

After you create the tables for your database and decide how the tables are related to one another, you are ready to build multiple-table queries to obtain information from several related tables. The query combines data from multiple tables and presents the data as if it existed in one large table.

The first step in creating a multiple-table query is to add the tables to the Query window:

1. **Create a new query by clicking the Query Design button on the Create tab.**
2. **Select `tblContacts`, `tblSales`, `tblSalesLineItems`, and `tblProducts` by double-clicking each table's name in the Show Table dialog box.**
3. **Click the Close button in the Show Table dialog box.**

NOTE You can also add each table by highlighting the table in the list separately and clicking Add.

Figure 36-20 shows the top pane of the Query Design window with the four tables you just added. Because the relationships were set at table level, the join lines are automatically added to the query.

FIGURE 36-20

The Query Design window with four tables added. Notice the join lines are already present.

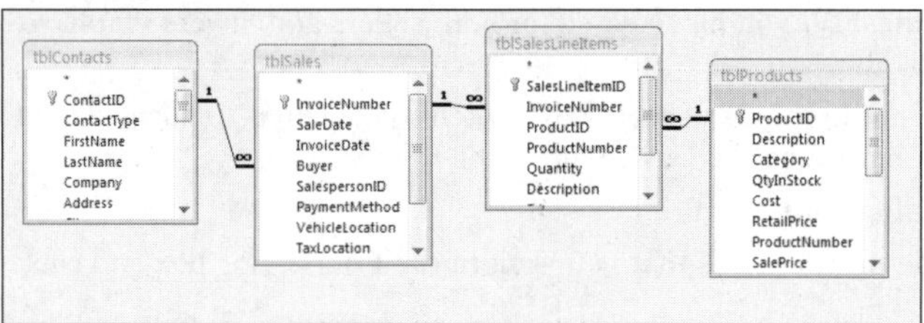

NOTE You can add more tables, at any time, by choosing Query Setup ➪ Show Table from the Design tab of the Query Design view. Then click Add in the dialog box that appears.

Working with the Table/Query Pane

As Figure 36-20 shows, a *join line* connects tables in the Query Designer. The join line connects the primary key in one table to the foreign key in another table.

CROSS-REF These lines were predrawn because you already set the relationships between the tables earlier in Chapter 34.

The join line

A *join line* represents the relationship between two tables in the Access database. In this example, a join line goes from `tblSales` to `tblContacts`, connecting `ContactID` in the `tblContacts` table to the `Buyer` field in `tblSales`. There are other join lines connecting the other tables in this query.

The join line is automatically created because relationships were set in the relationship builder. If Access already knows about the relationship, it adds the join line when the tables are added to a query.

If Referential Integrity is set on the relationship, Access displays a thicker line where the join line connects to the table in the Query Designer. This variation in line thickness tells you that Referential Integrity is set between the two tables. If a one-to-many relationship exists, the many-side table is indicated by an infinity symbol (∞).

Access will auto join to tables if the following conditions are met:

- Both tables have fields with the same name.
- The same-named fields are the same data type (text, numeric, and so on).
- One of the fields is a *primary key* in its table.

Access 2007 automatically attempts to join the tables if a relationship exists. Access cannot set referential integrity on the join line.

Manipulating the Field List window

Each Field List window begins at a fixed size, which shows approximately four fields and perhaps 12 characters for each field. Each Field List is a resizable window and can be moved within the Query Designer. If there are more fields than will show in the Field List window, a scroll bar enables you to scroll through the fields in the Field List.

NOTE **After a relationship is created between tables, the join line remains between the two fields. As you move through a table selecting fields, the line moves relative to the linked fields. For example, if the scroll box moves down (toward the bottom of the window) in `tblContacts`, the join line moves up with the customer number, eventually stopping at the top of the table window.**

When you're working with many tables, these join lines can become confusing as they cross or overlap. As you scroll through the table, the line eventually becomes visible, and the field it is linked to becomes obvious.

Moving a table

Move the Field Lists by grabbing the title bar of a Field List (where the name of the table is) with the mouse and dragging the Field List to a new location. You may want to move the Field Lists for a better working view or to clean up a confusing query diagram.

You can move and resize the Field Lists anywhere in the top pane. Access saves the arrangement when you save and close the query. Generally speaking, the Field Lists will appear in the same configuration the next time you open the query.

Removing a table

There are times when you need to remove tables from a query. Any table can be removed from the Query window. Use the mouse to select the table you want to remove in the top pane of the Query window and press the Delete key. Or right-click on the Field List and choose Removed Table from the shortcut menu.

CAUTION **When you delete a table, join lines to that table are deleted as well. When you delete a table, there is no warning or confirmation dialog box. The table is simply removed from the screen, along with any of the table's fields added to the QBE grid.**

Adding more tables

You may decide to add more tables to a query or you may accidentally delete a table and need to add it back. You accomplish this task by clicking on the Show Table button from the Query Setup group in the Design tab. The Show Table dialog box appears in response to this action.

Adding Fields from More Than One Table

You add fields from more than one table to the query in exactly the same way as when you're working with a single table. You can add fields one at a time, multiple fields as a group, or all the fields from a table.

CAUTION **If you type a field name in an empty Field cell that has the same name in more than one table, Access enters the field name from the first table that it finds containing the field name.**

If you select the field from the drop-down list in the Field cell, you see the name of the table first, followed by a period and the field name. For example, the `ProductID` in `tblSalesLineItems` is displayed as *tblSalesLineItems.ProductID.* This helps you select the right field name. Using this method, you can select a common field name from a specific table.

The easiest way to select fields is still to double-click the field names in the top half of the Query Designer. To do so, you may have to resize the Field Lists to see the fields that you want to select.

Viewing the table names

When you're working with two or more tables, the field names in the QBE grid can become confusing. You may find yourself asking, for example, just which table the field is from.

Access automatically maintains the table name that is associated with each field displayed in the QBE grid. Figure 36-21 shows the Query Designer with the name of each table displayed under the field name in the QBE grid.

FIGURE 36-21

The QBE grid with table names displayed. Notice that it shows all four table names.

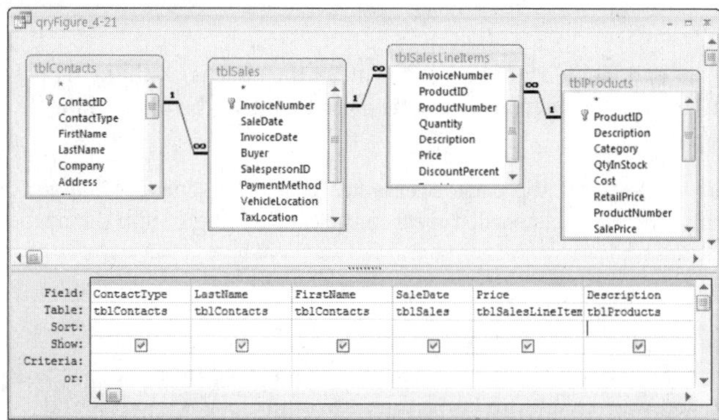

After you add fields to a query, you can view the returned records at any time. Figure 36-22 shows the data returned by the query in Figure 36-21.

FIGURE 36-22

Datasheet view of data from multiple tables. This resulting recordset, from the query, contains 84 records.

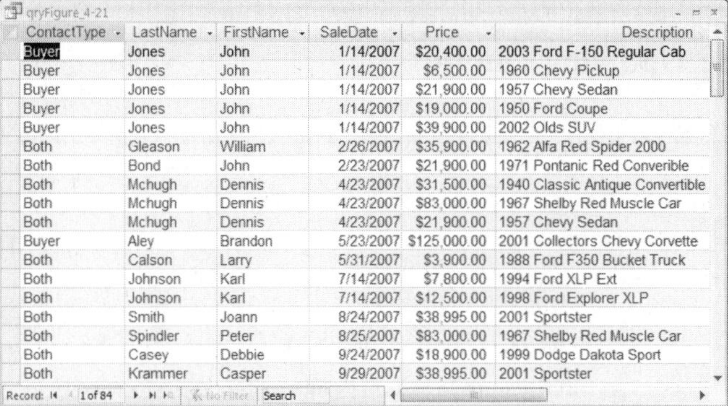
qryFigure_4-21

ContactType	LastName	FirstName	SaleDate	Price	Description
Buyer	Jones	John	1/14/2007	$20,400.00	2003 Ford F-150 Regular Cab
Buyer	Jones	John	1/14/2007	$6,500.00	1960 Chevy Pickup
Buyer	Jones	John	1/14/2007	$21,900.00	1957 Chevy Sedan
Buyer	Jones	John	1/14/2007	$19,000.00	1950 Ford Coupe
Buyer	Jones	John	1/14/2007	$39,900.00	2002 Olds SUV
Both	Gleason	William	2/26/2007	$35,900.00	1962 Alfa Red Spider 2000
Both	Bond	John	2/23/2007	$21,900.00	1971 Pontanic Red Converible
Both	Mchugh	Dennis	4/23/2007	$31,500.00	1940 Classic Antique Convertible
Both	Mchugh	Dennis	4/23/2007	$83,000.00	1967 Shelby Red Muscle Car
Both	Mchugh	Dennis	4/23/2007	$21,900.00	1957 Chevy Sedan
Buyer	Aley	Brandon	5/23/2007	$125,000.00	2001 Collectors Chevy Corvette
Both	Calson	Larry	5/31/2007	$3,900.00	1988 Ford F350 Bucket Truck
Both	Johnson	Karl	7/14/2007	$7,800.00	1994 Ford XLP Ext
Both	Johnson	Karl	7/14/2007	$12,500.00	1998 Ford Explorer XLP
Both	Smith	Joann	8/24/2007	$38,995.00	2001 Sportster
Both	Spindler	Peter	8/25/2007	$83,000.00	1967 Shelby Red Muscle Car
Both	Casey	Debbie	9/24/2007	$18,900.00	1999 Dodge Dakota Sport
Both	Krammer	Casper	9/29/2007	$38,995.00	2001 Sportster

Record: 1 of 84 No Filter Search

Adding multiple fields

The process of adding multiple fields in a multi-table query is identical to adding multiple fields in a single-table query. When you're adding multiple fields from several tables, you must add them from one table at a time. The easiest way to do this is to select multiple fields and drag them together down to the QBE grid.

You can select multiple contiguous fields by clicking the first field of the list and then clicking the last field while holding down the Shift key. You can also select noncontiguous fields in the list by holding down the Ctrl key while clicking individual fields with the mouse.

CAUTION **Selecting the * does have one drawback: You cannot specify criteria on the asterisk column itself. You have to add an individual field from the table and enter the criterion. If you add a field for a criterion (when using the *), the query displays the field twice — once for the * field and a second time for the criterion field. Therefore, you may want to deselect the Show cell of the criterion field.**

Understanding Multi-Table Query Limitations

When you create a query with multiple tables, there are limits to which fields can be edited. Generally, you can change data in a query's recordset, and your changes are saved in the underlying tables. The main exception is a table's primary key — a primary key value cannot be edited if referential integrity is in effect and if the field is part of a relationship.

To update a table from a query, a value in a specific record in the query must represent a single record in the underlying table. This means that you cannot update fields in a query that transforms data because most transformations group records and fields display aggregate information. Each field in a transformed recordset represents multiple fields in the underlying tables. There is no way to change the data in a transformed field and have it reflected in the underlying tables.

Updating limitations

In Access, the records in your tables may not always be updateable. Table 36-1 shows when a field in a table is updateable. As Table 36-1 shows, queries based on one-to-many relationships are updateable in both tables (depending on how the query was designed).

TABLE 36-1

Rules for Updating Queries

Type of Query or Field	Updateable	Comments
One table	Yes	
One-to-one relationship	Yes	
Results contains Memo field	Yes	Memo field updateable
Results contain Hyperlink	Yes	Hyperlink updateable
Results contain an OLE object	Yes	OLE object updateable
One-to-many relationship	Mostly	Restrictions based on design methodology (see text)
Many-to-one-to-many	No	Can update data in a form or data access page if RecordType = Recordset
Two or more tables with no join line	No	Must have a join to determine updateability
Crosstab	No	Creates a snapshot of the data
Totals Query (Sum, Avg, and so on)	No	Works with grouped data creating a snapshot
Unique Value property is Yes	No	Shows unique records only in a snapshot
SQL-specific queries	No	Union and pass-through work with ODBC data
Calculated field	No	Will recalculate automatically
Read-only fields	No	If opened read-only or on read-only drive (CD-ROM)
Permissions denied	No	Insert, replace, or delete are not granted
ODBC tables with no primary key	No	A primary key (unique index) must exist
Paradox table with no primary key	No	A primary key file must exist
Locked by another user	No	Cannot be updated while a field is locked by another

Overcoming query limitations

Table 36-1 shows that there are times when queries and fields in tables are not updateable. As a general rule, any query that performs aggregate operations or uses an ODBC (Open DataBase Connectivity) data source is not updateable. Most other queries can be updated. When your query has more than one table and some of the tables have a one-to-many relationship, there may be fields that are not updateable (depending on the design of the query).

Updating a unique index (primary key)

If a query uses two tables involved in a one-to-many relationship, the query must include the primary key from the one-side table. Access must have the primary key value so that they can find the related records in the two tables.

Replacing existing data in a query with a one-to-many relationship

Normally, all the fields in the many-side table (such as the `tblSales` table) are updateable in a one-to-many query. All the fields (*except* the primary key) in the one-side table (`tblCustomers`) can be updated. Normally, this is sufficient for most database application purposes. Also, the primary key field is rarely changed in the one-side table because it is the link to the records in the joined tables.

Design tips for updating fields in queries

If you want to add records to both tables of a one-to-many relationship, include the foreign key from the *many-side* table and show the field in the datasheet. After doing this, records can be added starting with either the one-side or many-side table. The *one* side's primary key field is automatically copied to the *many* side's join field.

If you want to add records to multiple tables in a form (covered in Chapter 37), remember to include all (or most) of the fields from both tables. Otherwise, you will not have a complete record of data in your form.

Summary

This chapter has taken on the major topic of building select queries. Without a doubt, query creation is a daunting task, and one that takes a lot of practice. Even simple queries can return unexpected results, depending on the criteria used to filter data in the underlying tables.

Queries are an integral and important part of any Access database application. Queries drive forms, reports, and many other aspects of Access applications.

Your best bet for mastering Access queries is to try increasingly difficult queries, and to always check your work. In the case of improperly joined tables, Access queries almost always under-report the data in the tables. You will discover the missing records only by carefully examining the data to ensure that your query is working properly.

Chapter 37

Presenting Data with Access Reports

IN THIS CHAPTER

Understanding the different types of Access reports

Knowing the differences between reports and forms

Understanding the process of building reports

Creating reports with a Report Wizard

Viewing reports onscreen

Printing reports

Saving reports

Reports provide the most flexible way of viewing and printing summarized information. Reports display information with the desired level of detail, while enabling you to view or print your information in almost any format. In this chapter, you learn to use Report Wizards as a starting point.

ON the WEB In this chapter, you create new reports using the report wizards and by creating a blank report without using a wizard. You use tables created previously. The `Chapter37.accdb` database file contains the completed reports described in this chapter. The example databases are available for download from `http://www.wiley.com/TOCOME`. When you open the file, you can click Options in the Security Warning bar, click Enable This Content in the Microsoft Office Security Options dialog box, and then click OK.

Understanding Reports

Reports present a customized view of your data. Report output is viewed onscreen or printed to provide a hard copy of the data. Reports provide summaries of the information contained in the database. Data can be grouped and sorted in any order and can create totals that add numbers, calculate averages or other statistics, and graphically display data. Reports can include pictures and other graphics as well as memo fields in a report. If you can think of a report you want, Access probably supports it.

Understanding report types

Four basic types of reports are used by businesses:

- **Tabular reports:** These print data in rows and columns with groupings and totals. Variations include summary and group/total reports.
- **Columnar reports:** These print data as a form and can include totals and graphs.

- **Mail-merge reports:** These create form letters.
- **Mailing labels:** These create multicolumn labels or snaked-column reports.
- **Graphs:** Visual representation of your data in a form such as a bar or a pie chart.

Tabular reports

Figure 37-1 is a typical tabular-type report (rptProductsSummary) displayed in print preview. *Tabular reports* (also known as *groups/totals reports*) are similar to a table that displays data in neat rows and columns. Tabular reports, unlike forms or datasheets, usually group data by one or more fields. Often, tabular reports calculate and display subtotals or statistical information for numeric fields in each group. Some reports include page totals and grand totals. You can even have multiple *snaked columns* so that you can create directories (such as telephone books). These types of reports often use page numbers, report dates, or lines and boxes to separate information. Reports may have color and shading and display pictures, business graphs, and memo fields. A special type of *summary* tabular report can have all the features of a *detail* tabular report but omit record details.

FIGURE 37-1

A tabular report (`rptProductsSummary`) displayed in Print Preview.

Products Summary

Access Auto Auctions

Category	Product ID	Description	Qty in Stock	Cost	Retail Price	Sale Price	Profit
Minivans							
	26	1992 Buick Roadmaster Estate Wag	1	$1,500.00	$1,850.00	$1,795.00	$295.00
	27	2003 Mini Van	2	$21,000.00	$24,000.00	$23,000.00	$2,000.00
	28	1992 Ford Conversion Van	1	$3,000.00	$5,500.00	$4,390.00	$1,390.00
	29	1999 Ford E350 Cargo Van	1	$4,500.00	$6,800.00	$5,990.00	$1,490.00
	30	2002 Ford Mini Van	1	$11,000.00	$14,500.00	$13,989.00	$2,989.00
	31	2002 Honda SUV	1	$29,000.00	$35,900.00	$34,900.00	$5,900.00
	32	2000 Dodge Minivan SEE	1	$6,000.00	$11,500.00	$8,999.00	$2,999.00
		Category Minivans Total:	8	$76,000.00	$100,050.00	$93,063.00	$17,063.00
Motor Homes							
	33	1973 Rare Popup Hard sided Indiar	1	$1,200.00	$1,750.00	$1,400.00	$200.00
		Category Motor Homes Total:	1	$1,200.00	$1,750.00	$1,400.00	$200.00
SUV							
	34	2002 Olds SUV	3	$35,900.00	$39,900.00	$38,900.00	$3,000.00
	35	1995 GMC Jimmie SLE	1	$5,000.00	$7,500.00	$6,990.00	$1,990.00
	36	1995 Jeep Laredo Red	1	$6,000.00	$8,900.00	$8,650.00	$2,650.00
	37	1998 Range Rover	1	$12,500.00	$0.00	$0.00	($12,500.00)

Columnar reports

Columnar reports generally display one or more records per page, but do so vertically. Columnar reports display data very much as a data-entry form does but are used strictly for viewing data and not for entering data. Figure 37-2 shows part of a columnar report (rptProducts) in Print Preview.

Another type of columnar report displays one main record per page (like a business form) but can show many records within embedded subforms. An invoice is a typical example. This type of report can have sections that display only one record and at the same time have sections that display multiple records from the *many* side of a one-to-many relationship — and even include totals.

Figure 37-3 shows an invoice report (rptInvoice) from the Access Auto Auctions database system in Report view.

FIGURE 37-2

A columnar report showing report controls distributed throughout the entire page.

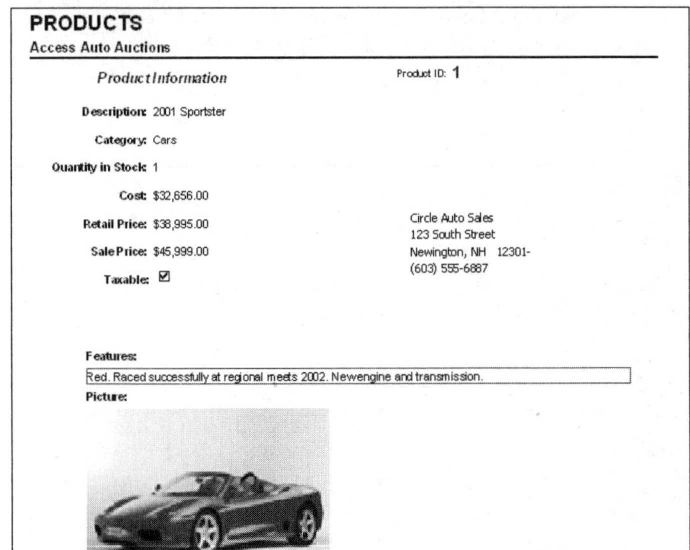

FIGURE 37-3

An invoice report (rptInvoice).

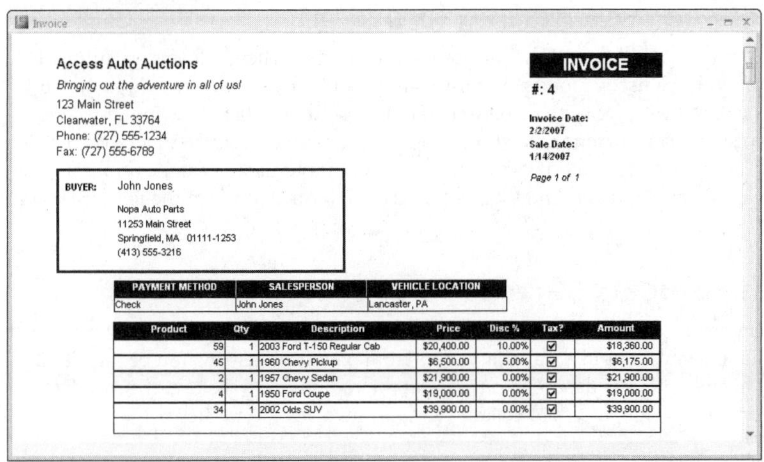

In Figure 37-3, the information in the top portion of the report is on the "main" part of the report, whereas the product details near the bottom of the figure are contained in a subreport embedded within the main report.

Mailing labels

Mailing labels are also a type of report. You can easily create mailing labels, shown in Figure 37-4, using the Label Wizard to create a report in Access. The Label Wizard enables you to select from a long list of Avery label (and other vendors) paper styles, after which Access correctly creates a report design based on the data you specify to create your label. After the label is created, you can open the report in Design mode and customize it as needed.

FIGURE 37-4

rptCustomerMailingLabels, a typical mailing-label report.

Brandon Aley Tip Top Chevy 1916 Erickson Drive Fairbanks, MA 12333-	Karen Bailey Sammy Fordman 59 West Church Westbourgh, MA 01581-
Ann Bond A-1 Auto Sales 54 South Main Colchester, CT 06415-	John Bright Pleasantville Monda Inc 46 Pleasantville RD West Bridgewater, MA 02379-
Harry Bush Bush Sales 100 State Street Mohegan Lake, NY 10547-	Larry Calson Chicota American Auto Sales 60 Mexico Drive Chicota, TX 75425-
Debbie Casey Jackhorn Monda, Inc 95 Elm Street Jackhorn, KY 41825-	Cindy Casey Circle Auto Sales 123 South Street Newington, NH 12301-

Distinguishing between reports and forms

The main difference between reports and forms is the purpose of the output. Whereas forms are primarily for data entry and interaction with the users, reports are for viewing data (either onscreen or in hard copy form). Calculated fields can be used with forms to display an amount based on other fields in the record. With reports, you typically perform calculations on a group of records, a page of records, or all the records processed during the report. Anything you can do with a form — except input data — can be duplicated by a report. In fact, you can save a form as a report and then customize the form controls in the Report Design window.

Understanding the process of creating a report

Planning a report begins long before you actually create the report design. The report process begins with your desire to view your data in a table, but in a way that differs from datasheet display. You begin with a design for this view; Access begins with raw data. The purpose of the report is to transform the raw data into a meaningful set of information. The process of creating a report involves several steps:

- Defining the report layout
- Assembling the data
- Creating the report design using the Access Report Design window
- Printing or viewing the report

Defining the report layout

You should begin by having a general idea of the layout of your report. You can define the layout in your mind, on paper, or interactively using the Access Report Designer. Good reports can first be laid out on paper, showing the controls needed and the placement of the controls. Very often, an Access report is expected to duplicate an existing paper report used by the application's consumers.

Assembling the data

After you have a general idea of the report layout, you should assemble the data needed for the report. Access reports use data from two primary sources: a single database table, or a recordset produced by the query. You can join many tables in a query and use the query's recordset as the record source for your report. A query's recordset appears to an Access report as if it were a single table.

As you learned earlier in the last chapter, you specify the fields, records, and sort order of the records in a query. Access treats this recordset data as a single table (for processing purposes) in datasheets, forms, and reports. The recordset becomes the source of data for the report and Access processes each record to create the report. When the report is run, Access matches data from the recordset or table against the fields specified in the report and uses the data available at that moment to produce the report.

In this example, you use data from `tblProducts` to create a relatively simple tabular report.

Creating a Report with Report Wizards

Access enables you to create virtually any type of report. Some reports, however, are easier to create than others, especially when a Report Wizard is used as a starting point. Like Form Wizards, Report Wizards give you a basic layout for your report, which you can then customize.

Report Wizards simplify the layout process of your controls by visually stepping you through a series of questions about the type of report that you want to create and then automatically creating the report for you. In this chapter, you use Report Wizards to create tabular and columnar reports. Feel free to use the database file you downloaded for this chapter to follow along with the actions described.

Creating a new report

The Access Ribbon contains several commands for creating new reports for your applications. The Create tab of the Ribbon includes a grouping called Reports containing several options such as Report, Labels, and Report Wizard. For this exercise, use the Report Wizard button to create a new report from tblProducts. Begin by clicking the Report Wizard button in the Reports group of the Create Ribbon tab. The Report Wizard dialog opens, as shown in Figure 37-5.

In Figure 37-5, `tblProducts` has been selected as the data source for the new report. Under the data source selection drop-down list is a list of available fields. Clicking on a field in this list and pressing the right pointing arrow moves the field from the Available Fields list to the Selected Fields list, adding it to the report. For this exercise, select `Product ID`, `Description`, `QtyInStock`, `RetailPrice`, and `SalePrice`.

TIP **Double-click any field in the Available Fields list to add it to the Selected Fields list. You can also double-click any field in the Selected Fields list to remove it from the box. Access then moves the field back to the Available Fields list.**

FIGURE 37-5

The first screen of the Report Wizard after selecting a data source and fields.

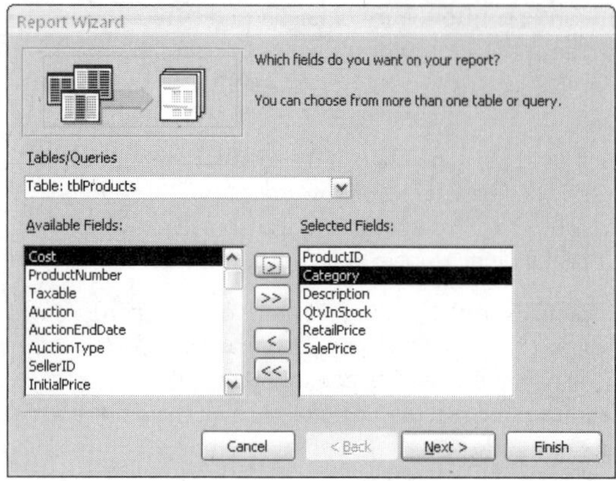

You are limited to selecting fields from the original record source you started with. You can select fields from other tables or queries by using the Tables/Queries drop-down list in the Report Wizard. As long as you have specified valid relationships so that Access properly links the data, these fields are added to your original selection and you use them on the report. If you choose fields from unrelated tables, a dialog box asks you to edit the relationship and join the tables. Or, you can return to the Report Wizard and remove the fields.

After you have selected your data, click the Next button to go to the next wizard dialog box.

Selecting the grouping levels

The next dialog box enables you to choose which field(s) to use for grouping data. Figure 37-6 shows the Category field selected as the data grouping field for the report. The field selected for grouping determines how data appears on the report, and the grouping fields appear as group headers and footers in the report. Groups are most often used to combine data that are logically related. For instance, you may choose to group on CustomerID so that each customer's sales history appears as a group on the report. You use the report's group headers and footers to display the customer name and any other information specific to each customer.

The Report Wizard lets you specify as many as four group fields for your report. You use the Priority buttons to change the grouping order on the report. The order you select for the group fields is the order of the grouping hierarchy.

Select the Category field as the grouping field and click (>) to specify a grouping based on category values. Notice that the picture changes to show Category as a grouping field, as shown in Figure 37-6. Each of the other fields (ProductID, Description, QtyInStock, RetailPrice, and SalesPrice) selected for the report will appear within the Category groups.

FIGURE 37-6

Specifying the report's grouping.

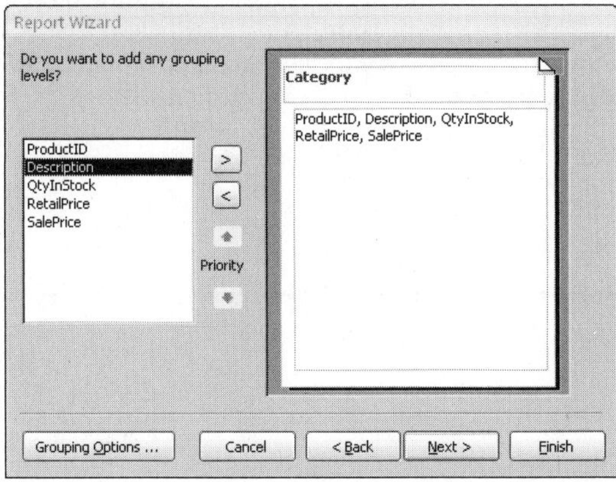

Defining the group data

After you select the group field(s), click the Grouping Options button at the bottom of the dialog box to display another dialog box, which enables you to further define how your report uses the group field.

For instance, you can choose to group by only the first character of a field chosen for grouping. This means that all records with the same first character in the grouping field are included as a single group. If you group a customers table by the CustomerName, and specify to group on the first character of the CustomerName field, a group header and footer appears for the set of all customers whose name begins with the same character. There would be a group for all records with a CustomerName beginning with the letter A, another group for all records with CustomerName beginning with the letter B, and so on.

The Grouping Options dialog box, which is displayed when you click the Grouping Options button in the lower-left corner of the Report Wizard screen, enables you to further define the grouping. This selection can vary in importance, depending on the data type.

The Grouping intervals list box displays different values for the various data types:

- **Text:** Normal, 1st Letter, 2 Initial Letters, 3 Initial Letters, 4 Initial Letters, 5 Initial letters
- **Numeric:** Normal, 10s, 50s, 100s, 500s, 1000s, 5000s, 10000s, 50000s, 100000s
- **Date:** Normal, Year, Quarter, Month, Week, Day, Hour, Minute

Normal means that the grouping is on the entire field. In this example, use the entire Customer Name field.

In this example, the default text-field grouping option of Normal is acceptable.

If you displayed the Grouping Options dialog box, click the OK button to return to the Grouping levels dialog box.

Click the Next button to move to the Sort order dialog box.

Selecting the sort order

By default, Access automatically sorts the grouped records in an order that helps the grouping make sense. For instance, after you have chosen the Customer Name field to group customer records, Access arranges the groups in alphabetical order by the CustomerName. However, for your purposes, it may be useful to specify a sort within each group. As an example, your users may want to see the customer records sorted by Order Date in descending order so that the newest orders appear near the top of each customer group.

In our example, Access sorts data by the Category field. As Figure 37-7 shows, the data is also sorted by Description within each group.

FIGURE 37-7

Selecting the field sorting order.

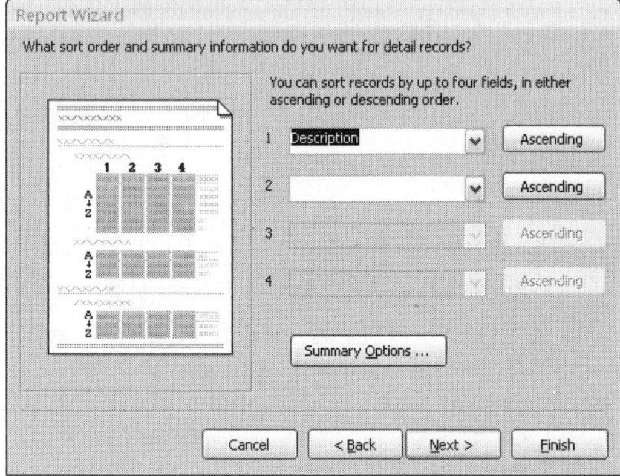

The sort fields are selected by the same method you use for grouping fields in the report. You can select fields that you have not already chosen to group and use these as sorting fields. The fields chosen in this dialog box do not affect grouping. Instead, they affect only the sorting order in the Detail section fields. You select ascending or descending sort by clicking the button to the right of each sort field.

Selecting summary options

At the bottom of the sorting dialog box is a Summary Options button. Clicking this button displays the dialog box shown in Figure 37-8. This dialog box provides additional display options for numeric fields. As you can see in Figure 37-8, all of the numeric and currency fields are displayed and specified to be summed. Additionally, you can display averages, minimums, and maximums.

You can also decide whether to show or hide the data in the Detail section. If you select Detail and Summary, the report shows the detail data, whereas selecting Summary Only hides the Detail section and shows only totals in the report.

Finally, checking the Calculate percent of total for sums box adds the percentage of the entire report that the total represents below the total in the group footer. If, for example, you have three products and their totals are 15, 25, and 10, respectively, 30%, 50%, and 20% show below their total (that is, 50) — indicating the percentage of the total sum (100%) represented by their sum.

Clicking the OK button in this dialog box returns you to the Sorting dialog box. There you can click the Next button to move to the next wizard dialog box.

FIGURE 37-8

Selecting the summary options.

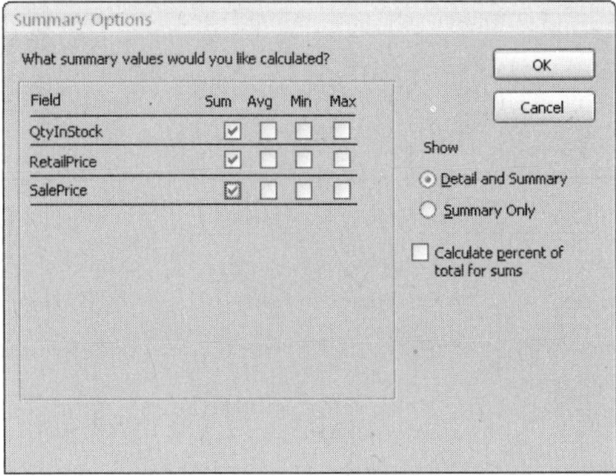

Selecting the layout

Two more dialog boxes affect the look of your report. The first (shown in Figure 37-9) enables you to determine the basic layout of the data. The Layout area provides six layout choices that tell Access whether to repeat the column headers, indent each grouping, and add lines or boxes between the detail lines. As you select each option, the picture on the left changes to show how the choice affects the report's appearance.

You choose between Portrait (up-and-down) and Landscape (across-the-page) layout for the report in the Orientation area. Finally, the Adjust the field width so all fields fit on a page checkbox enables you to cram a lot of data into a little area. (A magnifying glass may be necessary!)

For this example, choose Stepped and Landscape, as shown in Figure 37-9. Then click the Next button to move to the next dialog box.

FIGURE 37-9

Selecting the page layout.

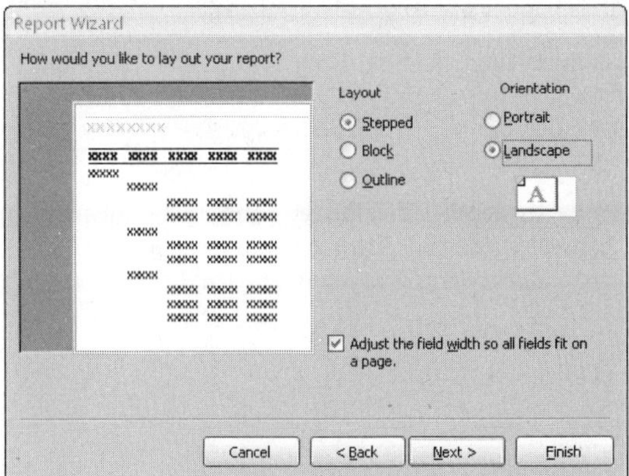

Choosing the style

After you choose the layout, select the style of your report from the dialog shown in Figure 37-10. Each style has different background shadings, font size, typeface, and other formatting. As each is selected, the picture on the left changes to show a preview. For this example, choose Opulent. Finally, click the Next button to move to the last dialog box.

FIGURE 37-10

Choosing the style of your report.

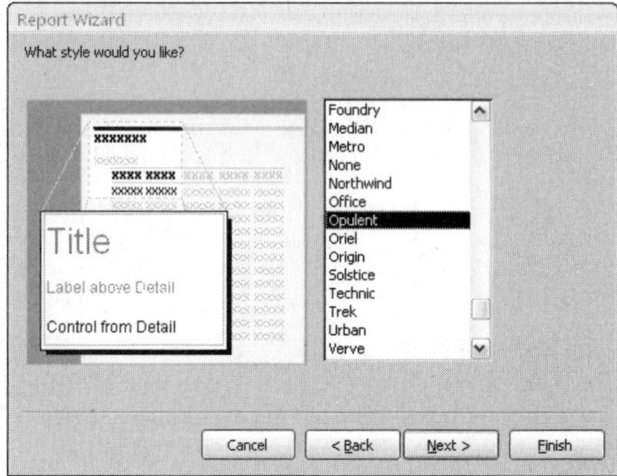

TIP **You can customize the styles, or add your own with the AutoFormat option on the Arrange tab of the Ribbon while in Design view of the Report.**

Opening the report design

The final Report Wizard dialog box contains a checkered flag, which lets you know that you're at the finish line. The first part of the dialog box enables you to enter a title for the report. This title appears only once, at the very beginning of the report, not at the top of each page. The report title also serves as the new report's name. The default title is the name of the table or query you initially specified as the report's data source. The report just created in `Chapter 37.accdb` is named `rptProducts_Wizard`.

Next, choose one of the option buttons at the bottom of the dialog box:

- Preview the report
- Modify the report's design

For this example, leave the default selection intact to preview the report. Clicking the Finish button displays the report in Report view. Click Finish to complete the Report Wizard and view the report (see Figure 37-11).

Report view provides an overall view of the report, but it does not show the margins, page numbering, and how the report will look when printed on a piece of paper. To get a good idea of how a report will look when printed, click the Office Button. Click the right arrow beside the Print choice, and then click Print Preview.

FIGURE 37-11

rptProducts_Wizard displayed in Report View.

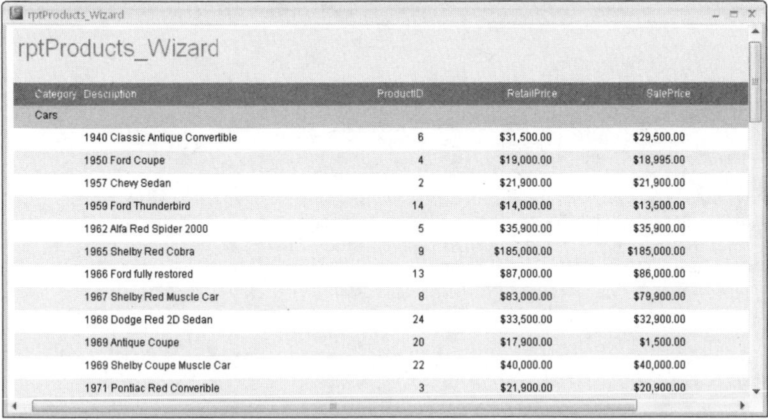

Using the Print Preview window

Figure 37-12 shows the Print Preview window in a zoomed view of rptProducts_Wizard. This view displays your report with the actual fonts, shading, lines, boxes, and data that will be on the printed report. Clicking the left mouse button changes the view to a *page preview* that shows the entire page.

NOTE **In the default tabbed view, each report will appear in a tab rather than a window. Figures were shown with the windowed method for screen shot purposes. To change this behavior, click Office Button ⇨ Access Options. Click Current Database at the left, and work with the Document Window Options settings.**

The Print Preview tab of Ribbon in the Print Preview view transforms to display controls relevant to viewing and printing the report. The Print Preview tab of the Access Ribbon includes controls for adjusting the size, page orientation (Portrait or Landscape), and other viewing options. The Print Preview tab also includes a handy Print button for printing the report.

You can move around the page by using the horizontal and vertical scrollbars. Use the Page controls (at the bottom-left corner of the window) to move from page to page. These controls include VCR-like navigation buttons to move from page to page or to the first or last page of the report. You can also go to a specific page of the report by entering a value in the text box between the previous and next controls.

FIGURE 37-12

Displaying rptProducts_Wizard in the zoomed preview mode.

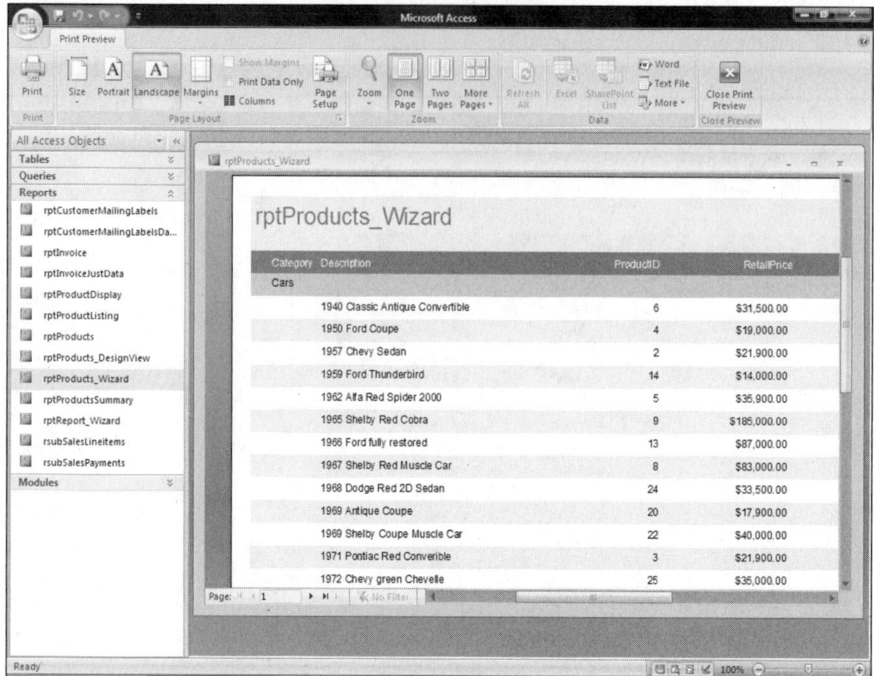

Right-clicking on the report and selecting the Multiple Pages option lets you view more than one page of the report in a single view. Figure 37-13 shows a view of the report in the Print Preview's multipage mode. Use the navigation buttons (in the lower-left section of the Print Preview window) to move between pages, just as you would to move between records in a datasheet. The Print Preview window has a toolbar with commonly used printing commands.

If, after examining the preview, you are satisfied with the report, click the Printer button on the toolbar to print the report. If you are dissatisfied, select the Close button to switch to the Report Design window and make further changes.

Viewing the Report Design window

Right-clicking the report's title bar and selecting Design View opens the Access Report Designer on the report. As shown in Figure 37-14, the report design reflects the choices you made using the Report Wizard. You can use this view to make manual changes to your report.

Return to the Print Preview mode by selecting the Print Preview button on the Report Design toolbar or by selecting the Print Preview option from the File menu. You can also select Print or Page Setup from the File menu. This menu also provides options for saving your report.

FIGURE 37-13

Displaying multiple pages of a report in Print Preview's page preview mode.

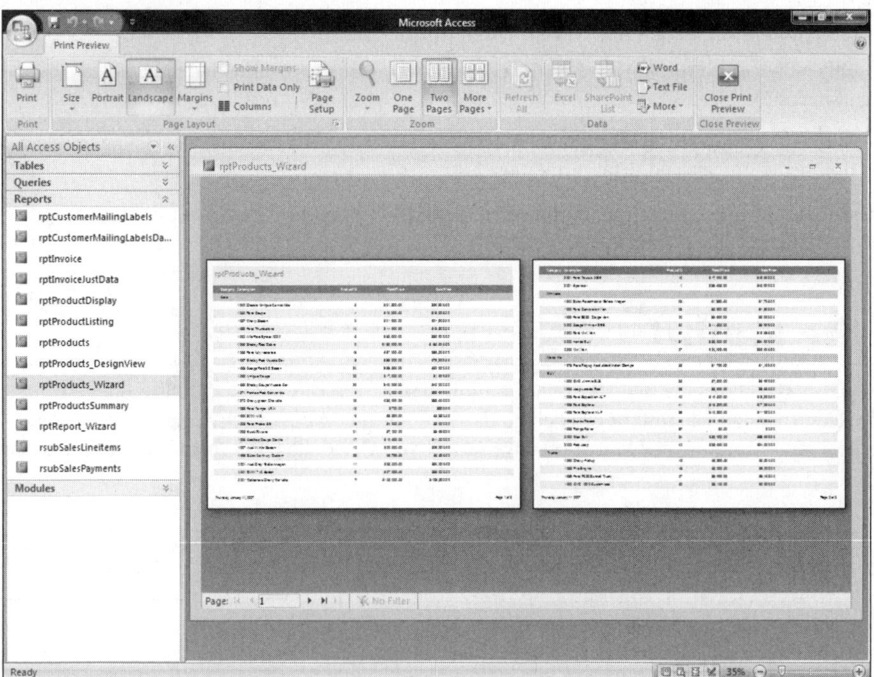

FIGURE 37-14

The Report Design window.

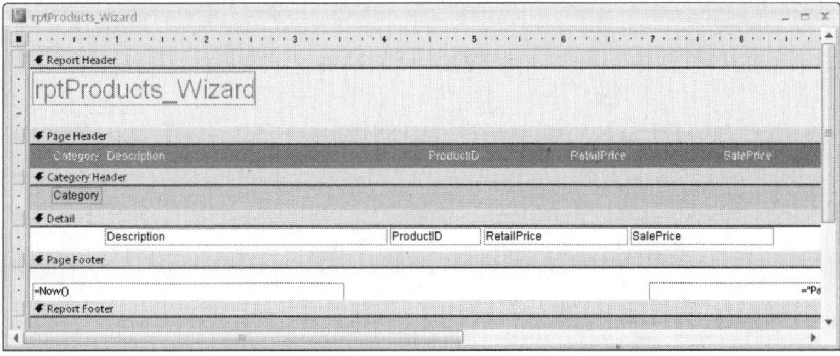

Printing a Report

There are several ways to print your report:

- Click the Print button in the Print Preview tab of the Ribbon.
- Click Office Button ➪ Print in the main Access window (with a report highlighted and the Navigation Pane).

Selecting Office Button ➪ Print opens the standard Windows Print dialog box. You use this dialog to select the print range, number of copies, and print properties.

Clicking the Print button in the Access ribbon immediately sends the report to the default printer without displaying a Print dialog box.

Saving the Report

Save the report design at any time by selecting Office Button ➪ Save, File ➪ Save As, or Office Button ➪ Export from the Report Design window, or by clicking the Save button on the Quick Access toolbar. The first time you save a report (or any time you select Save As or Export), a dialog box enables you to select or type a name.

Summary

Reports are an important and integral part of most Access applications. Very often reports are the most important aspect of Access applications, and are seen by people who never see the Access application running on a computer. In this chapter, you read about the different types of Access reports and learned how to use the Access Report Wizard to build reports.

Part VIII

Gathering Information

IN THIS PART

Chapter 38

Keeping Information at Hand with OneNote

IN THIS CHAPTER

Introducing OneNote

Learning how OneNote is organized

Adding notebooks, sections, and pages

Creating notes

Inserting Outlook tasks

Inserting pictures, files, or screen clips

Writing notes rather than typing

Saving and browsing your notebook

One of the challenges in managing any project is how to bring together all the information about the project so that it's at your fingertips. You typically make notes, track tasks, create data files, look at Web information, and handle all the other activities in different programs. Storing all the files or having many open program windows onscreen has never been a satisfactory way to manage your project's information. Microsoft OneNote 2007 provides that elusive solution, enabling you to bring together notes and other types of information in an accessible way. If you're ready to see how you can be better organized and more effective at anything you do, read this chapter and learn how to use OneNote.

Who Needs OneNote and Why

OneNote is designed to function as a digital three-ring binder. With a three-ring binder, you can add and rearrange pages, write on pages, paste clipped articles on a page, or even punch holes in a magazine or report page to add it to the binder. You also can add plastic sleeves that expand the notebook's versatility, enabling you to include nonpaper materials in the notebook.

OneNote brings the same type of versatility to tracking all sorts of digital information in a centralized location. You can add a variety of information to a OneNote *notebook* — notes, Outlook tasks, pictures, files, screen clips, audio or video recordings, details about an Outlook meeting, information copied from a Web page, and more. But the best part is that you can see and use *all* the information at the same time — you don't have to open multiple files and arrange multiple windows.

These capabilities make OneNote a perfect tool for managing information related to specific projects or clients, research or study subjects, or topical areas of interest. Although OneNote's versatility can make it useful to anyone, users in the following types of situations will find OneNote an especially valuable tool:

- If you attend many meetings that generate ideas and action items, OneNote can be perfect for tracking them. Because OneNote enables you to organize information quickly and flexibly, you can easily add the notes and tasks you need. You also can jump right to the information you need as a meeting discussion changes.
- If you often handle research projects in which you bring together information from a variety of sources, OneNote provides a great central storage location for statistics, citations, and useful documents.
- If you like to brainstorm or capture ideas about a topic over time, OneNote helps you keep that information together so that the big picture comes together. You can even capture your ideas as an audio recording so that you're not slowed down by your typing skills.
- If you're a student and need to keep together notes and information for each class, OneNote enables you to collect all the notes and schedule information that you need to stay prepared.
- If you need to use your notes on multiple computers or share them with other users, OneNote enables you to place a notebook on a shared network location or even a USB thumb drive. In this way, OneNote gives you the opportunity to take your work with you or keep others involved.

Touring OneNote

OneNote divides information into *notebooks*, *sections*, and *pages*. You can start OneNote from the Start menu (Start ➪ All Programs ➪ Microsoft Office ➪ Microsoft Office OneNote 2007). Rather than represent a file, each notebook is a separate subfolder within the Documents ➪ OneNote Notebooks folder within your Windows Vista user folder. (In XP, the My Documents\My Notebooks folder holds the notebook subfolders.) Each section you add to a notebook appears as a file within the folder for the notebook, and that file stores the information for the pages in the section.

In the OneNote Window, this arrangement translates to a Notebooks navigation bar at the left, where you can click a notebook's button to display the sections for that notebook (Figure 38-1). Tabs for the sections within the selected notebook appear above the page area. Clicking a section tab selects that section, displaying page tabs for the pages in the section at the right. Click a page tab to display the contents of that page. OneNote also includes Standard and Formatting toolbars onscreen by default, and as in some of the other Office applications, it includes additional toolbars that you can hide and redisplay on an as-needed basis by right-clicking an existing toolbar or choosing View ➪ Toolbars.

As Figure 38-1 also shows, OneNote by default includes three notebooks to help you get started. The top two notebooks, Work Notebook and Personal Notebook, include starter sections and pages. When you select each section tab, the default page that it contains provides ideas for the types of information you might include on a page in that section, as well as gives you help and shortcuts for adding that type of information.

FIGURE 38-1

Clicking selects a notebook, section, or page.

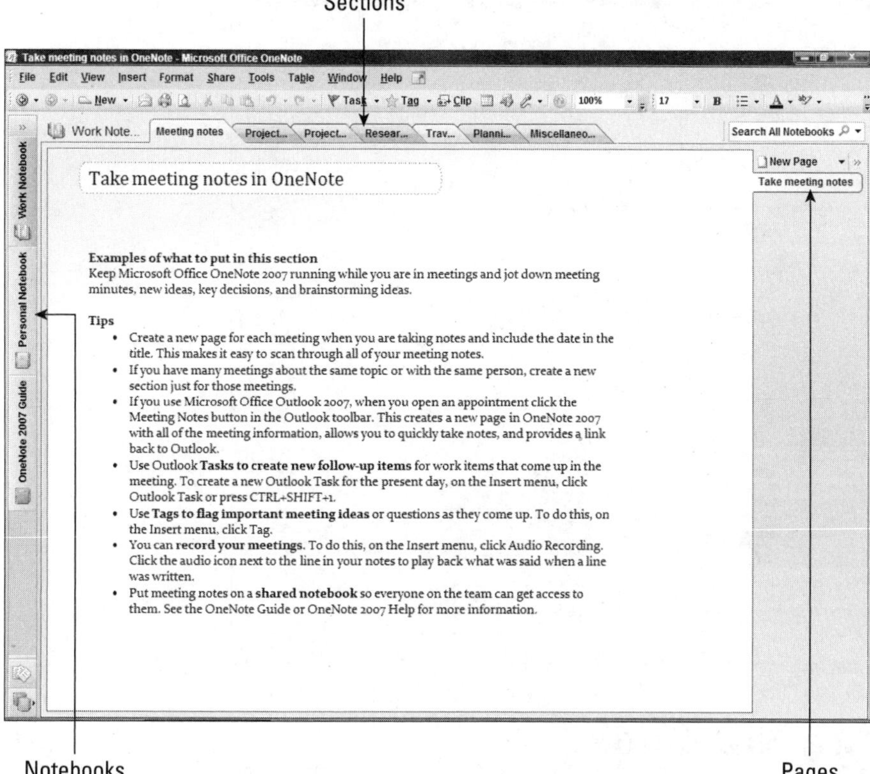

The bottom notebook, named OneNote 2007 Guide, includes two sections of information to help you learn how to use OneNote. As shown in Figure 38-2, the first page in the Getting Started with OneNote section even prompts you to practice adding a note.

If you want to close the starter notebooks that come with OneNote or any other notebook, right-click the notebook's name in the Notebooks navigation bar and then click Close This Notebook in the shortcut menu that appears. You can reopen a notebook at any time by choosing File ➪ Open ➪ Notebook, navigating to and clicking the notebook folder in the Folders list at the left side of the Open Notebook dialog box, and then clicking Open.

FIGURE 38-2

OneNote helps you practice taking a note.

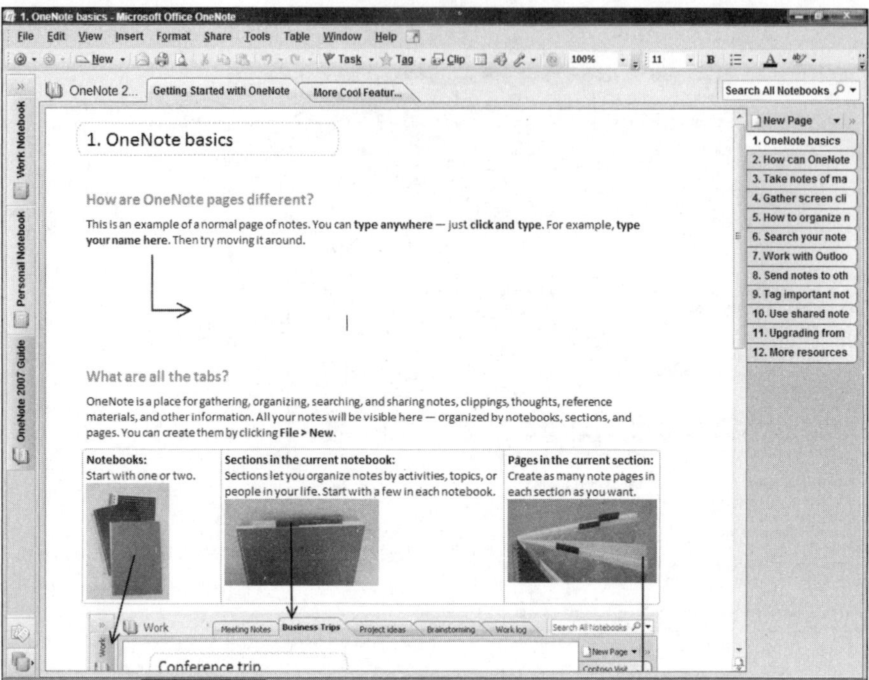

Creating a Notebook

You can create a notebook for any project, client, subject, research topic, or purpose that you want. Because each notebook represents a folder, you can create as many notebooks as your system has storage to handle. Follow these steps to create a new notebook in OneNote:

1. **Choose File ➪ New ➪ Notebook command or click the drop-down list arrow for the New button on the Standard toolbar, and then click Notebook.** The first New Notebook Wizard dialog box appears.
2. **Type a name for the notebook into the Name text box.**
3. **Choose a color for the notebook button using the Color drop-down list.**
4. **Click a template in the From Template list to use as the basis for the notebook.** As shown in Figure 38-3, OneNote does offer templates (in addition to the Blank template) to help you prepare a notebook geared for a particular use or subject matter.
5. **Click Next.** The next wizard screen appears, prompting you to specify how you intend to use the notebook.

FIGURE 38-3

Choose a template when creating a new notebook.

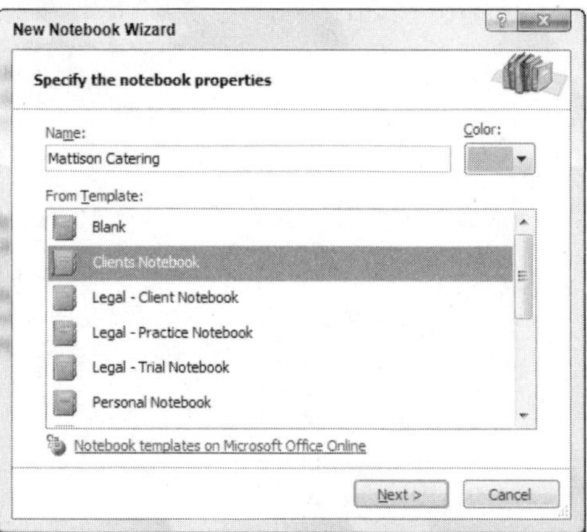

6. **Click the option button to specify how you want to use the notebook and then click Next.** The folder location that you specify, and whether there are additional wizard steps for creating the notebook, vary depending on your selection:
   - **I Will Use It on This Computer.** When you choose this option and click Next, the wizard prompts you to confirm the folder where the subfolder for the notebook will be created, as in Figure 38-4. If needed, click the Browse button and use the dialog box that appears to specify an alternate location for the notebook.
   - **I Will Use It on Multiple Computers.** As for the prior option, this choice prompts you to verify the storage location for the new notebook. A note in the dialog box informs you that in order to use the notebook if you copy it to another computer or a USB thumb drive and try to open it from there, you must be using the same username and password on the destination computer as on the computer where you created the notebook.
   - **Multiple People Will Share the Notebook.** Selecting this option enables the On a Server and In a Shared Folder on This Computer option buttons. If you click the first option button and click Next, you need to specify the path to the shared network folder, server, or SharePoint location where you want to create the notebook. Clicking In a Shared Folder on This Computer prompts you to specify the shared folder. Later you will see steps for setting permissions that enable other users to access the notebook.
7. **Click Create.** The new notebook appears onscreen, ready for your use.

If you used a template other than the Blank template, the new notebook may contain several suggested sections, with the first one typically being called Start Here. If you created a blank notebook, it will have a single section called New Section 1 that contains a single blank page called Untitled Page.

FIGURE 38-4

The new notebook becomes a subfolder of the specified folder.

NOTE You can rename a notebook later by right-clicking the Notebook and clicking Rename. Change the contents of the Display Name text box as needed and then click OK.

TIP If the notebook you want to use isn't visible on the Notebooks navigation bar, you can click the All Notebook List button at the very bottom of the bar to find it in the menu that appears. The button above it, Unfiled Notes, reveals a location that stores side notes created when you click the Open New Side Note icon in the taskbar notification area.

Creating a Section

Each new section in a notebook works much like a tabbed divider added into a three-ring binder. The section sets off the pages within and provides a label for them. If you create a notebook for client information, for example, you might create a new section for each client. If you create a notebook for school studies, you might create a section for each class during the current semester.

To add a new section to a notebook:

1. **In the Notebooks navigation bar, click the name of the notebook to which you want to add a section.** The contents of the selected notebook appear.
2. **Choose File ➪ New ➪ Section or click the drop-down list arrow for the New button on the Standard toolbar and then click Notebook.** The new section tab appears, with the temporary name highlighted, as shown in Figure 38-5.
3. **Type the name for the new section and press Enter.** The finished section appears, waiting for you to add pages, notes, and other content.

FIGURE 38-5

Type a name to replace the placeholder in the new section's tab.

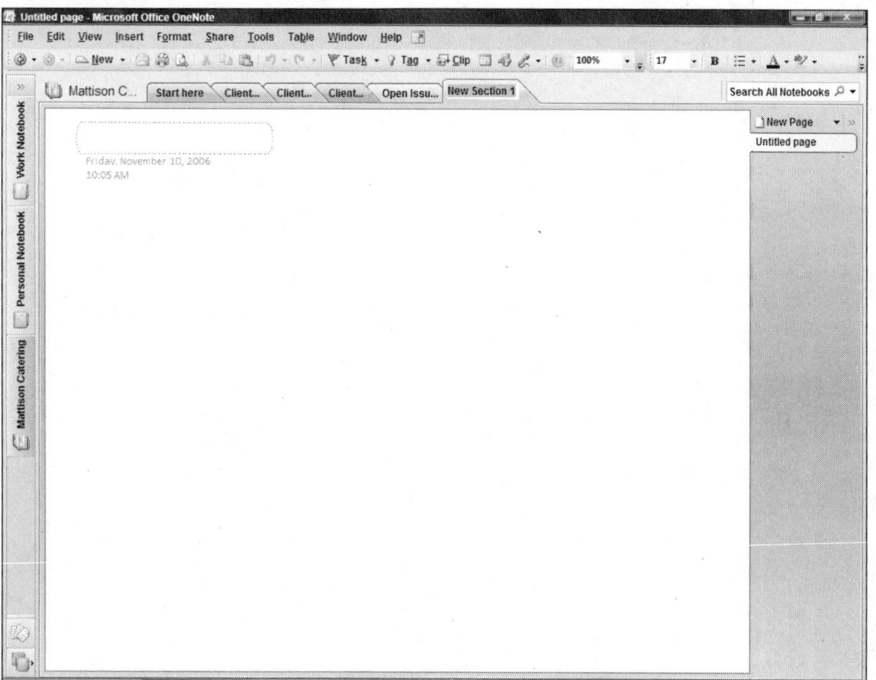

Creating a Page

Each new section you create includes by default a new, blank page called Untitled Page. You can add pages as needed to further organize the information in a notebook. For example, within a section for a client, you could have a page for each project you're handling for the client. Within a section for a class, you could have a page for each assignment, report, or exam. Because you can switch between pages simply by clicking a page tab, dividing your notes into more pages actually saves time because you can jump to the information you need by clicking a tab rather than having to scroll around in a lengthy document.

Use these steps to add a page:

1. **In the Notebooks navigation bar, click the name of the notebook to which you want to add a page.** The contents of the selected notebook appear.
2. **At the top of the notebook, click the section tab for the section into which you want to add a page.** The tabs for the pages in the section appear at the right.
3. **Click the New Page button at the top of the page tabs area or press Ctrl+N.** The new page tab appears.
4. **Type a new name for the page and then press Enter.** As shown in Figure 38-6, the name you type appears on both the page tab and in a title area on the new page.

FIGURE 38-6

The page name appears on the page tab and as a page title.

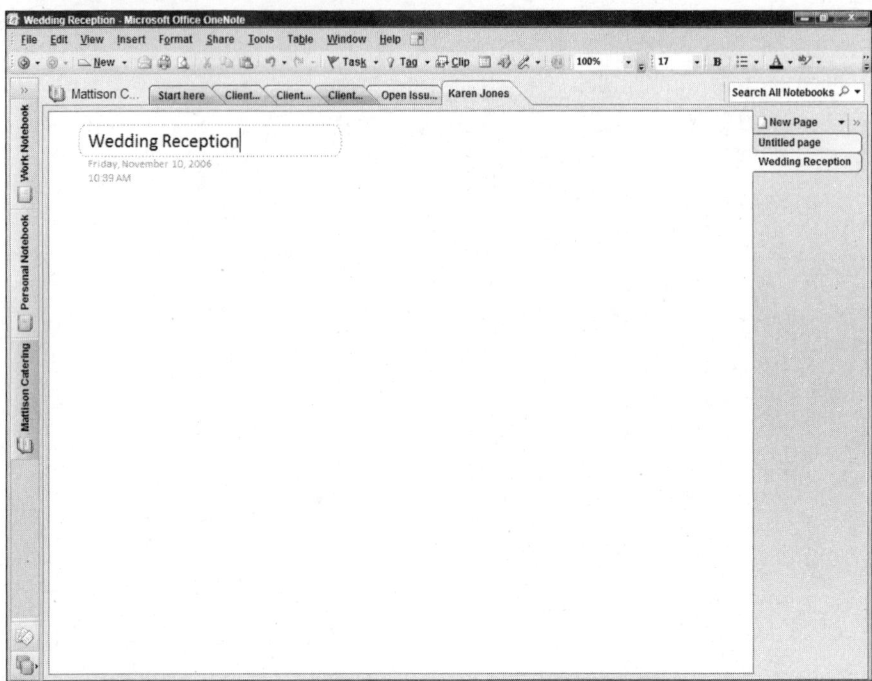

NOTE **You don't have to use the Save command to save your work in OneNote. The program saves automatically for you. You can use the Save As command on the File menu to make a copy of the current notebook file.**

Inserting Notes

Each new page you add to a notebook section is ready to go as a blank slate for your notes, doodles, tasks, and more. Adding notes to a notebook may be the feature you use the most. This section explains how OneNote trumps sticky notes in helping you capture key thoughts.

Plain notes

You can add a note anywhere on a page in OneNote. You're not bound by the tradition of starting at the top and working down to the bottom. Just click anywhere on the page, type the note text (Figure 38-7), and click outside the note when you've finished. You can press Enter as needed within a note, and pressing Tab after you enter at least one character of text creates table cells within the note. You also can click back on the note to place the insertion point within it to make changes to the note at any time.

FIGURE 38-7

Click and type a note anywhere on a page.

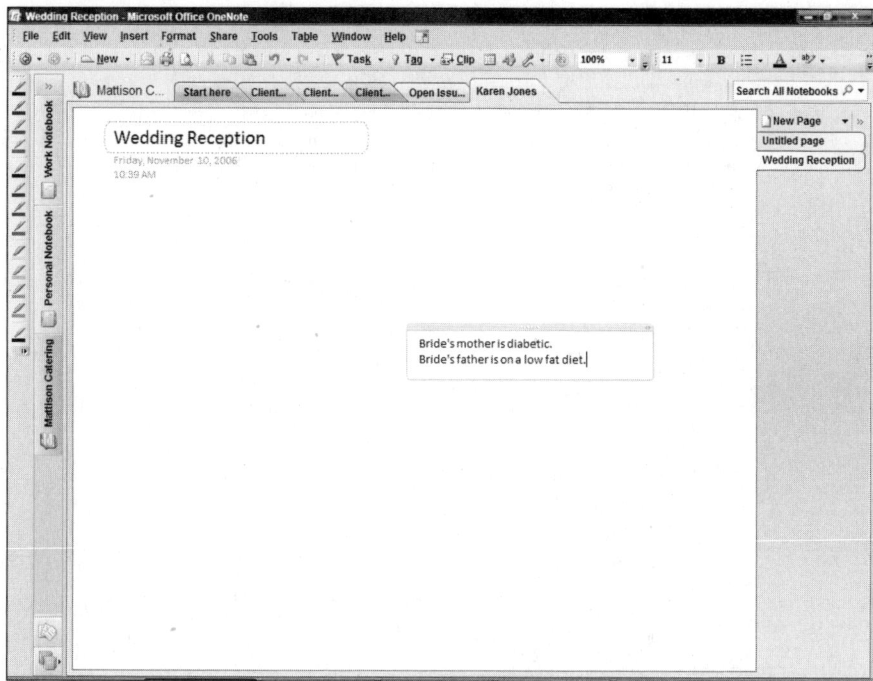

Tagged notes

Tagging a note assigns a category and icon to the note, such as the To Do tag, Important tag, Question tag, Phone number tag, or Idea tag. The tag icon appears beside the note so that you can determine what kind of information a note contains just by scanning the page. You also can view tagged notes by group, as described later in this chapter.

You can choose Insert ➪ Tag or click the Tag This Note button and its drop-down list on the Standard toolbar to assign a tag to a note. You can assign a tag when you create a note or at any later time. To assign the tag when you create the note, click in the page to position the insertion point where you want the note to appear. Choose Insert ➪ Tag and then click the desired tag type in the submenu. Or, click the drop-down list arrow for the Tag This Note button and then click the desired tag type in the list. A note container with the tag icon appears. Type your note text and then click away to finish.

To assign a tag to an existing note, click the note to display its note container. Then choose Insert ➪ Tag and click the tag type. Or, click the drop-down list arrow for the Tag This Note button, click the desired tag type in the list (Figure 38-8), and then click outside the note.

NOTE **If you click the Tag This Note button rather than its drop-down list arrow, OneNote applies the most recently used tag.**

FIGURE 38-8

Tagging a note identifies the type of information the note contains.

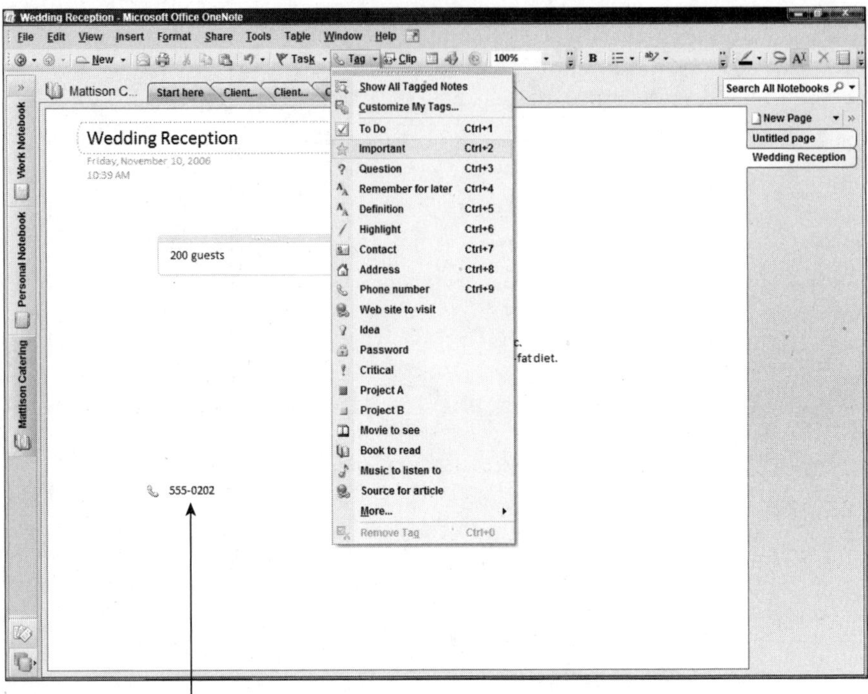

Extra writing space

Even though you certainly can make room for more information by creating a new page in a section, you also have the option of extending the space available in a page so that it can accommodate more notes or larger items. To add more writing space, choose Insert ➪ Extra Writing Space. Drag down the page until the down-arrow pointer changes from a single arrow to a layered arrow. Then click. OneNote adds more space on the page. If you scroll back up without adding anything to the new space, the extra space disappears.

Inserting an Outlook Task

Talk about keeping you on track! Any Outlook task you add on a OneNote page automatically appears in your To-Do list in Outlook. If you, like many people, have ever failed to follow through on an action item because you didn't copy it from your meeting notes to your calendar, this feature alone will make you more productive.

To add an Outlook Task into the notebook:

1. **Click in the page at the location where you want to insert the task.**
2. **Choose Insert ⇨ Outlook Task or click the drop-down list arrow for the Create Synched Outlook Task from This Note button on the Standard toolbar.** A submenu or list of the flags that you can use to schedule the task, such as Today, Tomorrow, or This Week, appears.
3. **Click the desired flag.** A note container with the specified flag appears.

NOTE If you click Custom, a Task window from Outlook opens so that you can enter a custom Start Date and Due Date to schedule the task in the Outlook To-Do List.

4. **Type the note text and then click outside the note.** The note appears with a flag icon beside it.

As shown in Figure 38-9, when you select the task in your Outlook To-Do list, Outlook identifies it as a task linked to OneNote. The two applications synch the task information. Marking the task as complete in Outlook, for example, identifies it as complete in OneNote, dimming the task flag for that note.

FIGURE 38-9

The selected task was created in OneNote and remains synched to the notebook.

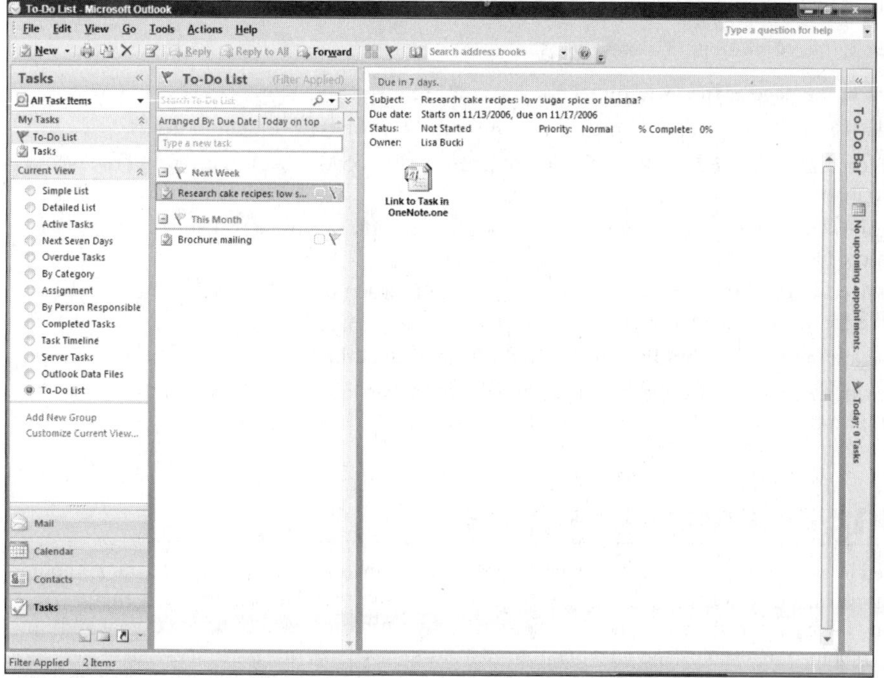

TIP If you mark a task as complete in Outlook but want to reinstate it in OneNote, deselecting the task in Outlook doesn't work. You have to select the OneNote task, open the Create Synched Outlook Task from This Note drop-down list and click Delete Outlook Task, and then use the drop-down list again to reapply a task flag. You can then delete the original task in Outlook.

Inserting a Picture or File

If the contents you want to capture already exist in a file outside OneNote, you can insert the information. Inserting information works much the same as opening a file: You give a command, navigate to the folder holding the file to insert, and select and insert the file.

When you insert a picture, the image appears on the OneNote page, where you can move or resize it as desired. You might insert a picture that shows a look or idea that you're after, or that you want to use to illustrate some other document at a later time. (You can copy and paste the picture from OneNote.)

There are two different ways in which you can insert a file. A regular insert operation displays a hyperlinked icon for the file on the page. Double-clicking the icon opens the file in its home application. Or, to display the file's contents on the OneNote page, insert the file as a printout. In that case, a special OneNote print driver outputs a version of the file's contents that display on the page along with an icon for the file and a hyperlink to the original document.

To insert a picture, file, or printout, use these steps:

1. **Click in the page at the location where you want to insert the item.**
2. **Click the Insert menu and then click the command for the type of item to insert.**
   - **Pictures ⇨ From Files.** Opens the Insert Picture dialog box so that you can select the picture to insert.
   - **Files.** Opens the Choose a File or Set of Files to Insert dialog box so that you can select one or more files to insert.
   - **Files as Printouts.** Opens the Choose Document to Insert dialog box so that you can choose the file to "print" and display.
3. **Navigate to the folder holding the desired file and select the file.**
4. **Click Insert.** The picture, file icon, or "printed" file appears on the page. Figure 38-10 shows an example of each.

Inserting a Screen Clipping

Adding a screen clipping to OneNote literally enables you to take a picture of something on your computer screen and place it on a OneNote page. You might use this feature to capture information that appears onscreen during a Webcast or shared online work session. Or you can capture information from a Web page, such as grabbing the headline and lead photo from a news site so that you remember where you saw the information. When you take a screen clipping from a Web page, OneNote also inserts a hyperlink to the Web page.

FIGURE 38-10

This page holds an icon for an inserted file, an inserted picture, and a "printout" of a file.

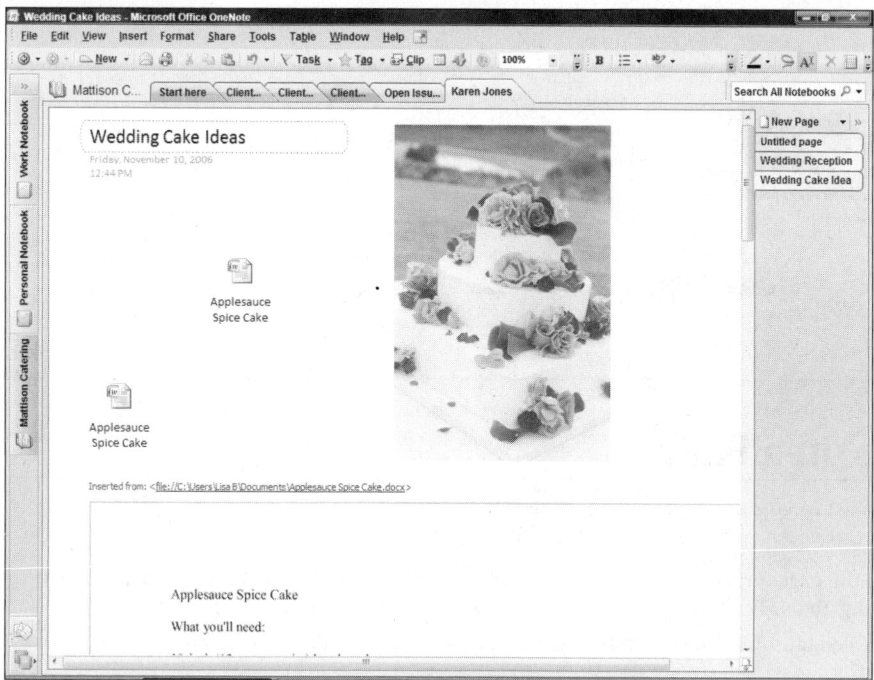

Here's how to create a screen clip in OneNote:

1. **Click in the page at the location where you want to insert the item in OneNote.**
2. **Switch to the location from which you want to clip the screen.** For example, display the desktop or launch your Web browser and brows to the page that holds the information to clip.
3. **Switch back to OneNote.**
4. **Choose Insert ➪ Screen Clipping.** OneNote minimizes, and the location you selected in Step 2 appears. The screen appears "grayed out" to indicate that OneNote is waiting for you to make your clip selection.
5. **Drag diagonally to make the selection.** When you release the mouse, the clip appears in a note container along with any hyperlink, as in the example in Figure 38-11.

NOTE If you want to insert a plain hyperlink rather than a file or screen clipping, choose Insert ➪ Hyperlink. Type the URL to link to in the Address text box of the Hyperlink dialog box, or click the Browse for File button to select a file to link to. If you want the hyperlink to appear as a label or descriptive text rather than a URL or file path, make an entry in the Text to Display text box. Then click OK. Use the Insert ➪ Audio Recording and Insert ➪ Video Recording commands to insert recorded content.

FIGURE 38-11

The screen clip appears as a new note.

Writing on a Page

If you have a Tablet PC or a pen input device attached to your computer, you can choose a pen and then use the stylus to create a handwritten note, also called *ink*, like this:

1. **With the page on which you want to add the note selected, right-click a toolbar and click Writing Tools.** The Writing tools toolbar appears at the upper right.
2. **Click Pen button's drop-down list arrow and then click the desired pen.** The pen becomes active for the stylus.
3. **Write on the tablet with the stylus to create the note.** The note text appears on the page, as in the example in Figure 38-12.
4. **Click the Pen button to turn off the pen (stylus) input.** The stylus resumes working like a mouse.

You also can use the ink feature with a regular mouse rather than a pen input device, but because writing with a mouse is rather difficult, you might change your mind after you try it.

If you want to convert the handwritten note to text, move the mouse over the note so that the *note container* appears. Click (or tap) the top edge of the note container to select all the note contents. Then choose Tools ⇨ Convert Handwriting to Text. Figure 38-13 shows a selected note container and the same note converted to text. Converting the note to text in this way makes it easier to edit later, if needed.

You also can create drawings on the page using a Tablet PC or pen input device.

FIGURE 38-12

Create handwritten notes on a Tablet PC or pen input device.

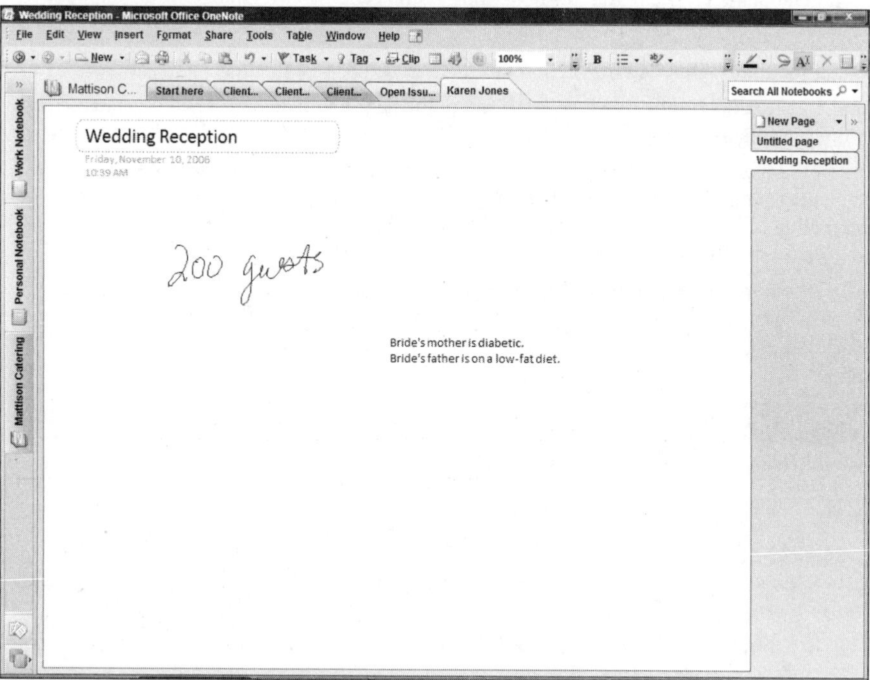

FIGURE 38-13

You can select a handwritten note and convert it to text.

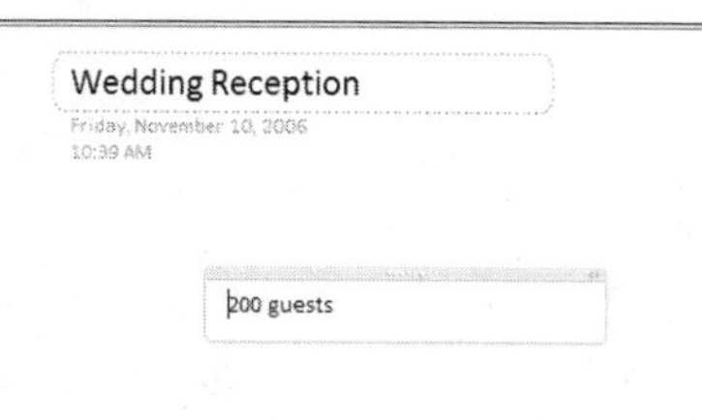

Organizing, Finding, and Sharing

Just as you can rearrange, change, and view pages in a three-ring binder, your OneNote notes remain flexible so that you can update, change, rearrange, and use them exactly as *you* need to. You can search for notes or even publish them for use by others. This last section in the chapter explains how you can get the most out of all the content that you pile in to your OneNote notebooks.

Reorganizing

You can tackle any of a number of tasks to reorganize and rearrange information on a page, between sections, and between notebooks. These are the most common actions you will use to keep your notebook information up-to-date:

- **Rename a section.** Right-click the section tab, click Rename, type the new name, and press Enter.
- **Rename a page.** Click in the title box at the top of the page and make the desired changes. The new name appears in the page tab, as well.
- **Move a note on a page.** Click the note, move the mouse pointer over the bar at the top of the note container until the four-headed arrow appears, and then drag. To move an icon, drag it. To move a picture or inserted file printout, place the mouse pointer over the picture or printout and then click the select button that appears; then, drag the picture.
- **Move a section to another notebook.** Right-click the section tab and click Move. In the Move Section To dialog box that appears (Figure 38-14), click the section near where you want to move the selected section and then click the Move Before or Move After button.

FIGURE 38-14

You can move a section into another notebook.

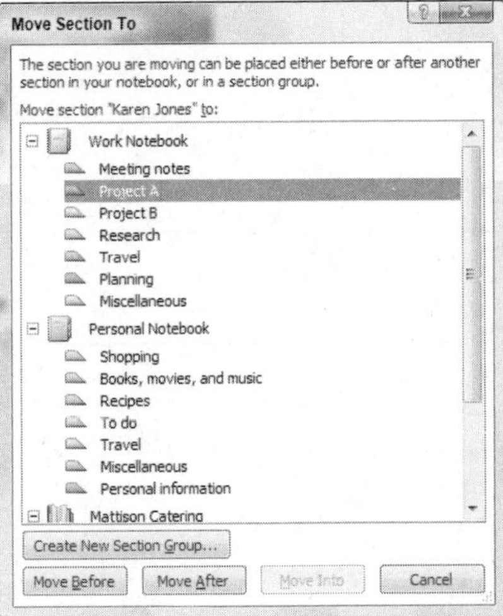

- **Move a section within the notebook.** Drag the section tag left or right until the black triangle appears in the desired destination and then release the mouse button.
- **Move or copy a page to another section.** Right-click the page tab, point to Move Page To, and then click Another Section. Select the desired section in the Move or Copy Pages dialog box that appears (it resembles the Move Section To dialog box in Figure 38-14), click the section into which you want to move or copy the page, and then click the Move or Copy button.

- **Move a page within its own section.** Drag the page tab until the black triangle appears at the desired destination location and then release the mouse button.
- **Delete a note or other item from the page.** Move the mouse pointer over the item or note container and then click the select button that appears. Press Delete.
- **Delete a page or section.** Right-click the page or section tab and then click Delete.

Viewing tagged notes

Taking the time to tag notes pays off when you need to view key note information later. OneNote can display a Tags Summary task pane (Figure 38-15), which displays the tagged notes from all your open notebooks. To open the Tags Summary task pane, choose View ➪ All Tagged Notes. To change how the task pane lists the notes, open the Group Tags By drop-down list at the top of the task pane and then click the desired grouping: Tag Name, Section, Title, Date, or Note Text. You can even add a new page listing the tagged notes to the current notebook by clicking the Create Summary Page button at the bottom of the task pane. Click the task pane's Close (X) button when you finish viewing the tagged notes.

FIGURE 38-15

Viewing tagged notes can help you find key information stored in your notebooks.

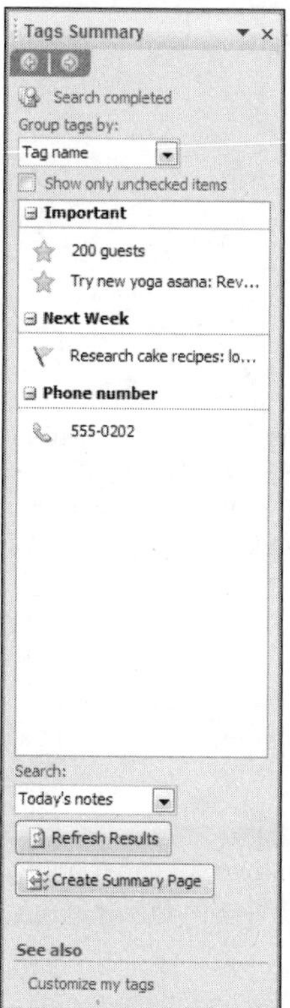

Searching notes

When you want to find a particular note, type a search word or phrase into the Search All Notebooks text box above the page tabs (Figure 38-16), and then press Enter. As shown in Figure 38-17, the search feature highlights every item on the page that holds matching text. The search results also highlight the tab for every page that holds the matching text; click page tabs or the arrows in the search text box area to view additional matches. To close the search, click the red X (Exit Search and Clear Match Highlighting) button at the right end of the search text box area.

FIGURE 38-16

Search for notes by making an entry in the Search All Notebooks text box.

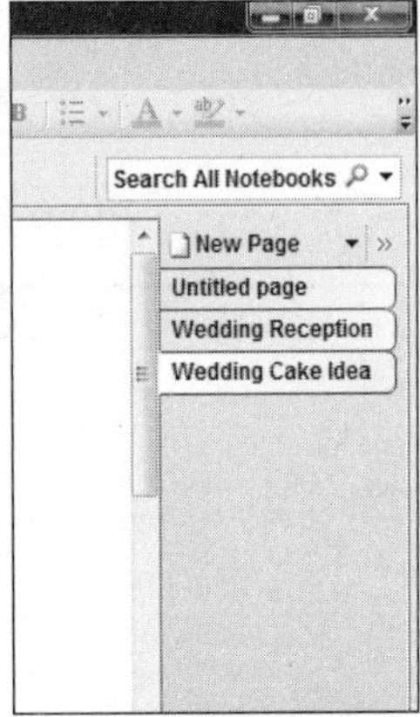

Publishing pages for others

You can *publish* one or more pages from a notebook to share the information on those pages with others who need the information but don't necessarily need to have access to your OneNote notebook. Publishing converts the page information to another format and saves it in a file of that format: Single File Web Page (viewable with a Web browser), OneNote Sections or OneNote Single File Package (for OneNote users), Microsoft Office XML Document (for Word 2007 users), and Microsoft Office Word Document (for users of an older Word version).

Use this process to publish pages to a file:

1. **Select the pages to publish using the page tabs.** To select a single page, click its tab. To select multiple pages, click the first tab and then Ctrl+click to add other pages or Shift+click to select a range of pages.
2. **Choose File ⇨ Publish Pages.** The Publish dialog box appears (Figure 38-18).
3. **Type a filename in the File Name text box.** Note that if you're using Windows XP rather than Vista, your Publish dialog box will look a little different.
4. **Select a file type from the Save As Type drop-down list.**
5. **Click Save.** OneNote creates the file, which you can then e-mail or otherwise provide to the desired recipients. The recipient can then double-click the file in Windows to open the file in its associated application.

FIGURE 38-17

Search highlights all instances of the search text, and highlights the tab for each page holding the search text.

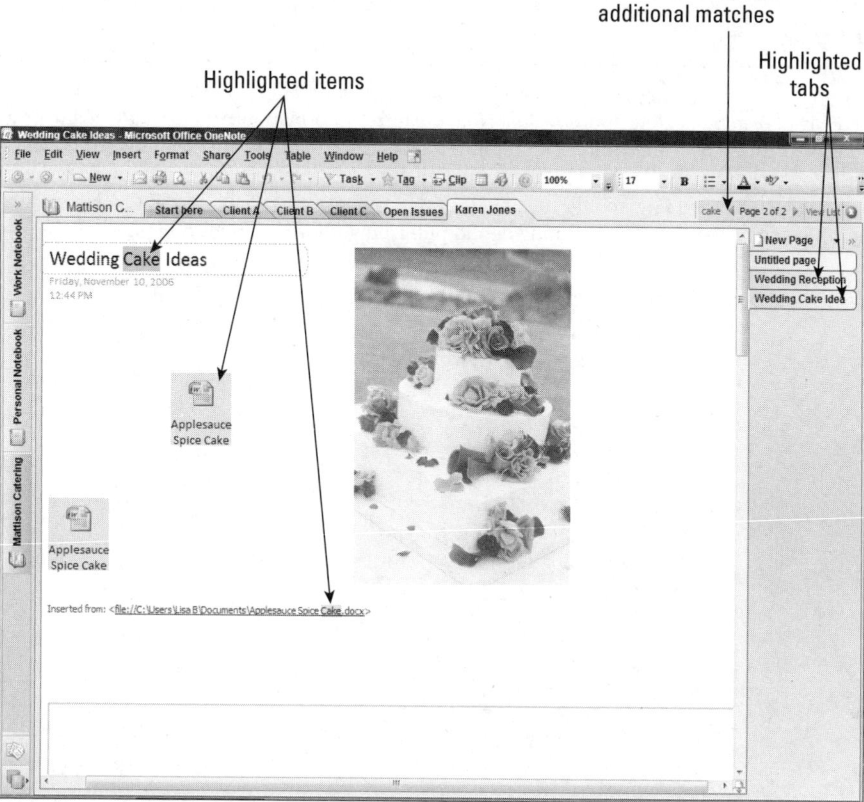

FIGURE 38-18

Publishing pages in another format enables other users to view your notes.

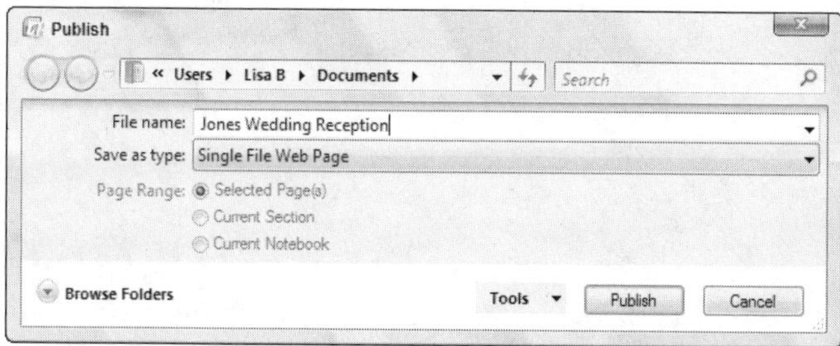

If you also have Microsoft Office Word 2007 installed, you can publish any note as a blog entry. Right-click a note and click Blog This to start the process. If you aren't already signed up with a blogging provider, you will be prompted to do so.

Summary

You're now well on your way to getting your life organized with Microsoft Office OneNote. This chapter explained the benefits of using OneNote and how OneNote organizes information. You saw how to create a notebook, sections, and pages to arrange information in the way that suits your needs. You learned how to add notes and tasks on a page, as well as how to insert a file, picture, or screen clipping and how to write on a page. From there, you learned how to take advantage of the content you've captured in OneNote by reorganizing and updating it, viewing and searching it, and publishing information for others.

Chapter 39

Making Data Forms with InfoPath

IN THIS CHAPTER

- Understanding what InfoPath does and how to use it
- Creating a new form template
- Adding layout items and controls to the template
- Working with the data source and publishing settings
- Distributing the form to users
- Filling out the form as a user

Microsoft Office InfoPath 2007 is included as part of the Ultimate, Professional Plus, and Enterprise versions of Microsoft Office. InfoPath enables you to create fill-in forms for gathering information from a variety of users inside and outside your organization. The good news is that you don't have to be a programmer to set up the form. This chapter teaches skills that anyone can use to create and distribute a basic InfoPath form. Although no office will ever be paperless, anyone who gathers data in his or her job can use InfoPath to cut down the amount of paper shuffling that eats up precious time.

Understanding InfoPath

InfoPath relies on Extensible Markup Language (XML) as a way to gather and transfer lists of information. You create a *form template* in InfoPath that defines and labels the various fields of information to gather. That form template file, which has an `.xsn` filename extension, is a type of container or cabinet file that holds other files such as an XML Schema (`.xsd`) and XSL Transformation (`.xslt`) file. Those other files within the template container give the form its functionality.

Each form template is connected to a *main data source*. For a form template created from a blank state, the data source is the XML definitions with the template itself, created by adding fields to the template. Each time an end user opens and fills out the form, he or she creates a new *instance* of the form. After filling in the form fields, the user can then save the new instance of the form as a separate XML file in the same folder as the template or another designated folder, from which the manager of the form can export the data from all the forms into a single Excel database. Or, if the form was sent by e-mail, the user can e-mail the results back to the form's distributor, who can consolidate the data in an InfoPath folder in Outlook.

If you take the reverse approach and set up a form with a data connection to an existing database, Web service, XML Schema, or other database connection, you add existing fields from that data source to the connected database. In this way, the form becomes a live "front end" that enables users to append information to an existing database file.

Figure 39-1 illustrates the stages in using an InfoPath template to gather data.

FIGURE 39-1

Each time the user opens the template, it spins off a separate forms instance. After the user fills out the form, he or she can save it as a separate XML file or submit it to a database.

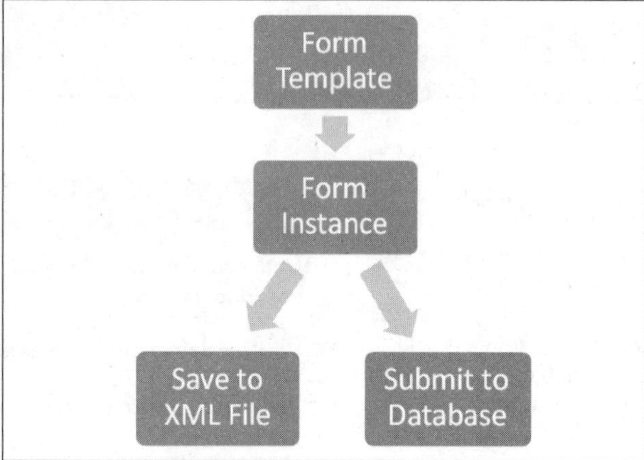

Designing a Form Template

When you start InfoPath by clicking Start and then choosing All Programs ➪ Microsoft Office ➪ Microsoft Office InfoPath 2007, InfoPath displays its Getting Started dialog box, shown in Figure 39-2. That dialog box gives you the option of filling out an existing form (as an end user) or designing a new form template. This section focuses on the latter, more challenging task.

Open a new form

If you just started InfoPath, click the Design a Form Template under Design a Form in the lower-left corner of the Getting Started dialog box to begin the design process. If you've already started working in InfoPath and want to start the process for creating a new form, choose File ➪ Design a Form Template. Either method of starting displays the Design a Form Template dialog box shown in Figure 39-3.

FIGURE 39-2

InfoPath opens this dialog box at startup, presenting you with the option to open or design (create) a form.

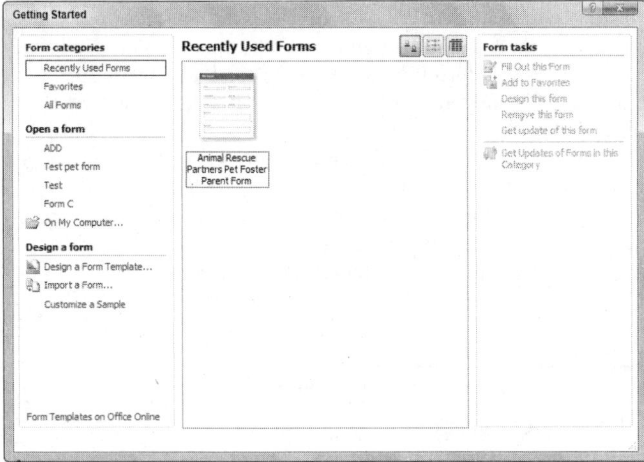

FIGURE 39-3

Choose whether to create a blank template or connect it to an existing data source.

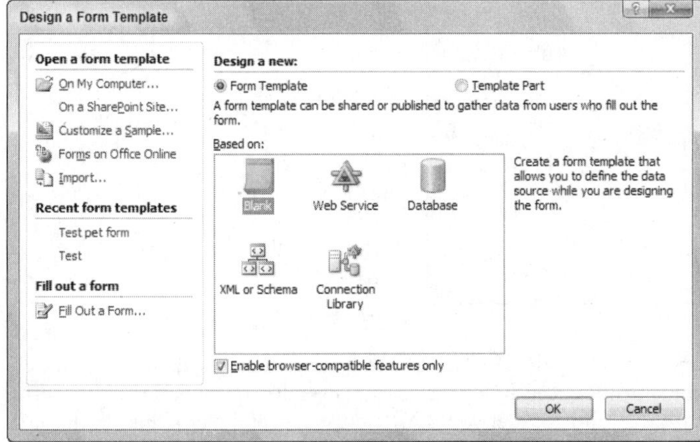

If you want to start with a totally blank template and design the data source by adding fields, leave the Blank icon selected in the Based On list. If you instead want to either use the form template to submit or retrieve data from an existing data source such as a database, click the icon for the desired type of data source. Then click OK.

If you opted to create a blank form template, the template appears right away onscreen. If you instead specified that the database should connect to a data source, InfoPath prompts you to specify information about the data source, such as the location of a database file and what tables to use from it. Fill out the Data Connection Wizard dialog boxes that appear to establish the connection. Figure 39-4 shows the wizard's dialog box that appears after you select Database in the dialog box shown in Figure 39-3, click the Change Database button to select a database, and then select a table or query to use in the Select Table dialog box. You can select which fields to use in the data source for the form and then click Next. In the next dialog box, enter names for the source data connection and connection for submitting information to the data source in the text boxes at the top; then click Finish to finish creating the data source connection.

FIGURE 39-4

Selecting the fields to use from an existing data source, and Access database in this example.

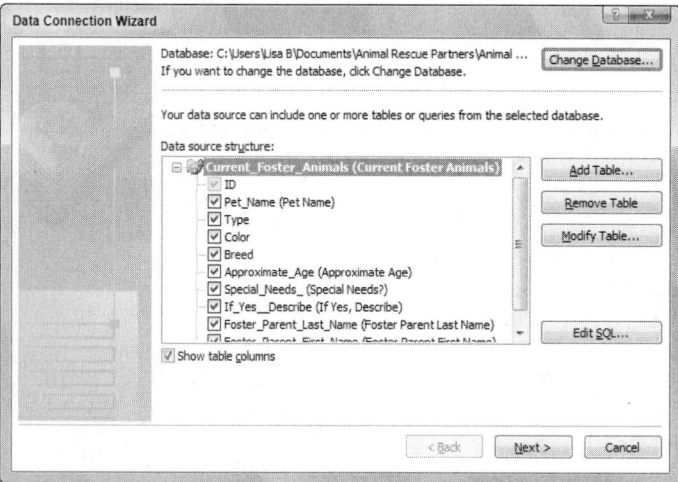

When the new form template appears in InfoPath, the Design Tasks task pane automatically opens at the right side of the screen. As shown in Figure 39-5, this task pane lists the overall steps of designing the form, so you can just follow its links to finish the process. After you click and use one of the task links in this task pane, click the Design Tasks link that appears at the top of the task pane to return to the initial list so that you can click the next link and continue the design process.

FIGURE 39-5

The Design Tasks task pane leads you through the overall steps of designing your form.

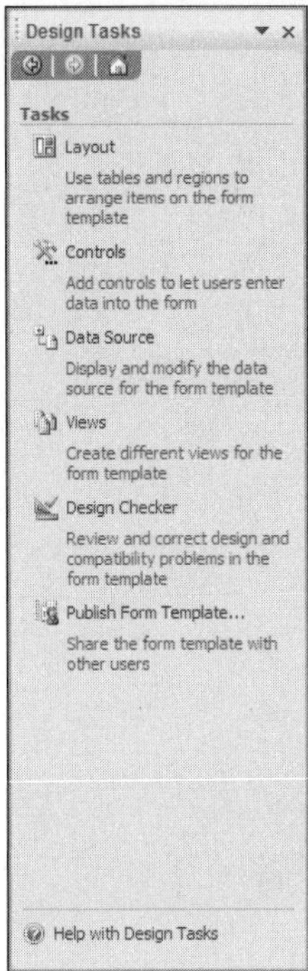

Adding layout items

Layout items help separate and label the fields of information in a form, both to give it an attractive appearance and to make it easy to navigate. When you click Layout in the Design Tasks task pane, the Layout task pane and its choices appear.

Click a choice in the Insert Layout Tables list in the upper part of the pane, and the initial table appears on the form, as shown in Figure 39-6. To continue building the content of such a table, you can click in the title area and type a title. You can then click in the Click to Add Form Content area and type text, or you can click another Insert Layout Tables choice to *nest* table cells within table cells. Figure 39-7 shows how doing so looks.

FIGURE 39-6

The Table with Title layout added to the form.

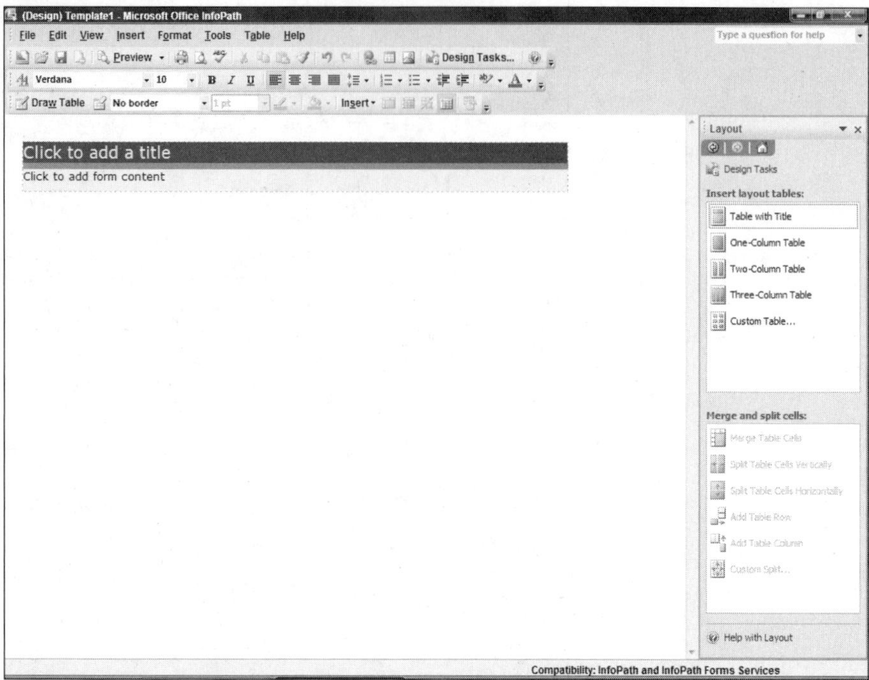

You also can click outside table cells and type text directly in the form background, as well as add single-cell tables by clicking the Draw Table button on the Tables toolbar to draw a table. When you click in a cell of a table that you've already drawn, you can use the Choices in the Merge and Split Cells list at the bottom of the Layout task pane to further determine how the table lays out.

After you finish arranging your table(s), click the Design Tasks link at the top of the Layout task pane to go back to the Design Tasks task pane.

Adding controls

Controls create the fields that accept the user input for your form. Click the Controls choice in the Design Tasks task pane to display the list of controls that you can insert into the table(s) on your form. If you based the form template on an existing data source such as a database, you can skip this process and move on to the next section, because you can add the controls simply by dragging fields from the Data Source task pane.

FIGURE 39-7

A Two-Column table nested within the bottom cell of a Table with Title.

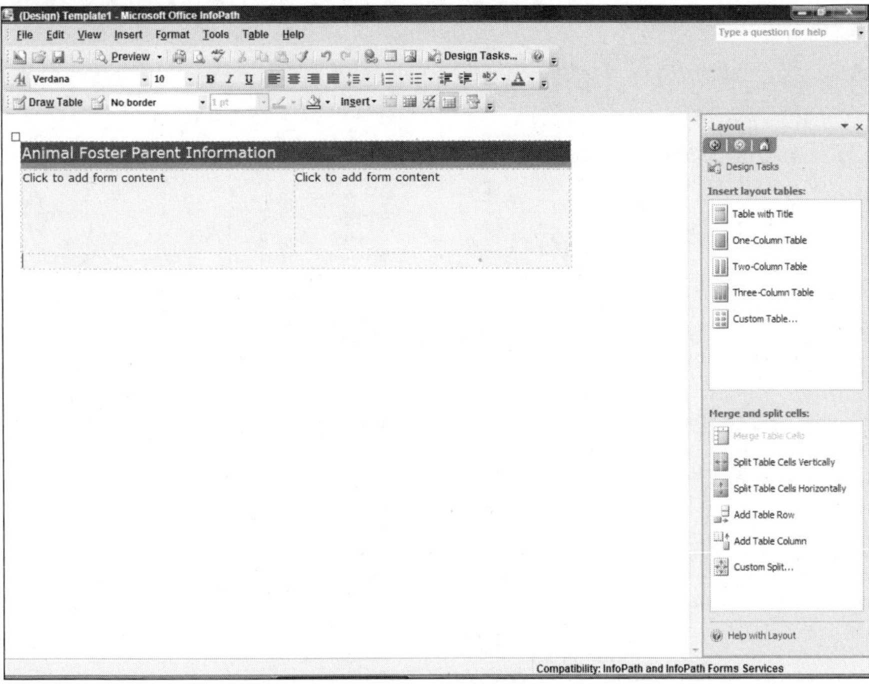

To add a control on a form template that you've created as a blank, use these steps:

1. **Click in the table cell into which you want to add the control.**
2. **Type any needed label text and press Enter if needed.**
3. **Click the desired control in the Insert Controls list.** The control appears at the insertion point location on the form.
4. **Double-click the control on the form.** The control's Properties dialog box appears. If the control appears with its own label, be sure to double-click the control itself, not the label, to open the Properties dialog box. You also need to edit the label manually.
5. **Specify the desired information for the control.** For example, type a field name to give the field a unique name in the data source, such as in the example shown in Figure 39-8. Note that you cannot include spaces in the field name.
6. **When you have applied the desired property settings to the control, click OK.**

Repeat the preceding process to add as many controls as needed to your form. When you finish, click the Design Tasks link at the top of the task pane to return to the design tasks task pane.

NOTE If you checked the Enable Browser Compatible Features Only checkbox when creating the template (refer to Figure 39-3), some controls will not be available to you and you will see the Some Controls Have Been Hidden Based on the Current Compatibility Settings message in the Controls task pane, as shown in Figure 39-8.

FIGURE 39-8

You should enter a friendly field name for each form to better identify the field in the data source.

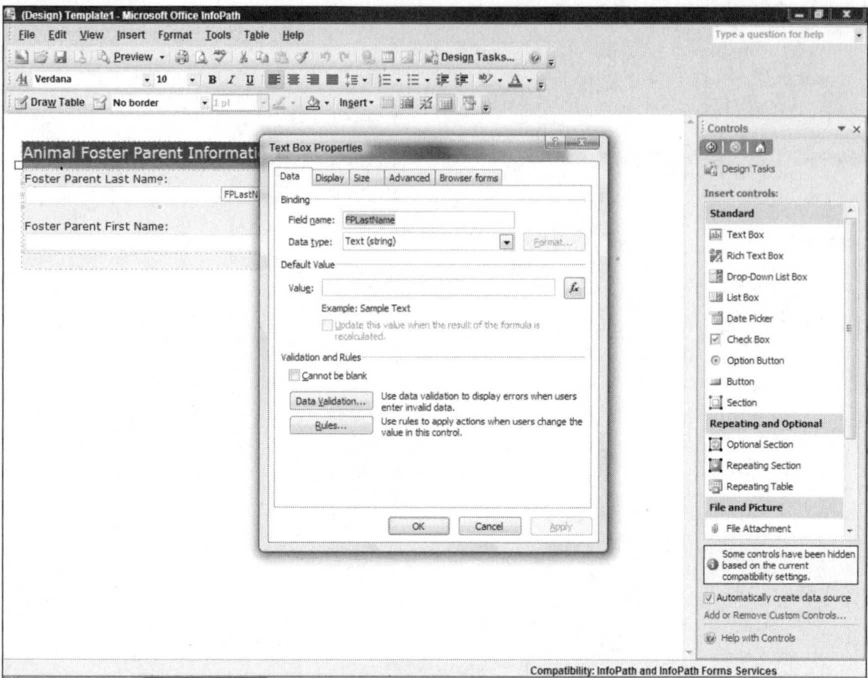

Working with the data source

If you created a form template from scratch, that process set up the fields in the data source — one field for every control you added. If, however, you based the form template on an existing database or data source, you need to come to this task pane to add the fields or controls to the template.

Click Data Source in the Design Tasks task pane to list the available fields from the connected data source. Drag the desired field onto the template and then size and position it as desired.

If you want to add a new field, click the Add a Field or Group link at the bottom of the Data Source task pane. Enter the desired field information in the Add a Field or Group dialog box that appears and then click OK. Click the Design Tasks link at the top of the task pane when you finish working with data source fields to return to the Design Tasks task pane.

NOTE **If you want to connect the template you're designing to a data source after the fact, click the Manage Data Connections link at the bottom of the Data Source task pane to open the Data Connections dialog box, in which you can click the Add button to open the Data Connection Wizard and choose the new connection. Keep in mind, however, that the data you make in this way will not be the main data connection for the form template.**

Checking and saving the template

As with files you create in most other Office applications, you should save your form template file to give it a unique name and preserve its information. Choose File ➪ Save or the Save button on the InfoPath Standard toolbar to perform the save as usual.

Then, click the Design Checker link in the Design Tasks task pane. This action displays the Design Checker task pane (Figure 39-9), which identifies any errors you need to correct before continuing. Clear up the errors and rerun the check, and then save any changes you made to the form template. Then click the Design Tasks link at the top of the task pane to return to the Design Tasks task pane.

FIGURE 39-9

Run the Design Checker to see whether your form template has errors before publishing.

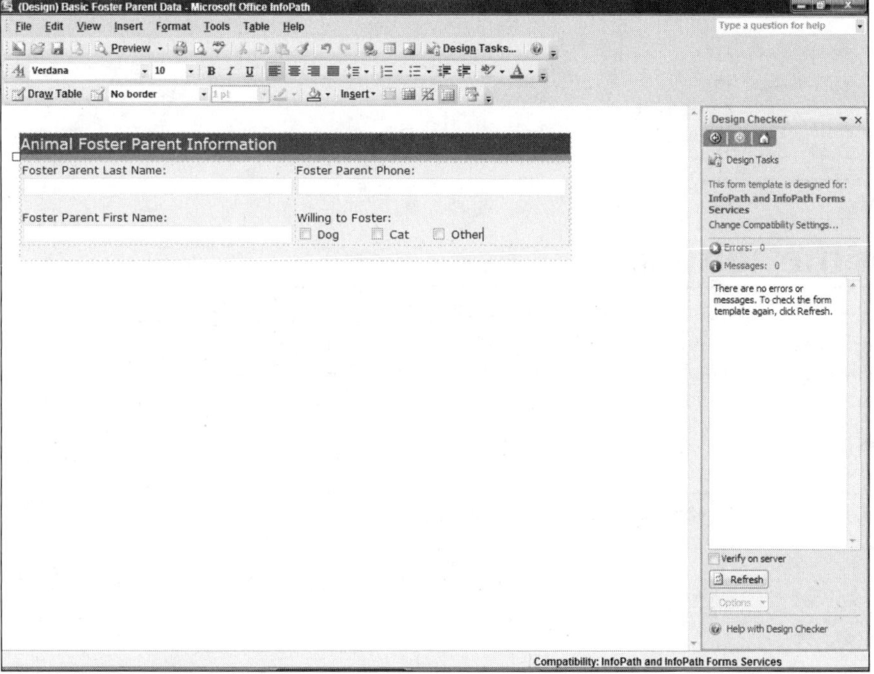

Setting up submit behavior

If you started with a blank form template, one last area to check before distributing the form template is the submit behavior — telling InfoPath to display a submit button and specifying what happens when the user clicks it after filling in the form. Choose Tools ➪ Submit Options to display the Submit Options dialog box. To set the submit behavior, click the All Users to Submit This Form checkbox to check it. Doing so enables the rest of the settings in the dialog box, as shown in Figure 39-10.

You can then choose what single destination the form results get sent to or add a data connection. You also can control whether the Submit button and menu item appear using the Show the Submit Menu Item and the Submit Toolbar Button checkbox. After you choose your settings in this dialog box, click OK to apply them.

Setting a submit behavior doesn't prevent the user from saving individual form instances as XML files so that you can merge them.

FIGURE 39-10

Set up submit behavior in this dialog box.

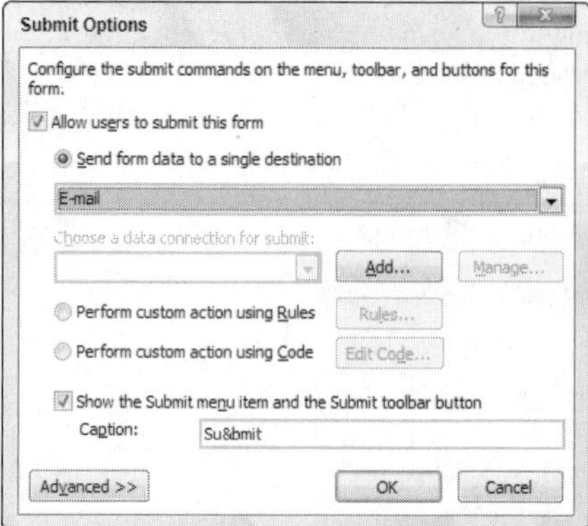

Publish the Template

Back in the Design Tasks task pane, one of the last tasks you can perform in creating the form template is to *publish* it to distribute it to form users. Click the Publish Form Template link at the bottom of the task pane to open the Publishing Wizard dialog box, shown in Figure 39-11. Follow the prompts to continue and publish the form. Two examples follow.

FIGURE 39-11

A wizard leads you through the steps for publishing the form template.

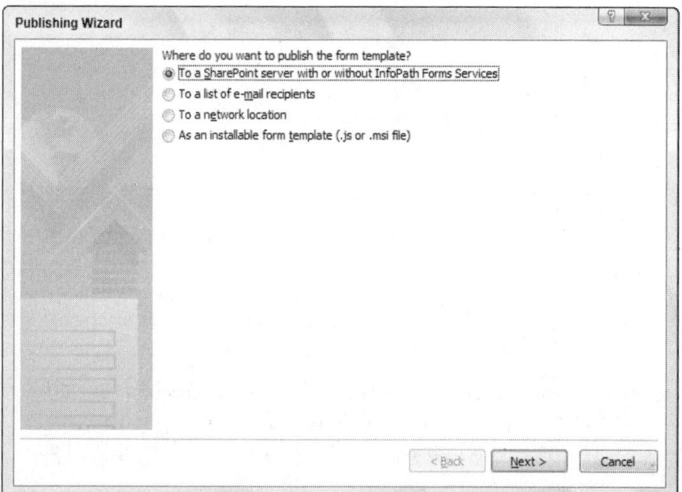

To a shared network location

If you click To a Network Location in the first Publishing Wizard dialog box and then click Next, the wizard prompts you to specify a shared network or Web server location to which to publish the file. Click the Browse button to open the Browse dialog box, in which you can brows to the desired shared network folder or other location, enter a filename in the File Name text box, and then click OK. The destination location appears in the Form Template and File Name text box, as shown in Figure 39-12.

FIGURE 39-12

Specifying the shared network location in which you want to publish the form.

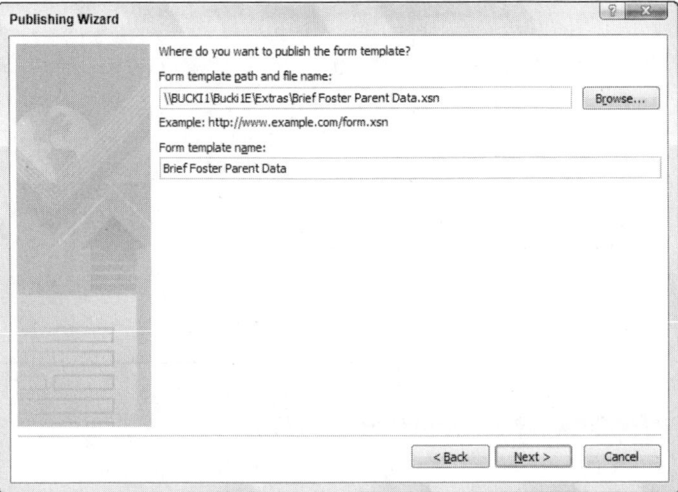

Click Next. The Publishing Wizard asks you to specify any alternate path that users might follow to access the form at the specified location. Type the path or use the Browse button to find it; then click Next. Verify the path settings in the next Publishing Wizard dialog box and then click Publish.

The final Publishing Wizard dialog box informs you that the form template published correctly. If you want to e-mail the form as well or open it immediately, check the Send the Form to E-mail Recipients or the Open this Form Template from the Published Location checkboxes (or you can check both) and then click Close.

Via e-mail

If you click the To a List of E-mail Recipients choice from the first Publishing Wizard dialog box and then click Next, you can confirm or edit the template name shown in the next dialog box, and then click Next. The next Publishing Wizard dialog box is more crucial. In it, you specify the fields that the users can see when they deal with the form in folders in Microsoft Outlook 2007. To add a field, click the Add button to open the Select a Field or Group dialog box. Click the desired field and then click OK. Repeat the process until you've added all the fields you want, as in Figure 39-13, and then click Next.

Click Publish. InfoPath hooks up with Outlook and opens the form in an Outlook e-mail message. Specify the message recipients in the To: field (Figure 39-14), enter optional Introduction field information, and then click Send. If needed, open Outlook and manually send and receive messages to make sure that the form leaves your Outbox.

FIGURE 39-13

Specifying the fields that will be visible to form users in Outlook.

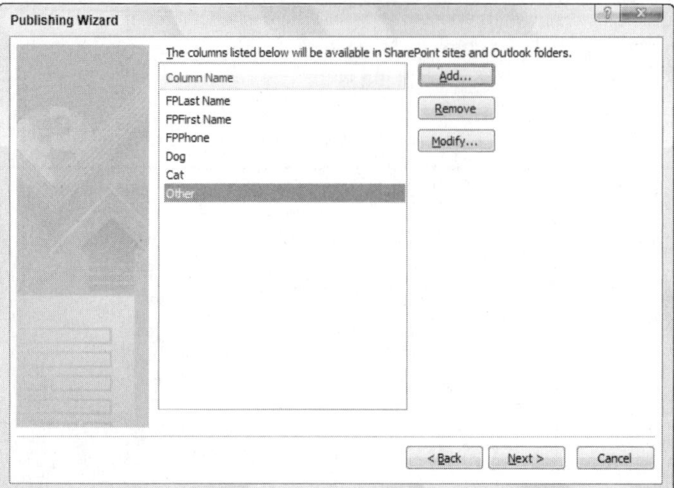

FIGURE 39-14

InfoPath can publish the form to an Outlook e-mail message.

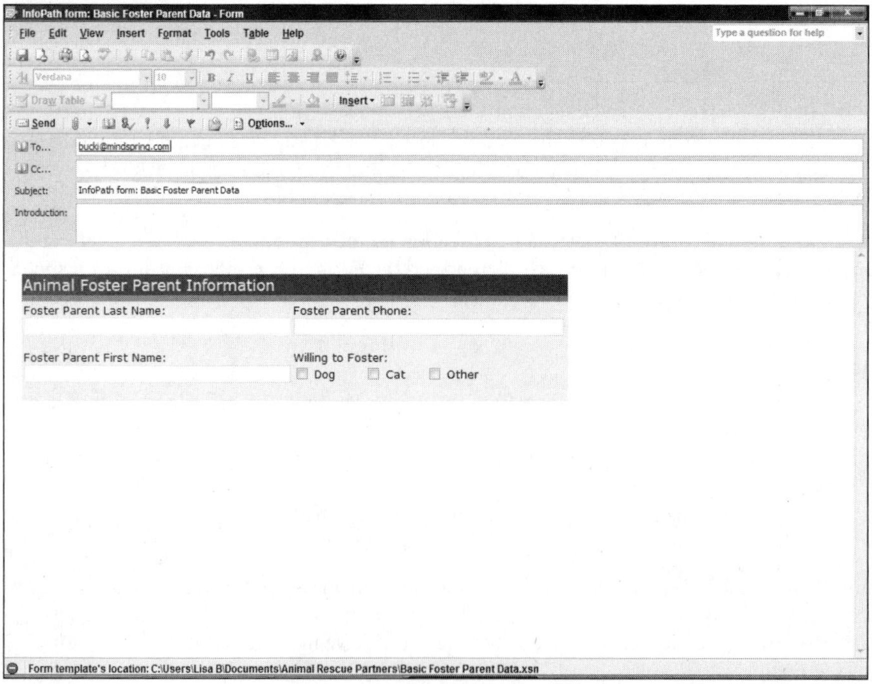

InfoPath is automatically compatible with Outlook 2007 but is not compatible with other e-mail programs.

Filling Out a Form

How the end user fills out a form depends on how the form was published. For example, if the form is connected to a database and published to a shared network location, the user opens the form template file to generate a copy of the form, fills in the form data, and clicks the Submit button to add his or her information to the database.

The process works a bit differently for forms not connected to a database. For a form that is published to a shared network location, each user should double-click the template file in the network folder or choose the File ➪ Fill Out a Form command in InfoPath to open an XML file instance of the form. The user should then fill in the form, choose File ➪ Save to save it under a unique name, and then close the file. The user can also submit the filled-in form by choosing the File ➪ Send to Mail Recipient command in InfoPath.

If the recipient receives the form via e-mail in Outlook, he or she can open the message, click Reply, fill in the form contents as shown in Figure 39-15, and then click Send.

FIGURE 39-15

Responding to a form received in e-mail.

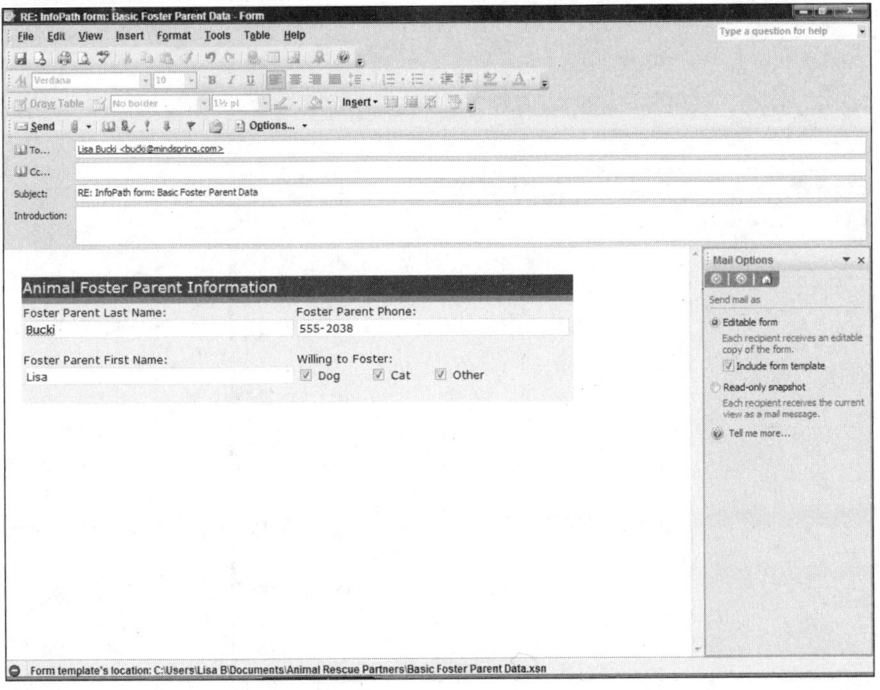

Note that the first time you fill out a form in Outlook, it asks you to confirm that you want to set up an InfoPath folder to store the form results, as shown in Figure 39-16. Click Create Form Folder to do so. Received form responses are placed in that folder automatically for your viewing, as shown in Figure 39-17.

FIGURE 39-16

Creating an InfoPath Form folder in Outlook sets up a location for received form responses.

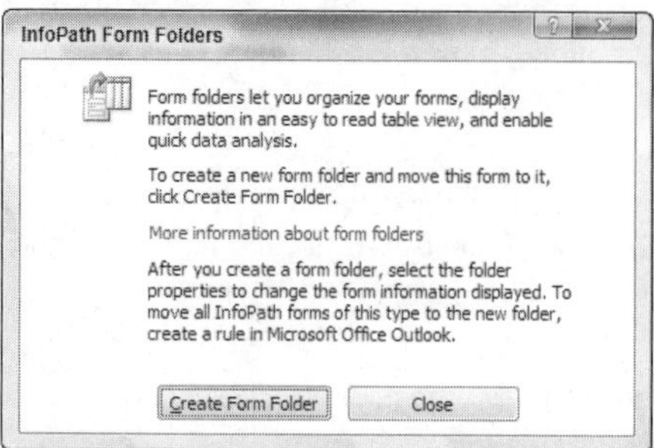

FIGURE 39-17

Viewing InfoPath data in Outlook.

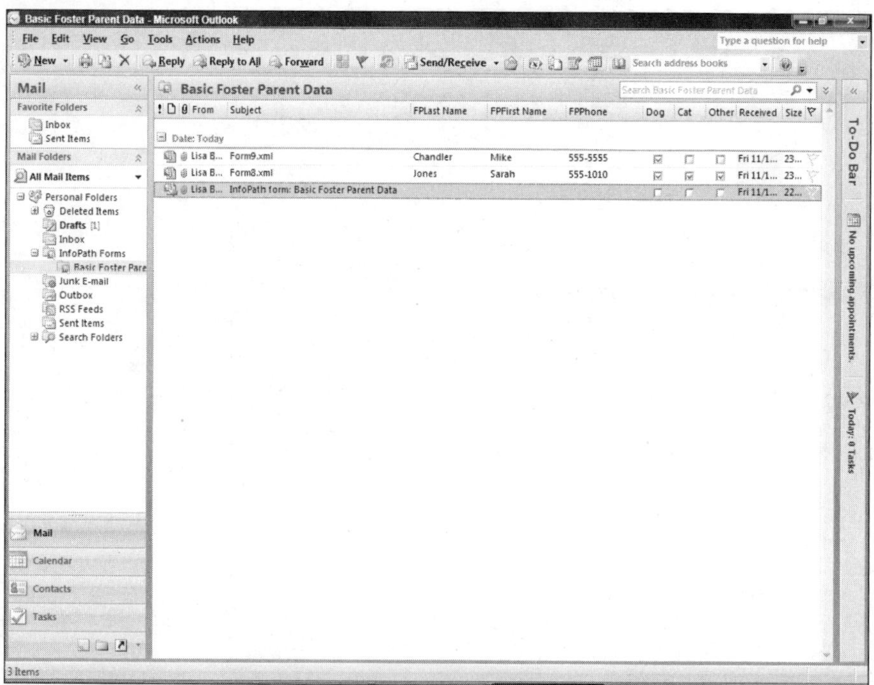

Exporting and Merging Form Data

When your form users save XML file instances of the form, you can easily export them to an Excel file or merge them into another XML copy of the form.

To start an export to Excel, open one of the filled-in form XML files and then choose File ➪ Export to ➪ Microsoft Office Excel in InfoPath. Click Next in the first Export to Excel Wizard dialog box. Leave All Form Data selected and click Next. Click the Export Data from This Form and These Additional forms option button, click the Add button, and use the Add Files to Export dialog box that appears to select the form files to export. Click Finish back in the wizard, and the exported data opens in a new Excel file (Figure 39-18), which you can save and use the same as any other Excel database.

Remember, use Shift+click or Ctrl+click to select multiple files in any dialog box where you select or open files.

FIGURE 39-18

Form data exported to Excel.

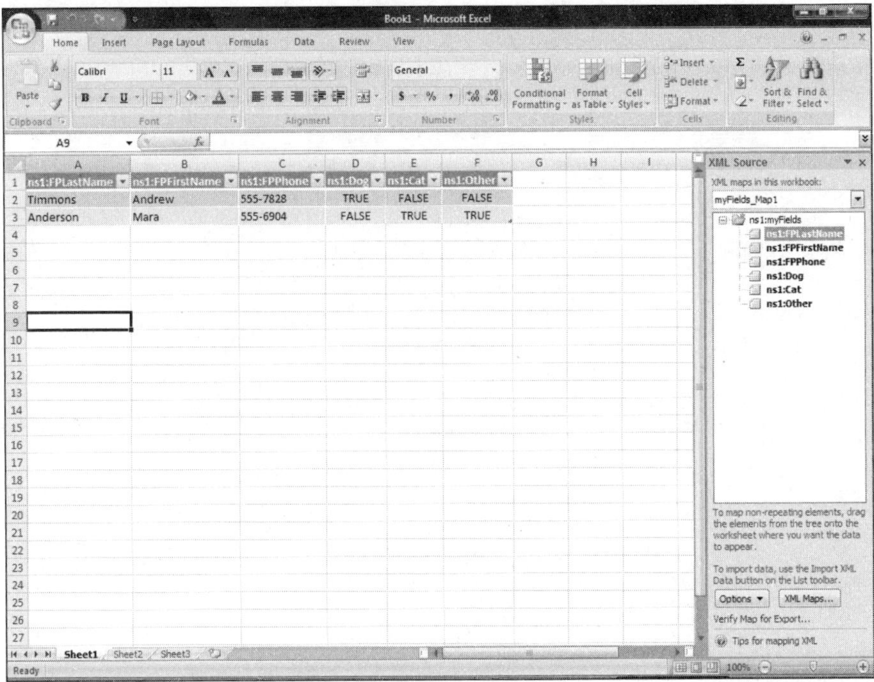

You must open a blank *target* copy of a form to merge data into it, choose File ➪ Fill Out a Form and then select File ➪ Merge Forms command in InfoPath. Use the Merge Forms dialog box that appears to select the XML form files; then click Open to finish the merge.

TIP

In Outlook, you can click the InfoPath folder for a form, right-click the list of e-mails, click InfoPath Actions in the shortcut menu that appears, and then click the Export Forms to Excel or Merge Forms command in that shortcut menu.

Summary

This chapter gave you a good taste of the power and flexibility of InfoPath forms. Although covering an entire application in a single chapter is impossible, this chapter brought you the good stuff, giving you an essential overview of how InfoPath works so that you know the lay of the land when using it. The chapter explained the essential steps for designing a form template, including creating the template, adding layout items, adding controls and setting their properties, adding data source fields for a form connected to an existing data source such as a database, and saving and checking the form template before publishing it.

Part IX

Sharing and Collaboration

IN THIS PART

Chapter 40

SharePoint

SharePoint is a program that helps businesses share access to files and information in a variety of ways. In essence, SharePoint is a special kind of Web site that provides controlled access to folders, documents, contact information, scheduling, and other resources related to documents and workflow management.

SharePoint works as a server that can be installed on your own company's computers. A server is a computer or computer program that provides services to client programs. Servers usually are connected to a network — such as the Internet or a local area network — and are available to respond to client applications, such as your Web browser, Microsoft Outlook, and even Microsoft Word. For example, Web sites are located on servers, and they respond to your browser requests to display information. When you send or receive e-mail, different kinds of server programs are used to deliver e-mail between you and your correspondents.

If you or your company doesn't have its own servers connected to the Internet, you can purchase SharePoint hosting services, just as you can purchase a hosting plan for other Web sites and services. Increasingly, the same companies that provide ordinary Web hosting are also offering SharePoint hosting, sometimes bundled into hosting plans as low as $10 per month or lower. You can discover such plans by searching for "sharepoint hosting" using a search engine such as Google or Yahoo!.

Word 2007 has features that are designed to work with a SharePoint server. You can access these features directly, using the Publish command from the Office menu, or you can access them indirectly by saving a file to a SharePoint server or by opening a file that resides on a SharePoint server. All you need is a SharePoint server and a user account.

IN THIS CHAPTER

Creating a SharePoint document workspace from Word

Publishing documents to a SharePoint server

Checking documents out from a SharePoint server

Creating and reviewing workflow tasks from Word

Adding new files and folders to a SharePoint document workspace

Accessing Your SharePoint Server

Accessing a SharePoint server from Word can be as easy as opening a file. First, you'll need the URL (Internet address), your user name, and a password. In Windows XP, choose Office Button ➪ Open, type the SharePoint Server URL into the File Name text box and press Enter. Yes, we know it's not a file. This is a shortcut method for navigating to a location, rather than using Look In or other methods when using Windows XP. In Vista, rather than use the File Name box, click in the Location field at the top of the Open dialog box and replace the current location with the SharePoint server's URL, and press Enter.

Assuming you typed the URL correctly, you're next prompted for a user name and password, as shown in Figure 40-1.

FIGURE 40-1

If you're the only user of your computer, you can save time if you click Remember My Password.

Type your user name and password. Note that a SharePoint user name format typically calls for a site/domain name in all uppercase letters, a backslash, and your user name. Type your password, click Remember My Password if you like, and then click OK. This opens the SharePoint site, as shown in Figure 40-2. SharePoint sites usually are organized into one or more libraries and document workspaces. A library is a collection of resources on a SharePoint site. Don't worry if your SharePoint site doesn't look like this one. Different organizations format sites differently, and appearances can vary wildly. A document workspace is a location on a SharePoint site that enables you to coordinate work on one or more documents with other team members.

TIP In Windows XP, once you've navigated to your SharePoint library, right-click in the Places Bar and choose Add *library URL*. Next time, you can come directly here without having to type the URL. Note that this trick doesn't work in Vista, although you can drag individual SharePoint folders into the Favorite Links collection. If you drag the SharePoint site link from the Location box into Favorite links, it does go, but promptly disappears. It will not appear in Word's Open or Save dialog box. Instead, you'll see it when you view Links in Windows Explorer, where it won't do you any good in Word.

FIGURE 40-2

Access documents using a SharePoint library.

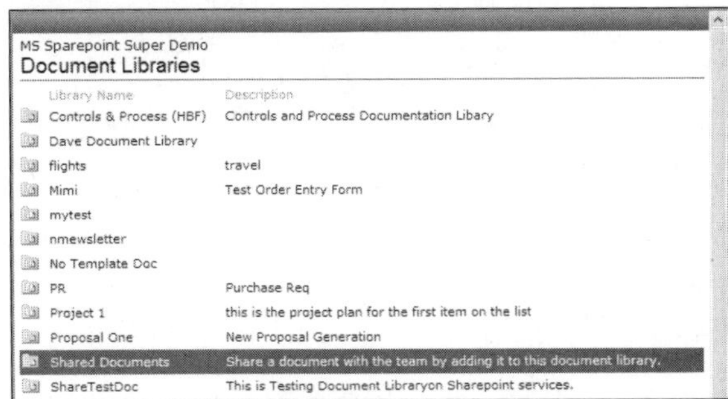

A document workspace provides a number of tools and facilities to share files, make updates available to team members, establish workflow by creating and managing tasks, and provide information about the status of documents and tasks. Earlier versions of SharePoint were called SharePoint Team Services, the idea being that you and other people working together form a team.

There are other ways to log on to your SharePoint server. Once you have checked out documents from the library, anytime you open a local copy of that file, Word attempts to log you on to the server to check for updates, etc. Using the URL, however, is a sure-fire direct route, especially when you're just getting started.

NOTE **With SharePoint, you can either work from the file that is stored in the document workspace or work on a local copy. When you choose the latter route, you are notified of changes to the workspace copy, and you can choose when and whether to publish your changes. The latter approach can be a bit tedious because you often have to compare your changes to those of others so you can integrate and coordinate changes. As a result, it's usually ultimately more efficient if work on a given document is done sequentially, rather than simultaneously. Nonetheless, if you choose the local route, choose Office Button ➪ Word Options ➪ Advanced ➪ Save section, enable the option Copy Remotely Stored Files onto Your Computer, and update the remote file when saving. See "Check Out" later in this chapter for the proper way to do it, however.**

Using Publish from the Office menu

You can also create and access SharePoint resources by choosing Office Button ➪ Publish ➪ Create Document Workspace, as shown in Figure 40-3.

Create Document Workspace

When you choose the Create option, the Document Workspace pane appears, as shown in Figure 40-4. Type a name for the document workspace and provide the URL (recent URLs can be selected from the drop-down list).

NOTE **When accessing a particular SharePoint site for the first time, Word might notify you that the site is not in your trusted locations. If you do indeed trust the site, copy the URL to the Clipboard, and then choose Office Button ➪ Word Options ➪ Trust Center ➪ Trust Center Settings ➪ Trusted Locations ➪ Add New Location. Paste the URL into the Path text box, enable the Subfolders option (if appropriate), type a Description, and click OK ➪ OK ➪ OK. This setting might not take effect until you close all Office 2007 applications.**

FIGURE 40-3

Use Office Button ➪ Publish to create a document workspace or to save the current file to the document management server (SharePoint site).

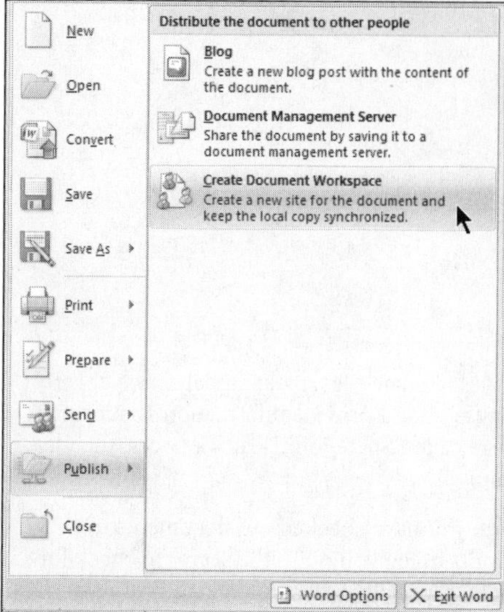

FIGURE 40-4

Create a new document workspace for managing Word documents on your SharePoint site.

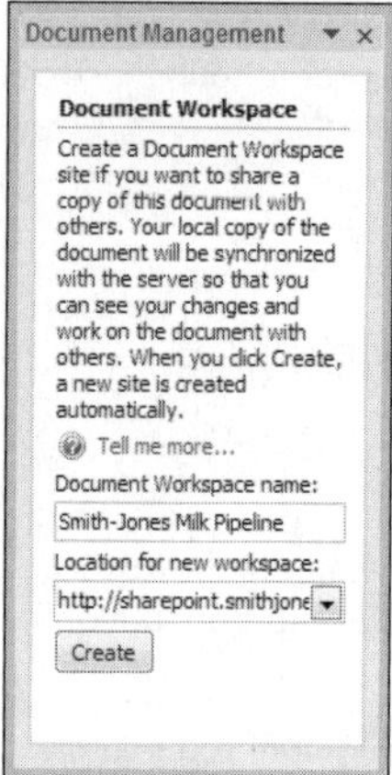

Opening and saving files on the server

To open a file on the server, in the Open dialog box, navigate to the desired library folder, select the file, and double-click it. Because it's located on a server that might not be where you are, there can be a noticeable lag before the file appears. When it does appear, the Document Management pane displays by default, as shown in Figure 40-5.

FIGURE 40-5

When a SharePoint Server file is open, Word displays the Document Management pane.

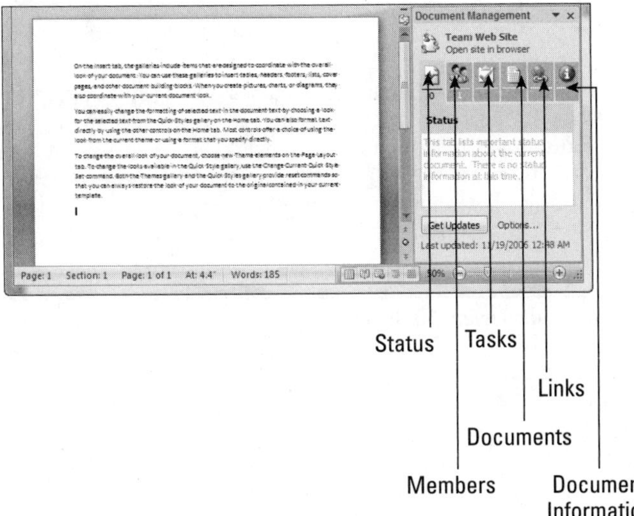

To save a file on the server, choose Office Button ➪ Publish ➪ Document Management Server (see Figure 40-3), use the Save As dialog box to navigate first to the SharePoint server's URL, then to the appropriate workspace and library, and click Save. Note that you can use Office Button ➪ Save As, instead. The only difference is that Save As uses your last saved folder as a starting point, whereas Document Management Server uses My Network Places (Windows XP) or Network Shortcuts (Windows Vista) as a starting point. Once you've successfully logged into your SharePoint Server using Word, the site's URL will be listed in My Network Places or Network Shortcuts. If you followed the Windows XP tip shown above, you can also go there by clicking the corresponding link in your Places Bar. Or, you can click the link to the target folder, if it's there, instead (in both XP and Vista). Once you're there, depending on your settings, the Document Management pane appears.

Workspace Management and Options

The Document Management pane provides six tools for keeping informed and managing your workspace documents:

- Status
- Members
- Tasks
- Documents
- Links
- Document Information

The sections that follow look at each of these. Notice at the bottom of the Document Management pane the Get Updates button and the Options link. Click Get Updates to refresh the information provided in the Document Management pane (for example, status information, number of members, and so on) as well as to get the latest updates for the currently opened document. Click the Options link to set your Document Management options using the Service Options dialog box, shown in Figure 40-6.

FIGURE 40-6

SharePoint defaults to updating status and other workspace data every 10 minutes. Other settings shown here are not necessarily the defaults.

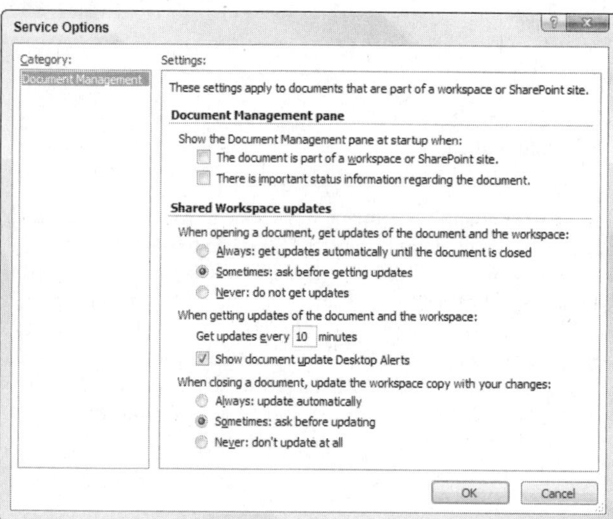

Status

The Status tool lists information about the current document. This information can be provided automatically, depending on your update interval, as shown in Figure 40-6.

Members

The Members tool shows the number of members online. You can send e-mail to all members, and, depending on your permission level, add new members. To add new members, click Add New Members. In Choose Members, shown in Figure 40-7, type e-mail addresses or user names, separated by semicolons. Notice the format for user names: DOMAIN\name.

FIGURE 40-7

You can add multiple new members at the same time.

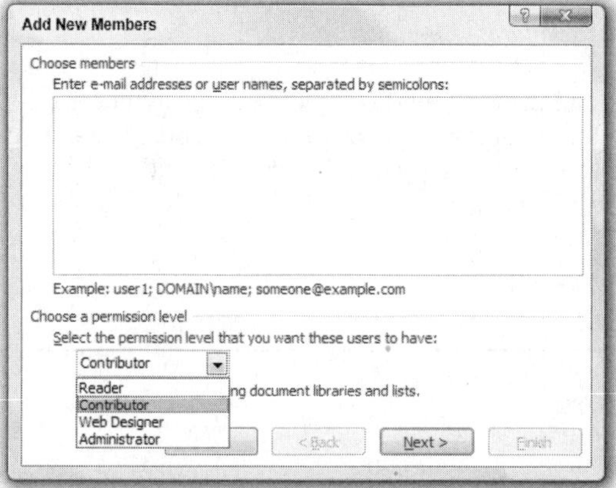

By default, SharePoint has five default permission levels you can assign:

- **Administrators (Full Control)** — These have complete control over the SharePoint Web site. They are able to configure settings, manage users and groups, and monitor usage statistics.
- **Web Designers (Design)** — Member of this group use SharePoint-compatible editors such as SharePoint Designer to customize the content of the SharePoint site and libraries.
- **Contributor (Contribute)** — These members can interact with different parts of the SharePoint Web, lists, and document libraries. They create and manage personal views and cross-site groups, and set up different parts of the Web.
- **Reader (Read)** — Readers can view items in lists and document libraries, view different SharePoint site pages, and create sites using the Self-Service Site Creation tools.
- **Guest** — This is a special custom permission level whereby users are given permissions for specific lists. This provides access to that list, but not to the entire site.

After adding members, SharePoint displays confirmation that they were added, as shown in Figure 40-8. If you opt to send an e-mail message, it will contain information about how to access the SharePoint server.

FIGURE 40-8

When adding new members, you can send them an e-mail.

Tasks

Use the Tasks tool, shown in Figure 40-9, to establish and manage workflow, control task/workflow alert settings, and view workflow. Note that clicking "Alert me about tasks" will open the appropriate settings in your browser. This is true for all of the different Alert links shown in each of the six different document workspace tools. The format and options for alerts vary by SharePoint site. Click View Workflow Tasks to see the status of existing tasks.

FIGURE 40-9

Use the Tasks tool to add tasks, set alerts, and view workflow.

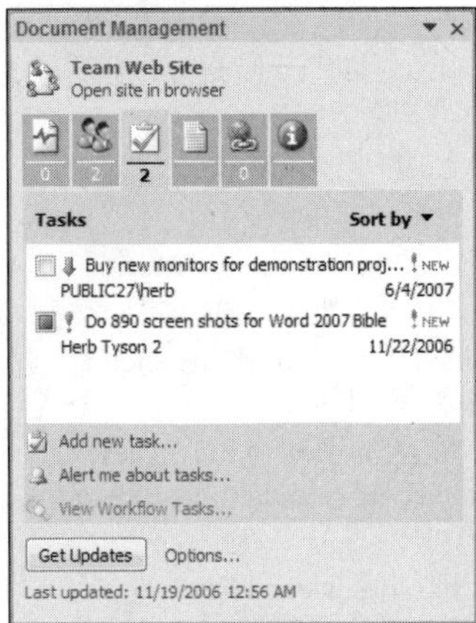

Adding tasks

To create a new task, click Add New Task. This opens the Task dialog box shown in Figure 40-10. Use the Task dialog box to create a title for the task, set task status and priority, assign the task to a specific team member (if appropriate), and set a due date and time. It's usually an excellent idea to type a description of the task as well, so that others (especially those to whom tasks are assigned) know what this is about. Include in the description enough information so that the assignee will know when the task is finished.

FIGURE 40-10

Assign tasks to establish project workflow.

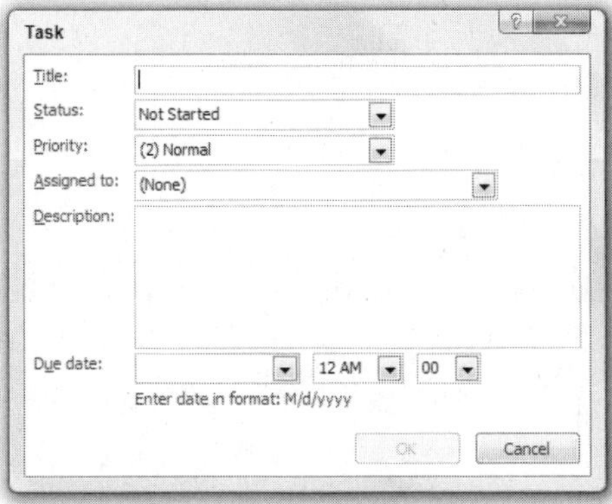

Use the Documents tool, shown in Figure 40-11, to display documents that are currently open by members, as well as to add new documents, add new folders, and set document alerts. Once again, as is the case for the other Document Management tools, alerts are managed using the Web interface.

FIGURE 40-11

Use the Documents tool to manage documents and alerts.

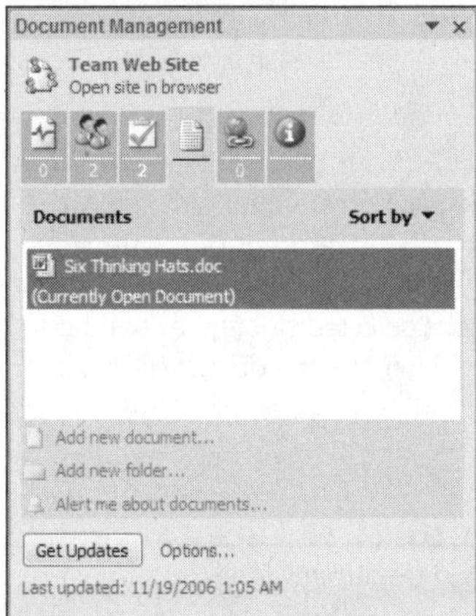

Adding New Documents

To add a new document to the current workspace folder, click the Add New Document link. Word displays the Add New Document dialog box. Click Browse to navigate to the file's local location; select the file and click Open. Back in Add New Document, click OK. Word saves the document to the SharePoint workspace, as shown in Figure 40-12.

FIGURE 40-12

Choosing Add New Document copies a local file to the SharePoint server.

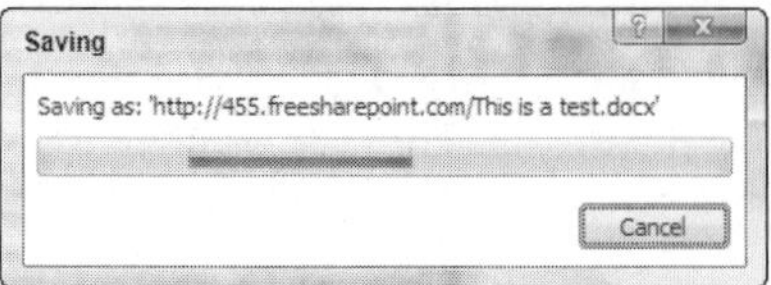

To delete or perform other actions on a document, hover the mouse over a document in the list and click the drop-down arrow next to a document to display document options, as shown in Figure 40-13. If a document is currently checked out (open) by a member, certain options will not be available (Open, Delete, Document Updates, Save Updatable Copy, and Publish Back to Source Location). Options that don't affect the document's current status, however, are available (Alert Me About This Document, Check Status, and Create Document Workspace).

FIGURE 40-13

Click a document's drop-down arrow to see a list of available options.

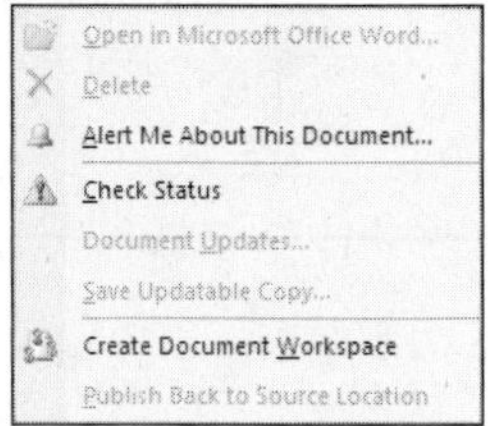

Creating a new document workspace

You've already seen at least one method for creating a new document workspace on a SharePoint site. In Figure 40-13, notice that you can create a new document workspace from a document's drop-down menu. Click Create Document Workspace. The dialog box shown in Figure 40-14 appears, explaining the purpose and implications of this option. If you create a new document workspace, the selected document will be stored there. However, you still retain the ability to automatically publish changes to the document back to its original location.

FIGURE 40-14

Right-click a document and choose Create Document Workspace to save the selected document to it.

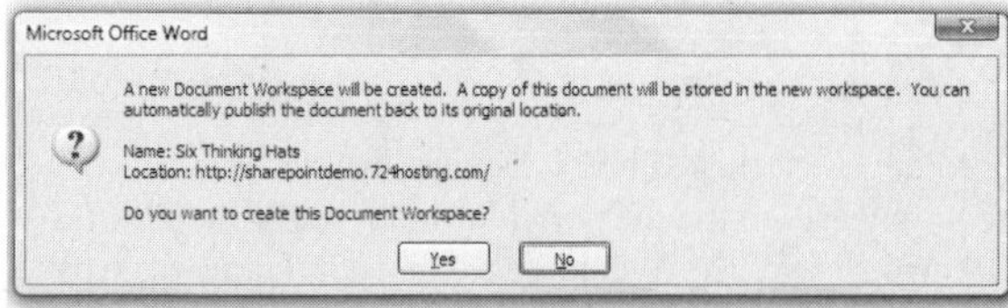

Adding new folders

To add a new folder in the current workspace, click Add New Folder. In Add New Folder, type a name for the folder. There is no facility for removing a folder in the Document Management pane. Instead, back in the document library view (refer to Figure 40-2), click the folder you want to delete, press the Delete key, and confirm the deletion. If other options are available, you can access them by clicking Tools in either the Open or the Save dialog box.

Links

Use the Links tool, shown in Figure 40-15, to display and add links relevant to the document workspace. If you or team members discover relevant articles, documents, data sources, or Web sites, click Add New Link. Type the URL, a succinct description, and any notes you have that might be useful to other team members. You and other members can see these details by hovering the mouse over a link, clicking the drop-down arrow, and choosing Edit Link. Additional options in the drop-down list are Delete Link and Alert Me About This Link.

FIGURE 40-15

Use the Links tool to provide information about related resources, data, and documents.

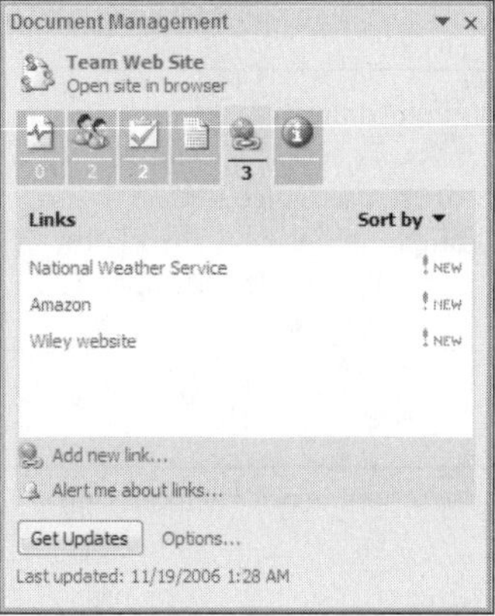

Document Information

Use the Document Information tool to obtain information about open documents. As shown in Figure 40-16, you can click the drop-down arrow next to a document to display additional information and options related to that document. If available, there's information on the owner/author of the document, a link for scheduling a meeting, as well as a variety of ways to contact the document owner. Rounding out integration in Office 2007, notice that the menu offers to let you add the document owner to Outlook contacts, as well as look at the Outlook properties for an existing contact. Notice the Additional Actions command. Whether this command actually contains additional actions will depend upon the designer of your SharePoint site.

FIGURE 40-16

The Document Information tool provides additional information about open documents.

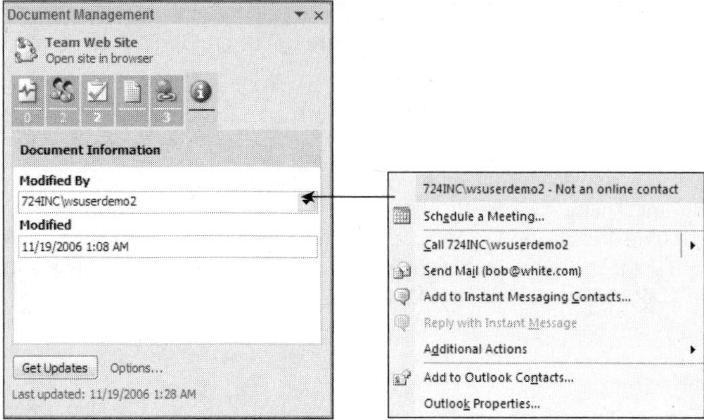

Server Tasks

Use Server Tasks options, in the Office menu, to perform a number of SharePoint-related tasks, such as checking in, checking out, viewing version history, and viewing workflow tasks. To access these options, a SharePoint document must be open. Either open a SharePoint document or choose Office Button ➪ Publish ➪ Create Document Workspace to create a workspace for the current document on a SharePoint server. Once a SharePoint document is open, choose Office Button ➪ Server Tasks to display the options shown in Figure 40-17.

FIGURE 40-17

If the document is checked out, then Check In is the top option in the menu; if the document is not checked out, then Check Out is the top option.

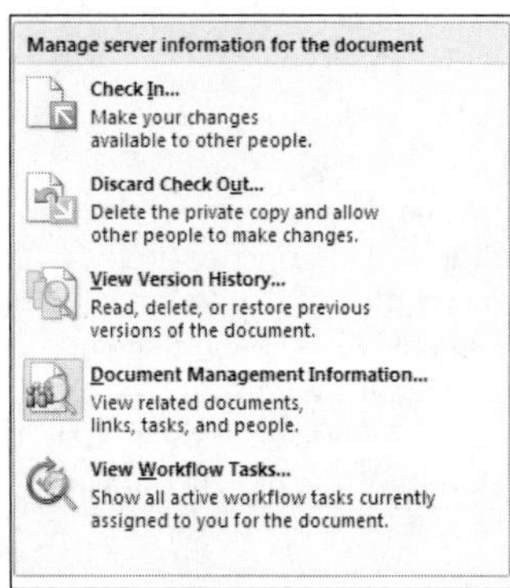

Check In

If the document in the current window is checked out, choose Office Button ➪ Server Tasks ➪ Check In to check the document back in so others can edit and view changes and updates. The Check In dialog box appears, as shown in Figure 40-18.

FIGURE 40-18

When checking in a document, add a comment indicating what kinds of changes you made.

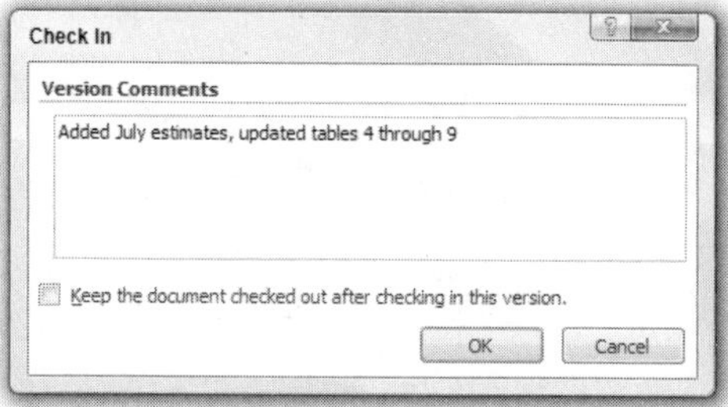

Under Version Comments, type a comment, if appropriate, indicating the nature of changes you made to the document. It's often even more useful, however, to enable tracking of changes on documents that are checked out, so other users can see directly what changes were made, who made them, and when.

Note that when checking a document in, you can also click "Keep the document checked out after checking in this version." Do this if you are making a series of unrelated changes, and want to preserve separate versions for each set of changes. Adding version comments is essential to letting other team members know what you did, and why.

Check Out

Use Check Out to prevent others from making changes while you are editing the document. Note that it's possible to save changes to the server (depending on server settings) even if you haven't checked the document out. For orderly and coordinated team editing, however, it's important to use the check-out and check-in systems to prevent team members from working at cross purposes.

Discard Check Out

Use this option at any time to abandon any changes that haven't been saved to the server and to delete your private local copy of the file. You might want to do this if you learn that your current efforts are moot or if you want to start over.

View Version History

Use version history to compare different versions of the same document and comments. Choose Office Button ➪ Server Tasks ➪ View Version History to display the dialog box shown in Figure 40-19. From here, you can select two versions and click Compare to see how the two versions differ. Or, select a single version and choose Open or Delete to open or remove the selected version. Click Restore to make the selected version the latest version for normal check-out procedures.

FIGURE 40-19

Use the Versions dialog box to manage and edit different versions of the same document.

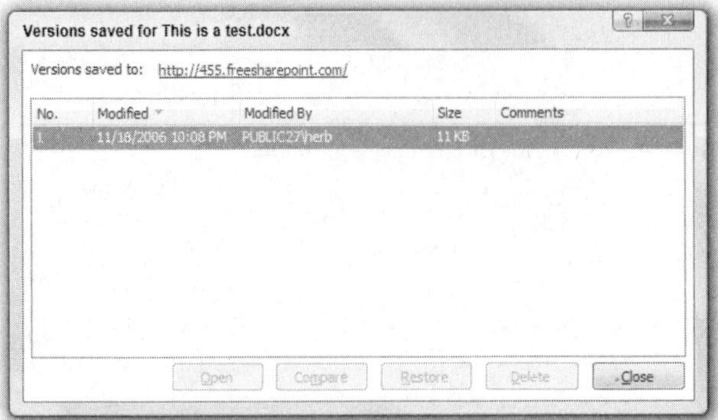

Document Management Information

Use the Document Management Information tool to toggle the Document Management pane. When a SharePoint document isn't open, the Document Workspace options are presented.

View Workflow Tasks

Use this tool to view workflow. This is another way to access the same information you can see in the Document Management pane.

Summary

In this chapter, you've seen how SharePoint integrates with Word 2007. You've learned how to initiate contact with a SharePoint site and create document workspaces, as well as use Word's Document Management pane to manage certain aspects of the SharePoint site. You should now be able to do the following:

- Publish a document to your SharePoint site
- Check out (open) a document from a SharePoint workspace
- Add new documents and folders to a SharePoint workspace
- Find the owner of a document and be able to contact them

Chapter 41

Groove

IN THIS CHAPTER

Groove versus SharePoint

Groove basics

Creating and deleting accounts

Creating and deleting workspaces

Sending workspace invitations

Working with workspace documents

Groove is a collaborative alternative to SharePoint (discussed in the previous chapter). One is tempted to call it a poor man's SharePoint, but Microsoft would be quick to point out that Groove offers a robust feature set that gives users advantages otherwise not available.

From an organizational standpoint, Groove 2007, a peer-to-peer collaboration tool, is less expensive and administratively easier than buying, setting up, and maintaining a SharePoint server. From the user's standpoint — particularly non-enterprise users — Groove 2007 offers some of the advantages you get from using SharePoint at a fraction of the cost. If what you really want to do is share Word documents so users can benefit from each other's updates without having to resort to e-mail, Groove 2007 might be all you need. Similarly, if you have work, home, and notebook computers on which you need to synchronize files, Groove 2007 might be just what the doctor ordered.

In this chapter, you'll learn how to use Groove as a way to manage shared Word documents. Groove 2007 has a lot of dimensions that are beyond the scope of *Office 2007 Bible,* so you won't end up being a Groove expert. However, if you have Groove 2007 and haven't even started it yet, this chapter will give you a basic sense of how to use it, and what it can do for you, a Word user.

Groove versus SharePoint

Does Groove replace SharePoint? In a word — no. If you need the collaborative and server facilities of SharePoint, Groove 2007 is not a substitute. The client Groove application does not provide for the following:

- Check-in and check-out of documents so that two people can't edit at cross purposes
- Server storage of shared workspace documents
- Access to documents and a managed workspace using Word's built-in features
- An enterprise-wide server location for managing a team project

Conversely, is SharePoint really what you want? Suppose for example, that you want to be able to edit a project's files from multiple locations, such as your work computer, your home computer, and your notebook computer. In addition, suppose some or all of those computers are sometimes offline. Groove enables you to do the following:

- Automatically (or on demand) synchronize a shared "workspace" when you are connected to the Internet
- Work on documents even when you aren't connected to the Internet, and then synchronize the next time you're connected
- Share a workspace with multiple peers who aren't on your work network or in the same Windows workgroup or domain
- Share multiple workspaces with multiple peers, including yourself (no need to pretend you're someone else) when you're using a different computer

For some users, it's not a choice between the two. SharePoint serves some needs best, and Groove serves other needs best. There are times, in fact, when SharePoint and Groove can work together, but when SharePoint isn't an option or when you have to choose between the two, Groove often comes out ahead in calculations centered on cost, convenience, and functionality — especially for small groups, and especially if you yourself comprise a small group.

Using the Groove 2007 Client

Unlike SharePoint, which is covered in Chapter 40, Groove does not add any extra features to Word or take special advantage of any of Word's existing features. Nor does Groove provide shared or coordinated access to the same files, for the most part (see "Working with groovy documents," later in this chapter). Instead, when sharing a workspace, each computer has its own local copy of the files in the workspace. This might seem redundant, but what it lacks in storage thriftiness it makes up for in convenience.

If you are working in an enterprise, you might have access to additional facilities through Groove Server or SharePoint. Because implementation can vary substantially, it would be impossible for this chapter to accurately or adequately describe how you interact with the environment created by your IT department. Instead, this chapter focuses on the individual user's Groove experience, and aspects common to all users of the Groove 2007 client application.

Groove basics

There are two main Groove windows: the Launchbar and the Workspace window. When you install Groove, two things happen. A Groove icon is added to the Windows notification area (the system tray), and the Launchbar opens. The Launchbar, shown in Figure 41-1, by default is displayed in tabbed view. It has two main tabs: Workspaces and Contacts. If you like seeing more information in one glance, choose Options, and remove the check next to Tabbed View. Groove then displays Workspaces and Contacts stacked on top of each other, with Command Tasks at the bottom. When you click in Workspace List or Contact List, the Common Tasks list changes to display tasks related to the selected list, just as it changes when you change tabs.

Use the Launchbar to create new workspaces, change workspace properties, control alerts, issue invitations, and add and remove contacts, among other things.

To display the Workspace window, right-click the Groove icon in the system tray and choose Open ➪ Workspace. In Select Workspace, click the workspace you want to open and then click OK. You will learn more about workspaces in "Workspaces," later in this chapter. The Workspace window offers a number of the same facilities as the Launchbar.

FIGURE 41-1

Use the Launchbar to access your Workspaces and Contacts lists.

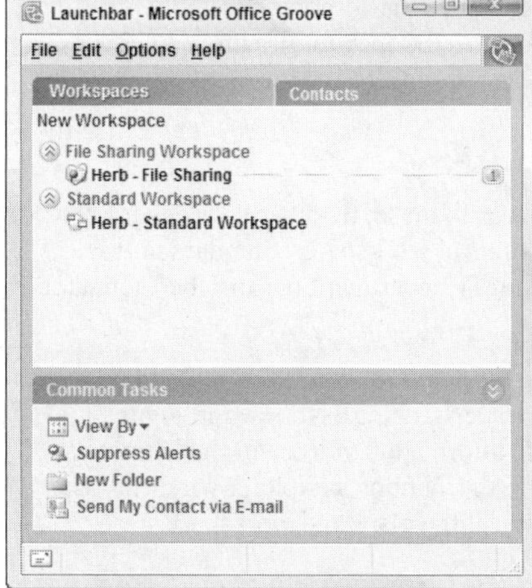

Account

In order to use Groove, you need an account. To create a new Groove account, right-click the Groove icon in the system tray and choose New Account. Choose Create a New Groove Account in the Account Configuration Wizard, and click Next to proceed. In the Groove Account Configuration Code step, if you don't know what a Groove Account Configuration Code is, choose I don't have a Groove Account Configuration Code, and proudly click Next. In the next Window, type your name and e-mail address (but read the following Tip before continuing).

TIP **Don't use the identical name when creating multiple Groove accounts for yourself. When you open a Groove window, your name is used to identify the accounts. If you use the identical name, you won't be able to tell which name is which account. Instead, include something about the e-mail address parenthetically. For example, I might have one account named Herb Tyson (MSN), another named Herb Tyson (Hotmail), and so on. That way, I can tell which is which when I log onto Groove.**

Type a password, confirm it, and provide a hint, if desired. Choose the desired password behavior/settings, and then click Next. Groove flashes the Create Account message box, and then asks whether to list you in the Public Groove Directory. If you want to be found, fine. If you don't, that's fine, too. Name Only is a nice compromise, particularly if you have multiple accounts using the same name.

NOTE **Groove accounts are *not* tied to .NET Passport or Windows Live ID. The e-mail address and password you type in Enter Groove Account Information have nothing to do with .NET Passport or Windows Live ID. The password you type is one you are creating for logging into Groove. It is not connected to your e-mail account. Your e-mail address is simply one way that other Groove members can contact you.**

Deleting an account

Deleting an account can be a little confusing because of the way information is presented. To delete an account, right-click the Groove icon on the system tray, click the account name you want to delete, and then click Launchbar. In the Launchbar window, choose Options ➪ Preferences ➪ Account tab. The lower part of the Account tab panel displays the name of your computer — not your Groove account name. That notwithstanding, this is the place to delete the account. It will not delete your computer name.

CAUTION Deleting an account will delete any Standard workspaces you have created and all data and files they contain (see "Workspaces," below). Back up anything you need to save before deleting an account.

Once you've backed up everything you need to save, click Delete. Notice the admonitions about what deleting does, and then click Yes to confirm Delete Account. Groove deletes the account, leaving any other accounts you have untouched. Click OK to complete this mindless wanton destruction.

Workspaces

To do anything useful with Groove, you need to create a workspace. To do so, in either Launchbar or the Workspace window, click New Workspace. There are two basic kinds of workspaces: Standard and File Sharing. The third, Template, will have templates listed only if your IT department has installed some for you to use. Do you have an IT department?

The Standard workspace, which has a Files tool and a Discussion tool (and to which you can add additional tools, such as Calendar, Pictures, Notepad, InfoPath Forms, and Issue Tracking), is shown in Figure 41-2. At the left, notice the Workspace List. This is the same workspace information you see in the Launchbar (unless there are shared folder workspaces, which are displayed in the Windows Explorer window). The "1" you see within an oval background indicates that one user is active in the displayed workspace.

FIGURE 41-2

A standard Workspace displays in the Workspace window.

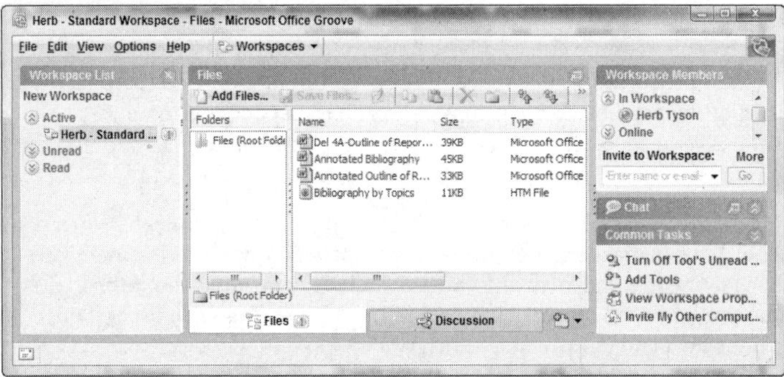

The second kind of workspace, File Sharing, is not displayed in Groove's Workspace window. Instead, it is displayed in a Windows Explorer window, with the Groove Folder Synchronization panel at the left. Exactly how this appears depends on whether you're running Windows XP or Vista, but the basic look of the panel itself should be the same. In the Windows Explorer toolbar, a Folder Sync tool will have been added. You can use the Folder Sync tool to turn the Groove Folder Synchronization panel on and off. It can be displayed for any folder, not just folders that have been shared using Groove.

If a folder has been shared using Groove, the Groove Folder Synchronization panel displays as shown in Figure 41-3. Otherwise, the Groove Folder Synchronization panel explains its *raison d'être*. It has one tool that lets you make the displayed folder Groovy (make it a Groove file-sharing workspace), and another tool that tells you what I just told you, basically. Another addition to Windows Explorer is a special folder icon that displays when a folder has been shared using Groove, also indicated in Figure 41-3. Note that this icon displays only when the account with which it is associated is active.

FIGURE 41-3

When you install Groove, groovy additions are made to Windows Explorer. The Groove Folder Synchronization panel is added, along with a new icon that lets you know a folder has been shared using Groove.

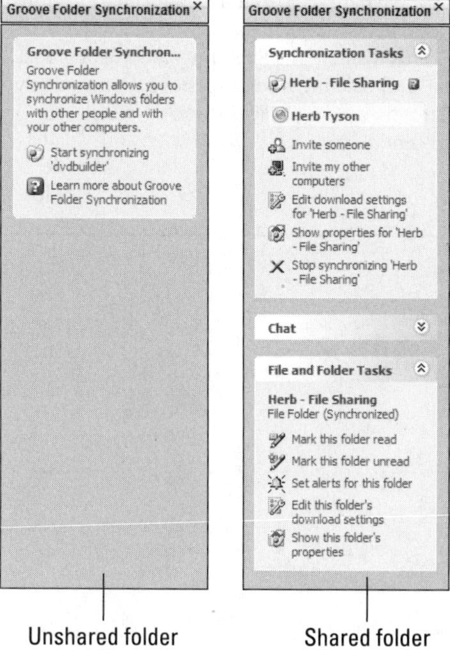

Removing workspaces

Because there are two different kinds of workspaces, there are two ways of removing or disassociating them from Groove. For Standard workspaces, you delete them. When you delete a Standard workspace, all of the files and other data it contains are deleted from your computer. If you have any files you need to save, do it before deleting a workspace or an account that contains workspaces.

To delete a Standard workspace, in the Launchbar or Workspace window, right-click the workspace you want to remove and click Delete. Notice the options provided, choose the course you want to follow, and proceed with caution. Again, make sure you've backed up anything you don't want to lose, because this action *will* remove the files from your computer such that they are no longer accessible.

To remove a File Sharing workspace, you aren't deleting it. Instead, you're simply telling Groove to stop synchronizing and sharing it. To do this, in the Launchbar, right-click the folder and choose Delete ➪ From this Computer or For All Members. If you choose the former, you're only de-Grooving the folder on your own computer. If you choose the latter, you're de-Grooving for all members. In neither case, however, are any actual files deleted. All that is removed is the association with Groove. The folder accepts its gold watch and goes home.

Sending workspace invitations

To be of any use, workspaces need to be used from different computers. One way to do that is to invite others, even if it's just yourself.

You can invite someone to use a shared folder or a standard workspace either from the Launchbar or from the Groove Folder Synchronization panel. To invite another user, in the Launchbar, click to select the workspace or File Sharing folder, and choose Invite to Workspace. This displays the Send Invitation dialog box, shown in Figure 41-4. Note the buttons for recording, playing, and deleting a voice message. Use this only if the user is already on your list of Groove contacts and is currently online. If the user isn't available, the invitation is sent by e-mail, and the recorded portion won't be sent.

FIGURE 41-4

You can type a message, record a message, or both.

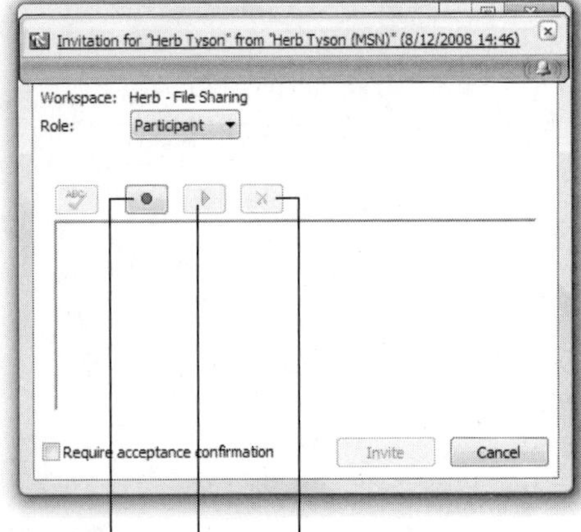

In the To field, type the name or e-mail address of the contact. Set Role to Manager, Participant, or Guest. Consult Groove's Help system to see how each is defined by default, and how to change the levels of access granted to each for a particular workspace.

In the space provided, type a message. If the contact is online and you've included a recording telling them what's what, the message needn't be too detailed. However, if the invitation will go by e-mail, then you can decide what level of information and detail the invitee needs, based on your assessment of their familiarity with Groove.

To invite additional contacts, click Add More. In the Add Recipients dialog box, type the name or e-mail address, or select it from cached contacts, if available. Click Add to List to send a name into the Recipients List. Click Search for User if you need help finding a name. When you're done, click OK. Back in the Send Invitation dialog box, decide whether to require acceptance confirmation, and then click Invite.

To invite your other computer to the shared folder, with the folder selected in the Launchbar, click Invite My Other Computers. Click OK to confirm the notice shown in Figure 41-5 Computers to which you've copied your Groove account information will automatically receive the shared folder information.

FIGURE 41-5

Inviting your other computers to use a shared folder is quick and easy.

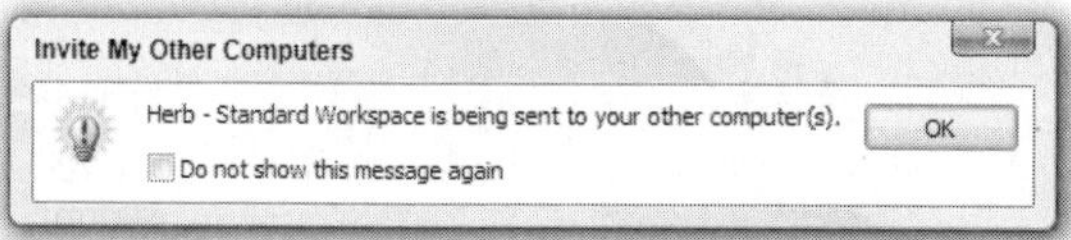

Canceling pending invitations

Once someone has been invited to join a workspace and has accepted, you cannot cancel their membership. You can, however, cancel invitations that have not yet been accepted. In the Launchbar, select the workspace and choose Options ➪ Cancel All Pending Invitations. Note that this cancels all pending invitations.

Accepting workspace invitations

You can receive a workspace invitation in either of two ways. If you are online and logged into Groove, the invitation shows up as a pop-up (or a pop-down, because it appears by the system tray), as shown in Figure 41-6. If the invitation disappears before you can get to it, hover the mouse over the Groove icon in the system tray to make the message reappear. Click the Invitation link.

FIGURE 41-6

If you're logged onto your Groove account, invitations arrive as pop-ups near your system tray.

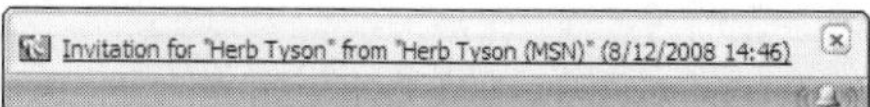

In Respond to Invitation, click Accept or Decline, as you wish, or Close to defer a decision. If you click Reply and send a reply, that is in effect a verbose acceptance.

If you're not logged onto your Groove account, the invitation will arrive as an e-mail. The e-mail will contain a link for you to click to accept the invitation.

NOTE **For some reason, the e-mail invitations sent by Groove sometimes contain broken links. Due to the way the lines are wrapped, part of the link occurs on a successive line and is not included as part of the link. When that happens, copy the orphaned portion to the Clipboard and then click on the non-orphaned portion. When your browser appears, press Esc to stop it from loading the broken link. Paste the orphaned portion at the end of the URL shown, to complete it, and then press Enter to load the link.**

Working with Groovy documents

As noted previously, Groove does not have facilities for version control or managing editing by multiple users at the same time. It does, however, check before saving changed files to the workspace. When working from a standard workspace, if there are changes, then Groove alerts you to that fact and asks if you want to save the changes to the Groove workspace, as shown in Figure 41-7.

FIGURE 41-7

When using a standard workspace, Word prompts before saving changes to Groove.

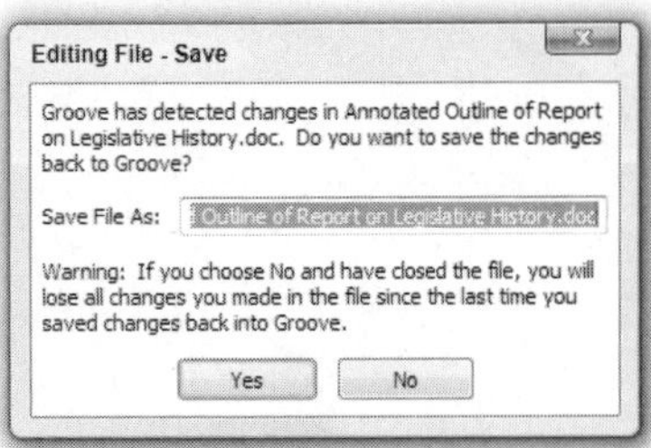

If the new version conflicts with an existing version — i.e., changes from another Groove user who is logged into the same workspace — Groove alerts you to the conflict. You can then use either Word's Compare or Combine commands to resolve the different changes.

When saving to a folder shared by Groove, each user works with his or her own local copies of files. Depending on the type of synchronization used, there often will be no warning about file conflicts. However, Groove does still detect whether there are conflicting versions of the same file. If there are, the last version saved is given a different name. As described earlier, the user's name is added to the document name, in parentheses. Use the Compare or Combine commands to resolve any differences.

Summary

In this chapter, you've been introduced to Groove. You now know how to create a Groove account, how to create workspaces, and how to share folders for use in Groove. You should now be able to do the following:

- Use Groove to synchronize files on different computers you own
- Use Groove to synchronize work performed by a project team, without using SharePoint
- Add contacts to Groove
- Send workspace invitations to contacts
- Recognize Groove's modified folder icons to determine that a folder has been shared by Groove

Chapter 42

Integration with Other Office Applications

In some ways, using Office 2007 is like using a single multipurpose program. Things mesh together almost seamlessly. For example, when you insert a chart into a Word 2007 document, if you don't pay close attention, you might not notice that the process starts Excel 2007. Back in the "olden days," you clearly knew you were using two programs.

Although integration is now better than ever for many things you do in Office 2007, some times you wonder whether the left hand knows what the right hand is doing. For example, when copying cells from an Excel spreadsheet into a Word table, you might wonder why the default action would paste a 100 × 100 selection into a single Word table cell.

In this chapter, you explore the ways in which Excel, PowerPoint, and Outlook communicate with Word. Some things are perfectly intuitive; others aren't. The casual PowerPoint user might never stumble on how to send outlines back and forth with Word. Do you ever wonder about the array of different picture options when copying images between Word and other programs? Which format should you use, and what are the consequences of using this one or that? How can pasting a 40K picture into a Word file add 900K to its size? In this chapter, the focus is on the less intuitive, to get you over some hurdles and stumbling blocks, and to make sense of some of those little mysteries that can make using Word seem to be a struggle.

IN THIS CHAPTER

Excel

Although sharing work between Word and Excel often works well, differences in how the two programs operate can produce confusing results. You can address this issue by becoming aware of those differences and working to accommodate them. This section looks at Word and Excel and ways to share text, data, tables, and graphics.

Using Excel content in Word

Word offers a variety of different ways to share and exchange content with Excel:

- **Clipboard:** Copy content to the Clipboard and then use Paste or Paste Special to insert the contents into Word or Excel. Commandment: When in doubt, use Paste Special.
- **Chart:** Use Office 2007's new Chart feature to create a chart inside Word using Excel's facilities.
- **Object:** Use Insert ➪ Text ➪ Object ➪ Object ➪ Create New or Create from File to embed all or part of an Excel worksheet into a Word document.
- **File:** Use Insert ➪ Text ➪ Object ➪ Text from File to insert content from an Excel worksheet into a Word file.

A common method that does not work, however, is drag and drop. You cannot select data or other content in Excel and drag it into Word. The reverse does work, however, as you'll see shortly.

Clipboard

Excel's Clipboard works differently from the Clipboard in most other Office programs. Why? Nobody seems to know for certain, although theories abound. If you're not an Excel veteran, however, it's likely to bother you. When you select cells in an Excel worksheet, they are highlighted as shown in Figure 42-1. At this point, they are merely highlighted and cannot be moved or otherwise acted upon. You also need to copy (or cut) the selection to the Clipboard, by pressing Ctrl+C, right-clicking, and choosing Copy, etc.

FIGURE 42-1

To move cells in Excel, it's not enough to select them; you have to copy them to the Clipboard.

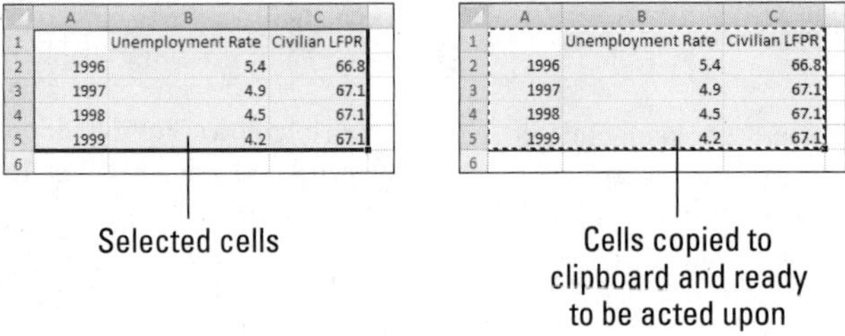

Even after you've copied the selection to the Clipboard, the Excel selection needs to remain highlighted as shown (surrounded by a dashed outline). If you press Esc in Excel or double-click elsewhere (or perform dozens of other actions in Excel), the Paste button dies. Even if the data has actually been copied to the Clipboard, you still can't use the Paste button unless the selection is still active in Excel. More to the point, the Paste Special feature is no longer available, and Paste Special often is the best way to deal with Excel data.

When the selection has been disturbed, and if the Clipboard was set up to automatically collect data, you can use the Clipboard pane itself to paste the selection into Word. However, the Paste Special options aren't available. The Office Clipboard develops a terrible case of amnesia about Excel's data unless the selection is still active. Therefore, don't get distracted in the middle of trying to copy data from Excel to Word.

With the selection active in Excel, click where you want the data to appear in Word, click the Paste button's drop-down arrow, and choose Paste Special (or press Ctrl+Alt+V). The Paste Special dialog box, shown in Figure 42-2, appears. Notice that the default is HTML format. Why is that the default, rather than Formatted Text (RTF), and does it make any difference?

FIGURE 42-2

When pasting a selection of cells from Excel into Word, you often have as many as eight options regarding how to paste.

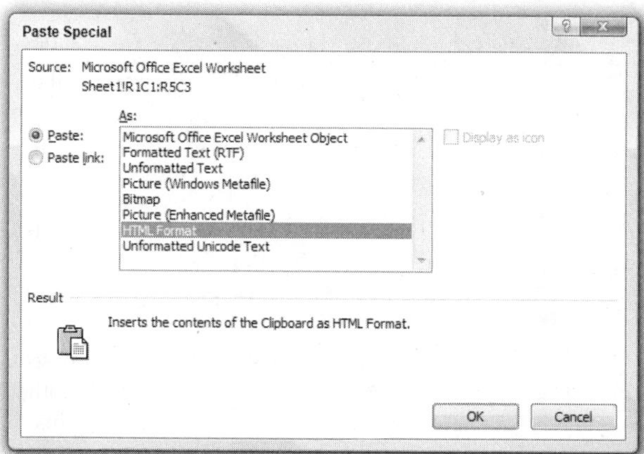

At the end of the day, both HTML and RTF retain both formatting and table structure, but there are differences. They might seem subtle, or they might seem substantial, depending on your needs. Note that nothing special was done in Excel to format the cells. Differences also exist among other options that might seemingly appear similar. Different paste special options are as follows:

- **Microsoft Office Excel Worksheet Object:** Inserts the selection as a complete mini-spreadsheet, complete with Excel facilities.
- **Formatted Text (RTF):** Inserts formatted text as a table, retaining the cell, column, and row formatting in effect in the Excel file. This option often misinterprets cell shading and other colors.
- **Unformatted Text:** Inserts plain text with no attributes.
- **Picture (Windows Metafile):** Inserts an `.emf` picture file that does not retain the cell divisions in the resulting picture, that is, it's just a picture of the text (larger than either Bitmap or Enhanced Metafile).
- **Bitmap:** Inserts a `.png` picture file (smaller than either of the other two picture options; this option retains the cell divisions in the picture).
- **Picture (Enhanced Metafile):** Inserts an `.emf` picture file that is essentially identical in appearance to the Windows Metafile, but is slightly smaller in size.
- **HTML Format:** Retains text formatting but doesn't retain all of the table formatting. This feature usually results in a table that is smaller in width than the RTF table. This option inserts cell shading and colors more accurately than RTF.
- **Unformatted Unicode Text:** Usually, this option yields the same result as Unformatted Text. Unicode goes well beyond ASCII and ANSI and provides for many more characters and languages. If you find that linguistic information is being lost when you're pasting as unformatted text, then switch to unformatted Unicode text.

When you copy graphics from Excel to Word, the rules change a bit and become more familiar. Right-click the graphic and choose Copy. This time, you don't get the dashed selection because you're not copying cells—so it's a bit simpler, and after something has been copied to the Clipboard, the Paste Special options remain available. Switch to Word and you'll see the options shown in Figure 42-3.

FIGURE 42-3

When copying pictures from Excel to Word, no special handling is required.

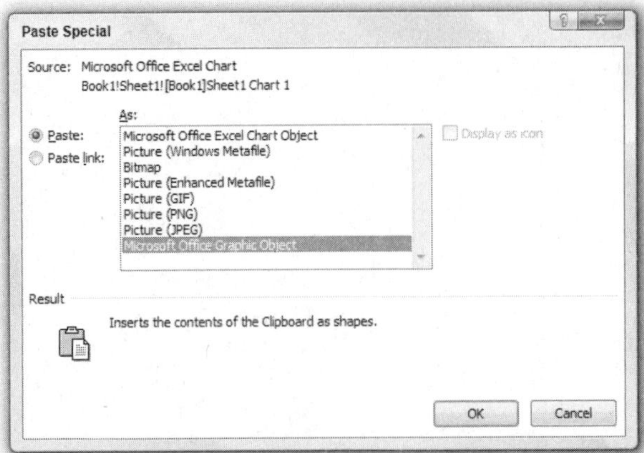

The simplicity stops there, however, because the choice you make can produce wildly varying file sizes. For example, a 40K `.jpg` file was inserted into an Excel worksheet. It was then copied to the Clipboard so that it could be pasted back into Word to see what difference the different Paste Special options make. The dramatic differences are shown in Table 42-1.

TABLE 42-1

Graphics Sizes When Using Different Paste Methods

Paste Special Method	File Extension	Size
Picture (Windows Metafile)	`.emf`	460K
Bitmap	`.bmp`	331K
Picture (Enhanced Metafile)	`.emf`	214K
Picture (GIF)	`.gif`	129K
Picture (PNG)	`.png`	821K
Picture (JPEG)	`.jpg`	47K
Microsoft Office Graphic Object (Default)	`.jpg`	40K

When using Paste Special, you might want to experiment to see which format gives you the best appearance in your document depending on how it is to be presented (online versus on paper). However, based on file size, Word's default option, Microsoft Office Graphic Object, is the best choice.

Chart

When you insert a chart using Insert ➪ Illustrations ➪ Chart, assuming that Excel 2007 is installed and available, Word starts Excel, uses a placeholder data set in an Excel worksheet, and creates a chart based on that data. The chart is embedded as an Excel object in Word. Use Excel to replace the data set with the data you want to use. The chart and all information taken from the data set are updated automatically.

Formatting is performed using the Chart Tools tabs on the Ribbon — Design, Layout, and Format. If you need to change the data, however, you use Excel, but don't start Excel directly. Instead, click inside the chart, choose the Chart Tools Design tab on the Ribbon, and then click Select Data or Edit Data in the Data section of the Ribbon, as shown in Figure 42-4.

FIGURE 42-4

You can swap rows and columns without resorting to Excel. To edit the data, however, you need Excel.

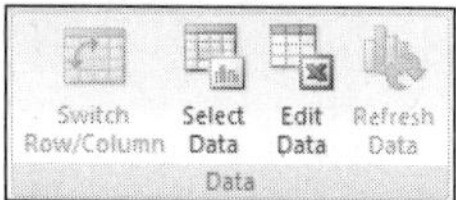

When you make changes to the data, the chart itself in Word is updated automatically. If you might need to undo changes, leave Excel open. As long as it remains open, Ctrl+Z will work. If you close Excel, changes to the chart and data set are saved automatically. However, Excel really does close, so Ctrl+Z will no longer undo changes you might have made.

Object

A third way to use Excel data in a Word document is as an object. In Word, choose Insert ➪ Text ➪ Object ➪ Object. To use an existing Excel worksheet, click Create from File. To create a new Excel object, click Create New.

Create from File

Use the Browse button to navigate to the target file. Choose Link to File or Display as Icon, according to your needs, and click OK.

NOTE **Typically, you would use Display as Icon when the purpose is to provide access to the contents of the Excel file rather than to display it. For example, suppose you have a number of tax tables that you want to provide to the reader. Some readers need one table, others need another, and so on. A document will be much less cluttered if users can click a link to open the data set of interest in Excel rather than make all readers look through all the data files to find the one they want.**

Create New

In the Create New tab of the Object dialog box, select the desired type of Excel object, as shown in Figure 42-5. Choose Display as Icon if desired (click Change Icon if appropriate) and then click OK. Use Excel's tools to create the desired object and then close Excel. When you close Excel, you will be prompted to save the changes in the Word document. Click Yes to save the changes; click No to keep working on the Excel object; or click No if you don't mind losing the work you've been doing.

FIGURE 42-5

You can create any of five types of Excel objects from Word.

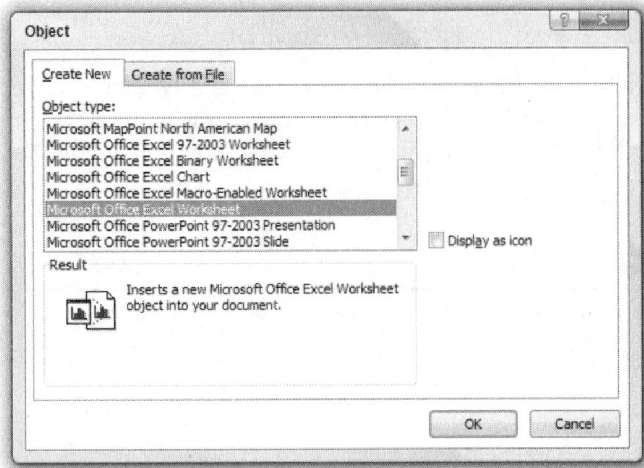

TIP **Notice that when working in Excel this way, you can't get inside the Excel object to save your work. Saving is controlled within the Word process. If you want to have an independent version of the Excel object that is accessible from Excel without using Word, copy the contents of the "objectized" Excel worksheet to the Clipboard, open the full Excel application, paste your work into it, and save it.**

To insert the contents of the file, click Insert. To link to the contents, click the drop-down arrow next to Insert and select Insert as Link. Word now issues a confirmation dialog box. If you're sure the Excel file you're opening is safe, click Yes.

From spreadsheet to table

When you use one of the methods shown to insert formatted Excel data into Word, a Word table is created automatically. Sometimes, however, you need to insert data into a table that already exists. Typically, two problems can occur. First, sometimes the pasted cells don't go exactly where you want them to go. Second, no matter what you do, the formatting in the table never ends up exactly as you want.

To handle the first problem, the dimensions (rows and columns) of the source must be identical to the destination, and the destination cells must be selected. For example, if you are pasting a selection of cells that contains five rows and four columns, the destination must also be 5 × 4, and you must select the destination cells. If you try to paste in the top-left cell (which seems logical, right?), Word pastes the entire selection into that cell, so you end up with a table within a table.

There is no perfect way to handle the second problem. Even if you choose the setting Office Button ➪ Word Options ➪ Advanced ➪ Pasting from other programs to Match Destination Formatting or Keep Text Only, *something* in the formatting will be messed up — usually the spacing.

Your best bet, assuming that you're using a style, is to choose Paste Special ➪ Unformatted Text and then reapply the style to the pasted cells. Alternatively, if some table cells contain the correct formatting, use the Format Painter to reformat the pasted cells as desired.

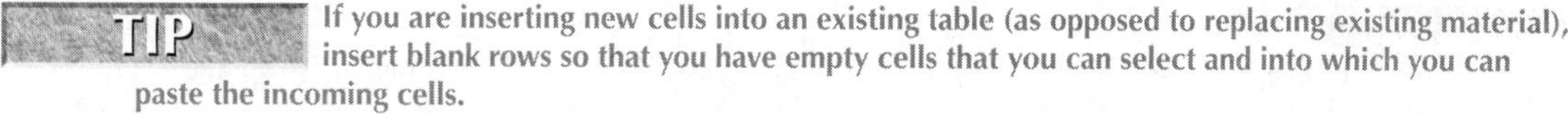

TIP If you are inserting new cells into an existing table (as opposed to replacing existing material), insert blank rows so that you have empty cells that you can select and into which you can paste the incoming cells.

Using Word content in Excel

Going from Word into Excel isn't quite as tricky as going from Excel into Word, although some quirks exist to be aware of.

Clipboard

When you paste content from Word into Excel — using the default Paste behavior — different kinds of content are handled differently. To see your options, make your selection in Word and copy or cut it to the Clipboard. In Excel, click the Paste drop-down arrow for the options shown in Figure 42-6.

FIGURE 42-6

When pasting text, table material, or both from Word into Excel, you can paste as a link, a picture (including text and tables), or a picture link.

NOTE When you paste a picture link, if the source text or tables material is updated, then it is automatically updated in Word. If you replace the picture, the picture will not be updated. If the source picture is updated (that is, it is linked and the original picture changes but it keeps the same name and location), the picture will be updated.

When you paste text that includes one or no paragraph marks, it is inserted into the selected cell. If the selection contains multiple paragraphs, it is inserted into consecutive cells in the target column. For example, if the Clipboard contains three paragraphs and you paste into Row 1 Column 1, the three paragraphs are inserted into Row 1 Column 1, Row 2 Column 1, and Row 3 Column 1, respectively.

When you paste all or part of a table into Excel, the cells are inserted into separate cells matching the original selection in Word. Destination cells do not need to be selected. For example, to copy a 5 × 4 table from Word to Excel, select the table and copy or cut it to the Clipboard. Right-click in the upper-left cell of the 5 × 4 area where you want the table to appear and choose Paste. Formatting and cell shading is copied to the destination unless you choose Paste Special ⇨ Text (or Unicode Text).

NOTE In Excel, when you choose Paste Special, unformatted text is indicated only as Text, without the word *unformatted.*

When you paste a picture from Word into Excel, it is inserted into Excel's drawing layer rather than into cells. Note that Excel does not have an In Line with Text option for graphics.

Drag and drop

In contrast to going from Excel to Word, when you go from Word to Excel, drag and drop does work, as long as drag and drop editing is enabled in Word (choose Office Button ➪ Word Options ➪ Advanced ➪ Editing Options ➪ Allow Text to Be Dragged and Dropped).

CAUTION **When you drag from one program to another, the normal default is for text to be copied. When you drag from Word to Excel, the default action is to move the selection. If you really want to move the text, fine. If you instead merely want to copy, then you need to press the Ctrl key when you drop the text. You don't need to press Ctrl when you begin the drag. However, you do need to press it when you drop. When you press the Ctrl key, notice that the drag icon suddenly gains a + sign, signifying that it will be copied.**

Object

You can insert a new or existing Word document into an Excel file as an object. To insert part of an existing Word file as an object, select the portion you want and copy it to the Clipboard. Click where you want it to reside, choose the Paste button's drop-down arrow, and then choose Paste Special. In the Paste Special dialog box, shown in Figure 42-7, choose Microsoft Office Word Document Object. Select Display as Icon and Paste or Paste Link, as needed, and then click OK. Note that when using the Clipboard approach, you often can't get the entire document, even if you press Ctrl+A (Select All). That's because Ctrl+A excludes contents such as headers, footers, and footnotes. To insert the entire file as an object, therefore, you need to use a different approach.

FIGURE 42-7

Use Paste Special to paste the Clipboard's contents as a Word object.

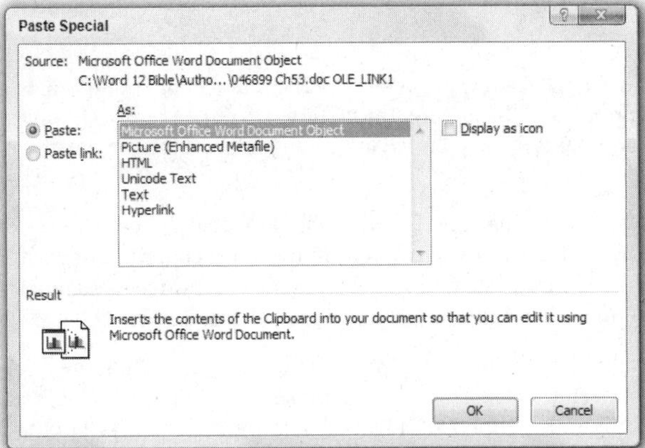

To insert the entire file as an object, in Excel, choose Insert ➪ Object. If you're using Create New or Create from File, proceed as shown earlier in this chapter.

PowerPoint

In some ways, Word and PowerPoint were meant to work together. That's because PowerPoint uses heading levels that are similar to Word's Heading styles. When creating a PowerPoint presentation, for example, it's a simple matter to convert a Word outline into a PowerPoint presentation (or at least the basis for one), or to use a PowerPoint presentation as an outline for a Word document.

Converting Word to PowerPoint presentations

Converting a Word document outline into a PowerPoint presentation is simple — as long as you've used Word's Heading styles for your outline, and as long as the outline contains no other text. Unfortunately, PowerPoint is not able to extract just the outline from a Word document, so you must manage that trick yourself if the document has already been written.

TIP **A quick way to obtain an outline from a Word document that was formatted using Heading levels is to insert a table of contents. Copy the table of contents to another document, press Ctrl+Shift+F9 to convert it to static text, save it, and then proceed.**

To convert a Word outline into a PowerPoint presentation, in PowerPoint, start a new PowerPoint presentation (Ctrl+N). In the Home tab of the Ribbon in PowerPoint, click the New Slide drop-down arrow in the Slides group and choose Slides from Outline, as shown in Figure 42-8. In the Insert Outline dialog box, find the document containing your outline, select it, and click Insert.

FIGURE 42-8

You can use a Word outline to create a PowerPoint presentation.

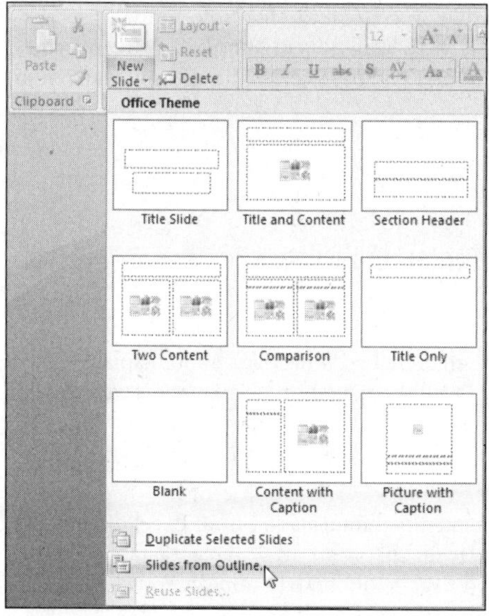

NOTE After you've inserted an outline into a PowerPoint presentation, you'll often discover that stray or extra paragraph marks insinuate themselves prominently in the PowerPoint presentation. You can fix them in PowerPoint, or, if it's easier, press Ctrl+Z to undo the insert, clean up the outline in Word, and then try again.

TIP In PowerPoint's Normal view, click the Outline tab. Working with a presentation in Outline view, you might find it as easy to clean up an imported outline there as it would be to go back to Word and start over. Note that some of Word's more useful outlining keystrokes, such as Alt+Shift+arrow keys, perform the same actions in PowerPoint as they do in Word — demoting, promoting, and moving selected outline headings.

Converting PowerPoint presentations to Word documents

You can also go in the other direction, using a PowerPoint presentation as a starting outline for a Word document. In PowerPoint, choose Office Button ➪ Save As. Set Save as Type to Outline/RTF (*.rtf) and click Save. Unlike Word, PowerPoint does not open or display the `.rtf` file, and it is immediately available for Word to open without your having to close anything in PowerPoint.

In Word, choose Office Button ➪ Open, navigate to the `.rtf` file you just created, and open it. Then switch to Outline view. Look, Ma! It's an outline! The top level for each slide was assigned Heading 1, the next level Heading 2, and so on.

You now have a Word outline of your document, and all you need to do now is fill in those petty details. You know — that stuff called content.

Exporting PowerPoint handouts to Word

Because PowerPoint gives you limited options for formatting the notes and handouts pages, you might want to create your handouts and other documents based on presentation content in Microsoft Word. To send your presentation to Word, choose Office Button ➪ Publish ➪ Create Handouts in Microsoft Office Word. The Send To Microsoft Office Word dialog box that appears enables you to select the format you want from among these choices:

- Notes Next to Slides
- Blank Lines Next to Slides
- Notes Below Slides
- Blank Lines Below Slides
- Outline Only

Click the format option that you prefer and then click OK. Word launches, if necessary, and displays the new handout document, as in the one shown in Figure 42-9. From there, you can format and save the document as you wish.

Using Excel to add a table that calculates

If you need to calculate values in a table in PowerPoint, you can embed information from Excel directly on a slide. With the slide where you want to insert the table displayed, choose Insert ➪ Tables ➪ Table ➪ Excel Spreadsheet. The cells appear as a new object on the slide, and Excel's Ribbon tabs appear. You can type labels, values, and formulas into cells as needed; resize and move the object; and use the tab choices for formatting and completing the embedded Excel table.

FIGURE 42-9

Handout content sent from PowerPoint to Word.

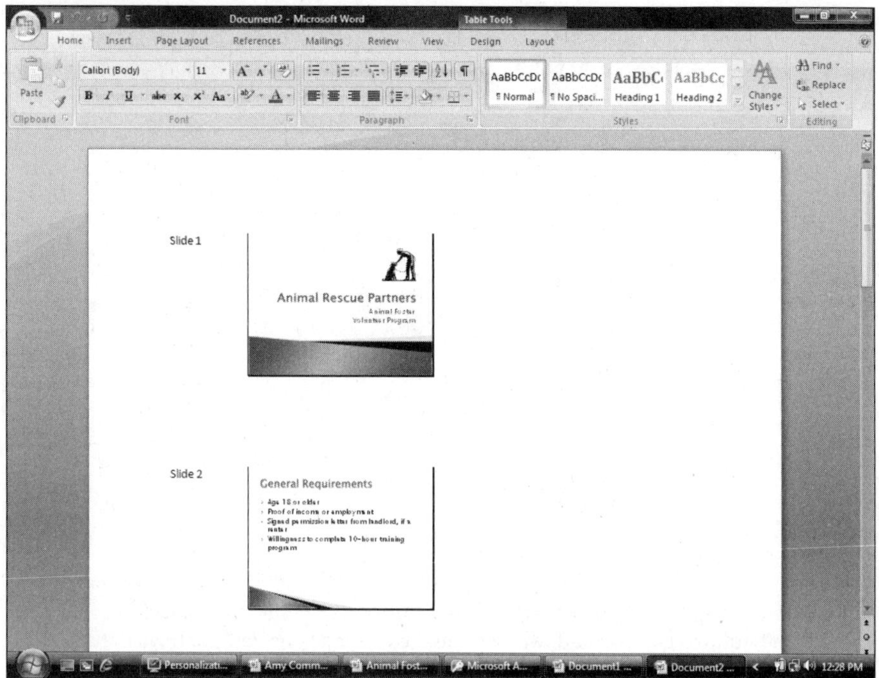

Outlook

In past versions, Outlook and Word had a potentially much more intimate connection than they have in Office 2007. That's because you could use Word itself to view, edit, and compose your e-mail. Although Outlook's e-mail editor might look a whole lot like Word, it's not Word anymore. Instead, it's a small, mostly independent subset of Word, borrowed from the Word programming team. If you have only Outlook 2007, you still have the same Word-like editor. In fact, if your word processing needs are fairly simple, you might not even need Word. But let's not be hasty. After all — we have an *Office 2007 Bible* we want to sell you!

We've already looked at how to use the Outlook address book to perform an e-mail merge. See Chapter 10 for the nitty-gritty details.

Using the Outlook Address Book in Word

One of the more conspicuous relationships between Word and Outlook is the use of the Outlook Address Book for addresses in Word documents — especially letters and envelopes. For example, in the Mailings tab of the Ribbon, click Envelopes or Labels in the Create group, and then click the Insert Address tool (see Figure 42-10).

FIGURE 42-10

You can access the Outlook Address Book using the Insert Address tool.

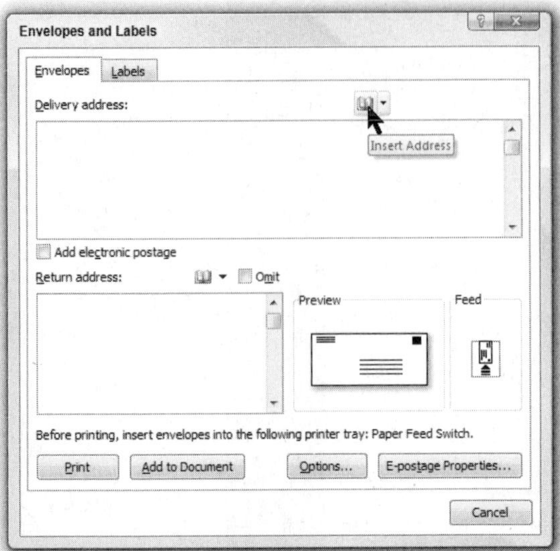

The Select Name dialog box appears, as shown in Figure 42-11. If you have multiple Contact folders set up as address books, click the Address Book drop-down arrow and choose the one you want. Note that the Search option enables you to search the Name Only or More columns. When you use Name Only, the dialog box displays only names that start with what you type.

Alternatively, click More Columns, type what you're looking for, and click Go. This search feature searches for occurrences of the search text anywhere in any contact field. If that search gives you too many hits, click Advanced Find. Use the Find dialog box to search for names containing text you type. When you find the person or business whose address you want, select it and click OK.

This method is great for envelopes and labels, but what about for inserting the address in the body of the letter, or what if you want to type "John's mailing address is . . ."? You could simply use the envelope or label feature, select the address from the dialog box, and then dismiss the Envelopes and Labels dialog box (unless your address book is set up to display the contact's name rather than name and e-mail address). Someone reading this does exactly that. Caught you, eh?

Rather than send you on a hunting expedition, let's save a little trouble right now. The Address Book or Insert Address tool does not exist in any freestanding Ribbon. The only way to get to it in the default ribbon is using the Envelopes and Labels dialog box.

However, there is a better way. If you were following along, dismiss the various dialog boxes, right-click the Quick Access Toolbar, and choose Customize Quick Access Toolbar. You probably saw this coming, right? To drive home the point, set Choose Commands From to Commands Not in the Ribbon. About halfway down the first page of A commands, locate Address Book. Click it and then click Add. If you don't like where it is, you can use the up or down buttons to move it.

NOTE **The only difference between this Address Book tool and the one in the Envelopes and Labels dialog box is that the latter has a drop-down arrow from which you can select recently inserted addresses.**

FIGURE 42-11

Insert addresses in Outlook using the Address Book.

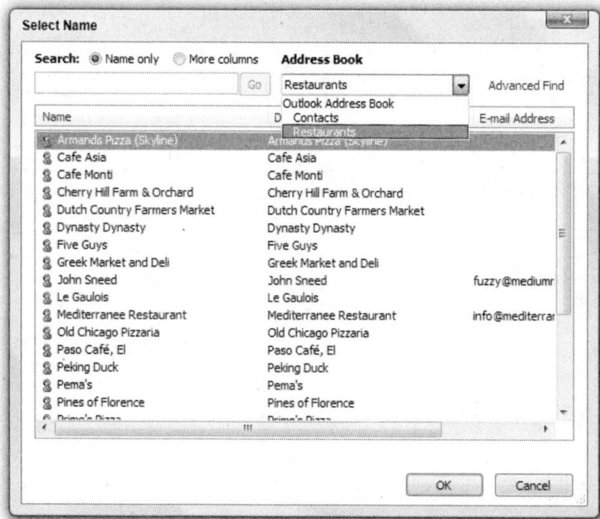

Smart Tags, Outlook, and Word

Another way in which Outlook rears its Outlookish head in Word is through the use of Smart Tags. If Smart Tags are enabled, when you type the name of someone in your Contact list, you can access that contact's information, as shown in Figure 42-12. Note the other options as well. You can initiate an e-mail, schedule a meeting, open the Outlook contact's record, insert the contact's address, or even create a new contact record if one doesn't already exist.

FIGURE 42-12

When Smart Tags are enabled, and Person Name (Outlook e-mail recipients) is enabled, you can access Outlook contacts from Smart tags in Word documents.

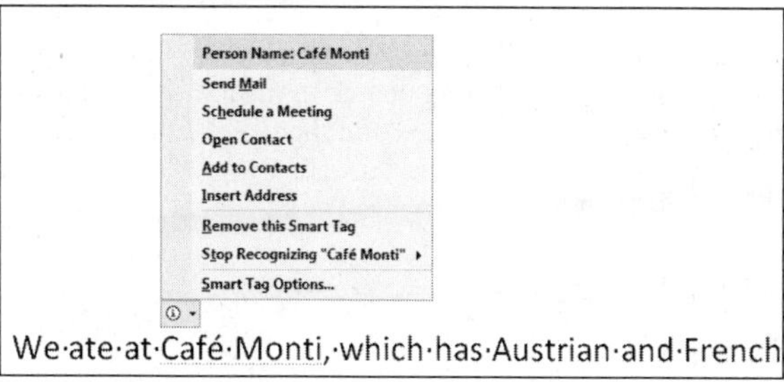

If people's names don't show up as Smart Tags, or if they do but you can't access Outlook information from them, then perhaps your options need adjusting. Hover over the Smart Tag, click the i button, and choose Smart Tag Options (refer to Figure 42-12). In the AutoCorrect dialog box, examine the options. (Note that you also can display Smart Tag options by choosing Office Button ➪ Word Options, clicking the Proofing category, clicking AutoCorrect Options, and then clicking the Smart Tags tab in the dialog box that appears.) Ensure that both the Label Text with Smart Tags checkbox and the Person Name (Outlook e-mail recipients) Recognizer are checked, as shown in Figure 42-13.

FIGURE 42-13

With Person Name (Outlook e-mail recipients) enabled, a number of Outlook-related actions are accessible from a Word document.

Access Imports and Exports

You can copy information from an Excel worksheet and paste it into an Access datasheet, and vice versa. However, to convert longer lists of data, an import or export operation might be more appropriate. To perform an import or export, use the External Data tab on the Ribbon in Access (Figure 42-14).

If you are exporting information, open the table or query with the data to export. Then, after clicking the External Data tab, you can click a button in the Import or Export group on the tab to display the Import or Export (Figure 42-14) dialog box. Make the needed choices in the dialog box and then click OK to perform the import or export.

FIGURE 42-14

Click a choice on the External data tab to start an Access import or export.

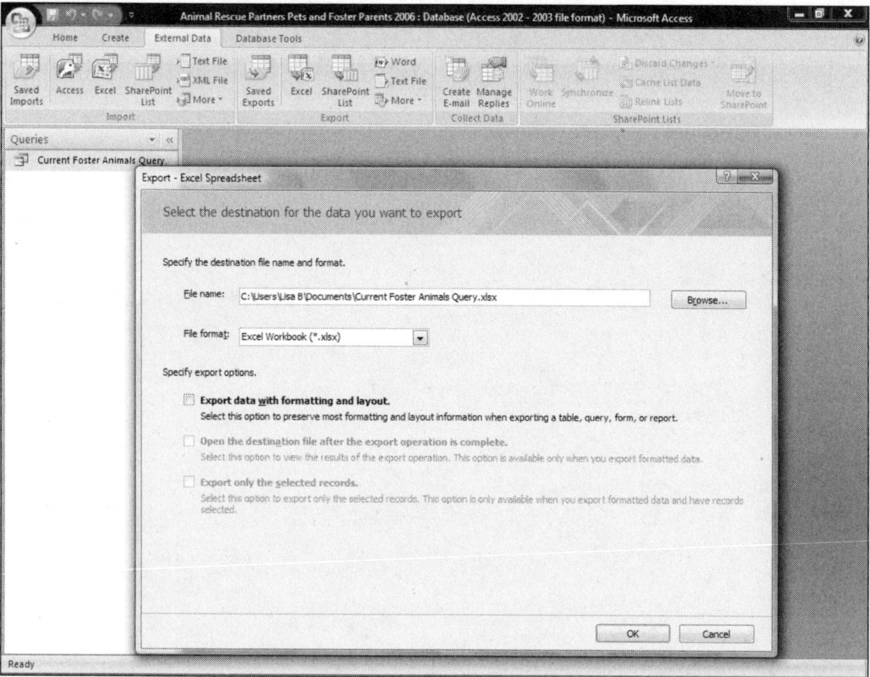

Summary

In this chapter, you've learned several ways to exchange data between Word and Excel. You've also seen how to convert Word outlines into PowerPoint presentations, how to create a Word outline or handouts using a PowerPoint presentation, and how to insert calculating cells from Excel on a slide. Additionally, you've looked at several ways that Outlook and Word stay in contact with, well, Contacts, and how to start an import or export in Access.

Index

SYMBOLS AND NUMERICS

A

B

C

D

E

F

G

J

K

L

M

N

O

P

Q

R

S

T

U

V

W

X

Y

Z

"I recommend this book f anyone who wants a stro foundation in Access."

—Jeff Lenamon, CIBC World Marke

Harness the power of Access 2007 with the expert guidance in this comprehensive reference. Beginners will appreciate the thorough attention to database fundamentals and terminology. Experienced users can jump right into Access 2007 enhancements like the all-new user interface and wider use of XML and Web services. Each of the book's six parts thoroughly focuses on key clements in a logical sequence, so you have what you need, when you need it. Designed as both a reference and a tutorial, *Access 2007 Bible* is a powerful tool for developers needing to make the most of the new features in Access 2007.

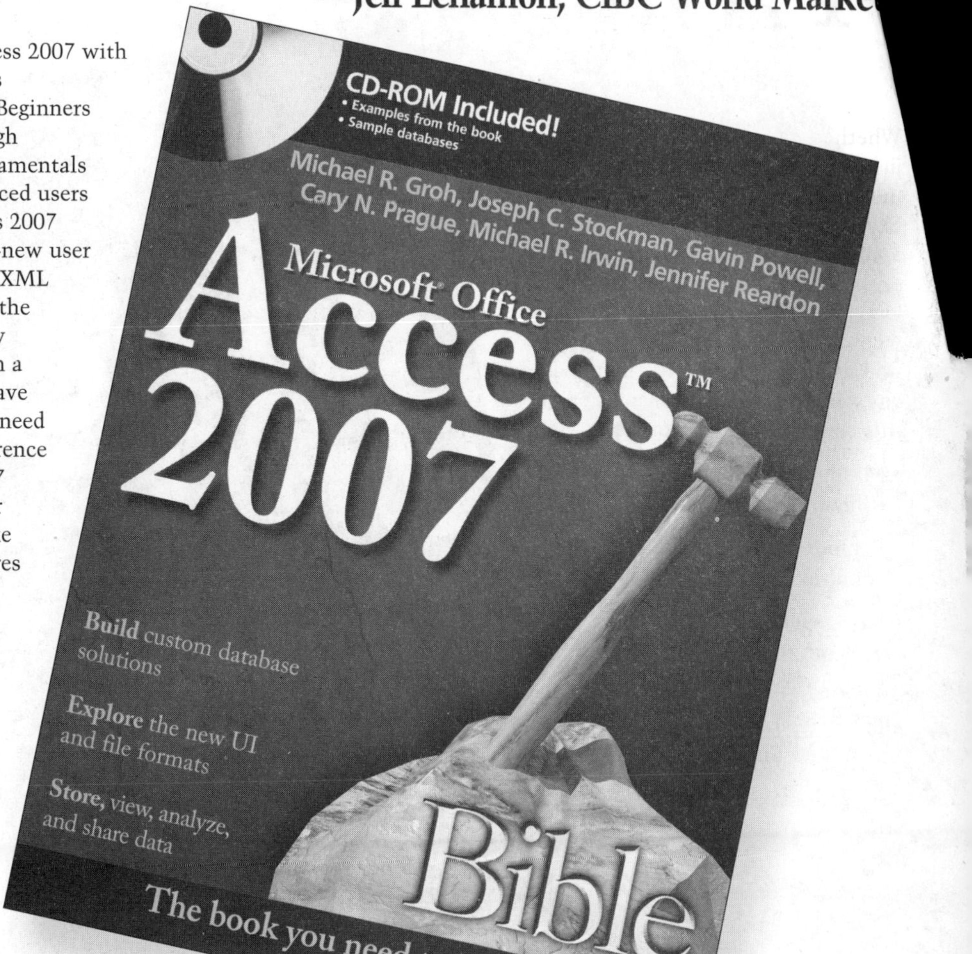

CD-ROM Included!
• Examples from the book
• Sample databases

Michael R. Groh, Joseph C. Stockman, Gavin Powell, Cary N. Prague, Michael R. Irwin, Jennifer Reardon

Microsoft® Office Access™ 2007 Bible

Build custom database solutions

Explore the new UI and file formats

Store, view, analyze, and share data

The book you need to succeed!

978-0-470-04673-9, 1416 pages, $49.99

Find out more at www.wiley.com/compbooks